ANDERSON'S
Law School Publications

Administrative Law Anthology
Thomas O. Sargentich

Administrative Law: Cases and Materials
Daniel J. Gifford

An Admiralty Law Anthology
Robert M. Jarvis

Alternative Dispute Resolution: Strategies for Law and Business
E. Wendy Trachte-Huber and Stephen K. Huber

The American Constitutional Order: History, Cases, and Philosophy
Douglas W. Kmiec and Stephen B. Presser

American Legal Systems: A Resource and Reference Guide
Toni M. Fine

Analytic Jurisprudence Anthology
Anthony D'Amato

An Antitrust Anthology
Andrew I. Gavil

Appellate Advocacy: Principles and Practice, *Third Edition*
Ursula Bentele and Eve Cary

Arbitration: Cases and Materials
Stephen K. Huber and E. Wendy Trachte-Huber

The Art and Science of Trial Advocacy
L. Timothy Perrin, H. Mitchell Caldwell, and Carol A. Chase

Bankruptcy Anthology
Charles J. Tabb

Basic Accounting Principles for Lawyers: With Present Value and Expected Value
C. Steven Bradford and Gary A. Ames

Basic Themes in Law and Jurisprudence
Charles W. Collier

The Best-Kept Secrets of Evidence Law: 101 Principles, Practices, and Pitfalls
Paul R. Rice

Business Associations, *Fourth Edition*
Larry E. Ribstein and Peter V. Letsou

A Capital Punishment Anthology (and Electronic Caselaw Appendix)
Victor L. Streib

Cases and Materials in Juvenile Law
J. Eric Smithburn

Cases and Materials on Corporations
Thomas R. Hurst and William A. Gregory

Cases and Materials on the Law Governing Lawyers
James E. Moliterno

Cases and Problems in California Criminal Law
Myron Moskovitz

Cases and Problems in Criminal Law, *Fourth Edition*
Myron Moskovitz

The Citation Workbook: How to Beat the Citation Blues, *Second Edition*
Maria L. Ciampi, Rivka Widerman, and Vicki Lutz

Civil Procedure Anthology
David I. Levine, Donald L. Doernberg, and Melissa L. Nelken

Civil Procedure: Cases, Materials, and Questions, *Third Edition*
Richard D. Freer and Wendy Collins Perdue

Civil Procedure for Federal and State Courts
Jeffrey A. Parness

Clinical Anthology: Readings for Live-Client Clinics
Alex J. Hurder, Frank S. Bloch, Susan L. Brooks, and Susan L. Kay

Clinical Legal Education–A Textbook for Law School Clinical Programs
David F. Chavkin

Communications Law: Media, Entertainment, and Regulation
Donald E. Lively, Allen S. Hammond, Blake D. Morant, and Russell L. Weaver

A Conflict-of-Laws Anthology
Gene R. Shreve

Constitutional Conflicts
Derrick A. Bell, Jr.

A Constitutional Law Anthology, *Second Edition*
Michael J. Glennon, Donald E. Lively, Phoebe A. Haddon, Dorothy E. Roberts, and Russell L. Weaver

Constitutional Law: Cases, History, and Dialogues, *Second Edition*
Donald E. Lively, Phoebe A. Haddon, Dorothy E. Roberts, Russell L. Weaver, and William D. Araiza

The Constitutional Law of the European Union
James D. Dinnage and John F. Murphy

The Constitutional Law of the European Union: Documentary Supplement
James D. Dinnage and John F. Murphy

Constitutional Torts
Sheldon H. Nahmod, Michael L. Wells, and Thomas A. Eaton

A Contracts Anthology, *Second Edition*
Peter Linzer

Contract Law and Practice
Gerald E. Berendt, Michael L. Closen, Doris Estelle Long, Marie A. Monahan, Robert J. Nye, and John H. Scheid

Contracts: Contemporary Cases, Comments, and Problems
Michael L. Closen, Richard M. Perlmutter, and Jeffrey D. Wittenberg

A Copyright Anthology: The Technology Frontier
Richard H. Chused

Corporate Law Anthology
Franklin A. Gevurtz

Corporate and White Collar Crime: An Anthology
Leonard Orland

Criminal Law: Cases and Materials, *Second Edition*
Arnold H. Loewy

Federal and State Civil Procedure Handbook, *Second Edition*
Jeffrey A. Parness

Federal Wealth Transfer Tax Anthology
Paul L. Caron, Grayson M.P. McCouch, Karen C. Burke

First Amendment Anthology
Donald E. Lively, Dorothy E. Roberts, and Russell L. Weaver

First Amendment Law: Cases, Comparative Perspectives, and Dialogues
Donald E. Lively, William D. Araiza, Phoebe A. Haddon, John C. Knechtle, and
    Dorothy E. Roberts

The History, Philosophy, and Structure of the American Constitution
Douglas W. Kmiec and Stephen B. Presser

Individual Rights and the American Constitution
Douglas W. Kmiec and Stephen B. Presser

International Human Rights: Law, Policy, and Process, *Third Edition*
David Weissbrodt, Joan Fitzpatrick, and Frank Newman

Selected International Human Rights Instruments and
    Bibliography for Research on International Human Rights Law, *Third Edition*
David Weissbrodt, Joan Fitzpatrick, Frank Newman, Marci Hoffman, and Mary Rumsey

International Intellectual Property Anthology
Anthony D'Amato and Doris Estelle Long

International Law Anthology
Anthony D'Amato

International Taxation: Cases, Materials, and Problems
Philip F. Postlewaite

Introduction to the Study of Law: Cases and Materials, *Second Edition*
John Makdisi

Judicial Externships: The Clinic Inside the Courthouse, *Second Edition*
Rebecca A. Cochran

A Land Use Anthology
Jon W. Bruce

Law and Economics Anthology
Kenneth G. Dau-Schmidt and Thomas S. Ulen

The Law of Disability Discrimination, *Third Edition*
Ruth Colker and Bonnie Poitras Tucker

The Law of Disability Discrimination Handbook:
    Statutes and Regulatory Guidance, *Third Edition*
Ruth Colker and Bonnie Poitras Tucker

The Lawyer's Craft: An Introduction to Legal Analysis, Writing, Research, and Advocacy
Cathy Glaser, Jethro K. Lieberman, Robert A. Ruescher, and Lynn Boepple Su

Lawyers and Fundamental Moral Responsibility
Daniel R. Coquillette

Mediation and Negotiation: Reaching Agreement in Law and Business
E. Wendy Trachte-Huber and Stephen K. Huber

Microeconomic Predicates to Law and Economics
Mark Seidenfeld

Natural Resources: Cases and Materials
Barlow Burke

Negotiable Instruments Under the UCC and the CIBN
Louis F. Del Duca, Egon Guttman, and Alphonse M. Squillante

Patients, Psychiatrists and Lawyers: Law and the Mental Health System, *Second Edition*
Raymond L. Spring, Roy B. Lacoursiere, and Glen Weissenberger

Preventive Law: Materials on a Non Adversarial Legal Process
Robert M. Hardaway

Principles of Evidence, *Fourth Edition*
Irving Younger, Michael Goldsmith, and David A. Sonenshein

Problems and Simulations in Evidence, *Second Edition*
Thomas F. Guernsey

A Products Liability Anthology
Anita Bernstein

Professional Responsibility Anthology
Thomas B. Metzloff

A Property Anthology, *Second Edition*
Richard H. Chused

Property Law: Cases, Materials, and Questions
Edward E. Chase

Public Choice and Public Law: Readings and Commentary
Maxwell L. Stearns

The Question Presented: Model Appellate Briefs
Maria L. Ciampi and William H. Manz

Readings in Criminal Law
Russell L. Weaver, John M. Burkoff, Catherine Hancock, Alan Reed, and Peter J. Seago

Sales Under the Uniform Commercial Code and the CISG
Louis F. Del Duca, Egon Guttman, and Alphonse M. Squillante

Science in Evidence
D.H. Kaye

A Section 1983 Civil Rights Anthology
Sheldon H. Nahmod

Secured Transactions Under the Uniform Commercial Code and International Commerce
Louis F. Del Duca, Egon Guttman, Frederick H. Miller, Peter Winship, and William H. Henning

Sports Law: Cases and Materials, *Fourth Edition*
Ray Yasser, James R. McCurdy, C. Peter Goplerud, and Maureen A. Weston

State and Local Government Law: A Transactional Approach
John Martinez and Michael E. Libonati

A Torts Anthology, *Second Edition*
Julie A. Davies, Lawrence C. Levine, and Edward J. Kionka

Torts: Cases, Problems, and Exercises
Russell L. Weaver, John H. Bauman, John T. Cross, Andrew R. Klein, Edward C. Martin, and Paul J. Zwier

Trial Practice
Lawrence A. Dubin and Thomas F. Guernsey

Understanding Negotiation
Melissa L. Nelken

Unincorporated Business Entities, *Second Edition*
Larry E. Ribstein

FORTHCOMING PUBLICATIONS

Administrative Law: Cases and Materials, *Second Edition*
Daniel J. Gifford

The American Constitutional Order: History, Cases, and Philosophy, *Second Edition*
Douglas W. Kmiec, Stephen B. Presser, and John C. Eastman

Bankruptcy Law: Principles, Policies, and Practice
Charles J. Tabb and Ralph Brubaker

Cases and Materials on Comparative Military Justice
Eugene R. Fidell, Michael F. Noone, and Elizabeth Lutes Hillman

Cases and Materials on the Law Governing Lawyers, *Second Edition*
James E. Moliterno

Conflict of Laws: Cases and Materials
Gene R. Shreve and Hannah L. Buxbaum

Constitutional Torts, *Second Edition*
Sheldon H. Nahmod, Michael L. Wells, and Thomas A. Eaton

Elder Law: Readings, Cases, and Materials, *Second Edition*
A. Kimberley Dayton, Thomas P. Gallanis, and Molly M. Wood

Elder Law: Statutes and Regulations, *Second Edition*
A. Kimberley Dayton, Thomas P. Gallanis, and Molly M. Wood

Judicial Externships: The Clinic Inside the Courthouse, *Third Edition*
Rebecca A. Cochran

The Law of Disability Discrimination, *Fourth Edition*
Ruth Colker, Bonnie Poitras Tucker, and Adam A. Milani

The Law of Disability Discrimination Handbook: Statutes and Regulatory Guidance,
    Fourth Edition
Ruth Colker, Bonnie Poitras Tucker, and Adam A. Milani

The Law and Ethics of Human Subject Research
Nancy N. Dubler, Carl H. Coleman, Jesse A. Goldner, and Jerry A. Menikoff

Negotiable Instruments: Problems and Materials
Wayne K. Lewis and Steven H. Resnicoff

Property: Cases, Documents, and Lawyering Skills
David Crump, David S. Caudill, and David Hricik

Sales Under the Uniform Commercial Code and the Convention on International Sale of Goods
Louis F. Del Duca, Egon Guttman, Frederick H. Miller, and Peter Winship

Securities Law and Practice: Cases, Problems, and Exercises
Russell L. Weaver, Douglas M. Branson, and Manning G. Warren, III

Sexual Orientation and the Law
Donald H.J. Hermann

Sports Law: Cases and Materials, *Fifth Edition*
Ray Yasser, James R. McCurdy, C. Peter Goplerud, and Maureen A. Weston

Taxation: Law, Planning, and Policy
Michael A. Livingston

BUSINESS ASSOCIATIONS
FOURTH EDITION

BUSINESS ASSOCIATIONS
FOURTH EDITION

LARRY E. RIBSTEIN
Richard & Marie Corman Professor of Law
University of Illinois College of Law

PETER V. LETSOU
Van Winkle Melton Professor of Law
Director, Law and Business Program
Willamette University College of Law

ANDERSON PUBLISHING CO.
CINCINNATI, OHIO

BUSINESS ASSOCIATIONS, FOURTH EDITION
LARRY E. RIBSTEIN AND PETER V. LETSOU

Anderson Publishing Co.
2035 Reading Road / Cincinnati, Ohio 45202
800-582-7295 / e-mail lawschool@andersonpublishing.com / Fax 513-562-5430
www.andersonpublishing.com

ISBN 1-58360-791-9

To Ann, Sarah and Susannah

and

To Felicity, William, Christina and Theodore

Table of Contents

Preface to Fourth Edition:
For Students and Teachers

In writing this fourth edition, we have followed the basic philosophy of the first three versions: to provide a comprehensive teaching tool that brings together the many disparate threads essential to a complete understanding of the law of business associations. Like the first three editions, this book is suitable for survey courses of any length up to six semester hours. The accompanying teacher's manual suggests ways to adapt the book to courses of less than six semester hours.

The following is a description of the important features of the fourth edition.

[1] Economics and Business Associations as a Contract

The fourth edition retains earlier editions' focus on business associations as a form of private contract. The focus is evident from the beginning, with Chapter 1 providing an introduction to the basic economic concepts that are relevant to contracting through business associations.

This focus is a natural outgrowth of the book's guiding principle of keeping the law of business associations in its "real world" context. An important part of this real world context is the developing study by economists and lawyers of why business associations are organized the way they are. Economists' theories have become more sophisticated and are now supported by extensive empirical evidence. Meanwhile, judges, lawyers and regulators have become more and more familiar with, and willing to use, economic analysis. As a result of these developments, complete preparation for entering law practice in the 21st century requires some familiarity with the economic theory of business associations.

Indeed, for the vast majority of business associations teachers, the question is not whether to teach economics, but how much economics to teach. Teachers usually ask students to evaluate as well as to understand legal rules. This evaluation usually entails a cost-benefit analysis. Economists' learning, which is informed by precise modeling and empirical verification, gives body to such a discussion. For example, it is impossible to evaluate, or even fully understand, the courts' "hands off" approach embodied in the business judgment rule without understanding agency costs, alternative devices for minimizing agency costs, and the tradeoffs inherent in selecting among these devices.

How much economics one brings into the course is obviously a close judgment call. We have tried to include all that we think law students can feasibly absorb in an introductory course. This edition continues work begun in the third edition of simplifying the presentation of this material.

The contract theory of business associations and the primacy of economic analysis are not universally accepted. We have tried to present a balanced view of the counterarguments in order to spur informed debate. But this book does present a point of view. There are strong pedagogical reasons for it to do so. First by bringing our views into the open, we do not risk shrouding them in false "objectivity." Second, we have provided students and teachers who disagree with the contractarian perspective a target at which they can shoot. In fact, we think this book will be more fun for those who disagree with the contractarian approach than for those who agree with it.

[2] Organization

The basic organization of the third edition has largely been retained. Accordingly, the fourth edition begins by considering issues that arise in the formation of business associations (Chapters 2 and 3); then proceeds to a discussion of topics connected with the operation of the firm, such as governance arrangements (Chapters 4, 5, 6 and 7); the authority of management (Chapter 8); fiduciary duties (Chapter 9); shareholder litigation (Chapter 10); distributions to owners (Chapter 11); and the sale and trading of ownership interests (Chapter 12); and concludes with a consideration of business acquisitions and combinations (Chapters 13-15).

We have adopted this issue-by-issue organizational approach, instead of completely segregating the discussions of different types of business associations, because it fits particularly well with the emphasis on the business association as a contract. "Standard forms," such as partnerships, corporations, and limited liability companies, should be viewed not as abstract and immutable sets of rules, but as alternative responses to underlying real-world contracting problems.

Like the third edition, the fourth edition departs to some extent from issue-by-issue presentation by dividing into separate chapters focusing on corporations and partnerships the materials dealing with the formation of business associations (see Chapters 2 and 3) and the materials on the governance of closely held businesses (see Chapters 4 and 5). These changes should reduce any student confusion that may have resulted from treating corporations and partnerships together in the same chapters.

The main organizational changes from the third edition are a significant shortening of the materials on federal securities regulation and some reordering of the materials on business acquisitions. Much of prior Chapter 12 dealing with regulation of the issuance of securities under the Securities Act of 1933, has been replaced by a summary at the beginning of Chapter 12, with the rest of the Chapter focusing on insider trading. We think this better aligns the book with the likely coverage of securities regulation in the basic course as distinguished from a separate securities regulation course. The reorganized chapters on business acquisitions clarify, simplify and shorten coverage after decades of significant takeover law. Chapter 13 now presents an overview of the area, Chapter 14 covers takeover defenses, and Chapter 15 covers mergers and acquisitions.

[3] Principles of Corporate Finance

In keeping with the book's coverage of economics, principles of corporate finance are summarized in Section 7.01. This is a shorter and simpler version of what was formerly the Finance Appendix. This approach better integrates the finance materials into the book. The materials have been inserted at the point at which most teachers are likely to cover them—that is, the beginning of coverage of publicly held firms. Of course, professors may continue to bring the material into the course at any time they deem appropriate or assign Section 7.01 as background reading.

[4] Cases

This fourth edition, like the first three, includes cases that provide recent examples of the law at work in modern business contexts and particularly good analyses of legal issues. The facts of these cases continue to be important in understanding and evaluating the law. Thus, we have tried not to edit out key facts, and have sometimes supplemented the facts with notes on the factual backgrounds. However, consistent with our general approach in this edition, some cases have been shortened or placed into notes. As in the prior editions, we have omitted some footnotes, and renumbered the remaining footnotes as in the original.

[5] Notes and Questions

Notes and questions are placed immediately following the principal cases. Some notes and questions are intended to bring out or elaborate important elements of the individual cases, thus providing a sort of roadmap that enhances students' understanding and ability to discuss long and complex opinions. Others are prepared on the assumption that teachers and students will want to do more than technically analyze principal cases. Notes and questions of this type summarize corporate statutes and cases on the larger legal issues in the course and often include economics, tax, and business materials.

The notes and questions are almost entirely our own, not excerpts from the writings of others. Excerpts have the virtue of presenting contrasting views, which encourages the students to think critically rather than accept the notes as "black letter." But the explosion of law and theory over the past few years has necessitated a clearer and more economical form of exposition. Excerpts rarely confine themselves to those points for which they are being excerpted, and so are usually longer than they need to be to make the relevant point. Also, excerpts from scholarly articles are often written for an advanced audience or omit necessary definitions and explanations. The "black letter" problem is offset to some extent through bibliographical references.

As in the third edition, we use short, numbered notes, with the issue covered in each note identified in boldface. This should make the text easier to follow.

[6] References

References for further student reading are now gathered together at the end of the particular sections and subsections. The appearance in the text of an author's name in boldface indicates that the work is listed in the immediately following Reference section.

[7] Problems

The fourth edition, like all previous editions, includes problems that provide a real-world context for applying both law and policy. Some of the problems have been updated and some others are new in this edition.

[8] Supplemental Materials

There is no statutory supplement designed for this book. Teachers have significant choice of comprehensive stand-alone supplements.

Table of Cases

xxxix

CHAPTER 1

Introduction

§ 1.01 Legal and Economic Views of Business Associations

A business association is a set of contracts among owners, creditors, executives, and workers. Economists often refer to the business association as a "firm" or "nexus of contracts." They loosely distinguish business associations from other types of contracts that accomplish similar purposes, such as long-term supply contracts, franchise agreements, and leases.

Courts and legislators have identified particular types of business associations to which they apply different sets of legal rules. These include sole proprietorships, general and limited partnerships, corporations, limited liability companies and partnerships, joint stock companies, joint ventures, business trusts, and professional associations. Economists, however, usually pay little attention to legal distinctions among types of business associations.

This Chapter discusses both the legal and economic views of business associations. It begins with the economic view in order to provide insight into the forces that have actually shaped business organizations. The Chapter then discusses the role legal rules can play in governing these contracts.

§ 1.02 Economic Theory and Business Associations

This Section summarizes some economic theories about why parties to business relationships select particular types of firms or other types of contracts that accomplish similar purposes. (For purposes of the following discussion, a "firm" is a contract for a hierarchical relationship in which certain people have control over resources contributed by others.) In general, these theories focus on the various kinds of costs that the parties try to minimize in organizing their business. In addition to these theories, basic concepts of corporate finance are very important to the study of business, including risk, return, portfolio diversification, and markets. These concepts will be discussed below in Section 7.01 in connection with publicly held firms, where they are particularly significant.

The parties to business transactions choose the form of contract that minimizes the total of costs in the parties' particular business, including the types of costs discussed in this Section. The choice is not limited to the different types of business associations that are considered in this book, but may also include different forms of long-term contracts, such as franchise agreements.

1

[A] Coase and Transaction Costs

Ronald Coase,[1] in his seminal 1937 article, *The Nature of the Firm*, discussed why goods are produced by "firms." Consider, for example, two ways to make a widget that consists of a bulb and two knobs: (1) A buys bulbs and sells them to B, who buys and affixes knobs and then sells the enhanced products to C, who buys and affixes second knobs and sells the completed widgets to consumers; or (2) A buys the bulbs and knobs, hires B and C as employees and has them affix the knobs to the bulbs, and then sells the completed widgets. Coase explained that it may be less costly to have somebody giving orders in a single firm (alternative 2) than to determine prices and negotiate the terms of repeated transactions (alternative 1). Indeed, pricing may be particularly difficult where, as is probably the case in this example, there is no developed market for the interim bulb with only one knob. These costs of entering into multiple transactions help explain the decision to organize firms.

Although Coase did not note the point, the explanatory power of his theory is not limited to the formation of firms. Parties to a business relationship could also avoid the costs of repeated contracts by negotiating a single long-term contract that provides in advance for prices and quantities. Thus, Coase's theory also suggests a purpose for the formation of other types of contractual relationships.

As is clear from the remainder of this Section, economists have not been entirely satisfied with Coase's explanation for firms. One problem with Coase's theory is that it fails to explain why parties would elect to form hierarchical or firm-type arrangements instead of entering into other types of contracts. Nonetheless, Coase started economists asking similar types of questions about the form of transactions.

[B] Shirking

A second concern that can influence parties' contracting choices is the problem of shirking. Shirking is a problem in situations involving "team production"—that is, where two or more people combine their resources to produce more than they could by working separately. Because the products of team production inherently result from joint rather than individual contributions, it is hard to measure each party's contribution to what they jointly produce. Some team members might try to contribute less effort or lower-quality resources in the hope that the others will pick up the slack. If the shirkers cannot be fully penalized for their shirking, they will come out ahead. But as a result of the group's inability to cooperate fully, its joint profit will decline.

For example, suppose five people—A, B, C, D and E—form a team to load the contents of a house onto a moving truck. The team is paid $100, which they divide equally. If they work hard, the team can move four houses in a working day for $400.

---

[1]   The appearance in the text or a footnote of an author's name in boldface type indicates the discussion of a work cited in the immediately following References section.

Now suppose A decides to slack off. If the others pick up the slack by lifting more or moving faster, the group's compensation will remain the same, but each other member's profit—that is, the difference between the member's compensation and the value of the member's effort —declines. If the other members also slack off, the group will do fewer moves and make less money.

As economists **Alchian & Demsetz** pointed out, one way that the group can reduce shirking is by hiring a "monitor" to observe the parties' effort and mete out rewards and punishments. But shirking by the monitor may be as hard to detect as shirking by the other team members. The members can reduce shirking by the monitor by giving the monitor a right to share in the profit left after subtracting payments to the team members, such as wages and interest. The more effort the monitor gets from the same resources, the higher the monitor's reward.

To translate these principles to a conventional business association, the "monitor" in a corporation or partnership is the common shareholders or partners who, in exchange for a right to the profits, oversee the contributions of team members, either directly or through hired managers, and adjust the latter's compensation and job tenure accordingly.

A second way that the members of the group can reduce shirking is by formally binding themselves together by contract. This contract can be quite detailed, specifying with precision the way in which each worker is to perform his or her job. In addition, the contract could provide for an automatic reduction in compensation for those workers who fail to live up to the specified standards.

Because effort is difficult to observe and contracts are costly to write, neither monitoring nor contracting will completely eliminate shirking.

[C] Bounded Rationality

Another factor that might influence the parties' contract form is the difficulty of planning for all possible contingencies. When contracting is difficult due to the inability to foresee and plan for contingencies, contracting parties may provide for a way to deal with contingencies as they arise by establishing a decision-making device such as voting by owners, allocating the power to decide to an executive or board of directors, or letting courts fill the blanks with fiduciary duty and good faith rules. This is the principle of "bounded rationality"—we know what we don't know and plan accordingly.

[D] Agency Costs

Many organizational devices, including firms, involve the creation of agency relationships—*i.e.*, relationships where one party (the "principal") delegates authority to another (the "agent"). ("Principal" and "agent" are used here to refer to any delegation of power, rather than only to the particular relationship governed by the law of agency.)

With the establishment of an agency relationship comes the potential for the sort of abuse that is referred to in the economics literature as "agency costs." Agency costs generally refer to the costs imposed on the principal when an agent with discretionary authority takes actions to help himself rather than the principal. Shirking by agents is one example of an agency cost.

The principal can try to reduce these costs by monitoring the agent. Alternatively, the principal may require that the agent give some sort of "bond." A "bond" in the economic sense is, like the cash posted by a criminal defendant, any kind of asset that can be lost if the one who posted the bond misbehaves. It can even include intangibles such as the agent's investment in developing a reputation for honesty. In general, therefore, agency costs include (1) monitoring costs; (2) bonding costs; and (3) residual losses imposed by agents on principals because of the agent's incentive to act contrary to the principal's interest, despite monitoring and bonding.[2]

[E] Opportunism

Even if contracting parties can spell out their arrangement in a non-firm-type long-term contract, they might still need to deal with the parties' inclination to seize advantages that are permitted by the literal terms of the contract, or to breach or threaten to breach the contract and take advantage of a slow legal system or weak damage remedies. Lawyers and economists sometimes refer to this natural human inclination as "opportunism," or the propensity to seize on the opportunity for gain.

Suppose, for example, that A, who owns a daily newspaper with a large daily circulation, regularly engages B, who owns a large press, to print the newspaper. Now suppose that B finds somebody who is willing to pay more than A for printing. B tells A, shortly before a deadline, that he wants more money to print A's newspaper. A may have to accede because there is no other press that can suddenly handle A's job. In other words, B can "hold up" A by demanding a share of the extra value that A's newspaper has if A has immediate access to B's press.

One solution to A's problem is for A to enter into a long-term contract with B, providing that B will print A's daily newspaper in a timely fashion. That agreement may further provide for penalties should B fail to perform. Contractual remedies, however, may be an imperfect solution to the problems of opportunistic behavior by B. This is because A cannot fully counter B's threat not to perform by litigating. Among other things, B's breach may not be clear: A might have breached by delaying payment of bills, or B might have some colorable excuse for not performing on time.

Another solution to the problem inherent in the A-B situation is for A to own its own press rather than contracting with the owner of a press. In fact, we observe that most daily newspapers do own their own presses. On the other hand, book publishers often do not own their own presses. Can you account for the difference?

---

[2] *See* **Jensen & Meckling**.

[F] Risk Bearing Costs

Finance theory assumes that people are "risk averse" and therefore must be paid to accept risk. "Risk" refers to the "variance" of possible outcomes from an investment or other endeavor. People can reduce risk (*i.e.,* make investment outcomes more predictable) by holding diversified portfolios of assets. Some organizational forms facilitate diversification of assets better than others. For example, personal liability for debts of the firm makes it difficult for owners to diversify (*see* Section 3.03[B]). The parties to a firm may therefore take this increased cost of risk into account in determining whether to adopt an organizational form that imposes this personal liability on owners. Also, it is obviously easier to diversify a portfolio that consists of a relatively large number of small investments than of a relatively small number of large ones; thus, size of required investment may also influence choices regarding organizational form.

REFERENCES

Alchian & Demsetz, *Production, Information Costs, and Economic Organization*, 62 AM. ECON. REV. 777 (1972).

Coase, *The Nature of the Firm*, 4 ECONOMICA 386 (1937), *reprinted in* THE NATURE OF THE FIRM: ORIGINS, EVOLUTION, AND DEVELOPMENT (O. Williamson & S. Winter, eds. 1991).

Jensen & Meckling, *Theory of the Firm: Managerial Behavior, Agency Costs and Ownership Structure*, 3 J. FIN. ECON. 305 (1976).

Klein, *The Modern Business Organization: Bargaining Under Constraints*, 91 YALE L.J. 1521 (1982).

Klein, *Fisher-General Motors and the Nature of the Firm,* 43 J.L. & ECON. 105 (2000).

Klein, Crawford & Alchian, *Vertical Integration, Appropriable Rents, and the Competitive Contracting Process,* 21 J.L. & ECON. 297 (1978).

Simon, *A Behavioral Model of Rational Choice*, 69 Q.J. ECON. 99 (1955).

Williamson, MARKETS AND HIERARCHIES: ANALYSIS AND ANTITRUST IMPLICATIONS 26-30 (1975).

§ 1.03 Types of Business Associations

This subsection briefly reviews the outlines of the most popular forms of business associations and discusses how these business forms provide alternative contractual solutions to the contracting problems inherent in particular types of businesses.

[A] Sole Proprietorship

In this type of firm, there is only one owner, or residual claimant, who has the exclusive claim to the profits of the business. She is the sole monitor of the other team members and has the power to buy and sell assets and to hire and fire workers. The sole proprietor is also personally liable for all debts of the business.

[B] General Partnership

A general partnership has two or more residual claimants who share the monitoring role. Like sole proprietors, partners are personally liable for the debts of the business. The differences between the sole proprietorship and the general partnership arise primarily from the fact of multiple owners. The owners must agree in advance how to make decisions in the future and how to share the profits and other assets of the business. Because the owners are generally actively involved in the business and liable for its debts, they would usually want to participate in management and have the power to veto important decisions, such as the admission of new partners. They would also want rules specifying the consequences of each party's withdrawing from (that is, dissolving) the relationship.

Why would two or more resource owners choose the general partnership form over, say, one or more sole proprietorships? Consider, for example, two people going into the restaurant business, one with funds and the other with culinary skills. The chef could own the restaurant as a sole proprietorship, with the other party loaning the money, or the capital-contributor could form a sole proprietorship and hire the chef as a salaried employee, or the two could form a partnership. What combination of circumstances would lead to each of these results? If the chef's skills are important to the relationship and the chef quits, the capital contributor's investment in the other assets may be substantially devalued. The chef may exploit this by demanding renegotiation of his contract backed by a threat to quit. The capital contributor therefore may want to tie the chef to the business by, for example, giving the chef an equity interest coupled with liability for debts and penalizing the chef's withdrawal from the business. In effect, the chef's equity investment serves as a kind of bond to ensure the continued contribution of his skills.

General partnerships are governed in virtually every state by the Uniform Partnership Act (UPA), which was completed in 1914, or the Revised Uniform Partnership Act (RUPA), which was completed in 1993 and revised in 1997. Both statutes were drafted by the National Conference of Commissions on Uniform State Laws (NCCUSL). General partnerships historically have been considered "aggregates," as distinguished from separate "entities," because rights, duties and liabilities connected with the business belong to individual partners and not to any separate legal person. Important "aggregate" features of the general partnership traditionally have included (1) personal liability of partners for debts of the business, (2) at least nominal ownership by individual partners of partnership property, (3) technical dissolution of the partnership upon any change in membership, and (4) flow-through taxation, whereby partnership income is taxed directly to the individual partners, not to the partnership. But general partnerships also have "entity"-like features, including (1) the increasingly recognized power to sue or be sued in the partnership's name, (2) the right to hold and convey title to property in the partnership's name, and (3) the ability to provide for continuance of the partnership by contract even when the partnership technically dissolves because of a change in membership.

[C] Corporation

A corporation, like a partnership, generally has many residual claimants who contract to allocate control and profits. The standard-form corporation differs from partnership in that owners are passive and delegate to the corporation's managers the responsibility for day-to-day operations. Because owners are not actively involved in management, they are essentially "fungible" capital-providers and, therefore, shares in the business can be freely transfered. Passive ownership is facilitated by "limited liability," which means that the owners are not personally liable for the debts of the business. As noted earlier, personal liability can make it difficult for owners to diversify risk, thus decreasing the amount an owner would be willing to pay for a share in the business. The limited liability contract is effectuated by a public filing that informs all creditors that the business is incorporated, so that creditors dealing with the firm impliedly agree not to hold the owners personally liable.

Many corporations are governed by the Delaware General Corporation Law. Other states have adopted variations on the Model Business Corporation Act (MBCA), promulgated by a committee of the American Bar Association.

A corporation is a separate legal entity that—like a natural person—has its own rights, powers and liabilities, separate from those of the persons who own or manage it. As a legal person, a corporation can own and hold title to property, the corporation's continued existence is unaffected by changes in its shareholders, and the corporation, not its shareholders, is liable for the debts of the business. Because a corporation is a separate entity, its income is subject to taxation separately from that of the shareholders. This means that corporate income will generally be taxed twice—once when earned by the corporation and once when distributed to the shareholders.

Characterizing a corporation as a legal entity separate from its owners makes practical sense in many contexts. But just because some corporate features are best described as entity-type attributes, it does not necessarily follow that a corporation should be treated as an entity for all purposes. Nevertheless, the entity concept has often determined results.[3]

One example of the misuse of the entity concept relates to duties of corporate managers and corporate attorneys. It is often said that these parties owe duties to the "corporation." But what does this mean? Where duties are concerned, it is helpful to articulate to whom these duties are owed. Since the "corporation" embraces such disparate interests as creditors, employees, consumers, and warring factions of sharehold-

---

[3] *See, e.g., Braswell v. United States,* 487 U.S. 99 (1988) (sole shareholder of corporation denied the protection of his Fifth Amendment privilege against compelled self-incrimination by being ordered to produce business documents).

ers, to say that managers owe duties to the "corporation" tends to attenuate or nullify these duties.

[D] Close Corporation

Sometimes the corporate contract combines partnership-type owner-management with corporate-type limited liability. This type of arrangement is called a "close corporation" because the membership is limited rather than open to all, as in a publicly held corporation with freely traded shares. Such corporations often include special shareholder agreements for allocating governance functions and controlling shirking. These agreements are designed to bring partnership-style management and governance to the corporate setting.

The main question regarding close corporations is why the parties to such a business would choose limited liability, which facilitates passive ownership, when all the owners are active in the firm's affairs. Creditors will demand that the owners compensate them for the extra credit risk involved in insulating the owners from liability. Why might the owners be willing pay this extra credit cost without obtaining an important benefit of limited liability—passive ownership? The answer might be that the owners receive an important benefit for which they do not need to pay—limited liability to nonconsensual creditors, such as tort victims.

The close corporation form is subject to statutory and common law restrictions on contracting that are not found in the law of general partnership. The owners may be constrained in setting up governance arrangements (*see* Sections 5.02-.03), and may be personally liable for business debts, notwithstanding their nominal incorporation, if they do not adhere to certain corporate norms (*see* Section 3.05).

[E] Limited Partnership

Limited partnerships combine attributes of both partnerships and corporations. Some owners are general partners and, like general partners in general partnerships, contract for active involvement in management and personal liability. Other owners are limited partners, and generally contract for non-management monitoring status and limited liability. However, limited partners can sometimes lose their limited liability if they take too active a role in the firm's affairs.

Limited partnership is usually viewed as a way to combine partnership-type taxation with corporate-type organization (*see* Section 6.03). But it may make sense even apart from tax considerations. Among other things, placing personal liability on the managers can reduce credit costs by ensuring creditors that the business will be managed in their interests.

Limited partnerships are governed by the Uniform Limited Partnership Act which was first completed by the NCCUSL in 1916 and then revised in 1976, 1985 and 2001.

[F] Limited Liability Company

In a limited liability company, or "LLC," the owners have the limited liability of limited partners and corporate shareholders, the flexibility to take on the management powers of general partners without jeopardizing their limited liability, and the flow-through taxation of general and limited partnerships. Over the last few years, this new form of business association has emerged rapidly through statutes passed in every state. *See* Section 6.04.

[G] Limited Liability Partnership

The newest type of business association is the registered limited liability partnership, or "LLP." This is essentially a general partnership whose owners, by filing a registration and complying with other formalities, obtain full or partial limited liability, depending on the statute. *See* Section 6.05.

REFERENCES

Bromberg & Ribstein, BROMBERG AND RIBSTEIN ON PARTNERSHIP § 1.03.
Comment, *The Personification of the Business Corporation in American Law*, 54 U. CHI. L. REV. 1441 (1987).
Ribstein, *The Evolving Partnership,* 26 J. CORP. L. 819 (2001).
Ribstein, *An Applied Theory of Limited Partnership*, 37 EMORY L.J. 837 (1988).
Rosin, *The Entity-Aggregate Dispute: Conceptualism and Functionalism in Partnership Law,* 42 ARK. L. REV. 395 (1989).

§ 1.04 A Short History of Business Associations

The first business association recognizable today as such was the general partnership. The general partnership first developed under English law during the Middle Ages. The early mercantile courts applied the body of custom cumulatively known as the "law merchant." They also borrowed from two business forms that had been developed in continental Europe—the Societa, equivalent to the general partnership, and the Commenda, or Societe en Commendite, equivalent to the limited partnership. Parliament first sanctioned the mercantile courts by the Statute of the Staple in 1353. By the early seventeenth century, mercantile cases were being heard in the common law courts, but no coherent commercial law was developed until the latter part of the eighteenth century.

The corporate form of business developed in response to the increasing business need to assemble large amounts of capital. In particular, the limited liability generally associated with the corporate form facilitates passive ownership. Also, the more property the business owns and the more extensive its activities, the greater the need to simplify property transfers and litigation by providing that the firm's property be owned by a legal entity separate from the individual participants.

Some of these features could be found in a variety of noncorporate business forms that were developed in the eighteenth century. For instance, "joint stock companies" provided for the separation of ownership and control, transferable shares and continuity of life, and "business trusts" provided for separation of management and control together with limited liability of owners. But all of the business features sought for larger aggregations of capital—separation of ownership and control, a separate legal entity, and limited liability—could be found in various legal forms developed in the Middle Ages, such as municipalities, monopoly franchises (such as the East India Company), and the church institution known as the "corporation sole" by which church property was separated from individuals (such as bishops) who held church title.

These latter, entity-based legal forms became the models for the private corporation. An important aspect of using these legal forms as models for the private corporation is that the creation of all these forms required government permission. Thus, very early on, corporate status came to be viewed as something that must be conferred by permission of the state even if the status was not combined with a monopoly franchise or other special public power. Under the first corporation statutes, firms secured this permission by buying "special charters" from state legislatures.

The nature of corporate law in the early nineteenth century is best exemplified by *Trustees of Dartmouth College v. Woodward,*[4] in which the United States Supreme Court invalidated under the Contract Clause (Art. I, § 10 of the Constitution) a New Hampshire statute that altered the terms of a British crown charter granted to Dartmouth College. Although the Court held that the charter was a contract, entitled like other contracts to protection from impairment by the state, Justice Marshall also described the corporation as:

> . . . an artificial being, invisible, intangible, and existing only in contemplation of law. Being the mere creature of law, it possesses only those properties which the charter of its creation confers upon it, either expressly, or as incidental to its very existence. These are such as are supposed best calculated to effect the object for which it was created.[5]

The era of special charters and tight state control over incorporation began to break down with the first general incorporation law in Massachusetts in 1830. General incorporation laws permitted formation of corporations without special permission from the legislature. But general incorporation did not immediately replace special chartering. For many years, the states employed a dual incorporation system, under which more expansive powers were available only through special charters.

---

[4]   17 U.S. (4 Wheat.) 518 (1819).

[5]   *Id.* at 636.

During the mid-nineteenth century there were many pressures toward liberalizing incorporation laws. Corporations—particularly those involved in building railroads and canals—began expanding outward from their states of incorporation. The courts held that the law of the state of incorporation governed the "internal affairs" of such multistate corporations, and the Supreme Court held that states could not discriminate against corporations selling in interstate commerce.[6] As a result of these developments, corporations could choose their states of incorporation without regard to where their business was located. It was only a short step to states competing for franchise tax revenues and filing fees by offering flexible and permissive corporation laws.

The first modern general incorporation statute was adopted in New Jersey in 1875. Delaware entered the competition with an 1899 law based closely on New Jersey's. After New Jersey passed a state antitrust law in 1913 that was hostile to business, Delaware became the undisputed leader in the state competition for incorporation business. Although New Jersey quickly realized its mistake and repealed its 1913 antitrust law, it never regained its advantage.

History has left its mark on the modern law of corporations. The special chartering origins of corporation law established the principle that the corporation is a "mere creature of law" rather than a product of private contract. A century of general incorporation laws has eroded but not completely erased this principle. Examples of this erosion are the decline of the doctrine of *ultra vires* (*see* Section 8.04) and of limitations on the form of governance of close corporations (*see* Chapter 5). But the vestiges of the special chartering era remain. A striking reminder is the recent decision in *CTS Corp. v. Dynamics Corp. of America*,[7] in which the Supreme Court quoted the 168-year-old Dartmouth College characterization of the corporation as a "mere creature of law" in support of state power to pass anti-takeover statutes.

REFERENCES

Bromberg & Ribstein, BROMBERG AND RIBSTEIN ON PARTNERSHIP, § 1.02.

Butler, *Nineteenth Century Jurisdictional Competition in the Granting of Corporate Privileges*, 14 J. LEG. STUD. 129 (1985).

Grandy, *New Jersey Chartermongering, 1875-1929*, 49 J. ECON. HIST. 677 (1989).

Hessen, IN DEFENSE OF THE CORPORATION (1979).

Hurst, THE LEGITIMACY OF THE BUSINESS CORPORATION 1780-1970 (1970).

Shughart & Tollison, *Corporate Chartering: An Exploration in the Economics of Legal Change*, 23 ECON. ING. 585 (1985).

Sowards & Mofsky, *Factors Affecting the Development of Corporation Law*, 23 U. MIAMI L. REV. 476 (1969).

---

[6] *Paul v. Virginia*, 75 U.S. 168 (1869).

[7] 481 U.S. 69, 89 (1987).

§ 1.05 The Role of Law

Before beginning to cover the law of business associations, it would be helpful to take a broad look at the major currents of thought in this area. This Section reviews the role of law in connection with business associations and poses the question to which we will return repeatedly in this book: To what extent should the law of business associations be left to private contract, and to what extent should the law regulate the terms on which the parties enter into business associations?

[A] The Contractarian View

Under what will be referred to as the "contractarian" view, a business association is viewed simply as a nexus of contracts. Under this view, which is supported by the economic theory discussed in Section 1.02 and by the many different types of private arrangements that have arisen to minimize the costs of productive activity, the law plays two basic roles.

First, the law provides a mechanism for enforcing the parties' arrangements. However, the courts are not the only enforcement mechanism. Because resort to judicial enforcement can be slow and costly, the parties may choose to rely on other enforcement devices. Second, the law provides a way of determining the parties' contract terms. It is costly to haggle over details, and contracts are inevitably ambiguous and incomplete. The law can minimize these costs by providing standard terms (*i.e.*, "gap-fillers") that the parties can opt into or that apply unless the parties opt out.

Statutes such as the Uniform Partnership Act, the Uniform Limited Partnership Act, the Delaware General Corporation Law and the Model Business Corporation Act can provide standard terms. In addition, standard terms can be provided by the common law, such as the law of agency and fiduciary duties.

The "gap-filling" function of the common law of corporations raises two important questions. First, when does a "gap" exist that needs to be filled? The courts can, in effect, provide quasi-mandatory terms by finding ambiguities in seemingly explicit contract provisions. Second, how should a court go about filling the gap? The approach most often discussed in the literature is to formulate a "hypothetical bargain" that informed parties would have entered into if they had contracted as to every detail. Keep in mind that, in formulating a "hypothetical bargain," the court is not determining an actual contract in the sense of terms upon which both parties agreed, but rather is establishing a rule that later parties may accept as part of their contract.

REFERENCE

Easterbrook & Fischel, THE ECONOMIC STRUCTURE OF CORPORATE LAW, Ch. 1 (1992).

[B] The Regulatory View

Under the opposing line of thinking, referred to here as the "regulatory" view, the law should dictate some of the terms of business associations. The regulatory view draws historical support from the corporation's origin as a state-conferred privilege, discussed above in Section 1.04. Although general incorporation under modern corporation statutes should have ended the "state creation" idea, this idea was heavily entrenched and dies hard. Among other things, the survival of the requirement of a state filing as a prerequisite of corporate organization preserves the appearance of state creation. However, that states have regulated the corporate form does not prove that they should do so.

There are several modern policy arguments for the regulatory view. First, government regulation is believed to be necessary to protect public corporation shareholders from terms to which they have not actually consented, and to rescue them from a position of weakness in the corporation. In a public corporation, the small holder of a few shares may appear to be a helpless cog in the great corporate apparatus. The shareholder rarely reads the contract terms to which she is subject, such as the corporate charter and bylaws. Even when terms are voted on, shareholders usually passively vote in accordance with management's recommendations, without paying attention to what is going on. The most important early expression of this view was by **Berle** and **Means** in their landmark 1932 book, THE MODERN CORPORATION AND PRIVATE PROPERTY. Berle & Means voiced concern about the separation of passive ownership and active control inherent in the structure of the public corporation. They believed that this left the managers effectively in control of property they did not own, and therefore without incentives to efficiently use the property.

A second argument for the regulatory view is that shareholders' contracts should not be enforced because of the need to protect the interests of non-shareholders who are affected by the firm. Some non-shareholders also contract with the firm, and all claimants contract in view of the contracts of others. But corporate managers might ignore some costs incurred by non-contracting parties, such as pollution, and by weak contracting parties, such as consumers. This "externalization" of costs may cause a misallocation of resources, with results such as more pollution than is socially optimal.

Third, regulation of contracts has been based on the inherent incompleteness of all corporate contracts, including those entered into by parties who are able to protect themselves. The parties cannot foresee and contract against every contingency that might occur over the very long term of the typical partnership or corporate arrangement. It is often difficult to categorize judicial intervention on this ground as contractarian or regulatory. The court may be imposing a mandatory duty, or it may simply be applying an expansive reading of the contract to include broad standard form duties in the absence of explicit contractual nullification of those duties.

An important extension of the regulatory view is a general distrust of state corporation law, most famously expressed in **Cary**. Professor Cary argued that Delaware had become the state of incorporation of a large percentage of the country's major corporations by fashioning rules that appeal to corporate managers, who effectively make the decision where to incorporate. Cary called this competition a "race for the bottom," referring to the quality of corporate duties that results from the competition. Cary's theory is obviously based on the helpless passivity of public corporation shareholders that underlies the regulatory position.

Because of its view of the effect of competition among the states, it is not surprising that the regulatory view is consistent with a strong federal law of business associations. One approach to federal regulation of business associations is to require minimum federal standards for corporate charters, enforced through the mechanism of federal chartering of corporations, as advocated by Professor Cary. Although the idea of federal chartering enjoyed considerable vogue in the early 1970s, there does not now appear to be strong support for the idea.

Another route to federal control of business associations is through the federal securities laws. These statutes were adopted beginning in 1933, spurred by the stock market crash of 1929. The Berle-Means theory discussed above formed a significant intellectual underpinning of the securities laws. The federal securities laws will be discussed in detail in Chapters 7 and 12 below. These laws do not purport to regulate corporate governance beyond requiring disclosure. However, during the late 1960s and early 1970s the federal courts began using the federal securities laws to broadly regulate internal corporate governance. This trend was nipped by the Supreme Court, most notably in *Santa Fe Industries, Inc. v. Green*.[8]

The contractarian answer to the regulatory view emphasizes the sophistication and variety of market and contract devices. Perhaps the most important of these is the efficient capital market hypothesis (EMH). EMH states that relevant information is quickly and accurately reflected in the prices of capital assets, including corporate securities. Market efficiency helps ensure that the costs of contracting in business associations are reflected in market prices, so that even passive, ignorant investors get what they pay for. Efficient capital markets also provide a contractarian answer to the Cary critique of Delaware law. If Delaware law is, indeed, less efficient than that of other states, the price of the stock of Delaware corporations will fall relative to comparable companies incorporated elsewhere, reducing the capital that can be attracted by these companies and making their managers more vulnerable to takeover. Thus, even if, as Professor Cary argues, Delaware competes for chartering business, it cannot win this competition by offering contracts that are unfavorable to investors.

We will return to a discussion of the arguments for and against the regulatory view throughout this book. In particular, the separation of ownership and control and the "race to the bottom" are discussed further in Section 7.02, and market discipline of corporate contract terms is discussed in Section 9.09.

An important modern arena for the contractarian-regulatory debate is the American Law Institute's *Principles of Corporate Governance: Analysis and Recommenda-*

---

[8]   430 U.S. 462 (1977).

*tion*s. Although the ALI *Principles* do not have the force of law, they may affect state legislation and judicial decisions.

QUESTION

The state of X has decided to eliminate all of its statutes dealing with corporations, limited partnerships, limited liability companies, general partnerships and other business associations and to replace them with a statute that provides: "A contract among the parties to a business association shall be enforceable according to its terms." Evaluate this approach.

REFERENCES

Berle & Means, THE MODERN CORPORATION AND PRIVATE PROPERTY (1932).

Black, *Is Corporate Law Trivial?: A Political and Economic Analysis*, 84 Nw. U. L. REV. 542 (1990).

Bratton, *The New Economic Theory of the Firm: Critical Perspectives From History*, 41 STAN. L. REV. 1471 (1989).

Butler & Ribstein, *Opting Out of Fiduciary Duties: A Response to the Anti-Contractarians*, 65 WASH. L. REV. 1 (1990).

Cary, *Federalism and Corporate Law: Reflections upon Delaware*, 83 YALE L.J. 663 (1974).

Easterbrook & Fischel, THE ECONOMIC STRUCTURE OF CORPORATE LAW, Ch. 1 (1992).

CHAPTER 2

Agency and Partnership: Introduction and Formation

This Chapter introduces the basic business relationships of agency and partnership and shows how these informal relationships are created. One of the most important aspects of these relationships is that those who are legally principals and partners are liable for the acts of their agents and co-partners. This means that unless the creditors and proprietor or partners agree otherwise, in a sole proprietorship, the proprietor is liable for the acts of her employees, and in a partnership, the partnership and all the partners are liable for the acts of all the partners.

§ 2.01 Creation of Agency Relationship

An agency relationship exists in the law whenever one party (the agent) works for and under the direction of another (the principal). As in the economic concept of agency discussed in Chapter 1, an agent is one who has the power to control resources owned by the principal. The legal agent-principal relationship is, in a sense, the basic standard form contract in the business association, of which all other standard forms—including the sole proprietorship, the general and limited partnership, the corporation, and the limited liability company and partnership—are variations.

Agency is an informal relationship that can be created without filing certificates or writing agreements. Parties therefore might stumble accidentally into agency if a court later decides that the terms of their relationship fit the legal definition of agency.

To illustrate the potential breadth and unexpectedness of agency, consider the following example. Kathy has experience managing a gourmet food store and wants to go into business for herself. This type of business requires inputs other than Kathy's skills, including capital for inventory, equipment and space, and the services of additional employees. Judy owns a building that would be an ideal location for the business, and is willing to invest money in the business, although she has no experience in the food business. Ray, a friend of Kathy's who also has experience in the food business, is interested in working in the store in a position of responsibility but has no money to invest.

What contracts should these people adopt? Kathy could form a sole proprietorship by renting space in Judy's building, borrowing Judy's money, and hiring Ray as an employee. In this hypothetical, Ray would be Kathy's agent, so that Kathy would be liable to third parties for Ray's acts within the scope of the agency. Based on these facts alone, there would probably be no agency relationship between Kathy and Judy.

Suppose, however, that Judy wants a share of the profits and a say in management because of the risk she is taking in associating with a start-up business. Might this create an agency relationship between Judy, Kathy and Ray? Consider the following case.

NICHOLS v. ARTHUR MURRAY, INC.
California Court of Appeal
248 Cal. App. 2d 610, 56 Cal. Rptr. 728 (1967)

COUGHLIN, J.:

Defendant appeals from a judgment awarding plaintiff the amount prepaid by the latter under contracts for dancing lessons which were not furnished.

Plaintiff had entered into five such contracts with "Arthur Murray School of Dancing" at San Diego, operated by Burkin, Inc., a corporation, under a franchise agreement with defendant Arthur Murray, Inc., a corporation.

Defendant Arthur Murray, Inc., was engaged in the business of licensing persons to operate dancing studios using its registered trade name "ARTHUR MURRAY" and the Arthur Murray method of dancing. The franchise agreement between defendant, therein referred to as Licensor, and Burkin, Inc., therein referred to as Licensee, conferred upon the latter a license "to use the 'ARTHUR MURRAY METHOD' and name in connection with a dancing school" to be conducted by it in San Diego.

The judgment herein is premised upon the conclusion defendant was the undisclosed principal in the transaction between plaintiff and the "Arthur Murray School of Dancing" in San Diego. An undisclosed principal is liable for the contractual obligations incurred by his agent in the course of the agency, even though the obligee did not know there was a principal at the time the obligations were incurred.

The issue on appeal is whether the evidence supports the conclusion, as found by the trial court, that Burkin, Inc., was the agent of defendant when the former executed the contracts for dancing lessons with plaintiff, and accepted the latter's prepayments on account of those contracts. Defendant contends Burkin, Inc., was only its licensee, and not its agent.

Whether the relationship between parties to a written agreement is that of principal and agent, at least insofar as this relationship affects a stranger to the agreement as in the case at bench, is dependent upon the intention of the parties determined from the writing and the accompanying circumstances.

* * *

In determining whether an agency relationship exists between parties to a business enterprise, which is the subject of an agreement between them, the right to control is an important factor. If, in practical effect, one of the parties has the right to exercise complete control over the operation by the other an agency relationship exists; the former is the principal and the latter the agent.

In the case at bench defendant depreciates the importance of the element of control, contending in a franchise agreement conferring the right to use a trade name controls are essential to the protection of the trade name; the controls provided by the instant agreement were for this purpose; the franchise holder was given some freedom of action; and, for these reasons, the court should have concluded the controls in question did not establish an agency relationship. . . .

In apparent response to this position, the trial court found:

> . . . the controls and rights to control retained by Arthur Murray, Inc. extended beyond those necessary to protect and maintain its trade mark, trade name and good will, and covered day to day details of the San Diego studio's operation.

* * *

The subject agreement, in substance, conferred upon defendant the right to control the employment of all employees of the franchise holder whether or not their duties related to teaching or supervising dancing instruction; to fix the minimum tuition rates to be charged; to select the financial institution handling, financing or discounting all pupil installment contracts; to designate the location of the studio, its layout and decoration; to make refunds to pupils and charge the amounts paid to the franchise holder; to settle and pay all claims against defendant arising out of the operation of the contemplated enterprise; to reimburse itself for the payment of any such refunds or claims, and the expense of any litigation in connection therewith, from a fund consisting of weekly payments by the franchise holder to defendant in an amount equal to 5% of the gross receipts; to invest the proceeds of this fund and pay the franchise holder only such portion of the income therefrom as defendant "shall determine should be properly allocated"; to control all advertising by the franchise holder, which was required to be submitted to defendant for approval prior to use; and to exercise a broad control over the operation of the enterprise under a provision requiring the franchise holder "to conduct the studio, to be maintained and managed by Licensee, in accordance with the general policies of the Licensor as established from time to time," and directing that failure to maintain such policies shall be sufficient cause for immediate cancellation of the agreement.

Other provisions evidencing the nature of the control vested in defendant were those requiring the franchise holder to honor unused lessons purchased by a pupil from another franchise holder at the rate of $2.50 per hour, and to pay that amount for unused lessons purchased from the former when furnished by the latter; also requiring the franchise holder to maintain records, and submit copies thereof weekly to defendant, setting forth the names and addresses of pupils enrolled during the week, the amounts paid by all pupils, number of lessons taken by each pupil, and the names of all pupils taking lessons; and further requiring the franchise holder to furnish defendant with duplicates of all social security and unemployment insurance reports, and all federal and state tax returns.

Many of the controls conferred were not related anywise to the protection of defendant's trade name, including its dancing and teaching methods, good will and business image. Other controls, although related to the protection of the trade name because the exercise thereof was not limited to effecting such purpose, enabled defendant to impose its will upon the franchise holder in areas wholly unrelated to that purpose.

Defendant directs attention to provisions in the agreement which it claims expressly declare the intention of the parties that no agency relationship is intended;[4] refers to the

---

[4]   There are two such provisions. One of them requires the licensee to post in the reception room of the studio a license certificate in the form prescribed by the licensor. The prescribed certificate states in part that the licensee is

established principle that agency is a consensual relationship; and contends these circumstances dictate the conclusion no agency was created by the subject agreement. This contention disregards the fact that the agreement, as such, was consensual; both parties consented to the provisions imposing controls; and the agency relationship was created by the legal effect of those provisions.

Defendant also emphasizes the importance of the franchise method of business to the economy; claims the decision of the trial court will destroy this type of business; deplores the plight of the independent small businessman who can operate only through franchise agreements; and urges a review of the interpretation placed upon the subject agreement in light of this situation. Our conclusion is that the controls imposed upon the franchise holder by defendant completely deprived the former of any independence in the business operation subject to the agreement.

The agreement provided, in substance, that Burkin, Inc., "shall solely be responsible" for all obligations incurred in the studio operation, and defendant "shall not be liable" for any thereof. Defendant asserts as a fact that by virtue of this provision it is not responsible for any obligation incurred by Burkin, Inc., and concludes this establishes the nonexistence of an agency relationship between them. However, the provision effected such non-responsibility only as between the parties to the agreement. . . .

Under the policy control provision of the subject agreement, defendant could have foreclosed the practice of executing multiple contracts, such as in the case at bench, and obtaining prepayments on account of lessons provided thereby far in advance of the time when those lessons would be given. Defendant received its share of the payments made by plaintiff upon such contracts under the provisions of the franchise agreement directing the weekly payment to it of 10% of the franchise holder's gross receipts, and an additional 5% thereof for the "fund" from which it was authorized to reimburse pupils for prepaid unused lessons.

The evidence adequately supports the conclusion that in executing the subject contract and receiving the prepayments thereon, Burkin, Inc., was acting as agent for defendant.

The judgment is affirmed.

NOTES AND QUESTIONS

(1) **Agency in the absence of an explicit contract.** Whether defendant is liable under an agency theory depends partly on the deal the parties have made. Suppose, to begin with, that Arthur Murray and Burkin have agreed to be agent and principal and have dealt with plaintiff on that basis, but have made no other arrangement regarding defendant's liability. In this situation, the court would fill in a term from the "standard

---

solely responsible for all obligations of any kind respecting the business of the studio. The other provision declares an understanding between the parties that the license does not authorize the licensee to sign the name "Arthur Murray" to any instrument in writing or "hold himself out" as agent for the licensor, *i.e.*, Arthur Murray, Inc., and that all contracts shall be in the name of the licensee and not in the name of "Arthur Murray." Neither of these provisions expressly declare the relationship of principal and agent does not exist between the licensee and licensor. They bear the interpretation and support an inference that the licensee is foreclosed from disclosing the existence of an agency relationship between the parties.

form" of the law of agency—namely, that the principal is liable for the agent's acts in the scope of the agency. If, as in *Nichols*, none of the parties has explicitly agreed on an agency relationship, the court also fills a gap, although it has a bigger gap to fill. Instead of starting with the agency agreement and filling in a term from agency law, the court has to decide whether to characterize the basic terms of the deal as an agency relationship.

(2) **Hypothetical bargains.** Why characterize the Arthur Murray-Burkin relationship as an agency, particularly since the parties themselves did not do so? The court might ask what deal the parties themselves would make if they were willing to incur the costs of agreeing on all the details. In other words, the courts could make up a "hypothetical bargain" for parties who have not made an explicit real bargain. In *Nichols*, for example, the court could assume that the franchisor would promise to back the franchisee's obligations, such as the obligation to return pre-payments for lessons, if the customer otherwise would demand a discount for prepayments that exceeds the franchisor's costs of assuming this obligation. These costs include the risk of loss and the cost of measures that would prevent the loss from occurring. Arthur Murray not only has superior information about the risk of insolvency, but can reduce its risk of liability for pre-payments by controlling the studio so as to ensure that it does not become insolvent. The plaintiff, on the other hand, can reduce the risk of non-repayment only by learning about or becoming involved in managing a business in which he currently has no role. From this standpoint, the law appropriately imposes the burden of agency on the basis of one party's power of control over another.

(3) **Actual contracts and undisclosed principals.** But is a hypothetical bargain analysis appropriate in *Nichols*? Arguably, there is no gap in the parties' contracts for the court to fill. The contract between Burkin and Arthur Murray provided expressly that Burkin "shall be solely responsible" for all the studio's obligations. Nichols did not contract with Arthur Murray, Inc., but rather with "Arthur Murray School of Dancing" (a non-existent entity). Moreover, Nichols may have been aware of the contents of the license certificate referred to in footnote 4 of the court's opinion. Why, then, should Nichols be able to recover from Arthur Murray? One possible reason is Arthur Murray's failure to make itself and the nature of its powers known to Nichols before contracting out of liability. This invokes the general rule of "undisclosed principal" liability. If principals were permitted to opt out of liability without fully informing third parties of their existence and the scope of their powers, they might secretly remain in the background calling the shots without bearing any liability for bad results. In this situation, principals may make risky decisions that compromise the agent's ability to repay third parties. Thus, the law imposes liability on an undisclosed principal in order to force the principal to come out into the open and clearly disclaim its liability, rather than forcing third parties to investigate whether this situation exists.[1]

---

[1]   Note that an undisclosed principal is liable even for unauthorized acts where the agent is in apparent charge of a business actually owned by the principal and has acted generally within the scope of the business. *See Watteau v. Fenwick* [1893] 1 Q.B. 346; RESTATEMENT (SECOND) OF AGENCY § 195 (1957). This gives the principal the incentive to come out into the open in order to avoid open-ended liability.

(4) **Franchising and standard forms.** *Nichols* illustrates the "franchising" form of business. In some types of business, the value of the product includes not only what is in the package but how the package is delivered to the consumer. McDonald's customers, for example, expect to get exactly the advertised experience at each outlet. Accordingly, McDonald's must try to protect its brand name by ensuring consistent quality of the delivered product. It can do this either by owning its restaurants and employing managers of individual outlets or by selling "franchises" to independent business people who own their own businesses and enter into long-term franchise agreements with the franchisor. These agreements may be quite detailed, covering every aspect of the franchisee's business. In making the choice, the brand name owner must balance the transaction costs discussed above in Section 1.02. For example, franchisees may try to shirk on services and materials and "free ride" off the franchisor's brand name and the high quality services rendered by other franchisees. Also, franchisees may find it difficult to diversify the risks associated with their business, and risk being subject to the franchisor's opportunism, like the newspaper in Section 1.02[E]. On the other hand, owning its outlets presents costs and risks for brand name owners, such as the need to monitor employees of all outlets through hired managers, who may lack adequate incentives to police shirking by employees. *See generally* **Brickley & Dark; Norton & Rubin**. Note that the rule applied in *Nichols* implicitly absolves typical franchisors from liability for acts of franchisees. Why should that be, in light of the significant controls present in typical franchise agreements? Perhaps a brand name owner franchises rather than owns outlets precisely in order to avoid the costs of directly monitoring employees. A franchise agreement therefore can be viewed as a "standard form" of limited liability contract which binds anyone who deals with a typical franchisee and is on notice of the non-agency nature of the relationship. What contract terms or other circumstances are and should be relevant in determining whether the relationship is franchise or agency?[2]

(5) **Apparent agency.** Even if there is no actual agency relationship, a party may be held liable under an "apparent agency" theory for negligently or intentionally causing or allowing a third party to believe the party was a principal. *See* RESTATEMENT (SECOND) OF AGENCY § 8B. Should an apparent agency be found on the basis of plaintiff's doing business with "Arthur Murray School of Dancing"?

REFERENCES

Barnett, *Squaring Undisclosed Agency Law with Contract Theory*, 75 CAL. L. REV. 1969 (1987).

Brickley & Dark, *The Choice of Organizational Form: The Case of Franchising*, 18 J. FIN. ECON. 401 (1987).

---

[2] For a contrasting case, discussing and distinguishing *Nichols* and finding no agent-principal relationship between the franchisor and store owner of a 7-11 store, see *Cislaw v. Southland Corp.*, 4 Cal. App. 4th 1284, 6 Cal. Rptr. 2d 386 (1992).

Hynes, *Lender Liability: The Dilemma of the Controlling Creditor,* 58 TENN. L. REV. 635
    (1991).
Norton, *Franchising, Labor Productivity, and the New Institutional Economics,* 145 J. INST.
    & THEOR. ECON. 578 (1989).
Rubin, *The Theory of the Firm and the Structure of the Franchise Contract,* 21 J.L. & ECON.
    223 (1978).
Sykes, *The Economics of Vicarious Liability,* 93 YALE L.J. 123 (1984).

§ 2.02 General Partnerships

Like agency, general partnership is an informal business relationship in the sense
that the parties need not follow any special procedures in order to form the partnership.
The parties therefore may be partners, with all the consequences that entails, even if
they never agreed to, or indeed never heard of, such a relationship. Any agreement
between the parties usually controls as between the partners, with the Uniform Partnership Act governing elements of the relationship upon which the parties have not
agreed, as well as the rights of third parties. Throughout this book, we will be discussing both the 1914 version of the Uniform Partnership Act (referred to as the Uniform Partnership Act or UPA), which is in effect in the vast majority of states, and the
1994 version (referred to as the Revised Uniform Partnership Act or RUPA), which is
in effect in a few states.

Subsection [A] provides an overview of the type of relationship outlined in the
uniform partnership statutes. Subsection [B] considers what relationships will be
deemed partnerships and therefore subject to the terms of the UPA or RUPA, as the case
may be. Subsection [C] discusses rules related to the partnership's financing.

[A] An Overview of UPA and RUPA

Both the Uniform Partnership Act and the Revised Uniform Partnership Act can
be understood as standard form contracts that the law provides in order to reduce the
costs of entering into agreements. The forms do not save contracting costs if they force
the kind of firms that would adopt them to draft around many of their terms. In other
words, the terms of the standard forms have to mesh with each other.

Both UPA and RUPA have a kind of internal consistency. The essence of the partnership relationship (as defined in UPA § 6(1) and RUPA §§ 101(6), 202) is that the
partners are co-owners. Consistent with this characterization, the statutes give each
partner the power to control the business and to share in the residual claim, or profits
(UPA § 18(a) and (e), RUPA § 401(b) and (f)). Thus, each partner is both a co-princi-
pal and an agent in a principal-agent relationship. Like other agents, each partner can
bind the business to acts within the scope of the agency (UPA §§ 9-14, RUPA § 301-
305); like other principals, each is personally liable for the acts of his agents (UPA § 15,
RUPA § 306). Because of the severe consequences of the partnership relationship, it fol-

lows that each partner should be able to veto important acts (UPA § 18(h), RUPA § 401(j)), including admission of new partners (UPA § 18(g), RUPA § 401(i)). The power to veto new members means that partners cannot freely transfer all of their partnership rights. This lack of free transferability and the severe consequences of partnership status make it important that partners be able to exit the relationship (UPA §§ 31, 38, RUPA §§ 601, 801).

Although both UPA and RUPA provide rules that generally suit "co-owners [of] a business for profit," not all of the rules suit all co-ownership situations. Consider the situation discussed in Section 2.01 above, involving Judy, Kathy and Ray. Assume that the parties have decided to form a partnership. Each will work full time in the store, which will be located in Judy's run-down building. The building is valued at $50,000 and mortgaged for $35,000. Judy will contribute $10,000 cash and Kathy $30,000. Ray will contribute no money or assets. Business funds will be used to convert the building into usable store space and to make mortgage payments and pay other expenses connected with the property.

As to each of the following questions, would the parties want (a) the terms given by the UPA; (b) the terms of RUPA; or (c) some different terms? In answering these questions, consider carefully how the parties would want to minimize the kinds of contracting costs discussed in Section 1.02[A].

(1) Who will own the building in which the store is located—Judy or the partnership?

(2) What will be each party's share of the revenues of the business? Will they share profits (revenues less expenses) equally? In addition to or instead of their profit shares, will any of the parties be entitled to receive salaries for working in the store? Will Judy or Kathy receive interest on their cash contributions? Will Judy receive rent?

(3) Suppose Ray orders an expensive kind of jelly from a supplier without conferring with Judy or Kathy. Will all three partners be individually liable to the supplier, even if Judy and Kathy vehemently oppose the order? If Ray pays the full price to the creditor, may he recover two thirds back from Judy and Kathy?

(4) Suppose one of the parties wishes to withdraw from the business. Can the other partners compel continuation of the business, or can the withdrawing partner require that the business be sold and the proceeds distributed? What can the withdrawing partner take out as his or her share?

[B] Informal Partnerships

A partnership may exist even if it is not planned, or even if the relationship is explicitly planned not to be a partnership. One of the main difficulties involved in determining the existence of partnership is that the parties can vary most elements of the UPA and RUPA standard forms in order to devise the set of contract terms that best suits their business relationship. It is often not clear whether the parties have entered into a partnership but opted out of a standard form term, or have entered into a non-partnership relationship, such as that of employer-employee or debtor-creditor. Consider what elements of the UPA and RUPA standard forms are necessary or sufficient for the existence of partnership. As with agency, the question is whether the terms of the UPA or RUPA provide a suitable hypothetical bargain for relationships that meet the definition of partnership.

The definition of partnership (UPA § 6, RUPA §§ 101(6), 202) compactly describes four elements of partnership:

(1) Membership. A partnership consists of "two or more persons." Note the broad definition of "person" in UPA § 2 and RUPA § 101(10). For example, two or more corporations can, and frequently do, form a partnership.

(2) "Association." This term implies an intentional relationship. Thus, the partners must intend to enter into a relationship that includes the legal elements of partnership. However, as stated in the last clause of RUPA § 202(a), the parties need not know that they are engaging in a "partnership."

(3) Form of activity. In order to comprise a partnership, the parties must "carry on . . . a business for profit." Many of the elements of the UPA standard form necessarily relate to a for-profit business relationship. The business/non-business distinction is emphasized in UPA § 7(2) and RUPA § 202(c)(1). This is one of the most important distinctions between partnership and agency.

(4) Type of participation in the activity. To be partners, the parties must be "co-owners." This is another important distinction from an ordinary agency relationship, where only the principal is an "owner." Co-ownership is the source of most difficulty in determining the existence of partnership. At one time, profit-sharing alone established co-ownership. In the leading case of *Waugh v. Carver*,[3] two ship agents who operated out of separate ports agreed to share commissions (which the court characterized as profits) received on ships that each recommended to the other. The court held one of the agents liable for trade debts of the other solely on the basis of the profit-sharing arrangement, even though the parties explicitly agreed among themselves that they would each be liable for their own losses. Why place such emphasis on profit-sharing? One reason is that profit-sharing is an important attribute of one who occupies a controlling or monitoring role, and therefore is in a good position to place loss-avoidance constraints on management.

Profit-sharing later came to be regarded only as important, but not conclusive, evidence of partnership. A leading early case for this view was *Cox v. Hickman*.[4] UPA § 7(4) and RUPA § 202(c)(3) provide that a profit-sharing arrangement is *prima facie*

---

[3]   2 H. Bl. 235, 126 Eng. Rep. 525 (Court of Common Pleas 1793).

[4]   8 H.L. Cas. 267, 11 Eng. Rep. 431 (House of Lords 1860).

evidence of partnership unless the party opposing the partnership characterization shows that the parties are in one of several specified relationships. Note that even if the relationship is within one of these "protected" categories, it may still be proved to be a partnership.

Consider carefully what facts the court stresses in determining whether partnerships exist in the following cases.

MINUTE MAID CORP. v. UNITED FOODS, INC.

United States Court of Appeals, Fifth Circuit
291 F.2d 577, *cert. denied,*
368 U.S. 928 (1961)

TUTTLE, Chief Judge.

This is an appeal from a judgment of the trial court, sitting without a jury, denying a recovery from United States Cold Storage Corporation by the appellant for the purchase price of commodities sold by it to the United Foods, Inc.

Appellant's theory of recovery was that United Foods, Inc., a direct purchaser from it, was engaged in a partnership operation with the Cold Storage Corporation, thus making Cold Storage liable for the unpaid purchase price.

There is no dispute about the fact that United Foods was indebted to Minute Maid Corporation in the sum of $143,141.66, representing the purchase price of frozen food products sold to United. The question whether Cold Storage is equally liable for this sum must be answered in the light of the following history of the relationship between the parties: Commencing November 1, 1956, United Foods was an authorized direct buyer of products packaged by Minute Maid; Minute Maid's terms of sale for retail size packages to authorized direct buyers, such as United Foods, included discounts based upon the volume of goods included in a single order, ...

United Foods did not have the financial ability from its own resources plus normal credit sources to finance the carrying of a large inventory of frozen food products; that means that there were certain substantial price benefits that it could not get; Cold Storage did have and was willing to make funds available to assist United Foods in buying Minute Maid products in quantities that permitted the maximum discounts; the market conditions affecting frozen food products are such that the price of such goods tends to rise from the month of May to the end of the year, and such increases in price as to citrus food products is as high as 50% in years when weather conditions adversely affect citrus production; at all times pertinent to this action a direct buyer of frozen foods products, such as United Foods, was protected against price declines to the extent of inventories representing goods received during the last thirty day period; United Foods, without the knowledge of Minute Maid, operated so as to obtain an additional thirty days protection against price declines by taking goods owned by Minute Maid from warehouses approximately thirty days prior to notifying Minute Maid of the withdrawal. The effect of this relationship made it possible for a direct buyer, by buying large quantities, to profit as much as 50% on inventories by receiving notice from Minute Maid of proposed price increases a considerable time in advance of the price increase, whereas there was practically no risk of a loss on such inventories by reason of the sixty days protection against price declines above referred to. It is undisputed that this made peculiarly attractive the speculation in inventories.

On May 1, 1957, United Foods and Cold Storage entered into an agreement which spelled out their relationship with each other. Since we conclude that the essential question presented by this appeal must be resolved by reference to this written agreement we consider it essential to print the relevant portions of it in full as follows:

"Memorandum of Agreement

"May 1, 1957

"Between—United Foods, Inc., referred to as United and United States Cold Storage Corporation, referred to as U.S.

"United is a broker of frozen foods in the Dallas, Texas, Area;

"U.S. operates cold storage plants at Dallas and Fort Worth, and will extend finance services to United on the following basis:

"1. Staple commodities bought by United, stored in U.S. plants, will be the collateral if acceptable to U.S., together with acceptable (to U.S.) accounts receivable resulting from sales of the commodities, for loans to be made by U.S. The aggregate amount of loans outstanding at both plants, taken together, shall not exceed $300,000.00.

"2. The amount of loan to United on any lot of product shall be United's gross cost delivered to the warehouse of U.S. The amount of the loan on any of United accounts receivable shall be the amount of the invoices.

"3. Notes to U.S. shall be given by United for each loan and shall bear interest at 6% until paid.

"4. Notes for loans on commodities shall be paid when product is ordered from warehouse.

"5. Notes for loans on accounts receivable shall be paid to U.S. by endorsement of check received from customer to U.S. provided that United will itself pay U.S. for any invoices not otherwise paid in 45 days from date of invoice.

"6. Warehouse charges on staple product on which loans are made on these terms shall be 15¢/100 lbs. handling and 12¢/100 lbs. per month storage, based on the gross weight of package and contents, and a lot delivery charge of 50¢ as current at each plant. Interest, interest service charges and insurance charges shall be at the rates current at each plant. Tariff rates will apply on all other products stored.

"7. All warehouse, interest and insurance charges shall be billed by U.S. monthly, and charged to the "Special Account" described below.

"8. The "Special Account" on the books of U.S. is to be set up to accumulate charges as set forth in Paragraph 7 and to accumulate credits as follows:

"a. United shall pay to U.S. the 6¢ per dozen packer allowance on retail merchandise or any other quantity allowance, advertising, freight, allowance, incentive and profit to the Special Account;

"b. United shall pay to U.S. for the Special Account the incentive from any packer special proposals, as for instance, in forward buying, in anticipating of a price raise, or other inducements to move special product items, such as fish, shrimp, poultry and the like;

"c. United is paid 20¢/100 lbs./month by Minute Maid on institutional merchandise and this allowance will be paid to U.S. for the Special Account to which also U.S. will debit the warehouse charges on this product;

* * *

"9. At the end of the calendar year, the Special Account shall be closed, and

"a. If there is a credit balance, 1/2 thereof shall be paid by U.S. to United within 20 days and the remainder shall be retained by U.S. as its property.

"b. If there is a debit balance, U.S. shall so notify United, who will pay U.S. 1/2 of the amount of such debit balance within 20 days of notification.

* * *

"11. In case of pending price increase, U.S. and United may agree on the volume to be purchased by United, and U.S. will loan, upon receipt of product in storage, the cost to United. When the price increase is effective, U.S. will loan United an additional amount equivalent to the price increase, and such amount shall be paid by United to U.S. for credit to the Special Account, as set forth in Paragraph 8 b.

"12. This agreement shall terminate January 1, 1958, but may be extended by written agreement of the parties hereto."

On June 24, 1957, the foregoing agreement was amended only to the extent of providing that instead of $300,000 the aggregate amount of loans outstanding was increased to $500,000.

All of the sales for which the purchase price is here in litigation were made while this contract was in effect. Subsequently, on December 9, 1957, at which time there was a credit balance of approximately $22,000 in the "special account," referred to in the contract, the parties entered into a termination agreement terminating the contract effective December 31, 1957. This contract further provides:

Any amounts due by United States Cold Storage Corporation to United Foods, Inc. under said contract and the provisions of paragraph nine thereof shall be retained by United States Cold Storage Corporation to apply against future storage and financing charges that may accrue on products stored with them by United Foods, Inc.

United Foods, as a food broker engaged in the business of selling Minute Maid products, and during the year 1957 handled in excess of $1,000,000 of these products. This business was carried on by United Foods at its own office, with its own employees, and at its own expense.

During the life of the contract, Cold Storage did advance 100% of the invoice price of Minute Maid products purchased and stored by United Foods in Cold Storage's warehouse; and United Foods deposited in the "special account" all of the allowances referred to in the written contract. This account, which was held by Cold Storage, paid Cold Storage interest at 6% on all advances and paid its warehouse and insurance charges monthly. At the end of the year the profits from the accumulated credits exceeded these expenses by some $22,000.

Minute Maid did not know of the relationship between United Foods and Cold Storage. It does not contend that it was misled into extending credit to United by reason of such relationship. It contends that the agreement between the parties and the course of dealing thereunder created a partnership relationship between United and Cold Storage and that Cold Storage became liable with United Foods for all debts of the partnership. Minute Maid distinguishes between the regular sales business of United Foods in selling Minute Maid products to the trade from what it considers to be the subject of the partnership. It says that the partnership consisted of a joint endeavor by United Foods and Cold Storage under which United Foods would take advantage of its position as a direct purchaser of Minute Maid products and of the financing afforded it by Cold Storage to buy products in the quantities that would yield the greatest amount in allowances and discounts and if the market appeared right, to speculate on a possible price increase; that in return for Cold Storage's agreement to finance the transaction to the extent of advancing 100% of the purchase price of the products it would store the products in Cold Storage's warehouse at a profitable rate, it would pay interest of 6% on all advances and it and Cold Storage would share equally the profits that could thus be anticipated from the discounts and from profitable speculation, if indulged in.

Cold Storage, on the other hand, contends that the agreement created only a relationship at most of debtor and creditor between it and United, or that the relationship was an ambiguous one which the trial court, on disputed evidence, found as a fact not to be a partnership.

* * *

A critical examination of the foregoing facts, most of which are made the basis of formal findings by the trial court, necessarily leads to the following conclusions:

(1) Cold Storage was to be repaid the principal amount of its advances to United regardless of the success or failure of the enterprise.

(2) Cold Storage was to receive its warehouse charges, its interest at 6% and reimbursement for the cost of insurance out of the "special fund" set up under the contract. It seems plain that there could be no failure of the special fund to provide sufficient sums to meet these obligations and provide a profit, because the parties could in advance know exactly how much by way of special allowances and discounts would be paid into the special fund, and, of course, the charges would bear a direct relation to these same items. However, if there was a deficit in this special fund, it was to be shared by the parties equally.

(3) The advance of 100% of the invoice price of the merchandise was not a normal credit arrangement which would be available to United by the payment of legal rates of interest.

(4) Both United and Cold Storage would profit by increasing the purchases of United made possible by the arrangement between the two parties. United's profit would come from its 50% participation in the profits in the special fund and Cold Storage's profit would come from the increasing of the inventory for which it received substantial warehouse fees, an increase in inventories for which it received its 6% interest and the anticipated profit aris-

ing by reason of the fact that it could be computed in advance that the special allowances and discounts paid into the fund would exceed the carrying charges. Cold Storage became the owner of one half of this excess.

(5) Cold Storage was undoubtedly in the relation of a creditor of United; it was also in the relation of a bailee for hire.

(6) It is also clear, however, that the operation that here produced the sale of the volume of Minute Maid products to United would not have occurred by reason of Cold Storage's willingness to engage in either or both of these two activities standing alone, and on normal terms—that is as a creditor receiving a legal rate of interest and a warehouseman receiving its stated warehouse charges.

(7) It is plain that Cold Storage was interested in assisting United to create a larger indebtedness on which it would receive its interest and a larger volume of inventory on which it would receive its warehouseman's fees and that in order to assist in creating this larger volume of business for itself it participated with United in making possible the larger purchases of Minute Maid products than United could otherwise have accomplished.

Does this analysis cause us to conclude that the two parties, acting to their mutual interest to make possible an increased purchase of Minute Maid products, created a joint venture or partnership between them?

* * *

Appellee is too preoccupied, we think, with its insistence that the relationship between United and Cold Storage was that of debtor and creditor. This is undoubtedly correct, but it is equally undoubtedly indecisive. Appellee also relies strongly on the contention that there was no express obligation assumed under the written contract whereby Cold Storage was to share in the overall losses of the enterprise. This, of course, is the very question that this Court has to decide, for if the relationship between the parties constituted them partners, then the law imposes upon them the obligation to pay the losses. No case has been cited from Texas or elsewhere to the effect that the mere failure to agree in the formal contract that the parties will share the losses prevents the relationship from being that of partners.

* * *

It is the burden of appellee's argument here that if there is nothing more than a lender relationship, coupled with an agreement that compensation for the loan is to be in the form of a sharing in profits, either in lieu of or in addition to normal interest, these facts are sufficient to rebut the presumption that arises by the profit sharing agreement. Appellee contends that additional indicia of an intent to create a partnership must be shown either in the nature of joint control by the person sought to be bound as a partner, or an express agreement to share in losses.

Assuming this position to be correct, we think it is undeniably true here that control over the particular enterprise in which these two parties were engaged was jointly held by United and Cold Storage. We must bear in mind exactly what this enterprise was. It was not the commission food business carried on by United. It was the arrangement whereby Cold Storage furnished the financing and warehouse facilities to make possible United's use of its relationship as a direct buyer of Minute Maid products in such quantities and under such terms as would turn a profit for both of them. There can be no question but that the parties had joint control over this enterprise. This follows from the fact that United initially determined how much to buy but such determination was subject to Cold Storage's right to determine whether the proposed collateral would be "acceptable." Also, it was provided that in case of pending price increases, which the court found would offer the opportunity to speculate on inventory, the parties would agree on the volume to be purchased. In point of fact the responsible officer for United testified that, "they [Cold Storage] could have stepped in and written me [United] off pretty damned fast."

* * *

We conclude that the relationship established by the written contract of the parties and by their conduct thereunder constituted a legal partnership or joint enterprise under the Texas law. . . . .

The judgment of the trial court is reversed and the case is remanded to the trial court for further proceedings not inconsistent with this opinion.

JOSEPH C. HUTCHESON, Circuit Judge (dissenting).

. . . [T]he question of whether or not a partnership is created depends entirely upon the intent, of the parties to the agreement, to create a partnership . . . not, however, their secret subjective intent but the intent manifested in what they agreed to, and did do. Here there was no such indication whatever of such an intent on the part of either United States Cold Storage or United Foods, Inc.

. . . [I]n Texas it is settled law that "In order for there to be a partnership, the parties must not only participate in the profits but *they must have an interest in the profits, as profits, and share them as joint owners or principals of the business or venture, as distinguished from having an interest therein as compensation under a profit sharing agreement*" (emphasis added). *LeBus v. LeBus*, Tex. Civ. App., 269 S.W.2d 506, 511. Here there was no agreement between United States Cold Storage and United Foods, Inc., that they should go into any kind of business together to share the profit thereof. The agreement was specifically that the United States Cold Storage, in connection with its warehousing business would lend money to United Foods and the money loaned would be paid back to United States Cold Storage at all events, primarily out of the special account provided for in the agreement, if there was accumulated enough in it to pay it, with the further understanding, however, that there was a chance that after the loan, with interest, was paid back by United Foods, there would be additional compensation to United States Cold Storage out of one-half of the special account, if there was a balance left in it after paying the proper expenses chargeable against it.

MARTIN v. PEYTON
New York Court of Appeals
246 N.Y. 213, 158 N.E. 77 (1927)

[In the following case, creditors of the K.N. & K., which is now bankrupt, are suing K.N. & K. as well as Peyton and others who had loaned money to K.N. & K. The lower courts had held that those who had loaned money to K.N. & K. were not partners.]

ANDREWS, J. Assuming some written contract between the parties, the question may arise whether it creates a partnership. If it be complete, if it expresses in good faith the full understanding and obligation of the parties, then it is for the court to say whether a partnership exists. It may, however, be a mere sham intended to hide the real relationship. Then other results follow. In passing upon it, effect is to be given to each provision. Mere words will not blind us to realities. Statements that no partnership is intended are not conclusive.

* * *

In the case before us the claim that the defendants became partners in the firm of Knauth, Nachod & Kuhne, doing business as bankers and brokers, depends upon the interpretation of certain instruments. There is nothing in their subsequent acts determinative of or indeed material upon this question. . . .

Remitted then, as we are, to the documents themselves, we refer to circumstances surrounding their execution only so far as is necessary to make them intelligible. And we are to remember that although the intention of the parties to avoid liability as partners is clear, although in language precise and definite they deny any design to then join the firm of K. N. & K.; although they say their interests in profits should be construed merely as a measure of compensation for loans, not an interest in profits as such; although they provide that they shall not be liable for any losses or treated as partners. . . , the question still remains whether in fact they agree to so associate themselves with the firm as to "carry on as co-owners a business for profit."

In the spring of 1921 the firm of K. N. & K. found itself in financial difficulties. John R. Hall was one of the partners. He was a friend of Mr. Peyton. From him he obtained the loan of almost $500,000 of Liberty bonds, which K. N. & K. might use as collateral to secure bank advances. This, however, was not sufficient. The firm and its members had engaged in unwise speculations, and it was deeply involved. Mr. Hall was also intimately acquainted with George W. Perkins, Jr., and with Edward W. Freeman. He also knew Mrs. Peyton and Mrs. Perkins and Mrs. Freeman. All were anxious to help him. He therefore, representing K. N. & K., entered into negotiations with them. While they were pending, a proposition was made that Mr. Peyton, Mr. Perkins, and Mr. Freeman, or some of them, should become partners. It met a decided refusal. Finally an agreement was reached. It is expressed in three documents, executed on the same day, all a part of the one transaction. They were drawn with care and are unambiguous. We shall refer to them as "the agreement," "the indenture," and "the option."

We have no doubt as to their general purpose. The respondents were to loan K. N. & K. $2,500,000 worth of liquid securities, which were to be returned to them on or before April 15, 1923. The firm might hypothecate them to secure loans totaling $2,000,000, using the proceeds as its business necessities required. To insure respondents against loss K. N. & K. were to turn over to them a large number of their own securities which may have been valuable, but which were of so speculative a nature that they could not be used as collateral for bank loans. In compensation for the loan the respondents were to receive 40 per cent. of the profits of the firm until the return was made, not exceeding, however, $500,000, and not less than $100,000. Merely because the transaction involved the transfer of securities and not of cash does not prevent its being a loan, within the meaning of section 11 [UPA § 7]. The respondents also were given an option to join the firm if they, or any of them, expressed a desire to do so before June 4, 1923.

Many other detailed agreements are contained in the papers. Are they such as may be properly inserted to protect the lenders? Or do they go further? Whatever their purpose, did they in truth associate the respondents with the firm so that they and it together thereafter carried on as co-owners a business for profit? The answer depends upon an analysis of these various provisions.

As representing the lenders, Mr. Peyton and Mr. Freeman are called "trustees." The loaned securities when used as collateral are not to be mingled with other securities of K. N. & K., and the trustees at all times are to be kept informed of all transactions affecting them. To them shall be paid all dividends and income accruing therefrom. They may also substitute for any of the securities loaned securities of equal value. With their consent the firm may sell any of its securities held by the respondents, the proceeds to go, however, to the trustees. In other similar ways the trustees may deal with these same securities, but the securities loaned shall always be sufficient in value to permit of their hypothecation for $2,000,000. If they rise in price, the excess may be withdrawn by the defendants. If they fall, they shall make good the deficiency.

So far, there is no hint that the transaction is not a loan of securities with a provision for compensation. Later a somewhat closer connection with the firm appears. Until the securities are returned, the directing management of the firm is to be in the hands of John R. Hall, and his life is to be insured for $1,000,000 and the policies are to be assigned as further collateral security to the trustees. These requirements are not unnatural. Hall was the one known and trusted by the defendants. Their acquaintance with the other members of the firm was of the slightest. These others had brought an old and established business to the verge of bankruptcy. As the respondents knew, they also had engaged in unsafe speculation. The respondents were about to loan $2,500,000 of good securities. As collateral they were to receive others of problematical value. What they required seems but ordinary caution. Nor does it imply an association in the business.

The trustees are to be kept advised as to the conduct of the business and consulted as to important matters. They may inspect the firm books and are entitled to any information they think important. Finally, they may veto any business they think highly speculative or injurious. Again we hold this but a proper precaution to safeguard the loan. The trustees may not initiate any transaction as a partner may do. They may not bind the firm by any action of their own. Under the circumstances the safety of the loan depended upon the business success of K. N. & K. This success was likely to be compromised by the inclination of its members to engage in speculation. No longer, if the respondents were to be protected, should it be allowed. The trustees therefore might prohibit it, and that their prohibition might be effective, information was to be furnished them. Not dissimilar agreements have been held proper to guard the interests of the lender.

As further security each member of K. N. & K. is to assign to the trustees their interest in the firm. No loan by the firm to any member is permitted and the amount each may draw is fixed. No other distribution of profits is to be made. So that realized profits may be calculated the existing capital is stated to be $700,000, and profits are to be realized as promptly as good business practice will permit. In case the trustees think this is not done, the question is left to them and to Mr. Hall, and if they differ then to an arbitrator. There is no obligation that the firm shall continue the business. It may dissolve at any time. Again we conclude there is nothing here not properly adapted to secure the interest of the respondents as lenders. If their compensation is dependent on a percentage of the profits, still provision must be made to define what these profits shall be.

The "indenture" is substantially a mortgage of the collateral delivered by K. N. & K. to the trustees to secure the performance of the "agreement." It certainly does not strengthen the claim that the respondents were partners.

Finally we have the "option." It permits the respondents, or any of them, or their assignees or nominees to enter the firm at a later date if they desire to do so by buying 50 per cent. or less of the interests therein of all or any of the members at a stated price. Or a corporation may, if the respondents and the members agree, be formed in place of the firm. Meanwhile, apparently with the design of protecting the firm business against improper or ill-judged action which might render the option valueless, each member of the firm is to place his resignation in the hands of Mr. Hall. If at any time he and the trustees agree that such resignation should be accepted, that member shall then retire, receiving the value of his interest calculated as of the date of such retirement.

This last provision is somewhat unusual, yet it is not enough in itself to show that on June 4, 1921, a present partnership was created, nor taking these various papers as a whole do we reach such a result. It is quite true that even if one or two or three like provisions contained in such a contract do not require this conclusion, yet it is also true that when taken together a point may come where stipulations immaterial separately cover so wide a field that we should hold a partnership exists. As in other branches of the law, a question of degree is often the determining factor. Here that point has not been reached. . . .

The judgment appealed from should be affirmed, with costs.

NOTES AND QUESTIONS

(1) **Rationale for holding in** *Minute Maid.* Why should Minute Maid be able to reach Cold Storage's assets when Minute Maid contracted only with United? Is *Minute Maid* an example of undisclosed principal liability discussed in Note 3 after *Nichols*?

(2) **Reconciling** *Minute Maid* **and** *Martin.* Why did the court find a partnership in *Minute Maid* but not in *Martin*? Are the different results attributable to economic differences between the relationships in the two cases or to the skills of the lawyers in drafting the agreements?

(3) **The role of intent.** Consider again the role of intent discussed in connection with the "association" element of partnership in the introduction to this subsection, 2.02[B]. The dissent in *Minute Maid* concluded that neither United States Cold Storage nor United Foods intended to form a partnership. In what sense did the court mean the word "intent"?

(4) **Consequence of finding partnership.** In determining the existence of partnership, should the consequences of the determination matter? In particular, should it make a difference whether the court is determining an alleged partner's share of the business' property, or the liability of the alleged partner to third party creditors? The policy argument discussed above in Section 2.02[B] concerning the relevance of profit-sharing relates only to the third-party liability case. However, UPA § 7(1) (which was removed from RUPA) says that the third-party and inter-partner cases should not be distinguished except in the estoppel situation discussed below in Note 7. If "partners" are not liable to third parties, should their agreement between each other be interpreted consistent with the default rules of partnership? Did the removal of § 7(1) from RUPA change the law in this regard?

(5) **Individual partner liability for partnership debts.** Under UPA § 15 and RUPA § 306, each partner is subject to liability to creditors for all of the partnership's obligations. Unlike most UPA and RUPA provisions, these are not subject to contrary agreement of the partners, although the partners may agree with individual creditors that the creditors will have recourse only against business assets (*see* Section 3.04[A] below).

(6) **Exhaustion.** Creditors may be required to exhaust their remedies against partnership assets before they can execute against partners' individual assets. In some cases, this may relieve partners of having to pay a judgment and then finding and executing against their co-partners. Exhaustion was traditionally required only in cases of "joint" liability—*i.e.*, liability based on contract—and not "joint and several" liability, based on tort. However, some jurisdictions require exhaustion as to both joint, and joint and several claims, and this is the rule adopted in RUPA § 307(d).

(7) **Partnership by estoppel.** Under UPA § 16 and RUPA § 308, partnership liability may be imposed for the benefit of a third-party creditor when the defendant is responsible for a representation of partnership status on which the creditor relied. This liability exists even where defendant would not be considered a partner for other purposes under the cases in this Section. Compare the "apparent agency" theory discussed in Note 5 following *Nichols*.

PROBLEMS

(1) Feedlot, Inc., operated a cattle feedlot. Bar K, Inc., owned some cattle. Feedlot and Bar K, Inc., entered into the following agreement: "Feedlot and Bar K hereby agree to engage in a joint venture with regard to servicing by Feedlot of Bar K's cattle.

Bar K will be charged Feedlot's going rate for services performed by Feedlot for Bar K's cattle. If Feedlot's actual expenditures for Bar K's cattle are less than the going rate, the resulting profit will be split 50-50 by Feedlot and Bar K." A grain seller that supplied grain to Feedlot seeks to hold Bar K liable for the cost of the grain. The grain seller was unaware of Bar K's participation in the deal at the time of the sale. What are Bar K's chances of losing this suit? What if the grain seller were aware of the Bar K-Feedlot agreement? Would it make a difference whether Bar K exercised control over the type of feed used by Feedlot for Bar K's cattle?[5]

(2) Assume that in the *Minute Maid* situation, Cold Storage had brought you the United Cold Storage agreement before it was signed. How would you have advised that it be redrafted?

(3) Assume that in the situation in Problem 1, Bar K had brought you the agreement set forth in the problem before it was signed. How would you have advised that it be redrafted?

REFERENCE

Bromberg & Ribstein, BROMBERG & RIBSTEIN ON PARTNERSHIP, Ch. 2.

[C] Financing the General Partnership

One of the most important issues in the formation of any new business is the firm's financing. Generally, a firm will raise money by borrowing from lenders and/or selling equity interests to owners. This subsection is concerned with financing that involves the sale of ownership interest to partners.

[1] Background

General partnerships raise equity capital by admitting new partners, who are entitled to full ownership rights and not merely financial rights (*see* Section 4.03 below), and by obtaining additional contributions from existing partners. The contributions to the firm's capital by the partners are reflected in the partnership's "balance sheet," so called because it consists of two columns of figures with equal sums. The assets of the partnership are usually disclosed on the left side of the balance sheet, the claims of creditors and partners on the right. The excess of assets over liabilities is the "net worth" of the firm. The partner's share of net worth is variously referred to as the partner's "equity" or "capital" (the latter term is used in §§ 18(a) and 40(b) of the UPA).

---

[5]   *See Tex-Co. Grain Co. v. Happy Wheat Growers, Inc.*, 542 S.W.2d 934 (Tex. Civ. App. 1976); *P & M Cattle Co. v. Holler*, 559 P.2d 1019 (Wyo. 1977).

For an example of balance sheet accounting in the partnership, assume that three partners, X, Y and Z, each contribute $2,000 cash to their firm. The initial balance sheet would look as follows:

Assets	Liabilities
Cash: $6000	Partners' Equity
	x: $2,000
	y: $2,000
	z: $2,000
$6,000	$6,000

Partners' equity is increased by additional contributions, including partners' contributions of portions of their shares of the profits, and is reduced by losses. *See* RUPA § 401(a). Upon liquidation, the capital accounts provide a basis for determining how much is to be distributed to each partner under UPA § 40(b) and RUPA § 807. A final note: the partners could agree to credit their capital accounts other than according to contributions. For example, the partners could agree that the capital account of each partner is to be credited as above even though X and Y each contributed $3,000 and Z contributed nothing.

[2] Legal Rules Regarding Admission of Partners

[a] Protection of Incoming Partners

An incoming owner could be harmed if the balance sheet or other financial records of the partnership failed to accurately disclose relevant facts concerning the value of the partnership. The incoming owner is protected from misrepresentation and nondisclosure in the partnership setting primarily by the common law of fraud, enhanced by a fiduciary duty to disclose relevant facts relating to the value of a partnership interest.

[b] Protection of Creditors

Creditors are not concerned with the amount that a particular partner contributes to the firm, since partners generally are personally liable for partnership debts. *See* UPA § 15; RUPA § 307. Accordingly, there are no regulations controlling the amount that incoming owners must pay for their partnership interests or requiring disclosure to creditors.

[c] Protection of Existing Partners

Existing partners have the greatest need for protection in connection with the sale of ownership interests in the partnership. Because each new partner has an equal vote and an equal share of the partnership's profits under UPA § 18 and RUPA § 401, the admission of new partners may significantly dilute the existing partners' votes and profit shares. Accordingly, UPA § 18(g) and RUPA § 401(i) give each partner the power to veto the admission of a new partner, subject to contrary agreement. Larger partnerships often alter this default rule by permitting the admission of new members upon a less than unanimous vote. But in these situations, the partnership agreement frequently provides for detailed protection of the existing partners.

CHAPTER 3

Forming the Corporation

This Chapter introduces the corporation, the most important example of a business association in which the liability of the owners is limited to their investment in the firm. Corporations are formed by filing a document known as the "certificate" or "articles" of incorporation with the appropriate state authorities. Most corporations share the following attributes: (1) they are owned by limited liability shareholders whose ownership interests in the firm are freely transferable; (2) they are managed by "directors" elected by the shareholders and "officers" chosen by the directors, with directors exercising general supervisory powers over the corporation's affairs and officers making most day-to-day decisions; and (3) they continue in existence notwithstanding changes in ownership. Because state corporation statutes generally permit the corporate form to be customized to meet the needs of the particular firm, some corporations may lack some of these attributes.

§ 3.01 Notes on Incorporation

The attorney advising a new business with respect to incorporation must consider a variety of questions. These questions include whether, where, and how to incorporate.

[A] Choosing the Appropriate Business Form

The most basic question that arises with respect to incorporation is whether the corporate form is appropriate for the client's business. The selection of a business form depends on a detailed evaluation of the needs of the particular business. General partnership often is best for the small, closely held business because the Uniform Partnership Act provides what owners of such businesses most often want: Co-equal management powers, ease of dissolution, flexible capital structure, and control over selection of associates. Also, partnerships, unlike corporations, do not have to pay a separate tax at the entity level. The corporate form, however, is more attractive to larger businesses. This is because corporate limited liability, free transferability of stock, and centralized management facilitate the aggregation of large amounts of capital from passive investors.

While small firms can adapt the corporate form to their needs under modern corporation statutes, the discussion in Section 3.05 and Chapter 5 shows that this involves many difficulties and much uncertainty, including the risk that courts will "pierce the corporate veil" and impose personal liability on the shareholders of closely held firms. Moreover, even small corporations that distribute much of their income as dividends must pay the separate corporate tax, unless they qualify as subchapter S corporations (*see* section 6.02). As discussed below in Section 3.03, small firms may want corporate-type limited liability despite these problems. They may be able to have the best of both the corporate and partnership worlds by forming a limited liability company or limited liability partnership. *See* Chapter 6.

[B] Choosing the State of Incorporation

As noted above in Section 1.04, the courts have held both that states cannot discriminate against foreign corporations selling in interstate commerce[1] and that the "internal affairs" of corporations are governed by the law of the state of incorporation.[2] A corporation therefore can choose its state of incorporation (and thus the law that will govern the corporation's internal affairs) without regard to where its business is located.

The appropriate state of incorporation depends, as does the decision whether to incorporate, upon the needs of the particular firm. For many relatively heavily capitalized corporations, Delaware incorporation may be advisable because Delaware law has been fine-tuned over the years to attract incorporation business, and there is a well-developed body of case law in Delaware that provides a measure of predictability. But a company that incorporates in Delaware and does business elsewhere must pay the franchise fee in Delaware and the costs associated with qualifying to do business as a foreign corporation where it does business. For many smaller corporations, "home state" incorporation may be more desirable because the double expense that accompanies incorporation outside the home state may outweigh any advantages obtained by securing the application of a different state's laws to the corporation's internal affairs.

[C] How to Incorporate

The act of legal creation is now quite simple under most state statutes. Under Delaware General Corporation Law §§ 101 and 103, for example, it is necessary only for one or more persons to prepare, acknowledge, and file with the Secretary of State a

---

[1]   *See, e.g., South Central Bell Telephone Co. v. Alabama*, 526 U.S. 160 (1999) (state franchise tax system charged foreign corporations five times more than domestic corporations).

[2]   *But see Havlicek v. Coast-to-Coast Analytical Services, Inc.*, 46 Cal. Rptr. 2d 696 (Cal. App. 1995) (applying California law to request by dissident directors to inspect the records of Delaware corporation, where the corporation maintained its principal office in California, employed California residents, and 40% of its stock and two of the five seats on its board of directors were controlled by California residents).

certificate of incorporation. After filing the certificate of incorporation, the initial directors or incorporators must, pursuant to G.C.L. § 108(a), "perfect the organization of the corporation" by, among other things, adopting bylaws and electing officers and directors.

In addition to creating the corporation, it is also necessary to prepare the foundation of the parties' business relationship. The terms of this relationship are set forth in the certificate of incorporation, bylaws, and any shareholders' agreements. The certificate (or the "articles" in some states) must contain the information specified in the applicable statute. *See*, for example, Del. G.C.L. § 102. Such required information generally includes the corporation's name, purposes, and capitalization. Details of the management of the corporation, including rules governing shareholder and director meetings, voting by shareholders and directors, and the powers of officers, are generally included in the bylaws, but may also be included in the certificate or shareholders' agreements.

There are many corporation forms, including those prepared by the secretary of state in the state of incorporation. The attorney may even buy "corporate outfits" that contain forms for stock certificates, bylaws, and even for minutes of meetings that need only be filled in with a little information when the meeting actually takes place. But the attorney should take the trouble to tailor the corporate documents to the needs of the client and the applicable law.

§ 3.02 The Capital Structure

This Section describes the basic agreements among contributors of capital and other resources, which are often referred to as the "capital structure" of the corporation. Every business, including partnership, has an equivalent set of agreements. The corporate "capital structure" is distinctive only in that certain standard form financial instruments, such as common and preferred stock, have been developed through business practice and their terms have been embodied in corporation statutes.

[A] Important Components

In very general terms, a corporation's capital structure consists of common stock, preferred stock, and debt. Each type of instrument is simply an agreement made between the purchaser or creditor and the corporation. The terms are contained in the applicable corporation statute, in the certificate or bylaws, or in instruments called "indentures" which govern the relationship between the corporation and holders of long-term debt.

The main terms of the agreement deal with the extent of control the security holder has over corporate affairs (that is, the holder's voting power); the rights of the security holder to receive a pre-dissolution distribution of assets in the form of interest, dividends, or repayment of principal; and the holder's priority in distribution of the corporation's assets on liquidation. In general, the higher the certainty of payback the agreement provides, the lower the amount of control. The ingenuity of corporate finance experts in meeting the shifting demands of the market place has resulted in the development of many different kinds of instruments, some of which blur distinctions between common stock, preferred stock, and debt. The following are only extremely general working definitions.

Common Stock

Common stockholders hold the most junior claims against the corporation's assets. Prior to liquidation, they have no right to receive any distributions of the corporation's assets, except for such dividends as the board of directors may decide to declare. On liquidation, common shareholders have a claim only on what is not distributed to all other claimants. Because common shareholders bear the greatest risk of failure and have the most to gain from success of the enterprise, they generally wield more voting power than other security holders in electing directors and approving corporate transactions.

Preferred Stock

Preferred stockholders hold the next most junior claims to the corporation's assets. Preferred stockholders are typically entitled to receive dividends at a specified rate (generally stated in terms of a percentage of the face amount of the investment per year) before any dividends are paid to common stockholders. But like common stockholders, preferred stockholders do not receive the dividends accrued on their stock until the corporation's board of directors determines that dividends should be paid. Holders of "cumulative" preferred stock are entitled to receive dividends earned but not paid in prior periods, together with dividends earned during the current period, before anything is paid to the common stockholders, while holders of "noncumulative" preferred generally lose any future right to dividends that are earned but not declared in a given year. On liquidation, holders of preferred stock are entitled to a specific amount (generally the face amount of their investment or some multiple of the face amount of their investment) before anything is paid to the common stockholders, subject to the prior rights of creditors. As a tradeoff for their greater security, preferred stockholders generally have fewer voting rights than common stockholders and no right to share in the corporation's earnings beyond the specified dividend and liquidation preference (although some preferred stock, referred to as "participating preferred," "preference" or "class A common," does give the holders some right to share in earnings with common shareholders).

Debt

Creditors are the senior claimants to the corporation's assets. Debt is distinguishable from common stock and preferred stock, which together comprise the corporation's "equity," in that creditors are entitled to regular payments of principal and interest, rather than to such distributions as the directors may declare. Further, if the corporation is liquidated before the creditors have been fully repaid, creditors are entitled to be repaid out of the assets of the company before any payments are made to equity holders. Because creditors are repaid out of the corporation's assets before any amounts are paid to equity holders, creditors are less likely to lose their investment if the corporation fails. Accordingly, creditors generally have no role in the governance of the corporation. However, long-term creditors often have substantial contractual rights which are set forth in a loan indenture and are enforceable by an indenture trustee.

[B] Disclosing the Capital Structure

The capital structure of the corporation is disclosed on the firm's balance sheet (*see* Section 2.02[C][1], above). The balance sheet (1) identifies and quantifies the corporation's assets and (2) shows how the claims against those assets are divided among creditors, holders of preferred stock, and holders of common stock. The balance sheet should be distinguished from the "income statement" which shows how much money the company earned during a period. Since the income statement shows how the company is performing, it may provide more direct information about the company's ability to repay the debt.

The following notes are intended to help you understand the balance sheet below.

1) *Book Value, Net Asset Value, and Shareholders' Equity*: Book or net asset value is determined by subtracting the claims of creditors (*i.e.*, the corporation's liabilities) from the value of the corporation's assets. Because it shows what is left over for the shareholders after the claims of creditors have been paid in full, it is sometimes referred to as "shareholders' equity." If a corporation has more than one type of equity security outstanding (*i.e.*, if its capital structure consists of both preferred stock and common stock), the corporation's total book value will frequently be allocated among the different classes of equity securities. In that case, the book value of a particular class of equity securities would be computed by determining what the holders of that class of securities would receive if the corporation were liquidated.

2) *The Debt-to-Equity Ratio*: As the name suggests, the debt-to-equity ratio is computed by dividing the value of the claims of the corporation's creditors by the value of the corporation's shareholders' equity. A very high ratio means that the company may have difficulty paying its debt since it indicates that the value of the company's assets does not greatly exceed the amount owed to the company's creditors.

3) *Current Assets, Current Liabilities, and Working Capital*: Current liabilities refer to those liabilities that the company must pay right away; current assets refer to those assets that are readily available to meet these current commitments. The excess of current assets over current liabilities is often referred to as working capital, and is a measure of the corporation's ability to pay its debts as they come due. The working capital ratio, which is computed by dividing current assets by current liabilities, is an alternative measure of a corporation's ability to pay its debts as they come due. The working capital ratio better indicates a corporation's ability to pay its debts on time, because it measures the relative size of current assets and current liabilities, not just the difference between the two.

4) *Stockholders' Equity Summary*: The stockholders' equity summary divides what the corporation's shareholders own among the holders of the preferred stock and the holders of the corporation's common stock. Shareholders' equity is subdivided into "par value," "capital in excess of par value," and "retained earnings." Capital and par value are discussed in greater detail in Subsection [D] below.

QUESTIONS

On the basis of the following balance sheet, what are the:

a) book value,
b) debt-equity ratio,
c) working capital, and
d) working capital ratio

as of the date of the balance sheet?

Manufacturing Corporation Balance Sheet

Assets		*Liabilities and Stockholders' Equity*	
Current Assets:		**Current Liabilities**:	
Cash	490,855	Short term debt	7,217,304
Inventories	26,871,706	Acct payable	3,142,119
Other	3,318,270	Accrued expenses	1,860,957
		Income taxes	874,742
Total	30,680,831	Total	13,095,122
		Long term debt	5,000,000
Property and Equipment		**Stockholders' equity**	
Machinery	1,866,666	Preferred $10 par,	
Furniture and	408,451	authorized 1,500,000	
Fixtures		outstanding 50,000	500,000
Improvements	1,349,304		
	3,624,421		
		Common stock $1 par	
Accumulated		authorized 6,000,000	
depreciation and		outstanding 3,479,560	3,479,560
amortization	(396,475)	Capital in excess of par	6,564,009
Other assets	75,536	Retained earnings	5,345,622
			15,889,191
	33,984,313		33,984,313

[C] Choosing the Capital Structure

When parties form corporations, they must decide how much of the firm's capital structure will consist of debt (*i.e.*, how much money will be raised through borrowing) and how much will consist of equity (*i.e.*, how much money will be raised through the sale of stock). Although a detailed consideration of the determinants of capital structure is beyond the scope of this book, three potential benefits from including debt in the corporation's capital structure should be noted.

First, by using debt in the capital structure (*i.e.*, borrowing funds instead of selling stock), shareholders can increase their individual shares in the residual after payment of fixed expenses. This is called "leveraging" because, just as the use of a longer lever permits lifting more weight with less force, debt can magnify the earning power of equity. Higher leverage means greater returns for shareholders in good years, but larger losses in bad ones.

Second, debt can be used to control the agency costs that arise from the separation of ownership and control of corporations (*see* Section 1.02[D]). By using debt in the capital structure, shareholders can ensure that revenues are paid out in the form of interest, rather than being used unprofitably by management for such things as fancy office furniture or corporate aircraft.

Finally, debt can be used as a way of reducing corporate income taxes. Most importantly in this regard, corporations may deduct interest payments on debt but not dividends on stock.

But debt also has its costs. In the leveraged firm, creditors must be concerned that shareholders, who elect the firm's managers, will choose excessively risky business strategies, because shareholders are, in effect, gambling with other people's (*i.e.*, the creditors') money. This risk becomes more severe as the proportion of debt in the firm's capital structure increases. In addition, highly leveraged firms are more susceptible to bankruptcy than are firms with less debt. Thus, as the firm's leverage increases, so will the interest rate charged by the firm's lenders. Indeed, this raises the question whether a firm's debt-equity ratio has any effect at all on its value (*see* Section 7.01[G], below).

The relative costs and benefits of debt can be expected to vary from firm to firm. Thus, the precise balance of debt and equity for a particular firm will depend on that firm's circumstances.

[D] Legal Rules Governing the Capital Structure

[1] Overview

The legal rules regarding governing the corporation's capital structure may best be understood by organizing them according to the following classes of persons they arguably protect:

(1) *Purchasers.* The primary function of the law insofar as purchasers of stock are concerned is to ensure full disclosure of the facts relating to value, thereby enabling pur-

chasers to make informed judgments. While some protection from misrepresentation and nondisclosure is provided by the state common law of fraud and promoter liability (*see* Section 3.04[C], below), these devices have been eclipsed in importance by the Securities Act of 1933, which is summarized in Section 12.02.

(2) *Creditors.* Corporate statutes include rules on what equity owners must pay for their shares and may also provide for some disclosure of the consideration paid. Many of these rules regarding the sale of equity are intended to protect creditors. Creditors of corporations are concerned with whether the corporation will have sufficient assets to pay its debts, since corporate shareholders are not individually liable for corporate debts. Thus, creditors who rely on disclosure documents such as balance sheets might be injured if these documents inflate the amounts the shareholders have paid for their stock. Also, shareholders may lack economic incentives to avoid reckless business decisions that could potentially harm creditors if they have paid very little for their power of control. But creditors who loan money after stock has been sold arguably do not care whether equity holders have paid very little for their shares, since creditors can adjust their price of credit to reflect the risk of reckless business decisions, assuming the consideration for the stock has been accurately disclosed.

(3) *Existing Stockholders.* When new stock is sold, existing stockholders may be adversely affected in that the sale may diminish their voice in the affairs of the firm and their share of the firm's assets and earnings. This problem is dealt with by giving existing stockholders some control over the sale of new ownership interests and some right to minimize the dilution of their interests by purchasing additional shares. Additionally, the courts have imposed fiduciary duties on managers and owners of businesses on behalf of other owners in connection with the sale of ownership interests.

The following subsections discuss in more detail the corporate law rules designed to protect creditors and existing stockholders.

[2] Rules Protecting Creditors

The contractual provisions that comprise the corporation's capital structure are usually set forth in the certificate or articles of incorporation. The certificate describes the various classes of stock and number of shares of each class the corporation is authorized to "issue" (*i.e.*, sell). *See* Del. G.C.L. §§ 102, 151(a). Since the certificate may be amended only upon approval of the shareholders (Del. G.C.L. § 242), the shareholders have some control over changes in the capital structure. But within the limits set forth in the certificate, and subject to the various statutory and common law rules to be discussed in other parts of the book (see, for example, Section 3.05 which discusses thin capitalization as a basis for "piercing the corporate veil" to impose personal liability on shareholders for corporate debts), the directors may vote to issue stock without further shareholder approval. This subsection discusses additional constraints on the directors' power to issue corporate stock which are designed to protect creditors.

The Delaware provisions controlling the amount that must be paid for shares exemplify the traditional "legal capital" approach that is followed in many statutes.

These statutes provide that stock may, but need not, have a "par" value. *See* Del. G.C.L. § 102(a)(4). Stock with par value must be issued for a consideration at least equal to par. *See* Del. G.C.L. § 153(a).

In the early history of corporations, stock had to have a par value, and par was generally the price for which the corporation sold its stock. In light of this practice, the par requirement ensured that all of the new shareholders were paying substantial consideration—indeed, that all holders of a given class paid the same consideration. This protected creditors from fraud and existing shareholders from dilution.

The requirement that shareholders pay par and the equating of par with purchase price caused a number of practical problems. First, fluctuations in market price sometimes made it difficult to sell stock at a preset par value. Second, non-cash property exchanged for stock had to be valued to ensure that the consideration was at least equal to par. Third, high par value reduced the corporation's flexibility in paying dividends (*see* Section 11.03). Fourth, a former federal statute and some current state statutes tax corporations on the basis of the par value of their stock.

These costs of high par value stock exceeded its benefits to creditors and shareholders. Par value is little help to creditors as compared with other available devices for assessing credit risks and ensuring that the corporation repays its debts. As for shareholders, dilution from new stock issues is not the problem it was once thought to be, and in any event shareholders are protected against dilution by pre-emptive rights, as discussed in subsection [3] below.

Par value has only vestigial importance today. Corporation statutes do not prevent firms from offering stock carrying a par value that is only a trivial fraction of the consideration paid. (However, some preferred stock is still high par, reflecting the debt-like character of preferred). And corporations may now offer "no par" stock. *See, e.g.,* Del. G.C.L. § 153(b). "No par" statutes became dominant as a result of the interstate competition for corporate charters discussed above in Section 7.02[B].[3] The concepts of par and legal capital have been eliminated from the Model Act. *See* MBCA § 6.21.

Most statutes limit how shareholders may pay for their stock. Del. G.C.L. § 152 excludes future services and limits the use of promissory notes to that part of the consideration which exceeds the amount allocated to capital. However, Del. G.C.L. § 156 permits the directors to issue "partly paid" shares in return for a promise to pay on the corporation's call in the future.

Permissible consideration is defined more expansively in MBCA § 6.21(b). Restrictions on permissible consideration, like those in the Delaware statute, prevent the corporation from representing values on the balance sheet which, in the event of insolvency, will prove to be of little help to creditors, and reduce valuation problems by eliminating from the category of eligible consideration commodities that are of speculative value. But these restrictions impose costs in terms of decreased financing flexibility that may outweigh any benefits to creditors.

---

    [3]   *See State ex rel. Standard Tank Car Co. v. Sullivan,* 221 S.W. 728 (Mo. 1920) (permitting a Delaware corporation with no par stock to do business in Missouri, which had not adopted no-par stock).

Shareholder contributions generally are not required to be disclosed in the corporation's certificate. The medium of disclosure is usually the corporation's balance sheet. *See* Section 3.02[B] above. Most corporations make their balance sheets available to creditors and others, although they are not legally required to do so unless they are subject to reporting requirements, such as those under federal and state securities laws.

The traditional "legal capital" type of provision requires part of the consideration received for stock to be segregated into a "capital" account that is reflected in the shareholders' equity portion of the balance sheet. *See* Del. G.C.L. § 154. As discussed in Chapter 11, the capital account restricts the amount which may be paid out as dividends. The following shows how § 154 operates.

Assume that the corporation begins with three shareholders, each contributing $2,000 and each receiving 200 shares of the single class of common stock:

(1) If the directors fix par at $10, the balance sheet would reflect the transaction in something like the following manner:

Assets	Liabilities
Cash: $6,000	
	Stockholders' Equity
	Capital: 600 shares common
	$10 par value = $6000
$6000	$6000

(2) If par value is $1:

Assets	Liabilities
Cash: $6,000	
	Stockholders' Equity
	Capital: 600 shares
	$1 par value = $600
	Capital surplus: $5400
$6000	$6000

Note that: "capital" and "surplus" are merely arbitrary figures designated by the directors and do not refer to real economic values. Surplus may also be referred to as "paid-in-surplus" or "additional paid-in capital" or "capital in excess of par value." See the balance sheet in Section 3.02[B].

(3) If the stock is "no par," Del. G.C.L. § 154 requires the directors to allocate part of the consideration received for the stock to capital and part to surplus. If the directors allocated $1 per share to capital, the balance sheet would look as follows:

Assets   Liabilities
Cash: $6,000

                                          Stockholders' Equity

                                          Stated Capital:
                                            600 Shares = $600

                                          Capital surplus: $5400
          $6000 $6000

Note that the capital could also have been designated as, for example, $10 per share, with the appropriate adjustments in the balance sheet.

A firm incorporated under the Model Act, which does not recognize the concept of legal capital, may disclose the entire amount of the consideration received for the stock ($6,000 in the example) as a single amount under "stockholders' equity," and need not segregate it into "capital" and "capital surplus." *See* MBCA § 6.21.

Where stock is issued for noncash consideration, the directors must generally determine the value of the consideration in dollars. The statutes often leave valuation very much to the discretion of the directors. *See* Del. G.C.L. § 152 ("fraud" standard). What if the directors breach their statutory duties in issuing stock? Illegally issued stock may be cancelled.[4] However, unless the statute specifically characterizes the stock as "void," the court may refuse to cancel the stock despite noncompliance with the statute.[5] Also, those who have extended credit to a corporation in reliance on a misstatement concerning the amount of consideration received for stock may recover under a fraud theory against directors and shareholders who were responsible for the misstatement, though only if the corporation has become insolvent. The most significant roadblocks to recovery under a fraud theory are the requirements that the plaintiff prove defendant's intent to defraud, or "scienter," and her own reliance. Since most creditors do not extend credit on the basis of representations concerning the consideration received for stock, the latter requirement may present a particular problem.[6]

Shareholders are liable at least for what they agreed to pay for their stock. *See* Del. G.C.L. § 162(a); MBCA § 6.22. *See also* Del. G.C.L. § 325 permitting recovery by creditors.[7]

---

[4]   *See, e.g., Stone v. Martin*, 85 N.C. App. 410, 355 S.E.2d 255 (1987) (directors failed to value stock).

[5]   *See Frasier v. Trans-Western Land Corp.*, 210 Neb. 681, 316 N.W.2d 612 (1982), where the court held that the plaintiff was a shareholder and entitled to statutory rights in connection with a sale of assets although plaintiff's stock was issued for future services. The court emphasized that the claim of invalidity was made by other shareholders rather than creditors. *See also Crowder v. Electro-Kinetics Corp.*, 228 Ga. 610, 187 S.E.2d 249 (1972) (directors' failure to value the stock did not require invalidation).

[6]   For a case imposing liability in favor of a creditor for a fraudulent statement in a balance sheet where the creditor was able to prove reliance on the balance sheet, see *Brown-Wales Co. v. Barber*, 88 N.H. 103, 184 A. 855 (1936).

[7]   For cases in which liability was imposed in favor of creditors for "partly paid" stock, see *Providence State Bank v. Bohannon*, 426 F. Supp. 886 (E.D. Mo. 1977), *aff'd*, 572 F.2d 617 (8th Cir. 1977); *Goff v. Henry Goff & Co.'s Assignee*, 257 Ky. 519, 78 S.W.2d 758 (1935).

An important question is whether the shareholders may be held liable for more than they agreed to pay for their stock. Provisions like Del. G.C.L. § 162(a) seem to say no, subject to the limitation on valid consideration in Del. G.C.L. § 152. This latter provision, and MBCA § 6.21(d), provide that the shareholder's stock is "nonassessable" if consideration of the prescribed type has been paid. There are, however, at least three other possible interpretations of provisions like those just referred to which cast some doubt on the scope of the purchasing shareholder's liability. "Consideration" under Del. G.C.L. § 162(a) could refer to the price that investors in general were charged for the same issue of stock. Under this interpretation, if shares were sold to twenty investors at $20 per share and, at the same time, to an additional investor who only agreed to pay $5 per share, the $5 investor would be liable for an additional $15 per share.[8] "Consideration" also could mean the amount for which the stock was stated on the balance sheet to have been sold, so that the shareholder would be liable for the difference between the amount stated and the amount actually paid, at least if the shareholder was aware of the difference.[9] Finally, "whole of the consideration payable for shares" in Del. G.C.L. § 162(a) could refer to the requirement in § 153(a) that par be paid for par value stock.

Two cases support limiting shareholders' liability to agreed consideration: *G. Loewus & Co. v. Highland Queen Packing Co.*,[10] and *Johnson v. Louisville Trust Co.*[11] But neither case involved any of the arguments discussed above supporting liability beyond the shareholders' agreement. In addition, in both cases, the stock was no par, and there was no clear misrepresentation of the consideration received for the stock.

The corporation clearly has a cause of action against a shareholder who fails to pay the agreed consideration for stock. Where the corporation is insolvent, the cause of action may be prosecuted by the trustee in bankruptcy for the benefit of the creditors. There are a few cases in which shareholders have recovered damages under legal capital provisions.[12]

Outside of bankruptcy, creditors may attempt to obtain direct recovery against defaulting shareholders. Some cases apply the so-called "trust fund" theory. These cases characterize the legal capital of the corporation as a trust fund so that shareholders who did not pay par held the unpaid amount as trustees for the benefit of creditors. But there is no actual trust fund since the whole problem in cases where shareholders have failed to pay par is that the would-be assets of the so-called trust never actually existed.

---

[8]   *See* I Folk, Ward & Welch, FOLK ON THE DELAWARE GENERAL CORPORATION LAW 312 (1988).

[9]   For a discussion of the possibility of statutory liability in this situation, see Israels, *Problems of Par and No Par Shares: A Reappraisal*, 47 COLUM. L. REV. 1279, 1300 (1947).

[10]   125 N.J. Eq. 534, 6 A.2d 545 (N.J. Ch. 1939). For a critique of *Loewus*, see Israels, *supra* footnote 9, at 1290-91.

[11]   293 F. 857 (6th Cir. 1923), *cert. denied*, 264 U.S. 585 (1924).

[12]   *See Scully v. Automobile Finance Co.*, 12 Del. Ch. 174, 109 A. 49 (1920), in which damages were awarded as a concession to the defendant to avoid the inequities created by cancellation. *See also Lewis v. Dansker*, 68 F.R.D. 184, 191-92 (S.D.N.Y. 1974), relying on New York Business Corporation Law § 628, which provides for such liability.

The trust fund theory was discredited in the leading case of *Hospes v. Northwestern Manufacturing & Car Co.*,[13] which held that shareholders who had received $1,500,000 par value stock for free would be liable, if at all, on the basis that creditors were misled by the overstatement of capital. Thus, those who extended credit before the stock issuance, or who knew of the inflation problem, were excluded from recovery. The court stated that creditors need not prove that they actually relied on the misleading balance sheet since those who extended credit after the issuance of the stock relied on the financial standing of the company which could be assumed to rest in part on its capital. But the *Hospes* theory is unlikely to lead to recoveries by creditors today, since creditors rarely base decisions as to the creditworthiness of a mature company on the consideration paid for its stock. Instead, creditors rely on the company's debt-paying habits, earnings, the ratio of debts to assets and other facts, and usually pay little attention to what the company received for its stock many years before. Moreover, the fact that some creditors are precluded from recovering hinders collective enforcement of creditor rights in bankruptcy.

Under the alternative "statutory obligation" theory, liability is imposed in favor of all creditors, irrespective of whether they were deceived as to the amount of a corporation's capital or when they extended credit. This is the theory that applies under the Delaware statute.[14] This theory in effect provides a workable way for creditors of a corporation in bankruptcy to enforce the contract between the corporation and the shareholder.

Consider, in light of the following Problem, how a careful legal planner can accomplish the planning objectives discussed above in Section 3.02[C] without risking liability under the statutory provisions discussed in this Section.

PROBLEM

Assume in the Judy, Kathy and Ray situation described in Section 2.01 that the parties have decided that Judy and Kathy will incorporate and loan their money to the business, that the corporation will rent space in Judy's building and that equal amounts of a single class of common stock will be issued to each shareholder. Advise the parties as to precisely how the issuance of stock should be handled to avoid shareholder liability to creditors under the legal rules discussed in this section. Assume Delaware law applies. What would the balance sheet look like? Consider the following specific alternatives, among others:

(1) Have Judy and Kathy make loans to the business and then allocate stock to all of the shareholders for free.

---

[13]   48 Minn. 174, 50 N.W. 1117 (1892).

[14]   *See Dupont v. Ball*, 11 Del. Ch. 430, 106 A. 39 (Sup. Ct. 1918); *Smith v. Mississippi Livestock Producers Association*, 188 So. 2d 758 (Miss. 1966); and *Easton National Bank v. American Brick and Tile*, 70 N.J. Eq. 732, 64 A. 917 (1906).

(2) Have Judy and Kathy make loans to the business and allocate stock to all of the shareholders for $.0001 per share.

(3) Same as (2), only place a value on the shares for balance sheet purposes at $1 share, with the difference between the cash payment and the consideration payable coming in the value of employment contracts entered into by the shareholders.

REFERENCE

Manning & Hanks, LEGAL CAPITAL (3d ed. 1990).

[3] Rules Protecting Existing Shareholders

Stock issuance may injure existing shareholders by diluting their voting power or their interests in the assets and earnings of the business. Dilution of voting rights depends on whether the new stock is of the same class as existing shares. For example, a new class of nonvoting stock does not dilute the voting power of any existing stock. Also, to the extent that shareholders vote as a class, each shareholder's voting power is measured as a percentage of her class and is unaffected by new shares of another class. For example, in *Lehrman v. Cohen*, discussed in Section 5.02[B][3], the classes voted together on all issues except the election of directors, so that issuing additional shares of either class would have diluted the shares of the other class.

Dilution of the right to share in earnings (through dividends) and in the assets of the corporation upon liquidation also depends partly on classification of the corporation's stock. Assume, for example, a corporation with classes of common and cumulative preferred stock, the latter entitling holders to a yearly dividend of 10% of the face amount of the stock and to the face amount of the stock plus accumulated dividends upon liquidation. Because both the dividend and liquidation amounts must be paid to the preferred stockholders before such payments are made on common shares, new common stock could not dilute the preferred. *Compare Thomas Branch & Co. v. Riverside & Dan River Cotton Mills*,[15] in which new common stock diluted existing stock that was preferred only as to dividends and not as to liquidation. To what extent would there be dilution of the rights of any of the shareholders in the above example by (a) additional preferred shares or (b) additional common shares?

Dilution may also occur in connection with warrants, options or convertible debt or securities. A warrant or option allows the holder to purchase a certain number of shares of a certain class at a given price (warrants are usually issued for longer periods than options). A holder of convertible securities may convert each share of stock or unit of debt into a given number of shares of stock of another class (generally common stock). Thus, new warrants, options or convertibles may dilute the classes of stock for which the new securities may be converted or exercised. Outstanding warrants, options

---

[15]   139 Va. 291, 123 S.E. 542 (1924).

and convertibles may, in turn, be diluted by new stock of the class obtainable by exercise or conversion.

The extent of dilution of assets and earnings depends on factors other than classification of the corporation's stock, including, in particular, the price paid for the new stock and the expected return on investment of the new capital.

Consider the following very simple illustrations:

(1) Corporation A has outstanding 100 shares of common stock selling for $10 per share. A's expected return in a year is $100, or 10%. A gives away 100 shares of new common stock. Assuming there are no changes in A's profitability, the expected per-share return on existing common will be diluted by 50% (200 shares will earn the same total amount as 100 shares did before the share issuance).

(2) Corporation A sells the 100 new common shares for $5 per share. If the expected return on the new capital is the same as that on the existing capital, 200 shares will earn only $50 more than 100 shares did. The common shares would have an expected return of $.75/share versus $1.00/share before the new issuance. If the actual return on the new capital is 20%, there is no reduction in earnings per share for the existing common. Does this mean the existing holders have not been injured by the sale?

(3) Corporation A sells the 100 new shares for $10 per share, but the return from investing the new capital is only 5%. Again, the common shares will earn only $.75/share instead of $1.00/share. But note that this does not result from the sale of new stock at too low a price, but because the present value of the projects in which the funds were invested was less than the company's cost of capital. In other words, the firm invested funds for which it was paying a 7.5% rate of return to invest in a project carrying a 5% rate of return. More technically, taking the cost of funds into account, the project had a negative net present value.

Even without misinvestment, the new issue may cause a decline in price if the market reads it as a signal that management believes the price is headed down because of undisclosed developments.

The above discussion shows that it is seldom possible to determine with any precision the existence or extent of dilution of liquidation value or dividends which will result from a new issue of stock.[16]

Shareholders may be protected from dilution in various ways:

(1) The corporate governance documents may give a class of shareholders the power to object to new stock issues.

(2) The shareholders may have a "preemptive right," discussed below, to purchase a portion of the new issue of stock.

---

[16] For an early discussion of this problem, see Frey, *Shareholders' Pre-Emptive Rights*, 38 YALE L.J. 563 (1929).

(3) The shareholders may have a cause of action for individual breach of fiduciary duty based on the dilution of their interest in the corporation. *See* Section 5.05[E], below.

(4) The shareholders may be able to sue derivatively on behalf of the corporation, claiming that the corporation was injured by the directors' decision to sell corporate property (its stock) for inadequate consideration, or to misinvest the proceeds of the sale. *See generally* Chapters 9 and 10 below.

The "preemptive right" refers to the right of existing shareholders to purchase part of a new issue of stock. This right helps protect shareholders from dilution by letting them maintain the same voting power and share of assets and dividends that they had prior to the issuance of the new stock.

The rules regarding the shareholders' exercise of their preemptive rights are left to the discretion of the board, subject to any restrictions in the corporation's governance documents and to general statutory guidelines. The preemptive right is available to shareholders who have purchased as of a particular date (the "record date") and is extended only for a limited time. If the shareholders do not exercise the right within the required time, the stock may then be offered for sale free of the preemptive right. Shareholders do not, however, lose their preemptive rights if there has been misrepresentation or nondisclosure of relevant facts or if the terms of the offer of rights are unfair.[17]

The practical considerations relevant to preemptive rights are different in public and close corporations. First, a preemptive right to buy stock in a public corporation, like the stock to which it applies, may be publicly traded as a separate security. The market price of the right depends largely on the difference between the price at which the underlying stock is trading and the price at which the holder of the right may purchase the stock, although the price is affected by other market considerations. Thus, the public corporation shareholder, unlike the close corporation shareholder, may protect himself against dilution either by selling the preemptive right or by exercising it and buying the underlying stock.

Second, preemptive rights involve both costs and benefits in connection with public marketing of securities. They may be burdensome because they interfere with the complex mechanisms for marketing publicly traded stock. The corporation generally sells its stock through an investment banker, which usually buys the stock from the corporation at a discount from the price at which it will be sold to the public, and takes the risk that the issue will not sell out. (For a more complete description of this distribution process, see Section 12.02 below.) If the shareholders have a preemptive right, this means that the investment banker's undertaking must be made contingent on the shareholders' exercise of their right. On the other hand, since the shareholders presumably know more about the corporation and are more favorably disposed to purchasing its

---

[17] *Compare Gord v. Iowana Farms Milk Co.*, 245 Iowa 1, 60 N.W.2d 820 (1953) (holding no waiver because of inadequate disclosure of facts), *with Fuller v. Krogh*, 15 Wis. 2d 412, 113 N.W.2d 25 (1962) (holding in favor of waiver).

stock than the general public, the corporation may be able to sell the issue directly to its shareholders at a higher net price than would be realized through an investment banker.

A third difference between public and close corporations concerning preemptive rights is that the protection afforded by such rights is needed more by close than by public corporation shareholders. The small voting interest of a public corporation shareholder usually will not be significantly affected by a new stock issue. And even if the new stock is sold cheaply, only a massive stock sale in a public corporation would seriously dilute the financial interests of the existing shares. On the other hand, new stock issues in close corporations are likely to have a significant effect on existing holders.

In general, therefore, preemptive rights are more burdensome to the corporation and less important to its shareholders in the public as compared with the close corporation. On the other hand, preemptive rights may prove less useful to the shareholders of close than of public corporations since, in the case of a close corporation, the preemptive right will not be publicly traded as a separate security and, therefore, the stockholder will not be able to protect himself against dilution by selling (as opposed to exercising) the right.

In early corporate history, the preemptive right was regarded as so basic that it was assumed to exist in most situations absent a contrary express agreement or charter provision. Moreover, amending the charter to eliminate preemptive rights would not affect the rights of existing shareholders.[18]

The preemptive right is no longer considered basic in most jurisdictions. This reflects the fact that, as discussed in the preceding subsection, the costs of preemptive rights may frequently exceed their benefits. Most statutes now provide that there is no preemptive right unless it is given by the articles of incorporation. *See, e.g.,* Del. G.C.L. § 102(b)(3). This shift in statutory law is another illustration of how states, competing for corporate chartering business, have adapted their statutes to meet the demands of corporations.

MBCA § 6.30 provides a "standard form" preemptive right provision that the corporation may opt into simply by providing in the articles of incorporation that "the corporation elects to have preemptive rights."

Even where the preemptive right has been granted by the articles of incorporation, modern cases have permitted amendment of the articles to remove the right, even with respect to existing shareholders.[19]

§ 3.03 Limited Liability: Theoretical Considerations

Corporate shareholders have "limited liability"—that is, they normally may not be called upon to use their own assets not invested in the business to pay business debts. This may be the most important reason why many people incorporate. The following section discusses the theory underlying limited liability.

---

[18] *See Stokes v. Continental Trust Co.,* 186 N.Y. 285, 78 N.E. 1090 (1906).

[19] *See, e.g., L.I. Minor Co., Inc. v. Perkins,* 246 Ga. 6, 268 S.E.2d 637 (1980).

[A] Introduction

Corporate shareholders have limited liability even if, but for incorporating, they would be personally liable as principals or partners under the rules discussed in Sections 2.01 and 2.02[B] above. This means that the shareholders are not liable for the debts of the corporation merely because they are shareholders, although they may be liable for their own torts or breaches of contract.

This is one of the most important corporate features. Indeed, at first glance, it might seem that all participants in business firms would want to incorporate in order to avoid the obligations of agency and partnership. Would anyone want a general partnership interest in Jurassic Park? The catch is that Jurassic Park's creditors, including its customers who are exposed to potential injuries, will demand compensation for the risk that they might eventually be left with an uncollectible damage claim. As discussed in Note 2 following *Nichols* in Section 2.01, this compensation might be more than the cost to the owners of bearing the risk.

To explain why firms adopt limited liability, therefore, one must explain how the benefits to the firm of limited liability outweigh the increase in the firms' cost of credit. The next subsections examine the principal benefits of limited liability.

[B] Minimizing the Cost of Capital

Perhaps the most important benefit of limited liability is that, for some, particularly larger, firms, it can result in a lower cost of capital than personal liability, all other things being equal. Limited liability accomplishes this result in several ways (**Easterbrook & Fischel**):

(1) *Reduced Costs of Risk Bearing*: Limited liability helps shareholders hold diversified portfolios of stock, an important risk-reduction strategy. For personally liable shareholders, owning more different stocks just creates more ways that the owners can lose their entire wealth. Personally liable shareholders are therefore less able to diversify their portfolios and demand greater compensation from firms for bearing risk.

(2) *Reduced Monitoring Costs*: Limited liability can reduce both owners' and creditors' monitoring costs. Personally liable owners need to monitor the managers' activities and the wealth of their fellow shareholders, since their entire wealth is at risk if the firm fails and their fellow shareholders are not able to bear their *pro rata* portion of the loss. Similarly, the firm's creditors need to know who owns the stock and how much they are worth in order to keep track of their cost of credit. When shareholders have limited liability, both shareholders and creditors have less need to monitor: shareholders have less reason to monitor managers' activities because their entire wealth is no longer at risk if the firm fails; and both shareholders and creditors can refrain from monitoring the identity and financial status of individual shareholders because their risk of loss no longer depends on shareholder wealth.

(3) *Increased Liquidity*: Limited liability facilitates free transfer of ownership interests. In order to reduce their monitoring costs (*see* (2)), creditors of personal-lia-

bility firms would want to keep shareholders from transferring their liability to low-asset holders when firms become insolvent. Even if shareholders are legally free to sell their stock, they may not easily find buyers willing to guarantee the firm's debts. These problems disappear when shareholders have limited liability. In that case, creditors have no reason to care about the identity of shareholders, since they have no recourse against the assets of those shareholders in the event that the firm fails. In addition, since buyers enjoy the same limited liability as sellers, shareholders seeking to sell their stock do not have to find a buyer who is willing to guarantee the firm's debts.

(4) *Market Efficiency*: Limited liability helps develop an efficient securities market (*see* Section 7.01). Frequent trading made possible by free transferability (*see* (3)) creates a market for information about stock values and prices. Also, limited liability makes it easier for the market to price securities, since market prices depend on the value of the firm's assets and not on the amount of wealth each shareholder exposes to liability. Efficient market valuation of the firm, among other benefits, helps outside shareholders monitor managers' use of corporate resources.

The value to shareholders of these benefits of limited liability may exceed the costs of limited liability to creditors. This is particularly likely in large firms for the following reasons: first, shareholders of large firms can expect to have more difficulty finding buyers willing to guarantee the firm's more substantial debts; second, firms with larger numbers of stockholders are much more likely than smaller firms to have sufficient trading volume to capture the benefits of free transferability of shares; and third, efficient markets are particularly important in large firms to help outside shareholders monitor managers. These features of large firms mean that shareholders of those firms are much more likely to profit from the benefits of limited liability discussed above—*i.e*, reduced risk bearing costs, reduced monitoring costs, increased liquidity, and market efficiency.

At the same time, the cost of limited liability to creditors of large firms with numerous investors may not be that great. For instance, shareholders' personal liability may not be worth much to creditors of such firms because it is too costly for creditors to keep track of and pursue shareholders' personal wealth. Firms with large amounts of capital are much more likely to be able to pay their debts without having to resort to their owners' personal assets. Moreover, creditors share in some benefits of limited liability. In particular, efficient market pricing of securities reduces creditors' need to investigate their debtors and limited liability eliminates the need to monitor the identity and wealth of individual shareholders.

It is important to emphasize that limited liability does not make sense for every business. In some firms, owners are particularly good monitors, so that it might pay for them to promise to bear the full risks of the firm. Thus, Lloyd's, the famous British insurance syndicate, has long been operated as a partnership (although this is changing). Its underwriters specialize in insuring unusual risks, and its investors (known as Names) stake their personal wealth on their willingness and ability to monitor the underwriters (**Winton**). Similarly, owners of smaller, closely held firms generally are active monitors. Moreover, if the firm's shares are not actively traded, the efficient market advantage of limited liability is unavailable. And it is important to keep in mind that, in very closely held firms, the owners may be directly liable for breach of contract or negligent acts or supervision, and therefore would not get much help from limited liability for the firm's debts.

Firms in which limited liability is excessively costly can organize as partnerships or some other type of firm in which the owners are personally liable. Alternatively, they can incorporate and contract out of the "default" corporate term of limited liability by expressly agreeing to be liable for the corporation's debts.

[C] The Problem of Involuntary Creditors

The foregoing analysis explains why shareholders—particularly shareholders of large firms—may opt for limited liability even though limited liability may increase the price of credit. However, the analysis does not, by itself, establish that limited liability is efficient. This is because the analysis fails to consider the interests of involuntary creditors (*i.e.*, tort victims) who are not in a position to demand compensation for the extra risks they take under limited liability. Thus, more is required to explain limited liability vis-a-vis involuntary creditors.

One explanation for limited liability vis-a-vis involuntary creditors is that the benefits to owners of limited liability discussed above outweigh the potential benefits to tort plaintiffs of personal liability. Whether this is actually the case depends on the extent to which limited liability lets firms' owners ignore potential risks to tort victims because they don't have to pay the full costs of these risks.

This problem of ignoring risks is not as serious as it might seem. For one thing, many corporations do insure against tort liability (**Easterbrook & Fischel**; **Ribstein**). Even with limited liability, shareholders have reason to be concerned about loss of corporate assets. Managers, who are charged with the decision whether to insure, may fear losing their jobs as a result of tort-induced insolvency. And the company may have to insure to appease unsecured contract creditors, who must share corporate assets with tort creditors. If the company does have to insure, its insurance rates, and the availability of insurance, depend on how carefully managers operate the business. Moreover, the inadequate insurance problem could be addressed directly through minimum insurance or bonding requirements for certain types of very risky firms rather than through mandatory unlimited liability.

[D] Closely Held Firms: Shifting Risk to Tort Victims?

The discussion in the preceding subsection explains why larger firms with numerous investors might opt for limited liability. It fails to explain, however, why smaller, closely held firms sometimes select limited liability. One explanation for limited liability in this situation is that the benefits to owners, while small, still outweigh the potential benefits to voluntary creditors and tort plaintiffs of personal liability. Another explanation for limited liability in this situation is that limited liability allows owners to shift part of the risk of their businesses to tort victims who are not in a position to demand extra compensation for the extra risks they undertake when businesses are run by limited liability owners who do not bear the full costs of their actions. It is this possible explanation that may underlie the historic unwillingness of policy-makers to allow limited liability to what are essentially partnerships. *See* Chapters 5 and 6.

REFERENCES

Alexander, *Unlimited Shareholder Liability Through A Procedural Lens*, 106 HARV. L. REV. 387 (1992).

Easterbrook & Fischel, THE ECONOMIC STRUCTURE OF CORPORATE LAW, Ch. 2 (1992).

Grundfest, *The Limited Future of Unlimited Liability: A Capital Markets Perspective*, 102 YALE L.J. 387 (1992).

Halpern, Trebilcock & Turnbull, *An Economic Analysis of Limited Liability in Corporation Law*, 30 U. TORONTO L.J. 117 (1980).

Hansmann & Kraakman, *Toward Unlimited Shareholder Liability for Corporate Torts*, 100 YALE L.J. 1879 (1991).

Hansmann & Kraakman, *The Essential Role of Organizational Law*, 110 YALE L.J. 387 (2000).

Leebron, *Limited Liability, Tort Victims, and Creditors*, 91 COLUM. L. REV. 1565 (1991).

Manne, *Our Two Corporation Systems: Law and Economics*, 53 VA. L. REV. 259 (1967).

Ribstein, *The Deregulation of Limited Liability and the Death of Partnership*, 70 WASH. U. L.Q. 417 (1992).

Ribstein, *Limited Liability and Theories of the Corporation*, 50 MD. L. REV. 80 (1991).

Thompson, *Unpacking Limited Liability: Direct and Vicarious Liability of Corporate Participants for Torts of the Enterprise*, 47 VAND. L. REV. 1 (1994).

Winton, *Limitation of Liability and the Ownership Structure of the Firm*, 48 J. FIN. 487 (1993).

Woodward, *Limited Liability and the Theory of the Firm*, 141 J. INST. & THEOR. ECON. 601 (1985).

§ 3.04 Limited Liability Without Incorporating

Incorporation provides a low-cost way of entering into a limited liability contract. Incorporating cheaply sends several messages to third parties: (1) the owners of the firm are not personally liable for its debts solely because they are shareholders; (2) the creditor has recourse against a specific set of assets owned in the name of the corporation; (3) certain information about the firm has been centrally filed in the articles or certificate of incorporation; and (4) the firm is bound by certain creditor-protection devices provided for by the corporation statute, such as limits on payment of dividends.

Although incorporation makes sense as a contracting device, it does not necessarily follow that investors should have to incorporate or form certain types of firms (such as limited partnerships or limited liability companies discussed below in Chapter 6) in order to obtain limited liability. This Section considers three types of private contracts in which this has been an issue: "nonrecourse" contracts wholly outside the corporate form; purported corporations; and promoter contracts.

[A] Nonrecourse Contracts

Partners or proprietors theoretically could simply agree with each of the firm's creditors not to hold the owners personally liable. This is known as a "nonrecourse" contract. Nonrecourse contracts give partners and proprietors the same limited liability enjoyed by corporate shareholders vis-a-vis voluntary creditors, but provide no protection in actions by involuntary creditors. Courts have generally enforced the liability limiting provisions of nonrecourse contracts, at least where the party alleged to be bound knew of the limitations and consented to them.[20]

What should be the result if the "nonrecourse" provision is contained in a publicly filed document that the third party fails to examine? In *Dominion National Bank v. Sundowner Joint Venture*,[21] the court refused to enforce the limited-recourse provisions of a publicly-filed joint venture agreement, finding that the plaintiffs had, at best, *constructive* knowledge of terms limiting the venturers' liability to their proportionate share of the venture's obligations. The joint venture agreement in *Dominion* had been filed in the Maryland real property records, but plaintiffs had never examined it. Why should a public filing be sufficient to create limited liability in the case of a corporation, but not in the case of a joint venture?

[B] Purported and Defective Corporations

Suppose a firm represents itself to creditors as a corporation, or the firm's owners believe they are incorporated, but the corporation has not actually been formed. Doesn't this solve the notice problem in *Dominion*? This is the logical counterpart to "apparent agency" (*see* Note 5 following *Nichols* in Section 2.01) and "partnership by estoppel" (*see* Note 7 following *Martin v. Peyton* in Section 2.02) theories of creating personal liability. But the law has not been that simple.

Early courts conferred corporate status where formalities had not fully been complied with only if a "*de facto*" corporation had been created. Courts in these cases exonerated would-be shareholders purportedly on the ground they had substantially complied in good faith with the prescribed incorporation procedures.[22] However, an

---

[20] *See, e.g., Union Trust Co. v. Poor & Alexander, Inc.*, 177 A. 923 (Md. 1935); *Demas v. Convention Motor Inns*, 232 S.E.2d 724 (S.C. 1977).

[21] 436 A.2d 501 (Md. App. 1981).

[22] *But cf. Fee Insurance Agency Inc. v. Snyder*, 930 P.2d 1054 (Kan. 1997) (stockholder held personally liable for unpaid corporate debt where copy of the articles of incorporation had not been filed with the local register of deeds).

early leading article (**Frey**) showed that many of these courts were really examining the dealings between the parties and their mutual expectations. The more modern "corporation by estoppel" approach explicitly adopts this view, focusing on the third party's belief that she was dealing with a corporation rather than on whether there was substantial compliance with formalities.[23] **McChesney**, applying a multiple regression analysis, determined that both the "substantial compliance" and "estoppel" arguments played a role in the cases relied on by Frey—that is, there is a unified "doctrine" of defective incorporation.

Statutes like Delaware G.C.L. § 106 and Model Business Corporation Act § 2.03 arguably preclude application of "*de facto*" incorporation by clarifying when the corporate existence begins, but do not entirely foreclose limited liability on grounds other than actual incorporation, particularly estoppel. However, MBCA § 2.04 goes further, abolishing incorporation by estoppel by explicitly imposing liability on parties who purport to act on behalf of a corporation without incorporating.[24]

Is MBCA § 2.04 right to impose individual liability when all parties expected that they were contracting for limited liability? The Official Comment to MBCA § 2.04 says that "to recognize limited liability in this situation threatens to undermine the incorporation process, since one then may obtain limited liability by consistently conducting business in the corporate name." But this just begs the question of whether "the incorporation process" is really necessary.

Evaluate the following reasons why the law might compel incorporation, or some similar formality, as a prerequisite for limited liability:

(A) To prevent particular types of firms from adopting limited liability—*i.e.,* where limited liability may impose excessive costs on creditors. For example, requiring incorporation might discourage closely held firms from adopting limited liability by forcing the firm to accept costly governance provisions, such as a board of directors, as a cost of limited liability (*see* Chapter 6). But do these rules actually protect creditors?

(B) To police misrepresentation. A firm that represents itself as an entity with limited liability owners without being incorporated misleads creditors into believing that creditor-protection terms and disclosures required by corporate statutes are in place. Several years ago a singer booked concerts under the name of "Elten John" in an effort to cash in on the British singer Elton John's popularity. Is this the same thing? How much protection do creditors get from corporate-type creditor protection rules? In any event, why not impose these rules on any firm that represents itself as an entity with limited liability owners?

---

[23] For a good discussion of the difference between the de facto and estoppel doctrines, see *Cranson v. International Business Machines Corp.*, 234 Md. 477, 200 A.2d 33 (1964).

[24] *See Booker Custom Packing Co., Inc. v. Sallomi*, 716 P.2d 1061 (Ariz. Ct. App. 1986); *T-K Distributors, Inc. v. Soldevere*, 704 P.2d 280 (Ariz. Ct. App. 1985); *Minish v. Gem State Developers, Inc.*, 99 Idaho 911, 591 P.2d 1078 (1979); *Thompson & Green Machinery Co., Inc. v. Music City Lumber Co.*, 683 S.W.2d 340 (Tenn. Ct. App. 1984).

(C) To police the terms of limited liability to involuntary creditors. Incorporation might be conditioned on minimum insurance requirements and other creditor-protection provisions, particularly for very risky firms, such as a single-owner taxicab corporation in which the owner has made little investment and there is no incentive to insure. But how convincing is this rationale if firms can form other types of limited liability entities without these requirements (*see* Chapter 6)?

(D) To facilitate taxation and regulation of businesses. This is a holdover from the early history of the corporate form, when incorporation was a state-conferred "privilege" (*see* Section 1.04). But it still makes some practical sense. If limited liability were freely available by private contract, there might be little remaining reason to incorporate. This would make it more difficult for the government to collect fees (*i.e.*, franchise taxes and corporate income taxes) as payment for corporate features, to regulate these features and to obtain information about firms. Of course, the question remains whether governments ought to impose such fees and regulation.

(E) To provide a clear rule about when limited liability is available in order to reduce uncertainty and the resulting litigation, such as the dispute in *Dominion*. But the parties to firms themselves can decide to clarify their situation by incorporating without being forced to do this. Also, consider whether mandating formalities really provides a clear rule in light of the rules discussed in this Section, granting limited liability even to imperfectly formed firms. Assuming there are real costs involved in recognizing limited liability absent compliance with formalities, are these costs greater than the uncertainty and extra litigation cost resulting from refusing to recognize corporate status because of noncompliance with formalities?

If the court imposes liability for defective incorporation, it is not always clear who should be liable—for example, all of the would-be shareholders, all large shareholders, all active participants, or all would-be officers and directors? The Official Comment to MBCA § 2.04 says liability is imposed on all those who contract "knowing" no corporation exists and approves a case[25] that imposes liability on "active" participants in the firm. A court also might recognize a partnership in this setting.[26]

REFERENCES

Frey, *Legal Analysis and the "De Facto" Doctrine*, 100 U. Pa. L. Rev. 1153 (1952).
McChesney, *Doctrinal Analysis and Statistical Modeling in Law: The Case of Defective Incorporation*, 71 Wash. U. L.Q. 493 (1993).
Ribstein, *Limited Liability and Theories of the Corporation*, 50 Md. L. Rev. 80 (1991).

---

[25] *Timberline Equipment Co. v. Davenport*, 267 Or. 64, 514 P.2d 1109 (1973).

[26] *See State ex rel. Carlton v. Triplett*, 213 Kan. 381, 517 P.2d 136 (1973).

[C] Promoter Cases

Suppose an entrepreneur now says that she is doing business on behalf of a corporation to be formed. This is arguably no longer the "assuming to act" situation because the promoter was not "purporting to act" as a present corporation,[27] but may trigger promoter liability. A "promoter" is someone who is involved in the preliminary steps of setting up a business. A promoter who is sued on a contract made prior to incorporation often argues that the plaintiff contracted neither with a nonexistent corporation nor with the promoter individually but rather with the promoter as the agent for the forming corporation. In effect, the promoter argues that, by acting as the agent for a forming corporation, he was contracting for "nonrecourse" liability. The promoter cases involve one or both of two separate issues: (1) the promoters' individual liability and (2) the liability of the corporation that is eventually formed.

[1] Promoter's Liability

The initial question is whether the promoter ever became individually bound to make payment to the creditor. Depending on the parties' intent, the contract may be only an option that the corporation can accept or reject. Assuming the promoter was bound initially, there is often the additional question (discussed in subsection [2] below) of whether the promoter is off the hook when the corporation is formed, adopts the contract, or becomes able to pay. This, too, depends on the parties' intent.

Binding the promoter may seem surprising in the face of contract language that the promoter was acting for "a corporation to be formed." But it may not be clear that the plaintiff intended both that no one be bound at first and that any corporation, regardless of how funded or formed, could be substituted for the promoter. Indeed, now that incorporation is so simple, the reason why it was not done at the time of the contract is probably because the underlying firm had not yet been formed.

Consider the leading case of *Stanley J. How & Assocs. v. Boss.*[28] Plaintiff architect contracted to furnish plans for a hotel. The contract was with "Owner: (s) Edw. A. Boss By: Edwin A Boss, agent for a Minnesota corporation to be formed who will be the obligor." Despite this seemingly clear language, the court held Boss individually liable. The court stressed that the contract called for plaintiff to begin work, and to begin receiving payments, soon after the contract was entered into. Moreover, only an Iowa corporation named "Minneapolis-Hunter Hotels Co." was formed, there was no evidence that this corporation had a charter or bylaws and it had no assets at the time of plaintiff's action.

---

[27] *See Sherwood & Roberts-Oregon, Inc. v. Alexander*, 269 Or. 389, 525 P.2d 135 (1974). However, the Official Comment to MBCA § 2.04 says that the statute applies except in the specific situation where the plaintiff urged defendant to contract in the name of the nonexistent corporation.

[28] 222 F. Supp. 936 (S.D. Iowa 1963).

[2] Corporation's Liability

In determining the corporation's liability, the courts have struggled with terms from agency and contract law by which new parties become bound to existing contracts, including ratification, adoption, and novation. Ratification and adoption both refer to the corporation's act of accepting the contract (*see* Section 8.01 below), though adoption is more properly applied to the situation in which the corporation did not exist at the time of the making of the contract. Novation, on the other hand, refers to the corporation's acceptance of the contract with the plaintiff's consent. The basic question in determining the corporation's liability for pre-incorporation contracts is whether the interests of the corporate shareholders, who will indirectly bear any liability imposed on the corporation, matter more than those of the plaintiff creditor.[29]

As discussed above, whether the corporation is bound by the contract can affect the promoter's liability. A court may conclude that the parties intended the promoter to be released if the corporation adopted or ratified the contract, or perhaps if there was a novation.[30] Therefore, a finding that the corporation is liable for the pre-incorporation contract may take the promoter off the hook.

Cases involving corporate successors to unincorporated firms present a related but distinguishable issue to corporate liability for pre-incorporation contracts. The plaintiff may have dealt with a partnership or sole proprietorship that later incorporated. Even if the corporation assumes the debts, the owners remain personally liable for pre-incorporation debts in the absence of a novation (*i.e.*, absent plaintiff's consent), and for some post-incorporation debts if the plaintiff had no notice of incorporation.[31]

§ 3.05 Personal Liability Despite Incorporation: Piercing the Corporate Veil

Now suppose that the entrepreneur has actually formed a corporation according to the statute. Is she now safe from liability? Even if the corporation has been formed in accordance with the statutory provisions discussed above, a court may "pierce the corporate veil"—that is, refuse to recognize the corporate entity and impose liability on individual shareholders for corporate debts.

Veil-piercing cases, and the theories they apply, are legion. It is important to pierce the linguistic veil in these cases and penetrate to the considerations that really matter. Sometimes the courts say that it is enough to pierce the veil that the corporation is an "instrumentality," "alter ego," or "dummy" of the shareholders. But the courts do not mean to say that they always pierce the veil in a one-person corporation, which is nec-

---

[29]   For a good opinion on this issue, see *Framingham Savings Bank v. Szabo*, 617 F.2d 897 (1st Cir. 1980).

[30]   *See Skandinavia, Inc. v. Cormier*, 514 A.2d 1250 (N.H. 1986) (promoter liable because corporation did not ratify).

[31]   *See* UPA §§ 35, 36, RUPA §§ 703-704, 804-805. Bromberg & Ribstein, BROMBERG AND RIBSTEIN ON PARTNERSHIP § 7.21(e).

essarily its owner's "dummy." Sometimes the courts say that the corporation is the shareholder's "agent." But the corporation is an "agent" only in the sense that the court has reached the legal conclusion, based on some other ground, that the shareholder, like a principal, should be held personally liable. In other cases the courts say that it is necessary to prove some kind of "fraud." That word is used here, as in other contexts, to refer to the conduct the court deems is necessary to reach a particular legal result. But what is the nature of that conduct?

No matter what the theory, the question always is: Under what circumstances should the court impose personal liability on corporate shareholders? Consider what role the following factors or distinctions should play in veil-piercing cases. For an extensive empirical examination of the role each of these factors plays in the cases, see **Thompson**.

[A] Voluntary Creditors

The discussion in Section 3.03 suggests that voluntary creditors are not injured by limited liability, and therefore should not be protected by veil-piercing, because they can raise their cost of credit to compensate them for the added risk. Some courts have suggested that some voluntary creditors, such as employees and trade creditors, should be treated differently from others because they are unable to negotiate for compensation.[32] But even "unsophisticated" creditors can seek assistance in negotiating deals. If, given the time and money involved in some deals, it is not worth it to the creditor to obtain assistance or more information, the uninformed or unsophisticated creditor is seemingly just as likely to overvalue as to undervalue the risk (*i.e.*, charge too much for credit, rather than too little), so that the corporation has the incentive to reduce the creditors' information or negotiation costs. If the problem is simply that the corporation has greater bargaining leverage than the creditor, should the courts be any more willing to rewrite this type of contract for this reason than they are any other types of contracts?

In cases involving voluntary creditors, the courts have often stressed whether there were misrepresentations to the creditors as to (i) the entity on which the creditor could rely for recovery or (ii) the extent of the corporation's assets.[33] The first sort of misrepresentation" is like a contract that is enforced by veil-piercing. Veil-piercing on the second ground, like other liability for deceit, arguably reduces information costs by ensuring disclosure by the party with the best access to information.

---

[32] *See Brunswick Corp. v. Waxman*, 459 F. Supp. 1222 (E.D.N.Y. 1978), *aff'd*, 599 F.2d 34 (2d Cir. 1979); *Bendix Home Systems, Inc. v. Hurston Enterprises, Inc.*, 566 F.2d 1039 (5th Cir. 1978); *Bartle v. Home Owners Cooperative, Inc.*, 309 N.Y. 103, 127 N.E.2d 832 (1955); *Angus v. Air Coils, Inc.*, 567 S.W.2d 931 (Tex. Civ. App. 1978); *Hanson Southwest Corp. v. Dal-Mac Construction Co.*, 554 S.W.2d 712 (Tex. Civ. App. 1977).

[33] *Compare Edwards Co., Inc. v. Monogram Industries, Inc.*, 730 F.2d 977 (5th Cir. 1984) (en banc) (denying liability where no misrepresentation), *and George Hyman Construction Co. v. Gateman*, 16 F. Supp. 2d 129 (D. Mass. 1998) (same), *with Mobridge Community Industries, Inc. v. Toure, Ltd.*, 273 N.W.2d 128 (S.D. 1978) (veil-piercing based primarily on misrepresentation).

[B] Involuntary Creditors

Thompson found that the courts rarely pierce the veil in tort cases. This might seem surprising in light of the fact that limited liability imposes costs on involuntary creditors. But keep in mind that any veil-piercing must be reconciled with the fact that corporation statutes do provide for limited liability in both tort and contract cases. Consider the *Walkovszky* case below in this light. Consider also the arguments against imposing unlimited liability on behalf of tort creditors discussed in Section 3.03.

[C] Undercapitalization

Walkovzsky illustrates the debate over the role of the firm's capitalization—that is, its ratio of debt to equity—in veil-piercing cases. As noted in the *Walkovzsky* dissent, there is California authority for shareholder liability on the basis of inadequate capitalization alone. But should small capitalization be a sufficient justification for piercing the veil in cases involving voluntary creditors, where the creditor can adjust the cost of credit based on the extent of capitalization? An alternative justification for veil piercing based on inadequate capitalization is to give corporations the incentive to disclose their capitalization to creditors before transacting (*see* **Easterbrook & Fischel**). But disclosure is arguably irrelevant to involuntary creditors who are not in a position to act on the disclosed information. Moreover, voluntary creditors can simply adjust their credit terms to reflect their higher information costs without disclosure. Veil piercing for undercapitalization is also difficult to reconcile with statutes allowing incorporation without imposing minimum capitalization requirements.

Assuming undercapitalization is a good reason to pierce the veil, what should be the test for whether a corporation is undercapitalized? As the principal policy justification for piercing the veil for undercapitalization is to prevent owners from shifting business risks to creditors, the amount of required capital should depend on the risks inherent in the particular business. Also, perhaps courts should distinguish initial undercapitalization (*i.e.*, undercapitalization at the time the corporation is formed), which may indicate a deliberate transfer of risks to creditors, from undercapitalization later in the corporation's history, which may simply reflect a poor business environment. On the other hand, voluntary creditors presumably can determine the capitalization at the time of the debt and fix their credit charges accordingly. Thus, maybe the relevant distinction should be between undercapitalization at the time a particular debt was incurred, which is reflected in the price that is charged for credit, and undercapitalization thereafter.

[D] Public versus Close Corporations

Limited liability may carry fewer benefits and greater costs for closely held than for publicly held firms (*see* Section 3.03). But even so, consider whether courts should pierce the veil more readily in cases involving closely held corporations under corporate statutes which make limited liability equally available to closely held and publicly held corporations.

[E] Parent-Subsidiary Cases

It might seem that the corporate veil should be pierced more readily in subsidiary firms that are wholly or mostly owned by a single parent corporation. **Blumberg, Landers** and **Posner** debate this point. First, limited liability is arguably unnecessary in this situation. Among other things, the subsidiary's shares are not actively traded, so the parent has little, if anything, to gain from the capacity of limited liability to facilitate transfers of ownership interests and to enhance market efficiency. Moreover, parent corporations actively monitor their subsidiaries and so do not benefit from the power of limited liability to facilitate passive investing. Second, corporate groups may be run as single firms, with each corporation supporting the others, rather than being run as independent entities. Parents therefore may deliberately undercapitalize the subsidiaries, or move assets around in such a complicated way that creditors cannot determine the creditworthiness of each corporation in the group. (On the other hand, many parents run their subsidiaries as independent "profit centers" so that they can determine the profitability of particular lines of business.)

In light of the above discussion, it might seem surprising that courts only rarely pierce the veil to reach parent corporations (**Thompson**). This could represent a judicial judgment that the risks of limited liability are not so great, or simply deference to corporation statutes that do not condition the availability of limited liability on whether the shareholders are individuals or corporations. On the latter point, **Blumberg** argues that limited liability was already well-established before the advent of corporate ownership of stock, and was applied to this situation without any real consideration of the costs and benefits.

[F] Observance of Formalities

The courts, in determining whether to pierce the veil, often stress whether the shareholders have disregarded formalities of decision making, such as director and shareholder meetings, and of record-keeping, as by commingling shareholder and corporate funds. Why should these facts be relevant?[34]

In light of the above considerations, evaluate whether the veil should be pierced in the following cases.

---

[34] For a recent case considering the observance of formalities, see *Lorenz v. Beltio Ltd.*, 963 P.2d 488 (Nev. 1998) (allowing veil to be pierced though corporation had been formed in accordance with law and generally adhered to corporate formalities, in part because owners commingled corporate and personal funds).

WALKOVSZKY v. CARLTON
New York Court of Appeals
18 N.Y.2d 414, 223 N.E.2d 6, 276 N.Y.S.2D 585 (1966)

FULD, Judge.

This case involves what appears to be a rather common practice in the taxicab industry of vesting the ownership of a taxi fleet in many corporations, each owning only one or two cabs.

The complaint alleges that the plaintiff was severely injured four years ago in New York City when he was run down by a taxicab owned by the defendant Seon Cab Corporation and negligently operated at the time by the defendant Marchese. The individual defendant, Carlton, is claimed to be a stockholder of 10 corporations, including Seon, each of which has but two cabs registered in its name, and it is implied that only the minimum automobile liability insurance required by law (in the amount of $10,000) is carried on any one cab. Although seemingly independent of one another, these corporations are alleged to be "operated . . . as a single entity, unit and enterprise" with regard to financing, supplies, repairs, employees, garaging, and all are named as defendants. The plaintiff asserts that he is also entitled to hold their stockholders personally liable for the damages sought because the multiple corporate structure constitutes an unlawful attempt "to defraud members of the general public" who might be injured by the cabs.

The defendant Carlton has moved, pursuant to CPLR 3211(a)(7), to dismiss the complaint on the ground that as to him it "fails to state a cause of action." The court at Special Term granted the motion but the Appellate Division, by a divided vote, reversed, holding that a valid cause of action was sufficiently stated. . . .

The law permits the incorporation of a business for the very purpose of enabling its proprietors to escape personal liability . . . but, manifestly, the privilege is not without its limits. Broadly speaking, the courts will disregard the corporate form, or, to use accepted terminology, "pierce the corporate veil," whenever necessary "to prevent fraud or to achieve equity." (*International Aircraft Trading Co. v. Manufacturers Trust Co.*, 297 N.Y. 285, 292, 79 N.E.2d 249, 252.) In determining whether liability should be extended to reach assets beyond those belonging to the corporation, we are guided, as Judge Cardozo noted, by "general rules of agency." (*Berkey v. Third Ave. Ry. Co.*, 244 N.Y. 84, 95, 155 N.E. 58, 61, 50 A.L.R. 599.) In other words, whenever anyone uses control of the corporation to further his own rather than the corporation's business, he will be liable for the corporation's acts "upon the principles of *respondeat superior* applicable even where the agent is a natural person . . . ." . . . Such liability, moreover, extends not only to the corporation's commercial dealings . . . but to its negligent acts as well. . . .

In the *Mangan* [*v. Terminal Transp. System*] case (247 A.D. 853, 286 N.Y.S. 666, *mot. for lv. to app. denied*, 272 N.Y. 676, 286 N.Y.S. 666, *supra*), the plaintiff was injured as a result of the negligent operation of a cab owned and operated by one of four corporations affiliated with the defendant Terminal. Although the defendant was not a stockholder of any of the operating companies, both the defendant and the operating companies were owned, for the most part, by the same parties. The defendant's name (Terminal) was conspicuously displayed on the sides of all of the taxis used in the enterprise and, in point of fact, the defendant actually serviced, inspected, repaired and dispatched them. These facts were deemed to provide sufficient cause for piercing the corporate veil of the operating company—the nominal owner of the cab which injured the plaintiff—and holding the defendant liable. The operating companies were simply instrumentalities for carrying on the business of the defendant without imposing upon it financial and other liabilities incident to the actual ownership and operation of the cabs.

* * *

In the case before us, the plaintiff has explicitly alleged that none of the corporations "had a separate existence of their own" and, as indicated above, all are named as defendants. However, it is one thing to assert that a corporation is a fragment of a larger corporate combine which actually conducts the business. (*See* Berle, *The Theory of Enterprise Entity*, 47 Col. L. Rev. 343, 348-350.) It is quite another to claim that the corporation is a "dummy" for its individual stockholders who are in reality carrying on the business in their personal capacities for purely personal rather than corporate ends. (*See African Metals Corp. v. Bullowa*, 288 N.Y. 78, 85, 41 N.E.2d 466, 469.) Either circumstance would justify treating the corporation as an agent and piercing the corporate veil to reach the principal but a different result would follow in each case. In the first, only a larger corporate entity would be held financially responsible . . . while, in the other, the stockholder would be personally liable.

. . . Either the stockholder is conducting the business in his individual capacity or he is not. If he is, he will be liable; if he is not, then it does not matter—insofar as his personal liability is concerned—that the enterprise is actually being carried on by a larger "enterprise entity." (*See* Berle, *The Theory of Enterprise Entity*, 47 COL. L. REV. 343.)

. . . Reading the complaint in this case most favorably and liberally, we do not believe that there can be gathered from its averments the allegations required to spell out a valid cause of action against the defendant Carlton.

The individual defendant is charged with having "organized, managed, dominated and controlled" a fragmented corporate entity but there are no allegations that he was conducting business in his individual capacity. Had the taxicab fleet been owned by a single corporation, it would be readily apparent that the plaintiff would face formidable barriers in attempting to establish personal liability on the part of the corporation's stockholders. The fact that the fleet ownership has been deliberately split up among many corporations does not ease the plaintiff's burden in that respect. The corporate form may not be disregarded merely because the assets of the corporation, together with the mandatory insurance coverage of the vehicle which struck the plaintiff, are insufficient to assure him the recovery sought. If Carlton were to be held individually liable on those facts alone, the decision would apply equally to the thousands of cabs which are owned by their individual drivers who conduct their businesses through corporations organized pursuant to section 401 of the Business Corporation Law, Consol. Laws, c. 4 and carry the minimum insurance required by subdivision 1 (par. [a]) of section 370 of the Vehicle and Traffic Law, Consol. Laws, c. 71. These taxi owner-operators are entitled to form such corporations . . . and we agree with the court at Special Term that, if the insurance coverage required by statute "is inadequate for the protection of the public, the remedy lies not with the courts but with the Legislature." . . .

This is not to say that it is impossible for the plaintiff to state a valid cause of action against the defendant Carlton. However, the simple fact is that the plaintiff has just not done so here. While the complaint alleges that the separate corporations were undercapitalized and that their assets have been intermingled, it is barren of any "sufficiently particular[ized] statements" (CPLR 3013; *see* 3 Weinstein-Korn-Miller, N.Y. Civ. Prac., par. 3013.01 *et seq.*, pp. 30-142 *et seq.*) that the defendant Carlton and his associates are actually doing business in their individual capacities, shuttling their personal funds in and out of the corporations "without regard to formality and to suit their immediate convenience." . . . Nothing of the sort has in fact been charged, and it cannot reasonably or logically be inferred from the happenstance that the business of Seon Cab Corporation may actually be carried on by a larger corporate entity composed of many corporations which, under general principles of agency, would be liable to each other's creditors in contract and in tort.

In point of fact, the principle relied upon in the complaint to sustain the imposition of personal liability is not agency but fraud. Such a cause of action cannot withstand analysis. If it is not fraudulent for the owner-operator of a single cab corporation to take out only the minimum required liability insurance, the enterprise does not become either illicit or fraudulent merely because it consists of many such corporations. The plaintiff's injuries are the same regardless of whether the cab which strikes him is owned by a single corporation or part of a fleet with ownership fragmented among many corporations. Whatever rights he may be able to assert against parties other than the registered owner of the vehicle come into being not because he has been defrauded but because, under the principle of *respondeat superior*, he is entitled to hold the whole enterprise responsible for the acts of its agents.

In sum, then, the complaint falls short of adequately stating a cause of action against the defendant Carlton in his individual capacity.

The order of the Appellate Division should be reversed, . . . with leave to serve an amended complaint.

KEATING, Judge (dissenting).

From their inception these corporations were intentionally undercapitalized for the purpose of avoiding responsibility for acts which were bound to arise as a result of the operation of a large taxi fleet having cars out on the street 24 hours a day and engaged in public transportation. And during the course of the corporations' existence all income was continually drained out of the corporations for the same purpose.

The issue presented by this action is whether the policy of this State, which affords those desiring to engage in a business enterprise the privilege of limited liability through the use of the corporate device, is so strong that it will permit that privilege to continue no matter how much it is abused, no matter how irresponsibly the corporation is operated, no matter what the cost to the public. I do not believe that it is.

Under the circumstances of this case the shareholders should all be held individually liable to this plaintiff for the injuries he suffered. . . . At least, the matter should not be disposed of on the pleadings by a dismissal of the complaint. "If a corporation is organized and carries on business without substantial capital in such a way that the corporation is likely to have no sufficient assets available to meet its debts, it is inequitable that shareholders should set up such a flimsy organization to escape personal liability. The attempt to do corporate business without providing any sufficient basis of financial responsibility to creditors is an abuse of the separate entity and will be ineffectual to exempt the shareholders from corporate debts. It is coming to be recognized as the policy of law that shareholders should in good faith put at the risk of the business unincumbered capital reasonably adequate for its prospective liabilities. If capital is illusory or trifling compared with the business to be done and the risks of loss, this is a ground for denying the separate entity privilege." (Ballantine, CORPORATIONS [rev. ed., 1946] § 129, pp. 302-303.)

In *Minton v. Cavaney*, 56 Cal. 2d 576, 15 Cal. Rptr. 641, 364 P.2d 473, the Supreme Court of California had occasion to discuss this problem in a negligence case. The corporation of which the defendant was an organizer, director and officer operated a public swimming pool. One afternoon the plaintiffs' daughter drowned in the pool as a result of the alleged negligence of the corporation.

Justice Roger Traynor, speaking for the court, outlined the applicable law in this area. "The figurative terminology 'alter ego' and 'disregard of the corporate entity,'" he wrote, "is generally used to refer to the various situations that are an abuse of the corporate privilege. . . . The equitable owners of a corporation, for example, are personally liable when they treat the assets of the corporation as their own and add or withdraw capital from the corporation at will . . .; when they hold themselves out as being personally liable for the debts of the corporation . . .; *or when they provide inadequate capitalization and actively participate in the conduct of corporate affairs.*" (56 Cal. 2d, p. 579, 15 Cal. Rptr., p. 643, 364 P.2d p. 475; italics supplied.)

Examining the facts of the case in light of the legal principles just enumerated, he found that "[it was] undisputed that there was no attempt to provide adequate capitalization. [The corporation] never had any substantial assets. It leased the pool that it operated, and the lease was forfeited for failure to pay the rent. Its capital was 'trifling compared with the business to be done and the risks of loss.'" (56 Cal. 2d, p. 580, 15 Cal. Rptr., p. 643, 364 P.2d p. 475.)

It seems obvious that one of "the risks of loss" referred to was the possibility of drownings due to the negligence of the corporation. And the defendant's failure to provide such assets or any fund for recovery resulted in his being held personally liable.

In *Anderson v. Abbott*, 321 U.S. 349, 64 S. Ct. 531, 88 L. Ed. 793, the defendant shareholders had organized a holding company and transferred to that company shares which they held in various national banks in return for shares in the holding company. The holding company did not have sufficient assets to meet the double liability requirements of the governing Federal statutes which provided that the owners of shares in national banks were personally liable for corporate obligations "to the extent of the amount of their stock therein, at the par value thereof, in addition to the amount invested in such shares" (U.S. Code, tit. 12, former § 63).

The court had found that these transfers were made in good faith, that other defendant shareholders who had purchased shares in the holding company had done so in good faith and that the organization of such a holding company was entirely legal. Despite this finding, the Supreme Court, speaking through Mr. Justice Douglas, pierced the corporate veil of the holding company and held all the shareholders, even those who had no part in the organization of the corporation, individually responsible for the corporate obligations as mandated by the statute.

"Limited liability," he wrote, "is the rule, not the exception; and on that assumption large undertakings are rested, vast enterprises are launched, and huge sums of capital attracted. But there are occasions when the limited liability sought to be obtained through the corporation will be qualified or denied. Mr. Chief Judge Cardozo stated that a surrender of that principle of limited liability would be made 'when the sacrifice is so essential to the end that some accepted public policy may be defended or upheld.' . . . The cases of fraud make up part of that exception. . . . But they do not exhaust it. *An obvious inadequacy of capital, measured by the nature and magnitude of the corporate undertaking, has frequently been an important factor in cases denying stockholders their defense of limited liability. . . . That rule has been invoked even in absence of a legislative policy which undercapitalization would defeat.* It becomes more important in a situation such as the present one where the statutory policy of double liability will be defeated if impecunious bank-stock holding companies are allowed to be interposed as non-conductors of liability. *It has often been held that the interposition of a corporation will not be allowed to defeat a legislative policy, whether that was the aim or only the result of the arrangement.* . . . 'the courts will not permit themselves to be blinded or deceived by mere forms of law' but will deal 'with the substance of the transaction involved as if the corporate agency did not exist and as the justice of the case may require.'" (321 U.S., pp. 362-363, 64 S. Ct., p. 537; emphasis added.)

The policy of this State has always been to provide and facilitate recovery for those injured through the negligence of others. The automobile, by its very nature, is capable of causing severe and costly injuries when not operated in a proper manner. The great increase in the number of automobile accidents combined with the frequent financial irresponsibility of the individual driving the car led to the adoption of section 388 of the Vehicle and Traffic Law which had the effect of imposing upon the owner of the vehicle the responsibility for its negligent operation. It is upon this very statute that the cause of action against both the corporation and the individual defendant is predicated.

In addition the Legislature, still concerned with the financial irresponsibility of those who owned and operated motor vehicles, enacted a statute requiring minimum liability coverage for all owners of automobiles. The important public policy represented by both these statutes is outlined in section 310 of the Vehicle and Traffic Law. That section provides that: "The legislature is concerned over the rising toll of motor vehicle accidents and the suffering and loss thereby inflicted. The legislature determines that it is a matter of grave concern that motorists shall be financially able to respond in damages for their negligent acts, so that innocent victims of motor vehicle accidents may be recompensed for the injury and financial loss inflicted upon them."

The defendant Carlton claims that, because the minimum amount of insurance required by the statute was obtained, the corporate veil cannot and should not be pierced despite the fact that the assets of the corporation which owned the cab were "trifling compared with the business to be done and the risks of loss" which were certain to be encountered. I do not agree.

The Legislature in requiring minimum liability insurance of $10,000, no doubt, intended to provide at least some small fund for recovery against those individuals and corporations who just did not have and were not able to raise or accumulate assets sufficient to satisfy the claims of those who were injured as a result of their negligence. It certainly could not have intended to shield those individuals who organized corporations, with the specific intent of avoiding responsibility to the public, where the operation of the corporate enterprise yielded profits sufficient to purchase additional insurance. More-over, it is reasonable to assume that the Legislature believed that those individuals and corporations having substantial assets would take out insurance far in excess of the minimum in order to protect those assets from depletion. Given the costs of hospital care and treatment and the nature of injuries sustained in auto collisions, it would be unreasonable to assume that the Legislature believed that the minimum provided in the statute would in and of itself be sufficient to recompense "innocent victims of motor vehicle accidents . . . for the injury and financial loss inflicted upon them."

The defendant contends that the court will be encroaching upon the legislative domain by ignoring the corporate veil and holding the individual shareholder. This argument was answered by Mr. Justice Douglas in *Anderson v. Abbott, supra*, pp. 366-367, 64 S. Ct. p. 540, where he wrote that: "In the field in which we are presently concerned, judicial power hardly oversteps the bounds when it refuses to lend its aid to a promotional project which would circumvent or undermine a legislative policy. To deny it that function would be to make it impotent in situations where historically it has made some of its most notable contributions. If the judicial power is helpless to protect a legislative program from schemes for easy avoidance, then indeed it has become a handy implement of high finance. Judicial interference to cripple or defeat a legislative policy is one thing; *judicial interference with the plans* of those whose corporate or other devices would circumvent that policy is quite another. Once the purpose or effect of the scheme is clear, once the legislative policy is plain, we would indeed forsake a great tradition to say we were helpless to fashion the instruments for appropriate relief." (Emphasis added.)

The defendant contends that a decision holding him personally liable would discourage people from engaging in corporate enterprise.

What I would merely hold is that a participating shareholder of a corporation vested with a public interest, organized with capital insufficient to meet liabilities which are certain to arise in the ordinary course of the corporation's business, may be held personally responsible for such liabilities. Where corporate income is not sufficient to cover the cost of insurance premiums above the statutory minimum or where initially adequate finances dwindle under the pressure of competition, bad times or extraordinary and unexpected liability, obviously the shareholder will not be held liable (Henn, CORPORATIONS, p. 208, n.7).

The only types of corporate enterprises that will be discouraged as a result of a decision allowing the individual shareholder to be sued will be those such as the one in question, designed solely to abuse the corporate privilege at the expense of the public interest.

For these reasons I would vote to affirm the order of the Appellate Division.

Order reversed, etc.

NOTES AND QUESTIONS

(1) **Pleading.** The plaintiff amended his complaint by adding an allegation that the defendant conducted business in his individual capacity. This was upheld by the Court of Appeals.[35] What must plaintiff prove at trial in order to recover from Carlton?

---

[35] 23 N.Y.2d 714, 244 N.E.2d 55, 296 N.Y.S.2d 362 (1968).

(2) **Liability of "sister" corporations.** The plaintiff sued not only Carlton, but also Carlton's other taxi corporations. Those corporations were not shareholders in the corporation that injured plaintiff, but rather were "sister" corporations under common ownership. What result if the motion to dismiss had been brought by these defendants? When should there be liability in this situation? In other words, when should the court permit suit against the "larger corporate combine"? Is it necessary or sufficient that there be a basis for veil-piercing liability against the dominating shareholder? Consider the *Walkovszky* majority's discussion of the *Mangan* case, as well as the *Zaist* case, below.

(3) **Liability of other non-shareholders.** Compare *Walkovszky* with *Wallace v. Tulsa Yellow Cab Taxi & Baggage Co.*[36] In that case, the defendant, which had operated profitably for some time and had substantial assets, was finding it difficult to obtain liability insurance. Three non-shareholder employees of defendant organized Yellow Cab Service Company ("Service"). They contributed $1,000 capital that they borrowed from defendant's president. Defendant leased all of its taxis to Service, retaining the right to terminate the lease at any time. Service paid out virtually all of its income in salaries, rental payments and other expenses. For most of its existence, and at the time of the accident, Service carried no liability insurance. A cab operated by Service injured plaintiff. Less than a month after plaintiff obtained a judgment from Service, Service ceased doing business and defendant took possession of its taxis. The court held that plaintiff could recover from defendant under a veil-piercing theory. Can this case be reconciled with *Walkovszky*?

(4) **Reverse veil-piercing.** In a traditional veil-piercing case, a creditor of a corporation seeks to reach the assets of a corporate shareholder to satisfy a corporate debt. If a court decides that veil-piercing is appropriate, should the corporation be held personally liable for the individual shareholders' liabilities? For a recent case considering the propriety of "reverse veil piercing" in the limited partnership setting, see *C.F. Trust Inc. v. First Flight Limited Partnership.*[37]

---

[36]   61 P.2d 645 (Okla. 1936).

[37]   306 F.3d 126 (4th Cir. 2002) (certifying "reverse veil piercing" question to Virginia Supreme Court).

ABRAHAM v. LAKE FOREST, INC.

Louisiana Court of Appeals

377 So. 2d 465 (1980)

Schott, Judge.

After taking a judgment against NEI Corporation, Alabama (hereinafter referred to as "Alabama") plaintiff brought this suit against Lake Forest, Inc., the owner of all the stock in Alabama and NEI Corporation, the owner of all of the stock in Lake Forest, attempting to pierce Alabama's corporate veil and to make the other corporations liable for Alabama's debt. Plaintiff has appealed from a dismissal of the suit and raises the issue that the facts and circumstances support the imposition of liability on Lake Forest and NEI as a matter of law.

On March 14, 1973, plaintiff purchased for $21,524 an option to purchase some 119 acres on Cody Road near Mobile, Alabama, for $389,382.50. Shortly thereafter plaintiff began to negotiate with a representative of Lake Forest to sell the option. These negotiations culminated with a sale and assignment of the option by Abraham to Lake Forest's newly formed subsidiary Alabama for $375,500. On the same date Abraham and Alabama jointly exercised the option to purchase the property and Alabama subsequently took title to the property for $389,382.50.

The price Alabama paid for the option consisted of $172,117.50 in cash paid to Abraham and his partner, and Alabama's note for $203,382.50. Between March 14, 1974, and January 10, 1975, payments amounting to $50,845.64 on the principal were made, leaving a balance of $152,536.86, the amount of the judgment taken by Abraham against Alabama and the amount sued on in this case, plus accrued interest.

In connection with Alabama's purchase of the property it borrowed $550,000 from the First National bank of Mobile, secured by a mortgage on the property. Its plans to develop the property into 385 residential sites and 14 acres of commercial property did not materialize and Alabama sold the property on November 4, 1975, for $490,000. After deduction of the mortgage balance and the closing costs Alabama received $33,185.36. It is Alabama's disposition of this sum which creates one of the principal issues raised by plaintiff and which will be discussed in detail hereafter.

NEI Corporation, one of the defendants in this case, is a large public corporation engaged in the real estate development and management business throughout the United States. It operates through numerous wholly owned subsidiaries, some of whose stock such as Lake Forest it directly owns while the stock of others, such as Alabama, is owned by other subsidiaries, such as Lake Forest in this case. Alabama was incorporated for the immediate purpose of acquiring the property on which Abraham had the option and for the long range purpose of developing that property residentially and commercially. It was incorporated with the minimum of $1,000 paid in capital and never generated any revenues of its own. All of the funds in excess of those realized by Alabama when it sold the property in November, 1975, were advanced by Lake Forest. This amounted to about $290,000 including the $172,117.50 originally paid by Alabama to Abraham and his partner, the $50,845.64 paid on the principal of the note held by Abraham, and interest payments amounting to $22,783.61. Although Alabama had its own bank account these transactions were handled by Lake Forest, but complete accounting records were kept to reflect that they were loans being made by Lake Forest to Alabama. Any operating expenses incurred by Alabama were likewise paid by Lake Forest with appropriate accounting entries made to show these as loans to Alabama. When Alabama sold the property the net proceeds of $33,185.36 were represented by a check payable to the order of Alabama, and although the check was endorsed by Alabama it was deposited in the Ohio bank account of NEI Corporation. Accounting entries were made in the books of Alabama showing its receipt of the funds, its payment of the funds to Lake Forest, and reduction of Alabama's debt to Lake Forest. Lake Forest's books reflected its receipt of the funds on account of Alabama's indebtedness and its payment on account of its indebtedness to NEI Corporation.

In the management of the corporate affairs of NEI, Lake Forest and Alabama, separate boards of directors and slates of officers were elected and separate minutes of meetings of the boards were maintained, although the same individuals for the most part sat on the boards and held office in each of the corporations.

Plaintiff argues primarily that he is entitled to the judgment against Lake Forest and NEI because Alabama is the alter ego and a mere business conduit of the other corporations. Alternatively, plaintiff contends that the receipt of the $33,185.36 by NEI from the sale of the property by Alabama constituted an unlawful dividend or distribution of assets under LSA R.S. 12:93D so that NEI and Lake Forest are liable to plaintiff for at least this amount.

Plaintiff's primary argument rests on legal principles recently considered by this court in *Dillman v. Nobles*, 351 So. 2d 210 (La. App. 4th Cir. 1977) where the following analysis was given: As a general rule a corporation is a distinct legal entity whose shareholders are not individually liable for its debts. However, this rule admits of the "alter ego" exception which, in turn, is supported either by a fraud or deceit practiced on a creditor by the shareholder acting through the corporation or even in the absence of fraud when the business of the corporation has been conducted under such circumstances where corporate formalities have been disregarded to the extent that the corporation ceases to be distinguishable from the shareholders.

* * *

However, although the court recognized these same principles in *Kingsman Enterprises v. Bakerfield Elec. Co.*, 339 So. 2d 1280 (La. App. 1st Cir. 1976), it reached the opposite result emphasizing that the separation of the corporate entity from its shareholders is the firmly established general rule and should be disregarded only in exceptional circumstances. . . .

The court repeatedly emphasized that the "totality of facts" in the case did not support the alter ego theory even though the plaintiff did establish a number of important factors tending to support the theory.

We have concluded that plaintiff in the instant case is in much the same position.

On plaintiff's side of the case, he established that all of Alabama's stock was owned by one shareholder, Lake Forest. In a sense it can be said that Alabama was under-capitalized in that it purchased property for $790,000 while having only $1,000 of capital stock. There was a commingling of funds in the sense that Alabama had practically no funds of its own, virtually all of the funds it used were put up by Lake Forest and/or NEI, and even the proceeds from the sale of the property were deposited in NEI's account and were never put into Alabama's bank account. Finally, almost all of the business of the corporation was accomplished by unanimous consent of the shareholders, which obviated the necessity of meetings of Alabama's share-holders and board of directors.

On the other hand everything Alabama did was in compliance with corporation law. Individuals are specifically authorized to assume only limited liability by setting up a minimally capitalized corporation. Furthermore, the law specifically authorizes the establishment of a corporation by a sole stockholder and the use of unanimous consent agreements among shareholders and directors in lieu of meetings. Since all of the funds paid to Abraham and his partner originated from NEI no practical purpose would have been served for NEI to write a check to Lake Forest, for Lake Forest to write a check to Alabama, and for Alabama to write a check to plaintiff with intervening deposits into separate corporate accounts. It was sufficient under these circumstances for the matter to be covered with bookkeeping entries. Separate minute books were kept, resolutions were adopted, elections were held, positions and offices were filled and all of the facets of a separate formal corporation were observed by Alabama.

In any event, even though plaintiff can isolate a number of factors which favor his position they lose their significance when considered as a part of the totality of facts in this case. Plaintiff was a sophisticated real estate entrepreneur who was quite familiar with the practice of undertaking separate real estate developments through separate minimally capitalized corporations. In fact, he admitted that he himself utilized this practice in his own business. Although his initial negotiations were with Lake Forest's representative he knew several months before the option was exercised by Alabama that it would purchase the option from him. . . .

In none of the cases cited by plaintiff where the corporate veil was pierced on the alter ego theory was there even a voluntary creditor, let alone one who was as knowledgeable and free to enter into a transaction as was the plaintiff in this case.

* * *

In the instant case the plaintiff made a business judgment which, at the time he accepted the note, seemed to be quite prudent. He had gotten appraisals on this property which indicated that it had a great potential and he was apparently convinced that Alabama could capitalize on the project. Needless to say, Alabama was equally optimistic because it and its parent corporations invested considerable sums in the purchase of the property. When plaintiff took the note he was obviously speculating on the success of the project itself and was not relying on the credit of the parent corporation. He was apparently satisfied to take the risk considering the fact that he stood to make a relatively quick profit on the option which he had purchased just six months previously. While we understand from the jurisprudence that it is not necessary to establish fraud in order to support the alter ego theory we are satisfied that the doctrine contains equitable features which require that the type of claim and the relative positions of the parties be considered before applying the doctrine. In the instant case, these considerations do not support the application of the theory.

Turning to plaintiff's alternate theory, he refers to R.S. 12:93D which provides as follows:

> Every shareholder who receives any unlawful dividend or other unlawful distribution of assets shall be liable to the corporation, or to creditors of the corpora-

tion, or to both, in an amount not exceeding the amount so received by him. An action to enforce this liability must be brought within two years from the date on which the unlawful distribution was received, and this time limit shall not be subject to suspension on any ground, nor to interruption except by timely suit.

* * *

When NEI collected the $33,185.36 from Alabama it was insolvent. This was its remaining asset while it owed over $200,000 to plaintiff and $290,000 to Lake Forest. With the sale of the Cody Road property no hope remained for the generation of any income in the immediate future. NEI was in a position to scoop up this remaining asset because it was in total control. Its decision through its directors and officers who were also the directors and officers of Alabama was altogether in its own interest and in total disregard of the rights and interests of Alabama's only other creditor, Abraham.

* * *

Accordingly, the judgment appealed from is reversed and set aside and there is judgment in favor of plaintiff Anthony P. Abraham and against defendants. Lake Forest, Inc. and NEI Corporation, jointly and *in solido* in the sum of $33,185.36, with legal interest from November 4, 1975, until paid and for all costs of these proceedings.
Reversed and Rendered.

ZAIST v. OLSON
Connecticut Supreme Court
154 Conn. 563, 227 A.2d 552 (1967)

[Beginning in 1954, plaintiff did clearing and grading of land in Groton, New London and Waterford, Connecticut, which was to be developed for shopping centers. This land was owned at various times by Martin Olson individually, as well as by various corporations owned by Olson, including Martin Olson, Inc. Plaintiff dealt with and was paid in part by East Haven Homes, Inc., which also employed other contractors for the various shopping center projects. East Haven had few assets, but was provided with funds with which to pay contractors by means of bank loans arranged by Martin Olson and secured by the New London land. By 1959, plaintiff was owed $23,000 for which he sued Martin Olson, The East Haven Homes, Inc. and Martin Olson, Inc. The court below rendered judgment against all defendants for plaintiff on the basis of a referee's report. Further facts appear in the opinion.]

ALCORN, Associate Justice.

* * *

The offices maintained by Olson, Olson, Inc., East Haven, The New London Shopping Center, Inc., and Viking, Inc., were all at the same address, and Olson's secretary was also secretary and bookkeeper for Olson, Inc., and East Haven. East Haven was originally formed for the purpose of building homes and, prior to 1954, engaged in that and other construction work on property of Olson and others. During the period covered by the plaintiffs' work, East Haven maintained an office and a checking account, kept corporate and financial records, filed corporation returns, and had employees. The record is completely silent as to any similar activity or conduct on the part of any of the other corporations involved except for the single meeting of Olson, Inc., at which that corporation voted to sell land to The New London Shopping Center, Inc., for $177,000, and the single meeting of Viking, Inc., which authorized Olson to borrow such sums as he deemed advisable. The only corporate action found to have been taken by East Haven relating to these projects consists of the two votes authorizing contracts with Olson, Inc., which were never consummated, to erect shopping centers in Groton and New London.

* * *

Although Olson was the person with whom the plaintiffs dealt, he directed them to look to East Haven for payment, and the plaintiffs did so. All checks issued in payment of bills rendered were East Haven checks signed by either its vice-president or by Olson, who was its president. East Haven was, as a corporation, a separate legal entity. It must be assumed, from the facts found, that the plaintiffs undertook to deal with this corporation. The facts indicate that they were unaware of, and probably indifferent to, the identity of the owners of the property, who were to receive the actual benefit of their work. Nothing is indicated to warrant the conclusion that Olson ever enlightened them on this subject or that they ever asked him to do so. These circumstances did not prevent the plaintiffs, once they learned that their undertaking was for the benefit of Olson and Olson, Inc., from seeking to hold them, as they did in this action. . . .

[T]his brings us to the basic question of the plaintiffs' right to look beyond East Haven, the corporate entity with which they dealt, to Olson and Olson, Inc., for a recovery of the amount due them.

The referee and the court based this right on agency. No express agency was found to exist, and, consequently, either an implied agency was meant, or the term "agency" was loosely used, as is sometimes done, to pierce the shield of immunity afforded by the corporate structure in a situation in which the corporate entity has been so controlled and dominated that justice requires liability to be imposed on the real actor. . . . The complaint alleged that East Haven was "the agent or instrumentality" of Olson and Olson, Inc. We think that it was the latter.

Courts will disregard the fiction of separate legal entity when a corporation "is a mere instrumentality or agent of another corporation or individual owning all or most of its stock." . . . The circumstance that control is exercised merely through dominating stock ownership, of course, is not enough. . . . There must be "such domination of finances, policies and practices that the controlled corporation has, so to speak, no separate mind, will or existence of its own and is but a business conduit for its principal." 1 Fletcher, [Corporations (Perm. Ed. 1963 Rev.)], p. 205.

In the present case, Olson, Inc., owned none of the stock of East Haven. On the other hand, Olson held a dominating stock interest in both East Haven and Olson, Inc., and was president, treasurer and a director of both corporations. It is not the fact that he held these positions which is controlling but rather the manner in which he utilized them. The essential purposes of the corporate structure, including stockholder immunity, must and will be protected when the corporation functions as an entity in the normal manner contemplated and permitted by law. When it functions in this manner, there is nothing insidious in stockholder control, interlocking directorates or identity of officers. When, however, the corporation is so manipulated by an individual or another corporate entity as to become a mere puppet or tool for the manipulator, justice may require the courts to disregard the corporate fiction and impose liability on the real actor. . . .

The facts in the present case are, beyond question, that Olson caused the creation of both East Haven and Olson, Inc., and thereafter completely dominated and controlled not only them but his other corporate creations. All shared the same office. All the work and material furnished by the plaintiffs went into land which, after being juggled about, came to rest in Olson or Olson, Inc. The record is significantly silent with regard to any formal corporate action by the directors or stockholders of any of the several corporations except in the insignificant instances specifically mentioned. . . . East Haven had no sufficient funds of its own and acquired no funds for the work on its own initiative. It had no proprietary interest in the property on which the work was done, and, so far as appears, it gained nothing from whatever part it played in the transaction. . . . With no showing of any responsible corporate action of its own, it was used by Olson for the benefit of Olson and Olson, Inc. On the facts established, the cause of justice would not be served by denying to the plaintiffs the amount found due them and unpaid because of the inadequate resources of East Haven.

We do not wish to be understood to countenance, by anything we have said here, the imposition of the legitimate indebtedness of a corporation upon a majority stockholder in derogation of his legal immunity merely because of the corporate control inherent in his stock ownership. The present case presents a set of circumstances far different from that.. . . The only reasonable meaning to attach to the transactions spread upon this record is that East Haven undertook no obligation of its own to the plaintiffs, was financially unable to cope with the actual transaction, and reaped no benefit from it. The undertaking throughout was Olson's, planned and carried out through his various other corporate creatures for his own and Olson, Inc.'s enrichment, a part of which, if the plaintiffs were to be denied a recovery, would consist of the amount which East Haven, as the plaintiffs' ostensible debtor, is unable to pay because Olson and Olson, Inc., have not provided the final necessary funds.

On the basis of the referee's report, the court could properly conclude that Olson so completely controlled East Haven that that corporation had "no separate mind, will or existence of its own"; see 1 Fletcher, CORPORATIONS (Perm. Ed. 1963 Rev.) p. 205; that the control was used to perpetrate an unjust act in contravention of the plaintiffs' rights; and that it caused the unjust loss complained of. Consequently, a judgment against Olson was warranted. The court could, with equal propriety, reach the conclusion that the identity of Olson and Olson, Inc., was such that judgment against Olson, Inc., was warranted. . . .

COTTER, Associate Justice (dissenting).

* * *

The practice of disregarding the corporate entity should be undertaken with great caution. . . . Persons dealing with such corporations may refuse to contract without a personal guarantee of payment from the principal. . . . The plaintiffs in the present case, however, elected to deal with the corporation and in fact were paid substantial sums by the corporation over a long period of time.

The underlying rationale behind the statutory granting of stockholder immunity from corporate debts has been stated as follows: "Obviously the useful and beneficial role of the corporate concept in the economic and business affairs of the modern day world would be destroyed if the rule of freedom from individual liability for corporate obligations did not obtain. The protection of limited liability for venture or investment capital is essential to the efficient operation of a system of free enterprise. Such protection from individual liability encourages and promotes business, commerce, manufacturing and industry which provides employment, creates sales of goods and commodities and adds to the nation's economic and financial growth, stability and prosperity." *Johnson v. Kinchen*, 160 So. 2d 296, 299 (La.). The majority opinion in the present case, although not directly undermining this principle, casts a doubtful shadow in its direction.

The new rule which the majority has adopted as the test of the personal liability of a corporation's dominant shareholder is a broad one, will be difficult to apply realistically and is not warranted by the record in the present case. Close corporations, although individual entities from a legal standpoint, are normally no more than vehicles for the goals and motives of their principals. The law is not necessarily advanced by adopting a rule which includes a presumption that this kind of corporation may have a "separate mind, will, or existence of its own." Under the circumstances of this case, I would reaffirm the "fraudulent or illegal purposes" test. . . .

NOTES AND QUESTIONS

(1) **Reconciling the cases.** Can *Zaist* be reconciled with *Walkovzsky* and *Abraham*? Didn't Zaist deliberately deal with East Haven, just as Abraham dealt with Alabama? Was undercapitalization any better a basis for veil-piercing in *Zaist* than in *Walkovzsky*?[38] What result in *Abraham* if plaintiff had been a tort creditor?

(2) **Other grounds for veil-piercing.** Courts often pierce the veil on grounds different from those discussed above. First, the veil may be pierced to effectuate specific statutory policies. For example, in *Sundaco, Inc. v. State*,[39] a corporation violated a law requiring closing on alternate weekends by incorporating a subsidiary and opening its stores on the weekends when the parent's stores were closed.[40] Second, individual liability may be imposed because of a direct wrong by the shareholder to the plaintiff,

---

[38] For another case discussing the grounds on which the corporate veil might be pierced on behalf of a voluntary creditor, see *Clinical Components, Inc. v. Leffler Industries, Inc.*, 1997 Ohio App. LEXIS 199, 1997 WL 28246 (Ohio Ct. App. 1997) (denying defendant's motion for summary judgment where complaint alleged that the corporation concealed substantial payments to the defendant during period when the corporation could not meet its obligations to its creditors, resulting in injury to plaintiff).

[39] 463 S.W.2d 528 (Tex. Civ. App. 1970).

[40] *See* Note, *Piercing the Corporate Law Veil: The Alter Ego Doctrine under Federal Common Law*, 95 HARV. L. REV. 853 (1982). For a more recent case allowing veil piercing to effectuate statutory policies, see *Love v. Texas*, 972 S.W.2d 114 (Tex. App. 1998) (state law environmental liabilities).

rather than because of a corporate wrong for which the shareholder is held responsible under a veil-piercing theory.[41] The "direct wrong" could include breach of a contract between the plaintiff and the shareholder defendant or a fraudulent misrepresentation by the shareholder defendant. Sometimes the "direct wrong" and the "corporate veil" theories almost merge. For example, where a creditor is misled as to the entity with which it is dealing, liability could be based either on direct fraud by the shareholder defendant or on a "corporate veil" theory (**Hackney & Benson**).

(3) **Other grounds of recovery.** As *Abraham v. Lake Forest* illustrates, even if creditors cannot reach shareholder assets through veil piercing, they may be able to reach shareholder assets under other theories. These theories include the unlawful dividend theory used in *Abraham*, as well as several remedies available to creditors of bankrupt corporations. The latter remedies include:

(A) *Subordination.* The bankruptcy court may subordinate shareholder loans to debts owed to other creditors in cases of shareholder misconduct (*i.e.*, debts to other creditors are paid in full before shareholder creditors receive anything), with the almost invariable effect that the shareholder loans are not paid. In federal bankruptcy proceedings, subordination is done pursuant to § 510(c) of the Bankruptcy Code. Subordination has been referred to as the "Deep Rock" doctrine, since a major early application of the doctrine, *Taylor v. Standard Gas & Electric Co.*,[42] involved a subsidiary called the Deep Rock Oil Corp.

(B) *Consolidation.* Where two or more related companies have gone into bankruptcy a court may not only combine the administration of the estates in one proceeding (this is referred to as procedural or administrative consolidation), but may also treat the corporations as one entity for purposes of payment of creditors' claims by combining both debts and assets of the separate bankrupt corporations (this is referred to as substantive consolidation). Unlike both piercing the corporate veil and subordination, the effect of substantive consolidation is to give creditors access to the assets of related corporations, not to the assets of shareholders. Accordingly, the courts emphasize not shareholder misconduct, but rather whether consolidation will be fair to the creditors of the separate enterprises.

(C) *Fraudulent Conveyances and Preferences.* A bankruptcy trustee may recover pre-bankruptcy payments made to shareholders and others if such payments constitute "fraudulent conveyances" or "voidable preferences." Fraudulent conveyances generally refer to payments made within one year of bankruptcy with actual intent to hinder, delay, or defraud credi-

---

[41]   *See Publicker Industries, Inc. v. Roman Ceramics Corp.*, 603 F.2d 1065 (3d Cir. 1979); *Donsco, Inc. v. Casper Corp.*, 587 F.2d 602 (3d Cir. 1978).

[42]   306 U.S. 307 (1939).

tors or for less than reasonably equivalent value;[43] voidable preferences generally refer to payments made to creditors within 90 days (or, in the case of insider creditors, one year) before the filing of a bankruptcy petition that enable creditors to receive more than they would have received in a bankruptcy liquidation.[44] Courts sometimes characterize eve-of-insolvency transfers as frauds that justify piercing the veil.[45]

(4) **Environmental liability.** The Comprehensive Environmental Response, Compensation, and Liability Act ("CERCLA"), 42 U.S.C. § 9601 *et seq.*, provides that "any person who at the time of disposal of any hazardous substance *owned* . . . any facility at which" disposal took place can be held liable for the costs of environmental clean-up, 42 U.S.C. § 9607(a)(2) (emphasis supplied). *United States v. Bestfoods*[46] held that "owner" liability could be imposed on parent corporations for the actions of their subsidiaries if veil-piercing would be appropriate under corporate law principles, but the Court refused to decide whether courts enforcing CERCLA liabilities "should borrow state law, or instead apply a federal common law of veil piercing."

(5) **Abolishing veil-piercing. Bainbridge** argues that the doctrine of veil-piercing should be abolished as arbitrary and unprincipled and replaced by direct consideration of whether shareholders have committed fraud or other wrong. Do you agree?

PROBLEMS

(1)(a) Gray ordered two cabs for his family by calling a number listed in the Yellow Pages under the "Black and White Taxi Company." Two cabs bearing "Black and White" insignia arrived. The cab in which plaintiff traveled crashed. This cab was owned by the "White and Black Company." "Black and White" and "White and Black" have the same three shareholders, directors and officers, and use the same dispatcher and telephone number. Each maintains the $5,000 of insurance required as a minimum by state law. Black and White Company owns ten cabs, while White and Black owns only two. The shareholders of the corporation have substantial personal assets. Gray has retained you to look into his case. White and Black has admitted liability and has made a settlement offer that is significantly less than Gray's damages but adequately reflects the value of the case assuming White and Black is the sole responsible party. The cab-

---

[43] Fraudulent conveyances are prohibited by state statutes, most of which are modeled on the Uniform Fraudulent Conveyance Act. A version of the Uniform Fraudulent Conveyance Act has been enacted as § 548 of the Federal Bankruptcy Code. For a recent case setting aside a transfer to a corporate insider as a violation of a state's fraudulent conveyance statute, see *New Horizon Enterprises, Inc. v. Contemporary Closet Design, Inc.*, 570 N.W.2d 12 (Minn. App. 1997).

[44] *See* § 547 of the Federal Bankruptcy Code.

[45] *See Camelot Carpets, Ltd. v. Metro Distributing Co.*, 607 S.W.2d 746 (Mo. Ct. App. 1980); *Tigrett v. Pointer*, 580 S.W.2d 375 (Tex. Civ. App. 1978).

[46] 524 U.S. 51 (1998).

driver is judgment-proof. Advise Gray whether to accept this offer or whether to attempt to reach the assets of Black and White and of the shareholders.

(b) How would each of the following changes in the facts, considered separately, affect your advice?

(i) The cabs that arrived at Gray's house were each marked with the names of their respective companies.[47]

(ii) The two companies were owned by wholly different individuals and simply decided to use the same dispatcher in order to save money.

(2)(a) Jones is a construction contractor who began by doing small remodeling jobs as a sole proprietorship and then decided to graduate to larger construction jobs. In connection with this plan, he formed Jones Corporation. Jones was the sole director, officer and shareholder of Jones Corporation. In forming the corporation, Jones complied with all statutory requirements, including paying the $1,000 minimum capital required by law. But Jones never held any meetings with himself and did not keep the financial records of Jones Corporation separate from those of his sole proprietorship. As a result of Jones' sloppy record keeping, an indeterminate amount of money earned on jobs contracted for by Jones Corporation was put into Jones' personal bank account, and an indeterminate amount of expenses on jobs done by the sole proprietorship were paid out of the Jones Corporation account.

Mrs. P. contracted with Jones Corporation to do a major addition to her house. The contract was written on the letterhead of Jones Corporation and signed by Jones as president of Jones Corporation. Jones Corporation became insolvent before completing the job, as a result of which Mrs. P. incurred $5,000 damages. She has retained you to represent her in this matter. Mrs. P's claim is worthless if she cannot reach Jones' personal assets. What would you advise Mrs. P. are her chances of success?[48]

(b) How would each of the following changes in the facts, considered separately, affect your advice?

(i) Jones kept perfect records that showed that the corporation was insolvent almost from its inception and prior to the making of the contract with Mrs. P.

(ii) Jones kept perfect records that showed that Jones transferred to the sole proprietorship without any consideration all of the $3,000 in revenues received by the Jones Corporation during the period following the making of the contract with Mrs. P, rendering the corporation insolvent.

(3) Hoyt owns three 18-wheel tractor-trailers that are worth a considerable amount of money. Since these trucks represent virtually all of his assets and his livelihood, Hoyt would like to insulate them from creditors' claims. He plans to form two corpo-

---

[47] *See Black and White, Inc v. Love*, 367 S.W.2d 427 (Ark 1963).

[48] *See Gallagher v. Reconco Builders*, 91 Ill. App. 3d 999, 415 N.E.2d 560 (1980).

rations in which he will be the sole shareholder, officer and director. Hoyt Leasing Corporation will take title to the trucks and rent them to Hoyt Trucking Corporation. Hoyt Trucking will buy the minimum amount of liability insurance required by law, and will have as assets only the $1,000 minimum capital required by law. Hoyt Trucking will contract with shippers and drivers. The rent Hoyt Trucking pays to Hoyt Leasing for the trucks will be equal to the income from the trucks less the expenses of running them. Hoyt will comply with all statutory formalities in forming and running the corporations. Hoyt figures that if he has an accident or if Hoyt Trucking breaches a contract the victim will be able to reach only Hoyt Trucking's minimal capital. He has retained you to advise him whether his plan will achieve its desired aim. What advice would you give?[49]

REFERENCES

Bainbridge, *Abolishing Veil Piercing*, 26 J. CORP. L. 479 (2001).

Blumberg, *Limited Liability and Corporate Groups*, 11 J. CORP. L. 573 (1986).

Easterbrook & Fischel, THE ECONOMIC STRUCTURE OF CORPORATE LAW, Ch. 2 (1992).

Hackney & Benson, *Shareholder Liability for Inadequate Capitalization*, 43 U. PITT. L. REV. 837 (1982).

Hamilton, *The Corporate Entity*, 49 TEX. L. REV. 979 (1971).

Presser, PIERCING THE CORPORATE VEIL (1991).

Thompson, *Piercing the Corporate Veil: An Empirical Study*, 76 CORNELL L. REV. 1036 (1991).

---

[49] *See Fisser v. International Bank*, 282 F.2d 231, 240 (2d Cir. 1960); *Luckenback S.S. Co. v. W.R. Grace & Co.*, 267 F. 676 (4th Cir. 1920).

CHAPTER 4

Partnership: Governance, Transfer and Dissolution

This Chapter begins the discussion of the management and control of business associations. In general, shareholders, partners and other "residual claimants," who have a claim to what is left after paying creditors, employees and other "fixed claimants," have the power to control the firm's affairs. Sometimes owners delegate day-to-day management power to agents, such as directors, officers and managing partners, and exercise control primarily by electing and retaining the power to remove their agents and by reserving the right to approve certain matters in advance. Most issues concerning the governance of business associations, therefore, relate to the allocation of power between the residual claimants and the managers.

This Chapter focuses on the governance of partnerships. It begins by discussing the general theory underlying voting rules in all business associations (Section 4.01). It then goes on to discuss the basic "standard form" of partnership governance (Section 4.02), as well as two other important aspects of the partnership relationship: (1) the limitations on the ability of partners to transfer their ownership interests (Section 4.03); and (2) the partners' rights to exit the firm through liquidation of the firm or buyout (Section 4.04). These latter aspects of the partnership relationship are discussed in connection with partnership governance because partners' ability to exit the firm is as much a part of their ability to control the firm as their power to vote.

Chapters 5 through 7 focus on governance issues relating to other forms of business associations—close corporations, hybrid limited liability firms, and public corporations.

§ 4.01 Theoretical Considerations Underlying Voting Rules

Business associations involve a "governance" form of contracting in which the parties establish general rules for making future decisions. Instead of a contract that says "deliver 100 widgets tomorrow here for $1 per widget," or "repay $100 in a year with 10% interest," owners contract to have managers "make ordinary decisions and let us vote on the rest." There are many variations on how much control the owners retain, each with its own set of costs and benefits.

Business association statutes and contracts must address the following basic governance questions: (1) what do the owners vote on? (2) how many votes control the outcome? and (3) how are the votes allocated among voters? These questions are discussed in general terms in the following subsections.

[A] What Issues Do Owners Vote on?

By delegating decision-making authority to managers, such as the directors or officers of a corporation or the managing partners of a partnership, owners can reduce the costs of decision-making by large numbers of people and take advantage of the managers' specialized knowledge. Which decisions should the managers make, and which should be reserved to the owners? This depends on both the costs of decision-making and the need to protect the owners' interests. For example, voting by owners on all ordinary business decisions may be quite expensive while the benefits to the owners may be limited because other mechanisms such as incentive compensation and fiduciary duties constrain managers. Owner voting might therefore be reserved for those instances where these other mechanisms do not function effectively.

[B] How Many Votes Control the Outcome?

Another issue that arises in setting up a governance structure is what proportion of affirmative votes to require for approval of a particular type of decision—unanimity, majority or some other rule? Also, who has the right to vote on a given issue? The costs and benefits of voting schemes were studied in **Buchanan & Tullock**'s path-breaking work, THE CALCULUS OF CONSENT. Although the book addressed the political context, its insights also relate to the governance of business associations. In general, the costs of reaching a decision, including the costs of bargaining among the voters to form coalitions, increase both with the size of the deciding group and with the percentage of a group who must vote to take action. Assume, for example, in our Judy-Kathy-Ray situation (Section 2.01 immediately preceding *Nichols*), that only two members must agree on any decision, and that Ray favors decision X. To prevail, Ray need only convince Judy or Kathy. But if all three must agree for the action to be taken, Ray must bargain with both Judy and Kathy. This increases not only the number of bargains to be made, but also the difficulty of bargaining, since each member has more incentive to hold out under a unanimity rule than under the 2/3 rule.

If decision-making costs were the only relevant consideration, the analysis so far suggests that dictatorship would always be the ideal form of governance. But one must also take into account the costs of a decision that are borne by parties other than the decision-makers. The smaller the percentage of voters authorized to make a given decision, the higher these "externalized" costs will be, other things being equal. The degree of externalization depends significantly on whether non-voting mechanisms such as incentive or monitoring devices cause the party or parties with decision-making power to act in the interests of the other members of the group. In designing a governance system for a business association, the members will therefore attempt to devise the voting rule that minimizes the combination of externalized costs and decisionmaking costs.

[C] How Are Votes Allocated Among Voters?

Even after the contracting parties settle who votes and how many votes control a given decision, they must still decide how to allocate votes—for example, one vote per member, as under the standard partnership form, or a number of votes proportionate with the member's financial investment in the firm, as under the standard corporate form. Many firms will allocate voting power according to the voters' capital investment because this tends to align votes with the firm's economic interests. But others, such as closely held general partnerships (*see* Section 4.02), may adopt alternative allocations because some of the owners have made significant non-financial investments in the firm.

REFERENCE

Buchanan & Tullock, THE CALCULUS OF CONSENT (1962).

§ 4.02 Partnership Governance

This Section discusses governance of the partnership. Section 4.02[A] covers the "standard form" of partnership governance provided for in the Uniform Partnership Act, and Section 4.02[B] discusses modification of the standard form in the partnership agreement.

[A] The Uniform Partnership Act

The Uniform Partnership Act (UPA § 18(e); RUPA § 401(f)), which controls in the absence of contrary agreement, sets forth the basic governance terms of partnership. It provides that partners have "equal rights in the management and conduct of the partnership business." This means that each partner has one vote regardless of her financial contribution and can participate actively in management decisions rather than merely voting to approve or disapprove actions taken by others. This "per capita" voting rule is consistent with the fact that the partners make service, credit and other contributions apart from their capital investment in the firm.

In the event of disagreement among the partners, a majority vote decides "ordinary" matters, while all partners must approve extraordinary matters, including amendments to the partnership agreement, admission of new partners and sale of all the firm's main assets (UPA § 18(g), (h); RUPA § 401(i), (j)).

There are also many borderline situations. For example, in the Judy, Kathy, and Ray partnership situation in Section 2.01 immediately before *Nichols*, if the partners have not otherwise agreed, would a two-thirds majority be sufficient to approve the following acts: 1) hiring a full-time employee? 2) borrowing $10,000 from a bank? 3) placing a $2,000 order for a new kind of expensive jam? 4) buying $5,000 of new cooking equipment for the store?

How should a court decide what voting rule to apply in a particular situation where the result is ambiguous under the parties' agreement? The court might ask what rule would result in the lowest total decision-making costs (*see* Section 4.01), on the assumption that this is the rule the parties would have adopted if they had thought about the matter. How might this approach work in the following situation?

PROBLEMS

(1) Paciaroni, Cassidy and Crane decided to go into partnership for the purpose of obtaining and racing a champion race horse. They bought a promising yearling named "Black Ace" for $35,000. Paciaroni contributed 50% of this amount, Cassidy and Crane 25% each. Although there was no formal partnership agreement, it was understood that each partner would contribute equally to the expense of upkeep, that Crane, an experienced trainer, would train the horse and be paid a salary for his services, that Paciaroni would have a "60% interest" in the partnership, and that Cassidy and Crane would each have a "20% interest." Black Ace became one of the top pacers in the country, winning almost $100,000 in his first few races. He is eligible for races with purses totaling $600,000. His current value is estimated at $500,000, but could easily reach $2,000,000 if he wins a few of these major races.

Despite the lack of a formal agreement, the partnership initially operated smoothly, with the other partners following Crane's decisions because he was the trainer. But recently there has been a disagreement. Black Ace has developed a ringbone problem, was running peculiarly, and even fell in one race. Although the problem has apparently been resolved and Black Ace has returned to his winning ways, Crane refuses to let the horse race for fear it will be seriously injured. Paciaroni and Cassidy, on the other hand, insist that this big chance for a considerable fortune is worth the risk.

Crane now holds Black Ace's eligibility papers without which he cannot be raced. Paciaroni and Cassidy have consulted you as to their chances of having a court require Crane to turn over the papers so that Black Ace may be raced. What advice would you give?[1]

(2) How, if at all, would your answer to Problem (1) differ if: (a) the partnership consisted only of Paciaroni and Crane, who owned equal shares? or (b) Crane wanted to race the horse but the other two, who held the eligibility papers, did not?

---

[1] *See Paciaroni v. Crane*, 408 A.2d 946 (Del. Ch. 1979).

REFERENCE

Bromberg & Ribstein, BROMBERG & RIBSTEIN ON PARTNERSHIP, § 6.03.

[B] Altering the "Standard Form" by Agreement

The form of management prescribed by the Uniform Partnership Act contemplates a few equal partners for whom the decision-making costs of a majority vote on ordinary matters and unanimity on other matters are less than the external costs imposed by giving more power to managers. But many partnerships, such as large law and accounting firms, do not fit this mold. Even small firms may want to grant decision-making power to a single managing partner to reduce decision costs, weigh the votes of some partners more heavily than others, or prevent the majority from enforcing its will over the minority even as to ordinary matters. This raises two questions: First, to what extent may the management and control provisions of the UPA be altered? Second, what considerations explain the governance provisions adopted in particular situations?

McCALLUM v. ASBURY
Oregon Supreme Court
238 Ore. 257, 393 P.2d 774 (1964)

GOODWIN, Justice.

This is a suit between individuals practicing medicine as partners. The plaintiff sued to dissolve the partnership and for other relief. The remaining partners answered with a counterclaim for an injunction to enforce against the plaintiff a restrictive covenant contained in the partnership agreement. The covenant, if enforced, would prohibit the plaintiff for ten years from practicing medicine in Corvallis or within 30 miles of that city.

The trial court entered a decree denying relief to the plaintiff in his suit for dissolution, and also denying injunctive relief to the defendants. All parties appeal.

The plaintiff is a surgeon formerly associated with the Corvallis Clinic. The Corvallis Clinic was organized by three doctors in 1947. By 1962 seventeen doctors, ten of whom were partners, were associated with the clinic. After having been employed by the clinic for almost two years, the plaintiff became a partner in 1953. Some of the defendant partners had entered the firm before the plaintiff did, and others entered after the plaintiff had become a partner. The provisions of the partnership agreement material to this case were renewed each time a new partner came into the firm.

Growth and prosperity did not produce harmony. Differences about the proper management of the clinic arose between the plaintiff and his fellow doctors. The areas of disagreement between the plaintiff and his partners grew, and the working relationship among the partners began to suffer. The disagreements involved honest differences of opinion about the best way to run a business, and did not reflect adversely upon the professional abilities of any of the parties.

The defendants seek to enforce a provision of the agreement which permits a majority of the partners to expel a partner and buy his interest. They also seek to enforce a restriction upon the right of the departing partner to compete with the partnership. Neither provision is ambiguous.

The trial court held that the plaintiff was released from his obligation to comply with the terms of the agreement because the defendants breached the agreement before he sought to dissolve the partnership. The majority, over the protest of the plaintiff, had created an executive committee to:

> . . . manage generally all affairs of the partnership except that the committee shall have no authority to enter into any employment contract with a physician for services as a medical doctor, shall not take any action which is discriminating against any partner or partners, and shall exercise no power expressly reserved to the partnership by the Partnership Agreement.

The court reasoned that the majority of the partners had no right to form the executive committee and to delegate to that committee the management of the business affairs of the clinic.

Section 8 of the partnership agreement reads as follows:

> All partners shall have an equal share in the management of the business and all decisions pertaining to the partnership, not herein specifically provided for, including amendment of this contract, shall be decided by a majority vote of the partners. Provided that any amendments of this agreement shall not be discriminating against any partner or partners.

ORS 68.310(8) provides as follows [same as UPA § 18(h)].
The public statute and the private agreement must be examined together.

* * *

Fundamental changes in a partnership agreement may not be made without the consent of all the parties. This is true even though the agreement may provide that it can be amended by majority vote. The power to amend is limited by the rule that, unless unanimous, no amendment may be in contravention of the agreement. ORS 68.310(8).

The plaintiff insists that even though he had agreed in advance that the majority of the partners could amend the agreement, the executive-committee amendment was so broad that it was inconsistent with the agreement between the partners and was beyond the scope of the power of amendment under the agreement.

The defendants insist that the institution of an executive committee was well within the terms of the agreement. They further contend that even if the creation of the committee was not within the expressed grant of power to the majority to amend the agreement, the right to delegate routine functions to a committee would have to be implied from the purposes for which the partners had associated themselves. At the heart of this dispute is the question of the scope of the management powers delegated to the committee.

The amendment provided that any action taken by the committee could be altered or cancelled by a majority vote of the partners. The majority of the partners retained the right to reconstitute the committee. All members of the partnership retained the right to attend all meetings of the committee. However, when attending a meeting, any partner who was not a member of the executive committee was not entitled to participate in committee deliberations unless given permission to do so.

A safeguard of the rights of all partners was provided in the requirement that ten days must elapse before any action, other than emergency action, taken by the committee would become effective. This delay gave a majority of the partners a power to override the committee at any time during the ten days that intervened between committee action and execution. There is no evidence that the emergency clause was intended to subvert the right of review. On the contrary, it is presumed that the clause was intended to be employed in good faith. We hold that these limitations upon the committee's powers kept the delegation well within the scope and intent of the original partnership agreement.

* * *

Reversed and remanded; costs to none of the parties.

QUESTIONS

(1) How was the UPA standard form varied by (a) the original *partnership agreement* and (b) the *amendment*? Why do you suppose the partners other than plaintiff passed the amendment?

(2) According to the court, precisely why did the amendment not violate the agreement?

(3) Plaintiff could, in effect, "veto" the amendment by dissolving the partnership by express will. *See* Section 4.04, below. Does it then matter whether he could veto the amendment by voting against it?

(4) Oregon's version of UPA § 18 was at the time of *McCallum* the same as the UPA, and this included the "subject to any agreement" language. Why, then, wasn't it clear that any amendment, including a "fundamental change," could be made by a majority vote pursuant to § 8 of the partnership agreement?

PROBLEMS

(1) Jones, formerly a high government official, joined a large law firm as a partner in its Washington, D.C. office. For several years, Jones had been in charge of that office. Many of his partners support a merger with another firm which also has a Washington office. The Washington offices of the two firms would merge into one office which would have "co-chairmen." Jones wants advice on whether he can veto the merger. What advice would you give, assuming the partnership agreement provides as follows:[2]

---

[2]   *See Day v. Sidley & Austin*, 394 F. Supp. 986 (D.D.C. 1975).

All questions of firm policy, including determination of salaries, expenses, partners' participation, required balances of partners, investment of funds, designation of counsel, and the admission and severance of partners, shall be decided by an Executive Committee. . . . Provided, however, that the determination of participation, admission and severance of partners shall require the approval of partners (whether or not members of the Executive Committee) then holding a majority of all voting percentages.

(2) What management provisions would you suggest in each of the following situations: (a) The Judy, Kathy and Ray partnership situation discussed at the beginning of Section 2.01 immediately before *Nichols*? and (b) A law firm agreement among six lawyers of approximately the same age and experience? Consider the following specific questions:

(a) Would you want to give some partners more voting power than others?
(b) Do you want to depart from the UPA unanimity rule with respect to certain important decisions? If so, which ones?
(c) Do you want to delegate power over decisions to a management committee? If so, which ones? What controls do you want to give to the non-managing partners?

§ 4.03 Transfer of Partnership Interests

A discussion of governance of the partnership would not be complete without a review of legal rules governing withdrawal from the business, because partners' power to exit the firm is an important part of their say in governance. This Section discusses limitations on the ability of partners to transfer their ownership interests and Section 4.04 discusses the partners' rights to exit the firm through liquidation of the firm or buyout.

Because partners are individually liable for debts of the business, and because they are co-managers of the firm under the standard form of partnership, it follows that they would want to control who their associates are. At the same time, partners would not want their investments to be completely locked in the firm. The Uniform Partnership Act, which applies in the absence of contrary agreement, accommodates both of these objectives by limiting the transfer of management rights while permitting free transferability of financial rights. *See* UPA §§ 18(g), 27(1); RUPA §§ 401(i), 502. These provisions are applied in the following case.

RAPOPORT v. 55 PERRY CO.
New York Supreme Court, Appellate Division
50 A.D.2d 54, 376 N.Y.S.2d 147 (1975)

TILZER, Justice.

In 1969, Simon, Genia and Ury Rapoport entered into a partnership agreement with Morton, Jerome and Burton Parnes, forming the partnership known as 55 Perry Company. Pursuant to the agreement, each of the families owned 50% of the partnership interests. In December of 1974 Simon and Genia Rapoport assigned a 10% interest of their share in the partnership to their adult children, Daniel and Kalia. The Parnes defendants were advised of the assignment and an amended partnership certificate was filed in the County Clerk's Office indicating the addition of Daniel and Kalia as partners. However, when the plaintiffs, thereafter, requested the Parnes defendants to execute an amended partnership agreement to reflect the above changes in the partnership, the Parnes refused, taking the position that the partnership agreement did not permit the introduction of new partners without consent of all the existing partners. Thereafter, the plaintiffs Rapoport brought this action seeking a declaration that Simon and Genia Rapoport had an absolute right to assign their interests to their adult children without consent of the defendants and that such assignment was authorized pursuant to Paragraph 12 of the partnership agreement. The plaintiffs further sought to have Daniel and Kalia be declared partners in 55 Perry Company and have their names entered upon the books of the partnership as partners. The defendants Parnes interposed an answer, taking the position that the partnership agreement did not permit admission of additional partners without consent of all the existing partners and that the filing of the amended certificate of partnership was unauthorized. After joinder of issue plaintiffs moved for summary judgment and although the defendants did not cross-move for similar relief, such was, nevertheless, requested in their answering papers.

* * *

[T]he Court below found that the agreement was ambiguous and that there was a triable issue with respect to the intent of the parties. We disagree and conclude that the agreement is without ambiguity and that pursuant to the terms of the agreement and of the Partnership Law, consent of the Parnes defendants was required in order to admit Daniel Rapoport and Kalia Shalleck to the partnership.

Plaintiffs, in support of their contention that they have an absolute right to assign their interests in the partnership to their adult children and that the children must be admitted to the partnership as partners rely on Paragraph 12 of the partnership agreement which provides as follows:

> No partner or partners shall have the authority to transfer, sell . . . assign or in any way dispose of the partnership realty and/or personalty and shall not have the authority to sell, transfer, assign . . . his or their share in this firm, nor enter into any agreement as a result of which any person shall become interested with him in this firm, unless the same is agreed to in writing by a majority of the partners as determined by the percentage of ownership . . ., except for members

of his immediate family who have attained majority, in which case no such consent shall be required.

As indicated, plaintiffs argue that the above provision expressly authorizes entry of their adult children into the partnership. Defendants, on the other hand, maintain that Paragraph 12 provides only for the right of a partner to assign or transfer a share of the profits in the partnership. We agree with that construction of the agreement.

A reading of the partnership agreement indicates that the parties intended to observe the differences, as set forth in the Partnership Law, between assignees of a partnership interest and the admission into the partnership itself of new partners. The Partnership Law provides that subject to any contrary agreement between the partners, "[n]o person can become a member of a partnership without the consent of all the partners." (Partnership Law Section 40(7) [UPA Section 18(g)].) Partnership Law Section 53 [UPA Section 27(1)] provides that an assignee of an interest in the partnership is not entitled "to interfere in the management or administration of the partnership business" but is merely entitled to receive "the profits to which the assigning partner would otherwise be entitled." . . . Additionally, Partnership Law Section 50 [UPA Section 24] indicates the differences between the rights of an assignee and a new partner. That section states that the "property rights of a partner are (a) his rights in specific partnership property, (b) his interest in the partnership, and (c) his right to participate in the management." On the other hand, as already indicated above, an assignee is excluded in the absence of agreement from interfering in the management of the partnership business and from access to the partnership books and information about partnership transactions. . . .

The effect, therefore, of the various provisions of the Partnership Law, above discussed, is that unless the parties have agreed otherwise, a person cannot become a member of a partnership without consent of all the partners whereas an assignment of a partnership interest may be made without consent, but the assignee is entitled only to receive the profits of the assigning partner. And, as already stated, the partnership agreement herein clearly took cognizance of the differences between an assignment of an interest in the partnership as compared to the full rights of a partner as set forth in Partnership Law Section 50. Paragraph 12 of the agreement by its language has reference to Partnership Law Section 53 dealing with an "assignment of partner's interest." It (Paragraph 12) refers to assignments, encumbrances and agreements "as a result of which any person shall become interested with (the assignor) in this firm." That paragraph does not contain language with respect to admitting a partner to the partnership with all rights to participate in the management of its affairs. Moreover, interpretation of Paragraph 12 in this manner is consistent with other provisions of the partnership agreement. For example, in Paragraph 15 of the agreement, the following is provided:

> In the event of the death of any partner the business of this firm shall continue with the heir, or distributee providing he has reached majority, or fiduciary of the deceased partner having the right to succeed the deceased partner with the same rights and privileges and the same obligations, pursuant to all of the terms hereof.

In that paragraph, therefore, there is specific provision to succeed to all the privileges and obligations of a partner—language which is completely absent from Paragraph 12.

Accordingly, it appears that contrary to plaintiffs' contention that Paragraph 12 was intended to give the parties the right to transfer a full partnership interest to adult children, without consent of all other partners (an agreement which would vary the rights otherwise existing pursuant to Partnership Law Section 40(7)), that paragraph was instead intended to limit a partner with respect to his right to assign a partnership interest as provided for under Partnership Law Section 53, *i.e.*, the right to profits—to the extent of prohibiting such assignments without consent of other partners except to children of the existing partners who have reached majority. Therefore, it must be concluded that pursuant to the terms of the partnership agreement, the plaintiffs could not transfer a full partnership interest to their children and that the children only have the rights as assignees to receive a share of the partnership income and profits of their assignors.

* * *

NUNEZ, Justice (dissenting).

I agree with Special Term that the written partnership agreement providing for the assignment of partners' shares to members of their immediate families without the consent of the other partners is ambiguous and that there is a triable issue as to intent. The agreement being ambiguous, construction is a mixed question of law and fact and resolution thereof to determine the parties' intent should await a trial. . . . Summary judgment was properly denied both parties. I would affirm.

NOTES AND QUESTIONS

(1) **Drafting the agreement.** On what basis could the dissent and Special Term conclude that the agreement was ambiguous? What should the partnership agreement have said in order to give the plaintiffs what they were seeking in *Rapoport*?

(2) **Effect of assignment: rights of assignee.** Unless otherwise agreed, partners can transfer financial but not management rights. Thus, an assignee normally has no management or information rights under the default provisions of the UPA, but rather only the right to receive such distributions as would have been paid to the assignor, and under some circumstances to seek dissolution of the partnership. *See* UPA § 27(1); RUPA § 503(a)-(b). Even an assignee with a significant financial interest may be helpless in the face of wasteful or selfish partner conduct.[3] The assignee's impotence obviously makes it hard to sell a financial interest in the firm. On the other hand, enabling transfer of management rights may create problems for the non-selling partners.

(3) **Effect of assignment: rights of assignor.** The assignor remains a partner, and therefore eligible to participate in management and liable for partnership debts. *See*

---

[3]   *See Bauer v. The Blomfield Company/Holden Joint Venture*, 849 P.2d 1365 (Alaska 1993) (assignee could not question the partners' decision to pay a large commission to a co-partner in order to stop making income payments to the assignee).

RUPA § 503(d). But the assignor gives up the right to partnership distributions to the extent these have been assigned. This creates a potential conflict between the incentives of the non-profit-sharing assignor partner and those of the other partners. Accordingly, UPA § 31(1)(c) lets the non-assigning partners dissolve the firm over the objection of the assignor, while RUPA § 601(4)(ii) allows the non-assignors to expel the assignor. Should the Act instead provide that the assignor is no longer a partner even without a dissolution or expulsion?

REFERENCE

Bromberg & Ribstein, BROMBERG & RIBSTEIN ON PARTNERSHIP § 3.04, 3.05(d)(3).

§ 4.04 Dissolution of the Partnership

As already indicated, partners cannot easily sell their partnership interests. This "illiquidity" means that partners need to substitute another form of exit—the ability to dissolve (*i.e.*, withdraw from) the partnership and thereby compel liquidation of the firm or buyout of the dissolving partners' interests. This Section discusses and evaluates the partner's dissolution right.

[A] Overview

Illiquidity of partnership interests is a function of both (1) the statutory and other contract terms regarding transferability discussed in Section 4.03, and (2) the conditions of markets where partnership interests are traded. First, parties are unlikely to wish to become "assignors" or "assignees" under the terms of the Uniform Partnership Act, as suggested in Note 2 following *Rapoport* above. The assignor retains liability for partnership debts but loses an offsetting profit share, and is subject to potential removal by the remaining non-assigning partners (*see* Note 3 following *Rapoport*). Second, the transferability of partnership interests is inherently limited by the absence of an active trading market in, and therefore cheaply available information about, partnership interests.

The Uniform Partnership Act addresses illiquidity by giving each partner the power at any time to dissolve the partnership and therefore compel liquidation of the firm or at least the purchase of the partner's interest. However, because a partner's power to dissolve the firm at any time engenders its own problems, whether to retain this power was a controversial issue in connection with the revision of the UPA. A discussion of RUPA § 801, which significantly dilutes the power to dissolve at will, is deferred until Subsection [F].

Dissolution is defined in UPA § 29 as a "change in the relation of the partners caused by any partner ceasing to be associated in the carrying on . . . of the business [of the partnership]." UPA §§ 31(1)(b) and 31(2) let a partner dissolve the partnership by "express will." Sections 31 and 32 provide for dissolution by several other events, including death (§ 31(4)), expulsion (§ 31(1)(d)), and court decree (§§ 31(6) and 32). On dissolution, the firm is either continued on payment to departing owners (except those who wrongfully dissolve) of the value of their investments, or is liquidated and the proceeds paid to the owners. In either event, departing owners are no longer liable for post-dissolution debts, subject to creditors' knowledge or notice of the dissolution (§ 35). Departing owners, however, remain personally liable for pre-dissolution debts unless there has been a novation or the departing partners are otherwise relieved of liability pursuant to § 36.

The key provision in determining the consequences of dissolution is UPA § 38, which provides that, if the dissolution is not "in contravention" of the agreement, any partner can compel liquidation of the firm. In other words, the firm continues in this situation only if all of the partners (including the dissolving partners) agree to do so at the time of dissolution or in the partnership agreement. A liquidating firm enters "winding up" under § 30, during which the firm is managed pursuant to § 37. There is a full accounting for assets and liabilities (§ 43) and assets are distributed pursuant to § 40. If the firm is continued by agreement, the departing partners are entitled to receive the value of their interests plus profits or interest from the time of dissolution under § 42. In other words, the firm "winds up" by paying off the exiting partner.

If dissolution has been caused "wrongfully" or "in contravention of the partnership agreement," § 38(2) provides that the non-"wrongful" partners can continue the firm on payment to the "wrongful" partner of the value of his interest, less goodwill and damages resulting from the wrongful dissolution. The wrongful partner is also entitled to profits or interests from the time of dissolution to the time of payment under § 42, as well as an indemnity against all present and future partnership liabilities (§ 38(2)(b)). "In contravention" and "wrongful" apparently refer both to dissolution prior to the expiration of an agreed term under § 31(2) and to judicial dissolution because of a partner's misconduct under § 32(1)(c) or (d).

The UPA therefore solves the liquidity problem by letting any partner leave the firm at any time and force a liquidation of the firm or a buy out of her interest. But partners who leave prior to the expiration of an agreed term or who otherwise act wrongfully may suffer a monetary penalty upon departure.

The UPA's dissolution provisions can be costly to the non-dissolving members in a number of ways:

(1) Dissolution of the partnership entity can cause confusion and discontinuity in the business by, for example, terminating executory contracts or making it difficult for creditors to collect debts from the dissolved firm.

(2) By letting any partner withdraw her financial capital and terminate her investments of personal credit and human capital, dissolution can help a partner withdraw property that is vital to the business and thereby reduce the value of the other partners' investments. Sometimes this property was developed at firm expense, such as the contacts and expertise of a lawyer or other partner in a professional firm. More generally, the other partners may have made their investments with some expectation of continuity.

(3) A partner who can compel liquidation of the firm may be able to use advantages of credit, wealth, or special information about the firm to outbid the other partners at the liquidation sale and purchase the firm's assets.[4] The "non-wrongful" partners' power to continue the firm under UPA § 38(2) is a partial antidote to these problems. As discussed above, the dissolution is "wrongful," at least where it occurs prior to expiration of an agreed term. By agreeing to a term, the parties have indicated that premature dissolution would be particularly harmful to the nondissolving partners. The wrongful partner is penalized by loss of a share in goodwill and is assessed damages caused by the premature dissolution. Also, the non-wrongful partners can avoid being bought out at a low price because they need not bid against their stronger partner at a liquidation sale.

REFERENCES

Carney, *The Theory of the Firm: Investor Coordination Costs, Control Premiums and Capital Structure*, 65 WASH. U. L.Q. 1 (1987).

DeMott, *Transatlantic Perspectives on Partnership Law: Risk and Instability*, 26 J. CORP. L. 879 (2001).

Ribstein, *A Statutory Approach to Partner Dissociation*, 65 WASH. U. L.Q. 357 (1987).

[B] Judicial Limitations on the Power to Dissolve

The following case illustrates the potential problems inherent in the dissolution power and how courts have attempted to mitigate these problems.

PAGE v. PAGE
California Supreme Court
55 Cal. 2d 192, 359 P.2d 41, 10 Cal. Rptr. 643 (1961)

TRAYNOR, Justice.

Plaintiff and defendant are partners in a linen supply business in Santa Maria, California. Plaintiff appeals from a judgment declaring the partnership to be for a term rather than at will.

The partners entered into an oral partnership agreement in 1949. Within the first two years each partner contributed approximately $43,000 for the purchase of land, machinery, and linen needed to begin the business. From 1949 to 1957 the enterprise was unprofitable, losing approximately $62,000. The partnership's major creditor is a corporation, wholly owned by plaintiff, that supplies the linen and machinery necessary for the day-to-day operation of the business. This corporation holds a $47,000 demand note of the partnership. The partnership operations began to improve in 1958. The partnership earned $3,824.41 in that

---

[4]   *See Prentiss v. Sheffel*, 20 Ariz. App. 411, 513 P.2d 949 (1973) (permitting the partners to bid against each other at the sale).

year and $2,282.30 in the first three months of 1959. Despite this improvement plaintiff wishes to terminate the partnership.

The Uniform Partnership Act provides that a partnership may be dissolved "By the express will of any partner when no definite term or particular undertaking is specified." [UPA § 31(1)(b)]. The trial court found that the partnership is for a term, namely, "such reasonable time as is necessary to enable said partnership to repay from partnership profits, indebtedness incurred for the purchase of land, buildings, laundry and delivery equipment and linen for the operation of said business . . . ." Plaintiff correctly contends that this finding is without support in the evidence.

Defendant testified that the terms of the partnership were to be similar to former partnerships of plaintiff and defendant, and that the understanding of these partnerships was that "we went into partnership to start the business and let the business operation pay for itself,—put in so much money, and let the business pay itself out." There was also testimony that one of the former partnership agreements provided in writing that the profits were to be retained until all obligations were paid.

Upon cross-examination defendant admitted that the former partnership in which the earnings were to be retained until the obligations were repaid was substantially different from the present partnership. The former partnership was a limited partnership and provided for a definite term of five years and a partnership at will thereafter. Defendant insists, however, that the method of operation of the former partnership showed an understanding that all obligations were to be repaid from profits. He nevertheless concedes that there was no understanding as to the term of the present partnership in the event of losses. He was asked: "[W]as there any discussion with reference to the continuation of the business in the event of losses?" He replied, "Not that I can remember." He was then asked, "Did you have any understanding with Mr. Page, your brother, the plaintiff in this action, as to how the obligations were to be paid if there were losses?" He replied, "Not that I can remember. I can't remember discussing that at all. We never figured on losing, I guess."

Viewing this evidence most favorably for defendant, it proves only that the partners expected to meet current expenses from current income and to recoup their investment if the business were successful.

Defendant contends that such an expectation is sufficient to create a partnership for a term under the rule of *Owen v. Cohen*, 19 Cal. 2d 147, 150, 119 P.2d 713. In that case we held that when a partner advances a sum of money to a partnership with the understanding that the amount contributed was to be a loan to the partnership and was to be repaid as soon as feasible from the prospective profits of the business, the partnership is for the term reasonably required to repay the loan. It is true that *Owen v. Cohen, supra*, and other cases hold that partners may impliedly agree to continue in business until a certain sum of money is earned (*Mervyn Investment Co. v. Biber*, 184 Cal. 637, 641-642, 194 P. 1037), or one or more partners recoup their investments (*Vangel v. Vangel*, 116 Cal. App. 2d 615, 625, 254 P.2d 919), or until certain debts are paid (*Owen v. Cohen, supra*, 19 Cal. 2d at page 150, 119 P.2d at page 714), or until certain property could be disposed of on favorable terms (*Shannon v. Hudson*, 161 Cal. App. 2d 44, 48, 325 P.2d 1022). In each of these cases, however, the implied agreement found support in the evidence.

In *Owen v. Cohen, supra*, the partners borrowed substantial amounts of money to launch the enterprise and there was an understanding that the loans would be repaid from partnership profits. In *Vangel v. Vangel, supra*, one partner loaned his co-partner money to invest in the partnership with the understanding that the money would be repaid from partnership profits. In *Mervyn Investment Co. v. Biber, supra*, one partner contributed all the capital, the other contributed his services, and it was understood that upon the repayment of the contributed capital from partnership profits the partner who contributed his services would receive a one-third interest in the partnership assets. In each of these cases the court properly held that the partners impliedly promised to continue the partnership for a term reasonably required to allow the partnership to earn sufficient money to accomplish the understood objective. In *Shannon v. Hudson, supra*, the parties entered into a joint venture to build and operate a motel until it could be sold upon favorable and mutually satisfactory terms, and the court held that the joint venture was for a reasonable term sufficient to accomplish the purpose of the joint venture.

In the instant case, however, defendant failed to prove any facts from which an agreement to continue the partnership for a term may be implied. The understanding to which defendant testified was no more than a common hope that the partnership earnings would pay for all the necessary expenses. Such a hope does not establish even by implication a "definite term or particular undertaking" as required by [UPA § 31(1)(b)]. All partnerships are ordinarily entered into with the hope that they will be profitable, but that alone does not make them all partnerships for a term and obligate the partners to continue in the partnerships until all of the losses over a period of many years have been recovered.

Defendant contends that plaintiff is acting in bad faith and is attempting to use his superior financial position to appropriate the now profitable business of the partnership. Defendant has invested $43,000 in the firm, and owing to the long period of losses his interest in the partnership assets is very small. The fact that plaintiff's wholly-owned corporation holds a $47,000 demand note of the partnership may make it difficult to sell the business as a going concern. Defendant fears that upon dissolution he will receive very little and that plaintiff, who is the managing partner and knows how to conduct the operations of the partnership, will receive a business that has become very profitable because of the establishment of Vandenberg Air Force Base in its vicinity. Defendant charges that plaintiff has been content to share the losses but now that the business has become profitable he wishes to keep all the gains.

There is no showing in the record of bad faith or that the improved profit situation is more than temporary. In any event these contentions are irrelevant to the issue whether the partnership is for a term or at will. Since, however, this action is for a declaratory judgment and will be the basis for future action by the parties, it is appropriate to point out that defendant is amply protected by the fiduciary duties of co-partners.

Even though the Uniform Partnership Act provides that a partnership at will may be dissolved by the express will of any partner [UPA § 31(1)(b)], this power, like any other power held by a fiduciary, must be exercised in good faith.

We have often stated that "partners are trustees for each other, and in all proceedings connected with the conduct of the partnership every partner is bound to act in the highest good faith to his co-partner, and may not obtain any advantage over him in the partnership affairs by the slightest misrepresentation, concealment, threat, or adverse pressure of any kind."

A partner at will is not bound to remain in a partnership, regardless of whether the business is profitable or unprofitable. A partner may not, however, by use of adverse pressure "freeze out" a co-partner and appropriate the business to his own use. A partner may not dissolve a partnership to gain the benefits of the business for himself, unless he fully compensates his co-partner for his share of the prospective business opportunity. In this regard his fiduciary duties are at least as great as those of a shareholder of a corporation.

In the case of *In re Security Finance Co.*, 49 Cal. 2d 370, 376-377, 317 P.2d 1, 5, we stated that although shareholders representing 50 per cent of the voting power have a right under Corporations Code, § 4600 to dissolve a corporation, they may not exercise such right in order "to defraud the other shareholders, to 'freeze out' minority shareholders, or to sell the assets of the dissolved corporation at an inadequate price."

Likewise in the instant case, plaintiff has the power to dissolve the partnership by express notice to defendant. If, however, it is proved that plaintiff acted in bad faith and violated his fiduciary duties by attempting to appropriate to his own use the new prosperity of the partnership without adequate compensation to his co-partner, the dissolution would be wrongful and the plaintiff would be liable as provided by [UPA § 38(2)(a)] for violation of the implied agreement not to exclude defendant wrongfully from the partnership business opportunity.

The judgment is reversed.

NOTES AND QUESTIONS

(1) **Note on** *Page.* Santa Maria, California is 17 miles from Vandenberg AFB, which was originally known as Camp Cooke and used actively during WWII. "[A]s of January 1957, the military reservation had reverted to its previous use for cattle and sheep grazing. Transformation of Camp Cooke into the nation's first space and ballistic missile operational and training base began in 1957 when it was transferred to the United States Air Force." *See* www.vandenberg.af.mil/30sw/history/index.asp. Camp Cooke's isolation made it ideal for ICBMs, which were established on the base beginning in January, 1957. This program was accelerated when, in October, 1957, Russia launched Sputnik. On October 4, 1958, the base was renamed Vandenberg AFB in honor of the late General Hoyt S. Vandenberg, the Air Force's second Chief of Staff. *See* http://www.vandenberg.af.mil/30sw/history/tanks_to_missiles/af_takes_charge/air_force _takes_charge.html.

(2) **Judicially qualifying the power to liquidate: "bad faith" dissolution.** Since the partnership was not for a term, it would seem to follow that plaintiff can compel liquidation of the partnership pursuant to UPA § 38(1) and buy the business at a liquidation sale. However, the last section of Justice Traynor's decision suggests that there may be a legal impediment to plaintiff's doing this. Assuming plaintiff may be able to appropriate the "gains" of the business, why don't these gains belong to plaintiff? Also, should these facts justify ignoring plaintiff's liquidation right under UPA § 38(1)? What do you suppose the partners expected in this case? Should their actual expectations be controlling?

(3) **Consequences of dissolution in bad faith.** If the dissolution is in bad faith, what, precisely, is defendant's remedy? Should the dissolution be deemed wrongful, triggering the remedies under UPA § 38(2)? What should be the measure of damages?

(4) **Death of a partner.** It is not clear whether the surviving partners have the right to continue the business after the death of a co-partner. Continuation is arguably consistent with UPA §§ 37 and 38(1), which give the right to force liquidation only to a "partner," as distinguished from the representative of a deceased's estate. But UPA § 41(3) implies that the estate's consent is required for continuation, and the estate's legal representative can obtain judicial winding up under UPA § 37. What should be the result as a matter of policy? On the one hand, a partner's death can occur unexpectedly, thus increasing the costs of liquidation for the surviving partners. On the other hand, inability to force a sale leaves the estate on the hook for pre-dissolution debts of the partnership. Whether the liquidation right is a problem for the surviving partners ultimately depends on, among other things, how hard it will be for them to buy the business as a going concern at auction, or negotiate with the estate for a buyout. For a more general discussion of the balancing process involved in determining the partners' liquidation rights, see Subsection [A] above.

REFERENCES

Bromberg & Ribstein, BROMBERG & RIBSTEIN ON PARTNERSHIP §§ 7.02-7.05.

Hillman, *The Dissatisfied Participant in the Solvent Business Venture: A Consideration of the Relative Permanence of Partnerships and Close Corporations*, 67 MINN. L. REV. 1 (1982).

Hillman, *Loyalty in the Firm: A Statement of General Principles on the Duties of Partners Withdrawing from Law Firms*, 55 WASH. & LEE L. REV. 997 (1998).

[C] The Consequences of Dissolution: Liquidation

Following dissolution, the partners can either compel the firm to liquidate or force a buyout of the dissolving partners' interests. Which result follows depends upon the circumstances surrounding the dissolution: if dissolution is not in contravention of the partnership agreement and the partnership agreement does not require continuation of the partnership, any partner may compel liquidation of the firm; if, on the other hand, dissolution has been caused wrongfully or in contravention of the partnership agreement, the non-wrongful partners can continue the partnership on payment to the wrongful partners of the value of their interests less goodwill and damages resulting from the wrongful dissolution. This subsection looks more closely at the details of liquidation, while subsection [D] examines the buyout right.

Liquidation (which may involve sale of the business as a going concern) generally involves sale of the partnership property and a cash distribution to the partners rather than a distribution "in kind" of partnership property to the partners. Sale and cash dis-

tribution avoid the need to value the assets, effectively terminate the partners' obligations to creditors, and ensure that the partners can go their separate ways rather than
remaining joint owners of some of the partnership assets. For an interesting illustration,
see Hill v. Brown,[5] in which the court ordered the sale of a cow belonging to a two-per-
son partnership, which had been used in an embryo transplant business, rather than
letting one of the partners maintain an interest in the cow by bidding on only [an unspec-
ified] half of it.

On liquidation, it is necessary to determine what each partner is entitled to take
away from the business. This involves consideration of two separate questions, covered
in the following two subsections: (1) determining what the partnership owns and (2)
determining each partner's share of assets and liabilities.

[1] What Does the Partnership Own?

Because of the informal nature of partnership, it may be difficult to distinguish
property the business owns from that retained by the individual partners. If the partners
do not specify in the partnership agreement what property each has contributed to the
partnership, the court must somehow discern their intention under the UPA. Section 8
of the UPA provides some loose rules for determining what property falls within the category of "partnership property." The courts have emphasized, among other things,
whether the property was purchased with partnership funds (*see* UPA § 8(2)) and the
language of deeds and other instruments. RUPA § 204 provides somewhat more guidance.

[2] Computing the Partner's Share

In the absence of contrary agreement, the UPA determines the partner's share on
liquidation by making up a "pot" under § 40(a) consisting of the partnership property
and any necessary additional contributions by the partners toward the firm's "liabilities,"
which are defined in § 40(b). Under §§ 40(d) and 18(a), partners must make up the
excess of liabilities over assets in proportion to their profit shares. Section 40(b) determines the order in which the firm's liabilities are paid out of this "pot"—amounts owed
to outside creditors first, then amounts owed to creditors who are partners, then partners' capital contributions, then partners' share of profits (note that the latter two are
technically "liabilities" of the partnership under § 40(b)).

Note that partners who contributed services rather than money to a losing firm
may find that they have not only sweated for nothing, but have to dig into their pockets
to pay off creditors. For example, if A and B form a 50/50 partnership with A contributing $100 in capital and B contributing expertise, and the partnership has $50 more

---

[5]   166 Ill. App. 3d 867, 520 N.E.2d 1038 (1988).

debts than assets on dissolution, B must contribute $25 to the partnership to help repay creditors. B might have expected that A would share the load by paying the debts out of his capital, but that is not what happens unless the agreement so provides.

If there are no losses, partners (in the absence of contrary agreement) are entitled to the full repayment of amounts they contributed ("capital") and to equal shares of the remaining surplus ("profits") under § 18(a). However, the partners might agree, for example, to give a large capital contributor a correspondingly large share of the profits.

[3] Partnership Accounts

The partners' shares on liquidation depend significantly on the partnership accounts. The partnership agreement and the capital portion of the partnership balance sheet (which is equivalent to the stockholders' equity portion of a corporation balance sheet) usually specify the partners' contributions of property to the partnership and the credit allowed each partner's capital account. If the partnership is worth more on dissolution than the amounts reflected in the capital accounts, this may leave a surplus to be divided according to the UPA and the parties' agreement. Conversely, depreciation in value may result in a loss to be shared by the partners. Individual partners keep all of the gain on property owned by them personally rather than by the partnership

Subject to contrary agreement, RUPA § 401 provides for establishment of capital accounts for partners. Section 807 provides for distribution of property according to amounts credited and charged to partners' accounts. If the partners have not maintained accounts, the court may have to construct them.

REFERENCE

Bromberg & Ribstein, BROMBERG & RIBSTEIN ON PARTNERSHIP § 7.10.

[D] Consequences of Dissolution: Buyout of Dissolving Partners

The partnership may be continued after dissolution rather than liquidated, where the partners have so agreed or by agreement of the non-wrongful partners in the event of dissolution in contravention of the agreement. If the partnership is continued, the partnership must buy the dissolving partners' interests. This Section discusses the partners' rights in connection with dissolutions that result in buyouts, rather than liquidations. In general, compare the positions of partners who leave with, and without, liquidation of the firm. Under the default provisions of the UPA and RUPA, is a leaving partner better off insisting on liquidation? Should these provisions be designed to encourage continuity of the firm?

When a partnership is continued, UPA § 42 (in the absence of contrary agreement) requires that the departing partner or estate be paid "the value of his interest at the date of dissolution." (As to the rights of the estate, see Note 4 following the *Page* case). That value ordinarily includes "goodwill," discussed in the following case.

IN RE BROWN
New York Court of Appeals
242 N.Y. 1, 150 N.E. 581 (1926)

CARDOZO, J., delivered the opinion of the court:

Vernon C. Brown & Co. were stockbrokers for many years in the city of New York. Stephen H. Brown, one of the partners, died. The survivors, denying that there was any good will to be accounted for, continued the business at the old stand and in the old name. The executors acquiesced. For so acquiescing they have been held to be at fault, and their accounts have been surcharged accordingly. The question is whether the decree may be sustained.

The Browns, Vernon and Stephen, were brothers. They began business in 1895 with one Watson, under the name of Watson & Brown. In 1901, Watson withdrew, and the brothers went on. "Vernon C. Brown & Co." became the name of the continued partnership. New members were admitted from time to time, but the firm name remained unchanged. Good will was not mentioned in the partnership articles or in any books of account. Incoming members did not pay anything for it. One member, Mr. Schoonmaker, retired while Stephen Brown was alive. If good will was an asset he was entitled to a share of it. The evidence is uncontradicted that nothing was paid him. We may infer that in the thought of the partners nothing was due.

At the outset, Stephen Brown, like his brother, was active in the business. He had a seat on the Exchange, and represented the firm upon the floor. Falling ill in 1912, he sold his seat, and, though leaving his capital intact, gave no services thereafter. His share of the profits, which before his illness had been 33 per cent, was gradually reduced till at his death in July, 1917, it was only 15 per cent. The business was lucrative, though it was run, one would gather, in a more or less old-fashioned and conservative way, without advertising in newspapers or solicitation of accounts. It had four branches or departments: (1) The general commission business; (2) the so-called "odd lot" business, which proved to be the most lucrative of all; (3) the so-called "two-dollar" business; and (4) speculative business transacted for the firm itself. There is a finding that all the branches of the business, except the last, had in them an element of good will for which the survivors were accountable. The net profits of the three branches were averaged for a period of three years; allowance being made for interest on capital and for the personal services rendered by the partners. The value of the good will was fixed at two years' purchase price of the profits so computed. On this basis, the value was $103,891.60 of which 15 per cent, $15,538.74, was the share due to the estate. The surrogate, confirming the report of a referee, held that the accounts of the executors were to be surcharged for failing to collect this amount from the survivors. The Appellate Division unanimously affirmed.

The books abound in definitions of good will. . . . There is no occasion to repeat them. Men will pay for any privilege that gives a reasonable expectancy of preference in the race of competition. . . . Such expectancy may come from succession in place or name or otherwise to a business that has won the favor of its customers. It is then known as good will. Many are the degrees of value. At one extreme there are expectancies so strong that the advantage derived from the economic opportunity may be said to be a certainty; at the other are expectancies so weak that for any rational mind they may be said to be illusory. We must know the facts in any case.

. . . We must consider at the outset what rights would have passed to a buyer of good will if the surviving partners had sold it in the course of liquidation. The chief elements of value upon any sale of a good will are first, continuity of place; and, second, continuity of name. . . . There may, indeed, at times be others, *e.g.*, continuity of organization. That element is of value in business of a complex order. Where the business is simple, the benefits of organization are slight and not so easily transmitted. Confining ourselves now to the two chief elements of value, we may assume that the buyer of this good will would have been reasonably assured of continuity of place. The firm offices were the same from the beginning of the business till the death of Stephen Brown and later. There is nothing to show that the survivors, genuinely endeavoring to dispose of the good will, would have been unable to deliver possession to a buyer of the lease. A more difficult question is presented when we ask to what extent there would have been continuity of name. "Vernon C. Brown & Co." was not an arbitrary symbol, like the Snyder Manufacturing Company, *e.g.*, in *Snyder Mfg. Co. v. Snyder*, 54 Ohio St. 86, 31 L.R.A. 657, 43 N.E. 325. It has not gained a secondary meaning supplanting a primary meaning which had been descriptive of a man or men, and instead identifying impersonally an organization or a product. Writ large in this style or title was the name of a living man who had done nothing by word or act to give the name a reality or a significance external to himself. A buyer of the good will gains no right to the use of any style or title whereby this man would be represented as still a partner in the business. We assume that in conducting the new business he would be privileged to describe himself, subject, however, to the rules of the Exchange, as the "successor" to the old one. *Moore v. Rawson*, 199 Mass. 493, 497, 499, 85 N.E. 586. He would not be suffered to go farther. One who writes his name at large in the style or title of a partnership does not dedicate to the partnership, by force of that act alone without other tokens of intention, the right to sell the name at auction upon every change of membership.

* * *

A name, which in popular thought is solely or predominantly the name of a living man, may not be sold against his protest as it might if it were the impersonal symbol of an organization or a product. The objection is not merely that the partner, whose name is thus appropriated, may be exposed to the risk of liability for debts of the continued business. . . . If that were all, he might be adequately protected by the certificate which his successors must file under the statute. . . . He would remain exposed to other perils though this one were averted. Business designed for him might be diverted to some one else. Worse than this, he might suffer in standing or good name "by reason of inferiority of goods or dishonorable business conduct, to which he is thereby made ostensibly a party." A different situation presents itself when the name is "arbitrary or fancy." . . . The like is true when, though it may once have designated a person, it has "practically become an artificial one, designating nothing but the establishment." . . .

This will happen oftener in trading partnerships than in those where the personal relation, even though not exclusive, counts for more. It will happen oftener where the title contains the surnames only of the members, than it will when individuals are identified more sharply. . . . The question in last analysis is one of probable intention. To answer it we must know whether by reasonable intendment, as gathered from the nature of the business and the course of dealing, the partner whose name is appropriated by a stranger has given consent to his associates to submit to an impersonation so disturbing and deceptive. In the record before us there is neither finding of consent nor evidence pointing to the conclusion that consent should be implied.

* * *

We conclude, then, that a buyer of this good will, if it had been put up for sale by the liquidating partners, would have had the benefit at most of continuity of place and of such continuity of name as would belong to a "successor." We have next to consider the relation of these benefits to the several branches or departments in which the business was conducted.

1. There is a finding, unanimously affirmed, that appurtenant to the general commission branch was an element of good will not incapable of conveyance. We cannot say that this finding is qualified by others to such an extent that as a matter of law it must be disregarded as erroneous. The buyer of the good will would take over the firm records, which would give the names of the old customers. He would be in a position to notify them that he had succeeded to the business. True, the old partners might send out notices that they were still in business for themselves. None the less, some customers might wander into the old place from forgetfulness or habit. Once there, inertia might lead them to give an order to brokers whom they found established in possession. The relation is not so distinctly personal or professional that good will is excluded either for reasons of public policy or as an inference of law. . . . We may doubt whether a privilege so uncertain would be worth a great deal. The surrogate would have been justified in placing the value at a much lower figure than he did, or even at a nominal amount. . . . The question is not whether the buyer would be willing to pay much or would be making a wise bargain. The question is whether a reasonable man would be willing to pay anything.

2. The odd lot business stands on a different basis. Its essential characteristics are established by the findings. There is a rule of the New York Stock Exchange by which the unit of trading on the floor of the Exchange is declared to be 100 shares. Dealings in smaller numbers of shares are known as odd lot transactions. Most stockbrokers do not transact an odd lot business, but there are some that do, and Vernon C. Brown & Co. was one of them. Orders for odd lots do not come through the office. They are given on the floor of the Exchange to the individual member or members of the firm who are its floor representatives. They come invariably from other brokers communicating with fellow members of the Exchange whom they know as individuals.

A buyer of the good will would gain nothing in respect of this branch of the business from continuity of place. There was no relation between such orders and the place where the firm business was transacted. He would gain nothing from the privilege of announcing himself the successor of the business without continuity of name. The individual brokers who had been accustomed to receive these orders from fellow members of the Exchange would still be on hand to receive them as before. The findings suggest no reason why business so individual and personal should be diverted or diminished. Very likely the new firm, when announcing its succession to the business, would advertise the fact that its board members, if there were any, would buy and sell odd lots. It might advertise a like readiness though the business it was starting had no relation of succession to any that had gone before. The appeal to favor would be hardly stronger in one case than in the other. The situation would be different if the old partners had been about to withdraw from the field of competition. While they remained in the arena, the tie of succession was too attenuated to give to the buyer in transactions so individual and personal a fair promise of advantage. One cannot gain a foothold upon a ledge of opportunity so narrow. Expectancy in such conditions may be said to have reached the vanishing point at which it merges in illusion.

3. The "two-dollar" or "specialist" business is personal and individual like the department just considered. The specialist is a broker who remains at one post of the Exchange where particular stocks are dealt in, and there executes orders received from other brokers. He receives a commission of $2.50 for every 100 shares. Good will does not attach to business of this order for the same reason that none attaches to dealings in odd lots.

Mention should be made in conclusion of a provision of the will of Stephen Brown, whereby his executors are relieved of responsibility for mistakes or errors of judgment. This provision may become important upon a rehearing in determining liability for the value of the good will, if any, incidental to the commission business. In the event that the value of such good will shall be found to be doubtful or insignificant, the surrogate may properly conclude that the failure to collect it was an error of judgment and nothing more. The order of the Appellate Division and the decree of the Surrogate's Court, so far as such decree is appealed from, should be reversed, and a rehearing ordered, with costs to abide the event.

* * *

NOTES AND QUESTIONS

(1) **What "goodwill" belongs to a leaving partner?** Why give the estate only the going concern value that would remain if the survivors sold the firm to third parties? Note that some more recent cases have been more liberal than *Brown* in finding goodwill, even in professional firms.[6] Is *Brown* justified in holding that the continuing mem-

---

[6]   *See, e.g., Dawson v. White & Case*, 88 N.Y.2d 666, 672 N.E.2d 589 (1996) (but finding an agreement not to pay goodwill); *Donahue v. Draper*, 22 Mass. App. 30, 491 N.E.2d 260 (1986) (value of "top-making" [a type of wool manufacturing] firm could include even value derived partly from the experience and contacts that one partner had before he joined the firm where he could be deemed to have "contributed" this to the business and where the business "was not an esoteric endeavor responsive to one virtuosic hand"); *Spayd v. Turner, Granzow & Hollenkamp*, 19 Oh. St. 3d 55, 482 N.E.2d 1232 (1985) (modern law firms, because of their size and extensive organization, are not precluded as a matter of law from having goodwill).

bers were entitled to most of the value of the income that would have been paid to Stephen had he survived? Is the result justified by the difficulty of valuing goodwill based on human capital?

(2) **The death of a string quartet.** A string quartet called the Audubon Quartet broke up because of differences between three of the members and a fourth member over the fourth member's effort to get a Bergonzi violin, which apparently would have enhanced his sound compared to the second violin and the viola, the latter of whom is the wife of the founder of the quartet. The group operated without an agreement on a supposed principle of equality in which the founder regarded himself as more equal than the others and owned the group's name. The group was organized as a Pennsylvania non-profit corporation. The fourth member sued, eventually winning over $600,000 in damages from the other three members based on the supposed value of the member's interest and attorneys' fees, forcing them to try to seek refuge in bankruptcy,[7] and ultimately resulting in the seizure of group members' personal assets.[8] The bitter dispute destroyed a popular string quartet and became a cause celebre in the music world.[9] Under *Brown,* how do you suppose the dissenting member's share would have been computed? Why do you suppose the court ruled that he was entitled to significant going concern value?

(3) **Effect of *Brown* rule on continuity.** Cases like *Brown* generally arise when the exiting member or estate agrees to continuation at the continuing partners' request. A highly conservative approach to valuation makes it cheaper for the continuing partners to carry on. On the other hand, the partners may not be able easily to agree on valuation, and the threat of a very conservative valuation by the court may lead the leaving partner or estate to insist on liquidation.

(4) **Agreements on valuation.** If the partners want a more realistic valuation of goodwill, they can draft for it. *Brown* illustrates why an agreement may be advisable, since the parties may not get the valuation they expect. Some facts in *Brown* indicate that there was at least an implied agreement to limit the payment of goodwill.

(5) **The effect of ethical rules.** Withdrawing law partners' rights to share in partnership goodwill are limited by ethical rules against fee-splitting. *See* Rule 1.5, Model Rules of Professional Conduct; DR 2-107(B), Model Code of Professional Responsibility.[10] But courts often hold that professional firms have goodwill for purposes of

---

[7]   *See In re Weincko*, (Bankr., W.D. Va., April 3, 2002) (dismissing Chapter 13 petition); *In re Audubon Quartet, Inc.* (Bankr., W.D. Va., April 3, 2002) (ordering corporate ratification of Chapter 7 petition); *Ehrlich v. Audubon Quartet, Inc.*, Court of Common Pleas of Allegheny County, Pennsylvania (October 16, 2001) (opinion, adjudication and decree).

[8]   For this and other recent history, see http://www.audubon4tet.com.

[9]   *See, e.g., Trial in Virginia*, CHAMBERMUSIC, April, 2002, at 29.

[10]   *See Fraser v. Bogucki*, 203 Cal. App. 3d 604, 250 Cal. Rptr. 41 (1988) (denying, partly on the basis of the fee-splitting rule, a law partner's claim against his former partners for appropriation of client relationships).

determining the amount owed the divorcing spouse of a partner. Is this situation distinguishable from the division of assets among partners on dissolution?

(6) **Work in process.** Professional partners may be entitled to share in "work in process," such as law cases, that is pending as of dissolution and completed afterward.[11] The main issue in these cases is whether partners (whether departing or continuing) who complete the work should be entitled to the full fee for their efforts. UPA § 18(f) provides for remuneration to partners for acting in the partnership business only when a "surviving partner" winds up the partnership's affairs. Under this rule, most courts have split the fee according to the partners' pre-dissolution profit share without allowing extra compensation to the completing partner, at least when the firm is dissolved other than by death of a partner.[12] This raises a question about whether the completing partner will work hard for the client when he only gets part of the fee—the same concern that makes referral fees ethically questionable. It also makes it harder for partners to leave. RUPA § 401(h) changes the UPA by providing, in the absence of contrary agreement, for remuneration in connection with winding up. The partners can, of course, always decide in their partnership agreement how to deal with work in process.[13]

(7) **Non-competition agreements.** If a partner agrees not to compete with her former firm, this in effect transfers the exiting partner's "personal" goodwill to the continuing partners. Conversely, if the leaving partner is paid for goodwill, this may imply the existence of a noncompetition agreement. Attorney non-competes may violate ethical rules against interference with clients' choice of counsel. *See* ABA Model Rules of Professional Conduct, Rule 1.8(h)(1). However, the firm may be able to provide for "two-tiered" severance pay that ties compensation of withdrawing partners to whether the partner will remain in the same line of practice or jurisdiction as the firm. The validity of these agreements under ethical rules is unclear.[14]

(8) **Effect of RUPA.** RUPA § 701(b) may change some of the rules regarding valuation. It provides that, when the firm is continued following partner withdrawal, the dissociated partner is entitled to a "buyout price" of "the greater of the liquidation value or the value based on a sale of the entire business as a going concern without the dissociated partner." It is not clear when, if ever, the "liquidation value" will differ from the "going concern" value, since the assets normally have "going concern" rather than scrap value. More importantly for present purposes, § 701(b) might change the rule

---

[11]   *See, e.g., Rosenfeld, Meyer & Susman v. Cohen*, 146 Cal. App. 3d 200, 194 Cal. Rptr. 180 (1983), and 191 Cal. App. 3d 1035, 237 Cal. Rptr. 14 (1987) (involving a multi-million dollar anti-trust settlement that was pending for years before dissolution and then settled shortly after two partners left the firm, taking the case with them).

[12]   *See, e.g., Frates v. Nichols*, 167 So. 2d 77 (Fla. Dist. Ct. App. 1964).

[13]   *See Meehan v. Shaughnessy*, 404 Mass. 419, 535 N.E.2d 1255 (1989).

[14]   *Compare Cohen v. Lord Day & Lord*, 75 N.Y.2d 95, 551 N.Y.S.2d 157, 550 N.E.2d 410 (1989) (invalidating agreement denying withdrawing law partner distributions from post-dissolution receipts), *with Howard v. Babcock*, 6 Cal. 4th 409, 25 Cal. Rptr. 2d 80, 863 P.2d 150 (1994) (upholding agreement that reduced payouts to partner who engaged in post-departure practice that might involve competition with the firm).

in cases like *Brown*: by providing for payment of going concern value determined "without the dissociated partner," § 701(b) seems to imply that the reputations of the non-dissociating partners are taken into account.

(9) **Effect of time lag between dissolution and paying off partner.** The value of the departing partner's interest is determined as of the time of dissolution or dissociation. *See* UPA §§ 38 and 42; RUPA § 701(b). In order to encourage quick payout and thereby reduce the time the departing partner is at risk, as well as to compensate the partner for the use of his capital, UPA § 42 lets departing partners elect the greater of interest on, or "profits attributable to," their share of the partnership. RUPA § 701, however, omits the profits option.

(10) **Liabilities of dissolved partnership.** A partner's dissociation does not in itself affect liabilities owed prior to the dissociation. Creditors can, of course, continue to collect these debts from the property of the pre-dissociation partnership. Under UPA § 41, creditors also may be able to collect the debts out of property transferred to a new successor partnership on the theory that successor partnerships essentially continue the original partnership despite a technical "dissolution." RUPA has no provision comparable to § 41 because RUPA assumes that, whenever the partnership is "dissolved," it is liquidated rather than continued. But this does not address the situation in which the partnership is sold as a going concern at liquidation.

(11) **Liabilities of partner of dissolved firm.** A partner who leaves a partnership continues to be personally liable for all the firm's liabilities as of the time of departure unless the creditor expressly or impliedly agrees not to continue to hold the partner liable (UPA § 36, RUPA § 703(c)-(d)). The partner also is liable for debts that arise following the partner's departure as to certain creditors who lacked knowledge or notice of the dissociation (UPA § 35, RUPA §§ 704-705). In other words, continuing the firm necessarily exposes the departing partner to a continued liability risk. The continuing partners may agree to indemnify the departing partner. Also, UPA § 38 requires the continuing partners to "discharge" expelled partners from liabilities and to indemnify wrongfully withdrawing partners "against all present or future liabilities" and "release" them from "existing liabilities." But the UPA does not provide for indemnification for rightfully dissolving partners, probably because they can use their ability to block continuation of the firm as leverage to obtain complete indemnification. RUPA § 701(d) provides more clearly for indemnification of *all* dissociated partners against present and future liabilities.

REFERENCES

Bromberg & Ribstein, BROMBERG & RIBSTEIN ON PARTNERSHIP §§ 4.05(g), 7.08, 7.12, 7.13, 7.22.

Hillman, *Law Firms and Their Partners: The Law & Ethics of Grabbing and Leaving*, 67 TEX. L. REV. 1 (1988).

Ribstein, *A Theoretical Analysis of Professional Partnership Goodwill*, 70 NEB. L. REV. 38 (1991).

Ribstein, *Ethical Rules, Agency Costs and Law Firm Structure*, 84 VA. L. REV. 1707 (1998).

[E] Altering the Consequences of Dissolution

The many problems indicated above in connection with dissolution of the partnership can be settled by the partnership agreement. While UPA § 31 provides that dissolution necessarily occurs upon one of the specified events, the parties' agreement can control many, if not all, of the consequences of dissolution. As discussed more fully below in Subsection [F], RUPA allows the partners to wholly avoid dissolution by advance agreement. The following case illustrates the potential problems in drafting for dissolution under the UPA.

PAV-SAVER CORPORATION v. VASSO CORPORATION
Illinois Appellate Court
143 Ill. App. 3d 1013, 97 Ill. Dec. 760, 493 N.E.2d 423 (1986)

Justice BARRY delivered the opinion of the court.

* * *

Plaintiff, Pav-Saver Corporation ("PSC"), is the owner of the Pav-Saver trademark and certain patents for the design and marketing of concrete paving machines. Harry Dale is the inventor of the Pav-Saver "slip-form" paver and the majority shareholder of PSC, located in Moline, Illinois. H. Moss Meersman is an attorney who is also the owner and sole shareholder of Vasso Corporation. In 1974 Dale, individually, together with PSC and Meersman formed Pav-Saver Manufacturing Company for the manufacture and sale of Pav-Saver machines. Dale agreed to contribute his services, PSC contributed the patents and trademark necessary to the proposed operation, and Meersman agreed to obtain financing for it. The partnership agreement was drafted by Meersman and approved by Attorney Charles Peart, president of PSC. The agreement contained two paragraphs which lie at the heart of the appeal and cross-appeal before us:

> 3. The duties, obligations and functions of the respective partners shall be:
>
> A. Meersman shall provide whatever financing is necessary for the joint venture, as required.
>
> B. (1) PAV-SAVER shall grant to the partnership without charge the exclusive right to use, on all machines manufactured and sold, its trademark "PAV-SAVER" during the term of this Agreement. In order to preserve and maintain the goodwill and other values of the trademark PAV-SAVER, it is agreed between the parties that PAV-SAVER Corporation shall have the right to inspect from time to time the quality of machines upon which the licensed trademark PAV-SAVER is used or applied on machines for laying concrete pavement where

such machines are manufactured and/or sold. Any significant changes in structure, materials or components shall be disclosed in writing or by drawings to
PAV-SAVER Corporation.

(2) PAV-SAVER grants to the partnership exclusive license without charge
for its patent rights in and to its Patent #3,377,933 for the term of this agreement
and exclusive license to use its specifications and drawings for the Slip-form
paving machine known as Model MX 6-33 .... It being understood and agreed
that same shall remain the property of PAV-SAVER and all copies shall be
returned to PAV-SAVER at the expiration of this partnership. ...

* * *

11. It is contemplated that this joint venture partnership shall be permanent
and same shall not be terminated or dissolved by either party except upon
mutual approval of both parties. If, however, either party shall terminate or dissolve said relationship, the terminating party shall pay to the other party, as liquidated damages, a sum equal to four (4) times the gross royalties received by
PAV-SAVER Corporation in the fiscal year ending July 31, 1973, as shown by
their corporate financial statement. Said liquidated damages to be paid over a ten
(10) year period next immediately following the termination, payable in equal
installments.

In 1976, upon mutual consent, the PSC/Dale/Meersman partnership was dissolved and
replaced with an identical one between PSC and Vasso, so as to eliminate the individual
partners.

It appears that the Pav-Saver Manufacturing Company operated and thrived according
to the parties' expectations until around 1981, when the economy slumped, sales of the
heavy machines dropped off significantly, and the principals could not agree on the direction that the partnership should take to survive. On March 17, 1983, Attorney Charles Peart,
on behalf of PSC, wrote a letter to Meersman terminating the partnership and invoking the
provisions of paragraph 11 of the parties' agreement.

In response, Meersman moved into an office on the business premises of the Pav-
Saver Manufacturing Company, physically ousted Dale, and assumed a position as the day-
to-day manager of the business. PSC then sued in the circuit court of Rock Island County
for a court-ordered dissolution of the partnership, return of its patents and trademark, and
an accounting. Vasso counterclaimed for declaratory judgment that PSC had wrongfully terminated the partnership and that Vasso was entitled to continue the partnership business, and
other relief pursuant to the Illinois Uniform Partnership Act. Other related suits were filed,
but need not be described as they are not relevant to the matters before us. After protracted
litigation, the trial court ruled that PSC had wrongfully terminated the partnership; that
Vasso was entitled to continue the partnership business and to possess the partnership assets,
including PSC's trademark and patents; that PSC's interest in the partnership was $165,000,
based on a $330,000 valuation for the business; and that Vasso was entitled to liquidated
damages in the amount of $384,612, payable pursuant to paragraph 11 of the partnership
agreement. Judgment as entered accordingly.

Both parties appealed. PSC takes issue with the trial court's failure to order the return of its patents and trademark or, in the alternative, to assign a value to them in determining the value of the partnership assets. Further, neither party agrees with the trial court's enforcement of their agreement for liquidated damages. In its cross-appeal, PSC argues that the amount determined by the formula in paragraph 11 is a penalty. Vasso, on the other hand, contends in its appeal that the amount is unobjectionable, but the installment method of pay-out should not be enforced.

In addition to the afore-cited paragraphs of the parties' partnership agreement, the resolution of this case is controlled by the dissolution provision of the Uniform Partnership Act (Ill. Rev. Stat. 1983, ch. 106-1/2, pars. 29-43 [UPA § 38(2)]).

* * *

Initially we must reject PSC's argument that the trial court erred in refusing to return Pav-Saver's patents and trademark pursuant to paragraph 3 of the partnership agreement, or in the alternative that the court erred in refusing to assign a value of PSC's property in valuing the partnership assets. The partnership agreement on its face contemplated a "permanent" partnership, terminable only upon mutual approval of the parties (paragraph 11). It is undisputed that PSC's unilateral termination was in contravention of the agreement. The wrongful termination necessarily invokes the provisions of the Uniform Partnership Act so far as they concern the rights of the partners. Upon PSC's notice terminating the partnership, Vasso elected to continue the business pursuant to section 38(2)(b) of the Uniform Partnership Act. As correctly noted by Vasso, the statute was enacted "to cover comprehensively the problem of dissolution . . . [and] to stabilize business." (*Kurtzon v. Kurtzon*, (1st Dist. 1950), 339 Ill. App. 431, 437, 90 N.E.2d 245, 248.) Ergo, despite the parties contractual direction that PSC's patents would be returned to it upon the mutually approved expiration of the partnership (paragraph 3), the right to possess the partnership property and continue in business upon a wrongful termination must be derived from and is controlled by the statute. Evidence at trial clearly established the Pav-Saver machines being manufactured by the partnership could not be produced or marketed without PSC's patents and trademark. Thus, to continue in business pursuant to the statutorily-granted right of the party not causing the wrongful dissolution, it is essential that paragraph 3 of the parties' agreement—the return to PSC of its patents—not be honored.

Similarly, we find no merit in PSC's argument that the trial court erred in not assigning a value to the patents and trademark. The only evidence adduced at trial to show value of this property was testimony relating to goodwill. It was unrefuted that the name Pav-Saver enjoys a good reputation for a good product and reliable service. However, inasmuch as the Uniform Partnership Act specifically states that "the value of the goodwill of the business shall not be considered" (Ill. Rev. Stat. 1983, ch. 106-1/2, par. 38(2)(c)(II)), we find that the trial court properly rejected PSC's goodwill evidence of the value of its patents and trademark in valuing its interest in the partnership business.

Next, we find no support for PSC's argument that the amount of liquidated damages awarded to Vasso pursuant to the formula contained in paragraph 11 of the parties' agreement is a "penalty." . . .

It appears clear from the record that Meersman, with some insecurity about his partner's long-term loyalty to the newly-formed partnership, insisted on a liquidated damaged provision to protect his financial interests. Nonetheless, the record discloses that the agreement was reviewed by Peart and not signed until it was acceptable to both parties. As of December 31, 1982, the date of its last financial statement prior to trial, Pav-Saver Manufacturing Company carried liability on notes owed to various banks amounting to $269,060. As of December 31, 1981, the loans outstanding amounted to $347,487. These loans, the record shows, were obtained primarily on the basis of Meersman's financial ability to repay and over his signature individually. The amount of liquidated damages computed according to the formula in the parties agreement—$384,612—does not appear too greatly disproportionate to the liability. As earlier stated, the slip-form Pav-Saver machines could not be manufactured and marketed as such without the patents and trademarks contributed by Pav-Saver Corporation. Likewise, the services of Dale were of considerable value to the business.

In sum, we find there is no evidence tending to prove that the amount of liquidated damages as determined by the formula was unreasonable. Nor can we say, based on the evidence of record, that actual damages (as distinguished from a mere accounting) were readily susceptible to proof at the time the parties entered into their agreement. Suffice it to say, the liquidated damages clause in the parties' agreement appears to have been a legitimate matter bargained for between parties on equal footing and enforceable upon an unilateral termination of the partnership. We will not disturb the trial court's award of damages to Vasso pursuant to the liquidated damages formula.

We turn next to Vasso's arguments urging reversal of the trial court's decision to enforce paragraph 11 of the parties' agreement with respect to the manner of paying out the amount of damages determined by the formula. The paragraph provides for the liquidated sum to be paid out in equal installments over a 10-year period. The trial court held that the $384,612 owed by PSC should be paid in 120 monthly installments of $3,205.10 each commencing with March 17, 1983. In support of its argument that it was entitled to a set-off of the full amount of liquidated damages, including the unaccrued balance, Vasso argues that the doctrine of equitable set-off should apply on these facts and further urges that such set-off is required by statute.

In considering whether the liquidated damages formula contained in paragraph 11 of the partnership agreement was enforceable, we necessarily scrutinized the totality of the agreement—not merely the dollar figure so determined. Certainly at first blush the formula appears to yield a suspiciously high amount that is not directly related to any anticipated damages that either party might incur upon a wrongful termination of the agreement by the other. The manner of pay-out however—equal installments over a.10-year period—appears to temper the effect that the amount of liquidated damages so determined would have on the party who breached the agreement. In our opinion, the validity of the clause is greatly influenced by the pay-out provision. What might have been a penalty appears to be a fairly bargained-for, judicially enforceable liquidated damages provision. While, in hindsight, Vasso may sense the same insecurity in enforcement of the paragraph in toto that Meersman had hoped to avoid by insisting on the provision in 1974 and 1976, Vasso's concerns of PSC's potential insolvency are neither concrete nor sufficiently persuasive to entitle it to a right of set-off. . . .

For the foregoing reasons, we affirm the judgment of the circuit court of Rock Island County.

Affirmed.

Justice STOUDER concurring in part—dissenting in part.

I generally agree with the result of the majority. I cannot, however, accept the majority's conclusion the defendant is entitled to retention of the patents.

The Uniform Partnership Act is the result of an attempt to codify and make uniform the common law. Partners must act pursuant to the provisions of the Act which apply when partners have not agreed how they will organize and govern their ventures. These UPA provisions are best viewed as "default" standards because they apply in the absence of contrary agreements. The scope of the Act is to be determined by its provisions and is not to be construed to extend beyond its own proper boundaries. When the partnership contract contains provisions, imposing on one or more of the partners obligations differing from those which the law ordinarily infers from the partnership relation, the courts should strive to construe these provisions so as to give effect to the honest intentions of the partners as shown by the language of the contract and their conduct under it. . . .

Here, express terms of the partnership agreement deal with the status of the patents and measure of damages, the question is settled thereby. I think it clear the parties agreed the partnership only be allowed the use of the patents during the term of the agreement. The agreement having been terminated, the right to use the patents is terminated. The provisions in the contract do not conflict with the statutory option to continue the business and even if there were a conflict the provisions of the contract should prevail. The option to continue the business does not carry with it any guarantee or assurance of success and it may often well be that liquidation rather than continuation would be the better option for a partner not at fault.

As additional support for my conclusion, it appears the liquidated damages clause was insisted upon by the defendant because of earlier conduct of the plaintiff withdrawing from a former partnership. Thus, the existence of the liquidated damages clause recognizes the right of plaintiff to withdraw the use of his patents in accordance with the specific terms of the partnership agreement. Since liquidated damages depends on return of the patents, I would vacate that part of the judgment providing defendant is entitled to continue use of the patents and provide that use shall remain with plaintiff.

NOTES AND QUESTIONS

(1) **Interpreting the agreement.** If the dissent is correct and the UPA provision on wrongful dissolution can be varied by contrary agreement, is the majority's result nevertheless consistent with the parties' intent? Note that a contrary result lets Dale put Meersman out of business. But did the parties intend to let Dale do this as long as he paid liquidated damages? How might the partnership agreement have been drafted to better effectuate the parties' intent? Should it have provided that Dale was free to leave the partnership at any time and take the patents with him, so long as he paid liquidated damages? Should Dale's rights on leaving have been pegged to the time of his departure?

(2) **Precluding termination.** Meersman might have been better off if the agreement had provided that the agreement was not terminable, consistent with the parties'

underlying intent. Would such an agreement have been enforceable? Should it be enforceable?

[F] RUPA and Dissolution at Will

In light of the potential costs of the dissolution power, statutory provisions should balance the benefits of the power in providing liquidity for minority partners against its potential costs to the majority. At one extreme, a partner would have no right to exit the firm apart from the limited ability to assign financial rights, as discussed in *Rapoport* in Section 4.03. At the other extreme, represented by the UPA's dissolution provisions, each partner would have the power to liquidate the firm, pay off the creditors, and withdraw the remaining cash. An intermediate approach would provide that a leaving partner normally receives only the value of her interest and indemnification against liabilities.

In light of the above materials, do the UPA dissolution provisions achieve an appropriate balance between the benefits of providing a means of exit from the partnership and the costs of permitting dissolution at will? If the UPA provisions impose excessive costs on most partnerships, most partners will have to draft around the statute, thereby negating any potential transaction cost savings from having a partnership statute.

The main question is whether the statute should give the benefit of the doubt to the exiting partner or, instead, to the continuing partners. From the exiting partner's standpoint, dissolution may be to get out of the firm. Even a buyout right may not be enough given the problems of valuing a partnership interest (see *Brown* and related notes) and of protecting the dissociating partner from continued exposure to partnership liabilities. On the other hand, as *Page* illustrates, giving any exiting partner the power to compel liquidation lets each partner time her departure to maximize her own gain regardless of the others' loss.

In balancing these considerations, it is important to keep in mind that the parties have made open-ended investments of their human and financial capital and personal credit in an ongoing business. It arguably follows that the partners normally would rather not give each member a continuing option to force the other partners to buy the right to continue. Moreover, since the dissolution power invites opportunistic conduct by dissolving partners, perhaps the default rule should be designed to force partners who want such a power to identify themselves and negotiate for the power. Accordingly, perhaps the UPA should provide, subject to contrary agreement, merely for a right of partner buyout and indemnification in most situations, or at least that the majority of the partners can avoid dissolution. In exceptional situations, including wrongdoing by the other partners, a withdrawing partner could compel liquidation of the firm as under current UPA § 38(1).

In any event, the partners normally should be able to draft around the statute. However, under UPA § 31(2), a partner can compel dissolution no matter what the partnership agreement says. Moreover, § 29 apparently lets the partner withdraw irrespective of the agreement.[15] *Pav-Saver* shows that partners cannot necessarily solve all exit problems through drafting.

Despite the concerns raised by the UPA dissolution provisions, RUPA § 801 continues to provide that a partnership at will is dissolved, and its business must be wound up if, among other circumstances, a partner withdraws. However, as a concession to the problems caused by dissolution at will, a partnership for a definite term or particular undertaking is not dissolved after a partner's dissociation prior to expiration of the term unless within 90 days after the partner's withdrawal, a majority in interest of the remaining partners, including those who have rightfully dissociated, agree to dissolve the partnership.

REFERENCES

Ribstein, *The Revised Uniform Partnership Act: Not Ready for Prime Time*, 49 Bus. Law. 45 (1993).

Ribstein, *A Statutory Approach to Partner Dissociation*, 65 Wash. U. L.Q. 357 (1987).

---

[15] *See Infusaid Corp. v. Intermedics Infusaid, Inc.*, 739 F.2d 661 (1st Cir. 1984) (indicating that the right to withdrawal does not exist in all cases under the UPA).

CHAPTER 5

Enforcement of Governance Arrangements in Close Corporations

The Uniform Partnership Act provides that owners directly participate in management, are personally liable, cannot freely transfer management rights, and have the power to dissolve the partnership. As discussed in Chapter 4, this statutory scheme suits closely held firms. By contrast, corporation statutes provide that shareholders have limited liability, management is by a board of directors monitored by shareholders, ownership rights are freely transferable and the firm generally can be dissolved only by majority vote of both members and managers. This statutory scheme is appropriate for firms with many members.

This Chapter discusses the extent to which the corporate form can be adapted for closely held firms, just as the partnership standard form may be substantially altered by agreement in, for example, large law firms. Section 5.01 sets the stage by discussing the "standard form" of management and control set forth in the corporate statutes. Sections 5.02 through 5.04 then discuss limitations on contracting in the corporation for the partnership features of *per capita* voting, direct management and limited transferability. As these latter sections discuss, courts and legislatures have gradually permitted corporations to adopt a partnership management structure. However, with such a structure come the problems of partnership-type illiquidity discussed in Section 4.03. Accordingly, Section 5.05 discusses the extent to which the partnership solution to this problem—easy dissolution—has been applied to close corporations.

Courts and legislatures traditionally have been less willing to allow corporations to opt out of the corporate form than they have been to allow partnerships to adopt corporate features. This may be partly a holdover from the early view that a corporation is a "concession" of the state (*see* Section 1.04 above), and therefore subject to its control. Even some modern writers have argued that the state should not permit substantial variation of the corporate form to suit small businesses (*see* **Fessler, Mitchell** and **Rosenberry**). Some practical considerations that might underlie restrictions on contracting are discussed below in Section 5.02[A]. Other commentators (*see* **Bradley**) have advocated increased flexibility in corporate legislation to respond to the needs of close corporations.

Modern courts have pushed legislative and judicial limits in order to allow the parties to closely held corporations to adapt the corporate form to their needs. As one court said: "[W]e think the correct rule is that [a] stockholder control agreement is valid where it is for the benefit of the corporation, where it works no fraud upon creditors or other stockholders, and where it violates no statute or recognized public policy."[1] Legislatures have responded with special legislation for close corporations (*see* **Karjala**).

In general, this Chapter shows that legal and practical problems remain even after courts and legislatures have recognized that the standard corporate form may be varied in close corporations. Modern statutes, despite their flexibility, still impose limitations on what the parties to a close corporation may agree to. Also, unexpected problems result from trying to fit the closely held business into the corporate mold.

REFERENCES

Bradley, *Toward a More Perfect Close Corporation—The Need for More and Improved Legislation*, 54 Geo. L.J. 1145 (1966).

Fessler, *The Fate of Closely Held Business Associations: The Debatable Wisdom of "Incorporation,"* 13 U. Cal. Davis L. Rev. 473 (1980).

Karjala, *A Second Look at Special Close Corporation Legislation*, 58 Tex. L. Rev. 1207 (1980).

Mitchell, *Close Corporations Reconsidered*, 63 Tul. L. Rev. 1143 (1989).

Rosenberry, *Traditional Corporate Concepts in Light of Demands for Elastic Norms for the Family or Closely Held Corporation*, 5 J. Corp. L. 455 (1980).

§ 5.01 The Standard Form of Corporate Governance

This section discusses the corporate "standard form" of management and control set forth in the statute.

[A] General Considerations

The standard corporate form is suited to firms with many dispersed, passive owners in three important respects:

(1) *Decisionmaking by Agents.* Many corporate decisions are made by directors and officers, who act as agents of generally passive shareholders, rather than by the shareholders themselves.

(2) *Majority Vote Decision Rule.* When shareholders do make decisions, such decisions typically are made by majority vote rather than unanimously as with important partnership decisions.

(3) *Votes Allocated According to Financial Contributions.* Members vote according to their financial contributions, as contrasted with the one-partner-one-vote model.

---

[1]   *E.K. Buck Retail Stores v. Harkert*, 157 Neb. 867, 62 N.W.2d 288, 299 (1954).

Passive shareholders with limited liability make only financial contributions, unlike partners who also contribute services and credit.

[B] Allocating Power Between Board and Shareholders

Many of the questions concerning corporate governance involve allocating decision-making authority between the directors and officers, on the one hand, and the shareholders, on the other. In general, there is a question of how much to rely on shareholder voting as a way to minimize the agency costs associated with delegating decision making authority to officers and directors. While shareholder voting is an important constraint on management power, that does not mean that more voting is necessarily better. At some point, the cost of an additional unit of direct shareholder participation exceeds the benefit in terms of reducing agency costs. Not only would deciding everything General Motors does by direct shareholder vote be prohibitively expensive, but it wouldn't even reduce agency costs very much, because individual shareholders would devote little attention to monitoring managers. Corporations therefore substitute lower-cost alternative methods of ensuring that the managers act in the shareholders' interests, including incentive compensation, auditing by accountants, and fiduciary duties.

The following materials examine in greater detail the principal statutory provisions bearing on the allocation of authority between the board of directors and the shareholders.

[1] Management by the Board and Officers

As noted above, the standard corporate form provides for management by the board of directors and officers. More specifically, Del. G.C.L. § 141(a) provides for management "by *or under* the direction of a board of directors" (emphasis added). In general, the board exercises its authority to manage under provisions like Del. G.C.L. § 141(a) by electing corporate officers and then delegating to those officers substantial power to execute corporate policies set by the board. The duties and authority of officers are commonly matters for the corporate bylaws. *See* Del. G.C.L. § 142.

While the shareholders generally meet annually to elect the directors (*see* Del. G.C.L. § 211(b)), the certificate of incorporation or the bylaws may provide for the election of only a fraction of the directors at each annual shareholders meeting, so that the term of each director is more than one year. *See* Del. G.C.L. § 141(d). Such "staggered" boards obviously limit the shareholders' ability to change management in a given year, thereby reducing the monitoring of management. Staggered boards do, however, have potential benefits, such as encouraging managers to invest their time and skills in long-range corporate projects, and ensuring continuity of management.

If a director fails to serve a complete term, the directors can call a special shareholders' meeting to elect a successor. Because this is cumbersome, many statutes give directors the power to fill board vacancies. Del. G.C.L. § 223 even lets the directors fill newly-created positions. This is particularly significant since these statutes also permit the number of directors to be fixed by bylaws (Del. G.C.L. § 141(b)) which can be amended by the directors (*see* Del. G.C.L. § 109(a)). The Delaware Act therefore permits charter or bylaw provisions that allow the directors to create a board that is radically different from the one elected by the shareholders at the last annual meeting.

Shareholders may remove directors for cause, even where the statute and articles of incorporation do not specifically so provide.[2] Many corporation statutes also authorize the shareholders to remove directors without cause. *See* Del. G.C.L. § 141(k).[3] Delaware G.C.L. § 141(k) limits the power to remove without cause for "classified" (*i.e.*, staggered) boards. This limitation does not extend to the removal of directors by shareholders who can vote for particular directors—that is, where shares rather than directors, are classified.[4] Classified stock is discussed below (*see* Note 4 following *Oceanic* in Section 5.02[B][3]). MBCA § 8.08(a) permits the certificate of incorporation to provide for removal only for cause, even where the board is not classified.

Rohe v. Reliance Training Network, Inc.[5] held that the right to remove directors is a "fundamental element of stockholder authority" that "[can] not be impaired by either the certificate or the bylaws."

[2] Voting by Shareholders

While corporate statutes give the board of directors general management authority, those statutes do not leave the shareholders without a voice in corporate governance. Among other things, corporate statutes generally (a) reserve for the shareholders the power to select the corporation's directors (subject to the directors' power to fill vacancies and newly-created directorships that occur between shareholder meetings); (b) give the shareholders power over the corporation's bylaws concurrently with the board of directors (*see* Del. G.C.L. § 109(a)); and (c) specify some decisions that must be approved by vote of the shareholders.

One type of decision on which shareholders may vote is an amendment of the articles of incorporation. Under the Delaware Act, for example, a certificate amendment must first be adopted by the board of directors and then approved by a majority vote of the shareholders (Del. G.C.L. § 242(b)(1)) or of the class of shareholders particularly affected by the amendment (Del. G.C.L. § 242(b)(2)), unless a larger margin of approval is required by the certificate of incorporation (Del. G.C.L. § 242(b)(4)). Similar procedures apply when the corporation is merged with another (Del. G.C.L. § 251(a)-(c)); when the corporation sells all or substantially all of its assets (Del. G.C.L. § 271); and when the corporation is voluntarily dissolved (Del. G.C.L. § 275). Objecting share-

---

[2] *See Campbell v. Loew's Inc.*, 36 Del. Ch. 563, 134 A.2d 852 (1957).

[3] *See Scott County Tobacco Warehouses, Inc. v. Harris*, 214 Va. 508, 201 S.E.2d 780 (1974).

[4] *See Insituform of N.A., Inc. v. Chandler*, 534 A.2d 257 (Del. Ch. 1987).

[5] 2000 Del. Ch. LEXIS 108, 2000 WL 1038190 (Del. Ch. 2000).

holders sometimes can receive the appraised value of their shares (*see* Del. G.C.L. § 262). In addition to the matters discussed above, the board may also seek shareholder approval of some transactions which the board technically has the legal authority to enter into on its own in order to reduce the risk of being held liable for breach of fiduciary duty or to comply with stock exchange listing requirements.

Traditionally, courts have not permitted shareholders to use their franchise to dictate ordinary business decisions delegated to management pursuant to provisions like Del. G.C.L. § 141(a). But under Securities and Exchange Commission rules discussed *infra* (*see* Section 7.03), shareholders have been permitted to vote on *precatory* proposals touching on ordinary business matters, provided such proposals are significantly related to the corporation's business and involve substantial policy or other considerations. In addition, at least one court has allowed shareholders to use their power to amend the corporate bylaws to include provisions *mandating* board action.[6]

[C] Decisionmaking Procedures

[1] Directors' Meetings

Directors' decisions normally must be made at meetings after notice to the directors of the time and place of the meetings and of the matters which will be discussed. These details are generally referred by statute to the bylaws. The statutes specify a minimum quorum of directors who must attend directors' meetings in order for business to be transacted. *See* Del. G.C.L. § 141(b).

Some corporation statutes allow the directors to decide matters without a meeting if they *unanimously* consent to the action to be taken, and if the charter does not require a meeting. *See* Del. G.C.L. § 141(f). Also, § 141(i) allows the directors to meet by telephone or through other communications equipment.

If a majority of the directors agree to a matter without having complied with a statutory meeting requirement, it is not clear why their decision should be any less effective than one taken at a meeting. While director action without a meeting has resulted in invalidation of the decision,[7] more recent cases have tended to look the other way.[8]

---

[6]   See *International Brotherhood of Teamsters General Fund v. Fleming Companies*, 975 P.2d 907 (Okla. 1999) (approving bylaw requiring board to remove defenses against hostile takeovers).

[7]   See *Mosell Realty Corp. v. Schofield*, 183 Va. 782, 33 S.E.2d 774 (1945).

[8]   See *American Center for Education, Inc. v. Cavnar*, 80 Cal. App. 3d 476, 145 Cal. Rptr. 736 (1978) (upholding the action of a committee of the board of directors where the third member of the committee showed up at a bank where he knew the other two would be and stayed long enough to argue about the action being taken). *But see Moore Business Forms, Inc. v. Cordant Holdings*, 1998 Del. Ch. LEXIS 25, 1998 WL 71836 (Del. Ch. 1998) (voiding action taken at special board meeting where one director was deliberately not given notice of the meeting).

[2] Shareholders' Meetings: General Rules

Like directors, shareholders also generally may act only at meetings, although some modern statutes (*see* Del. G.C.L. § 228) permit shareholders to act by written consent without a meeting. The shareholders normally act by a vote of a majority of the shares represented at the meeting (*see* Del. G.C.L. § 216), though special rules apply in connection with the election of directors (*see* Subsection [3] immediately below). In addition, a majority of *all shares eligible to vote* is typically necessary to approve fundamental changes, such as amendments to the certificate of incorporation, mergers, sales of all or substantially all of a corporation's assets, or dissolutions.

Shareholders' meetings are held annually at a time and place and upon such notice as provided in the bylaws. The board can call a meeting at other times, although this power may be shared with the shareholders under the statute and bylaws. *See* Del. G.C.L. § 211(d). As a practical matter, the directors' power over the bylaws means that, even if the shareholders technically have the power to take action on an issue, the directors can thwart this power to some extent by making it difficult for the shareholders to meet.

Public corporation shareholders usually do not personally attend shareholders' meetings, but rather vote by filling out proxy cards they get from the corporation that list the items to be voted on at the meeting. The proxy forms are accompanied by a proxy statement which explains the issues to be voted on at the shareholders' meeting and, in the case of an annual meeting, an annual report that describes the company and its business (*see* Section 7.03 below).

Different types of securities in the corporation's capital structure carry different voting rights. Some preferred shareholders may only be able to vote on matters particularly affecting their securities. *See* Del. G.C.L. § 242(b)(2). Shareholders who do vote normally are entitled to one vote per share of stock owned. *See* Del. G.C.L. § 212(a). This system gives the greatest voting power to those who have made the largest financial investment in the corporation and therefore have the most incentive to use their vote to maximize corporate wealth.

[3] Shareholder Meetings: Voting on Directors

The corporation statutes provide for two principal methods of voting on directors. The usual method is "straight" voting. Under this method, shareholders cast their total allotted votes for each of the directorships being voted on, just as they would in an election for public office, resulting in the election of the nominee winning the plurality of votes cast for a particular directorship (*see* Del. G.C.L. § 216). A straight voting system lets a shareholder who owns a bare majority of the shares elect all of the directors.

Some corporations elect directors by "cumulative" voting. Under this system, each shareholder voting in a director election may cast a total number of votes computed by multiplying the number of votes she could vote for each director under a "straight" voting system by the number of directorships being voted on. The shareholder may allocate this total among the candidates in any way she sees fit—that is, she may "cumulate" votes on a selected candidate or candidates and disregard the others to enhance the impact of her votes. Under a cumulative voting system, a shareholder who owns less than a majority of the shares may be able to elect one or more directors.

In understanding how cumulative voting helps increase the power of minority shareholders, the following formula is helpful (X = number of shares needed to elect one director; Y = number of shares voted at the meeting; N = number of directors elected):

$$X = [Y/(N + 1)] + 1$$

Thus, if there are one million shares voted at the meeting and nine directors to be voted on, a minority shareholder with 100,001 votes will be able to elect one director under a cumulative voting regime. In contrast, a minority shareholder with 100,001 votes would not be able to elect any directors in a corporation which employed a straight voting system.

REFERENCE

Easterbrook & Fischel, THE ECONOMIC STRUCTURE OF CORPORATE LAW, Ch. 3 (1992).

§ 5.02 Shareholder Voting Arrangements in Close Corporations

[A] Introduction

As noted in Section 5.01[A], under the standard corporate form of management, shareholder votes are normally allocated according to the number of shares owned—that is, by the extent of financial investment in the firm. In addition, a majority vote usually is enough to approve corporate changes and (in the absence of cumulative voting) to elect the entire board of directors. This standard form can create problems in close corporations.

First, the parties might have made investments of services, expertise and personal credit (through guarantees of corporate debts) in addition to, or in lieu of, any financial contributions to the firm's capital. Therefore, like partners, they may insist on the power to control the firm's management that is out of proportion to their financial investments—that is, something more like the one-partner-one-vote model than one-share-one-vote.

Second, since the shareholders cannot easily sell their investments, they may be concerned about conflicts with other shareholders concerning investment objectives. Therefore, each close corporation shareholder may want to be able to veto the firm's decisions.

Third, because closely held firms typically have a relatively small total capital-ization, voting control in a closely held firm can easily be concentrated in the hands of a single shareholder or tight control group. Accordingly, minority shareholders in close corporations may need protection from the majority group.

For these reasons, close corporation shareholders may wish to draft around the standard corporate form through agreements and bylaw and charter provisions. As dis-cussed in subsection [B] below, shareholder voting arrangements come in several vari-eties, including irrevocable proxies, agreements to vote in a particular way, voting trusts, classified shares, and high vote and high quorum requirements.

Shareholder voting arrangements are generally enforceable today.[9] However, as indicated in *Ringling* and *Abercrombie*, below, this was not always the case. Courts have cited one or more of the following policy reasons for refusing to enforce share-holder voting arrangements:

(1) *Contrary to principles of representative government.* Shareholder voting arrangements contradict the standard "representative government, with vot-ing conducted conformably to the statutes, and the power of decision lodged in certain fractions, always more than half, of the stock."[10] But this reason-ing does not provide a practical explanation of why the parties should not be able to contract around the statutory standard form.

(2) *Lack of consideration.* There is no consideration apart from the mutual promises of the shareholders.[11] However, the parties' mutual promises could be considered sufficient consideration.

(3) *Analogy to personal service agreements.* A shareholder voting agree-ment involves "an ongoing, intimate, personal, consensual relation" that, like a personal service agreement, is not easily enforceable in court.[12] How-ever, enforcing voting arrangements, unlike compelling personal services, does not involve the court in difficult long-term supervision of performance.

(4) *Reconciling with other aspects of the corporate form.* Enforcing a vot-ing arrangement can cause paralyzing deadlock if, for instance, it confers blocking power on a minority shareholder. But giving each party a judicial way out of an agreement that creates a deadlock could provide an incentive to precipitate deadlock in the first place. Indeed, the parties might have formed a corporation rather than a partnership precisely in order to protect against easy exit from the agreement.

---

[9]   *See, e.g., Weil v. Beresth,* 154 Conn. 12, 220 A.2d 456 (1966); *E.K. Buck Retail Stores v. Harkert,* 157 Neb. 867, 62 N.W.2d 288 (1954).

[10]   *Benintendi v. Kenton Hotel,* 294 N.Y. 112, 60 N.E.2d 829, 831 (1945). *See also Roberts v. Whitson,* 188 S.W.2d 875 (Tex. Civ. App. 1945).

[11]   *See Johnson v. Spartanburg County Fair Ass'n,* 210 S.C. 56, 41 S.E.2d 599 (1947).

[12]   *See* Abraham Chayes, *Madame Wagner and the Close Corporation,* 73 HARV. L. REV. 1532, 1535 (1960).

(5) *Misalignment of incentives.* Enforcing voting agreements makes control disproportionate to the shareholders' financial stake in the enterprise, so that those who control do not necessarily have the incentive to act consistently with the firm's welfare. But recall that a reason for departing from the one-share-one-vote rule is to align voting power with total investment, including service and credit commitments. In all events, it is not clear why the shareholders should not be able to allocate voting power other than in accordance with financial stakes. Third-party creditors also may be injured if the agreement gives control to owners who lack appropriate incentives to maximize the value of the firm. But this is a risk that the creditors, too, can take into account when contracting with the firm, as long as the arrangement is disclosed.

(6) *Third-party effects.* A voting arrangement can lock in a coalition and let it consistently extract gains from the other shareholders who are not parties to the agreement.[13] But it is important to distinguish the situation in which third parties buy into the corporation with knowledge of the voting agreement from one in which the agreement is hidden or entered into without the consent of the other existing shareholders. In the former case, any costs that the agreement imposes on the corporation can be reflected in the price the non-participants pay for their stock. Rules requiring public disclosure of voting arrangements protect incoming investors.

The following subsection discusses particular types of shareholder voting arrangements and some of the leading cases on enforcement of these arrangements.

[B] Types of Shareholder Voting Arrangements

[1] Irrevocable Proxies

Close corporation shareholders have attempted to increase the security of voting arrangements through the device of the irrevocable proxy. The attraction of the irrevocable proxy is that the proxy-givers do not merely promise to vote in a particular way, but actually give up their vote to the proxy-holder to be exercised in accordance with the agreement.

For a proxy to be irrevocable, it must so state[14] and be "coupled with an interest." *See* Del. G.C.L. § 212(e). The latter rule is derived from the agency law rule that a principal generally has the power to terminate an agency relationship at will (although the termination may trigger a right to damages) except where the agent holds a power to act

---

[13]   *See* Easterbrook & Fischel, *Voting in Corporate Law,* 26 J.L. & Econ. 395, 406 (1983).

[14]   *See Eliason v. Englehart,* 733 A.2d 944 (Del. 1999) (proxy not irrevocable under Del. G.C.L. § 212(e) because the word "irrevocable" did not appear in the body of the proxy but only in the acknowledgment of the shareholder's signature).

for the principal as security to protect the agent's interest in the subject matter of the agency. This is "a power given as security."[15]

One commentator has argued that the "interest" necessary to support irrevocability "must center around a security need comparable to a proprietary incentive to maximize the overall welfare of the corporation so that abuse of his power is rendered highly unlikely."[16] But the interest need not be an interest in the stock itself.[17]

Proxies given by shareholders of public corporations (like those discussed in Section 5.01[C][2] above) are generally revocable.

[2] Voting Agreements

The most direct way for shareholders to control voting is simply to agree with each other that they will vote in a particular way. For example, a group of shareholders could agree that they will all vote together or that they will all vote for particular candidates for board or executive positions. Such an arrangement gives each party a power to block corporate action that is disproportionate to the shareholder's financial investment. For example, assume a corporation has five shareholders, each owning 20% of the stock. If three shareholders agree that they will vote together, any one of these three could block corporate action because each party to the agreement has the power of a 60% holder. On the other hand, each member's power to *initiate* actions is reduced because of the need to secure the agreement of the other two parties to the agreement, rather than of any two other shareholders.

Shareholder voting agreements are generally enforceable today.[18] However, as indicated in *Ringling*, below, this was not always the case.

Background Note on
Ringling v. Ringling Bros.-Barnum & Bailey Combined Shows, Inc.

The original Ringling brothers were Charlie, John, Alf and Al. Beginning humbly with dancing and juggling, the brothers built a fortune. By 1906, the brothers had bought Barnum & Bailey. By 1924, John, by then the leader of the clan, was reputed to be one of the wealthiest men in the world. However, in 1929 John's reckless management brought on a disastrous $1,700,000 debt. The default on this loan in 1932 resulted

---

[15] *See* RESTATEMENT (SECOND) OF AGENCY § 138 (1958).

[16] Comment, *Irrevocable Proxies*, 43 TEX. L. REV. 733, 747 (1965).

[17] *See Haft v. Haft*, 671 A.2d 413 (Del. Ch. 1995) (interest may be either "an interest in the stock itself or an interest in the corporation generally," so proxy holder's status as a senior executive of company was sufficient to support irrevocability).

[18] *See, e.g., Weil v. Beresth*, 154 Conn. 12, 220 A.2d 456 (1966); *E.K. Buck Retail Stores v. Harkert*, 157 Neb. 867, 62 N.W.2d 288 (1954).

in the transfer of the business to a Delaware corporation and the Ringling family temporarily lost control. John Ringling died in 1936.

At this point, the Ringling family is best viewed as three discrete factions—in fact, a three-ring circus—whose quarreling was to be a central theme of the history of the circus over the following decade:

1) *Edith Conway Ringling and her son Robert, who were the wife and son of the original Ringling brother, Charlie.* Robert was a stocky opera singer, a baritone, whose career reached its peak at the Civic Opera in Chicago.

2) *Ida Ringling North and her son, John Ringling North, the sister and nephew of the original Ringling brothers.* North was a shrewd go-getter whose shrewdness had antagonized John Ringling. Because of this antagonism, and despite the fact that they were his closest relatives, John cut the Norths out of his will. John's carelessness extended to his estate, however, and he forgot to remove the Norths as executors. As a result, they controlled a 37% voting interest in the circus.

3) *Aubrey Ringling, the widow of Alf's son, Richard.* Aubrey later married Haley, who was brought in as an accountant to untangle the mess left by John's poor estate planning.

In 1937, John Ringling North managed to refinance the debt which had resulted in the Ringling family's losing control of the circus. In connection with the refinancing, a voting trust was established by whose terms North was to name three of the seven directors, the bank one, and Edith and Aubrey the other three. The bank's nominee was Dunn, a bank vice president. The voting trust put North into effective control and he became president.

Under North, some changes were made in the circus. North put a big gorilla in an air-conditioned cage and had its toenails painted; had the designer Norman Bell Geddes modernize the circus' decor; and brought in a ballet composed by Stravinsky and choreographed by Balanchine. These changes, combined with North's apparent abrasiveness, irritated the Edith and Aubrey factions. In 1941 they entered into the agreement that is the subject of the following case. The agreement took effect in 1943 when the debt was paid off and the voting trust ended. The agreement provided, in part:

> 1. Neither party will sell any shares of stock or any voting trust certificates in either of said corporations to any other person whomsoever, without first making a written offer to the other party hereto of all of the shares or voting trust certificates proposed to be sold, for the same price and upon the same terms and conditions as in such proposed sale, and allowing such other party a time of not less than 180 days from the date of such written offer within which to accept same.
>
> 2. In exercising any voting rights to which either party may be entitled by virtue of ownership of stock or voting trust certificates held by them in either of said corporation [sic], each party will consult and confer with the other and the parties will act jointly in exercising such voting rights in accor-

dance with such agreement as they may reach with respect to any matter calling for the exercise of such voting rights.

3. In the event the parties fail to agree with respect to any matter covered
by paragraph 2 above, the question in disagreement shall be submitted for
arbitration to Karl D. Loos, of Washington, D.C., as arbitrator and his decision thereon shall be binding upon the parties hereto. Such arbitration shall
be exercised to the end of assuring for the respective corporations good management and such participation therein by the members of the Ringling family as the experience, capacity and ability of each may warrant. The parties
may at any time by written agreement designate any other individual to act
as arbitrator in lieu of said Loos.

4. Each of the parties hereto will enter into and execute such voting
trust agreement or agreements and such other instruments as, from time to
time they may deem advisable and as they may be advised by counsel are
appropriate to effectuate the purposes and objects of this agreement.

5. This agreement shall be in effect from the date hereof and shall continue in effect for a period of ten years unless sooner terminated by mutual
agreement in writing by the parties hereto.

When the voting agreement went into effect, Edith and Aubrey elected five of the
seven directors, including Dunn. Edith's son Robert became president, and Haley first
vice president. During Robert's tenure the circus became more traditional but did not
entirely return to the old days. Among other things, Robert introduced some operatic
production numbers and an elephant version of the changing of the guards at Bucking-
ham Palace.

In 1944 the Big Top caught fire in Hartford, Connecticut, and crashed down on the
audience. There were 168 deaths and 487 injuries and a total liability of four million
dollars. This fire was to have a substantial effect on the alignment of the Ringling factions. Haley, the executive on the scene, went to jail on an involuntary manslaughter
charge. Robert did not serve any time because he happened not to be around at the time
of the fire. He refused to testify at Haley's sentencing that the latter was indispensible
to the circus and did not write to Haley or visit him in prison. All of this considerably
upset Haley. North also did not support Haley at trial but did visit him in jail and managed to turn all of Haley's anger toward Robert. North was able to work out a deal
whereby Haley would be vindicated by having the presidency for a year while North
was to have the real authority and then take over the presidency. The following occurred
at and in connection with the 1946 stockholders' meeting (from Judge Pearson's
Supreme Court opinion):

> The Mr. Loos mentioned in the agreement is an attorney and has repre-
> sented both parties since 1937, and, before and after the voting trust was ter-
> minated in late 1942, advised them with respect to the exercise of their
> voting rights. At the annual meetings in 1943 and the two following years,
> the parties voted their shares in accordance with mutual understandings

arrived at as a result of discussions. In each of these years, they elected five of the seven directors. Mrs. Ringling and Mrs. Haley each had sufficient votes, independently of the other, to elect two of the seven directors. By both voting for an additional candidate, they could be sure of his election regardless of how Mr. North, the remaining stockholder, might vote.[1]

Some weeks before the 1946 meeting, they discussed with Mr. Loos the matter of voting for directors. They were in accord that Mrs. Ringling should cast sufficient votes to elect herself and her son; and that Mrs. Haley should elect herself and her husband; but they did not agree upon a fifth director. The day before the meeting, the discussions were continued, Mrs. Haley being represented by her husband since she could not be present because of illness. In a conversation with Mr. Loos, Mr. Haley indicated that he would make a motion for an adjournment of the meeting for sixty days, in order to give the ladies additional time to come to an agreement about their voting. On the morning of the meeting, however, he stated that because of something Mrs. Ringling had done, he would not consent to a postponement. Mrs. Ringling then made a demand upon Mr. Loos to act under the third paragraph of the agreement "to arbitrate the disagreement" between her and Mrs. Haley in connection with the manner in which the stock of the two ladies should be voted. At the opening of the meeting, Mr. Loos read the written demand and stated that he determined and directed that the stock of both ladies be voted for an adjournment of sixty days. Mrs. Ringling then made a motion for adjournment and voted for it. Mr. Haley, as proxy for his wife, and Mr. North voted against the motion. Mrs. Ringling (herself or through her attorney, it is immaterial which objected to the voting of Mrs. Haley's stock in any manner other than in accordance with Mr. Loos' direction. The chairman ruled that the stock could not be voted contrary to such direction, and declared the motion for adjournment had carried. Nevertheless, the meeting proceeded to the election of directors. Mrs. Ringling stated that she would continue in the meeting "but without prejudice to her position with respect to the voting of the stock and the fact that adjournment had not been taken." Mr. Loos directed Mrs. Ringling to cast her votes.

882 for Mrs. Ringling,
882 for her son, Robert, and
441 for a Mr. Dunn,

---

[1] Each lady was entitled to cast 2205 votes (since each had the cumulative voting rights of 315 shares, and there were 7 vacancies in the directorate). The sum of the votes of both is 4410, which is sufficient to allow 882 votes for each of 5 persons. Mr. North, holding 370 shares, was entitled to cast 2590 votes, which obviously cannot be divided so as to give to more than two candidates as many as 882 votes each. It will be observed that in order for Mrs. Ringling and Mrs. Haley to be sure to elect five directors (regardless of how Mr. North might vote) they must act together in the sense that their combined votes must be divided among five different candidates and at least one of the five must be voted for by both Mrs. Ringling and Mrs. Haley.

who had been a member of the board for several years. She complied. Mr. Loos directed that Mrs. Haley's votes be cast

> 882 for Mrs. Haley,
> 882 for Mr. Haley, and
> 441 for Mr. Dunn.

Instead of complying, Mr. Haley attempted to vote his wife's shares
> 1103 for Mrs. Haley, and
> 1102 for Mr. Haley.

Mr. North votes his shares

> 864 for a Mr. Woods,
> 863 for a Mr. Griffin, and
> 863 for Mr. North.

The chairman ruled that the five candidates proposed by Mr. Loos, together with Messrs. Wood and North, were elected. The Haley-North group disputed this ruling insofar as it declared the election of Mr. Dunn and insisted that Mr. Griffin, instead, had been elected. A directors' meeting followed in which Mrs. Ringling participated after stating that she would do so "without prejudice to her position that the stockholders' meeting had been adjourned and that the directors' meeting was not properly held." Mr. Dunn and Mr. Griffin, although each was challenged by an opposing faction, attempted to join in voting as directors for different slates of officers. Soon after the meeting, Mrs. Ringling instituted this proceeding.

At the directors' meeting referred to by Judge Pearson, Robert was replaced by Haley as president. (In fact, when Robert appeared at the next show after the directors' meeting to direct the circus he found that his seat had been replaced by a tub from the elephant act and was asked to leave.) Edith brought suit. Excerpts from the two Delaware opinions follow.[19]

---

[19]   The above and the two succeeding notes on *Ringling* are based on North & Hatch, THE CIRCUS KINGS, OUR RINGLING FAMILY STORY (1960); BUSINESS WEEK, Apr. 7, 1945 at 24-26; *Id.*, Apr. 14, 1945 at 46; *Id.*, Apr. 20, 1946 at 18-19; *Id.*, June 14, 1947 at 24-28; NEWSWEEK, April 22, 1946 at 75; FORTUNE, July, 1947 at 114-15, 162-67; CURRENT BIOGRAPHY, 1945 at 500-03. For a riveting account of the fire, *see* O'Nan, THE CIRCUS FIRE (2000).

RINGLING v. RINGLING BROTHERS-BARNUM & BAILEY COMBINED SHOWS, INC.

Delaware Court of Chancery

29 Del. Ch. 318, 49 A.2d 603 (1946)

SEITZ, Vice Chancellor.

It is at once apparent that the right of Loos to direct the voting of the stock of the parties to the Agreement is the crucial point for decision. . . .

* * *

. . . [Defendants contend] that the Agreement is unenforceable under Delaware law . . . because it involves an attempted delegation of irrevocable control over voting rights in a manner which is against the public policy of this state.

* * *

The law with respect to agreements of the general type with which we are here concerned is fairly stated as follows in 5 FLETCHER CYC. CORP. (Perm. Ed.) § 2064, at page 194: "Generally, agreements and combinations to vote stock or control corporate action and policy are valid, if they seek without fraud to accomplish only what the parties might do as stockholders and do not attempt it by illegal proxies, trusts, or other means in contravention of statutes or law."

The principle of law stated seems to be sound and I think it is applicable here with respect to the legality of the Agreement under consideration. In the first place, there is no constitutional or statutory objection to the Agreement and defendants do not seriously challenge the legality of its objects. Indeed, in my opinion the objects and purposes of the Agreement as they are recited in the Agreement are lawful in principle and no evidence was introduced which tended to show that they were unlawful in operation.

The only serious question presented under this point arises from the defendants' contention that the arbitration provision has the effect of providing for an irrevocable separation of voting power from stock ownership and that such a provision is contrary to the public policy of this state. Perhaps in no field of the law are the precedents more varied and irreconcilable than those dealing with this phase of the case.

By adhering to strict literalism, it can be said that the present Agreement does not separate voting rights from ownership because the arbitrator only directs the parties as to how they shall vote in case of disagreement. However, recognizing substance rather than form, it is apparent that the arbitrator has voting control of the shares in the instances when he directs the parties as to how they shall vote since, if the Agreement is to be binding, they are also bound by his direction. . . .

* * *

. . . [W]hat vice exists in having an arbitrator agreed upon by the parties decide how their stock shall be voted in the event they are unable to agree? The parties obviously decided to contract with respect to this very situation and to appoint as arbitrator one in whom both had confidence. The cases which strike down agreements on the ground that some public policy prohibits the severance of ownership and voting control argue that there is something very wrong about a person "who has no beneficial interest or title in or to the stock" directing how it shall be voted. Such a person, according to these cases, has "no interest in the general prosperity of the corporation" and moreover, the stockholder himself has a duty to vote. *See Bostwick et al. v. Chapman et al. (Shepaug Voting Trust Cases)*, 60 Conn. 553, 24 A. 32. Such reasons ignore the realities because obviously the person designated to determine how the shares shall be voted has the confidence of such shareholders. Quite naturally they would not want to place such power over their investment in the hands of one whom they felt would not be concerned with the welfare of the corporation. The objection based on the so-called duty of the stockholders to vote, presumably in person, is ludicrous when considered in the light of present day corporate practice. Thus, precedents from other jurisdictions which are based on reasons which have, in my opinion, lost their substance under present day conditions cannot be accorded favorable recognition. No public policy of this state requires a different conclusion.

* * *

Defendants say that even if the Agreement is valid under the statutes and public policy of this state, it is, nevertheless, to be governed by "principles applicable to proxy delegations and, hence, would be revocable." Defendants go on to show how, in their opinion, the alleged proxy was revoked and conclude therefrom that the Agreement was not violated. It is perfectly obvious that the construction of the Agreement contended for by defendants, if accepted, would in effect render it meaningless. The answer to this contention of the defendants must be that we are not here concerned with a proxy situation as between the parties to the Agreement on one hand, and the arbitrator Loos on the other. The Agreement does not contemplate such a proxy either in form or in substance.

* * *

I conclude that the stock held under the Agreement should have been voted pursuant to the direction of the arbitrator Loos to the parties or their representatives. When a party or her representative refuses to comply with the direction of the arbitrator, while he is properly acting under its provisions (as did Aubrey B. Haley's proxy here), then I believe the Agreement constitutes the willing party to the Agreement an implied agent possessing the irrevocable proxy of the recalcitrant party for the purpose of casting the particular vote. Here an implied agency based on an irrevocable proxy is fully justified to implement the Agreement without doing violence to its terms. Moreover, the provisions of the Agreement make it clear that the proxy may be treated as one coupled with an interest so as to render it irrevocable under the circumstances. *In re Chilson, supra.* . . .

It is the opinion of the court that the nature of the Agreement does not preclude the granting of specific performance. . . . Indeed, the granting of such relief here is well within the spirit of certain principles laid down by our courts in cases granting specific performance of contracts to sell stock which would give the vendee voting control. . . . Obviously, to deny specific performance here would be tantamount to declaring the Agreement invalid. Since petitioner's rights in this respect were properly preserved at the stockholders' meeting, the meeting was a nullity to the extent that it failed to give effect to the provisions of the Agreement here involved. However, I believe it preferable to hold a new election rather than attempt to reconstruct the contested meeting. In this way the parties will be acting with explicit knowledge of their rights.

. . . It must and should be assumed that the so-called arbitrator, if called upon to act, will bring to bear that sense of duty and impartiality which doubtless motivated the parties in selecting him for such an important role. In any event, the master in conducting the election will be bound to recognize and to give effect to the Agreement here involved, if its terms are properly invoked.

NOTES AND QUESTIONS

(1) **Decision of the Delaware Supreme Court.** On appeal, Justice Pearson upheld the lower court's determination that the Ringling voting agreement could not be invalidated on grounds of public policy, fraud or illegality.[20] He wrote that groups of shareholders "may lawfully contract with each other to vote in the future in such a way as they, or a majority of them, from time to time determine" and that "[r]easonable provisions for cases of failure of the group to reach a determination because of an even division in their ranks seem unobjectionable," particularly where "[i]t does not appear that the agreement enables the parties to take any unlawful advantage of the outside shareholder, or of any other person."[21] He concluded that Mrs. Haley's refusal to vote her shares in accordance with the arbitrator's direction was a breach of contract. But Justice Pearson refused to read the agreement, as Vice Chancellor Seitz had, to give the complying party (Mrs. Ringling) an implied proxy to vote the non-complying party's (Mrs. Haley's) shares:

> The agreement expresses no other function of the arbitrator than that of deciding questions in disagreement which prevent the effectuation of the purpose "to act jointly." The power to enforce a decision does not seem a necessary or usual incident of such a function. Mr. Loos is not a party to the agreement. It does not contemplate the transfer of any shares or interest in shares to him, or that he should undertake any duties which the parties might compel him to perform. They provided that they might designate any other individual to act instead of Mr. Loos. The agreement does not attempt to make the arbitrator a trustee of an express trust. What the arbitrator is to do is for the benefit of the parties, not for his own benefit. Whether the parties accept or reject his decision is no concern of his, so far as the agreement or the surrounding circumstances reveal. We think the parties sought to bind each other, but to be bound only to each other, and not to empower the arbitrator to enforce decisions he might make.

---

[20] *Ringling Bros.-Barnum & Bailey Combined Shows, Inc. v. Ringling*, 53 A.2d 441 (Del. 1947).

[21] *Id.* at 447.

From this conclusion, it follows necessarily that no decision of the arbitrator could ever be enforced if both parties to the agreement were unwilling that it be enforced, for the obvious reason that there would be no one to enforce it. Under the agreement, something more is required after the arbitrator has given his decision in order that it should become compulsory: at least one of the parties must determine that such decision shall be carried into effect. Thus, any "control" of the voting of the shares, which is reposed in the arbitrator, is substantially limited in action under the agreement in that it is subject to the overriding power of the parties themselves. The agreement does not describe the undertaking of each party with respect to a decision of the arbitrator other than to provide that it "shall be binding upon the parties." It seems to us that this language, considered with relation to its context and the situations to which it is applicable, means that each party promised the other to exercise her own voting rights in accordance with the arbitrator's decision. The agreement is silent about any exercise of the voting rights of one party by the other. The language with reference to situations where the parties arrive at an understanding as to voting plainly suggests "action" by each, and "exercising" voting rights by each, rather than by one for the other. There is no intimation that this method should be different where the arbitrator's decision is to be carried into effect. Assuming that a power in each party to exercise the voting rights of the other might be a relatively more effective or convenient means of enforcing a decision of the arbitrator than would be available without the power, this would not justify implying a delegation of the power in the absence of some indication that the parties bargained for that means. The method of voting actually employed by the parties tends to show that they did not construe the agreement as creating powers to vote each other's shares; for at meetings prior to 1946 each party apparently exercised her own voting rights, and at the 1946 meeting, Mrs. Ringling, who wished to enforce the agreement, did not attempt to cast a ballot in exercise of any voting rights of Mrs. Haley. We do not find enough in the agreement or in the circumstances to justify a construction that either party was empowered to exercise voting rights of the other.

Rather than literally enforcing Loos' vote, Justice Pearson proposed a different remedy:

It seems to us that upon the application of Mrs. Ringling, the injured party, the votes representing Mrs. Haley's shares should not be counted. Since no infirmity in Mr. North's voting has been demonstrated, his right to recognition of what he did at the meeting should be considered in granting any relief to Mrs. Ringling; for her rights arose under a contract to which Mr. North was not a party. With this in mind, we have concluded that the election should not be declared invalid, but that effect should be given to a rejection of the votes representing Mrs. Haley's shares. No other relief seems appropriate in this proceeding. Mr. North's vote against the motion for adjournment was sufficient to defeat it. With respect to the election of directors, the return of the inspectors should be corrected to show a rejection of Mrs. Haley's votes, and to declare the election of the six persons for whom Mr. North and Mrs. Ringling voted.

This leaves one vacancy in the directorate. The question of what to do about such a vacancy was not considered by the court below and has not been argued here. For this reason, and because an election of directors at the 1947 annual meeting (which presumably will be held in the near future) may make a determination of the question unimportant, we shall not decide it on this appeal. If a decision of the point appears important to the parties, any of them may apply to raise it in the Court of Chancery, after the mandate of this court is received there.

An order should be entered directing a modification of the order of the Court of Chancery in accordance with this opinion.[22]

Do you agree with Justice Pearson's interpretation of the voting agreement? What else do you suppose might explain Justice Pearson's reluctance to enforce Loos' vote?

(2) **Subsequent events.** Following the Chancery Court opinion, Robert was back as president. This, however, only lasted for three weeks. North was able to obtain an injunction temporarily restoring Haley and North to power. Then Robert had a stroke. Even before the Supreme Court opinion, the tenuous Haley-North alliance fell apart when Haley announced that he wanted to retain his office beyond the agreed term. Also, North won a preliminary victory in a $5,000,000 suit against Robert. North worked out a compromise with the Edith-Robert faction whereby pending litigation between North and Robert was dropped, North became president, and Robert became executive vice president and chairman of the board. Thereafter, the Haleys sold out to the other two factions, and North obtained 51% control. Robert died of a second stroke in 1950. In 1967, the circus was sold to the Feld family and Judge Roy Hofheinz (who built the Houston Astrodome). The circus was sold to Mattel, Inc., in 1974, and then resold to the Felds in 1982.[23] Haley ended up with a successful career in politics, serving in the U.S. Congress from 1953-1977. He died in 1981.

(3) **Statutory provisions.** Voting agreements are now expressly permitted by many statutes. *See, e.g.,* Del. G.C.L. § 218(c) & (d); Model Business Corporation Act § 7.31. Are any voting agreements prohibited under Del. G.C.L. § 218 as currently drafted?

---

[22]　*Id.* at 448.

[23]　*See* WALL ST. J., March 19, 1982, at 15.

[3] Voting Trusts

Shareholders who want the advantages of agreements like those discussed in the previous subsection might also consider the voting trust. A voting trust, like a voting agreement, combines the voting power of two or more shareholders to achieve a voting block. The main conceptual difference between a voting trust and an ordinary voting agreement is that the voting trust, like trusts generally, involves the transfer of legal title.

It is not clear why the courts have been more willing to approve voting trusts than other voting agreements, since the severing of legal title fails to solve many of the supposed policy problems discussed above. One writer referred to this as an example of "protective coloring" in the law.[24] It is somewhat like the incident in the movie "Five Easy Pieces" in which a waitress refused to serve toast to Jack Nicholson, but would serve chicken salad sandwich on toast without the chicken salad.

Perhaps voting trusts are distinguished from voting agreements because the former are subject to some restrictions and formal requirements under the corporation statutes that do not apply to voting agreements, including the filing of the voting trust at the corporation's registered office, where it can be inspected by the corporation's stockholders and by any beneficiaries of the trust. *See* Del. G.C.L. § 218.

Apart from statutory formalities, the fact that title to the stock is transferred to a trustee results in some substantive differences between voting trusts and voting agreements. In the first place, the voting trustee, unlike those holding powers under other voting arrangements, bears special fiduciary duties to the beneficiaries.[25]

Second, while parties to a stockholders' agreement may retain their stock and all the rights and privileges of shareholders in the corporation, beneficiaries of voting trusts have few of the governance rights of shareholders. This latter feature of voting trusts makes them particularly attractive where it is desired that the beneficial owners of the corporation not make any important decisions or select directors. Such situations include temporary control of a corporation by creditors; ensuring professional management of a family-owned corporation after the founder's death, where the heirs are not involved in the business; where, as under an antitrust decree, the owner of the stock must temporarily divest control; and transfer of stock in connection with the dissolution of a marriage.[26]

The voting trust involves potential advantages and disadvantages as compared with *Ringling*-type voting agreements. The main advantages are that validity is more certain because voting trusts are more often specifically provided for by statute than are voting agreements; trustees clearly owe a fiduciary duty to beneficiaries; and the ben-

---

[24] *See* Ballantine, *Voting Trusts, Their Abuses and Regulation*, 21 TEX. L. REV. 139, 147-48 (1942).

[25] *See Brown v. McLanahan*, 149 F.2d 703 (4th Cir. 1945). For a recent case discussing the fiduciary duties of voting trustees, *see Warehime v. Warehime*, 761 A.2d 1138 (Pa. 2000) (fiduciary obligations of voting trustee controlled by terms and conditions of voting trust agreement).

[26] *See Castonguay v. Castonguay*, 306 N.W.2d 143 (Minn. 1982).

eficiary of the trust is insulated from a say in the corporation. The disadvantages include the latter feature, where such insulation is not desired, as well as the formalities and requirements (including public disclosure) involved in voting trusts.

Although voting trusts are more legally secure than other voting agreements, a court may invalidate even a technically complying voting trust if it is established for an "improper purpose," meaning that it involves some kind of unfairness or breach of fiduciary duty to the nonparticipating shareholders.[27] In addition, while the statutory requirements for voting trusts may provide greater security for arrangements that comply with the requirements, the following cases show that these provisions may threaten the validity of voting agreements and other arrangements which are similar to voting trusts but do not comply. Precisely what differences between the arrangements involved in these cases justify the difference in outcome?

ABERCROMBIE v. DAVIES
Delaware Supreme Court
36 Del. Ch. 371, 130 A.2d 338 (1957)

SOUTHERLAND, Chief Justice.

The pertinent facts are as follows:

American Independent Oil Company ("American") is a Delaware corporation. It was formed to develop an oil concession in the Kuwait-Saudi Arabian neutral zone. The organizers were James S. Abercrombie, Sunray Oil Corporation ("Sunray"), Phillips Petroleum Company ("Phillips"), Ralph K. Davies, Signal Oil and Gas Company ("Signal"), The Hancock Oil Company ("Hancock"), The Globe Oil and Refining Company ("Globe"), Lario Oil and Gas Company ("Lario"), Ashland Oil & Refining Company ("Ashland"), Deep Rock Oil Corporation ("Deep Rock"), and Allied Oil Company (later acquired by Ashland). The organizers subscribed in varying proportions to American's original issue of stock. Additional stock was later issued, and there are now outstanding 150,000 shares.

The organization agreement provided that the Board of Directors of American should consist of one director for each 5,000 shares held, and that the directors should be elected by cumulative voting. In effect, each stockholder has been permitted to name the director or directors to represent on the board his or its interests. Davies represents his own interest and is president of the corporation. At all times the number of directors has been fifteen. No one stockholder holds a majority of stock, and no one stockholder is represented by more than four directors. Obviously, smooth functioning of such a board was dependent either upon substantial harmony among the interests represented on it or upon an effective coalition of the interests of a majority.

On March 30, 1950, six of the stockholders took steps to form such a coalition. On that date an agreement was executed between eight individuals designated "Agents," and the six stockholders—Davies, Ashland, Globe, Lario, Hancock and Signal. These stockholders

---

[27] *See Grogan v. Grogan*, 315 S.W.2d 34 (Tex. Civ. App. 1958).

hold about 54½% of the shares. They are represented on the board by eight of the fifteen directors. The Agents named in the agreement were at the time the eight directors representing these six stockholders.

The obvious purpose of the agreement was to achieve effective control of the board and thus control of corporate policy. The motive for the agreement, according to the defendants, was to prevent acquisition of control by Phillips, which was the largest single stockholder, holding about one-third of the stock. In the view we take of the case, only the purpose is material.

The Agents' Agreement is an unusual one. In effect, it transfers voting control of the stock of the six stockholders to the eight Agents for a period of ten years (subject to termination by seven of the Agents). The Agents are to be, as far as possible, identical with the directors. The agreement of seven of the eight is required to vote the stock and elaborate provisions are added for the choice of an arbitrator to resolve disagreements. Somewhat similar provisions attempt to control the action of the directors. . . . At the moment we note that the majority of the board secured by this agreement (eight of the fifteen) comprised Davies, the two Signal directors, the two Hancock directors, the director representing Globe and Lario, and the two Ashland directors.

The effective control thus sought to be achieved apparently lasted until December 9, 1954. On that date a meeting of the Board of Directors was held in Chicago. A resolution was adopted calling a special meeting of the board for December 16, to consider and take action upon certain amendments to the by-laws and other matters. This resolution was adopted by a vote of nine to six. This majority consisted of Abercrombie, the four Phillips directors, the Sunray director, the Deep Rock director, and the two Ashland directors. The minority consisted of Davies and the Globe, Lario, Hancock and Signal directors. The nature of the action to be considered at the proposed meeting was such as to indicate to the minority that the control of the board set up by the Agents' Agreement was seriously threatened. The Ashland directors, it was charged, had violated the Agents' Agreement. Counter moves were made by Davies. Litigation was instituted in California by Davies, Signal, Hancock, Globe and Lario against Ashland and its two directors. American, named as a defendant, was preliminarily enjoined from recognizing any action taken at a board meeting of December 16, and Ashland was enjoined from violating the Agents' Agreement.

In the meantime, the suit below was filed by Abercrombie, Phillips and Sunray against the other shareholders and the Agents. Davies, Signal, Hancock, Lario, Globe and six of the Agents appeared and answered. Plaintiffs filed a motion for summary judgment. Several contentions arose out of the hearings on this motion. The Chancellor made the following rulings of law:

> (1) Certain provisions of the Agents' Agreement attempting to control directorate action are invalid on their face;
> (2) The agreement is not a voting trust;
> (3) The provisions respecting stockholder action are severable from the illegal provisions, and constitute a valid stockholders' pooling agreement.

See 123 A.2d 893, 900 and 903.

Both sides appeal. All of the issues argued below have been presented here.

* * *

[The Agent's] agreement, plaintiffs assert, is invalid on its face. Among other contentions they say that in substance, though not in form, it is a voting trust, and that it is void because it does not comply with the provisions of our voting trust statute. Defendants reply that it is not, and was not intended to be, a voting trust, and is a mere pooling agreement of the kind recognized as legal in Delaware by the decision in *Ringling Bros.-Barnum & Bailey Combined Shows v. Ringling*, 29 Del. Ch. 610, 53 A.2d 441.

* * *

In *Perry v. Missouri-Kansas Pipe Line Co.*, 22 Del. Ch. 33, 191 A. 823, it was determined that in Delaware, as in New York, voting trusts derive their validity solely from the statute. "The test of validity is the rule of the statute. When the field was entered by the Legislature it was fully occupied and no place was left for other voting trusts." Quoted by the Chancellor with approval from *Matter of Morse*, 247 N.Y. 290, 160 N.E. 374, 376. The statute lays down for voting trusts "the law of their life"; compliance with its provisions is mandatory. Voting trusts not so complying are illegal.

* * *

The correctness of the holding in the *Missouri-Kansas* case has never been questioned in Delaware, so far as we know. It has a direct bearing upon the instant case. If any stockholders' agreement provided for joint or concerted voting is so drawn as in effect to occupy the field reserved for the statutory voting trust, it is illegal, whatever mechanics may be devised to attain the result. The provisions of the instrument determine its legal effect, and if they clearly create a voting trust, any intention of the parties to the contrary is immaterial.

. . . A review of the Delaware decisions upon the subject of voting trusts shows that our courts have indicated that one essential feature that characterizes a voting trust is the separation of the voting rights of the stock from the other attributes of ownership.

* * *

When we apply these tests to the Agents' Agreement we find: (1) that the voting rights of the pooled stock have been divorced from the beneficial ownership, which is retained by the stockholders; (2) that the voting rights have been transferred to fiduciaries denominated Agents; (3) that the transfer of such rights is, through the medium of irrevocable proxies, effective for a period of ten years; (4) that all voting rights in respect of all the stock are pooled in the Agents as a group, through the device of proxies running to the agents jointly and severally, and no stockholder retains the right to vote his or its shares; and (5) that on its face the agreement has for its principal object voting control of American.

These elements, under our decisions, are the elements of a voting trust.

We find one other significant circumstance.

Paragraph 7 of the Agents' Agreement gives any seven of the eight agents the power to withdraw the stock from escrow and to transform the Agreement into a formal voting trust. Any one of the agents is authorized to sign the voting trust agreement for any shareholder who fails to do so upon the request of any seven of the agents. A form of a voting trust agreement is attached as an exhibit to the Agents' Agreement. A comparison of this form with the provisions of the Agents' Agreement shows that upon the execution of the Voting Trust Agreement the scheme of control functions just as it functions under the Agents' Agreement. Without pausing for a detailed analysis, we note that Paragraphs 2, 4, 5 and 6 of the Agents' Agreement are paralleled (in some cases almost verbatim) by Paragraphs 2, 5, 8 and 10, respectively, of the Voting Trust Agreement. Paragraph 3 of the Agents' Agreement is paralleled in part by Paragraph 3 of the Voting Trust Agreement. The provisions of Paragraph 3 of the Agents' Agreement controlling directorate action remain in effect as part of the Voting Trust Agreement.

Thus the only significant changes made in transforming the Agents' Agreement into a Voting Trust Agreement are the provisions formalizing the trust, viz.: (1) the Agents become Trustees—a change of name and nothing more; (2) the stock with irrevocable stock powers running to the Agents becomes stock registered in their names as Trustees; and (3) voting trust certificates instead of receipts are issued to the stockholders.

To sum up: the substance of the voting trust already existed; the transformation added only the special mechanics that the statute requires.

Now, the provisions of the statute that were not complied with are the requirement that the shares be transferred on the books and the requirement that a copy of the agreement shall be filed in the corporation's principal office in Delaware. The effect was to create a secret voting trust. The provision respecting the filing of a copy in the principal office in Delaware "open to the inspection of any stockholder . . . or any beneficiary of the trust" is a provision obviously for the benefit of all stockholders and of all beneficiaries of the trust, who are entitled to know where voting control of a corporation resides. And the provision for transfer of the stock on the corporate books necessarily serves, though perhaps only incidentally, a similar purpose with respect to the officers and directors. If the validity of a stockholders' pooling agreement of the kind here presented were to be sustained, the way is clear for the creation of secret voting trusts. The statute clearly forbids them.

The Chancellor took the contrary view. He held the Agents' Agreement not to be a voting trust because (1) title to the stock did not pass to the Agents, and (2) because the Agents are in fact the agents and are subject to the directions of their principals.

The failure to transfer the stock on the books is not a sufficient reason in this case for holding the Agents' Agreement not a voting trust. It is an indication that the parties did not intend to create a voting trust; but that subjective intention is unimportant. The stock here was endorsed in blank and delivered to the agents for deposit in escrow with irrevocable proxies. Transfer of the stock on the books is not essential to effect an irrevocable transfer of voting rights to fiduciaries, divorced from the other attributes of the stock, in order to secure voting control, as the Agents' Agreement demonstrates. It is such a transfer that is the characteristic feature of a voting trust.

The fact that the Agents are subject to control by their respective principals does not prevent the agreement from constituting a voting trust. The stock is voted by the Agents as a group. No one stockholder retains complete control over the voting of its stock. It cannot vote its own stock directly; all it can do is to direct its Agent how to vote on a decision to be made by the Agents as a group. The stock of any corporate stockholder may at any time be voted against its will by the vote of the seven other agents. The control of the agents rests upon the provisions that they are severally chosen by the respective stockholders and each may be removed and replaced by the stockholder he represents. In effect, these provisions come to this: that each corporate stockholder participating in the agreement reserves the right to name and remove the fiduciary or fiduciaries representing him. Such a provision is not inconsistent with a voting trust. In fact, the scheme is carried forward to the voting trust set out as "Exhibit A" to the Agents' Agreement. See Paragraphs 3 and 5, paralleling Paragraphs 3 and 4 of the Agents' Agreement. And the alleged continuing control of the Agent by the stockholder clearly would not exist in the event of the death, removal or resignation of Davies in his capacity of Agent. In that case his successor, whether Agent or Trustee, is named by a majority of the remaining Agents or Trustees, as the case may be, and his estate has no control whatever over the Agent so named.

Defendants stress the contention that the parties to the Agents' Agreement did not intend to create a voting trust. As above noted, the intent that governs is the intent derived from the instrument itself. A desire to avoid the legal consequences of the language used is immaterial. Additional arguments (1) that the fiduciaries vested with voting rights are called agents instead of trustees, and (2) that title to the stock did not pass to the agents, have already been noticed.

In support of their argument that the Agents' Agreement creates only a stockholders' pooling agreement and not a voting trust, defendants lean heavily on the decision of this Court in *Ringling Bros.-Barnum & Bailey Combined Shows v. Ringling*, 29 Del. Ch. 610, 53 A.2d 441. That case involved a true pooling agreement, far short of a voting trust. Two stockholders agreed to act jointly in exercising their voting rights. There was no deposit of the stock with irrevocable stock powers conferring upon a group of fiduciaries exclusive voting powers over the pooled stock. Indeed, the Supreme Court (modifying the decision below) held that the agreement did not provide, either expressly or impliedly, for a proxy to either stockholder to vote the other's shares. The *Ringling* case is clearly distinguishable on the facts.

* * *

[A]s a pooling agreement in substance and purpose approaches more and more nearly the substance and purpose of the statute, there comes a point at which, if the statute is not complied with, the agreement is illegal. A pooling agreement may not escape the statutory controls by calling the trustees agents and giving to the stockholders receipts instead of voting trust certificates. If this were not so, stockholders could, through the device of an agreement such as the one before us, accept for themselves the chief benefits of the statute: unified voting control through fiduciaries for an appreciable period of time; and escape its burdens: the requirements for making an open record of the matter, and the limitations in respect of time. If the agreement before us is upheld, what is there to prevent a similar agreement for 15 years—or 25 years?

* * *

For the foregoing reasons, we are compelled to disagree with the holding of the Chancellor upon the question discussed. We are of opinion that the Agents' Agreement is void as an illegal voting trust.

Our conclusion upon this question makes it unnecessary to discuss any of the other questions raised on the appeal.

The cause is remanded to the Court of Chancery of New Castle County, with instructions to vacate paragraphs (2) to (5) inclusive of the order of October 24, 1956, and to enter a further order consistent with this opinion, with such provisions for injunctive relief, if any, as the Chancellor may determine to be appropriate.

NOTES AND QUESTIONS

(1) **Relevance of intent.** Why isn't it enough to validate the agreement in *Abercrombie* that the parties did not intend a voting trust? In other words, what is wrong with a rule that the parties must comply with the voting trust statute only when they enter into an arrangement that they want to be characterized as a voting trust? Who would be hurt by such a rule, and how?

(2) *Lehrman v. Cohen.*[28] In *Lehrman v. Cohen*, the corporation was controlled by Lehrman and the Cohen family. The corporate charter provided for two controlling classes of stock, AL common (held by Lehrman) and AC common (held by the Cohen family), each with the power to elect two directors. The corporate charter also provided for Class AD common stock which was held by the long-time corporate counsel, Danzansky. Although Class AD stock had no equity in the corporation, it could elect one director and the stock was voted over a long period of time for Danzansky. Class AD stock therefore served as a mechanism for breaking deadlocks between Lehrman and the Cohen family. After more than fourteen years of operation under this arrangement, the holders of the AD and AC stock and their directors joined forces over the opposition of Lehrman, the holder of the AL stock, and his directors to replace Cohen with Danzansky as president. Lehrman sued, claiming primarily that the Class AD voting arrangement was in effect a voting trust under *Abercrombie*, because it separated voting and other ownership rights by granting 20% of the voting power of the company to Danzansky. But the court distinguished *Abercrombie*, holding that the arrangement was not a voting trust because it did not separate voting rights from ownership. The court also noted that the arrangement did not violate the "main purpose" of the voting trust statute "to avoid secret, uncontrolled combinations of stockholders," an argument the court repeated in its later decision in *Oceanic Exploration Co. v. Grynberg*, below.

(3) **Statutory provisions.** How effectively is the *Abercrombie* problem dealt with by Del. G.C.L. § 218(d)? By MBCA § 7.31?

---

[28]   43 Del. Ch. 222, 222 A.2d 800 (Del. 1966).

OCEANIC EXPLORATION CO. v. GRYNBERG
Delaware Supreme Court
428 A.2d 1 (1981)

[Majority shareholders entered into an agreement whereby, among other things, voting rights were transferred to voting trustees and the corporation was given an option to purchase the stock which was the subject of the agreement. Pursuant to this agreement, the majority shareholders effectively relinquished control of the corporation in exchange for benefits including indemnity for large liabilities. One purpose of the agreement was to head off a creditor's suit which threatened to put the company into bankruptcy if the majority shareholders remained in control. The majority shareholders sued to invalidate the agreement and thereby regain control of the corporation. On plaintiff's motion for summary judgment, the Chancery Court held that the agreement constituted an illegal voting trust because the agreement had been extended more than two years prior to its expiration, in violation of the then-applicable version of Del. G.C.L. § 218(b), which limited the initial term of a voting trust to ten years and permitted extensions only during the final two years.[29] The court also held that the pledge of the subject shares prevented their deposit in compliance with Del. G.C.L. § 218(a). On appeal, the Delaware Supreme Court reversed.]

QUILLEN, Justice:

. . . In determining the applicability of § 218(a) and (b), the test is whether the substance and purpose of the stock arrangement is "sufficiently close to the substance and the purpose of [the statute] to warrant its being subject to the restrictions and conditions imposed by that statute." *Lehrman v. Cohen*, Del. Supr., 222 A.2d 800, 806 (1966). As did the Vice Chancellor, we take a frontal tack and direct our attention to the same threshold question. Is the voting trust arrangement here governed by § 218(a) and (b)?

Without attempting to resolve factual disputes, we note the defendant alleges, with some record support, evidence of the following factors:

(1) The final overall contract is one of internal corporate reorganization with integrated portions of which the voting trust is merely one.

(2) The final contract here, including the voting trust feature, is an agreement between the majority shareholder group and the corporation.

(3) While the voting trust portion of the contract is important, it is basically an enforcement provision to a purchase option agreement involving the sale of the majority interest and incidents connected with such sale such as change in management and an agreement not to compete.

(4) The contract is open and notorious within the corporation. Not only was the contract with the corporation itself and not only did it occasion fundamental changes in corporate management but it was prominently featured and positively represented in the proxy statement dated October 14, 1976 and in the 1975 annual report. The operations of the company and the involvement of minority shareholders, officers and employees proceeded in reliance on the contract.

---

[29]   The ten-year limit on voting trusts was eliminated from the Delaware statute in 1993.

(5) The contract serves a valid corporate purpose, being designed to end financial hardship, and perhaps to end financial ruin.

(6) The contract has been significantly performed by the corporation, its officers and employees.

(7) A substantial benefit has been conferred on the depositing majority shareholder group.

(8) The contemplated benefit to the corporation and the minority shareholders remains largely executory.

(9) The party seeking a declaration that the agreement is void is the depositing majority shareholder group itself.

In such a factual setting, if established or substantially established at trial, we do not find that the Vice Chancellor should be legally prohibited from specifically enforcing the "voting trust agreement" in issue here as a consequence of the statutory provisions contained in § 218(a) and (b). Our reasons are simple: statutory language, statutory purpose and public policy.

First, even viewed historically, § 218, from its original enactment in 1925, was designed to regulate agreements by "[o]ne or more stockholders." . . .

* * *

. . . While we do not suggest that the mere fact that the corporation is a party removes a trust from the statute, we do find that the final contract in issue here, with its multifaceted aspects including a stock purchase option agreement running from an already unified majority shareholder group to the corporation may be so foreign to the stockholder voting trust agreement to which the language used by the General Assembly was directed that it is beyond the contemplated scope of the statute. Given the scope of this agreement it may be that the voting rights are not separated from the other retained attributes of ownership. In short, the agreement here may not be a voting trust as that term is used in our law.

Second, our case law makes it clear that the main purpose of a voting trust statute is "to avoid secret, uncontrolled combinations of stockholders formed to acquire control of the corporation to the possible detriment of non-participating shareholders." *Lehrman*, 222 A.2d at 807. The contract involved in this case, given the factual contentions of the defendants, may be so far divorced from that purpose that it makes the contemplated regulation unnecessary and irrelevant.

Third, it is important to recognize there has been a significant change from the days of our original 1925 statute. Voting trusts were viewed with "disfavor" or "looked upon . . . with indulgence" by the courts. . . . Other contractual arrangements interfering with stock ownership, such as irrevocable proxies, were viewed with suspicion. The desire for flexibility in modern society has altered such restrictive thinking. . . . The trend of liberalization was markedly apparent in the 1967 changes to our own § 218. Voting or other agreements and irrevocable proxies were given favorable treatment and restrictive judicial interpretations as to the absolute voiding of voting trusts for terms beyond the statutory limit were changed by statute. The trend was not to extend the voting trust restrictions beyond the class of trust being regulated and beyond the reasons for statutory regulation. That public policy cannot be ignored here.

Thus we are faced with a "voting trust agreement" which: (1) may not fit into the situation contemplated by the language of the restrictive statute, (2) may have little, if any, connection with the purpose for which the statute was enacted, and (3) may have no evil or improper aspects under any current ascertainable public policy. Given such circumstances, we are hard pressed to see why § 218(a) and (b) should be a legal bar to a factual inquiry and a discretionary consideration by the Court of Chancery of full enforcement of the contract in this case. We conclude the Vice Chancellor erred in holding the voting trust aspect of the contract in this case to be, as a matter of law, a § 218(a) and (b) voting trust.

NOTES AND QUESTIONS

(1) **What difference does it make if it's a voting trust?** In Lewis Carroll's ALICE'S ADVENTURES IN WONDERLAND, Alice met a pigeon who accused her of being a serpent bent on eating the eggs the pigeon was hatching.

> "But I'm not a serpent, I tell you!" said Alice; "I'm a . . . little girl."
> "A likely story indeed!" said the Pigeon in a tone of the deepest contempt.
> ". . . I suppose you'll be telling me next that you never tasted an egg."
> "I have tasted eggs, certainly," said Alice, who was a very truthful child; "but little girls eat eggs quite as much as serpents do, you know."
> "I don't believe it," said the Pigeon; "but if they do, why, then they're a kind of serpent, that's all I can say."
> This was such a new idea to Alice that she was quite silent for a minute or two, which gave the Pigeon the opportunity of adding, "You're looking for eggs, I know that well enough; and what does it matter to me whether you're a little girl or a serpent?"

Is the real issue in the above cases whether the instrument is a "voting trust" (*i.e.*, is a serpent) or poses some other underlying problem (*i.e.*, is an egg-eater). If the latter, what problems were the courts concerned about?

(2) **The role of disclosure.** Is the real problem a lack of disclosure? If so, why not require all "voting agreements," not just voting trusts, to be publicly filed? Would disclosure have helped the excluded parties in *Ringling* and *Abercrombie* (North and Phillips, respectively)? Should voting agreements and trusts among fewer than all the shareholders be prohibited, or do shareholders take the risk that their co-owners will enter into such arrangements?

(3) **Survival of *Abercrombie*.** Does the argument accepted in *Abercrombie* for invalidating shareholder voting agreements survive the Delaware Supreme Court's decision in *Oceanic*?

(4) **Other devices for reallocating voting power: Classified stock.** As *Lerman v. Cohen, supra,* illustrates (*see* Note 2 following *Abercrombie*), voting power also can be reallocated through an arrangement known as "classified stock," in which different

classes of stock are issued to the shareholders, with each class carrying different voting rights that are spelled out in the articles of incorporation. For example, assume a corporation has four 25% shareholders and majority voting. Without classification, corporate action can be taken by any three shareholders. If the stock is divided into two classes of two holders each, with a requirement that all actions be approved by a majority vote of each class, corporate action would require the votes of all four holders. The effect is to confer blocking power out of proportion to financial investment, just as if the four holders had formed voting agreements or trusts. Because classified stock is created by a charter provision rather than by private agreement, the courts have been more willing to recognize the validity of classified stock than other shareholder voting arrangements.

(5) **Other devices for reallocating voting power: High vote and high quorum provisions.** The usual quorum and required vote at both shareholders' and directors' meetings is a majority (*see* Del. G.C.L. §§ 141(b) and 216). Shareholders can, by requiring higher than majority votes and quorums, increase the power of minority shareholders—precisely the effect that is accomplished through the other shareholder voting arrangements discussed in this section. For example, four shareholders, each holding 25% of the stock can provide in the certificate that business cannot be conducted at the shareholder level without all members of the body present or that corporate actions must be approved by an 80% vote. High vote and quorum requirements have been invalidated where they were not expressly authorized by statute and where they created a high probability of deadlock by permitting a veto as to all matters.[30] But many states now have statutes specifically authorizing such requirements (*see, e.g.,* Del. G.C.L. §§ 102(b)(4), 141(b) and 216), usually by a provision included in the corporation's charter. Such statutes raise a question analogous to that raised by *Abercrombie* concerning the voting trust statute: does a statute that validates a shareholder arrangement provided for in the certificate of incorporation invalidate similar arrangements that are not provided for in the articles?[31]

PROBLEM

Assume you are an attorney who is confronted by the same fact situation that confronted the attorney who drafted the agreement in *Abercrombie*. What agreement would you draft today? In answering this question, consider both the parties' objectives and what you must do to ensure validity and enforceability of the agreement under the current state of Delaware law.

---

[30]   *See Benintendi v. Kenton Hotel,* 294 N.Y. 112, 60 N.E.2d 829 (1945); *Kaplan v. Block,* 183 Va. 327, 31 S.E.2d 893 (1944).

[31]   For a case answering this question in the negative where the parties had expressly agreed to make any charter amendments necessary to validate the shareholder veto, see *Beresovski v. Warszawski,* 28 N.Y.2d 419, 322 N.Y.S.2d 673, 271 N.E.2d 520 (1971).

§ 5.03 Agreements Controlling Action by the Board of Directors

Section 5.02 discussed arrangements by which shareholders controlled decisions made by the shareholders. Under the corporate standard form, these decisions relate to such things as election of directors and approval of certain important corporate acts (*see* Section 5.01[B][2], above). But in a closely held firm, the shareholders may want to take a greater role in management. Where there are relatively few owners and decision-making is relatively simple, total decision-making and agency costs can be minimized by placing management power directly in the owners (*i.e.*, the shareholders). Also, shareholders may have interests apart from their financial investments that they want to protect.

The parties theoretically could achieve the above objectives within the corporate form by, among other things, (1) agreeing as shareholders to have themselves elected directors and either (a) agreeing as directors to make particular decisions on certain matters or (b) providing for high vote or high quorum requirements at the director level which would give each of them a veto power over these matters; or (2) partially or completely dispensing with the directors and providing that some or all management decisions will be made by the shareholders directly, perhaps coupled with one or more of the shareholder voting arrangements discussed above in Section 5.02. Each of these alternatives, and particularly the second, approximates the type of agreement that would be made in the partnership situation where there is no board of directors.

As discussed in this section, however, the law has restricted these types of arrangements.

[A] Common Law

Early corporation statutes generally explicitly required management by a board of directors, and judicial decisions, including *McQuade* and *Manson* discussed in *Clark*, below, literally interpreted these statutes by refusing to enforce arrangements that weakened or eliminated the board. Why this limitation on private contracting? Evaluate the following arguments:

(1) *The "concession" theory of the corporation, which holds that the corporation is a creature of, and controlled by, state law.* Since the board of directors is the single most distinctive feature of the corporate form—that which, more than anything else, distinguishes corporations from partnerships—pushing aside the board is a more significant deviation from the norm than arrangements concerning voting at the shareholder level. However, this attitude does not explain why contracting should be restricted.

(2) *To ensure that the board can protect minority shareholders from opportunistic conduct by the majority.* Yet the board is presumably elected and controlled by the majority, and there is nothing other than fiduciary duties—the same duties that could be applied directly to the majority shareholders—that protects the minority from the board.

Moreover, it is not clear why the minority shareholders should not be allowed to make a different deal.

(3) *To ensure that the board can protect third-party creditors from shareholders.* Shareholders may decide to impose excessive risks on the creditors while they (the shareholders) reap the potential rewards if the conduct pays off (*see* Section 3.02[C]). Once again, however, the board is controlled by the shareholders, and nothing prevents shareholders in closely held firms from punishing directors who favor creditors. Indeed, in a closely held firm the board members are likely to be shareholders themselves. If so, the creditors would be no better off with the directors in charge than with direct management by the shareholders.[32]

For whatever reason, the law has become more tolerant of arrangements that either bind directors to make particular decisions on certain matters or transfer authority over some or all management decisions to shareholders or non-board managers (collectively, "director control arrangements"). Two leading cases sustaining director control arrangements are *Clark*, below, and *Galler v. Galler.*[33] Additionally, some courts have held that where the parties incorporated a preexisting joint venture or partnership and intended to continue to be bound by their partnership agreement, the parties' rights would be controlled by the agreement and by partnership law even after incorporation.[34]

CLARK v. DODGE
New York Court of Appeals
269 N.Y. 410, 199 N.E. 641 (1936)

CROUCH, Judge.

The action is for the specific performance of a contract between the plaintiff, Clark, and the defendant Dodge, relating to the affairs of the two defendant corporations. . . . The defendant . . . moved to dismiss the complaint. We shall deal . . . with the questions here presented in the light of the facts most favorable to plaintiff appearing in the pleadings only.

Those facts, briefly stated, are as follows: The two corporate defendants are New Jersey corporations manufacturing medicinal preparations by secret formulae. The main office, factory, and assets of both corporations are located in the state of New York. In 1921, and at all times since, Clark owned 25 per cent. and Dodge 75 per cent. of the stock of each corporation. Dodge took no active part in the business, although he was a director, and through

---

[32]   Compare the "control rule" in limited partnerships, discussed in Section 6.03[B] below, which can impose personal liability on limited partners who override the usual authority of the general partners and take part in control of the business.

[33]   32 Ill. 2d 16, 203 N.E.2d 577 (1964).

[34]   *See Arditi v. Dubitzky*, 354 F.2d 483 (2d Cir. 1965); *De Boy v. Harris*, 207 Md. 212, 113 A.2d 903 (1955); *Boyd, Payne, Gates & Farthing, P.C. v. Payne, Gates, Farthing & Radd, P.C.*, 422 S.E.2d 784 (Va. 1992); Note, *Corporations: Does a Joint Adventure Agreement to Use the Corporation as a Medium Survive Incorporation?*, 44 CAL. L. REV. 590 (1956).

ownership of their qualifying shares, controlled the other directors of both corporations. He was the president of Bell & Co., Inc., and nominally general manager of Hollings-Smith Company, Inc. The plaintiff, Clark, was a director and held the offices of treasurer and general manager of Bell & Co., Inc., and also had charge of the major portion of the business of Hollings-Smith Company, Inc. The formulae and methods of manufacture of the medicinal preparations were known to him alone. Under date of February 15, 1921, Dodge and Clark, the sole owners of the stock of both corporations, entered into a written agreement under seal, which after reciting the stock ownership of both parties, the desire of Dodge that Clark should continue in the efficient management and control of the business of Bell & Co., Inc., so long as he should "remain faithful, efficient and competent to so manage and control the said business"; and his further desire that Clark should not be the sole custodian of a specified formula, but should share his knowledge thereof and of the method of manufacture with a son of Dodge, provided, in substance, as follows: That Dodge during his lifetime and, after his death, a trustee to be appointed by his will, would so vote his stock and so vote as a director that the plaintiff (a) should continue to be a director of Bell & Co., Inc.; and (b) should continue as its general manager so long as he should be "faithful, efficient and competent"; (c) should during his life receive one-fourth of the net income of the corporations either by way of salary or dividends; and (d) that no unreasonable or incommensurate salaries should be paid to other officers or agents which would so reduce the net income as materially to affect Clark's profits. Clark on his part agreed to disclose the specified formula to the son and to instruct him in the details and methods of manufacture; and, further, at the end of his life to bequeath his stock—if no issue survived him—to the wife and children of Dodge.

It was further provided that the provisions in regard to the division of net profits and the regulation of salaries should also apply to the Hollings-Smith Company.

The complaint alleges due performance of the contract by Clark and breach thereof by Dodge in that he has failed to use his stock control to continue Clark as a director and as general manager, and has prevented Clark from receiving his proportion of the income, while taking his own, by causing the employment of incompetent persons at excessive salaries, and otherwise.

The relief sought is reinstatement as director and general manager and an accounting by Dodge and by the corporations for waste and for the proportion of net income due plaintiff, with an injunction against further violations.

The only question which need be discussed is whether the contract is illegal as against public policy within the decision in *McQuade v. Stoneham*, 263 N.Y. 323, 189 N.E. 234, upon the authority of which the complaint was dismissed by the Appellate Division.

"The business of a corporation shall be managed by its board of directors." General Corporation Law (Consol. Laws, c. 23) § 27. That is the statutory norm. Are we committed by the *McQuade* case to the doctrine that there may be no variation, however slight or innocuous, from that norm, where salaries or policies or the retention of individuals in office are concerned? There is ample authority supporting that doctrine . . . and something may be said for it, since it furnishes a simple, if arbitrary, test. Apart from its practical administrative convenience, the reasons upon which it is said to rest are more or less nebulous. Public policy, the intention of the Legislature, detriment to the corporation, are phrases which in this connection mean little. Possible harm to *bona fide* purchasers of stock or to creditors or to stockholding minorities have more substance; but such harms are absent in many instances. If the enforcement of a particular contract damages nobody—not even, in any perceptible degree, the public—one sees no reason for holding it illegal, even though it impinges slightly upon the broad provision of § 27. Damage suffered or threatened is a logical and practical test, and has come to be the one generally adopted by the courts. . . . Where the directors are the sole stockholders, there seems to be no objection to enforcing an agreement among them to vote for certain people as officers. There is no direct decision to that effect in this court, yet there are strong indications that such a rule has long been recognized. The opinion in *Manson v. Curtis*, 223 N.Y. 313, 325, 119 N.E. 559, 562, Ann. Cas. 1918E, 247, closed its discussion by saying: "The rule that all the stockholders by their universal consent may do as they choose with the corporate concerns and assets, provided the interests of creditors are not affected, because they are the complete owners of the corporation, cannot be invoked here." That was because all the stockholders were not parties to the agreement there in question. So, where the public was not affected, "the parties in interest, might, by their original agreement of incorporation, limit their respective rights and powers," even where there was a conflicting statutory standard.

* * *

Except for the broad dicta in the *McQuade* opinion, we think there can be no doubt that the agreement here in question was legal and that the complaint states a cause of action. There was no attempt to sterilize the board of directors, as in the *Manson* and *McQuade* cases. The only restrictions on Dodge were (a) that as a stockholder he should vote for Clark as a director—a perfectly legal contract; (b) that as director he should continue Clark as general manager, so long as he proved faithful, efficient, and competent—an agreement which could harm nobody; (c) that Clark should always receive as salary or dividends one-fourth of the "net income." For the purposes of this motion, it is only just to construe that phrase as meaning whatever was left for distribution after the directors had in good faith set aside whatever they deemed wise; (d) that no salaries to other officers should be paid, unreasonable in amount or incommensurate with services rendered—a beneficial and not a harmful agreement.

If there was any invasion of the powers of the directorate under that agreement, it is so slight as to be negligible; and certainly there is no damage suffered by or threatened to anybody. The broad statements in the *McQuade* opinion, applicable to the facts there, should be confined to those facts.

The judgment of the Appellate Division should be reversed and the order of the Special Term affirmed, with costs in this court and in the Appellate Division.

NOTES AND QUESTIONS

(1) **Later history in *Clark*.** After the above opinion, the case went to trial. The evidence showed that following the entry of Dodge's son into the business in 1926 there was friction between Clark and the younger Dodge and that Clark refused to reveal the formulae as required by the contract. The court therefore upheld Clark's dis-

charge. Clark was, however, held entitled to one-fourth of the net income of the corporation since his discharge.[35]

(2) **Interpreting the corporation statute.** Was permitting the arrangement in *Clark* consistent with the statutory language requiring management by the board? If not, can and should the court simply ignore the statute? Consider the following argument: Legislators did not contemplate at the time of the original corporation statutes that these statutes would be used by firms that were essentially partnerships. After these statutes were passed, new circumstances arose which made the corporate form attractive to closely held firms, including the expansion of tort law which increased the benefit of limited liability. The courts interpreted the statutory language as simply omissions of inattentive legislatures rather than intentional restrictions on form. *See* **Ayres**.

(3) ***Long Park.*** What kinds of director-control agreements are invalid? In *Long Park, Inc. v. Trenton-New Brunswick Theatres Co.,*[36] the court invalidated a contract agreed to by all of the shareholders which delegated full management power to one of the shareholders for 19 years. The manager could not be removed by the other shareholders for a year, and after that only by an arbitrator. Why not enforce the agreement by all of the shareholders? Should it make a difference if the manager is removable by the shareholders for cause?

PROBLEM

A, B and C have pooled their skill and resources in a real estate development venture. For some time they have been operating as a partnership. Under the parties' loose agreement, each has equal rights to management and a right to receive one-third of net profits and important decisions must be made unanimously. In all material respects the rules governing the parties' relationship are those set forth in the Uniform Partnership Act. The parties have decided to incorporate in order to obtain the advantages of limited liability but would like to continue operating as they have to the extent possible. What changes would you advise in how the business is organized, assuming the relevant law is *Clark* and the New York statute that was in effect at that time? Assume there are no ethical problems in rendering the requested advice.

[B] Modern Statutory Provisions

As discussed in Section 5.02, corporation statutes generally permit such variations in the standard corporate form as shareholder voting agreements, classified stock, and supermajority voting and quorum requirements. Many of these statutory provisions

---

[35] *See* 28 N.Y.S.2d 442 (Sup. Ct. 1939), *aff'd mem.* 261 A.D. 1086, 28 N.Y.S.2d 464 (1941), *aff'd mem.* 287 N.Y. 833, 41 N.E.2d 102 (1942).

[36] 297 N.Y. 174, 77 N.E.2d 633 (1948).

apply to all businesses incorporated under the general corporation statute. A more recent phenomenon has been statutory provisions permitting arrangements that apply only to close corporations. Many of these statutes allow parties to covered firms to restrict the authority of or eliminate the board of directors. Some go beyond this and provide for share transfer restrictions (*see* Section 5.04) and remedies for misconduct (*see* Section 5.05). These provisions may apply to "close corporations," defined in terms of number of shareholders, absence of a public offering or listing on a securities exchange, and use of stock transfer restrictions (*see* N.Y. Bus. Corp. L. § 620; MBCA § 7.32); any corporation that elects coverage (Maryland Corps. & Ass'ns Code §§ 4-101 to 4-603; Tex. Bus. Corp. Act Arts. 12.01 *et seq.*); or corporations that both elect to be covered and meet a statutory definition of a "close corporation." *See* Del. G.C.L. §§ 341-356.

Many corporation statutes include provisions that loosen the requirement for management by a board of directors as to corporations generally. *See* for example, the "except" clause in the first sentence of Del. G.C.L. § 141(a). Often, as in Delaware, this type of provision coexists with those applying only to certain corporations. But statutes authorizing departures from management by a board of directors may render non-statutory methods for limiting board powers invalid.[37]

NOTES AND QUESTIONS

(1) **Effect of general authorization.** Where a statute contains only a general authorization of charter provisions like Delaware G.C.L. § 141(a), what types of arrangements are permitted? Does such a provision let the parties dispense with the board of directors?

(2) **Qualification requirement.** Special close corporation provisions requiring election by a certificate provision obviously help notify shareholders and creditors of non-standard governance structures that might present risks, such as those discussed in the Introduction to this Section. But why also require *qualification—i.e.*, that the firm be a "close corporation"? In other words, why should General Motors not be able to enter into the governance provisions permitted by these statutes? Are such provisions justified by the concern that otherwise judicial precedents in close corporation cases may be applied inappropriately in the public corporation context? *See* **Ayres**.

(3) **Effect of failure to elect or qualify.** Under statutes that apply only to corporations that elect or qualify or both, what is the effect of director control agreements in non-qualifying or non-electing corporations? In *Lehrman v. Cohen*, discussed in Note 2 following *Abercrombie* above, the Delaware Supreme Court upheld a deadlock-break-

---

[37]   *See Quickturn Design Systems, Inc. v. Shapiro*, 721 A.2d 1281 (Del. 1998) (invalidating limitation on board's fundamental power to negotiate a sale of the corporation where the limitation was not included in the certificate of incorporation pursuant to Del. G.C.L. § 141(a)).

ing arrangement in a public corporation against the contention that it constituted a delegation of management authority. But *Lehrman* noted that the device in question—the use of classified stock—was provided for in the certificate of corporation and therefore was authorized by the "except" clause of Del. G.C.L. § 141(a). Courts may invalidate delegations of board authority not specifically authorized under Del. G.C.L. § 141(a) or Delaware's special close corporation provisions, at least where the delegations "restrict[] the board's power in an area of fundamental importance to the shareholders."[38] Delaware G.C.L. § 356 implies that this case law remains available to nonqualifying corporations despite the enactment of the special close corporation provisions. To the extent that qualification is essential to the validity of a director control agreement, it is necessary to protect the parties from inadvertent termination of the agreement as a result of loss of qualification. *See* Del. G.C.L. §§ 345(b) and 348.

(4) **Limitations on flexibility.** What sorts of agreements are not permitted by the provisions discussed above? *See* Del. G.C.L. §§ 350-51; MBCA § 7.32. For example, note that MBCA § 7.32(a)(8) precludes agreements that are "contrary to public policy." The Official Comment to this section says that this qualification includes, among others, agreements that eliminate dissenters' rights, derivative actions, or inspection rights. Why not permit shareholders to agree on these matters?

(5) **Non-consenting shareholders.** To what extent do the provisions permit binding of non-consenting shareholders to a director control agreement? *See* Del. G.C.L. § 350, which provides that an agreement among majority shareholders "is not invalid, *as between the parties to the agreement,* on the ground that it so relates to the conduct of the business and affairs of the corporation as to restrict or interfere with the discretion or powers of the board of directors" (emphasis added).

ZION v. KURTZ
New York Court of Appeals
50 N.Y.2d 92, 428 N.Y.S.2d 199, 405 N.E.2d 681 (1980)

MEYER, Judge.
On these appeals we conclude that when all of the stockholders of a Delaware corporation agree that, except as specified in their agreement, no "business or activities" of the corporation shall be conducted without the consent of a minority stockholder, the agreement is, as between the original parties to it, enforceable even though all formal steps required by the statute have not been taken. We hold further that the agreement made by the parties to this action was violated when the corporation entered into two agreements without the minority stockholder's consent. . . . The order of the Appellate Division should, therefore, be modified, with costs to plaintiffs, as hereafter indicated.
Defendant Lombard-Wall Incorporated ("Lombard") was owned by Equimark Corporation. Wishing to acquire Lombard, defendant Kurtz, a dealer in unregistered securities,

---

[38] *See id.*

caused a corporation originally known as H-K Enterprises, Inc., the name of which was later changed to Lombard-Wall Group, Inc. ("Group"), to be formed under Delaware law. Kurtz was the sole stockholder of Group, but neither Kurtz nor Group could provide the $4,000,000 needed to acquire Lombard from Equimark. It was in fact acquired with a short-term loan from a Swiss bank, shortly thereafter repaid from Lombard's cash, loaned by Lombard to Group on Group's noninterest bearing note.

Since Lombard's business required book assets at the full value of $4,000,000 and Group had no assets other than Lombard's stock, Group's note to Lombard was secured by a nonrecourse guarantee from Half Moon Land Corporation, of which plaintiff Zion is the principal shareholder, collateralized by California lands owned by Half Moon. The loan agreement recited that Half Moon had made no presentation as to the value of the land and Lombard and Group agreed that should Lombard's accountants require additional acts or documents in order to maintain the value of the note, they would pay to Half Moon in advance all expenditures necessary to meet the accountants' requirements.

At the time the note, loan agreement and guarantee were entered into Zion, Kurtz and Group entered into a stockholders' agreement. Zion and Kurtz were the sole stockholders of Group at that time, Zion holding class A stock and Kurtz, class B. § 3.01(a) of the agreement expressly provided that without the consent of the holders of class A stock:

> Anything in its Certificate of Incorporation or By-Laws to the contrary notwithstanding, the Corporation shall not:
>
> (a) Engage in any business or activities of any kind, directly or indirectly, whether through any Subsidiary or by way of a loan, guarantee or otherwise, other than the acquisition and ownership of the stock of L-W as contemplated by this Agreement; provided, however, that the Corporation or L-W may obtain and pay premiums for, and shall be the beneficiary of, term life insurance, if obtainable, on the lives of the Purchaser, Kurtz and such other executive personnel of the Corporation and/or L-W, and in such amounts, as the directors of the Corporation or L-W may from time to time approve or as otherwise expressly provided in this Agreement.

Notwithstanding that provision, Group and Lombard some eight months thereafter, at the suggestion of Group's accountants, entered into an agreement which made the previously noninterest bearing loan from Lombard to Group bear interest provided interest could be paid out of earnings, and an escrow agreement with Chase Manhattan Bank pursuant to which Group deposited $580,000 in bonds to secure payment of the note. The two agreements were authorized by Group's board over Zion's objection.

* * *

Plaintiffs thereafter began this action for declaratory and injunctive relief, asking in their first cause of action that the interest and escrow agreements executed without Zion's consent be declared in violation of the stockholders' agreement and annulled[.] . . .

* * *

. . . Subdivision (a) of § 141 of the General Corporation Law of Delaware provides that the business and affairs of a corporation organized under that law "shall be managed by a board of directors, except as may be otherwise provided in this chapter or in its certificate of incorporation." Included in the chapter referred to are provisions relating to close corporations, which explicitly state that a written agreement between the holders of a majority of such a corporation's stock "is not invalid, as between the parties to the agreement, on the ground that it so relates to the conduct of the business and affairs of the corporation as to restrict or interfere with the discretion or powers of the board of directors" (§ 350) or "on the ground that it is an attempt by the parties to the agreement or by the stockholders of the corporation to treat the corporation as if it were a partnership" (§ 354), and further provides that "The certificate of incorporation of a close corporation may provide that the business of the corporation shall be managed by the stockholders of the corporation rather than the board of directors" and that such a provision may be inserted in the certificate by amendment if "all holders of record of all of the outstanding stock" so authorize (§ 351).

Clear from those provisions is the fact that the public policy of Delaware does not proscribe a provision such as that contained in the shareholders' agreement here in issue even though it takes all management functions away from the directors. Folk, in his work on the Delaware Corporation Law, states concerning § 350 that "Although some decisions outside Delaware have sustained 'reasonable' restrictions upon director discretion contained in stockholder agreements, the theory of § 350 is to declare unequivocally, as a matter of public policy, that stockholder agreements of this character are not invalid" (at p. 518), that § 351 "recognizes a special subclass of close corporations which operate by direct stockholder management" (at p. 520), and with respect to § 354 that it "should be liberally construed to authorize all sorts of internal agreements and arrangements which are not affirmatively improper or, more particularly, injurious to third parties" (at p. 526).

Defendants argue, however, that Group was not incorporated as a close corporation and the stockholders' agreement provision was never incorporated in its certificate. The answer is that any Delaware corporation can elect to become a close corporation by filing an appropriate certificate of amendment (Del. General Corporation Law, § 344) and by such amendment approved by the holders of all of its outstanding stock may include in its certificate provisions restricting directors' authority (*ibid.*, § 351). Here, not only did defendant Kurtz agree in paragraph 8.05(b) of the stockholders' agreement to "without further consideration, do, execute and deliver, or cause to be done, executed and delivered, all such further acts, things and instruments as may be reasonably required more effectively to evidence and give effect to the provisions and the intent and purposes of this Agreement", but also as part of the transaction by which the Half Moon guarantee was made and Zion became a Group stockholder, defendant Kurtz, while he was still the sole stockholder and sole director of Group, executed a consent to the various parts of the transaction under which he was "authorized and empowered to execute and deliver, or cause to be executed and delivered, all such other and further instruments and documents and take, or cause to be taken, all such other and further action as he may deem necessary, appropriate or desirable to implement and give effect to the Stockholders Agreement and the transactions provided for therein." Since there are no intervening rights of third persons, the agreement requires nothing that is not permitted by statute, and all of the stockholders of the corporation assented to it, the certificate of incorporation may be ordered reformed, by requiring Kurtz to file the appropriate amendments, or more directly he may be held estopped to rely upon the absence of those amendments from the corporate charter.[3]

The result thus reached accords with the weight of authority which text-writer F. Hodge O'Neal tells us sustains agreements made by all shareholders dealing with matters normally within the province of the directors (1 CLOSE CORPORATIONS § 5.24, p.83), even though the shareholders could have, but had not, provided similarly by charter or by-law provision sanctioned by statute (*ibid.*, § 5.19, pp. 73-74). Moreover, though we have not yet had occasion to construe subdivision (b) of § 620 of the Business Corporation Law, which did not become effective until September 1, 1963, it is worthy of note that in adopting that provision that Legislature had before it the Revisers' Comment that: "Paragraph (b) expands the ruling in *Clark v. Dodge*, 269 N.Y. 410, 199 N.E. 637 [641] (1936), and, to the extent therein provided, overrules *Long Park, Inc. v. Trenton-New Brunswick Theatres Co.*, 297 N.Y. 174, 77 N.E.2d 633 (1948); *Manson v. Curtis*, 223 N.Y. 313, 119 N.E. 559 (1919), and *McQuade v. Stoneham*, 263 N.Y. 323, 189 N.E. 234 (1934)." Thus it is clear that no New York public policy stands in the way of our application of the Delaware statute and decisional law above referred to[.]

* * *

GABRIELLI, Judge (dissenting in part).

* * *

By its holding today, the majority has, in effect, rendered inoperative both the language and the underlying purpose of the relevant Delaware and New York statutes governing "close corporations." According to the majority's reasoning, the only requirements for upholding an otherwise unlawful shareholder agreement which concededly deprives the directors of all discretionary authority are that all of the shareholders concur in the agreement and that no "intervening rights of third persons" exist at the time enforcement of the agreement is sought. The statutes in question also recognize these factors as conditions precedent to the enforcement of shareholder agreements to "sterilize" a corporate board of directors (Del. General Corporation Law, § 351; BUSINESS CORPORATION LAW, § 620, subd. [b], pars. [1]-[2]; subd. [g]). But the laws of both jurisdictions go further, requiring in each case that the "close corporation" give notice of its unorthodox management structure through its filed certificate of incorporation. The obvious purpose of such a requirement is to prevent harm to the public before it occurs. If, as the majority's holding suggests, this requirement of notice to the public through the certificate of incorporation is without legal effect unless and until a third party's interests have actually been impaired, then the prophylactic purposes of the statutes governing "close corporations" would effectively be defeated. It is this aspect of the majority's ruling that I find most difficult to accept.

* * *

---

[3]   The fallacy of the dissent is that it converts a shield into a sword. The notice devices on which the concept of the dissent turns are wholly unnecessary to protect the original parties, who may be presumed to have known what they agreed to. To protect an original party who has not been hurt (indeed, has expressly agreed to the limitation he is being protected against and affirmatively covenanted to see to it that all necessary steps to validate the agreement were taken) because a third party without notice could have been hurt had he been involved can only be characterized as a perversion of the liberal legislative purpose demonstrated by the Delaware statutes quoted in the text above.

NOTES AND QUESTIONS

(1) **Judicial liberalization of statutory requirements.** Other cases have, like *Zion*, taken a generous view of agreements which failed to comply with a close corporation statute. *Triggs v. Triggs*,[39] again over Judge Gabrielli's dissent, enforced a share transfer provision of a shareholder agreement although the agreement also included director control provisions which were invalid because they had not been approved by all of the shareholders. The court reasoned that the director control provisions had never actually operated to restrict director discretion and that in all events, these provisions were severable from the share transfer provisions at issue. *Boyd, Payne, Gates & Farthing, P.C. v. Payne, Gates, Farthing & Radd, P.C.*[40] held that law partners who formed a professional corporation for tax purposes but who continued to conduct themselves as partners could have their rights determined according to partnership law. The court reasoned that statutory close corporation provisions merely codified prior law and that the partnership did not wrongfully eliminate the board mandated under the professional corporation act because the corporate board continued to perform tax functions.

(2) **Policy considerations.** Do you agree with the majority or dissent in *Zion*? What types of harm to third parties could result from enforcing agreements like the one in *Zion* without a charter election of close corporation status? See the discussion in subsection [A] above of the rationales for restricting these types of agreements.

(3) **Courts versus legislatures.** Irrespective of whether restrictions on contracting in close corporations are appropriate, once the legislature has seemingly required formalities, on what ground can the courts justify enforcing non-complying agreements? Is this the same sort of interpretation issue as that concerning the New York statute in *Clark*? *See* Note 2, after *Clark v. Dodge, supra.*

PROBLEMS

(1) How would you respond to the Problem (1) at the end of Section 5.02[B][3] under (a) the Delaware Act? (b) MBCA § 7.32?

(2) Smith, Jones and Brown are the only three stockholders and directors of the SJB Corporation. Smith is the president and chief executive officer and owns 40 percent of the stock, and Jones and Brown own 40 percent and 20 percent respectively. Smith worries that Jones and Brown will combine votes to elect Brown president. In order to prevent this, Smith persuades Jones to cooperate with him. Jones agrees to help Smith retain the presidency in exchange for Smith's promise that dividends will remain at their present level. Brown will certainly not agree to this arrangement. Smith and Jones seek your advice as to how they can best effectuate their arrangement. Assume that the

---

[39] 46 N.Y.2d 305, 413 N.Y.S. 325, 385 N.E.2d 1254 (1978).

[40] 422 S.E.2d 784 (Va. 1992).

corporation has not been formed as a close corporation under Del. G.C.L. § 343. What advice would you give under (a) the Delaware Act (*see* Del. G.C.L. §§ 141(a), 242, 344, 350, and 351)? (b) MBCA § 7.32?

REFERENCES

Ayres, *Judging Close Corporations in the Age of Statutes*, 70 Wash. U. L.Q. 365 (1992).

Easterbrook & Fischel, The Economic Structure of Corporate Law, Ch. 9 (1991).

Karjala, *An Analysis of Close Corporation Legislation in the United States*, 21 Ariz. St. L.J. 663 (1989).

Karjala, *A Second Look at Special Close Corporation Legislation*, 58 Tex. L. Rev. 1207 (1980).

O'Neal & Thompson, O'Neal's Close Corporations § 1.18 (3d ed. 1986).

Romano, *State Competition for Close Corporation Charters: A Commentary*, 70 Wash. U. L.Q. 409 (1992).

§ 5.04 Share Transfer Restrictions

As in partnerships (*see* Section 4.03), shareholders of close corporations may want to restrict transferability of their stock to avoid introducing strangers and potential conflicts of interest and to avoid shifts in control. Once again, however, corporate law has not always accommodated shareholder wishes. The courts may invalidate restrictions on transferability, as in the following case, or, as discussed in subsection [C], may limit their effectiveness by restrictive interpretation. As with director control agreements, these judicial restrictions have been alleviated by statute.

[A] Validity of the Restriction

RAFE v. HINDIN
New York Supreme Court, Appellate Division
29 A.D.2d 481, 288 N.Y.S.2d 662,
aff'd mem. 23 N.Y.2d 759, 244, N.E.2d 469, 296 N.Y.S.2d 955 (1968)

Beldock, Presiding Justice.

On November 1, 1963 the plaintiff and the individual defendant organized the corporate defendant for the purpose of purchasing and developing a parcel of real property in Port Jefferson Station, New York. Each owned one certificate for 50% of the outstanding stock. There was a legend on each certificate, signed by the parties, which made it non-transferable except to the other stockholder; and written permission from the other stockholder was required to transfer the stock to a third party on the books of the corporation.

In April, 1967, being in financial difficulties, the plaintiff found a prospective purchaser for his stock for $44,000. The plaintiff offered to sell his stock to the individual defendant at that price. The latter refused to buy the stock and also refused to consent to the sale thereof to the plaintiff's prospective purchaser.

The plaintiff then instituted this action for a judgment declaring void the legend on the certificate, declaring the stock transferable to a third party without the consent of the individual defendant, and granting other incidental relief.

* * *

The plaintiff moved for summary judgment. . . .

* * *

The legend contained two separate restrictions: (a) each stockholder is required to sell to the other stockholder, but no price is stated at which the offeror is required to sell or the offeree to purchase, and no time limit is set for the offeree to exercise his option to purchase; and (b) each stockholder is required to obtain the consent of the other stockholder to a proposed transfer of the stock to a third party, but there is no provision that the second stockholder may not unreasonably withhold his consent. We are concerned on this appeal solely with the validity of the second restriction.

There is a conflict of authority in other States on the subject of the validity of a restriction on the transfer of stock in a close corporation without the consent of either all or a stated percentage of the other stockholders or the board of directors of the corporation.

* * *

In New York certificates of stock are regarded as personal property and are subject to the rule that there be no unreasonable restraint on alienation (*Allen v. Biltmore Tissue Corp.*, 2 N.Y.2d 534, 540, 161 N.Y.S.2d 418, 421, 141 N.E.2d 812, 814, 61 A.L.R.2d 1309). In *Penthouse Properties v. 1158 Fifth Ave.*, 256 App. Div. 685, 690-691, 11 N.Y.S.2d 417, [quoted with approval in *Allen* (*supra*), 2 N.Y.2d at pp. 541-542, 161 N.Y.S.2d at p. 423, 141 N.E.2d 816], the court declared that "[t]he general rule that ownership of property cannot exist in one person and the right of alienation in another . . . has in this State been frequently applied to shares of corporate stock . . . and cognizance has been taken of the principle that 'the right of transfer is a right of property, and if another has the arbitrary power to forbid a transfer of property by the owner that amounts to annihilation of property.'"

* * *

The legend on the stock certificate at bar contains no provision that the individual defendant's consent may not be unreasonably withheld. Since the individual defendant is thus given the arbitrary power to forbid a transfer of the shares of stock by the plaintiff, the restriction amounts to annihilation of property. The restriction is not only not reasonable, but it is against public policy and, therefore, illegal. It is an unwarrantable and unlawful restraint on the sale of personal property, the sale and interchange of which the law favors, and in restraint of trade.

The individual defendant argues that there was an oral agreement between the parties that his consent would not be unreasonably withheld and that, in fact, the withholding of his consent to the transfer to the plaintiff's prospective purchaser was reasonable. Assuming that there was such an oral agreement prior to the issuance of the shares of stock and assuming further that the inclusion of such a provision in the written legend on the stock certificate would make reasonable what we hold to be an unreasonable restraint on alienation, it is our opinion that proof of such an oral agreement would be inadmissible at the trial as in violation of the parol evidence rule. Such an agreement relates so closely to the stockholder relationship and the subject dealt with in the written legend that it would be expected to be embodied in the writing; therefore, if it is contained merely in an oral agreement, it may not be proved.

* * *

It is further noted that, because the individual defendant is given by the legend on the stock certificate the arbitrary right to refuse for any reason or for no reason to consent to the transfer of the plaintiff's stock to a prospective purchaser, and since no price is stated at which the plaintiff must sell to the individual defendant and which the latter is required to pay to the plaintiff for the plaintiff's stock, the legend may be construed as rendering the sale of the plaintiff's stock impossible to anyone except to the individual defendant at whatever price he wishes to pay. This construction makes the restriction illegal (*Allen v. Biltmore Tissue Corp.*, 2 N.Y.2d 534, 542, 161 N.Y.S.2d 418, 423, 141 N.E.2d 812, 816, *supra*).

In the *Penthouse Properties* case (256 A.D. 685, 11 N.Y.S.2d 417, *supra*), it was held that a provision in stock certificates of a corporation operating a cooperative apartment house and in the proprietary leases of apartments therein, barring the transfer of any certificate or the assignment of any lease without the written consent of the board of directors of the corporation or of two-thirds of its stockholders, is neither invalid nor unenforceable as in restraint of alienation, where it appeared that the restrictions imposed, viewed in the light of the permanency of the individual occupants as tenant owners, were legal, reasonable, and appropriate to the lawful purpose to be attained; and that the special nature of the ownership of cooperative apartment houses by tenant owners required that they not be included in the general rule against restraint on the sale of stock of corporations organized for profit. The case at bar involves the sale of stock of a corporation organized for profit and, therefore, does not come within the principle of that holding.

The order denying the plaintiff's motion for summary judgment should be reversed; the motion should be granted; and judgment should be directed to be entered (1) declaring void the legend on the certificate requiring the consent of the individual defendant to the transfer of the plaintiff's stock to a third-party and (2) directing the corporate defendant, upon submission to it of a properly endorsed assignment of the stock and appropriate payment to it on account of any taxes on the transfer, to record the transfer in its stock transfer book, to cancel the plaintiff's stock certificate, to issue a new stock certificate to the plaintiff's transferee, and to record the plaintiff's transferee in its stock book as the present holder of the stock.

NOTES AND QUESTIONS

(1) **Nonenforcement of consent restrictions.** What "public policy" justifies nonenforcement of a contract between two experienced business people? What about the argument that share transfer restrictions prevent allocation of property to its most valuable use? Then why distinguish the *Penthouse Properties* case, discussed in *Rafe*, in which a consent restriction was enforced?[41] Can the result in *Rafe* be explained as effectuating the parties' intent or preventing oppressive conduct? Note, in the latter regard, that share transfer restrictions have a different effect in corporations than in partnerships (*see Rapoport* in Section 4.03): a partner who cannot transfer her shares usually has the power to dissolve the firm. Indeed, courts sometimes resolve this problem in close corporations not by refusing to enforce the agreement, but by invoking a statutory dissolution or buyout procedure. *See In re Pace Photographers, Ltd.*[42]

(2) **Enforcement of price restrictions.** The courts usually have enforced share transfer restrictions providing for the purchase of the exiting shareholder's shares at a price determined in accordance with the agreement. For example, in *Allen v. Biltmore Tissue Corp.*,[43] the New York Court of Appeals upheld a bylaw that gave the corporation an option to repurchase stock at its original purchase price whenever the shareholder wished to sell or upon the shareholder's death. The court distinguished between a "restriction" and a "prohibition" on share transfer, approving the former. The court reasoned that some definite formula was necessary to permit a restriction to operate without expensive litigation, and stated that "[t]o be invalid, more than mere disparity between option price and current value of the stock must be shown."[44] But where the buyout price is a small fraction of market value, the restriction on transfer effectively

---

[41]　For other cases enforcing consent restrictions, see *Fayard v. Fayard*, 293 So. 2d 421 (Miss. 1974); *Gray v. Harris Land & Cattle Co.*, 737 P.2d 475 (Mont. 1987). For a case refusing to enforce a consent restriction, relying partly on *Rafe*, see *Hill v. Warner, Berman & Spitz, P.A.*, 197 N.J. Super. 152, 484 A.2d 344 (App. Div. 1984).

[42]　71 N.Y.2d 737, 530 N.Y.S.2d 67, 525 N.E.2d 713 (1988) (discussed in Note 7 after *Gardstein v. Kemp & Beatley* in Section 5.05[C], below).

[43]　2 N.Y.2d 534, 161 N.Y.S.2d 418, 141 N.E.2d 812 (1957).

[44]　2 N.Y.2d at 543, 161 N.Y.S.2d at 424, 141 N.E.22d at 817. For cases sustaining share transfer restrictions that provide for the purchase of the restricted shares at a price significantly below market value, see *Di Loreto v. Tiber Holding Corp.*, 2001 Del. Ch. LEXIS 26, 2001 WL 221001 (Del. Ch.) (enforcing buyout price of less than $27,500/share where unaudited balance sheet showed value of $158,000/share), *aff'd*, 804 A.2d 1055 (Del. 2001); *Sennerikuppam v. Datel Eng'g Co.*, 156 F.3d 1232 (6th Cir. 1998) (upholding option to buy shares of deceased shareholder or shareholder who elected to sell for $2500 per share where plaintiff alleged that fair value of shares exceeded $27,000); *Hardy v. South Bend Sash & Door Co.*, 603 N.E.2d 895 (Ind. Ct. App. 1993) (enforcing fixed price provision although price was not revised annually per agreement, noting the need for fixing a price in light of difficulty of determining market value of close corporation shares); *Rosiny v. Schmidt*, 185 A.D.2d 727, 587 N.Y.S.2d 929 (1992) (upholding post-mortem buyout despite huge disparity between contract price—$200 per share—and market price—$41,500 per share—and fact that plaintiffs were approximately 40 years or younger and were guaranteed to outlive decedents); *Renberg v. Zarrow*, 667 P.2d 465 (Okla. 1983) (option to buy deceased shareholder's shares at price less than 1/100 of market value); *In re Mather's Estate*, 410 Pa. 361, 189 A.2d 586 (1963) (option to buy shares of holder who died or wished to sell at $1 per share; current value is $1,000 per share). For a case refusing to enforce share transfer agreements where the price was far below market, see *Swanson v. Shockley*, 364 N.W.2d 252 (Iowa 1985) (agreement provided for buyout of shareholder

functions as a prohibition. Why, then, are the courts apparently more willing to enforce these agreements than consent restrictions like the one involved in *Rafe*?

(3) **Statutory provisions.** The validity of share transfer restrictions is now explicitly provided for by some statutory provisions. *See* Del. G.C.L. § 202. How would *Rafe* and the cases discussed in the preceding notes be decided under this section? Also, close corporation statutes may provide "standard form" statutory share transfer restrictions (*see* Section 5.04[E]).

PROBLEM

A corporation consists of three shareholders, A, B and C. At the time of formation of the corporation, there was no provision restricting the transfer of stock and the articles of incorporation provided for amendment upon a 2/3 vote of the shareholders. Three years after forming the corporation, A and B became concerned that C might sell his shares to an undesirable outsider. A and B voted to amend the charter to provide that no shareholder could sell his stock without giving the corporation an opportunity to buy it at book value, which at all relevant times was 50% percent of market value. Six months after the amendment, C has found a purchaser for his stock at market value. Can C sell to the outsider under (a) the case law discussed above in this subsection? or (b) Del. G.C.L. § 202?[45]

[B] Planning Corporate Share Transfer Agreements

The share transfer agreement must not only be enforceable, but must accomplish the parties' goals. This involves planning how and when the restriction should operate and drafting the agreement so that it actually does what the parties want it to do. The first problem is discussed below; the second problem is discussed in Subsection [C].

[1] Choosing the Type of Agreement

We have so far focused on only one function of share transfer agreements: restricting the ability of owners to transfer their interests so as to prevent unwanted outsiders from entering the firm and to prevent shifts in control from transfers among existing owners. But share transfer agreements can serve other purposes as well. Among other things, share transfer agreements can be used (1) to provide a market for shareholders' otherwise illiquid stock and (2) to provide for the elimination of shareholders when, for

---

who wishes to sell at 8% of fair market value; plaintiff, who was not even aware of the restriction when he bought into the corporation, would receive a windfall from enforcement of the agreement).

[45] *See B & H Warehouse, Inc. v. Atlas Van Lines, Inc.*, 490 F.2d 818 (5th Cir. 1974); *Tu-Vu Drive-In Corp. v. Ashkins*, 61 Cal. 2d 283, 38 Cal. Rptr. 348, 391 P.2d 828 (1964).

example, they are no longer employed by the company. The type of share transfer agreement selected by the parties therefore depends upon their particular goals.

The following are some important varieties of share transfer agreements, together with the goals they serve.

(a) *Consent Provisions.* The shareholder may sell only if the directors or the other shareholders consent, as in *Rafe*. This type of agreement prevents parties from transferring their interests to others. It may be particularly useful in family close corporations.

(b) *Call Provisions.* The corporation or the other shareholders may purchase (or "call") stock at a price determined in accordance with a particular formula when a shareholder wishes to sell, upon the happening of a specified contingency, such as the death or termination of employment of a shareholder, or at any time. This type of agreement can be used to prevent shares from being transferred to unwanted outsiders (such as inactive heirs of insiders). In addition, this type of agreement can be used to eliminate shareholders when they are no longer employed by the firm. As demonstrated by the discussion in the next subsection, specifying the circumstances that trigger operation of the restriction may present formidable drafting problems.

(c) *Rights of First Refusal.* The corporation or the other shareholders may purchase stock when a shareholder wishes to sell to a third party upon the terms that the third party buyer is ready, willing, and able to accept. This type of agreement, like the call provisions discussed above, can be used to prevent shares from being transferred to an unwanted outsider. Unlike call provisions, however, there is no need for the parties to bargain in advance over the price that the corporation or other shareholders will pay to the shareholder who wishes to sell. Thus, rights of first refusal may be easier to negotiate.[46]

(d) *Put Provisions.* The corporation or the other shareholders must purchase stock at the option of a shareholder or upon the happening of a specified contingency, such as a shareholder's death (*i.e.*, the shareholder can "put" his shares to the company or the other shareholders). This type of agreement can be used to provide a market for a shareholders stock and may be used in conjunction share transfer agreements that prevent a shareholder from transferring shares to an outsider. See the discussion of price restrictions in *Rafe* (*see* Section 5.04[A]) and in Note 2 following *Rafe*.

[2] Availability of Funds for Purchase

If the corporation or other shareholders are required or permitted to purchase a shareholder's stock, it is important to ensure that the prospective purchasers are financially able to make the purchase. A corporate purchaser in financial trouble may be pre-

---

[46] For a case upholding a right of first refusal, see *Agranoff v. Miller*, 1999 Del. Ch. LEXIS 78, 1999 WL 219650 (Del. Ch., Apr. 12, 1999) (right of first refusal on transfer of shares of closely held corporation not invalid as an unreasonable restraint on alienation, even though it lacks termination date).

cluded from purchasing the stock by statutes that are intended to protect corporate creditors (*see* Section 11.07). Among the possible solutions to this problem are insurance, sinking funds and installment contracts.[47]

[3] Ensuring the Effectiveness of the Restriction

In order to bind shareholders who owned stock prior to adoption of a transfer restriction but who did not consent to the restriction, it will be necessary, at least, to place the restriction in the charter or bylaws of the corporation. Even in that situation, the restriction may not bind such shareholders. *See* Del. G.C.L. § 202(b) and the Problem in Section 5.04[A].

Shareholders who buy into the corporation after the adoption of a restriction on transfer may be bound only if the restriction is noted conspicuously on the stock certificate itself or if they have actual notice of the provision. *See* Uniform Commercial Code § 8-204(a); Del. G.C.L. § 202(a).[48]

[4] Price

In the case of transfer agreements that make use of "puts" and "calls," the transfer price is probably the most difficult term in a share transfer agreement. This problem is discussed in subsection [D], below.

[C] Drafting and Interpretation of Share Transfer Agreements

Shareholders must take particular care in drafting share transfer agreements, because the courts often apply a rule of strict construction requiring the narrow interpretation of share transfer restrictions. This rule has been employed to reject the application of transfer restrictions to particular events not specifically covered by the agreement, such as transfers among the shareholders[49] and involuntary transfers, as to an executor by will.[50] For example, in *Frandsen v. Jensen-Sundquist Agency*,

---

[47] For a case refusing to let a stockholder enforce a contractual right of redemption because of statutory limitations on share repurchases, see *McAlister v. Peregrine Enterprises Inc.*, 1997 Tenn. App. LEXIS 848, 1997 WL 746373 (Tenn. Ct. App. 1997).

[48] For interpretations of the conspicuousness requirement, see *Allen v. Biltmore Tissue Corp.*, discussed in Note 2 following *Rafe* in Section 5.04[A], and *Ling & Co. v. Trinity Savings & Loan Ass'n*, 482 S.W.2d 841 (Tex. 1972).

[49] *Compare Birmingham Artificial Limb Co. v. Allen*, 280 Ala. 445, 194 So. 2d 848 (1967) (applicable only to transfers to ousiders), *with Frickert v. Deiter Bros. Fuel Co.*, 464 Pa. 596, 347 A.2d 701 (1975) (applicable to inter-shareholder transfers).

[50] For cases holding that the agreement did not apply to testamentary transfers, see *In re Estate of Riggs*, 36 Colo. App. 302, 540 P.2d 361 (1975); *Avrett and Ledbetter Roofing & Heating Co. v. Phillips*, 85 N.C. App. 248, 354 S.E.2d 321 (1987); *Glenn v. Seaview Country Club*, 154 N.J. Super. 69, 380 A.2d 1175 (Ch. Div. 1977); *In re Estate of Spaziani*, 125 Misc. 2d 901, 480 N.Y.S.2d 854 (Surr. Ct. Jefferson Co. 1984). *Contra, see Murray Van & Storage, Inc. v. Murray*, 364 So. 2d 68 (Fla. Dist. Ct. App. 1978). *See generally*, Annot., 61 A.L.R.3d 1090 (1975). For cases holding

Inc.,[51] Judge Posner interpreted a restriction on the ability of majority shareholders to offer to sell "their stock" not to apply to a transaction where the majority shareholders offered to engage in a merger-type transaction that would result in the conversion of the corporation's shares into cash "but not by sale, for in a merger the shares of the acquired firm are not bought, they are extinguished."[52]

In some cases, the effect of the restriction may be consistent with the parties' intent. Thus, in *Frandsen*, Judge Posner noted evidence that the party opposing the restriction sought to protect himself from being a frozen-out minority holder. But the parties' intent may not be clear. For example, in *Frandsen*, the party opposing enforcement also may have been concerned that the other shareholders would receive side benefits in a merger. Thus, the court's non-enforcement may be attributable to a rule of strict construction of share transfer restrictions. If so, the question then becomes what might justify such a rule, which is also evident in the *Rafe* case. Judge Posner opined in *Frandsen*:

> Any lingering doubts [about the application of the transfer restrictions] are dispelled by the rule that rights of first refusal are to be interpreted narrowly. This may seem to be one of those fusty "canons of construction" that invite ridicule because they have no basis and contradict each other and are advanced simply as rhetorical flourishes to embellish decisions reached on other, more practical grounds. But actually it makes some sense. The effect of a right of first refusal is to add a party to a transaction, for the right is triggered by an offer of sale, and the effect is therefore to inject the holder of the right into the sale transaction. Adding a party to a transaction increases the costs of transacting exponentially; the formula for the number of links required to connect up all the members of an n-member set is $n(n-1)/2$, meaning that, for example, increasing the number of parties to a transaction from three to four increases the number of required linkages from three to six. Certainly the claim of a right of first refusal complicated the transaction here! If all the costs of the more complicated transaction were borne by the parties, it would hardly be a matter of social concern. But some of the costs are borne by the taxpayers who support the court system, and the courts are not enthusiastic about this, and have decided not to be hospitable to such rights. *The right is enforceable but only if the contract clearly confers it.*[53]

---

that the agreement did not apply to transfers by order of court in divorce proceedings, see *Durkee v. Durkee Mower, Inc.*, 384 Mass. 628, 428 N.E.2d 139 (1981); *Castonguay v. Castonguay*, 306 N.W.2d 143 (Minn. 1981); *Witte v. Beverly Lakes Investment Co.*, 715 S.W.2d 286 (Mo. Ct. App. 1986); *Bryan-Barber Realty Inc. v. Fryar*, 461 S.E.2d 29 (N.C. App. 1995) ("[u]nder rule of strict construction, a restriction on the transfer of stock does not apply to [an interspousal transfer of shares incident to an equitable distribution] absent an express provision prohibiting such transfers"). For a holding that the agreement triggered by inheritance of stock did not apply to an *inter vivos* donation, see *In re Succession of Elise Lowe Baltazor*, 540 So. 2d 1295 (La. Ct. App. 1989).

[51]   802 F.2d 941 (7th Cir. 1986).

[52]   *Id.* at 944.

[53]   *Id.* at 946.

Do you agree with Judge Posner's rationale for the narrow interpretation of first refusal rights? To the extent such rights impose costs, is this problem worse for close corporation transfer restrictions than, for example, for first refusal rights in real property leases? Finally, even if litigation concerning this type of contract is costly, does giving a party a ground for invalidating the agreement reduce potential litigation? *Bruns v. Rennebohm Drugstores, Inc.*[54] held that "sale" in a share transfer agreement included a merger. The court criticized the strict construction rule as anachronistic, noting the special need for share transfer restrictions in close corporations.[55]

Assuming a share transfer restriction is triggered, there may be an issue as to how it operates. In *Burt v. Burt Boiler Works, Inc.*,[56] the agreement in a family-owned corporation provided that, on a stockholder's death, "the corporation" might buy the deceased's shares at book value and that, if it did not, "the remaining stockholders shall have the same privilege of purchase in proportion to their respective stock ownership in the corporation." The majority shareholder died, leaving his stock by will to his children. The other shareholders (brothers and sisters of the deceased) voted as directors to exercise the corporation's option to buy the deceased's shares. The executors of the deceased's estate then called and held a shareholders' meeting at which they removed the old board and replaced it with a new board consisting of the deceased's children, which voted to rescind the old board's exercise of the option. The court held that whether to exercise the option was properly to be decided by the majority shareholders and accordingly declared the children's actions to be valid. Assuming the majority shareholders were the appropriate decision-makers, who were the majority shareholders? Why not say that the brothers and sisters validly prevented the children from becoming majority shareholders by voting to exercise the option on behalf of the corporation? Is this what was intended in the agreement? Assuming the exercise of the option was validly rescinded, can the brothers and sisters now buy any or all of the stock of the children of the deceased shareholder? Must they buy all or none?[57]

What is the status of a party to a share transfer agreement after another party to the agreement elects to exercise its option to purchase the first party's shares? In *Stephenson v. Drever*,[58] the company's chief financial officer entered into an agreement that gave the company the right to repurchase his shares at fair market value within 90 days of his termination. Upon his termination in 1994, the CFO and the company agreed that the CFO's shares would be repurchased at their fair market value as of May 1, 1994, but the repurchase never took place because the parties failed to agree on the value of the shares as of the selected date. In May, 1995, the former CFO sued the company's major-

---

[54]   442 N.W.2d 591 (Wis. Ct. App. 1989).

[55]   For a recent case agreeing with *Frandsen* and distinguishing *Bruns*, see *Seven Springs Farm, Inc. v. Croker*, 801 A.2d 1212 (Pa. 2002) (cash-for-stock merger is "corporate act" which does not trigger right of first refusal under closely held corporation's buy-sell agreement).

[56]   360 So. 2d 327 (Ala. 1978).

[57]   For a discussion of this issue, *see Rainwater v. Milfeld*, 485 S.W.2d 831 (Tex. Civ. App. 1972).

[58]   947 P.2d 1301 (Cal. 1997).

ity shareholder for breach of fiduciary duty, alleging, among other things, that the majority shareholder had received excessive compensation. The lower courts dismissed the complaint, reasoning that the former CFO was no longer a shareholder after the company elected to repurchase his shares, but the California Supreme Court reversed on the ground that the former CFO would remain a shareholder until such time as his shares were actually repurchased. A dissenting opinion argued that the action should have been dismissed because the plaintiff shared no risk of the venture after May 1, 1994. Which position is correct?

PROBLEM

Assume, in the Judy, Kathy, and Ray situation (described in the introduction to Section 2.01) that the parties have formed a corporation. The certificate of incorporation provides for one class of common shares, divided equally among the shareholders, and also includes the following provision:

> No holder of shares of stock in this corporation shall sell, assign, transfer, pledge, hypothecate or in any other manner dispose of any of them, without first giving written notice to the corporation. If the corporation—or in case of its failure or refusal, the remaining shareholders of the corporation— shall fail to pay the holder the book value of the shares desired to be disposed of, exclusive of good will (and the determination of book value of the shares by regular accountant then and there acting for the corporation shall be final and conclusive) within 6 months from receipt of notice, then the holder may dispose of them as he shall see fit.

Consider each of the following questions separately.

(1) Ray died in a motorcycle accident. Under Ray's will, all of his property, including his interest in the food store, is to pass to his wife Annie, whom Judy and Kathy detest. They seek your advice as to whether they can purchase Ray's stock over the objections of Annie and the executor. What advice would you give? How would it affect your advice if the provision contained the following additional language: "This provision is binding on the parties' executors, heirs, and personal representatives"?[59]

(2) Ray would like to leave the business, and Judy would like to run the food store. Ray offers his stock to the corporation. Ray (who dislikes Kathy) and Judy vote as directors against exercise of the option, and Ray thereupon offers his stock to Judy, who purchases it. Kathy seeks your advice as to whether she can maintain her equal position with Judy. What advice would you give?[60]

---

[59] *See Vogel v. Melish*, 31 Ill. 2d 620, 203 N.E.2d 411 (1965).

[60] *See Lash v. Lash Furniture Co. of Barre, Inc.*, 130 Vt. 517, 296 A.2d 207 (1972).

[D] Price Provisions

Perhaps the most difficult problem in drafting share transfer agreements is providing for the price at which the stock must be purchased. Agreements on price are important for close corporation share transfer agreements because there is no market price that reflects significant information about the firm's stock. *See* Section 7.01[F]. Thus, the parties must devise alternative valuation methods. The problems of drafting a suitable price provision are dealt with in the following case and Notes.

PIEDMONT PUBLISHING CO. v. ROGERS
California Court of Appeal
193 Cal. App. 2d 171, 14 Cal. Rptr. 133 (1961)

DRAPEAU, Justice Pro Tem.

[Piedmont Publishing Company, a North Carolina corporation that owned newspapers and a radio station in Winston-Salem, and Mary Pickford Rogers, a silent film star, were rival applicants for a single television station license to be awarded in Winston-Salem. They decided to avoid a time-consuming battle and organize a new North Carolina corporation (Triangle Broadcasting Corporation) to apply for the license. When the owner of another radio station in Winston-Salem also applied for a license, Triangle agreed to pay the new applicant $20,000 over a 12-month period, for advertising Triangle's television station on the latter applicant's radio station in return for his withdrawing his application. Triangle was awarded the license to station WSJS-TV and an exclusive local contract with National Broadcasting Company. Pickford was represented by a business adviser and a lawyer who negotiated on her behalf.

[In a May 25, 1953 agreement Piedmont subscribed for 2/3 (1,000 shares) of Triangle's stock, for which it paid $100,000, while Pickford bought 1/3 (500 shares) for $50,000. The parties' agreement gave Piedmont an option to purchase Pickford's stock at the end of any one of Triangle's fiscal years 1956, 1957, 1958, and 1959 for a price to be determined by a formula to be applied by Triangle's "regularly employed independent certified public accountants." If Piedmont did not exercise its option within those years, Pickford was to have an option to purchase one-half of Piedmont's stock in Triangle. The court summarized the agreement as follows:

[The formula to determine the purchase price to be paid by Piedmont for the Pickford stock was as follows:

An amount per share of stock equal to the sum of the two following items, divided by the number of outstanding shares of the corporation:

1. An amount equal to the total book value at the beginning of any such period of Triangle's common stock (total amount of issued and outstanding common stock at par plus the amount of earned and other surplus or less the amount of deficit, if any) adjusted to reflect an annual depreciation and obsolescence charge of not over 10% against such tangible assets as have been depreciated on the books of Triangle at a higher rate; and

2. An amount determined by multiplying the average net annual profits of Triangle by five.

Five was the multiplier agreed upon for 1956, the year in which Piedmont exercised its option. If the option had been exercised in 1957 it would have been four; in 1958 three; and in 1959 two.

"Average annual net profits" was defined as follows:

> "Average annual net profits shall be determined by dividing the number of fiscal years for the period involved, as described in column (2) above, into the sum of the annual net profits during such fiscal years less the sum of the annual net losses, if any, during such fiscal years, as shown by the annual financial reports of Triangle as prepared by Triangle's regularly employed independent certified public accountants, and after provision for all taxes, including federal and state income and excess profits taxes."

[On July 20, 1956, Piedmont exercised its option and tendered the purchase price, as computed by the accountants. After attempting to have Pickford and her husband comply with the agreement, Piedmont sued for specific performance and declaratory relief. Triangle claimed that the purchase price under the formula was $85,461.00 but, because of unusual expenditures caused by relocating Triangle's transmitting station to transmit to a wider area, the Pickfords were entitled to an additional amount of $41,351.36, which Piedmont "voluntarily and gratuitously" tendered. The Pickfords claimed the sum tendered by Piedmont ($126,812.36) was inadequate. The trial court agreed with Piedmont, except it also ordered payment of $6,431.59 in additional amounts, including advertising charges for the radio station that withdrew its application.]

Did Piedmont offer a correct and adequate price for the Pickford stock?

* * *

At the trial, a witness testified that the market value of Triangle's television station when the option was exercised was $1,270,548.23. This would make the Pickfords' one-third interest in Triangle worth something more than $400,000.00. It follows that in computing the option price neither the accountants nor the trial court included good will in "total book value" as used in the formula.

Component parts of that good will would be:

    a. The fair market value of the telecasting license, which the parties worked so hard to secure.

    b. The fair market value of the television station, as its listening audience grew in numbers, and as the value of its advertising contracts consequently became greater.

    c. The fair market value of Triangle's contract with National Broadcasting Company.

* * *

When we come to the question whether or not good will must be included in book value, we find the decisions in conflict. In *Early v. Moor*, 249 Mass. 223, 144 N.E. 108, 33

A.L.R. 362, it was held that unless good will was included in an agreement for sale of corporate stock it was not included in the term book value. But in *Lindsay's Estate*, 210 Pa. 224, 59 A. 1074, 1076, the court took a contrary view. The agreement in that case speaks of the book value, and also the fair value, of the stock. The court said:

> "It is therefore manifest, as stated by the court below, that the contemplation of the parties was a fair value of the stock as a basis upon which it could be taken, and whatever contributes to such value must be taken into consideration as an element of it. It is a matter of common knowledge that, beyond the actual value of the tangible assets of a successful partnership or corporation, there is also a substantial value in the patronage enjoyed, due to the reputation of the firm or company for excellence in its business. Such value is recognized by the law as 'good will'"

In California "good will" is defined by § 14100 of our Business and Professions Code: "The good will of a business is the expectation of continued public patronage."

* * *

Let us now consider the agreement, the circumstances surrounding its making, and what happened afterwards, to see what the contracting parties intended to include in their formula to compute the option price of the stock.

They used the words "total book value" in the formula. WEBSTER'S NEW INTERNATIONAL DICTIONARY, 2d Ed. defines the word as follows:

> 1. Of, pertaining to, or referring to the whole of a thing, specified or implied, or the entire number of things concerned; not partial; as a total eclipse or wreck.
>
> 2. Comprising or constituting a whole, or the sum of all parts, items, instances, etc., entire; the total amount, revenue, output, disbursements, mileage, or membership.

So we think the conclusion necessarily follows that by adding the word "total" to "book value" the parties meant to include the value of Triangle's intangible assets,—the license to telecast, the advertising value of the station, and Triangle's contract with National Broadcasting Company.

When they provided a limitation of 10% on charges for depreciation and obsolescence in clause 1 of the formula, they used the words "against such *tangible* assets as have been depreciated on the books of Triangle at a higher rate." (Emphasis added.) This language indicates that they had in mind not only tangible but intangible assets as well.

The method of accounting points to the same conclusion. For example, take the item of $20,000 paid for advertising to the radio man who made and withdrew his application for the television license. This was charged on Triangle's books to "expense." That charge on the books, like the Kernersville charge, affected the option price, and reduced it $6,666.67.

We do not believe that gentlemen in control of Piedmont's policies, with their standing in their community and state, meant to use an accounting method that would cut down the fair value of Miss Pickford's stock, if they exercised their option. We think, rather, they intended to pay her a fair price for her participation in securing the television license, and in making the television station an outstanding success.

Sounder and safer principles of equity and fair dealing dictate the conclusion that when the contract was made every one intended to include the value of the good will of the television station, as we have defined it, in computing the price of the Pickford stock when the time came for Piedmont to exercise its option; or if Piedmont did not exercise its option, the price Miss Pickford was to pay if she exercised her option.

The Piedmont people and Miss Pickford combined their interests and applied jointly for a federal license because they feared a competing station would capture the television audience while they were engaged in a long procedure before the Federal Communications Commission on contested applications. They joined in a business enterprise that would have been worthless without an audience for the television station.

As the audience grew, the advertising worth of the station and of its earnings increased enormously. One of the primary purposes of the venture was to secure, and then to build up these elements of good will. After the station was in operation, the relocation of the Kernersville transmitter evidenced the major purpose of all concerned,—to expand their television audience, to increase the advertising value of their telecasting station, and thus to increase the value of these intangible but nonetheless real assets of good will. So when Piedmont determined to exercise its option, every one recognized the inequity of the accountants' computation of $85,561.00 as the option price. They knew it wasn't fair to include the Kernersville losses in the computation. It wasn't fair because while that expenditure increased the value of the television station, the accountants gave the Pickfords no credit for it. Instead, they charged them for the cost of moving the transmitter. They transferred value to the intangible asset of good will of the television station, and reduced book profits that would otherwise have been used to compute the option price, using the multiplier.

The "gratuitous" offer of an additional $41,357.36 emphasizes the point. Piedmont's directors' minutes recite that its officers and directors doubted whether under all the circumstances it was within the spirit of the contract of May 25, 1953, to charge these losses as expenses in the fiscal year ending April 30, 1956, and requested Ernst & Ernst to make the further computation. They struck at the effect of the Ernst & Ernst computation but failed to perceive the cause. And the way Piedmont treated this item becomes in our opinion a weighted factor for the consideration of a court of equity called upon to say what the parties meant to include in the formula.

The definition of "total book value" contained within the parenthesis in clause 1 of the formula—"(total amount of earned and other surplus or less the amount of deficit, if any)"—also supports this construction. The words "other surplus" again indicate that the parties intended to include intangible as well as tangible assets.

Mr. Borthwick testified that there was no "other surplus" shown in any of the financial statements of Triangle. Ballentine defines "surplus" as: "The term 'surplus' means the excess of assets at book value (all proper deductions having been made), over liabilities plus stated capital." (Ballentine, 1949, Ed., Par. 136, p. 184.)

Mr. Borthwick testified that in computing the option price he gave no consideration to the intangible items of value we have been talking about. He testified:

"Q. Will you state your reasons therefore?

"A. Yes, because it was not purchased. Such things, if purchased, might be added to the assets as an intangible asset, but since they were not purchased or bought or paid for, there is no requirement in generally accepted accounting principles that they be entered in the books, and in fact, quite the contrary."

* * *

But we are not dealing here with rules for accounting in corporate bookkeeping. Our problem here is to determine what the parties meant to include in their formula. That problem is one of law and fact, and is not to be determined solely upon principles of accounting. We include the value of the telecasting license, the value of the television station, and the value of the National Broadcasting Company contract in the term "total book value" as used in the formula for the purposes of this case only. We do not hold that good will must necessarily include such items in all corporate accounting.

* * *

The case is to be re-tried on the sole issue of the fair market value of the total good will of Triangle, as we have defined its three component parts, viz.:

1. The fair market value of the telecasting license.
2. The fair market value of the television station.
3. The fair market value of the contract with National Broadcasting Company.

We agree with the trial court's finding that the option price, not including the items of good will specified, was $133,243.95. To that sum shall be added one-third of the value of these three items of good will, to be ascertained by the Superior Court, and the total sum shall be adjudged to be paid to the Pickfords as a condition of specific performance. All other findings are approved and affirmed.

NOTES AND QUESTIONS

(1) **Interpreting the agreement.** Was the result consistent with the parties' agreement? Did the court have a good reason for rejecting the accountants' judgment that goodwill was not properly a part of "total book value"? If the parties did not intend to include good will, should the court nevertheless protect defendants from a bad result? Did the defendants need protecting? After becoming one of the greatest silent film stars ("The World's Sweetheart") at the age of 27, Mary Pickford helped found United Artists (along with Douglas Fairbanks, D.W. Griffith, and Charlie Chaplin), and became one of the world's richest women. She was also instrumental in forming the city of Beverly Hills. Pickford's and United Artists' "Pollyanna" was the first film ever sold on a percentage basis. Around the time of this case, Pickford reportedly owned the world's largest jewelry collection.

(2) **Valuation and the relevance of context.** This book discusses legal approaches to business valuation in several different contexts, including partnership and close corporation dissolution, appraisal rights in mergers and, here, share transfer agreements. You should understand legal valuation against the background of general economic principles of valuing productive assets discussed in Section 7.01, below. It is

important to keep in mind that policy and practical considerations associated with particular types of transactions may justify legal values that differ from market values. For example, the law may not recognize the extra value of controlling stock or discount the value of minority stock even if contrary results seem warranted from the standpoint of general principles of valuation. There are several reasons why the parties may have intended accuracy to give way to other practical concerns: to minimize costly litigation by sacrificing accuracy for clarity; to avoid the need to sell assets to pay off the exiting shareholder; or to bind the members to the firm by making exit financially difficult.

(3) **Balance sheet valuation.** One valuation method is to use a document virtually every firm prepares in the ordinary course of business—the balance sheet (*see* Section 3.02[B]). The balance sheet discloses one measure of the value of a business: the "net worth" or "book value"—that is, assets minus liabilities as of the date of the balance sheet.

Balance sheet values, however, do not generally reflect the market value of the company as of the date of the document. First, balance sheet value, as a rule, only counts up the "hard" assets of the company—the tables, chairs, land, and buildings. Intangible assets are not generally reflected. The balance sheet therefore excludes, among other things, the value of a favorable reputation among customers, a group of employees and managers who work well together, a good training program, location, and favorable relations with suppliers.

Second, the balance sheet generally values assets based on historical cost. When an asset is first acquired by a company, it is recorded on the firm's books at cost. Each year thereafter, a portion of the asset's cost is offset as an expense against revenues on the corporation's income statement. The asset side of the balance sheet shows these annual expenses as accumulated depreciation, an offset or subtraction from the cost of the asset. Through this process, net income roughly reflects the cost of the use of the asset in producing the earnings of a given year. Thus, assets as reflected on the balance sheet are merely future expenses to be "passed through" the income statement. Under this method, appreciation in the value of the asset is not reflected on the balance sheet.

Despite the defects of book value, the parties may use this approach for simplicity or clarity. After all, balance sheet "value" already exists on accounting documents the firm must prepare for other purposes. However, there is no universally accepted method of arriving at book value. Therefore, if the parties want clarity, or want to avoid accounting definitions, they must provide for the accounting treatment of specific items in their agreement. Consider, for example, the provision in the *Piedmont* agreement for depreciation and obsolescence charges.

(4) **Definitions of goodwill.** The intangible value of the business that is excluded by the balance sheet is often referred to as "goodwill." Goodwill is also sometimes defined very generally as the difference between the net worth and actual value of the business. Under this definition, goodwill includes not only all value that is too intangible to be recorded, but also the difference between the depreciated historical cost and

current value of tangible assets. Accountants generally define goodwill more narrowly as the unusual earning power of the business—that is, the difference between the typical productivity of the tangible and quantifiable intangible assets of the business and that of the particular business (*see* Brown, Section 4.04[D]). Under the accounting definition of goodwill, there is often a question as to what value is attributable to assets that are intangible but quantifiable and what constitutes the "extra" asset of goodwill. For example, should favorable relationships with customers be valued separately as a trade name or placed in the "extra" earning power category? How does the legal definition of goodwill applied in *Piedmont* fit with the above discussion?

(5) **Capitalized earnings.** Another way to measure the entire value of the firm, including intangible value, is by capitalizing earnings. Under this method, the firm's historical earnings, typically averaged over several previous years, are used as an approximation of future earnings. A "capitalizer" is then applied to these earnings to determine the value of the company. Thus, $V = C \times e$, where V is the value of the stock, C is the capitalizer, and e is the earnings from the investment.

Earnings capitalization can be seen as a kind of rough proxy for risk and return elements of market valuation. (These concepts are discussed in more detail below in § 7.01.) For example, a low risk associated with the continuation of a particular level of earnings will be reflected in a high capitalizer, which means low risk investments will be valued more highly than high risk investments. While this approach may be more accurate than using book value, it is subject to a great deal of uncertainty in application. There will be questions as to the amount of earnings to be capitalized and as to what the capitalizing figure should be.

With respect to the amount of earnings, consider the questions raised in *Piedmont* concerning the treatment of the cost of moving the transmitter and for advertising on the radio station that withdrew its application. To begin with, it is unclear if these costs should be viewed as expenses in the current year, or as the purchase price for durable assets and applied against revenues in future years and, if the latter, how this should be done. In general, if a company erects a building for a $1 million, incurs $500,000 of other expenses, and earns revenues of $1 million during a given period, this clearly does not mean that it has lost $500,000 because although the company has spent money for the building, it still has the building. The building's cost is allocated as expenses over future periods (that is, "depreciated"). There are further questions as to, for example, how quickly the building should be depreciated, and whether the depreciation be done evenly (that is, "straight line") or bunched at the beginning (*i.e.*, "accelerated").

These and many other matters are dealt with under fairly loose accounting conventions that may produce accounting earnings that are different from economic cash flows and that are subject to manipulation. Thus, in the WorldCom accounting scandal in 2002, expenses apparently were transformed willy-nilly into assets.

The accountants in *Piedmont* endorsed the view that moving the transmitter created an asset. (Can you see why?) Once the "asset" view is accepted, there was a second question as to the appropriate period over which the expenses should be amortized or depreciated (*i.e.*, taken as expenses against revenues). In *Piedmont*, for example, the court changed the amortization period for the advertising expense from two to five years.

A second source of ambiguity in capitalized earnings valuation is the determination of the capitalizer. The capitalizer is often borrowed from a "comparable" public company, or company whose value was recently determined in an arms' length transaction. There are always questions about the degree of comparability. Consider, for example, the valuation of professional sports teams. In 1986, a planned public offering for the Boston Celtics basketball team placed the value of the team at $130 million on $5.4 million in profit for the previous year, for a capitalizer of about 25. Meanwhile, a bid had been made for 95% of the New York Mets for $80 million on $19.5 in revenue for the previous year, a capitalizer of about 4.[61]

Finally, note how the *Piedmont* agreement combined capitalization of earnings with book value. In light of that provision, was the court justified in expanding "total book value" to include goodwill?

(6) **Offer price.** If the transfer agreement is triggered by a prospective sale of the stock, the parties may decide to let the offer price control. Under this approach, the parties must ensure that the offer is *bona fide* and not concocted for purposes of triggering a buyout.

(7) **Appraised value.** The parties may simply give up trying to decide on a specific formula and throw the entire matter into the hands of an appraiser. In that case, they must agree on the method of selecting the appraiser, and determine the guidelines the appraiser must apply.

[E] Statutory Close Corporation Provisions

Some statutes provide for standard form share transfer agreements. See the following provisions from the Maryland Act.

Maryland Code Annotated
Corporations and Associations

§ 4-503. Restrictions on transfer of stock
(a) "Transfer" Defined.
(1) In this section, "transfer" means the transfer of any interest in the stock of a close corporation, except:
(i) A transfer by operation of law to a personal representative, trustee in bankruptcy, receiver, guardian, or similar legal representative;

---

[61] *See* Wong, *Boston Celtics Set Price for 40% Stake at over $50 Million*, WALL ST. J., Oct. 29, 1986.

(ii) The acquisition of a lien or power of sale by an attachment, levy, or similar procedure; or

(iii) The creation or assignment of a security interest.

(2) A foreclosure sale or other transfer by a person who acquired his interest or power in a transaction described in paragraph (1) of this sub-section is a transfer subject to all the provisions of this section. For purposes of the transfer, the person effecting the foreclosure sale or other transfer shall be treated as and have the rights of a holder of the stock under this section and § 4-602(b) of this title.

(b) Enumeration of Restrictions. A transfer of the stock of a close corporation is invalid unless:

(1) Every stockholder of the corporation consents to the transfer in writing within the 90 days before the date of the transfer; or

(2) The transfer is made under a provision of a unanimous stockholders' agreement permitting the transfer to the corporation or to or in trust for the principal benefit of:

(i) One or more of the stockholders or security holders of the corporation or their wives, children, or grandchildren; or

(ii) One or more persons named in the agreement.

§ 4-602. Involuntary dissolution

* * *

(b) Dissolution by Stockholder Desiring to Transfer Stock.

(1) Unless a unanimous stockholders' agreement provides otherwise, a stockholder of a close corporation has the right to require dissolution of the corporation if:

(i) The stockholder made a written request for consent to a proposed bona fide transfer of his stock in accordance with the provisions of § 4-503(b)(1) of this title, specifying the proposed transferee and the consideration, and the consent was not received by him within 30 days after the date of the request; or

(ii) Another party to a unanimous stockholders' agreement defaulted in an obligation, set forth in or arising under the agreement, to purchase or cause to be purchased stock of the stockholder, and the default was not remedied within 30 days after the date for performance of the obligation.

(2) A petition for dissolution under this subsection shall be filed within 60 days after the date of the request or the default, as the case may be.

* * *

§ 4-603. Avoidance of dissolution by purchase of petitioner's stock

(a) Stockholder's Right to Avoid Dissolution. Any one or more stockholders who desire to continue the business of a close corporation may avoid the dissolution of the corporation or the appointment of a receiver by electing to purchase the stock owned by the petitioner at a price equal to its fair value.

(b) Court to Determine Fair Value of Stock. (1) If a stockholder who makes the election is unable to reach an agreement with the petitioner as to the fair value of the stock, then, if the electing stockholder gives bond or other security sufficient to assure payment to the petitioner of the fair value of the stock, the court shall stay the proceeding and determine the fair value of the stock.

* * *

QUESTIONS

(1) **Standard forms.** Are the Maryland provisions a suitable standard form? In other words, do you suppose a substantial proportion of close corporations would be likely to adopt these provisions without substantial modification?

(2) **Customizing statutory provisions.** Are the restrictions in the Maryland statute on customized share transfer provisions appropriate? In particular, why shouldn't the parties to a close corporation be able to agree in advance to permit transfers other than to the parties listed in § 4-503(b)(2)?

§ 5.05 Dissolution, Buyout, and Related Remedies in the Close Corporation

Previous Sections have shown how courts and legislatures increasingly have allowed the parties to close corporations to agree to a partnership-like management structure within the corporate framework. Nevertheless, standard corporation statutes are designed for publicly held, centrally managed firms. So, unless the parties agree otherwise, the firm can be dissolved only by a majority vote of the board of directors followed by a majority vote of the shareholders (*see* Del. G.C.L. § 275). Unlike partners, corporate minority shareholders have no absolute power to dissolve the corporation at will and cash out of the business.

All of this means that shareholders who form a close corporation under standard form corporate statutory provisions may find that they have created a monster unless they have been prescient enough to foresee difficulties and disagreements. Although they may have contemplated co-equal partner-like management, a majority group may be able to seize power and, for example, fire shareholder-employees and cut them off from ongoing participation in the finances and management of the business. Minority shareholders may find themselves bound to the firm by share transfer restrictions or by the lack of a market for their shares. Or equal factions may find themselves locked in bitter disagreement but without partners' dissolution escape valve.

Legislatures and courts have responded to close corporation shareholders' predicament by formulating special close corporation remedies, particularly dissolution and buyout. Unlike the rules discussed in the preceding chapters on close corporations, these are not simply rules that let the parties vary the corporate standard form by agreement. Rather, these are rules that often are applied to close corporations even if the parties have not agreed to them, and perhaps even if they have agreed that these rules should not apply.[62] In evaluating such rules, it is natural to think of close corporations as partnerships under a corporate facade. From this standpoint, empowering the minority to dissolve the corporation simply completes the parties' partnership-like arrangement by adding partnership-like dissolution-at-will.

On the other hand, the parties' decision to incorporate may be an important clue to their intent. Given the significant costs of dissolution, perhaps the courts should not assume too readily from the fact that close corporation shareholders have adopted some partnership-like features that they wanted the whole package. Indeed, as this Section makes clear, close corporations are not as dissolvable as partnerships.

Subsections [A] through [C] discuss dissolution for deadlock and oppression under statutory provisions. Subsections [D] and [E] then discuss remedies, apart from these statutes, that courts have developed for close corporations.

[A] Overview of Statutory Provisions

The following New York statutory provisions are examples of those dealing with judicial dissolution, and are interpreted in the cases in subsections [B] and [C]. For additional provisions, see MBCA §§ 14.30(2) and 14.34. Contrast Delaware G.C.L. § 273, which provides for involuntary dissolution only in limited situations.

NEW YORK BUSINESS CORPORATION LAW

§ 1104. Petition in case of deadlock among directors or shareholders

(a) Except as otherwise provided in the certificate of incorporation under section 613 (Limitations on right to vote), the holders of one-half of all outstanding shares of a corporation entitled to vote in an election of directors may present a petition for dissolution on one or more of the following grounds:.

(1) That the directors are so divided respecting the management of the corporation's affairs that the votes required for action by the board cannot be obtained.

(2) That the shareholders are so divided that the votes required for the election of directors cannot be obtained.

(3) That there is internal dissension and two or more factions of shareholders are so divided that dissolution would be beneficial to the shareholders.

(b) If the certificate of incorporation provides that the proportion of votes required for action by the board, or the proportion of votes of shareholders required for election

---

[62] See, e.g., In re Validation Review Assocs., Inc., 646 N.Y.S.2d 149 (App. Div. 1996) (refusing to enforce provision in shareholders' agreement that waived statutory and common law right to petition for judicial dissolution of closely held corporation, even though there is "no absolute prohibition against the parties entering into some form of agreement as to how the dissolution of a closely held corporation might be effected"); see also In re Pace Photographers, Ltd., discussed in Note 7 following Gardstein v. Kemp & Beatley, in Section 5.05[C], below.

of directors, shall be greater than that otherwise required by this chapter, such a petition may be presented by the holders of more than one-third of all outstanding shares entitled to vote on non-judicial dissolution under section 1001 (Authorization of dissolution).

(c) Notwithstanding any provision in the certificate of incorporation, any holder of shares entitled to vote at an election of directors of a corporation, may present a petition for its dissolution on the ground that the shareholders are so divided that they have failed, for a period which includes at least two consecutive annual meeting dates, to elect successors to directors whose terms have expired or would have expired upon the election and qualification of their successors.

§ 1104-a. Petition for judicial dissolution under special circumstances

(a) The holders of twenty percent or more of all outstanding shares of a corporation, other than a corporation registered as an investment company under an act of congress entitled "Investment Company Act of 1940", no shares of which are listed on a national securities exchange or regularly quoted in an over-the-counter market by one or more members of a national or an affiliated securities association, who are entitled to vote in an election of directors may present a petition of dissolution on one or more of the following grounds:

(1) The directors or those in control of the corporation have been guilty of illegal, fraudulent or oppressive actions toward the complaining shareholders;

(2) The property or assets of the corporation are being looted, wasted, or diverted for non-corporate purposes by its directors, officers or those in control of the corporation.

(b) The court, in determining whether to proceed with involuntary dissolution pursuant to this section, shall take into account:

(1) Whether liquidation of the corporation is the only feasible means whereby the petitioners may reasonably expect to obtain a fair return on their investment; and.

(2) Whether liquidation of the corporation is reasonably necessary for the protection of the rights and interests of any substantial number of shareholders or of the petitioners.

* * *

§ 1111. Judgment or final order of dissolution

(a) In an action or special proceeding under this article if, in the court's discretion, it shall appear that the corporation should be dissolved, it shall make a judgment or final order dissolving the corporation.

(b) In making its decision, the court shall take into consideration the following criteria:

(1) In an action brought by the attorney-general, the interest of the public is of paramount importance.

(2) In a special proceeding brought by directors or shareholders, the benefit to the shareholders of a dissolution is of paramount importance.

(3) In a special proceeding brought under section 1104 (Petition in case of deadlock among directors or shareholders) or section 1104-a (Petition for judicial disso-

lution under special circumstances) dissolution is not to be denied merely because it is found that the corporate business has been or could be conducted at a profit.

(c) If the judgment or final order shall provide for a dissolution of the corporation, the court may, in its discretion, provide therein for the distribution of the property of the corporation to those entitled thereto according to their respective rights.

(d) The clerk of the court or such other person as the court may direct shall transmit certified copies of the judgment or final order of dissolution to the department of state and to the clerk of the county in which the office of the corporation was located at the date of the judgment or order. Upon filing by the department of state, the corporation shall be dissolved.

(e) The corporation shall promptly thereafter transmit a certified copy of the judgment or final order to the clerk of each other county in which its certificate of incorporation was filed.

§ 1118. Purchase of petitioner's shares; valuation

(a) In any proceeding brought pursuant to section 1104-a of this chapter, any other shareholder or shareholders or the corporation may, at any time within ninety days after the filing of such petition or at such later time as the court in its discretion may allow, elect to purchase the shares owned by the petitioners at their fair value and upon such terms and conditions as may be approved by the court . . . .

(b) If one or more shareholders or the corporation elect to purchase the shares owned by the petitioner but are unable to agree with the petitioner upon the fair value of such shares, the court, upon the application of such prospective purchaser or purchasers, may stay the proceedings brought pursuant to section 1104-a of this chapter and determine the fair value of the petitioner's shares as of the day prior to the date on which such petition was filed, exclusive of any element of value arising from such filing . . . .

[1] The Scope of Judicial Power

An important question raised by statutes like the New York and MBCA provisions is what discretion the court has in ordering remedies. Sometimes the statute makes it clear that the court has significant power. Sometimes the courts have gone far without statutory authorization. Some specific issues are discussed in this subsection.

A court may have inherent equitable power to order dissolution in situations not covered by the applicable statute. In *Leibert v. Clapp*,[63] the court held that dissolution could be granted for oppressive conduct by the majority even though the statute provided for dissolution only upon deadlock. The same court later took a narrow view of its inherent power to order dissolution.[64] More recently, a lower New York court ordered "equitable" dissolution on the petition of a plaintiff who lacked standing even under the

---

[63]   13 N.Y.2d 313, 247 N.Y.S.2d 102, 196 N.E.2d 540 (1963).

[64]   *See Kruger v. Gerth*, 16 N.Y.2d 802, 263 N.Y.S.2d 1, 210 N.E.2d 355 (1965).

expanded New York statute.[65] On the other hand, the Delaware supreme court has refused to establish special remedies for non-statutory close corporations, reasoning that the shareholders can contract for such remedies if they want them.

Some statutes authorize remedies instead of dissolution, particularly including buyout, but also including enjoining or ordering particular acts, if the grounds for statutory dissolution are present.[66] Others allow these remedies even without a showing of the statutory grounds for dissolution.[67] Delaware G.C.L. §§ 226, 352, and 353 authorize appointment of provisional directors and custodians *instead* of dissolution (*see Hoban*, discussed in Note 2 following *Weiss v. Gordon*, below).

Most courts have held that they have the power to order such relief even if not specifically authorized by statute. An often-cited case espousing an expansive view of judicial power, *Baker v. Commercial Body Builders, Inc.*,[68] held that the court's options included, among other remedies, affirmative relief, appointment of a receiver, and an order that the majority buy out the minority's stock. Some courts have ordered relief short of dissolution where the statutory grounds for dissolution were not shown.[69] In *Smith v. Atlantic Properties, Inc.*,[70] the lower court had retained jurisdiction for five years in order to supervise the dividends paid by the corporation, and the appellate court indicated that it might instead order the payment of specified dividends. But a Virginia court refused to order payment of a dividend or other affirmative relief under a statute that permitted only dissolution or the appointment of a custodian, although the custodian could have granted the same relief.[71]

---

[65] *See Lewis v. Jones*, 107 A.D.2d 931, 483 N.Y.S.2d 868 (1985).

[66] *See, e.g.,* Ill. Rev. Stat. ch. 32, ¶ 12.56 (2002); Mich. Comp. Laws Ann. § 450.1489 (2002); *see also* N.J. Stat. Ann. 14A:12-7 (2002). *Muellenberg v. Bikon Corp.*, 669 A.2d 1382 (N.J. 1996), interpreted the New Jersey statute to permit the courts not only to order majority shareholders to buy out minority shareholders, but also to order minority shareholders to buy out majority shareholders. Although the court said that a "minority buyout of the majority is an uncommon remedy," it found it appropriate under the facts, since the minority shareholder was the only shareholder who worked full time for the company, the company had been the minority shareholder's only source of income for over 10 years, and the minority shareholder was primarily responsible for developing most of the company's contacts.

[67] *See* S.C. Code Ann. § 33-14-310 (2002). For a recent case making use of this power, see *Kreischer v. Kerrison Dry Goods Company*, 172 F.3d 863 (4th Cir. 1999) (ordering the majority shareholder to buy out the minority even though the majority shareholder was not guilty of oppressive, illegal, or fraudulent conduct).

[68] 264 Or. 614, 507 P.2d 387 (1973).

[69] *See Gimpel v. Bolstein*, 125 Misc. 2d 45, 477 N.Y.S.2d 1014 (1984); *see also Schirmer v. Bear*, 672 N.E.2d 1171, 1176 (Ill. 1996) ("plaintiff need not prove that the defendant's wrongdoing was so severe that it would justify dissolving the corporation" when he seeks a buyout under Ill. Rev. Stat. ch. 32, ¶ 12.55). *But see Matter of Farega Realty Corp.*, 132 A.D.2d 797, 517 N.Y.S.2d 610 (1987) (*contra*). In *Brenner v. Berkowitz*, 134 N.J. 488, 634 A.2d 1019 (1993), the court held that it could compel an involuntary buyout, although the statute literally authorizes only voluntary purchases. However, the trial court's injunction against future misconduct and reinstatement of minority shareholder as director were sufficient under the circumstances.

[70] 422 N.E.2d 798 (Mass. App. Ct. 1981).

[71] *White v. Perkins*, 213 Va. 129, 189 S.E.2d 315 (1972).

The statute may or may not empower the court not to order any relief where the statutory grounds are present.[72] Some statutes, including N.Y. Bus. Corp. L. §§ 1104-a(b) and 1111(a), make it clear that the court must exercise discretion as to whether to dissolve.

[2] Policy Issues

To what extent *should* courts and legislatures provide for dissolution or other relief in closely held firms? The minority's power to dissolve the business entails costs and benefits similar to those in the partnership context (*see* Section 4.04[B]). On the benefit side, dissolution gives the members a right of exit to replace the efficient market available to owners of publicly held firms—one that is particularly important in light of the high risk of deadlock occasioned by direct management by passive owners. On the cost side, among other things, the power to dissolve facilitates opportunistic conduct by the dissolving owner, as in *Page v. Page* (Section 4.04[B]). Moreover, permitting dissolution or other relief on such vague grounds as "oppression" can provoke costly litigation.

One might conclude that, because the parties have entered into a closely held firm with partnership-like attributes, it follows that they would want the partnership-like attribute of easy dissolution. However, as **Easterbrook & Fischel** caution, that is not necessarily the case. The benefits of dissolution (that is, the costs of illiquidity) are somewhat lower in the corporation because corporate shareholders who have limited liability do not need to have the firm liquidated and debts paid off in order to be relieved of further exposure to personal liability (unless, of course, they have given personal guarantees). Thus, the risk of opportunistic conduct by dissolving owners may outweigh the benefit of dissolution more often in corporations than in partnerships. **Rock & Wachter** reach a similar conclusion, focusing on the risk of opportunism by insiders in closely held venture capital firms whose early departure could destroy the value of the firm. In any event, the important point is that the parties have chosen the corporate form. They may have done so not merely for tax advantages or limited liability, but at least partly in order to avoid the easy dissolution of partnership.

The issue of whether the dissolution remedy applies to close corporations could, of course, be settled by contract. The parties to close corporations could contract for easy dissolution by, for example, electing to be covered by a standard form statute that provides for this remedy. For example, Del. G.C.L. § 355 permits the certificate of incorporation of any close corporation to grant any stockholder, or the holders of any specified number or percentage of shares, an option to have the corporation dissolved at will or upon the occurrence of any specified event or contingency.[73] Conversely, if the

---

[72]   *Compare Strong v. Fromm Laboratories, Inc.*, 273 Wis. 159, 77 N.W.2d 389 (1956) (court compelled to order dissolution of deadlocked corporation under § 97 of the Model Act), *with Jackson v. Nicholai-Neppach Co.*, 219 Or. 560, 348 P.2d 9 (1959) (dissolution not compelled).

[73]   However, as discussed more fully below (Note 5 following *Gardstein v. Kemp & Beatley* in Section 5.05[C], below), close corporation dissolution provisions are mandatory under some statutes.

applicable statute does not provide for dissolution, or provides only for dissolution and not for other remedies, a court that orders non-statutory relief might in effect be altering contracts made in light of the statute.

If dissolution is too drastic, perhaps the court should order buyout. But since a plaintiff may be able to use a buyout right opportunistically, as where the plaintiff owns crucial assets or has critical skills, as in *Page* or the venture capital situation, the availability of this alternative does not eliminate the potential costs of dissolution. *See* **Chayes**, approving the court's refusal to dissolve a deadlocked business in the famous case of *In re Radom & Neidorff, Inc.*[74] N.Y. Bus. Corp. L. § 1118 quoted above and Model Act § 14.34 deal with this problem by allowing defendants to buy the plaintiff's interest at a judicially determined "fair value."[75] But this, too, may not be a complete solution given the difficulties of valuing close corporation stock.

Even without a judicial or statutory buyout right, owners who wish to continue the business in the face of a petition for dissolution can always attempt to settle the litigation by negotiating for a buyout of the plaintiff. **Hetherington & Dooley**'s survey of reported dissolution cases between 1960 and 1976 reports that the likely result of a dissolution order in the case of an economically viable business is continuation through purchase by one or more of the members or a third party.

As noted above, the court might try to keep the parties together by ordering specific relief, or installing a custodian or provisional director. The custodian takes charge of the corporation, usually supplanting the existing board of directors, while the provisional director is simply added to the existing board. Both the custodian and provisional director remedies have the unfortunate effect of wresting control from the original owner-managers and placing it in those who may not have the right incentives and information to make the proper management decisions. Installing a custodian or provisional director may even thwart governance devices the parties have installed to maximize management efficiency. As a result, the costs of preserving the corporate entity may be high.

[3] Drafting and Planning to Avoid Problems

Many of the problems in the cases below might have been avoided by better planning and drafting at the outset of the relationship. Indeed, the courts in the dissolution and buyout cases often are trying to supply terms the parties should have thought of themselves. Consider the following devices, among others:

(a) *Shareholder management arrangements* (*see* Sections 5.02 and 5.03).

(b) *Share transfer agreements* (*see* Section 5.04) *or partnership-type dissolution provisions* (*see* Del. G.C.L. § 355). Share transfer agreements

---

[74]   307 N.Y. 1, 119 N.E.2d 563 (1954).

[75]   This is available only in cases brought under § 1104-a, and therefore not where dissolution is brought for deadlock. *See Greer v. Greer*, 124 A.D.2d 707, 508 N.Y.S.2d 217 (1986).

that provide for buyouts under specific circumstances are particularly useful in eliminating family members who enter the corporation through inheritance or divorce and whose interests differ from those whose stock they now own. These agreements also guard against unwanted shifts in control among the original shareholders. As noted above, Delaware G.C.L. § 355 allows shareholders of close corporations to provide for partnership-type dissolution provisions in their certificate of incorporation.

(c) *Arbitration*. The courts were initially hostile to this device on the corporate law ground that the arbitrator usurped the proper role of the board of directors. More liberal legislation and court decisions in some jurisdictions have broadened the possible uses of agreements to arbitrate.[76] Now the main question is whether agreements to arbitrate are of practical value. On the benefit side, arbitrators have great flexibility in terms of remedies, and the parties can select arbitrators who will resolve problems along common sense rather than legal lines. On the other hand, arbitration may only prolong a bad situation where the parties have reached a fundamental parting of the ways.

In light of the foregoing discussion, consider these questions in connection with the cases in the following sections: (1) What is the role of the applicable statutory dissolution provisions? (2) What is the best solution to the parties' problems from a policy standpoint? Consider, in this regard, the role of any actual agreements the parties have made. (3) How might the parties' problems have been avoided by better drafting?

REFERENCES

Ayres, *Judging Close Corporations,* 70 WASH. U. L.Q. 365 (1992).

Chayes, *Madame Wagner and the Close Corporation,* 73 HARV. L. REV. 1532 (1960).

Easterbrook & Fischel, THE ECONOMIC STRUCTURE OF CORPORATE LAW, Ch. 9 (1991).

Hetherington & Dooley, *Illiquidity and Exploitation: A Proposed Statutory Solution to the Remaining Close Corporation Problem,* 63 VA. L. REV. 1 (1977).

O'Kelley, *Filling Gaps in the Close Corporation Contract: A Transaction Cost Analysis,* 87 NW. U. L. REV. 216 (1992).

Rock & Wachter, *Waiting for the Omelet to Set: Match-Specific Assets and Minority Oppression in Close Corporations,* 24 J. CORP. L. 913 (1999).

---

[76] *See, e.g., Petition of Levitt,* 109A.D.2d 502, 492 N.Y.S.2d 736 (1985); *Application of Vogel,* 25 A.D.2d 212, 268 N.Y.S.2d 237 (1966), *aff'd,* 19 N.Y.2d 589, 278 N.Y.S.2d 236, 224 N.E.2d 738 (1967).

[B] Deadlock

This subsection discusses judicial enforcement of statutory remedies for dead-lock in close corporations.

WEISS v. GORDON
New York Supreme Court, Appellate Division
32 A.D.2d 279, 301 N.Y.S.2d 839 (1969)

[The trial court summarily ordered dissolution of a two-shareholder corporation.]

STEUER, Justice.

The first objection to the order is that no dissolution can be ordered in any event without a hearing. The statutory proceeding for a dissolution (Business Corporation Law Section 1104 *et seq.*) does provide for a hearing but this provision is not jurisdictional. It could not be maintained that a dissolution otherwise properly granted was a nullity because there was no hearing. A hearing is only required where there is some contested issue deter-minative of the validity of the application. . . . Absent such an issue there is nothing in the nature of the proceeding that distinguishes it from any other litigated proceeding in this respect.

Appellant further contends that there is such an issue, namely, the good faith of the petitioner. His claim in this respect is that dissolution is sought to squeeze him out of the business for an inadequate consideration. While his averments do show that petitioner had embarked on a course of conduct which did have that end in view, the institution of this pro-ceeding precludes it. Whatever respondent's share of the business is, he will get it. Instead of forcing respondent to accept an inadequate consideration for his share of the business, petitioner now applies to the court to make the distribution.

However, this is not the complete answer to appellant's contention in regard to good faith. He contends that the real reason why petitioner seeks a dissolution is that he does not wish to continue in business with respondent. If this constitutes bad faith, he has undoubt-edly raised an issue.

We do not believe it does. This is a service corporation. The services for the clients are performed by the two parties to this proceeding. It is not disputed that they are not working together. The Board of Directors admittedly does not function because there is either a deadlock or by purposeful absence a quorum cannot meet. No significant corporate action is possible. There has been a consequent decrease in profits and loss of personnel. Regard-less of which of the parties is ultimately responsible, that is the situation.

In the instance of the close corporation, both the legislature and the courts have come closer to treating the situation as it exists in fact rather than in theory. The enactment of sec-tion 1111(b)(3), providing that in cases of deadlock among directors and shareholders dis-solution should not "be denied merely because it is found that the corporate business has been or could be conducted at a profit" reflects that change. The earlier thinking stressed the distinction between the corporation as an entity and the shareholders, and as long as the for-mer could continue to function profitably the relationship between the shareholders was of no moment (*cf. Matter of Radom & Neidorff, Inc.*, 307 N.Y. 1, 119 N.E.2d 563). It is being increasingly realized that the relationship between the stockholders in a close corporation vis-a-vis each other in practice closely approximates the relationship between partners. . . . As a consequence, when a point is reached where the shareholders who are actively conducting the business of the corporation cannot agree, it becomes in the best interests of those shareholders to order a dissolution. . . . The so-called issue here presented is not whether this condition exists but rather why it exists. That being of no relevance, there is no issue.

As noted, the order provides that the receiver is charged with the duty of formulating a plan of dissolution and distribution of assets, which plan shall be subject to the final approval of the court.

* * *

McCivern, Justice (dissenting).

On the most basic grounds, I disagree with the majority. We are dealing with a statutory proceeding, principally involving Sections 1104 and 1109 of the Business Corporation Law. Pursuant to these sections, the court may entertain the petition or dismiss it. It can do no other. *See Matter of Radom & Neidorff, Inc.*, 307 N.Y. 1, 119 N.E.2d 563, particularly the analysis of predecessor statutes contained in the dissenting opinion of then Judge, now Chief Judge Fuld. In contravention of the statutes, in the instant case, a judicial thunderbolt has sundered the corporation. I can find no case in the Court of Appeals or in any Appellate Division that would sanction such sudden and unprovided for death without a preliminary hearing. The statute, Section 1109, does not permit it. A hearing is mandated.

* * *

In my judgment, the respondent herein has showed more than enough to command a hearing and an opportunity to present his proof, particularly regarding his claim that petitioner, in bad faith, is attempting to squeeze him out of a profitable venture without fair compensation. We cannot ignore the contention that petitioner's own accountant evaluated the enterprise as having a book value alone of approximately $300,000, less only some undetermined amount which would be required for payment of income taxes, yet petitioner's apparently best offer to the respondent is $60,000. This, notwithstanding the alleged suggestion by petitioner's attorney that respondent be offered a $250,000 "package." Again, according to the cases, unless the petitioner acts in good faith, or if his bald purpose is to squeeze out his erstwhile partner without fair compensation, the courts will turn him back. . . .

This petitioner has already been rejected thrice by various Special Terms, the last time in an opinion that explicitly impugned his good faith. In the first instance, Special Term (Mr. Justice Flynn) nullified a Board of Directors meeting convoked by petitioner, directed a restoration of funds improperly diverted, and made permanent a restraint against petitioner and others, preventing them from interference with respondent's rights and privileges. In the second instance, Special Term (Mr. Justice Geller) enjoined petitioner and one Aczel from any attempts to vote the non-voting stock of the latter. In the third instance, Special Term (Mr. Justice Spector) dismissed an action ostensibly brought by Aczel, as nominal plaintiff but apparently inspired by petitioner, to compel respondent to attend a specially noticed Directors' meeting, one of whose purposes was to consider the removal of respondent and

reduction of the quorum required for meetings. Although the dismissal of the latter proceeding against respondent was on the ground he had not been validly served, the court also
observed "serious doubts are raised with respect to the bona fides of plaintiff's application."

Accordingly, in my view, the granting of an order of dissolution without the holding
of the required statutory hearing was erroneous, as was the appointment of a Receiver,
which was premature and unwarranted. . . . I would reverse the order appealed from and
remand the matter for a hearing, pursuant to the provisions of Section 1109, Business Corporation Law.

NOTES AND QUESTIONS

(1) **Alternatives to dissolution for deadlock.** Suppose at a hearing the defendant
in *Weiss* proved that a dissolution would permit plaintiff to appropriate business assets.
Should the court refuse to order dissolution? Alternatively, should it (a) dissolve but
award damages for breach of fiduciary duty[77] or (b) order an alternative remedy short
of dissolution, such as the appointment of a custodian, assuming the statute permits it?
In *Wollman v. Littman*,[78] a faction holding 50% of the stock sued for dissolution under
the New York statute, claiming that dissension precluded effective management. The
Appellate Division refused to summarily order dissolution, noting that since the plaintiffs controlled the source of the product that was sold by the corporation, dissolution
would permit the plaintiff faction to squeeze out the defendants.[79]

(2) **Appointment of a custodian.** Delaware has restricted the dissolution remedy
to cases where shareholders of close corporations have expressly opted for that remedy
under Del. G.C.L. § 355. The remedy for deadlock is otherwise limited to the appointment of a custodian (*see* Del. G.C.L. § 226) or, in the case of a statutory close corporation, a provisional director (*see* Del. G.C.L. §§ 352 and 353). In *Hoban v. Dardanella
Electric Corporation*,[80] Hoban and Rensberger each owned 50% of the firm's stock

---

[77] *See In re Security Finance Co.*, 49 Cal. 2d 370, 317 P.2d 1 (1957), holding that a power to voluntarily dissolve granted by statute to 50% or more holders was subject to a fiduciary duty on the part of the party seeking dissolution.

[78] 35 A.D.2d 935, 316 N.Y.S.2d 526 (1970).

[79] To the same effect, see *In re Arthur Treacher's Fish & Chips*, 386 A.2d 1162 (Del. Ch. 1978) (holding, in an
action for dissolution of a two-shareholder joint venture under Delaware G.C.L. § 273, that dissolution was not compelled and that the court would hear evidence on respondent's claim that petitioner was conspiring to remove him from
the business); *Callier v. Callier*, 61 Ill. App. 3d 1011, 278 N.E.2d 405 (1978) (reversing a decree of dissolution under
a provision similar to N.Y. Bus. Corp. Law § 1104, noting that dissolution would allow plaintiff, who had established a
successor corporation, to "siphon off the going concern value" of the corporation). *In re McKinney-Ringham Corp.*, 1998
Del. Ch. LEXIS 34, 1998 WL 118035 (Del. Ch. 1998), held that, in an action for dissolution of a two-shareholder joint
venture under Delaware G.C.L. § 273, the court would exercise its "narrow" discretion to refuse to dissolve the corporation only when "the actual foundation for [the] action is something other than a genuine inability to agree upon the
desirability of discontinuing [the] joint venture." The court then determined that allegations that the petitioner "'brought
the petition in bad faith as part of a scheme to marginalize [Respondent]' and to give greater control over [the corpora-
tion] to Petitioner's sons" were irrelevant so long as "the facts support[ed] a genuine dispute over the desirability of continuing the business enterprise as a joint venture."

[80] 9 DEL. J. CORP. L. 470 (Del. Ch. 1984).

and each had a position on the corporation's two-member board of directors. To force Hoban to address certain concerns over how the business was being operated, Rensberger refused to vote as a director to authorize a new banking arrangement that would increase the corporation's credit line, decrease its interest rate, and provide funds necessary to meet certain future obligations. The court granted Hoban's petition for a custodian under the director deadlock provisions of Del. G.C.L. § 226(a)(2), finding that Hoban had successfully shown a division in the board of directors that could not be cured by shareholder action and that threatened the corporation with irreparable injury (*i.e.*, the inability of the 145-employee corporation to operate when the current banking arrangement expired). Why do you suppose "irreparable injury" must be shown in cases of director deadlock under Del. G.C.L. § 226(a)(2), but not where the shareholders are deadlocked under § 226(a)(1)? *See Guiricich v. Emtrol Corp.*[81]

PROBLEM

Drug Corporation is owned equally by two factions. One faction originally consisted of A, who was the chief executive of the corporation, and the other consisted of the B family, who were also active in the business. The board of directors originally included the two members of the B family, A, and A's personal attorney, C, to whom A had assigned one share. The bylaws of the corporation provide that the board is to consist of four persons and that, if a vacancy occurs on the board, the shareholders must meet and select another director, until which time the board may transact no other business. The stock is subject to a restriction that the other shareholders are to have a first option to purchase it at book value if a shareholder wishes to sell. Assume there are no other relevant provisions in the certificate of incorporation or bylaws.

A dies, leaving his shares by will in trust to his niece, D, who had no previous business experience. C is trustee and, as such, votes all of A's stock. After A's death, the two factions failed for two years to agree on a fourth director. C wants to put the niece on the board, while the B faction wants one of its own on the board. C sues for appropriate relief. The corporation is very profitable.

(a) Assume you are the trial judge. What relief would you grant under

   (i) Delaware law; or

   (ii) the New York statute?

(b) How could the problem have been avoided through planning or drafting at the outset of the relationship?[82]

---

[81]   449 A.2d 232 (Del. 1982). For a case refusing to appoint a custodian under Del. G.C.L. § 226(a)(2), see *Francotyp-Postalia AG & Co. v. On Target Technology, Inc.*, 24 DEL. J. CORP. L. 649 (Del. Ch. 1998) (since corporation was still able to pay its debts as they became due, there was no threat of irreparable injury from dispute over capital call and therefore an absence of statutory authority to appoint a custodian under Del. G.C.L. § 226(a)(2)). For a case construing Del. G.C.L. § 226(a)(1), see *Bentas v. Haseotes*, 769 A.2d 70 (Del. Ch. 2000) (court can appoint custodian under Del. G.C.L. § 226(a)(1) where, because of deadlock, the shareholders fail to elect a sufficient number of directors to constitute a quorum; complete failure to elect directors is not required).

[83]   *See Strong v. Fromm Laboratories, Inc.*, 273 Wis. 159, 77 N.W.2d 389 (1956).

[C] Dissolution for Oppression or Other Misconduct

GARDSTEIN v. KEMP & BEATLEY
New York Court of Appeals
64 N.Y.2d 63, 484 N.Y.S.2d 799, 473 N.E.2d 1173 (1984)

COOKE, Chief Judge.

When the majority shareholders of a close corporation award de facto dividends to all shareholders except a class of minority shareholders, such a policy may constitute "oppressive actions" and serve as a basis for an order made pursuant to section 1104-a of the Business Corporation Law dissolving the corporation. In the instant matter, there is sufficient evidence to support the lower courts' conclusion that the majority shareholders had altered a long-standing policy to distribute corporate earnings on the basis of stock ownership, as against petitioners only. Moreover, the courts did not abuse their discretion by concluding that dissolution was the only means by which petitioners could gain a fair return on their investment.

I

The business concern of Kemp & Beatley, incorporated under the laws of New York, designs and manufactures table linens and sundry tabletop items. The company's stock consists of 1,500 outstanding shares held by eight shareholders. Petitioner Dissin had been employed by the company for 42 years when, in June 1979, he resigned. Prior to resignation, Dissin served as vice-president and a director of Kemp & Beatley. Over the course of his employment, Dissin had acquired stock in the company and currently owns 200 shares.

Petitioner Gardstein, like Dissin, had been a long-time employee of the company. Hired in 1944, Gardstein was for the next 35 years involved in various aspects of the business including material procurement, product design, and plant management. His employment was terminated by the company in December 1980. He currently owns 105 shares of Kemp & Beatley stock.

Apparent unhappiness surrounded petitioners' leaving the employ of the company. Of particular concern was that they no longer received any distribution of the company's earnings. Petitioners considered themselves to be "frozen out" of the company; whereas it had been their experience when with the company to receive a distribution of the company's earnings according to their stockholdings, in the form of either dividends or extra compensation, that distribution was no longer forthcoming.

Gardstein and Dissin, together holding 20.33% of the company's outstanding stock, commenced the instant proceeding in June 1981, seeking dissolution of Kemp & Beatley pursuant to section 1104-a of the Business Corporation Law. Their petition alleged "fraudulent and oppressive" conduct by the company's board of directors such as to render petitioner's stock "a virtually worthless asset."

* * *

At issue in this appeal is the scope of section 1104-a of the Business Corporation Law. Specifically, this court must determine whether the provision for involuntary dissolution when the "directors or those in control of the corporation have been guilty of . . . oppressive actions toward the complaining shareholders" was properly applied in the circumstances of this case. We hold that it was, and therefore affirm.

II

* * *

The statutory concept of "oppressive actions" can, perhaps, best be understood by examining the characteristics of close corporations and the Legislature's general purpose in creating this involuntary-dissolution statute. It is widely understood that, in addition to supplying capital to a contemplated or ongoing enterprise and expecting a fair and equal return, parties comprising the ownership of a close corporation may expect to be actively involved in its management and operation.

As a leading commentator in the field has observed: "Unlike the typical shareholder in a publicly held corporation, who may be simply an investor or a speculator and cares nothing for the responsibilities of management, the shareholder in a close corporation is a co-owner of the business and wants the privileges and powers that go with ownership. His participation in that particular corporation is often his principal or sole source of income. As a matter of fact, providing employment for himself may have been the principal reason why he participated in organizing the corporation. He may or may not anticipate an ultimate profit from the sale of his interest, but he normally draws very little from the corporation as dividends. In his capacity as an officer or employee of the corporation, he looks to his salary for the principal return on his capital investment, because earnings of a close corporation, as is well known, are distributed in major part in salaries, bonuses and retirement benefits." (O'NEAL'S CLOSE CORPORATIONS [2d ed.], Sec. 1.07, at pp. 21-22.)

Shareholders enjoy flexibility in memorializing these expectations through agreements setting forth each party's rights and obligations in corporate governance. In the absence of such an agreement, however, ultimate decision-making power respecting corporate policy will be reposed in the holders of a majority interest in the corporation. A wielding of this power by any group controlling a corporation may serve to destroy a stockholder's vital interests and expectations.

As the stock of closely held corporations generally is not readily salable, a minority shareholder at odds with management policies may be without either a voice in protecting his or her interests or any reasonable means of withdrawing his or her investment. This predicament may fairly be considered the legislative concern underlying the provision at issue in this case; inclusion of the criteria that the corporation's stock not be traded on securities markets and that the complaining shareholder be subject to oppressive actions supports this conclusion.

Defining oppressive conduct as distinct from illegality in the present context has been considered in other forums. The question has been resolved by considering oppressive actions to refer to conduct that substantially defeats the "reasonable expectations" held by minority shareholders in committing their capital to the particular enterprise. This concept is consistent with the apparent purpose underlying the provision under review. A shareholder who reasonably expected that ownership in the corporation would entitle him or her to a job, a share of corporate earnings, a place in corporate management, or some other form of security, would be oppressed in a very real sense when others in the corporation seek to defeat those expectations and there exists no effective means of salvaging the investment.

Given the nature of close corporations and the remedial purpose of the statute, this court holds that utilizing a complaining shareholder's "reasonable expectations" as a means of identifying and measuring conduct alleged to be oppressive is appropriate. A court considering a petition alleging oppressive conduct must investigate what the majority shareholders knew, or should have known, to be the petitioner's expectations in entering the particular enterprise. Majority conduct should not be deemed oppressive simply because the petitioner's subjective hopes and desires in joining the venture are not fulfilled. Disappointment alone should not necessarily be equated with oppression.

Rather, oppression should be deemed to arise only when the majority conduct substantially defeats expectations that, objectively viewed, were both reasonable under the circumstances and were central to the petitioner's decision to join the venture. It would be inappropriate, however, for us in this case to delineate the contours of the courts' consideration in determining whether directors have been guilty of oppressive conduct. As in other areas of the law, much will depend on the circumstances in the individual case.

The appropriateness of an order of dissolution is in every case vested in the sound discretion of the court considering the application (*see* Business Corporation Law Sec. 1111, subd. [a]). Under the terms of this statute, courts are instructed to consider both whether "liquidation of the corporation is the only feasible means" to protect the complaining shareholder's expectation of a fair return on his or her investment and whether dissolution "is reasonably necessary" to protect "the rights or interests of any substantial number of shareholders" not limited to those complaining (Business Corporation Law, Sec. 1104-a, subd. [b], pars. [1], [2]). Implicit in this direction is that, once oppressive conduct is found, consideration must be given to the totality of circumstances surrounding the current state of corporate affairs and relations to determine whether some remedy short of or other than dissolution constitutes a feasible means of satisfying both the petitioner's expectations and the rights and interests of any other substantial group of shareholders (*see also* Business Corporation Law, Sec. 1111, subd. [b], par. [1]).

By invoking the statute, a petitioner has manifested his or her belief that dissolution may be the only appropriate remedy. Assuming the petitioner has set forth a prima facie case of oppressive conduct, it should be incumbent upon the parties seeking to forestall dissolution to demonstrate to the court the existence of an adequate, alternative remedy. A court has broad latitude in fashioning alternative relief, but when fulfillment of the oppressed petitioner's expectations by these means is doubtful, such as when there has been a complete deterioration of relations between the parties, a court should not hesitate to order dissolution. Every order of dissolution, however, must be conditioned upon permitting any shareholder of the corporation to elect to purchase the complaining shareholder's stock at fair value (*see* Business Corporation Law, Sec. 1118).

One further observation is in order. The purpose of this involuntary dissolution statute is to provide protection to the minority shareholder whose reasonable expectations in undertaking the venture have been frustrated and who has no adequate means of recovering his or her investment. It would be contrary to this remedial purpose to permit its use by minority shareholders as merely a coercive tool. Therefore, the minority shareholder whose own acts, made in bad faith and undertaken with a view toward forcing an involuntary dissolution, give rise to the complained-of oppression should be given no quarter in the statutory protection.

III

There was sufficient evidence presented at the hearing to support the conclusion that Kemp & Beatley had a long-standing policy of awarding *de facto* dividends based on stock ownership in the form of "extra compensation bonuses." Petitioners, both of whom had extensive experience in the management of the company, testified to this effect. Moreover, both related that receipt of this compensation, whether as true dividends or disguised as "extra compensation," was a known incident to ownership of the company's stock understood by all the company's principals. Finally, there was uncontroverted proof that this policy was changed either shortly before or shortly after petitioners' employment ended. Extra compensation was still awarded by the company. The only difference was that stock ownership was no longer a basis for the payments; it was asserted that the basis became services rendered to the corporation. It was not unreasonable for the fact finder to have determined that this change in policy amounted to nothing less than an attempt to exclude petitioners from gaining any return on their investment through the mere recharacterization of distributions of corporate income. Under the circumstances of this case, there was no error in determining that this conduct constituted oppressive action within the meaning of section 1104-a of the Business Corporation Law.[2]

Nor may it be said that the Supreme Court abused its discretion in ordering Kemp & Beatley's dissolution, subject to an opportunity for a buy-out of petitioners' shares. After the referee had found that the controlling faction of the company was, in effect, attempting to "squeeze-out" petitioners by offering them no return on their investment and increasing other executive compensation, respondents, in opposing the report's confirmation, attempted only to controvert the factual basis of the report. They suggested no feasible alternative remedy to the forced dissolution. In light of an apparent deterioration in relations between petitioners and the governing shareholders of Kemp & Beatley, it was not unreasonable for the court to have determined that a forced buy-out of petitioners' shares or liquidation of the corporation's assets was the only means by which petitioners could be guaranteed a fair return on their investments.

Accordingly, the order of the Appellate Division should be modified, with costs to petitioners-respondents, by affirming the substantive determination of that court but extending the time for exercising the option to purchase petitioners-respondents' shares to 30 days following this court's determination.

---

[2]   Respondent is correct in arguing that there is no basis in the record for the referee's conclusion that the corporation had an established policy to buy-out the shares of employees when they left the company. Although the record reflects that petitioners intended to offer proof on this issue, the referee erroneously concluded that the issue was beyond the scope of the reference. He considered such evidence only as "background." In light of this limitation of the issues under consideration, which neither side objected to, the referee could not then properly ground his decision on a failure by respondent to abide by any buy-out policy. The referee's reliance on this ground is irrelevant for the purposes of this appeal, however, as Supreme Court's confirmation of the report was based solely on the principal ground for the finding of oppression, the company's failure to award dividends.

NOTES AND QUESTIONS

(1) **The "reasonable expectations" test.** The "reasonable expectations" test of oppression discussed in *Gardstein* has been applied in many other cases. For discussions of various tests applied by the courts in determining whether there has been the requisite misconduct for dissolution or related relief, see the articles by **Thompson** and **Hillman**. For another leading elaboration of the "reasonable expectations" test, see *Meiselman v. Meiselman*:

> These "reasonable expectations" are to be ascertained by examining the entire history of the participants' relationship. That history will include the "reasonable expectations" created at the inception of the participants' relationship; those "reasonable expectations" as altered over time; and the "reasonable expectations" which develop as the participants engage in a course of dealing in conducting the affairs of the corporation. The interests and views of the other participants must be considered in determining "reasonable expectations." The key is "reasonable." In order for plaintiffs' expectations to be reasonable, they must be known to or assumed by the other shareholders and concurred in by them. . . . Also, only substantial expectations should be considered and this must be determined on a case-by-ease basis.[83]

A Minnesota statute requires a court, in ordering dissolution or other relief involving a closely held corporation, to consider "the reasonable expectations of the shareholders as they exist at the inception and develop during the course of the shareholders' relationship with the corporation and with each other."[84]

(2) **Application of the test in *Gardstein*.** Is it clear that petitioners in *Gardstein* reasonably could expect payouts on their shares to continue after they left the company? Could you make a counter-argument as to the parties' reasonable expectations? Note that salary bonuses are tax-deductible by the corporation, but dividends are not. On the other hand, was there an implied term that plaintiffs would not be deprived entirely of the value of their investment if they left the firm?

(3) **Judicial discretion to dissolve.** As discussed in *Gardstein*, assuming the statutory standard for dissolution has been met, the court then must determine whether it should exercise its discretion not to dissolve the corporation. The *Meiselman* case discussed in Note 1 above held that, although N.C.G.S. § 55-125(a)(4) permitted liquidation only if "reasonably necessary," the court could consider whether any other relief, including any of the alternative remedies listed in N.C.G.S. § 55-125.1 is more appropriate than liquidation and order such relief if "reasonably necessary" to protect the plaintiff.

---

[83] 309 N.C. 279, 298-99, 307 S.E.2d 551, 563 (1983).

[84] Minn. Stat. 302A.751, subd. 3a (West 2002). *See also* N.D. Cent. Code § 10-19.1-115 (2001).

(4) **Alternative tests for dissolution.** Although more than thirty states' statutes include "oppression"-type language similar to that in the New York statute, a few states allow dissolution under significantly broader standards. California Corporation Code § 1800(b)(5) and North Carolina Gen. Stat. § 55-14-30 permit dissolution and other relief whenever "reasonably necessary" for the protection of complaining shareholders. As an indication how such a test might go beyond reasonable expectations, *Stumpf v. C.E. Stumpf & Sons, Inc.*[85] interpreted this language to permit dissolution where a disgruntled son voluntarily left the employment of a family corporation following hostility between him and the rest of his family.

(5) **Electing and opting out of oppression remedy.** Many statutes that provide for dissolution or related remedies in close corporations apply to corporations that fit within the defined close corporation category whether or not the parties to the corporation explicitly elect coverage. This is arguably supported by the parties' inability to foresee and plan for potential risks of oppression. But should the right to seek involuntary dissolution be non-waivable? *See Pace*, discussed below in Note 7. *Compare* California Corporation Code § 300(c) (making the agreement unwaivable). Does it make sense to permit parties to generally elect to have their relationship governed by special close corporation statutes, but not to opt out of particular provisions of those statutes? Like oppression, oppression litigation may involve potential costs and risks. Could the parties reasonably conclude that they would be better off relying on alternative contractual and market constraints on majority conduct?

(6) **"Reasonable expectations" and the parties' agreement.** Even if the parties cannot contract out of the oppression remedy, perhaps their agreement should determine their "reasonable expectations" under a *Gardstein*-type oppression test. The Minnesota provision referred to in Note 1 provides that "any written agreements . . . between or among shareholders or between or among one or more shareholders and the corporation are presumed to reflect the parties' reasonable expectations concerning matters dealt with in the agreements." In *Capitol Toyota, Inc. v. Gervin*,[86] Gervin had been hired to manage an automobile dealership. The parties agreed to give Gervin a 25% interest in the business at the time of the retirement of certain indebtedness. The parties further agreed that "[i]f at any time after the . . . indebtedness . . . is retired, . . . [Gervin] ceases to be employed by Capitol Toyota, Inc., for any reason whatsoever, then [Coleman and Polk] agree . . . to acquire said share of stock [25%] at book value." Gervin did a reasonably good but not outstanding job managing and, relying on his ultimately receiving an interest in the business, turned down another job offering a higher salary. Nevertheless, the dealership was sold and the new owners fired Gervin. The state supreme court reversed the trial court's order of dissolution, holding that while Gervin should be deemed to have acquired the 25% interest although the note had not been retired, he was

---

[85]   147 Cal. App. 3d 230, 120 Cal. Rptr. 671 (1975).
[86]   381 So. 2d 1038 (Miss. 1980).

not entitled to dissolution but rather was limited to buyout pursuant to the agreement. What do you suppose the result would have been in *Capitol Toyota* if plaintiff had been fired solely in order to take advantage of the buyout provision?

(7) **Share transfer agreements and the buyout price.** Even if the parties' agreement does not determine whether an oppression remedy is available, perhaps the parties' share transfer agreement (assuming one exists) should control the price of the buyout to which plaintiff is entitled. In *In re Pace Photographers, Ltd.*,[87] a shareholders' agreement provided that, for five years, no shareholder shall "sell, hypothecate, transfer, encumber or otherwise dispose of any of his shares" without the consent of the other shareholders, except that a stockholder who "desires to sell his shares" could sell to the other stockholders at a formula price that was a fraction of the value of the shares, and was then bound by a three-year non-compete. The parties fell out and petitioner sued to dissolve for oppression. The respondents offered, pursuant to N.Y. Bus. Corp. Law § 1118, to buy petitioner's stock for the agreed price. The Court of Appeals held that, despite a trial court finding that there was no proof of oppression against the petitioner, respondents were bound by their § 1118 election. The Court of Appeals further held that the price provisions of the agreement and the restrictive covenant were inapplicable, reasoning as to the price provisions as follows:

> As an abstract matter, it may well be that shareholders can agree in advance that an 1104-a dissolution proceeding will be deemed a voluntary offer to sell, or fix "fair value" in the event of judicial dissolution, and that their agreement would be enforced. Participants in business ventures are free to express their understandings in written agreements, and such consensual arrangements are generally favored and upheld by the courts.
>
> But in the absence of explicit agreement, a shareholders' agreement fixing the terms of a sale does not equally control when the sale is the result of claimed majority oppression or other wrongdoing—in effect, a forced buyout. Here, the shareholders' agreement neither provided that an 1104-a dissolution proceeding would be deemed a voluntary offer to sell, nor fixed fair value in the event of an 1118 election. The buy-out provisions were explicitly limited to the desire of any party to "sell, hypothecate, transfer, encumber or otherwise dispose of" his shares. The only event otherwise deemed a voluntary sale was the death of a stock-holder. The provisions of the shareholders' agreement regarding buyout within the first five years, at a 50% discount, were expressly limited to the situation where "a stockholder desires to sell his shares of the stock to the other stockholders" (para. 12 [e]), contemplating a voluntary sale at the convenience of and for the benefit of the selling shareholder, without regard to the inconvenience or detriment inflicted on the corporation or other shareholders. Similarly, paragraph 14 and sched-

---

[87]　71 N.Y.2d 737, 530 N.Y.S.2d 67, 525 N.E.2d 713 (1988).

ule A by their terms dealt with the value of shares for shareholders "retiring or withdrawing from the business." It is plain from these cited provisions that a sale occasioned by an 1104-a petition premised on abuse by the majority does not fall within the contemplation of this shareholders' agreement regarding a sale of stock by a shareholder to the corporation.

We therefore conclude that the stipulated price of "one-half of the formula as set forth in paragraph 15" does not in and of itself dictate the "fair value" of petitioner's shares under section 1118, and that it was error to impose those terms without further inquiry regarding valuation.

Does plaintiff's decision to sue for dissolution show that he "desires to sell" his stock, thus triggering paragraph 12(e) of the agreement? Note that there was no determination that defendants engaged in oppressive conduct that, in effect, forced plaintiff to sue. In any event, isn't the agreement at least relevant in determining "fair value" under the statute? The Minnesota statute referred to in Notes 1 and 6 provides that the court must order the transfer of shares at the price fixed by a share-transfer agreement unless the court determines that the price is unreasonable.[88]

(8) **Determining "fair value" under buyout provisions.** The most important issues under provisions like N.Y. § 1118 and MBCA § 14.34 concern the method of determining "fair value." These issues arise whenever the court orders a buyout of petitioner whether or not by respondent's election. A court may use the "capitalized earnings" approach discussed above in connection with share transfer agreements (*see* Note 5 following *Piedmont* in Section 5.04[D], above).[89]

(9) **The "minority discount."** A much-contested issue is whether the value of petitioner's shares should be reduced by a "minority discount"—that is, should be less than the petitioner's *pro rata* share of the value of the entire firm because of the petitioner's lack of control. New York courts have refused to apply the minority discount in buyouts under § 1118.[90] A minority discount arguably would be required if the relevant standard were fair market value, since control shares are valued more highly than minority shares in the market place. Among other things, the power to make payout decisions is valuable in a close corporation because owners usually cannot readily cash in their

---

[88]   Minn. Stat. Ann. § 302A.751(2). For a more recent case reaching the same result as *Pace Photographers*, see *Hayes v. Olmsted & Associates, Inc.*, 21 P.3d 178 (Or. App. 2001) (declining to use buyback price in stockholders agreement, after finding majority had oppressed majority, even though buyback provision applied to any employee "whose employment with Corporation is terminated *for any reason*").

[89]   *See In re Raskin v. Walter Karl, Inc.*, 129 A.D.2d 642, 514 N.Y.S.2d 120 (1987). *But see Ronald v. 4-C's Electronic Packaging, Inc.*, 168 Cal. App. 3d 290, 214 Cal. Rptr. 225 (1985) (error to rely exclusively on the capitalized earnings approach and suggested application of five valuation approaches, including adjusted net worth, capitalization of earnings before interest and taxes and discounted cash flow).

[90]   *See Raskin v. Walter Karl, Inc.*, 129 A.D.2d 642, 514 N.Y.S.2d 120 (1987); *Matter of Fleischer*, (Sup. Ct. App. Div.), N.Y.L.J. March 11, 1985, page 1, col. 7; *Matter of Blake* (Sup. Ct. App. Div.), N.Y.L.J., March 15, 1985, page 1, col. 6. *See also Ronald*, above. *But see McCauley v. Tom McCauley & Son, Inc.*, 104 N.M. 523, 724 P.2d 232 (1986) (holding in favor of the discount).

shares. But the test under N.Y. § 1118 is "fair value" which seems to permit some departure from a strict market test. Because § 1118 is invoked in the context of petitioner's suit to remedy majority oppression, it arguably follows that petitioner should not have her minority status thrown back at her on valuation. This raises the question of the minority holder's substantive right to be treated equally with the majority (*see* Subsection [D] below). Does refusing the minority discount unfairly thwart the majority's expectations based on its power of control? Assuming the courts are correct in not applying a minority discount in cases where the majority is guilty of oppression, should a different rule apply when a court decides to exercise its inherent or statutory power to order a buyout absent any showing of majority wrongdoing (*see* Section 5.05[A][1])?[91]

PROBLEMS

(1) Herbert was retired and bored in Florida after having sold his drug store in New York. He jumped at the suggestion by two brothers, Bill and George, who were casual but long-standing business acquaintances, that the three open another drug store in New York, with Herbert as manager, Bill as pharmacist, and George as passive investor. All three associates invested much of their savings and personally guaranteed business loans. Herbert and his wife moved back to New York.

The three associates comprised the board of directors. Bill and Herbert each owned 45% of the one class of common stock, with George owning the remaining 10%. The three associates each invested the same amount of money in the business, with George's investment being mostly in the form of a long-term loan and Bill's and Herbert's mostly in common stock. There were no special governance arrangements. The shares voted on a one-share-one-vote basis with straight voting for directors, and there was majority voting at both the shareholder and director level. The company paid no dividends. Herbert and Bill drew large salaries, and all three were paid interest on their loans.

The business was immediately successful, but the parties—particularly Bill and Herbert—never got along. Herbert wanted to expand the non-pharmacy part of the business, and Bill resisted adamantly. Also, Herbert was "laid back"—although still responsible—while Bill was somewhat younger and more active and aggressive. Bill finally convinced George to vote with him to fire Herbert and get another manager. After Herbert was fired, he had only the interest and principal payments on his loan to show for his life savings.

Advise Herbert as to his legal options under (a) New York law and (b) Delaware law.[92]

---

[91] *See Kreischer v. Kerrison Dry Goods Co.*, 172 F.3d 863 (4th Cir. 1999) (rejecting majority shareholder's argument that a minority discount would be appropriate in such circumstances under South Carolina law).

[92] *See Application of Topper*, 107 Misc. 2d 25, 433 N.Y.S.2d 359 (1980).

(2) How, if at all, would it affect your answer to Problem (1) if (a) Herbert had turned out to be an obnoxious loud-mouth who had an unfortunate tendency to irritate customers? or (b) Herbert had not made any personal investment in the business, but had been invited in as Bill's son and given a directorship, salary and stock? or (c) both (a) and (b) were true?[93]

(3) How, if at all, would it affect your answers to Problems (1) and (2) if the parties had agreed that, if one of them left the business for any reason, the other parties or the corporation would have the option to buy his shares for one-half book value?

REFERENCES

Hillman, *The Dissatisfied Participant in the Solvent Business Venture: A Consideration of the Relative Performance of Partnerships and Close Corporations*, 67 MINN. L. REV. 1 (1982).

Moll, *Shareholder Oppression in Close Corporations: The Unanswered Question of Perspective*, 53 VAND. L. REV. 750 (2000).

O'Kelley, *Filling Gaps in the Close Corporation Contract: A Transaction Cost Analysis*, 87 NW. U. L. REV. 216 (1992).

Olson, *A Statutory Elixir for the Oppression Malady*, 36 MERCER L. REV. 627 (1984).

Thompson, *Corporate Dissolution and Shareholders' Reasonable Expectations*, 66 WASH. U. L.Q. 193 (1988) (Thompson I).

Thompson, *The Shareholder's Cause of Action for Oppression*, 48 BUS. LAW. 699 (1993) (Thompson II).

[D] Judicial Buyout Rights

The cases discussed in this Section have so far involved the interpretation of statutory provisions permitting dissolution and related remedies. There has been some judicial recognition, led by *Donahue*, below, of a common law right of minority shareholders to exit the corporation.

---

[93]   *See Exadaktilos v. Cinnaminson Realty Co.*, 167 N.J. Super. 141, 400 A.2d 554, *aff'd, mem.*, 173 N.J. Super. 559 (App. Div. 1979); *Gimpel v. Bolstein*, 125 Misc. 2d 45, 477 N.Y.S.2d 1014 (1984); *see also Willis v. Bydalek*, 997 S.W.2d 798 (Tex. Ct. App. 1999).

DONAHUE v. RODD ELECTROTYPE CO.

Massachusetts Supreme Judicial Court

367 Mass. 578, 328 N.E.2d 505 (1975)

TAURO, Chief Justice.

[Plaintiff, a minority stockholder in Rodd Electrotype, a Massachusetts corporation, and widow of a former long-time employee sued Rodd Electrotype, Rodd's directors and Harry C. Rodd, the former controlling shareholder, to rescind Rodd Electrotype's purchase of Harry Rodd's shares in Rodd Electrotype and to compel Harry Rodd to repay the purchase price to the corporation, alleging breach of fiduciary duty in the corporation's purchase of the shares. The lower courts denied relief.

[Rodd and plaintiff's husband, Joseph Donahue, had started work with Royal of New England, then a wholly-owned subsidiary of Royal Electrotype, in 1935 and 1936, respectively. Rodd rose rapidly to become the general manager and treasurer of Royal of New England, while Donahue remained a plant worker throughout his career who never participated in management. In the years preceding 1955, Rodd acquired from the parent 200 shares in the subsidiary for $20 a share, while Donahue bought fifty shares at the same price. In 1955, the subsidary bought all of the remaining 725 of its shares owned by its parent company for $135,000, using promissory notes and $75,000 in cash, most of which had been loaned to the company by Rodd, who mortgaged his house in connection with the transaction. As a result of the purchase, Rodd became president of the subsidiary and an 80% shareholder, while Donahue, the sole minority shareholder, was left with a 20% stake. In 1960, after the promissory notes issued to cover a portion of the purchase price were discharged, the company was renamed the Rodd Electrotype Company of New England, Inc. In 1962, Rodd's son Charles became corporate vice president, joining the board in 1963 and succeeding Harry as president and general manager in 1965. From 1959 to 1967, Harry Rodd distributed a large portion of his shares equally among his two sons and his daughter, with each child receiving 39 shares, two shares being returned to the corporate treasury, and 81 shares being retained by Harry.

[In May, 1970, Harry Rodd, in poor health and seeking to retire, negotiated with Charles the sale to the company of forty-five shares at what Charles testified was the book and liquidating value of the shares. At a special board meeting on July 13, 1970, Harry Rodd resigned as director. The remaining directors, Charles Rodd and a Harold E. Magnuson, the company's clerk and defense attorney in this case, elected Frederick Rodd (Harry's other son) as a replacement, after which the three directors authorized Charles to execute the stock purchase agreement between Harry and the company providing for the company's purchase of forty-five shares for $800 a share ($36,000). Harry Rodd then completed the divestiture of his Rodd Electrotype stock to his children, maintaining equal holdings among the three, by selling two shares to each child on July 15, 1970, for $800 a share and then giving each child ten shares in March, 1971. As a result of these transfers, the three children each held fifty-one shares and the Donahues fifty shares.

[The Donahues first learned of the company's purchase of Harry Rodd's shares at a shareholders' meeting on March 30, 1971. A few weeks later, the Donahues offered their shares to the corporation on the same terms given to Harry Rodd. Magnuson said the corporation would not, and financially could not, do so. The Donahues had rejected the company's earlier offers (made between 1965 and 1969) to buy their fifty shares for $2,000 to $10,000 ($40 to $200 a share).]

On her argument before this court, the plaintiff has characterized the corporate purchase of Harry Rodd's shares as an unlawful distribution of corporate assets to controlling stockholders. She urges that the distribution constitutes a breach of the fiduciary duty owed by the Rodds, as controlling stockholders, to her, a minority stockholder in the enterprise, because the Rodds failed to accord her an equal opportunity to sell her shares to the corporation. . . . [W]e agree with the plaintiff and reverse the decree of the Superior Court. However, we limit the applicability of our holding to "close corporations," as hereinafter defined. Whether the holding should apply to other corporations is left for decision in another case, on a proper record.

A. Close Corporations. In previous opinions, we have alluded to the distinctive nature of the close corporation. . . . We deem a close corporation to be typified by: (1) a small number of stockholders; (2) no ready market for the corporate stock; and (3) substantial majority stockholder participation in the management, direction and operations of the corporation.

As thus defined, the close corporation bears striking resemblance to a partnership. Commentators and courts have noted that the close corporation is often little more than an "incorporated" or "chartered" partnership. . . . Just as in a partnership, the relationship among the stockholders must be one of trust, confidence and absolute loyalty if the enterprise is to succeed. Close corporations with substantial assets and with more numerous stockholders are no different from smaller close corporations in this regard. All participants rely on the fidelity and abilities of those stockholders who hold office. Disloyalty and self-seeking conduct on the part of any stockholder will engender bickering, corporate stalemates, and, perhaps, efforts to achieve dissolution.

* * *

Although the corporate form provides the above-mentioned advantages for the stockholders (limited liability, perpetuity, and so forth), it also supplies an opportunity for the majority stockholders to oppress or disadvantage minority stockholders. The minority is vulnerable to a variety of oppressive devices, termed "freeze-outs," which the majority may employ.

* * *

The minority can, of course, initiate suit against the majority and their directors. Self-serving conduct by directors is proscribed by the director's fiduciary obligation to the corporation. . . . However, in practice, the plaintiff will find difficulty in challenging dividend or employment policies. Such policies are considered to be within the judgment of the directors.

* * *

Thus, when these types of "freeze-outs" are attempted by the majority stockholders, the minority stockholders, cut off from all corporation-related revenues, must either suffer their losses or seek a buyer for their shares. Many minority stockholders will be unwilling or unable to wait for an alteration in majority policy. Typically, the minority stockholder in a close corporation has a substantial percentage of his personal assets invested in the corporation. . . . The stockholder may have anticipated that his salary from his position with the corporation would be his livelihood. Thus, he cannot afford to wait passively. He must liquidate his investment in the close corporation in order to reinvest the funds in income-producing enterprises.

At this point, the true plight of the minority stockholder in a close corporation becomes manifest. He cannot easily reclaim his capital. In a large public corporation, the oppressed or dissident minority stockholder could sell his stock in order to extricate some of his invested capital. By definition, this market is not available for shares in the close corporation. In a partnership, a partner who feels abused by his fellow partners may cause dissolution by his "express will . . . at any time" (G.L. c. 108A, 31[1][b] and [2]) and recover his share of partnership assets and accumulated profits. . . . By contrast, the stockholder in the close corporation or "incorporated partnership" may achieve dissolution and recovery of his share of the enterprise assets only by compliance with the rigorous terms of the applicable chapter of the General Laws. To secure dissolution of the ordinary close corporation subject to G.L. c. 156B, the stockholder, in the absence of corporate deadlock, must own at least fifty per cent of the shares (G.L. c. 156B, 99[a]) or have the advantage of a favorable provision in the articles of organization (G.L. c. 156B, 100[a][2]). The minority stockholder, by definition lacking fifty per cent of the corporate shares, can never "authorize" the corporation to file a petition for dissolution under G.L. c. 156B 99(a), by his own vote. He will seldom have at his disposal the requisite favorable provision in the articles of organization.

* * *

Thus, in a close corporation, the minority stockholders may be trapped in a disadvantageous situation. No outsider would knowingly assume the position of the disadvantaged minority. The outsider would have the same difficulties. To cut losses, the minority stockholder may be compelled to deal with the majority. This is the capstone of the majority plan. Majority "freeze-out" schemes which withhold dividends are designed to compel the minority to relinquish stock at inadequate prices.

* * *

Because of the fundamental resemblance of the close corporation to the partnership, the trust and confidence which are essential to this scale and manner of enterprise, and the inherent danger to minority interests in the close corporation, we hold that stockholders[17] in the close corporation owe one another substantially the same fiduciary duty in the operation of the enterprise[18] that partners owe to one another. In our previous decisions, we have

---

[17]　We do not limit our holding to majority stockholders. In the close corporation, the minority may do equal damage through unscrupulous and improper "sharp dealings" with an unsuspecting majority. See *Helms v. Duckworth*, 101 U.S. App. D.C. 390, 249 F.2d 482 (1957).

[18]　We stress that the strict fiduciary duty which we apply to stockholders in a close corporation in this opinion governs only their actions relative to the operations of the enterprise and the effects of that operation on the rights and investments of other stockholders. We express no opinion as to the standard of duty applicable to transactions in the shares of the close corporation when the corporation is not a party to the transaction. *Cf.* Andrews, *The Stockholder's Right to Equal Opportunity in the Sale of Shares*, 78 HARV. L. REV. 505 (1965). *Compare Perlman v. Feldmann*, 219 F.2d 173 (2d Cir.), *cert. denied*, 349 U.S. 952, 75 S. Ct. 880, 99 L. Ed. 1277 (1955), *with Zahn v. Transamerica Corp.*, 162 F.2d 36 (3d Cir. 1947).

defined the standard of duty owed by partners to one another as the "utmost good faith and loyalty." Stockholders in close corporations must discharge their management and stock-holder responsibilities in conformity with this strict good faith standard. They may not act out of avarice, expediency or self-interest in derogation of their duty of loyalty to the other stockholders and to the corporation.

We contrast this strict good faith standard with the somewhat less stringent standard of fiduciary duty to which directors and stockholders of all corporations must adhere in the discharge of their corporate responsibilities.

* * *

The more rigorous duty of partners and participants in a joint adventure, here extended to stockholders in a close corporation, was described by then Chief Judge Cardozo of the New York Court of Appeals in *Meinhard v. Salmon*, 249 N.Y. 458, 164 N.E. 545 (1928): "Joint adventurers, like copartners, owe to one another, while the enterprise continues, the duty of the finest loyalty. Many forms of conduct permissible in a workaday world for those acting at arm's length, are forbidden to those bound by fiduciary ties. . . . Not honesty alone, but the punctilio of an honor the most sensitive, is then the standard of behavior." *Id.* at 463-464, 164 N.E. at 546.

Application of this strict standard of duty to stockholders in close corporations is a nat-ural outgrowth of the prior case law. In a number of cases involving close corporations, we have held stockholders participating in management to a standard of fiduciary duty more exacting than the traditional good faith and inherent fairness standard because of the trust and confidence reposed in them by the other stockholders.

* * *

B. Equal Opportunity in a Close Corporation. Under settled Massachusetts law, a domestic corporation, unless forbidden by statute, has the power to purchase its own shares. . . . When the corporation reacquiring its own stock is a close corporation, the purchase is subject to the additional requirement, in the light of our holding in this opinion, that the stockholders, who, as directors or controlling stockholders, caused the corporation to enter into the stock purchase agreement, must have acted with the utmost good faith and loyalty to the other stockholders.

To meet this test, if the stockholder whose shares were purchased was a member of the controlling group, the controlling stockholders must cause the corporation to offer each stockholder an equal opportunity to sell a ratable number of his shares to the corporation at an identical price.[24] Purchase by the corporation confers substantial benefits on the mem-bers of the controlling group whose shares were purchased. These benefits are not available to the minority stockholders if the corporation does not also offer them an opportunity to sell their shares. The controlling group may not, consistent with its strict duty to the minority,

---

[24] Of course, a close corporation may purchase shares from one stockholder without offering the others an equal opportunity if all other stockholders give advance consent to the stock purchase arrangements through acceptance of an appropriate provision in the articles of organization, the corporate bylaws, or a stockholder's agreement. Similarly, all other shareholders may ratify the purchase.

utilize its control of the corporation to obtain special advantages and disproportionate benefit from its share ownership.

* * *

The benefits conferred by the purchase are twofold: (1) provision of a market for shares; (2) access to corporate assets for personal use. By definition, there is no ready market for shares of a close corporation. The purchase creates a market for shares which previously had been unmarketable. It transforms a previously illiquid investment into a liquid one. If the close corporation purchases shares only from a member of the controlling group, the controlling stockholder can convert his shares into cash at a time when none of the other stockholders can. Consistent with its strict fiduciary duty, the controlling group may not utilize its control of the corporation to establish an exclusive market in previously unmarketable shares from which the minority stockholders are excluded.

* * *

The purchase also distributes corporate assets to the stockholder whose shares were purchased. Unless an equal opportunity is given to all stockholders, the purchase of shares from a member of the controlling group operates as a preferential distribution of assets. In exchange for his shares, he receives a percentage of the contributed capital and accumulated profits of the enterprise. The funds he so receives are available for his personal use. The other stockholders benefit from no such access to corporate property and cannot withdraw their shares of the corporate profits and capital in this manner unless the controlling group acquiesces. Although the purchase price for the controlling stockholder's shares may seem fair to the corporation and other stockholders under the tests established in the prior case law . . . the controlling stockholder whose stock has been purchased has still received a relative advantage over his fellow stockholders, inconsistent with his strict fiduciary duty—an opportunity to turn corporate funds to personal use.

The rule of equal opportunity in stock purchases by close corporations provides equal access to these benefits for all stockholders. We hold that, in any case in which the controlling stockholders have exercised their power over the corporation to deny the minority such equal opportunity, the minority shall be entitled to appropriate relief.

* * *

C. Application of the Law to this Case. We turn now to the application of the learning set forth above to the facts of the instant case.

The strict standard of duty is plainly applicable to the stockholders in Rodd Electrotype. Rodd Electrotype is a close corporation. Members of the Rodd and Donahue families are the sole owners of the corporation's stock. In actual numbers, the corporation, immediately prior to the corporate purchase of Harry Rodd's shares, had six stockholders. The shares have not been traded, and no market for them seems to exist. Harry Rodd, Charles Rodd, Frederick Rodd, William G. Mason (Phyllis Mason's husband), and the plaintiff's husband all worked for the corporation. The Rodds have retained the paramount management positions.

Through their control of these management positions and of the majority of the Rodd Electrotype stock, the Rodds effectively controlled the corporation. In testing the stock purchase from Harry Rodd against the applicable strict fiduciary standard, we treat the Rodd family as a single controlling group. We reject the defendants' contention that the Rodd family cannot be treated as a unit for this purpose. From the evidence, it is clear that the Rodd family was a close-knit one with strong community of interest. . . . Harry Rodd had hired his sons to work in the family business, Rodd Electrotype. As he aged, he transferred portions of his stock holdings to his children. Charles Rodd and Frederick Rodd were given positions of responsibility in the business as he withdrew from active management. In these circumstances, it is realistic to assume that appreciation, gratitude, and filial devotion would prevent the younger Rodds from opposing a plan which would provide funds for their father's retirement.

Moreover, a strong motive of interest requires that the Rodds be considered a controlling group. When Charles Rodd and Frederick Rodd were called on to represent the corporation in its dealings with their father, they must have known that further advancement within the corporation and benefits would follow their father's retirement and the purchase of his stock. The corporate purchase would take only forty-five of Harry Rodd's eighty-one shares. The remaining thirty-six shares were to be divided among Harry Rodd's children in equal amounts by gift and sale.[28] Receipt of their portion of the thirty-six shares and purchase by the corporation of forty-five shares would effectively transfer full control of the corporation to Frederick Rodd and Charles Rodd, if they chose to act in concert with each other or if one of them chose to ally with his sister. Moreover, Frederick Rodd was the obvious successor to his father as director and corporate treasurer when those posts became vacant after his father's retirement. Failure to complete the corporate purchase (in other words, impeding their father's retirement plan) would have delayed, and perhaps have suspended indefinitely, the transfer of these benefits to the younger Rodds. They could not be expected to oppose their father's wishes in this matter. Although the defendants are correct when they assert that no express agreement involving a quid pro quo—subsequent stock gifts for votes from the directors—was proved, no express agreement is necessary to demonstrate the identity of interest which disciplines a controlling group acting in unison.

* * *

On its face, then, the purchase of Harry Rodd's shares by the corporation is a breach of the duty which the controlling stockholders, the Rodds, owed to the minority stockholders, the plaintiff and her son. The purchase distributed a portion of the corporate assets to Harry Rodd, a member of the controlling group, in exchange for his shares. The plaintiff and her son were not offered an equal opportunity to sell their shares to the corporation. In fact, their efforts to obtain an equal opportunity were rebuffed by the corporate representative. As the trial judge found, they did not, in any manner, ratify the transaction with Harry Rodd.

Because of the foregoing, we hold that the plaintiff is entitled to relief. Two forms of suitable relief are set out hereinafter. The judge below is to enter an appropriate judgment.

---

[28]   Charles Rodd admitted in his trial testimony that the parties to the negotiations which led to the stock purchase agreement structured subsequent transactions so that each of the Rodd children would eventually own fifty-one shares of corporate stock. The plaintiff points out that this was precisely the number of shares which would permit any two of Harry Rodd's children to outvote the third child and the remaining stockholders.

The judgment may require Harry Rodd to remit $36,000 with interest at the legal rate from July 15, 1970, to Rodd Electrotype in exchange for forty-five shares of Rodd Electrotype treasury stock. This, in substance, is the specific relief requested in the plaintiff's bill of complaint. Interest is manifestly appropriate. A stockholder, who, in violation of his fiduciary duty to the other stockholders, has obtained assets from his corporation and has had those assets available for his own use, must pay for that use. . . . In the alternative, the judgment may require Rodd Electrotype to purchase all of the plaintiff's shares for $36,000 without interest. In the circumstances of this case, we view this as the equal opportunity which the plaintiff should have received. Harry Rodd's retention of thirty-six shares, which were to be sold and given to his children within a year of the Rodd Electrotype purchase, cannot disguise the fact that the corporation acquired one hundred per cent of that portion of his holdings (forty-five shares) which he did not intend his children to own. The plaintiff is entitled to have one hundred per cent of her forty-five shares similarly purchased.

    WILKINS, Justice (concurring).

    I agree with much of what the Chief Justice says in support of granting relief to the plaintiff. However, I do not join in any implication (*see, e.g.*, footnote 18 and the associated text) that the rule concerning a close corporation's purchase of a controlling stockholder's shares applies to all operations of the corporation as they affect minority stockholders. That broader issue, which is apt to arise in connection with salaries and dividend policy, is not involved in this case. The analogy to partnerships may not be a complete one.

NOTES AND QUESTIONS

    (1) **Critique of *Donahue*. Easterbrook & Fischel** (at 246) suggest that *Donahue* "overlooked . . . the basic question—which outcome would the parties have selected had they contracted in anticipation of this contingency?" Shouldn't this question be answered based on the contract the parties have actually made—in this case, incorporation under a statute that did not provide for the right the court gave the Donahues? *See* Section 5.05[A][2]. Should it be significant whether the parties believed themselves to be partners? Should the court have considered evidence of whether sophisticated parties in situations like this generally negotiate for equal rights to be bought out with corporate funds?

    (2) **Business purpose.** *Wilkes v. Springside Nursing Home, Inc.*[94] tempered *Donahue* by permitting controlling shareholders to identify a legitimate business purpose for the unequal treatment of minority shareholders. The court wrote:

> [W]hen minority stockholders in a close corporation bring suit against the majority alleging breach of the strict good faith duty owed to them by the majority, we must carefully analyze the action taken by the controlling stockholders in the individual case. It must be asked whether the controlling group

---

[94]   353 N.E.2d 657 (Ma. 1976).

can demonstrate a legitimate business purpose for its action. . . . In asking this question, we acknowledge the fact that the controlling group in a close corporation must have some room to maneuver in establishing the business policy of the corporation. It must have a large measure of discretion, for example, in declaring or withholding dividends, deciding whether to merge or consolidate, establishing the salaries of corporate officers, dismissing directors with or without cause, and hiring and firing corporate employees.

When an asserted business purpose for their action is advanced by the majority, however, we think it is open to minority stockholders to demonstrate that the same legitimate objective could have been achieved through an alternative course of action less harmful to the minority's interest.[95]

Toner v. The Baltimore Envelope Co.[96] followed *Wilkes*, holding that controlling shareholders must be given the opportunity to show that a selective repurchase of corporate stock advanced the corporation's legitimate interests by removing a shareholder who might otherwise have triggered an involuntary dissolution under Maryland's deadlock provision. The court said "[a] strict equal opportunity rule would not even consider the evaluations, projections, and judgments involved in that possible explanation of the known facts. These factors should not be relegated to the legal dustbin."[97] Consider what the result might have been in *Donahue* if the defendants established that the corporation's purchase of Rodd's stock was necessary to effect the transition in management.

(3) **Scope of *Donahue*.** Should a minority shareholder in a close corporation have a common law right of buyout or some other remedy whenever a controlling shareholder causes the corporation to take action *other than a buyout* that disadvantages a minority shareholder without a *bona fide* business purpose? See the concurring opinion in *Donahue* and footnote 18 to the court's opinion. *Merola v. Exergen Corp.*[98] found no breach of duty for terminating a minority shareholder without good cause.

(4) **Interrelation with statutory remedies.** In addition to agreeing with the *Wilkes* business purpose defense, the *Toner* court added:

> We reject the proposition that failure to accord strict "equal opportunity" is a breach of duty by the majority for the further reason that it is inconsistent with the legislative approach to the problems of closely held corporations. We refer to the Maryland Close Corporation Title, 1/2 4-101 to -603, which was first enacted by Ch. 649 of the Acts of 1967. The statutory close corporation is a corporation which has elected close corporation status. 4-101(b). Envelope Co., whose existence ante-dated the adoption of the close corporation statute, could have elected that status by unanimous stockholder

---

[95]   *Id.* at 663.

[96]   498 A.2d 642 (Md. 1985).

[97]   *Id.* at 652-53.

[98]   668 N.E.2d 351 (Mass. 1996).

action. 4-201(b)(2)(ii). It did not do so. Thus, adoption of Toner's "equal opportunity" argument would oblige us judicially to create a close corporation subclass out of all of the general business corporations governed by Titles 1, 2, and 3. That subclass would be distinct from the legislatively created class of close corporations governed by Title 4. From the standpoint of substance a strict equal opportunity rule is philosophically at odds with the statutory approach to disagreement among shareholders in a close corporation. We can compare the statutory approach to Toner's position by walking the subject transaction through the Maryland Close Corporation Title as if Envelope Co. had elected that status. When members of the Elma Branch agreed to sell their stock [to the corporation], consummation of that agreement required unanimous shareholder approval because of the absence of a shareholder agreement. 4-503(b)(1). Toner could have objected. Significantly, however, the result of a Toner objection would not have been that Envelope Co. would have been required to purchase Toner's stock. Rather Toner's protest would have allowed the Elma Branch to require dissolution of Envelope Co. under 4-602(b)(1)(i) unless other stockholders purchased the stock of the members of the Elma Branch at an independently appraised value pursuant to 4-603. The Maryland Close Corporation Title thereby more closely follows an analogy to partnerships than does the strict equal opportunity theory. Under the statute disagreements are primarily resolved by corporate dissolution if the selling stockholders' shares are not purchased by other stockholders at appraised value.[99]

Should the *Donahue* court similarly have held that relief was precluded by the limited Massachusetts statute? *Sundberg v. Lampert Lumber Co.*[100] held that a Minnesota statute permitting buyouts in defined close corporations precluded application of a common law buyout right to a corporation that was too "public" to fit within the definition. The court noted that applying the buyout right even to a corporation that did not fit within the statutory theory would nullify a broader subsection of the same statute that provided for just and equitable relief for "unfairly prejudicial" conduct in all corporations. What should be the result if the statute provided only for the broader remedy and applied only to close corporations?

(5) *Nixon v. Blackwell.*[101] *Nixon v. Blackwell* held that the corporation could establish a stock option program for key employees even if this meant that non-employee shareholders would be treated differently. In addressing the question of "[w]hether there should be any special, judicially-created rules to 'protect' minority stockholders of closely-held Delaware corporations," the court said, in part:[102]

---

[99] *Id.* at 653-54.

[100] 390 N.W.2d 352 (Minn. App. 1986).

[101] 626 A.2d 1366 (Del. 1993).

[102] *Id.* at 1379-81.

It is not difficult to be sympathetic, in the abstract, to a stockholder who finds himself or herself in that position. A stockholder who bargains for stock in a closely-held corporation and who pays for those shares . . . can make a business judgment whether to buy into such a minority position, and if so on what terms. One could bargain for definitive provisions of self-ordering permitted to a Delaware corporation through the certificate of incorporation or by-laws by reason of the provisions in 8 Del. C. §§ 102, 109, and 141(a). Moreover, in addition to such mechanisms, a stockholder intending to buy into a minority position in a Delaware corporation may enter into definitive stockholder agreements, and such agreements may provide for elaborate earnings tests, buy-out provisions, voting trusts, or other voting agreements. The tools of good corporate practice are designed to give a purchasing minority stockholder the opportunity to bargain for protection before parting with consideration. It would do violence to normal corporate practice and our corporation law to fashion an ad hoc ruling which would result in a court-imposed stockholder buy-out for which the parties had not contracted.

In 1967, when the Delaware General Corporation Law was significantly revised, a new Subchapter XIV entitled "Close Corporations; Special Provisions," became a part of that law for the first time. While these provisions were patterned in theory after close corporation statutes in Florida and Maryland, "the Delaware provisions were unique and influenced the development of similar legislation in a number of other states . . . ." Subchapter XIV is a narrowly constructed statute which applies only to a corporation which is designated as a "close corporation" in its certificate of incorporation, and which fulfills other requirements, including a limitation to 30 on the number of stockholders, that all classes of stock have to have at least one restriction on transfer, and that there be no "public offering." 8 Del. C. § 342. Accordingly, subchapter XIV applies only to "close corporations," as defined in section 342. "Unless a corporation elects to become a close corporation under this subchapter in the manner prescribed in this subchapter, it shall be subject in all respects to this chapter, except this subchapter." 8 Del. C. § 341. The corporation before the Court in this matter, is not a "close corporation." Therefore it is not governed by the provisions of Subchapter XIV.[19]

One cannot read into the situation presented in the case at bar any special relief for the minority stockholders in this closely-held, but not statutory "close corporation" because the provisions of Subchapter XIV relating to close corporations and other statutory schemes preempt the field in their respective areas. It would run counter to the spirit of the doctrine of inde-

---

[19]   We do not intend to imply that, if the Corporation had been a close corporation under Subchapter XIV, the result in this case would have been different.

pendent legal significance, and would be inappropriate judicial legislation for this Court to fashion a special judicially-created rule for minority investors when the entity does not fall within those statutes, or when there are no negotiated special provisions in the certificate of incorporation, by-laws, or stockholder agreements.

(6) **Effect of the agreement.** In a jurisdiction that applies the *Donahue* rule, what should be the effect of (a) an explicit agreement providing that minority holders shall not have an "equal opportunity" right of buyout or (b) a share transfer agreement that gives the corporation the option to buy a shareholder's stock when the shareholder desires to sell? See footnote 24 to the *Donahue* opinion. *Sennerikuppam v. Datel Engineering Company*,[103] while holding under Ohio law that the fiduciary duty of a majority shareholder "might well extend beyond the equal opportunity principal of [*Donahue*]," refused to hold a majority shareholder liable merely for failing to compensate plaintiff for the true value of his shares, where plaintiff had freely consented to an agreement that set a different price.

(7) **Hetherington & Dooley proposal.**[104] These authors suggest that corporation statutes be amended to provide that any minority shareholder in a close corporation may require the corporation to purchase his stock at any time for fair value as long as the corporation would not be rendered insolvent by the purchase. This right would not be subject to contrary agreement after two years from the date of incorporation. Evaluate this proposal in light of the above discussion.

PROBLEMS

(1) Widget Corporation had three shareholders, A and B who were brothers and 37½ percent shareholders, and C, an outside investor who owned the remaining 25 percent. One day C casually mentioned to A that he might be interested in selling his stock. This led to further negotiations and, ultimately, to A's purchase of C's stock. B, suddenly a minority shareholder, seeks your advice as to whether he may compel the corporation to buy his stock. What advice would you give? Assume that the applicable jurisdiction has a statute identical to that in *Donahue* but has not taken a position with respect to the *Donahue* rule, and that there are no relevant agreements or charter or bylaw provisions.[105]

(2) String Corporation had three shareholders, A, B, and C, who were brothers. A and B each owned 375 shares, C the remaining 250. After C died, A purchased 10 shares from his estate. Shortly thereafter, the String Corporation board of directors,

---

[103] 156 F.3d 1232 (6th Cir. 1998).

[104] Hetherington & Dooley, *Illiquidity and Exploitation: A Proposed Statutory Solution to the Remaining Close Corporation Problem*, 63 Va. L. Rev. 1 (1977).

[105] *See Kennedy v. Titcomb*, 553 A.2d 1322 (N.H. 1989); *Zidell v. Zidell, Inc.*, 277 Or. 423, 560 P.2d 1091 (1977); *Johns v. Caldwell*, 601 S.W.2d 37 (Tenn. Ct. App. 1980).

which consisted of A, B and C's widow, approved the Corporation's purchase of the remainder of C's stock with A and C's widow voting in favor of the purchase and B against. The purchase was at a price determined by an independent appraiser, and was for the purpose of eliminating a shareholder who was not actively participating in the business. B seeks your advice as to whether he can compel the corporation to buy his stock. What advice would you give? Assume the same applicable law as in Problem (1).

(3) How might the difficulties of the minority shareholders in Problems (1) and (2) have been avoided by planning or drafting at the outset of the relationship?

REFERENCES

Easterbrook & Fischel, THE ECONOMIC STRUCTURE OF CORPORATE LAW, Ch. 9 (1991).
Note, *Contractual Disclaimer of the* Donahue *Fiduciary Duty: The Efficacy of the Anti-*Donahue *Clause*, 26 B.C. L. REV. 1215 (1985).

[E] Breach of Fiduciary Duty in the Issuance of Stock

The following cases show how the courts have protected existing shareholders in closely held corporations in connection with the issuance of stock. These remedies are in addition to or instead of any preemptive rights that may be available under corporate statutes (*see* Section 3.02[D], above). In reading these cases, consider carefully the role of the following factors in the court's decision: (1) whether preemptive rights were offered by the corporation; (2) the price at which the stock was sold; (3) the effect of the offer on the voting power of the existing shareholders; (4) whether the corporation's stock was publicly or closely held; and (5) the existence of a "business purpose" for the issuance of new stock.

SCHWARTZ v. MARIEN
New York Court of Appeals
37 N.Y.2d 487, 373 N.Y.S.2d 122, 335 N.E.2d 334 (1975)

JONES, Judge.

Plaintiff-appellant claims that the three defendant directors of Superior Engraving Co., Inc. violated their fiduciary duty to her when they sold shares of treasury stock to themselves and to two corporate employees without at the same time granting her the opportunity to purchase treasury shares on the same terms in proportion to her stockholding. We conclude that on this record questions of fact are raised which preclude granting plaintiff-appellant's motion for summary judgment.

All of the outstanding stock of the corporation at one time had been owned in equal 50-share lots by Albert Smith, August A. Marien, and Girard Dietrich. Smith died in 1959 and his 50 shares were purchased by the corporation and thereafter held in treasury. Following Marien's death in 1961 his 50 shares were held as follows: 26 by his widow, Clara, and 8 shares each by his sons Robert, Edward, and August, Jr. Just prior to the death of the third founder, Girard Dietrich, on March 15, 1968, there were four members of the board of directors—Dietrich, his daughter Margaret A. Schwartz, Robert Marien, and August Marien, Jr.

Following Dietrich's death, on the admission of his will to probate, letters testamentary were issued to his daughter, here plaintiff-appellant.

August and Edward Marien gave notice of a special meeting of the board of directors to be held on May 6, 1968 to fill the vacancy on the board created by Dietrich's death and to consider the purchase of the Dietrich stock and the sale of treasury stock. At the meeting, by the affirmative votes of Robert and August Marien, Edward Marien was elected to fill the Dietrich vacancy on the board. Thereupon after authorizing negotiations for the purchase of the Dietrich stock, with no word of explanation the three Marien directors voted to sell five shares of stock held in treasury, one share each to the three Marien brothers and one share apiece to two long-time corporate employees, Edward L. Kasprzak and Louis A. Zimmerman.*

Following such sales there were 105 corporate shares outstanding: 50 held by the Dietrich estate, 53 by the Marien family, and one each by the two corporate employees. Thus, corporate control was assured to the Marien family by a margin of one share even if both employee-stockholders were to join the Dietrich camp.

Following oral protest on the day after the special board meeting, plaintiff-appellant's attorney wrote to the three Marien brothers on May 16 protesting the sales of the treasury stock as illegal and demanding that they be rescinded. This was followed on May 20 by a second letter containing plaintiff-appellant's offer to purchase five shares of treasury stock at the same price at which the other five treasury shares had been sold. Pursuant to plaintiff-appellant's demand a second special meeting of the board of directors was held on June 20 to act on her purchase offer. Although her attorney asserted plaintiff-appellant's right to purchase five treasury shares to preserve her proportion-ate stock ownership in the corporation, the board rejected her offer. The only explanation then given for such rejection was that it was "not consistent" and not "in the best interests of the corporation" to sell more shares to the Dietrich estate at a time when the estate was negotiating to sell the shares it already held to the corporation.

Plaintiff-appellant's attorney asserted that failure to enable her to maintain her proportionate position would be a breach of the fiduciary responsibility owed by the directors. Plaintiff-appellant's related request that the sales of the first five shares of treasury stock be rescinded was ruled out of order, and the meeting adjourned.

After her demands were ignored, plaintiff-appellant called a special meeting of the corporate shareholders to be held on July 25, 1968, for the election of directors. Thereafter, sensing the numerical predicament she was in, plaintiff-appellant instituted the present action alleging conspiracy and fraud on the part of defendants to deprive the Dietrich estate of its 50% stock ownership position and sought to enjoin the holding of the proposed meeting of shareholders. Her application for injunctive relief was denied and the meeting was

---

* The two employees were originally named party defendants but the action was subsequently dismissed on the merits as to each of them.

held at which Edward Kasprzak was elected to replace plaintiff-appellant on the board of directors.

Nothing had been said to plaintiff-appellant or her attorney prior to the special board meeting on May 6, 1968 of any sale of treasury stock to the Marien brothers or to the corporate employees. No explanation was offered at the May 6 meeting or at the later meeting on May 20. The only articulated basis for the refusal to sell five shares of treasury stock to plaintiff-appellant was that it was inconsistent for her to purchase more shares when she was already negotiating for the sale of the shares she already held. This was an irrelevant rejoinder to her announced objective of regaining her 50% stock ownership position.

It was not until an examination before trial, three years after the sales of treasury stock to the corporate employees, that mention was first made of Mr. Kasprzak's desire to purchase stock following Dietrich's death and of Robert Marien's purported apprehension that Kasprzak might leave the company's employ. To his affidavit sworn to March 16, 1972, Edward Marien attached a copy of minutes of a special meeting of stockholders and directors held on December 28, 1955 in which reference was made to a possible stock purchasing plan, concededly abandoned in 1959, in which two of the Marien brothers and Mr. Kasprzak were then listed as prospective beneficiaries.

Supreme Court denied cross motions for summary judgment, concluding that a trial must be held to resolve material issues of fact. The Appellate Division affirmed with one dissenting Justice disposed to grant summary judgment for plaintiff-appellant. We agree that there is sufficient evidence in this record to raise issues of fact, precluding summary judgment in plaintiff's favor.

While it is conceded that pre-emptive rights as such do not attach to treasury stock in the absence of specific provision in the certificate of incorporation (Business Corporations Law, § 622, subd. [e], par. [4]), members of a corporate board of directors nevertheless, owe a fiduciary responsibility to the shareholders in general and to individual shareholders in particular to treat all shareholders fairly and evenly.

* * *

Departure from precisely uniform treatment of stockholders may be justified, of course, where a bona fide business purpose indicates that the best interests of the corporation would be served by such departure. The burden of coming forward with proof of such justification shifts to the directors where, as here, a prima facie case of unequal stockholder treatment is made out. Particularly is this so when it appears that members of the board of directors favored themselves individually over the complaining shareholder. Additionally, disturbance of equality of stock ownership in a corporation closely held for several years by the members of two families calls for special justification in the corporate interest; not only must it be shown that it was sought to achieve a bona fide independent business objective, but as well that such objective could not have been accomplished substantially as effectively by other means which would not have disturbed proportionate stock ownership. Similarly, should the proof disclose double motivation on the part of the directors, that is, both to advance an independent corporate interest and at the same time to place a complaining shareholder at a disadvantage, the directors could then be absolved, if at all, of breach of fiduciary responsibilities only by accompanying proof that no other means were available appropriate to the accomplishment of the corporate objective.

There is evidence to support plaintiff-appellant's contention that no independent corporate interest was served in the sale of the five shares of treasury stock to the Marien directors and the two long-time employees and that there was here only a program to vest corporate control in the Marien family to the obvious disadvantage of the Dietrich family. On the other hand, there is also some evidence that prior to Dietrich's death the directors had given consideration to an employee stock purchase plan, and it appears that Kasprzak and Zimmerman had each been corporate employees for 37 years and that August, Edward, and Robert Marien had been employed for 24, 22, and 19 years respectively.

Plaintiff's right to relief does not depend on proof of fraud or conspiracy on the part of the Marien members of the board of directors, although this is plaintiff's pleading. . . . Rather, plaintiff's right of recovery depends on proof of breach of the fiduciary duty owed by the directors to plaintiff-appellant stockholder. This would follow, in the circumstances of this case, if it were found that the actions of defendants were not, in objective and accomplishment, in good faith furtherance of an independent, significant corporate purpose sufficient to override the obviously legitimate interest in the corporation and which purpose could not have been substantially accomplished by other means which would not have disturbed the equality of the two-family ownership.

Determinations as to whether the activities of defendants were undertaken in good faith for a legitimate corporate purpose and whether other means were available depend not only on an analysis of the objective facts but as well in part on an appraisal of defendants' motives, involving as it will issues of credibility: "Good faith or bad faith as the guide or the test of fiduciary conduct is a state or condition of mind—a fact—which can be proved or judged only through evidence." (*Kavanaugh v. Kavanaugh Knitting Co.*, [226 N.Y. 185, 198, 123 N.E. 148, 152].) Accordingly it is appropriate that this case go before triers of fact.

The order of the Appellate Division should be affirmed and the case proceed to trial.

KATZOWITZ v. SIDLER
New York Court of Appeals
24 N.Y.2d 512, 301 N.Y.S.2d 470, 249 N.E.2d 359 (1969)

KEATING, Judge.

Isador Katzowitz is a director and stockholder of a close corporation. Two other persons, Jacob Sidler and Max Lasker, own the remaining securities and, with Katzowitz, comprise Sulburn Holding Corp.'s board of directors. Sulburn was organized in 1955 to supply propane gas to three other corporations controlled by these men. Sulburn's certificate of incorporation authorized it to issue 1,000 shares of no par value stock for which the incorporators established a $100 selling price. Katzowitz, Sidler and Lasker each invested $500 and received five shares of the corporation's stock.

The three men had been jointly engaged in several corporate ventures for more than 25 years. In this period they had always been equal partners and received identical compensation from the corporations they controlled. Though all the corporations controlled by these three men prospered, disenchantment with their inter-personal relationship flared into the open in 1956. At this time, Sidler and Lasker joined forces to oust Katzowitz from any role in managing the corporations. They first voted to replace Katzowitz as a director of Sullivan County Gas Company with the corporation's private counsel. Notice of directors' meetings was then caused to be sent out by Lasker and Sidler for Burnwell Gas Corporation. Sidler and Lasker advised Katzowitz that they intended to vote for a new board of directors. Katzowitz at this time held the position of manager of the Burnwell facility.

Katzowitz sought a temporary injunction to prevent the meeting until his rights could be judicially determined. A temporary injunction was granted to maintain the status quo until trial. The order was affirmed by the Appellate Division (*Katzowitz v. Sidler*, 8 A.D.2d 726, 187 N.Y.S.2d 986).

Before the issue could be tried, the three men entered into a stipulation in 1959 whereby Katzowitz withdrew from active participation in the day-to-day operations of the business. The agreement provided that he would remain on the boards of all the corporations, and each board would be limited to three members composed of the three stockholders or their designees. Katzowitz was to receive the same compensation and other fringe benefits which the controlled corporations paid Lasker and Sidler. The stipulation also provided that Katzowitz, Sidler and Lasker were "equal stockholders and each of said parties now owns the same number of shares of stock in each of the defendant.corporations and that such shares of stock shall continue to be in full force and effect and unaffected by this stipulation, except as hereby otherwise expressly provided." The stipulation contained no other provision affecting equal stock interests.

The business relationship established by the stipulation was fully complied with. Sidler and Lasker, however, were still interested in disassociating themselves from Katzowitz and purchased his interest in one of the gas distribution corporations and approached him with regard to the purchase of his interest in another.

In December of 1961 Sulburn was indebted to each stockholder to the extent of $2,500 for fees and commissions earned up until September 1961. Instead of paying this debt, Sidler and Lasker wanted Sulburn to loan the money to another corporation which all three men controlled. Sidler and Lasker called a meeting of the board of directors to propose that additional securities be offered at $100 per share to substitute for the money owed to the directors. The notice of meeting for October 30, 1961 had on its agenda "a proposition that the corporation issue common stock of its unissued common capital stock, *the total par value which shall equal the total sum of the fees and commissions now owing by the corporation to its ... directors.*" [Emphasis in *Katzowitz*.] Katzowitz made it quite clear at the meeting that he would not invest any additional funds in Sulburn in order for it to make a loan to this other corporation. The only resolution passed at the meeting was that the corporation would pay the sum of $2,500 to each director.

With full knowledge that Katzowitz expected to be paid his fees and commissions and that he did not want to participate in any new stock issuance, the other two directors called a special meeting of the board on December 1, 1961. The only item on the agenda for this special meeting was the issuance of 75 shares of the corporation's common stock at $100 per share. The offer was to be made to stockholders in "accordance with their respective preemptive rights for the purpose of acquiring additional working capital." The amount to be raised was the exact amount owed by the corporation to its shareholders. The offering price for the securities was 1/18 the book value of the stock. Only Sidler and Lasker attended the special board meeting. They approved the issuance of the 75 shares.

Notice was mailed to each stockholder that they had the right to purchase 25 shares of the corporation's stock at $100 a share. The offer was to expire on December 27, 1961. Failure to act by that date was stated to constitute a waiver. At about the same time Katzowitz received the notice, he received a check for $2,500 from the corporation for his fees and commissions. Katzowitz did not exercise his option to buy the additional shares. Sidler and Lasker purchased their full complement, 25 shares each. This purchase by Sidler and Lasker caused an immediate dilution of the book value of the outstanding securities.

On August 25, 1962 the principal asset of Sulburn, a tractor trailer truck, was destroyed. On August 31, 1962 the directors unanimously voted to dissolve the corporation. Upon dissolution, Sidler and Lasker each received $18,885.52 but Katzowitz only received $3,147.59.

The plaintiff instituted a declaratory judgment action to establish his right to the proportional interest in the assets of Sulburn in liquidation less the $5,000 which Sidler and Lasker used to purchase their shares in December 1961. [The lower courts held that plaintiff's share in the assets was limited to what he had already received.]

* * *

The concept of pre-emptive rights was fashioned by the judiciary to safeguard two distinct interests of stockholders—the right to protection against dilution of their equity in the corporation and protection against dilution of their proportionate voting control. . . . After early decisions . . . legislation fixed the right enunciated with respect to proportionate voting but left to the judiciary the role of protecting existing shareholders from the dilution of their equity. . . .

It is clear that directors of a corporation have no discretion in the choice of those to whom the earnings and assets of the corporation should be distributed. Directors, being fiduciaries of the corporation, must, in issuing new stock, treat existing shareholders fairly. . . . Though there is very little statutory control over the price which a corporation must receive for new shares (Stock Corporation Law §§ 12, 27, 69, 74; Business Corporation Law § 504) the power to determine price must be exercised for the benefit of the corporation and in the interest of all the stockholders. . . .

Issuing stock for less than fair value can injure existing shareholders by diluting their interest in the corporation's surplus, in current and future earnings and in the assets upon liquidation. Normally, a stockholder is protected from the loss of his equity from dilution, even though the stock is being offered at less than fair value, because the shareholder receives rights which he may either exercise or sell. If he exercises, he has protected his interest and, if not, he can sell the rights, thereby compensating himself for the dilution of his remaining shares in the equity of the corporation. . . .[2]

---

[2]   There is little justification for issuing stock far below its fair value. The only reason for issuing stock below fair value exists in publicly held corporations where the problem of floating new issues through subscription is concerned. The reasons [sic] advanced in this situation is that it insures the success of the issue or that it has the same psychological effect as a dividend (Guthman and Dagell, CORPORATE FINANCIAL POLICY [3d ed., 1955], p. 369).

On rare occasions stock will be issued below book value because this indicia of value is not reflective of the actual worth of the corporation. The book value of the corporation's assets may be inflated or the company may be under the direction of poor management. In these circumstances there may be a business justification for a major disparity in issuing price and book value in order to inject new capital into the corporation. . . .

When new shares are issued, however, at prices far below fair value in a close corporation or a corporation with only a limited market for its shares, existing stockholders, who do not want to invest or do not have the capacity to invest additional funds, can have their equity interest in the corporation diluted to the vanishing point.

* * *

The protection afforded by stock rights is illusory in close corporations. Even if a buyer could be found for the rights, they would have to be sold at an inadequate price because of the nature of a close corporation. Outsiders are normally discouraged from acquiring minority interests after a close corporation has been organized. Certainly a stockholder in a close corporation is at a total loss to safeguard his equity from dilution if no rights are offered and he does not want to invest additional funds.

Though it is difficult to determine fair value for a corporation's securities and courts are therefore reluctant to get into the thicket, when the issuing price is shown to be markedly below book value in a close corporation and when the remaining shareholder-directors benefit from the issuance, a case for judicial relief has been established. In that instance, the corporation's directors must show that the issuing price falls within some range which can be justified on the basis of valid business reasons. . . . If no such showing is made by the directors, there is no reason for the judiciary to abdicate its function to a majority of the board or stockholders who have not seen fit to come forward and justify the propriety of diverting property from the corporation and allow the issuance of securities to become an oppressive device permitting the dilution of the equity of dissident stockholders.

The defendant directors here make no claim that the price set was a fair one. No business justification is offered to sustain it. . . . Admittedly, the stock was sold at less than book value. The defendants simply contend that, as long as all stockholders were given an equal opportunity to purchase additional shares, no stockholder can complain simply because the offering dilutes his interest in the corporation.

The defendants' argument is fallacious.

The corollary of a stockholder's right to maintain his proportionate equity in a corporation by purchasing additional shares is the right not to purchase additional shares without being confronted with dilution of his existing equity if no valid business justification exists for the dilution.

* * *

A stockholder's right not to purchase is seriously undermined if the stock offered is worth substantially more than the offering price. Any purchase at this price dilutes his interest and impairs the value of his original holding. . . . Judicial review in this area is limited to whether under all the circumstances, including the disparity between issuing price of the stock and its true value, the nature of the corporation, the business necessity for establishing an offering price at a certain amount to facilitate raising new capital, and the ability of stockholders to sell rights, the additional offering of securities should be condemned because the directors in establishing the sale price did not fix it with reference to financial considerations with respect to the ready disposition of securities.

Here the obvious disparity in selling price and book value was calculated to force the dissident stockholder into investing additional sums. No valid business justification was advanced for the disparity in price, and the only beneficiaries of the disparity were the two director-stock-holders who were eager to have additional capital in the business.

It is no answer to Katzowitz' action that he was also given a chance to purchase additional shares at this bargain rate. The price was not so much a bargain as it was a tactic, conscious or unconscious on the part of the directors, to place Katzowitz in a compromising situation. The price was so fixed to make the failure to invest costly. However, Katzowitz at the time might not have been aware of the dilution because no notice of the effect of the issuance of the new shares on the already outstanding shares was disclosed (*Gord v. Iowana Farms Milk Co., supra*, 245 Iowa p. 18, 60 N.W.2d 820). In addition, since the stipulation entitled Katzowitz to the same compensation as Sidler and Lasker, the disparity in equity interest caused by their purchase of additional securities in 1961 did not affect stockholder income from Sulburn and, therefore, Katzowitz possibly was not aware of the effect of the stock issuance on his interest in the corporation until dissolution.

No reason exists at this time to permit Sidler and Lasker to benefit from their course of conduct. Katzowitz' delay in commencing the action did not prejudice the defendants. By permitting the defendants to recover their additional investment in Sulburn before the remaining assets of Sulburn are distributed to the stockholders upon dissolution, all the stockholders will be treated equitably. Katzowitz, therefore, should receive his aliquot share of the assets of Sulburn less the amount invested by Sidler and Lasker for their purchase of stock on December 27, 1961.

Accordingly, the order of the Appellate Division should be reversed, with costs, and judgment granted in favor of the plaintiff against the individual defendants.

BURKE, SCILEPPI, BERGAN, BREITEL and JASEN, JJ., concur with KEATING, J.

FULD, C.J., dissents and votes to affirm on the opinion at the Appellate Division.

NOTES AND QUESTIONS

(1) **The dilution problem.** To understand precisely how Katzowitz' shares were diluted by the new stock, try constructing two balance sheets, one reflecting the company's financial situation and capital structure before the issuance of the new shares, and the other reflecting the post-issuance situation, in each case using as the value of the assets the ultimate liquidation value of the company ($40,917).

(2) **Inadequacy of preemptive rights.** Precisely why isn't it enough that the defendants offered Katzowitz an opportunity to buy new stock? Why shouldn't Katzowitz be forced to bear the consequences of his decision not to buy? For another case in which the court found a breach of fiduciary duty in connection with the issuance of stock even though plaintiff was offered a preemptive right, see *Browning v. C & C Plywood Corp.*[106] There, the court struck down the issuance of stock in a close corporation at significantly below market value where the plaintiff was financially unable to exer-

---

[106] 248 Or. 574, 434 P.2d 339 (1967).

cise the option to buy the stock and the purpose of the issuance was found to be to freeze the plaintiff, a minority shareholder, out of the corporation. On the other hand, in *Herbik v. Rand*,[107] the court reversed the trial court's injunction against a *pro rata* share sale to existing holders where the company needed additional capital, the company's bank and others approved the price at which the stock was sold, and there was no evidence the objecting shareholder could not buy his *pro rata* share of the stock.

---

[107] 732 S.W.2d 232 (Mo. Ct. App. 1987).

CHAPTER 6

The Search for "Incorporated" Partnership: Hybrid Limited Liability Firms

Chapters 4 and 5 show that both of the two most important business forms—the general partnership and the corporation—have problems and advantages for closely held firms. The partnership form offers a governance structure that fits the needs of closely held businesses—direct owner participation in management, restrictions on the transfer of ownership interests, and easy dissolution. However, partners are personally liable for the debts of the business, which can be a drawback for many firms (*see* Section 3.03). Corporations, on the other hand, provide owners of closely held firms with easy access to limited liability. But, at the same time, corporations subject those owners to substantial costs: first, the parties must adapt the default rules of corporate law, which provide for free transferability of ownership interests, centralized management and continuity of life, to meet the needs of closely held businesses (a task which Chapter 5 shows creates an open-ended potential for litigation); and second, the parties must bear the detrimental tax consequences (discussed more fully below) that arise because corporations, unlike partnerships, are treated as separate taxpaying entities.

Writers thinking about the awkwardness of closely held corporations have long wondered why we could not simply allow firms to have all of the features of partnerships combined with the basic corporate feature of limited liability (*see* **Kessler**).

This Chapter shows how impediments to the incorporated partnership have been disappearing in recent years. It begins in Section 6.01 by discussing the tax consequences of organizational form. It then discusses in Sections 6.02 and 6.03 two important tax-driven approaches to the incorporated partnership—the Subchapter S corporation and the limited partnership. Next, Section 6.04 discusses the realization of the incorporated partnership in the form of the "limited liability company." Finally, Section 6.05 discusses even newer entities, particularly the "limited liability partnership." This proliferation of business forms has brought new questions concerning choice of organizational form (*see* **Ribstein & Kobayashi**).

REFERENCES

Kessler, *With Limited Liability for All: Why Not a Partnership Corporation?*, 36 FORDHAM L. REV. 235 (1967).

Ribstein, *The Deregulation of Limited Liability and the Death of Partnership*, 70 WASH. U. L.Q. 417 (1992).

Ribstein, *Limited Liability and Theories of the Firm,* 50 MD. L. REV. 80 (1991).
Ribstein, *The Evolving Partnership,* 26 J. CORP. L. 819 (2001).
Ribstein & Kobayashi, *Choice of Form and Network Externalities,* 43 WM. & MARY L. REV. 79 (2001).

§ 6.01 Tax Considerations in Choice of Form

This Section discusses the tax consequences of organizational form. Because of the sometimes considerable differences in the tax treatment of various types of firms, an understanding of tax rules is essential both in choosing the form of organization that is appropriate for a particular firm and in understanding how and why particular organizational forms have been developed.

[A] Tax Consequences of Partnership

The tax treatment of partnerships is more favorable for some investors in some situations than that of corporations. Put simply, a corporation is a separate taxpaying entity, but a partnership is not. This distinction has several important consequences:

(1) Where the business earns money and distributes it to the owners:

(A) If the business is a corporation (with the major exception of Subchapter S corporations discussed in Section 6.02), the profits are subject to what is, in effect, a double tax: the corporation is usually taxed on profits when they are earned by the business at the corporate tax rate, a rate that may be higher than the rate applicable to an individual investor; and the shareholders are taxed on the profits when they are distributed as dividends.

(B) If the business is a partnership, the profits are generally only taxed once. The income is usually treated as if it were earned directly by the partners. Thus, it is taxed to the partners when generated by the business, but not again when it is distributed.

(2) Where the business earns money and retains it:

(A) If the business is a corporation, the profits are still taxed twice, though the second tax is deferred until the investor's disposition of shares. The corporation is taxed on the profits when they are earned by the business and the shareholders are taxed on any increase in the value of their shares when they sell.

(B) If the business is a partnership, the profits are only taxed once and at a rate that may be lower than the rate applicable to corporations. The income is treated as if it were earned directly by the partners, even if it is used entirely in the business and the individual partners never see a dime of it.

(3) Where the business loses money:

(A) If the business is a corporation, ordinary business losses are only deductible against income generated by the business. If ordinary losses exceed income in a particular year, the excess can, to some extent, be carried back or forth to previous or succeeding years. Shareholders may also be able to deduct capital losses resulting from sales of shares at prices that reflect a decrease in share value.

(B) If the business is a partnership, business losses are often deductible against (and therefore may "shelter") income of the partner apart from income generated by the partnership's business. This is because partnership losses are generally treated as incurred directly by the partners. However, there are limitations on the deductibility of partnership losses, including restrictions for losses incurred by investors who are not active in the business (*i.e.*, "passive" losses).[1]

It follows from the above discussion that the partnership form of business may have tax advantages for many types of firms, particularly those which do not expect to retain earnings.

[B] Rules for Characterizing Firms

Whether a business is taxed as a corporation or a partnership once was determined according to what the IRS believed to be the characteristics that distinguished corporations from partnerships: continuity of life, corporate-type centralized management, limited liability, and free transferability of ownership interests (with an entity with at least three of these four attributes being classified as a corporation). However, the rationale for these rigid distinctions was hard to discern.

In recognition of the problems with the classification rules, the I.R.S. gradually made the rules more flexible and ultimately decided to let unincorporated firms choose to be taxed as either corporations or partnerships—that is, to "check a box." *See* Treas. Reg. § 301.7701-1-3. The rules provide that a domestic "eligible entity" (foreign entities are covered separately), which includes business firms other than corporations, joint stock companies, insurance companies or banks, is not treated as a corporation for income tax purposes unless it elects this treatment. An eligible entity with two or more members is a partnership for income tax purposes unless it elects to be a corporation. An eligible entity with one member is taxed directly and the entity is ignored unless the entity elects to be a corporation for tax purposes.

But even under the new "check a box" rules, a basic policy question remains: why tax unincorporated firms, like partnerships, differently from corporations? One

---

[1]   *See* I.R.C. § 469.

possible answer is that corporate features make a firm look more like an "entity" and therefore more appropriate for "entity"-like tax treatment. But even partnerships are "entities" in many critical respects, as RUPA § 201 recognizes. In any event, "aggregate" and "entity" are descriptions of, rather than rationales for, statutory features.

Even if it makes sense to base the corporate tax on "corporate," as distinguished from partnership-like, characteristics, in evaluating this approach it is also necessary to take into account possible costs of the system. In particular, the tax rules encourage firms to adopt non-corporate organizational forms that might not suit them apart from tax consequences. So the firm may "pay," in the form of increased costs of management for its tax advantages. This payment is simply a cost to the members as a whole and, therefore, to society, rather than a social benefit that would offset the reduced tax. Congress' recognition of Subchapter S corporations (*i.e.*, a subclass of corporations which are taxed as partnerships) eases these concerns, but does not eliminate them because of Subchapter S' tight eligibility requirements (*see* Section 6.02).

REFERENCES

Ribstein, *The Deregulation of Limited Liability and the Death of Partnership*, 70 WASH. U. L.Q. 417 (1992).

Ribstein & Sargent (eds.), *Check-the-Box and Beyond: The Future of Limited Liability Entities*, 52 BUS. LAW. 605 (1997).

§ 6.02 Subchapter S Corporations

Subchapter S, first enacted in 1958, was an important early step toward the "incorporated partnership" concept since it allowed firms that were essentially partnerships to do business in the corporate form (*i.e.*, to enjoy the benefits of limited liability) without forfeiting all the tax advantages of partnership. However, under Subchapter S as originally enacted there were important differences between the taxation of Subchapter S corporations and of partnerships, and several traps for the unwary. The Subchapter S Revision Act of 1982 eliminated many of these problems.

Income and losses in a Subchapter S corporation "flow through" to the shareholders almost exactly as they do in a partnership. Subchapter S therefore provides an important tax feature of partnership. However, it must compete with the other limited liability forms discussed in the remainder of this Chapter in the light of the "check-the-box" rule discussed immediately above. Also, Subchapter S status may not be available because of the eligibility rules discussed below.

The shareholders in a close corporation may elect Subchapter S status if they vote unanimously to do so and meet certain qualifications: (1) there can be no more than seventy-five shareholders (husband-wife shareholders counting as one); (2) all of the shareholders must be either individuals, estates, or certain types of trusts; (3) there can only be one class of stock; and (4) no shareholder can be a nonresident alien.

The "one class of stock" requirement is particularly important for close corporation planning. Under the original version of Subchapter S, all stock was required to be identical as to voting, dividend and liquidation rights. The revised version of Subchapter S permits differences in voting rights and therefore facilitates giving all management and control powers to certain participants, as in family corporations where some family members are active in the business and others are not. But Subchapter S retains the prohibition against differences in dividend and liquidation rights. Thus, the parties may not give some shareholders preferred stock with liquidation or dividend preferences or both, instead of common stock, to allocate interests among entrepreneurs who have made different contributions to the business. However, Subchapter S at least includes a "safe harbor" of "straight debt" which will not be considered a separate class of stock for Subchapter S purposes.

A firm loses Subchapter S status if: (1) stock is transferred to a shareholder who does not meet the qualifications of Subchapter S;[2] (2) stock is transferred so as to create more than the maximum number of shareholders (including when the stock is distributed to legatees under a will or split up between spouses pursuant to a divorce decree); or (3) the corporation creates an additional class of stock.

REFERENCE

Kantor, *To Elect or Not to Elect Subchapter S—That is a Question*, 60 TAXES 882 (1982).

§ 6.03 Limited Partnerships

The limited partnership form combines elements of both the corporate and partnership forms. A limited partnership must include one or more general partners who, like general partners in a general partnership, are co-managers with personal liability. A limited partnership also includes one or more limited partners who, like corporate shareholders, do not actively participate in management and have limited liability.

An important reason for selecting limited over general partnership is, of course, limited liability. But there are other ways to get limited liability. Limited partnerships once were uniquely suited to combining the tax advantages of partnership with limited liability, but that is no longer the case since adoption of the "check-the-box" rules discussed in Section 6.01 made it possible to have partnership taxation in more flexible forms, particularly including the limited liability company. Yet the limited partnership remains an important business form. What advantages does it now offer over the alternatives?

An investor could avoid personal liability by contributing money as a creditor. However, a court might characterize the association as a general partnership or the

---

[2]   *But see A.W. Chesterton Company, Inc. v. Chesterton*, 128 F.3d 1 (1st Cir. 1997) (minority shareholder enjoined from transferring shares in a way that would cause the subchapter S status to terminate automatically, even though the transfer was not expressly prohibited by transfer restrictions in the corporation's articles of organization).

creditor as a principal and thereby leave the creditor personally liable for the firm's obligations (*see* Section 2.02[B]), particular if the investor receives a share of the profits as consideration for the loan (*see* UPA § 7(4), RUPA § 202) or participates in the management or control of the debtor's business. The limited partnership provides such investors with a legislative "safe harbor" from the uncertainties of the common law, although the "control rule" discussed in subsection [B] reduces some of the safety.

Investors seeking limited liability also could incorporate or form limited liability companies. A possible advantage of the limited partnership form is that the general partners' personal liability lowers the firm's cost of credit by aligning the interests of the general partners (who manage the firm) with those of the creditors. As discussed below in subsection [B], this helps explain why control is locked into the general partners by means of the "control rule."

Most states have adopted the Revised Uniform Limited Partnership Act (1985) (RULPA), although some still have the original Uniform Limited Partnership Act (1976) (ULPA). In the summer of 2001 the National Conference of Commissioners on Uniform State Laws promulgated the Uniform Limited Partnership Act (2001) (ULPA (2001)), which ultimately may become the dominant law of limited partnerships. A key feature of the 2001 Act is that, rather than relying on some general partnership provisions as in prior limited partnership acts, a process often referred to as "linkage," the new act includes a complete set of provisions relating to limited partnerships. Another important feature is the elimination of the "control rule," as discussed in Note 2 following *Gast,* below.

[A] Formation of a Limited Partnership

As in general partnerships, a limited partnership begins with an agreement that outlines such things as partners' management powers, contributions of capital and income shares. Unlike a general partnership, but like a corporation, forming a limited partnership requires the additional step of filing a certificate with the state. Like corporate certificates, limited partnership certificates provide notice to the world of the firm's limited liability status. A limited partnership certificate serves the additional purpose of identifying for creditors the general partners to whom they can look for satisfaction of debts. Note that a person listed in the certificate as a general partner probably would be liable as such under UPA § 16 and RUPA § 308 even apart from the limited partnership statute.

Despite the similarities between corporations and limited partnerships, there are several differences regarding the formalities of formation that are not easily explained (*see* **Ribstein 1** at 843-46):

(1) ULPA § 2 requires disclosure of limited partners and their contributions. It is not clear why limited partners, but not corporate shareholders, need be disclosed. This disclosure requirement was dropped from the RULPA § 201 and ULPA (2001) § 201.

(2) ULPA § 11, RULPA § 304 and ULPA (2001) § 306 provide protection for "erroneous" limited partners—*i.e.*, parties who have contributed to the capital of a partnership erroneously believing that they have become limited partners. The closest corporate analog to these provisions is MBCA § 2.04, which provides that parties acting on behalf of a defectively formed corporation will be held personally liable for the corporation's obligations only if they knew of the defect in formation.

(3) ULPA §§ 6 and 24, RULPA §§ 202 and 207 and ULPA (2001) §§ 202 and 208 provide for the duty to amend, and for liability for, false partnership certificates. It is not clear why there is no similar duty and liability regarding corporate certificates.

[B] Management and Control and the "Control Rule"

The governance of limited partnerships mixes the partnership and corporate standard forms. General partners have the same power to control the partnership in a limited partnership as they do in a general partnership (ULPA § 9; RULPA § 403; ULPA (2001) §§ 402 and 406), except that the limited partners may be able to vote on certain matters. Limited partners have a passive role similar to that of corporate shareholders.

There are, however, important differences between limited partners and shareholders. Neither ULPA nor RULPA explicitly gives limited partners the power to remove general partners who manage the firm, and RULPA § 302 contemplates that limited partners could be entirely denied any voting rights (although most limited partnership agreements do provide for limited partner voting rights, including a power of removal). ULPA (2001) § 406(b) provides for a short list of limited partner voting rights. Corporate statutes, on the other hand, grant shareholders wide voting rights, particularly including the right to replace the corporation's directors every year (*see* Section 5.01[B][2]).

These differences between corporate shareholders and limited partners are explained, at least in part, by the general partners' personal liability for the debts of the business. Removing general partners is probably costlier than removing directors because general partners have continuing personal obligations to the firm's creditors and ownership interests. Moreover, the general partners' ownership interests and personal obligations help ensure that they will not manage the firm into insolvency, arguably making limited partner voting rights less necessary (*see* **Ribstein 1** at 880-82). But note that limited partners have fewer voting rights than shareholders even in a limited partnership with a corporate general partner. Also, even if general partners have an incentive not to mismanage the firm into bankruptcy, limited partners still need to be able to keep the general partners from grabbing more than their share of the firm's wealth or managing more conservatively than the limited partners would want.

The most striking difference between management and control rules in limited partnerships and corporations concerns the power to alter the standard form rules by agreement. In closely held corporations, the shareholders may, and often do, participate directly in management without jeopardizing their limited liability (*see* Section 5.03). By contrast, under the rule traditionally applicable to limited partnerships, the limited partners may not participate in management without risking personal liability for the firm's debts. Specifically, under ULPA § 7, a limited partner will be denied limited liability if "in addition to the exercise of his rights and powers as a limited partner, he takes part in the control of the business." This provision, and the successor provision in RULPA § 303, are applied and explained in the following case and notes.

GAST v. PETSINGER
Pennsylvania Superior Court
288 Pa. Super. 394, 323 A.2d 371 (1974)

HOFFMAN, Judge.

This appeal is from a summary judgment involving a contract dispute. Appellant charges in his Complaint that he was employed by LNG Services as a project engineer in 1968. For over a year, he was paid his agreed salary of $15,000.00 per year. From October of 1969 until March of 1971, when he severed his employment from the business, he continued in his capacity without pay. Upon tendering notice of termination of employment, appellant submitted a claim for back pay and expenses. This amount was never paid and a suit in assumpsit was thereupon instituted. The Complaint states that the business known as LNG Services is formally a limited partnership. The only named general partner is the defendant, Robert E. Petsinger. Nevertheless, appellant claims that the other named individual defendants, while ostensibly limited partners, were, by virtue of their participation in the enterprise, acting as general partners, and should therefore be liable for the monies due him.

* * *

[T]he Court entered an Order granting defendants' Motion of Summary Judgment. The plaintiff-appellant has appealed to this Court asserting that the Answers to Interrogatories and his own Deposition supported by documentary evidence establish certain involvement in the partnership by the named defendants that presents a factual dispute on the question of "control" which should be submitted to a jury.

We have examined the record in this case and find the following to be the degree and kind of participation of the Limited Partners in LNG Services:

1. All Limited Partners have the following rights and powers as described in the Limited Partnership Agreement:

    (a) the right to receive distributions from time-to-time and upon dissolution;

    (b) the right to prevent the transfer of assets and other acts "outside the ordinary business of the partnership" unless an aggregate of 50% in interest give written consent to the transfers or acts;

    (c) the right to examine the books and records of the partnership at the principal office of the partnership;.

    (d) the right to attend meetings "for the purpose of receiving the report of the General Partner and for taking any action referred to . . ." in clause (b), *supra*;

    (e) the right to transfer, sell or assign their interests to third parties;

(f) and, upon the death of a Limited Partner, to have his or her share of the profits and distributions inure to his or her Estate.

2. According to the Limited Partnership Agreement, "the management and control of the Partnership's day-to-day operation and maintenance of the property of the Partnership shall rest exclusively with the General Partner." Consistent with statutes regulating limited partnerships, the Agreement places the "control" of the business in the hands of the General Partner. The Limited Partners, by virtue of their capital contributions, have the powers mentioned above, and are prohibited from taking any "part in the conduct or control of the Partnership and its business and shall have no right or authority to act for, or bind, the Partnership."

* * *

The organization of LNG Services is in conformance with the Uniform Limited Partnership Act (59 P.S. § 171 *et seq.*). The certificate is in good order, and the Agreement delineates the powers, rights and liabilities of the General and Limited Partners in express terms. None of the powers mentioned therein exceed the degree of "control" which converts the status of a limited partner to that of general partner.

* * *

Only Dr. Garwin and Jerome Apt, Jr., appear to have acted in capacities which require some discussion and evaluation. In addition to receiving reports and attending meetings wherein status reports and additional capital investments were discussed, Dr. Garwin was employed by the Partnership as an independent engineering consultant with respect to certain projects undertaken by LNG Services for which service he was retained by the General Partner and in which, he and the General Partner assert, he remained subject to the supervision and control of Petsinger, the General Partner. Apt was also engaged from time to time as an independent consultant on certain projects. These individuals were described as "Project Managers" on several booklets which were attached to appellant's deposition as exhibits.

Accepting all the facts as asserted by the plaintiff as true, as we must do in determining the propriety of a summary judgment, we do not believe that, at least with respect to several of the appellees, this case so clearly was devoid of a single factual issue as to remove the matter from the deliberation of a jury.

* * *

The key issue before the lower court was whether the appellant had presented an arguable case demonstrating that some or all of the appellees had "take[n] part in the control of the business." The question of "control" has not been squarely met in Pennsylvania. We are, however, guided by decisions in a number of jurisdictions following the ULPA which have construed the term in various factual contexts. One excellent Harvard Law Review article examining this problem identifies the problem and the important factors to consider. "Investing Partners want to limit their liability in connection with the enterprise. They will not participate in managing the partnership's ordinary investment activities. . . . [H]owever, as a practical matter, it is unlikely that major commitments of capital would be made without informing and perhaps consulting with Investing Partners." Alan L. Feld, *The "Control" Test for Limited Partnerships*, 82 HARV. L.R. 1471, 1474.

State and federal courts have taken a similar view. The courts have held, without satisfactorily describing the standards by which to judge a limited partner's activities, that the following did not constitute taking part in the "control" of the business: acting as a foreman in the employ of the partnership, with the power to purchase parts as necessary without consulting the general partner, but without the power to extend credit without prior approval from the general partner or deal with the partnership account, *Silvola v. Rowlett*, 129 Colo. 522, 272 P.2d 287 (1954); acting as a member of the board of directors of the partnership (although the Court noted that he never did actually serve as such), *Rathke v. Griffith*, 36 Wash. 2d 394, 218 P.2d 757 (1950); acting as sales manager in a new car sales department of the partnership without power to hire or fire, and, with power to order cars only with the general partner's approval, *Grainger v. Antoyan*, 48 Cal. 2d 805, 313 P.2d 848 (1957); and, participating in the choice of key employees and giving a certain degree of "advice," *Plasteel Products Corporation v. Helman*, 271 F.2d 354 (1st Cir. 1959).

An analysis of each of the cases reveals that they were decided on their own facts and are of little use in forming rules or standards. In each case, it was not the position of the limited partner that was stated as permissible, but the actual role and degree of participation that each had in relation to the general partner. A reading of those cases reinforces the belief of this Court that the determination must be made on an ad hoc basis, and while employment may not be conflicting with the status of a limited partner, the "control" that partner has in the day-to-day functions and operations of the business is the key question. Does the limited partner have decision-making authority that may not be checked or nullified by the general partner? As Alan Feld notes in his article: "[While] some cases would permit the limited partner to 'advise' the general partners . . . it is not at all clear that Investing Partners may do so without fear of liability in view of the weight their advice is likely to carry, both because of the size of their investment and because they are 'carrying' Managing Partners' interests. The determination of control is a factual one and this relationship may, as a practical matter, give any 'advice' the color of a command in the partnership." 81 HARV. L.R. 1471, 1477.

Here, the appellant testified that partners Apt and Garwin acted in the partnership as "Project Managers." He stated in his deposition that the appearance of their names on brochures and reports, the obvious weight their "advice" carried in their recommendations and report on key projects, and their managerial responsibilities, all contributed to a belief that they exercised "control." The defendant Petsinger, the General Partner, confirms the fact that these two individuals acted as independent "consultants" on various "projects." He denies their authority or right to control the business decisions. His statement as defendant is conclusionary, and since we are reviewing this appeal on a summary judgment, the inference most favorable to the plaintiff must be made.

It may be true that once all the facts are in the appellees, Apt and Garwin, will have been found not to have exercised the degree of "control" necessary to impose general liability upon them. We agree that the nature of the business of LNG Services, described as having as its purposes "the management of the development, engineering, and technical advice relating to the development or uses for liquefied natural gas, etc.," required the utilization of expert opinion of technical minds. It is not apparent from the face of the record that the technical skills and training of Apt and Garwin did not by virtue of their retention as "Project Managers" place them in a position where their "advice" did influence and perhaps, control the decisions of the General Partner, whose particular expertise is unknown.

With respect to the appellees, John J. McMullen Associates, Inc., J. Judson Brooks, John C. Oliver, Jr., W. D. George, Jr., Alexander M. Laughlin, Charles Manning, and Joan M. Apt, we affirm the order of the court below granting defendants' motion for summary judgment. None of the above-named partners is shown to have engaged in any activity or participated beyond those lawfully and expressly stated in the Limited Partnership Agreement. With respect to the appellees, Jerome Apt, Jr., and Dr. Leo Garwin, we reverse the order and judgment of the court below, and remand the case for further proceedings consistent with this opinion.

NOTES AND QUESTIONS

(1) **Explaining the control rule.** Possible explanations of the bases of the control rule applied in *Gast* are discussed in **Abrams, Basile, Feld** and **Ribstein**, below. Does it follow that just because limited partners are acting like general partners they should be liable as such? Note that corporate shareholders are not liable merely for participating in control. Compare the far more elaborate tests for piercing the corporate veil discussed in Section 3.05.

(a) **Misleading about general partner status.** The control rule may be designed to ensure that a limited partner's participation in control does not mislead creditors into believing that the limited partner is really a general partner. *See* RULPA § 303, which provides that limited partners who participate in control of the business are "liable only to persons who transact business with the limited partnership reasonably believing, based upon the limited partner's conduct, that the limited partner is a general partner." But ULPA § 7 appears to hold limited partners who participate in control liable regardless of whether any third parties are misled.[3] If the potential for misleading explains control liability, RULPA § 303 is unnecessary since a limited partner may be held liable on estoppel grounds under UPA § 16 or RUPA § 308.

(b) **Ensuring that managers are liable.** Another potential explanation for the control rule is that it ensures that the managers of the firm, whoever they are, will be liable for the firms' debts, and thereby aligned with creditors' interests. Unlike simply forbidding the limited partners from managing,

---

[3]   *See Delaney v. Fidelity Lease Ltd.*, 526 S.W.2d 543 (Tex. 1975) (the mere fact that plaintiffs were not misled into thinking that the limited partners were really general partners did not preclude "control" liability). There is authority for a reliance test under this provision. *See Frigidaire Sales Corp. v. Union Properties, Inc.*, 88 Wyo. 2d 400, 562 P.2d 244 (1977). For an application of the reliance test under ULPA, see *In re Ridge II*, 158 B.R. 1016 (C.D. Cal. 1993) (even if there was substantial participation in control by limited partners, there was still an issue of fact whether creditors could recover deficiency because under California law reliance theory, creditor must prove it was led to believe limiteds were generals).

the control rule gives the limited partners the flexibility to take over management when they must, as where the firm is nearing insolvency, while protecting both third parties and the general partners by ensuring that, when the limited partners do take over, they take on personal liability as well. Note that the control rule applies only when the limited partners take over the business, and not when the general partners give up management to non-owners, such as a management company. Can you explain this limitation?

(2) **Elimination of the control rule.** The Georgia and Missouri versions of RULPA § 303[4] and ULPA (2001) provide that a limited partner does not become liable for the debts of the limited partnership "by participating in the management or control of the business." ULPA (2001) § 303.

(3) **The control rule and choice of form.** The advent of the limited liability company (*see* Section 6.04, below) provides, in effect, a way of opting into or out of the control rule in that parties who want the control rule can choose the limited partnership, while parties who do not can choose the limited liability company. Requiring all limited partnerships to adopt the control rule helps ensure that the owners of the firm cannot change rules in midstream, possibly frustrating third parties' expectations, without changing the form of their business. This might be one reason why states adopted limited liability company statutes rather than simply amending their limited partnership statutes to eliminate the control rule or make it optional. Note that the choice-of-form argument depends to some extent on how easy it is to change forms through merger or conversion. For an additional argument for maintaining distinct limited partnership and LLC business forms, see Note 3 in Section 6.04.

PROBLEMS

(1) A group of business people engaged in real estate development have formed a limited partnership under RULPA. Some will contribute management skills and receive a fee for their services, while others will contribute substantially all of the money and receive a share of the profits. In order to protect their capital, and in order to be able to use their substantial expertise in real estate matters, the capital contributors want to have certain powers. Specifically, they seek your advice as to whether the following powers given to limited partners in the partnership agreement and exercised by the partners will create problems: (a) The power to remove the general partners; (b) The power to control the salaries of the general partners; (c) The power to veto the purchase or sale of any property; and (d) The power to select, and to prevent the general partners from firing, any general contractors employed by the partnership. In giving your advice, consider which of these provisions will present the most problems and which the least so that the limited partners can decide on that basis what to include in the agreement.

---

[4]   Ga. Code Ann. § 14-9-303; Mo. Rev. Stat. § 359.201.

(2) How would your answer to Problem (1) change if the parties' agreement provided that all contracts between the limited partnership and third parties must contain a clause in which the third party acknowledges that he or she is dealing with a limited partnership having certain named limited partners?

[C] Transfer of Interests and Dissolution

Limited partnership rules regarding transfer of interests and dissolution differ somewhat from those in general partnerships. UPA § 6(2) and RULPA §§ 403 and 1105 provide that general partnership provisions apply to limited partnerships unless the limited partnership statute provides for different rules. ULPA (2001) provides comprehensively for limited partnerships without "linkage" to the general partnership statutes.

With respect to transfer of interests, RULPA §§ 701-705 and ULPA (2001) §§ 301, 401, 701-704 provide for rules that are similar to those in the partnership statutes—*i.e.*, financial rights are freely transferable but members must approve transfer of management rights or admission of partners. While it makes sense to apply the same rules to general partners in both types of firms, the rationale for restricting transferability of limited partners' management rights is less clear. In ULPA and RULPA it might have been best explained on the basis that it avoided corporate-type free transferability for tax purposes. However, with the loosening of tax classification rules discussed in Section 6.01, this is no longer a complete explanation. Preservation of restrictions on limited partners' management rights in ULPA (2001) is, however, consistent with the greater recognition of such rights in that Act, including by elimination of the "control" rule and provision for default consent rights in § 406(b).

Dissociation of a limited partner does not dissolve the partnership. Moreover, RULPA § 801(4), unlike the UPA, provides that dissociation of a general partner does not dissolve the partnership if the partners vote to continue it. ULPA (2001) § 801(3) continues this trend toward greater continuity in limited partnerships by providing that the limited partnership does not dissolve in this situation except by further affirmative vote unless the dissociating general partner was the last.

REFERENCES

Basile, *Limited Liability for Limited Partners: An Argument for the Abolition of the Control Rule*, 38 VAND. L. REV. 1199 (1985).

Feld, *The Control Test for Limited Partnerships*, 82 HARV. L. REV. 1472 (1969).

Ribstein, *An Applied Theory of Limited Partnership*, 37 EMORY L.J. 837 (1988) (Ribstein 1).

Ribstein, *Limited Partnerships Revisited*, 67 U. CIN. L. REV. 953 (1999) (Ribstein 2).

§ 6.04 Limited Liability Companies

All states have statutes providing for "limited liability companies" ("LLCs"), which were passed in the wake of the loosening of the tax classification rules described in Section 6.01. Over a half million LLCs filed returns in the 1999 tax year—significantly more than the number of limited partnerships, and over 30% of the total number of tax partnerships.[5]

In general, LLCs under most statutes are distinguished from close corporations and limited partnerships in that the members have complete flexibility to adopt partnership-style management and control provisions while retaining limited liability. In other words, there is no "control rule" (*see* Section 6.03) or judicial or legislative hostility to partnership-type management as in closely held corporations (*see* Section 5.03). Instead, the statutes generally provide for direct participation by the members in management as a default provision that can be varied by contrary agreement.

The following Sections summarize the developing law on LLCs. It is important to keep in mind that LLC statutes are a work in process, with the precise outlines of the LLC form changing as states adopt new and amended statutes. The tables in **Ribstein & Keatinge** provide a detailed review of the statutes.

[A] Formation

All LLC statutes require the firm to publicly file articles or a certificate, just as limited partnerships and corporations must do. The provisions on contents of the filed document are generally similar to those under RULPA § 201. Some LLC statutes provide for consequences to owners of defectively formed firms that are based on MBCA-type "assuming to act" provisions found in corporation statutes, rather than the "erroneous partner" provisions found in limited partnership statutes (*see* ULPA § 11, RULPA § 304, and MBCA § 2.04)—*i.e.*, owners of defectively formed LLCs generally are only personally liable for the defective LLC's obligations if they purport to act for the LLC, knowing it has not been properly formed.

[B] Management and Control

As noted at the beginning of this Section, a critical difference between LLC statutes and limited partnership and corporation statutes is that there are few statutory limitations on the form of management. All but a few of the LLC statutes provide that, like partnerships, LLC's are managed by members unless they agree otherwise. Most statutes provide that LLCs that are managed by managers must so provide in the articles or certificate or at least in a written operating agreement. Most statutes limit the power

---

[5]   *See* Zempel & Wheeler, *Partnership Returns, 1999, from Statistics of Income Bulletin,* Fall 2001, Figure F, at 53.

of non-managing members of manager-managed LLCs to bind the firm in transactions with third parties. As discussed below in Chapter 8 (*see* Note 6 following *Burns v. Gonzalez* in Section 8.02, below), this is an important distinction between LLCs and general partnerships.

[C] Transfer of Interests and Dissolution

LLC statutory provisions on transferability of interests are similar to those in partnership statutes (*see* Section 4.03). The transferability provisions were originally designed to avoid the "corporate" tax characteristic of free transferability (*see* Section 6.01), but also reflect the greater default management power of LLC members as compared with limited partners. The statutes permit the members to contract around these limitations.

LLC statutes originally mimicked partnership statutes regarding dissolution and dissociation, again with an eye on the tax classification rules. They generally provided that, unless the agreement or certificate provides otherwise, a member has a right to at least exit the firm and be paid the value of her interest, although unlike the UPA these statutes also provided for dissociation of members without necessarily causing winding up of the firm. Later statutes allowed the LLC to provide in the operating agreement for continuation after a member's dissociation. The "check-the-box" rule eliminates any tax-classification need for LLCs to avoid corporate-type continuity of life. Many statutes have been amended to provide that the LLC does not dissolve on dissociation of a member, as well as to eliminate the members' default power to dissociate.

NOTES AND QUESTIONS

(1) **The function of the LLC: a new standard form.** As discussed in Chapter 5, corporate statutory default rules do not fit most closely held firms. Although such firms can contract around these default rules, contracting in detail for every rule is costly. Thus, firms still may be left with ill-fitting default rules that they have neglected to alter. In particular, such firms may neglect to provide an "out" for disgruntled owners. When this happens, courts and statutes may supply exit routes in the form of oppression and buyout remedies (*see* Section 5.05). Yet the application of these remedies sometimes raises questions about whether the parties are getting rights they did not contract for. Making available a new standard form that combines partnership rules with limited liability lets closely held firms select the set of default rules that fits their needs (*see* **Ribstein 2**). Since the firms can now choose between corporate and partnership defaults while retaining limited liability, courts no longer need to assume that the firms chose the corporate set only for limited liability. This makes it clearer what rules firms want to have applied. Thus, in denying special relief in a non-statutory close corporation, the Delaware Supreme Court has pointed out that "Delaware statutory law provides

for many forms of business enterprise: partnerships . . .; limited partnerships . . .; limited liability companies . . .; business trusts . . . ."[6]

(2) **LLCs and close corporation statutes.** Why a new standard form for closely held firms in light of the availability of special close corporation statutes (*see* Section 5.04[E])? Although these statutes seem to provide the same sort of special standard form that is provided by LLC statutes, they also add new formalities and qualifications to those already provided for in the corporation statute, and invoke standard corporate default rules with respect to issues not specifically covered by the statute or the parties' agreement. Moreover, firms formed under special close corporation provisions are still taxed as corporations unless they comply with Subchapter S. Finally, special close corporation statutes, because they have never been very popular, have not undergone the process of innovation and evolution that has occurred for LLCs.

(3) **LLCs and limited partnerships.** Now that the LLC has become an accepted form of business, what should become of the limited partnership? Note that, in contrast to LLCs, limited partnership statutes traditionally provide for centralized management by general partners enforced by the "control rule" (*see* Section 6.03[B]). As discussed in Note 3 following *Gast,* permitting the parties to choose between LLCs and limited partnerships increases the justification for the control rule. In particular, limited partnerships are suitable for family firms in which the founder gives equity interests in the firm to her children but seeks to ensure that the children are locked out of control.

As noted in this Subsection, both LLC and limited partnership statutes are being revised to eliminate members' right to exit at will, which has the advantage of reducing the tax valuation of the members' interests under I.R.C. § 2704. A problem with this type of provision is that it may bring back the very "oppression" type problems partnership-type firms, including LLCs, are supposed to solve (*see* Note 1, above). But the limitations on exit may make more sense in family limited partnerships, where the parties want to create an "estate freeze" that locks in the junior family members.

REFERENCES

Ribstein & Keatinge, RIBSTEIN & KEATINGE ON LIMITED LIABILITY COMPANIES (1992 & Supp.).

Ribstein, *The Emergence of the Limited Liability Company*, 51 BUS. LAW. 1 (1995) (Ribstein 1).

Ribstein, *Statutory Forms for Closely Held Firms: Theories and Evidence from LLCs*, 73 WASH. U. L.Q. 369 (1995) (Ribstein 2).

---

[6]   *Nixon v. Blackwell*, 626 A.2d 1366, 1380, n.20 (Del. 1993).

§ 6.05 Limited Liability Partnerships

Statutes have now taken what would seem to be the ultimate step toward the "incorporated partnership." Beginning in 1992 with Texas and Louisiana, most states have now adopted "registered limited liability partnership" (LLP) provisions as part of their general partnership statutes. In general, LLP provisions allow general partnerships to adopt a form of limited liability. All of the statutes provide that a general partnership may become an LLP by filing a certificate. Notwithstanding the filing, the statutes define LLPs as general partnerships. Some statutes, including New York's, apply only to professional firms.

All LLP statutes provide that LLP partners are not personally liable for the negligence or other misconduct of other partners or employees unless the partner participated in or supervised the wrongdoing. Under some statutes, LLP partners are liable for several categories of conduct, including misconduct in which they are involved directly or indirectly involved through supervision; and conduct that is no more than a breach of contract. In other words, some LLPs have "limited limited liability." Most recently enacted LLP statutes limit the liability of LLP partners for both contract-type and tort-type liabilities. For a detailed analysis of the statutes, see **Bromberg & Ribstein**, ch. 3.

In return for their limited liability, LLP members sacrifice some of the informality of general partnership. LLP provisions prescribe registration formalities, restrict the name of the LLP, and, in some cases, require the firm to insure or purchase a bond.

NOTES AND QUESTIONS

(1) **Choosing between LLP or LLC: the transition factor.** Why would a firm become an LLP rather than an LLC? Indeed, given the availability of LLCs, why bother to enact LLP provisions in the first place? One possible answer may be that a firm that is now a general partnership does not have to formally convert into or merge with a different type of firm in order to obtain limited liability. Among other things, this means that the firm continues to be subject to the same set of default rules and so does not need to change its agreement; and the firm need not cash out members or pay off creditors. However, creditors have the benefit of the partners' vicarious liability at least for debts as of the time of the registration. Also, just because the statutory default rules remain the same, it does not necessarily follow that the members would not want a new agreement in some respects to reflect their new-found limited liability. Among other things, LLP registration may transfer liability risk from the partners as a whole to those who are involved in supervising or monitoring high-risk activities, and still may be subject to individual liability under the LLP statute (*see* Note 7, below).

(2) **Choosing between LLP and LLC: the regulatory factor.** Another reason why firms may want to be LLPs rather than LLCs is that the partnership form of business may create fewer problems with regulators and taxing authorities (*see* **Ribstein &**

Kobayashi). Among other things, a partnership interest may be less likely to be regulated under the federal securities laws than an LLC interest (*see* Section 12.02, below).

(3) **Voting on the LLP registration.** LLP statutes that address the issue provide that registration may be authorized by a majority vote of the partners. It is not clear what happens when the statute does not provide for voting on the registration. Should this be regarded as an "ordinary" matter that can be approved by a mere majority in the absence of contrary agreement, or as an extraordinary matter or amendment of the agreement which requires unanimity, again in the absence of contrary agreement? Consider these questions in light of the general theoretical discussion of voting rules in Section 4.01. Although a unanimity rule will impose high decision-making costs, a majority-vote rule could impose heavy costs on dissenting partners, particularly under liability rules which reallocate liability from the partners as a whole to those involved in monitoring high-risk activities (*see* Note 7, below).

(4) **Policy considerations concerning members' limited liability.** Is the limitation of LLP partners' liability troubling from a policy standpoint? Consider the theoretical discussion of limited liability in Section 3.03. Does a limitation of partners' liability raise policy issues that are not raised by limiting liability of corporate shareholders or LLC members? One possible problem is that there are no creditor-protection limitations on distributions and contributions in general partnership statutes as there are in statutes providing for other types of limited liability firms. Some LLP statutes replace this protection with mandatory insurance. Note that the LLP form may come under increased policy scrutiny as large accounting firms, which generally are organized as LLPs, are sued in connection with Enron and other corporate frauds that emerged in 2002.

(5) **Scope of limited liability: distinction between "contract-type" and "misconduct" liabilities.** Why do you suppose many LLP statutes limit LLP partners' personal liability only for misconduct-type debts and not for debts that arise out of ordinary contracts? One might argue that the limitation is unnecessary for contract-type debts, since the firm can contract with such creditors to limit liability. But if the firm usually will contract for limited liability, this should be provided by default. Conversely, if firms usually will not contract to limit liability, this suggests that limiting liability as to involuntary creditors is inefficient. Even if partners' personal liability is appropriate with respect to some creditors, it is not necessarily the right default rule. The theoretical discussion in Section 3.03 suggests that partners' personal liability will be most valuable for large creditors. These creditors are in a position to contract for personal liability. On the other hand, under a default rule of personal liability, the firm would be forced to contract to limit liability precisely in those small-claim situations where the cost of bargaining is likely to outweigh the benefits. An additional problem is that, where contract-type creditors have the benefit of personal liability, they will not have an incentive to monitor the firm and insist that it insure as will creditors in other limited-liability firms. Of course, the partners may have an incentive to insure and guard against excessive risk if they will be personally liable to contract creditors when tort claims absorb

the firm's assets. Consider, in that light, the discussion in Note 6, below, of priority of payment of claims. In the final analysis, is the distinction between contract-type and tort-type claims justified, or at least explained, by the concern that a complete limited liability entity would not be a true "partnership" for tax and regulatory purposes?

(6) **The scope of limited liability: contribution liability.** Most LLP statutes provide that the liability limitation applies not only to suits by creditors directly against partners, but also to the partners' duty to contribute on dissolution to make up any shortfall of assets to liabilities. This is an important point, since creditors often are barred from recovering directly from partners and so must rely on partners' contribution obligation. Yet this can create troublesome problems. Suppose, for example, that a partnership has $50,000 in assets, and $100,000 in debts divided equally between "contract" debts, for which partners retain individual liability, and "tort" debts, for which they do not. Should the $50,000 in assets be used to pay tort debts, leaving partners with their full contribution liability? Although this seems inconsistent with the partners' limitation of liability, denying any recovery to the tort creditors also seems inconsistent with their continued right of action against the partnership entity. The courts might deal with this problem by requiring that the partners be personally responsible at least for the portion of total claims that is represented by the "contract-type" claims for which partners' liability is not limited. But note that, subject to bankruptcy rules regarding "preferences," partners threatened with tort liabilities may have some flexibility to deplete the firm's assets by paying off contract-type claims. Problems similar to those discussed above in this Note apply in allocating payments among those who extended credit before and after the partnership registered as an LLP.

(7) **The scope of member liability: personal wrongdoing.** LLP statutes do not, of course, limit partners' liability for their own wrongdoing. Such wrongdoing could include a negligent failure to supervise a co-partner. Most LLP statutes go further and explicitly impose liability for failing to monitor or supervise. For example, the New York statute provides that partners "shall be personally and fully liable and accountable for any negligent or wrongful act or misconduct committed by him or her or by any person under his or her direct supervision and control." The effect of both statutory and common law liability of individual partners may be to reallocate liability from the partners as a whole to the partners who have the misfortune of being involved in the riskier aspects of the business (such as the bank regulation department of a law firm). These partners may demand to be compensated for this risk if they have the power to veto the registration (*see* Note 3, above). Supervisory liability also could have the perverse effect of discouraging partners from supervising, as where they are asked for help on a matter in another department.

(8) **Application of partnership rules to LLPs.** Should general partnership default rules apply to limited-liability partners? For example, should LLP partners who make no credit contributions share voting and financial rights according to their capital contributions rather than equally, as under general partnership law? Should partners who do not have personal exposure to the firm's liabilities have the same exit right as

non-LLP partners? In analyzing these issues, keep in mind that providing special rules for LLPs can reduce or eliminate the advantages of providing for limited liability in the partnership form.

(9) **A new twist: the LLLP.** Some LLP statutes provide that a limited partnership can register as an LLP, thereby producing an "LLLP"—*i.e.,* a limited liability limited partnership. This firm would be a limited partnership in all respects except that the general partner would have the limited liability of a partner in an LLP. Although the firm could achieve a similar result by incorporating the general partner, this would subject the general partner to corporate tax treatment. The LLP mechanism also may be better than reorganizing the general partner as an LLC, which would involve creating a new entity, with potential tax and liability consequences. ULPA (2001) helps bring the LLLP into the mainstream of limited partnership law by requiring all limited partnerships to elect in their certificates whether they will be LLLPs or non-LLLPs.

(10) **Limited liability as the default rule.** In light of the expansion and liberalization of limited liability forms of business, might limited liability become the default form of business—*i.e.,* that even general partnerships will have limited liability?

REFERENCES

BROMBERG & RIBSTEIN ON LLPs, RUPA AND ULPA (2001) (2002).
Ribstein & Kobayashi, *Choice of Form and Network Externalities,* 43 WM. & MARY L. REV. 79 (2001).

CHAPTER 7

Governance of the Publicly Held Business

We turn now to the distinct issues concerning the governance of publicly held businesses, characterized by numerous owners and freely traded shares. Publicly held businesses are generally governed in the manner explained in Section 5.01, above: (1) most business decisions are made by corporate officers and directors, who act as agents for generally passive shareholders, rather than by the shareholders themselves; (2) when shareholders do make decisions (such as when they elect directors or vote to approve fundamental corporate changes like mergers or sales of all or substantially all the firm's assets), decisions are typically made by a majority vote; and (3) votes are allocated among shareholders according to their financial contributions to the firm—*i.e.*, one-share-one-vote, not one-shareholder-one-vote.

The chapter begins in Section 7.01 by briefly discussing some issues concerning corporate finance. Although these issues are relevant throughout corporate law, they are particularly important in publicly held firms, where efficient capital markets and the greater ability to diversify portfolios fundamentally affect how governance issues should be addressed.

Section 7.02 discusses some of the basic issues that arise by virtue of the delegation of authority from shareholders to directors and officers. Sections 7.03-7.06 then examine some of the principal state and federal regulations aimed at protecting shareholders and others from managers of publicly held firms—federal proxy regulation (Section 7.03), the shareholder proposal rule (Section 7.04), state laws granting shareholders access to shareholder lists (Section 7.05), and state laws providing for cumulative voting (Section 7.06). Finally, Section 7.07 discusses some alternative methods to ensure that shareholder and other interests are respected by corporate officers and directors, including internal management devices, the "monitoring board," and boards that include representatives of constituencies other than shareholders.

§ 7.01 An Introduction to Finance in the Publicly Held Firm

"Corporate finance" is basically the study of the markets in which financial instruments are traded. These various instruments can be seen as ways of allocating "cash flows," or cash generated by firms. Financial markets accommodate investors' and firms' varying preferences for consumption and spending. In other words, the markets let firms invest for future returns even if their shareholders want to be able to spend now.

In addition, financial markets help corporate managers value business projects and other investments, and therefore decide how best to use the firm's assets.

Some lawyers may believe that these complicated matters can be left to the finance experts. However, Enron and other corporate scandals that emerged in 2002 demonstrated clearly the dangers to lawyers and their clients of deferring to these experts.

[A] The Starting Point: Present Value of Expected Future Cash Flows

The value of cash to be received in the future is referred to as present value. To take a simple example, consider a U.S. treasury bill offering a "cash flow" in a year of $110—that is, a repayment of principal plus interest. Finance theory tells us that the present value of the treasury bill can be determined from the following equation: **PV = $110/(1 + r)** where PV is the present value, or the value today, of the $110 to be received in a year, and r is the rate of interest that the buyer would charge—that is, the buyer's "time value" of money.

The time value of money is determined by the laws of supply and demand. For example, the time value of a t-bill is largely attributable to the fact that, all things being equal, people would rather have money available for spending than give it to someone else and defer spending. At the same time, some people and organizations (like the U.S. government) have more uses for money than they have money. Those who need more money will pay those who have it to defer their spending. The time value of money is also affected by inflation—that is, the expectation that things will cost more in a year than they do today.

As a practical matter, "r" in the above equation would be filled in by the actual bids of investors. If investors demand a 10% interest rate to compensate them for not being able to spend money now and for the risk of inflation, the present value of a t-bill offering a "cash flow" in one year of $110 would be $100 ($110/(1 + .10)). We can guess "r" by looking at the interest rates investors demand for comparable investments.

Now consider an investment in a firm's common stock. The cash flow of that stock in a year is the price for which the stock is expected to sell in a year—the value of the stock today (V) plus the appreciation in one year (A1)—plus any distributions (that is, dividends or repurchases of stock) during that time (D1). Using the formula above, **PV = (V + A1 + D1)/(1 + r)**, where r is the rate of return or time value of money demanded by investors. (Distributions and appreciation will be referred to collectively as the stock's "return.") Thus, if the stock is expected to increase in value from $100 to $110 in one year and to produce dividends of $10 and we decide r = 20%, PV = $100.

Coming up with a value is considerably trickier in this situation than it was for the t-bill because we know neither the appropriate interest rate (r) nor the expected return (D1 + A1). This brings up the subjects of expected value and risk.

[B] Expected Value

To calculate D1 + A1 we would need to ask, what might happen to our stock over the next year? The answer any securities expert will give you is: maybe some good things, maybe some bad things, and maybe not much either way. Consider, for example, a film company, Fine Pictures, that has some very expensive films in production. Production difficulties could drive the films way over budget, the films could flop, or the films could each be another "Titanic," or some combination of the above. We have some idea of the probabilities of each of these occurrences because we know the personnel involved and their track records.

The net result of all this figuring could look like this:

Probability	Return	Weighted value
20%	−10	−2
20%	50	10
30%	−20	−6
30%	60	<u>18</u>
		20

This chart shows the values of the potential returns for Fine stock (appreciation + dividends) over the next year, and the percentage probabilities of each. The chart arrives at a single expected return, which is the probability-weighted average of the four possible outcomes.

[C] Risk

We now have a value to insert for D1 + A1, but we need a value for r. Should we borrow this number from the going t-bill rate? Obviously not, because the t-bill is certain to generate its expected return of $10, while the stock may have a return of -10, 50, -20, or 60, depending upon which outcome occurs. Investors must be paid not only to defer spending and for inflation, but also for the risk that D1 + A1 will turn out to be something other than expected return. In other words, investors must be compensated for the "variance" between possible outcomes.

To understand risk, compare the above expected value chart with the following one for Cosmic Pictures, which specializes in expensive pictures with quirky scripts:

Probability	Return	Weighted value
20%	−50	−10
20%	90	18
30%	−40	−12
30%	80	<u>24</u>
		20

Note that the probability-weighted average of possible outcomes is precisely the same for Cosmic as for Fine Pictures. But there is an important difference between the two investments: The spread, or more technically the "variance" between possible outcomes is greater for Cosmic than for Fine. Financial theory assumes that investors don't like "variance" (sometimes referred to in financial theory as "risk"), and therefore that investors will apply a greater discount rate, r, to the Cosmic investment than to the Fine investment. The result will be a lower present value for Cosmic than for Fine, even though the expected values of the cash flows of the two firms are the same.

Variance can be defined mathematically: For each possible outcome, the amount by which the outcome differs from the expected value is squared and then multiplied by the probability of that outcome. Variance is the sum of the resulting numbers for all possible outcomes. Another way of quantifying risk is to compute the standard deviation, which is the square root of the variance.

Assuming a normal (i.e., bell-shaped) distribution, there is a probability of about 2/3 that results will fall within one standard deviation above or below the expected value. So if the expected value is 10 and the standard deviation is 11, there is a 2/3 probability that the actual result will fall between -1 and 21. The greater the variance, the greater the standard deviation—that is, the wider the range of results that is expected to occur with a 2/3 probability.

[D] Another Look at Risk: The Portfolio Theory and CAPM

To fully understand risk and return, it is vital to appreciate that investors do not buy only individual stocks, but rather hold portfolios of investments. Investors are therefore primarily concerned with the risk and return characteristics of their portfolios, not the risk and return characteristics of particular securities.

Expected *portfolio return* can be calculated quite simply by computing the weighted average of the expected returns of all of the stocks in the portfolio. Thus, the portfolio return of a portfolio consisting half of stock A with return 15% and half of stock B with return 5% is 10%. Calculating portfolio risk—the combined risk of all of the securities in a portfolio—is more difficult.

To determine *portfolio risk* one must determine the "covariance" of the securities. Covariance is the relationship of the risk of the stocks held *together* in the portfolio to the risk of the two stocks held *separately* in two portfolios. A standard example would be umbrella and swimsuit stocks. An investor who owned only one would suffer financially more from bad weather or gain more from good weather than one who held both. The seminal work on this idea is **Markowitz**.

The concept of covariance is the basic principle underlying selection of stocks for a portfolio. But it doesn't tell us precisely which stocks to select, and in what proportions. You cannot put together a portfolio of common stocks that has no risk. For example, in the October, 1987 and July, 2002 "crashes," almost all common stocks fell. You can achieve this maximum diversification by holding the portfolio of all risky stocks, or what is called the "market portfolio," or close to this maximum diversification by holding only a few stocks.

[E] The Separation Theorem and CAPM

The limit on portfolio diversification leads to a fundamental distinction between types of risk. The risk that cannot be eliminated through diversification is referred to as "market" or "systematic" risk, or "beta"; the risk that can be "diversified away" is referred to as "unsystematic" or "unique" risk. The beta of a stock is its co-variance with the market portfolio. Thus, a stock with a beta of 1 varies as much as the market portfolio, a stock with a beta of 2 fluctuates twice as much as the market portfolio, and a stock with a beta of 1/2 fluctuates half as much. Riskless securities like government t-bills have 0 beta.

You could put together a portfolio of risky assets that achieves maximum diversification but yet offers a higher or lower expected return by combining this portfolio with risk-free debt or credit. If you want a lower expected return and less risk, lend some of your money at the risk free rate of interest (that is, buy government bonds). If you do that, you reduce risk and return in direct proportion. In other words, if you put half your assets into government bonds, you have cut your risk in half, and reduced your risk premium by half the difference between the return of the market portfolio and the risk-free rate. For example, if the risk of the market portfolio, measured in terms of standard deviation, is 12, the return is 10%, and government bonds are trading for 5%, you will now have a portfolio with a risk of 6 and a return of 7½%. You can achieve commensurate increases in risk and return by investing double your assets in the market portfolio and borrowing the necessary extra money at the risk-free rate. In other words, under the same assumptions as above, your risk will be 24 (because for every unit of fluctuation of the portfolio, you now incur a fluctuation both of your initial pile of assets and of your borrowed funds) and your expected return will be 15%.

This discussion has a very important implication: Every investor who wants to own an efficient portfolio can do this in the same way, by owning the market portfolio and either lending or borrowing at the risk-free rate of interest. Another way to state this is that the decision of which risky securities to own is separate from the decision of how much risk to bear. This is the "separation theorem" first stated in **Tobin**.

The separation theorem is important not simply because all investors should or do invest this way, but because they *can*. If enough investors can take advantage of this opportunity, the prices of all securities will be priced on this basis. Suppose, for example, that a security were offered bearing the risk and expected return associated with an incompletely diversified portfolio. Smart investors would not buy this stock because they could get a better expected return at the same risk level by owning a well-diversified portfolio and lending at the risk-free rate. The market would eventually catch on and bid down the price of the stock until it offered a lower price for the same expected return.

All this leads to an even more important insight: The expected return of *every* stock is directly proportional (that is, bears a straight-line relationship) to the return of the market portfolio. More specifically, the expected risk premium of any stock is directly proportional to its beta—its market risk compared to that of the market portfolio. Mathematically, the expected risk premium of a risky stock is the beta of the stock times the risk premium of the market portfolio, or $r - rf = B(rm - rf)$, where r is the expected return on the stock, rf is the expected risk-free return, B is the stock's beta, and rm is the expected return on the market portfolio. This is consistent with the separation theorem, which holds that investors can maximize their return at a given level of risk by taking only market risk—that is, by holding the market portfolio. So investors are not paid for taking risk that they could eliminate by holding that portfolio. By analogy, consumers can not buy tires more cheaply just by telling the seller that they plan to use them for coffee tables rather than transportation. This is the "capital asset pricing model," or "CAPM."

The capital asset pricing model can be demonstrated by the following series of statements: (1) the market portfolio offers the highest expected return at a given degree of risk; (2) therefore you would not buy a stock unless its contribution to the risk of the portfolio was directly proportional to its expected return; (3) therefore the expected return of every risky stock (that is, every stock in the market portfolio) must be directly proportional to the stock's contribution to the risk of the market portfolio; (4) the contribution of a stock to the risk of the market portfolio is its beta; (5) therefore the expected return of every stock is directly proportional to its beta. The seminal works on the capital assets pricing model are **Lintner** and **Sharpe**.

As a practical matter, CAPM means that you can calculate a stock's expected return by determining (1) the stock's beta by plotting the stock's past return in comparison with that of the market portfolio; (2) the expected return of the market portfolio by referring to a standard market index (like the S & P 500); and (3) the risk-free rate of interest.

CAPM has been used as a way of testing other theories, including theories concerning corporate governance (**Bhagat & Romano**) and, as we shall see, market efficiency. If beta determines the expected risk premium of a stock, any actual return in excess of the return predicted by a stock's beta must be for something other than risk. The return predicted by the stock's beta is referred to as "normal" return, and the excess is "abnormal" return. The abnormal return could be attributable, for example, to the effect of new data or events, such as the passage of an anti-takeover statute. An investor who consistently earns abnormal returns may have information that was not reflected in the price of the stock.

There are a number of possible arguments against CAPM and questions about empirical tests purporting to confirm it, including the following: (1) Securities prices do not perfectly align with CAPM's prediction, indicating that variables other than beta determine expected returns; (2) CAPM is a statement about investors' expected returns, which there is no way to measure other than assuming that investors initially priced the security on the basis of a "rational expectation" that returns would align with beta, which turned out to be correct; (3) it is impossible to test CAPM based on the portfolio of all risky assets, which includes such diverse assets as human capital and interests in closely held firms. But despite these problems, CAPM is currently the most widely used model of the relationship between risk and return.

[F] The Efficient Market Hypothesis

Investors don't normally calculate return and risk when they buy or sell stock. Instead, they simply "accept" the market price as accurately reflecting current risk-return information about the stock. This investor behavior is supported by the "efficient capital market hypothesis," or EMH. The best guide to the theory and evidence of market efficiency continues to be **Malkiel,** which is updated periodically.

EMH originally was broken down into three "forms": "weak," "semi-strong" and "strong," based on the types of tests that have been done of the theory (**Fama (1970)**). Although the theory has become considerably more nuanced over the years to reflect more recent evidence (*see, e.g.,* **Fama (1991)**) the traditional form at least illustrates the range of results. The "weak" form of the theory says that the current price of the stock is an unbiased minimum variance estimate of the future price. This means that an investor cannot reduce the variance of expected returns, and therefore cannot make a profit, by analyzing historical price data and devising a trading rule based on that data. To put this in the commonly used jargon, securities prices take a "random walk." While prices are rational in the sense that they constantly react to new information, future stock prices will not correspond to any pattern that traders can discern by studying "charts" of historical price data. For an early empirical test of the weak form of the EMH, see **Fama (1965)**.

The "semi-strong" form of the theory states that investors cannot earn profits by learning publicly disclosed data. An important test of this theory was **Fama, Fisher, Jensen & Roll,** in which the authors analyzed the extent of "abnormal" returns from stock "splits." By studying price data of stocks that split, beginning 30 months before and ending 30 months after the split, the authors found positive abnormal returns beginning long before there could have been any information available about the split, until the month of the split. Thereafter, returns were generally close to normal, although there were slight positive abnormal returns on stocks that increased their dividends in the post-split period. The authors concluded from this evidence that the splits communicated information about the prosperity of the company—that there would later be dividend increases but that all of this information was fully incorporated in stock price by the month of the split. The subsequent positive returns from actual dividend increases were attributable to the elimination of any uncertainty about whether the dividends "promised" by the split would actually be forthcoming.

The "strong-form" of EMH states that no one can consistently earn positive abnormal returns from access to information (although people may occasionally profit from inside information). Perhaps the best-known empirical study is **Jensen (1968)**, which found that mutual funds did not consistently outperform portfolios of randomly selected stocks compiled to represent different proportions of the market portfolio (defined as the S & P Composite Index).

Although there is significant evidence supporting EMH, the evidence is not conclusive. The following are some "holes" in evidence of EMH:

(1) Evidence that you cannot earn abnormal returns from securities *trading* does not mean you cannot make or lose money by trading in the underlying assets represented by the securities—that is, by buying and selling entire companies. In other words, even if the market price of a company's stock is an unbiased guess as to its future market price, it may understate the value of the company. This has been referred to as the difference between "information-arbitrage" or "speculative" efficiency and "fundamental-valuation" or "allocative" efficiency. In other words, "irrational" traders may buy and sell other than on the basis of stock fundamentals. Many people have long believed that stock price movements are influenced to some extent by mob psychology, fashions, or bubbles. Such stock price movements are sometimes collectively referred to as "noise." The stock market's wild gyrations in October, 1987 and July, 2002 seemed to confirm that market movements had nothing to do with fundamental values. But note that even if stock prices are influenced by "noise," this "noisy" price may be a better guess about future returns than any person can make, so that decision-makers should trust the market price anyway. A related point is that it is never clear whether the "fundamental" value that is compared with market price is accurate. For example, earnings and dividends, which are often used as benchmarks of value, may be manipulated or misleading in the short run.

(2) Stock prices can exhibit "chaotic" behavior, the most important characteristic of which is that a seemingly unimportant event can cause great fluctuations. Chaos researchers have discerned patterns in very long term studies of stock price, which is seemingly inconsistent with the notion of the "random walk." But the seemingly chaotic behavior of stock prices does not necessarily rebut market efficiency. First, stock prices can be quite volatile without actually being chaotic. Second, and most importantly, the patterns found by chaos researchers were apparent only long after the fact and do not provide a way to "beat the market." For an entertaining look at someone who thought he found a way to do this, see the movie "Pi."

(3) The proof of "information-arbitrage" or "speculative" efficiency is flawed. The important studies supporting EMH measure whether certain types of information can produce returns that are "abnormal" as compared with the "normal" returns predicted by CAPM. But if CAPM is wrong—that is, if expected returns depend on factors other than a stock's beta—this eliminates the benchmark by which the studies have tested EMH. As discussed above, there is debate as to the validity of CAPM.

(4) EMH creates an interesting paradox: investment analysis persists although market efficiency supposedly prevents gains from research. Indeed, without this research, the market probably would not be as efficient as it is. This paradox does not generally refute market efficiency, but merely reinforces the point made earlier about the various levels or forms of market efficiency.

To see the efficient market paradox, consider the example of the analyst (named "Alexander") in Michael Lewis' LIAR'S POKER (at 176)[1] who continually thought of new

---

[1]   Copyright © 1990 by Norton & Co. Reprinted with permission.

ways to make money by investing on the heels of major events. Immediately after Chernobyl exploded, he called Lewis (a securities broker) and told him to buy oil futures, figuring that less nuclear power meant more need for oil.

> Minutes after I had persuaded a few clients to buy some oil, Alexander called back. "Buy potatoes," he said. "Gotta hop." Then he hung up. Of course, a cloud of fallout would threaten European food and water supplies, including the potato crop, placing a premium on uncontaminated American substitutes. Perhaps a few folks other than potato farmers think of the price of potatoes in America minutes after the explosion of a nuclear reactor in Russia, but I have never met them.

So market prices are efficient partly because of the Alexanders of the world. Yet if Alexander believed in perfectly efficient markets, he would not have bothered, instead figuring that the market had beaten him to it.

In short, the theory and evidence favoring the proposition that market prices are the best available guesses about future market prices and underlying values are, therefore, inconclusive. Should legal rules assume the validity of a theory that is still subject to some debate? Ultimately this depends on the projected costs and benefits of second-guessing the market. Since the evidence of market efficiency is great and the counter-theories inconclusive, policy-makers should be careful about second-guessing the market, particularly where the costs of doing so are likely to be substantial.

EMH has several important policy ramifications:

(1) Securities markets that are "fundamental-value" efficient allocate capital to its best uses. It follows that regulation that promotes market efficiency may be desirable, and regulation that interferes with market allocation of resources may be suspect. For a contrary argument, see **Stout.**

(2) Together with the separation theorem and CAPM, EMH tells us that the expected return of a security turns only on its beta, or market risk. In other words, investors in public firms should not attempt to pick good deals based on a determination that a stock is "underpriced," and should choose securities based solely on their preference for risk. This argues against compelling delivery of detailed disclosure documents to investors. Even if sophisticated analysts like Alexander can make money because of the paradox of market efficiency, it is highly unlikely that ordinary investors can gain by studying the stale information that appears in mandatory disclosure documents.

(3) EMH should make us wary of anyone who says she can determine whether the market is "overpricing" or "underpricing" particular securities, including corporate managers who defend against tender offers on the ground that the bid is "too low." This is true even if markets are only "information-arbitrage" efficient. To the extent that capital markets are also "fundamental-value" efficient, the price of a security is an accurate "report card" on the quality of management. It follows that if there is a profit opportunity in a hostile takeover, this is a good sign that the managers should be

replaced. This is obviously important in determining the appropriate scope of manager's power to defend against takeovers. *See* Chapter 14, below.

(4) The importance of market efficiency underscores the differences between publicly and closely held firms. Governance of closely held firms can be analyzed largely as a set of devices that substitute for the monitoring and easy exit provided by efficient trading markets. These include management-control, share transfer and dissolution provisions.

[G] Implications for leverage

The above discussion has implications for firms' debt-equity ratios, or leverage. Specifically, does a firm's capital structure matter in determining its value? According to the **Modigliani-Miller** theory (MM), the answer is no. In short, Modigliani and Miller suggest that, if you view a firm's total cash flow—that is, the total returns to all investors—as a "pie," the way in which the pie is divided among equity holders and creditors does not affect the value of the firm as a whole; it will still produce the same total cash flow. As discussed above in Section 3.02[C]), the increased return to shareholders from taking on more debt does not necessarily increase the value of their holdings after return is adjusted for risk. That more of the firm's cash flows are allocated to fixed claimants means not only that percentage returns to equity rise when total returns rise, but also that they commensurately decrease when the firm's total returns fall. In other words, leverage increases both the expected return to equity and the variance in the expected return.

Mathematically, the beta of any portfolio is a weighted average of the betas of the securities in the portfolio. (This follows from the fact that beta is directly proportional to expected return, and the expected return of a portfolio is a weighted average of the expected returns of the individual securities in the portfolio.) Thus, $Ba = [D/(D + E)$ x $Bd] + [E/(D + E)$ x $Be]$ where Ba is the beta of the firm's assets, Bd is the beta of the debt, Be is the beta of the equity, D is the total amount of debt and E is the total amount of equity. This can be restated as $Be = Ba + D/E (Ba - Bd)$. Thus, increasing a firm's debt increases the beta of its equity, and therefore the risk premium that shareholders would demand for holding this stock.

It might be argued that increasing a firm's leverage increases its value because some security holders prefer debt to equity. Suppose, for example, that an all-equity firm worth $1.2 million is capitalized at 10% and so is expected to earn $120,000. Suppose the firm offers debt, so that creditors have a claim on the first $60,000, and equity on the second $60,000. Because the first $60,000 is less risky, the creditors would presumably pay a premium in the form of accepting a lower interest rate—say, 9%, or a capitalizer of 11. This would make their investment worth about $660,000. Under MM, the value of equity must be $540,000, for a capitalizer of 9 to reflect the higher risk.

But what if some investors are risk-preferring, and so would not insist on an interest rate premium that fully adjusts for the added debt? Perhaps the equity holders would be willing to pay $550,000 for the firm's equity, with a commensurate reduction in their rate of return. If this is true, the firm would be worth $1,210,000 if it is leveraged, as compared with only $1,200,000 if it is not. However, this proposition runs up against the concept of "homemade leverage": The risk-preferring investors could have created precisely the same opportunity for themselves by buying the unlevered firm for $1,200,000 and borrowing $660,000 of the purchase price of their stock from a bank for an interest rate that reflects its risk (*i.e.*, 9%). (It is not unrealistic to assume that the shareholders can borrow from a bank at this interest rate since they can probably put up their shares as security.) These cagey investors would end up with equity carrying precisely the same return as in the previous example, but they would pay only $1,200,000 − $660,000 (the amount loaned by the bank) = $540,000. Moreover, given the opportunity of risk-preferring investors to produce "homemade leverage," the market will ensure that the price of stock of the levered firm does not exceed $540,000. The final lesson, therefore, is that a firm cannot increase its value simply by changing its capital structure to appeal to a market of risk-preferring investors.

MM works only under certain assumptions. First, it assumes efficient securities markets. Without efficient markets, "homemade leverage" doesn't work. Stock is less valuable as collateral if it doesn't reflect available information about the firm. Thus an outside (bank) lender would demand a higher interest rate than would the insiders (equity).

Second, "irrelevance" does not take taxes into account. Because interest payments on debt are tax-deductible to the firm, corporate debt may increase the value of the firm by decreasing the government's share of corporate earnings. Tax effects depend on a number of factors, including the amount of the tax on capital gains and a comparison between the corporation's marginal rate and that of its shareholders. If the shareholders are taxed at a higher rate than the corporation and are taxed heavily on capital gains, leverage may not increase the value of the firm even when taxes are taken into account.

Third, MM does not take transaction costs into account, including the costs of bankruptcy and the costs of resolving conflict of interest problems between shareholders and creditors. These conflicts become severe where the firm is close to bankruptcy, and the shareholders can readily transfer risks to creditors. Creditors charge up front to bear these risks. Thus, equityholders may want to avoid the credit charges resulting from a highly leveraged capital structure.

REFERENCES

Bhagat & Romano, Event Studies and the Law: *Part I: Technique and Corporate Litigation*, 4 AMER. L. & ECON. REV. __ (2002); *Part II: Empirical Studies of Corporate Law* (2001), http://papers.ssrn.com/paper.taf?abstract_id=268285.

Fama, *Efficient Capital Markets: II*, 46 J. FIN. 1575 (1991).

Fama, *Efficient Capital Markets: A Review of Theory and Empirical Work*, 25 J. FIN. 383 (1970).

Fama, Fisher, Jensen & Roll, *The Adjustment of Stock Prices to New Information*, 10 INT'L
    ECON. REV. 1 (1969).
Fama, *The Behavior of Stock Market Prices*, 38 J. BUS. 34 (1965).
Fama & MacBeth, *Risk, Return and Equilibrium: Empirical Tests*, 81 J. POL. ECON. 607
    (1973)
Jensen, *The Performance of Mutual Funds in the Period 1945-64*, 23 J. FIN. 389 (1968).
Lintner, *The Valuation of Risk Assets and the Selection of Risky Investments in Stock Port-
    folios and Capital Budgets*, 47 REV. ECON. & STATISTICS 13 (Feb. 1965).
Malkiel, A RANDOM WALK DOWN WALL STREET.
Modigliani & Miller, *The Cost of Capital, Corporation Finance and the Theory of Invest-
    ment*, 48 AM. ECON. REV. 261 (1958).
Markowitz, *Portfolio Selection*, 7 J. FIN. 77 (1952).
Sharpe, *Capital Asset Prices: A Theory of Market Equilibrium Under Conditions of Risk*, 19
    J. FIN. 425 (1964).
Tobin, *Liquidity Preference as Behavior Toward Risk*, 25 REV. ECON. STUD. 64 (Feb. 1958).

§ 7.02 The Separation of Ownership and Control in the Publicly Held Business

This Section discusses three important issues that arise in connection from the delegation of authority from shareholders of public corporations to management: (1)
whether shareholders need legal protections to ensure that managers act consistently
with shareholder interests; (2) whether the relationship between shareholders and managers should be governed by state or federal law; and (3) whether legal protections are
necessary to ensure that managers act consistently with societal interests.

[A] Do Shareholders Need Legal Protections to Constrain Managers?: The Berle-Means Thesis and Rebuttal

Berle & Means revolutionized thinking about the modern public corporation by
arguing that this institution separated ownership from control, raising questions about
whether the large amount of property controlled by such corporations was being used
in shareholders' interests. The Berle-Means theory is based on their observation that
managers, not shareholders, seem to be in control of public corporations. Berle and
Means found that each individual shareholder in the 200 largest nonfinancial corporations owned no more than a small fraction of the company's stock. With many small
share-holders widely scattered throughout the country, management could virtually
perpetuate itself by using corporate funds to solicit from the firm's shareholders the
power to vote their shares at corporate elections. Anyone wishing to unseat the incumbents would be faced with the enormously risky and expensive task of either acquiring
a controlling bloc of stock or soliciting from thousands of widely-scattered, individual
shareholders proxies to vote their shares.

Two significant economic problems of corporate governance are implicit in the Berle-Means thesis that managers, not shareholders, control public corporations. First, managers who act for shareholders rather than for their own benefit may try to further their own interests rather than those of their principals: as Adam Smith noted in 1776, "directors . . . being the managers rather of other people's money than of their own, it cannot well be expected that they should watch over it with the same anxious vigilance with which the partners in a private copartnery frequently watch over their own."[2] Second, shareholders who own small lots of a corporation's stock may be unable to monitor management effectively to minimize these agency costs. Because each shareholder can capture only a small portion of the gain from monitoring management, the other shareholders will "free ride" on the efforts of any monitoring shareholder. It follows that no shareholder will undertake monitoring unless this "free rider" problem can be solved. This problem cannot be remedied by giving shareholders more legal power because it simply will not make economic sense for the average shareholder to spend the time and energy necessary to watch over management (see **Manning** for an often-cited statement of this view).

The Berle-Means view was immediately influential, and its influence persists today. An important implication of the Berle-Means theory is that government regulation is necessary to make corporate managers more accountable to shareholders and ensure efficient use of corporate resources. Indeed, Berle-Means was an important intellectual basis for federal securities laws (*see* Section 7.03) adopted soon after the publication of the Berle-Means book.

Although the Berle-Means view has been widely accepted, much recent economic and legal scholarship is critical of the theory. The rebuttal to Berle and Means emphasizes that competition between firms for investment dollars leads companies to adopt market and organizational devices to constrain managers to act consistently with shareholder interests. In other words, the rebuttal to Berle and Means emphasizes private contracting rather than regulation as the best approach to the agency cost and free rider problems discussed above.

The following discussion outlines some of the organizational and market devices that mitigate the problems discussed by Berle and Means, as well as some of the trade-offs involved in selecting governance devices for particular firms. In reviewing the following materials, it should be kept in mind that the optimal mix of organizational and market devices to constrain managers may vary from firm to firm.

[1] Devices that Overcome Free Rider Problems

In corporations where ownership is dispersed in small lots among widely scattered shareholders, free-rider problems generally prevent shareholders from effectively monitoring management. The free-rider problem, however, can be overcome by two main

---

[2]   WEALTH OF NATIONS, Vol. 2, p. 741 (Glasgow ed. 1976).

devices: the takeover, where a single shareholder acquires *ownership* of a controlling block of stock, and the proxy contest, where a single shareholder obtains the *right to vote* a controlling block of stock. Thus, shareholder oversight remains a possibility even in firms where share ownership is widely dispersed. As noted above, however, takeovers and proxy contests are both risky and expensive; therefore, they may only be useful to police more extreme forms of managerial misconduct.

[a] Takeovers

The corporate takeover is perhaps the most important shareholder monitoring device. The quality of management is reflected in the price of the corporation's securities. A firm's selection of a new chief executive officer or adoption or elimination of a device for constraining management discretion is likely to affect the firm's expected returns and, in turn, according to the Efficient Capital Markets Hypothesis (*see* Section 7.01[F]), the firm's stock price. An outsider or existing shareholder can cash in on the difference between the current price and the value of the company under better management by buying control, often through a hostile tender offer, and making changes. This "market for corporate control" forces management to run the corporation consistently with shareholder interests or risk being replaced.

The active market for control obviously causes job insecurity for managers and other employees. Managers may respond by developing skills that will have market value outside the firm. To encourage managers to invest more time and effort in developing skills that are valuable to the firm but relatively unmarketable, the firm may choose to adopt governance devices that entrench managers, even if this reduces the effectiveness of the takeover market as a device for policing managers. Moreover, regulation in the wake of the 1980s takeover boom has curtailed the use of the hostile takeover as a governance mechanism. This has increased the importance of the other monitoring mechanisms discussed below.

[b] Proxy Contests

In a proxy contest, a shareholder or a group of shareholders solicits "proxies" (*i.e.,* the legal authority to vote shares owned by another) from the firm's shareholders (*see* Section 7.03). Proxy contests may occur in connection with a hostile tender offer (when, for instance, a hostile bidder seeks to replace existing managers with ones who will dismantle the target firm's takeover defenses), or they may be waged by shareholders, including institutional investors, who own only a fraction of the shares and do not intend to buy control. While proxy contests are an important monitoring device, they can also divert managers' energies. Thus, more proxy contests are not necessarily better, and firms may choose to adopt devices that discourage proxy contests.

[2] Monitoring by Large Shareholders

Unlike the Berle and Means paradigm, many public corporations have shareholders who own substantial percentages of the firm's stock. These large shareholders can capture much of the gain from effecting corporate changes and therefore may actively monitor the firm's affairs. This sort of oversight is obviously more direct than the threat that a shareholder or outsider will aggregate substantial votes through a proxy contest or tender offer. The References indicate the large amount of empirical and theoretical work that has been done on the role of institutional and other large investors, particularly in the wake of the decline in monitoring by the market for control. But concentrated shareholding has costs as well as benefits. Dispersion of ownership lets shareholders reduce risk by holding diversified portfolios of shares; shareholders therefore demand less compensation from the firm for "risk bearing." This benefit is lost when ownership is concentrated in a few holders.

Monitoring by large shareholders is not necessarily effective. **Romano (2001)**, reviewing empirical studies, concludes that institutional shareholder activism has not had much effect in improving firms' performance. There are several possible reasons for this ineffectiveness. First, large shareholders reduce but do not overcome free rider problems (*i.e.*, while large shareholders will monitor more than small shareholders, they still will not monitor to the same extent as a single shareholder who holds 100% of the firm's stock). Second, institutional investors often have reasons of their own to vote with incumbent managers, even when they believe others might do a better job. For example, banks and insurance companies have commercial contacts with the firms in which they invest that make them wary of alienating management. State pension plans are controlled by public officials subject to political pressures. These public officials may hesitate to vote pension plan stock against incumbent managers for fear of alienating their constituents. Finally, **Roe** has shown that regulation impedes institutional investors from taking large positions in companies and active roles in management. For example, mutual funds must diversify their investments in order to be entitled to "pass-through" tax treatment under Subchapter M of the Internal Revenue Code; and active pension fund managers face close scrutiny under the "prudent man" rule.

Demsetz & Lehn, in a pathbreaking study, explore the tradeoffs inherent in concentration of ownership in publicly held firms. They show how the degree to which ownership is concentrated in large shareholders depends on a variety of factors. First, large firm size discourages concentration of ownership because a given level of control requires greater sacrifice of the benefits of diversification of risk. Second, the greater the payoff to owners from monitoring, the more efficient it is for the owners to concentrate ownership to facilitate monitoring. For example, government-regulated firms tend to have more dispersed ownership because the owners have less ability to control management and suffer fewer costs as a result of mismanagement. It follows that dispersion of ownership interests and owner passivity are not inherently worse than concentration of ownership and institutional investor activism.

[3] Monitoring by Creditors

Agency costs between managers and shareholders can be minimized by simply reducing the amount of cash that is controlled by the managers—*i.e.*, by forcing managers to pay out cash flow in the form of mandatory interest payments, rather than letting them decide whether to pay dividends or retain earnings. Creditors also monitor managers. They can enforce covenants and governance mechanisms in debt instruments, even including forcing management turnover. They can also adjust the interest rate for, or impose restrictions on, new debt depending on the managers' past performance.

[4] Monitoring by Directors and Auditors

The firm can hire outside directors and outside auditors to monitor managers. But while monitoring by outside directors can be beneficial for many firms, it also introduces a costly procedural layer that makes it inappropriate for others.[3] In addition, recent events, such as the collapse of Enron and the indictment and conviction of the firm's accountants (Arthur Andersen), have caused some to question the effectiveness of these monitoring mechanisms.

[5] Employment Contracts and Managerial Markets

Manager and shareholder incentives can be aligned by compensation devices such as stock, stock option, and bonus plans (*see* Section 9.05). Compensation that rises or declines with the company's fortunes gives managers incentives to manage the company consistently with the interests of shareholders. But incentive compensation can create problems for managers who are at the mercy of the market for control, since termination can cause managers to lose deferred benefits. Managers therefore may insist on protection from this risk such as expensive "golden parachutes" (*see* Section 9.05[B][6]). Alternatively, firms may choose not to key compensation solely to managers' performance, even if this causes the firm to forego some agency cost reduction.

Incentive compensation, particularly the heavy use of stock options during the late 1990s, has come under increased fire in the wake of the Enron scandal. Critics of stock option compensation contend that such compensation creates incentives for managers to manipulate reported results in order to maximize personal income. These perceived problems have lead to calls for reform, including, among other things, new stock exchange rules requiring nearly all option compensation to be approved by the corpo-

---

[3]   Judge Posner, in a controversial opinion, held that auditors are not liable for failing to detect managerial fraud. *See Cenco Inc. v. Seidman & Seidman*, 686 F.2d 449 (7th Cir. 1982). While this case seems inconsistent with auditors' monitoring function, it more likely reflects the problems inherent in imposing civil liability for auditors' failure to monitor.

ration's shareholders. But, as always, it is not clear that the cost of the proposed reforms will be less than the benefits.

Even if managers' contracts do not provide for pay according to the quality of their services, managers still have an incentive to maximize profits because the market for managerial services rewards managers for their track records as they climb up the corporate ladder or jump from job to job.[4]

REFERENCES

Berle & Means, THE MODERN CORPORATION AND PRIVATE PROPERTY (1932).

Black, *Agents Watching Agents: The Promise of Institutional Investor Voice*, 39 UCLA L. REV. 811 (1992).

Black, *Shareholder Passivity Reexamined*, 89 MICH. L. REV. 520 (1990).

Black, *The Value of Institutional Investor Monitoring; The Empirical Evidence*, 29 UCLA L. REV. 895 (1992).

Brickley, Lease & Smith, *Ownership Structure and the Monitoring of Managers*, 20 J. FIN. ECON. 267 (1988).

Coffee, *Liquidity vs. Control: The Institutional Investor as Corporate Monitor*, 91 COLUM. L. REV. 1277 (1991).

Demsetz & Lehn, *The Structure of Corporate Ownership: Causes and Consequences*, 93 J. POL. ECON. 1155 (1985).

Downs, ECONOMIC THEORY OF DEMOCRACY (1957).

Fama & Jensen, *Separation of Ownership and Control*, 26 J. L. & ECON. 301 (1983).

Fama, *Agency Problems and the Theory of the Firm*, 88 J. POL. ECON. 288 (1980).

Gilson, *Management Turnover and Financial Distress*, 25 J. FIN. ECON. 241 (1989).

Gilson & Vetsuypens, *CEO Compensation in Financially Distressed Firms: An Empirical Analysis*, 48 J. FIN. 425 (1993).

Grundfest, *Just Say No: A Minimalist Strategy for Dealing with Barbarians Inside the Gates*, 45 STAN. L.J. 857 (1993).

Heard & Sherman, CONFLICTS OF INTEREST IN THE PROXY VOTING SYSTEM (1987).

Jensen, *Eclipse of the Public Corporation*, HARVARD BUS. REV., Sept.-Oct. 1989.

Manne, *Our Two Corporation Systems: Law and Economics*, 53 VA. L. REV. 259 (1967).

Manne, *Mergers and the Market for Corporate Control*, 73 J. POL. ECON. 110 (1965).

Manne, *Some Theoretical Aspects of Share Voting: An Essay in Honor of Adolf A. Berle*, 64 COLUM. L. REV. 1427 (1964).

Manning, *Review of Livingstone*, THE AMERICAN STOCKHOLDER (1958), 67 YALE L.J. 1477 (1958).

Mayers & Smith, *Ownership Structure and Control—The Mutualization of Stock Life Insurance Companies*, 16 J. FIN. ECON. 73 (1986).

---

[4]   Although market constraints on managers may not work perfectly, they may work when it matters most—in financially distressed firms. For example, **Gilson & Vetsuypens** report that a third of the chief executive officers of publicly traded financially distressed firms are replaced, while those who remain have their pay cut. Replacements from inside the firm earn 35% less than their predecessors, and the replacements' pay is fixed so that it better reflects shareholder and creditor welfare.

Pound, *The Efficiency of Shareholder Voting: Evidence from Proxy Contests,* 20 J. FIN.
    ECON. 237 (1988).
Rock, *The Logic and (Uncertain) Significance of Institutional Shareholder Activism,* 79
    GEO. L.J. 445 (1991).
Roe, STRONG MANAGERS, WEAK OWNERS (1994).
Roe, *A Political Theory of American Corporate Finance,* 91 COLUM. L. REV. 10 (1991).
Romano, *Public Pension Fund Activism in Corporate Governance Reconsidered,* 93 COLUM.
    L. REV. 795 (1993).
Romano, *Less Is More: Making Shareholder Activism a Valuable Mechanism of Corporate
    Governance,* 18 YALE J. REG. 174 (2001).
Stigler & Friedlander, *The Literature of Economics: The Case of Berle and Means,* 26 J.L.
    & ECON. 237 (1983).

[B] Federal versus State Regulation of Public Corporations

The debate over the Berle-Means thesis raises questions concerning the adequacy of state corporation law—in particular, whether the relationship between shareholders and corporate managers should continue to be governed largely by the law of the state of incorporation or whether the federal government should play a greater role. This debate is examined below.

State corporation law evolved from its early "concession" origins, in which corporate charters were state-granted franchises that controlled corporate size and activities, to the present enabling statutes that permit such matters as managerial power to be decided by the shareholders through the articles of incorporation (*see* Section 1.04). According to **Cary**'s provocative article, state law evolution has been a "race" in which corporations "shop" among the states for favorable charter provisions, and states compete for franchise tax revenues from out-of-state firms by offering attractive terms. Cary concluded that tiny Delaware won the competition by tailoring its corporation law to attract a huge percentage of major corporations. Delaware judges cooperate with legislators in this policy because the bar, judiciary and legislature are all selected from the same close-knit group of people.

Berle-Means adherents and market-oriented theorists agree that there is a competition for corporate charters, but disagree about whether the competition is bad. Cary, aligned with the Berle-Means position, argues that corporate managers are able to use their power in the corporation to choose state laws that favor them, rather than the shareholders. Under this view, the competition among the states for corporate charters is a "race for the bottom" from which shareholders need to be protected by federal law—including the federal securities laws and, perhaps, federal chartering of corporations.

The opposing group, led by **Winter**, and sometimes referred to as "corporate federalists," argues that the same market forces that discipline corporate management's selection of governance terms also discipline corporate management's selection of the state of incorporation. For example, incorporation under a state law that offers terms that are unfavorable to shareholders will depress the stock price of firms incorporated in the state, spurring action by the market for control to change the state of incorporation. States that want to attract corporate managers therefore will compete by offering corporate laws that are favorable to shareholders. The result, then, is a race for the top in corporate law, not a race for the bottom.

In support of the corporate federalists, there are, indeed, some real benefits of incorporating in Delaware that should appeal to both managers and investors. The Delaware courts are the most expert in the country on corporate matters. These courts have developed a large body of what is, in effect, a national case law on corporations, so that outcomes of cases are relatively predictable. Delaware statutes are developed exclusively by expert corporate lawyers. Stability of the law is ensured by the 2/3 vote of the legislature required for amendment. Further, Delaware's unique dependence on franchise tax receipts bonds Delaware to continue to offer high-quality and stable corporate law in the future. **Romano (1985)** argues that this is why Delaware is able to hang onto its huge share of the business of incorporating the nation's largest firms when states seemingly could out-compete it by mimicking Delaware's law at a lower price. **Romano (2001)** summarizes recent evidence on the efficiency of state corporate law competition.

An important qualification of the corporate federalist position relates to interest groups. Even if the market for charters works well, so that it is in the interests of Delaware *taxpayers* for their state to maximize franchise tax revenues by offering efficient corporation laws, the standard economic theory of interest groups suggests that legislators sometimes will serve concentrated interest groups rather than dispersed taxpayers. Relying on this theory, **Macey & Miller** argue that *lawyers* rather than *taxpayers* are the dominant interest group in Delaware regarding corporate law.[5] Not surprisingly, then, Delaware law sometimes favors lawyers' interests, as by adopting rules that promote litigation, even at the risk of reducing the state's franchise tax revenues. Also, state anti-takeover statutes, which most market-oriented theorists agree are contrary to shareholder interests, suggest that managers do sometimes get legislators' attention, just as Cary said they did (**Bebchuk & Farrell**).

In the end, however, the important question is not whether state competition generates perfect corporate laws, but whether state competition is better than the alternatives, including federal chartering of all large corporations. In this regard, it is important to note that, even if the states sometimes get it wrong, the mistakes are self-correcting to some extent through jurisdictional competition. No similar self-correction device operates at the federal level.

---

[5]   Indeed, **Alva** shows that Delaware lawyers *are* the Delaware legislature, at least insofar as corporate law is concerned. Delaware has one of the three smallest legislatures in the country, its legislative committees are virtually inactive, and, most strikingly, few of its legislators are lawyers. Virtually all of Delaware corporate law is proposed by the Delaware bar, and the bar's proposals invariably pass the legislature. *See* Alva at 900.

REFERENCES

Alva, *Delaware and the Market for Corporate Charters: History and Agency*, 15 DEL. J.
CORP. L. 885 (1990).

Baysinger & Butler, *Race for the Bottom v. Climb to the Top: The ALI Project and Uniformity in Corporate Law*, 10 J. CORP. L. 431 (1985).

Bebchuk, *Federalism and the Corporation: The Desirable Limits on State Competition in
Corporate Law*, 105 HARV. L. REV. 1435 (1992).

Bebchuk & Ferrell, *Federalism and Takeover Law: The Race to Protect Managers from
Takeovers*, 99 COLUM. L. REV. 1168 (1999).

Cary, *Federalism and Corporate Law: Reflections upon Delaware*, 83 YALE L.J. 663 (1974).

Coffee, *The Future of Corporate Federalism: State Competition and the New Trend Toward
De Facto Federal Minimum Standards*, 8 CARDOZO L. REV. 759 (1987).

Daniels, *Should Provinces Compete? The Case for a Competitive Corporate Law Market*, 36
MCGILL L.J. 130 (1991).

Dodd & Leftwich, *The Market for Corporate Charters: "Unhealthy Competition" Versus
Federal Regulation*, 53 J. BUS. L. 259 (1980).

Easterbrook & Fischel, THE ECONOMIC STRUCTURE OF CORPORATE LAW, Ch. 8 (1991).

Macey & Miller, *Toward an Interest-Group Theory of Delaware Corporate Law*, 65 TEX. L.
REV. 469 (1987).

Manning & Moore, *State Competition: Panel Response*, 8 CARDOZO L. REV. 779 (1987).

Romano, THE GENIUS OF AMERICAN CORPORATE LAW (1993).

Romano, *Law as a Product: Some Pieces of the Incorporation Puzzle*, 1 J.L. ECON. & ORG.
225 (1985).

Romano, *The Need for Competition in International Securities Regulation*, 2 THEO.
INQUIRIES IN LAW 387 (2001)

Schwartz, *Federal Chartering of Corporations: An Introduction*, 61 GEO. L.J. 71 (1972).

Weiss & White, *Of Econometrics and Indeterminacy: A Study of Investors' Reactions to
"Changes" in Corporate Law*, 75 CAL. L. REV. 551 (1987).

Winter, GOVERNMENT AND THE CORPORATION (1978).

[C] Corporate Social Responsibility

A third issue that arises in connection with the delegation of authority from shareholders to managers is whether public corporation managers should be more "socially
responsible"—that is, whether public corporation managers should be required to consider, in addition to the interests of shareholders, the interests of such groups as consumers of corporate products, people affected by corporate pollution, employees, and
communities that are economically dependent on the corporation.

Some advocates of more corporate responsibility sometimes emphasize the "ille-
gitimacy" of corporate power. They point out that large corporations resemble nations
in terms of their resources and ability to affect society as a whole.[6] Thus, these com-

---

[6]   *See, e.g.*, Nader, Green & Seligman, TAMING THE GIANT CORPORATION 16 (1976).

mentators argue that it is necessary to regulate corporate governance in order to ensure that managers serve the non-shareholder interests affected by their decisions.

Will corporate managers chosen by shareholders to maximize corporate profits necessarily ignore the interests of non-shareholders, like consumers, workers, and people affected by corporate pollution? Advocates of the "free-market position" say no, pointing to the constraining effects of market forces. **Friedman** has said:

> The view . . . that corporate officials and labor leaders have a "social responsibility" that goes beyond serving the interests of their stockholders or their members . . . shows a fundamental misconception of the character and nature of a free economy. In such an economy, there is one and only one social responsibility of business—to use its resources and engage in activities designed to increase its profits so long as it stays within the rules of the game, which is to say, engages in open and free competition, without deception or fraud. Similarly, the "social responsibility" of labor leaders is to serve the interests of the members of their unions. It is the responsibility of the rest of us to establish a framework of law such that an individual in pursuing his own interest is, to quote Adam Smith again, "led by an invisible hand to promote an end which was no part of his intention. Nor is it always the worse for the society that it was no part of it. By pursuing his own interest, he frequently promotes that of the society more effectually than when he really intends to promote it. I have never known much good done by those who affected to trade for the public good."
>
> Few trends could so thoroughly undermine the very foundations of our free society as the acceptance by corporate officials of a social responsibility other than to make as much money for their stockholders as possible. This is a fundamentally subversive doctrine. If businessmen do have a social responsibility other than making maximum profits for stockholders, how are they to know what it is? Can self-selected private individuals decide what the social interest is? Can they decide how great a burden they are justified in placing on themselves or their stockholders to serve that social interest? Is it tolerable that these public functions of taxation, expenditure, and control be exercised by the people who happen at the moment to be in charge of particular enterprises, chosen for those posts by strictly private groups? If businessmen are civil servants rather than the employees of their stockholders then in a democracy they will, sooner or later, be chosen by the public techniques of election and appointment.[7]

Kenneth Arrow has observed that "[t]he forces of competition prevent the firms from engrossing too large a share of the social benefit. For example, if a firm tries to reduce the quality of its goods, it will sooner or later have to lower the price which it

---

[7]   Friedman, Capitalism and Freedom 133-36, by permission of the University of Chicago Press. Copyright © 1962.

charges because the purchaser will no longer find it worthwhile to pay the high price. Hence, the consumers will gain from price reduction at the same time as they are losing through quality deterioration. On detailed analysis it appears the firm will find it privately profitable to reduce quality under these circumstances only if, in fact, quality reduction is a net social benefit, that is, if the saving in cost is worth more to the consumer than the quality reduction."[8]

But, as **Stone** points out, markets do not always function perfectly:

> One ought to be clear that those who have faith that profit orientation is an adequate guarantee of corporations realizing socially desirable consumer goals are implicitly assuming . . . that the persons who are going to withdraw patronage know the fact that they are being "injured" (where injury refers to a whole range of possible grievances, from getting a worse deal than they might get elsewhere, to purchasing a product that is defective or below warranted standards, to getting something that produces actual physical injury)
> . . . .
>
> [But] . . . over a range of important cases the person who, under this model, should be shifting his patronage, does not even know that he is being "injured" (in the broad sense referred to above). For example, from our vantage point in the present, we can look back on history and appreciate some of the dangers of smoking on a cigarette consumer's health, or of coal dust on a worker's lungs. But the basis for these doubts was not adequately appreciated by the earlier consumer, who might have wanted to shift his patronage from, say, non filter to filter cigarettes, or to the worker who might have shifted his career from coal mining to something else. It hardly strains the imagination to believe that we today, as consumers, employees, investors, and so forth, are being subjected by corporations to all sorts of injuries that we will learn about only in time. But we are not able to translate these general misgivings into market preferences because we simply do not know enough about where dangers lie.

* * *

> [Further], the [free-market] model presupposes the existence of some negotiating interface between the corporation and the person disaffected with it. Such a relationship is available for a worker who is a member of a union recognized by the corporation, and for a person who is directly a consumer of the corporation's products or services. But consider, for example, a person whose grievance is with an aluminum company that is showering his land with pollutants, or that is, in his estimate, exercising objectionable influences in Latin America. If, as is likely, he is not a direct purchaser of

---

[8]   Arrow, *Responsibility and Economic Efficiency,* Pub. Pol. 303, 304-05 (1973), Copyright © 1973. Reprinted by permission of John Wiley & Sons.

aluminum, what recourse does he have: to do a study of all the products he is contemplating buying that contain aluminum so as to determine the "percentage" of their aluminum components and know which of them to boycott? . . .[9]

Does Stone's argument mean that corporate managers will necessarily ignore the interests of groups that have no direct dealings with the corporation? Consider the following:

> Rational enterprise managers judge the yield of outlays for social purposes by their long-run effect upon profits. They measure the return on the "investment" in each social program. Each social outlay is tested by a cost/benefit analysis. Among the benefits may be a reduction in the costs of defending the firm's actions before the legislative or executive agencies of government, an avoidance of onerous governmental regulations, or a reduction in property damage at the hands of activists. Social pressures generate costs, the amount of which can be minimized by appropriate corporate outlays. When viewed in the perspective of our model, there is no conflict between profit maximization and corporate social activity. The popular notion that a company which pursues profit must eschew a social role, or that social involvement means a sacrifice of profit, is unfounded. On the contrary, the contemporary corporation must become socially involved in order to maximize its profits.[10]

The dramatic collapses of Enron and WorldCom in 2001 and 2002 resulted in large losses, not only for shareholders, but also for employees and other corporate stakeholders. These losses are certain to trigger renewed focus on the social responsibility of corporate managers. For an early discussion of corporate social responsibility in the post-Enron world, see the **Symposium** cited in the References below.

NOTES AND QUESTIONS

(1) **Social responsibility and the contract view of the corporation.** There is no reason under the contract view of the corporation why employees and other groups could not also be shareholders to whom directors would owe a contractual duty. A Reporter's Note to the provision in the American Law Institute's *Principles of Corporate Governance* states that "there is little doubt that such limitations would normally be permissible if agreed to by all the shareholders."[11] The idea that corporations should be

---

[9]   Stone, WHERE THE LAW ENDS 88-91 (1975). Copyright © 1975 by Christopher Stone. Reprinted by permission of Harper & Row.

[10]   Jacoby, CORPORATE POWER AND SOCIAL RESPONSIBILITY 194-97 (1973). Copyright © 1973 by The Trustees of Columbia University in the City of New York.

[11]   American Law Institute, Principles of Corporate Governance: Analysis and Recommendations, Reporter's Note 6 to § 2.01 (1994).

managed in a "socially responsible" way (*i.e.*, in the interests of non-shareholder groups) therefore reduces to the contention that the shareholders should not be allowed to enter into enforceable contracts for exclusive ownership of the firm's profits and for exclusive control, but rather should be forced to accept at least a limited form of cooperative ownership despite its potential costs. Do the arguments discussed above support this result?

(2) **Social responsibility and "team production."** As a kind of compromise between the contractarian and social responsibility views of corporate governance, **Blair & Stout** suggest that corporate boards of directors serve as a way of mediating among the various corporate constituencies, or "team members," including workers, shareholders and others. The board's representation of these various interests, by ensuring all that they will be treated fairly, arguably reduces contracting costs in the firm, including the shirking, agency and opportunism costs discussed above in Section 1.02. In other words, rather than viewing corporate social responsibility as a reallocation of wealth from shareholders to "society," Blair and Stout see this approach as maximizing the wealth of all participants in the firm. This raises at least two questions. First, how can the various groups be sure that the board will work for them? Second, since this proposal maximizes everybody's joint wealth, isn't this the structure that we would have expected firms already to have adopted? Is that the case? If not, why not?

(3) **The costs of "social responsibility."** Markets surely do not always ensure that every group affected by the corporation gets what it wants. However, it does not necessarily follow that managers should act in a non-profit-maximizing, "socially responsible," way. As **Friedman** notes in the above excerpt, this approach offers little guidance as to how managers should act. For example, should managers favor pollutees who live near the plant over employees? Should managers assume that consumers want crash-proof cars, even if they do not seem to be willing to pay for crash protection? If these questions cannot be easily answered, then managers may be able to use the power to behave in a "socially responsible" way as a shield for actions that further the managers' own interests. For example, managers who oppose takeovers in order to protect their own jobs may defend their actions as necessary to protect workers or the communities in which the company operates.

(4) **Social responsibility and government regulation.** If managers themselves cannot be relied upon to do anything more than maximize profits, can government do a better job? In determining whether transferring power from corporate managers to government officials will produce "socially responsible" decisions, consider how government regulation is produced. Under standard interest group theory, interest groups pay politicians (in the form of votes, contributions, expenditures, junkets, employment for politicians' associates and so forth) to effect wealth transfers from other groups through such means as subsidies, tax reductions, and trade barriers. Wealth transfers occur because some interest groups face higher organizational costs, such as the costs of identifying and communicating with other potential group members, than others and therefore are able to devote a greater percentage of their wealth to the payments that pro-

duce favorable legislation.[12] For example, relatively small groups that have built-in organizational advantages, such as the American Manufacturers Association, the AFL-CIO, or the Sierra Club, may be able to "outbid" larger, but more poorly organized groups, such as taxpayers generally, for legislation. In other words, government regulation of corporate governance may not be any more socially efficient than profit-maximization.

(5) **Corporate social responsibility and the law.** What role should the law play in ensuring corporate power is exercised in a "socially responsible" manner? It has been suggested that managers be permitted and encouraged to exercise their power for the good of society. This view has come to be known as "managerialism." Modern corporate managers who adhere to the managerialist view generally attempt to reconcile corporate social responsibility and the shareholders' interest in maximizing corporate profits. But as Note 3 indicates, this may be difficult, if not impossible. We will return to the question of whether corporate managers should be required (or, indeed, permitted) to act in "socially responsible" fashion in discussing managers' fiduciary duties to shareholders in Chapter 9.

Another route to corporate social responsibility is to facilitate expression of shareholder views so that society's viewpoint will be brought home to management through the shareholder "electorate." This Chapter discusses three legal rules relating to this alternative: disclosure in corporate proxy materials of information concerning social problems (Section 7.03[C]); use of corporate proxy materials by shareholders to discuss social issues (Section 7.04); and access to shareholder lists for the purposes of communicating with other shareholders on social issues (Section 7.05).

A third alternative route to increased corporate social responsibility discussed in this Chapter is requiring corporations to include on their boards of directors representatives of constituencies other than the shareholders, including labor union leaders and consumer advocates (Section 7.07).

REFERENCES

Allen, *Our Schizophrenic Conception of the Business Corporation*, 14 CARDOZO L. REV. 261 (1992).

Berle, *Corporate Powers as Powers in Trust*, 44 HARV. L. REV. 1049 (1931).

Blair, *A Contractarian Defense of Corporate Philanthropy*, 28 STETSON L. REV. 27 (1998).

Blair & Stout, *A Team Production Theory of Corporate Law*, 85 VA. L. REV. 247 (1999).

Brudney & Farrell, *Corporate Charitable Giving*, 69 U. CHI. L. REV. 1191 (2002).

Carney, *Does Defining Constituencies Matter?*, 59 U. CIN. L. REV. 385 (1990).

Dodd, *For Whom are Corporate Managers Trustees?*, 45 HARV. L. REV. 1145 (1932).

---

[12]   *See generally* McCormick & Tollison, POLITICIANS, LEGISLATION AND THE ECONOMY 17 (1981); Stigler, *The Theory of Economic Regulation*, 2 BELL J. ECON. & MGT. SCI. 3, 10-13 (1971); Olson, THE LOGIC OF COLLECTIVE ACTION (1965).

Eisenberg, *Corporate Conduct that Does Not Maximize Shareholder Gain,* 28 STETSON L. REV. 1 (1998).

Engel, *An Approach to Corporate Social Responsibility,* 32 STAN. L. REV. 1 (1979).

Hansmann, *Ownership of the Firm,* 4 J. LAW, ECON. & ORG. 267 (1988).

Hazen & Buckley, *Models of Corporate Conduct,* 58 NEB. L. REV. 100 (1978).

Kahn, *Pandora's Box: Managerial Discretion and the Problem of Corporate Philanthropy,* 44 UCLA L. REV. 579 (1997).

Macey, *An Economic Analysis of the Various Rationales for Making Shareholders the Exclusive Beneficiaries of Corporate Fiduciary Duties,* 21 STETSON L. REV. 23 (1991).

Manne, *Should Corporations Assume More Social Responsibilities?, in* THE ATTACK ON CORPORATE AMERICA: THE CORPORATE ISSUES SOURCEBOOK (M. Johnson, ed., 1978).

Rostow, *To Whom and For What Ends is Corporate Management Responsible?, in* THE CORPORATION IN MODERN SOCIETY (E. Mason, ed., 1960).

Soderquist, *Reconciling Shareholders' Rights and Corporate Responsibility: Close and Small Public Corporations,* 33 VAND. L. REV. 1387 (1980).

Stone, *The Place of Enterprise Liability in the Control of Corporate Conduct,* 90 YALE L.J. 1 (1980).

Stone, WHERE THE LAW ENDS (1975).

Symposium, *The New Corporate Social Responsibility,* 76 TUL. L. REV. 1187 (2002).

Weiner, *The Berle-Dodd Dialogue on the Concept of the Corporation,* 64 COLUM. L. REV. 1458 (1964).

Williams, *Corporate Compliance with the Law in the Era of Efficiency,* 76 N.C. L. REV. 1265 (1998).

§ 7.03 Federal Regulation of Proxy Solicitations

During the 1930s, Congress passed several laws that were intended to deal with abuses it found to be contributing causes of the 1929 stock market crash. This course is concerned primarily with two of those laws: the Securities Act of 1933 (the "1933 Act") and the Securities Exchange Act of 1934 (the "1934 Act"). The 1933 Act requires disclosures primarily in connection with the *initial* issuance of securities by corporations and other types of businesses. The 1934 Act requires periodic disclosures to markets *after* the securities have been distributed to the public. It also regulates representations and nondisclosures by issuers and others (including representations and nondisclosures that occur in connection with proxy solicitations), insider trading, and tender offers, among other things. Periodic disclosure requirements and insider trading regulation are covered in Chapter 12, and tender offer regulation is discussed in Chapter 13. This Section covers regulation of solicitations of proxies from shareholders of public corporations under § 14 of the 1934 Act

[A] Introduction to Federal Proxy Regulation

A *proxy* refers to an instrument by which a shareholder entitled to vote at a meeting authorizes another person (frequently the corporation's managers) to act for him at that meeting. Before 1934, the solicitation of proxies from shareholders of public corporations was governed solely by state corporation law. Since 1934, however, federal regulation of the proxy solicitation process has become paramount. It is, therefore, the focus of the following discussion. Nonetheless, it should be noted that states have continued to regulate proxy solicitations despite the advent of the federal law,[13] with the lack of full disclosure to shareholders granting proxies being a common state law ground for overturning shareholder-approved corporate transactions.[14]

Federal regulation of proxy solicitation can traced to the Berle-Means thesis (*see* Section 7.02[A]) that public corporations are controlled by managers who are free from effective monitoring because shareholders are passive and uninformed, and the related distrust of state regulation (*see* Section 7.02[B]). Federal proxy regulation is intended to remedy the problems identified by Berle and Means by ensuring, first, that shareholders are well-informed about the matters to be voted on before they grant proxies to others; and, second, that shareholders are given an opportunity to direct how their shares will be voted by the holder of the proxy. The main devices through which federal proxy regulation operates are the "proxy statement," the document which explains in detail the matters to be voted on by the shareholders, and the "form of proxy," the instrument used by a shareholder to authorize another person to vote his stock.

The key federal statutory provisions concerning proxies are §§ 14(a)-(c) of the 1934 Act. Section 14(a), the most important of these provisions, empowers the Securities and Exchange Commission, the federal agency charged with administering the federal securities laws, to promulgate rules and regulations dealing with proxy solicitations. Under this authority, the Commission has promulgated a series of proxy rules,[15] some of which will be discussed below.

[B] Overview of the Federal Proxy Solicitation Rules

The federal proxy rules generally require that any "solicitation" of a proxy from a shareholder of a public corporation be accompanied or preceded by a proxy statement explaining the matters to be voted on by shareholders (*see* SEC Rule 14a-3). But under amendments adopted in 1999, delivery of the proxy statement may generally be deferred until the form of proxy (*i.e.*, the corporate ballot) is given to the shareholders (*see* SEC Rule 14a-12).

---

[13] *See, e.g., Campbell v. Loew's, Inc.*, 36 Del. Ch. 563, 134 A.2d 852 (1957).

[14] *See, e.g., Smith v. Van Gorkom*, Section 9.03[B], and *Weinberger v. UOP, Inc.*, Section 15.02[D].

[15] *See* 17 C.F.R. § 250.14.

The proxy statement must comply as to form and content with SEC regulations (*see* SEC Rules 14a-3 and 14a-5). The federal proxy regulations also control the form of proxy used in connection with the solicitation. Among other things, the form of proxy must permit shareholders to direct how their shares will be voted separately on specific matters clearly identified in the proxy (*see* SEC Rule 14a-4). In order to ensure compliance with SEC rules, both the proxy statement and the form of proxy generally must be filed with the SEC at least ten days before copies are sent or given to shareholders (*see* SEC Rule 14a-6).

The materials that follow explore the federal proxy rules in somewhat greater detail. These issues covered include: (1) the meaning of "solicitation," the term which triggers the application of the federal proxy rules; (2) the required content of the proxy statements; (3) who beyond shareholders must receive a proxy statement; and (4) exemptions from the proxy rules.

[1] What Is a Solicitation?

The requirement that a proxy statement be sent to shareholders applies only when there has been a "solicitation." That term is defined quite broadly in Rule 14a-1(l) to include, among other things, a "communication to security holders under circumstances reasonably calculated to result in the procurement, withholding or revocation of a proxy."

In *Studebaker Corp. v. Gittlin*,[16] the court held that a solicitation of shareholders to join in a request for a shareholder list was a proxy solicitation. Although this was a solicitation of an "authorization" by the shareholders to inspect the list, and so was technically included in the SEC's definition of "proxy," the court's decision was based on the broader rationale that the solicitation was "intended to prepare the way for" the success of a later solicitation of proxies.[17] This case indicates, therefore, that any communication that aids a planned proxy solicitation is subject to the proxy rules.

Other cases, however, have refused to go as far as *Gittlin*. In *Brown v. Chicago, Rock Island & Pacific Railroad*,[18] a newspaper advertisement was held not to be a proxy solicitation. Although one purpose of the advertisement was to stir public sentiment against a proposed railroad merger, and thereby to influence the Interstate Commerce Commission hearings on the merger, another purpose, or at least foreseeable result, of the advertisement was to aid in the later solicitation of proxies against the merger. Nevertheless, the court may have feared that application of the proxy rules to this situation would dampen free debate of public issues. Cases like *Brown* indicate that the courts will balance the need for a proxy statement against other considerations where it is not clear that a "solicitation" has taken place.

---

[16]   360 F.2d 692 (2d Cir. 1966).

[17]   *Id.* at 696.

[18]   328 F.2d 122 (7th Cir. 1964).

In 1992, the SEC amended the proxy rules to facilitate shareholder activism by, among other things, changing the definition of a "solicitation" and adding exemptions for certain types of solicitations. The new definition of "solicitation" now makes clear that shareholders can publicly announce how they intend to vote and provide reasons for that decision without triggering the application of the SEC's proxy rules (Rule 14a-1(l)(2)(iv)).[19]

[2] Disclosure Obligations

The most important requirement of federal proxy regulation is that substantial information be furnished to shareholders who are the subject of a solicitation. SEC rules spell out what must be disclosed. Rule 14a-3 provides that a proxy statement that contains the information specified in Schedule 14A ordinarily must accompany or precede a solicitation of proxies or shareholder consents. Schedule 14A provides for disclosures of such matters as: (a) the date, time, and place of the shareholders meeting related to the solicitation; (b) the names of the participants in the solicitation; (c) any interest of those participants in the matter to be voted upon by the shareholders; (d) the "record date" set by the board of directors to determine the shareholders entitled to vote at the meeting (*see* Delaware G.C.L. § 213), and (e) specific disclosures tailored to the precise matters to be voted upon at the shareholders' meeting.

The federal proxy rules mandate the delivery of an especially comprehensive disclosure package when management is soliciting proxies in connection with an annual or special meeting at which directors are to be elected. In that case, Schedule 14A requires detailed information concerning the firm's senior executives, including their names, ages, business backgrounds, legal problems, potential conflicts of interest, and, in the case of the company's five most highly compensated officers, detailed compensation information. In addition, Rule 14a-3(b) requires proxy statements related to director elections to be accompanied by an annual report which provides an overview of the corporation's business, management's discussion and analysis of the corporation's financial condition and results of operations, and audited financial statements. Many public corporations use the annual report as a glossy public relations device for selling the company to shareholders and to the general public.

Even if management is not soliciting proxies, § 14(c) of the 1934 Act requires it to send to shareholders an information statement and (if the meeting is one at which directors are to be elected) an annual report. The information required to be furnished in the information statement is specified in Schedule 14C. Schedule 14C includes many of the same requirements as Schedule 14A.

The proxy rules require that both the proxy statement and the information statement be filed with the SEC (Rule 14a-6, Rule 14c-5). The proxy rules also require that

---

[19] For a case holding that this exemption is not available when the press release is a step in a campaign likely to end in the solicitation of proxies, see *Capital Real Estate Investors Tax Exempt Fund LP v. Schwartzberg*, 917 F. Supp. 1050 (S.D.N.Y. 1996).

any annual report accompanying the proxy statement or information statement be mailed to the SEC (Rule 14a-3(c), Rule 14c-3(b)). The annual report, however, is not deemed to be "filed" with the SEC and so is not subject to the civil liability provisions in Section 18 of the 1934 Act.

[3] Proxy Form and Dissemination

Proxy solicitation is complicated by the fact that many of those listed as shareholders on the corporation's records ("record holders") are institutional holders or brokers who are only nominees for the beneficial owners. Although this practice facilitates securities trading, it makes it possible for nominees to wield substantial power by voting stock they hold for others, as record holders can do under state law.[20] The SEC's concern with this practice resulted in its "Street Name Study,"[21] and ultimately in revised rules on dissemination of proxy materials, voting by nominees and identification of beneficial owners.

Rules 14b-1 and 14b-2 require brokers, banks, and others who hold securities for investors to forward proxy materials (at the corporation's expense) to their customers. Rule 14b-2 also requires banks to forward to their customers executed proxies or requests for voting instructions so as to ensure that the beneficial holders (not nominal record holders) make voting decisions. Rule 14b-1 subjects brokers to similar requirements. Subject to state law, banks can vote uninstructed shares. Brokers may vote customers' stock subject to the rules of the stock exchanges and of the National Association of Securities Dealers. Brokers must vote customers' stock as instructed by the customers and, in general, may vote "uninstructed" stock only as to routine issues and only if proxy material has been transmitted to the shareholders before a specified time.[22]

[4] Exemptions

The federal proxy rules contain a variety of exemptions from all, or a portion of, the federal proxy rules. Many of these exemptions are found in Rule 14a-2, which covers, among other things, solicitations (other than on behalf of the company) of not more than ten shareholders and communications where the soliciting shareholder is not seeking proxy authority and does not have a substantial interest in the matter that is the subject of the solicitation. Solicitations included in Rule 14a-2 are generally exempt from all requirements of the federal proxy rules, except (in the case of solicitations covered by paragraph (b) of the Rule) the prohibitions on material misleading statements found in Rule 14a-9.

---

[20] *See American Hardware Corp. v. Savage Arms Corp.*, 136 A.2d 690 (Del. 1957).

[21] Fed. Sec. L. Rep. (CCH) Sp. Report No. 672 (1976).

[22] For descriptions of how these rules operate, see *Report of the Advisory Committee on Shareholder Communications*, Fed. Sec. L. Rep. (CCH) ¶ 83,224 at 85, 165-66 (1982).

Rule 14a-12 provides for a limited exemption from the requirement of furnishing a full-fledged proxy statement with or prior to the first communication in a proxy contest. Under Rule 14a-12, oral and written communications prior to the delivery of a proxy contest are generally permissible so long as all written communications related to the solicitation are filed with the SEC on the date of first use and include both the identity of the participants in the solicitation and a prominent legend advising security holders to read the proxy statement when it becomes available. Rule 14a-12, however, continues to forbid the furnishing of a *form of proxy* (*i.e.*, the ballot) until a written proxy statement meeting the requirements of the proxy rules has been provided.

Rule 14a-12 has changed the way proxy contests are fought, permitting contestants to begin their electioneering well before a proxy statement is filed with the SEC or delivered to shareholders.

REFERENCES

Brown, *The Shareholder Communication Rules and the Securities and Exchange Commission: An Exercise in Regulatory Utility or Futility?*, 13 J. CORP. L. 683 (1988).
Comment, *Solicitation under the Proxy Rules: The Need for a More Precise Definition of Solicitation*, 8 SW. U. L. REV. 1019 (1976).

[C] Misleading Proxy Statements

Rule 14a-9 prohibits proxy statements that are "false or misleading with respect to any material fact, or which omit[] to state any material fact necessary in order to make the statements therein not false of misleading." In addition, Rule 14a-5 requires that information included in a proxy statement be "clearly presented." Thus, even if all items specifically required to be disclosed by Schedule 14A are set forth in the proxy materials, the materials may still violate the proxy rules.

The starting point for determining whether a proxy statement is *materially* misleading is the Supreme Court's decision in *TSC Industries, Inc. v. Northway, Inc.*,[23] where the Court stated:

> An omitted fact is material if there is a substantial likelihood that a reasonable shareholder would consider it important in deciding how to vote. This standard is fully consistent with Mills' general description of materiality as a requirement that "the defect have a significant *propensity* to affect the voting process." It does not require proof of a substantial likelihood that disclosure of the omitted fact would have caused the reasonable investor to change his vote. What the standard does contemplate is a showing of a substantial likelihood that, under all the circumstances, the omitted fact would have assumed actual significance in the deliberations of the reasonable

---

[23]   426 U.S. 438 (1975).

shareholder. Put another way, there must be a substantial likelihood that the disclosure of the omitted fact would have been viewed by the reasonable investor as having significantly altered the "total mix" of information made available.[24]

The *TSC* standard recognizes that more information is not necessarily better, since "[s]ome information is of such dubious significance that insistence on its disclosure may accomplish more harm than good."[25] In other words, firms are not required to disclose so much that investors will be unable to separate the wheat from the chaff.

The proxy rules regulate not only what is disclosed, but how. See, for example, Rule 14a-5(a), which requires that information in a proxy statement be "clearly presented." The difficult question is how far the proxy statement must go toward clarifying the facts or bringing their importance home to the reader. Also, since *TSC* requires an evaluation of the disclosure in light of the "'total mix' of information made available," it is important to keep in mind that information is available about publicly traded companies from many different sources, including other SEC filings (such as a public corporation's annual filing with the SEC on Form 10-K, which is required under Section 13 of the 1934 Act), press reports and so forth. These "presentation" issues are discussed in the following case.

UNITED PAPERWORKERS INTERNATIONAL UNION v. INTERNATIONAL PAPER COMPANY
United States Court of Appeals, Second Circuit
985 F.2d 1190 (1993)

KEARSE, Circuit Judge:

[International Paper Company ("Paper Co."), is a large paper and paper products manufacturer whose shares are traded on the New York Stock Exchange. At the request of the Presbyterian Church (USA) of Louisville, Kentucky, which owned 31,000 shares of the Company's stock, and the Sisters of Saint Dominic of Blauvelt, New York, the Company included the following shareholder proposal in the proxy statement for its 1992 annual meeting:

> [RESOLVED, that shareholders request our company to: 1. sign and actively implement the Valdez Principles; and 2. engage with shareholders, CERES, and affected communities in a continuing process to achieve a genuine and publicly trusted measure of public environmental accountability.

[In its Proxy Statement, Paper Co. opposed the resolution, saying that the Company had already addressed environmental matters "in an appropriate and timely manner" and

---

[24]   *Id.* at 449.

[25]   *Id.* at 448.

was in the "forefront" with respect to environmental protection; and that its Board had adopted a comprehensive statement of Environmental, Health and Safety Principles ("Company Principles"), which it described as "the most recent articulation of the Company's longstanding commitment to the protection of the environment, which has been an explicit Company policy for many years." The company said it had made hundreds of millions of dollars of investments in environmental protection and detailed its various environmental audits and reviews, concluding that the Valdez Principles would simply impose duplicative audit and reporting requirements. Its Company Principles appended to the Proxy Statement stated that "International Paper is dedicated to safe and environmentally sound products, packaging and operations"; that "[e]nvironmental stewardship has always been an important part of International Paper's business"; that "[t]he principles are consistent with International Paper's long-standing policies on environment, health and safety"; and that the Company had a "strong environmental compliance program."

[The response was submitted to the sponsors of the shareholder proposal prior to mailing and they did not object to it. However, the Union, which the court described as having had "an unusually tense relationship with the Company" and which owned 25 shares of the Company's stock, commenced this suit, contending that the Company's response violated the proxy rules by containing false and misleading representations and omissions in that, as disclosed in the company's Form 10-K Report, which was filed with the SEC but not distributed to shareholders, the Company had been accused of numerous environmental offenses, had pleaded guilty to felonies, had agreed to pay huge fines, and had been the target of numerous administrative complaints. The Union unsuccessfully sought to delay the meeting to force revised disclosures. At the meeting, the Valdez Resolution was defeated, receiving only 5.937% of the votes cast.]

* * *

Following its denial of the preliminary injunction motion, the district court, with the consent of the parties, converted that motion into cross-motions for summary judgment. The Company, in support of judgment in its favor, argued, inter alia, (1) that its Proxy Statement was not misleading standing alone, and (2) that, in any event, that statement was not misleading when read in conjunction with (a) its annual report, which was mentioned in its Proxy Statement, had been mailed to all shareholders, and contained a segment entitled "Environmental Issues" that summarized various environmental proceedings involving the Company, (b) its 10-K Report filed with the SEC, which the annual report informed shareholders they could obtain free of charge, and various news reports. The Company's annual report stated as follows with respect to environmental litigation:

> In late 1990 and early 1991, several lawsuits were filed against paper producers alleging property damage or risk of personal injury resulting from the presence of dioxin in mill discharges. International Paper is named in some of these lawsuits. As anticipated, aggressive solicitation methods utilized by plaintiffs' attorneys led to the filing of several additional lawsuits in 1991, with the result that at year end, cumulative damages sought totaled more than $6 billion. Recent scientific studies indicate that earlier concerns about the adverse effects of dioxin on human health were significantly overstated. Management believes these suits

are without merit and expects to prevail upon final resolution. Pursuant to an agreement with the U.S. Attorney in Maine, the Company pled guilty in July 1991 to five criminal charges associated with environmental violations at its Androscoggin mill and paid a $2.2 million fine. The Imaging Products Division is currently conducting soil, groundwater and air testing at its Binghamton, N.Y., Anitec facility under a consent order with the State of New York to determine the extent of contamination and remedial action required due to accidental discharges. The Division's film base production process, which was a principal source of the environmental impact, was shut down in 1991. Environmental reviews are also under way at other locations, including certain Arizona Chemical and Masonite facilities. . . . International Paper is also a party to other environmental remedial action under various federal and state laws.

Though some of the Company's involvement in environmental litigation was thus adverted to in the annual report, the Union pointed out that a number of unfavorable details were not mentioned. For example, the five criminal charges to which the Company had pleaded guilty in July 1991 in federal court in Maine were felonies; they involved not only violations of hazardous-waste laws but also the falsification of required environmental reports; and the $2.2 million criminal fine to which the Company agreed was the second largest fine ever assessed for violation of the hazardous-waste laws. Though the annual report mentioned that Paper Co. was conducting air, soil, and ground-water testing at its Binghamton plant pursuant to a consent order, it did not mention that the Company anticipated additional orders and fines relating to environmental matters at that facility. And though the annual report noted that "several" private environmental lawsuits had been filed against paper producers and that the Company was named in "some" of those suits, in fact as of January 1992 the Company was a defendant in 43 civil actions relating to pollution of three rivers in Mississippi alone.

In addition, neither the Proxy Statement nor the annual report mentioned several other matters, including (a) that though in April 1991, the Company settled a civil suit brought by the State of Maine and the Maine Board of Environmental Protection for violations of state environmental laws and regulations, the Company had failed to perform its obligations under the settlement agreement and the State had returned to court seeking substantial penalties for noncompliance; (b) that as of March 30, 1992, the Company had been named in a large number of administrative proceedings to enforce environmental and safety laws or regulations, including approximately 50 proceedings brought under the Comprehensive Environmental Response, Compensation, and Liability Act ("CERCLA"), 42 U.S.C. § 9601 *et seq.* (1988), and comparable state laws, relating to hazardous wastes at commercial landfills; and that in February 1992, the United States Environmental Protection Agency ("EPA") had initiated proceedings to bar the Company from doing business with the federal government for a period of three years.

[The district court held that the proxy statement was materially misleading and ordered the Board to resubmit the proposal at the company's next annual meeting.]

* * *

II. THE RULING THAT THE PROXY STATEMENT WAS MISLEADING

* * *

Section 14(a) of the Act makes it unlawful to solicit proxies in contravention of any rule or regulation promulgated by the SEC. 15 U.S.C. § 78n(a). Rule 14a-9 promulgated thereunder prohibits the inclusion in a proxy statement of any statement which, at the time and in the light of the circumstances under which it is made, is false or misleading with respect to any material fact, or which omits to state any material fact necessary in order to make the statements therein not false or misleading. 17 C.F.R § 240.14a-9 (emphasis added). A fact is material for purposes of Rule 14a-9 "'if there is a substantial likelihood that a reasonable shareholder would consider it important in deciding how to vote.'" *Virginia Bankshares, Inc. v. Sandberg*, 115 L. Ed. 2d 929, 111 S. Ct. 2749, 2757 (1991) (*quoting TSC Industries, Inc. v. Northway, Inc.*, 426 U.S. 438, 449, 48 L. Ed. 2d 757, 96 S. Ct. 2126 (1976)). "'Once the proxy statement purports to disclose the factors considered [by the board of directors] . . ., there is an obligation to portray them accurately.'" *Virginia Bankshares, Inc. v. Sandberg*, 111 S. Ct. at 2761 n.7 (*quoting Berg v. First American Bankshares, Inc.*, 254 U.S. App. D.C. 198, 796 F.2d 489, 496 (D.C. Cir. 1986)).

In the present case, Paper Co. responded to the shareholder proposal in the Proxy Statement with a rather glowing description of the Company's environmental spirit, performance, and sense of responsibility. Plainly, a reasonable shareholder would consider the Company's actual record important in assessing the merits of the Company's response to the shareholder proposal. The response was, therefore, misleading absent a description of the Company's record of environmental derelictions or non-compliance.

In considering a claim of material omission in violation of Rule 14a-9, however, the court ordinarily should not consider the proxy statement alone. To succeed on such a claim, the plaintiff must show that there was "a substantial likelihood that the disclosure of the omitted fact would have been viewed by the reasonable investor as having significantly altered the 'total mix' of information made available." *TSC Industries, Inc. v. Northway, Inc.*, 426 U.S. at 449, 96 S. Ct. at 2132.

A. "Total Mix" and the 10-K and Press Reports

The "total mix" of information may include data sent to shareholders by a company in addition to its proxy materials. . . .

The "total mix" of information may also include "information already in the public domain and facts known or reasonably available to the shareholders." Thus, when the subject of a proxy solicitation has been widely reported in readily available media, shareholders may be deemed to have constructive notice of the facts reported, and the court may take this into consideration in determining whether representations in or omissions from the proxy statement are materially misleading. . . . However, the mere presence in the media of sporadic news reports does not give shareholders sufficient notice that proxy solicitation statements sent directly to them by the company may be misleading, and such reports should not be considered to be part of the total mix of information that would clarify or place in proper context the company's representations in its proxy materials.

In the present case, the district court properly rejected Paper Co.'s contention that public press reports and its 10-K Report should be viewed as part of the total mix of information reasonably available to shareholders.

Though the Company argued that news articles should be considered, the articles were few in number, narrow in focus, and remote in time. The Company pointed to only eight articles, and they apparently dealt only with the Company's litigation in the states of Maine and Mississippi, reporting its plea of guilty in the former and ongoing lawsuits in the latter. Further, these articles were not published in the context of this proxy contest. Rather, they spanned more than a year; the latest of them had appeared more than two months before the Company's Proxy Statement was even issued; and all but one had appeared more than six months earlier. These articles were properly considered not to be part of the information that was reasonably available to shareholders.

Nor was the Company's 10-K Report part of the reasonably available mix. That report was filed with the SEC, not distributed to shareholders. Nothing in any of the documents sent to shareholders highlighted the 10-K Report. The Proxy Statement did not mention it at all; and the annual report made no reference to it in its description of the Company's environmental record. Indeed, in each link of the chain of references on which the Company now relies the pertinent reference was a general one widely separated from any environmental discussion. Thus, the Proxy Statement's mention of the annual report appeared only as a general reference on page 2 of the Proxy Statement; the annual report's reference to the availability of the 10-K Report appeared only as an unenlightening statement on the inside of the annual report's back cover:

> This Annual Report includes most of the *financial* information required to be on file with the Securities and Exchange Commission and is incorporated in our Form 10-K. The Company will be pleased to provide a copy of its 1991 Annual Report or Form 10-K free of charge upon request. (Emphasis added.)

Nothing in this reference or in the annual report's description of environmental matters suggested that there existed additional environmental facts and proceedings adverse to the Company, much less that they could be learned from the Company's 10-K Report. In short, a reasonable shareholder who was interested in the Valdez Principles and had read both the Proxy Statement and the annual report would have received no indication that additional information pertinent to the Valdez Resolution was available in the 10-K Report.

We conclude that the district court correctly ruled that the press reports and the Company's 10-K Report to the SEC were not part of the total mix of information reasonably available to shareholders about to vote on the Valdez Resolution.

B. The Proxy Statement and the Annual Report

There can be no serious question here that the Proxy Statement standing alone was materially misleading with respect to the Company's environmental record. The stated purpose of the Valdez Principles was to "achieve a genuine and publicly trusted measure of public environmental accountability." The Company's representations, in opposition, that it had a longstanding commitment to the protection of the environment, that it was a leader in environmental protection, that it had a vigorous compliance program, and that it had addressed such issues appropriately, conveyed an impression that was entirely false.

The annual report, which the district court treated as part of the total mix reasonably available to shareholders, presents its own special problems. Had the Company's misleadingly self-laudatory statements not been made, and had the disclosures made in the annual report appeared in the Proxy Statement, we would likely consider the disclosures not to be materially incomplete. On the other hand, given the unqualifiedly glowing statements that were actually made in the Proxy Statement, we consider it a close question whether such disclosures as were made in the annual report should be deemed part of the total mix available to shareholders or should instead be deemed buried in a part of the report where one seeking environmental information, might not think to look. The major headings in the annual report were "Financial Highlights," "To Our Shareholders," "International Paper in the 1990s," and about a dozen others, none of which mentioned the environment. In the section boldly headed "International Paper in the 1990s," there were smaller subheadings, to wit, "Customers," "Value Added Products," "Global Presence," "Manufacturing Efficiency," and "The Environment: Steadily Improving Performance." This environmental section, though not quite as self-laudatory as the Proxy Statement, was nonetheless unqualifiedly positive. Such negative information as was included in the annual report was set out some 20 pages later in a section that bore the heading "Environmental Issues" in less prominent type and was placed in an untitled financial summary section describing the Company's investment activities, capital resources, and capital expenditures. This more informative "Environmental Issues" section was sandwiched between sections headed "Other Financial Statement Items and Accounting Standards Changes" and "Effects of Inflation."

We need not decide, however, whether the annual report should have been ruled not part of the total mix here, for we agree with the district court that even such disclosures as could be found in that report were not sufficient in light of the pristine picture painted by the Proxy Statement. Shareholders could have viewed the disclosures made in the annual report as not being inconsistent with the Company's "achieve[ment of] a genuine and publicly trusted measure of public environmental accountability" had they read only the Proxy Statement and the information disclosed in the annual report. For example, reading only the annual report, they could have believed that the five pleas of guilty were for minor infractions that did not bespeak a lack of corporate responsibility; they would likely have viewed the Company's statements in a different light had they known that the charges were not minor but felonies, that the $2.2 million fine was the second largest ever assessed for violation of hazardous-waste laws, and that some of the felonies involved falsification of required environmental reports. They would undoubtedly have been considerably enlightened as to the sincerity of the Company's claimed explicit policy and firm longstanding commitment for protection of the environment had they known the facts, undisclosed by the annual report, that the Company had falsified environmental reports and breached the settlement agreement it had reached in the Maine civil litigation. Shareholders could have believed the Company's claimed "strong compliance program" was not belied by the mere fact that the Company had been sued in "some" of "several" lawsuits as described in the annual report; they would have had a decidedly different picture had they also known facts not disclosed in that report, including that there were 43 such suits charging the Company with having dumped chemically contaminated waste in three rivers in one state alone, that the Company had been named in more than 50 administrative proceedings to enforce federal and state laws governing treatment of hazardous wastes, and that the Company's record was such that the EPA was seeking to prohibit it from doing business with the federal government for three years.

In sum, the disclosures contained in the annual report failed to cure the materially misleading representations and omissions in the Proxy Statement. The district court properly ruled that the Company had violated § 14(a) and Rule 14a-9.

NOTES AND QUESTIONS

(1) **The "total mix" and efficient markets.** Since the Company's stock was very widely traded in a well-developed securities market, the information that the company claimed was part of the "total mix" had probably been made sufficiently public that it was reflected in the price of the company's stock (*see* Section 7.01[F]). Assuming that is the case, have the shareholders been injured by the misstatements in the proxy statement? How?[26]

(2) **Buried facts.** One issue in *International Paper* concerned *how* facts were disclosed in the annual report. For another case involving "buried facts," see *Gould v. American-Hamilton Steamship Co.*,[27] in which the proxy statement stated that the directors had unanimously approved the merger and recommended that the shareholders do so. Companies represented by three of the directors, and one of those directors himself, were being treated more favorably than the other shareholders by receiving cash rather than stock in the merger. Although these facts could be found in various parts of the proxy statement, the disclosure was held inadequate. The district court said that the proxy rules do not allow drafters to "avoid blatant fraud and still keep the stockholder from discovering which shell the pea is under."[28] The appellate court added:

> While we find ourselves in general accord with Judge Mansfield's statement in *Richland v. Crandall*, 262 F. Supp. 538, 554 (S.D.N.Y. 1967), that "corporations are not required to address their stockholders as if they were children in kindergarten," we also bear in mind Judge Friendly's admonition in *Gerstle v. Gamble-Skogmo, Inc.*, 478 F.2d 1281, 1297 (2d Cir. 1973), who, after quoting Judge Mansfield's statement, said that "it is not sufficient that overtones might have been picked up by the sensitive antennae of investment analysts." In the present case many of the statements upon which the defendant-appellants rely are scattered through and rather buried in the lengthy proxy statement. There is nowhere a statement giving emphasis to the con-

---

[26] *Compare Klein v. PDG Remediation, Inc.*, 937 F. Supp. 323 (S.D.N.Y. 1996) (public information about a Florida environmental clean-up fund not considered part of the "total mix" because the "inquiry into whether information is part of the 'total mix' does not end with the revelation that the information was public, rather the inquiry must turn to whether the investors could have reasonable been aware of the information").

[27] 319 F. Supp. 795 (D. Del. 1970), *aff'd*, 535 F.2d 761 (3d Cir. 1976). *See also Feit v. Leasco Data Processing Corp.*, 332 F. Supp. 544, 565-66 (E.D.N.Y. 1971).

[28] 319 F. Supp. at 810.

flicts of interest similar to that given to the board's approval of the merger agreement. We conclude that the district court did not err in holding on summary judgment that the proxy materials were materially deficient in this respect.[29]

(3) **Distorted presentation.** Issuers also may not deliberately distort facts by misleading presentation. See *Gillette Co. v. RB Partners*,[30] in which the target of a proxy contest issued a misleading organizational chart of the insurgents which exaggerated the prominence of foreign investors in the insurgent organization.

(4) **Disclosures concerning social issues.** *International Paper* relates to broader issues concerning companies' obligations to disclose in proxy statements matters that arguably are unconnected with corporate profits, and therefore are not of concern to most shareholders. Should social disclosures that are of little interest to most investors (other than "ethical investors" such as church groups and universities) nonetheless be considered "material" for purposes of the federal securities laws? If so, how should the "materiality" of such social disclosures be determined? Should "ethical investors" be treated as "reasonable investors" for purposes of the *TSC* standard? Or should courts insist that ethical disclosures relate to the corporation's financial well-being?

The controversy over social disclosures was the subject of a round of lawsuits and rulemaking proceedings involving the SEC and several public interest groups in *Natural Resources Defense Council, Inc. v. SEC*,[31] The public interest groups had petitioned the SEC in 1971 to promulgate a rule requiring disclosure of information concerning environmental damage by the corporation and employment discrimination. The result of the NRDC proceedings was SEC rules requiring disclosure of projected costs of compliance with environmental laws and other environmental matters having a material economic effect on the company.

The SEC has treated disclosures concerning illegal corporate payments somewhat differently from other "social" disclosures. The SEC has persistently sued companies that have failed to disclose such information in proxy materials, contending that such payments reflect on the integrity of management and also may be "economically" material if the payments affect a substantial percentage of the company's business. See *SEC v. Joseph Schlitz Brewing Co.*,[32] in which the Commission sued Schlitz for failing to disclose in various disclosure documents a scheme to induce sales by bribing beer retailers in violation of federal, state and local liquor laws and for failing to disclose transactions with Spanish affiliates that violated Spanish laws. The court denied defendant's motion to dismiss, accepting the SEC's integrity-of-management and effect-on-

---

[29]   535 F.2d at 774.

[30]   693 F. Supp. 1266 (D. Mass. 1988).

[31]   389 F. Supp. 689 (D.D.C. 1974) and 432 F. Supp. 1190 (D.D.C. 1977) (hearing after rule-making proceeding), *rev'd*, 606 F.2d 1031 (D.C. Cir. 1979).

[32]   452 F. Supp. 824 (E.D. Wis. 1978).

business arguments. The SEC pointed out, among other things, that the illegal practices could threaten Schlitz's liquor licenses. Although improper payments are now illegal under the Foreign Corrupt Practices Act,[33] the extent to which they must be disclosed under § 14(a) is not clear. From the standpoint of the duty to disclose, are improper payments distinguishable from other illegal or antisocial activities?

Note, finally, that a broad duty to disclose illegal or antisocial conduct that has not yet given rise to litigation might convert the securities laws from disclosure rules to a system of regulation of internal corporate misconduct. In light of these concerns, most courts have, in fact, hesitated to impose liability in civil cases under § 14(a) for failure to disclose in proxy materials violations of law which have not given rise to litigation.[34]

(5) **Opinions.** Rule 14-9 speaks of statements that are false or misleading "with respect to any material fact." Are statements of a person's opinions, reasons for acting, or beliefs statements of material *fact* for purposes of Rule 14-9? In *Virginia Bankshares, Inc. v. Sandberg,*[35] the Supreme Court addressed this question in connection with a proxy statement that stated: "The Plan of Merger has been approved by the Board of Directors because it provides an opportunity for the Bank's public shareholders to achieve a high value for their shares." The Court held that, although directors' statements of reasons or belief are factual both "as statements that directors do act for the reason given or hold the belief stated and as statements about the subject matter of the reason or belief expressed,"[36] they are actionable under Rule 14-9 only if they are misleading in the latter sense. Accordingly, in a case like *Virginia Bankshares,* the plaintiffs would have to show that the price offered for their shares was not "high," as the directors had asserted, rather than that the directors approved the merger for a different reason—for instance, to preserve their own jobs. One ground for the holding was a concern for the potential of abusive litigation resting on the shaky foundation of director motivation. Another concerned the appropriate dividing line between federal and state law. Imposing liability for improperly characterizing a transaction as fair comes dangerously close to turning fairness, normally a state issue, into a federal issue. On this point, the Court wrote:

> Petitioners are also wrong to argue that construing the statute to allow recovery for a misleading statement that the merger was "fair" to the minority shareholders is tantamount to assuming federal authority to bar corporate transactions thought to be unfair to some group of shareholders. . . . Although a corporate transaction's "fairness" is not, as such, a federal con-

---

[33]   15 U.S.C.A. §§ 78dd-1, 78dd-2.

[34]   *See Gaines v. Haughton,* 645 F.2d 761 (9th Cir. 1981); *Cowin v. Bresler,* Fed. Sec. L. Rep. (CCH) ¶ 98,393 (D.D.C. 1981); *Amalgamated Clothing & Textile Workers Union v. J.P. Stevens & Co., Inc.,* 475 F. Supp. 328 (S.D.N.Y. 1979).

[35]   501 U.S. 1083 (1991).

[36]   *Id.* at 1092.

cern, a proxy statement's claim of fairness presupposes a factual integrity that federal law is expressly concerned to preserve.[37]

(6) **Application of the First Amendment.** Is SEC regulation of proxy disclosures consistent with the First Amendment? Note that SEC rules prescribe what issuers and others can and must say in their proxy materials. Should a newspaper ad raising questions about those seeking control of Gillette (*see* Note 3 above) be treated differently from the New York Times ad that protested racial abuse in the landmark First Amendment case, *New York Times v. Sullivan?*[38] Some SEC-regulated speech may fall within the broad category of "commercial speech." The Court has held that commercial speech will be accorded somewhat less protection than non-"commercial" speech. Although the Court has said that commercial speech may include the broad category of speech "related solely to the economic interests of the speaker and its audience,"[39] more recently the Court has apparently narrowed the category to include speech that proposes a commercial transaction.[40] Although some SEC regulation, such as that regarding the initial sale of securities, would seem to be "commercial,"[41] proxy solicitations are not classic commercial speech in the sense of advertising. Among other things, they sometimes bear a striking similarity to political debate, particularly with respect to "social" disclosures (*see* Note 4 above) and shareholder proposals (*see* Section 7.04). For example, in *Long Island Lighting Co. v. Barbash,*[42] the solicitation involved the question of municipal ownership of a utility.[43]

The main indication of how the Court might rule on a proxy issue is *Pacific Gas & Electric Co. v. Public Utilities Commission,*[44] in which the Court held unconstitutional under the First Amendment a state utility commission requirement that a utility company provide space in its billing envelope for opposing political viewpoints. This is very similar to the shareholder proposal rule discussed below in Section 7.04, which requires managers to give space to shareholder proposals in corporate proxy solicitation material. However, the Court distinguished the shareholder proposal rule on the ground that managers have no interest in corporate property that would justify constitutionally protecting their internal governance speech.[45] The Court, therefore, failed to consider the interests of shareholders and others besides managers that are potentially at stake in

---

[37]   *Id.* at 1094 n.6.

[38]   376 U.S. 254 (1964)

[39]   *Central Hudson Gas & Elec. Corp. v. Public Service Comm'n of New York*, 447 U.S. 557, 561 (1980).

[40]   *See Board of Trustees of State Univ. of New York v. Fox*, 492 U.S. 60, 66-67 (1983). *See also City of Cincinnati v. Discovery Network, Inc.*, 507 U.S. 410 (1993) (assuming but not deciding that this is the test).

[41]   This regulation is not necessarily constitutional under the First Amendment. *See* **Schoeman**.

[42]   779 F.2d 793 (2d Cir. 1985).

[43]   The court avoided the First Amendment issue by focusing on whether the ad was a "solicitation."

[44]   475 U.S. 1 (1986).

[45]   475 U.S. at 14, n.10. Justice Stevens, dissenting, concluded that the two situations could not be distinguished. *Id.* at 39-40.

the manipulation of corporate debate. Assuming proxy speech is "commercial," it will be judged under *Central Hudson Gas & Elec. Corp. v. Public Serv. Comm'n*:[46]

> For commercial speech to come within [First Amendment protection], it at least must concern lawful activity and not be misleading. Next, we ask whether the asserted governmental interest is substantial. If both inquiries yield positive answers, we must determine whether the regulation directly advances the governmental interest asserted, and whether it is not more extensive than is necessary to serve that interest.

Board of Trustees of State University v. Fox[47] held that the "not more extensive than is necessary" language in the *Central Hudson* test does not necessarily compel the government to adopt the least restrictive means of achieving the governmental interest, but rather only requires a reasonable fit between ends and means. At the same time, however, the Court has made it clear in recent commercial speech cases such as *City of Cincinnati v. Discovery Network*[48] and *Edenfield v. Fane*,[49] that "reasonable fit" requires a careful cost/benefit analysis rather than merely a showing that a substantial purpose is furthered in some way by the restriction. For example, in *Edenfield*, the Court struck down a ban on solicitations by CPA's, reasoning that the state had not shown a sufficient likelihood that permitting such solicitation would compromise the independence of CPA's or result in fraud or overreaching.

In applying these standards to proxy solicitations, note that some proxy rules, such as those requiring filings, prescribing the form of proxies, and requiring inclusion of shareholder proposals in proxy materials, do not involve regulation of "misleading" statements. As to whether proxy regulation reasonably advances a substantial governmental interest, consider the arguments against federal proxy regulation discussed in Section 7.03[E]: mandatory disclosure to public corporation shareholders is unnecessary because they are rationally apathetic, disclosures and firms' rules can be tested in efficient securities markets, and disclosure would emerge in unregulated markets if investors wanted it.

The most direct First Amendment pronouncement in a securities case is *SEC v. Wall Street Publishing Institute, Inc.*,[50] in which the court held that the First Amendment did not prevent the SEC from enjoining, under the Securities Act of 1933, publication of monthly magazines by an investment adviser because the adviser failed to disclose that the publisher received consideration in the form of free text from the subject firms. The court emphasized that the case did not involve prior restraint without review of the contents, there were misleading statements, and the SEC was only requiring additional

---

[46]   447 U.S. 557, 566 (1980).

[47]   492 U.S. 469 (1989).

[48]   507 U.S. 410 (1993).

[49]   507 U.S. 761 (1993).

[50]   851 F.2d 365 (D.C. Cir. 1988).

disclosure rather than censoring contents. Perhaps most significantly, the court upheld the regulation despite characterizing the speech as not clearly "commercial," but more like a news story.

REFERENCES

Brudney, *Business Corporations and Stockholders' Rights under the First Amendment*, 91 YALE L.J. 235 (1981).

Butler & Ribstein, *Corporate Governance Speech and the First Amendment*, 43 KANS. L. REV. 163 (1994).

Coffee, *Beyond the Shut-Eyed Sentry: Toward a Theoretical View of Corporate Misconduct and an Effective Legal Response*, 63 VA. L. REV. 1099 (1977).

Stevenson, *The SEC and the New Disclosure*, 62 CORNELL L. REV. 50 (1976).

Symposium, *The First Amendment and Federal Securities Regulation*, 20 CONN. L. REV. 2 (1988).

Williams, *The Securities and Exchange Commission and Corporate Social Transparency*, 112 HARV. L. REV. 1197 (1999).

Wolfson, THE FIRST AMENDMENT AND THE SEC (1990).

[D] Remedies for Misleading Proxy Statements

The only express remedy in the 1934 Act that applies to proxy statements is § 18 which provides that investors who have purchased or sold securities in reliance on misstatements in a document filed with the SEC may sue for damages caused by such reliance. While proxy statements are "filed" with the SEC within the meaning of Section 18, the annual report required by Rule 14a-3 is not, although Section 18 may apply if the proxy statement incorporates the annual report by reference (Rule 14a-3(c)).

There is also an implied civil remedy under § 14 of the 1934 Act. In *J.I. Case Co. v. Borak*,[51] the Court reasoned that implied civil remedies for private parties aid enforcement of § 14, thereby effectuating the congressional purpose underlying the securities laws—to protect investors. More recently, the Supreme Court has moved toward a much more restrictive rule regarding implied rights of action.[52] But *Borak* is still good law as far as § 14(a) and Rule 14a-9 are concerned.[53]

Because § 14(a) does not expressly provide for a civil remedy for private investors, there are several questions concerning the extent of liability under that Section. First, it

---

[51]   377 U.S. 426 (1964).

[52]   *See Transamerica Mortgage Advisors, Inc. v. Lewis*, 444 U.S. 11 (1979); *Touche Ross & Co. v. Redington*, 442 U.S. 560 (1979).

[53]   For a case upholding a shareholder's implied right of action to sue to enforce the shareholder proposal rule (SEC Rule 14a-8, discussed in Section 7.04), see *Roosevelt v. E.I. DuPont de Nemours & Co.*, 958 F.2d 416 (D.C. Cir. 1992). For a case upholding an implied right of action to enforce SEC Rule 14a-4's requirement that shareholders be permitted to vote separately on separate issues, see *Koppel v. 4987 Corp.*, 167 F.3d 125 (2d Cir. 1999).

is not settled whether it is necessary to prove that the defendant had knowledge of the falsity of the misrepresentations or omissions when a private action is based on a violation of Rule 14a-9. In *Ernst & Ernst v. Hochfelder*,[54] the Supreme Court held that knowledge of falsity, or scienter, was required in a cause of action implied under § 10(b) of the 1934 Act. However, the courts have divided concerning this requirement's application to actions under § 14(a).[55]

Second, there is a question concerning the requisite causal link between the violation of § 14(a)—the misrepresentations or omissions in the proxy statement in violation of Rule 14a-9—and the injury to the shareholders. For example, management may hold enough votes to prevail even without the proxies solicited by the defective statement. In this situation, some courts have held that the proxy statement might still have caused injury because a properly informed electorate could have sought other remedies under state law, such as appraisal rights or an injunction. The Court, in a part of *Virginia Bankshares* not discussed above, casts some doubt on this theory. There may also be an issue concerning whether nondisclosure of illegal transactions in director election proxy materials caused additional illegal transactions because of the reelection of the directors who approved the transactions. The courts have uniformly denied relief in this situation.[56]

Finally, what is the significance of the fairness of the transaction that is approved by a tainted solicitation? In *Mills v. Electric Auto-Lite Co.*,[57] the Supreme Court held that a remedy under § 14(a) might lie for materially misleading statements in a proxy statement issued in connection with a merger, even if the defendants could show that the merger was fair. Ultimately, some 14 years after the suit was first filed, relief was denied because the plaintiff was unable to prove that the shareholders were damaged.[58]

[E] Evaluation and Revision of Federal Proxy Regulation

This Section concludes with an overall evaluation of federal proxy regulation, and with a discussion of recent revisions of the proxy rules in response to some recent criticism.

---

[54] 425 U.S. 185 (1976).

[55] *Compare Gerstle v. Gamble-Skogmo, Inc.*, 478 F.2d 1281 (2d Cir. 1973) (holding that negligence is enough for liability under § 14(a)), *and Herskowitz v. Nutri/System, Inc.*, 857 F.2d 179 (3d Cir. 1988) (applying negligence standard to outside advisers such as accountants and investment bankers), *with Adams v. Standard Knitting Mills, Inc.*, 623 F.2d 422 (6th Cir.), *cert. denied*, 449 U.S. 1067 (1980) (contra).

[56] *See, e.g., Herman v. Beretta*, Fed. Sec. L. Rep. (CCH) ¶ 97,685 (S.D.N.Y. 1980). *See also Royal Business Group, Inc. v. Realist, Inc.*, 933 F.2d 1056 (1st Cir. 1991) (denying standing to sue under § 14(a) for a proxy contestant because its right to an informed vote was not denied and there was no causal nexus with corporate transaction resulting from misleading proxy statement)

[57] 396 U.S. 375 (1970).

[58] *Mills v. Electronic Auto-Lite Co.*, 552 F.2d 1239 (7th Cir.), *cert. denied*, 434 U.S. 922 (1977).

[1] Proxy Regulation and Shareholder Passivity

Does the scheme of federal regulation of the proxy solicitation process discussed in this section make sense in light of the economics of the publicly held corporation?

The principle underlying the federal proxy rules regime is that providing information to the shareholders at proxy time enables them to control corporate managers more effectively. Contrast this principle with the theory discussed in Section 7.02[A] that shareholder passivity is inherent in dispersed ownership of public corporation shares. Because each shareholder owns only a small piece of the firm, the cost to each shareholder of becoming well-informed about the corporation outweighs the benefits. Even if the vote (such as on a merger or asset sale) has substantial economic consequences to each shareholder, a small shareholder is likely to conclude that her vote is inconsequential, and therefore not worth the costs of understanding the proxy material. And even if the information would actually have a substantial impact on each shareholder, the ignorant shareholder would not necessarily expend resources to discover that fact. In other words, the average shareholder is not merely ignorant, but rationally ignorant about corporate affairs. This basic fact cannot be changed by giving shareholders even more information.

As discussed in Section 7.02[A], the fact that shareholders are rationally ignorant does not necessarily mean that they are defenseless. For example, a shareholder or outsider who believes he can improve on the transaction being submitted to the shareholders or provide better management than the incumbent directors can bid for control and reap a profit from entering into the transaction or effecting the change once control is obtained. Because this process is driven by sophisticated investors, it does not depend for its success on mandatory disclosure to individual investors.

It does not necessarily follow, however, that no shareholders benefit from proxy disclosures. Institutions often own substantial portions of public corporations and can benefit from proxy disclosures. While these large shareholders could obtain their own information, requiring them to do so would cause a wasteful duplication of effort. Requiring disclosure of information by management thus can minimize the costs of obtaining voting information.

But even if disclosure is worthwhile for *some* shareholders, why require delivery to *all* shareholders? Institutional investors and analysts who may benefit from disclosure easily can access centrally filed disclosures.

Related questions concern the appropriate standard of materiality: If most shareholders are rationally ignorant about corporate affairs, what sorts of facts would be likely to affect the shareholders' votes? If small shareholders are passive, perhaps materiality should be based on the voting behavior of large shareholders such as institutions for whom it pays to be well informed. Under that theory, are cases like *United Paperworkers*, which hold that disclosure duties are not satisfied by information that is available in the market or which is obscurely present in public disclosures, rightly decided? What about cases which require "social disclosure" that does not affect stock price?

[2] The Mandatory Nature of Proxy Regulation

Even if giving information to the shareholders at proxy time is a good idea, this does not necessarily justify the mandatory rules requiring disclosure of information found in federal proxy regulation. Suppose, for example, that Corporation X wanted to opt out of the federal disclosure system. Should it be prevented from doing so? If harm to existing shareholders is a concern, opt-out could be limited to new firms, or to companies that obtain 100% shareholder consent. To the extent that investors value the disclosures required by federal law as a way of minimizing agency costs, the market price of the stock would be bid down in an efficient market, so that investors would get what they paid for. If so, firms would have the incentive to opt out only if the benefits of doing so outweighed the cost.

A possible argument for a mandatory system is that new investors would not be aware of the opt-out or its consequences. However, analysts should be able to ferret out this information, as they do many other bits of arcane information about, for example, the technology underlying the company's products or the details of state corporation law. Thus, a company's election to opt out of proxy regulation would be reflected in the company's share price, even if the individual investor was not aware of the opt out.

Even if permitting opting out may entail some costs, it might be justified if the benefits outweigh the costs. Corporations are put to considerable expense to compile and distribute disclosure documents that are ignored by the vast majority of addressees. Also, rigid proxy rules may actually interfere with shareholder monitoring by discouraging proxy initiatives, communications among institutional shareholders, and dissemination of information to shareholders by independent advisors (*see* subsection [3] below). An important advantage of a voluntary system is that it would permit the evolution of efficient proxy rules under state law and private contract.

[3] Proxy Rules and Shareholder Monitoring

Prior to the most recent major revision of the federal proxy rules in 1992, some shareholder groups and institutional investors, led by the California Public Employees' Retirement System ("CalPERS"), complained that the proxy rules interfered with effective monitoring by large shareholders. This is consistent with the theory that government regulation has consistently constrained the power of large investors (*see* Section 7.02[A]). In response to this criticism, the SEC adopted new rules that, among other things, (1) exempted from coverage solicitations by people who do not seek proxy authority and do not have a substantial interest in the matter subject to a vote, (2) amended the definition of "solicitation" to specify that a shareholder can publicly announce how it intends to vote and provide the reasons for that decision without having to comply with the proxy rules, and (3) allowed soliciting parties to commence a solicitation on the basis of a preliminary proxy statement publicly filed with the Commission, so long as no form of proxy is provided to the solicited shareholders until the dissemination of a definitive proxy statement. These rules, including an expanded power under Rule 14a-12 to communicate with investors prior to the filing or dissemination of proxy statements, are discussed above in Section 7.03[B].

REFERENCES

Black, *Disclosure, Not Censorship: The Case for Proxy Reform*, 17 J. CORP. L. 49 (1991).
Easterbrook & Fischel, THE ECONOMIC STRUCTURE OF CORPORATE LAW (1991).
Hornstein, *Proxy Solicitation Redefined*, 71 WASH. U. L.Q. 1129 (1993).
Pound, *Proxy Voting and the SEC: Investor Protection versus Market Efficiency*, 29 J. FIN. ECON. 241 (1991).
Sharara & Hoke-Witherspoon, *The Evolution of the 1992 Shareholder Communication Proxy Rules and their Impact on Corporate Governance*, 49 BUS. LAW. 327 (1993).

§ 7.04 Shareholder Proposals

As we have already seen in the *United Paperworkers* case in Section 7.03[C], SEC Rule 14a-8 lets a shareholder in a public corporation force management to include her proposal in the proxy statement that management distributes to all the corporation's shareholders. Motivated by the Berle-Means thesis that public corporations are controlled by managers who are free from effective monitoring because shareholders are passive and uninformed, the shareholder proposal rule is designed to give the small shareholder a chance to air ideas in the corporate forum. Without the shareholder proposal rule, a shareholder who wished to communicate with her fellow shareholders on a particular matter would be faced with two equally unattractive options: raising the matter at a shareholders' meeting attended in person by few of the corporation's shareholders or conducting a full-blown proxy solicitation.

[A] Types of Shareholder Proposals

Shareholder proposals fall in three general categories. The first includes proposals made by shareholder activists, sometimes referred to as gadflies, such as John and Lewis Gilbert, who purport to speak for the smaller shareholders of large, management-controlled corporations. These proposals have a "populist" flavor, protesting things like management compensation and perquisites. A colorful fictional example was the character played by Judy Holliday in "The Solid Gold Cadillac" (1956).

A second type of shareholder proposal is concerned with the corporation's social responsibilities. An important early example was "Campaign GM," in which the Project on Corporate Responsibility sought to expand the General Motors board to include three "public interest" directors and to create a Shareholders Committee for Corporate Responsibility that would perform a "social audit" on General Motors. Social activists have also offered shareholder resolutions on such matters as economic support of South Africa and animal rights.

A third type of shareholder proposal includes those offered by institutional and other large shareholders. These proposals seek to maximize shareholder value by proposing or opposing specific corporate transactions. For example, proposals by institutional investors have suggested that the company be sold in pieces or opposed anti-takeover devices, such as "poison pills." Unlike proposals in the first two categories, which ordinarily attract little shareholder support, proposals in this third category frequently garner a significant percentage of shareholder votes, though few are actually approved.[59]

[B] Procedures

Under Rule 14a-8, if the proponent meets the eligibility requirements of subsection (b) and complies with the rules as number of proposals, length and time of submission set forth in subsections (c)-(e), and the proposal does not fall within one of the categories of subsection (i), an issuer must include in its proxy statement both the shareholder's proposal and, if the proponent so requests, a supporting statement of up to 500 words. In addition, Rule 14a-8 requires the issuer to include the proposal on its form of proxy and provide means by which shareholders can separately express their approval, disapproval, or abstention. Under Rule 14a-8(j), an issuer asserting that the proposal may be omitted must file with the SEC the proposal, the supporting statement, if any, and a statement of the issuer's reasons for believing the proposal may be omitted. The SEC may respond by stating that it will take no action against the issuer if it omits the proposal or by stating that, in the SEC's view, there is no basis on which the proposal can be excluded.[60] If management decides to include the proposal in its proxy materials, it may state its position in opposition. In doing so, as discussed in *United Paperworkers*, management is subject to restrictions on misleading proxy statements.[61]

---

[59] For a recent discussion of two successful campaigns, see Jerry Guidera, *EMC and Mentor Graphics Lose Proxy Fights Over Independence of Directors and Stock Options*, WALL ST. J., May 9, 2002, at C1. See also Section 14.03[A][2][d], discussing the success of some proposals to eliminate "poison pill" takeover defenses.

[60] Although a "no action" statement was held reviewable in *Medical Committee*, below, this holding was repudiated by the same court in *Kixmiller v. SEC*, 492 F.2d 641 (D.C. Cir. 1974). *See also Amalgamated Clothing and Textile Workers Union v. SEC*, 15 F.3d 254 (2d Cir. 1994) (federal appeals court lacked jurisdiction to review SEC's letter affirming SEC Corporate Finance Division's position that company could exclude shareholder resolution requiring evaluation of health care reform proposals because this was not a final order). Compare the procedure used in NYCERS, immediately below, in which the shareholders sued the company for not including the proposal. Note that the SEC's position in a "no-action" statement does not legally bind the shareholder proponent or the issuer.

[61] *See also New England Anti-Vivisection Society, Inc. v. U.S. Surgical Corp., Inc.*, 889 F.2d 1198 (1st Cir. 1989) (held not misleading).

[C] Categories of Excludable Proposals

The most important questions concerning shareholder proposals involve the categories of excludable proposals under Rule 14a-8(i). These categories have changed substantially since Rule 14a-8 was first promulgated in 1942. Two of the more controversial exclusions in the 1970 version of the rule are interpreted in the following case.[62]

MEDICAL COMMITTEE FOR HUMAN RIGHTS v. SEC
United States Court of Appeals, District of Columbia Circuit
432 F.2d 659 (1970), *vacated*, 404 U.S. 403 (1972)

TAMM, Circuit Judge:

The instant petition presents novel and significant questions concerning implementation of the concepts of corporate democracy embodied in section 14 of the Securities Exchange Act of 1934, and of the power of this court to review determinations of the Securities and Exchange Commission made pursuant to its proxy rules. For reasons to be stated more fully below, we hold that the Commission's action in the present case is reviewable, and that the cause must be remanded for further administrative proceedings.

I. Procedural History of the Case

On March 11, 1968, Dr. Quentin D. Young, National Chairman of the Medical Committee for Human Rights, wrote to the Secretary of the Dow Chemical Company, stating that the Medical Committee had obtained by gift several shares of Dow stock and expressing concern regarding the company's manufacture of the chemical substance napalm.

In part, Dr. Young's letter said:

> After consultation with the executive body of the Medical Committee, I have been instructed to request an amendment to the charter of our company, Dow Chemical. We have learned that we are technically late in asking for an amendment at this date, but we wish to observe that it is a matter of such great urgency that we think it is imperative not to delay until the shareholders' meeting next year.

* * *

We respectfully propose the following wording to be sent to the shareholders:

> "RESOLVED, that the shareholders of the Dow Chemical Company request the Board of Directors, in accordance with the laws of the State of Delaware, and the Composite Certificate of Incorporation of the Dow Chemical Company, to adopt a resolution setting forth an amendment to

---

[62] Prior to 1998, when the shareholder proposal rule was recast in its current question and answer format, categories of excludable proposals were found in subsection (c) of Rule 14a-8. Accordingly, many of the older cases and materials below refer to subsection (c), rather than subsection (i).

the Composite Certificate of Incorporation of the Dow Chemical Company that napalm shall not be sold to any buyer unless that buyer gives reasonable assurance that the substance will not be used on or against human beings."

The letter concluded with the following statement:

Finally, we wish to note that our objections to the sale of this product [are] primarily based on the concerns for human life inherent in our organization's credo. However, we are further informed by our investment advisers that this product is also bad for our company's business as it is being used in the Vietnamese War. It is now clear from company statements and press reports that it is increasingly hard to recruit the highly intelligent, well-motivated, young college man so important for company growth. There is, as well, an adverse impact on our global business, which our advisers indicate, suffers as a result of the public reaction to this product.

Copies of this letter were forwarded to the President and the General Counsel of Dow Chemical Company, and to the Securities and Exchange Commission.

By letter dated March 21, 1968, the General Counsel of Dow Chemical replied to the Medical Committee's letter, stating that the proposal had arrived too late for inclusion in the 1968 proxy statement, but promising that the company would "study the matter and . . . communicate with you later this year" regarding inclusion of the resolution in proxy materials circulated by management in 1969. Copies of this letter, and of all subsequent correspondence, were duly filed with the Commission.

The next significant item of record is a letter dated January 6, 1969, noting that the Medical Committee was "distressed that 1968 has passed without our having received a single word from you on this important matter," and again requesting that the resolution be included in management's 1969 proxy materials. The Secretary of Dow Chemical replied to this letter on January 17, informing the Medical Committee that Dow intended to omit the resolution from its proxy statement and enclosing an opinion memorandum from Dow's General Counsel, the contents of which will be discussed in detail in part III, *infra*. On February 3 the Medical Committee responded to Dow's General Counsel, asserting that he had misconstrued the nature of their proposal in his opinion memorandum, and averring that the Medical Committee would not "presume to serve as draftsmen for an amendment to the corporate charter." The letter continued:

We are willing to bend . . . to your belief that the management should be allowed to decide to whom and under what circumstances it will sell its products. Nevertheless, we are certain that you would agree that the company's owners have not only the legal power but also the historic and economic obligation to determine what products their company will manufacture. Therefore, [we submit] . . . our revised proposal . . . requesting the Directors to consider the advisability of adopting an amendment to the corporate charter, forbidding the company to make napalm (any such amendment would, of course, be subject to the requirements of the "Defense Production Act of 1950," as are the corporate charters and management decisions of all United States Corporations), [and] we request that the following resolution be included in this year's proxy statement:

> "RESOLVED, that the shareholders of the Dow Chemical Company request that the Board of Directors, in accordance with the laws [sic] of the Dow Chemical Company, consider the advisability of adopting a resolution setting forth an amendment to the composite certificate of incorporation of the Dow Chemical Company that the company shall not make napalm."

On the same date, a letter was sent to the Securities and Exchange Commission, requesting a staff review of Dow's decision if it still intended to omit the proposal, and requesting oral argument before the Commission if the staff agreed with Dow.

. . . [O]n February 18, 1969, the Commission's Chief Counsel of the Division of Corporation Finance sent a letter to Dow, with copies to the Medical Committee, concluding that "[f]or reasons stated in your letter and the accompanying opinion of counsel, both dated January 17, 1969, this Division will not recommend any action . . . if this proposal is omitted from the management's proxy material . . . ." . . . [O]n April 2, 1969, both parties were informed that "[t]he Commission has approved the recommendation of the Division of Corporation Finance that no objection be raised if the Company omits the proposals from its proxy statements for the forthcoming meeting of shareholders." The petitioners thereupon instituted the present action, and on July 10, 1969, the Commission moved to dismiss the petition for lack of jurisdiction. On October 13 we denied the motion "without prejudice to renewal thereof in the briefs and at the argument on the merits."

* * *

II. Jurisdiction to Review

* * *

. . . We hold the Commission's decision in this case is presently reviewable, and turn our attention to an investigation of the proper scope of this review.

. . . We conclude that partial review of the merits of this controversy will not project us into an area which is committed by law to agency discretion.

III. The Merits of Petitioner's Proposal

The Medical Committee's sole substantive contention in this petition is that its proposed resolution could not, consistently with the Congressional intent underlying section 14(a), be properly deemed a proposal which is either motivated by general political and moral concerns, or related to the conduct of Dow's ordinary business operations. These criteria are two of the established exceptions to the general rule that management must include all properly submitted shareholder proposals in its proxy materials. They are contained in Rule 14a-8(c), 17 C.F.R. § 240.14a-8(c)(1970), which provides in relevant part:

> . . . [M]anagement may omit a proposal . . . from its proxy statement and form of proxy under any of the following circumstances:

* * *

(2) If it clearly appears that the proposal is submitted by the security holder ... primarily for the purpose of promoting general economic, political, racial, religious, social or similar causes; or

* * *

(5) If the proposal consists of a recommendation or request that the management take action with respect to a matter relating to the conduct of the ordinary business operations of the issuer.

... [T]he Commission has not deigned to address itself to any possible grounds for allowing management to exclude this proposal from its proxy statement. We confess to a similar puzzlement as to how the Commission reached the result which it did, and thus we are forced to remand the controversy for a more illuminating consideration and decision.

* * *

In aid of this consideration on remand, we feel constrained to explain our difficulties with the position taken by the company and endorsed by the Commission.

It is obvious to the point of banality to restate the proposition that Congress intended by its enactment of section 14 of the Securities Exchange Act of 1934 to give true vitality to the concept of corporate democracy.

* * *

In striving to implement this open-ended mandate, the Commission has gradually evolved its present proxy rules. Early exercises of the rule-making power were directed primarily toward the achievement of full and fair corporate disclosure regarding management proxy materials[.] ... The rationale underlying this development was the Commission's belief that the corporate practice of circulating proxy materials which failed to make reference to the fact that a shareholder intended to present a proposal at the annual meeting rendered the solicitation inherently misleading. From this position, it was only a short step to a formal rule requiring management to include in its proxy statement any shareholder proposal which was "a proper subject for action by the security holders." 7 Fed. Reg. 10,659 (1942). It eventually became clear that the question of what constituted a "proper subject" for shareholder action was to be resolved by recourse to the law of the state in which the company had been incorporated; however, the paucity of applicable state law giving content to the concept of "proper subject" led the Commission to seek guidance from precedent existing in jurisdictions which had a highly developed commercial and corporate law and to develop its own "common law" relating to proper subjects for shareholder action.

Further areas of difficulty became apparent as experience was gained in administering the "proper subject" test, and these conflicts provided the Commission with opportunities to put a detailed gloss upon the general phraseology of its rules. Thus, in 1945 the Commission issued a release containing an opinion of the Director of the Division of Corporation Finance that was rendered in response to a management request to omit shareholder resolutions which bore little or no relationship to the company's affairs; for example, these shareholder resolutions included proposals "that the anti-trust laws and the enforcement thereof be revised," and "that all Federal legislation hereafter enacted providing for workers and farmers to be represented should be made to apply equally to investors." The Commission's release endorsed the Director's conclusion that "proposals which deal with general political, social or economic matters are not, within the meaning of the rule, 'proper subjects for action by security holders.'" The reason for this conclusion was summarized as follows in the Director's opinion:

> Speaking generally, *it is the purpose of Rule X-14A-7 to place stockholders in a position to bring before their fellow stockholders matters of concern to them as stockholders in such corporation*; that is, such matters relating to the affairs of the company concerned as are proper subjects for stockholders' action under the laws of the state under which it was organized. It was not the intent of Rule X-14A-7 to permit stockholders to obtain the consensus of other stockholders with respect to matters which are of a general political, social or economic nature. *Other forums exist for the presentation of such views.*

Several years after the Commission issued this release, it was confronted with the same kind of problem when the management of a national bus company sought to omit a shareholder proposal phrased as "A Recommendation that Management Consider the Advisability of Abolishing the Segregated Seating System in the South"—a proposal which, on its face, was ambiguous with respect to whether it was limited solely to company policy rather than attacking all segregated seating, and which quite likely would have brought the company into violation of state laws then assumed to be valid. The Commission staff approved management's decision to omit the proposal, and the shareholder then sought a temporary injunction against the company's solicitation in a federal district court. The injunction was denied because the plaintiff had failed to exhaust his administrative remedies or to show that he would be irreparably harmed by refusal to grant the requested relief. *Peck v. Greyhound Corp.*, 97 F. Supp. 679 (S.D.N.Y. 1951). The Commission amended its rules the following year to encompass the above-quoted exception for situations in which "it clearly appears that the proposal is submitted by the security holder . . . primarily for the purpose of promoting general economic, political, racial, religious, social or similar causes." 17 Fed. Reg. 11,433 (1952); *see also id.* at 11,431. So far as we have been able to determine, the Commission's interpretation or application of this rule has not been considered by the courts.

The origins and genesis of the exception for proposals "relating to the conduct of the ordinary business operations of the issuer" are somewhat more obscure. This provision was introduced into the proxy rules in 1954, as part of amendments which were made to clarify the general proposition that the primary source of authority for determining whether a proposal is a proper subject for shareholder action is state law. *See* 19 Fed. Reg. 246 (1954). Shortly after the rule was adopted, the Commission explained its purpose to Congress in the following terms:

> The policy motivating the Commission in adopting the rule . . . is basically the same as the underlying policy of most State corporation laws to confine the solution of ordinary business problems to the board of directors and place such problems beyond the competence and direction of the shareholders. The basic reason for this policy is that it is manifestly impracticable in most cases for stockholders to decide management problems at corporate meetings.

* * *

. . . While Rule X-14A-8 does not require that the ordinary business operations be determined on the basis of State law, the premise of Rule X-14A-8 is that the propriety of . . . proposals for inclusion in the proxy statement is to be determined in general by the law of the State of incorporation. . . . Consistency with this premise requires that the phrase "ordinary business operations" in Rule X-14A-8 have the meaning attributed to it under applicable State law. To hold otherwise would be to introduce into the rule the possibility of endless and narrow interpretations based on no ascertainable standards.

It also appears that no administrative interpretation of this exception has yet been scrutinized by the courts.

These two exceptions are, on their face, consistent with the legislative purpose underlying section 14; for it seems fair to infer that Congress desired to make proxy solicitations a vehicle for *corporate* democracy rather than an all-purpose forum for malcontented shareholders to vent their spleen about irrelevant matters,[26] and also realized that management cannot exercise its specialized talents effectively if corporate investors assert the power to dictate the minutiae of daily business decisions. However, it is also apparent that the two exceptions which these rules carve out of the general requirement of inclusion can be construed so as to permit the exclusion of practically any shareholder proposal on the grounds that it is either "too general" or "too specific." Indeed, in the present case Dow Chemical Company attempted to impale the Medical Committee's proposal on both horns of this dilemma: in its memorandum of counsel, it argued that the Medical Committee's proposal was a matter of ordinary business operations properly within the sphere of management expertise and, at the same time, that the proposal clearly had been submitted primarily for the purpose of promoting general political or social causes. As noted above, the Division of Corporation Finance made no attempt to choose between these potentially conflicting arguments, but rather merely accepted Dow Chemical's decision to omit the proposal "[f]or reasons stated in [the company's] letter and the accompanying opinion of counsel, both dated January 17, 1969"; this determination was then adopted by the full Commission. Close examination of the company's arguments only increases doubt as to the reasoning processes which led the Commission to this result.

---

[26] *See, e.g.,* the following colloquy, which appears in House Hearings at 162-63:

Mr. Boren. So one man, if he owned one share in A.T. & T. . . . and another share in R.C.A. . . . if he decided deliberately . . . to become a professional stockholder in each one of the companies—he could have a hundred-word propaganda statement prepared and he could put it in every one of these proxy statements. Suppose he were a Communist. Commissioner Purcell. That is possible. We have never seen such a case. Mr. Boren. Suppose a man were a Communist and he wanted to send to all of the stockholders of all of these firms, a philosophic statement of 100 words in length, or a propaganda statement. . . . He could by the mere device of buying one share of stock . . . have available to him the mailing list of all the stockholders in the Radio Corporation of America.

* * *

Commissioner Purcell. Of course, we have never seen such a case; and if such a case came before us, then we would have to deal with it and make such appropriate changes as might seem necessary. . . .

In contending that the Medical Committee's proposal was properly excludable under Rule 14a-8(c)(5), Dow's counsel asserted:

> It is my opinion that *the determination of the products which the company shall manufacture*, the customers to which it shall sell the products, and the conditions under which it shall make such sales are related to the conduct of the ordinary business operations of the Company and that any attempt to amend the Certificate of Incorporation to define the circumstances under which the management of the Company shall make such determinations is contrary to the concept of corporate management, which is inherent in the Delaware General Corporation Act under which the Company is organized.

In the first place, it seems extremely dubious that this superficial analysis complies with the Commission's longstanding requirements that management must sustain the burden of proof when asserting that a shareholder proposal may properly be omitted from the proxy statement, and that "[w]here management contends that a proposal may be omitted because it is not proper under State law, it will be incumbent upon management to refer to the applicable statute or case law." 19 Fed. Reg. 246 (1954). As noted above, the Commission has formally represented to Congress that Rule 14a-8(c)(5) is intended to make state law the governing authority in determining what matters are ordinary business operations immune from shareholder control; yet, the Delaware General Corporation law provides that a company's Certificate of Incorporation may be amended to "change, substitute, enlarge or diminish the nature of [the company's] business." If there are valid reasons why the Medical Committee's proposal does not fit within the language and spirit of this provision, they certainly do not appear in the record.

The possibility that the Medical Committee's proposal could properly be omitted under Rule 14a-8(c)(2) appears somewhat more substantial in the circumstances of the instant case, although once again it may fairly be asked how Dow Chemical's arguments on this point could be deemed a rational basis for such a result: the paragraph in the company's memorandum of counsel purporting to deal with this issue, . . . consists entirely of a fundamentally irrelevant recitation of some of the political protests which had been directed at the company because of its manufacture of napalm, followed by the abrupt conclusion that management is therefore entitled to exclude the Medical Committee's proposal from its proxy statement. Our own examination of the issue raises substantial questions as to whether an interpretation of Rule 14a-8(c)(2) which permitted omission of this proposal as one motivated primarily by general political or social concerns would conflict with the congressional intent underlying section 14(a) of the Act.

As our earlier discussion indicates, the clear import of the language, legislative history, and record of administration of section 14(a) is that its overriding purpose is to assure to corporate shareholders the ability to exercise their right—some would say their duty—to control the important decisions which affect them in their capacity as stockholders and owners of the corporation. Thus, the Third Circuit has cogently summarized the philosophy of section 14(a) in the statement that "[a] corporation is run for the benefit of its stockholders and not for that of its managers." *SEC v. Transamerica Corp.*, 163 F.2d 511, 517 (3d Cir. 1947), *cert. denied*, 332 U.S. 847, 68 S. Ct. 351, 92 L.Ed. 418 (1948). Here, in contrast to the situations detailed above which led to the promulgation of Rule 14a-8(c)(2), the proposal relates solely to a matter that is completely within the accepted sphere of corporate activity and control. No reason has been advanced in the present proceedings which leads to the conclusion that management may properly place obstacles in the path of shareholders who wish to present to their co-owners, in accord with applicable state law, the question of whether they wish to have their assets used in a manner which they believe to be more socially responsible but possibly less profitable than that which is dictated by present company policy. Thus, even accepting Dow's characterization of the purpose and intent of the Medical Committee's proposal, there is a strong argument that permitting the company to exclude it would contravene the purpose of section 14(a).

However, the record in this case contains indications that we are confronted with quite a different situation. The management of Dow Chemical Company is repeatedly quoted in sources which include the company's own publications as proclaiming that the decision to continue manufacturing and marketing napalm was made not *because* of business considerations, but *in spite* of them; that management in essence decided to pursue a course of activity which generated little profit for the shareholders and actively impaired the company's public relations and recruitment activities because management considered this action morally and politically desirable. . . . The proper political and social role of modern corporations is, of course, a matter of philosophical argument extending far beyond the scope of our present concern; the substantive wisdom or propriety of particular corporate political decisions is also completely irrelevant to the resolution of the present controversy. What is of immediate concern, however, is the question of whether the corporate proxy rules can be employed as a shield to isolate such managerial decisions from shareholder control. After all, it must be remembered that "[t]he control of great corporations by a very few persons was the abuse at which Congress struck in enacting Section 14(a)." *SEC v. Transamerica Corp.*, *supra*, 163 F.2d at 518. We think that there is a clear and compelling distinction between management's legitimate need for freedom to apply its expertise in matters of day-to-day business judgment, and management's patently illegitimate claim of power to treat modern corporations with their vast resources as personal satrapies implementing personal political or moral predilections. It could scarcely be argued that management is more qualified or more entitled to make these kinds of decisions than the shareholders who are the true beneficial owners of the corporation; and it seems equally implausible that an application of the proxy rules which permitted such a result could be harmonized with the philosophy of corporate democracy which Congress embodied in section 14(a) of the Securities Exchange Act of 1934.

In light of these considerations, therefore, the cause must be remanded to the Commission so that it may reconsider petitioner's claim within the proper limits of its discretionary authority as set forth above, and so that "the basis for [its] decision [may] appear clearly on the record, not in conclusory terms but in sufficient detail to permit prompt and effective review."[33]

---

[33]   [The Supreme Court granted *certiorari* to review the decision of the D.C. Circuit but then vacated and remanded on the ground of mootness. 404 U.S. 403 (1972). As to reviewability of the SEC's "no action" position, see Section 7.04[B], n.60—Eds.].

NOTES AND QUESTIONS

(1) **Napalm.** Napalm is essentially slow-burning gasoline. In World War II, the Allied forces used jellied gasoline primarily to dislodge stubborn Japanese soldiers from their bunkers. Napalm was an "improvement" on this idea in that it incorporated polystyrene, a kind of plastic, which increased both the area covered and the stickiness of the substance.

(2) **Dow.** Dow Chemical Company is publicly held but, as of 1966, the Dow family held or controlled by far the largest block of stock. Industrial, as distinguished from consumer, products contributed over 90% of the company's sales. Dow's principal consumer product was Saran Wrap. Although Dow did very little direct defense work, many of its products were purchased by defense contractors. The company's headquarters were in the small (population approximately 35,000) middle-class community of Midland, Michigan. Dow, then the largest manufacturer of polystyrene, received its first napalm contract in 1965. The napalm contract represented only .5% of Dow's sales at that time.

(3) **Dow and napalm.** Dow was in hot water over napalm almost from the beginning of production. The first demonstration at Dow's napalm factory in Torrence, California was held in May, 1966. By 1968, there were protests against Dow recruiters at a large number of campuses. One recruiter was cornered in a room at Harvard for seven hours. There was some question as to Dow's ability during this time to compete for the best chemical engineers in a highly competitive job market. In 1969, Dow's corporate headquarters were vandalized by antiwar demonstrators and some embarrassing documents were made public. Much top executive time was being consumed with the napalm problem. On NBC's July 9, 1969 "Today" show, Herbert Dow Doan, president and grandson of the founder, stated:

> We feel that, in the first place, like everyone else, we don't like wars of any type. We wish this one would end. But our people are over there, they need the best weapons they can get. This napalm is a good discriminate, strategic weapon, and we feel those folks ought to have it. I think we should say that in back of our judgment to stay here is this kind of thinking: that our country is a democracy, a viable democracy—a morally viable democracy. We believe in its operation. We feel that we must do the things that this country asks of itself. We are individually responsible for the things that happen in this country, this war, and all of it is part of this. As long as we're that kind of government, we should supply the materials that our people need. . . .[63]

---

[63] The above account is based on Friedman, *This Napalm Business, in* IN THE NAME OF PROFIT (1972); *Why Dow Continues to Make Napalm*, BUSINESS WEEK, Feb. 10, 1968, at 118; *The Garbage Burner*, NEW REPUBLIC, July 26, 1969, at 7; *Dow Chemical Company: Sales and Worries are Up*, SCIENCE, Nov. 24, 1967, at 1031.

(4) **Subsequent history.** In 1969, after substantial debate within the company, Dow "lost" the napalm contract by not bidding aggressively against American Electric Company. Still later, Dow changed its image to that of a more "socially conscious" company, coincidentally with its increasing specialization in consumer products.[64] It also reportedly had fewer problems recruiting students in the tougher job market of the 1980s than it had in the low-unemployment 60s.[65]

(5) **Excludable proposals: 14a-8(i)(1)—"Not a proper subject for action."** Following *Medical Committee*, the categories of excludable proposals were revised in 1972, 1976 and 1983. There are now thirteen separate bases on which shareholder proposals can be excluded from management's proxy materials (*see* Rule 14a-8, subsections (i)(1) through (i)(13)).[66] Rule 14a-8(i)(1) permits the exclusion of shareholder proposals which are "not a proper subject for action" by shareholders under state law. This is a potentially broad exclusion if it is interpreted to permit only proposals relating to matters over which state corporate law gives shareholders decisionmaking authority. But Rule 14a-8(i)(1) has not been so interpreted. As the SEC's note to 14a-8(i)(1) states, the shareholders can always *recommend* that the board take certain action even if they cannot decide the issue under state law.[67] In addition, since shareholders generally share the power to alter the corporation's bylaws with the corporation's directors (*see* Section 5.01 above), shareholders may be able to circumvent 14a-8(i)(1) by phrasing proposals concerning matters committed to director discretion as amendments to the corporation's bylaws. See, for example, *International Brotherhood of Teamsters General Fund v. Fleming Companies*,[68] where the Oklahoma Supreme Court upheld a shareholder-proposed bylaw requiring the company's board of directors to dismantle the firm's takeover defenses, and the SEC's *General DataComm Industries No-Action Letter*,[69] where the Commission refused to authorize the corporation to omit a shareholder proposal that would amend the corporation's bylaws to limit stock option re-pricing.

Can the board thwart shareholder efforts by passing a bylaw explicitly precluding shareholder proposals? *SEC v. Transamerica Corp.*[70] held that the corporation could not exclude a proposal to amend a bylaw despite the fact that the corporation's bylaws provided for amendment only after a favorable resolution by the board of directors and the proposed amendment had not received this approval. The court held that permitting the directors to block the proposal in this way would unduly frustrate the purpose of Rule 14a-8.

---

[64] *See Dow Chemical Tries to Shed Tough Image and Court the Public*, WALL ST. J., Nov. 20, 1987, at 1.

[65] *See* Hirshey, *Desperately Seeking Employment*, WASHINGTON POST MAGAZINE, Jan. 3, 1988, at 20, 25.

[66] Prior to 1998, the thirteen exclusions were found in subsections (c)(1) through (c)(13).

[67] *See Auer v. Dressel*, 306 N.Y. 427, 11 N.E.2d 590 (1954).

[68] 975 P.2d 907 (Okla. 1999) (Oklahoma law).

[69] 1998 SEC No-Act. LEXIS 1037, 1998 WL 883796 (Dec. 9, 1998).

[70] 163 F.2d 511 (3d Cir. 1947).

(6) **14a-8(i)(5)—"Not significantly related to the issuer's business."** The 1976 version of Rule 14a-8(i)(5), then designated (c)(5), permitted exclusion "if the proposal deals with a matter that is not significantly related to the issuer's business." The following is excerpted from the Commission's comments concerning the 1976 version:[71]

> [T]he Commission does not believe that subparagraph (c)(5) should be hinged solely on the economic relativity of a proposal, since there are many instances in which the matter involved in a proposal is significant to an issuer's business, even though such significance is not apparent from an economic viewpoint. For example, proposals dealing with cumulative voting rights or the ratification of auditors in a sense may not be economically significant to an issuer's business but they nevertheless have a significance to security holders that would preclude their being omitted under this provision. And proposals relating to ethical issues such as political contributions also may be significant to the issuer's business, when viewed from a standpoint other than a purely economic one.
>
> Notwithstanding the foregoing, the Commission recognizes that there are circumstances in which economic data may indicate a valid basis for omitting a proposal under this provision. The Commission wishes to emphasize, however, that the significance of a particular matter to an issuer's present or prospective business depends upon that issuer's individual circumstances, and that there is no specific quantitative standard that is applicable in all instances. Moreover, as previously indicated, the burden is on the issuer to demonstrate that this or any other provision of Rule 14a-8 may properly be relied upon to omit a proposal.

The current version of this exclusion differs from the 1976 version by establishing a quantitative standard for determining when a proposal may *not* be omitted under 14a-8(i)(5). Under the current version of the rule, if a proposal relates to operations that account for more than five percent of the issuer's total assets or more than five percent of its net earnings or gross sales, it cannot be excluded under 14a-8(i)(5). If, however, the proposal fails to satisfy any of the five percent tests, it *may* be excluded under (i)(5), but only if the issuer shows that the proposal is not "otherwise significantly related to the [issuer's] business."

In 1998, the SEC rejected a proposal that would have converted the "relevance" test of 14a-8(i)(5) into a purely economic test permitting exclusion of any proposal relating to less than (a) $10 million or less in gross revenue or total costs for the company's most recently completed fiscal year, or (b) 3% of the company's gross revenue

---

[71] Exchange Act Release No. 12999, Fed. Sec. L. Rep. (CCH) ¶ 80,812 (1976-77 Transfer Binder).

or total assets (whichever is higher) for its most recently completed fiscal year, if that resulted in a number lower than $10 million

(7) **14a-8(i)(7)—"Ordinary business operations."** Rule 14a-8(i)(7) allows the exclusion of proposals that deal with matters "relating to the conduct of the ordinary business operations of the [issuer]." The following is another excerpt from the release concerning the 1976 version of Rule 14a-8(i)(7), then designated (c)(7), which is identical to the current version:

> The Commission recognizes that this standard for omission has created some difficulties in the past, and that, on occasion, it has been relied upon to omit proposals of considerable importance to security holders.

* * *

> The Commission is of the view that the provision adopted today can be effective in the future if it is interpreted somewhat more flexibly than in the past. Specifically, the term "ordinary business operations" has been deemed on occasion to include certain matters which have significant policy, economic or other implications inherent in them. For instance, a proposal that a utility company not construct a proposed nuclear power plant has in the past been considered excludable under former subparagraph (c)(5). In retrospect, however, it seems apparent that the economic and safety considerations attendant to nuclear power plants are of such magnitude that a determination whether to construct one is not an "ordinary" business matter. Accordingly, proposals of that nature, as well as others that have major implications, will in the future be considered beyond the realm of an issuer's ordinary business operations, and future interpretative letters of the Commission's staff will reflect that view.
>
> Although subparagraph (c)(7) will be subject to a more restrictive interpretation in the future than its predecessor, former subparagraph (c)(5), this should not be construed to mean that the provision will not be available for the omission of proposals that deal with truly "ordinary" business matters. Thus, where proposals involve business matters that are mundane in nature and do not involve any substantial policy or other considerations, the subparagraph may be relied upon to omit them.

Current interpretations of the "ordinary business operations" exclusion are discussed below (*see* Notes 1 and 2 following *Dole*, below).

(8) **14a-8(i)(8)—"Relates to an election to office."** Rule 14a-8(i)(8) permits the exclusion of proposals that relate to an election to corporate office. It may seem surprising that, under 14a-8(i)(8), shareholders may not use management's proxy statement to propose director candidates. A rationale for this provision is that someone must screen candidates who are given the prominence of being mentioned in the corporation's

proxy statement. Is it possible to accommodate this concern while limiting management's control over the nomination process?

Several of the current exclusions in Rule 14a-8(i) are interpreted in the following case.

NEW YORK CITY EMPLOYEES' RETIREMENT SYSTEM v. DOLE FOOD COMPANY, INC.

United States District Court, Southern District of New York

795 F. Supp. 95, *dismissed as moot*, 969 F.2d 1430 (2d. Cir. 1992)

CONBOY, District Judge:

Proceeding by an order to show cause, the New York City Employees' Retirement System ("NYCERS") brings this action for a preliminary injunction that would enjoin defendant Dole Food Company, Inc. ("Dole") from the solicitation of shareholder proxies for Dole's upcoming annual meeting without informing shareholders of NYCERS' shareholder proposal. In the alternative, NYCERS seeks inclusion of the proposal on a supplemental mailing prior to the annual meeting.

I. Background

NYCERS is a public pension fund that owns approximately 164,841 shares of common stock in Dole Food Company, Inc. ("Dole"). . . . On December 12, 1991, New York City Comptroller Elizabeth Holtzman, in her capacity as the custodian of NYCERS' assets, wrote to the executive vice president of Dole, requesting Dole to include the following proposal ("the NYCERS proposal") in its proxy statement prior to its annual meeting:

NEW YORK CITY EMPLOYEE'S [sic] RETIREMENT SYSTEM
SHAREHOLDER RESOLUTION ON HEALTH CARE TO
DOLE FOOD COMPANY, INC.

WHEREAS: The Dole Food Company is concerned with remaining competitive in the domestic and world marketplace, acknowledging the positive relationship between the health and well being of its employees and productivity, and the resulting effect on corporate growth and financial stability; and

WHEREAS: Sustained double-digit increases in health care costs have put severe financial pressure on a company attempting to continue to provide adequate health care for its employees and their dependents; and

WHEREAS: The company has a societal obligation to conduct its affairs in a way which promotes the health and well being of all;

BE IT THEREFORE RESOLVED: That the shareholders request the Board of Directors to establish a committee of the Board consisting of outside and independent directors for the purpose of evaluating the impact of a representative cross section of the various health care reform proposals being considered by national policy makers on the company and their [sic] competitive standing in domestic and international markets. These various proposals can be grouped in three generic categories; the single payor model (as in the Canadian plan), the limited payor (as in the Pepper Commission Report) and the employer mandated (as in the Kennedy-Waxman legislation). Further, the aforementioned committee should be directed to prepare a report of its findings. The report should be prepared in a reasonable time, at a reasonable cost and should be made available to any shareholder upon written request.

SUPPORTING STATEMENT

Our nation is now at a crossroads on health care. Because of cutbacks in public programs, jobs that offer no benefits and efforts by employers to shift health care costs to workers, 50 million Americans have health care coverage that is inadequate to meet their needs and another 37 million have no protection at all.

The United States spends $2 billion a day, or eleven percent of its gross national product, on health care. As insurance premiums increase 18 to 30 percent a year, basic health care has moved well beyond the reach of a growing number of working families. This increase also places heavy pressure on employer labor costs. There is no end in sight to this trend.

As a result and because of the significant social and public policy issues attendant to operations involving health care, we urge shareholders to SUPPORT the resolution. Holtzman Afft., Exhibit B (emphasis in original).

On January 16, 1992, J. Brett Tibbitts, deputy general counsel of Dole Food Company, Inc., wrote to the office of chief counsel of the Securities & Exchange Commission's ("SEC") division of corporation finance and stated Dole's position that Dole could exclude the NYCERS proposal from its proxy statement because the proposal concerned employee benefits, an assertedly "ordinary business operation," and both SEC regulations and the law of the Dole's state of incorporation relegate such ordinary business operations to management, not shareholder, control.

On February 10, 1992, John Brousseau, special counsel to the SEC's division of corporation finance, responded to Tibbitts' letter with the following written statement:

The proposal relates to the preparation of a report by a Committee of the Company's Board of Directors to evaluate various health-care proposals being considered by national policy makers.

There appears to be some basis for your view that the proposal may be excluded pursuant to rule 14a-8(c)(7) because the proposal is directed at involving the Company in the political or legislative process relating to an aspect of the Company's operations. Accordingly, we will not recommend enforcement action to the Commission if the proposal is omitted from the Company's proxy materials. In reaching a position, the staff has not found it necessary to address the alternative basis for omission on which the Company relies. Holtzman Afft., Exhibit D.

. . . On April 9, 1992, NYCERS brought the instant action. In conjunction with NYCERS' request for an order to show cause, NYCERS submitted an affidavit of Theodore R.

Marmor, a professor of political science and public policy at Yale University. In his affidavit, Professor Marmor averred, inter alia, that (1) at least 37 million Americans have no health insurance; (2) the United States spends more on health per capita than any other developed nation; (3) health care expenditures in 1989 represented 56 percent of pre-tax company profits in 1989, as compared to 8 percent in 1985; and (4) the national average cost for health care per employee is $3,200, and some large companies pay $5,000 or more per employee. Professor Marmor also defined and explained the three major categories of national health care proposals pending in Congress. . . .

II. Discussion

* * *

[F]or the reasons stated below, we find that NYCERS has met its burden of showing that it is substantially likely that Dole would fail to show on the merits that the proposal falls within one of the enumerated exceptions.

1. Rule 14a-8(c)(7): "Ordinary Business Operations"

* * *

The term "ordinary business operations" is neither self-explanatory nor easy to explain. The exception does not elaborate on whether "business operations" encompass merely certain routine internal functions or whether they can extend to cost-benefit analyses or profit-making activity. The SEC's commentary on the current version of the "ordinary business operations" exception states, "[W]here proposals involve business matters that are mundane in nature *and* do not involve any substantial policy or other considerations, the sub-paragraph may be relied upon to omit them." Adoption of Amendments Relating to Proposals by Security Holders, 41 Fed. Reg. 52,994, 52,998 (1976) (emphasis added).

This commentary indicates that even if the proposal touches on the way daily business matters are conducted, the statement may not be excluded if it involves a significant strategic decision as to those daily business matters, i.e., one that will significantly affect the manner in which a company does business. One Court has held that the purpose of the "ordinary business exception" is to prevent shareholders from seeking to "assert the power to dictate the minutiae of daily business decisions." *Grimes v. Centerior Energy Corp.*, 909 F.2d 529, 531 (D.C. Cir. 1990), *cert. denied*, 498 U.S. 1073, 111 S. Ct. 799, 112 L. Ed. 2d 860 (1991).

While we give due deference to the SEC staff opinion letter in this case and other similar cases, we find that NYCERS has shown under that the proposal does not relate to "ordinary business operations." If one aspect of "ordinary business operations" is certain, it is that the outcome of close cases such as the instant one are largely fact-dependent. Nevertheless, Dole has not provided the Court with any information on (1) whether Dole has a health insurance program; (2) if such a program exists at Dole, how it operates; and (3) the amount of corporate financial resources that Dole devotes to health insurance. Instead, Dole argues, "To the extent [the NYCER proposal] relates to Dole's business at all, it relates to its employee relations and health care benefits, a matter traditionally within the 'ordinary business' category." . . . In support of its position, Dole cites several SEC "No-Action" letters relating to proposals similar to the instant one. However, the SEC "No-Action" letters contain scarcely any analysis, and, while they are entitled to deference, they do not bind this

Court. We note that the SEC itself has changed its reasoning as to why proposals relating to national employee health insurance relate to "ordinary business relations." The SEC has shifted rationales for rejecting proposals such as this one, initially stressing the "employee relations" aspect of national health insurance and then emphasizing its "political [and] legislative" dimensions.

We further find that the principal cases relied upon by Dole are distinguishable from the instant case. *Austin v. Consolidated Edison Co. of New York*, 788 F. Supp. 192 (S.D.N.Y. 1992), involved an internal, relatively mundane plan to change the eligibility criteria of a company's specific retirement benefits policy, a subject of union collective bargaining. *Austin*, at 193. As Professor Marmor's affidavit demonstrates, however, the proposals in the instant case relate to a strategic policy choice as to the prospect of a major outlay to the federal treasury, as well as possible internal changes that may affect the entire scope of Dole's employee health insurance policy. The question of which plan, if any, that Dole should support, and how Dole would choose to function under the plans (*e.g.*, "pay or play") could have large financial consequences on Dole. The instant case is also distinguishable from *New York.City Employees' Retirement System v. Brunswick Corporation*, 789 F. Supp. 144 (S.D.N.Y. 1992).

In *Brunswick*, the NYCERS submitted a vague proposal that the company 1) study the national health plans in those countries in which the company had subsidiaries and 2) describe any aspect of these foreign health plans that should be included in the development of a national health insurance plan in the United States. Unlike the proposal in *Brunswick*, the proposal in the instant case does not seek to involve the corporation in making abstract political proposals but rather requests the corporation to study existing, concrete plans before Congress that affect the scope of Dole's health insurance operations.

The proposed report primarily relates to Dole's policy making on an issue of social significance that, while not relating to a specific health care policy at Dole, nevertheless relates to a distinct type of operations that Dole has undoubtedly grappled with in the past. Accordingly, we do not find that the instant proposal relates to "ordinary business operations."

2. Rule 14a-8(c)(5): "Insignificant Relationship" Exception

Rule 14a-8(c)(5) states that a corporation may exclude a shareholder proposal from a proxy statement "[i]f the proposal relates to operations which account for less than 5 percent of the registrant's total assets at the end of its most recent fiscal year, and for less than 5 percent of its net earnings and gross sales for its most recent fiscal year, *and* is not otherwise significantly related to the registrant's business." (emphasis supplied).

Dole does not dispute that the clear language of the NYCERS proposal in large part relates to national health insurance's impact on Dole. Without specific reference to Rule 14a-8(c)(5), Dole argues that the NYCERS proposal lacked a discrete nexus to Dole's distinct line of business, presumably the manufacture of food products. Dole's argument is essentially made under the exception referred to in the last phrase of Rule 14a-8(c)(5), *i.e.*, that the proposal is "not otherwise significantly related to the registrant's business."

. . . We need not address Dole's "nexus" argument because we find the activity addressed by the NYCERS proposal relates to activities that likely occupy outlays more than five percent of Dole's income. It is substantially likely that Dole's health insurance outlays constitute more than five percent of its income.[7] Dole has offered no information on the percentage of its income that it devotes to employee health insurance. In his affidavit, Professor Marmor stated that nationwide, 1989 health care expenditures represented 56 percent of pre-tax company profits. . . . We find it substantially likely that this figure applies to Dole to a greater or lesser extent. Because the subject of the proposed study likely relate to a significant aspect of Dole's business, we find that the proposal does not fall within the exception stated in Rule 14(a)-8(c)(5).

* * *

3. Rule 14(a)-8(c)(6): "Beyond Power to Effectuate" Exception

Rule 14(a)-8(c)(6) states that a corporation need not include a shareholder proposal on a proxy statement "[i]f the proposal deals with a matter beyond the registrant's power to effectuate . . . ."

Dole argues, "The NYCERS proposal requests the analysis of, and implicitly suggests that Dole should attempt to influence the selection of, national health care reform proposals." . . . However, Dole does not point to any language that suggests that a necessary consequence of the proposal is political lobbying. While couched in language that clearly supports a national solution to the problems of growing health insurance costs, the NYCERS proposal merely calls for the commission of a research report on national health insurance proposals and their impact on Dole's competitive standing. Moreover, we fail to see why such a study necessarily "deals with a matter beyond the registrant's power to effectuate." For example, a decision that Dole's interests mandate a choice to "pay" rather than "play" under two of the three major proposals would clearly be within Dole's power to effectuate if these proposals are enacted. Moreover, Dole might conceivably find that it is in its interests to draft such a proposal and lobby for its enactment. For the reasons stated above, we disagree with Dole's argument that the political aspect of this proposal means that it does not relate to Dole's business in a substantial way. . . .

Having found that the required showing has been met, this Court directs Dole to include in its proxy materials for its June 4, 1992 annual meeting NYCERS' shareholder proposal submitted to Dole by letter dated December 12, 1991.

---

[7]   However, even if we did address Dole's "nexus" argument, we note there is no authority that establishes that a proposal that does not relate to a corporation's distinct line of business automatically falls within the Rule 14a-8(c)(5) exception. The SEC commentary on the unacceptable nature of abstract political proposals, such as against anti-trust laws in general, see Securities Exchange Act Release No. 3638, (January 3, 1945), cited in *Medical Committee for Human Rights v. Securities & Exchange Commission*, 432 F.2d 659, 677 (D.C. Cir. 1970), *vacated as moot*, 404 U.S. 403, 92 S. Ct. 577, 30 L. Ed. 2d 560 (1972), does not address a proposal such as the instant one, which expressly seeks to study national health insurance's impact on Dole. The cases that discuss Rule 14a-8(c)(5) also do not reach this question, because the proposals in those cases directly involved the product manufactured by the corporation. *See Medical Committee*, 432 F.2d at 662 (proposal relating to chemical corporation's production of napalm used against human beings); *Lovenheim v. Iroquois Brands, Ltd.*, 618 F. Supp. 554, 561 (D.D.C. 1985) (proposal relating to pate de fois gras produced by force-feeding geese).

NOTES AND QUESTIONS

(1) **Recent interpretations of the "ordinary business operations" exclusion.** The courts and the SEC often have, as in *Dole*, liberally required inclusion of proposals that seem more relevant to non-shareholder than to shareholder interests, including affirmative action[72] and animal rights.[73] On the other hand, the courts sometimes have excluded proposals that have an obvious bearing on shareholder welfare, including capital spending limits.[74] Does it make sense to hold that capital spending proposals clearly relating to corporate financial welfare are excludable, while a proposal relating to general health care policy must be included? The SEC has been more tolerant of "shareholder welfare" proposals.[75]

(2) *Cracker Barrel.* In 1992, the SEC appeared to broaden its interpretation of the "ordinary business operations" exclusion by holding that Cracker Barrel Old Country Store, Inc. could omit a proposal requesting, among other things, the implementation of hiring policies relating to sexual orientation, despite the proposal's apparent social policy implications.[76] Rejecting the position it had taken in past no-action letters and, apparently, in its 1976 Release on the exclusion (*see* Note 7 following *Medical Committee*), the SEC stated that "the fact that a shareholder proposal concerning a company's employment policies and practices for the general workforce is tied to a social issue will no longer be viewed as removing the proposal from the realm of ordinary business operations of the registrant." The SEC returned to its pre-*Cracker Barrel* position when, in adopting its 1998 amendments to the shareholder proposal rule, it announced it would no longer permit the exclusion of employment-related proposals that raise significant social policy matters.

(3) **The 1998 amendments.** As originally proposed, the 1998 amendments would have curtailed use of the shareholder proposal rule by, among other things, (a) making it more difficult for shareholders to resubmit proposals by requiring shareholder support

---

[72] *See Amalgamated Clothing and Textile Workers Union v. Wal-Mart Stores, Inc.*, 821 F. Supp. 877 (S.D.N.Y. 1993) (proposal requiring the company to report on equal employment and affirmative action policies was not excludable).

[73] *See Lovenheim v. Iroquois Brands, Ltd.*, 618 F. Supp. 554 (D.D.C. 1985) (enjoining exclusion of a proposal seeking study of the practice of one of the issuer's divisions of force-feeding geese to make pate where the pate business generated a net loss of $3,121 on $78 million in sales for the last fiscal year, and involved less than .05% of the company's total assets).

[74] *See, e.g., Grimes v. Centerior Energy Corp.*, 909 F.2d 529 (D.C. Cir. 1990), *cert. denied*, 498 U.S. 1073 (1991) (earlier proposal to generally limit capital spending).

[75] *See, e.g., SEC Division of Corporate Finance: Staff Legal Bulletin 14A* (July 12, 2002) (public companies can no longer rely on the "ordinary business matters" exclusion to omit certain shareholder proposals related to equity compensation plans, because "public debate [regarding such plans] has become significant"). *But cf. National Semiconductor Corp.*, SEC No-Action Letter, 2002 WL 1611592 (July 19, 2002) (company may exclude proposal that directors establish a policy of expensing costs of all future stock options issued to company executives). The staff bulletin is available at http://www.sec.gov/interps/legal/cfslb14a.htm.

[76] *Cracker Barrel Old Country Store, Inc.*, SEC No-Action Letter, 1992 SEC No-Act. LEXIS 984, 1992 WL 289095 (Oct. 13, 1992).

of 5%, 15%, and 30% for proposals that have been submitted at one, two, and three meetings, respectively; (b) converting the "relevance" test of 14a-8(i)(5) into a purely economic test permiting exclusion of any proposal relating to less than (i) $10 million or less in gross revenue or total costs for the company's most recently completed fiscal year; or (ii) 3% of the company's gross revenue or total assets (whichever is higher) for its most recently completed fiscal year, if that results in a number lower than $10 million; and (c) introducing an "override" mechanism permitting 3% of the share ownership to override a company's decision to exclude a proposal under 14a-8(i)(5) or 14a-8(i)(7).[77] The final rules, adopted in May 1998, recast the shareholder proposal rule in question and answer format, but rejected the proposed substantive amendments.[78]

[D] An Appraisal and Critique of Shareholder Proposals

Medical Committee and Rule 14a-8 have encouraged hundreds of shareholder proposals a year. Deciding whether to include these proposals in proxy statements engages the time of corporate executives and counsel and SEC staff, and these added proposals increase postage and printing costs. Nevertheless, only a few of these proposals are ever supported by more than a small percentage of the shareholders' votes. Is the time and money spent on these proposals justified?

Corporate management has reacted vigorously against shareholder proposals. Consider the following, from a December 11, 1981, speech by SEC Commissioner Longstreth to the National Association of Manufacturers:[79]

> Something peculiar to this process touches a corporate nerve. Perhaps the answer lies in the perspective which the typical corporate executive brings to the situation. From the corporate viewpoint, the overriding truth is that, without management support, shareholder proposals practically never attract a majority vote, yet they still demand the time and personal attention of corporate officials and attorneys. This distaste is sharpened by the fact that traditional management prerogatives are often challenged and social concerns promoted through the process. Management tends to be portrayed in an unfavorable light—an acutely distressing result when one remembers that management is people, with egos, sensitivity and human concerns.
>
> To this injury add the insult that a company is forced, at its own expense, to dignify proposals by including them in its proxy materials. Management knows that the proxy statement places these proposals squarely on the desks

---

[77]   *See* Securities Exchange Act Release No. 34-39093 (Sept. 19, 1997).

[78]   *See* Securities Exchange Act Release No. 34-40018 (May 19, 1998).

[79]   Fed. Sec. L. Rep. (CCH) (1981-82 Transfer Binder) ¶ 83,067, pages 84, 704-705. Reproduced with permission from FEDERAL SECURITIES LAW REPORTER, published and copyrighted by Commerce Clearing House, Inc., 4025 W. Peterson Ave., Chicago, Ill. 60646.

of the top management of corporate fiduciaries holding stock in the company, and attracts their careful attention. It could not be otherwise, since proxy voting, as one of the bundle of rights accorded to stockholders, must be carried on by fiduciaries with due care.

Add the rare, but popularized instances where shareholders have clearly abused the process to attempt to harass or blackmail a company, and the feelings of management become more comprehensible.

Academic commentators (*see* **Dent**, **Easterbrook & Fischel**, and **Manne**) have criticized the shareholder proposal rule on the ground that it forces the vast majority of shareholders to subsidize publicity for groups purporting to represent the public interest—even those whose goals are contrary to the profit-maximization aims of most shareholders. This forced speech may even raise questions about the constitutionality of the shareholder proposal under the First Amendment.[80] **Romano** concludes that restricting shareholder proposals that fail to receive substantial support would save hundreds of millions of dollars.

Despite these criticisms of the shareholder proposal rule, shareholder proposals arguably do have some role in the public corporation. First, they provide managers with information relevant both to the corporation's social responsibilities and to long-run profit maximization. For example, the shareholder proposals of "Campaign GM" attracted less than 3% of the shareholder vote but resulted in the adoption of some of the aims of the proponents. Second, the vote on economically oriented proposals such as those suggesting liquidation of the corporation or opposing anti-takeover measures can signal shareholder discontent to potential bidders for control, and therefore are a useful adjunct to the market for control.[81]

Even if issuer-financed shareholder proposals are desirable in some situations, there is an additional question whether they should be *required*. Not only is the shareholder proposal rule mandatory in terms, but the *Transamerica* case (Note 5 following the *Medical Committee* excerpt), appears to limit corporations' power under state law to avoid the effect of the Rule by adopting certificate or bylaw provisions that define proper subjects for shareholder action. Should shareholders be able to decide, by certificate provision or otherwise, whether and under what circumstances shareholder proposals will be permitted? Waivers of the Rule may be reflected in stock price, and therefore are subject to market constraints. Moreover, **Palmiter** notes that the SEC's sudden policy shifts on shareholder proposals over the years indicate that an outside administrative agency is unlikely to do a better job than the shareholders themselves in determining the content of shareholder speech.

---

[80]   *See* Butler & Ribstein, *Corporate Governance Speech and the First Amendment*, 43 Kans. L. Rev. 163, 184-86 (1994).

[81]   For evidence suggesting that voting on shareholder proposals is informed and varies based on ownership structure and nature of proposal, see Gordon & Pound, *Information, Ownership Structure, and Shareholder Voting: Evidence from Shareholder-Sponsored Corporate Governance Proposals*, 48 J. Fin. 697 (1993).

On the other hand, the real concern about shareholder waiver may be that the shareholder proposal rule protects *non-shareholders*. But if shareholder proposals, while socially desirable, are not a net economic benefit for shareholders, should shareholders be forced to pay for them?

In 1982, prior to ultimately retaining the current approach to shareholder proposals, the SEC suggested permitting issuers to adopt their own procedures by shareholder vote subject to periodic reapproval.[82] Commentary on the proposal opposed this alternative. Perhaps a mandatory shareholder proposal rule is in the interest of the SEC because it increases the work, and therefore the staff requirements, of the Commission (*see* **Dent** at 31). Although corporate managers would seem to be a powerful opposition force, they did not mobilize for an optional rule. What might explain this?

PROBLEMS

Assume your corporate client has received each of the following proposals. In light of the above materials, how would you advise the company with respect to its duty to include the proposal in its proxy statement?

(1) A recommendation to the board of directors that it commit more than 5% of corporate assets and earnings to ending the fighting in Israel. Assume the company has no business connections with Israel.

(2) A recommendation to the board that it increase production of a certain detergent made by the company which has caught on with consumers but is not available in many stores.

(3) A recommendation proposed by an animal rights group that a drug corporation change its procedures for experimenting on animals in developing drugs.[83]

(4) A recommendation to the board that it increase by 5% the company's contributions to charity.

(5) A recommendation to the board that it increase the safety of the company's automobiles by relocating the gas tank.

(6) A recommendation that the board nominate for election to the board of directors a certain prominent member of the community in which the company's main factory is located in order to bring the community's viewpoint onto the board of directors.

REFERENCES

Black & Sparks, *SEC Rule 14a-8: Some Changes in the Way the SEC Staff Interprets the Rule*, 11 U. TOL. L. REV. 957 (1980).

---

[82]   *See* Exchange Act Rel. 19135, Fed. Sec. L. Rep.(CCH) ¶ 83,262 (1982 Trans. Binder).

[83]   For cases dealing with animal rights proposals see *New England Anti-Vivisection Society, Inc. v. United States Surgical Corp.*, 889 F.2d 1198 (1st Cir. 1989); *Lovenheim v. Iroquois Brands, Inc.*, 618 F. Supp. 554 (D.D.C. 1985); Note, *Challenging Objectionable Animal Treatment With the Shareholder Proxy Proposal Rule*, 1988 U. ILL. L. REV. 119.

Dent, *SEC Rule 14a-8: A Study in Regulatory Failure*, 30 N.Y.L. Sch. L. Rev. 1 (1985).

Easterbrook & Fischel, *Voting in Corporate Law*, 26 J.L. & Econ. 395 (1983).

Manne, *Shareholder Social Proposals Viewed by an Opponent*, 24 Stan. L. Rev. 481 (1972).

Palmiter, *The Shareholder Proposal Rule: A Failed Experiment in Merit Regulation*, 45 Ala. L. Rev. 879 (1994).

Romano, *Less Is More: Making Shareholder Activism a Valuable Mechanism of Corporate Governance*, 18 Yale J. Reg. 174 (2001).

Ryan, *Rule 14a-8, Institutional Shareholder Proposals and Corporate Democracy*, 23 Ga. L. Rev. 97 (1988).

Schwartz, *The Public-Interest Proxy Contest: Reflections on Campaign GM*, 69 Mich L. Rev. 419 (1971).

Thomas & Martin, *Should Labor Be Allowed to Make Shareholder Proposals?*, 73 Wash. L. Rev. 41 (1998).

Thomas & Martin, *The Effect of Shareholder Proposals on Executive Compensation*, 67 U. Cin. L. Rev. 1021 (1999).

§ 7.05   Inspection of Shareholder Lists

To help shareholders monitor managers and communicate with their fellow shareholders, both the common law and statutes have provided shareholders rights to inspect corporate books and records and lists of shareholders. It is important at the outset to distinguish three types of inspection rights. First, shareholders have the right to inspect books and records. This inspection can be quite burdensome to the company and accordingly has been the most restricted of shareholders' inspection rights.[84] Second, shareholders have the right to inspect lists of shareholders prepared by managers in anticipation of particular shareholders' meetings. *See* Del. G.C.L. § 219 (inspection right only for the ten days preceding the meeting); MBCA § 7.20 (permitting inspection of the list beginning two business days after notice of the meeting is given). Third, shareholders have the right to inspect shareholder lists other than those prepared for particular meetings. *See* Del. G.C.L. § 220; MBCA §§ 16.01(c), 16.02.

[A] Statutory and Common Law Rights

If the statute provides for a qualified right of inspection and the shareholder fails to qualify, the courts typically have enforced a common law right to inspect so long as the inspection is for a "proper purpose."[85] (See subsection [C], below, for a discussion

---

[84]   *See Goldman v. Trans-United Industries, Inc.*, 404 Pa. 288, 171 A.2d 788 (1961).

[85]   *See Rockwell v. SCM Corp.*, 496 F. Supp. 1123 (S.D.N.Y. 1980); *Crane Co. v. Anaconda Co.*, 39 N.Y.2d 14, 382 N.Y.S.2d 707, 346 N.E.2d 507 (1976) (both holding that the common law right of inspection survived N.Y. Bus. Corp. Law § 624, permitting inspection by 5% or 6-month shareholders). *But see Caspary v. The Louisiana Land and Exploration Company*, 707 F.2d 785 (4th Cir. 1983).

of the meaning of "proper purpose.") Non-statutory inspection rights are explicitly preserved by MBCA § 16.02(e)(2).

[B] Who May Inspect?

The common law right of inspection extends generally to shareholders. Many statutes commonly limit the right to shareholders *of record*, thus excluding beneficial owners. *See* Del. G.C.L. § 220. Compare MBCA § 7.20, granting rights to any "shareholder," defined in § 1.40(22) to include a "beneficial owner of shares to the extent of the rights granted by a nominee certificate on file with a corporation"; with § 16.02(f), which extends general inspection rights to beneficial owners. Some statutes are further limited to shareholders who own a certain amount of stock (often 5%) or who have owned stock for a given length of time (often six months).

[C] Proper Purpose

Both statutory and common law rights of inspection are commonly hedged with the requirement that they be for a "proper purpose." Note that Del. G.C.L. § 219 permits inspection of the list prepared for particular shareholders' meetings "for any purpose germane to the meeting." MBCA § 7.20 has no "purpose" requirement for inspection of the list prepared for the meeting, but MBCA § 16.02(c) has a "proper purpose" requirement for inspection of other records, and for *copying* the list prepared for the meeting.

Purposes that have been held sufficient to justify an inspection of a corporation's books and records include the desire of a minority shareholder in a closely held corporation to value its shares and the desire of a shareholder to investigate possible waste and mismanagement if the shareholder can "present some credible basis from which the court can infer that waste or mismanagement may have occurred."[86] *Security First Corp. v. U.S. Die Casting and Development Co.*[87] held that "the plaintiff must show the credible basis [from which a court may infer managerial misconduct] by a preponderance of the evidence," though "actual wrongdoing itself need not be proved."[88] The court further noted that, if a proper purpose is established, the "plaintiff bears the burden of proving that each category of books and records is essential to the accomplishment of the stockholder's articulated purpose for the inspection."[89] *Saito v. McKesson HBOC, Inc.*[90] permits the inspection of company records dated before the shareholder

---

[86] *Thomas & Betts Corp. v. Leviton Mfg. Co.*, 681 A.2d 1026, 1031 (Del. 1996); *see also Everett v. Hollywood Park, Inc.*, 1996 Del. Ch. LEXIS 2, 1996 WL 32171 (Del. Ch. 1996); *Towle v. Robinson Springs Corp*, 719 A.2d 880 (Vt. 1998).

[87] 687 A.2d 563 (Del. 1997).

[88] *Id*. at 567. The Kansas Supreme Court adopted the same standard in *Arctic Financial Corp. v. OTR Express, Inc.*, 38 P.3d 701 (Kan. 2002).

[89] *Security First Corp.*, 687 A.2d at 569.

[90] 806 A.2d 113 (Del. 2002).

bought his stock, even though standing rules prevent the shareholder from suing for events that took place at that time (see the discussion of the "contemporaneous shareholder requirement" in Section 10.03[B][1], below).

A purpose unrelated to the corporation is not "proper."[91] But if the shareholder is seeking the list for a purpose related to corporate governance, such as to solicit proxies from the shareholders in connection with a director election, the shareholder cannot be denied the list simply because she may also be seeking personal gain[92] or might be involved in some wrongdoing.[93] Also, a shareholder who otherwise has a proper purpose is entitled to the list even if the shareholder plans to turn the list over to a hostile bidder who may not have a direct right to the list.[94]

The following cases revisit the corporate social responsibility debate discussed above in this Chapter by examining the issue of whether "proper purpose" can be interpreted to exclude requests that are governance-related but are connected with the requester's "social" agenda.

STATE ex rel. PILLSBURY v. HONEYWELL, INC.
Minnesota Supreme Court
291 Minn. 322, 191 N.W.2d 406 (1971)

[Petitioner Pillsbury, who opposed the war in Viet Nam, learned that Honeywell, Inc. was producing anti-personnel fragmentation bombs for use in that war. Pillsbury requested production by the corporation of shareholder lists and corporate records dealing with munitions manufacture. When this request was denied, Pillsbury petitioned for a writ of mandamus which was denied by the trial court under Delaware law, the law of the state of incorporation. The Minnesota Supreme Court affirmed. The following is a brief excerpt from that court's opinion.]

---

[91]   See Shabshelowitz v. Fall River Gas Co., 588 N.E.2d 630 (Mass. App. 1991) (improper purpose if list used solely to identify people who might sell petitioner more stock); Bergmann v. Lee Data Corp., 467 N.W.2d 636 (Minn. App. 1991) (corporate records denied to former employee whose real, although not stated, purpose was related to his wrongful termination litigation); Advance Concrete Form, Inc. v. Accuform, Inc., 462 N.W.2d 271 (Wis. App. 1990) (records denied to competitor because of ulterior purpose). For examples of other decisions finding that the petitioner lacked a proper purpose for inspection, see Golden Cycle LLC v. Global Motorsport Group Inc., Civ. Action No. 16292 (Del. Ch., June 18, 1998) (improper purpose where shareholder sought access to evaluate corporation for potential acquisition); Leviton Mfg. Co., Inc. v. Blumberg, 660 N.Y.S.2d 726 (N.Y. App. Div. 1997) (improper purpose where petitioner sought access to books and records to facilitate third party's takeover of corporation); Berkowitz v. Legal Sea Foods Inc., 1997 Del. Ch. LEXIS 35, 1997 WL 153815 (Del. Ch. 1997) (improper purpose where petitioner sought to obtain discovery denied in a Massachusetts lawsuit commenced by the shareholder against the corporation); Retail Property Investors Inc. v. Skeens, 471 S.E.2d 181 (Va. 1996) (improper purpose where petitioner sought shareholder list for the purpose of determining whether other shareholders would join in a lawsuit against the corporation).

[92]   See Alex Brown & Sons v. Latrobe Steel Co., 376 F. Supp. 1373 (W.D. Pa. 1974); E.L. Bruce Co. v. State ex rel. Gilbert, 51 Del. 252, 144 A.2d 533 (1958).

[93]   See General Time Corp. v. Talley Industries, Inc., 43 Del. Ch. 531, 240 A.2d 755 (1968).

[94]   See Sadler v. NCR Corp., 928 F.2d 48 (2d Cir. 1991); Davey v. Unitil Corp., 585 A.2d 858 (N.H. 1991).

KELLY, Justice:

* * *

Petitioner's standing as a shareholder is quite tenuous. He only owns one share in his own name, bought for the purposes of this suit. He had previously ordered his agent to buy 100 shares, but there is no showing of investment intent. While his agent had a cash balance in the $400,000 portfolio, petitioner made no attempt to determine whether Honeywell was a good investment or whether more profitable shares would have to be sold to finance the Honeywell purchase. Furthermore, petitioner's agent had the power to sell the Honeywell shares without his consent. Petitioner also had a contingent beneficial interest in 242 shares. Courts are split on the question of whether an equitable interest entitles one to inspection. *See* 5 Fletcher, PRIVATE CORPORATIONS, § 2230 at 862 (Perm. ed. rev. vol. 1967). Indicative of petitioner's concern regarding his equitable holdings is the fact that he was unaware of them until he had decided to bring this suit.

* * *

But for his opposition to Honeywell's policy, petitioner probably would not have bought Honeywell stock, would not be interested in Honeywell's profits and would not desire to communicate with Honeywell's shareholders. His avowed purpose in buying Honeywell stock was to place himself in a position to try to impress his opinions favoring a reordering of priorities upon Honeywell management and its other shareholders. Such a motivation can hardly be deemed a proper purpose germane to his economic interest as a shareholder.[5]

* * *

We do not mean to imply that a shareholder with a bona fide investment interest could not bring this suit if motivated by concern with the long-or short-term economic effects on Honeywell resulting from the production of war munitions. Similarly, this suit might be appropriate when a shareholder has a bona fide concern about the adverse effects of abstention from profitable war contracts on his investment in Honeywell.

In the instant case, however, the trial court, in effect, has found from all the facts that petitioner was not interested in even the long-term well-being of Honeywell or the enhancement of the value of his shares. His sole purpose was to persuade the company to adopt his social and political concerns, irrespective of any economic benefit to himself or Honeywell.

---

[5]   We do not question petitioner's good faith incident to his political and social philosophy; nor did the trial court. In a well-prepared memorandum, the lower court stated: By enumerating the foregoing this Court does not mean to belittle or to be derisive of Petitioner's motivations and intentions because this Court cannot but draw the conclusion that the Petitioner is sincere in his political and social philosophy, but this Court does not feel that this is a proper forum for the advancement of these political-social views by way of direct contact with the stockholders of Honeywell Company or any other company. If the courts were to grant these rights on the basis of the foregoing, anyone who has a political-social philosophy which differs with that of a company in which he becomes a shareholder can secure a writ and any company can be faced with a rash and multitude of these types of actions which are not bona fide efforts to engage in a proxy fight for the purpose of taking over the company or electing directors, which the courts have recognized as being perfectly legitimate and acceptable.

This purpose on the part of one buying into the corporation does not entitle the petitioner to inspect Honeywell's books and records.[7]

Petitioner argues that he wishes to inspect the stockholder ledger in order that he may correspond with other shareholders with the hope of electing to the board one or more directors who represent his particular viewpoint. On p. 30 of his brief he states that this purpose alone compels inspection:

> . . . [T]his Court has said that a stockholder's motives or "good faith" are not a test of his right of inspection, except as "bad faith" actually manifests some recognized "improper purpose"—such as vexation of the corporation, or purely destructive plans, or *nothing specific*, just pure idle curiosity, or necessarily illegal ends, or nothing germane to his interests. *State ex rel. G.M. Gustafson Co. v. Crookston Trust Co.* [222 Minn. 17, 22 N.W.2d 911 (1946)]. . . . (Italics supplied.)

While a plan to elect one or more directors is specific and the election of directors normally would be a proper purpose, here the purpose was not germane to petitioner's or Honeywell's economic interest. Instead, the plan was designed to further petitioner's political and social beliefs. Since the requisite propriety of purpose germane to his or Honeywell's economic interest is not present, the allegation that petitioner seeks to elect a new board of directors is insufficient to compel inspection.

* * *

The order of the trial court denying the writ of mandamus is affirmed.

---

[7]   Petitioner cites *Medical Committee for Human Rights v. SEC,* 139 App. D.C. 226, 432 F.2d 659 (1970), for the proposition that economic benefit and community service may, in the motives of a shareholder, blend together. We have ruled that petitioner does not meet this test because he has no investment motivation for his inspection demands. The *Medical Committee* case did not reach the merits, the court ruling only that S.E.C. actions concerning the inclusion of proxy statements are reviewable. It is interesting to note, however, that the Dow Chemical Company's manufacture of napalm on grounds that management had "decided to pursue a course of activity which generated little profit . . . and actively impaired the company's public relations and recruitment activities because *management considered the action morally and politically desirable."* 139 App. D.C. 249, 432 F.2d 681 (Italics supplied.) The court, in dictum, expressed its disapproval of Dow's claim that it could use its power to impose management's personal politics and moral prejudices. It would be even more anomalous if an outsider with no economic concern for the corporation could attempt to adapt Honeywell's policies to his own social convictions.

FOOD AND ALLIED SERVICE TRADES DEPARTMENT v. WAL-MART STORES, INC.
Delaware Court of Chancery
18 DEL. J. CORP. L. 651 (1992)

ALLEN, Chancellor.

This is an action under Section 220 of the Delaware General Corporation law for an order compelling defendant to permit plaintiff to inspect defendant's stockholder list and related materials. Plaintiff "Food and Allied Service Trades Department, AFL-CIO" ("FAST") is an unincorporated labor organization. It was established as a department of the AFL-CIO by that organization's sixteen, affiliated labor unions for the purpose of addressing the affiliates' common concerns by means of research, public relations and, apparently, litigation. Significantly, it also is the owner of 23 shares of the defendant's common stock.

Defendant Wal-Mart Stores, Inc. ("Wal-Mart"), a Delaware corporation, is the largest retailer in the United States.

On April 24 of this year, FAST delivered to Wal-Mart a written demand under oath for a list of the corporation's shareholders and other related documents customarily demanded in connection with such inspection requests.

That demand stated the purpose of the inspection request to be: to permit the undersigned to communicate with other stockholders of the Company on matters relating to their interest as stockholders, including communicating with such stockholders regarding a solicitation of proxies to be conducted by the undersigned in connection with the Company's 1992 Annual Meeting of Shareholders, scheduled for June 5, 1992, in support of an independent shareholders' resolution recommending that the Board of Directors establish a Special Committee to study and report to the Board of Directors and to the shareholders on the Company's buying policies and practices in China, with special attention to ensuring that no products purchased directly and/or indirectly from sources in China are produced wholly or in part by forced labor. The purpose of this demand for a stocklist is also to permit the undersigned to furnish the Company's stockholders with copies of proxy materials relating to that resolution and to solicit proxies from those stockholders.

* * *

Wal-Mart . . . contend[s] that the stated purpose is not "proper" as required by Section 220 because it is not "reasonably related to [FAST's] interest as a stockholder," 8 Del. C. § 220, as required by that section. . . .

* * *

Following Wal-Mart's refusal to comply with FAST's demand, FAST filed this suit on May 5, 1992. On May 18, a trial was held at which the court heard the direct and cross-examination testimony of plaintiff's witness, FAST's president, Robert F. Harbrant, and received documentary evidence from both parties.

Mr. Harbrant described the events leading up to FAST's proposal of its resolution in the following manner. Sometime during 1991, particularly following the massacre in Tianamen Square and the related government arrests of students and workers, FAST grew concerned about the abuse of civil rights by the government of the People's Republic of China. FAST then heard that the Chinese government was using forced prison labor in the manufacture of goods for export. Mr. Harbrant testified that the sale of goods produced by forced labor is not only morally repugnant, but a violation of United States law. He added that FAST, as a labor organization, sympathizes with workers throughout the world and thus has an interest in eliminating the worldwide.purchase of goods produced by forced labor. Accordingly, FAST began to investigate the use of forced labor in China.

A FAST board member, Jeffrey Fiedler, travelled to China once during 1991 as part of a Congressional fact finding mission and has travelled there twice subsequently in search of more information about the production of goods by forced labor. In his capacity as a FAST board member, Fiedler testified on the subject of Chinese forced labor before various Congressional committees in September, October and November of 1991.

In late 1991, FAST helped organize a boycott of toys made in China and allegedly sold in the United States by "Toys R Us" and defendant Wal-Mart.

Also in 1991, FAST took issue with announcements by Wal-Mart, as part of its "Buy American" campaign, suggesting that its products were made in America.

According to Harbrant, FAST did not believe Wal-Mart in fact acted consistently with its own public statements. FAST thus circulated to consumers leaflets explaining how to determine where a product is made from the "RN" number displayed on its label.

Finally, Harbrant testified that the impetus for the resolution now proposed by FAST came during Wal-Mart's 1991 shareholders' meeting where, in response to a question from a FAST representative, Wal-Mart's president, now chief executive officer, appeared to be too little concerned, in FAST's opinion, with the possibility that Wal-Mart was importing and selling in the United States a significant number of products that were produced by captive laborers in China. According to Harbrant, Wal-Mart had and still has no system in place for determining which, if any, of the Chinese products it sells are produced by forced labor. FAST believes that its proposed resolution calling, as it does, for a report to the shareholders by a special board committee, will rectify this situation.

* * *

The principal argument of defendant is factual. It is that the proxy solicitation purpose is a pretext to get the shareholder list for an inappropriate purpose (organizing [Wal-Mart, which is not unionized]) and that, in all events, the purpose is to injure Wal-Mart, to the advantage of competitors who employ union workers.

Defendant has not met its burden of proof on this assertion. The willingness of the plaintiff to agree . . . [that it be ordered not to use the list for any purpose other than soliciting proxies for the present resolution and to return the list following the meeting] and the limitation of the names to be disclosed makes defendant's first supposition unlikely. But, even if those proposals had not been made, too little has been shown to justify that inference. The second explanation advanced is equally unsupported in the record. On cross-examination, Mr. Harbrant's testimony did not establish that FAST's largest union sponsor, the United Food and Commercial Workers International Union ("UFCW"), would have a motive to harm Wal-Mart. It did establish that the UFCW and FAST have been urging consumers to "buy American" and have been teaching them, as Harbrant also noted on direct, how to identify foreign made goods. Finally, Harbrant's testimony established that some of the efforts of FAST and the UFCW in this regard have been targeted at Wal-Mart. However, in my opinion, Wal-Mart has not met its burden of proof in establishing that FAST is seeking to harm Wal-Mart.

The more plausible explanation is the one that FAST offers: that it is motivated by a desire to try to combat the importation of goods made with forced labor both as a matter of international labor solidarity and as a self-interested effort to keep low-price foreign goods out of competitive American markets. Thus, I accept as truthful Mr. Harbrant's testimony that FAST's principal purpose in seeking the stockholder list is to facilitate its solicitation of proxies from Wal-Mart stockholders so that it more easily can get its proposed resolution adopted at the June 5 stockholders' meeting or, if unsuccessful then, at some later date. As the owner of just 23 shares which it purchased for about $300, FAST cannot persuasively argue that its effort to see the resolution adopted is pursued in order to benefit its interest as a stockholder.

* * *

This leaves the question whether Section 220 permits a stockholder to inspect a corporation's stockholder list if that stockholder's purpose in seeking such inspection is to solicit proxies in support of a resolution that it has proposed solely for moral and political reasons.

While as a matter of public policy interesting arguments could be made on either side of this question, such an exercise, by this court, is no longer useful. The question is not an open one. It once was held that shareholders have no right to inspect their corporation's stockholder list unless their ultimate aim is the enhancement of the economic value of the corporation. *See Pillsbury v. Honeywell, Inc.*, Minn. Supr., 191 N.W.2d 406 (1971) (applying Delaware law). However, this result was disapproved by the Delaware Supreme Court. In *Credit Bureau Reports, Inc. v. Credit Bureau of St. Paul, Inc.*, Del. Supr., 290 A.2d 691 (1972), the Supreme Court of Delaware affirmed this court's order requiring the defendant corporation to permit inspection of its stockholder list by a stockholder whose purpose in seeking the list was to solicit proxies with the ultimate aim of inducing the corporation to deal more generously with its suppliers of which the stockholder was one.

I believe *Credit Bureau Reports* is controlling here. There, as here, the plaintiff sought the stockholder list for the immediate purpose of soliciting proxies to be voted at an annual meeting. And there, as here, plaintiff's ultimate aim was not to enhance the value of the corporation's shares. In fact, in that case, the plaintiff's ultimate aim was even further removed from enhancement of share value than is FAST's aim which on some attenuated basis might arguably be said to foster corporate profit. Rather than seeking to benefit itself and certain nonshareholders at the expense of the corporation, FAST seeks to ensure that the corporation complies with its legal obligations in the interest of forced laborers in China. This purpose, while principally directed towards other interests, is consistent with management's conception of the corporation's long-term interest. I therefore conclude that FAST's purpose in seeking inspection is no less proper than was that of the plaintiff in the Credit Bureau case.

* * *

NOTES AND QUESTIONS

(1) **Who is Pillsbury?** Charlie Pillsbury was a Green Party candidate for Congress from Connecticut in 2002. According to his website (http://pillsbury.ctgreens.org/faq.htmland) he was Garry Trudeau's roommate at Yale from 1968-1970 and a model for Doonesbury. His great-grandfather founded the Pillsbury Company in 1869.

(2) **Moral or political purposes.** For another case which involved the question of whether shareholders could obtain shareholder lists in order to raise moral or political issues in a board election, see *Conservative Caucus v. Chevron Corp.*,[95] in which a shareholder who owned thirty shares in a major public corporation wanted a shareholder list in order to communicate with fellow shareholders in support of another shareholder's petition calling for termination of the corporation's business in Angola unless that country abandoned Communism. The court said the purpose was proper and distinguished *Pillsbury* by noting that plaintiff sought to call attention to the economic risks of dealing with this regime. Consider, in this light, footnote 7 to the *Pillsbury* court's opinion and its distinction of *Medical Committee.*

(3) **Economic purposes.** Should the shareholder have to find an economic "hook" for her request? If not, why should requests for shareholder lists be treated differently from shareholder proposals?

[D] Certificate Restrictions

It has been held that, due to the fundamental nature of the right, the certificate of incorporation may not deny shareholders a right of inspection.[96] This is made explicit by MBCA § 16.02(d). Why shouldn't the shareholders be able to agree to limit the inspection right?

§ 7.06 Cumulative Voting

Cumulative voting ensures that a minority holder can elect one or more directors (*see* Section 5.01, above). In contrast, under straight voting, the holder of a majority of the votes, whether a majority shareholder or the proxy-voting managers of a corporation with diffuse shareholdings, can elect all directors by casting its votes in favor of each director being nominated.

Cumulative voting has mixed implications for publicly held corporations. On the one hand, cumulative voting may enhance shareholder monitoring of publicly held firms, thus helping shareholders overcome the problems of public ownership identified by Berle and Means. Large dissident shareholders can gain board representation through

---

[95]   525 A.2d 569 (Del. Ch. 1987).

[96]   *See State ex rel. Cochran v. Penn-Beaver Oil Co.,* 34 Del. 81, 143 A. 247 (1926).

cumulative voting by concentrating their minority of votes on one or two director slots. They will then be in a position to urge a wealth-increasing sale of the company or other corporate changes. Cumulative voting may also facilitate participation in governance by institutional investors (*see* **Gordon**). On the other hand, cumulatively elected directors can be counterproductive in a publicly held firm. Since a minority of directors cannot actually take action, the cumulatively voted directors can only introduce time-wasting dissension into the board's deliberative processes. In addition, cumulative voting can make full-fledged corporate control contests more difficult by preventing a bidder who has acquired a majority of the stock from taking complete control of the board.

Because the costs and benefits of cumulative voting vary among publicly held corporations, individual firms arguably should be able to decide whether to adopt cumulative voting. This is the rule in most states. However, some states adhere to a regulatory view of cumulative voting and require cumulative voting by constitutional or statutory provision. The rationale for such provisions is that cumulative voting is an important aspect of shareholder governance and that management, if left to its own devices, would block adoption of cumulative voting. In contrast, a contractarian approach to corporate governance would rely on the capital markets to bid down the stock price of companies that unwisely reject cumulative voting.

Even in states where cumulative voting is "mandatory," firms have some ability to opt out. First, they can reincorporate in jurisdictions that do not require cumulative voting. Second, they can adopt other corporate governance devices, including "staggered" boards (*i.e.*, election of only a fraction of the board at each annual meeting), that reduce the effectiveness of cumulative voting.

To understand how staggered boards affect cumulative voting, it is helpful to apply the formula discussed above in Section 5.01[C][3]: $X = (Y \times N')/(N + 1) + 1$, where X = number of shares needed to elect a given number of directors; Y = number of shares voted at the meeting; N' = number of directors a shareholder wishes to elect; and N = number of directors elected. If there are a million shares voted at the meeting, nine directors to be voted on, and a minority shareholder seeks to elect one director, the shareholder will need 100,001 votes. On the other hand, if only three of the nine directors were to be voted on at a given meeting, X would increase to 250,001.

Because of their impact on cumulative voting, courts sometimes have invalidated staggered board provisions. For example, in *Wolfson v. Avery*,[97] the court invalidated a staggered board provision on the ground that it conflicted with mandatory cumulative voting by lessening its effect. The adoption of a staggered board was also enjoined in *CAPUR v. Engels*.[98] There, the directors, knowing that a minority shareholder was planning to attempt to place a "public interest" director on the board, amended the bylaws approximately three months prior to the annual meeting to reduce the size of the board from 14 to 12 and to stagger the remaining directors into three terms. The directors then

---

[97] 6 Ill. 2d 78, 126 N.E.2d 701 (1955).

[98] 364 F. Supp. 1202 (D. Minn. 1973).

failed to disclose the changes until about four weeks prior to the meeting. As a result of these actions, plaintiff discovered late in its proxy compaign that it would need more votes than it previously thought.[99] The majority of courts, however, have upheld staggered boards despite their effect on cumulative voting—a sort of implicit adoption of a contractarian approach.[100]

REFERENCES

Bhagat & Brickley, *Cumulative Voting: The Value of Minority Shareholder Voting Rights*, 27 J.L. & Econ. 339 (1984).

Gordon, *Institutions as Relational Investors: A New Look at Cumulative Voting*, 94 Colum. L. Rev. 124 (1994).

QUESTION

An argument for "mandatory" rules. As noted above, corporations can choose their state of incorporation, and therefore choose to be bound by "mandatory" cumulative voting. They might adopt cumulative voting in order to ensure spots on boards for useful shareholder "monitors." They might want *mandatory* cumulative voting to ensure that managers cannot remove or thwart cumulative voting. Firms' share prices arguably reflect this choice of corporate rule. Under the "race to the top" theory of state corporate law (*see* Section 7.02[B]), this effectively disciplines firms that choose to adopt mandatory cumulative voting for the "wrong" reasons, such as to insulate inefficient managers from takeovers. In light of these facts, are mandatory cumulative voting rules efficient?

§ 7.07 Internal Management of the Public Corporation

The preceding sections have considered how to ensure that managers act consistently with shareholder and social interests through devices designed to increase shareholder participation in corporate governance. This section considers alternative methods of ensuring that shareholder and social interests are respected by managers, such as internal monitoring devices (subsection [A]), the "monitoring board" (subsection [B]), and boards that include representatives of constituencies other than shareholders (subsection [C]).

---

[99] For another case concerning the effect of bylaw changes on cumulative voting, see *Whetstone v. Hossfeld Manufacturing Co.*, 457 N.W.2d 380 (Minn. 1990).

[100] *See Bohannan v. Corporation Commission*, 82 Ariz. 299, 313 P.2d 379 (1957); *Humphreys v. Winous Co.*, 165 Ohio St. 45, 133 N.E.2d 780 (1956); *Janney v. Philadelphia Transportation Co.*, 387 Pa. 282, 128 A.2d 76 (1956).

[A] Devices for Monitoring Management

As discussed in Section 7.02, because a widely dispersed shareholder body is unable effectively to control a tightly knit management group which has access to the corporation's proxy solicitation machinery, there is a danger that management will run the corporation in its own interests rather than those of the shareholders. Increasing the shareholders' power through proxy disclosures and other mechanisms is one possible approach to forcing management to respond to the needs of shareholders. Another way is to establish mechanisms within the corporation that protect the interests of shareholders by overseeing management's performance. Firms, in fact, have developed such mechanisms. This is not surprising because, in order to compete effectively, firms must deliver their products at the lowest possible cost, including agency and other organizational costs.

A prominent example of internal monitoring of management is the "M (or multi-divisional)-form" of management developed by DuPont and General Motors during the 1920s and analyzed by Oliver Williamson. This device involves the operation of separate divisions by a general office. This device does not grant complete autonomy to the divisions, as may be the case with a holding company, or attempt to centralize all operating decisions. Rather, it separates operational decisions, made at the divisional level, from strategic planning, done at the general-office level. One effect of this device is to facilitate monitoring of operational managers by the policy-makers at the top—in particular, by the board of directors.

As discussed in Section 7.02[A], there are other internal monitoring mechanisms. Corporate managers compete with each other to get good corporate jobs through promotion in the firm or through inter-firm hiring. These decisions are made on the basis of the managers' productivity. Outside auditors provide additional oversight of financial performance. Auditing firms sell not only their services but their reputations. Thus, in order to be able to charge more, the auditors must protect their reputations by not serving as "tools" of management. The consequences for an auditor that fails to adequately protect its reputation can be severe. Consider the fate of Arthur Andersen, once one of the nation's leading auditors, as a result of its role in the Enron scandal.

[B] The Monitoring Board

The board of directors is intended to supervise the performance of management to ensure that the corporation is run consistently with shareholder interests. But some commentators have questioned the effectiveness of the board of directors because of the extent to which it is controlled by those whom it is supposed to be overseeing—the management of the corporation. Their antidote to this problem is to staff corporate boards with "outside" directors—that is, directors who are not full-time executives of the company. A leading advocate of change is **Eisenberg**, who has advocated restructuring the board so as to enhance its central monitoring function. The "monitoring board" as envisioned by Eisenberg and others includes the following basic features: a majority of independent directors in the sense that they are neither employed full-time by the company nor are otherwise subservient to corporate executives; an "audit" committee composed of outside directors that works directly with the corporation's outside auditing firm to ensure that the board of directors receives accurate information about the company's operation; and a "nominating" committee composed of outside directors that removes control of the election of directors from the insiders.

Pressures toward adoption by corporations of the "monitoring" board have come from several directions. The Committee on Corporate Law of the Section of Corporation, Banking & Business Law, American Bar Association, has advocated this model in its influential CORPORATE DIRECTOR'S GUIDEBOOK,[101] the SEC urged the adoption of the monitoring model and insisted on the adoption of monitoring boards in consent decrees entered into with some securities law violators;[102] and the New York Stock Exchange requires listed companies to have audit committees composed of outside directors.[103] New and increased pressures to increase the effectiveness and independence of corporate boards are almost certain in light of the apparent failure of the Enron board to detect or prevent the problematic transactions that ultimately lead to the firm's demise.

Potentially the most influential proposal for change is the American Law Institute's PRINCIPLES OF CORPORATE GOVERNANCE. The first Draft recommended legislative adoption of a full panoply of monitoring board devices applying to public corporations.[104] The ALI's second draft retreated somewhat from this broad regulatory approach and suggested legislative adoption only of an audit committee requirement for very large public companies.[105] Audit committees for smaller public firms, and nominating and compensation committees became merely "Recommendations of Corporate Practice Concerning the Board and Principal Oversight Committees." This structure has been retained in the final version of the *Principles*.

In 1999, the SEC adopted new rules designed to encourage public companies to increase the effectiveness of their audit committees. The new rules require, among other things, that:

> (1) the proxy statement include a report from the audit committee stating whether the committee (a) reviewed and discussed the audited financial statements with management, (b) discussed certain important matters, such as the selection of significant accounting policies, with the independent auditors, (c) received disclosures from the auditors regarding auditor inde-

---

[101] 33 BUS. LAW. 1595, 1607-10 (1978); 1994 Edition, 49 BUS. LAW. 1243 (1994).

[102] *See* Second Amended Judgment and Order of Permanent Injunction and Ancillary Relief in *SEC v. Mattel, Inc.*, Civ. Action No. 74-2958-FW (C.D. Cal. 1974), discussed in Solomon, *Restructuring the Board of Directors: Fond Hope-Faint Promise?*, 76 MICH. L. REV. 581 (1978).

[103] *See* NYSE Guide, CCH Fed. Sec. L. Rep. ¶ 2501 (1988).

[104] Tentative Draft 1, Part III, Ch. 1 (1982).

[105] Tenative Draft 2, Section 3.03 (1984).

pendence, and (d) recommended to the board of directors that the audited financial statements be included in the company's annual report;

(2) the proxy statement disclose whether the board of directors has adopted a written charter for the audit committee, and if so, include a copy of that charter at least once every three years; and

(3) the proxy statement disclose whether the audit committee's members are "independent," together with certain information about any director on the audit committee who is not independent.[106]

In the wake of Enron, the New York Stock Exchange proposed new rules regarding board independence[107] and Congress enacted requirements regarding the activities and composition of board audit committees that oversee the firms' relationships with their auditors.[108]

Even if monitoring boards theoretically are a good idea, a famous study by **Miles Mace** showed that the reality of modern public corporations limits how much monitoring such boards are likely to do in practice. Mace says that outside directors lack the *time, information* and *inclination* to participate effectively in management.

With respect to the *time* factor, outside directors are generally top executives of other companies. They are chosen in large measure because they add prestige to the board. **Mace** quotes an executive as saying (page 90):

> You've got to have the names of outside directors who look impressive in the annual report. They are, after all, nothing more or less than ornaments on the corporate Christmas tree. You want good names, you want attractive ornaments. You want to communicate to the various publics that if any company is good enough to attract the president of a large New York bank as a director, for example, it just has to be a great company.[109]

According to one "ornament" quoted by Mace (page 92):

> I don't do much as an outside director. I know I should do more, but the facts of life are that the other outside directors and I have full-time jobs with a lot of responsibilities to our respective companies. The problem is not the lack of motivation because of the low fees—the problem basically is that I've got more than I can do right here on this job. Presidents of large companies

---

[106] *See* SEC Release No. 34-42266 (Dec. 22, 1999).

[107] *See* Report of the New York Stock Exchange Corporate Accountability and Listing Standards Committee to the NYSE's Board of Directors, June 6, 2002.

[108] *See* Sarbanes-Oxley Act of 2002, § 301, adding Securities Exchange Act of 1934 § 10A(m) requiring securities exchanges and associations to amend listing standards to require issuers' audit committees to be responsible for hiring and supervising the firm's auditor and restricting members from receiving fees from or being affiliated persons of the issuer.

[109] Copyright © 1971 by the President and Fellows of Harvard College; all rights reserved.

are busy people, with careers that typically occupy 110 percent of their working hours. And they have a primary set of responsibilities. They and I tend to look at outside directorships as being an extra burden. It certainly doesn't have the same importance in their priority list as the primary job they have, so naturally it gets less attention. The reason I don't get involved, as an outside board member, is that I don't have time to get the facts, and I prefer not to look stupid. Silence is a marvelous cover.

The time problem can be more fully appreciated by considering Mace's description of how the business of a corporation is "managed" at a typical board of directors meeting (pages 11-12):

> Board meetings are usually held monthly, except for August, and last anywhere from one to two-and-a-half hours, but quarterly meetings are quite common. The practice in some companies is to follow or precede the meeting with a luncheon to which insiders who are not members of the board are invited. Frequently at the luncheon a company division manager— not necessarily on the board—will make a brief presentation of his divisional operations, describing the product line, method of distribution, product developments, sales, profits, competition, and organizational relationships to other divisions in the company. The purpose of the presentation is to help outside directors learn the operations of the company and get acquainted with the key executives, and, as one president stated, "To build the morale of key divisional people by inviting them to meet informally with the board."
>
> Each position at the board table will have a book, usually leather bound with the director's name embossed in gold, containing the agenda, information and financial results for the period, and memoranda pertinent to the topics to be covered. There are many and varied approaches to the seating of directors, for instance the simple and controversy-avoiding technique of arranging the directors around the table alphabetically starting at the chairman's right, or perhaps assigning the seats closest to the chairman to outside members who have been on the board longest—an arrangement similar to that used in the United States Supreme Court.
>
> After approval by the board of the minutes of the previous meeting, the next item on the agenda is usually a review of operations for the last period—month or quarter. This may be given by the president or the vice president of finance. Divisional or functional managers may report on their respective operations or elaborate on the comments made by their superiors. Depending upon the size and complexity of the company, the financial report will take from thirty minutes to an hour.
>
> This is followed by board approvals of actions of the executive committee taken since the last meeting. The next item is often concerned with capital appropriations requiring board approval—the standard may be that requests for anything over, say, $100,000 or $300,000 are required to come

to the board. Brief explanations of the capital appropriations are made by the president or by the interested operating vice president, and a motion for approval is customarily made by one of the outsiders.

A particular agenda might include one or more of the following items:

- Consideration of a refinancing plan.
- Liquidation of obsolete or surplus plants.
- Dividend action.
- Consideration of an acquisition proposed by management.
- Company's position and risks of devaluation abroad.
- A report of research and development programs and products.

There are also constraints on *information*. Even if outside directors had more time, they lack direct access to the detailed information necessary to manage a large corporation. Given their control over the day-to-day affairs of the corporation, top management can control what information reaches the directors. Proposals for monitoring boards attempt to deal with this informational problem by establishing "audit" committees composed of independent directors to work with the corporation's outside auditors.

An illustration of time and information constraints on the performance of outside directors is provided by the American Telephone and Telegraph Company's decision to offer to settle the U.S. Government's huge antitrust suit against it by agreeing to divest itself of its local operating companies in return for the ability to go into new high-technology lines of business. The basic decision to completely change the nature of one of the world's largest corporations was made by Charles L. Brown, the chairman of the board and chief executive officer. The board authorized negotiations along these lines at a regular monthly meeting. The matter was not on the agenda, and there was no advance notice of any discussion of a divestiture plan. The meeting lasted the usual two hours.[110]

Finally, outside directors lack the *inclination* to take over direct management. This is particularly true where "inside" directors control who is nominated as an outside director. The insiders may want as directors those who will gently provide them with wise advice, but not "boatrockers" who will probe and ask embarrassing questions. So the insiders choose those who will be sympathetic, including personal friends, friends of friends, and executives of companies which do business with the corporation.[111] Consider the following quotes from **Mace**, at 99:

> "In selecting new outside directors," one president said, "I pick them very much like a trial lawyer goes about the selection of a jury."

* * *

---

[110] *See* WALL STREET JOURNAL, Jan. 19, 1982, at 1, 10.

[111] For some current statistics on who these outsiders are, see Herman, CORPORATE CONTROL, CORPORATE POWER 39-40 (1981).

"Here in New York it's a systems club. There is a group of companies that you can see, and you know them as well as I do, where the chief executive of Company A has B and C and D on his board. They are chief executive officers of B, C, and D, and he is on their boards. They are all members of the Brook Club, the Links Club, or the Union League Club. Everybody is washing everybody else's hands."[112]

* * *

The retired chairman of a medium-sized company in the midwest stated: "In the companies I know, the outside directors always agree with management. That's why they are there. I have one friend that's just the greatest agreer that ever was, and he is on a dozen boards. . . ."

Even if the insiders lacked the ability to control the selection of board members, as would be the case under proposals for "monitoring" boards, outside directors probably would not be the sort of people who would be inclined to second-guess management. That is because, once it is accepted that the function of the board is to maximize profits, the best outside directors are other corporate executives who are experts on making money. These directors are likely to be sympathetic with the insiders even if they have no other link with the insiders or with the company. Consider the following statement of a corporate president quoted in Mace, *supra* at 93:

[T]hese outside-director presidents don't get involved, because there is sort of an unwritten code—they don't want outside directors bothering them in their operations, and therefore they don't bother the management of companies they serve as outside directors. By "bothering operations" I mean understanding enough about the company and industry to be able to ask some sensible questions.

Moreover, the sympathies of the directors can be affected in other ways. In the recent best-seller, BARBARIANS AT THE GATE,[113] the authors tell how Ross Johnson, the chief executive of RJR Nabisco, quashed a possible coup attempt led by the board chairman Paul Sticht, who objected to Johnson's lavish spending of corporate cash. Johnson had Sticht removed as chairman.

[T]here was no ground swell of protest from Sticht's board allies. In contrast to their treatment under Wilson [the previous chief executive], the directors found that all their needs were now attended to in detail. Bill Anderson of NCR slid into Sticht's chairmanship of the International Advisory

---

[112] [In Vance, CORPORATE LEADERSHIP: BOARDS, DIRECTORS & STRATEGY 81 (1983), the author notes that according to a 1966 study a Harvard, Yale or Princeton graduate had a 1/49 chance of being on a board, compared to 1/818 for graduates of ten large public universities.—Ed.]

[113] Burrough & Helyar, BARBARIANS AT THE GATE: THE FALL OF RJR NABISCO 97 (1990). Excerpts Copyright © 1990 by Bryan Burrough and John Helyar. Reprinted by permission of HarperCollins, Inc.

Board and was slipped an $80,000 contract for his services. Johnson disbanded RJR Nabisco's shareholder services department and contracted its work out to John Medlin's Wachovia Bank. Juanita Kreps was given $2 million to endow two chairs at Duke, one of them named after herself. For another $2 million, Duke's business school named a wing of a new building "Horrigan Hall . . . ."

Holdovers from Johnson's Nabisco board did especially well. Bob Schaeberle was given a six-year $180,000-a-year consulting contract for ill-defined duties. Andy Sage received $250,000 a year for his efforts with financial R & D. In an unusual move, Charlie Hugel took Sticht's post as the ceremonial "nonexecutive" chairman of RJR Nabisco, for which he recieved a $150,000 contract. By naming him chairman, Johnson hoped Hugel would cement his increasingly close ties with the board.

At the same time, the number of board meetings was slashed, and directors' fees were boosted to $50,000. Wilson had allowed board members to use company jets only for official business. Johnson encouraged them to use the [company's jets] anytime, anywhere, at no charge. "I sometimes feel like the director of transportation," he once sighed after arranging yet another director's flight. "But I know if I'm there for them they'll be there for me."

That the presence of outside directors on the board is not a panacea is illustrated by the misfortune of the collapse of the Penn Central Company. The SEC cast much of the blame there on the passive non-management directors who gave inadequate consideration to the ramifications of the Pennsylvania-New York Central merger and who failed to stop substantial financial misconduct by insiders.[114] Other examples include the criminal conduct of E.F. Hutton, the deterioration of Eastern Air Lines under Frank Borman, and the collapse of Enron.

There is some anecdotal evidence that outside board members are becoming more aggressive, perhaps chastened by the liability imposed on outside directors in *Smith v. Van Gorkom*, Section 9.03[B]. For example, BARBARIANS AT THE GATE tells how the same RJR Nabisco board that Ross Johnson pampered so well finally balked at a leveraged buyout proposal that would have greatly enriched Johnson and agreed to sell the company to Kohlberg, Kravis, which had made a virtually identical bid.

The data on monitoring boards, some of which is presented in articles listed in the References, is ambiguous. The **MacAvoy** study found no correlation between profitability and adoption by firms of an ALI-type board. Reviews by **Bhagat & Black** find no positive correlation between board independence and corporate performance. On the other hand, **Morck, Shleifer & Vishny** and **Weisbach** found a correlation between outsider-dominated boards and forced management changes in firms that were doing poorly. This tends to support the hypothesis that outsider boards serve a useful monitoring function. Other studies of monitoring boards include **Baysinger & Butler**, **Byrd**

---

[114] *See* Staff Report, *The Financial Collapse of the Penn Central Company*, 157-72 (1972).

& Hickman, and **Rosenstein & Wyatt**. These studies indicate that "monitoring" boards may be beneficial for *some* companies, but they also suggest that more independence is not necessarily better.

NOTES AND QUESTIONS

(1) **Professional directors.** Professors **Gilson & Kraakman** suggest solving the problems discussed above concerning lack of time, information, and inclination by having professional directors who serve on several boards at the instance of institutional shareholders. They argue that well-compensated, professional directors who are monitored by large shareholders would better represent shareholder interests than outside directors selected by managers. Consider the possible advantages and disadvantages of this proposal in the light of the above discussion.

(2) **Equity compensation of directors. Elson (1996)** has argued that independent directors would be more attentive to corporate interests if they held stock in their companies. There is evidence that firms with independent boards that get incentive compensation are more likely to fire bad managers.[115]

REFERENCES

Andrews, *Rigid Rules Will Not Make Good Boards*, HARV. BUS. REV., Nov.-Dec. 1982, at 34.

Baysinger & Butler, *Revolution versus Evolution in Corporate Law: The ALI's Project and the Independent Director*, 52 GEO. WASH. L. REV. 557 (1984).

Bhagat & Black, *The Non-Correlation Between Board Independence and Long-Term Firm Performance*, 27 J. CORP. L. 231 (2002)

Bhagat & Black, *The Uncertain Relationship Between Board Composition and Firm Performance*, 54 BUS. LAW. 921 (1999).

Byrd & Hickman, *Do Outside Directors Monitor Managers? Evidence from Tender Offer Bids*, 32 J. FIN. ECON. 195 (1992).

Eisenberg, THE STRUCTURE OF THE MODERN CORPORATION (1976).

Elson, *Director Compensation and the Management-Capital Board: The History of a Symptom and a Cure*, 50 SMU L. REV. 127 (1996).

Faith, Higgins & Tollison, *Managerial Rents and Outside Recruitment in the Coasian Firm*, 74 AM. ECON. REV. 60 (1984).

Gilson & Kraakman, *Reinventing the Outside Director: An Agenda for Institutional Investors*, 43 STAN. L. REV. 863 (1991).

Kaplan & Reishus, *Outside Directorships and Corporate Performance*, 27 J. FIN. ECON. 389 (1990).

MacAvoy, Cantor, Dana & Peck, *ALI Proposals for Increased Control of the Corporation by the Board of Directors: An Economic Analysis*, Statement of the Business Round-

---

[115] *See* Perry, *Incentive Compensation for Outside Directors and CEO Turnover* (SSRN) (June 2000).

table on the American Law Institute's Proposed "Principles of Corporate Governance and Structure: Restatement and Recommendations" (1983).

Mace, DIRECTORS: MYTH AND REALITY (1971).

Millstein & MacAvoy, *The Active Board of Directors and Performance of the Large Publicly Traded Corporation,* 98 COLUM. L. REV. 1283 (1998).

Morck, Shleifer & Vishny, *Management Ownership and Market Valuation: An Empirical Analysis,* 20 J. FIN. ECON. 293 (1988).

Rosenstein & Wyatt, *Outside Directors, Board Independence and Shareholder Wealth,* 26 J. FIN. ECON. 175 (1990).

Watts & Zimmerman, *Agency Problems, Auditors, and the Theory of the Firm: Some Evidence,* 26 J.L. & ECON. 613 (1983).

Weisbach, *Outside Directors and CEO Turnover,* 20 J. FIN. ECON. 431 (1988).

Williamson, *The Modern Corporation: Origins, Evolution, Attributes,* 19 J. ECON. LITERATURE 1537 (1981).

[C] Representing Other Constituencies

The monitoring board discussed in the preceding subsection has been proposed primarily as a way to protect the shareholders. It has also been suggested that boards of directors should balance the conflicting claims of various corporate constituencies, including workers. *See* Note 2 in Section 7.02[C] and **Blair and Stout**.

One way to be sure that the board represents multiple constituencies is to actually put these constituencies on the board. Some commentators, including **Stone** and **Nader**, have suggested including publicly appointed directors on the board. Others, like **Chayes**, have suggested that the board include representatives of constituencies other than the shareholders. But these proposals have been sharply criticized. Critics, such as **Coffee**, have pointed out that public directors would have an "adversarial relationship" with the other directors which might discourage the disclosure of information to the board. Also, the presence of antithetical points of view on the board may inhibit the decision-making process. If the "social" representatives are in a minority, management will continue to wield the real power and the bickering is likely to accomplish little. If, on the other hand, the "social" directors can outvote management, this may lead to decision-making by a process of compromise of the various positions. This process is not much more likely to lead to the decision that is best for society than is the present profit orientation.

Finally, there will be problems in determining how representatives of various interest groups are to be selected. For example, after the Exxon Valdez oil spill in Alaska, Exxon responded to pressure from environmentalists by appointing a prominent marine scientist to its board. Environmentalists sharply criticized this selection on the ground that the new board member had inadequate environmentalist credentials.[116] It is

---

[116] *See* Sullivan, *Exxon Names Marine Scientist to Board in Response to Demands from Activists,* WALL STREET JOURNAL, Aug. 31, 1989, at A6, col. 3.

questionable whether all these problems are worth the benefits of more non-share-holder representation. Even without such representation, boards cannot ignore non-shareholder constituencies because the corporation must perform contracts and compete in capital and product markets.

The most noteworthy moves in the direction of including representatives of non-shareholder groups on the boards of public corporations are the elections in 1980 of Douglas Fraser, president of the United Automobile Workers, to the Chrysler board, and in 1982 of a union representative to the Pan Am board. Employees long have constituted nearly 50% of the voting power of the boards of directors of German public corporations under the German system of "codeterminism," which now applies to Daimler/Chrysler. There is, of course, a problem in this situation to the extent that employees and shareholders are competing claimants for corporate resources.

Compare employee *ownership* of the firm, as has occurred in the case of United Airlines. Here there is seemingly less conflict between owners and employees. However, there may be other conflicts between groups of employees, as between the skilled and unskilled, between employee and non-employee shareholders where the company has both types, and between employee-owners and their union-leader representatives on the board. These conflicts may have hindered United's adjustment to a changing industry and led to its fall into bankruptcy.[117]

REFERENCES

Blair & Stout, *Director Accountability and the Mediating Role of the Corporate Board*, 79 WASH. U. L.Q. 403 (2001).

Chayes, *The Modern Corporation and the Rule of Law, in* THE CORPORATION IN MODERN SOCIETY (E. Mason ed., 1960).

Coffee, *Beyond the Shut-Eyed Sentry: Toward a Theoretical View of Corporate Misconduct and an Effective Legal Response*, 63 VA. L. REV. 1099 (1977).

Conard, *Reflections on Public Interest Directors*, 75 MICH. L. REV. 941 (1977).

Herman, CORPORATE CONTROL, CORPORATE POWER (1981).

Nader, Green & Seligman, TAMING THE GIANT CORPORATION (1976).

Stone, WHERE THE LAW ENDS (1975).

---

[117] *See* Holman W. Jenkins, Jr., *Business World: To Save United, Pull the Plug on Employee Ownership*, WALL ST. J., December 4, 2002 at A19.

CHAPTER 8

The Authority of Management

This Chapter deals with management from the perspective of third parties. It applies some general principles of agency law concerning the managers' powers to bind the business association in dealings with third parties. The chapter begins with a discussion of general principles of authority (Section 8.01). It then goes on to discuss how those principles apply to partnerships (Section 8.02) and corporations (Section 8.03). The chapter concludes with a discussion of the corporate law *ultra vires* doctrine (Section 8.04).

§ 8.01 Introduction to Authority and Related Concepts

A principal is bound by the acts of an agent who has authority, apparent authority, or inherent agency power. Each of these concepts is explained briefly below. Most of the summary below is based on the RESTATEMENT (SECOND) OF AGENCY (1965), but, where appropriate, references to the tentative draft of the RESTATEMENT (THIRD) OF AGENCY (Tent. Draft No. 2, 2001) are also included.

Authority is sometimes referred to as "actual" or "real" authority.[1] The principal creates such authority by manifesting *to the agent* consent to be bound by the agent's acts. Section 2.01 of Tentative Draft No. 2 of the RESTATEMENT (THIRD) OF AGENCY makes clear that the focus of actual authority is on the *agent's understanding* of her authority at the time she acts.[2] Real authority can be either *express* or *implied* from the course of dealings between the principal and agent.

Apparent authority exists when the *principal's* acts create an appearance of authority from the perspective of third parties dealing with the agent.[3] Apparent authority can exist even if the principal lacks real authority—*i.e.*, even if the principal has not manifested to the agent consent to be bound by the agent's acts. In general, an agent's *apparent* authority will only differ from the agent's *real* authority when the principal restricts the agent's real authority by instructions which are not communicated to third parties.

Inherent agency power arises from the general power the principal has conferred on the agent.[4] Like apparent authority, inherent agency power can exist in situations

---

[1] *See* RESTATEMENT (SECOND) OF AGENCY § 7 (1965); *see also* RESTATEMENT (THIRD) OF AGENCY § 2.01 (Tent. Draft No. 2, 2001).

[2] *Id.*

[3] RESTATEMENT (SECOND) OF AGENCY § 8 (1965); *see also* RESTATEMENT (THIRD) OF AGENCY § 2.03 (Tent. Draft No.2, 2001).

[4] RESTATEMENT (SECOND) OF AGENCY § 8A (1965).

where the principal has not explicitly manifested to the agent his consent to be bound by the agent's acts, as where the agent acts beyond express authority in entering into contracts or making conveyances. Tentative Draft No. 2 of the RESTATEMENT (THIRD) OF AGENCY eliminates the concept of inherent agency power, stating that "[o]ther doctrines stated in this *Restatement* encompass the justifications underpinning [inherent agency authority], including the importance of interpretation by the agent in the agent's relationship with the principal," as well as the doctrine of apparent authority and the other doctrines discussed below.[5]

Even a transaction that is not authorized in any of the senses of the term discussed above may bind the principal under one or more of several legal theories. For example, the principal may be *estopped* from denying authority by carelessly letting a third party rely to its detriment on the agent's assertion of authority. An example is where the boss learns that the janitor is secretly dressing in a business suit and contracting with third parties but fails to stop the masquerade. Estoppel differs from apparent authority in that the principal is liable even though she did not create the appearance of authority.[6]

A general theory appears to underlie the rules discussed so far: the principal is liable if she either consented to be bound or was in a better position than the third party to protect against mistaken reliance on authority. This is the same "cheaper loss avoider" idea behind the creation of the agency relationship (*see* Note 2 following *Nichols* in Section 2.01). For example, where the agent does not even appear to have authority, the third party bears the risk of loss because it is usually cheaper for the third party to check on the agent's power in unusual situations than it is to force the principal to keep watch over the agent. However, estoppel liability makes sense because a principal who knows the agent is misleading the third party is in a relatively good position to correct the third party's mistake. More broadly, these rules permit firms to deal with third parties through agents when this is efficient, while minimizing the costs to third parties of such dealings.

Some grounds for holding principals liable for their actual or purported agents' acts do not fit neatly into this general theory. One such ground is *restitution*. Pursuant to that doctrine, a third party may be entitled to recover from the principal if it conferred a benefit on the principal for which the principal should be required to pay, whether or not the principal was responsible for the third party's being misled.[7] The principal's retention of the benefit creates a sort of contract to pay for it.

Section 2.07 of Tentative Draft No. 2 of the RESTATEMENT (THIRD) OF AGENCY limits recovery for restitution under the law of agency to situations where the benefit was conferred "by the action of an agent or a person who appears to be an agent," tying the restitution theory of recovery more closely to the law of agency. But recovery on broader

---

[5] RESTATEMENT (THIRD) OF AGENCY § 2.01 Comment b (Tent. Draft No. 2, 2001).

[6] RESTATEMENT (SECOND) OF AGENCY § 8B (1965); *see also* RESTATEMENT (THIRD) OF AGENCY § 2.05 (Tent. Draft No. 2, 2001).

[7] RESTATEMENT (SECOND) OF AGENCY § 8C (1965).

grounds may still be available under the law of contracts. *See* RESTATEMENT (SECOND) OF CONTRACTS § 370 ("[a] party is entitled to restitution under the rules stated in this Restatement only to the extent that he has conferred a benefit on the other party by way of past performance or reliance").

A more puzzling basis of liability for unauthorized transactions is the peculiar agency doctrine of *ratification*. Ratification is an "affirmance" of an earlier unauthorized act,[8] which includes any conduct manifesting consent to be bound by the transaction.[9] A principal may be held responsible for an unauthorized transaction by, for example, failing to say anything about it under circumstances in which silence may be interpreted as consent, even though the third party did not rely on the consent (or, indeed, even know about it) and did not confer a benefit on the principal. Consider the following illustrations:[10]

> 1. Purporting to act for P but without power to bind him, A buys goods from T and pays the purchase price out of his own money. P, learning of this, does nothing. There is not sufficient evidence of affirmance.

> 2. Purporting to represent P but without power to bind him, A contracts to take care of T's horse for a year. A places the horse in P's stable and feeds it from P's bin. P learns the facts, and does nothing for a week. There is evidence of affirmance.

> 3. A, a clerk employed by P but having nothing to do with advertising, places an order with T for advertising in P's name for a period of six months. P learns of the act and although knowing that T is preparing copy, does nothing. There is evidence of affirmance.

The RESTATEMENT (SECOND) OF AGENCY says "the best defense of ratification is pragmatic; that it is needed in the prosecution of business. It operates normally to cure minor defects in an agent's authority, minimizing technical defenses and preventing unnecessary law suits."[11] Are you satisfied with this rationale?

The ratification provisions of Tentative Draft No. 2 of the RESTATEMENT (THIRD) OF AGENCY are substantively similar to those found in the RESTATEMENT (SECOND) OF AGENCY. But the terminology is different, referring to conduct "manifesting assent,"[12] rather than to "affirmance."[13]

---

[8]   *Id.* at § 82.

[9]   *Id.* at § 93.

[10] *Id.* at § 94, comment a. Copyright © 1965, American Law Institute. Reprinted with permission.

[11] *Id.* at § 82, comment d.

[12] RESTATEMENT (THIRD) OF AGENCY § 4.01 (Tent. Draft No. 2, 2001).

[13] RESTATEMENT (SECOND) OF AGENCY § 82 (1965).

REFERENCE

Hetherington, *Trends in Enterprise Liability: Law and the Unauthorized Agent,* 19 STAN. L. REV. 76 (1966).

§ 8.02 Partners' Authority

The principles discussed above are generally applicable to all business associations—that is, they show how the acts of partners or corporate officers come to bind partnerships and corporations. But statutes and case law relating to specific forms of business associations fill in and alter some details. Statutes and case law relating to partnerships are discussed below.

Uniform Partnership Act §§ 9-14 and RUPA §§ 301-305 determine when acts of partners bind the partnership and thus incorporate the concepts of real authority, apparent authority, and inherent agency power. The key provisions are UPA § 9 and RUPA § 301, which establish a set of presumptions: A partner's act that is "for apparently carrying on in the usual way the business of the partnership" presumptively binds the partnership unless it can show that the third party was aware of specific limitations on the partner's authority. Where, on the other hand, the act was not "apparently . . . usual," UPA § 9(2) and RUPA § 301(2) provide that the act does not bind the partnership, unless authority can be shown in some other way, implicitly placing on the third party the burden to show real authority, inherent agency power or an act giving rise to apparent authority. (In the absence of any contrary agreement, the rules set forth in UPA § 18(h) and RUPA § 401(j) determine whether the partnership has conferred real authority on a partner.) UPA § 9(3) (for which there is no equivalent in RUPA) gives examples of acts which are not in the "apparently . . . usual" category, and thus are not presumptively authorized. The following case illustrates the operation of the UPA presumptions.

BURNS v. GONZALEZ
Texas Court of Civil Appeals
439 S.W.2d 128 (1969)

CADENA, Justice:

* * *

Plaintiff, William G. Burns, sued Arturo C. Gonzalez and Ramon D. Bosquez, individually and as sole partners in Inter-American Advertising Agency (herein called "the partnership"), to recover on a $40,000.00 promissory note executed by Bosquez in his own name and in the name of the partnership. After an interlocutory default judgment had been entered in favor of plaintiff against Bosquez, the trial court, sitting without a jury, entered the judgment appealed from, denying Burns any recovery against Gonzalez.

The sole business of the partnership was the sale, on a commission basis, of broadcast time on XERF, a radio station located in Ciudad Acuna, Mexico, and owned and operated by a Mexican corporation, Compania Radiodifusora de Coahuila, S.A. (herein called "Radiodifusora"). Bosquez and Gonzalez each owned 50% of the Radiodifusora stock, with Bosquez acting as president of the corporation.

The events culminating in this litigation began in 1957 when a written contract was entered into between Radiodifusora and the partnership, on the one hand, and Roloff Evangelistic Enterprises, Inc., and Burns, on the other. Under this contract, Radiodifusora and the partnership, in consideration of the payment of $100,000.00 by Roloff and Burns, agreed to make available to them two 15-minute segments of broadcast time daily over XERF so long as the franchise of the radio station remained in force, beginning July 1, 1957. In accordance with the terms of the contract, Roloff and Burns paid the $100,000.00 in four equal installments on July 1, 1957, November 1, 1957, March 1, 1958, and July 1, 1958, with Burns retaining 15% of such payments as his commission, as he had a right to do under the terms of the contract.

Subsequently, Roloff assigned all of its rights under this contract to Burns, effective June 16, 1962. Both Radiodifusora and the partnership approved such assignment.

Because of labor disputes and other circumstances, the radio station was shut down at various times. With some exceptions, the broadcast periods described in the 1957 contract were not made available to Burns or to persons to whom he sold such broadcast periods, after June 16, 1962.

On November 28, 1962, Bosquez, purporting to act on his own behalf and on behalf of the partnership, executed the note in question, payable to Burns on November 28, 1964. According to a separate instrument signed by Bosquez on the same date, the radio station was in receivership and it was unlikely that the broadcast periods to which Burns was entitled under the 1957 contract would be made available to him for the two-year period ending November 28, 1964, the date on which the note was payable. This instrument recited that since Burns would derive an income of $20,000.00 a year from sale of such broadcast periods, the note in the amount of $40,000.00 had been executed and delivered to Burns to compensate him for the income which he would have derived during the two-year period ending November 28, 1964. Bosquez testified, and Burns does not deny, that "one of the reasons" why he executed the note was the promise by Burns not to sue Radiodifusora.

* * *

. . . In this case, in fact, Bosquez had no authority to bind the partnership by executing a negotiable instrument. But, since this express limitation on the authority of Bosquez was unknown to Burns, then, under the language of Sec. 9(1), his act in executing the note would bind the partnership if such act can be classified as an act "for apparently carrying on in the usual way the business of the partnership."

As we interpret Sec. 9(1), the act of a partner binds the firm, absent an express limitation of authority known to the party dealing with such partner, if such act is for the purpose of "apparently carrying on" the business of the partnership in the way in which other firms engaged in the same business in the locality usually transact business, or in the way in which the particular partnership usually transacts its business. In this case, there is no evidence relating to the manner in which firms engaged in the sale of advertising time on radio stations usually transact business. Specifically, there is no evidence as to whether or not the borrowing of money, or the execution of negotiable instruments, was incidental to the transaction of business, "in the usual way," by other advertising agencies or by this partnership, Inter-American Advertising Agency. It becomes important, therefore, to determine the location of the burden of proof concerning the "usual way" of transacting business by advertising agencies.

Sec. 9(1) states that the act of a partner "for apparently carrying on in the usual way the business of the partnership" binds the firm. This language does not place the burden of proof on the non-participating partner to establish the nonexistence of the facts which operate to impose liability on the firm. If the Legislature had intended to place the burden of proof on the non-participating partner, it could have done so easily. The statute could have been drafted to declare that the act of a partner binds the firm "unless it is shown that such act was not for apparently carrying on in the usual way the business of the partnership." Actually, the liability-imposing language of Sec. 9(1) indicates that the burden of proof is on the person seeking to hold the non-participating partner accountable. It is not couched in terms appropriate for the establishment of a presumption, "administrative" or otherwise. The language relating to carrying on in the usual way the business of the partnership is no more than a statement of the rule concerning vicarious liability based on "apparent" authority.

* * *

We conclude that, under a reasonable interpretation of the language of Sec. 9(1), . . . the burden of proving the "usual way" in which advertising agencies transact business was upon Burns.

Our conclusion is supported by the fact that the liability of partners with respect to third persons is largely determined by reference to the principles of the law of agency. Restatement 2d, Agency Sec. 14 (1958); UPA, Sec. 4(3). One who asserts that the particular act of an agent is within the scope of the agent's authority has the burden of proving the extent of such authority. . . .We recognize, of course, that there are aspects in which the partner-agent differs from the "ordinary" agent. But we know of no distinction which compels application of different rules concerning the burden of proof in connection with establishment of the extent of the agent's power. The principle for imposing liability on the non-acting party, be he partner or ordinary principal, is that he has "held out" the actor as being empowered to perform acts of the nature of the act in question. If A seeks to impose liability on B for the act of C on the theory that B held C out as having power to do such act, clearly the burden of establishing the facts which constitute such holding out is on A.

In the case of an ordinary agent, "holding out" is established by showing that the principal placed the agent in a position which ordinarily carries with it generally recognized powers. The agent will then have, as far as third parties are concerned, the power to do the things ordinarily done by one occupying such a position, unless the third party has knowledge of limitations on the powers of the agent. In *Collins v. Cooper*, 65 Tex. 460, 464 (1886), the Supreme Court said that in determining the extent of an agent's power, it "becomes necessary, to consider the character of the business, the manner in which it is usual to carry on such a business, and, where the agency has continued for a long time, the manner in which the particular business was carried on . . . ." This is the same principle which is made applicable to problems concerning the power of partners by Sec. 9(1).

* * *

We are aware of the language in *Crozier, Rhea & Co. v. Kirker*, 4 Tex. 252, 258-259 (1849), to the effect that every partner has implied power to bind his co-partners by executing notes for commercial purposes consistent with the object of the partnership. Similar language is found in *Brewer v. Big Lake State Bank*, 378 S.W.2d 948, 951 (Tex. Civ. App.— El Paso 1964, no writ), and *Ft. Dearborn Nat. Bank v. Berrott*, 23 Tex. Civ. App. 662, 57 S.W. 340, 341 (San Antonio, 1900, no writ). But in each of these cases the partnership business contemplated "the periodical or continuous or frequent purchasing, not as incidental to an occupation, but for the purpose of selling again the thing purchased." Where the partnership business is of that nature, it is usual and customary to purchase on credit and to execute paper evidencing the existence of the partnership debt. That is, to use the language of Sec. 9(1), in such partnership, "carrying on in the usual way the business of the partnership" involves borrowing and the issuance of commercial paper.

* * *

The only thing we know of the nature of the partnership here is that it was restricted to the sale of broadcast time over XERF on a commission basis. There is nothing to show that the transaction of such business required "periodical or continuous or frequent purchasing" or made "frequent resort to borrowing a necessity, not existing by reason of embarrassments, or on account of some fortuitous event, but for the advantageous prosecution of even a prosperous business." The assets of the partnership consisted of a few desks, chairs, typewriters and office supplies.

We disagree with the contention put forward by Burns to the effect that Bosquez was the managing partner. At best, the record reflects that both Bosquez and Gonzalez were active in the management of the business. As a matter of fact, with the exception of the transactions involving the 1962 note and [one other] agreement, the record discloses that all instruments significantly affecting the relations between the partners and Burns were signed by both Bosquez and Gonzalez.

Since the evidence does not disclose that Bosquez, in executing the 1962 note, was performing an act "for apparently carrying on in the usual way the business of the partnership," there is no basis for holding that the note sued on was a partnership obligation.

* * *

The judgment of the trial court is affirmed.

NOTES AND QUESTIONS

(1) **Mexican Radio.** XERF was started by a flamboyant entrepreneur named John Romulus Brinkley, who used it, among other things, to sell nostrums (such as a goat gland operation) and carry on a political career all the way back to Kansas (yes, the station's signal could reach back there). Following the events in this case, the station broadcast the famous disk jockey Wolfman Jack, who went on from XERF to XERB. These stations were commemorated in the songs "I Heard it on the X" (ZZ Top) and "Mexican Radio" (Wall of Voodoo), and in the film *American Graffiti*.

(2) **Scope of partner authority.** What would be the result under *Burns*, the UPA and RUPA under each of the following variations (considered separately) on the facts in *Burns*?

(a) Plaintiff sued the partnership for damages for breach of the advertising contract described in the case and proved only that he had contracted with the partnership through Bosquez who represented that he was acting on behalf of the firm. (For purposes of this question, disregard the $40,000 note.) Why distinguish this case from a note arising out of a breach of the advertising contract?

(b) Plaintiff proved that Bosquez, without the knowledge of either plaintiff or Gonzalez, had entered into five other loans of the type plaintiff was suing on with other frustrated advertisers during the six months preceding the execution of plaintiff's note.

(c) Plaintiff proved that before he entered into the loan transaction, Bosquez showed him a document with Gonzalez' signature which stated that Bosquez had full authority to represent the partnership in any transactions in connection with selling advertising time. Gonzalez proved in rebuttal that although the document is authentic, he had made it clear to Bosquez that Bosquez was not to enter into transactions like the loan arrangement with plaintiff.

(3) **Post-dissolution authority.** Authority may be complicated by the dissociation of a member from the partnership, with or without dissolution or liquidation of the firm. Under UPA § 35, acts of partners following the dissociation of a member continue to bind the "old" partnership, including dissociated members, if those acts are in connection with "winding up" the partnership (and so presumably benefited both leaving and staying partners) or if creditors lack notice of the dissociation. RUPA treats situations where dissociation leads to liquidation (§§ 804-805) separately from situations where dissociation leads to continuation of the partnership's business by the non-dissociating partners (§§ 702-705). In both cases liability depends on the notice or knowledge of the third party and, in the case of dissolution, on whether the transaction is appropriate for winding up.

(4) **Public filings.** Given the uncertainties about the scope of partner authority, both the partnership and third parties may want a device that clarifies this authority. RUPA authorizes public filings that clarify partners' authority in ongoing partnerships (§ 303), following partner dissociation (§ 704), and following dissolution (§ 805). Should third parties be bound to look at public records before they enter into transactions with partnerships?

(5) **Authority in limited partnerships.** A general partner in a limited partnership appears to have the same authority to bind the firm as does a general partner in general partnership. RULPA § 403 gives a general partner the rights and powers of a partner in a general partnership. Also, because neither ULPA nor RULPA include provisions on partners' agency power, the UPA and RUPA provisions would apply under statutory pro-

visions generally applying partnership law to limited partnerships.[14] By contrast, ULPA § 402(a) (2001) provides expressly that a general partner's act "for apparently carrying on in the ordinary course the limited partnership's activities or activities of the kind carried on by the limited partnership binds the limited partnership," unless the general partner lacked authority and the person with which the general partner dealt was aware of that lack of authority; an act outside § 402(a)'s grant of authority binds the limited partnership "only if the act was actually authorized by all the other partners."[15] In the absence of a provision like UPLA § 402 (2001), should courts apply the general partnership rule to limited partnerships? In light of limited partners' passivity, third parties would expect general partners to have greater power to manage the firm *vis a vis* the limited partners than does each general partner *vis a vis* her co-partners in a general partnership. A general partner therefore should be able to take all but the most extraordinary actions on behalf of the partnership without limited partner approval.[16] Limited partnership cases have, in fact, restricted general partners' authority mainly in cases in which the third party had specific reason to know under the circumstances that the general partner's act was unauthorized, as where the general partner was obviously self-dealing.[17] This appears to be the rule specifically provided for under ULPA § 9, which requires limited partner consent only to particular types of acts, including acts which would make it impossible to carry on the partnership's ordinary business.

(6) **Authority in limited liability companies.** Many LLC statutes provide that a member of a member-managed LLC, and a manager of a manager-managed LLC, have authority to bind the firm which is phrased in terms similar or identical to UPA § 9. Such statutes also generally provide that a member of a manager-managed LLC has no authority as such to bind the LLC. Consider the following questions:

(a) Under what circumstances might a member of a manager-managed LLC have *apparent authority* to bind the firm?

(b) When is a member considered a manager? Note that while LLC statutes generally require the LLC's election to be manager-managed to be set forth in a filed cer-

---

[14]   *See* UPA § 6(2); RULPA § 1106. Note that neither RUPA nor ULPA have such "linkage" language, so it is not clear what rules apply in a limited partnership that is subject to both of these statutes.

[15]   ULPA § 402(b) (2001).

[16]   For a case broadly construing a general partner's authority in a limited partnership, see *In re Hunt's Pier Associates*, 162 B.R. 442 (E.D. Pa. 1993) (contracting to install amusement park ride was within usual business of amusement pier despite large size of project, and despite the fact that the general partner apparently acted for himself, where the contract was within the expressly authorized purpose of acquiring the ride).

[17]   *See, e.g., Fox Hill Office Investors, Ltd. v. Mercantile Bank, N.A.*, 926 F.2d 752 (8th Cir. 1991) (limited partnership not bound by loan because partner's broad authority was limited by restrictions regarding recourse loans and commingling; even if creditor had no duty to examine partnership agreement, it was on notice of restrictions once it did examine agreement) (Kansas law); *Anchor Centre Partners, Ltd. v. Mercantile Bank, N.A.*, 803 S.W.2d 23 (Mo. 1991) (limited partnership not bound by loan where creditor knew from the partnership agreement that the partners' consent was required for an assignment of assets as security for non-partnership debt); *Luddington v. Bodenvest Ltd.*, 855 P.2d 204 (Utah 1993) (partnership not bound by loan to general partner rather than to limited partnership, despite general authority to hypothecate partnership assets for loans).

tificate, they do not require a formal listing of managers as do limited partnership statutes.[18] Is a "member" a "manager" whenever she engages in management activities? If so, it might follow that *all* member acts bind the firm despite the statutory distinction between members and managers.

(c) Should the partnership-type authority provisions in LLCs be interpreted the same as identical language in partnership statutes? Is it significant that an act which binds the LLC has less drastic consequences in a limited-liability firm than in a general partnership?

PROBLEM

Assume the same basic facts as the problems at the end of Section 4.02[A]. Suppose Paciaroni and Cassidy decide to race Black Ace at an exhibition. When Crane learns about the negotiations with the race promoter, he contacts the promoter and tells him that he (Crane) is the trainer and one of the three partners in the firm that owns Black Ace, that he objects to racing the horse, and that any contract made without his consent would be unauthorized. After the execution of the contract but before the race, the three partners finally agree to withdraw Black Ace from the race. Would the withdrawal be a breach of contract under the partnership law described above? How could the race promoter determine before entering into the contract whether it is authorized? Would it be enough for the promoter to contact Paciaroni and Cassidy and get confirmation from them?

§ 8.03 Authority of Corporate Officers

While the basic decision-making power resides in the board, corporations *act* through their officers (*see* Del. G.C.L. § 142) and employees. The actual authority of some of the officers of the company is often spelled out in the bylaws of the corporation. Actual authority of officers or other agents may also be derived from resolutions of the board of directors (acting, where necessary, with shareholder approval) which grant authority to enter into specific transactions. In addition to the express real authority provided by the corporate bylaws and resolutions, officers or other agents may have implied real authority, apparent authority or inherent agency power to bind the corporation if they are acting within the scope of powers they have exercised in the past or which holders of their titles normally possess.

---

[18] For discussions of agency and management issues in LLCs and citations to specific statutes, see generally, Ribstein & Keatinge, RIBSTEIN & KEATINGE ON LIMITED LIABILITY COMPANIES, Ch. 8 (1992 & Supp.).

The following case involves the authority of a corporate president. Is the court discussing real authority, apparent authority, inherent agency power, or some combination of the three?

LEE v. JENKINS BROS.

United States Court of Appeals, Second Circuit
268 F.2d 357, *cert. denied*, 361 U.S. 913 (1959)

MEDINA, Circuit Judge.

[Bernard J. Lee sued Jenkins Brothers, a corporation, and Farnham Yardley to recover pension payments allegedly due under an oral agreement by Yardley on behalf of the corporation and for his own account, made in 1920. The trial judge held that the claim was barred by the Statute of Frauds and, as to the corporate defendant, was unauthorized. The Court of Appeals upheld dismissal on the ground that there was insufficient proof that the alleged agreements were made. It then went on to hold that, if the evidence of the making of the agreements had been sufficient, the claim would not be barred by the Statute of Frauds. The Court of Appeals then considered the question of authority.]

* * *

The following is a summary of Lee's testimony. At the time of the alleged contract Lee was in the employ of the Crane Company, a large manufacturer of valves, fittings and plumbing supplies, at the company's Bridgeport plant. He had been with the Crane Company for thirteen years and had risen to the post of business manager, earning a salary of $4,000 per year. In December, 1919, the Crane Company agreed to sell its Bridgeport plant to Jenkins Brothers, a New Jersey corporation and a defendant in one of these actions. The transaction was consummated June 1, 1920 when Jenkins took over Crane's Bridgeport plant.

According to Lee's testimony this was the first venture into the manufacturing phase of the business for Jenkins, which was formerly content to be merely a customer of Crane. Jenkins was therefore extremely anxious to secure competent personnel, particularly the old Crane employees, in order to insure as smooth a transition as possible in view of the change to a relatively inexperienced management.

With this in mind Charles V. Barrington, Vice President of Jenkins in charge of manufacturing, approached Lee in February, 1920, in an attempt to induce him to join Jenkins. Lee, however, was reluctant to do so. He felt his prospects with Crane were good and he had accumulated thirteen years of pension rights under the Crane Company plan which he did not want to give up. Some time after this conversation but before June 1, 1920, Barrington arranged a meeting for Lee at his hotel suite in Bridgeport with the co-defendant Yardley, president of Jenkins, chairman of the board of directors, a substantial stockholder, son-in-law of Mr. Jenkins, and co-trustee of the Jenkins estate. Present at this meeting besides Lee and Yardley were Barrington and his wife. However, at the time of the trial in October, 1957, only Lee was alive to describe the conversation.

Yardley convinced Lee of his fine prospects with Jenkins, of the company's need for him as assistant to Barrington, and allegedly made a promise on behalf of Jenkins and a promise on his own behalf with respect to Lee's pension rights. Since the content of these promises is so vital to the determination of the various aspects of this case, we set out in full the various versions of the conversation with Yardley as given by Lee.

First, Lee testified:

> As far as the pension that I had earned with Crane Company he said the company [Jenkins Brothers] would pay that pension (and) if they didn't or, if anything came up, he would assume the liability himself, he would guarantee payment of the pension; and in consideration of that promise I agreed to go to work for Jenkins Bros. on June 1, 1920.
>
> The amount of the pension referred to by Mr. Yardley was a maximum of $1500 a year and that would be paid me when I reached the age of 60 years; regardless of what happened in the meantime, if I were with the company or not, I would be given a credit for those 13 years of service with the maximum pension of $1500.

Later Lee put it this way:

> Mr. Farnham Yardley said that Jenkins would assume the obligation for my credit pension record with Crane Company and, if anything happened and they did not pay it, he would guarantee it himself.
>
> Mr. Yardley's words were "regardless of what happens, you will get that pension if you join our company."

Finally, Lee summarized his position:

> My claim is that the company through the chairman of the board of directors and the president, promised me credit for my 13 years of service with Crane Company, regardless of what happened I would receive a pension at the age of 60, not to exceed $1,500 a year. If I was discharged in 1921 or 1922 or left I would still get that pension. That is what I am asking for.

This agreement was never reduced to writing.

Lee's prospects with Jenkins turned out to be just about as bright as he had hoped. He subsequently became vice president and general manager in charge of manufacturing and a director of the company. At that time he was receiving a salary of $25,000 from Jenkins, $8,000 more from an affiliate, plus an annual 10 per cent bonus. In 1945, however, after 25 years with Jenkins, Lee was discharged at the age of 55 and his pension rights under the company's established plan were settled in full.

In 1950 the payments under the alleged pension agreement became due. Although nothing was paid under this agreement Lee waited until 1955 to institute suit against Jenkins, joining Yardley eight and one-half months later.

The Crane Company pension plan prior to June 1, 1920, to which Lee said Yardley "referred," was a gratuitous or voluntary one whereby male employees could be retired by the company at 60 or apply for retirement at 65, if they had 25 years of service. Under the plan each employee would receive 2% of his salary for each year of service at retirement, with a maximum pension of $1500 a year. Lee admits it was a condition of eligibility under the Crane plan that the employee had to be in the employ of the company at the time of his retirement.

Although at the start of operations on June 1, 1920 Jenkins did not have a pension plan, it soon adopted one effective as of June 1, 1920 incorporating all the features of the Crane plan. The 350 former Crane employees, including Lee, who transferred over to Jenkins were all given credit under the Jenkins plan for service with the Crane Company. Lee, however, asserts that Yardley's promise was not fulfilled by the adoption of the Jenkins plan since he had been assured of pension payments "regardless of what happened." Moreover, although Jenkins revised its plan in 1932 and Lee voluntarily took coverage thereunder, all this he claims was "over and above" the rights promised by Yardley. Lee, a member of the pension committee, admits no other employee was given such pension rights.

* * *

The Scope of Yardley's Authority

In the discussion which follows we assume arguendo, that there was evidence sufficient to support a finding that Yardley orally agreed on behalf of the corporation that Lee would be paid at the age of 60 a pension not to exceed $1500, and that Yardley's words "regardless of what happens" were, as Lee contends, to be interpreted as meaning that Lee would receive this pension even if he were not working for Jenkins at the time the pension became payable. Jenkins asserts that Yardley had no authority to bind it to such an "extraordinary" contract, express, implied, or apparent and the trial court so found. There is nothing in the proofs submitted by Lee to warrant any finding of actual authority in Yardley. The Certificate of Incorporation and By-Laws of Jenkins are not in evidence nor was any course of conduct shown as between the corporation and Yardley. Accordingly, on the phase of the case now under discussion, we are dealing only with apparent authority.

* * *

. . . [T]he law reads into the agreement an obligation on the part of Lee to work for Jenkins for a "reasonable" period of time, if he wished to qualify for the pension. Ordinarily this would be determined by a variety of attendant circumstances. We are not now called upon to make this appraisal as it is clear that Lee's twenty-five years of continuous employment with Jenkins was more than a "reasonable" period.

Our question on this phase of the case then boils itself down to the following: can it be said as a matter of law that Yardley as president, chairman of the board, substantial stockholder and trustee and son-in-law of the estate of the major stockholder, had no power in the presence of the company's most interested vice president to secure for a "reasonable" length of time badly needed key personnel by promising an experienced local executive a life pension to commence in 30 years at the age of 60, even if Lee were not then working for the corporation, when the maximum liability to Jenkins under such a pension was $1500 per year.

A survey of the law on the authority of corporate officers does not reveal a completely consistent pattern. For the most part the courts perhaps have taken a rather restrictive view on the extent of powers of corporate officials, but the dissatisfaction with such an approach has been manifested in a variety of exceptions such as ratification, estoppel, and promissory estoppel. . . . For the most part also there has been limited discussion of the problem of apparent authority, perhaps on the assumption that if authority could not be implied from a continuing course of action between the corporation and the officer, it could not have been apparent to third parties either.

Such an assumption is ill-founded. The circumstances and facts known to exist between officer and corporation, from which actual authority may be implied, may be entirely different from those circumstances known to exist as between the third party and the corporation. The two concepts are separate and distinct even though the state of the proofs in a given case may cause considerable overlap.

* * *

The rule most widely cited is that the president only has authority to bind his company by acts arising in the usual and regular course of business but not for contracts of an "extraordinary" nature. The substance of such a rule lies in the content of the term "extraordinary" which is subject to a broad range of interpretation.

The growth and development of this rule occurred during the late nineteenth and early twentieth centuries when the potentialities of the corporate form of enterprise were just being realized. As the corporation became a more common vehicle for the conduct of business it became increasingly evident that many corporations, particularly small closely held ones, did not normally function in the formal ritualistic manner hitherto envisaged. While the boards of directors still nominally controlled corporate affairs, in reality officers and managers frequently ran the business with little, if any, board supervision. The natural consequence of such a development was that third parties commonly relied on the authority of such officials in almost all the multifarious transactions in which corporations engaged. The pace of modern business life was too swift to insist on the approval by the board of directors of every transaction that was in any way "unusual."

The judicial recognition given to these developments has varied considerably. Whether termed "apparent authority" or an "estoppel" to deny authority, many courts have noted the injustice caused by the practice of permitting corporations to act commonly through their executives and then allowing them to disclaim an agreement as beyond the authority of the contracting officer, when the contract no longer suited its convenience. Other courts, however, continued to cling to the past with little attempt to discuss the unconscionable results obtained or the doctrine of apparent authority. Such restrictive views have been generally condemned by the commentators.

The summary of holdings pro and con in general on the subject of what are and what are not "extraordinary" agreements is inconclusive at best, as shown by the authorities collected in the footnote.[16] But the pattern becomes more distinct when we turn to the more limited area of employment contracts.

---

[16] We note that the following acts have been held to be within either the implied or apparent authority of a corporate president or manager: borrowing money and executing a corporate note, *Petition of Mulco Products*, Super. Ct., 1956, 11 Terry 28, 50 Del. 28, 123 A.2d 95, *affirmed Mulco Products, Inc. v. Black*, 11 Terry 246, 50 Del. 246, 127 A.2d 851; *Shircliff v. Dixie Drive-in Theatre*, 1955, 7 Ill. App. 2d 370, 129 N.E.2d 346; *Kraft v. Freeman Printing & Publishing Ass'n*, 1881, 87 N.Y. 628; even though the moneys obtained might not be used for the benefit of the corporation, *Chestnut St. Trust & Savings Fund Co. v. Record Pub. Co.*, 1910, 227 Pa. 235, 75 A. 1067; pledging security for a loan, *Williams v. Hall*, 1926, 30 Ariz. 581, 249 P. 755; guaranteeing the note of another corporation, *Allis-Chalmers Mfg. Co. v. Citizens Bank & Trust Co.*, D.C.D. Idaho, 1924, 3 F.2d 316; purchasing merchandise, *Blackstone Theatre Corporation*

It is generally settled that the president as part of the regular course of business has authority to hire and discharge employees and fix their compensation. In so doing he may agree to hire them for a specific number of years if the term selected is deemed reasonable. But employment contracts for life or on a "permanent" basis are generally regarded as "extraordinary" and beyond the authority of any corporate executive if the only consideration for the promise is the employee's promise to work for that period. Jenkins would have us analogize the pension agreement involved herein to these generally condemned lifetime employment contracts because it extends over a long period of time, is of indefinite duration, and involves an indefinite liability on the part of the corporation.

It is not surprising that lifetime employment contracts have met with substantial hostility in the courts, for these contracts are often oral, uncorroborated, vague in important details and highly improbable. Accordingly, the courts have erected a veritable array of obstacles to their enforcement. They have been construed as terminable at will, too indefinite to enforce, *ultra vires*, lacking in mutuality or consideration, abandoned or breached by subsequent acts, and the supporting evidence deemed insufficient to go to the jury, as well as made without proper authority.

---

v. Goldwyn Distributing Corp., 1925, 86 Ind. App. 277, 146 N.E. 217; *White v. Elgin Creamery Co.*, 1899, 108 Iowa 522, 79 N.W. 283; authorizing an attorney to sue on a corporate claim, *Elblum Holding Corp. v. Mintz*, 1938, 120 N.J.L. 604, 1 A.2d 204; compromising a corporate claim, *Fair Mercantile Co. v. Union-May-Stern Co.*, 1949, 359 Mo. 385, 221 S.W.2d 751; making a tax closing agreement, *E. Van Noorden & Co. v. United States*, D.C.D. Mass, 1934, 8 F. Supp. 279; executing a time limitations waiver, *Philip Carey Mfg. Co. v. Dean*, 6 Cir., 1932, 58 F.2d 737, *certiorari denied*, 287 U.S. 623, 53 S. Ct. 78, 77 L. Ed. 541: *St. Clair v. Rutledge*, 1902, 115 Wis. 583, 92 N.W. 234; pledging a substantial contribution to a hospital, *Memorial Hospital Ass'n of Stanislaus County v. Pacific Grape Products Co.*, 1955, 45 Cal. 2d 634, 290 P.2d 481, 50 A.L.R.2d 442; licensing a factory spur track, *Anglim v. Sears-Roebuck Shoe Factories*, 1926, 255 Mass. 334, 151 N.E. 313; sale of the corporation's only property, *Jeppi v. Brockman Holding Co.*, 1949, 34 Cal. 2d 11, 206 P.2d 847, 9 A.L.R.2d 1299: of all its merchandise and fixtures, *Magowan v. Groneweg*, 1902, 16 S.D. 29, 91 N.W. 335; or its real estate, *Domestic Bldg. Ass'n v. Guadiano*, 1902, 195 Ill. 222, 63 N.E. 98.

On the other courts have left the question to the jury when the matter involved was: execution of a corporate note, *Citizens' Bank v. Public Drug Co.*, 1921, 190 Iowa 983, 181 N.W. 274; a promise of additional service, *Wichita Falls Electric Co. v. Huey*, Tex. Civ. App.1923, 246 S.W. 692; a promise to pay a stale debt, *Renault v. L. N. Renault & Sons, Inc.*, 3 Cir., 1951, 188 F.2d 317; entering a joint venture, *Lane v. National Ins. Agency*, 1934, 148 Or. 589, 37 P.2d 365; oral waiver of written contract provisions, *Van Dusen Aircraft Supplies v. Terminal Construction Corp.*, 1949, 3 N.J. 321, 70 A.2d 65; and sale of the corporation's sole asset, *C. B. Snyder Realty Co. v. National Newark & Essex Banking Co.*, 1953, 14 N.J. 146, 101 A.2d 544.

On the other hand authority has been found lacking in the following instances: sale of all the company's assets or its major asset, *Winsted Hosiery Co. v. New Britain Knitting Co.*, 1897, 69 Conn. 565, 38 A. 310; *Plant v. White River Lumber Co.*, 8 Cir., 1935, 76 F.2d 155; *Gabriel v. Auf Der-Heide-Aragona, Inc.*, 1951, 14 N.J. Super. 558, 82 A.2d 644; a brokerage contract to effectuate a merger, *Abraham Lincoln Life Ins. Co. v. Hopwood*, 6 Cir., 1936, 81 F.2d 284, *certiorari denied*, 298 U.S. 687, 56 S. Ct. 955, 80 L. Ed. 1406; modification of directors' resolutions, *McMillan v. Dozier*, 1952, 257 Ala. 435, 59 So. 2d 563; *Miller v. Wick Bldg. Co.*, 1950, 154 Ohio St. 93, 93 N.E.2d 467; *Foley v. Wabasha-Nelson Bridge Co.*, 1940, 207 Minn. 399, 291 N.W. 903; *Sattler v. Howe Rubber Corp.*, Ct. Err. & App. 1923, 98 N.J.L. 460, 121 A. 523; employing an architect in a major construction project, *Colish v. Brandywine Raceway Ass'n, Inc.*, Super. Ct., 1955, 10 Terry 493, 49 Del. 493, 119 A.2d 887; giving away corporate property, *Fawcett v. New Haven Organ Co.*, 1879, 47 Conn. 224; *Sayre Land Co. v. Borough of Sayre*, 1956, 384 Pa. 534, 121 A.2d 579; postponing a mortgage foreclosure, *Myrtle Ave. Corp. v. Mt. Prospect B. & L. Ass'n*, Ct. Err. & App., 1934, 112 N.J.L. 60, 169 A. 707; suing the corporation's chief stockholder, *Ney v. Eastern Iowa Telephone Co.*, 1913, 162 Iowa 525, 144 N.W. 383; guaranteeing the debt of another, *First National Bank of Mason City v. Cement Products Co.*, 1929, 209 Iowa 358, 227 N.W. 908; and contracts deemed unconscionable from the corporation's point of view, *Bowditch, Furniture Co. v. Jones*, 1901, 74 Conn. 149, 50 A. 41; *Schwartz v. United Merchants & Manufacturers*, 2 Cir., 1934, 72 F.2d 256; *Bassick v. Aetna Explosives Co.*, D.C.S.D.N.Y. 1917, 246 F. 974.

However, at times such contracts have been enforced where the circumstances tended to support the plausibility of plaintiff's testimony. Thus when the plaintiff was injured in the course of employment and he agreed to settle his claim of negligence against the company for a lifetime job, authority has been generally found and the barrage of other objections adequately disposed of. And where additional consideration was given such as quitting other employment, giving up a competing business, or where the services were "peculiarly necessary" to the corporation, the courts have divided on the enforceability of the contract.

What makes the point now under discussion particularly interesting is the failure of the courts denying authority to make lifetime contracts to evolve any guiding principle. More often than not we find a mere statement that the contract is "extraordinary" with a citation of cases which say the same thing, without giving reasons. And even in some of the leading cases the question of apparent authority is not even mentioned. All this is a not uncommon indication that the law in a particular area is in a state of evolution, and there seems every reason to believe that the law affecting numerous features of employer-employee relationship, is far from static.

Where reasons have been given to support the conclusion that lifetime employments are "extraordinary," and hence made without authority, a scrutiny of these reasons may be helpful for their bearing on the analogous field of pension agreements. It is said that: they unduly restrict the power of the shareholders and future boards of directors on questions of managerial policy; they subject the corporation to an inordinately substantial amount of liability; they run for long and indefinite periods of time. Of these reasons the only one applicable to pension agreements is that they run for long and indefinite periods of time. There the likeness stops. Future director or shareholder control is in no way impeded; the amount of liability is not disproportionate; the agreement was not only not unreasonable but beneficial and necessary to the corporation; and pension contracts are commonly used fringe benefits in employment contracts. Moreover, unlike the case with life employment contracts, courts have often gone out of their way to find pension promises binding and definite even when labeled gratuitous by the employer. The consideration given to the employee involved is not at all dependent on profits or sales, nor does it involve some other variable suggesting director discretion.

In this case Lee was hired at a starting salary of $4,000 per year plus a contemplated pension of $1500 per year in thirty years. Had Lee been hired at a starting salary of $10,000 per year the cost to the corporation over the long run would have been substantially greater, yet no one could plausibly contend that such an employment contract was beyond Yardley's authority.

* * *

Apparent authority is essentially a question of fact. It depends not only on the nature of the contract involved, but the officer negotiating it, the corporation's usual manner of conducting business, the size of the corporation and the number of its stockholders, the circumstances that give rise to the contract, the reasonableness of the contract, the amounts involved, and who the contracting third party is, to list a few but not all of the relevant factors. In certain instances a given contract may be so important to the welfare of the corporation that outsiders would naturally suppose that only the board of directors (or even the shareholders) could properly handle it. It is in this light that the "ordinary course of business" rule should be given its content. Beyond such "extraordinary" acts, whether or not apparent authority exists is simply a matter of fact.

Accordingly, we hold that, assuming there was sufficient proof of the making of the pension agreement, Connecticut, in the particular circumstances of this case, would probably take the view that reasonable men could differ on the subject of whether or not Yardley had apparent authority to make the contract, and that the trial court erred in deciding the question as a matter of law. We do not think Connecticut would adopt any hard and fast rule against apparent authority to make pension agreements generally, on the theory that they were in the same category as lifetime employment contracts.

* * *

HAND, Circuit Judge (concurring in part and dissenting in part).

* * *

I cannot agree that Yardley, as president of the corporation, had authority to make a contract that was to last for the life of the promisee. I have not indeed found any decision in Connecticut that decides that question; but in New York, New Jersey, Maryland, Iowa, Wyoming and West Virginia the law is settled and in Texas the same limitation was even imposed on the president's authority to make a contract for three years. . . . Since the Connecticut courts have indicated no disposition to the contrary, I assume that they would follow so generally accepted a doctrine. There being no relevant corporate by-law, I would say that the accepted doctrine is the law of Connecticut. . . . For this reason I think that the complaint in the action against the corporation was rightly dismissed.

* * *

NOTES AND QUESTIONS

(1) **Other illustrations.** *Management Technologies, Inc. v. Morris*[19] held that, although the CEO's filing of insolvency proceedings for two subsidiaries is a major and unusual step that cannot be characterized as in the ordinary course of business, the law of agency suggests that "corporate officers, acting in good faith and with reasonable discretion, implicitly are empowered to protect the corporation where emergency or necessity requires action beyond their usual and regular authority."[20] *Grimes v. Alteon*[21] invalidated a CEO's promise of 10% of the corporation's future private stock offering to a stockholder, where there had been no approval of the agreement by the board of directors under Del. G.C.L. § 157 and the promise was not memorialized in a written instrument.

---

[19]   961 F. Supp. 640 (S.D.N.Y. 1997).

[20]   *Id.* at 648.

[21]   804 A.2d 256 (Del. 2002).

(2) **Variations on *Jenkins*.** What result in *Jenkins* if Lee were suing Jenkins to enforce an alleged promise by Yardley to employ Lee for five years at his current salary plus 20% of the profits of the business? Could Yardley bind Jenkins to a contract to sell the Bridgeport plant even without express authorization from the board of directors?

PROBLEMS

(1) The Jones Coal Mining Company owns ten coal-bearing properties and leases them to firms which extract the coal. Your client, Black Gold, is a coal mining company that wishes to lease one of these properties. The president of Black Gold negotiates a five-year lease upon terms which are standard in the industry with Robert Jones, the president and 50% shareholder of Jones. The lease is in writing and signed by Robert Jones as president of Jones Coal Mining Company. Robert Jones has assured Black Gold that he has authority to enter into the lease and has produced as proof of this a copy of the bylaws of the company that state: "The President shall be the chief executive officer of the Corporation and shall give general supervision and direction to the affairs of the Corporation, subject to the direction of the Board of Directors." When your client requested more proof of authority from Jones' board of directors, Robert Jones responded by saying that the board could not be convened for at least another month. Black Gold asks your advice as to the possibility that the contract may not be binding on Jones Coal. The client does not want to wait a month and possibly lose this lease. At the same time, it is worried that after it moves equipment onto the site, Jones Coal may try to back out and renegotiate in a rising coal market. What advice would you give?[22]

(2) How would it affect your answer to Problem (1) if Robert Jones had said that the board had approved the transaction and produced a copy of a resolution of the board of directors, certified by the secretary of the corporation, which authorized the lease with Black Gold?[23]

REFERENCES

Kempin, *The Corporate Officer and the Law of Agency,* 44 VA. L. REV. 1273 (1958).
Note, *Inherent Power as a Basis of a Corporate Officer's Authority to Contract,* 57 COLUM. L. REV. 868 (1957).

---

[22] *See Har-Bel Coal Co. v. Asher Coal Mining Co.,* 414 S.W.2d 128 (Ky. Ct. App. 1967).

[23] *See In re Drive-In Development Corp.,* 371 F.2d 215 (7th Cir. 1966), *cert. denied sub nom. Creditors' Committee of Drive-In Development Corp. v. National Boulevard Bank,* 387 U.S. 909 (1967).

§ 8.04 The *Ultra Vires* Doctrine

Certificates of incorporation and corporation statutes generally limit the purposes for which the corporation is being formed and include a statement of the powers it can exercise. An *ultra vires* act by a corporate officer or agent is one which goes beyond these purposes and powers. This Section considers the consequences of *ultra vires* acts, particularly for third parties dealing with corporations.

In the earliest cases, an *ultra vires* act by a corporate officer or agent could have disastrous consequences for third parties. For example, in *Ashbury Railway Carriage & Iron Co. v. Riche*,[24] the court let a corporation escape liability on an *ultra vires* contract, even though the contract had been unanimously ratified by the shareholders. These early cases can be best understood by placing them in their historical context. Early corporations, with their fictional legal personality and unlimited liability, were viewed suspiciously. Limiting powers and purposes was one way to keep early corporations on a leash. In other words, the law of *ultra vires* was regarded not as a limitation on management's authority to act *vis-a-vis* the shareholders, but as a limitation on the state's permission to do business.

During the last hundred years, judicial decisions have greatly eroded the importance of the law of *ultra vires*, especially for third parties doing business with the corporation. First, courts have minimized the likelihood of finding an act *ultra vires* to the corporation by, for example, reading into corporate charters broad implied powers to do things in aid of the stated purposes, such as letting a company organized to do railway business operate a resort hotel[25] and an automobile manufacturer operate a smelting plant.[26] Second, even when courts have found particular acts to be *ultra vires*, they have taken steps to prevent corporations from using those acts as a basis for escaping their obligations to third parties. For example, courts have enforced fully executed *ultra vires* contracts, as well as contracts that were unanimously approved by the shareholders (so long as there is no harm to nonconsenting creditors). As a result, the law of *ultra vires* has come to be regarded as a limitation on management's authority to act *vis-a-vis* the shareholders, not as a limitation on the corporation's power to do business.

The diminished importance and changed nature of the law of *ultra vires* that evolved through judicial decisions is now reflected in modern corporate statutes in effect in many states. Among other things, these statutory provisions obviate the *ultra vires* problem by very generally setting forth corporate powers (*see* Del. G.C.L. §§ 121-123) and by permitting corporations to broadly state their purpose in their charters (*see* Del. G.C.L. § 102(a)(3)).[27] In addition, these statutes clarify to some extent the consequences of *ultra vires* acts, making clear that corporations will rarely, if ever, be

---

[24] 7 L.R.-E. & I. App. 653 (1875).

[25] *Jacksonville, Mayport, Pablo Railway & Navigation Co. v. Hooper*, 160 U.S. 514 (1896).

[26] *Dodge v. Ford Motor Co.*, 204 Mich. 459, 170 N.W. 668 (1919).

[27] Corporations may draft narrower purpose clauses, as where two corporations form a limited joint venture. However, it may be risky to limit the corporation's *powers*, since a court could find that a power not mentioned was

permitted to assert *ultra vires* acts as a basis for escaping obligations to third parties doing business with the corporation. *See* Del. G.C.L. § 124; MBCA § 3.04; and the *Goodman* case, below.[28] Finally, these statutes underscore the modern role of the law of *ultra vires* as a limitation on management's authority by expressly leaving shareholders free to sue officers or directors responsible for *ultra vires* acts under the common law by analogy to an agent's liability for unauthorized acts (*see* RESTATEMENT (SECOND) OF AGENCY, § 401 (1965)) or under a breach of fiduciary duty theory (*see* Chapter 9).

Despite the advent of common law doctrines and corporate statutes that reduce the importance of the law of *ultra vires*, the *ultra vires* issue might still arise today in connection with certain types of transactions that are inconsistent with the general profit-making purpose of the corporation: (1) suits by shareholders against management concerning charitable contributions by the corporation; (2) pension payments to former employees or their families; and (3) credit transactions obligating the corporation for the benefit of a third party.

In charitable gift cases, the courts have upheld the payment as against an *ultra vires* claim (usually brought by a shareholder against the responsible officers or directors) if the gift was not very large in relation to the corporation's assets and was at least of some incidental benefit to the corporation. A leading case is *A.P. Smith Manufacturing Co. v. Barlow*[29] in which the court upheld a $1500 gift by a valve manufacturer to Princeton University. This matter is now covered by statute in many jurisdictions, including Del. G.C.L. § 122(10) which confers the power to "[m]ake donations for the public welfare or for charitable, scientific or educational purposes."

As in charitable gift cases, *ultra vires* claims in pension cases usually have been brought by a shareholder against the directors. For example, in *Moore v. Keystone Macaroni Manufacturing Co.*,[30] the court invalidated a board resolution authorizing large payments to the widow of the deceased founder of the company. While pensions, like charity, involve at least a remote benefit to the corporation (in the form of incentives to current employees) there may be a clearer conflict of interest on the part of the board of directors, which raises a fiduciary duty issue.

The following case deals with the third category of *ultra vires* transactions— credit transactions obligating the corporation for the benefit of a third party.

---

implicitly excluded even if the power was exercised in aid of one of the corporation's purposes. *See* Bromberg, *Corporate Organizational Documents and Securities—Forms and Comments Revised,* 30 Sw. L.J. 961, 964-965, nn. 7-8 (1976).

[28] *But see Inter-Continental Corp. v. Moody*, 411 S.W.2d 578 (Tex. Civ. App. 1967) (suggesting that an *ultra vires* debt may be reduced to the extent of the objecting shareholder's interest in the corporation).

[29] 13 N.J. 145, 98 A.2d 581, *app. dism.*, 346 U.S. 861 (1953).

[30] 370 Pa. 172, 87 A.2d 295 (1952).

GOODMAN v. LADD ESTATE CO.
Oregon Supreme Court
246 Or. 621, 427 P.2d 102 (1967)

LUSK, Justice.

Plaintiffs brought this suit to enjoin the defendant Ladd Estate Company, a Washington corporation, from enforcing a guaranty agreement executed by Westover Tower, Inc., a corporation, in favor of Ladd Estate. From a decree dismissing the suit plaintiffs appeal.

In 1961 the defendant Walter T. Liles held all the common shares of Westover and he, Dr. Edmond F. Wheatley and Samuel H. Martin were its directors.

On September 8, 1961, Dr. Wheatley borrowed $10,000 from Citizens Bank of Oregon and gave his promissory note therefor, which was endorsed by Ladd Estate. Contemporaneously with this transaction Liles, individually, and Westover, by Liles as president, and Martin, as secretary, executed an agreement in writing by which they unconditionally guaranteed Ladd Estate against loss arising out of the latter's endorsement of the Wheatley note to Citizens Bank. The agreement was also signed by Ladd Estate. It recited that it was made at the request of Liles and Westover and that Ladd Estate would not have guaranteed payment of the Wheatley note without the guarantee of Liles and Westover to Ladd Estate.

Wheatley defaulted on his note, Ladd Estate paid to Citizens Bank the amount owing thereon, $9,583.61, and demanded reimbursement from Westover. Upon the latter's rejection of the demand Ladd filed an action at law upon the guaranty agreement against Liles and Westover.

The plaintiffs Morton J. Goodman and Edith Goodman, husband and wife, came into the case in this manner: On September 27, 1963, plaintiffs purchased all the common shares of Westover from a receiver appointed by the Circuit Court for Multnomah County who was duly authorized to make such sale. At the time of such purchase, plaintiffs were fully aware of the guaranty agreement given by Westover and Liles to Ladd Estate. It is conceded that the guaranty agreement was *ultra vires* the corporation. Plaintiffs, as stockholders, brought this suit pursuant to the provisions of ORS 57.040 [which was identical to Del. G.C.L. § 124].

* * *

It will be noticed that the court may set aside and enjoin the performance of the *ultra vires* contract if it deems such a course equitable. Plaintiffs argue that to deny them the relief they seek would be "shocking," because Westover executed the guaranty agreement in order to enable one of its directors, Wheatley, to obtain a loan of money to be used for purposes entirely foreign to any corporate purpose. We see nothing shocking or even inequitable about it. The corporation was organized for the purposes, among others, to engage in the business of providing housing for rent or sale and to obtain contracts of mortgage insurance from the Federal Housing Commissioner, pursuant to the provisions of the National Housing Act, 12 U.S.C.A. § 1701 *et seq.* Authorized capital stock comprised 30,100 shares of which 100 shares, having a par value of $1 per share and designated preferred stock, were issued to the Commissioner, pursuant to § 1743(b)(1), U.S.C.A. and 30,000 shares, having a par value of $1 per share and designated common stock, were issued to Liles. Voting rights of the shareholders were vested exclusively in the holders of the common stock. The guaranty agreement recites that, at the request of Liles and Westover, Ladd Estate guaranteed payment of the Wheatley note. Ladd Estate made good on its endorsement when Wheatley defaulted and now calls upon Westover to honor its obligation. The agent of the plaintiffs, who purchased the shares for them, testified that he considered the question whether the guaranty was a valid obligation of the corporation before making the purchase and concluded that it was not. The fact that he guessed wrong does not in any way enhance plaintiffs' claims to equitable consideration.

Neither would it be inequitable to enforce the agreement because of the purpose which the guaranty was intended to serve. Even before the enactment of ORS 57.040 a corporation might properly enter into a guaranty agreement in the legitimate furtherance of its business or purposes[.] . . . That the agreement does not further such purposes is what makes it *ultra vires*. But the statute says the agreement is enforceable even though *ultra vires*, and to accept the plaintiffs' argument would be to say that because it is *ultra vires* the agreement is inequitable and, therefore, unenforceable. This would effectually emasculate the statute.

Moreover, plaintiffs are in no position to invoke the aid of a court of equity. Liles, the former holder of their shares—all the voting shares of Westover—induced Ladd Estate to endorse Wheatley's note by procuring Westover to execute the guaranty agreement. If a shareholder himself has participated in the ultra vires act he cannot thereafter attack it as *ultra vires*. . . . This would seem to be emphatically so of a shareholder who exercises the entire voting power of the corporation. Plaintiffs, as purchasers of Liles' shares, are in no better position than he would have been to raise the question.

* * *

It should be added that no rights of creditors of Westover are involved and there is nothing to indicate that the security of any mortgage guaranteed by the Federal Housing Commissioner would be impaired by enforcement of the agreement here in question.

* * *

We are of the opinion that plaintiffs are not entitled to equitable relief. The decree is affirmed.

PROBLEMS

What result under *Goodman* in each of the following situations?

(1) The plaintiffs had been minority shareholders of Westover at the time of the guaranty but were wholly unaware of the transaction until sometime later.

(2) The plaintiffs had purchased, with full knowledge of the guaranty, the interest of a minority shareholder who was unaware of the guaranty at the time it was entered into.

(3) The plaintiffs were unaware of the guaranty at the time they purchased Liles' interest.

(4) The plaintiff had been the FHA, which claimed that the security of its guaranteed mortgages had been impaired by the corporation's guarantee.

REFERENCE

Note, Ultra Vires *Corporate Credit Transactions,* 83 U. PA. L. REV. 479 (1935).

CHAPTER 9

Fiduciary Duties of Managers

As discussed in Chapters 4 through 8, partners and corporate managers often can commit their firms to acts or transactions without the consent of some, or even a majority, of the owners. As a result, decision-makers in firms may not bear the full effects of their decisions. Economists call this an "agency cost" problem (*see* Section 1.02[D]). This problem is pervasive, and is not limited to corporations or other firms. For example, a doctor who decides whether to operate on someone else's knee acts as an agent in the economic sense that the owner of the knee has delegated discretion over the use of the owner's "property" to the doctor. In firms, agency costs are constrained by such methods as the owners' power to fire managers or to exit the firm. These mechanisms alone usually do not, however, reduce agency costs to zero.

This gives rise to an additional agency-cost-reducing device—a legally enforceable "fiduciary duty" to act selflessly on the beneficiary's behalf. This Chapter discusses the extent of that duty, while Chapter 10 discusses liability for its breach.

§ 9.01 Introduction to Fiduciary Duties

[A] The Nature of Fiduciary Duties

[1] What Is a Fiduciary Duty?

The precise terms of fiduciary duties, at least as they have been defined in the business association context, will be described throughout this Chapter. For present purposes it is enough to note the general nature of the duty by quoting the most famous description, from Justice Cardozo's opinion in *Meinhard v. Salmon*:[1]

> Many forms of conduct permissible in a workaday world for those acting at arm's length, are forbidden to those bound by fiduciary ties. A trustee is held to something stricter than the morals of the market place. Not honesty alone, but the punctilio of an honor the most sensitive, is then the standard of behavior.

In other words, while non-fiduciaries who contract with each other can engage in "conduct permissible in a workaday world for those acting at arm's length," a *fiduciary* must act selflessly, with the "finest loyalty" to the beneficiary's interests.

---

[1] 164 N.E. 545 (N.Y. 1928).

As discussed throughout this Chapter, the line between the selfless conduct of a fiduciary and the selfish conduct of ordinary contracting parties may not be evident in many cases. But Justice Cardozo's language at least states the general nature of the duty.

[2] The Contractual Nature of Fiduciary Duties

Fiduciary duties can be viewed as a default, or "standard form," term that courts add to certain types of agency-type relationships. This raises the question whether fiduciary duties are basically contractual in nature, like other types of default terms. Commentators have hotly debated the "contractual" nature of fiduciary duties. On the one hand, fiduciary duties are not usually hammered out in one-on-one negotiations. Rather, they are usually imposed by courts through application of general rules that, at least on the surface, appear to have little to do with the parties' bargain.

On the other hand, fiduciary duties arguably are fundamentally contractual in the sense that, irrespective of how they arise or are characterized by the courts, they are ultimately determined by the parties' agreement. This is evident from the fact that courts recognize "fiduciary duties" only when parties have elected to enter into certain types of agency-like or trust-like contracts where it is appropriate to require a party who controls another's property to act in the other's interests.[2] The contractual nature of fiduciary duties also is evident from the fact that fiduciary duties are often determined by the express and implied terms of the particular contract. This insight underlies Justice Frankfurter's famous phrase that characterizing a person as a fiduciary "only begins analysis; it gives direction to further inquiry."[3]

[3] What Is a Fiduciary Relationship?

Fiduciary duties exist only in fiduciary relationships. Many contractual relationships at least resemble fiduciary relationships in the critical respect that one party delegates significant power over her property that would seem to require some fiduciary-type constraint. This could include, for example, the doctor-patient situation mentioned in the introduction to this Chapter, lawyer-client, franchiser-franchisee (*see* the *Nichols* case in Section 2.01, above), and so forth. The question in these cases is not whether there should be some duty, but whether the duty should be the sort of *fiduciary* duty of selfless conduct this Chapter describes. In answering this question it is necessary to consider not only the benefits of a fiduciary constraint, but also the costs. In particular, fiduciary duties are onerous responsibilities that one would ordinarily not

---

[2]   *See United States v. Chestman*, 947 F.2d 551 (2d Cir. 1991) (*en banc*) (Winter, J., concurring and dissenting), *cert. den.*, 112 S. Ct. 1759 (1992).

[3]   *SEC v. Chenery Corp.*, 318 U.S. 80, 85 (1943).

undertake without some reward or compensation. Imposing this cost is inefficient if other, less potent, constraints would provide adequate protection.

An example of a relationship in the business association setting that does *not* trigger fiduciary duties is the lender-borrower relationship (*see* Section 11.04).[4] Among the reasons suggested for distinguishing owners from creditors with respect to fiduciary duties is that creditors have alternative contractual protections, such as the right to specific payouts, to help ensure that debtors do not misuse the money lent to them. This suggests that courts considering fiduciary duties are attempting to anticipate the cost-benefit tradeoffs for which the parties themselves would have contracted in the absence of transaction costs.

[4] Distinguishing Fiduciary Duties from the Obligation of "Good Faith"

Fiduciary duties should be distinguished from the general contractual obligation of "good faith" which is studied in most contracts courses. These are recognized particularly in long-term, open-ended, contractual relationships. The duty of "good faith" bars contracting parties from opportunistically pressing contract terms to their advantage in order to free contracting parties from the need to take costly self-protective action. Unlike fiduciary duties, the "good faith" obligation does not generally force contracting parties to sacrifice their own interests in making or enforcing bargains. For example, in *Market Street Associates Limited Partnership v. Frey*,[5] Judge Posner held that a lessee had no duty to point out to a lessor that its turning down financing would trigger an obligation under the lease to sell the property for less than market value.

REFERENCES

Coffee, *The Mandatory/Enabling Balance in Corporate Law: An Essay on the Judicial Role*, 89 COLUM. L. REV. 1618 (1989).

Cooter & Freedman, *The Fiduciary Relationship: Its Economic Character and Legal Consequences*, 66 N.Y.U. L. REV. 1045 (1991).

DeMott, *Beyond Metaphor: An Analysis of Fiduciary Obligation*, 1988 DUKE L.J. 879.

Easterbrook & Fischel, *Contract and Fiduciary Duty*, 36 J.L. & ECON. 425 (1993).

Frankel, *Fiduciary Law*, 71 CALIF. L. REV. 795 (1983).

Ribstein, *Fiduciary Duty Contracts In Unincorporated Firms*, 54 WASH. & LEE L. REV. 537 (1997).

---

[4] *See Kham & Nate's Shoes No. 2 v. First Bank of Whiting*, 908 F.2d 1351 (7th Cir. 1990).

[5] 941 F.2d 58 (7th Cir. 1991).

[B] The Appropriate Scope of Fiduciary Duties

This Chapter deals with relationships between corporate managers and share-holders that are clearly fiduciary in nature. The main question in such cases is the scope of fiduciary duties rather than their existence. As a basis for answering this question, this section analyzes the potential benefits and costs of implying legally enforceable fiduciary duties in the corporate context.

[1] Benefits of Fiduciary Duties

In general, the function of fiduciary duties is to help ensure that agents act con-sistently with their principals' interests—that is, to reduce agency costs. More specifi-cally, because shareholders and other equity owners are entitled to what is left after paying fixed claims, they want the managers of the firm's assets to maximize the value of the firm and minimize the amounts paid to other claimants (including creditors and the managers themselves). A legally enforceable fiduciary duty of managers helps own-ers achieve this goal. It does so by providing a general contractual term—a requirement that managers act on behalf of owners—that courts can define on a case-by-case basis, thereby freeing owners from having to draft detailed contracts specifying the huge vari-ety of actions that managers can and cannot take.

[2] Alternatives to Fiduciary Duties

In assessing the benefits of fiduciary duties, it is important to note that agents' dis-cretion can be constrained by devices other than fiduciary duties—*i.e.*, that managers will not necessarily wholly disregard owner interests in the absence of legally enforce-able fiduciary duties. The question, then, is whether fiduciary duties (operating alone or in tandem with other devices) are a better cost-benefit tradeoff than the alternative devices, including the following:

(a) **The Market for Corporate Control and the Power to Dissolve the Firm.** In publicly held firms, the combination of owner voting rights and the efficient stock mar-ket put inefficient or dishonest managers at risk of being replaced by tender offer (*see* Section 7.02[A]). Comparable discipline is provided in closely held firms by the minor-ity's power to exit and dissolve the firm (*see* Sections 4.04 (partnerships) and 5.05 (close corporations)).

(b) **Capital Markets.** Managers are also disciplined by the capital markets. Lax governance can reduce the price of a firm's stock and increase the interest it must pay on its debt. This makes it more difficult for managers to finance projects by selling equity or borrowing money. In other words, the capital markets can punish bad man-agers not only by removing them from office (*see* (a), above), but also by reducing the assets under their control.

(c) **Internal and External Monitoring.** Management inefficiency is checked by monitoring within the managerial hierarchy by other managers, outside directors and auditors (*see* Section 7.07[A]).

(d) **Incentive Compensation.** Executive compensation can be structured to align the interests of owners and managers. For example, managers compensated by stock options gain, along with the firm's shareholders, as the firm does better and its stock price rises (*see* Section 9.05).

(e) **Reputational Constraints.** Executives spend a lifetime developing a reputation for probity and efficiency which has value in the market for managerial services. This investment in reputation is lost if managers act dishonestly or carelessly.

(f) **Shareholder Voting.** Managers' power in connection with certain matters is limited to recommending them. See Section 5.01, above, discussing the power of shareholders to approve certificate amendments, mergers, dissolutions, or sales of all or substantially all of the corporate assets. Thus, shareholders can, in effect, withdraw discretion from managers by voting directly on these corporate acts.

[3] Costs of Fiduciary Duties

Even if agency costs cannot be effectively reduced by the other mechanisms discussed above, fiduciary duties still may not be appropriate. This is because the costs of enforcing fiduciary duties may exceed the benefits of reduced agency costs. Some of the costs connected with the enforcement of fiduciary duties are considered below:

(a) **Managerial Risk Aversion.** Fiduciary duties can negate the potential benefits from specialization of managerial and risk-bearing functions in the standard corporate form. This specialization of functions places risk on those who can bear it most efficiently—passive investors with diversified investment portfolios—and gives management powers to those with specialized management skills. Managers cannot effectively diversify away the substantial risk of liability for business decisions that accompanies vague and unpredictable liability rules. Legally enforceable fiduciary duties therefore may make managers more risk-averse in their decisionmaking than the fully diversified owners would want them to be. Among other things, managers may tend to do only those things that have received a judicial stamp of approval and shy away from exercising their own judgment. Alternatively, managers may be willing to exercise discretion in decisionmaking, but demand extra compensation for their services.

(b) **Litigation Costs.** Litigation enforcing fiduciary duties absorbs executive and staff time and energy and can strain the relationship between the firm and managers who are crucial to the firm's success. Litigation can be so costly that minority owners may be able to, in effect, veto corporate transactions by threatening to sue.

(c) **Interference with Other Monitoring Mechanisms.** Fiduciary duties may, in effect, frustrate the sensitive tradeoffs the parties have made in their contracts. For example, the parties may have provided for costly monitoring by auditors or incentive compensation, or for shareholder control of certain decisions, as an alternative to fiduciary duties. Imposing fiduciary duties on top of these constraints in effect wastes the resources spent on these other mechanisms. Also, fear of potential fiduciary duty liability may prevent the firm from allocating benefits to the managers as part of an incentive compensation package.

[4] Balancing Costs and Benefits

Mechanisms like those discussed in [2] above leave some "slack" for managers that may be taken up by fiduciary duties. However, fiduciary duties are not justified merely because other incentive and monitoring devices fail to cause managers to act entirely in owners' interests, since the costs of fiduciary duties may still outweigh the benefits. The balance between costs and benefits of legally enforceable fiduciary duties may differ depending upon the context (*i.e.*, the type of manager, the type of firm, or the type of potential misconduct). Three contrasting situations illustrate this principle.

First, it might seem necessary to impose fiduciary duties on managers who are working in a "final period" before retirement. Because these managers need not fear the loss of their jobs, they may act so as to increase their immediate compensation (*e.g.*, by increasing short-term accounting earnings used for computing bonuses) but contrary to the firm's long-run interests.

Second, consider the case of "one-shot" fraud—that is, the manager who decides to take a once-in-a-lifetime chance for riches whatever the risk to her career. This manager is obviously not much deterred by the threat of being fired or of losing a bonus or payoff from stock options. Moreover, a clever enough thief can "fly below the radar" of the standard monitoring devices, such as the market for corporate control. Legally enforceable fiduciary duties crafted to address this kind of misconduct—for example, a rule creating legal liability for intentional fraud—may therefore be appropriate.

Third, consider the manager who takes steps to insulate herself from the market for control by unilaterally acting to prevent shareholders from transferring control. The manager's job retention motive may outweigh any fears about reduction in compensation. A rule that creates legal liability whenever managers engage in moves of this sort may, therefore, be consistent with shareholder interests (*see* Chapter 14).

In general, therefore, "standard form" fiduciary duties may be an appropriate constraint on management. But the appropriate level of such duties and the precise circumstances under which they should be applied depends on the costs and benefits of both fiduciary duties and other agency-cost-reducing mechanisms.

[C] Overview of Chapter

Most of this Chapter is concerned with showing what duties courts imply in particular corporate and non-corporate contexts. It first discusses the principal situations in which "standard form" duties of managers of business firms have been recognized: (1) failure to exercise due care in supervising conduct of others in the corporation (Section 9.02); (2) failure to exercise due care in connection with disinterested business decisions (Section 9.03); (3) transactions in which managers engage in self dealing (Sections 9.04 and 9.05); (4) diversions by managers of business opportunities that properly belong to the firm (Section 9.06); and (5) parent-subsidiary transactions (Section 9.07). These sections emphasize corporate officers and directors, while Section 9.08 discusses some parallel issues in unincorporated firms. The Chapter concludes, in Section 9.09, with a discussion of the important question of the extent to which investors and managers can write contracts that opt out of standard form fiduciary duties.

REFERENCES

Brudney, *Corporate Governance, Agency Costs, and the Rhetoric of Contract*, 85 COLUM. L. REV. 1403 (1985).

Butler & Ribstein, *Opting out of Fiduciary Duties: A Response to the Anti-Contractarians*, 65 WASH. L. REV. 1 (1990).

Clark, *Agency Costs versus Fiduciary Duties*, in PRINCIPALS AND AGENTS: THE STRUCTURE OF BUSINESS (Pratt and Zeckhauser, eds., 1985).

Coffee, *No Exit?: Opting Out, The Contractual Theory of the Corporation, and the Special Case of Remedies*, 53 BROOK. L. REV. 919 (1988).

DeMott, *Beyond Metaphor: An Analysis of Fiduciary Obligation*, 1988 DUKE L.J. 879.

Easterbrook & Fischel, *Contract and Fiduciary Duty*, 36 J.L. & ECON. 425 (1993).

Eisenberg, *The Structure of Corporation Law*, 89 COLUM. L. REV. 1461 (1989).

Fischel & Bradley, *The Role of Liability Rules and the Derivative Suit in Corporate Law: A Theoretical and Empirical Analysis*, 71 CORNELL L. REV. 261 (1986).

Romano, *The Shareholder Suit: Litigation Without Foundation?*, 7 J.L. ECON. & ORG. 55 (1991).

§ 9.02 The Duty of Care: Failure to Supervise

The *duty of care* of corporate directors and officers is usually defined in terms that are similar to those used in negligence cases, including cases involving professional malpractice. For example, ALI *Principles* § 4.01(a) provides that a director or officer shall perform her "functions in good faith, in a manner that . . . she reasonably believes to be in the best interests of the corporation, and with the care that an ordinarily prudent person would reasonably be expected to exercise in a like position and under similar circumstances."

The MBCA, however, rejects an "ordinarily prudent person" standard. The drafters contend that such a standard mistakenly implies that duties of corporate managers are governed by ordinary tort law principles.[6] Accordingly, the MBCA requires directors to discharge their duties "with the care that *a person in a like position* would reasonably believe appropriate under similar circumstances."[7]

This Section discusses the application of the duty of care to cases in which the directors, rather than making a mistake in something they did, failed to supervise the conduct of others in the corporation (including co-directors). Section 9.03 discusses the application of the duty of care to conscious "disinterested business decisions" of directors.

FEDERAL DEPOSIT INSURANCE CORPORATION v. BIERMAN
United States Court of Appeals, Seventh Circuit
2 F.3d 1424 (1993)

RIPPLE, Circuit Judge.

In November 1985, after a lengthy investigation of the faltering Allen County Bank (ACB) in Fort Wayne, Indiana, the Indiana Department of Financial Institutions (DFI) began liquidation proceedings and the Federal Deposit Insurance Corporation (FDIC) was appointed receiver. On November 27, 1987, the FDIC filed suit against seven former directors and officers of ACB. It alleged breaches of common law and statutory duties that resulted in losses to the bank. The case was tried to the bench in July 1991, and judgment was entered in the amount of $574,809.36 against the defendants, jointly and severally, with regard to three of the eight groups of loans that were at issue. *Federal Deposit Ins. Corp. v. Stanley*, 770 F. Supp. 1281(N.D. Ind. 1991). For the reasons that follow, we affirm the judgment of the district court.

I. BACKGROUND

A. *Pre-Closure and Closure Events*

As early as August 1981, the FDIC began to examine ACB's financial condition and issued a Report of Examination indicating that the classified assets of the bank had risen to 124.2% of total capital and reserves. The FDIC termed this state of affairs "staggering" and cautioned ACB that its loan portfolio was in poor condition, that better quality loans must be acquired, and that the directors must "adequately monitor the lending function." *Stanley*, 770 F. Supp. at 1285. On February 10, 1982, the FDIC and the DFI entered into a Memorandum of Understanding with ACB requiring, among other things, a 50% reduction of substandard loans within 360 days and the provision of loan servicing and collection policies.

Despite these warnings, ACB continued to deteriorate. On September 11, 1982, the FDIC began to examine ACB.[4] The FDIC Report of Examination was issued on November

---

[6]   MBCA § 8.30(b), Official Comment 2.

[7]   MBCA § 8.30(b) (emphasis added).

[4]   The FDIC's concerns were discussed at a meeting of the ACB Board of Directors held on October 5, 1982.

18, 1982, and showed a loan delinquency rate of more than 25% and many loans that were not supported by current credit information. The Report stressed poor lending practices, including poor supervision, incomplete credit information, self-dealing, and overlending generally. The Report specifically mentioned that little or no credit information had been maintained for commercial loans, including participation loans purchased from affiliated banks.

On February 22, 1983, the FDIC and the DFI entered into a second Memorandum of Understanding with ACB under which ACB agreed to implement an amended written loan policy and to reduce its substandard assets by $1,200,000 by December 31, 1983. ACB did not fulfill its agreement, and on November 22, 1985, liquidation proceedings were initiated pursuant to Indiana Code § 28-1-3.1-1 *et seq.*, and the FDIC was appointed receiver of ACB pursuant to Indiana Code § 28-1-3.1-5. On the same date, the FDIC, as receiver, sold certain ACB assets to the FDIC in its corporate capacity pursuant to Indiana Code § 28-1-3.1-7 and 12 U.S.C. § 1823(c)(2)(A). Among these assets were the claims against ACB directors and officers for failing to perform or poorly performing their duties.

B. *The Appellants*

The appellants are former directors and officers of ACB. V. Edgar (Ed) Stanley and Robert Marcuccilli sat on the ACB Board of Directors (Board) from March 24, 1982, until May 22, 1984; Ed Stanley served as president from March 24, 1982, until September 13, 1983. Judith Stanley sat on the Board between March 24, 1982, and May 8, 1984; Dan Stanley served between May 25, 1982, and May 8, 1984; and John Boley served between 1970 and June 16, 1983. Finally, Dr. Gilbert Bierman served from May 1978 until April 9, 1984. During the period when they were ACB directors, the defendants were also shareholders of the bank.

In addition to serving on the Board, Ed Stanley and Judith Stanley also served as directors of Leiters Ford State Bank (Leiters Ford), Counting House Bank, and Western State Bank. Mr. Marcuccilli served concurrently as director of Counting House Bank and Western State Bank, and he served until January 1983 as a director of Leiters Ford.

Mr. Boley attended only one Board meeting between November 9, 1982, and his resignation in June 1983. Dr. Bierman was advised by Ed Stanley in 1982 that he need not attend Board meetings, but that ACB wished to retain his name as director. Accordingly, Dr. Bierman attended no Board meetings after the October 5, 1982 meeting.

C. *The District Court*

In its extensive opinion, the district court dealt with both the legal and factual issues presented by the parties. . . .

We shall summarize each of the transactions in which the district court determined that the directors had breached their duty of care to ACB.

a. *Abbott Coal and Energy Loans (Abbott)*

On December 30, 1982, ACB was assigned without recourse an installment lease in the amount of $130,484 between Northern Indiana Leasing and Abbott, which was secured by a bulldozer. Ed Stanley and Mr. Marcuccilli were "interested directors" because they were vice-presidents of Northern Indiana Leasing when the lease was sold to ACB. On

February 12, 1983, ACB purchased a $60,000 commercial loan to Abbott from Counting House Bank. At the time, Ed Stanley, Judith Stanley, and Mr. Marcuccilli were "interested directors." The district court found that Abbott's financial condition at the time ACB acquired the lease and loan was very poor. *Id*. at 1288. Indeed, Abbott filed Chapter 11 bankruptcy on June 25, 1985.

* * *

The court found that the directors were liable on both the loan and the lease because they had failed to take sufficient collateral. . . .

b. *Sidney DeVries and DeVries Hog and Grain Farm Loans*

On March 24, 1983, ACB purchased a $70,000 note from Leiters Ford. The district court found, however, that the security interest that had been granted to Leiters Ford was, for all intents and purposes, worthless because LaSalle National Bank had a prior interest in it dating from a March 1980 pledge.

* * *

. . . On April 11, 1983, ACB purchased a $40,000 loan to DeVries Hog and Grain Farm from Leiters Ford. Ed Stanley and Judith Stanley were "interested directors." This loan was secured by collateral that had previously been pledged to LaSalle National Bank. In addition, the court found that there was no evidence that a futures contract pledged to secure this loan had any value.

Finally, the district court found that, on June 14, 1983, ACB had participated in a loan of $35,000 to Sidney DeVries from Leiters Ford. Of the original loan, ACB's participation was $34,000; Leiters Ford kept $1,000. The defendants claimed that this debt was secured by two indemnifying mortgages and four security agreements that covered DeVries' livestock, equipment, and machinery, as well as his futures account. All of this security had previously been pledged to LaSalle National Bank to cover other debts.

After reviewing all of the evidence, the district court concluded that, at least as early as February 1983, Sidney DeVries and DeVries Hog and Grain Farm were facing severe financial difficulties. . . . The court determined that a reasonably prudent banker would not have participated in these loans. . . .

c. *Conn loans*

On June 24, 1983, Leiters Ford issued to ACB a participation of $144,755 in a $147,262 loan that it had earlier made to James and June Conn, grain farmers. Ed Stanley and Judith Stanley were "interested directors" because they were directors of both Leiters Ford and ACB at the time. On July 19, 1983, Leiters Ford issued to ACB a participation of $13,000 in a $33,530.19 loan made to the Conns. The district court found that, at the time the loans were made, the Conns had a debt-to-net worth ratio of 2.23 to 1 (or a ratio of 9.51 to 1 after the Conns' inflated valuation of their farm land was taken into account). The district court concluded that a prudent banker would not have participated in the Conn loans.

. . .

II. *ANALYSIS*

A. *Standards of Review*

. . . Questions of law are, of course, subject to our de novo review. By contrast, we may disturb the district court's findings of fact only if we determine that they are clearly erroneous. . . .

B. *Director Liability*

1. *General principles*

a. *Standard of care*[6]

The parties do not dispute the basic principles governing bank director responsibilities:

[D]irectors must exercise ordinary care and prudence in the administration of the affairs of a bank, and [] this includes something more than officiating as figureheads. They are entitled under the law to commit the banking business, as defined, to their duly-authorized officers, but this does not absolve them from the duty of reasonable supervision, nor ought they to be permitted to be shielded from liability because of want of wrongdoing, if that ignorance is the result of gross inattention. . . .

* * *

A director may not rely on the judgment of others, especially when there is notice of mismanagement. Certainly, when an investment poses an obvious risk, a director cannot rely blindly on the judgment of others. In *Rankin* [*v. Cooper,* 149 F. 1010, 1013 (W.D. Ark. 1907], the court specifically recognized a heightened responsibility among those directors who have an inkling of trouble brewing:

If nothing has come to the knowledge to awaken suspicion that something is going wrong, ordinary attention to the affairs of the institution is sufficient. If, upon the other hand, directors know, or by the exercise of ordinary care should have known, any facts which would awaken suspicion and put a prudent man on his guard, then a degree of care commensurate with the evil to be avoided is required, and a want of that care makes them responsible.

* * *

---

[6]   FIRREA, 12 U.S.C. § 1821(k), enacted subsequent to the events that gave rise to this appeal, now provides that the FDIC in its capacity as conservator, receiver, or assignee may bring suit against a director or officer of an insured depository institution

for gross negligence, including any similar conduct or conduct that demonstrates a greater disregard of a duty of care (than gross negligence) including intentional tortious conduct, as such terms are defined and determined under applicable State law. Nothing in this paragraph shall impair or affect any right to the Corporation under other applicable law.

This provision has been interpreted by at least two appellate courts as not preempting state law claims based on a lesser degree of culpability. . . . Neither party has argued before us or in the district court that FIRREA ought to be retroactively applied in this case.

Reliance arguments are especially weak when regulators have told directors to take action. Finally, when insider transactions are being contemplated, "[t]he director's duty of inquiry cannot be met by representations of propriety from interested parties; he must be personally satisfied that there was an adequate independent investigation showing the propriety of the transaction." *Fitzpatrick v. FDIC*, 765 F.2d 569, 577 (6th Cir. 1985).

b. *Proximate cause*

It is well-settled that a director will not be liable for losses to the corporation absent a showing that his act or omission proximately caused the subsequent losses.

* * *

2. *Application to this case*

After a thorough study of the opinion of the district court, we are convinced that the court understood completely the governing legal principles that we have just set forth. We therefore turn to the question of whether the court applied those principles correctly in this case. . . .

* * *

The directors who were not involved in the daily operations of the bank add additional arguments that we shall now address. Mr. Boley and Dr. Bierman concede that they failed to attend Board meetings during the period when the poor loan acquisitions were being made. They attempt to use this inattention, however, as a shield against liability. Dr. Bierman, in fact, attended no Board meetings after October 5, 1982. Similarly, Mr. Boley attended only one meeting between November 9, 1982, and his resignation in June 1983.

* * *

Against this background, we shall first examine, on the basis of the record before us, what the outsiders should have known about the condition of the bank and whether that knowledge should have put them on notice that heightened vigilance on their part was indicated. Next, we must consider whether, if the outsiders had exercised the degree of vigilance expected of a prudent bank director under the circumstances, they would have learned of the poor loans and could have avoided them.

There can be no question that both Mr. Boley and Dr. Bierman were well aware that the ACB was being scrutinized by regulators as early as August 1981 and that the subsequent FDIC Report had criticized lending practices and had stressed the need for the Board to monitor loans more carefully. Dr. Bierman was present at the January 26, 1982 meeting when the first Memorandum of Understanding with the FDIC and the DFI was under discussion and then again at the October 5th meeting when the FDIC's September 1982 Report of Examination was under discussion (indeed, that meeting was Dr. Bierman's last). At that time, participation loans with affiliated banks and poor lending policy were under discussion. In addition, by the October 1982 meeting, it was abundantly clear that the initial concerns of the bank examiners were not being allayed. The danger signals were obvious. Instead of recognizing a renewed responsibility to the bank or choosing to resign from the Board, Mr. Boley and Dr. Bierman chose to absent themselves. Had they continued to attend the meetings, they would have learned of the continued FDIC correspondence and would have had access to the actual correspondence.

Even though they were not actively engaged in Board activities at the time, Mr. Boley and Dr. Bierman had an obligation to become familiar with the second Memorandum of Understanding executed in February 1983, which again stressed poor lending policies and practices. In addition, the Minutes of the March 6, 1984 Board meeting stated explicitly that the percentage of substandard loans was higher than it had been in September 1982. At this meeting (which included a number of FDIC representatives), the lamentable condition of the ACB was detailed and specific mention was made about Dr. Bierman's lack of attendance.

It should be noted also that Dr. Bierman's and Mr. Boley's memberships on the Board pre-dated those of the other Board members; consequently, the outsiders were on notice, or should have known, that a number of the newcomers to the Board were also affiliated with other banks and that the potential for insider dealings was real. Even if they had not had actual notice of insider status, the subsequent FDIC reports could have left them in no doubt that insider abuses might be occurring. Nevertheless, there is no indication that Dr. Bierman and Mr. Boley took any steps to monitor this situation.

Directors are also charged with knowledge of the loan policies in effect during their watch. The loan policy in effect from 1978 to 1983 indicated that all participation loans were to go to the Board for approval as well as other loans if the aggregate was more than $60,000. There was testimony that this policy was regularly ignored. However, a new loan policy manual was circulated on March 29, 1983, that authorized both Ed Stanley and Mr. Marcuccilli to approve all loans up to the bank lending limits.

Under the circumstances that faced the ACB, Mr. Boley and Dr. Bierman should have been put on notice that the possibility for abuse was heightened by the new loan policy, which cut the Board of Directors out of loan approval matters in many circumstances.

Dr. Bierman maintains that, even if he had been present at the meetings, he would not have been in a better position to intervene with problematic loans because they were not discussed and the papers that were distributed to directors in the form of minutes or reports did not contain the necessary data. Board reports were distributed to the directors with details of the monthly business of the bank. On this court's request, the parties supplemented the appellate record with the Board reports that had been part of the trial record. The "New Loans" sections of these reports do no more than list in summary fashion the loans that had apparently already been effected. Indeed, there was testimony that the particular loans were presented to the Board as "done deals."

There would be little to excite interest in these entries save for the fact that the February 12, 1983 $60,000 loan to Abbott was the largest loan made during that month. Likewise, the March 14, 1983 $70,000 DeVries loan was the largest on that report. The listing of the large aggregates for the April 11, 1983 DeVries loan and the July 19, 1983 Conn loan should have excited some interest. In addition, the fact that the large June 24, 1983 Conn loan was identified as a participation loan should have sparked some interest, in light of the bank's track record on such loans. . . .

. . . [T]he district court was entitled to conclude that Mr. Boley and Dr. Bierman abdicated their directorial responsibilities to ACB by their sheer inattention. The outsiders knew full well that the bank was in serious trouble. They knew that there had been risky loans; they knew that the insiders were affiliated with other area institutions; they received only summary reports of new loans; and they could see that the bank's condition was not improving. Under these circumstances, they had a duty to make further inquiries and either involve themselves in bank activities or resign.

The district court made a specific finding of proximate cause regarding the outside directors on the basis of Ed Stanley's comment that if a Board member objected to a loan, members "weren't going to cram anything down anybody's throat." *Stanley*, 770 F. Supp. at 1312. We see no reason to question the district court's determination that Mr. Stanley was credible. An attentive outside director would have found much about which to be suspicious in the large loans that appeared on the monthly reports with only spare collateral information. Consequently, we see no reason to disturb the district court's ruling that the outsiders shared responsibility with the insiders for the improvident loans (with the exception, as we have said above, that Mr. Boley is not responsible for the Conn loans).

* * *

Conclusion

For the foregoing reasons, we affirm the judgment of the district court.

NOTES AND QUESTIONS

(1) **Standard of care: notice of fraud.** Compare with *Bierman* the older case of *Bates v. Dresser*[8] in which outside directors were held not liable for a fraud by a cashier who took essentially the entire assets of the bank by drawing checks on the bank and falsely charging the checks to various accounts (including the president's) or by falsifying the deposits ledger. The Court upheld liability on the part of the president who had more notice of the fraud than the other directors, but refused to fault the remaining directors who accepted the cashier's statement of liabilities without inspecting the depositors' ledger. The Court noted that the outside directors were justified in having confidence in the cashier who committed the fraud because the cashier's work had been validated "by the semi-annual examinations by the government examiner" and by the supervision of the president "whose responsibility, as executive officer; interest, as large stockholder and depositor; and knowledge from long daily presence in the bank, were greater than theirs." Accordingly, the court concluded that the outside directors "were not bound by virtue of the office gratuitously assumed by them to call in the passbooks and compare them with the ledger, and until the event showed the possibility they hardly could have seen that their failure to look at the ledger opened a way to fraud." Should the outside directors have been liable on these facts? Can this case be reconciled with *Bierman*?

(2) **Standard of care: reliance on others.** Whether directors may rely on the assurances of others that there are no problems in the corporation largely depends on whether the directors have notice of facts which puts them under a duty of further

---

[8]   251 U.S. 524 (1920).

inquiry. In *Graham v. Allis-Chalmers Manufacturing Co.*,[9] directors were held not liable for failing to discover and prevent anti-trust violations by employees of the company. The court relied on the fact that Allis-Chalmers was a giant, decentralized corporation and that the illegal pricing decisions were made by the relevant division rather than by the board. Plaintiff claimed that the directors had breached a duty of inquiry because twenty years earlier a consent decree had been entered against the company concerning similar acts. The court rejected this argument, noting that none of the defendant directors had held a position of responsibility at the time of the earlier decree and that those who knew of the decree were told that the company had not in fact been guilty of the earlier violations.[10]

(3) **The emerging duty to maintain information and reporting systems.** An important counterpoint to *Graham* is *In re Caremark International Inc. Derivative Litigation*,[11] where directors were alleged to have failed to adequately supervise employees who were indicted for violating the terms of the Federal Anti-Referral Payments Law, which prohibits healthcare providers from paying to induce referral of Medicare or Medicaid patients. Commenting on *Graham*, Chancellor Allen wrote:

> How does one generalize this holding today? Can it be said today that, absent some ground giving rise to suspicion of violation of law, that corporate directors have no duty to assure that a corporate information gathering and reporting system exists which represents a good faith attempt to provide senior management and the Board with information respecting material acts, events or conditions within the corporation, including compliance with applicable statutes and regulations? I certainly do not believe so. . . .

Chancellor Allen concluded that the director's obligation includes a duty to assure himself that "information and reporting systems exist in the organization that are reasonably designed to provide to senior management and to the board itself timely, accurate information sufficient to allow management and the board, each within its scope, to reach informed judgments concerning both the corporation's compliance with law and its business performance." Failure to maintain such a system could "render a director liable for losses caused by non-compliance."

The duty to maintain information and reporting systems is likely to assume greater importance in the wake of Enron, WorldCom and similar scandals that have come to light since the fall of 2001, where firms apparently significantly misrepresented their financial condition. Among other things, § 404 of the Sarbanes-Oxley Act of 2002 requires companies to file disclosures stating management's responsibilities for establishing and maintaining an adequate internal control structure and procedures for finan-

---

[9]   41 Del. Ch. 78, 188 A.2d 125 (1963).

[10]   For prominent criticism of *Graham*, see Cary, *Federalism and Corporate Law: Reflections Upon Delaware*, 83 YALE L.J. 663, 683 (1974).

[11]   698 A.2d 959 (Del. Ch. 1996).

cial reporting and an assessment of the effectiveness of the structure, which are attested to by the firm's auditor. This duty to disclose may provide federal pressure for internal monitoring systems.

(4) **Nominal directors.** May a director ever be wholly excused from the duty to supervise? Compare with *Bierman, Allied Freightways, Inc. v. Cholfin*,[12] in which an "ordinary housewife with no business experience" who was "hardly any more than a nominal director" was held not liable for her husband's looting of the business.[13] The ALI *Principles*, § 4.01(a)(1), Comment (h) sides with the position in *Bierman*, as does *Francis v. United Jersey Bank*, discussed in Note 6 below. Why wasn't Bierman's "effective resignation," through his failure to attend any meetings after October 5, 1982, enough to let him off the hook? What should be the result if a director is explicitly designated as "nominal" and given reduced duties in the bylaws? Alternatively, what should be the result if directors do not formally abdicate their duties, but enter into contracts with non-director managers that have the practical effect of preventing the directors from fulfilling their statutory and common law duties? *See Grimes v. Donald*, excerpted in Section 9.05[D] below.

(5) **Subjective standards of care.** To what extent should the individual characteristics of the director be taken into account in determining whether a director has satisfied her duty of care? The court in *Cholfin*, discussed in Note 4, clearly took into consideration the defendant wife's limited directorial ability. But the court in *Hoye v. Meek*[14] said: "There is no separate standard for an ordinarily prudent non-resident director or an ordinarily prudent semi-retired director."

(6) **The relevance of the type of corporation:** *Francis v. United Jersey Bank.*[15] *Francis* is a notorious non-banking case in which a sick, elderly and disengaged outside director was held liable to creditors for not stopping her sons' massive misappropriation of the funds of her family's reinsurance brokerage firm. The court characterized the directors' duty in terms similar to those in *Bierman*. It also stressed the peculiar nature of the reinsurance brokerage industry, in which the broker receives and pays out very large sums of money to insurance companies, holding funds largely on trust. This ready availability of cash in the reinsurance brokerage industry may create the same potential for fraud that is present in banks, thereby increasing the benefits of legally enforceable fiduciary duties. Consider whether the court in *Francis* would have reached the same result if the corporation had engaged in manufacturing rather than reinsurance brokerage.[16]

---

[12]   325 Mass. 630, 633, 91 N.E.2d 765, 768 (1950), compared with *Francis* in Note, 12 SETON HALL L. REV. 581 (1982).

[13]   *See also Berman v. LeBeau Inter-America, Inc.*, 509 F. Supp. 156, 161 (S.D.N.Y.), *aff'd mem.* 679 F.2d 879 (2d Cir. 1981) (exonerating "figurehead" director).

[14]   795 F.2d 893 (10th Cir. 1986).

[15]   87 N.J. 15, 432 A.2d 814 (1981).

[16]   For a case similar to and relying on *Francis*, which also arises out of the insurance industry, and which also imposed liability on a director for a failure to supervise a family member (here, husband) which permitted his massive diversion of funds, see *Senn v. Washington State Insurance Comm'r*, 74 Wash. App. 408, 875 P.2d 637 (1994).

(7) **The relevance of the type of corporation: standards for bank directors.** It has been said that directors of banks are held to a higher standard than those of other types of corporations.[17] However, the ALI *Principles* reject distinctions between banks or other financial institutions and industrial corporations with respect to the duty of care. In particular, Introductory Note [d] to Section 4.01 states that "whatever merits they may have had near the turn of the century, today differentiations based solely on the distinction between a 'financial institution' and an 'industrial corporation' are unjustified and anachronistic." Do you agree? The special treatment may, to some extent, reflect the fact that the ready availability of liquid assets serves notice of the omnipresent potential for fraud. Also, the presence of federal deposit insurance removes some market scrutiny that might uncover fraud. As discussed in Section 9.01, the costs and benefits of legally enforceable fiduciary duties differ depending upon the context.

(8) **Other relevant characteristics of firms.** Are there any other distinctions among types of corporations that should be taken into account in determining the appropriate level of the directors' duty of care? For example, should it make a difference to the level of the duty of care whether the corporation is publicly or closely held?

(9) **Proximate cause.** Even a grossly negligent director is not liable unless the breach of duty was the proximate cause of the harm. The *Francis* court distinguished *Barnes v. Andrews,*[18] which exonerated a figurehead director for liability for general mismanagement. The court reasoned that because the mother was the only one reviewing the sons' transactions, her neglect "contributed to the climate of corruption."[19] The causation issue involves two questions: First, would the director have discovered the misconduct upon due investigation? Second, could the director have prevented some or all of the damage claimed if the misconduct had been discovered? Both questions require the court to determine precisely what the director had a duty to do. The answer to the first question depends on the degree to which the misconduct has been hidden. Both *Bierman* and *Francis* appear to place on the plaintiff the burden of showing that the defendant director's breach of duty was the proximate cause of the plaintiff's harm. ALI *Principles* §§ 4.01(d) and 7.18(b) adopt this position explicitly. For a different view on the allocation of the burden of proof, see *Cede & Co. v. Technicolor, Inc.,*[20] discussed in Section 9.03[D].

---

[17] For a discussion of older cases also reflecting a different treatment between banks and non-banks, see Bishop, *Sitting Ducks and Decoy Ducks: New Trends in Indemnification of Corporate Directors and Officers,* 77 YALE L.J. 1078, 1095 (1968).

[18] 298 F.2d 614 (S.D.N.Y. 1924).

[19] 87 N.J. at 44, 432 A.2d at 829. The *Senn* case in footnote 16 above also found proximate cause, relying on *Francis.*

[20] 634 A.2d 345 (Del. 1993).

PROBLEMS

(1) Frank was one of three directors of the Shelbyville Finance Company, which was in the business of making commercial, consumer and homeowner loans. One of the other directors was Pete, who was the president of the company, and the third director was Pete's wife. Frank had invested a substantial amount of money in the company on the basis of Pete's reputation in the community as an honest, up-and-coming go-getter. Frank worked full-time as the president of a local lumberyard and had no time to devote to the business of Shelbyville. Furthermore, Frank had little expertise with respect to finance companies.

Pete owned several construction companies. Frank was aware of this, but did not know the names of the companies. Pete caused Shelbyville to loan its funds to his other companies. The loans were quite substantial in relation to Shelbyville's assets, were unsecured and were repaid much more slowly than Shelbyville's regular loans. As a result of this substantial outflow of funds, Shelbyville's regular loan business decreased considerably, as was clearly reflected on Shelbyville's books. Frank was unaware of these facts. There were no director meetings. Frank asked Pete from time to time how the business was going, and Pete responded that "things are great."

The Shelbyville Finance Company ultimately became bankrupt. The trustee in bankruptcy, representing a number of banks that had loaned money to Shelbyville, is considering suing Frank to recover the losses resulting from Pete's misconduct. (Pete and all of his other businesses are bankrupt and have insufficient assets to repay the loans.) Assume you are representing the trustee. What advice would you give as to the possibility of winning this suit?[21]

(2) Bob Harris has been an officer and director of the Acme Widget Corporation, a closely held manufacturing company, for 40 years. He now wishes to retire and spend the rest of his days sailing in the West Indies. The corporation has offered to name Mr. Harris "Permanent Honorary Director" in appreciation of his long service to the company. Mr. Harris will have no duties. The bylaws will be amended upon unanimous director and shareholder vote to reflect the addition of this position to the board. You are Mr. Harris' personal attorney. Would you advise him to accept this position?

REFERENCE

Carney, *Section 4.01 of the American Law Institute's Corporate Governance Project: Restatement or Misstatement?*, 66 WASH. U. L.Q. 239 (1988).

---

[21] For a somewhat similar case, see *Harman v. Willbern*, 374 F. Supp. 1149 (D. Kan. 1974). *See also* Stern, *Chicanery at Phar-Mor Ran Deep, Close Look at Discounter Shows*, WALL ST. J., Jan. 20, 1994 at 1, 6, col. 6 (executives may have had notice of massive fraud).

§ 9.03 The Duty of Care: Disinterested Business Decisions

Section 9.02 discussed the directors' duty of care in cases where directors either abdicated their function or simply failed to act. This Section discusses the officers' and directors' duty of care in connection with disinterested business decisions—*i.e.* business decisions where the corporate officers or directors making the decision have no personal interest that conflicts with the interest of the corporation and its shareholders. Courts deal with these decisions under the so-called "business judgment rule," one version of which is summarized in § 4.01(c) of the ALI *Principles*.[22] Under the business judgment rule, as formulated by the drafters of the ALI *Principles*:

> A director or officer who makes a business judgment in good faith fulfills the [duty of care to the corporation] if the director or officer:
>
> (1) is not interested in the subject of the business judgment;
>
> (2) is informed with respect to the subject of the business judgment to the extent the director or officer reasonably believes to be appropriate under the circumstances; and
>
> (3) rationally believes that the business judgment is in the best interests of the corporation.

The ALI *Principles* make clear that the business judgment rule is a rule of judicial decision making: Courts normally will not second-guess directors' disinterested business decisions as long as they are informed. As so formulated, the business judgment rule appears to contemplate two levels of review of disinterested business decisions: first, the court reviews business decisions to see whether they pass substantive scrutiny—*i.e.*, in the terms of the ALI *Principles*, to see whether the directors' belief that the decision is in the best interests of the corporation is "rational"; and second, the court reviews business decisions to see whether they pass procedural scrutiny—*i.e.*, in the ALI's terms, to see whether the directors were adequately informed with respect to the subject of the business decision. Subsection [A] considers the substantive review of business decisions under the business judgment rule—that is, when, if ever, the courts will second-guess a disinterested business judgment that was reached by adequately informed directors. Subsection [B] then discusses the procedural review of business decisions under the business judgment rule. Finally, Subsection [C] considers statutory limitations on director liability and subsection [D] examines the consequences if a court determines that a disinterested business decision is not entitled to the protection of the business judgment rule.

---

[22] For another version, see the Model Business Corporation Act provision discussed in Note 3 following *Brehm v. Eisner*, below.

[A] Substantive Review of Disinterested Decisions

SHLENSKY v. WRIGLEY
Illinois Appellate Court
95 Ill. App. 2d 173, 237 N.E.2d 776 (1968)

SULLIVAN, Justice:

This is an appeal from a dismissal of plaintiff's amended complaint on motion of the defendants. The action was a stockholders' derivative suit against the directors for negligence and mismanagement. The corporation was also made a defendant. Plaintiff sought damages and an order that defendants cause the installation of lights in Wrigley Field and the scheduling of night baseball games.

Plaintiff is a minority stockholder of defendant corporation, Chicago National League Ball Club (Inc.), a Delaware corporation with its principal place of business in Chicago, Illinois. Defendant corporation owns and operates the major league professional baseball team known as the Chicago Cubs. . . . The individual defendants are directors of the Cubs and have served for varying periods of years. Defendant Philip K. Wrigley is also president of the corporation and owner of approximately 80% of the stock therein.

Plaintiff alleges that since night baseball was first played in 1935 nineteen of the twenty major league teams have scheduled night games. In 1966, out of a total of 1620 games in the major leagues, 932 were played at night. Plaintiff alleges that every member of the major leagues, other than the Cubs, scheduled substantially all of its home games in 1966 at night, exclusive of opening days, Saturdays, Sundays, holidays and days prohibited by league rules. Allegedly this has been done for the specific purpose of maximizing attendance and thereby maximizing revenue and income.

The Cubs, in the years 1961-65, sustained operating losses from its direct baseball operations. Plaintiff attributes those losses to inadequate attendance at Cubs' home games. He concludes that if the directors continue to refuse to install lights at Wrigley Field and schedule night baseball games, the Cubs will continue to sustain comparable losses and its financial condition will continue to deteriorate.

Plaintiff alleges that, except for the year 1963, attendance at Cubs' home games has been substantially below that at their road games, many of which were played at night.

Plaintiff compares attendance at Cubs' games with that of the Chicago White Sox, an American League club, whose weekday games were generally played at night. The weekend attendance figures for the two teams was similar; however, the White Sox week-night games drew many more patrons than did the Cubs' weekday games.

Plaintiff alleges that the funds for the installation of lights can be readily obtained through financing and the cost of installation would be far more than offset and recaptured by increased revenues and incomes resulting from the increased attendance.

Plaintiff further alleges that defendant Wrigley has refused to install lights, not because of interest in the welfare of the corporation but because of his personal opinions "that baseball is a 'daytime sport' and that the installation of lights and night baseball games will have a deteriorating effect upon the surrounding neighborhood." It is alleged that he has admitted that he is not interested in whether the Cubs would benefit financially from such action because of his concern for the neighborhood, and that he would be willing for the team to play night games if a new stadium were built in Chicago.

Plaintiff alleges that the other defendant directors, with full knowledge of the foregoing matters, have acquiesced in the policy laid down by Wrigley and have permitted him to dominate the board of directors in matters involving the installation of lights and scheduling of night games, even though they knew he was not motivated by a good faith concern as to the best interests of defendant corporation, but solely by his personal views set forth above. It is charged that the directors are acting for a reason or reasons contrary and wholly unrelated to the business interests of the corporation; that such arbitrary and capricious acts constitute mismanagement and waste of corporate assets, and that the directors have been negligent in failing to exercise reasonable care and prudence in the management of the corporate affairs.

The question on appeal is whether plaintiff's amended complaint states a cause of action. It is plaintiff's position that fraud, illegality and conflict of interest are not the only bases for a stockholder's derivative action against the directors. Contrariwise, defendants argue that the courts will not step in and interfere with honest business judgment of the directors unless there is a showing of fraud, illegality or conflict of interest.

Plaintiff argues that the allegations of his amended complaint are sufficient to set forth a cause of action under the principles set out in *Dodge v. Ford Motor Co.*, 204 Mich. 459, 170 N.W. 668. In that case plaintiff, owner of about 10% of the outstanding stock, brought suit against the directors seeking payment of additional dividends and the enjoining of further business expansion. In ruling on the request for dividends the court indicated that the motives of Ford in keeping so much money in the corporation for expansion and security were to benefit the public generally and spread the profits out by means of more jobs, etc. The court felt that these were not only far from related to the good of the stockholders, but amounted to a change in the ends of the corporation and that this was not a purpose contemplated or allowed by the corporate charter. The court relied on language found in *Hunter v. Roberts, Throp & Co.*, 83 Mich. 63, 47 N.W. 131, 134, wherein it was said:

> Courts of equity will not interfere in the management of the directors unless it is clearly made to appear that they are guilty of fraud or misappropriation of the corporate funds, or refuse to declare a dividend when the corporation has a surplus of net profits which it can, without detriment to its business, divide among its stockholders, and when a refusal to do so would amount to such an abuse of discretion as would constitute a fraud or breach of that good faith which they are bound to exercise toward the stockholders.

From the authority relied upon in that case it is clear that the court felt that there must be fraud or a breach of that good faith which directors are bound to exercise toward the stockholders in order to justify the courts entering into the internal affairs of corporations. This is made clear when the court refused to interfere with the directors' decision to expand the business. The following appears on page 684 of 170 N.W.:

We are not, however, persuaded that we should interfere with the proposed expansion of the business of the Ford Motor Company. In view of the fact that the selling price of products may be increased at any time, the ultimate results of the larger business cannot be certainly estimated. *The judges are not business experts.* It is recognized that plans must often be made for a long future, for expected competition, for a continuing as well as an immediately profitable venture. . . . We are not satisfied that the alleged motives of the directors, in so far as they are reflected in the conduct of business, menace the interests of the shareholders. (Emphasis supplied)

Plaintiff in the instant case argues that the directors are acting for reasons unrelated to the financial interest and welfare of the Cubs. However, we are not satisfied that the motives assigned to Philip K. Wrigley, and through him to the other directors, are contrary to the best interests of the corporation and the stockholders. For example, it appears to us that the effect on the surrounding neighborhood might well be considered by a director who was considering the patrons who would or would not attend the games if the park were in a poor neighborhood. Furthermore, the long run interest of the corporation in its property value at Wrigley Field might demand all efforts to keep the neighborhood from deteriorating. By these thoughts we do not mean to say that we have decided that the decision of the directors was a correct one. That is beyond our jurisdiction and ability. We are merely saying that the decision is one properly before directors and the motives alleged in the amended complaint showed no fraud, illegality or conflict of interest in their making of that decision.

While all the courts do not insist that one or more of the three elements must be present for a stockholder's derivative action to lie, nevertheless we feel that unless the conduct of the defendants at least borders on one of the elements, the courts should not interfere. The trial court in the instant case acted properly in dismissing plaintiff's amended complaint.

* * *

Finally, we do not agree with plaintiff's contention that failure to follow the example of the other major league clubs in scheduling night games constituted negligence. Plaintiff made no allegation that these teams' night schedules were profitable or that the purpose for which night baseball had been undertaken was fulfilled. Furthermore, it cannot be said that directors, even those of corporations that are losing money, must follow the lead of the other corporations in the field. Directors are elected for their business capabilities and judgment and the courts cannot require them to forego their judgment because of the decisions of directors of other companies. Courts may not decide these questions in the absence of a clear showing of dereliction of duty on the part of the specific directors and mere failure to "follow the crowd" is not such a dereliction.

For the foregoing reasons the order of dismissal entered by the trial court is affirmed.

NOTES

(1) **Da Cubs.** Wrigley Field is located in a heavily residential neighborhood on the north side of Chicago not far from Lake Michigan. There are approximately 50,000 people living within one mile of the ball park. The neighborhood has never been fancy,

but recently it has been revitalized by an influx of young professionals. Access to Wrigley Field is primarily through city streets, and much of the parking is on side streets. Night games at Wrigley Field bring a substantial amount of traffic and noise to the neighborhood. The public address system, organ, and crowd cheers can be heard a long way outside the ball park.

The Cubs have a record of failure unparalleled in the history of major league baseball. They have not won a National League championship since 1945, are the only team of all those that existed in 1949 not to win a league championship, won more games than they lost only once in the fourteen seasons from 1974-1987, from 1946 to 1966 finished seventh or eighth 13 times, and were the first of the old National League teams to finish behind an expansion team.

Yet the Cubs have a very loyal following. As political columnist and Cub fan George Will has said:[23]

> Scholars concede but cannot explain the amazing chemistry of Cub fans' loyalty. But their unique steadfastness through thin and thin has something to do with the Team's Franciscan simplicity.
>
> The Cubs play on real grass, under real sunlight. Their scoreboard does not explode and they do not wear gaudy uniforms like those that have the Pittsburgh Pirates looking like the softball team from Ralph's Bar and Grill.

Other reasons for the Cubs' success in attracting fans include the facts that day games draw children who can come by themselves and be home before dark, and out-of-towners whose principal day-time activity in Chicago is to watch baseball.

Perhaps the Cubs draw fans because they are not only mediocre, but a symbol of mediocrity. Some Cub fans formed an organization called the Emil Verban Memorial Society. George Will said of Emil Verban: "His most notable achievement was a remarkable ratio of home runs (one) to times at bat (291). Today he is a patron saint of Cub fans because he symbolizes mediocrity under pressure."[24]

Why have the Cubs been so bad? Cub fans have said that playing in the hot sun with fewer games in the cooler night causes the Cubs to tire early in the season. Also, the Cubs had to show up in the park early after partaking of Chicago night life the night before (or, even worse, dispense with the night life), and like ordinary mortals must fight morning traffic to make it to batting practice and evening traffic to make it home after the game. All this exhaustion would not explain why the Cubs usually started to lose on the very first day in April, but may explain the Cubs' famous fold in 1969 when they blew a substantial lead to lose the pennant to the New York Mets.

Mike Royko, who was a columnist for the Chicago Tribune, suggested that a reason for the Cubs' perennial failure is that they must continually change their "biologi-

---

[23]   PURSUIT OF HAPPINESS AND OTHER SOBERING THOUGHTS 313 (1978). Copyright © 1978 by The Washington Post Company. Reprinted by permission of Harper & Row, Publishers, Inc.

[24]   *Id.* at 310.

cal clocks" from day to nightwork which causes, among other things, constipation. Royko asked Cub fans to participate in a "Prunes for Bruins" campaign.[25] And in 1945, the owner of the Billy Goat Tavern put a hex on the Cubs when the guards would not let him into the park with his pet goat. The hex was lifted when saloon-keeper and goat were permitted to parade around the field.

An economic analysis of the Cubs might reveal another reason for the Cubs' mediocrity: Fan loyalty means that the Cubs lack product market discipline, or are disciplined in a different way from other teams in that their "product" is mediocre baseball.

In 1981, the Cubs were purchased by the Tribune Company. In 1984, new management and a willingness to pay higher salaries produced the first Cub division championship in forty years. However, tradition prevailed, and the Cubs snatched defeat from the jaws of victory by losing the last three games of the five-game National League division playoffs to San Diego. In 1989 the Cubs again won their division. They again lost the playoffs in five games, but this time the playoffs were best of seven. The 1989 World Series was interrupted by a massive earthquake which was probably not caused by the Cubs' non-participation in the Series.

The Tribune Company, in addition to publishing the Chicago Tribune, owns WGN-TV and WGN-Radio. These stations broadcast Cub games throughout the country. In fact, it was estimated that in 1982, $6 million of a total of $40 million of WGN's broadcast revenues were from commercials during Cubs games. It is a safe bet that the Tribune bought the Cubs for their broadcast revenues.[26]

Of course, a larger television audience may be expected from night games. Moreover, light-less Cubs would lose potential revenue from hosting All-Star games, which are played at night, and maybe even in some faraway era, from World Series games, most of which are now played at night. Considerable community pressure led by a group called Citizens United for Baseball in Sunshine forestalled night games for seven years after the Tribune bought the team.

The inexorable tide of progress finally brought lights to Wrigley Field in 1988. The first night game was scheduled for August 8, 1988. Scalpers charged up to $1000 per ticket. There were 1.5 million telephone calls to a ticket agency in 3½ hours to purchase the last 13,000 tickets to go on sale. Cub greats Billy Williams and Ernie Banks threw out the first pitches. Thunderstorms accompanied by fierce and dramatic lightning stopped the game in the fourth inning. Speculation as to the cause of the storm is beyond the scope of this book.

George Will has written that when he sought to buy stock in the Cubs, he was advised by a substantial Cub shareholder to ignore "price-earnings ratios, return on capital, and a bunch of other hogwash which has no place in a transaction between two true sportsmen."[27]

---

[25]   *See* Mike Royko, *Relieving the Cubs*, CHICAGO SUN-TIMES, June 16, 1982 at 2.

[26]   *See* Moore, *Why Tribune Co. is Feeding the Chicago Cubs*, FORTUNE, June 28, 1982, at 44-50.

[27]   Will, *supra* note 23, at 311.

(2) *Dodge v. Ford Motor Co.*[28] This case, distinguished in *Shlensky*, is an application of the business judgment rule. Minority shareholders in Ford Motor Company sued to compel the payment of a dividend. As of the time of the suit (1916), Ford Motor Company had enjoyed phenomenal success. The company's profits had grown from about $4.5 million in 1910 to approximately $25 million for the first ten months of 1915. As a result of this growth the company was able to pay $41 million in special dividends from December, 1911, through October, 1915, in addition to a regular dividend of 5% per month on the $2,000,000 capital. The plaintiffs sued when, in 1916, Henry Ford, who owned 58.5% of the stock and controlled the board of directors, announced that the company would pay no more special dividends, would retain earnings for expansion (primarily involving the addition of a smelter) and would reduce the selling price of the car from $440 to $360 despite the fact that the company was already selling all the cars it could produce. At the time of this plan, the company had a total surplus legally available for distribution of dividends of $112 million, of which $54 million consisted of cash and other liquid assets.

The plaintiffs had asked for an injunction against the planned expansion, for distribution of 75% of the $54 million cash surplus, and for distribution of all future earnings except for what was required to provide against emergencies. The Michigan courts held against plaintiffs' claims that the corporation had illegally expanded beyond the capital authorized in the corporation statute and that an investment in a smelting plant was *ultra vires* the corporation. (As to the latter claim, see Section 8.04, above.) The courts also held that the expansion was within the business judgment of the directors (see the excerpts from the opinion of the Michigan Supreme Court quoted in *Shlensky*). However, the Michigan Supreme Court affirmed the trial court's order requiring the distribution of approximately $20 million of the cash surplus. The court stated:[29]

> [Ford's] testimony creates the impression . . . that he thinks the Ford Motor Company has made too much money, has had too large profits, and that, although large profits might be still earned, a sharing of them with the public, by reducing the price of the output of the company, ought to be undertaken. We have no doubt that certain sentiments, philanthropic and altruistic, creditable to Mr. Ford, had large influence in determining the policy to be pursued by the Ford Motor Company—the policy which has been herein referred to.
>
> It is said by his counsel that—
>
> Although a manufacturing corporation cannot engage in humanitarian works as its principal business, the fact that it is organized for profit does not prevent the existence of implied powers to carry on

---

[28]   204 Mich. 459, 170 N.W. 668 (1919).

[29]   204 Mich. at 505-07, 170 N.W. at 683-84.

with humanitarian motives such charitable works as are incidental to the main business of the corporation.

And again:

As the expenditures complained of are being made in an expansion of the business which the company is organized to carry on, and for purposes within the powers of the corporation as herein before shown, the question is as to whether such expenditures are rendered illegal because influenced to some extent by humanitarian motives and purposes on the part of the members of the board of directors.

In discussing this proposition, counsel have referred to decisions such as *Hawes v. Oakland*, 104 U.S. 450, 26 L. Ed. 827; *Taunton v. Royal Ins. Co.*, 2 Hem. & Miller, 135; *Henderson v. Bank of Australia*, L. R. 40 Ch. Div. 170; *Steinway v. Steinway & Sons*, 17 Misc. Rep. 43, 40 N.Y. Supp. 718; *People v. Hotchkiss*, 136 App. Div. 150, 120 N.Y. Supp. 649. These cases, after all, like all others in which the subject is treated, turn finally upon the point, the question, whether it appears that the directors were not acting for the best interests of the corporation. We do not draw in question, nor do counsel for the plaintiffs do so, the validity of the general proposition stated by counsel nor the soundness of the opinions delivered in the cases cited. The case presented here is not like any of them. The difference between an incidental humanitarian expenditure of corporate funds for the benefit of the employees, like the building of a hospital for their use and the employment of agencies for the betterment of their condition, and a general purpose and plan to benefit mankind at the expense of others, is obvious. There should be no confusion (of which there is evidence) of the duties which Mr. Ford conceives that he and the stockholders owe to the general public and the duties which in law he and his codirectors owe to protesting, minority stockholders. A business corporation is organized and carried on primarily for the profit of the stockholders. The powers of the directors are to be employed for that end. The discretion of directors is to be exercised in the choice of means to attain that end, and does not extend to a change in the end itself, to the reduction of profits, or to the nondistribution of profits among stockholders in order to devote them to other purposes.

There is committed to the discretion of directors, a discretion to be exercised in good faith, the infinite details of business, including the wages which shall be paid to employees, the number of hours they shall work, the conditions under which labor shall be carried on, and the price for which products shall be offered to the public.

It is said by appellants that the motives of the board members are not material and will not be inquired into by the court so long as their acts are within their lawful powers. As we have pointed out, and the proposition does not require argument to sustain it, it is not within the lawful powers of a board of directors to shape and conduct the affairs of a corporation for the merely incidental benefit of shareholders and for the primary purpose of benefiting others, and no one will contend that, if the avowed purpose of the defendant directors was to sacrifice the interests of shareholders, it would not be the duty of the courts to interfere.

It is of possible interest that the principal plaintiffs, the Dodge brothers, had initially manufactured the Ford chassis. In 1912 Ford started making its own chassis, and the Dodges started making their own automobile. Before the suit was brought, John Dodge had sought to sell the Dodges' stock to Henry Ford for $35 million. After the Supreme Court opinion, Ford stated that he intended to form another company that would produce a $250 automobile. The Dodges finally sold their interest to Ford in April, 1919, for $25 million, after which the remaining minority shareholders also sold out to Ford.[30]

BREHM v. EISNER
Delaware Supreme Court
746 A.2d 244 (2000)

VEASEY, Chief Justice:

* * *

The claims before us are that: (a) the board of directors of The Walt Disney Company ("Disney") as it was constituted in 1995 (the "Old Board") breached its fiduciary duty in approving an extravagant and wasteful Employment Agreement of Michael S. Ovitz as president of Disney; (b) the Disney board of directors as it was constituted in 1996 (the "New Board") breached its fiduciary duty in agreeing to a "non-fault" termination of the Ovitz Employment Agreement, a decision that was extravagant and wasteful; and (c) the directors were not disinterested and independent. [The third claim is not considered in this excerpt.—Ed.]

* * *

Facts

* * *

A. The 1995 Ovitz Employment Agreement

By an agreement dated October 1, 1995, Disney hired Ovitz as its president. He was a long-time friend of Disney Chairman and CEO Michael Eisner. At the time, Ovitz was an important talent broker in Hollywood. Although he lacked experience managing a diversi-

---

[30] For an interesting perspective on *Dodge,* see Rock, *Corporate Law Through an Antitrust Lens*, 92 COLUM. L. REV. 562, 619-23 (1992) (characterizing *Dodge* as a restraint on competition that may be actionable under the antitrust laws).

fied public company, other companies with entertainment operations had been interested in hiring him for high-level executive positions. The Employment Agreement was unilaterally negotiated by Eisner and approved by the Old Board. Their judgment was that Ovitz was a valuable person to hire as president of Disney, and they agreed ultimately with Eisner's recommendation in awarding him an extraordinarily lucrative contract.

Ovitz' Employment Agreement had an initial term of five years and required that Ovitz "devote his full time and best efforts exclusively to the Company," with exceptions for volunteer work, service on the board of another company, and managing his passive investments. In return, Disney agreed to give Ovitz a base salary of $1 million per year, a discretionary bonus, and two sets of stock options (the "A" options and the "B" options) that collectively would enable Ovitz to purchase 5 million shares of Disney common stock.

* * *

The Employment Agreement provided for three ways by which Ovitz' employment might end. He might serve his five years and Disney might decide against offering him a new contract. If so, Disney would owe Ovitz a $10 million termination payment. Before the end of the initial term, Disney could terminate Ovitz for "good cause" only if Ovitz committed gross negligence or malfeasance, or if Ovitz resigned voluntarily. Disney would owe Ovitz no additional compensation if it terminated him for "good cause." Termination without cause (non-fault termination) would entitle Ovitz to the present value of his remaining salary payments through September 30, 2000, a $10 million severance payment, an additional $7.5 million for each fiscal year remaining under the agreement, and the immediate vesting of the first 3 million stock options (the "A" Options).

* * *

B. The New Board's Actions in Approving the Non-Fault Termination

Soon after Ovitz began work, problems surfaced and the situation continued to deteriorate during the first year of his employment. To support this allegation, the plaintiffs cite various media reports detailing internal complaints and providing external examples of alleged business mistakes. The Complaint uses these reports to suggest that the New Board had reason to believe that Ovitz' performance and lack of commitment met the gross negligence or malfeasance standards of the termination-for-cause provisions of the contract.

The deteriorating situation, according to the Complaint, led Ovitz to begin seeking alternative employment and to send Eisner a letter in September 1996 that the Complaint paraphrases as stating his dissatisfaction with his role and expressing his desire to leave the Company. The Complaint also admits that Ovitz would not actually resign before negotiating a non-fault severance agreement because he did not want to jeopardize his rights to a lucrative severance in the form of a "non-fault termination" under the terms of the 1995 Employment Agreement.

On December 11, 1996, Eisner and Ovitz agreed to arrange for Ovitz to leave Disney on the non-fault basis provided for in the 1995 Employment Agreement. Eisner then "caused" the New Board "to rubber-stamp his decision (by 'mutual consent')." This decision was implemented by a December 27, 1996 letter to Ovitz from defendant Sanford M. Litvack, an officer and director of Disney. . . .

* * *

Although the non-fault termination left Ovitz with what essentially was a very lucrative severance agreement, it is important to note that Ovitz and Disney had negotiated for that severance payment at the time they initially contracted in 1995, and in the end the payout to Ovitz did not exceed the 1995 contractual benefits. Consequently, Ovitz received the $10 million termination payment, $7.5 million for part of the fiscal year remaining under the agreement and the immediate vesting of the 3 million stock options (the "A" options). As a result of his termination Ovitz would not receive the 2 million "B" options that he would have been entitled to if he had completed the full term of the Employment Agreement and if his contract were renewed.

The Complaint charges the New Board with waste, computing the value of the severance package agreed to by the Board at over $140 million, consisting of cash payments of about $39 million and the value of the immediately vesting "A" options of over $101 million. The Complaint quotes Crystal, the Old Board's expert, as saying in January 1997 that Ovitz' severance package was a "shocking amount of severance."

* * *

Plaintiffs' Contention that the Old Board Violated "Substantive Due Care" Requirements and Committed Waste Ab Initio with Ovitz' Employment Agreement

* * *

Plaintiffs' principal theory is that the 1995 Ovitz Employment Agreement was a "wasteful transaction for Disney *ab initio*" because it was structured to "incentivize" Ovitz to seek an early non-fault termination. The Court of Chancery correctly dismissed this theory as failing to meet the stringent requirements of the waste test, *i.e.*, "'an exchange that is so one sided that no business person of ordinary, sound judgment could conclude that the corporation has received adequate consideration.'" Moreover, the Court concluded that a board's decision on executive compensation is entitled to great deference. It is the essence of business judgment for a board to determine if "a 'particular individual warrant[s] large amounts of money, whether in the form of current salary or severance provisions.'"

Specifically, the Court of Chancery inferred from a reading of the Complaint that the Board determined it had to offer an expensive compensation package to attract Ovitz and that they determined he would be valuable to the Company. The Court also concluded that the vesting schedule of the options actually was a disincentive for Ovitz to leave Disney. When he did leave pursuant to the non-fault termination, the Court noted that he left 2 million options (the "B" options) "on the table." Although we agree with the conclusion of the Court of Chancery that this particular Complaint is deficient, we do not foreclose the possibility that a properly framed complaint could pass muster.

. . . We agree with the analysis of the Court of Chancery that the size and structure of executive compensation are inherently matters of judgment. . . .

To be sure, there are outer limits, but they are confined to unconscionable cases where directors irrationally squander or give away corporate assets. Here, however, we find no error in the decision of the Court of Chancery on the waste test.

As for the plaintiffs' contention that the directors failed to exercise "substantive due care," we should note that such a concept is foreign to the business judgment rule. Courts do not measure, weigh or quantify directors' judgments. We do not even decide if they are reasonable in this context. Due care in the decisionmaking context is process due care only. Irrationality is the outer limit of the business judgment rule. Irrationality may be the functional equivalent of the waste test or it may tend to show that the decision is not made in good faith, which is a key ingredient of the business judgment rule.

Plaintiffs' Contention that the New Board Committed Waste in Its Decision That Ovitz' Contract Should be Terminated on a "Non-Fault" Basis

The plaintiffs contend in this Court that Ovitz resigned or committed acts of gross negligence or malfeasance that constituted grounds to terminate him for cause. In either event, they argue that the Company had no obligation to Ovitz and that the directors wasted the Company's assets by causing it to make an unnecessary and enormous payout of cash and stock options when it permitted Ovitz to terminate his employment on a "non-fault" basis. We have concluded, however, that the Complaint currently before us does not set forth particularized facts that he resigned or unarguably breached his Employment Agreement.

The Complaint does not allege facts that would show that Ovitz had, in fact, resigned before the Board acted on his non-fault termination. Plaintiffs contend, in effect, that the sum total of Ovitz' actions constituted a de facto resignation. But the Complaint does not allege that Ovitz had actually resigned. It alleges merely that he: (a) was dissatisfied with his role; (b) was underperforming; (c) was seeking and entertaining other job offers; and (d) had written to Eisner on September 5, 1996, "express[ing] his desire to quit." These are not particularized allegations that he resigned, either actually or constructively.

* * *

The Complaint alleges that it was waste for the Board to pay Ovitz essentially the full amount he was due on the non-fault termination basis because he should have been fired for cause. Ovitz' contract provided that he could be fired for cause only if he was grossly negligent or committed acts of malfeasance. Plaintiffs contend that ample grounds existed to fire Ovitz for cause under these terms. . . .

Construed most favorably to plaintiffs, the facts in the Complaint (disregarding conclusory allegations) show that Ovitz' performance as president was disappointing at best, that Eisner admitted it had been a mistake to hire him, that Ovitz lacked commitment to the Company, that he performed services for his old company, and that he negotiated for other jobs (some very lucrative) while being required under the contract to devote his full time and energy to Disney.

All this shows is that the Board had arguable grounds to fire Ovitz for cause. But what is alleged is only an argument—perhaps a good one—that Ovitz' conduct constituted gross negligence or malfeasance. First, given the facts as alleged, Disney would have had to persuade a trier of fact and law of this argument in any litigated dispute with Ovitz. Second, that process of persuasion could involve expensive litigation, distraction of executive time and company resources, lost opportunity costs, more bad publicity and an outcome that was uncertain at best and, at worst, could have resulted in damages against the Company.

The Complaint, in sum, contends that the Board committed waste by agreeing to the very lucrative payout to Ovitz under the non-fault termination provision because it had no obligation to him, thus taking the Board's decision outside the protection of the business judgment rule. Construed most favorably to plaintiffs, the Complaint contends that, by reason of the New Board's available arguments of resignation and good cause, it had the leverage to negotiate Ovitz down to a more reasonable payout than that guaranteed by his Employment Agreement. But the Complaint fails on its face to meet the waste test because it does not allege with particularity facts tending to show that no reasonable business person would have made the decision that the New Board made under these circumstances.

* * *

To rule otherwise would invite courts to become super-directors, measuring matters of degree in business decisionmaking and executive compensation. Such a rule would run counter to the foundation of our jurisprudence.

Nevertheless, plaintiffs will have another opportunity—if they are able to do so consistent with Chancery Rule 11—to file a short and plain statement alleging particularized facts creating a reasonable doubt that the New Board's decision regarding the Ovitz nonfault termination was protected by the business judgment rule.

* * *

HARTNETT, Justice, concurring:

I agree that the complaint leaves much to be desired and that plaintiffs be given an opportunity to file an amended complaint. In my view, however, the present complaint is adequate as to some of the asserted claims, if only barely so. . . .

Brushing aside technicalities, the issue here is whether this suit should have been dismissed by the Court of Chancery at this stage of the litigation without any discovery or whether the allegations in the complaint were sufficient to justify at least some discovery. In my opinion, the complaint already sufficiently alleges facts to warrant some limited discovery as to some of the claims.

NOTES AND QUESTIONS

(1) **The standard of liability.** What test does the *Shlensky* court adopt as the standard of liability? One way to understand *Shlensky* is to compare the *Dodge* case, which the court attempts to distinguish. Is second-guessing the board's decision in *Dodge* consistent with the *Shlensky* court's statement that liability will lie only if the defendants' conduct "at least borders on [fraud, illegality or conflict of interest]"? Does *Eisner* make it easier for plaintiffs to challenge disinterested business decisions or does it merely restate the *Shlensky* rule?

(2) **Policy basis of the business judgment rule.** Why shouldn't the courts second-guess business decisions that seem as clearly out of line as the ones in *Shlensky* and *Eisner*? Note that the plaintiffs in *Shlensky* and *Eisner* were not permitted even to present evidence on their claims. The rule can be understood in terms of the general fiduciary duty policies discussed above in Section 9.01: in the light of the availability of other monitoring devices and the costs of fiduciary duty liability (especially with respect to managerial risk aversion), the costs of overly intensive judicial scrutiny of

business transactions are likely to exceed the benefits. If managers were broadly liable for "unreasonable" transactions, they would tend to err on the side of caution in making decisions because they could not diversify away the substantial, firm-specific liability risk. Their shareholders would not favor this cautious approach because most hold diversified portfolios and therefore prefer managers who ignore firm-specific risk.[31] Also, courts do not have enough business skills or information to be, in the *Brehm* court's words, "super-directors."

(3) **Articulating the standard: the ALI and the RMBCA.** The business judgment rule has sparked considerable debate in connection with the formulation of director duties in the Revised Model Business Corporation Act and the ALI *Principles*. The first ALI draft provided in § 4.01(c) that a director or officer would be insulated from liability for the consequences of a disinterested business judgment if, in addition to acting on an informed basis and in good faith, he "had a rational basis for the business judgment." The Comments (at 144) said that "rational basis" insulated decisions that were unreasonable "but not egregiously unreasonable." The third draft changed this language to read: "had a rational basis for believing that the business judgment was in the best interests of the corporation," and the Comments (at 10) were changed to say that "rational basis" permitted "a significantly wider range of discretion than the term 'reasonable . . . .'" The final version, quoted on page 375, replaced "rational basis for believing" with "rationally believes."

Section 8.31(a) of the Model Business Corporation Act provides that disinterested directors shall not be liable to the corporation or its shareholders "unless the party asserting liability . . . establishes that . . . the challenged conduct consisted or was the result of: (i) action not in good faith; or (ii) a decision . . . which the director did not reasonably believe to be in the best interests of the corporation." The Official Comment to MBCA § 8.31 provides additional guidance as to when courts may second guess disinterested business decisions: "where a decision respecting the corporation's best interests is so removed from the realm of reason (*e.g.,* corporate waste) . . . , the director's judgment will not be sustained." How different is the MBCA approach from that of the ALI or *Eisner*?

Prior versions of the MBCA had set forth duties of directors in § 8.30, but had left the question of liability for violations of those duties to the courts. Section 8.31 now makes clear that not all violations of § 8.30 duties will result in liability. Why set forth duties in § 8.30 if there is no remedy for their violation under § 8.31?

(4) **Articulating the standard: Delaware.** The leading formulation of Delaware's business judgment rule appears in *Aronson v. Lewis*:[32]

---

[31] For a good judicial discussion of the policy basis underlying the business judgment rule, see *Gagliardi v. Tri-Foods International, Inc.*, 683 A.2d 1049, 1052-53 (Del. Ch. 1996).

[32] 473 A.2d 805, 812 (Del. 1984).

> . . . The business judgment rule is an acknowledgment of the manage-
> rial prerogatives of Delaware directors under Section 141(a). *See Zapata
> Corp. v. Maldonado.* . . . It is a presumption that in making a business deci-
> sion the directors of a corporation acted on an informed basis, in good faith
> and in the honest belief that the action taken was in the best interests of the
> company. Absent an abuse of discretion, that judgment will be respected by
> the courts. The burden is on the party challenging the decision to establish
> facts rebutting the presumption. *See Puma v. Marriott*, Del. Ch., 283 A.2d
> 693, 695 (1971). . . .

Does *Aronson* permit directors to be held liable for an erroneous but careful judgment short of conflict of interest or other fraud? A long line of cases, including *Eisner*,
suggests that liability is at least possible in such situations.[33] But cases ruling against
directors are extremely rare.

An older example is *Gimbel v. The Signal Companies.*[34] In *Gimbel*, the chancery
court held that the directors' decision to sell a subsidiary for $480 million could be pre-
liminarily enjoined based, in part, on evidence that the actual value of the subsidiary was
at least $761 million. The court reasoned as follows:

> Actual fraud, whether resulting from self-dealing or otherwise, is not
> necessary to challenge a sale of assets. And, although the language of "con-
> structive fraud" or "badge of fraud" has frequently and almost traditionally
> been used, such language is not very helpful when fraud admittedly has not
> been established. There are limits on the business judgment rule which fall
> short of intentional or inferred fraudulent misconduct and which are based
> simply on gross inadequacy of price. This is clear even if language of fraud
> is used. . . .

More recently, *Parnes v. Bally Entertainment Corporation*[35] considered whether
directors of Bally Entertainment Corporation were entitled to the protection of the business judgment rule for their role in approving a merger with Hilton. The plaintiff
alleged, among other things, that the merger transaction was tainted by demands of
Bally's CEO, Goldberg, for personal payments and asset transfers in exchange for his

---

[33] *See, e.g., In re 3COM Corporation Shareholders Litigation*, 1999 Del. Ch. LEXIS 215, 1999 WL 1009210
(Del. Ch., Oct. 25, 1999) (to establish a claim of waste the plaintiff must "establish a complete failure of consideration"
or acts that were "so blatant that no ordinary business person would ever consider the transaction to be fair to the corporation"); *Zupnick v. Goizueta*, 698 A.2d 384 (Del. Ch. 1997) (test for liability is "an extreme [one], very rarely satisfied by a shareholder plaintiff," because "if under the circumstances any reasonable person might conclude that the deal
made sense, then the judicial inquiry ends"); *Gagliardi v. TriFoods International, Inc.*, 683 A.2d 1049 (Del. Ch. 1996)
("There is a theoretical exception to this general statement that holds that some decisions may be so 'egregious' that liability for losses they cause may follow even in the absence of proof of conflict of interest or improper motivation. The
exception, however, has resulted in no awards of money judgments against corporate officers or directors in this jurisdiction . . . .").

[34]   316 A.2d 599, 610 (Del. Ch. 1974).

[35]   722 A.2d 1243 (Del. 1999).

consent. Assuming the independence of Bally's directors for purposes of its decision, the court said:

> The presumptive validity of a business judgment is rebutted in those rare cases where the decision under attack is "so far beyond the bounds of reasonable judgment that it seems essentially inexplicable on any ground other than bad faith." We are satisfied that the facts alleged in the Parnes complaint meet this test. Goldberg allegedly demanded that any potential acquiror pay Goldberg for his approval of the merger. Parnes supports that allegation by listing several substantial cash payments and asset transfers that allegedly lacked any consideration and were conditioned upon the completion of the merger. . . . If, as Parnes claims, Goldberg tainted the entire process of finding an interested merger partner and negotiating the transaction by demanding a bribe, then it is inexplicable that independent directors, acting in good faith, could approve the deal.[36]

The alleged payments and transfer to Goldberg in connection with the merger included:

> 1) a termination payment of $21 million (which exceeds the amount arguably due to Goldberg by approximately $14.4 million); 2) the transfer to Goldberg for $250,000 of a warrant worth $5 million for the purchase of 20% of Bally Total Fitness Holding Corporation's common stock and the forgiveness of $15.2 million of Bally Fitness indebtedness to Bally; 3) the merger of Bally's Casino Holdings, Inc., a shell corporation, into Bally and the conversion of the Casino Holdings preferred stock, all owned by Goldberg, into Bally and Bally Total Fitness stock worth approximately $43 million; 4) the transfer to Goldberg of 20% of Bally's interest in a Maryland race track project; and 5) the transfer to Goldberg of 40% of Bally's interest in a proposed Mexican gaming venture.[37]

How is this transaction distinguishable from the one in *Brehm*? In light of *Brehm* and *Parnes,* how might a court resolve under the business judgment rule a claim arising out of the contract Jack Welch, General Electric's long-time and very successful CEO, made before retiring to provide him with retirement benefits including an $80,000 a month apartment in Manhattan, $86,000 a year in consulting fees, use of a Boeing jet valued at $291,869 a month, flowers, wine, faxes, postage, food, autos and electronics, country club membership, tickets to sports and cultural events, security, financial planning, satellite TV, and access to the GE box at Fenway Park?

(5) **Need for a conscious decision.** The business judgment rule comes into play only when the directors have made a decision,[38] although the decision may be one to

---

[36]   *Id*. at 1246-47.

[37]   *Id*. at 1246.

[38]   *See Kaplan v. Centex Corp.*, 284 A.2d 119, 124 (Del. Ch. 1971).

refrain from acting (*see* MBCA § 8.31(a)). So the courts may be more likely to second-guess directors who have failed adequately to exercise their duty of supervision (*see* Section 9.02). MBCA § 8.31(a)(2)(iv) makes this distinction explicit, withdrawing the protection of the business judgment rule in cases of "a sustained failure of the director to devote attention to ongoing oversight of the business and affairs of the corporation." Is this distinction realistic? Doesn't the board exercise its business judgment about what to do, and what not to do?[39] For example, does the decision in *Bierman* (Section 9.02) involve a bad business judgment or a failure to supervise?

(6) **Corporate social responsibility and the business judgment rule.** To what extent does the business judgment rule's protection depend on whether the transaction is intended solely to maximize corporate profit or, as was arguably the case in *Shlensky* and *Dodge*, partly to benefit society?[40] ALI *Principles* § 2.01, purporting to codify these cases, provides that "a corporation should have as its objective the conduct of business activities with a view to enhancing shareholder gain." Some state statutes passed in the wake of the heated takeover activity of the 1980s explicitly permit directors to consider *non-shareholder* constituencies.[41] Do these statutory provisions give directors more leeway to benefit society than to be simply wrongheaded or careless? If so, is this appropriate in light of the discussion in Section 7.02[C] above? Note that some statutes, such as those in Connecticut, Indiana, Iowa and Pennsylvania, actually *require* directors to consider the interests of other constituencies, permit their interests to *dominate* those of shareholders, or *require* shareholder interests *not* to dominate. Such statutes may even allow non-shareholder groups to sue boards that make shareholder-oriented decisions.

(7) **Liability versus injunctive relief.** The business judgment rule may only insulate the directors from personal liability, rather than precluding injunctive relief. This distinction has been rejected by the Delaware Supreme Court,[42] but recognized in the ALI *Principles*, § 4.01. Should the standard to which director decisions are held depend

---

[39]   *See* **Manning** at 1485

[40]   For more recent cases that make clear the directors' wide discretion to make charitable gifts, see *Kahn v. Sullivan*, 594 A.2d 48 (Del. 1991) (Occidental's donation of art museum not unreasonably large gift given size of corporation); *Hanrahan v. Kruidenier*, 473 N.W.2d 184 (Iowa 1991) (donation of $250,000 to art museum within business judgment rule although made by dissolving company newspaper).

[41]   *See, e.g.*, Ohio Rev. Code Ann. § 1701.59:

Authority of directors; bylaws; standard of care.

* * *

(E) For purposes of this section, a director, in determining what he reasonably believes to be in the best interests of the corporation, shall consider the interests of the corporation's shareholders and, in his discretion, may consider any of the following: (1) The interests of the corporation's employees, suppliers, creditors, and customers; (2) The economy of the state and nation; (3) Community and societal considerations; (4) The long-term as well as short-term interests of the corporation and its shareholders, including the possibility that these interests may be best served by the continued independence of the corporation.

[42]   *See Revlon, Inc. v. MacAndrews & Forbes Holdings, Inc.*, 506 A.2d 173, 180 n.10 (1986).

on the relief the plaintiff is seeking? Many of the considerations discussed in Section 9.01, such as managerial risk aversion, underlying judicial deference to director decisions relate to the problems of holding directors individually liable. But the problem of the courts' *ability* to second-guess director decisions remains, whatever the relief. Moreover, as the court recognized in *Gimbel*, discussed in Note 4 above, overturning a transaction can have substantial adverse consequences for the shareholders and may even trump a majority vote in favor of the transaction. In *Gimbel*, the court held that the plaintiffs were entitled to a preliminary injunction blocking the sale of a subsidiary, but required the plaintiffs to post a $25 million bond to secure the risk that a preliminary injunction might lead the prospective buyer to abandon the transaction.

(8) **Illegality.** The business judgment rule may not insulate directors from liability for the corporation's illegal acts. In *Miller v. American Telephone & Telegraph Co.*,[43] the court reversed and remanded the dismissal of a stockholder's complaint alleging that AT&T directors had failed to collect a debt from the Democratic National Committee in violation of a federal law prohibiting certain corporate political contributions. The court reasoned that liability would be consistent with the legislature's intent to protect shareholders from spending corporate funds for political purposes.[44] But does it make sense to police corporate violations of law through shareholder suits?

The *Miller* liability theory raises some questions. First, the court noted that, under controlling New York law, damage to the corporation was an essential element of plaintiff's claim.[45] Thus, it is not clear whether the amount of the contribution would be offset against any benefit resulting from the contribution, such as favorable political action. ALI *Principles* § 7.18(c) lets the defendant offset the corporation's gains and losses in *the same transaction* except to the extent this would frustrate "public policy." Second, it is unclear whether the *Miller* theory makes the business judgment rule inapplicable whenever any law is violated, or only in the event of certain types of statutory violations. *Miller* emphasized that the statute at issue was specifically intended to protect shareholders.[46] It is not clear whether the same result would have been reached under, for example, anti-pollution legislation. What do you suppose is the effect on this issue of ALI *Principles*, § 2.01(B)(1), quoted above? Also, is any violation of law necessarily in "bad faith" and therefore not insulated by the business judgment rule (*see* **Arsht** at 129-30)? Third, to what extent are the directors liable if they failed to discover that the

---

[43]   507 F.2d 759 (3d Cir. 1974).

[44]   For a case going the other way, see *Stern v. General Electric Company*, 924 F.2d 472 (2d Cir. 1992) (dismissing complaint based on board approval of alleged illegal campaign contributions for failure sufficiently to allege fraud or bad faith).

[45]   507 F.2d at 763 n.5.

[46]   Note that in *Cort v. Ash*, 422 U.S. 66 (1975), the Supreme Court denied an implied right of action in favor of corporate shareholders under the statute involved in *Miller*, reasoning in part that the statute was not intended to benefit shareholders.

corporation was violating the law? See the *Graham* case, discussed in Note 2 following the *Bierman* excerpt in Section 9.02.

REFERENCES

Arsht & Hinsey, *Codified Standard—Same Harbor but Charted Channel: A Response*, 35 Bus. Law. ix (1980).

Hansen, *Other Constituency Statutes: A Search for Perspective*, 46 Bus. Law. 1355 (1991).

Hinsey, *Business Judgment and the American Law Institute's Corporate Governance Project: The Rule, the Doctrine and the Reality*, 52 Geo. Wash. L. Rev. 609 (1984).

Letsou, *Implications of Shareholder Diversification on Corporate Law and Organization: The Case of the Business Judgment Rule*, 77 Chi.-Kent L. Rev. 179 (2001).

Macey, *An Economic Analysis of the Various Rationales for Making Shareholders the Exclusive Beneficiaries of Corporate Fiduciary Duties*, 21 Stetson L. Rev. 23 (1991)

Manning, *The Business Judgment Rule and the Director's Duty of Attention: Time for Reality*, 39 Bus. Law. 1477 (1984).

Schwartz, *Defining the Corporate Objective: Section 2.01 of the American Law Institute's Principles*, 52 Geo. Wash. L. Rev. 511 (1984).

Veasey & Manning, *Codified Standard—Safe Harbor or Uncharted Reef? An Analysis of the Model Act Standard of Care Compared with Delaware Law*, 35 Bus. Law. 919 (1980).

[B] Procedural Review of Disinterested Decisions

As the ALI *Principles* make clear (see the introduction to Section 9.03), the business judgment rule protects only informed business decisions. The following materials discuss the meaning of this requirement.

SMITH v. VAN GORKOM
Delaware Supreme Court
488 A.2d 858 (1985)

Horsey, Justice:

This appeal from the Court of Chancery involves a class action brought by shareholders of the defendant Trans Union Corporation ("Trans Union" or "the Company"), originally seeking rescission of a cash-out merger of Trans Union into the defendant New T Company ("New T"), a wholly-owned subsidiary of the defendant, Marmon Group, Inc. ("Marmon"). Alternate relief in the form of damages is sought against the defendant members of the Board of Directors of Trans Union, New T, and Jay A. Pritzker and Robert A. Pritzker, owners of Marmon.[1]

---

[1] The plaintiff, Alden Smith, originally sought to enjoin the merger, but, following extensive discovery, the Trial Court denied the plaintiff's motion for preliminary injunction by unreported letter opinion dated February 3, 1981. On February 10, 1981, the proposed merger was approved by Trans Union's stockholders at a special meeting and

* * *

We hold . . . that the Board's decision, reached September 20, 1980, to approve the proposed cash-out merger was not the product of an informed business judgment . . . .

I.

The nature of this case requires a detailed factual statement. The following facts are essentially uncontradicted:

-A-

Trans Union was a publicly-traded, diversified holding company, the principal earnings of which were generated by its railcar leasing business. During the period here involved, the Company had a cash flow of hundreds of millions of dollars annually. However, the Company had difficulty in generating sufficient taxable income to offset increasingly large investment tax credits (ITCs). . . .

-B-

On August 27, 1980, Van Gorkom met with Senior Management of Trans Union. Van Gorkom reported on . . . his desire to find a solution to the tax credit problem more permanent than a continued program of acquisitions. Various alternatives were suggested and discussed preliminarily, including the sale of Trans Union to a company with a large amount of taxable income.

Donald Romans, Chief Financial Officer of Trans Union, stated that his department had done a "very brief bit of work on the possibility of a leveraged buy-out." This work had been prompted by a media article which Romans had seen regarding a leveraged buy-out by management. The work consisted of a "preliminary study" of the cash which could be generated by the Company if it participated in a leveraged buy-out. As Romans stated, this analysis "was very first and rough cut at seeing whether a cash flow would support what might be considered a high price for this type of transaction."

On September 5, at another Senior Management meeting which Van Gorkom attended, Romans again brought up the idea of a leveraged buy-out as a "possible strategic alternative" to the Company's acquisition program. Romans and Bruce S. Chelberg, President and Chief Operating Officer of Trans Union, had been working on the matter in preparation for the meeting. According to Romans: They did not "come up" with a price for the Company. They merely "ran the numbers" at $50 a share and at $60 a share with the "rough form" of their cash figures at the time. Their "figures indicated that $50 would be very easy to do but $60 would be very difficult to do under those figures." This work did not purport to establish a fair price for either the Company or 100% of the stock. It was intended to determine the cash flow needed to service the debt that would "probably" be incurred in a leveraged buy-out, based on "rough calculations" without "any benefit of experts to identify what the

---

the merger became effective on that date. Thereafter, John W. Gosselin was permitted to intervene as an additional plaintiff, and Smith and Gosselin were certified as representing a class consisting of all persons, other than defendants, who held shares of Trans Union common stock on all relevant dates. At the time of the merger, Smith owned 54,000 shares of Trans Union stock, Gosselin owned 23,600 shares, and members of Gosselin's family owned 20,000 shares.

limits were to that, and so forth." These computations were not considered extensive and no conclusion was reached.

At this meeting, Van Gorkom stated that he would be willing to take $55 per share for his own 75,000 shares. He vetoed the suggestion of a leveraged buy-out by Management, however, as involving a potential conflict of interest for Management. Van Gorkom, a certified public accountant and lawyer, had been an officer of Trans Union for 24 years, its Chief Executive Officer for more than 17 years, and Chairman of its Board for 2 years. It is noteworthy in this connection that he was then approaching 65 years of age and mandatory retirement.

For several days following the September 5 meeting Van Gorkom pondered the idea of a sale. He had participated in many acquisitions as a manager and director of Trans Union and as a director of other companies. He was familiar with acquisition procedures, valuation methods, and negotiations; and he privately considered the pros and cons of whether Trans Union should seek a privately or publicly-held purchaser.

Van Gorkom decided to meet with Jay A. Pritzker, a well-known corporate takeover specialist and a social acquaintance. However, rather than approaching Pritzker simply to determine his interest in acquiring Trans Union, Van Gorkom assembled a proposed per share price for sale of the Company and a financing structure by which to accomplish the sale. Van Gorkom did so without consulting either his Board or any members of Senior Management except one: Carl Peterson, Trans Union's Controller. Telling Peterson that he wanted no other person on his staff to know what he was doing, but without telling him why, Van Gorkom directed Peterson to calculate the feasibility of a leveraged buy-out at an assumed price per share of $55. Apart from the Company's historic stock market price,[5] and Van Gorkom's long association with Trans Union, the record is devoid of any competent evidence that $55 represented the per share intrinsic value of the Company.

Having thus chosen the $55 figure, based solely on the availability of a leveraged buy-out, Van Gorkom multiplied the price per share by the number of shares outstanding to reach a total value of the Company of $690 million. Van Gorkom told Peterson to use this $690 million figure and to assume a $200 million equity contribution by the buyer. Based on these assumptions, Van Gorkom directed Peterson to determine whether the debt portion of the purchase price could be paid off in five years or less if financed by Trans Union's cash flow as projected in the Five Year Forecast, and by the sale of certain weaker divisions identified in a study done for Trans Union by the Boston Consulting Group ("BCG study"). Peterson reported that, of the purchase price, approximately $50-80 million would remain outstanding after five years. Van Gorkom was disappointed, but decided to meet with Pritzker nevertheless.

Van Gorkom arranged a meeting with Pritzker at the latter's home on Saturday, September 13, 1980. Van Gorkom prefaced his presentation by stating to Pritzker "Now as far as you are concerned, I can, I think, show how you can pay a substantial premium over the

---

[5] The common stock of Trans Union was traded on the New York Stock Exchange. Over the five year period from 1975 through 1979, Trans Union's stock had traded within a range of a high of $39½ and a low of $24¼. Its high and low range for 1980 through September 19 (the last trading day before announcement of the merger) was $38¼ - $29½.

present stock price and pay off most of the loan in the first five years. . . . If you could pay $55 for this Company, here is a way in which I think it can be financed."

Van Gorkom then reviewed with Pritzker his calculations based upon his proposed price of $55 per share. Although Pritzker mentioned $50 as a more attractive figure, no other price was mentioned. However, Van Gorkom stated that to be sure that $55 was the best price obtainable, Trans Union should be free to accept any better offer. Pritzker demurred, stating that his organization would serve as a "Stalking horse" for an "auction contest" only if Trans Union would permit Pritzker to buy 1,750,000 shares of Trans Union stock at market price which Pritzker could then sell to any higher bidder. After further discussion on this point, Pritzker told Van Gorkom that he would give him a more definite reaction soon.

On Monday, September 15, Pritzker advised Van Gorkom that he was interested in the $55 cash-out merger proposed and requested more information on Trans Union. Van Gorkom agreed to meet privately with Pritzker, accompanied by Peterson, Chelberg and Michael Carpenter, Trans Union's consultant from the Boston Consulting Group. The meetings took place on September 16 and 17. Van Gorkom was "astounded that events were moving with such amazing rapidity."

On Thursday, September 18, Van Gorkom met again with Pritzker. At that time, Van Gorkom knew that Pritzker intended to make a cash-out merger offer at Van Gorkom's proposed $55 per share. Pritzker instructed his attorney, a merger and acquisition specialist, to begin drafting merger documents. There was no further discussion of the $55 price. However, the number of shares of Trans Union's treasury stock to be offered to Pritzker was negotiated down to one million shares; the price was set at $38—75 cents above the per share price at the close of the market on September 19. At this point, Pritzker insisted that the Trans Union Board act on his merger proposal within the next three days, stating to Van Gorkom: "We have to have a decision by no later than Sunday [evening, September 21] before the opening of the English stock exchange on Monday morning." Pritzker's lawyer was then instructed to draft the merger documents, to be reviewed by Van Gorkom's lawyer, "sometimes with discussion and sometimes not, in the haste to get it finished."

On Friday, September 19, Van Gorkom, Chelberg, and Pritzker consulted with Trans Union's lead bank regarding the financing of Pritzker's purchase of Trans Union. The bank indicated that it could form a syndicate of banks that would finance the transaction. On the same day, Van Gorkom retained James Brennan, Esquire, to advise Trans Union on the legal aspects of the merger. Van Gorkom did not consult with William Browder, a Vice-President and director of Trans Union and former head of its legal department, or with William Moore, then the head of Trans Union's legal staff.

On Friday, September 19, Van Gorkom called a special meeting of the Trans Union Board for noon the following day. He also called a meeting of the Company's Senior Management to convene at 11:00 a.m., prior to the meeting of the Board. No one, except Chelberg and Peterson, was told the purpose of the meetings. Van Gorkom did not invite Trans Union's investment banker, Salomon Brothers or its Chicago-based partner, to attend.

Of those present at the Senior Management meeting on September 20, only Chelberg and Peterson had prior knowledge of Pritzker's offer. Van Gorkom disclosed the offer and described its terms, but he furnished no copies of the proposed Merger Agreement. Romans announced that his department had done a second study which showed that, for a leveraged buy-out, the price range for Trans Union stock was between $55 and $65 per share. Van Gorkom neither saw the study nor asked Romans to make it available for the Board meeting.

Senior Management's reaction to the Pritzker proposal was completely negative. No member of Management, except Chelberg and Peterson, supported the proposal. Romans objected to the price as being too low;[6] he was critical of the timing and suggested that consideration should be given to the adverse tax consequences of an all-cash deal for low-basis shareholders; and he took the position that the agreement to sell Pritzker one million newly-issued shares at market price would inhibit other offers, as would the prohibitions against soliciting bids and furnishing inside information to other bidders. Romans argued that the Pritzker proposal was a "lock up" and amounted to "an agreed merger as opposed to an offer." Nevertheless, Van Gorkom proceeded to the Board meeting as scheduled without further delay.

Ten directors served on the Trans Union Board, five inside (defendants Bonser, O'Boyle, Browder, Chelberg, and Van Gorkom) and five outside (defendants Wadis, Johnson, Lanterman, Morgan and Reneker). All directors were present at the meeting, except O'Boyle who was ill. Of the outside directors, four were corporate chief executive officers and one was the former Dean of the University of Chicago Business School. None was an investment banker or trained financial analyst. All members of the Board were well informed about the Company and its operations as a going concern. They were familiar with the current financial condition of the Company, as well as operating and earnings projections reported in the recent Five Year Forecast. The Board generally received regular and detailed reports and was kept abreast of the accumulated investment tax credit and accelerated depreciation problem.

Van Gorkom began the Special Meeting of the Board with a twenty-minute oral presentation. Copies of the proposed Merger Agreement were delivered too late for study before or during the meeting.[7] He reviewed the Company's ITC and depreciation problems and the efforts theretofore made to solve them. He discussed his initial meeting with Pritzker and his motivation in arranging that meeting. Van Gorkom did not disclose to the Board, however, the methodology by which he alone had arrived at the $55 figure, or the fact that he first proposed the $55 price in his negotiations with Pritzker.

Van Gorkom outlined the terms of the Pritzker offer as follows: Pritzker would pay $55 in cash for all outstanding shares of Trans Union stock upon completion of which Trans Union would be merged into New T Company, a subsidiary wholly-owned by Pritzker and formed to implement the merger; for a period of 90 days, Trans Union could receive, but could not actively solicit, competing offers; the offer had to be acted on by the next evening, Sunday, September 21; Trans Union could only furnish to competing bidders published

---

[6]   Van Gorkom asked Romans to express his opinion as to the $55 price. Romans stated that he "thought the price was too low in relation to what he could derive for the company in a cash sale, particularly one which enabled us to realize the values of certain subsidiaries and independent entities."

[7]   The record is not clear as to the terms of the Merger agreement. The Agreement, as originally presented to the Board on September 20, was never produced by defendants despite demands by the plaintiffs. Nor is it clear that the directors were given an opportunity to study the Merger Agreement before voting on it. All that can be said is that Brennan had the Agreement before him during the meeting.

information, and not proprietary information; the offer was subject to Pritzker obtaining the necessary financing by October 10, 1980; if the financing contingency were met or waived by Pritzker, Trans Union was required to sell to Pritzker one million newly-issued shares of Trans Union at $38 per share.

Van Gorkom took the position that putting Trans Union "up for auction" through a 90-day market test would validate a decision by the Board that $55 was a fair price. He told the Board that the "free market will have an opportunity to judge whether $55 is a fair price." Van Gorkom framed the decision before the Board not as whether $55 per share was the highest price that could be obtained, but as whether the $55 price was a fair price that the stockholders should be given the opportunity to accept or reject.

Attorney Brennan advised the members of the Board that they might be sued if they failed to accept the offer and that a fairness opinion was not required as a matter of law.

Romans attended the meeting as chief financial officer of the Company. He told the Board that he had not been involved in the negotiations with Pritzker and knew nothing about the merger proposal until the morning of the meeting; that his studies did not indicate either a fair price for the stock or a valuation of the Company; that he did not see his role as directly addressing the fairness issue; and that he and his people "were trying to search for ways to justify a price in connection with such a [leveraged buy-out] transaction, rather than to say what the shares are worth." Romans testified:

> I told the Board that the study ran the numbers at 50 and 60, and then the subsequent study at 55 and 65, and that was not the same thing as saying that I have a valuation of the company at X dollars. But it was a way—a first step towards reaching that conclusion.

Romans told the Board that, in his opinion, $55 was "in the range of a fair price," but "at the beginning of the range."

Chelberg, Trans Union's President, supported Van Gorkom's presentation and representations. He testified that he "participated to make sure that the Board members collectively were clear on the details of the agreement or offer from Pritzker"; that he "participated in the discussion with Mr. Brennan, inquiring of him about the necessity for valuation opinions in spite of the way in which this particular offer was couched"; and that he was otherwise actively involved in supporting the positions being taken by Van Gorkom before the Board about "the necessity to act immediately on this offer," and about "the adequacy of the $55 and the question of how that would be tested."

The Board meeting of September 20 lasted about two hours. Based solely upon Van Gorkom's oral presentation, Chelberg's supporting representations, Romans' oral statement, Brennan's legal advice, and their knowledge of the market history of the Company's stock,[9]

---

[9] The Trial Court stated the premium relationship of the $55 price to the market history of the Company's stock as follows:

> . . . the merger price offered to the stockholders of Trans Union represented a premium of 62% over the average of the high and low prices at which Trans Union stock had traded in 1980, a premium of 48% over the last closing price, and a premium of 39% over the highest price at which the stock of Trans Union had traded any time during the prior six years.

the directors approved the proposed Merger Agreement. However, the Board later claimed to have attached two conditions to its acceptance: (1) that Trans Union reserved the right to accept any better offer that was made during the market test period; and (2) that Trans Union could share its proprietary information with any other potential bidders. While the Board now claims to have reserved the right to accept any better offer received after the announcement of the Pritzker agreement (even though the minutes of the meeting do not reflect this), it is undisputed that the Board did not reserve the right to actively solicit alternate offers.

The Merger Agreement was executed by Van Gorkom during the evening of September 20 at a formal social event that he hosted for the opening of the Chicago Lyric Opera. Neither he nor any other director read the agreement prior to its signing and delivery to Pritzker. . . .

On Monday, September 22, the Company issued a press release announcing that Trans Union had entered into a "definitive" Merger Agreement with an affiliate of the Marmon Group, Inc., a Pritzker holding company. Within 10 days of the public announcement, dissent among Senior Management over the merger had become widespread. Faced with threatened resignations of key officers, Van Gorkom met with Pritzker who agreed to several modifications of the Agreement. Pritzker was willing to do so provided that Van Gorkom could persuade the dissidents to remain on the Company payroll for at least six months after consummation of the merger.

Van Gorkom reconvened the Board on October 8 and secured the directors' approval of the proposed amendments—sight unseen. The Board also authorized the employment of Salomon Brothers, its investment banker, to solicit other offers for Trans Union during the proposed "market test" period.

The next day, October 9, Trans Union issued a press release announcing: (1) that Pritzker had obtained "the financing commitments necessary to consummate" the merger with Trans Union; (2) that Pritzker had acquired one million shares of Trans Union common stock at $38 per share; (3) that Trans Union was now permitted to actively seek other offers and had retained Salomon Brothers for that purpose; and (4) that if a more favorable offer were not received before February 1, 1981, Trans Union's shareholders would thereafter meet to vote on the Pritzker proposal.

It was not until the following day, October 10, that the actual amendments to the Merger Agreement were prepared by Pritzker and delivered to Van Gorkom for execution. As will be seen, the amendments were considerably at variance with Van Gorkom's representations of the amendments to the Board on October 8; and the amendments placed serious constraints on Trans Union's ability to negotiate a better deal and withdraw from the Pritzker agreement. Nevertheless, Van Gorkom proceeded to execute what became the October 10 amendments to the Merger Agreement without conferring further with the Board members and apparently without comprehending the actual implications of the amendments. . . .

Salomon Brothers' efforts over a three-month period from October 21 to January 21 produced only one serious suitor for Trans Union—General Electric Credit Corporation ("GE Credit"), a subsidiary of the General Electric Company. However, GE Credit was unwilling to make an offer for Trans Union unless Trans Union first rescinded its Merger

Agreement with Pritzker. When Pritzker refused, GE Credit terminated further discussions with Trans Union in early January.

In the meantime, in early December, the investment firm of Kohlberg, Kravis, Roberts & Co. ("KKR"), the only other concern to make a firm offer for Trans Union, withdrew its offer under circumstances hereinafter detailed.

On December 19, this litigation was commenced and, within four weeks, the plaintiffs had deposed eight of the ten directors of Trans Union, including Van Gorkom, Chelberg and Romans, its Chief Financial Officer. On January 21, Management's Proxy Statement for the February 10 shareholder meeting was mailed to Trans Union's stockholders. On January 26, Trans Union's Board met and, after a lengthy meeting, voted to proceed with the Pritzker merger. The Board also approved for mailing, "on or about January 27," a Supplement to its Proxy Statement. The Supplement purportedly set forth all information relevant to the Pritzker Merger Agreement, which had not been divulged in the first Proxy Statement. . . .

On February 10, the stockholders of Trans Union approved the Pritzker merger proposal. Of the outstanding shares, 69.9% were voted in favor of the merger, 7.25% were voted against the merger and 22.85% were not voted.

II.

We turn to the issue of the application of the business judgment rule to the September 20 meeting of the Board.

The Court of Chancery concluded from the evidence that the Board of Directors' approval of the Pritzker merger proposal fell within the protection of the business judgment rule. . . .

* * *

. . . [W]e conclude that the Court's ultimate finding that the Board's conduct was not "reckless or imprudent" is contrary to the record and not the product of a logical and deductive reasoning process. . . .

Under the business judgment rule there is no protection for directors who have made "an unintelligent or unadvised judgment . . . ." Representation of the financial interests of others imposes on a director an affirmative duty to protect those interests and to proceed with a critical eye in assessing information of the type and under the circumstances present here.

Thus, a director's duty to exercise an informed business judgment is in the nature of a duty of care, as distinguished from a duty of loyalty. . . .

The standard of care applicable to a director's duty of care has also been recently restated by this Court. In *Aronson v. Lewis*, [473 A.2d 805 (1984)], we stated:

> While the Delaware cases use a variety of terms to describe the applicable standard of care, our analysis satisfies us that under the business judgment rule director liability is predicated upon concepts of gross negligence.

473 A.2d at 812.

We again confirm that view. We think the concept of gross negligence is also the proper standard for determining whether a business judgment reached by a board of directors was an informed one.

* * *

III

* * *

-A-

On the record before us, we must conclude that the Board of Directors did not reach an informed business judgment on September 20, 1980 in voting to "sell" the Company for $55 per share pursuant to the Pritzker cash-out merger proposal. Our reasons, in summary, are as follows:

The directors (1) did not adequately inform themselves as to Van Gorkom's role in forcing the "sale" of the Company and in establishing the per share purchase price; (2) were uninformed as to the intrinsic value of the Company; and (3) given these circumstances, at a minimum, were grossly negligent in approving the "sale" of the Company upon two hours' consideration, without prior notice, and without the exigency of a crisis or emergency.

As has been noted, the Board based its September 20 decision to approve the cash-out merger primarily on Van Gorkom's representations. None of the directors, other than Van Gorkom and Chelberg, had any prior knowledge that the purpose of the meeting was to propose a cash-out merger of Trans Union. No members of Senior Management were present, other than Chelberg, Romans and Peterson; and the latter two had only learned of the proposed sale an hour earlier. Both general counsel Moore and former general counsel Browder attended the meeting, but were equally uninformed as to the purpose of the meeting and the documents to be acted upon.

Without any documents before them concerning the proposed transaction, the members of the Board were required to rely entirely upon Van Gorkom's 20-minute oral presentation of the proposal. No written summary of the terms of the merger was presented; the directors were given no documentation to support the adequacy of $55 price per share for sale of the Company; and the Board had before it nothing more than Van Gorkom's statement of his understanding of the substance of an agreement which he admittedly had never read, nor which any member of the Board had ever seen.

Under 8 Del. C. § 141(e), "directors are fully protected in relying in good faith on reports made by officers . . . ." However, there is no evidence that any "report," as defined under § 141(e), concerning the Pritzker proposal, was presented to the Board on September 20. Van Gorkom's oral presentation of his understanding of the terms of the proposed Merger Agreement, which he had not seen, and Romans' brief oral statement of his preliminary study regarding the feasibility of a leveraged buy-out of Trans Union do not qualify as § 141(e) "reports" for these reasons: The former lacked substance because Van Gorkom was basically uninformed as to the essential provisions of the very document about which he was talking. Romans' statement was irrelevant to the issues before the Board since it did not purport to be a valuation study. At a minimum for a report to enjoy the status conferred by § 141(e), it must be pertinent to the subject matter, upon which a board is called to act, and otherwise be entitled to good faith, not blind, reliance. Considering all of the surrounding circumstances—hastily calling the meeting without prior notice of its subject matter, the proposed sale of the Company without any prior consideration of the issue or necessity therefor, the urgent time constraints imposed by Pritzker, and the total absence of any documentation whatsoever the directors were duty bound to make reasonable inquiry of Van Gorkom and Romans, and if they had done so, the inadequacy of that upon which they now claim to have relied would have been apparent.

The defendants rely on the following factors to sustain the Trial Court's finding that the Board's decision was an informed one: (1) the magnitude of the premium or spread between the $55 Pritzker offering price and Trans Union's current market price of $38 per share; (2) the amendment of the Agreement as submitted on September 20 to permit the Board to accept any better offer during the "market test" period; (3) the collective experience and expertise of the Board's "inside" and "outside" directors; and (4) their reliance on Brennan's legal advice that the directors might be sued if they rejected the Pritzker proposal. We discuss each of these grounds seriatim:

(1)

. . . Using market price as a basis for concluding that the premium adequately reflected the true value of the Company was a clearly faulty, indeed fallacious, premise, as the defendants' own evidence demonstrates.

The record is clear that before September 20, Van Gorkom and other members of Trans Union's Board knew that the market had consistently undervalued the worth of Trans Union's stock, despite steady increases in the Company's operating income in the seven years preceding the merger. The Board related this occurrence in large part to Trans Union's inability to use its ITCs as previously noted. Van Gorkom testified that he did not believe the market price accurately reflected Trans Union's true worth; and several of the directors testified that, as a general rule, most chief executives think that the market undervalues their companies' stock. Yet, on September 20, Trans Union's Board apparently believed that the market stock price accurately reflected the value of the Company for the purpose of determining the adequacy of the premium for its sale.

In the Proxy Statement, however, the directors reversed their position. There, they stated that, although the earnings prospects for Trans Union were "excellent," they found no basis for believing that this would be reflected in future stock prices. With regard to past trading, the Board stated that the prices at which the Company's common stock had traded in recent years did not reflect the "inherent" value of the Company. But having referred to the "inherent" value of Trans Union, the directors ascribed no number to it. Moreover, nowhere did they disclose that they had no basis on which to fix "inherent" worth beyond an impressionistic reaction to the premium over market and an unsubstantiated belief that the value of the assets was "significantly greater" than book value. By their own admission they could not rely on the stock price as an accurate measure of value. Yet, also by their own admission, the Board members assumed that Trans Union's market price was adequate to serve as a basis upon which to assess the adequacy of the premium for purposes of the September 20 meeting. The parties do not dispute that a publicly-traded stock price is solely a measure of the value of a minority position and, thus, market price represents only the value of a single share. Nevertheless, on September 20, the Board assessed the adequacy of the premium over market, offered by Pritzker, solely by comparing it with Trans Union's current and historical stock price. (*See supra* Note 5.)

Indeed, as of September 20, the Board had no other information on which to base a determination of the intrinsic value of Trans Union as a going concern. As of September 20, the Board had made no evaluation of the Company designed to value the entire enterprise, nor had the Board ever previously considered selling the Company or consenting to a buy-out merger. Thus, the adequacy of a premium is indeterminate unless it is assessed in terms of other competent and sound valuation information that reflects the value of the particular business.

Despite the foregoing facts and circumstances, there was no call by the Board, either on September 20 or thereafter, for any valuation study or documentation of the $55 price per share as a measure of the fair value of the Company in a cash-out context. It is undisputed that the major asset of Trans Union was its cash flow. Yet, at no time did the Board call for a valuation study taking into account that highly significant element of the Company's assets.

We do not imply that an outside valuation study is essential to support an informed business judgment; nor do we state that fairness opinions by independent investment bankers are required as a matter of law. Often insiders familiar with the business of a going concern are in a better position than are outsiders to gather relevant information; and under appropriate circumstances, such directors may be fully protected in relying in good faith upon the valuation reports of their management. *See* 8 [Del. C.] § 141(e).

Here, the record establishes that the Board did not request its Chief Financial Officer, Romans, to make any valuation study or review of the proposal to determine the adequacy of $55 per share for sale of the Company. On the record before us: The Board rested on Romans' elicited response that the $55 figure was within a "fair price range" within the context of a leveraged buy-out. No director sought any further information from Romans. No director asked him why he put $55 at the bottom of his range. No director asked Romans for any details as to his study, the reason why it had been undertaken or its depth. No director asked to see the study; and no director asked Romans whether Trans Union's finance department could do a fairness study within the remaining 36-hour period available under the Pritzker offer.

Had the Board, or any member, made an inquiry of Romans, he presumably would have responded as he testified: that his calculations were rough and preliminary; and, that the study was not designed to determine the fair value of the Company, but rather to assess the feasibility of a leveraged buy-out financed by the Company's projected cash flow, making certain assumptions as to the purchaser's borrowing needs. Romans would have presumably also informed the Board of his view, and the widespread view of Senior Management, that the timing of the offer was wrong and the offer inadequate.

The record also establishes that the Board accepted without scrutiny Van Gorkom's representation as to the fairness of the $55 price per share for sale of the Company—a subject that the Board had never previously considered. The Board thereby failed to discover that Van Gorkom had suggested the $55 price to Pritzker and, most crucially, that Van Gorkom had arrived at the $55 figure based on calculations designed solely to determine the feasibility of a leveraged buy-out.[19] No questions were raised either as to the tax implica-

---

[19] As of September 20, the directors did not know: that Van Gorkom had arrived at the $55 figure alone, and subjectively, as the figure to be used by the Controller Peterson in creating a feasible structure for a leveraged buy-out

tions of a cash-out merger or how the price for the one million share option granted Pritzker was calculated.

We do not say that the Board of Directors was not entitled to give some credence to Van Gorkom's representation that $55 was an adequate or fair price. Under § 141(e), the directors were entitled to rely upon their chairman's opinion of value and adequacy, provided that such opinion was reached on a sound basis. Here, the issue is whether the directors informed themselves as to all information that was reasonably available to them. Had they done so, they would have learned of the source and derivation of the $55 price and could not reasonably have relied thereupon in good faith.

None of the directors, Management or outside, were investment bankers or financial analysts. Yet the Board did not consider recessing the meeting until a later hour that day (or requesting an extension of Pritzker's Sunday evening deadline) to give it time to elicit more information as to the sufficiency of the offer, either from inside Management (in particular Romans) or from Trans Union's own investment banker, Salomon Brothers, whose Chicago specialist in merger and acquisitions was known to the Board and familiar with Trans Union's affairs.

Thus, the record compels the conclusion that on September 20 the Board lacked valuation information adequate to reach an informed business judgment as to the fairness of $55 per share for sale of the Company.

(2)

This brings us to the post-September 20 "market test" upon which the defendants ultimately rely to confirm the reasonableness of their September 20 decision to accept the Pritzker proposal. In this connection, the directors present a two-part argument: (a) that by making a "market test" of Pritzker's $55 per share offer a condition of their September 20 decision to accept his offer, they cannot be found to have acted impulsively or in an uninformed manner on September 20; and (b) that the adequacy of the $17 premium for sale of the Company was conclusively established over the following 90 to 120 days by the most reliable evidence available—the marketplace. Thus, the defendants impliedly contend that the "market test" eliminated the need for the Board to perform any other form of fairness test either on September 20, or thereafter.

Again, the facts of record do not support the defendants' argument. There is no evidence: (a) that the Merger Agreement was effectively amended to give the Board freedom to put Trans Union up for auction sale to the highest bidder; or (b) that a public auction was in fact permitted to occur. The minutes of the Board meeting make no reference to any of this. Indeed, the record compels the conclusion that the directors had no rational basis for expecting that a market test was attainable, given the terms of the Agreement as executed during the evening of September 20.

---

by a prospective purchaser, that Van Gorkom had not sought advice, information or assistance from either inside or outside Trans Union directors as to the value of the Company as an entity or the fair price per share for 100% of its stock; that Van Gorkom had not consulted with the Company's investment bankers or other financial analysts; that Van Gorkom had not consulted with or confided in any officer or director of the Company except Chelberg; and that Van Gorkom had deliberately chosen to ignore the advice and opinion of the members of his Senior Management group regarding the adequacy of the $55 price.

* * *

The defendants attempt to downplay the significance of the prohibition against Trans Union's actively soliciting competing offers by arguing that the directors "understood that the entire financial community would know that Trans Union was for sale upon the announcement of the Pritzker offer, and anyone desiring to make a better offer was free to do so." Yet, the press release issued on September 22, with the authorization of the Board, stated that Trans Union had entered into "definitive agreements" with the Pritzkers; and the press release did not even disclose Trans Union's limited right to receive and accept higher offers. Accompanying this press release was a further public announcement that Pritzker had been granted an option to purchase at any time one million shares of Trans Union's capital stock at 75 cents above the then-current price per share.

Thus, notwithstanding what several of the outside directors later claimed to have "thought" occurred at the meeting, the record compels the conclusion that Trans Union's Board had no rational basis to conclude on September 20 or in the days immediately following, that the Board's acceptance of Pritzker's offer was conditioned on (1) a "market test" of the offer, and (2) the Board's right to withdraw from the Pritzker Agreement and accept any higher offer received before the shareholder meeting.

(3)

The directors' unfounded reliance on both the premium and the market test as the basis for accepting the Pritzker proposal undermines the defendants' remaining contention that the Board's collective experience and sophistication was a sufficient basis for finding that it reached its September 20 decision with informed, reasonable deliberation.[21] . . .

(4)

Part of the defense is based on a claim that the directors relied on legal advice rendered at the September 20 meeting by James Brennan, Esquire, who was present at Van Gorkom's request.

* * *

Several defendants testified that Brennan advised them that Delaware law did not require a fairness opinion or an outside valuation of the Company before the Board could act on the Pritzker proposal. If given, the advice was correct. However, that did not end the matter. Unless the directors had before them adequate information regarding the intrinsic value of the Company, upon which a proper exercise of business judgment could be made,

---

[21] Trans Union's five "inside" directors had backgrounds in law and accounting, 116 years of collective employment by the Company and 68 years of combined experience on its Board. Trans Union's five "outside" directors included four chief executives of major corporations and an economist who was a former dean of a major school of business and chancellor of a university. The "outside" directors had 78 years of combined experience as chief executive officers of major corporations and 50 years of cumulative experience as directors of Trans Union. Thus, defendants argue that the Board was eminently qualified to reach an informed judgment on the proposed "sale" of Trans Union notwithstanding their lack of any advance notice of the proposal, the shortness of their deliberation, and their determination not to consult with their investment banker or to obtain a fairness opinion.

mere advice of this type is meaningless; and, given this record of the defendants' failures, it constitutes no defense here.[22]

* * *

We conclude that Trans Union's Board was grossly negligent in that it failed to act with informed reasonable deliberation in agreeing to the Pritzker merger proposal on September 20 . . . .

A second claim is that counsel advised the Board it would be subject to lawsuits if it rejected the $55 per share offer. It is, of course, a fact of corporate life that today when faced with difficult or sensitive issues, directors often are subject to suit, irrespective of the decisions they make. However, counsel's mere acknowledgement of this circumstance cannot be rationally translated into a justification for a board permitting itself to be stampeded into a patently unadvised act. While suit might result from the rejection of a merger or tender offer, Delaware law makes clear that a board acting within the ambit of the business judgment rule faces no ultimate liability. Thus, we cannot conclude that the mere threat of litigation, acknowledged by counsel, constitutes either legal advice or any valid basis upon which to pursue an uninformed course.

Since we conclude that Brennan's purported advice is of no consequence to the defense of this case, it is unnecessary for us to invoke the adverse inferences which may be attributable to one failing to appear at trial and testify.

-B-

We now examine the Board's post-September 20 conduct for the purpose of determining first, whether it was informed and not grossly negligent; and second, if informed, whether it was sufficient to legally rectify and cure the Board's derelictions of September 20.

(1)

. . . [T]he primary purpose of the October 8 Board meeting was to amend the Merger Agreement, in a manner agreeable to Pritzker, to permit Trans Union to conduct a "market test." Van Gorkom understood that the proposed amendments were intended to give the Company an unfettered "right to openly solicit offers down through January 31." Van Gorkom presumably so represented the amendments to Trans Union's Board members on October 8. In a brief session, the directors approved Van Gorkom's oral presentation of the substance of the proposed amendments, the terms of which were not reduced to writing until October 10. But rather than waiting to review the amendments, the Board again approved them sight unseen and adjourned, giving Van Gorkom authority to execute the papers when he received them.[25]

---

[22]   Nonetheless, we are satisfied that in an appropriate factual context a proper exercise of business judgment may include, as one of its aspects, reasonable reliance upon the advice of counsel. This is wholly outside the statutory protections of 8 Del. C. § 141(e) involving reliance upon reports of officers, certain experts and books and records of the company.

[25]   We do not suggest that a board must read *in haec verba* every contract or legal document which it approves, but if it is to successfully absolve itself from charges of the type made here, there must be some credible contemporary evidence demonstrating that the directors knew what they were doing and ensured that their purported action was given effect. That is the consistent failure which cast this Board upon its unredeemable course.

* * *

The October 10 amendments to the Merger Agreement did authorize Trans Union to solicit competing offers, but the amendments had more far-reaching effects. The more significant change was in the definition of the third-party "offer" available to Trans Union as a possible basis for withdrawal from its Merger Agreement with Pritzker. Under the October 10 amendments, a better offer was no longer sufficient to permit Trans Union's withdrawal. Trans Union was now permitted to terminate the Pritzker Agreement and abandon the merger only if, prior to February 10, 1981, Trans Union had either consummated a merger (or sale of assets) with a third party or had entered into a "definitive" merger agreement more favorable than Pritzker's and for a greater consideration—subject only to stockholder approval. . . .

We conclude that the Board acted in a grossly negligent manner on October 8; and that Van Gorkom's representations on which the Board based its actions do not constitute "reports" under § 141(e) on which the directors could reasonably have relied. . . .

The October 9 press release, coupled with the October 10 amendments, had the clear effect of locking Trans Union's Board into the Pritzker Agreement. Pritzker had thereby foreclosed Trans Union's Board from negotiating any better "definitive" agreement over the remaining eight weeks before Trans Union was required to clear the Proxy Statement submitting the Pritzker proposal to its shareholders.

(2)

Next, as to the "curative" effects of the Board's post-September 20 conduct, we review in more detail the reaction of Van Gorkom to the KKR proposal and the results of the Board-sponsored "market test."

The KKR proposal was the first and only offer received subsequent to the Pritzker Merger Agreement. The offer resulted primarily from the efforts of Romans and other senior officers to propose an alternative to Pritzker's acquisition of Trans Union. . . .

On December 2, Kravis and Romans hand-delivered to Van Gorkom a formal letter-offer to purchase all of Trans Union's assets and to assume all of its liabilities for an aggregate cash consideration equivalent to $60 per share. The offer was contingent upon completing equity and bank financing of $650 million, which Kravis represented as 80% complete. The KKR letter made reference to discussions with major banks regarding the loan portion of the buy-out cost and stated that KKR was "confident that commitments for the bank financing . . . can be obtained within two or three weeks." The purchasing group was to include certain named key members of Trans Union's Senior Management, excluding Van Gorkom, and a major Canadian company. Kravis stated that they were willing to enter into a "definitive agreement" under terms and conditions "substantially the same" as those contained in Trans Union's agreement with Pritzker. The offer was addressed to Trans Union's Board of Directors and a meeting with the Board, scheduled for that afternoon, was requested.

Van Gorkom's reaction to the KKR proposal was completely negative; he did not view the offer as being firm because of its financing condition. It was pointed out, to no avail, that Pritzker's offer had not only been similarly conditioned, but accepted on an expedited basis. Van Gorkom refused Kravis' request that Trans Union issue a press release announcing KKR's offer, on the ground that it might "chill" any other offer. Romans and Kravis left with the understanding that their proposal would be presented to Trans Union's Board that afternoon.

Within a matter of hours and shortly before the scheduled Board meeting, Kravis withdrew his letter-offer. He gave as his reason a sudden decision by the Chief Officer of Trans Union's rail car leasing operation to withdraw from the KKR purchasing group. Van Gorkom had spoken to that officer about his participation in the KKR proposal immediately after his meeting with Romans and Kravis. However, Van Gorkom denied any responsibility for the officer's change of mind.

At the Board meeting later that afternoon, Van Gorkom did not inform the directors of the KKR proposal because he considered it "dead." Van Gorkom did not contact KKR again until January 20, when faced with the realities of this lawsuit, he then attempted to reopen negotiations. KKR declined due to the imminence of the February 10 stockholder meeting.

GE Credit Corporation's interest in Trans Union did not develop until November; and it made no written proposal until mid-January. Even then, its proposal was not in the form of an offer. Had there been time to do so, GE Credit was prepared to offer between $2 and $5 per share above the $55 per share price which Pritzker offered. But GE Credit needed an additional 60 to 90 days; and it was unwilling to make a formal offer without a concession from Pritzker extending the February 10 "deadline" for Trans Union's stock-holder meeting. As previously stated, Pritzker refused to grant such extension; and on January 21, GE Credit terminated further negotiations with Trans Union. Its stated reasons, among others, were its "unwillingness to become involved in a bidding contest with Pritzker in the absence of the willingness of [the Pritzker interests] to terminate the proposed $55 cash merger."

* * *

In the absence of any explicit finding by the Trial Court as to the reasonableness of Trans Union's directors' reliance on a market test and its feasibility, we may make our own findings based on the record. Our review of the record compels a finding that confirmation of the appropriateness of the Pritzker offer by an unfettered or free market test was virtually meaningless in the face of the terms and time limitations of Trans Union's Merger Agreement with Pritzker as amended October 10, 1980.

(3)

Finally, we turn to the Board's meeting of January 26, 1981. The defendant directors rely upon the action there taken to refute the contention that they did not reach an informed business judgment in approving the Pritzker merger. The defendants contend that the Trial Court correctly concluded that Trans Union's directors were, in effect, as "free to turn down the Pritzker proposal" on January 26, as they were on September 20. . . .

Johnson's [an outside director] testimony and the Board Minutes of January 26 are remarkably consistent. Both clearly indicate recognition that the question of the alternative courses of action, available to the Board on January 26 with respect to the Pritzker merger, was a legal question, presenting to the Board (after its review of the full record developed through pre-trial discovery) three options: (1) to "continue to recommend" the Pritzker merger, (2) to "recommend that the stockholders vote against" the Pritzker merger, or (3) to take a noncommittal position on the merger and "simply leave the decision to [the] share-holders."

We must conclude from the foregoing that the Board was mistaken as a matter of law regarding its available courses of action on January 26, 1981. Options (2) and (3) were not viable or legally available to the Board under 8 Del. C. § 251(b). The Board could not remain committed to the Pritzker merger and yet recommend that its stockholders vote it down; nor could it take a neutral position and delegate to the stockholders the unadvised decision as to whether to accept or reject the merger. Under § 251(b), the Board had but two options: (1) to proceed with the merger and the stockholder meeting with the Board's recommendation of approval; or (2) to rescind its agreement with Pritzker, withdraw its approval of the merger, and notify its stockholders that the proposed shareholder meeting was cancelled. There is no evidence that the Board gave any consideration to these, its only legally viable alternative courses of action.

But the second course of action would have clearly involved a substantial risk—that the Board would be faced with suit by Pritzker for breach of contract based on its September 20 agreement as amended October 10. As previously noted, under the terms of the October 10 amendment, the Board's only ground for release from its agreement with Pritzker was its entry into a more favorable definitive agreement to sell the Company to a third party. Thus, in reality, the Board was not "free to turn down the Pritzker proposal" as the Trial Court found. Indeed, short of negotiating a better agreement with a third party, the Board's only basis for release from the Pritzker Agreement without liability would have been to establish fundamental wrongdoing by Pritzker. Clearly, the Board was not "free" to withdraw from its agreement with Pritzker on January 26 by simply relying on its self-induced failure to have reached an informed business judgment at the time of its original agreement.

Therefore, the Trial Court's conclusion that the Board reached an informed business judgment on January 26 in determining whether to turn down the Pritzker "proposal" on that day cannot be sustained. The Court's conclusion is not supported by the record; it is contrary to the provisions of § 251(b) and basic principles of contract law; and it is not the product of a logical and deductive reasoning process. . . .

Upon the basis of the foregoing, we hold that the defendants' post-September conduct did not cure the deficiencies of their September 20 conduct; and that, accordingly, the Trial Court erred in according to the defendants the benefits of the business judgment rule.

IV.

Whether the directors of Trans Union should be treated as one or individually in terms of invoking the protection of the business judgment rule and the applicability of 8 Del. C. § 141(c) are questions which were not originally addressed by the parties in their briefing of this case. This resulted in a supplemental briefing and a second rehearing en banc on two basic questions: (a) whether one or more of the directors were deprived of the protection of the business judgment rule by evidence of an absence of good faith; and (b) whether one or more of the outside directors were entitled to invoke the protection of 8 Del. C. § 141(e) by evidence of a reasonable, good faith reliance on "reports," including legal advice, rendered the Board by certain inside directors and the Board's special counsel, Brennan.

The parties' response, including reargument, has led the majority of the Court to conclude: (1) that since all of the defendant directors, outside as well as inside, take a unified position, we are required to treat all of the directors as one as to whether they are entitled to the protection of the business judgment rule; and (2) that considerations of good faith, including the presumption that the directors acted in good faith, are irrelevant in determining the threshold issue of whether the directors as a Board exercised an informed business judgment. For the same reason, we must reject defense counsel's ad hominem argument for affirmance: that reversal may result in a multi-million dollar class award against the defendants for having made an allegedly uninformed business judgment in a transaction not involving any personal gain, self-dealing or claim of bad faith.

In their brief the defendants similarly mistake the business judgment rule's application to this case by erroneously invoking presumptions of good faith and "wide discretion" . . . .

[P]laintiffs have not claimed, nor did the Trial Court decide, that $55 was a grossly inadequate price per share for sale of the Company. That being so, the presumption that a board's judgment as to adequacy of price represents an honest exercise of business judgment (absent proof that the sale price was grossly inadequate) is irrelevant to the threshold question of whether an informed judgment was reached.

V.

The defendants ultimately rely on the stockholder vote of February 10 for exoneration. The defendants contend that the stockholders' "overwhelming" vote approving the Pritzker Merger Agreement had the legal effect of curing any failure of the Board to reach an informed business judgment in its approval of the merger.

The parties tacitly agree that a discovered failure of the Board to reach an informed business judgment in approving the merger constitutes a voidable, rather than a void, act. Hence, the merger can be sustained, notwithstanding the infirmity of the Board's action, if its approval by majority vote of the shareholders is found to have been based on an informed electorate.

[The court found that the proxy statement and supplemental proxy statement failed to disclose that the Board lacked adequate information as to the value of the company, and instead created the misimpression that it was informed as to this value; that the supplemental proxy statement misleadingly disclosed Romans' preliminary finding as to the $55-$65 range without stating that he had done so only to justify a leveraged buyout price; that the proxy statement misleadingly referred to the "substantial" premium without disclosing the Board's failure to determine the value of the company; and that the supplemental proxy statement failed to disclose that Van Gorkom suggested $55 per share to Pritzer as a price at which Pritzker could do a leveraged buy-out and repay the loan out of five years' cash flow.] . . .

We find that Trans Union's stockholders were not fully informed of all facts material to their vote on the Pritzker Merger and that the Trial Court's ruling to the contrary is clearly erroneous. . . .

VI.

. . . We hold, therefore, that the Trial Court committed reversible error or in applying the business judgment rule in favor of the director defendants in this case.

On remand, the Court of Chancery shall conduct an evidentiary hearing to determine the fair value of the shares represented by the plaintiffs' class, based on the intrinsic value of Trans Union on September 20, 1980. . . . Thereafter, an award of damages may be entered to the extent that the fair value of Trans Union exceeds $55 per share. . . .

MCNEILLY, Justice, dissenting:

. . . At the time of the September 20 meeting the 10 members of Trans Union's Board of Directors were highly qualified and well informed about the affairs and prospects of Trans Union. These directors were acutely aware of the historical problems facing Trans Union which were caused by the tax laws. They had discussed these problems ad nauseam. In fact, within two months of the September 20 meeting the board had reviewed and discussed an outside study of the company done by The Boston Consulting Group and an internal five year forecast prepared by management. At the September 20 meeting Van Gorkom presented the Pritzker offer, and the board then heard from James Brennan, the company's counsel in this matter, who discussed the legal documents. Following this, the Board directed that certain changes be made in the merger documents. These changes made it clear that the Board was free to accept a better offer than Pritzker's if one was made. The above facts reveal that the Board did not act in a grossly negligent manner in informing themselves of the relevant and available facts before passing on the merger. To the contrary, this record reveals that the directors acted with the utmost care in informing themselves of the relevant and available facts before passing on the merger. . . .

NOTES AND QUESTIONS

(1) **Aftermath of *Van Gorkom*.** The defendants agreed to a $23.5 million settlement, of which the directors' liability insurance carrier paid about $10 million.[47] The Pritzkers paid the remainder of the settlement.[48] In September, 1982, President Reagan appointed Van Gorkom undersecretary for management of the State Department. Five years after the transaction, the Pritzkers reportedly were struggling with the company because a decline in tank car sales made it difficult to finance the acquisition debt. But the successor to Van Gorkom's company, TransUnion, is now a major supplier of consumer credit information.

(2) **The legacy of *Van Gorkom*.** This case has become one of the most famous, controversial and written-about cases in the history of Delaware corporate law, as indicated by the **Symposium** and some of the articles from that Symposium listed in the References below. The following notes indicate some of the nuances that have intrigued corporate law scholars. Moreover, the impact of the case may have been quite different from what one might have expected when the decision was rendered. As **Macey and Miller** recognized not long after the case was decided, and as **Black and Kraakman**

---

[47]   *See* WALL ST. J., Aug. 2, 1985, at 18.

[48]   *See* N.Y. TIMES, Dec. 14, 1985, at 13. Pritzker says he paid the settlement because he did not think the directors had done anything wrong, and some did not have the funds to pay it. *See* William J. Carney, et al., *Roundtable Discussion: Corporate Governance*, 77 CHI. KENT L. REV. 235, 240 (2001). In the same discussion, Pritzker said that Van Gorkom, not Pritzker, had initiated the quick timetable, in part because he did not want an auction. *Id*. at 238.

elaborated more recently, *Van Gorkom*'s main significance may be in its implicit recognition of directors' power to screen takeover proposals, discussed briefly in Note 8 and in more detail below in Chapter 14.

(3) **Process versus substance.** Cases like *Van Gorkom* make clear that the courts are much more willing to second-guess the process by which director decisions were reached than the substance of the decisions themselves. Yet the selection of the appropriate decision-making process is clearly a type of business decision in itself. Whether managers should have gotten more information depends on the tricky question of whether the cost of doing so is exceeded by the expected benefits.[49] Where the transaction is recommended by a chief executive officer who has been reliable in the past, or where because of their experience, the board members have a strong sense of the merits of the transaction, the expected benefits of further inquiries often may be less than the costs. Thus, whether managers should inquire further involves a sensitive decision not only as to what will be lost by seeking more information, but what can be gained by doing so. Courts might think that they have greater expertise regarding decision making procedures. But, judicial second-guessing of board procedures can involve a clash of contrasting decision-making styles. Business people do not necessarily arrive at decisions in a deliberative manner as courts do. Moreover, directors, unlike courts, are engaged in an ongoing decision process involving interrelated rather than isolated decisions (*see* **Manning**). Finally, because the board of directors is a collegial body, board members cannot aggressively question each other and inside managers on every decision and still expect to function smoothly. In general, these criticisms of the procedural approach arguably support the theory that Delaware law has been designed to further the interests of lawyers and others who gain from this style of decision-making rather than those of shareholders (*see* Section 7.02[B], above).

Evaluate the decision in *Van Gorkom* in light of this critique of the court's emphasis on procedure. Was Van Gorkom careless in packaging an offer to sell the company at a substantial premium over current market in such a way that Pritzker accepted it, despite the reservations of Van Gorkom's own man, Peterson? Did the opposition of Trans Union's senior management, whose jobs were jeopardized by the sale of the company and who might have gained from an alternative management buyout, make the offer questionable? Was it careless for a board as experienced as Trans Union's to accept the recommendation of its most knowledgeable member, Van Gorkom? Note that Delaware G.C.L. § 141(e) explicitly permits directors to rely on others.[50]

---

[49]   *See generally* George Stigler, *The Economics of Information*, 69 J. POL. ECON. 213 (1961).

[50]   *See also* MBCA § 8.30(c) and ALI *Principles* §§ 4.01(b), 4.02, and 4.03. For recent decisions concerning the ability of directors to rely on others, see *Klang v. Smith's Food & Drug Centers*, 1997 Del. Ch. LEXIS 73, 1997 WL 257463 (Del. Ch. May 13, 1997) (permitting directors to rely on solvency opinion of firm that was selected with reasonable care based upon recommendation of legal counsel and investment banker); *In re Healthco International, Inc.*, 208 B.R. 288 (Bankr. D. Mass. 1997) (refusing to permit directors to rely on solvency opinion where firm rendering opinion had been selected by the party purchasing the corporation, rather than by directors themselves).

Indeed, might it have been careless for the board to *reject* the deal, given its relatively high price (*see* Note 6, below)? As **McChesney** discusses, the question is whether the board reasonably could have expected that a better deal would come along if they rejected Pritzker's deal, or delayed beyond the time he was willing to wait in order to undertake a valuation study. Under McChesney's analysis, assuming the board was really in the dark about whether $55 was a good price, the chances of no better offer (and therefore no premium for the shareholders) and of a better offer were about equal. In order to balance these two possibilities, the better offer would have to be *much* better. But only a very small percentage of firms during the relevant period sold for as much over current market as did Trans Union.

On the other hand, as **Macey** discusses, the board knew that Van Gorkom's interests differed from those of most of the shareholders, who had a much lower tax basis (because they had been shareholders in companies that merged into Trans Union) and who did not share Van Gorkom's interest in retiring and walking away from the company. Moreover, Van Gorkom had autocratically excluded the board from the negotiations, which should have made the board skeptical of the deal. And an important fact countering McChesney's analysis is that KKR actually *had* made a higher bid, indicating that others might have been forthcoming.

(4) **Post-*Van Gorkom* procedures.** Perhaps the business judgment rule only requires the board to follow specific procedures—judicially created "rules of the road"—that, if followed, give directors the benefit of the business judgment presumption. A clear, rule-oriented approach that emphasizes specific procedures arguably would serve the business judgment rule's basic functions of encouraging managers to act carefully while not causing them to become over-cautious. So what procedures should the board follow in the wake of *Van Gorkom*? Consider *Citron v. Fairchild Camera & Inst. Corp.*,[51] which held against liability under *Van Gorkom,* noting that the board had been considering the possibility of sale for two years, was advised by four leading investment banking firms, shopped the company to approximately 75 potential buyers, and discussed the sale of the company at three separate board meetings over a three-week period.

Assuming these procedures really do protect directors from liability, are they likely to be cost-effective? Consider the requirement that directors obtain an outside evaluation. Is such an evaluation sufficiently more reliable than *Van Gorkom*'s proposal to justify the added cost? **Fischel** (at 1453) says, "I wish someone would pay me several hundred thousand dollars to state that $55 is greater than $35." On the other hand, the board's use of such experts as independent appraisers does help ensure that someone with specialized expertise and a specific reputation to protect is involved in the decision-making process.

(5) **Type of director.** Should the application of the business judgment rule depend on the directors' particular characteristics? To begin with, should it matter whether the

---

[51]   569 A.2d 53 (Del. 1989).

defendant is an "insider"—that is, an officer or other full-time employee—or an outside director? MBCA § 8.42 provides for a very similar standard of conduct for officers as for directors, but the Official Comment states that the officer's "ability to rely on information, reports, or statements, may, depending upon the circumstances of the particular case, be more limited than in the case of a director in view of the greater obligation he may have to be familiar with the affairs of the corporation."[52] Similarly, ALI *Principles* § 4.01(a) provides that both officers and directors shall perform their functions "with the care that an ordinarily prudent person would reasonably be expected to exercise *in a like position* and *under similar circumstances*" (emphasis added). Comment (e) to § 4.01(a) makes clear that "in a like position" is "intended to recognize that the special skills, background, or expertise of a director or officer may entail greater responsibility." Comment (e) further notes that "[a] director's length of service on the board may also be relevant in evaluating the director's conduct." Is the result in *Van Gorkom* consistent with these positions?

Other director characteristics that might matter include whether the director was a substantial shareholder, as was Van Gorkom (*see* **Elson & Thompson**) and the directors' expertise, as stressed by the dissent. Yet, as **Macey** asks, is it feasible for courts to set standards of conduct based on the characteristics of individual directors?

(6) **Reliance on market prices.** Why weren't the abbreviated procedures employed by the board in *Van Gorkom* good enough given that the price offered, $55 per share, was "39% over the highest price at which the stock of Trans Union had traded any time during the prior six years" (note 9 to the court's opinion)? Is the opinion persuasive as to why the directors could not rely on this price? In light of the Efficient Capital Markets Hypothesis (*see* Section 7.01) how could the market have "undervalued" Trans Union stock? For comments on this point, see the **Fischel** articles. Perhaps the answer is that the market did not "undervalue" the company, but fully reflected its value under current management and mode of operation. Although the company would be worth more if it was combined with another company, refinanced or sold, the company's share price reflected only the *possibility* of these changes. Thus, current share price is only a clue to what the company's assets might be worth in their highest-value use.

(7) **The "market test."** Even if it the market price does not alone validate the *Van Gorkom* board's opinion, why wasn't the "market test" enough? Note that Salomon Brothers had been offered a finder's fee of more than $2.5 million if they came up with an alternative buyer, and they tried for four months to do so. Doesn't this validate the directors' decision? The court emphasized how the acquisition agreement hampered the board in submitting a higher price to the shareholders (*i.e.*, the merger agreement restricted the ability of the *board* to negotiate a merger with other potential bidders), as well as Van Gorkom's role in squelching the KKR deal. Despite these problems, a third party could have made a tender offer directly to the *shareholders* prior to the share-

---

[52]   2 Revised MBCA Annotated, 1067 (1985).

holder vote on the Pritzker deal. If the third party offered enough, this might persuade the shareholders to reject the Pritzker deal. Should the adequacy of Pritzker's bid be assumed from the absence of such a third party offer? Note that third party bids are significantly affected by the availability of information about the company and management's willingness to cooperate after the takeover. Consider also how the million-share sale to Pritzker might have deterred a third-party bid.

(8) **Director liability for negligent recommendations.** The *Van Gorkom* transaction could be accomplished only with shareholder approval. Should the board be liable for negligently *recommending* the sale to the shareholders? For example, should the directors be held liable if they had clearly disclosed that they didn't have any idea what the company was worth but thought that $55 per share was a good enough offer to warrant submission to the shareholders? This question should be analyzed in light of the general function of the business judgment rule to encourage directors to exercise their discretion for the benefit of the company. Holding the directors liable for negligently recommending a sale to the shareholders carries the potential cost of deterring managers from generating and submitting sale proposals. Can you think of arguments favoring a duty of careful recommendation?

(9) **Fiduciary outs.** The *Van Gorkom* court assumed that the board was legally bound to recommend the Pritzker deal to the shareholders as of January 26. Is that clear? Or does the board have an overriding, non-waivable duty to the shareholders to withdraw its recommendations (and, perhaps, cancel a scheduled shareholder vote) if changed circumstances make the proposed transaction inconsistent with the shareholders' best interests? In other words, did the board have the agency power to bind the corporation to the deal and themselves to recommend it regardless of what happened prior to the shareholder vote? Suppose, for example, that a third party had indicated a willingness to pay $75 per share, but had not entered into a definitive agreement by the time of the shareholder vote. Do you think the directors would have been legally bound to recommend the Pritzker deal? For a further discussion of this issue, see *Paramount Communications Inc. v. QVC Network Inc.*, and *Omnicare v. NCS Healthcare,* Section 14.03[D] below.

(10) **The effect of shareholder approval.** As discussed in *Van Gorkom*, even a careless director act may be "validated" by shareholder approval. Did it make sense to invalidate the shareholder vote in *Van Gorkom*? Is it likely the shareholders would have voted differently if they had known how the $55 price had been arrived at?

REFERENCES

Symposium: Van Gorkom *and the Corporate Board: Problem, Solution, or Placebo?*, 96 Nw. U. L. Rev. 449 (2002).

Black & Kraakman, *Delaware's Takeover Law: The Uncertain Search for Hidden Value*, 96 Nw. U. L. Rev. 521 (2002).

Elson & Thompson, Van Gorkom's *Legacy: The Limits of Judicially Enforced Constraints and the Promise of Proprietary Incentives*, 96 Nw. U. L. Rev. 579 (2002).

Fischel, *Market Evidence in Corporate Law*, 69 U. Chi. L. Rev. 941 (2002).

Fischel, *The Business Judgment Rule and the* Trans Union *Case*, 40 Bus. Law. 1437 (1985).

Macey, Smith v. Van Gorkom*: Insights about C.E.O.s, Corporate Law Rules, and the Jurisdictional Competition for Corporate Charters*, 96 Nw. U. L. Rev. 607 (2002).

Macey & Miller, Trans Union *Reconsidered,* 98 Yale L.J. 127 (1988).

McChesney, *A Bird in the Hand and Liability in the Bush: Why* Van Gorkom *Still Rankles, Probably,* 96 Nw. U. L. Rev. 631 (2002).

The following case provides a more recent illustration of the board's duty to inform itself before acting. Consider whether the standards have changed since *Van Gorkom*.

BREHM v. EISNER
Delaware Supreme Court
746 A.2d 244 (2000)

Veasey, Chief Justice:

* * *

Facts

[Further facts are reproduced in the earlier excerpt of this case in Section 9.03[A].]

A. The 1995 Ovitz Employment Agreement

* * *

The Complaint . . . alleges that the Old Board failed properly to inform itself about the total costs and incentives of the Ovitz Employment Agreement, especially the severance package. . . . Specifically, plaintiffs allege that the Board failed to realize that the contract gave Ovitz an incentive to find a way to exit the Company via a non-fault termination as soon as possible because doing so would permit him to earn more than he could by fulfilling his contract. The Complaint alleges, however, that the Old Board had been advised by a corporate compensation expert, Graef Crystal, in connection with its decision to approve the Ovitz Employment Agreement. Two public statements by Crystal form the basis of the allegation that the Old Board failed to consider the incentives and the total cost of the severance provisions, but these statements by Crystal were not made until after Ovitz left Disney in December 1996, approximately 14½ months after being hired.

The first statement, published in a December 23, 1996 article in the web-based magazine Slate, quoted Crystal as saying, in part, "Of course, the overall costs of the package would go up sharply in the event of Ovitz's termination (and I wish now that I'd made a spreadsheet showing just what the deal would total if Ovitz had been fired at any time)." The second published statement appeared in an article about three weeks later in the January 13, 1997 edition of California Law Business. The article appears first to paraphrase

Crystal: "With no one expecting failure, the sleeper clauses in Ovitz's contract seemed innocuous, Crystal says, explaining that no one added up the total cost of the severance package." The article then quotes Crystal as saying that the amount of Ovitz' severance was "shocking" and that "[n]obody quantified this and I wish we had." One of the charging paragraphs of the Complaint concludes:

> 57. As has been conceded by Graef Crystal, the executive compensation consultant who advised the Old Board with respect to the Ovitz Employment Agreement, the Old Board never considered the costs that would be incurred by Disney in the event Ovitz was terminated from the Company for a reason other than cause prior to the natural expiration of the Ovtiz Employment Agreement.

Although repeated in various forms in the Complaint, these quoted admissions by Crystal constitute the extent of the factual support for the allegation that the Old Board failed properly to consider the severance elements of the agreement. This Court, however, must juxtapose these allegations with the legal presumption that the Old Board's conduct was a proper exercise of business judgment. That presumption includes the statutory protection [under Del. G.C.L. §141(e)] for a board that relies in good faith on an expert advising the Board. We must decide whether plaintiffs' factual allegations, if proven, would rebut that presumption.

Principles of Corporation Law Compared with Good Corporate Governance Practices

This is a case about whether there should be personal liability of the directors of a Delaware corporation to the corporation for lack of due care in the decisionmaking process. . . . This case is not about the failure of the directors to establish and carry out ideal corporate governance practices.

All good corporate governance practices include compliance with statutory law and case law establishing fiduciary duties. But the law of corporate fiduciary duties and remedies for violation of those duties are distinct from the aspirational goals of ideal corporate governance practices. Aspirational ideals of good corporate governance practices for boards of directors that go beyond the minimal legal requirements of the corporation law are highly desirable, often tend to benefit stockholders, sometimes reduce litigation and can usually help directors avoid liability. But they are not required by the corporation law and do not define standards of liability.

* * *

Plaintiffs' Contention that the Old Board Violated the Process Duty of Care
in Approving the Ovitz Employment Agreement

Certainly in this case the economic exposure of the corporation to the payout scenarios of the Ovitz contract was material, particularly given its large size, for purposes of the directors' decisionmaking process.[49] And those dollar exposure numbers were reasonably

---

[49] The term "material" is used in this context to mean relevant and of a magnitude to be important to directors in carrying out their fiduciary duty of care in decisionmaking.

available because the logical inference from plaintiffs' allegations is that Crystal or the New Board could have calculated the numbers. Thus, the objective tests of reasonable availability and materiality were satisfied by this Complaint. But that is not the end of the inquiry for liability purposes.

* * *

. . . The Complaint, fairly construed, admits that the directors were advised by Crystal as an expert and that they relied on his expertise. Accordingly, the question here is whether the directors are to be "fully protected" (*i.e.*, not held liable) on the basis that they relied in good faith on a qualified expert under Section 141(e) of the Delaware General Corporation Law. The Old Board is entitled to the presumption that it exercised proper business judgment, including proper reliance on the expert. In fact, the Court of Chancery refers to the "Board's reliance on Crystal and his decision not to fully calculate the amount of severance." The Court's invocation here of the concept of the protection accorded directors who rely on experts, even though no reference is made to the statute itself, is on the right track, but the Court's analysis is unclear and incomplete.[54]

Although the Court of Chancery did not expressly predicate its decision on Section 141(e), Crystal is presumed to be an expert on whom the Board was entitled to rely in good faith under Section 141(e) in order to be "fully protected." Plaintiffs must rebut the presumption that the directors properly exercised their business judgment, including their good faith reliance on Crystal's expertise. What Crystal now believes in hindsight that he and the Board should have done in 1995 does not provide that rebuttal. That is not to say, however, that a rebuttal of the presumption of proper reliance on the expert under Section 141(e) cannot be pleaded consistent with Rule 23.1 in a properly framed complaint setting forth particularized facts creating reason to believe that the Old Board's conduct was grossly negligent.

To survive a . . . motion to dismiss in a due care case where an expert has advised the board in its decisionmaking process, the complaint must allege particularized facts (not conclusions) that, if proved, would show, for example, that: (a) the directors did not in fact rely on the expert; (b) their reliance was not in good faith; (c) they did not reasonably believe that the expert's advice was within the expert's professional competence; (d) the expert was not selected with reasonable care by or on behalf of the corporation, and the faulty selection process was attributable to the directors; (e) the subject matter (in this case

---

[54] The Court of Chancery seemed, however, to key the reliance issue not to the statute but to the lack of "egregiousness," a concept that is misplaced in this context. The Court said:

> It is the essence of the business judgment rule that a court will not apply 20/20 hindsight to second guess a board's decision, except "in rare cases [where] a transaction may be so egregious on its face that the board approval cannot meet the test of business judgment." Because the Board's reliance on Crystal and his decision not to fully calculate the amount of severance lack "egregiousness," this is not that rare case. I think it a correct statement of law that the duty of care is still fulfilled even if a Board does not know the exact amount of a severance payout but nonetheless is fully informed about the manner in which such a payout would be calculated. A board is not required to be informed of every fact, but rather is required to be reasonably informed.

Id.

the cost calculation) that was material and reasonably available was so obvious that the board's failure to consider it was grossly negligent regardless of the expert's advice or lack of advice; or (f) that the decision of the Board was so unconscionable as to constitute waste or fraud. This Complaint includes no particular allegations of this nature, and therefore it was subject to dismissal as drafted.

Plaintiffs also contend that Crystal's latter-day admission is "valid and binding" on the Old Board. This argument is without merit. Crystal was the Board's expert ex ante for purposes of advising the directors on the Ovitz Employment Agreement. He was not their agent ex post to make binding admissions.

We conclude that . . . [the Complaint], as drafted, fails to create a reasonable doubt that the Old Board's decision in approving the Ovitz Employment Agreement was protected by the business judgment rule. Plaintiffs will be provided an opportunity to replead on this issue.

* * *

HARTNETT, Justice, concurring:

* * *

. . . In my opinion, . . . from the totality of the factual allegations in the complaint, a reasonable doubt that the business judgment rule precludes judicial inquiry already exists as to some of the other claims, such as whether the directors were aware of the total cost of Ovitz' compensation package when they approved it . . . .

NOTES AND QUESTIONS

(1) **Reconciling *Van Gorkom* and *Eisner*.** Why let the Disney directors rely on the admittedly deficient advice of Crystal, while not letting the Trans Union directors rely on the advice of Van Gorkom and Romans? In both cases, the directors could have learned additional, pertinent information had they asked additional questions of the experts. Can the two cases be reconciled based on the significance of the transaction under consideration—that is, sale of an entire business vs. an employment contract?

(2) **Aspirational goals of ideal practice and the MBCA.** *Eisner* distinguishes between "aspirational goals of ideal practice for boards of directors" and legally enforceable duties. If the adoption of ideal practices "often benefit shareholders" as the *Eisner* court states, why not make the failure to abide by such practices legally actionable? Consider, once again, the policy basis for the business judgment rule discussed in Note 2 following the first *Eisner* excerpt in Section 9.03[A]. Note that the MBCA draws the line suggested in *Eisner* explicitly: MBCA § 8.30 sets forth duties of directors, while MBCA § 8.31 sets out the circumstances in which violations of those duties can result in legal liability.

[C] Statutory Responses to Director Liability

Van Gorkom moved the directors' duty-of-care from the theoretical to the real and vivid. At the same time, insurance against directors' and officers' liability became more expensive and less comprehensive. Among other things, insurers began excluding claims relating to takeover defenses, lowering the maximum payout, and making coverage unavailable to some risky companies. These highly publicized developments had the unsurprising effect of making it more difficult for companies to find outside directors.[53] Statutes passed in the wake of *Van Gorkom* that were intended to ameliorate the effects of that decision. The statutes and the policy issues they raise are discussed further below in Section 9.09.

The first response to *Van Gorkom* came in Delaware, the scene of the "crime." The legislature adopted Del. G.C.L. § 102(b)(7), which permits the certificate of incorporation to contain a provision eliminating or limiting directors' personal liability for breach of the duty of care. Some states, rather than simply letting the shareholders approve a change in the standard of care, changed the standard of care applicable to all firms incorporated in the state. For example, the Virginia act provides that a "director shall discharge his duties as a director . . . in accordance with his good faith business judgment of the best interests of the corporation."[54] Other states, including Florida, Maine, Ohio and Wisconsin, adopted provisions eliminating duty of care liability for money damages. Unlike the Delaware statute, these anti-*Van Gorkom* provisions limit director liability without the need for shareholder action. An alternative approach to protecting corporate officials from liability (through shareholder or legislative action) is to allow shareholders to limit the amount of liability as distinguished from modifying the duty. ALI *Principles* § 7.19 embodies this approach. That section permits the certificate of incorporation to include a provision "that limits damages against an officer or a director . . . to an amount not less than such person's annual compensation from the corporation," so long as that provision "may be repealed by the shareholders at any annual meeting without prior action by the board."

There are many variations and issues regarding the types of suits to which these statutes apply, including the nature of the plaintiff (*e.g.*, are creditors covered?); of the defendant (*e.g.*, are officers protected?); and the types of conduct protected from liability. Perhaps the most important question is what type of director conduct is (or can be) protected from liability under anti-*Van Gorkom* provisions. Statutory limits on anti-*Van Gorkom* provisions provide, for example, that the director must act in "good faith" and refrain from "intentional misconduct," "knowing violation of law" or "breach of the . . . duty of loyalty." Is it clear that the director conduct condemned by the Delaware

---

[53] *See* Shatz, *Directors Feel the Legal Heat*, N.Y. TIMES, Dec. 15, 1985, at 34; Bennett, *Hot Seats: Board Members Draw Fire, and Some Think Twice About Serving*, WALL ST. J., Feb. 5, 1986, at 1; Lewin, *Director Insurance Drying Up*, N.Y. TIMES, March 7, 1986, at D-1.

[54] Va. Code Ann. § 13.1-690(A).

Supreme Court in *Van Gorkom* was in "good faith" and was not "intentional misconduct." Couldn't a court conclude that the deliberate failure to obtain the appropriate facts in connection with a major corporate transaction triggered liability even under a charter provision that limited officer and director liability to the fullest extent permitted by Delaware law?[55]

[D] The Consequences of Failing Substantive or Procedural Review under the Business Judgment Rule

What happens when officers or directors who make a disinterested business decision are found not to satisfy the substantive or procedural standards of care under the business judgment rule? That issue is considered in the following case.

CEDE & CO. v. TECHNICOLOR, INC.
Delaware Supreme Court
634 A.2d 345 (1993)

Before HORSEY, MOORE and HOLLAND, JJ.

[On October 29, 1982, the nine-member board of Technicolor approved the sale of the company to MacAndrews and Forbes Group, Inc. ("MAF") for $23 per share. Although the price represented more than a 100% premium over the pre-acquisition price for Technicolor shares, the Chancery Court adopted a "presumed finding" that the Technicolor board had breached its duty of care by approving the sale of the company without adequately informing itself under *Van Gorkom*. The court, however, dismissed the action on the ground that the plaintiff, Cinerama, could not prove injury because the $23 price exceeded the fair value of the shares, as determined in plaintiff's parallel action asserting dissenters' rights under Del. G.C.L. § 262. An excerpt from the Delaware Supreme Court's disposition of plaintiff's appeal follows:]

---

[55] *Cf. Zirn v. VLI Corp.*, 681 A.2d 1050 (Del. 1996) (directors shielded under § 102(b)(7) from liability for breach of the duty of disclosure where directors acted in good faith and misstatements or omissions were not intentional); *see also Arnold v. Society for Savings Bancorp, Inc*, 650 A.2d 1270 (Del. 1994) (directors shielded from liability for proxy omissions because non-disclosure not intentional).

Horsey:

* * *

APPLICATION OF THE BUSINESS JUDGMENT RULE

* * *

Principal Rulings Below/Issues on Appeal

. . . [T]he court ruled that it was not sufficient for Cinerama to prove that the defendant directors had collectively, as a board, breached their duty of care. Cinerama was required to prove that it had suffered a monetary loss from such breach and to quantify that loss. The court expressed "grave doubts" that the Technicolor board "as a whole" had met that duty in approving the terms of the merger/sale of the company. The court, in effect, read into the business judgment presumption of due care the legal maxim that proof of negligence without proof of injury is not actionable. . . .

DIRECTOR AND BOARD DUTY OF CARE

. . . [W]e find the Chancellor's restatement of the duty of care requirement of the rule and a shareholder plaintiff's burden of proof for rebuttal thereof, in the context of a good faith, arms-length sale of the company, to be erroneous as a matter of law. We adopt the court's presumed findings that the defendant directors were grossly negligent in failing to reach an informed decision when they approved the agreement of merger, and to have thereby breached their duty of care. Those findings are fully supported by the record. The formulation and application of the duty of care element of the rule, as applied to a third-party transaction, is explicated in *Van Gorkom*. . . .

Applying *Van Gorkom* to the trial court's presumed findings of director and board gross negligence, we find the defendant directors, as a board, to have breached their duty of care by reaching an uninformed decision on October 29, 1982, to approve the sale of the company to MAF for a per-share sale price of $23. . . . We hold that the plan of merger approved by the defendant directors on October 29, 1982, must, on remand, be reviewed for its entire fairness. . . .

We think it patently clear that the question presented is not one of first impression, as the court below appears to have assumed. Applying controlling precedent of this Court, we hold that the record evidence establishes that Cinerama met its burden of proof for overcoming the rule's presumption of board duty of care in approving the sale of the company to MAF. The Chancellor's restatement of the rule—to require Cinerama to prove a proximate cause relationship between the Technicolor board's presumed breach of its duty of care and the shareholder's resultant loss—is contrary to well-established Delaware precedent . . . .

Director Duty of Care and Board Presumption of Care

* * *

The judicial presumption accorded director and board action which underlies the business judgment rule is "of paramount significance in the context of a derivative action." *Aronson*, 473 A.2d at 812. As *Aronson* states, the presumption may only be invoked by directors who are found to be not only "disinterested" directors, but directors who have both adequately informed themselves before voting on the business transaction at hand *and* acted with the requisite care. There we also stated that, for the rule to apply and attach to a particular transaction, directors "have a duty to inform themselves, prior to making a business decision, of all material information reasonably available to them. Having become so informed, they must *then* act with requisite care in the discharge of their duties." *Id.* at 812 (emphasis added).

The duty of the directors of a company to act on an informed basis, as that term has been defined by this Court numerous times, forms the duty of care element of the business judgment rule. . . .

Applying the rule, a trial court will not find a board to have breached its duty of care unless the directors individually and the board collectively have failed to inform themselves fully and in a deliberate manner before voting as a board upon a transaction as significant as a proposed merger or sale of the company. *See Van Gorkom*, 488 A.2d at 873; *Aronson*, 473 A.2d at 812. Only on such a judicial finding will a board lose the protection of the business judgment rule under the duty of care element and will a trial court be required to scrutinize the challenged transaction under an entire fairness standard of review.

The Chancellor held that "the questions of due care . . . need not be addressed in this case, because even if a lapse of care is assumed, plaintiff is not entitled to a *judgment on this record*." . . . Having assumed that the Technicolor board was grossly negligent in failing to exercise due care, the court avoided the business judgment rule's rebuttal by adding to the rule a requirement of proof of injury. The court then found that requirement not met and, indeed, injury not provable due to its earlier finding of fair value for statutory appraisal purposes. . . .

The court found authority for its requirement of proof of injury in an obscure seventy-year-old decision that none of the parties had relied on or felt pertinent. The trial court ruled: "because the board as a deliberate body was disinterested in the transaction and operating in good faith, plaintiff bears the burden to show that any such innocent, though regrettable, lapse was likely to have injured it. *See, e.g., Barnes v. Andrews*, 298 F. 614 (S.D.N.Y.1924)." The Chancellor concluded that the "fatal weakness in plaintifff's case" was plaintiff's failure to prove that it had been injured as a result of the defendant's negligence. . . .

As defendants concede, this Court has never interposed, for purposes of the rule's rebuttal, a requirement that a shareholder asserting a claim of director breach of duty of care (or duty of loyalty) must prove not only a breach of such duty, but that an injury has resulted from the breach and quantify that injury at that juncture of the case. No Delaware court has, until this case, imposed such a condition upon a shareholder plaintiff. That should not be surprising. The purpose of a trial court's application of an entire fairness standard of review to a challenged business transaction is simply to shift to the defendant directors the burden of demonstrating to the court the entire fairness of the transaction to the shareholder plaintiff[.] . . . Requiring a plaintiff to show injury through unfair price would effectively relieve director defendants of establishing the entire fairness of a challenged transaction.

* * *

*The Chancellor's Enlargement of the Rule to Require Cinerama to Prove Resultant Injury
from the Board's Presumed Failure to Exercise Due Care*

* * *

The Chancellor's reliance on *Barnes* is misguided.[39] While *Barnes* may still be "good law," *Barnes*, a tort action, does not control a claim for breach of fiduciary duty. In *Barnes*, the court found no actionable negligence or proof of loss—and granted defendant's motion for a nonsuit or grant of judgment for defendant on the merits. Here, the court was determining the appropriate standard of review of a business decision and whether it was protected by the judicial presumption accorded board action. The tort principles of *Barnes* have no place in a business judgment rule standard of review analysis.

To inject a requirement of proof of injury into the rule's formulation for burden shifting purposes is to lose sight of the underlying purpose of the rule. Burden shifting does not create per se liability on the part of the directors; rather, it is a procedure by which Delaware courts of equity determine under what standard of review director liability is to be judged. To require proof of injury as a component of the proof necessary to rebut the business judgment presumption would be to convert the burden shifting process from a threshold determination of the appropriate standard of review to a dispositive adjudication on the merits.

This Court has consistently held that the breach of the duty of care, without any requirement of proof of injury, is sufficient to rebut the business judgment rule. . . . A [breach] of either the duty of loyalty or the duty of care rebuts the presumption that the directors have acted in the best interests of the shareholders, and requires the directors to prove that the transaction was entirely fair. . . . Cinerama clearly met its burden of proof for the purpose of rebutting the rule's presumption by showing that the defendant directors of Technicolor failed to inform themselves fully concerning all material information prior to approving the merger agreement. . . .

. . . Thus, we must reverse and remand the case to the trial court with directions to apply the entire fairness standard of review to the challenged transaction. . . .

---

[39] In *Barnes*, the receiver of a failed corporation brought suit against Andrews, who was one of the corporation's former directors, for negligence in the performance of his duties. Andrews was charged with taking little, if any, active role as a director because he attended only part of one of two important meetings. The court found Andrews to have been negligent in his inattention to his directorial duties but not liable for damages since plaintiff failed to prove that the company's insolvency actually resulted from Andrews' negligence rather than the negligence of his fellow directors. Then District Judge Learned Hand ruled:

> Therefore I cannot acquit Andrews of misprision in his office, though his integrity is unquestioned. The plaintiff must, however, go further than to show that he should have been more active in his duties. *This cause of action rests upon a tort,* as much though it be a tort of omission as though it had rested upon a positive act. The plaintiff must accept the burden of showing that the performance of the defendant's duties would have avoided the loss, and what loss it would have avoided.

Barnes, 298 F. at 616 (emphasis added).

NOTES AND QUESTIONS

(1) **Holding in *Cede*.** What is the effect of showing an absence of due care in Delaware? *Cede* suggests that the effect of such a showing is to shift to the defendant officers and directors the burden of showing that their actions satisfy the "entire fairness" test[56] of *Weinberger v. UOP*.[57] This means, among other things, that the plaintiffs need not show that the defendants' conduct caused them any loss in order to overcome the presumption of the business judgment rule.

(2) **Proof of causation outside of Delaware.** ALI *Principles* § 4.01(d) provides that "[a] person challenging the conduct of a director has . . . the burden of proving that the breach was the legal cause of damage to the corporation." In addition, ALI *Principles* § 7.18(c) states that "[a] plaintiff bears the burden of proving causation and the amount of damages suffered by . . . the corporation . . . as a result of a defendant's violation of the [duty of care] . . . ." The Comments to § 7.18 note that "Section 7.18(c) follows the well-established rule that the plaintiff bears the burden of proving loss and causation." To the same effect, MBCA § 8.31(b) provides that a party seeking to hold directors liable for money damages "shall also have the burden of establishing that . . . the harm suffered was proximately caused by the director's challenged conduct." *Cede* thus appears to be a minority position.

(3) **The meaning of fairness.** Even with their victory in the Supreme Court, could the plaintiffs in *Cede* expect ultimately to prevail given the Chancery Court's finding that the merger consideration ($23 per share) exceeded the "fair value" of the Technicolor shares ($21.60)? The $21.60 "fair value" was set in connection with an action seeking an appraisal of the plaintiffs' shares under Del. G.C.L. § 262, rather than in connection with the plaintiffs' breach of fiduciary duty case. Indeed, on remand, Chancellor Allen again upheld the transaction, reasoning that despite the fact that the board was inadequately informed, in light of the evidence of substantial negotiations, the price achieved and the evidence of value, the transaction was fair even if a few dollars more might have been "financially rational."[58] The Delaware Supreme Court affirmed the Chancery Court's finding of entire fairness in *Cinerama v. Technicolor*.[59]

As applied in the *Cinerama* opinions, the entire fairness analysis included consideration of "fair dealing" and "fair price." With respect to fair dealing, the courts examined (1) the timing of the transaction; (2) how the transaction was initiated (*i.e.*, by the third party or by defendants); (3) the extent and effectiveness of price negotiations; (4) the structure of the transaction in terms of whether it invited or precluded compet-

---

[56] This test is discussed further in *Weinberger v. UOP*, 457 A.2d 701 (Del. 1983), excerpted below in Section 15.02[D].

[57] 457 A.2d 701 (Del. 1983).

[58] *Cinerama, Inc. v. Technicolor, Inc.*, 663 A.2d 1134 (Del. Ch. 1994).

[59] 663 A.2d 1156 (Del. 1995).

ing bids; (5) disclosure; (6) the director approval process—that is, whether it was "orderly" and "deductive;" and (7) the extent of shareholder approval (in *Cinerama*, 75% of the shareholders tendered their shares). With respect to fair price, the court noted that insiders sold their own stock, that Goldman, Sachs had undertaken a fairness analysis, and that the directors got the highest value reasonably available.

The final result in *Cinerama* is somewhat puzzling because, while Technicolor's directors are held to have been "grossly negligent" in informing themselves about the sale of the company, the plaintiff gets no remedy. Can this be reconciled with *Van Gorkom* where the Delaware Supreme Court determined that the plaintiff shareholders were entitled to an award of damages based *solely* on their showing that the Trans Union board breached its duty of care in approving the sale of the company? Or is the Delaware Supreme Court simply having second thoughts about the demanding nature of the duties imposed by *Van Gorkom*? *Cinerama* distinguished *Van Gorkom* by noting that the *Van Gorkom* Court had "also concluded that the directors had violated the duty of disclosure" to the Trans Union shareholders. The Court then noted that "the compound breaches of the duties of care and disclosure [in *Van Gorkom*] could not withstand an entire fairness analysis."[60] Therefore, "the only issue to remand [in *Van Gorkom*] was the amount of damages the Court of Chancery should assess."[61]

(4) **The directors' duty of disclosure.** The directors' duty of disclosure is particularly significant in light of the "virtual *per se* rule of damages for breach of the fiduciary duty of disclosure" in *In re Tri-Star Pictures, Inc. Litigation*.[62] However, *Loudon v. Archer-Daniels Midland Company* characterized the "*per se*" language from *Tri-Star* as "*dictum*" in rejecting a claim for damages where the alleged disclosure violations related solely to the election of directors. The court said that "*Tri-Star* stands only for the narrow proposition that, where directors have breached their disclosure duties in a corporate transaction that has in turn caused impairment *to the economic or voting rights of stockholders*, there must at least be an award of nominal damages."[63] *Malone v. Brincat*[64] confirmed the directors' fiduciary duty of disclosure, even for directors who "are not seeking shareholder action, but are deliberately misinforming shareholders about the business of the corporation, either directly or by public statement.[65]

(5) **Waiver of the duty of disclosure.** The Delaware Supreme Court has held that Del. G.C.L. § 102(b)(7) permits opting out of liability for breach of the fiduciary

---

[60] *Id.* at 1166.

[61] *Id.*

[62] 634 A.2d 319, 333 (Del. 1993).

[63] 700 A.2d 135, 142 (Del. 1997).

[64] 722 A.2d 5, 12-14 (Del. 1998).

[65] *Id.* at 14.

duty of disclosure, and that the opt-out cannot be avoided by suing the corporation, which is a beneficiary of the duty.[66]

(6) **The effect of shareholder approval revisited.** As noted above (Note 10 after the *Van Gorkom* excerpt), *Van Gorkom* suggested that shareholder approval might validate a careless board's act. Chancellor Allen so held in *In re Wheelabrator Technologies, Inc., Shareholders Litigation.*[67] Is this consistent with *Cinerama*, where "tacit approval" through tender of more than 75% of Technicolor's shares to MAF only "constituted *substantial evidence* of fairness."[68]

PROBLEM

Second Securities Corporation (S.S.), a securities firm with hundreds of retail offices throughout the country, pleaded guilty to two thousand counts of mail fraud based on intentional overdrafting at the many bank accounts used by its branches, and paid a ten million dollar fine.

An extensive investigation revealed the following facts: Branch and regional managers had for several years applied a system of cash management that involved writing checks on various accounts so as to minimize the balances at its various checking accounts and maximize the balance in interest-bearing accounts. As a part of the system, checks were written so as to produce negative balances on S.S.'s ledgers, but not necessarily in its checking accounts. The purpose of this technique was to anticipate delays in crediting S.S.'s deposits that contributed to the "float" on S.S.'s funds—that is, the time during which S.S. did not have control of its funds but was not earning interest on the funds. An inherent result of the system was the production of occasional overdrafts.

The overdrafting problem was caused by a number of factors: Branch and regional managers were continually exhorted by managers in the central office to maximize interest income, sometimes being directly instructed to engage in overdrafting; branch managers were paid 10% of net profits; there was no system for monitoring overdrafting by branch offices; and there was no effective system in place for monitoring overdrafting at the branch level.

S.S.'s board of directors consisted of a minority of outside directors, all of whom were aware of the company's policy of maximizing interest income, the lack of internal controls, and the method of compensating branch managers. None of the directors was actually aware of intentional overdrafting. At least two of the directors were aware of occasional overdrafting problems and were involved in exhorting branch and regional personnel to maximize interest income. All of the directors received approximately 20

---

[66] *See Arnold v. Society for Savings Bancorp, Inc.*, 650 A.2d 1270 (Del. 1994) (*Arnold I*); *see also Zirn v. VLI Corporation*, 681 A.2d 1050 (Del. 1996).

[67] 663 A.2d 1194 (Del. Ch. 1995).

[68] 663 A.2d at 1176 (emphasis added).

pages of monthly printouts showing, among other things, net income by type of income (including interest) at each branch. By looking at the printouts, the directors could have seen, for example, that at one branch interest income was up to 167.4% of total product revenues.

(a) A shareholder sues all members of the board to recover on behalf of the corporation the fines it paid to settle the mail fraud indictments. Assess the possibility that personal liability will be imposed under the case law discussed in this section.

(b) How would your answer to (a) differ if the corporation had adopted the charter provision permitted by Delaware G.C.L. § 102(b)(7)?[69]

REFERENCES

Arsht, *The Business Judgment Rule Revisited*, 8 HOFSTRA L. REV. 93 (1979).

Carney, *Section 4.01 of the American Law Institute's Corporate Governance Project: Restatement or Misstatement?*, 66 WASH. U. L.Q. 239 (1988).

Conard, *A Behavioral Analysis of Directors' Liability for Negligence*, 1972 DUKE L.J. 895.

DeMott, *Limiting Directors' Liability*, 66 WASH. U. L.Q. 295 (1988).

Fischel, *The Business Judgment Rule and the* Trans Union *Case*, 40 BUS. LAW. 1437 (1985).

Gelb, *Director Due Care Liability: An Assessment of the New Statutes*, 61 TEMPLE L. REV. 13 (1988).

Symposium: Van Gorkom *and the Corporate Board: Problem, Solution, or Placebo?*, 96 Nw. U. L. Rev. 449-693 (2002).

Veasey & Seitz, *The Business Judgment Rule in the Revised Model Act, the* Trans Union *Case, and the ALI Project—A Strange Porridge*, 63 TEX. L. REV. 1483 (1985).

§ 9.04 The Duty of Loyalty: "Interested" Transactions

This Section discusses court review of directors' business decisions where one or more board members has a personal interest in the outcome that is sufficient to rebut the presumption of loyalty underlying the business judgment rule (*see* Section 9.03[A]).

The legal rules regarding court review of such "interested transactions" have evolved considerably since the mid-19th century. Initially, the director's duty of loyalty was as strict as a trustee's, so that any contract between a corporation and one of its directors or a company with which a director was affiliated was voidable by the corporation. Gradually the courts came to uphold transactions in which directors were personally interested as long as the transactions were approved by a disinterested majority of the board of directors or a disinterested majority of the shareholders or were otherwise shown to be fair to the shareholders. For an often-cited history of the development of the modern rule, see **Marsh.**

---

[69] *See* Bell, *The Hutton Report: A Special Investigation into the Conduct of E.F. Hutton & Company Inc. That Gave Rise to the Plea of Guilty Entered on May 2, 1985* (1985).

The following subsections examine the legal rules governing interested transactions. Subsection [A] considers the types of interests that are sufficient to rebut the board's presumption of loyalty and, thereby, remove the protections of the business judgment rule. Subsection [B] considers the legal rules that apply once the presumption of loyalty has been lifted.

[A] Rebutting the Presumption of Loyalty

Statutory provisions like Del. G.C.L. § 144 indicate that the board's presumption of loyalty is withdrawn when a corporation engages in a transaction with one or more of its directors or with a business entity in which one or more of its directors has a financial interest. But should the size or degree of the director's personal interest matter? Also, what rules should apply when the corporate transaction doesn't directly involve a director or an entity in which a director is interested, but instead provides a more subtle personal benefit to the director such as a finder's fee? These and similar issues are considered below.

CEDE & CO. v. TECHNICOLOR, INC.
Delaware Supreme Court
634 A.2d 345 (1993)

Before HORSEY, MOORE and HOLLAND, JJ.
HORSEY.
[This is another part of the opinion excerpted in §9.03[D], above. Some additional facts relate to the following excerpt. At the October 29, 1982 meeting of Technicolor's nine-member board of directors Kamerman, Technicolor's CEO and board chairman, disclosed, among other things, the terms of his proposed employment contract with MAF and that another Technicolor director, Sullivan, would receive a $150,000 finder's fee if MAF acquired Technicolor. Following these disclosures and further discussion, the Technicolor board unanimously approved the proposed acquisition by MAF. Cinerama claims that Technicolor's board was not entitled to the business judgment rule's presumption of loyalty.]

* * *

[T]he Chancellor found that "the Board as a whole" had not breached its collective duty of loyalty, notwithstanding the court's finding that at least one director, Sullivan, if not a second director, Ryan, had breached his duty of loyalty.[24] . . . The Chancellor found the evidence sufficient to conclude that Director Sullivan had been disloyal because of his interest in the transaction. The court also questioned whether Director Ryan was also disloyal due to a conflict of interest. Notwithstanding, the Chancellor ruled that Cinerama had

---

[24] [Ryan was Technicolor's President and Chief Operating Officer. He had a poor working relationship with Technicolor's President and allegedly hoped for better employment opportunities if MAF acquired Technicolor.—Ed.]

failed to rebut the business judgment rule's presumption of loyalty accorded the Technicolor board's decision of October 29. The court held that the shareholder, to rebut the rule, was required to prove that the disloyal director either dominated the board or in some way tainted the presumed independence of the remaining board members voting to approve the challenged transaction. Thus, it was Cinerama's burden to establish that any director's self-interest was individually, or collectively, so "material" as to persuade a trier of fact that the independence of the board "as a whole" had been compromised. Applying this test, the court found that Cinerama had not rebutted the business judgment rule's presumption of director independence. . . .

Cinerama . . . contends that the Chancellor has placed upon a shareholder plaintiff [a] burden[] of proof for breach of duty of loyalty . . . that [is] foreign to equity and to Delaware law. Cinerama further contends that, even under the court's restatement of the duty of loyalty element of the rule, the court has clearly erred in finding that there is insufficient record evidence that a majority of the directors had breached their duty of loyalty to rebut the business judgment rule. . . .

IV. DIRECTOR DUTY OF LOYALTY/BOARD DUTY OF LOYALTY

Presumption of Loyalty/Duty of Loyalty

This Court has traditionally and consistently defined the duty of loyalty of officers and directors to their corporation and its shareholders in broad and unyielding terms: Corporate officers and directors are not permitted to use their position of trust and confidence to further their private interests. A public policy, existing through the years, and derived from a profound knowledge of human characteristics and motives, has established a rule that demands of a corporate officer or director, peremptorily and inexorably, the most scrupulous observance of his duty, not only affirmatively to protect the interests of the corporation committed to his charge, but also to refrain from doing anything that would work injury to the corporation, or to deprive it of profit or advantage which his skill and ability might properly bring to it, or to enable it to make in the reasonable and lawful exercise of its powers. The rule that requires an undivided and unselfish loyalty to the corporation demands that there be no conflict between duty and self-interest. Essentially, the duty of loyalty mandates that the best interest of the corporation and its shareholders takes precedence over any interest possessed by a director, officer or controlling shareholder and not shared by the stockholders generally. . . .

The Chancellor's Requirement that a Director's Self-Interest Must be Material

The Chancellor articulated a two-part test for finding a self-interest significant enough to rebut the presumption of director and board independence. This two-part test requires that a shareholder show: (1) the materiality of a director's self-interest to the given director's independence; and (2) the materiality of any such self-interest to the collective independence of the board. Proof of materiality under either part requires a showing that such an interest is reasonably likely to affect the decision-making process of a reasonable person on a board composed of such persons.

* * *

The First Part of the Chancellor's Materiality Test: Proof of Interest Material to Individual Director(s) Independence

. . . Cinerama contends that one director's receipt of any tangible benefit not shared by the stockholders generally is sufficient to overcome the business judgment presumption of director and board independence. . . .

We agree with defendants that the question of when director self-interest translates into board disloyalty is a fact-dominated question, the answer to which will necessarily vary from case to case. A trial court must have flexibility in determining whether an officer's or director's interest in a challenged board-approved transaction is sufficiently material to find the director to have breached his duty of loyalty and to have infected the board's decision. Therefore, we reject Cinerama's contention that "any" found director self-interest, standing alone and without evidence of disloyalty, is sufficient to rebut the presumption of loyalty of our business judgment rule.

Cinerama also takes exception to the Chancellor's use of a reasonable person standard for determining the materiality of a given director's self-interest in a challenged corporate transaction. We agree that the Chancellor's use of the reasonable person standard is unhelpful and, indeed, confusing. Therefore, we reject its use in resolving whether evidence of director self-interest is sufficient to rebut the rule.

The Second Part of the Chancellor's Materiality Test: Proof of Interest Material to the Independence of Entire Board

The Chancellor ruled that, for purposes of rebutting the business judgment rule, any found director self-interest affecting director independence must also be found to have tainted, influenced or otherwise undermined the board's deliberative process. . . .

. . . [W]e find the Chancellor's requirement that a director's self-interest translate into board self-interest to be an apparent borrowing of precepts embodied in 8 Del. C. § 144(a). . . . At the very least, section 144(a) protects corporate actions from invalidation on grounds of director self-interest if such self-interest is: (1) disclosed to and approved by a majority of disinterested directors; (2) disclosed to and approved by the shareholders; or (3) the contract or transaction is found to be fair "as to the corporation." . . .

Largely without explanation, the Court of Chancery concluded that Sullivan's finder's fee, while materially affecting his own independent business judgment, was not a material interest affecting the transaction overall because the board had approved the transaction after Sullivan's interest had been disclosed. Section 144(a) may arguably sustain this finding. . . . Unfortunately, neither the court below nor the parties have brought section 144(a) into their reasoning or analysis.

* * *

VII. CONCLUSION

We find no error in the Chancellor's reformulation of a materiality test for determining director self-interest. We find error in the trial court's adoption of the reasonable person standard. We decline to determine the correctness of the second part of the court's materiality test, for the reasons stated. We remand that issue to the trial court to consider the relevance and effect of section 144(a) on such standard . . .

CINERAMA v. TECHNICOLOR, INC.
Delaware Supreme Court
663 A.2d 1156 (1995).

[This is the appeal of the Chancery Court's decision after remand.]

Before HOLLAND, RIDGELY, and HORSEY.
HOLLAND, Justice:

* * *

DUTY OF LOYALTY ISSUES ON REMAND

* * *

Materiality Standard and Legitimacy

This Court asked the Court of Chancery to resolve two issues relating to the "second part" of the director interest materiality test: (1) the precise standard of proof required; and (2) the legitimacy of such a standard under Delaware law and the relevance of Section 144(a). *Cede II*, 634 A.2d at 366. The Court of Chancery began by acknowledging that this Court's rejection of the objective "reasonable director" formulation required it to apply a different standard upon remand for determining when an individual director's financial interest is material, before it addressed the remanded question of *board* independence.

The Court of Chancery reasoned that the logical alternative was a subjective "actual person" standard. We agree. . . .

The Court of Chancery stated that "under such a test of materiality [it] would be required to determine *not* how or whether a reasonable person in the same or similar circumstances . . . would be affected by a financial interest of the same sort as present in the case, but whether *this* director in fact was or would likely be affected." *Cinerama*, 20 Del. J. Corp. L. at 313-14. Thus, the "actual person" test requires an independent judicial determination regarding the materiality of the "*given*" director's self-interest . . . .

Cinerama contended on remand, and continues to contend in this appeal, that five of Technicolor's nine directors were "disabled" by conflicts of interest. The Court of Chancery, however, found every director, except Sullivan, to be free of any material conflict. . . .

The Court of Chancery concluded that, "with respect to each of the corporate directors treated in this court's opinion, analysis of actual interference with the directors' good faith judgment seeking the shareholders' best benefit does not produce a different result than does the 'reasonable person' analysis." *Id.* at 315. Thus, after applying the enhanced scrutiny required by the subjective "actual person" standard, the Court of Chancery reached the same determinations regarding the materiality of the alleged *individual* director self-interests as it had previously by applying the objective "reasonable person" standard. *Id.* Those conclusions, as to each director, are supported by the record.

The Court of Chancery then addressed the remanded issue of *board* independence. The Court of Chancery framed the issue as follows:

Has the presence of the found material self-interest of one or more directors on the board that acted upon a transaction so infected or affected the deliberative process of the board as to disarm the board of its presumption of regularity and respect and cast upon the directors the burden (and the heightened risks) of the entire fairness form of judicial review.

Id. at 317 [citations omitted] The Court of Chancery assumed that if actual self-interest is present and affects a majority of directors approving a transaction, the entire fairness standard applies.

The Court of Chancery concluded that a material interest of "one or more directors less than a majority of those voting" would rebut the application of the business judgment rule if the plaintiff proved that "the interested director controls or dominates the board as a whole or [that] the interested director failed to disclose his interest in the transaction to the board and a reasonable board member would have regarded the existence of the material interest as a significant fact in the evaluation of the proposed transaction." *Cinerama*, 20 Del. J. Corp. L. at 317. We hold that the Court of Chancery's conclusion is correct, as a matter of law. Thus, we affirm its ruling on the effect of director material self-interest as it was related to the requirement of board independence.

* * *

Technicolor Board Loyal

The Court of Chancery found as an ultimate fact regarding the issues of loyalty that "a large majority of the board of Technicolor was disinterested and independent with respect to this transaction and neither of those two directors found [Sullivan] or assumed [Ryan] to be interested, dominated or manipulated the process of board consideration. *See Paramount Communications, Inc. v. QVC Network, Inc.*, Del. Supr., 637 A.2d 34 (1994)." That finding must be affirmed as supported by the record . . . .

Section 144(a)'s Relevance

In accordance with this Court's mandate, the Court of Chancery then considered the relevance of 8 Del. C. § 144(a) to this case. The concern Section 144 addresses is self-dealing; for example, when a director deals directly with the corporation, or has a stake in or is an officer or director of a firm that deals with the corporation. [citations omitted] Traditionally, the term "self-dealing" describes the "situation when a [corporate fiduciary] is on both sides of a transaction . . . ." *Sinclair Oil Corp. v. Levien*, Del. Supr., 280 A.2d 717, 720 (1971). In *Cede II*, this Court distinguished classic self-dealing from incidental director interest. To be disqualifying, the nature of the director interest must be substantial. *Cede II*, 634 A.2d at 362-63 [citation omitted].

The Court of Chancery properly began its consideration of Section 144 with the following comment:

> [Section 144] does not deal with the question of when will a financial interest of one or more directors cast on the board the burdens and risks of the entire fairness form of judicial review. Rather it deals with the related problem of the conditions under which a corporate contract can be rendered "un-voidable" solely by reason of a director interest. These two problems—when will a director interest replace the business judgment form of review with the entire

fairness form of review and when are interested contracts not necessarily void-able—are related in that both focus upon an affect of action by an "independent" corporate decision maker. But as construed by our Supreme Court recently compliance with the terms of Section 144 does not restore to the board the presumption of the business judgment rule; it simply shifts the burden to plaintiff to prove unfairness. *See Kahn v. Lynch Communication Systems*, Del. Supr., 638 A.2d 1110 (1994).

The inquiry whether a board is independent and disinterested, etc. for purposes of determining whether it qualified for the business judgment rule presumption is somewhat similar to this Section 144 analysis but can't be the same, since the business judgment form of review analysis inquiry must admit of the possibility that, if there is no material interference with the independence of the board's process, that business judgment review is possible.

Cinerama, 20 Del. J. Corp. L. at 318.

In this appeal, Cinerama acknowledges that Section 144 is not directly applicable to this case.[24] Nevertheless, according to Cinerama, by analogy the safe harbor provisions in Section 144(a) for *disclosed financial* interests would not apply in this case because, allegedly, "many of the material conflicts were not disclosed."

When a board of directors loyalty is questioned, Delaware courts determine whether a conflict has deprived stockholders of a "*neutral* decision-making body." *Oberly v. Kirby*, Del. Supr., 592 A.2d 445, 467 (1991).[25] . . . In *Oberly*, even though Section 144(a) did not apply to the action being contested, this Court relied upon the provisions in that statute to illustrate the general principle that, as to the duty of loyalty, approval of a transaction by a board of which a majority of directors is disinterested and independent "brings it within the scope of the business judgment rule." *Id*. at 466.

Similarly, notwithstanding Section 144(a)'s inapplicability to this case, the Court of Chancery concluded that its "materiality" approach to individual director interest and board independence "is highly consistent with" the policy of Section 144. The Court of Chancery then concluded that "the interest of Mr. Sullivan was disclosed and a majority of the non-interested directors approved the transaction in good faith." *Cinerama*, 20 Del. J. Corp. L. at 318. As to the assumed interest of Mr. Ryan, the Court of Chancery concluded that, pur-

---

[24]   In a footnote in its opening brief in this appeal, Cinerama states:

On its face, Section 144 applies only to contracts or transactions between (i) a corporation and one or more of its directors or officers, or (ii) a corporation and any other corporation or entity in which there are directors or officers in common or in which the directors or officers have a financial interest. Here the merger was neither a transaction between Technicolor and its directors nor between Technicolor and another corporation in which any of the Technicolor directors were directors, officers, or had a financial interest. Although interests of a financial nature existed, those interests resulted *from the transaction itself*. Such interests are not contemplated by the statute. By its terms Section 144 would only apply if Kamerman, Sullivan, Ryan and the others had a financial interest in MAF . . . . Moreover, the statute speaks only to "financial interests" and conflicts arising from fiduciaries appearing on both sides of the transaction. On its face the statute does not encompass transactions tainted by influences affecting a director's independence . . . .

[25]   A board of which a majority of directors is interested is not a "neutral decision-making body." . . .

suant to the language of the statute, "the alleged hope of better employment opportunities does not constitute the kind of interest covered by Section 144." *Id*. We agree with each of the Court of Chancery's conclusions.

* * *

CONCLUSION

On remand, the Court of Chancery properly addressed each of the issues identified by this Court in its mandate. The judgment of the Court of Chancery, in favor of the defendants, is AFFIRMED.

NOTES AND QUESTIONS

(1) **Defining conflicts of interest: the Delaware approach.** Under *Cede* and *Cinerama*, a shareholder seeking to rebut the presumption of loyalty afforded by the business judgment rule must show the "materiality of a director's self interest to the given director's independence" and the "materiality of any such self interest to the collective independence of the board." The second prong of the test is satisfied by showing that a majority of those voting are individually interested or by proving that "the interested director controls or dominates the board as a whole or that the interested director failed to disclose his interest in the transaction to the board and a reasonable board member would have regarded the existence of the material interest as a significant fact in the evaluation of the proposed transaction." However, in *HMG/Courtland Properties, Inc. v. Gray*,[70] involving the corporation's sale of property to an entity affiliated with a director (Gray), approved by the board without knowledge of the director's relationship, the court said "Gray's undisclosed, buy-side interest in the Transactions is a classic case of self-dealing. Under *Cede II* and *Cinerama*, proof of such undisclosed self-dealing, in itself, is sufficient to rebut the presumption of the business judgment rule and invoke entire fairness review." [citation omitted] Section 144 of the Delaware General Corporation Law dictates this conclusion. That statute is implicated whenever a corporation and "1 or more of its directors or officers . . . or partnership . . . or other organization in which 1 or more of its directors or officers . . . have a financial interest" engage in a transaction." Should self dealing always rebut the presumption of loyalty, without regard to the two-part materiality of *Cede* and *Cinerama*?[71]

---

[70]   749 A.2d 94 (Del. Ch. 1999).

[71]   For cases considering the materiality of director self interest, see *Chaffin v. GNI Group, Inc.*, 1999 Del. Ch. LEXIS 182, 1999 WL 721569 (Del. Ch., Sept. 3, 1999) (father of director who would continue in management if acquisition proposal was approved not disinterested in connection with proposal, because "most parents would find it highly difficult, if not impossible, to maintain a completely neutral, disinterested position on an issue, where his or her own child would benefit substantially if the parent decides the issue a certain way"); *Krim v. Pronet, Inc.*, 744 A.2d 523 (Del. Ch. 1999) (directors who approved stock-for-stock merger *not* conflicted with respect to merger because neither the vesting of their stock options nor the retention of their board seats represented a "substantial conflict" of interest); and *Official Committee of the Unsecured Creditors of Color Tile, Inc. v. Investcorp. S.A.*, 1999 U.S. Dist. LEXIS 14826,

(2) **Defining conflicts of interest: the MBCA and ALI approaches.** Compare the Delaware approach to defining conflict of interest transactions to those taken by the MBCA and the ALI. MBCA § 8.60 defines "conflicting interest" transactions to include transactions in which a director or "related person" linked to the director is a party or has a financial interest of such significance that the transaction "would reasonably be expected to exert an influence on the director's judgment if he were called upon to vote on the transaction." ALI *Principles* § 1.23 is similar to the MBCA, but includes as "interested" transactions in which a director is shown to have a "business, financial, or familial relationship with a party [that] . . . would reasonably be expected to affect the director's . . . judgment with respect to the transaction," and in which a director is subject to a controlling influence "by a party to the transaction . . . or a person who has a material pecuniary interest in the transaction . . . that . . . could reasonably be expected to affect the director's . . . judgment . . . ." These approaches are both narrower and broader than Delaware's approach—narrower because they always require a connection between the conflicting interest and the director's judgment, and broader because they forego any required connection between the interest of the individual director and the board's collective decision-making.

(3) **Establishing dominance of otherwise disinterested directors.** *Cede* and *Cinerama* suggest that the *board* may be interested if interested directors dominate the board. ALI *Principles* § 1.23 similarly provides that a director will be considered "interested" if he is subject to a "controlling influence" by an interested party. Compare the more limited definition of "conflicting interest" in MBCA § 8.60. What should be enough domination or controlling influence to taint the approval of otherwise disinterested directors? Recall from the discussion above in Section 7.07[B] the pervasive influence of executives of public corporations over supposedly independent directors. The Comment to ALI *Principles* § 1.23 provides that "[i]t is not intended that a person would be treated as subject to a controlling influence, and therefore interested, solely because of a long-time friendship or other social relationship, or solely because of a long-time business association through service on the same board of directors . . . ."

[B] Rules Governing Conflict of Interest Transactions

As noted in the introduction to Section 9.04, conflict of interest transaction could, at one time, be voided by the corporation or its shareholders. Under modern statutes like Del. G.C.L. § 144, a conflict of interest transaction can no longer be voided solely on the grounds of interest, provided the transaction is approved by a majority of the disinterested directors, a majority of disinterested shareholders, or is otherwise shown by the

---

1999 WL 754015 (S.D.N.Y., Sept. 24, 1999) (Delaware law; "fact that the entire Color Tile board could have been replaced by the company's controlling shareholder group, while relevant, is not sufficient to support an inference that the board as a whole lacked independence").

directors to be fair to the corporation's shareholders. The following subsections generally follow the format of Delaware-type statutory provisions.

[1] No Disinterested Director or Shareholder Approval

Under the modern rule, where there is no disinterested director or shareholder
approval, the court may nevertheless uphold the transaction if it is fair to the corporation. *See* Del. G.C.L. § 144(a)(3); MBCA § 8.61(b)(3); ALI *Principles* § 5.02(a)(2)(A).
This rule is applied in the following case.

LEWIS v. S.L. & E., INC.
United States Court of Appeals, Second Circuit
629 F.2d 764 (1980)

KEARSE, Circuit Judge.

This case arises out of an intra-family dispute over the management of two closely-
held affiliated corporations. Plaintiff Donald E. Lewis ("Donald"), a shareholder of S.L. &
E., Inc. ("SLE"), appeals from judgments entered against him in the United States District
Court for the Western District of New York, Harold P. Burke, Judge, after a bench trial of his
derivative claim against directors of SLE, and of a claim asserted against him by the other
corporation, Lewis General Tires, Inc. ("LGT"), which intervened in the suit. The defendants Alan E. Lewis ("Alan"), Leon E. Lewis, Jr. ("Leon, Jr."), and Richard E. Lewis
("Richard"), are the brothers of Donald; they were, at pertinent times herein, directors of
SLE and officers, directors and shareholders of LGT. Donald charged that his brothers had
wasted the assets of SLE by causing SLE to lease business premises to LGT from 1966 to
1972 at an unreasonably low rental. LGT was permitted to intervene in the action, and filed
a complaint seeking specific performance of an agreement by Donald to sell his SLE stock
to LGT in 1972. The district court held that Donald had failed to prove waste by the defendant directors, and entered judgment in their favor. The court also awarded attorneys' fees
to the defendant directors and to SLE, and granted LGT specific performance of Donald's
agreement to sell his SLE stock.

On appeal, Donald argues that the district court improperly allocated to him the burden of proving his claims of waste, and that since defendants failed to prove that the transactions in question were fair and reasonable, he was entitled to judgment. . . . We agree with
each of these contentions, and therefore reverse and remand.

I

For many years Leon Lewis, Sr., the father of Donald and the defendant directors, was
the principal shareholder of SLE and LGT. LGT, formed in 1933, operated a tire dealership
in Rochester, New York. SLE, formed in 1943, owned the land and complex of buildings at
260 East Avenue in Rochester. This property was SLE's only significant asset. Prior to 1956
LGT occupied SLE's premises without benefit of a lease; the rent paid was initially $200 per
month, and had increased over the years to $800 per month by 1956, when additional parcels

were added. On February 28, 1956, SLE granted LGT a 10-year lease on the newly expanded property ("the Property"), for a rent of $1200 per month, or $14,400 per year. Under the terms of the lease, SLE was responsible for payment of real estate taxes on the Property, while all other current expenses were to be borne by the tenant, LGT.[1]

In 1962, Leon Lewis, Sr., transferred his SLE stock, 90 shares in all, to his six children (defendants Richard, Alan and Leon, Jr., plaintiff Donald, and two daughters, Margaret and Carol), giving 15 shares to each.[2]

At that time Richard, Alan and Leon, Jr., were already shareholders, officers and directors of LGT. Contemporaneously with their receipt of SLE stock, all six of the children entered into a "shareholders' agreement" with LGT, under which each child who was not a shareholder of LGT on June 1, 1972 would be required to sell his or her SLE shares to LGT, within 30 days of that date, at a price equal to the book value of the SLE stock as of June 1, 1972.

LGT's lease on the SLE property expired on February 28, 1966. At that time the directors of SLE were Richard, Alan, Leon, Jr., Leon, Sr., and Henry Etsberger; these five were also the directors of LGT. In 1966 Alan owned 44% of LGT, Richard owned 30%, Leon, Jr., owned 19%, and Leon, Sr., owned 7%. From 1967 to 1972 Richard owned 61% of LGT and Leon, Jr., owned the remaining 39%. When the lease expired in 1966, no new lease was entered into. LGT nonetheless continued to occupy the property and to pay SLE at the old rate, $14,400 per year. According to the defendants' testimony at trial, there was never any thought or discussion among the SLE directors of entering into a new lease or of increasing the rent. Richard testified: "We never gave consideration to a new lease." From all that appears, the defendant directors viewed SLE as existing purely for the benefit of LGT. Richard testified, for example, that although real estate taxes rose sharply during the period 1966-1971, from approximately $7,800 to more than $11,000, to be paid by SLE out of its constant $14,400 rental income, raising the rent was never mentioned. He testified that SLE was "only a shell to protect the operating company [LGT]." When this suit was commenced there had not been a formal meeting of either the shareholders or the directors of SLE since 1962. Richard, Alan and Leon, Jr., had largely ignored SLE's separate corporate existence and disregarded the fact that SLE had shareholders who were not shareholders of LGT and who therefore could not profit from actions that used SLE solely for the benefit of LGT.

Neither Donald nor his sisters ever owned LGT stock. As the June 1972 date approached for the required sale of their SLE stock to LGT, Donald apparently came to believe that SLE's book value was lower than it should have been. He sought SLE financial information from Richard, who had been president of SLE since 1967. Richard refused to provide information. Donald therefore refused to sell his SLE shares in 1972,[6] and com-

---

[1]   It appears that SLE was also responsible for payments due on a mortgage on the Property. In addition, LGT charged SLE for the costs of certain capital improvements, such as the major structural repairs to the principal building's facade, carried out in 1969.

[2]   SLE had 150 shares outstanding, and each child thus received a ten percent interest. At the same time LGT purchased the remaining 60 outstanding shares from the elder Lewis's business partner, Henry Etsberger.

[6]   Donald's sisters Carol and Margaret sold their SLE shares to LGT in 1972 and 1973 respectively Alan, who had sold his LGT stock in 1967, sold his SLE stock to LGT in 1972.

menced this shareholders' derivative action in the district court in August 1973. . . . The sole claim raised in the complaint was that the defendant directors had wasted the assets of SLE by "grossly undercharging" LGT for the latter's occupancy and use of the Property. Although the complaint charged such mismanagement for the period 1962 to 1973, plaintiff subsequently limited this claim to the period between February 28, 1966, the date on which the lease expired, and June 1, 1972, the date contractually set for valuation of the SLE shares which plaintiff had agreed to sell to LGT. LGT intervened and demanded specific performance of Donald's agreement to sell his SLE stock. Donald did not contest his ultimate obligation to sell, but took the position that since the book value of the shares would be increased if he prevailed on his derivative claim, specific performance should be granted only after adjudication of that claim.

There ensued an eight-day bench trial, at which plaintiff sought to prove, by the testimony of several expert witnesses, that the fair rental value of the Property was greater than the $14,400 per year that SLE had been paid by LGT. Defendants sought to show that the rental paid was reasonable, by offering evidence concerning the financial straits of LGT, the cost to LGT of operating the Property, the general economic decline of the East Avenue neighborhood, and rentals paid on two other properties in that neighborhood. LGT presented expert testimony that the value of plaintiff's stock as of June 1972, assuming a successful defense of the derivative claims, was $15,650.

The district court . . . held that Donald had failed to establish the rental value of the Property during the period at issue, and that defendants were therefore entitled to judgment on the derivative claims. Implicit in the district court's ruling, granting judgment for defendants upon plaintiff's failure to prove waste, was a determination that plaintiff bore the burden of proof on that issue.

* * *

II

Turning first to the question of burden of proof, we conclude that the district court erred in placing upon plaintiff the burden of proving waste. Because the directors of SLE were also officers, directors and/or shareholders of LGT, the burden was on the defendant directors to demonstrate that the transactions between SLE and LGT were fair and reasonable.

* * *

Under normal circumstances the directors of a corporation may determine, in the exercise of their business judgment, what contracts the corporation will enter into and what consideration is adequate, without review of the merits of their decisions by the courts. The business judgment rule places a heavy burden on shareholders who would attack corporate transactions. . . . But the business judgment rule presupposes that the directors have no conflict of interest. When a shareholder attacks a transaction in which the directors have an interest other than as directors of the corporation, the directors may not escape review of the merits of the transaction. At common law such a transaction was voidable unless shown by its proponent to be fair, and reasonable to the corporation. BCL § 713, in both its current and its prior versions, carries forward this common law principle, and provides special rules for scrutiny of a transaction between the corporation and an entity in which its directors are directors or officers or have a substantial financial interest.

The current version of § 713, which became effective on September 1, 1971, and governs at least so much of the dealing between SLE and LGT as occurred after that date, expressly provides that a contract between a corporation and an entity in which its directors are interested may be set aside unless the proponent of the contract "shall establish affirmatively that the contract or transaction was fair and reasonable as to the corporation at the time it was approved by the board . . . ." § 713(b). Thus when the transaction is challenged in a derivative action against the interested directors, they have the burden of proving that the transaction was fair and reasonable to the corporation.

The same was true under the predecessor to § 713(b), former § 713(a)(3), which was in effect prior to September 1, 1971. Section 713(a)(3) was not explicit as to the burden of proof, but simply stated that a transaction with interested directors would not be voidable "If the contract of transaction is fair and reasonable as to the corporation at the time it is approved by the board . . . ." The consensus among the commentators was that § 713(a)(3) carried forward the common law rule, which placed the burden of proof as to fairness on the interested directors. . . . We agree with this construction.

* * *

During the entire period 1966-1972, Richard, Alan and Leon, Jr., were directors of both SLE and LGT;[14] there were no SLE directors who were not also directors of LGT. Richard, Alan and Leon, Jr., were all shareholders of LGT in 1966, and from 1967 to 1972 Richard and Leon, Jr., were the sole shareholders of LGT. Under BCL § 713, therefore, Richard, Alan and Leon, Jr., had the burden of proving that $14,400 was a fair and reasonable annual rent for the SLE property for the period February 28, 1966 through June 1, 1972.

Our review of the record convinces us that defendants failed to carry their burden. At trial, there was no direct testimony as to what would have been a fair rental during the relevant period, *i.e.*, 1966 to 1972, and the evidence that was introduced fell far short of establishing that $14,400 was a fair annual rental value for those years.

Quite clearly Richard, Alan and Leon, Jr., had made no effort to determine contemporaneously what rental would be fair during the years 1966-1972. Their view was that the rent should simply cover expenses and that SLE existed for the benefit of LGT. During this period no appraisals were made; no attempts were made to sell or rent the Property; no thought whatever was given to whether $14,400 was a fair and reasonable rent even when real estate taxes had risen to consume nearly all of that amount.

Defendants offered instead evidence of rents paid on other properties. Among their best evidence was the expert testimony of Harvey Rosenbloom, a real estate appraiser. Rosenbloom testified that two other East Avenue buildings, which the district court found to be comparable to the 260 East Avenue premises, were leased at lower per-square-foot rentals than was paid by LGT to SLE. However, as to one of these properties, Rosenbloom

---

[14]   Alan ceased to be a director in November 1972; Leon Jr., ceased to be a director in 1977. Richard remains a director.

testified only to rent paid in 1973 and 1974, and did not consider the 1966-1972 period. As to the other property, Rosenbloom described a fifteen year lease that was entered into in 1961. This testimony, while perhaps not wholly irrelevant to the issues in this suit, fell far short of demonstrating what rental the Property could have fetched in 1966, or in any other of the relevant years. Indeed, Rosenbloom himself testified that rental value could well be different for each year of the period. Thus, rentals that Rosenbloom testified were agreed to in 1961 or 1973 might well have been unfair in 1966 or 1967. This evidence thus could not support a finding that defendants acted fairly in maintaining an annual rental of $14,400 during the years from 1966 to 1972.[16]

Defendants also produced considerable evidence that over the relevant period, the East End neighborhood had been on an economic decline; that businesses had been leaving the area; that urban renewal projects and increased crime had depressed property values there; and that the area had, in general, become a less desirable place to do business. There was also evidence of specific developments that had an adverse effect on the Property: for example, the street running along one side of the Property was made a one-way street, thus limiting customers' access to LGT's premises. The district court credited all of this testimony, and it is fair to say that defendants proved that there was a general downward trend in the value of the Property. However, as noted above, defendants did not establish what was a fair rental value for the Property in 1966. Absent such a point of reference, a general downward trend in value is of no assistance in determining whether the rental actually paid was fair and reasonable during the ensuing years.

Moreover, working in reverse, some of defendants' own evidence as to the value of the Property at the end of the relevant period suggested that $14,400 was less than a fair rental in 1966, and that the figure of $38,099, estimated by plaintiff's expert, was perhaps not far off the mark.[17]

First, there was a variety of evidence suggesting that in 1972 the Property was worth more than $200,000. An appraisal by defense witness Harold Grunert in 1972 set the fair market value of the Property as of June 30, 1972, at $200,000. In 1972 Leon, Jr., had offered personally to buy the Property for $200,000, an offer which Richard had rejected. And in 1971, Richard had informed Donald that evaluations by another appraiser, Harold Galloway, had set the value of the Property at $200,000 and $236,000. Second, defendants' expert witness Rosenbloom, asked what he would consider a fair rent for the property, given Grunert's 1972 valuation of $220,000, stated that ten percent of the value would be inadequate and that fifteen to seventeen percent would be closer to adequate. Fifteen percent of $220,000 would have yielded a rent of $33,000 on the basis of the 1972 valuation. Grunert's own expert testimony was entirely consistent with this. While he had made no estimate as to the fair rental value of the property for 1966-1972, he opined that a fair rental as

---

[16] Defendant Richard E. Lewis testified that defendants tried, without success, to sell the Property in 1975, listing it with a realtor for $200,000. In addition he testified that an effort was made to rent the Property in 1973, and that only one offer, for $700 per month, was forthcoming. Since these efforts were made in 1973 and 1975, the evidence, like the evidence as to rentals of other property, was too remote as to the earlier years of the 1966-1972 period.

[17] Plaintiff's expert made his evaluation as of February 1973. He did not make any evaluation for the period 1966-1972.

of June 30, 1972, would be $20-21,000 with the tenant paying all expenses including real estate taxes. According to Richard, SLE's real estate taxes in 1972 were about $12,000. Thus Grunert's testimony, too, suggests about $33,000 as the fair rental value in 1972. Finally, consistent with their view of the general downward economic trend, Richard and Alan conceded that, whatever the Property was worth in 1972, it was worth more in 1966. Thus the evidence presented by defendants, far from carrying their burden of showing that $14,400 was a fair and reasonable annual rental in 1966-1972, suggested that the fair rental value of the Property throughout that period exceeded $33,000 per year.

The defendants argued, however, that LGT could not have afforded to pay SLE rent higher than $14,400. They produced evidence designed to show that LGT had made little profit; that this low profitability was due to the expenses of maintenance and upkeep of the 260 East Avenue property; and that LGT therefore would not have been able to pay a higher rent to SLE. The district court credited this evidence, finding that LGT had "experienced a number of years of very severe losses," that during the period from 1962-1973, LGT's overall profit was only $53,876, and that payment of rent at the rate of $39,099 per year during this period could have led to the "demise" of LGT. These findings have only a distorted relationship to this lawsuit.

. . . [E]ven on paper, LGT could have "afforded" to double its rent payments to SLE during the period in question.

Moreover, the proposition that LGT could not afford to pay as rent more than what its own books showed as profits ignores the fact that LGT was owned and managed by members of the Lewis family, some of whom were also employees of that corporation. It is entirely possible that these family members granted to themselves unusually high salaries or other perquisites, thus reducing LGT's paper profits.

* * *

Finally, even if we were to assume that LGT's financial records provided a fair basis for evaluating the SLE-LGT transactions, defendants would not have carried their burden of proof. Defendants did not demonstrate that SLE could not have found some other tenant, stronger financially than LGT, which would have been willing and able to pay a higher rental. Even given the general downward trend of the East Avenue neighborhood, it is entirely possible that at least during the early years of the 1966-1972 period, such a tenant might have been secured. No effort was made during that period to rent to anyone other than LGT.

We conclude, therefore, that defendants failed to prove that the rental paid by LGT to SLE for the years 1966-1972 was fair and reasonable. Thus, Donald is not required to sell his SLE shares to LGT without such upward adjustment in the June 1, 1972, book value of SLE as may be necessary to reflect the amount by which the fair rental value of the Property exceeded $14,400 in any of the years 1966-1972.

* * *

We remand to the district court (a) for the entry of judgment in favor of SLE against Richard, Alan and Leon, Jr., jointly and severally, in such amount as the district court shall determine to be equal to the amounts by which the annual fair rental value of the Property exceeded $14,400 in the period February 28, 1966-June 1, 1972, (b) for an accounting as to the value of Donald's SLE shares as of June 1, 1972, in light of such judgment, (c) for an order, following such accounting, of specific performance of the shareholders' agreement, and (d) for such other proceedings as are not inconsistent with this opinion.

NOTES AND QUESTIONS

(1) **Policy basis for duty of loyalty.** Why have different legal rules for interested and disinterested transactions—that is, why distinguish between the duty of care and the duty of loyalty? Evaluate the following statement:

> [T]here is no difference between working less hard than promised at a given level of compensation (a breach of the duty of care) and being compensated more than promised at a given level of work (a breach of the duty of loyalty). Both are examples of agency costs (conflicts of interest in an economic sense) that reduce shareholders' wealth.[72]

The propriety of the distinction depends on the costs and benefits of self-dealing liability. On the one hand, aggressively policing self-dealing presents a risk of what is known in statistics as "Type 1 error" (*i.e.*, avoiding "good" transactions). Because an insider is usually well-informed about her firm's needs, and the board knows and trusts the insider, it may be cheaper for the firm to deal with an insider than with an outsider, other things being equal. Thus, many self-dealing transactions may be beneficial for the firm. This risk of Type 1 error, however, may not be that great if self-dealing that is contrary to the corporation's interest is easy for courts to spot. On the other hand, lenient rules against self-dealing present a risk of so-called "Type 2 error" (*i.e.*, entering into "bad transactions"). This is because it may be hard for firms to control self-dealing by incentive compensation and internal monitoring since agents have strong incentives to act selfishly. But if self-dealing that conflicts with the firm's interests is easy to spot but hard to control through incentive compensation and internal monitoring, does it follow that fiduciary duties are superior to internal monitoring by other managers and auditors?

(2) **Proving fairness.** What test of "fairness" does *Lewis* apply? Would the proof of fair rental value that failed to exonerate the *Lewis* defendants have passed muster under a "business judgment" test like that applied in *Shlensky* (*see* Section 9.03[A])?

(3) **Effect of non-disclosure of conflict.** The Delaware provision could be interpreted as wholly precluding liability for transactions defendant proves are substantively "fair" even if the board did not know of the director's interest in the transaction. However, at least one court has held that "non-disclosure by an interested director or officer is, in itself, unfair."[73] The ALI *Principles* § 5.02(a)(1) adopts the latter approach, requiring "disclosure concerning the conflict of interest . . . and the transaction" in addition

---

[72] **Fischel & Bradley** at 291.

[73] *Washington ex rel. Hayes Oyster Co. v. Keypoint Oyster Co.*, 64 Wash. 2d 375, 391 P.2d 979, 984 (1964).

to proof that the transaction is substantively fair. If the price is substantively fair, is there any damage to the corporation from the interested transaction? See, in this regard, the Comment to ALI *Principles* § 5.02(a)(1) which provides that, "[e]ven though a transaction may be subject to rescission due to failure of the director . . . to make the required disclosure under § 5.02(a)(1), the director . . . will not be subject to personal liability for damages if the burden of proving the transaction was fair to the corporation is sustained." Is the potential cost of a rule holding directors personally liable for substantively fair transactions in terms of deterring beneficial transactions (*i.e.*, increasing Type 1 error) likely to be worth the benefit of ensuring that the voting directors are well informed (*i.e.*, reducing Type 2 error)?

(4) **Varying the standard form.** The rule applied in *Lewis* is only a general procedure that is applied in a wide variety of cases. Should the "standard form" interested director analysis have been qualified in *Lewis* by the parties' expectations in this family business? Even if LGT clearly could not have paid more rent than it was being charged by SLE, is it clear that the SLE directors should be required to find another tenant that could pay the full market rent?

REFERENCES

Anderson, *Conflicts of Interest: Efficiency, Fairness and Corporate Structure*, 25 UCLA L. REV. 738 (1978).

Barnard, *Curbing Management Conflicts of Interest—The Search for an Effective Deterrent*, 40 RUTGERS L.J. 369 (1988).

Cooter & Freedman, *The Fiduciary Relationship: Its Economic Character and Legal Consequences*, 66 N.Y.U. L. REV. 1045 (1991).

Fischel & Bradley, *The Role of Liability Rules and the Derivative Suit in Corporate Law: A Theoretical and Empirical Analysis*, 71 CORNELL L. REV. 261 (1986).

Marsh, *Are Directors Trustees? Conflict of Interest and Corporate Morality*, 22 BUS. LAW. 35 (1966).

Scott, *Corporate Law and the ALI Corporate Governance Project*, 35 STAN. L. REV. 927, 939 (1983).

Weiss, *Economic Analysis, Corporate Law and the ALI Corporate Governance Project*, 70 CORNELL L. REV. 1 (1984).

[2] Approval by Disinterested Directors

Interested director statutes commonly provide that a transaction is not voidable by reason of director self-interest if it was approved by a majority of the disinterested directors. *See* Del. G.C.L. § 144(a)(1), MBCA §§ 8.61(b)(1) and 8.62; ALI *Principles* § 5.02(a)(2)(B). The question of when the directors may be considered disinterested is discussed in the following cases.

PUMA v. MARRIOTT
Delaware Court of Chancery
283 A.2d 693 (1971)

SHORT, Vice Chancellor.

This is a stockholder's derivative action which challenges the fairness of a transaction entered into by Marriott Corporation (Marriott), a Delaware corporation, whereby Marriott, in exchange for 313,000 shares of its common stock, acquired all of the stock of six corporations principally owned by members of the Marriott family. Defendants are those members of the Marriott family and others (Marriott Group) whose stock was acquired, four of whom were directors of Marriott (inside directors), and four of the remaining five directors (outside directors), one having died before commencement of the action. This is the decision after final hearing.

Marriott, originally wholly owned and operated by the Marriott family, was incorporated in 1929 under the name of Hot Shoppes, Inc., later changed to Marriott-Hot Shoppes, Inc., and then to its present name. Over the years the corporation's restaurant and related business expanded rapidly. In March 1953 when its stock was first sold to the public Marriott was operating at 45 locations with gross sales at the end of the fiscal year, July 31, 1952, in excess of $19,000,000 and net after-tax profit exceeding $532,000. At fiscal year end July 31, 1969 it was operating at 324 locations with gross sales exceeding $257,000,000 and net after-tax profit in excess of $10,000,000. From March 1953 Marriott stock was traded on the over-the-counter market until 1968 when it was listed on the New York Stock Exchange.

The acquisition of which plaintiff complains was consummated on January 4, 1966. It was authorized on September 10, 1965 by unanimous resolution of Marriott's outside directors, none of whom were officers or employees of Marriott and all of whom were prominent in legal, financial or business affairs in and about the City of Washington, D.C. The corporations acquired (property companies) were the owners or lessees of real property leased or subleased to Marriott. Each of the leases required Marriott to pay all real estate taxes, insurance, costs of repairs, replacement and utilities together with a fixed guaranteed minimum rental subject to increases based on sales. Since the property companies were principally owned by the Marriott Group there had long been a feeling among the directors that possible conflicts of interest could be avoided by severing the related interests. This feeling was accentuated when Marriott in 1964 inquired of the New York Stock Exchange concerning requirements for the listing of its stock and was informed that it would qualify if its relationship with the property companies was severed. The desire for such listing coupled with the belief that the acquisition would be for the benefit of Marriott led the outside directors to explore the possibility of acquiring the property companies.

The Marriott family initially was not interested in disposing of their real estate holdings for Marriott stock, the testimony indicating that they considered these interests as investment diversification in increasingly valuable assets and further that the additional Marriott shares which they would receive would not substantially increase their 44% ownership of the corporation's stock. At the urging of management officials and the outside directors the family ultimately agreed to a stock exchange. In the meantime, the outside directors had obtained from independent real estate appraisers appraisals of the real estate of the property companies. At least two appraisals were obtained on each property. Independent counsel, tax experts and accountants to advise the outside directors were retained. An independent firm of analysts was employed at the instance of independent counsel to value the Marriott stock. Company officials, none of whom were members of the Marriott Group, furnished information to and correlated data for the outside directors.

On August 10, 1965 at a meeting of Marriott's board the outside directors formally approved acquisition of the stock of the property companies on a non-taxable basis but determination of the number of Marriott shares to be exchanged was postponed until the next monthly board meeting scheduled for September 10, 1965. On the latter date, based on the appraisals, the analysts' computation of the value of Marriott stock, other data and the recommendation of independent counsel, the outside directors authorized, subject to the approval of Marriott stockholders, 375,000 unregistered shares of Marriott stock to be issued in exchange for the shares of the property companies owned by the Marriott Group. The number of Marriott shares to be exchanged was computed by taking the high appraisal for each of the properties adjusted by other assets and liabilities of the property companies and dividing into the figure thus obtained ($7,760,006) the per share value ($20.69) of Marriott stock as determined by the directors. The stockholders of the property companies agreed to the exchange on this basis.

In October 1965 the trading price of Marriott stock having risen from 2 to 3 points over the price prevailing on September 10, 1965, at the instance or with the approval of the Marriott Group, the number of shares of Marriott stock to be exchanged was recomputed and reduced to 313,000. This figure was arrived at by using the average of the high and low appraisals. On this basis the net value of the property companies was determined to be $7,086,007 and this figure was divided by $22 5/8, the recomputed value of a share of Marriott stock.

At the annual meeting of shareholders of Marriott on November 9, 1965 the acquisition of the stock of the property companies for 313,000 shares of Marriott stock was presented to and approved by the stockholders including the plaintiff. The closing of the transaction took place on January 4, 1966.

Plaintiff contends that since the case involves insiders dealing with their corporation the test of validity of the transaction is fairness. That our courts have frequently so held is without question. Thus in *Sterling v. Mayflower Hotel Corp.*, 33 Del. Ch. 20, 93 A.2d 107, the Supreme Court said: "Since they stand on both sides of the transaction, they bear the burden of establishing its entire fairness." And in *David J. Greene & Co. v. Dunhill International*, Del. Ch., 249 A.2d 427, the Chancellor stated that it is unquestionably the substance of our decisions that "when the persons, be they stockholders or directors, who control the making of a transaction and the fixing of its terms, are on both sides, then the presumption and deference to sound business judgment are no longer present." . . . In each of the cited cases, however, it either affirmatively appeared that the insider or insiders dominated the board of directors or the court found such to be the fact. Except to point out that the Marriott Group owned some 46% of the Marriott stock plaintiff here has utterly failed to make any showing of domination of the outside directors. No attempt was made to impugn the integrity or good faith of these directors, all of whom were men of experience in the business and financial world. There is no testimony which even tends to show that the terms of the transaction were dictated by the Marriott Group or any member thereof. On the contrary, the valuations of the property companies and the Marriott stock were made by a majority of Marriott directors, whose independence is unchallenged, based upon appraisals, analysis, information and opinions provided by independent experts, whose qualifications are not questioned. In these circumstances it cannot be said that the Marriott Group stood "on both sides of the transaction" within the meaning of the rule followed in the cases above cited. Therefore, the test here applicable is that of business judgment, there being no showing of fraud.

* * *

Plaintiff argues that the methods used by the appraisers and analysts resulted in over-valuation of the property companies and undervaluation of the Marriott stock. The expert testimony and legal analysis on these issues are in hopeless conflict. But since I am satisfied that in any event the methods of valuation used were not so clearly wrong as to result in an unconscionable advantage secured to the Marriott Group, resolution of these issues is not required.

I conclude that since the transaction complained of was accomplished as a result of the exercise of independent business judgment of the outside, independent directors whose sole interest was the furtherance of the corporate enterprise, the court is precluded from sub-stituting its uninformed opinion for that of the experienced, independent board members of Marriott. . . . Having so decided it is unnecessary to consider defendants' contention that rat-ification of the transaction by Marriott's stockholders effectively barred this action.

* * *

Judgment will be entered for defendants. An order accordingly may, on notice, be sub-mitted.

NOTES AND QUESTIONS

(1) **How many disinterested directors must approve interested transactions?** Delaware G.C.L. § 144, MBCA § 8.62, and ALI *Principles* § 1.15 provide that the dis-interested directors voting on the self-dealing transaction need not constitute a quorum. But the Delaware provision does not clarify whether a majority of disinterested direc-tors present, or of all disinterested directors, must approve the transaction. MBCA § 8.62(a) requires the affirmative vote of a majority, but not less than two, of *voting* "qualified" (disinterested) directors; ALI *Principles* § 1.15 requires the affirmative vote of a majority, but not less than two, of *all* the disinterested directors on the board or the appropriate committee.

(2) **Judicial review of transactions approved by disinterested directors.** MBCA § 8.61(b)(1) prohibits judicial action (injunction, damages or other relief) in connection with a "conflicting interest transaction" that has been approved by qualified directors under MBCA § 8.62. By contrast, Del. G.C.L. § 144 simply provides that a transaction approved by disinterested directors shall not be void or voidable solely on interest grounds. Although this section and *Puma* imply that decisions by disinterested

board members to approve self dealing transactions are entitled to the substantial protections of the business judgment rule, *Cinerama* (excerpted in Section 9.04[A] above) rejects this view. Specifically, the *Cinerama* court characterizes as "proper[]" the Chancery Court's statement that "compliance with the terms of Section 144 does not restore to the board the presumption of the business judgment rule; it simply shifts the burden to plaintiff to prove unfairness." To bring a decision by a board whose loyalty is questioned within the scope of the business judgment rule, a court must determine that a conflict has not deprived the stockholders of a "neutral decision-making body."[74]

Footnote 25 of the *Cinerama* opinion makes clear that the full board of directors qualifies as a "neutral decision-making body" only when (1) a majority of directors is disinterested, (2) interested directors do not dominate the disinterested majority, and (3) interested directors do not manipulate the disinterested majority. Could a board that fails to satisfy these conditions obtain the protection of the business judgment rule by entrusting the particular decision to a special committee composed of the board's disinterested members who are not dominated or manipulated by the interested directors? *Kahn v. Tremont Corp.*[75] held that the delegation to a special committee of independent directors would not alter the standard of review from fairness to business judgment where the corporation purchased property from its controlling shareholder. The court reasoned that, while the burden of proof "may be shifted from the defendants to the plaintiffs through the use of a well functioning committee of independent directors . . . , when a controlling shareholder stands on both sides of the transaction the conduct of the parties will be viewed under the more exacting standard of entire fairness as opposed to the more deferential business judgment standard." The court based this determination on the reality that . . . the controlling shareholder will continue to dominate the company regardless of the outcome of the transaction. The risk is thus created that those who pass upon the propriety of the transaction might perceive that disapproval may result in retaliation by the controlling shareholder. Consequently, even when a transaction is negotiated by a special committee of independent directors, "no court could be certain whether the transaction fully approximate[d] what truly independent parties would have achieved in an arm's length negotiation."

This rationale suggests that the Court might reach a different conclusion as to the effect of disinterested director approval if no controlling shareholder is involved.[76] ALI *Principles* § 5.02(a)(2)(B) provides for a remedy if the challenging party proves that the disinterested directors "could not reasonably have concluded that the transaction was fair to the corporation." The Comment to § 5.02(a)(2)(B) makes clear that judicial scrutiny under this standard is stricter than that required by the business judgment rule.

---

[74]   *Id.* at 1169-70.

[75]   694 A.2d 422 (Del. 1997).

[76]   For a subsequent Chancery Court decision so holding, see *Cooke v. Oolie*, 26 Del. J. Corp. L. 609 (Del. Ch. 2000) ("[T]his Court will apply the business judgment rule to the action of an interested director, who is not the majority shareholder, if the interested director fully discloses his interest and a majority of the disinterested directors ratify the interested transaction.").

(3) **Liability of individual directors.** Even if a transaction cannot be attacked on interest or fairness grounds because it has been approved by disinterested directors after full disclosure, it may still give rise to liability on the part of both interested and disinterested directors under the business judgment rule if, for example, they did not act with due care (*see* Sections 9.02-9.03).[77] Conversely, if the interest of a particular director in a transaction results in the rebuttal of the presumption of loyalty, some directors still may have the protection of the business judgment rule. The Comment to ALI *Principles* § 5.02(a)(2)(B) provides that the "disinterested director's conduct . . . will be protected by the business judgment rule [§ 4.01(c)], if the disinterested director acts in good faith and otherwise satisfies the requirements of § 4.01(c)." But if the directors are "dominated," should they be protected by the business judgment rule?

(4) **Disclosure.** The effectiveness of the disinterested directors' approval depends on disclosure. Delaware § 144(a)(1), ALI *Principles* § 5.02(a)(1) and MBCA § 8.60(4) require disclosure both of the director's interest and of the facts as to the transaction being approved.[78] Should insiders have a duty to disclose the material facts *regarding the transaction*? Such a duty goes considerably beyond the general common law duty of disclosure required from an outsider (*see* Section 12.04). In addition, such a duty is arguably unnecessary since board members who know of the insider's interest arguably can question the insider sharply and discount her recommendation. On the other hand, such questioning is not suited to the need to maintain a collegial atmosphere in board deliberations. *Kahn v. Tremont Corp.*, discussed above in Note 2, held that a controlling shareholder had no duty to disclose an investment banker's advice as to the appropriate illiquidity discount for shares to be sold to the controlled corporation. The court reasoned that a controlling shareholder need not "disclose information which might be adverse to its interests because the normal standards of arms-length bargaining do not mandate a disclosure of weakness."

REFERENCES

Barnard, *Curbing Management Conflicts of Interest—The Search for an Effective Deterrent*, 40 RUTGERS L.J. 369 (1988).

Bratton, *Self-Regulation, Normative Choice, and the Structure of Corporate Fiduciary Law*, 61 GEO. WASH. L. REV. 1084 (1993).

Brudney, *The Independent Director—Heavenly City or Potemkin Village?*, 95 HARV. L. REV. 597 (1982).

---

[77] For examples of cases imposing liability in this situation, see *DePinto v. Provident Security Life Insurance Co.*, 374 F.2d 37 (9th Cir.), *cert. denied*, 389 U.S. 822 (1967); *Doyle v. Union Insurance Co.*, 202 Neb. 599, 277 N.W.2d 36 (1979).

[78] For a case applying this standard, see *Globe Woolen Co. v. Utica Gas & Electric Co.*, 224 N.Y. 483, 121 N.E. 378 (1918).

[3] Shareholder Approval

Under interested director statutes like Del. G.C.L. § 144, MBCA § 8.61(2), and ALI *Principles* § 5.02(a)(2)(C), an interested transaction is not necessarily voidable if it was approved by the shareholders. The effect of shareholder approval under this type of provision is discussed in the following case and notes.

FLIEGLER v. LAWRENCE
Delaware Supreme Court
361 A.2d 218 (1976)

McNEILLY, Justice.

In this shareholder derivative action brought on behalf of Agau Mines, Inc., a Delaware corporation, (Agau) against its officers and directors and United States Antimony Corporation, a Montana corporation (USAC), we are asked to decide whether the individual defendants, in their capacity as directors and officers of both corporations, wrongfully usurped a corporate opportunity belonging to Agau, and whether all defendants wrongfully profited by causing Agau to exercise an option to purchase that opportunity. The Court of Chancery found in favor of the defendants on both issues. . . .

I

In November, 1969, defendant, John C. Lawrence (then president of Agau, a publicly held corporation engaged in a dual-phased gold and silver exploratory venture) in his individual capacity, acquired certain antimony properties under a lease-option for $60,000. Lawrence offered to transfer the properties, which were then "a raw prospect," to Agau, but after consulting with other members of Agau's board of directors, he and they agreed that the corporation's legal and financial position would not permit acquisition and development of the properties at that time. Thus, it was decided to transfer the properties to USAC, (a closely held corporation formed just for this purpose and a majority of whose stock was owned by the individual defendants) where capital necessary for development of the properties could be raised without risk to Agau through the sale of USAC stock; it was also decided to grant Agau a long-term option to acquire USAC if the properties proved to be of commercial value.

In January, 1970, the option agreement was executed by Agau and USAC. Upon its exercise and approval by Agau shareholders, Agau was to deliver 800,000 shares of its restricted investment stock for all authorized and issued shares of USAC. The exchange was calculated on the basis of reimbursement to USAC and its shareholders for their costs in developing the properties to a point where it could be ascertained if they had commercial value. Such costs were anticipated to range from $250,000 to $500,000. At the time the plan was conceived, Agau shares traded over-the-counter, bid at $5/8 to $3/4 and asked at $1 to $1 1/4. Applying to these quotations a 50% discount for the investment restrictions, the parties agreed that 800,000 Agau shares would reflect the range of anticipated costs in developing USAC and, accordingly, that figure was adopted.

In July, 1970, the Agau board resolved to exercise the option, an action which was approved by majority vote of the shareholders in October, 1970. Subsequently, plaintiff instituted this suit on behalf of Agau to recover the 800,000 shares and for an accounting.

II

The Vice-Chancellor determined that the chance to acquire the antimony claims was a corporate opportunity which should have been (and was) offered to Agau, but because the corporation was not in a position, either financially or legally, to accept the opportunity at that time, the individual defendants were entitled to acquire it for themselves after Agau rejected it.

We agree with these conclusions[.] . . . Accordingly, Agau was not entitled to the properties without consideration.

* * *

III

. . . [T]he individual defendants stood on both sides of the transaction in implementing and fixing the terms of the option agreement. Accordingly, the burden is upon them to demonstrate its intrinsic fairness[.] . . . We agree with the Vice-Chancellor that the record reveals no bad faith on the part of the individual defendants. But that is not determinative. The issue is whether the 800,000 restricted investment shares of Agau stock, objectively, was a fair price for Agau to pay for USAC as a wholly-owned subsidiary.[2]

A.

Preliminarily, defendants argue that they have been relieved of the burden of proving fairness by reason of shareholder ratification of the Board's decision to exercise the option. They rely on 8 Del. C. § 144(a)(2) and *Gottlieb v. Heyden Chemical Corp.*, Del. Supr., 33 Del. Ch. 177, 91 A.2d 57 (1952).

In *Gottlieb*, this Court stated that shareholder ratification of an "interested transaction," although less than unanimous, shifts the burden of proof to an objecting shareholder to demonstrate that the terms are so unequal as to amount to a gift or waste of corporate assets. . . . The court explained:

> [T]he entire atmosphere is freshened and a new set of rules invoked where formal approval has been given by a majority of independent, fully informed [share]holders.

91 A.2d at 59.

---

[2] The date at which the transaction must be scrutinized for intrinsic fairness is critical to the resolution of this question. We agree with the Vice-Chancellor that as of January 28, 1970, when the option was formally executed, that the transaction was one which would have commended itself to an independent corporation in Agau's position. *Johnston v. Greene, supra.* However, we are not concerned so much with Agau's acquisition of the option, but rather with the exercise thereof and implementation of its terms. In other words, the focus must be on the actual exchange of Agau's stock for USAC's stock and the test is whether that which Agau received was a fair quid pro quo for that which it had to pay. Since that exchange did not and could not, in fact occur until shareholder approval had been given in October, 1970, we must examine the transaction as of that point in time.

The purported ratification by the Agau shareholders would not affect the burden of proof in this case because the majority of shares voted in favor of exercising the option were cast by defendants in their capacity as Agau shareholders. Only about one-third of the "disinterested" shareholders voted, and we cannot assume that such non-voting shareholders either approved or disapproved. Under these circumstances, we cannot say that "the entire atmosphere has been freshened" and that departure from the objective fairness test is permissible. . . . In short, defendants have not established factually a basis for applying *Gottlieb*.

Nor do we believe the Legislature intended a contrary policy and rule to prevail by enacting 8 Del. C. § 144[.]

Defendants argue that the transaction here in question is protected by § 144(a)(2) which, they contend, does not require that ratifying shareholders be "disinterested" or "independent"; nor, they argue, is there warrant for reading such a requirement into the statute. . . . We do not read the statute as providing the broad immunity for which defendants contend. It merely removes an "interested director" cloud when its terms are met and provides against invalidation of an agreement "solely" because such a director or officer is involved. Nothing in the statute sanctions unfairness to Agau or removes the transaction from judicial scrutiny.

B.

Turning to the transaction itself, we note at the outset that from the time the option arrangement was conceived until the time it was implemented, there occurred marked changes in several of the factors which formed the basis for the terms of the exchange. As of the critical date, the market value of Agau shares had risen and shares were being traded at about $3.00 per share; thus, while initially the maximum discounted market value of the 800,000 was considered to be $500,000, by the time in question it was $1.2 million. Development expenses, originally anticipated to range from $250,000-$500,000, but as actually incurred, were towards the lower end of that scale. Further, while only equity investment was anticipated as the means of raising the capital to finance exploration and development, an original subscriber for 1,500 shares for $250,000. cancelled his subscription and USAC found itself unable to obtain sufficient capital through sale of stock; thus it was forced to borrow $300,000, the debt being secured by USAC property as well as by Agau stock purchase warrants.[4] It also appears that only $83,000 in cash was actually received through sales of stock.

On the basis of these changed conditions and in light of the fact that the exchange price was originally calculated simply to reimburse the USAC shareholders for their costs, plaintiff argues that the issuance of 800,000 shares of Agau stock, having a market value of at least 1.2 million dollars, to acquire a corporation in which only $83,000 in cash had been invested, and whose property was subject to loans of $300,000, is patently unfair.

The difficulty with this argument for purposes of the fairness test is that it impermissibly attempts to equate and compare two different standards of value (if indeed USAC's debt/equity ratio is a standard of value) in order to demonstrate the inadequacy of the con-

---

[4]   These warrants apparently were demanded by the lenders because of Agau's option rights in USAC and were issued after the Agau Board of Directors had resolved that the option be exercised.

sideration Agau received. *See Sterling v. Mayflower Hotel Corp., supra*. In fact, a reference to market sales of the stock involved, might support a finding of fairness. It appears that, although USAC was closely held, there was one arms-length sale of 75 USAC shares to non-affiliated investors for $160 per share. At this rate, the value of the 10,000 USAC shares would be 1.6 million, $400,000 more than the value of the shares given up by USAC. Furthermore, the market value of Agau's stock, even discounted, is an unrealistic indicator of the true value of what Agau gave up as it was clearly inflated due to Agau's possession of the option to acquire USAC whose properties were increasing in value largely as a result of the time and efforts expended by the individual defendants. As stated by the Vice-Chancellor:

> Thus, I think it is without question that if Lawrence and the other defendant shareholders of USAC had not granted the option to Agau, the value of the consideration originally established would not have risen. In other words, the very fact that Agau had the option increased the value of the consideration it was committed to give in the event it chose to exercise it, and this, in turn, was due to the fact that as USAC continued its efforts it became increasingly obvious that it had something that Agau would want to acquire.

The book value of 800,000 Agau shares reinforces this conclusion. Saleable assets (at cost less depreciation) less liabilities (excluding accrued salary due Lawrence) yielded an equity totaling about $113,000. On this basis, the 800,000 shares, which when issued represented a 28.6% interest in the corporation,[5] thus had a value of about $32,000. In this sense, Agau paid little; but, USAC's book position was no better, with assets and liabilities about equal. This comparison, however, is likewise unrealistic for it ignores the true value of USAC's most valuable asset, the antimony properties themselves. While the properties were carried on the books at cost ($60,000), the record indicates their value was considerably higher. In late 1969 or early 1970, when the properties were still considered to be a "raw prospect," USAC received two offers (subsequently confirmed in writing) of $200,000 for a 50% interest in the properties and their future development and yield. Further, Lawrence, a qualified expert, testified that in his opinion, the properties had a net value of between 3.5-70 million dollars as of August 31, 1970.

Viewing the two corporations as going concerns from the standpoint of their current and potential operational status presents a clearer and more realistic picture not only of what Agau gave up, but of what it received.

Agau was organized solely for the purpose of developing and exploring certain properties for potentially mineable gold and silver ore. The bulk of its cash, raised through a public offering, had been expended in "Phase I" exploration of the properties which failed to establish a commercial ore body, although it did reveal "interesting" zones of mineralization which indicated to Lawrence that "Phase II" development and exploration might eventually be desirable. However, plans for further development had been temporarily abandoned as being economically unfeasible due to Agau's lack of sufficient funds to adequately explore the properties, as well as to the falling market price of silver. It further appears that other

---

[5]   Prior to the exchange, there were approximately two million shares outstanding. Adding to that the 800,000 shares paid to defendants, their consequential share was 800,000/2,800,000, or 28.57%.

than a few outstanding unexercised stock purchase warrants, Agau did not have any ready sources of capital. Thus, as the Vice-Chancellor found, had the option not been exercised, Agau might well have gone out of business.

By comparison, the record shows that USAC, while still considered to be in the exploratory and development stage, could reasonably be expected to produce substantial profits. At the time in question, the corporation had established a sizeable commercial ore body, had proven markets for its product, and was in the midst of constructing a major ore separation facility expected to produce a high grade ore concentrate for market.

* * *

Considering all of the above factors, we conclude that defendants have proven the intrinsic fairness of the transaction. Agau received properties which by themselves were clearly of substantial value. But more importantly, it received a promising, potentially self-financing and profit generating enterprise with proven markets and commercial capability which could well be expected to provide Agau at the very least with the cash it sorely needed to undertake further exploration and development of its own properties if not to stay in existence. For those reasons, we believe that the interest given to the USAC shareholders was a fair price to pay. Accordingly, we have no doubt but that this transaction was one which at that time would have commended itself to an independent corporation in Agau's position.

Affirmed.

NOTES AND QUESTIONS

(1) **Appropriateness of reviewing fairness.** Why did *Fliegler* hold that the statute permitted judicial review of fairness despite shareholder approval? Does such an interpretation make redundant the fairness subsection, Del. G.C.L. § 144(a)(3)? As discussed in Note 2 following *Puma*, compliance with Del. G.C.L. § 144 alone only precludes voiding of the transaction solely on the grounds of interest.[79]

(2) **Effect of disinterested shareholder approval.** If the transaction is approved[80] by *disinterested* shareholders, and the corporation is not dealing with a controlling shareholder, the courts apply a "waste" standard, which one court characterized as applying its business judgment only insofar that "a man does not need to be a 'judge of horse-flesh' to refrain from buying a Clydesdale for racing."[81] ALI *Principles* § 5.02(a)(2)(D) also adopts this standard. Is this any different from the business judgment

---

[79] For a case reaching the same result as *Fliegler* under a similar statutory provision, see *Remillard Brick Co. v. Remillard-Dandini Co.*, 109 Cal. App. 2d 405, 241 P.2d 66 (1952).

[80] It may not be clear if the shareholders have approved a transaction if they have merely acquiesced in it after disclosure. *See Robert A. Wachsler, Inc. v. Florafax Intern., Inc.*, 778 F.2d 547 (10th Cir. 1985) (no shareholder ratification by acquiescence without knowledge of facts).

[81] *Gottlieb v. Heyden Chemical Corp.*, 33 Del. Ch. 177, 91 A.2d 57, 58 (1952); *see also In re Wheelabrator Technologies, Inc. Shareholders Litigation*, 663 A.2d 1194 (Del. Ch. 1995). For applications of the *Gottlieb* rule, see *Michelson v. Duncan*, 407 A.2d 211 (Del. 1979); *Schreiber v. Pennzoil Co.*, 419 A.2d 952 (Del. Ch. 1980).

rule applied to disinterested transactions? The ALI *Principles* fail to resolve this issue, noting only that both the business judgment rule and the "waste" standard "provide a limited scope of review."[82] *Should* courts have greater discretion to review shareholder-approved self-dealing transactions than ordinary transactions approved by disinterested directors? Can disinterested shareholders constitute a "neutral decision-making body" under *Cinerama*? Evaluate the following questions commentators have raised concerning the efficacy of shareholder voting. (See, for example, **Bebchuk** and **Coffee**.)

(a) Shareholders in public corporations are "rationally apathetic" in the sense that a transaction is unlikely to change the value of a shareholder's investment's enough to justify a large expenditure in information or persuading other shareholders to oppose the transaction (*see* Section 7.02[A]). On the other hand, even uninformed shareholders can pick up signals from the market price reaction to announcements of corporate transactions. Uninformed shareholders can even vote yes or no at random, thereby increasing the importance of the votes of informed shareholders (*see* **Romano** at 1607-11).

(b) Managers can exert influence on institutional holders, who face conflicts of interest, to vote with them. But such conflicts exist only for certain types of large holders who have business relationships with the firms in which they invest, such as banks, insurance companies and corporate pension plans. Other large holders, particularly including public pension plans, have strong incentives to vote knowledgeably and only for profit-maximizing proposals. Moreover, even "conflicted" shareholders have both fiduciary obligations and market incentives to oppose wealth-reducing proposals.

(c) Managers control the "agenda" in the sense that they can decide which proposals are presented to the shareholders. Thus, they can structure shareholder votes so as to maximize the chance of approval. For example, they can limit the shareholders' choices to self-dealing transactions when other, better, transactions are available (see the discussion in Section 14.03[A][1][c] of "dual class recapitalizations"). On the other hand, informed and disinterested shareholders can to some extent discern when they are being short-changed.

Assuming these problems are potentially serious, does the reduction in cost of potential Type II error by shareholders outweigh the costs of increased judicial scrutiny?

Should the effect of disinterested shareholder approval be different when the corporation deals with a controlling shareholder? In *In re Wheelabrator Technologies Shareholder Litigation*,[83] Chancellor Allen generally considered the impact of an informed vote of disinterested shareholders on duty of loyalty claims. For transactions *not* involving controlling shareholders, the Chancellor agreed that a fully informed, disinterested shareholder vote invokes "the business judgment rule and limits judicial review to issues of gift or waste with the burden of proof upon the party attacking the transaction." But for transactions with controlling shareholders, the court held that a fully, informed vote of disinterested shareholders had a more limited impact. In that

---

[82]   *See* ALI *Principles* § 1.42, Comment.

[83]   663 A.2d 1194 (Del. Ch. 1995).

case, the operative effect of the vote would be to "leave 'entire fairness' as the review standard, but shift the burden of proof to the plaintiff." The Chancellor explained that "participation of the controlling interested stockholder is critical to the application of the entire fairness standard because . . . the potential for process manipulation by the controlling stockholder, and the concern that the controlling stockholder's continued presence might influence even a fully informed shareholder vote, justify the need for the exacting judicial scrutiny and procedural protection afforded by the entire fairness form of review." Compare *Kahn v. Tremont Corp.*, discussed in Note 2 following *Puma*, regarding the limited effect of disinterested *director* approval on the review of transactions with controlling shareholders.

(3) **Effect of interested shareholder approval.** Where, as in *Fliegler*, the outcome of the vote is determined by interested shareholders, should the defendant have to establish fairness just as if there had been no shareholder ratification? Also, why shouldn't it be determinative that disinterested shareholders in *Fliegler* had sufficient shares to disapprove the transaction but chose not to vote? *Did* the *Fliegler* court apply the same level of review as was applied in *Lewis* (Section 9.04[B][1])—*i.e.*, did it give no effect to the vote of the interested shareholders approving the transaction?

(4) **Disclosure.** As with respect to disinterested director approval, the effect of shareholder approval depends on full disclosure.[84] (See Note 4 following the *Puma* excerpt in Section 9.04[B][2], discussing the type of disclosure which must be made to make effective a shareholder or director vote authorizing a self-dealing transaction.) Inadequate disclosure to shareholders in connection with an interested director transaction may also serve as the basis of a cause of action under § 14(a) of the 1934 Act (*see* Section 7.03[C]) if the company in question is a publicly held corporation.

REFERENCES

Bebchuk, *Limiting Contractual Freedom in Corporate Law: The Desirable Constraints on Charter Amendments*, 102 HARV. L. REV. 1820 (1989).

Coffee, *The Mandatory/Enabling Balance in Corporate Law: An Essay on the Judicial Role*, 89 COLUM. L. REV. 1618.

Eisenberg, *The Structure of Corporation Law*, 89 COLUM. L. REV. 1461 (1989).

Gilson, *Evaluating Dual Class Common Stock: The Relevance of Substitutes*, 73 VA. L. REV. 807 (1987).

Gordon, *The Mandatory Structure of Corporate Law*, 89 COLUM. L. REV. 1549 (1989).

Marsh, *Are Directors Trustees? Conflict of Interest and Corporate Morality*, 22 BUS. LAW. 35 (1966).

---

[84] For examples of cases decided under state law in which the adequacy of disclosure to the shareholders was at issue, see *Michelson* and *Schreiber, supra* footnote 81.

Romano, *Answering the Wrong Question: The Tenuous Case for Mandatory Corporate Laws*, 89 COLUM. L. REV. 1599 (1989).

Ruback, *Coercive Dual Class Exchange Offers*, 20 J. FIN. ECON. 153 (1988).

[C] The Interplay of Substance and Procedure

As is discussed in the preceding subsections, neither disinterested director nor shareholder approval completely insulates self-dealing transactions from judicial scrutiny; such approval only alters the level of judicial review—in other words, the placement and weight of the burden of persuasion as to the substantive fairness of the transaction. Thus, liability in a given case depends both on how the transaction was approved and on the proof adduced as to the fairness of the terms of the transaction. Liability also may depend on whether the conflict of interest transaction involved a controlling shareholder.

PROBLEM

Answer this problem in light of all of the materials in Section 9.04.

Carter owns a 35% interest in Bank, a medium-sized publicly held corporation. During the past year Bank lost a substantial amount of money as a result of sharply rising interest rates, and the price of its stock has fallen from an all-time high to an all-time low. However, the corporation still has a strong capital position; interest rates have begun to fall, and the Bank's outlook is good.

Bank needs an additional $25 million in order to pursue more aggressively new loan business in accordance with a recently formulated long-term financial plan. Carter has offered to loan Bank the funds. Carter would receive an unsecured convertible debenture under the terms of which Carter could convert the debt into $25 million of common stock at any time within the next five years at a price of $12.50 per share. The current market price of the stock is $11. Bank could borrow the same amount of money from a federal agency. Both the federal and Carter notes would be repayable over the same period. However, the federal note would be secured and would not be convertible. Interest would be 11½% on the federal note and 11% on the Carter note.

The Bank board of directors consists of nine members. Three of the members are Carter's representatives; one is a representative of a brokerage firm which would receive a fee for arranging the loan and which regularly performs investment banking services for Carter; three are Bank executives; one is a representative of a large shareholder who is opposed to the Carter transaction; and one is not otherwise affiliated in any way with the corporation or its shareholders.

Management favors the Carter transaction. They have asked for your advice, as counsel for Bank, as to the possibility that the transaction will be successfully challenged in court if it is approved, and as to what procedures should be employed in order to minimize this possibility. Management would like to avoid securing shareholder approval if possible, since calling a special shareholders' meeting and printing and distributing proxy materials would be quite expensive. However, management will take this step if it will clearly enhance the probability that the transaction will withstand court scrutiny. What advice would you give? Assume Delaware law applies.[85]

§ 9.05 The Duty of Loyalty: Executive Compensation

Executive compensation is an important fiduciary duty issue, particularly recently in the light of allegations of excessive compensation in Enron and other corporate scandals. Where the board of directors votes compensation for directors or senior executives, this is an interested business decision to which the general rules discussed in Section 9.04 apply. However, because several special considerations bear on judicial review of executive compensation decisions, this topic deserves separate treatment. Consistent with this view, the ALI *Principles* subject compensation decisions to the special rules in § 5.03, rather than the general rules on interested transactions in § 5.02.

[A] General Considerations

This Section reviews some considerations courts should and do take into account in evaluating executive compensation plans.

[1] Competing in the Market for Managers

Firms obviously must pay executives enough to buy them from competing bidders. In other words, an executive's worth, like that of any commodity, is determined by the market.

[2] Determining the Market Value of Managers

If the courts are to second-guess the board's appraisal of the market for an executive's services, they must make their own determination of what an executive is worth. This involves determining what others would pay for the executive's services and whether the executive has unique value to a particular firm. This raises difficult questions. Consider the following quote:

> If comparisons are to be made, with whose compensation are they to be made—executives? Those connected with the motion picture industry? Radio artists? Justices of the Supreme Court of the United States? The Pres-

---

[85] For a description of a similar transaction, see *Gibraltar Savings Holder Steinberg Irks Other Owners by a Purchase of Warrants*, WALL ST. J., Jan. 27, 1982 at 8.

ident of the United States? Manifestly, the material at hand is not of adequate plasticity for fashioning into a pattern or standard. Many instances of positive underpayment will come to mind, just as instances of apparent rank overpayment abound. Haplessly, intrinsic worth is not always the criterion. A classic might perhaps produce trifling compensation for its author, whereas a popular novel might yield a titanic fortune. Merit is not always commensurately rewarded, whilst mediocrity sometimes unjustly brings incredibly lavish returns. Nothing is so divergent and contentious and inexplicable as values.[86]

An executive's market value may be what some people consider "a lot" of money. Michael Milken, the former head of Drexel Burnham Lambert's junk-bond (high yield debt) department, was paid $550 million in salary and bonuses in 1987. This worked out to about $107,000 an hour based on a 14-hour day, more than 100 times the combined 1987 salaries of the chairmen of ITT, IBM and Chrysler, more than three times the SEC's annual budget, $100 million more than Guyana's gross national product, ten times the total pay for all members of Congress, and more than 2/3 the value of Pablo Picasso's life work. Many people were horrified by Milken's pay. (Comedian Steven Wright supposedly objected only to Milken's $50 million year-end bonus, saying, "I think $500 million is plenty.") But Milken was uniquely responsible for the development of the high-yield bond market, and particularly for the revolution these instruments caused in the takeover market. According to the Wall Street Journal, Milken's department was responsible for up to 80% of Drexel's total 1986 revenues of $4 billion.[87] So was Milken, perhaps, underpaid? Was Milken worth less per hour than, say, Barbra Streisand, who made a large amount of money for a brief Las Vegas stint?[88]

[3] Designing Incentive Compensation

Executive compensation must be designed not only to attract a particular executive to the company, but also to provide appropriate incentives for optimal executive performance. Yet appropriately designing incentive compensation is not easy. For example, one writer has suggested that the Mets—at the time both the worst and the highest paid team in baseball—should have been paid on the basis of attendance and concession sales rather than merely individual performance.[89] But such pay could encourage cheat-

---

[86] *Heller v. Boylan*, 29 N.Y.S.2d 653, 679-80 (N.Y. Sup. Ct. 1941), *aff'd without opinion*, 263 A.D. 814, 32 N.Y.S.2d 131 (1941).

[87] The above facts are drawn from Swartz, *Why Mike Milken Stands to Qualify for Guinness Book*, WALL ST. J., March 31, 1989, p. A1, col. 3.

[88] *See Editorial*, WALL ST. J., Oct. 14, 1993 at A16 (comparing Barbra Streisand's pay to executive compensation).

[89] Birnbach, *Mets Memo: Pay'em When they Win*, N.Y. TIMES, sec. 3, p. 3, June 13, 1993. For an attempt to measure the performance of managers of baseball teams, *see* Scully, THE BUSINESS OF MAJOR LEAGUE BASEBALL 182-90 (1989) (Earl Weaver was the best).

ing since it might lead Mets players to push games into extra innings to collect the extra beer sales. More generally, depending on how it is structured, incentive compensation can either force employees to bear risks which they cannot effectively reduce through diversification, or offset other risks employees are required to bear.

[4] Other Considerations

The problems of designing compensation levels are complicated by additional considerations, which are discussed in more detail in Subsection [C] below. First, the executive's employment and the compensation package continue over a period of time. Therefore, a compensation plan that appeared appropriate when first approved may appear excessive in operation. Second, compensation plans have varying tax consequences for firms and employees. It is therefore necessary to consider after-tax costs and benefits.

[B] Specific Types of Compensation

This subsection discusses the general problems identified above in the context of the features of particular types of compensation.

[1] Salary

A basic component of any compensation package is regular payments in predetermined amounts. These payments are taxed to the employee at ordinary income rates and, except as discussed below, are deductible by the corporation as business expenses.[90] Note that the corporation's deduction may be denied, particularly in the close corporation setting, if the Internal Revenue Service determines that the payments are actually dividends rather than compensation for services. Some relevant factors in making this determination are: whether the salary is comparable to that generally paid for similar services; whether amounts of salaries correspond with size of shareholdings; whether salaries exhaust earnings leaving nothing left over for dividends; and whether salaries are fixed at the end of the year in relation to available earnings.[91] Tax law also limits the ability of corporations to deduct compensation of corporate managers: compensation in

---

[90]   *See* I.R.C. § 162(a)(1).

[91]   *See Trinity Quarries, Inc. v. United States*, 679 F.2d 205 (11th Cir. 1982); 6 J. Merten, LAW OF FEDERAL INCOME TAXATION, § 25E.12 (1989). In *Exacto Spring Corporation v. Commissioner of Internal Revenue*, 196 F.3d 833 (7th Cir. 1999), Judge Posner criticized the multi-factor test traditionally used by the Tax Court to determine whether shareholders of closely held corporations paid themselves excessive salaries to avoid corporate taxes, reasoning that when "investors in [a] company are obtaining a far higher return than they had any reason to expect, [an executive's] salary is presumptively reasonable," but that presumption can be rebutted by showing that the return was due to outside factors unrelated to the executive's performance.

excess of $1,000,000 unless the compensation is payable only if the corporation meets performance goals that are determined by outside directors on a board compensation committee and are approved in advance by a majority shareholder vote.[92]

[2] Executive Perquisites

A corporation often provides its employees, and particularly its executives, with a number of valuable amenities. Typically these consist of such things as a dining room and a company automobile. Other "perks" include low-interest loans to executives (*see* **Barnard**) and the funding of large legacies by directors to charities of their choice.[93] Loans to executives became particularly controversial in the wake of disclosures of favorable insider loans such as Bernhard Ebbers' $366 million loan from WorldCom. Section 402(a) of the Sarbanes-Oxley Act of 2002 adds Securities Exchange Act of 1934 §13(k) making it unlawful for any public company "to extend or maintain credit, to arrange for the extension of credit, or to renew an extension of credit, in the form of a personal loan to or for any director or executive officer." Some types of "perks" may have tax advantages. For instance, amenities that help executives in their jobs or constitute compensation are deductible by the corporation as business expenses[94] but may not be taxable to the employees.[95]

[3] Bonuses

Payments under bonus plans are often tied to an indicator of the company's performance, such as earnings. The effect of bonuses from a tax standpoint is the same as that of salary (*i.e.*, bonus payments are taxed to the employee at ordinary income rates and are deductible by the corporation as business expenses). The advantage of bonuses over salaries is that, if the plan is properly formulated, the compensation provides an incentive for better performance.

There are, however, limits on the accuracy with which contingent compensation plans can be structured to reflect the quality of the employee's performance. A bonus that is simply a percentage of earnings may escalate enormously because of factors unrelated to the employee's performance, such as inflation. For example, the Supreme Court held that a bonus of $842,507.72 to the president of the American Tobacco Company in 1930 was excessive.[96] Moreover, basing bonuses on earnings may create per-

---

[92] *See* I.R.C. § 162(m).

[93] *See* Gibson, *Lure of Legacies Perks Up Directors*, Wall St. J., Sept. 28, 1990, p. B1.

[94] *See* I.R.C. § 162.

[95] *See id.* § 132.

[96] *See Rogers v. Hill*, 289 U.S. 582 (1993). However, in *Heller v. Boylan*, 29 N.Y.S2d 653 (N.Y. Sup. Ct. 1941), *aff'd*, 263 A.D. 814, 32 N.Y.S.2d 131 (1941), payment of $420,000 to the same executive under a modified version of the plan was held not to be *per se* excessive.

verse incentives for the executives to engage in actions that will generate profits over the short term but which hurt the firm in the long run because of expenses that accrue after the executive's tenure. Conversely, the executive may perversely avoid beneficial expenditures such as research and development that generate near-term losses and produce profits only over the long run. There are various ways of linking bonus compensation with the employee's accomplishments—for example, basing the bonus on the amount by which the corporation's profit exceeds that of its competitors, or on the company's stock price. But even these methods are subject to manipulation, since senior executives can adopt accounting policies (or engage in outright fraud) to keep reported profits and the company's stock price high, as may have happened in some of the corporate scandals emerging in late 2001 and 2002.[97]

[4] Deferred Compensation and Pension Plans

Compensation that is promised at a later date, such as after the employee's retirement, may be more cost-effective for the corporation than an equal amount (on a present-value basis) of current salaries and bonuses. First, deferred compensation such as a pension that is linked to years of service helps ensure retention of the executive's services. Second, deferred compensation may be advantageous from a tax standpoint. For example, the corporation can make certain types of payments for life insurance, annuities or pensions that are currently deductible business expenses but that do not produce taxable income for the employee until after retirement. Since the executive can expect to be in a lower tax bracket after retirement, this method enables the corporation to provide after-tax compensation at lower cost than if the compensation were in the form of current salary or bonus. Payments voted at or near retirement or after the employee's death raise cost/benefit issues. The plans may be *ultra vires* to the corporation (*see* Section 8.04 above) or a breach of fiduciary duty[98] unless the pension is tied to future obligations on the executive's part, such as agreements to consult and not to compete with the corporation.

[5] Stock Options

Employees may be compensated with stock, or with options that entitle them to buy stock from the corporation for a certain period at a certain price. Employees may hold their options and wait for the market price to rise above the exercise price of the option, at which point they can exercise their options and buy the underlying stock.

---

[97] *See, e.g.,* Guidera, *Probe of Computer Associates Centers on Firm's Revenue,* WALL ST. J., May 20, 2002, p. A3 (discussing allegations that three senior executives at Computer Associates engaged in accounting fraud to keep stock prices above levels necessary to trigger a special incentive stock award valued at $1 billion).

[98] *See, e.g., Fogelson v. American Woolen Co.,* 170 F.2d 660 (2d Cir. 1948).

Modern corporation statutes give the board the power to formulate stock option plans. *See, e.g.*, Del. G.C.L. § 157 and MBCA § 6.24.

With respect to the tax effects of stock options, if the option is actively traded on an established market, employees are generally taxed on the fair market value of the option at the time ownership of the option is no longer conditioned on the future performance of substantial services.[99] If the option is not so traded, generally the employee is taxed on the difference between the option exercise price and the value of the stock at the time the option is exercised or, if the option is sold rather than exercised, on the sale price of the option. The corporation may deduct the amount included in the employee's income.[100] The granting of stock options is, in general, similar to the payment of current salary, while the corporation's sale of the underlying stock to the employee when the option is exercised is similar in its incentive effect to the payment of a bonus based on earnings.

With respect to incentive effects, stock-based compensation arguably offers a more effective incentive than bonuses based on earnings because stock market prices may reflect the corporation's long-range performance more accurately than measures based on accounting earnings. On the other hand, stock-based compensation is subject to the criticism that the risk or fall in stock prices does not necessarily reflect the employee's own efforts.

The incentive effects of stock options may differ from those of stock compensation. Because stock options expire, executives may have an incentive to focus on short-term results, and even to manipulate accounting information. This is exacerbated by the fact that executives holding stock options may be particularly susceptible to downside risk that reduces stock price below the option price during the option period.

Stock option compensation became an increasingly important component of executive compensation during the 1990s with high-end plans sometimes giving senior executives annual stock profits in the hundreds of millions of dollars. Critics of option compensation have pointed to the apparent excessiveness of many grants, as well as to the above incentive effects. These criticisms have lead to calls for reform, including proposed stock exchange rules requiring option compensation to be submitted to a shareholder vote[101] and proposals to require companies to treat stock options as an expense against earnings, just as they do other forms of compensation.

[6] Golden Parachutes

Many executive employment contracts include severance payments, sometimes referred to as "golden parachutes," which are triggered by a change in or termination of the executive's employment as a result of a takeover of the company. The contracts can

---

[99] *See* Treas. Reg. § 1.83-7.

[100] *Id.* § 1.83-7.

[101] *See* Report of the New York Stock Exchange Corporate Accountability and Listing Standards Committee to the NYSE's Board of Directors, June 6, 2002, available at www.nyse.com.

benefit the corporation in several ways. First, they reduce management's incentive to defeat takeovers that benefit the shareholders.[102] Second, they encourage employees to develop skills (sometimes referred to as firm-specific human capital) that can be used only in the company and therefore would be valueless if the employee were terminated. Third, they replace deferred compensation that the employee would otherwise lose in a takeover. This last factor is important in motivating performance and in retaining and attracting employees.

There are several potential criticisms of golden parachutes, depending on how they are structured. Plans that are adopted in the midst of a takeover obviously do little to attract and ensure retention of employees or to encourage the development of firm-specific human capital.[103] In addition, parachutes with huge payoffs may give managers perverse incentives to embrace takeovers that hurt shareholders or to render the company vulnerable to takeover. Is it a sufficient answer to the perverse incentive problem that executives are constrained by various forces, including their investment in reputation, shareholder voting and fiduciary duties, from embracing value-decreasing takeovers or otherwise mismanaging the company? Finally, golden parachutes arguably do not benefit the corporation because they reward employees for performing a pre-existing duty (such as the development of firm-specific human capital or non-opposition to value-increasing takeover bids). But doesn't this criticism depend on whether the parachutes motivate performance that is not already subject to the discipline of an action for fiduciary breach or some other device designed to align managerial and shareholder interests? Indeed, isn't the same criticism potentially applicable to all incentive devices?

Most cases have upheld the granting of golden parachutes.[104] However, the usefulness of golden parachutes has been somewhat diminished by tax penalties that are now applied to "excessive parachute payments."[105]

---

[102] See Machlin, Choe & Miles, *The Effects of Golden Parachutes on Takeover Activity*, 36 J.L. & ECON. 861 (1993) (finding that golden parachutes positively influence the likelihood of takeover, and that the size of the parachute is correlated with multiple bids and with the size of the premium paid for the company, indicating that parachutes cause managers to maximize shareholder interests).

[103] *Gaillard v. Natomas Co.*, 208 Cal. App. 3d 1250, 256 Cal. Rptr. 702 (1989), held that inside directors were not entitled to the protection of the business judgment rule, and that there was a triable issue as to whether outside directors fulfilled their duties under the business judgment rule, in amending executive employment agreement in the course of a friendly merger to provide substantial payments to executives who left after the merger. The court noted, among other things, that the agreements were not structured to fulfill their stated purposes of attracting executives and ensuring that they would stay on after the merger.

[104] *See International Insurance Co. v. Johns*, 874 F.2d 1447 (11th Cir. 1989); *Buckhorn, Inc. v. Ropak Corp.*, 656 F. Supp. 209 (S.D. Ohio 1987); *Royal Crown Companies, Inc. v. McMahon*, 183 Ga. App. 543, 359 S.E.2d 379 (1987); *Worth v. Huntington Bancshares, Inc.*, 43 Oh. St. 3d 192, 540 N.E.2d 249 (1989); *Koenings v. Joseph Schlitz Brewing Co.*, 126 Wis. 2d 349, 377 N.W.2d 593 (1985). *But see Gaillard v. Natomas Co.*, note 103, above.

[105] *See* 26 U.S.C. §§ 280G, 4999 (payments subject to 20% excise tax and may not be deducted by the corporation).

[C] Fiduciary Duty Liability for Excessive Compensation

As noted above, compensation decisions can be thought of as a special type of "interested transaction." Indeed, **Bebchuk** et al. argue that many executive compensation arrangements, such as golden parachutes and stock options exercisable at current market price, are symptoms inadequate market discipline of executive compensation. Accordingly, the same general rules discussed in Section 9.04 apply in determining whether directors will be liable for excessive compensation. In general, the executives covered by the compensation arrangement have the burden of proving that the particular compensation package is fair to the corporation when there is no disinterested director or shareholder approval of the compensation plan. If, however, the compensation plan has been approved by disinterested directors or shareholders,[106] the burden of proof shifts to the complaining shareholder[107] and the substantive standard of judicial review becomes the business judgment rule (in the case of disinterested director approval) or waste (in the case of shareholder approval). There is a question whether approval of a compensation plan by directors who are "disinterested" in the sense of not being covered by the plan should be enough in itself to shift the burden of proof to the complaining shareholder. In addition, shareholder approval raises the question of sufficiency of disclosure to the shareholders who were asked to vote on the plan (*see* Section 7.03[C]).[108]

ALI *Principles* § 5.03 is generally consistent with the approach described in the preceding paragraph, except that it gives a little more protection to corporate decision makers than do the standards generally applied to interested transactions under § 5.02. For instance, a compensation arrangement that is approved by disinterested directors under § 5.03(a)(2) will be upheld if it satisfies the standards of the business judgment rule. By contrast, a self-dealing transaction approved by disinterested directors under § 5.02(a)(2)(B) will only be upheld if the disinterested directors "could reasonably have concluded that the transaction was fair to the corporation . . . ." The ALI *Principles* justify this less intense scrutiny of compensation decisions on a number of grounds including (1) unlike most other self interested transactions that can be foregone, "compensation

---

[106] As to the situation where the board is allegedly "dominated" by the key executives whose pay is at issue, see *Ash v. Brunswick Corp.*, 405 F. Supp. 234 (D. Del. 1975).

[107] *See Beard v. Elster*, 39 Del. Ch. 153, 160 A.2d 731 (1960); *Gottlieb v. Heyden Chem. Corp.*, 33 Del. Ch. 82, 90 A.2d 660 (1952); *Kerbs v. California Eastern Airways*, 33 Del. Ch. 69, 90 A.2d 652 (1952). *See generally Lewis v. Vogelstein*, 699 A.2d 327 (Del. Ch. 1997) (discussing the history of the Delaware law treating shareholder ratification of corporate plans that authorize the granting of stock options to corporate officers and directors).

[108] *See Lewis v. Vogelstein*, 669 A.2d 327, 333 (Del. Ch. 1997) (holding that "[w]here shareholder ratification of a plan of option compensation is involved, the duty of disclosure is satisfied by the disclosure or fair summary of all of the relevant terms and conditions of the proposed plan of compensation, together with any material extrinsic fact within the board's knowledge bearing on the issue. The directors' fiduciary duty of disclosure does not mandate that the board disclose one or more estimates of present value of options that may be granted under the plan."); *see also In re 3COM Corporation Shareholders Litigation*, 1999 Del. Ch. LEXIS 215, 1999 WL 1009210 (Del. Ch., Oct. 25, 1999) (while fiduciaries have an "obligation to disclose all material facts when seeking shareholder [approval of stock option plans]," they are not required to disclose the value of the options granted under the Black-Scholes Option Pricing Model).

arrangements with executives are necessary in all cases," (2) "compensation arrangements are sufficiently recurring and well publicized in public corporations that there is a greater opportunity for comparison of compensation arrangements and a corresponding deterrent to over-reaching," and (3) "institutional arrangements, like the use of compensation committees composed of disinterested directors, make unfair arrangements less likely."[109] Are these justifications for distinguishing compensation arrangements from other interested transactions convincing?

Publicly held corporations must disclose management remuneration in proxy statements and other disclosure documents even where shareholder approval is not solicited. For the substance of the required disclosure, see Item 402 of Regulation S-K. With the escalation of popular concern about generous compensation of corporate executives, the SEC responded by permitting shareholder proposals on executive pay (*see* Section 7.04) and by adopting proxy rules requiring clear disclosure of compensation and of the factors the board's compensation committee relied on in making compensation awards.[110] A shareholder can sue the corporation and its managers under the proxy rules for inaccurate or incomplete disclosure (*see* Section 7.03[D]).

In a close corporation, it may not be possible to obtain disinterested director or disinterested shareholder approval of executive compensation. In this situation, applying *Fliegler* (Section 9.04[B][3]), directors may have the burden of proving the fairness of their compensation. To avoid this problem, such firms may include a provision in the articles of incorporation giving the executives the authority to fix their own compensation. In the face of such a provision, some courts have put the burden on the shareholder to prove unfairness.[111]

PROBLEM

Fine Pictures, Inc., a large, publicly held company, is planning to revise its executive compensation package by offering some executives the opportunity to purchase interests in Fine's motion pictures. Under the new plan, certain senior executives will be able to contribute 2% of the equity investment in a movie and receive 6% of the film's profits. These executives already receive a compensation package consisting of salary, bonus, stock options, and pension which is comparable to that offered to executives of other motion picture companies. Fine does not offer investments in its movies to any other investors.

You are asked to advise the board as to the possibility that the new plan will be successfully challenged in court if the plan is approved unanimously by members of the board who are not involved in the compensation plan. Assume Delaware law applies. What advice would you give? Would you need additional facts?

---

[109] ALI *Principles* § 5.03 Comment (c).

[110] SEC Release No. 34-31327, Oct. 16, 1992.

[111] *See O'Malley v. Casey*, 42 Colo. App. 85, 589 P.2d 1388 (1979); *Coleman v. Plantation Golf Club, Inc.*, 212 So. 2d 806 (Fla. App. 1968).

REFERENCES

Barnard, *Corporate Loans to Directors and Officers: Every Business Now a Bank?*, 1988
     WIS. L. REV. 237.

Bebchuk, et. al, *Managerial Power and Rent Extraction in the Design of Executive Com-
     pensation*, 69 U. CHI. L. REV. 751 (2002)

Jensen & Murphy, *Performance Pay and Top Management Incentives*, 98 J. POL. ECON. 225
     (1990).

Levmore, *Puzzling Stock Options and Compensation Norms,* 149 U. PA. L. REV. 1901
     (2001).

Murphy, *Explaining Executive Compensation: Managerial Power Versus the Perceived Cost
     of Stock Options*, 69 U. CHI. L. REV. 847 (2002).

Scholes, *Stock and Compensation*, 46 J. FIN. 803 (1991).

Comment, *The Executive Compensation Contract: Creating Incentives to Reduce Agency
     Costs*, 37 STAN. L. REV. 1147 (1985).

[D] Other Legal Challenges to Compensation Arrangements

GRIMES v. DONALD
Delaware Supreme Court
673 A.2d 1207 (1996)

VEASEY, Chief Justice:

* * *

I. The Facts

C.L. Grimes ("Grimes"), plaintiff below-appellant, appeals from the dismissal, for failure to state a claim, of his complaint against James L. Donald ("Donald") (the CEO) and the Board of Directors (the "Board") of DSC Communications Corporation ("DSC" or the "Company"). Grimes seeks a declaration of the invalidity of the Agreements between Donald and the Company. . . . He alleges that the Board has breached its fiduciary duties by abdicating its authority . . . .

The following facts have been drawn from the face of the complaint. The Company is a Delaware corporation . . . . The Company, whose shares are traded on the Nasdaq National Market System, designs, manufactures, markets and services telecommunication systems.

The Agreements, executed during 1990, are the focus of the complaint. The Employment Agreement provides that Donald "shall be responsible for the general management of the affairs of the company . . . ," and that Donald "shall report to the Board." The Employment Agreement runs until the earlier of Donald's 75th birthday or his termination (1) by reason of death or disability; (2) for cause; or (3) without cause. Under the Employment Agreement, Donald can declare a "Constructive Termination Without Cause" by the Company of his employment as a result of, *inter alia,* "unreasonable interference, in the good-faith judgment of . . . [Donald], by the Board or a substantial stockholder of the Company, in [Donald's] carrying out his duties and responsibilities under the [Employment] Agreement." A Constructive Termination Without Cause takes effect after delivery of notice by Donald and the failure by the Board to remedy such interference.

In the event of a Termination Without Cause, constructive or otherwise, Donald is entitled to the following:

> 1. Continued payment of his "Base Salary" at the level in effect immediately prior to termination for the remainder of his "Term of Employment," which, as stated, will be 6½ years unless Donald dies or turns 75 first. In 1992, Donald's Base Salary exceeded $650,000.
>
> 2. Annual incentive awards for the remainder of the Term of Employment equal to the average of the three highest annual bonuses awarded to Donald during his last ten years as CEO. In 1992, such award allegedly equaled $300,000.
>
> 3. Medical benefits for Donald and his wife for life, as well as his children until the age of 23.
>
> 4. Continued participation in all employee benefit plans in which Donald is participating on the date of termination until the earlier of the expiration of the Term of Employment or the date on which he receives equivalent benefits from a subsequent employer.
>
> 5. Other (unidentified) benefits in accordance with DSC's plans and programs. *See* Am.Cplt.Ex. 1 § 11(d).

Grimes v. Donald, Del. Ch., 20 DEL. J. CORP. L. 757, 765 (1995).

The Income Continuation Plan provides, *inter alia*, that after Base Salary payments cease under the Employment Agreement, Donald is entitled to receive, for the remainder of his life, annual payments equal to the average of the sum of his Base Salary plus bonuses in the three highest years, multiplied by 3%, multiplied by his years of service. Donald has also been awarded 200,000 "units" under the Long Term Incentive Plan. In the event of a Change of Control, as defined in the Incentive Plan, Donald will have the right to cash payments for his units, which Grimes alleges could total $60,000,000 at the stock price in effect at the time the complaint was filed.

[The complaint alleged that the effect of the above-described agreements, particularly the provision giving Donald the right to unilaterally declare a "constructive termination without cause" whenever he determined that the Board had "unreasonably interfered" with his general management of the affairs of the company, was to impermissibly delegate the duties and responsibilities of the Board of Directors to Donald.]

* * *

II. Grimes Has Not Stated a Claim for Abdication of Directorial Duty.

* * *

C. Analysis of Grimes' Abdication Claim

In the case before us, the abdication claim fails as a matter of law. Grimes claims that the potentially severe financial penalties which the Company would incur in the event that the Board attempts to interfere in Donald's management of the Company will inhibit and deter the Board from exercising its duties under Section 141(a). The Court of Chancery assumed that, if a contract could have the practical effect of preventing a board from exercising its duties, it would amount to a *de facto* abdication of directorial authority.[2] The Chancellor concluded, however, that Grimes has not set forth well-pleaded allegations which would establish such a situation. We agree.

Putting aside the payments which would result from a change of control, Grimes has pleaded, at most, that Donald would be entitled to $20 million in the event of a Constructive Termination. The Chancellor found, in light of the financial size of DSC reflected in the exhibits to the complaint, that this amount would not constitute a *de facto* abdication. Grimes contends, however, that the payments could amount to a *de facto* abdication in possible future circumstances. Such a set of facts has not been pleaded, is not before this Court, is based on speculation, and is not ripe for adjudication.[3]

Directors may not delegate duties which lie "at the heart of the management of the corporation." *Chapin v. Benwood*, Del. Ch., 402 A.2d 1205, 1210 (1979), *aff'd sub nom. Harrison v. Chapin*, Del. Supr., 415 A.2d 1068 (1980). A court "cannot give legal sanction to agreements which have the effect of removing from directors in a very substantial way their duty to use their own best judgment on management matters." *Abercrombie v. Davies*, Del. Ch., 35 Del. Ch. 599, 123 A.2d 893, 899 (1956), *rev'd on other grounds*, Del. Supr., 130 A.2d 338 (1957). Distinguishing these cases, however, the Court of Chancery stated: "Unlike the agreements considered in *Abercrombie* and *Chapin*, the Donald Agreements do not formally preclude the DSC board from exercising its statutory powers and fulfilling its fiduciary duty." *Grimes*, 20 Del. J. Corp. L. at 774-775 . . . .

With certain exceptions, "an informed decision to delegate a task is as much an exercise of business judgment as any other." *Rosenblatt*, 493 A.2d at 943. Likewise, business decisions are not an abdication of directorial authority merely because they limit a board's freedom of future action. A board which has decided to manufacture bricks has less freedom to decide to make bottles. In a world of scarcity, a decision to do one thing will commit a board to a certain course of action and make it costly and difficult (indeed, sometimes impossible) to change course and do another. This is an inevitable fact of life and is not an abdication of directorial duty.

If the market for senior management, in the business judgment of a board, demands significant severance packages, boards will inevitably limit their future range of action by entering into employment agreements. Large severance payments will deter boards, to some extent, from dismissing senior officers. If an independent and informed board, acting in good faith, determines that the services of a particular individual warrant large amounts of money, whether in the form of current salary or severance provisions, the board has made

---

[2]　The cases cited by Grimes involve *formal* abdication by a board of directors. *See Chapin v. Benwood Foundation, Inc.*, Del. Ch., 402 A.2d 1205 (1979) (trustees agreed to appoint particular person to future vacancy on board); *Abercrombie v. Davies*, Del. Ch., 35 Del. Ch. 599, 123 A.2d 893 (1956), *rev'd on other grounds*, Del. Supr., 130 A.2d 338 (1957) (directors agreed to vote unanimously or submit to outside arbitrator).

[3]　The Chancellor perceptively notes that "an even more difficult case would be presented where the terms of a CEO's employment contract came to have the practical effect of precluding the board from exercising its statutory powers and satisfying its fiduciary duty, but that effect was not reasonably foreseeable at the time the contract rights were negotiated at arm's-length." *Grimes*, 20 Del. J. Corp. L. at 775 n.8.

a business judgment. That judgment normally will receive the protection of the business judgment rule unless the facts show that such amounts, compared with the services to be received in exchange, constitute waste or could not otherwise be the product of a valid exercise of business judgment. *See, e.g., Saxe v. Brady*, Del. Ch., 40 Del. Ch. 474, 184 A.2d 602, 610 (1962).

The Board of DSC retains the ultimate freedom to direct the strategy and affairs of the Company. If Donald disagrees with the Board, the Company may or may not (depending on the circumstances) be required to pay him a substantial sum of money in order to pursue its chosen course of action. So far, we have only a rather unusual contract, but not a case of abdication.[4] The Chancellor correctly dismissed the abdication claim.

NOTE

In *In re Bally's Grand Derivative Litigation*,[112] the corporation and a management company entered into a management agreement that gave the management company "uninterrupted control of and responsibility for the operation" of the casino which was the corporation's only material business, subject (1) "to exercise of the fiduciary duties under applicable law of [the corporation's] board of directors," and (2) to the corporation's right to terminate the management agreement if the board of directors "determine[d], based upon the written opinion of counsel, that in the exercise of the Board's fiduciary duties under applicable law it is necessary and in the best interests of [the corporation] to terminate [the] Agreement." The Chancery Court refused to dismiss a shareholder complaint alleging that the management agreement constituted an impermissible delegation of board powers. The Court reasoned that very broad delegations of duties might be upheld so long as directors retained the "unfettered" ability to terminate the delegation at will. But the Court was "unable to conclude as a matter of law that the board retained sufficient termination powers to validate the Management Agreement."

---

[4]   The unfortunate choice of language in the Employment Agreement should not obscure the fact that, in many cases, large severance payments do not necessarily preclude a formerly passive board from asserting its power over a CEO. The Court of Chancery, in dismissing the claim, nonetheless disparaged as "foolish" and "ill-conceived" the language of the agreement introducing the concept of the Board committing "unreasonable interference" in the discharge of Donald's duties, "in the good faith judgment of the Executive . . . ." 20 DEL. J. CORP. L. at 777. We agree that, on the surface, this unfortunate choice of words is "badly flawed" in terms of traditional concepts of corporate governance. *Id.* When the Employment Agreement is read as a whole, however, the initial perception of unlawful delegation gives way to the reality that the Agreement is not—on its face—a wrongful delegation. This poor choice of language in the Agreement is not actionable *per se*. What actually may happen in the future may or may not ever become a litigable issue that is ripe for adjudication.

[112]   1997 Del. Ch. LEXIS 77, 1997 WL 305803 (Del. Ch. 1997).

§ 9.06 The Duty of Loyalty: Corporate Opportunities and Competition

Sections 9.02 through 9.05 deal with managers' duties in connection with transactions by the corporation. This Section concerns managers' duties in connection with their business dealings outside the corporation. The most important limitation on these dealings is that managers may not take for their own benefit business that is deemed a "corporate opportunity" of their firms. This doctrine is discussed in the following cases and notes.

BROZ v. CELLULAR INFORMATION SYSTEMS, INC.
Delaware Supreme Court
673 A.2d 148 (1996)

VEASEY, Chief Justice:

[The defendant, Broz, was the sole stockholder of RFB Cellular, Inc. ("RFBC"), and was also a member of the board of the plaintiff, Cellular Information Systems, Inc. ("CIS"), a publicly held Delaware corporation that competed with RFBC in the provision of cellular telephone service in the Midwestern United States. In April, 1994, Mackinac Cellular Corp. ("Mackinac") sought to divest itself of a service license ("Michigan-2") authorizing the holder to provide cellular telephone service in an area immediately adjacent to an area covered by a license already owned by RFBC. In May, Mackinac offered the license to a list of prospects that included RFBC but not CIS, apparently because CIS was not considered a viable purchaser in light of its recent financial difficulties. (CIS had had recently emerged from Chapter 11, was subject to a loan agreement which substantially impaired its ability to incur new debt or take on new acquisitions, and was in the process of divesting itself of many of its cellular license systems.) Broz informed three CIS directors, including CIS's chief executive officer, of the Michigan-2 opportunity presented by Mackinac, but these directors indicated that CIS had neither the wherewithal nor the inclination to purchase the license, and the testimony of other CIS directors at trial confirmed that view. On August 2, 1994, PriCellular, Inc. ("PriCellular"), an unrelated cellular communications company, which was also interested in the Michigan-2 license, commenced a tender offer for all outstanding shares of CIS. Before PriCellular's tender offer for CIS closed, both Broz and PriCellular negotiated for the purchase of the Michigan-2 license offered by Mackinac. In late September, PriCellular agreed with Mackinac on an option to purchase the license for $6.7 million, but that agreement gave Mackinac the right to sell the license to any other party who was willing to exceed the exercise price of the option by at least $500,000. On November 14, 1994, Broz agreed to pay Mackinac $7.2 million for the Michigan-2 license, thereby meeting the terms of the option agreement. An asset purchase agreement was thereafter executed by Mackinac and RFBC. After PriCellular completed its acquisition of CIS, CIS brought suit against Broz, arguing that Broz's purchase of the Michigan-2 license constituted the impermissible usurpation of a corporate opportunity.]

In this appeal, we consider the application of the doctrine of corporate opportunity. The Court of Chancery decided that the defendant, a corporate director, breached his fiduciary duty by not formally presenting to the corporation an opportunity which had come to the director individually and independent of the director's relationship with the corporation. . . .

* * *

IV. APPLICATION OF THE CORPORATE OPPORTUNITY DOCTRINE

The doctrine of corporate opportunity represents but one species of the broad fiduciary duties assumed by a corporate director or officer. A corporate fiduciary agrees to place the interests of the corporation before his or her own in appropriate circumstances. In light of the diverse and often competing obligations faced by directors and officers, however, the corporate opportunity doctrine arose as a means of defining the parameters of fiduciary duty in instances of potential conflict. The classic statement of the doctrine is derived from the venerable case of *Guth v. Loft, Inc.* [5 A.2d 503 (Del. 1939)]. . . .

The corporate opportunity doctrine, as delineated by *Guth* and its progeny, holds that a corporate officer or director may not take a business opportunity for his own if: (1) the corporation is financially able to exploit the opportunity; (2) the opportunity is within the corporation's line of business; (3) the corporation has an interest or expectancy in the opportunity; and (4) by taking the opportunity for his own, the corporate fiduciary will thereby be placed in a position inimicable to his duties to the corporation. The Court in *Guth* also derived a corollary which states that a director or officer may take a corporate opportunity if: (1) the opportunity is presented to the director or officer in his individual and not his corporate capacity; (2) the opportunity is not essential to the corporation; (3) the corporation holds no interest or expectancy in the opportunity; and (4) the director or officer has not wrongfully employed the resources of the corporation in pursuing or exploiting the opportunity. *Guth*, 5 A.2d at 509.

Thus, the contours of this doctrine are well established. It is important to note, however, that the tests enunciated in *Guth* and subsequent cases provide guidelines to be considered by a reviewing court in balancing the equities of an individual case. No one factor is dispositive and all factors must be taken into account insofar as they are applicable . . . . In the instant case, we find that the facts do not support the conclusion that Broz misappropriated a corporate opportunity.

We note at the outset that Broz became aware of the Michigan-2 opportunity in his individual and not his corporate capacity. As the Court of Chancery found, "Broz did not misuse proprietary information that came to him in a corporate capacity nor did he otherwise use any power he might have over the governance of the corporation to advance his own interests." 663 A.2d at 1185. This fact is not the subject of serious dispute. In fact, it is clear from the record that Mackinac did not consider CIS a viable candidate for the acquisition of Michigan-2. Accordingly, Mackinac did not offer the property to CIS. In this factual posture, many of the fundamental concerns undergirding the law of corporate opportunity are not present (*e.g.,* misappropriation of the corporation's proprietary information). The burden imposed upon Broz to show adherence to his fiduciary duties to CIS is thus lessened to some extent. . . . Nevertheless, this fact is not dispositive. The determination of whether a particular fiduciary has usurped a corporate opportunity necessitates a careful examination of the circumstances, giving due credence to the factors enunciated in *Guth* and subsequent cases.

We turn now to an analysis of the factors relied on by the trial court. First, we find that CIS was not financially capable of exploiting the Michigan-2 opportunity. Although the Court of Chancery concluded otherwise, we hold that this finding was not supported by the evidence. *Levitt*, 287 A.2d at 673. The record shows that CIS was in a precarious financial position at the time Mackinac presented the Michigan-2 opportunity to Broz. Having recently emerged from lengthy and contentious bankruptcy proceedings, CIS was not in a position to commit capital to the acquisition of new assets. Further, the loan agreement entered into by CIS and its creditors severely limited the discretion of CIS as to the acquisition of new assets and substantially restricted the ability of CIS to incur new debt.

* * *

Second, while it may be said with some certainty that the Michigan-2 opportunity was within CIS' line of business, it is not equally clear that CIS had a cognizable interest or expectancy in the license. Under the third factor laid down by this Court in *Guth*, for an opportunity to be deemed to belong to the fiduciary's corporation, the corporation must have an interest or expectancy in that opportunity. As this Court stated in *Johnston*, 121 A.2d at 924, "for the corporation to have an actual or expectant interest in any specific property, there must be some tie between that property and the nature of the corporate business." Despite the fact that the nature of the Michigan-2 opportunity was historically close to the core operations of CIS, changes were in process. At the time the opportunity was presented, CIS was actively engaged in the process of divesting its cellular license holdings. CIS' articulated business plan did not involve any new acquisitions. Further, as indicated by the testimony of the entire CIS board, the Michigan-2 license would not have been of interest to CIS even absent CIS' financial difficulties and CIS' then current desire to liquidate its cellular license holdings. Thus, CIS had no interest or expectancy in the Michigan-2 opportunity. *Cf. Guth*, 5 A.2d at 514 (holding that Loft had an interest or expectancy in the Pepsi opportunity by virtue of its need for cola syrup for use in its retail stores).

Finally, the corporate opportunity doctrine is implicated only in cases where the fiduciary's seizure of an opportunity results in a conflict between the fiduciary's duties to the corporation and the self-interest of the director as actualized by the exploitation of the opportunity. In the instant case, Broz' interest in acquiring and profiting from Michigan-2 created no duties that were inimicable to his obligations to CIS. Broz, at all times relevant to the instant appeal, was the sole party in interest in RFBC, a competitor of CIS. CIS was fully aware of Broz' potentially conflicting duties. Broz, however, comported himself in a manner that was wholly in accord with his obligations to CIS. Broz took care not to usurp any opportunity which CIS was willing and able to pursue. Broz sought only to compete with an outside entity, PriCellular, for acquisition of an opportunity which both sought to possess. Broz was not obligated to refrain from competition with PriCellular. Therefore, the totality of the circumstances indicates that Broz did not usurp an opportunity that properly belonged to CIS.

A. Presentation to the Board:

In concluding that Broz had usurped a corporate opportunity, the Court of Chancery placed great emphasis on the fact that Broz had not formally presented the matter to the CIS board. The court held that "in such circumstances as existed at the latest after October 14, 1994 (date of PriCellular's option contract on Michigan-2 RSA) it was the obligation of Mr. Broz as a director of CIS to take the transaction to the CIS board for its formal action . . . ." 663 A.2d at 1185. In so holding, the trial court erroneously grafted a new requirement onto the law of corporate opportunity, *viz.*, the requirement of formal presentation under circumstances where the corporation does not have an interest, expectancy or financial ability.

The teaching of *Guth* and its progeny is that the director or officer must analyze the situation *ex ante* to determine whether the opportunity is one rightfully belonging to the corporation. If the director or officer believes, based on one of the factors articulated above, that the corporation is not entitled to the opportunity, then he may take it for himself. Of course, presenting the opportunity to the board creates a kind of "safe harbor" for the director, which removes the specter of a *post hoc* judicial determination that the director or officer has improperly usurped a corporate opportunity. Thus, presentation avoids the possibility that an error in the fiduciary's assessment of the situation will create future liability for breach of fiduciary duty. It is not the law of Delaware that presentation to the board is a necessary prerequisite to a finding that a corporate opportunity has not been usurped.

* * *

Thus, we hold that Broz was not required to make formal presentation of the Michigan-2 opportunity to the CIS board prior to taking the opportunity for his own.

* * *

B. Alignment of Interests Between CIS and PriCellular:

In concluding that Broz usurped an opportunity properly belonging to CIS, the Court of Chancery held that "for practical business reasons CIS' interests with respect to the Mackinac transaction came to merge with those of PriCellular, even before the closing of its tender offer for CIS stock." Based on this fact, the trial court concluded that Broz was required to consider PriCellular's prospective, post-acquisition plans for CIS in determining whether to forego the opportunity or seize it for himself. Had Broz done this, the Court of Chancery determined that he would have concluded that CIS was entitled to the opportunity by virtue of the alignment of its interests with those of PriCellular.

We disagree. Broz was under no duty to consider the interests of PriCellular when he chose to purchase Michigan-2. As stated in *Guth*, a director's right to "appropriate [an] . . . opportunity depends on the circumstances existing at the time it presented itself to him without regard to subsequent events." *Guth*, 5 A.2d at 513. At the time Broz purchased Michigan-2, PriCellular had not yet acquired CIS. Any plans to do so would still have been wholly speculative. Accordingly, Broz was not required to consider the contingent and uncertain plans of PriCellular in reaching his determination of how to proceed.

* * *

In reaching our conclusion on this point, we note that certainty and predictability are values to be promoted in our corporation law. *See Williams v. Geier*, Del. Supr., __ A.2d __, slip op. at 46 n.36 (Jan. 23, 1996). . . . In order for a director to engage meaningfully in business unrelated to his or her corporate role, the director must be allowed to make decisions based on the situation as it exists at the time a given opportunity is presented. Absent such a rule, the corporate fiduciary would be constrained to refrain from exploiting any opportunity for fear of liability based on the occurrence of subsequent events. This state of affairs would unduly restrict officers and directors and would be antithetical to certainty in corporation law.

VI. CONCLUSION

* * *

. . . Accordingly, we REVERSE the judgment of the Court of Chancery holding that Broz diverted a corporate opportunity properly belonging to CIS and imposing a constructive trust.

FARBER v. SERVAN LAND CO., INC.
United States Court of Appeals, Fifth Circuit
662 F.2d 371 (1981)

Tjoflat, Circuit Judge.

This is the second appeal of a stockholder's derivative suit against two corporate directors for preemption of a corporate opportunity. We find that the directors violated their fiduciary duties to the corporation and that they are liable for damages. We remand the case to the district court so that damages may be assessed.

I

In 1959, Charles Serianni, a Broward County, Florida, businessman, initiated a plan to build and operate a golf course and country club near Ft. Lauderdale. With the assistance of several other investors he formed a corporation, the Servan Land Company, Inc. (the corporation), which was to own and operate the enterprise. The corporation acquired 160 acres of land on which to build the course. Shortly thereafter it acquired from James Farquhar twenty additional acres abutting the golf course, to be used as a dump site for top soil and as a nursery.

Serianni held 180 shares of the corporation's stock and served as President of the corporation throughout its existence. A.I. Savin, a resident of Connecticut, owned 216½ shares of stock, and served as the corporation's Vice President. There were eight other stockholders, including Jack Farber, the plaintiff in this action. Farber owned sixty shares.

At one point, the corporation sold four of the twenty acres it had acquired from Mr. Farquhar to BD&L Corporation, which built a sixty-eight-unit lodge on the land. When BD&L was unable to meet its obligations, Servan Land bought the land and lodge, and subsequently held and operated it through a wholly-owned subsidiary.

On several occasions the directors and stockholders discussed the possibility of acquiring more land abutting the golf course, but the corporation took no action. Then, at the 1968 annual stockholders' meeting, Servan Land Company director and stockholder Hamilton Forman informed his associates that James Farquhar was willing to sell 160 acres of abutting land to the corporation. This land was suitable for use as an additional golf course. At the time he made the statement, the stockholders were discussing refinancing the mortgage on the country club in order to obtain funds to redeem the corporation's preferred stock and pay debts owed to several stockholders. Forman suggested that the proceeds the stockholders received from the redemption could be used to buy additional stock in the corporation, thus generating the funds necessary for the corporation to acquire the Farquhar property. According to the corporate minutes, "[t]he stockholders seemed to feel that this possibility should certainly be investigated and would be made financially feasible by the refinancing . . . ." The stockholders decided, however, to vote on the refinancing question without an amendment providing for purchase of the property. They passed the motion to refinance.

A few months later, Serianni and Savin met with James Farquhar and negotiated to buy, in their individual capacities, the same 160 acres abutting the golf course that had been discussed at the corporation's annual stockholders' meeting. They closed the transaction in March 1969.

* * *

Three years later, in 1973, Serianni, Savin and the corporation entered into an agreement with a purchaser to sell as a package the corporation's assets and the 160 acres of adjoining land Serianni and Savin had bought; each contract of sale was conditioned upon execution of the other. Of the aggregate sales price, the defendants allocated $5,000,000 to the corporation and $3,353,700 to Savin and Serianni, though this division was not based on any appraisal of the respective properties.

At a special directors' and stockholders' meeting, all the members of the corporation but Farber approved the sale and voted to liquidate Servan Land Company. After the sale was completed Farber brought a stockholders' derivative suit in the district court, based on diversity jurisdiction, alleging that Savin and Serianni had preempted a corporate opportunity by acquiring the 160 acres adjacent to the golf course. He also sought appointment of an appraiser to determine the proper allocation of the purchase price.

The district court, sitting without a jury . . . found, *inter alia*, that the initial investors had created the golf course and country club "as a bit of an ego trip and partially out of vanity considerations" because they were tired of waiting for starting times at other golf courses, and wanted a course of their own when they were in the Ft. Lauderdale area. The court found that Serianni had been the "driving force," *id.*, of the venture from its inception, though apparently this was at least partly due to the lack of interest of the other stockholders or because most of the others lived in distant states. The court then noted that Serianni had engaged in "questionable tactic[s]" in running the corporation but that "this golf course was not operated with an eye to investment in the sense that many of the real estate promotional ventures have been developed in this country." The court continued:

> Mr. Forman's testimony is persuasive, that the golf course should not have
> been built without acquiring all the perimeter land. It is persuasive in the sense

of the business aspects of the development; but it is also supportive of the Court's earlier findings that this matter was not originally designed exclusively as a real estate venture but had other goals which have been previously indicated.

The Court finds that the possibility of real estate development was certainly present. For example, Mr. Forman testified, via deposition, that scarcely ever a meeting of the stockholders occurred without discussing the acquiring of additional property of Mr. Farquhar.

. . . [T]he court found that Farber was entitled to an appraisal to determine whether the corporation should have received a larger portion of the total sale price of the properties than the $5 million allocated by Serianni and Savin. It withheld final judgment pending the completion of the appraisal. From the dialogue between the court and counsel following the court's findings of fact it is clear that the court considered the question of damages to ride entirely on the results of the appraisal as requested in Count II of the complaint, and not on the existence of a breach of fiduciary duty as charged in Count I. This, apparently, was because Serianni and Savin's cooperation in selling their 160 acres as a package with the corporation's assets enhanced the overall value of the deal, thus resulting in a benefit to the corporation.

The appraiser subsequently valued the corporation's properties at $4,065,915, and the Serianni-Savin property at $3,950,925. Serianni and Savin had allotted to the corporation a greater percentage of the proceeds of the sale than would have been allocated using the appraiser's figures. . . .

Farber appealed the district court's decision, and this court vacated and remanded it for clarification, stating: "if, as seems to be clearly expressed, there was no corporate opportunity, why should, as is three times stated, Serianni and Savin have offered the 160 adjacent acres to the corporation? The holdings are inconsistent." *Farber v. Servan Land Co., Inc.,* 541 F.2d 1086, 1088 (5th Cir. 1976). This court also questioned the district court's reliance on the theory that Savin and Serianni benefited the corporation by selling their 160 acres along with the corporation's assets. We stated:

> If the corporate opportunity doctrine is otherwise applicable it is not made inapplicable by the realization of a substantial gain from a fortuitous sale of its assets at the same time as the sale of the property asserted to be a corporate opportunity to a lone buyer who would not have bought either property without the other. If a corporate opportunity existed the corporation and its stockholders would have been entitled to the profits from the sale of both parcels. *Id.*

On remand, the district court failed to explain why it found that Serianni and Savin had a duty to offer the opportunity to purchase the 160 acres to the corporation, but it reaffirmed its finding that "Seriani [sic] and Savin had satisfactorily sustained the burden of establishing the propriety of the transaction." It stated that it based this conclusion on three grounds: "(1) the corporation, although it discussed Mr. Farquhar's abutting land . . . took no action to acquire it at a previous annual meeting of the corporation; (2) the action of Seriani [sic] and Savin in purchasing the abutting land was ratified and approved by a special meeting of the stockholders on May 9th, 1973" and (3) Serianni and Savin were generous in valuing the corporation's assets above their worth when apportioning the proceeds of the package sale. The third fact, the court held, indicated that the defendants were not taking advantage of the corporation.

Farber appeals once again.

II

In reviewing the district court's decision we must evaluate its resolution of four key issues: whether a corporate opportunity existed; whether the stockholders declined the opportunity by failing to act; whether the stockholders ratified Serianni and Savin's purchase; and whether the subsequent benefit the corporation received in selling its assets in conjunction with Serianni and Savin's 160 acres rectifies any wrong it might have suffered through the defendants' initial purchase of the land.

A. *The Existence of a Corporate Opportunity*

. . . If one occupying a fiduciary relationship to a corporation acquires, "in opposition to the corporation, property in which the corporation has an interest or tangible expectancy or which is essential to its existence," he violates what has come to be known as the "doctrine of 'corporate opportunity.'" [citation omitted] . . .

* * *

It should be noted that the district court not only found that the stockholders frequently discussed acquisition of Mr. Farquhar's land at their meetings; it also found that the stockholders had discussed this matter at the last meeting, just shortly before Serianni and Savin made their purchase, and that they had "indicated a sense of approval to the idea of acquiring abutting land from Mr. Farquhar." Further, the court heard testimony that the corporation needed the land on the perimeter of the golf course, and evidence that the corporation had bought additional land from Mr. Farquhar in the past and that it had bought and operated a lodge located on part of that land. These facts make it clear that the opportunity to acquire the Farquhar land was an advantageous one that fit into a present, significant corporate purpose, as well as an ongoing corporate policy, and that the corporation had an active interest in it. Accordingly, the opportunity to buy the land constituted a corporate opportunity. . . .

B. *Whether the Stockholders Declined the Opportunity*

In addition to finding that no corporate opportunity existed, the district court found that if one did exist, "it was rejected by the corporation." The court apparently reached this conclusion because after deciding at their annual meeting that the opportunity to purchase the land should be investigated, the stockholders did not vote, at that meeting, to commit the funds available from the refinancing to purchase of the Farquhar property. *See Farber*, 393 F. Supp. at 635, 638. We find that this failure does not indicate a decision to refrain from pursuing the opportunity to purchase. Indeed, since the stockholders apparently lacked specific information about Mr. Farquhar's terms of sale, it would have been illogical to make a commitment of funds at that time. It is true that there is no evidence to indicate that the stockholders undertook formal investigation of the potential purchase between the time of the meeting and the time of Serianni and Savin's purchase. It should be noted, however, that Serianni was the president of the corporation and the only active director. The other stockholders customarily relied upon him to exercise the executive powers of the corporation, since most of them resided in other states. *See Farber*, 393 F. Supp. at 634. Because the other stockholders relied upon Serianni to initiate the investigation on the corporation's behalf, he may not now translate his own inaction into a corporate rejection of the opportunity, thus allowing him to buy the land personally. The district court's finding that the corporation rejected the opportunity is clearly erroneous.[8]

C. *Ratification of the Purchase*

As another ground for its decision, the district court held that the stockholders ratified Serianni and Savin's purchase at their May 9, 1970 meeting. . . .

. . . We do not need to decide whether ratification was possible here . . . because even if it was, the manner of ratification in this case renders the ratification a nullity.

According to the corporate minutes, all of the directors present at the annual meeting, except the plaintiff, voted to ratify the land purchase. Both of the purchasing directors were present, and between the two of them, they held four-sevenths of the stock. While it is true that directors ordinarily may vote their stock on measures in which they have a personal interest, most authorities agree that "[t]he violation of their duty by corporate directors cannot be ratified by the action of those who were guilty of participation in the wrongful acts, even though they constitute a majority of the directors or of the stockholders." Thus, Serianni and Savin may not bind Farber by ratifying their own inappropriate acts. Farber is entitled to bring a derivative action. . . .

III

We find that the opportunity to buy Mr. Farquhar's 160 acres constituted a corporate opportunity and that the defendants, Serianni and Savin, breached their fiduciary duties to the corporation by preempting that opportunity. We also find that the attempted ratification of the preemption does not preclude Farber from bringing a derivative suit on behalf of the corporation.

The corporation is entitled to the profits of the directors' subsequent sale of the 160 acres. We remand the case to the district court to determine the proper amount of damages and the appropriate method for distributing those damages.

REVERSED AND REMANDED.

BURG v. HORN
United States Court of Appeals, Second Circuit
380 F.2d 897 (1967)

LUMBARD, Chief Judge.

This appeal in a diversity action by the plaintiff, Lillian Burg, a citizen of California and a one-third stockholder of Darand Realty Corp., a New York corporation which owns and operates low-rent rooming and apartment buildings in Brooklyn, from a judgment of

---

[8]   Further, it is inappropriate, under the circumstances, to attempt to second-guess the reaction of the stockholders, had Serianni and Savin presented their proposal to purchase the land before the sale was completed.

Judge Dooling in the Eastern District dismissing her derivative complaint insofar as it alleged that nine similar buildings in Brooklyn acquired by the defendants George and Max Horn, citizens of New York and holders of the remaining stock of Darand, were corporate opportunities belonging to Darand, requires us to consider the scope of the duty imposed by New York law on directors and majority stockholders not to appropriate for themselves opportunities which would be advantageous to their corporation. We hold that Judge Dooling correctly concluded that, under New York law, the properties acquired by defendants were not corporate opportunities of Darand, and we affirm the judgment below.

Darand was incorporated in September 1953 with a capital of $5500, subscribed equally by the three stockholders, Mrs. Burg and George and Max Horn, all of whom became directors, and immediately purchased a low-rent building in Brooklyn. The Horns, who were engaged in the produce business and had already acquired three similar buildings in Brooklyn through wholly-owned corporations, urged the Burgs, who were close friends then also residing in Brooklyn, to "get their feet wet" in real estate, and the result was the formation of Darand. The Burgs testified that they expected the Horns to offer any low-rent properties they found in Brooklyn to Darand, but that there was no discussion or agreement to that effect. The Horns carried on the active management of Darand's properties, and the plaintiff's husband, Louis Burg, an accountant who became an attorney in 1957, handled its accounting and tax planning. The stockholders generally drew equal amounts from Darand at the end of each taxable year, and then immediately repaid them to "loan accounts," from which they could draw when they desired.

Darand sold its first property and acquired another in 1956, and purchased two more buildings in 1959. From 1953 to 1963, nine similar properties were purchased by the Horns, individually or through wholly-owned corporations. . . .

In 1962 the Burgs moved to California, and disagreements thereafter arose between them and the Horns concerning the accounting for rent receipts and expenditures of Darand. This action seeking an accounting for receipts and expenditures and the imposition of a constructive trust on the alleged corporate opportunities was brought in 1967. . . . [Judge Dooling found] that there was no agreement that all low-rent buildings found by the Horns should be offered to Darand, and that the Burgs were aware of the purposes of the loans from Darand and Louis Burg and of at least some of the Horns' post-1953 acquisitions. He therefore declined to hold that those acquisitions were corporate opportunities of Darand.

. . . Under New York law, property acquired by a corporate director will be impressed with a constructive trust as a corporate opportunity only if the corporation had an interest or a "tangible expectancy" in the property when it was acquired. . . .

. . . [T]here is no evidence that the properties [plaintiff] seeks for Darand were offered to or sought by Darand, came to the Horns' attention through Darand, or were necessary to Darand's success.

Plaintiff apparently contends that defendants were as a matter of law under a duty to acquire for Darand further properties like those it was operating. She is seemingly supported by several commentators, who have stated that any opportunity within a corporation's "line of business" is a corporate opportunity. . . . This statement seems to us too broad a generalization. We think that under New York law a court must determine in each case, by considering the relationship between the director and the corporation, whether a duty to offer the corporation all opportunities within its "line of business" is fairly to be implied. Had the

Horns been full-time employees of Darand with no prior real estate ventures of their own, New York law might well uphold a finding that they were subject to such an implied duty. But as they spent most of their time in unrelated produce and real estate enterprises and already owned corporations holding similar properties when Darand was formed, as plaintiff knew, we agree with Judge Dooling that a duty to offer Darand all such properties coming to their attention cannot be implied absent some further evidence of an agreement or understanding to that effect.[2] Judge Dooling's finding that there was no such understanding is not clearly erroneous.

Although we have found no New York case involving similar facts, our holding that the scope of a director's duty to offer opportunities he has found to his corporation must be measured by the facts of each case seems more consistent than any other with the holdings of New York courts applying the "interest or expectancy" test. Moreover, the decisions of other courts in analogous cases support our conclusion. The Supreme Court of Delaware held in *Johnston v. Greene*, 35 Del. Ch. 479, 121 A.2d 919 (1956), that a director of several corporations who was offered the patents and stock of a corporation engaged in an unrelated business and who arranged for the purchase of the stock by one of the corporations of which he was a director did not appropriate a corporate opportunity of that corporation by retaining the patents. The court recognized that a corporation's need to invest funds and a director's duty to seek investments for it might convert an investment opportunity offered to the director into a corporate opportunity, but held that

> [W]hether it does . . ., in any particular case, depends on the facts—upon the existence of special circumstances that would make it unfair for him to take the opportunity for himself.

35 Del. Ch. at 488, 121 A.2d at 924.

The court found especially persuasive against the existence of such special circumstances the fact that the director served on several boards. . . . It has been urged that the reasoning of *Johnston v. Greene* is fallacious because the fact that a director may be under fiduciary obligations to more than one corporation should lead a court to find and enforce the strongest obligation, not to allow the director to disregard them all. This criticism seems to us to miss the point underscored by the facts of this case, that a person's involvement in more than one venture of the same kind may negate the obligation which might otherwise be implied to offer similar opportunities to any one of them, absent some contrary understanding. . . . Thus we affirm Judge Dooling's holding that the properties acquired by defendants were not corporate opportunities of Darand.[3]

A director may be barred from competing with his corporation even though he does not by doing so appropriate a corporate opportunity. . . . But the duty not to compete, like the duty to offer opportunities to the corporation, is measured by the circumstances of each

---

[2]   This conclusion is reinforced by the small initial capitalization of Darand, which made a plowback of profits or further capital contributions by its stockholders necessary for acquisition of additional properties.

[3]   Plaintiff has not argued, and the record does not suggest, that the properties the Horns offered to Darand were less profitable or more speculative than those they retained. Therefore we do not decide whether such a showing would establish a breach by the Horns of their duty to Darand.

case, so that the considerations which led us to hold that the properties acquired by the Horns were not corporate opportunities strongly suggest a finding that the Horns were free to compete by acquiring them. In any event, there is no evidence in the record suggesting that Darand has been harmed by the Horns' ownership and operation of the properties they acquired. . . .

HAYS, Circuit Judge.
I dissent.

* * *

. . . [I]t seems clear that in the absence of a contrary agreement or understanding between the parties, the Horns, who were majority stockholders and managing officers of the Darand Corporation and whose primary function was to locate suitable properties for the company, were under a fiduciary obligation to offer such properties to Darand before buying the properties for themselves.

NOTES AND QUESTIONS

(1) **Traditional tests for corporate opportunity.** The courts have employed a variety of tests in determining what is a corporate opportunity, ranging from the narrowest test requiring that the alleged opportunity be "necessary" to the corporation, through the broader "interest or expectancy" test requiring that the opportunity be one in which the corporation has expressed an interest or has some sort of claim,[113] to the broadest "line of business" test under which directors or executives are liable for engaging in opportunities of the same general type as those engaged in by the corporation.[114] The tests overlap. For example, whether an opportunity is within a corporation's "line of business" may determine whether the corporation has an "interest or expectancy" in it.[115] What tests were applied in the above cases?

(2) **The ALI *Principles*.** ALI *Principles* § 5.05 defines corporate opportunities differently for outside directors and for full-time senior executives. For *outside directors*, corporate opportunities include only those activities of which a director becomes aware either (A) "[i]n connection with the performance of functions as a director . . ., or under circumstances that should reasonably lead the director . . . to believe the person offering the opportunity expects it to be offered to the corporation; or (B) [t]hrough the use of corporate information or property, if the resulting opportunity is one that the director . . . should reasonably be expected to believe would be of interest to the corporation." For *senior executives*, corporate opportunities include those opportunities that

---

[113] *See Southeast Consultants, Inc. v. McCrary Engineering Corp.*, 246 Ga. 503, 273 S.E.2d 112 (1980); *Comedy Cottage, Inc. v. Berk*, 145 Ill. App. 3d 355, 495 N.E.2d 1006 (1986).

[114] *See Guth v. Loft, Inc.*, 23 Del. Ch. 255, 5 A.2d 503 (1939); *Miller v. Miller*, 301 Minn. 207, 222 N.W.2d 71 (1974); *Imperial Group (Texas) Inc. v. Scholnick*, 709 S.W.2d 358 (Tex. Civ. App. 1986).

[115] *See Lindehurst Drugs, Inc. v. Becker*, 154 Ill. App. 3d 61, 506 N.E.2d 645 (1987).

would be corporate opportunities for outside directors as well as any opportunity that a senior executive "knows . . . is closely related to a business in which the corporation is engaged or expects to engage." Comment (b)(2) to § 5.05(b) notes that the "closely related" test is broader than the traditional "line of business" test because it includes, as a corporate opportunity, "contemplated activity in which the corporation may subsequently engage." Would the Michigan-2 license at issue in *Broz* have been a corporate opportunity under the ALI test? What if Broz had been a senior executive of CIS, rather than just an outside director?

(3) **Close versus public corporations. Brudney & Clark** advocate distinguishing between close corporations and public corporations. They argue that the latter type of firm involves more potential opportunities, and therefore a greater possibility that an outside business will involve the executive in a potential conflict with the interests of the firm. They also maintain that in the public corporation there is less possibility of viable consent by the shareholders to the insider's engaging in the opportunity. Therefore, while the authors would permit close corporation executives to escape liability for outside business dealings if they can prove that there was no relationship between the outside business and their corporation and no use of corporate assets, they would impose nearly absolute liability on executives in public corporations. Do you agree with this distinction?

(4) **Policy considerations.** Giving corporations the right to business opportunities their agents find helps ensure that employees will devote their full efforts to the firm. On the other hand, employees can be expected to seek compensation for foregoing outside business opportunities, and it may sometimes be cheaper for the corporation to let employees keep the opportunities for themselves. Accordingly, if firms and employees bargained in advance over the proper scope of the corporate opportunity doctrine, they would likely agree to allocate opportunities according to who could be expected to make the most of the opportunities (*see* **Davis**). The applicable rule arguably should minimize the need for customized contracts by matching the bargain firms and employees usually would make. Does a "line-of-business"-type rule reflect the bargain most employees and firms would reach in light of these considerations? If not, does some other test, such as the ALI *Principles* "closely related" test, come closer?

(5) **Extent of employee's outside business.** As noted in *Burg*, the courts have sometimes taken into consideration the nature of the agent's relationship with the company and the extent of her outside business dealings in determining the scope of corporate opportunity liability. An outside director commonly serves on several boards. The costs to these individuals of being required to forego opportunities of all the companies they serve would be considerable, and would have to be offset by higher direct compensation. Would it be worth it to the companies to provide this compensation in order to obtain the benefit of the director's deals? If more than one company contracted for the opportunities, how would they be allocated?[116] Finally, if the firm's managers or direc-

---

[116] *See* Note, 74 HARV. L. REV. 765, 770-71 (1971).

tors know of the employee's outside activities at the time of her hiring (as was the case in *Broz*) and do not restrict these activities by agreement, should this establish an implied agreement allocating benefits from outside activities to the employee?

(6) **Authorizing appropriation of corporate opportunities.** Even if a particular opportunity appropriated by a director is a corporate opportunity under the tests discussed above, the director may escape liability if the opportunity is effectively rejected by the corporation *after full disclosure*. The firm may reject the opportunity by a director or shareholder vote on a specific transaction, by after-the-fact ratification or by implied acceptance of the employee's conduct, such as where the corporation fails to accept the opportunity within a reasonable time after the opportunity has been offered to the corporation. The standard used to determine the effectiveness of a corporation's rejection generally depends upon the manner in which the corporation rejects the particular opportunity. For example, under ALI *Principles* § 5.05, a rejection is effective if it is by disinterested directors in a manner that satisfies the business judgment rule, by disinterested shareholders if it is not a waste of corporate assets, or otherwise if it is fair to the corporation.[117] *Telxon Corp. v. Meyerson*[118] holds that "[r]ejection of a corporate opportunity by the CEO is not a valid substitute for consideration by the full board of directors." Why did the courts find insufficient evidence of notification and rejection in *Farber* and *Broz*?[119]

(7) **Fairness of appropriation.** In some jurisdictions, the insider may be permitted to appropriate a corporate opportunity, even if the opportunity has not been offered to the firm first if the appropriation is otherwise "fair."[120] In particular, the appropriation may be allowed if the corporation could not have taken advantage of the opportunity. Factors indicating that a corporation could not take advantage of a particular opportunity include the corporation's financial inability to acquire the opportunity, legal restrictions on the corporation's ability to accept the opportunity, and unwillingness of a third party to deal with the corporation. The courts are usually skeptical of defendants' claims about their own firm's financial inability,[121] although some courts, particularly in recent cases, have sided with insiders (and, in cases like *Broz*, outsiders)

---

[117] For an application of the ALI rules, see *Klinicki v. Lundgren*, 298 Or. 662, 695 P.2d 906 (1985).

[118] 802 A.2d 257, 263 (Del. 2002).

[119] For a recent case on the adequacy of a corporation's rejection of a corporate opportunity, see *Ostrowski v. Avery*, 703 A.2d 117 (Conn. 1997) (consent by 54% shareholder to appropriation of opportunity by shareholder's own son not effective).

[120] *See Ostrowski v. Avery, supra* footnote 119; *Miller v. Miller, supra* footnote 114; *Southeast Consultants, Inc. v. McCrary Engineering Corp., supra* footnote 113 (decided under a Georgia statute which provided for liability only where the defendant usurped a corporate opportunity "in violation of his duties").

[121] *See Borden v. Sinskey*, 530 F.2d 478 (3d Cir. 1976); *Irving Trust Co. v. Deutsch*, 73 F.2d 121 (2d Cir. 1934); *Morad v. Coupounas*, 361 So. 2d 6 (Ala. 1978); *Ellzey v. Fyr-Pruf, Inc.*, 376 So. 2d 1328 (Miss. 1979); *Imperial Group (Texas), Inc. v. Scholnick*, 709 S.W.2d 358 (Tex. Civ. App. 1986); *Nicholson v. Evans*, 642 P.2d 727 (Utah 1982); *Suburban Motors of Grafton, Inc. v. Forester*, 134 Wis. 2d 183, 396 N.W.2d 351 (Wis. App. 1986).

who make a clear showing of financial inability.[122] What is the appropriate approach in this type of case? Note that the employee may be able to obtain financing on behalf of the firm even if the firm's other resources are low, or to try to ameliorate any ill will between the third party and the firm. On the other hand, the employee probably can do little about a structural incapacity, such as legal restrictions on the firm's activities.[123]

Even if there is little chance the firm can use the opportunity, why not require the insider at least to disclose and let the corporation decide whether to take advantage of the opportunity? The ALI *Principles* adopt this position in Section 5.05(a).[124] *Yiannatsis v. Stephanis*[125] appeared to suggest a duty formally to present even those opportunities that a corporation was not financially able to acquire. In that case, the Court stated: "There is no need for us to consider . . . the Court of Chancery's findings of financial inability. . . . [W]e hold that [the stockholder-directors] breached the fiduciary duties they owed to [the corporation] by *failing to present properly the opportunity* to [the corporation] . . . ." *Broz* distinguished *Yiannatsis* on the ground that the defendants in the latter case acted in "bad faith" by "act[ing] surreptitiously to keep the opportunity from being exercised by the corporation, when they had no reasonable grounds to believe that the corporation would not be interested therein." *Thorpe v. CERBCO,*[126] decided by the Delaware Supreme Court less than one month after *Broz,* held that controlling shareholders impermissibly usurped a corporate opportunity by entering into negotiations to sell their stock to a third party who had contacted them to discuss the possibility of acquiring substantially all the corporation's assets. The Court held that the controlling shareholders should have presented the opportunity to the corporation before commencing negotiations to sell their own stock, even though the controlling shareholders could have vetoed an asset sale under Del. G.C.L. § 271. Can *CERBCO* be reconciled with *Broz*? Does it make sense to require presentation of a corporate opportunity where the corporation may be *legally* incapable of taking advantage of the opportunity but not where the corporation may be *financially* incapable of taking advan-

---

[122] *See In re McCalla Interiors, Inc.*, 228 B.R. 657 (Bankr. N.D. Ohio 1998) (defendant's consultations with accountant and other professionals established that corporation was no longer a viable entity); *Orchard v. Covelli*, 590 F. Supp. 1548 (W.D. Pa. 1984) (franchisor would not have renewed franchise for passive investor like plaintiff); *Peterson Welding Supply Co. v. Cryogas Prods., Inc.*, 126 Ill. App. 3d 759, 467 N.E.2d 1068 (1984) (retail distributors would not deal with plaintiff, who sold at wholesale); *A.C. Petters Co. v. St. Cloud Enterprises*, 301 Minn. 261, 222 N.W.2d 83 (1974); **Chew** at 469-77 (discerning a "corporate capability" approach in some recent cases).

[123] *See Warren v. Century Bankcorp., Inc.*, 741 P.2d 846, 847-48 n.1, 854 (Okla. 1987); **Chew** at 471-72.

[124] For case adopting the Restatement position, see *Hanover Insurance Company v. Sutton*, 705 N.E.2d 279 (Mass. App. Ct. 1999); *Northeast Harbor Golf Club Inc. v. Harris*, 661 A.2d 1146 (Me. 1995). *But see A. Teixeira & Co. v. Teixeira*, 699 A.2d 1383 (R.I. 1997) (accepting a financial inability defense over dissent which argued that the defendant should have been required to present the opportunity to the corporation first).

[125] 653 A.2d 275, 279 (Del. 1995).

[126] 676 A.2d 436 (Del. 1996).

tage of the opportunity?[127] *Havens v. Attar*[128] reconciles *Broz* and *Thorpe* by character-izing the latter case as involving breach of an *independent duty* to accurately present the opportunity to the corporation. This may reflect a distinction between the executive's duties as a *fiduciary* and as an *owner* of the firm. Consider in this respect the discussion in Section 9.07, below. But the question remains why directors should be required to present opportunities that the corporation is legally precluded from taking. The answer may have to do with the difficulty of assessing evidence of inability and the executive's unique access to facts on this issue (*see* **Talley**).

(8) **Remedy.** The remedy for engaging in a corporate opportunity is based on the defendants' profits rather than the harm to the corporation.[129] A gains-based test fre-quently leaves the corporation in a better position than a harm-based approach. For example, if the corporation was unable to take advantage of the opportunity (and that inability is not recognized as a defense), a gains-based standard gives the corporation damages even though it suffered no harm. A gains-based measure also may exceed actual harm in cases where the corporation might have taken advantage of the corporate opportunity, since the gains-based approach does not require a reduction in damages for profits earned by the corporation by investing its funds in alternative activities. The gains-based remedy is arguably based on deterrence, because the agent's actual gains are easier to show than the corporation's would-be gain. Can you think of any other justi-fications? If the employee injured the corporation by *competing* with it, she may be liable for harm to the corporation even if she earned no profits (*see* Note 11, below).

(9) **The role of express contracts.** The "standard form" contract supplied by the corporate opportunity rule may be superseded by an employment agreement or by char-ter or bylaw provisions. See, for example, Del. G.C.L. § 122(17), which provides that any corporation may "[r]enounce, in its certificate of incorporation or by action of its board of directors, any interest or expectancy of the corporation in, or in being offered an opportunity to participate in, specified business opportunities or specified classes or categories of business opportunities that are presented to the corporation or 1 or more of its officers, directors or stockholders." The enforceability of express provisions super-seding the corporate opportunity doctrine is discussed in Section 9.09. Alternatively, "opportunities" may be defined by the parties' expectations, as is implicit in the "inter-est or expectancy" test. Are the results in *Broz, Farber* and *Burg* best explained under the "standard form" corporate opportunities doctrine or by the parties' actual deals?

---

[127] *Compare Maxus Investment Group v. Bull & Bear Group, Inc.*, 1996 U.S. Dist. LEXIS 4696, 1996 WL 175044 (S.D.N.Y. 1996) (rejecting shareholder-plaintiffs' complaint that directors of corporation breached their fiduciary duties when they declined to accept plaintiffs' offers to purchase certain of the corporation's businesses because the cor-poration's controlling shareholder had no duty to vote his stock in favor of an extraordinary transaction and, therefore, it would "have been a complete waste of time for the defendant-directors to engage in any inquiry as to the value of the plaintiffs' offer").

[128] 1997 Del. Ch. LEXIS 12, 1997 WL 55957 (Del. Ch. 1997).

[129] *See, e.g., Farber, supra.*

(10) **Other bases of director liability for outside business dealings.** The corporate opportunity theory is not the only basis of director or executive liability for outside business dealings. In particular, directors and officers can be held liable for engaging in business activities that bring the director into competition with the corporation or for using corporate information or property for their personal advantage. These alternative bases for liability are examined in the following Notes.

(11) **Competition.** Even outside business that is not a corporate opportunity can bring the employee into competition with the corporation. See ALI *Principles* § 5.06 subjecting directors and senior executives to a duty not to compete with the corporation unless, among other things, the harm to the corporation from the competition is offset by benefits that the corporation can expect to derive from such competition or such competition is authorized in advance by disinterested directors or shareholders. Competition with the corporation is inconsistent with the employee's agreement to devote her services to the firm. The competition theory is particularly important where the transaction involves the executive in an ongoing enterprise, as distinguished, for example, from the purchase of vacant land.[130]

(12) **Competition by former employees.** Ex-employees generally can compete with their former firms.[131] However, the former employee often utilizes information she gained while working for her former employer. If the employee is allowed to use the information, this increases the cost (or decreases the net value) to the firm of employing the agent. Accordingly, the parties often opt out of the standard form by entering into post-employment non-competition agreements. These agreements have costs as well as benefits and may not be appropriate in all cases. For example, barring competition could effectively prevent the employee from using her human capital outside the firm. More-over, the employer could take advantage of the employee's lack of alternatives to chisel on compensation and working conditions.[132] For other discussions of the post-employment competition problem, see Notes 6-7 following *In re Brown* in Section 4.04[D] (work-in-process and noncompetition agreements).

---

[130] For a discussion and illustration of the distinction between the competition and corporate opportunity theories, see *Lincoln Stores, Inc. v. Grant*, 309 Mass. 417, 34 N.E.2d 704 (1941).

[131] *See, e.g., Riggs Investment Management Corp. v. Columbia Partners*, 966 F. Supp. 1250 (D.D.C. 1997) (CEO who set out to establish new business which competed with employer did not breach duty to his employer when he sent "feelers" to possible investors in his new venture or when, following his departure, he solicited his former employer's clients, since "agent may make arrangements or plan to go into competition with his principal before terminating his agency, 'provided no unfair acts are committed or injury done his principal'"; but CEO did breach a duty to his employer when he shared confidential information with outsiders and solicited employees to join his new venture, all while he was still CEO).

[132] The courts have struck down some non-competition agreements as "unreasonable." *See* RESTATEMENT (SECOND) CONTRACTS § 188; Closius & Schaffer, *Involuntary Nonservitude: The Current Judicial Enforcement of Employee Covenants Not to Compete—A Proposal for Reform*, 57 S. CAL. L. REV. 531 (1984).

(13) **Use of firm property.** Employees implicitly agree that they will use firm property only for corporate purposes, unless the parties agree otherwise. The employee violates this principle by diverting funds and other tangible resources to her outside business, and less obviously by using corporate information and time during working hours, even when the employee's outside business activity is itself permissible.[133] See ALI *Principles* § 5.04, imposing on directors and senior executives a duty not to use corporate property or information to secure a pecuniary benefit, unless, among other things, the use does not harm the corporation or the use is authorized by disinterested directors or shareholders. The misuse of corporate property or information also could be a basis of corporate opportunity or competition liability,[134] since the use of corporate resources bears on whether the opportunity is related to the corporation or its business under one or more of the tests for corporate opportunities discussed above.

PROBLEM

Ajax Real Estate Corporation is a large national firm in the business of purchasing land and developing it into apartment and condominium complexes. The company does not generally speculate in raw land. However, in isolated cases it has bought raw land intending to develop it and then sold the land for a profit when the development possibilities did not work out. Ajax has fallen on hard times as a number of its projects have failed to perform up to expectations. Ajax has lost considerable money over the last five years, and it is in danger of defaulting on some of its loans.

Bill is an expert in real estate evaluation and acquisition who is in charge of land acquisition for Ajax in the major urban center of Metropolis. Ajax hired Bill away from a competitor for a large salary and perks about a year ago, and is hoping he will help lift Ajax out of its doldrums.

While scouting for deals for Ajax, Bill negotiated for a parcel of land in Metropolis owned by Sam. Sam did not want to sell the Metropolis land, but told Bill he had a parcel of raw land in nearby Gotham he wanted to sell. Sam had had some unpleasant dealings with Ajax a few years before and said that he absolutely would not sell to Ajax. However, he had some pressing expenses and was willing to make a deal with Bill personally. Bill saw an opportunity for a quick profit on a resale because Sam's price was, in his expert view, quite low. He did not think Ajax would be interested (even if Sam wanted to sell to Ajax) because the land was not suitable for apartment buildings and, anyway, Ajax was in no financial condition to be developing new tracts. So Bill bought the land himself and made a killing when he resold it more than a year later, after spending considerable time taking care of a zoning problem that would have sharply reduced the resale price.

What should be the result in a suit by Ajax against Bill for his profit on the deal?

---

[133] *See, e.g., Maryland Metals, Inc. v. Metzner*, 282 Md. 31, 382 A.2d 564 (1978) (employees liable for use of corporate materials and facilities).

[134] For a notorious example, see *Guth v. Loft, Inc.*, 23 Del. Ch. 255, 5 A.2d 503 (1939).

REFERENCES

Brudney & Clark, *A New Look at Corporate Opportunities*, 94 HARV. L. REV. 997 (1981).

Chew, *Competing Interests in the Corporate Opportunity Doctrine*, 67 N.C. L. REV. 435 (1989).

Comment, *The Corporate Opportunity Doctrine and Outside Business Interests*, 56 U. CHI. L. REV. 827 (1989).

Davis, *Corporate Opportunity and Comparative Advantage*, 84 IOWA L. REV. 211 (1989).

Talley, *Turning Servile Opportunities to Gold: A Strategic Analysis of the Corporate Opportunities Doctrine*, 108 YALE L.J. 277 (1998).

§ 9.07 Parent-Subsidiary Transactions and Duties of Majority Shareholders

Transactions between controlling shareholders, including "parent" corporations, and the corporations they control (*i.e.*, subsidiaries) are interested director transactions in the sense that the subsidiary's directors have a conflicting self-interest to serve the interests of their employer, the controlling shareholder. In addition, because parent corporations and subsidiaries may often engage in related lines of business, the business opportunities that parent corporations take for themselves may frequently bring the parent into competition with the subsidiary or involve opportunities that may appear appropriate for the subsidiary.

Despite the potential for self-dealing in these transactions, the same rules applicable to other transactions raising duty of loyalty problems discussed in Sections 9.04 and 9.06 above may not work well here. Because the transactions usually cannot be approved by truly "disinterested" directors, strict application of the duty of loyalty principles would require either disinterested shareholder approval or heightened judicial review of all transactions entered into by the controlling shareholder that relate to the subsidiary's business. This could increase the governance costs of the parent/partially-owned-subsidiary type of business association to the point where this structure might rarely be feasible.

SINCLAIR OIL CORP. v. LEVIEN
Delaware Supreme Court
280 A.2d 717 (1971)

WOLCOTT, Chief Justice.

This is an appeal by the defendant, Sinclair Oil Corporation (hereafter Sinclair), from an order of the Court of Chancery, 261 A.2d 911 in a derivative action requiring Sinclair to account for damages sustained by its subsidiary, Sinclair Venezuelan Oil Company (hereafter Sinven), organized by Sinclair for the purpose of operating in Venezuela, as a result of dividends paid by Sinven, the denial to Sinven of industrial development, and a breach of contract between Sinclair's wholly-owned subsidiary, Sinclair International Oil Company, and Sinven.

Sinclair, operating primarily as a holding company, is in the business of exploring for oil and of producing and marketing crude oil and oil products. At all times relevant to this litigation, it owned about 97% of Sinven's stock. The plaintiff owns about 3000 of 120,000 publicly held shares of Sinven. Sinven, incorporated in 1922, has been engaged in petroleum operations primarily in Venezuela and since 1959 has operated exclusively in Venezuela.

Sinclair nominates all members of Sinven's board of directors. The Chancellor found as a fact that the directors were not independent of Sinclair. Almost without exception, they were officers, directors, or employees of corporations in the Sinclair complex. By reason of Sinclair's domination, it is clear that Sinclair owed Sinven a fiduciary duty. . . .

The Chancellor held that because of Sinclair's fiduciary duty and its control over Sinven, its relationship with Sinven must meet the test of intrinsic fairness. The standard of intrinsic fairness involves both a high degree of fairness and a shift in the burden of proof. Under this standard the burden is on Sinclair to prove, subject to careful judicial scrutiny, that its transactions with Sinven were objectively fair. . . .

Sinclair argues that the transactions between it and Sinven should be tested, not by the test of intrinsic fairness with the accompanying shift of the burden of proof, but by the business judgment rule under which a court will not interfere with the judgment of a board of directors unless there is a showing of gross and palpable overreaching. . . .

We think, however, that Sinclair's argument in this respect is misconceived. When the situation involves a parent and a subsidiary, with the parent controlling the transaction and fixing the terms, the test of intrinsic fairness, with its resulting shifting of the burden of proof, is applied. . . . The basic situation for the application of the rule is the one in which the parent has received a benefit to the exclusion and at the expense of the subsidiary.

Recently, this court dealt with the question of fairness in parent-subsidiary dealings in *Getty Oil Co. v. Skelly Oil Co.*, [267 A.2d 883 (Del. 1970)].

In that case, both parent and subsidiary were in the business of refining and marketing crude oil and crude oil products. The Oil Import Board ruled that the subsidiary, because it was controlled by the parent, was no longer entitled to a separate allocation of imported crude oil. The subsidiary then contended that it had a right to share the quota of crude oil allotted to the parent. We ruled that the business judgment standard should be applied to determine this contention. Although the subsidiary suffered a loss through the administration of the oil import quotas, the parent gained nothing. The parent's quota was derived solely from its own past use. The past use of the subsidiary did not cause an increase in the parent's quota. Nor did the parent usurp a quota of the subsidiary. Since the parent received nothing from the subsidiary to the exclusion of the minority stockholders of the subsidiary, there was no self-dealing. Therefore, the business judgment standard was properly applied.

A parent does indeed owe a fiduciary duty to its subsidiary when there are parent-subsidiary dealings. However, this alone will not evoke the intrinsic fairness standard. This standard will be applied only when the fiduciary duty is accompanied by self-dealing—the situation when a parent is on both sides of a transaction with its subsidiary. Self-dealing occurs when the parent, by virtue of its domination of the subsidiary, causes the subsidiary to act in such a way that the parent receives something from the subsidiary to the exclusion of, and detriment to, the minority stockholders of the subsidiary.

We turn now to the facts. The plaintiff argues that, from 1960 through 1966, Sinclair caused Sinven to pay out such excessive dividends that the industrial development of Sinven was effectively prevented, and it became in reality a corporation in dissolution.

From 1960 through 1966, Sinven paid out $108,000,000 in dividends ($38,000,000 in excess of Sinven's earnings during the same period). The Chancellor held that Sinclair caused these dividends to be paid during a period when it had a need for large amounts of cash. Although the dividends paid exceeded earnings, the plaintiff concedes that the payments were made in compliance with 8 Del. C. § 170, authorizing payment of dividends out of surplus or net profits. However, the plaintiff attacks these dividends on the ground that they resulted from an improper motive—Sinclair's need for cash. The Chancellor, applying the intrinsic fairness standard, held that Sinclair did not sustain its burden of proving that these dividends were intrinsically fair to the minority stockholders of Sinven.

* * *

We do not accept the argument that the intrinsic fairness test can never be applied to a dividend declaration by a dominated board, although a dividend declaration by a dominated board will not inevitably demand the application of the intrinsic fairness standard. . . .

If such a dividend is in essence self-dealing by the parent, then the intrinsic fairness standard is the proper standard. For example, suppose a parent dominates a subsidiary and its board of directors. The subsidiary has outstanding two classes of stock, X and Y. Class X is owned by the parent and Class Y is owned by minority stockholders of the subsidiary. If the subsidiary, at the direction of the parent, declares a dividend on its Class X stock only, this might well be self-dealing by the parent. It would be receiving something from the subsidiary to the exclusion of and detrimental to its minority stockholders. This self-dealing, coupled with the parent's fiduciary duty, would make intrinsic fairness the proper standard by which to evaluate the dividend payments.

Consequently it must be determined whether the dividend payments by Sinven were, in essence, self-dealing by Sinclair. The dividends resulted in great sums of money being transferred from Sinven to Sinclair. However, a proportionate share of this money was received by the minority shareholders of Sinven. Sinclair received nothing from Sinven to the exclusion of its minority stockholders. As such, these dividends were not self-dealing. We hold therefore that the Chancellor erred in applying the intrinsic fairness test as to these dividend payments. The business judgment standard should have been applied.

. . . The plaintiff contends only that the dividend payments drained Sinven of cash to such an extent that it was prevented from expanding.

The plaintiff proved no business opportunities which came to Sinven independently and which Sinclair either took to itself or denied to Sinven. As a matter of fact, with two minor exceptions which resulted in losses, all of Sinven's operations have been conducted in Venezuela, and Sinclair had a policy of exploiting its oil properties located in different countries by subsidiaries located in the particular countries.

From 1960 to 1966 Sinclair purchased or developed oil fields in Alaska, Canada, Paraguay, and other places around the world. The plaintiff contends that these were all opportunities which could have been taken by Sinven. The Chancellor concluded that Sinclair had not proved that its denial of expansion opportunities to Sinven was intrinsically fair. He based this conclusion on the following findings of fact. Sinclair made no real effort to expand Sinven. The excessive dividends paid by Sinven resulted in so great a cash drain as to effectively deny to Sinven any ability to expand. During this same period Sinclair actively pursued a company-wide policy of developing through its subsidiaries new sources of revenue, but Sinven was not permitted to participate and was confined in its activities to Venezuela.

However, the plaintiff could point to no opportunities which came to Sinven. Therefore, Sinclair usurped no business opportunity belonging to Sinven. Since Sinclair received nothing from Sinven to the exclusion of and detriment to Sinven's minority stockholders, there was no self-dealing. Therefore, business judgment is the proper standard by which to evaluate Sinclair's expansion policies.

Since there is no proof of self-dealing on the part of Sinclair, it follows that the expansion policy of Sinclair and the methods used to achieve the desired result must, as far as Sinclair's treatment of Sinven is concerned, be tested by the standards of the business judgment rule. Accordingly, Sinclair's decision, absent fraud or gross overreaching, to achieve expansion through the medium of its subsidiaries, other than Sinven, must be upheld.

Even if Sinclair was wrong in developing these opportunities as it did, the question arises, with which subsidiaries should these opportunities have been shared? No evidence indicates a unique need or ability of Sinven to develop these opportunities. The decision of which subsidiaries would be used to implement Sinclair's expansion policy was one of business judgment with which a court will not interfere absent a showing of gross and palpable overreaching. *Meyerson v. El Paso Natural Gas Co.*, 246 A.2d 789 (Del. Ch. 1967). No such showing has been made here.

Next, Sinclair argues that the Chancellor committed error when he held it liable to Sinven for breach of contract.

In 1961 Sinclair created Sinclair International Oil Company (hereafter International), a wholly owned subsidiary used for the purpose of coordinating all of Sinclair's foreign operations. All crude purchases by Sinclair were made thereafter through International.

On September 28, 1961, Sinclair caused Sinven to contract with International whereby Sinven agreed to sell all of its crude oil and refined products to International at specified prices. The contract provided for minimum and maximum quantities and prices. The plaintiff contends that Sinclair caused this contract to be breached in two respects. Although the contract called for payment on receipt, International's payments lagged as much as 30 days after receipt. Also, the contract required International to purchase at least a fixed minimum amount of crude and refined products from Sinven. International did not comply with this requirement.

Clearly, Sinclair's act of contracting with its dominated subsidiary was self-dealing. Under the contract Sinclair received the products produced by Sinven, and of course the minority shareholders of Sinven were not able to share in the receipt of these products. If the contract was breached, then Sinclair received these products to the detriment of Sinven's minority shareholders. We agree with the Chancellor's finding that the contract was breached by Sinclair, both as to the time of payments and the amounts purchased.

Although a parent need not bind itself by a contract with its dominated subsidiary, Sinclair chose to operate in this manner. As Sinclair has received the benefits of this contract, so must it comply with the contractual duties.

Under the intrinsic fairness standard, Sinclair must prove that its causing Sinven not to enforce the contract was intrinsically fair to the minority shareholders of Sinven. Sinclair has failed to meet this burden. Late payments were clearly breaches for which Sinven should have sought and received adequate damages. As to the quantities purchased, Sinclair argues that it purchased all the products produced by Sinven. This, however, does not satisfy the standard of intrinsic fairness. Sinclair has failed to prove that Sinven could not possibly have produced or some way have obtained the contract minimums. As such, Sinclair must account on this claim.

We will therefore reverse that part of the Chancellor's order that requires Sinclair to account to Sinven for damages sustained as a result of dividends paid between 1960 and 1966, and by reason of the denial to Sinven of expansion during that period. We will affirm the remaining portion of that order and remand the cause for further proceedings.

NOTES AND QUESTIONS

(1) **Policy considerations.** *Sinclair* makes it easier for controlling shareholders to engage in transactions that relate to the subsidiary's business by restricting the instances in which courts will apply "fairness" review to such transactions. As a result, minority shareholders are put at greater risk of exploitation by controlling shareholders than might otherwise be the case. What benefit do minority shareholders receive under *Sinclair* to compensate them for this increased risk of exploitation? The answer is that, by making it easier for controlling shareholders to engage in transactions that relate to a subsidiary's business, *Sinclair* makes the acquisition of a controlling stake more desirable. This ameliorates the "free rider" problem inherent in dispersed share ownership (*see* Section 7.02[A]) and encourages monitoring of management both by the market for corporate control, and by large shareholders after they acquire control. Thus, under *Sinclair*, shareholders trade off greater protection from exploitation by controlling shareholders *ex post* for increased monitoring of managers.

(2) **When does *Sinclair* apply?** A court may treat a transaction between a controlling shareholder and the corporation it controls as a conflict of interest transaction even when the corporation's directors are independent of the controlling shareholder. May a controlling parent avoid a fairness review on the ground that the board is independent despite the controlling interest? *In re Dairy Mart Convenience Stores, Inc.*[135] stated:

> Even if the board harbored deepseated contempt for [the controlling shareholders] because of their competing strategic vision (or for any other reason), that lack of personal domination would not take this case outside the rubric of this Court's controlling shareholder law. Under our jurisprudence, where a controlling shareholder has the power to influence the competing

---

[135] 1999 Del. Ch. LEXIS 94, 1999 WL 350473 (Del. Ch., May 24, 1999).

sides of a bargaining process, and where there are claims of actual abuse of that power to the benefit of the controlling shareholder at the corporation's expense, it is well established that the Court subjects the transactions in question to entire fairness review. While a dominating influence that causes directors to be beholden to an officer, director, or controlling shareholder may be enough to exert effective control over a transaction, that domination is certainly not an independent requirement for triggering entire fairness review.

(3) **When must the parent prove fairness?** Under the *Sinclair* test, the court must determine that the parent is earning a benefit to the exclusion and detriment of the minority before the fairness test applies. Note that the *Sinclair* court apparently required Sinclair to establish the fairness of its handling of the contract between Sinven and Sinclair's wholly owned subsidiary, Sinclair International, but did not require Sinclair to establish the fairness of the Sinven dividend payments. Can these apparently divergent holdings be reconciled? Does the claim in connection with the purchase contract involve something more than a breach of contract?

(4) **How can the parent prove fairness?** Assuming the parent is earning a benefit to the exclusion of, and detriment to, the minority, how can the parent prove the benefit was "intrinsically fair" under *Sinclair*? In *Burton v. Exxon Corp.*,[136] the subsidiary declared a dividend of funds received as compensation for nationalization of its properties to the parent as holder of first preferred stock, but not to the plaintiffs, holders of second preferred. This is the specific situation described in *Sinclair* where the "intrinsic fairness" test should be applied. The court held that the parent passed the test because the subsidiary's charter gave the first preferred absolute priority as to dividends, because retaining funds until enough had been accumulated to pay the second preferred would have deferred payment on the first preferred until the next century, and because the parent's shareholders might have been able to challenge a decision *not* to pay dividends.

(5) **The ALI** *Principles.* The ALI *Principles* §§ 5.10-.14 deal with the fiduciary duties of controlling shareholders. Like *Sinclair*, these sections subject controlling shareholders to somewhat lesser duties than directors or senior executives. For example, while § 5.10 generally requires that controlling shareholders establish the fairness of transactions between a controlling shareholder and the corporation in the absence of disinterested shareholder approval, subsection (c) places the burden of *coming forward* with evidence of unfairness on the party challenging the transaction. Similarly, § 5.12 provides that an opportunity not developed or received through a controlling shareholder's relationship with the corporation only becomes a corporate opportunity if it is held out by or on behalf of the controlling shareholder as "being the type of business activity that will be within the scope of the business in which the corporation is engaged

---

[136] 583 F. Supp. 405 (S.D.N.Y. 1984).

or expects to engage and will not be within the scope of the controlling shareholder's business." By contrast, § 5.05 holds that, in the case of senior executives, an opportunity is a corporate opportunity whenever it is "closely related" to the business in which the corporation is engaged or expects to engage. Finally, the ALI *Principles* do not subject controlling shareholders to any duty in respect of competition with the controlled corporation.

(6) **Parent-subsidiary mergers.** The rules that apply to parent-subsidiary *transactions* are closely related and similar to those which apply to parent-subsidiary *mergers*—that is, transactions in which the parent uses its control of the subsidiary to force the minority shareholders to exchange their shares for some combination of cash and securities other than common stock in the subsidiary. These transactions are considered below in Section 15.02.

PROBLEM

Corporation A owns 51% of Corporation B and wholly controls the B board of directors. The tax laws provide that a parent that owns 80% or more of a subsidiary may file a consolidated tax return with the subsidiary. Since A is incurring substantial losses and B is earning substantial income, a consolidated return would enable A to offset its losses against B's gains. A therefore plans to acquire enough additional stock in B to enable it to file a consolidated return. Prior to acquiring the stock, A plans to enter into an agreement with the B board pursuant to which B agrees to pay to A 90% of any taxes it saves as a result of the filing of a consolidated return.

You are counsel for Corporation A. Management seeks your advice as to the possibility that minority shareholders of B will be able to obtain relief from the proposed contract. If there is a substantial possibility that the arrangement will be overturned in court, it would be financially unwise for A to acquire the additional interest in B. What advice would you give?[137]

§ 9.08 Fiduciary Duties in Unincorporated Firms

The fiduciary duty issues discussed so far arise in unincorporated firms as well as in corporations. A significant difference between the two contexts is that the duties of non-owner managers in centrally-managed corporations described in this Chapter may not apply in firms that are managed directly by the owners. Moreover, the great variety of management arrangements in such firms illustrates the point discussed in Section 9.01, that fiduciary duties can and do differ according to the specific contractual arrangements in each firm.

---

[137] *See In re All Products Co.*, 32 B.R. 811 (E.D. Mich. 1983); *Case v. New York Central Railroad Co.*, 15 N.Y.2d 150, 256 N.Y.S. 607, 204 N.E.2d 643 (1965); *see also Smith v. Tele-Communication, Inc.*, 134 Cal. App. 3d 338, 184 Cal. Rptr. 571 (1982).

[A] General Partnerships

The most frequently cited description of partners' duties is Judge Cardozo's in *Meinhard v. Salmon*, quoted at the beginning of the Chapter. The partners' duty is embodied in UPA § 21, which provides generally that a partner must account for a benefit derived without the consent of the other partners from a transaction connected with the partnership or use of partnership property. This section covers at least self-dealing, use of partnership assets for personal benefit, usurping partnership opportunities, and competition with the partnership. Some cases have also recognized at least a limited duty of care among partners in connection with business decisions.[138]

Revised UPA § 404 has significantly changed the articulation of partners' fiduciary duties by elaborating on the partners' duty of loyalty, adding an explicit duty of care and obligation of good faith and fair dealing, and clarifying that the section is an exclusive list of fiduciary duties. Specifically, RUPA's fiduciary duty provision includes not only the UPA's language (§ 404(b)(1)), but also specific duties to refrain from self-dealing and competition (§ 404(b)(2)-(3)), to act carefully (§ 404(c)), and to discharge duties to the partnership and the partners consistently with the obligation of good faith and fair dealing (§ 404(d)). RUPA also provides that a partner does not violate a duty merely by furthering the partner's own interest (§ 404(e)) and that a partner may lend money and transact business with the partnership (§ 404(f)). Finally, RUPA makes clear that Section 404 is an exclusive list of a partner's fiduciary duties (§ 404(a)).

What is the appropriate scope of partners' fiduciary duties? Although Judge Cardozo's description of partners' duties sounds very fine, it may not correctly describe what the courts are, or should be, doing. Recall from Section 9.01 above that the appropriate "standard form" of fiduciary duties depends partly on the effectiveness of alternative constraints on management exercise of discretion. While corporate shareholders commonly delegate control to non-owner managers, control in partnerships is normally retained by the partners themselves. Thus, the managers in standard-form partnerships are constrained from the worst kinds of misconduct by their contingent compensation, personal liability for debts, and their co-partners' close monitoring and power to withdraw at any time. Accordingly, the need for monitoring in partnerships by means of fiduciary duties or other devices is reduced. Consistent with this view, courts have held, for example, that a partner who loans money to the partnership does not necessarily have a duty to refinance the loan,[139] and that a partner may buy partnership property on her own behalf at a liquidation sale.[140] Two prominent commentators have said that in a partnership the "[d]uty of loyalty [is] commonly relaxed. . . . Partners are treated more as co-owners than as each others' keepers."[141]

---

[138] *See* **Bromberg & Ribstein** § 6.07(f).

[139] *See Riveredge Assocs. v. Metropolitan Life Ins. Co.*, 774 F. Supp. 892 (D.N.J. 1991) (N.J. law).

[140] *See Prentiss v. Sheffel*, 20 Ariz. App. 411, 513 P.2d 949 (1973); *Mandell v. Centrum Frontier Corp.*, 86 Ill. App. 3d 437, 407 N.E.2d 821 (1980); *Cude v. Couch*, 588 S.W.2d 554 (Tenn. 1979).

[141] Easterbrook & Fischel, *Contract and Fiduciary Duty*, 36 J.L. & Econ. 425, 436 (1993).

Although monitoring and incentives address agency problems, they do not neces-sarily resolve problems of oppression and opportunistic conduct. Majority oppression is taken care of to some extent by the partners' power to dissolve the firm at will (*see* Section 4.04). But the potential for opportunistic exercise of the power to dissolve at will may give rise to special duties in partnerships. Recall *Page v. Page*, Section 4.04[B], in which the court recognized the existence of a remedy to discipline a partner's use of dissolution to grab the business from his co-partner. However, there is a question whether these duties should be regarded as *fiduciary* in nature, since they arise among co-owners rather than in the typical fiduciary context of delegated powers (*see* Section 9.01[A][3], above).

The foregoing analysis focuses on the standard form partnership where all partners participate in management. However, the situation may change when partnerships depart from the standard form and management is delegated to managing partners. It is not clear, however, whether even this kind of partnership resembles a corporation, since even managing partners are likely to be co-owners.

It follows from this analysis that RUPA arguably goes too far in imposing fidu-ciary duties on all partners in all partnerships. (*see* **Ribstein**, *Prime Time*). Indeed, RUPA itself seems to recognize this by providing in § 404(e) that partners can act in their own self interest. On the other hand, some commentators, including **Dickerson** and **Vestal**, argue that RUPA § 404(e) goes too far in relieving partners of fiduciary duties in light of such factors as the inadvertent nature of partnership and partners' personal liabilities.

[B] Limited Partnerships

ULPA and RULPA do not provide for fiduciary duties. However, RULPA § 404 provides that that general partners in limited partnerships have rights, powers, duties and liabilities of general partners in general partnerships, and both UPA § 6(2) and RULPA § 1106 provide for application of general partnership rules where the limited partnership act is silent. It seems to follow that UPA § 21 and RUPA § 404 govern the fiduciary duties of general partners in limited partnerships under both ULPA and RULPA.

ULPA (2001), on the other hand, includes specific provisions governing the fidu-ciary duties of both general and limited partners. ULPA (2001) § 408 states that general partners owe the partnership duties of both loyalty and care. The duty of loyalty includes, among other things, a duty to refrain from usurping partnership opportunities and a duty not to compete with the partnership; the duty of care requires the general partner to "refrain[] from engaging in grossly negligent or reckless conduct, intentional misconduct, or a knowing violation of law." In contrast, ULPA (2001) § 305 provides that limited partners owe no fiduciary duties to the partnership, though they remain sub-ject to the general obligations of good faith and fair dealing.

It is not clear that general partnership rules *should* apply to limited partnerships as ULPA and RULPA appear to require. Limited partnerships are characterized by manda-tory delegation of control by limited partners to general partners (*see* Section 6.03[B]).

This suggests that general partners in limited partnerships should have corporate-type fiduciary duties, while limited partners should not. Indeed, several courts do recognize such duties.[142] But the analogy is not complete.

In some respects, fiduciary duties may not be as important in limited partnerships as in corporations. As in general partnerships with managing partners, limited partnerships may differ from corporations in that they are managed by owner-managers who are personally liable for the debts of the business, and therefore motivated by constraints other than fiduciary duties to act in the firm's interests. Limited partners also normally have the right to exit at any time and to sell their shares to the firm.

In other respects, however, fiduciary duties may be more important in limited partnerships than corporations. Limited partners are locked out of management by the "control rule" (*see* Section 6.03[B]) and usually cannot sell their shares into an efficient market. Moreover, the general partners' personal liability may itself increase agency costs, since it gives the general partners an incentive to avoid business risks the limited partners would willingly take.

Just as it is not clear that general partners should be subject to fiduciary duties, it is not clear that limited partners should be free of them. The differing interests of limited and general partners due to limited liability can be just as much a problem for the general partners as for the limited partners. Perhaps limited partners should have a duty not to abuse their limited veto or removal power by selfishly acting contrary to the general partners' interests. For example, limited partners of financially strapped firms could block asset sales that would forestall bankruptcy and a large personal liability for the general partner, preferring to "roll the dice" with their own limited stakes in the firm. The potential conflict of interest between general partners and limited partners is illustrated by *KE Property Management Inc. v. 275 Madison Management Corp.*,[143] which held that a limited partner may have a fiduciary duty to the extent that he exercises the power to remove a general partner. The court held that the duty was not breached in that case because, regardless of the limited partner's selfish motive to prevent bankruptcy filing, the agreement permitted removal for cause. On the other hand, since limited partners have no managerial responsibilities, any duties of limited partners are those of *owners* and are not fiduciary in character. The parties could protect against opportunistic use of the limited partners' veto power by specific contractual provisions.

[C] Limited Liability Companies

As discussed in Section 6.04[B], LLCs can be either centrally managed or managed directly by owners, but most LLC statutes provide by default for the latter form of

---

[142] Some cases have applied the duties of corporate directors to general partners in limited partnerships. *See Wyler v. Feuer*, 85 Cal. App. 3d 392, 149 Cal. Rptr. 626 (1979); *Trustees of General Electric Pension Trust v. Levenson*, 1992 WL 41820, 18 DEL. J. CORP. L. 364 (Del. Ch. 1992) (no gross negligence for breach of duty of care, applying corporate director standard).

[143] 1993 WL 285900, 19 DEL. J. CORP. L. 805 (Del. Ch. 1993).

management as a default. A *member-managed* LLC closely resembles a partnership, so perhaps partnership fiduciary rules should apply. *Compare* ULLCA § 409, RUPA § 404, and UPA § 21.

A *manager-managed* LLC resembles a limited partnership except that, unlike general partners in limited partnerships, the LLC managers have default limited liability. Should managers of centrally managed LLCs be treated like corporate managers, general partners of limited partnerships, or managing general partners of general partnerships, limited partners, or none of the above? While the partnership-type rule in the Uniform Act also applies to managers of manager-managed firms, many LLC statutes include corporate-director-style duties for LLC managers (*see* **Ribstein & Keatinge**). Which approach is appropriate? Members of centrally managed LLCs arguably should not have the sort of corporate-type fiduciary duties discussed in this Chapter. Unlike corporations and limited partnerships, there is likely to be a wide variety of types of management, ranging from corporate-style boards to significant owner retention of control. Also, like limited and general partners, but unlike corporate shareholders, LLC owners normally have a right to a buyout but no ability to sell their shares into an efficient market (*see* Section 6.04[C]-[D]). Finally, LLC owners do not have the same type of conflict of interest arising out of limited and personal liability that may exist between limited and general partners.

QUESTION

Should general partners in limited liability partnerships (*see* Section 6.05) be subject to the same duties as general partners in non-LLP partnerships?

REFERENCES

Bromberg & Ribstein, BROMBERG & RIBSTEIN ON PARTNERSHIP § 6.07 (1988 & Supp.).

Dickerson, *Is It Appropriate to Appropriate Corporate Concepts: Fiduciary Duties and the Revised Uniform Partnership Act*, 64 U. COLO. L. REV. 111 (1993).

Ribstein, *Fiduciary Duty Contracts in Unincorporated Firms*, 54 WASH. & LEE L. REV. 537 (1997).

Ribstein, *Limited Partnerships Revisited*, 67 U. CIN. L. REV. 953 (1999).

Ribstein, *The Revised Uniform Partnership Act: Not Ready for Prime Time*, 45 BUS. LAW. 49 (1993).

Ribstein & Keatinge, RIBSTEIN & KEATINGE ON LIMITED LIABILITY COMPANIES, Chap. 9 (1992 & Supp.)

Vestal, *Fundamental Contractarian Error in the Revised Uniform Partnership Act of 1992*, 73 B.U. L. REV. 523 (1993).

§ 9.09 Opting Out of Fiduciary Duties

So far this Chapter has focused on "standard form" fiduciary duties supplied by case and statutory law. This Section discusses the extent to which corporate shareholders and other owners of firms can, and should be able to, "opt out" of fiduciary duties. This issue has been made prominent by the "opt-out" type statutes passed in response to the *Van Gorkom* case (*see* Section 9.03[C]). Subsections [A]-[C] consider some general policy considerations relating to opt-out, while the remainder of this Section evaluates specific statutory provisions on opt-out.

[A] Policy Considerations: Closely Held Firms

Is there any reason not to enforce waivers of fiduciary duties in closely held general partnerships, corporations and limited liability companies in which investors often have negotiated and explicitly agreed to the term? Waivers may be particularly valuable in closely held firms. A duty of care may be unnecessary to ensure careful conduct from co-owners who have their wealth on the line, and strictly requiring disinterested director or shareholder approval could hamstring governance where all managers and shareholders are closely connected with each other. In any event, even if a legislature or court disagrees with the contract, is there any reason why the parties to this sort of contract need extra protection from unconscionable clauses that does not apply to parties to other types of business arrangements?

One argument for refusing to enforce the contract in this situation is that the parties to a long-term business association cannot foresee at the time of contracting all of the possible applications of the contract. Fiduciary duties are a mechanism for dealing with the unexpected (see the discussion of "bounded rationality" in Section 1.02[C]). But it does not necessarily follow that fiduciary duties belong in *every* long-term contract. Because costs of fiduciary duties may be just as hard to anticipate as benefits, the parties might prefer to substitute other mechanisms to deal with the unexpected, such as voting rights or outside auditors.

Another argument for mandatory fiduciary duties in both closely and publicly held firms is that allowing parties to contract out of fiduciary duties reduces beneficial trust in firms. For discussions and critiques of this argument, see **Blair & Stout**, **Mitchell**, and **Ribstein** (2001).

Even if parties to closely held firms need protection from fiduciary duty waivers, it follows from the discussion in Section 9.01[A] of the inherently contractual nature of fiduciary duties that prohibiting one specific type of contract clause will not provide that protection because the parties can always contract for alternative mechanisms that achieve equivalent results. For example, a promoter who cannot effectively waive fiduciary duties can simply bargain for more compensation, for a type of clause that is not considered a fiduciary duty waiver, or for a non-"fiduciary" relationship such as debtor-creditor or franchisor-franchisee. Thus, limitations on fiduciary duty waivers in closely held firms may simply have the effect of forcing the parties to adopt business forms or contract terms they would not have chosen if the statute had not restricted contracting.

[B] Policy Considerations: Publicly Held Firms

Assuming waivers should be generally enforceable in closely held firms, is there some additional reason why they should not be enforced in publicly held firms? Consider the arguments below.

[1] Public Corporations as Adhesion Contracts

One argument is that the public corporation is not the product of one-on-one bargaining between shareholders and managers. Most public corporation shareholders have never read the charter or bylaws of their investments, and certainly would not know if these instruments contained an "opt out" provision. And even if investors did know what was in their "contracts," they must accept them in a lump, without any ability to negotiate individual terms.

Although these features make corporations look unlike "typical" contracts, the absence of individualized bargaining does not, itself, establish that fiduciary duties should be mandatory. Many transactions that are conventionally regarded as contracts are formed by one party's acceptance of standardized terms, such as sales warranties. Standardized terms often reduce transaction costs compared with customized terms by eliminating the need for costly bargaining and providing certainty and predictability.

A more serious concern is that investor ignorance of contractual provisions may permit managers to foist overly lenient terms on investors. Such concerns have given rise to regulation of product warranties, even though they are generally regarded as contractual in nature. But there is a significant difference between corporate securities and other types of contracts that have been regulated because of buyer ignorance. Public corporation securities are traded in the securities markets, to which the Efficient Markets Hypothesis (*see* Section 7.01[F]) applies. Information about corporate contract terms is therefore reflected in stock prices. As a result, even if managers succeed in foisting overly lenient terms on investors, investors are not harmed because stock prices adjust to reflect the impact of these terms.

Perhaps more importantly, this mechanism of stock price adjustment provides pressure for beneficial changes in contract terms. Any disparity between current market price and a higher price resulting from an "improved" contract provides a profit opportunity for a bidder for control and therefore threatens the job security of incumbent managers. Also, a stock price depressed by low investor expectations of future performance commensurately raises the firm's cost of capital, directly affecting the firm's ability to compete and therefore managers' power and compensation.

[2] The Efficient Securities Markets Do Not Protect Investors from Management Misconduct

Market efficiency is a potent argument favoring private ordering in the publicly held firm. Recognizing this, critics of the contract approach have made a number of arguments why the efficient securities markets do not adequately protect investors.

[a] Securities Markets Are Not Completely Efficient

Some economists have argued that stock prices are affected by "noise" rather than merely fundamental information about firms. Also, securities prices, like many other phenomena, may be "chaotic": Inexplicable patterns appear in long-term analysis of stock prices and seemingly insignificant events may have great consequences for stock prices. (For more discussion of these points, see § 7.01[F].) But even if securities markets are not completely efficient, the question remains whether the degree of inefficiency is sufficient to support mandatory corporate terms. Even if stock prices are somewhat "chaotic" and "noisy," they may contain information about firms' varying governance terms, including fiduciary duty opt outs.

[b] Expected Agency Costs Are Not Reflected in Share Price

Managers and other insiders know more about their firms than do outside shareholders. Most importantly, they know more than the shareholders about the likelihood that they will engage in discretionary behavior that harms shareholders. It follows that share prices will never accurately reflect expected agency costs—*i.e.*, that the market will undervalue firms with "good" managers (in which agency costs are low) and overvalue firms with "bad" managers (in which agency costs are high). As a result, managers will lack adequate incentives to be good, and some agency costs of "bad" firms will be borne by "good" firms.

Stock prices certainly do not reflect all potential agency costs. An efficient market is not a perfect predictor of corporate performance, but only the best available predictor of future events given available information. Therefore, even if the market cannot know whether a given executive is likely to take all the money and run to Brazil, it can assess the different probabilities of this resulting from weak or strong monitoring devices (such as outside boards and auditing), the reputation and track record of the firm's executives, and the presence or absence of "back-up" liability rules. A firm that hires shady characters as executives, puts stooges on its board, hires the managers' brothers-in-law as accountants, *and* waives fiduciary duties is unlikely to perform well on the securities market. Thus, a firm has some incentive to adopt an efficient mix of liability rules and constraints on management conduct, even if the market lacks full information about the propensity of managers to engage in behavior that harms shareholders. If it does not, the capital markets can reduce the capital under the managers' control by depressing the firm's stock price, and the control market can improve the firm's governance arrangement by throwing out the bums, stooges, and brothers-in-law. Moreover, "good" managers have incentives to inform, or in economic parlance, "signal," the market that they are not "bad" managers in order to avoid the punishment the market inflicts on "bad" managers,[144] thus ameliorating, to some extent, the informational problems that lead markets to overvalue "bad" firms and undervalue "good" firms.

[c] Governance Terms Are Not Reflected in Stock Prices

As the discussion in [a] makes clear, the "efficient market" argument against mandatory rules depends on governance terms being reflected in stock prices. Some studies cast doubt on whether this occurs. For instance, one study **(Weiss & White)** found no evidence of abnormal returns in a study of market price reactions to several significant Delaware Supreme Court fiduciary duty cases, while two others **(Janjigian & Bolster** and **Romano)** found that stock prices do not react adversely to the adoption of opt-out charter provisions.[145] On the other hand, another study **(Bradley & Schiapani)** found that enactment of Delaware G.C.L. § 102(b)(7), the "anti-*Van Gorkom*" provision, did affect the market prices of Delaware firms, although *Van Gorkom* itself did not.

While these studies arguably indicate that the intensity of fiduciary duties in a firm's governance contract—and more indirectly, governance provisions generally—are not reflected in stock prices, it is important to keep in mind the limitations on the studies. First, the studies attempt to compare firms that are affected by changes in Delaware law with those that are not. Not only are Delaware firms a significant portion of the market, but Delaware law is quickly followed in other jurisdictions. Therefore, the studies do not necessarily establish that the market would not react to governance changes in a single firm. Second, it may be very difficult to determine the period in which changes in the law affected stock prices, since the changes may have been anticipated even before they were announced. Therefore, the studies may simply have focused on the wrong period of time. Finally, common law fiduciary rules are inherently vague and carry several possible meanings. The same problem may not affect less ambiguous control and incentive mechanisms.

---

[144] Ross, *Disclosure Regulation in Financial Markets: Implications of Modern Finance Theory and Signaling Theory, in* ISSUES IN FINANCIAL REGULATION 177 (Edwards ed., 1979).

[145] Although Romano notes that stock prices of Delaware firms rose on the effective date of Delaware G.C.L. § 102(b)(7), she reports negative or insignificant stock price reactions on earlier dates when passage of the statute became likely, and cannot explain why the market would have taken so long to react.

[3] Shareholder Voting on Opt-Out Is Flawed

The discussion so far applies to the investor who has bought into the corporation with an opt-out provision already in place. What about those who are shareholders as of the time the corporation approves an opt-out provision? At first glance there doesn't seem to be a problem because the shareholders have an opportunity to vote on the opt-out.

There are, however, some potential problems with shareholder voting as a check on opt-out provisions that fail to advance shareholder interests. Managers who hold a majority of the stock may be able to impose unfair opt-outs on the minority. To be sure, this is an unusual situation in a publicly held firm. But even where managers do not own a majority of the stock, shareholder voting is arguably flawed because of investor apathy, conflicting interests of institutional investors, and management's ability to structure the vote so as obtain approval even of provisions that are not in the investors' interests (*see* Section 9.04[C]).

Mandatory rules obviously eliminate the problems associated with shareholder voting on opt-outs by committing the corporation to particular rules. But there may be less drastic solutions. Corporate charters could protect against wealth-decreasing opt-outs by, among other things, forbidding certain types of amendments, such as those involving opting out of particular fiduciary duties; special voting requirements, such as requiring votes in two or more succeeding years or forbidding agenda-manipulation tactics by managers; or giving shareholders the right to "cash out" of the corporation when opt-outs are approved over their objections. Such provisions would be priced in the market just as are other types of charter provisions.

[4] Optimal versus Complete Discipline of Managers

Commentators who favor mandatory fiduciary duties point out that the securities markets and contractual incentive and monitoring devices such as incentive compensation and outside directors do not completely prevent management misconduct. This is undoubtedly correct. But it makes sense to adopt monitoring and incentive devices, including fiduciary duties, only up to the point where an additional dollar spent on these devices produces equal or greater savings in terms of managerial disloyalty prevented. In other words, the goal is *optimal*, not *complete*, deterrence of management misconduct. Therefore, whether fiduciary duties should be mandatory depends not on the existence of gaps in other constraints on management, but on whether the parties to a corporation should be required to fill those gaps with fiduciary duties. The answer to this question depends on the other arguments discussed in this Section, particularly including whether the securities markets adequately discipline the parties' choice of contract terms.

[C] Policy Considerations: The Costs of Mandatory Rules

Even if it would be costly to allow firms to opt out of fiduciary duties, there is an additional question whether the costs of mandatory rules outweigh those of optional duties. First, it is unlikely that the rules discussed in this Chapter are suitable for *all* firms. For example, some firms may gain little from a duty of care. This is borne out by **Romano**'s finding that corporations gained little or nothing from duty-of-care litigation.

Second, even assuming that a perfect set of mandatory rules for all firms exists, courts and legislatures are unlikely to adopt them. The adversary system and *stare decisis* make it difficult for courts to formulate and promulgate general rules. Legislators are subject to interest group pressures, and public corporation shareholders are a relatively ineffective interest group. In any event, even mandatory rules formulated by all-wise and perfectly motivated public servants would still be unable to take into account differences among firms or react quickly to changing business conditions.

QUESTION

If there are costs associated with both mandatory and optional rules, and the evidence is unclear which regime is preferable, which regime should be adopted? In other words, who should have the burden of proof—proponents of mandatory rules, or those of optional rules?

[D] The Scope of Permissible Opt-Out

The following is a description and evaluation of some of the limitations on opting out of fiduciary duties including those in Del. G.C.L. § 102(b)(7); MBCA § 202(b)(4); ALI *Principles* § 7.19, and the opt-out statutes discussed in Section 9.03[C].

[1] Face-to-Face Contracting: Opt-Out in the Partnership and Close Corporation

UPA § 21 provides that a partner is accountable only for benefits "derived by him without the consent of the other partners." Courts have held that partners may effectively authorize self-interested conduct by provisions in the partnership agreement (*see* **Bromberg & Ribstein** §§ 6.07(h), 16.07(h)). For example, in *Singer v. Singer*,[146] the court upheld a partner's purchase of land within the area of the partnership's interest under the following provision in the partnership agreement:

> Each partner shall be free to enter into business and other transactions
> for his or her own separate individual account, even though such business or

---

[146] 634 P.2d 766 (Okla. App. 1981).

other transaction may be in conflict with and/or competition with the business of the partnership. Neither the partnership nor any individual member of this partnership shall be entitled to claim or receive any part of or interest in such transactions, it being the intention and agreement that any partner will be free to deal on his or her own account to the same extent and with the same force and effect as if he or she were not and never had been members of this partnership.[147]

Delaware has amended its limited partnership statute to broadly permit opting out of legal duties, explicitly including fiduciary duties.[148]

There are, however, limitations on opting out even in the partnership.[149] For example, in *Froemming v. Gate City Federal Savings & Loan Ass'n*,[150] the court applied general fiduciary duties to a limited partnership despite a provision in the partnership agreement permitting partners to engage in other business and to benefit from the partnership without accounting to the partnership. The court apparently was concerned that the provision was too open-ended—that is, it did not explicitly provide for any partner duties. Should the parties be able to contract out of *all* fiduciary duties? Alternatively, do the parties expect some fiduciary duty limitation even when they enter into an apparently complete waiver?

RUPA § 103(b)(3)-(5) limits the extent to which partners can opt out of fiduciary duties. This provision emphasizes the specificity of the opt-out.

[2] The Care/Loyalty Distinction

All of the opt-out provisions limit opting out of liability for self-dealing. The Delaware statute prohibits opt-out for breach of the duty of loyalty, acts not in good faith or involving intentional misconduct, or transactions from which the director received an "improper personal benefit."[151] Some states, including Georgia[152] and North Car-

---

[147] *See also U.S. West, Inc. v. Time Warner Inc.*, 1996 Del. Ch. LEXIS 55, 1996 WL 307445 (Del. Ch. 1996) (noting that the doctrine of corporate opportunity extends to partnership law, but stating that "partnerships are amenable to greater freedom contractually to shape the set of legal relationships that constitute the partnership than are corporations").

[148] *See* Del. Code Ann. tit. 6, § 17-1101(c)-(d) (1990 Cum. Supp.), discussed in **Ribstein** (1993). For cases applying this provision, see **Bromberg & Ribstein** §16.07(h)(5).

[149] *See* **Bromberg & Ribstein** §§ 6.07(h), 16.07(h).

[150] 822 F.2d 723 (8th Cir. 1986).

[151] *Emerald Partners v. Berlin*, 726 A.2d 1215, 1223-24 (Del. 1999), held that the burden of establishing good faith for purposes of coming within Delaware § 102(b)(7) is on "the party seeking the protection of the statute." *In re Frederick's of Hollywood, Inc. Shareholders Litigation,* 2000 Del. Ch. LEXIS 19, 2000 WL 130630 (Del. Ch., Jan. 31, 2000), held under this case that "where a complaint alleges actionable disloyalty the burden will shift to the defendants to show the immunizing effect of the charter provision, but where the complaint only alleges a breach of the duty of care, that claim may be dismissed at the pleading stage."

[152] Ga. Code Ann. § 14-2-202(b)(4).

olina,[153] permit exculpation for liability for breach of the duty of loyalty as long as the directors' conduct meets other standards, such as good faith or no improper personal benefit. ALI *Principles* § 7.19 and MBCA § 202(b)(4) refer to personal benefit rather than broadly to the duty of loyalty.

There is an obvious problem in interpreting statutes that preclude the taking of an "improper benefit" or a taking not in "good faith." ALI *Principles* § 5.09 clarifies the extent to which the corporation can prevent insider transactions from being "improper." Section 5.09 effectuates a charter or bylaw provision or other "standard of the corporation" that was approved by disinterested directors or disinterested shareholders and that authorizes certain "specified types" of transactions that are likely to "recur in the ordinary course of business of the corporation." Transactions under such a provision are treated as if they were approved in advance by disinterested shareholders or directors. While § 5.09 does not let the corporation generally authorize insiders to take corporate opportunities or to compete with the corporation, the firm can "define" its business so that certain business activities outside the definition would not be corporate opportunities or competition. Along the same lines, Del. G.C.L. § 122(17) provides that any corporation may "[r]enounce, in its certificate of incorporation or by action of its board of directors, any interest or expectancy of the corporation in, or in being offered an opportunity to participate in, specified business opportunities or specified classes or categories of business opportunities that are presented to the corporation or one or more of its officers, directors or stockholders."

Does it make sense to limit shareholders' power to opt out of self-dealing liability? Assuming there is some justification for the care-loyalty distinction in formulating the standard form rule (*see* Section 9.04[A]), should these distinctions carry over to limitations on the opt-out power? To put this another way, are market constraints on opt-out provisions likely to be less effective for opt-outs of self-dealing liability than for opt outs of due care liability?

Comment (d) to ALI *Principles* § 7.19 rationalizes the care-loyalty distinction concerning opt-out in this way:[154]

> If corporate managers were to ask shareholders to approve a charter provision that limits or exculpates them from liability for duty of loyalty violations, a fundamental problem of asymmetric information would arise because investors would face substantial uncertainty and could not accurately price the cost to them of this discretionary power. This same imbalance in information is not as likely to result from exculpatory provisions that reduce liability for duty of care violations because in any real world setting it is highly unlikely that corporate officials are negotiating for the right to be

---

[153] N.C. Gen. Stat. § 55-2-02(b)(3).

[154] Copyright © 1994 by the American Law Institute. Reprinted with the permission of the American Law Institute.

negligent. In part, this is because they themselves bear much of the loss from their own negligence.

Assuming there is an "asymmetric information" problem, does it justify limiting opt-out? Consider the following arguments. First, investors can judge the quality of bonding, monitoring or incentive devices that are in place even if they cannot know the insiders' intentions. This suggests that the market price will reflect the extent of the "asymmetry" problem. And even if the market price does not adjust accurately in all cases, there is no reason to assume that it will under-discount the problem rather than over-discount. Second, investors' information problems can be mitigated through monitoring devices such as outside directors and auditors and through "good" managers' incentives to inform the market that they are not "bad" in order to avoid the punishment the market inflicts on "bad" managers. Thus, perhaps the parties should be permitted to decide on the mix between fiduciary duties and other constraints on management, even though they lack perfect information about the propensity of managers to engage in self dealing.

[3] Specific versus General Opt-Outs

The cases have distinguished between specific opt-outs and general opt-outs, enforcing the former but not always the latter. Similarly, RUPA § 103(b)(3) permits opting out of the duty of loyalty only for "specific types or categories of activities." Some arguments which have already been discussed bear on the "specific/general" distinction. For example, it has been suggested that shareholders cannot foresee the effect of broad waivers (*see* Section 9.09[A]) and that the stock market cannot "price" a general waiver (*see* Section 9.09[B][2]).

Another argument against enforcing general opt-outs is that shareholders might not expect the provision to be interpreted literally. Surely they did not agree to let insiders appropriate all of the assets of the company. Therefore, because the provision is ambiguous, the courts apply standard form limitations on insider conduct. But this may not be a correct reading of the parties' intent. Perhaps the owners really do intend the opt-out literally, at least for all but the most egregious misconduct, and assume that non-judicial constraints (*i.e.*, implicit bargains) will be effective and cheaper than fiduciary duties.

[4] Damages versus Injunctive Relief

Neither damage-limiting provisions like ALI *Principles* § 7.19 nor Delaware-type opt-out statutes permit opting out of fiduciary *duties*, as distinguished from personal liability. Thus, a court could still enjoin a transaction notwithstanding the existence of an opt-out provision. Does this distinction make sense? If a firm may opt out of personal liability where the costs exceed the benefits for that firm, why not permit opt-out of the duties themselves on the same basis? Is market discipline of opt-out provisions likely to be less where the provision concerns the basic duty than where it concerns personal liability?

[5] Other Limits on Opt-Out

ALI *Principles* § 7.19(3) prevents opting out of liability for conduct that "consti-tute[s] a sustained and unexcused pattern of inattention that amounted to an abdication of the defendant's duty to the corporation." What explains this limitation? Why shouldn't a corporation be able to hire a person to be a nominal or figurehead director, as long as the director's status was fully disclosed and agreed to by the shareholders? *See* Problem 2 at the end of Section 9.02.

Delaware G.C.L. § 102(b)(7)(ii), MBCA § 202(b)(4) and ALI *Principles* § 7.19(1) prevent exculpation for knowing violations of law. Thus, shareholders could not autho-rize managers to engage in profit-maximizing but illegal conduct. *See* Note 8 following *Eisner* in Section 9.03[A]. This limitation seems logical once it is recognized that a function of a shareholders' suit based on illegal board actions is to police conduct that injures non-shareholders, who do not have a vote on the opt-out provision. The problem with this explanation is that a waiver of a fiduciary duty action affects only remedies sought on behalf of the shareholders, not those sought on behalf of injured third parties. Moreover, in many states illegal management actions do not give rise to damages if the profits from the illegality outweighed the cost. So the end result of suits based on ille-gal conduct may be nothing more than costly litigation. This suggests that shareholders should be able to enter into an agreement that would preclude such suits.

Many statutes, including the Delaware, ALI and MBCA provisions, do not permit exculpation of intentional or reckless misconduct. MBCA § 202(b)(4) refers to "inten-tional infliction of harm" and ALI *Principles* § 7.19(2) refers to acts the director or offi-cer "was aware . . . created an unjustified risk of serious injury to the corporation." This "catch-all" sort of exception seems unremarkable. But note the problems, discussed in Section 9.03[C], of defining the scope of the exception to clearly exclude merely neg-ligent conduct.

[E] The Role of Statutory Authorization

ALI *Principles* § 7.19 would let a corporation adopt the provision even in the absence of statutory authorization, presumably because it merely codifies current law. This raises the question whether Del. G.C.L. § 102(b)(7) was necessary. There is some question whether a provision that went further than ALI § 7.19, particularly regarding opting out of the duty of loyalty, would be consistent with prior law. Should statutory authorization be sufficient to validate such provisions? Does prior law embody the par-ties' agreement, so that any statutory change applying to existing firms would retroac-tively change the parties' contract?

PROBLEMS

(1) Suppose in the situation in the *Lewis* case, Section 9.04[B][1], you were Leon Sr.'s attorney, and he consulted you in 1962 concerning the transfer of SLE shares to his children. What corporate agreements would best effectuate the expectations of Lewis, Sr. at this time concerning the governance of LGT and SLE? Would such agreements be enforceable under the law discussed in Section 9.09[D]?

(2) Suppose you represent the Horns in the situation in *Burg v. Horn*, Section 9.06. They are about to enter into the arrangement with Lillian Burg that was involved in that case, but they would like to make sure that the arrangement does not prevent them from pursuing interests outside their dealings with Burg. What agreements or charter or bylaw provisions would you draft? Keep in mind that you must secure Burg's consent to the provision. Is the provision excerpted from the *Singer* case discussed above in Section 9.09[D] a useful form? Would it be enforceable in Delaware?

REFERENCES

Black, *Is Corporate Law Trivial?: A Political And Economic Analysis*, 84 Nw. U. L. Rev. 542 (1990).

Blair & Stout, *Trust, Trustworthiness, and the Behavioral Foundations of Corporate Law*, 149 U. Pa. L. Rev. 1735 (2001).

Bradley & Schiapani, *The Relevance of the Duty of Care Standard in Corporate Governance: An Analysis of the* Trans Union *Decision and Subsequent Delaware Legislation*, 75 Iowa L. Rev. 1 (1989).

Bratton, *The New Economic Theory of the Firm: Critical Perspectives From History, II*, 41 Stan. L. Rev. 1471 (1989).

Bromberg & Ribstein, Bromberg & Ribstein on Partnership.

Brudney, *Corporate Governance, Agency Costs, and the Rhetoric of Contract*, 85 Colum. L. Rev. 1403 (1985).

Butler & Ribstein, *Opting Out of Fiduciary Duties—A Response to the Anti-Contractarians*, 65 Wash. L. Rev. 1 (1990).

Carney, *The ALI's Corporate Governance Project: The Death of Property Rights?*, 61 Geo. Wash. L. Rev. 898 (1993).

Coffee, *No Exit?: Opting Out, The Contractual Theory of the Corporation, and the Special Case of Remedies*, 53 Brook. L. Rev. 919 (1988).

Cox, *Compensation, Deterrence, and the Market as Boundaries for Derivative Suit Procedures*, 52 Geo. Wash. L. Rev. 745 (1985).

DeMott, *Fiduciary Obligation under Intellectual Siege: Contemporary Challenges to the Duty to be Loyal*, 30 Osgoode Hall L.J. 471 (1992).

Easterbrook & Fischel, *Contract and Fiduciary Duty*, 36 J.L. & Econ. 425 (1993).

Easterbrook & Fischel, The Economic Structure of Corporate Law, Chap. 1 (1991).

Eisenberg, *The Structure of Corporation Law*, 89 Colum. L. Rev. 1461 (1989).

Gordon, *The Mandatory Structure of Corporate Law*, 89 Colum. L. Rev. 1599 (1989).

Janjigian & Bolster, *The Elimination of Director Liability and Stockholder Returns: An Empirical Investigation*, 13 J. Fin. Res. 53 (1990).

McChesney, *Economics, Law, and Science in the Corporate Field: A Critique of Eisenberg*, 89 Colum. L. Rev. 1530 (1989).

Mitchell, *Trust. Contract. Process*, in PROGRESSIVE CORPORATE LAW 185 (Mitchell, ed., 1995).

Ribstein, *Law v. Trust,* 81 B.U. L. REV. 553 (2001).

Ribstein, *Fiduciary Duty Contracts in Unincorporated Firms,* 54 WASH. & LEE L. REV. 537 (1997).

Ribstein, *The Revised Uniform Partnership Act: Not Ready for Prime Time*, 49 BUS. LAW. 45 (1993).

Ribstein, *Unlimited Contracting in the Delaware Limited Partnership and Its Implications for Corporate Law*, 16 J. CORP. L. 299 (1991).

Romano, *Corporate Governance and the Aftermath of the Insurance Crisis, in* TORT LAW AND THE PUBLIC INTEREST: COMPETITION, INNOVATION, AND CONSUMER WELFARE (P. Schuck, ed. 1990), *extended and revised in* Romano, *Corporate Governance in the Aftermath of the Insurance Crisis*, 39 EMORY L.J. 1155 (1990).

Romano, *Answering the Wrong Question: The Tenuous Case for Mandatory Corporate Laws*, 89 COLUM. L. REV. 1599 (1989).

Weiss & White, *Of Econometrics and Indeterminacy: A Study of Investors' Reactions to "Changes" in Corporate Law*, 75 CAL. L. REV. 551 (1987).

CHAPTER 10

Corporate Litigation: Shareholder Suits

This Chapter discusses the procedural aspects of suits by corporate shareholders. It emphasizes the rules regarding suits to enforce the duties of directors, officers, and controlling shareholders. As will become clear in this Chapter, issues in shareholder suits are closely related to other matters that are central to the study of business associations, such as the allocation of management and control rights between shareholders and managers and fiduciary duties.

§ 10.01 Introduction to Shareholder Litigation

Shareholders can bring both "direct" actions, which enforce causes of action that are personal to the shareholders, and "derivative" actions which enforce corporate rights. For example, as discussed in more detail in Section 10.02, shareholders would generally bring a "derivative" action against a director who allegedly reaped excessive profits in a transaction with the corporation, since the primary harm in such a case is suffered by the corporation through a depletion of its assets, and a "direct" action for damages they suffered as a result of buying stock at too high a price due to a misleading prospectus. This Section provides a brief overview of each of these types of shareholder litigation. It also provides a survey of the policy debate connected with derivative actions—*i.e.*, whether individual shareholders should be allowed to control the assertion of corporate (as opposed to personal) rights.

[A] Direct Actions

In direct actions, the plaintiff shareholders assert their own rights against defendants who may include the corporation itself, the corporation's officers and directors, or any other person whose conduct allegedly harmed the plaintiff. A direct action may be brought by one or a few individually named shareholders on their own behalf or as a class action on behalf of all similarly situated shareholders. (Class actions, by permitting prosecution of many claims by the same lawyer in the same proceeding, facilitate a remedy for claims that might not have been worth pursuing on an individual basis.) If brought as a class action, special procedural rules will apply to the case largely to ensure that the class representatives act in the interests of the class members.

For instance, under Rule 23 of the Federal Rules of Civil Procedure, which governs class actions brought in federal courts and which serves as the model for many state class action statutes, the court must determine whether a complaint brought as a class action is appropriate for class adjudication and is likely to be capably prosecuted by the plaintiff-representative. In addition, in a so-called "common questions" class action under Rule 23(b)(3) (*i.e.*, class actions based upon the existence of questions of law or fact common to the members of the class), the court must give class members an opportunity to opt out of the action. Once commenced, class actions may not be settled without notice to the class and court approval. In addition, any judgment in the case binds all members of the class (except those who opted out).

[B] Derivative Suits

In a derivative suit, the nominal plaintiff shareholder sues on a right derived from the corporation. Derivative suits are generally brought against the corporation's officers or directors or other parties whose conduct allegedly harmed the corporation. The corporation is made a party to the suit so that it may be bound by the judgment. Although derivative suits assert corporate rights, the corporation is normally aligned as a party defendant because the suit is generally prosecuted over the opposition of the corporation's management. Like direct suits that are brought as class actions, derivative suits are subject to a number of procedural rules, discussed throughout this Chapter, which are designed to ensure that the nominal plaintiff shareholder acts in the interest of shareholders as a group.

In a successful derivative suit, damages are paid to the corporation, not the shareholders. Even though the right being asserted in a derivative suit "belongs" to the corporation, it is not immediately obvious why the recovery is not paid to the shareholders as the corporation's owners. One reason is that, if the corporation has been injured, awarding recovery only to the shareholders would bypass the creditors, whose securities have been devalued by the breach. Indeed, if the corporate assets have been severely depleted, giving the damages directly to the shareholders could have the same effect as an illegal dividend by an insolvent corporation. On the other hand, applying this theory to a solvent corporation would seem to be inconsistent with the theory that the directors owe fiduciary duties only to shareholders and not to creditors.

A second rationale for the peculiar aspect of the derivative suit which gives the damages to the corporation rather than directly to the shareholders (*i.e.*, the nominal plaintiff) is that this avoids the problems involved in fashioning direct relief to shareholders. Public corporation shares trade at various times before or after disclosure of the wrong at prices that may or may not reflect the full extent of the loss or the probability of recovering damages. If shareholders were to be paid directly, the court would have to undertake the difficult task of determining which shareholders were harmed by the wrong and by how much. The derivative remedy avoids these complications.

[C] The Policy Debate on Derivative Suits

The merits and drawbacks of allowing individual shareholders to take control of corporate litigation in derivative suits have been hotly debated in recent years, particularly in connection with the American Law Institute Corporate Governance project. This subsection reviews some of the arguments for and against derivative suits.

[1] The Benefits of Derivative Suits

The main benefit of the derivative suit is that it provides a legal remedy for breaches of fiduciary duty by corporate managers: since managers are presumably reluctant to sue themselves on the corporation's behalf, the corporation's rights against managers may only be asserted if individual shareholders are allowed to take control of corporate litigation. On the other hand, as noted above in Section 9.01[B], corporate managers are constrained to act consistently with shareholder interests by devices other than legally enforceable fiduciary duties. Thus, assuming these other devices work well, the benefits of derivative litigation may not be that great.

[2] Costs of Derivative Suits

Even if derivative suits serve a useful purpose, they are also potentially costly because shareholder plaintiffs can be expected to commence some "bad" derivative suits (often referred to generically as "strike" suits), where the costs to the corporation exceed the benefits. Some of the reasons for this are examined below.

First, even a perfectly motivated plaintiff often lacks detailed information about the underlying transaction. For instance, plaintiffs sometimes sue solely on the basis of a Wall Street Journal story reporting difficulties at a company.[1]

Second, derivative plaintiffs often are not perfectly motivated. Although the interests of individual shareholders will generally be aligned with those of the rest of the class, there may be cases where derivative plaintiffs have private interests that diverge from those of the non-plaintiff shareholders. In this regard, many derivative suits are facially suspect because they are brought by shareholders who own only a few shares in the company and therefore cannot possibly gain enough from a derivative recovery to offset their investment in the suit. Indeed, hundreds of suits have been brought by one person—Harry Lewis.[2] One writer has wryly commented that "[o]ne might well wonder about Mr. Lewis's technique for portfolio selection."[3]

---

[1]   See, e.g., Blumenthal v. Teets, 155 Ariz. 123, 745 P.2d 181 (Ariz. Ct. App. 1987) (suit against corporate directors for negligently permitting loans by a subsidiary was based only on Wall Street Journal article about the loans, that contained no information about director negligence).

[2]   See Branson, The American Law Institute Principles of Corporate Governance and the Derivative Action: A View from the Other Side, 43 WASH. & LEE L. REV. 399, 418, n.108 (1986).

[3]   DeMott, Demand in Derivative Actions: Problems of Interpretation and Function, 19 U.C. DAVIS L. REV. 461, 495, n.154 (1986).

Third, even if derivative plaintiffs are perfectly motivated, their attorneys might not be. The attorney can gain individually and handsomely from a payment in the form of a fee award if the derivative suit results in a judgment for the plaintiffs or if the defendants agree to a settlement that provides for such an award. But if the attorney gains only from a successful outcome in a derivative suit, why would the prospect of a fee award result in non-meritorious lawsuits? One possible reason is that insider defendants may be willing to settle even frivolous claims in order to avoid the costs involved with getting the derivative litigation dismissed. But since pursuing litigation is also quite expensive for plaintiffs, it is not clear why defendants do not pursue a policy of vigorous resistance in order to deter future "strike" suits. Another reason that insider defendants may agree to settle non-meritorious suits is that they may have more to lose than plaintiffs from litigating: directors are exposed to substantial personal liability and embarrassment should their defense prove unsuccessful, while plaintiffs' lawyers can afford to press many ultimately losing causes by holding a diversified portfolio of suits.

The prospect that defendants will agree to settle non-meritorious suits is even greater in the context of derivative suits than it is in the context of ordinary class actions. While a class action attorney must at least establish a particular fund for the plaintiffs for a fee award to be approved, that is not necessarily so in a derivative suit: since such a suit is brought for the "corporation," the benefit which justifies the fee may be in the form of a mostly cosmetic change in corporate governance. Moreover, under most corporate statutes, derivative defendants are eligible for indemnification for expenses, such as attorneys' fees (though generally not for amounts paid in settlement) if they settle, but not if adjudged liable by a court (*see* Section 10.12). Putting these factors together, the incentives of derivative defendants to settle even non-meritorious suits before trial (and therefore the incentives of derivative attorneys to bring such cases in the first instance) are likely to be great.

The divergence of interests between plaintiff's counsel and shareholders involves not only the risk of "strike" suits discussed above, but also the risk of under prosecution of meritorious claims. Plaintiff's attorneys, who are paid on a contingency basis, have an incentive to accept relatively small settlements on their client's behalf in order to avoid the risk of not receiving any compensation if the defendants ultimately prevail. Ways to motivate plaintiff's counsel to act in the shareholders' interests are discussed in Section 10.11.

[D] Overview of Chapter

Many of the rules regarding derivative suits can best be understood in light of the above discussion. For instance, much of the law relating to derivative suits reflects a search for effective screening devices that block "bad" derivative suits while letting through "good" suits, and for ways to align the interests of plaintiff and plaintiff's counsel with those of the shareholders. Therefore, throughout the Chapter, you should keep in mind the following two questions. First, how well do the rules discussed operate to minimize the costs and maximize the benefits of derivative suits and, second, is the game worth the candle? In other words, would the best approach be simply to scrap the derivative remedy and rely on other market and internal monitoring devices, such as the control market and manager prosecution of corporate remedies for breach of fiduciary duty, to deter managerial misconduct?

REFERENCES

Coffee, *Litigation and Corporate Governance: An Essay on Steering Between Scylla and Charybdis*, 52 GEO. WASH. L. REV. 789 (1984).

Coffee & Schwartz, *The Survival of the Derivative Suit: An Evaluation and a Proposal for Legislative Reform*, 81 COLUM. L. REV. 261 (1981).

Cox, *Compensation, Deterrence, and the Market*, 52 GEO. WASH. L. REV. 745 (1984).

Fischel & Bradley, *The Role of Liability Rules and the Derivative Suit in Corporate Law: A Theoretical and Empirical Analysis*, 71 CORNELL L. REV. 261 (1986).

§ 10.02 Characterizing the Action: Derivative or Direct?

The rules on derivative suits discussed in this Chapter are designed to deal with suits in which shareholder plaintiffs assert corporate, rather than personal, rights. But it is sometimes not clear whether a particular right is a corporate right that must be pursued in a derivative action or a personal right that can be pursued directly (*i.e.*, without compliance with the special rules that apply to derivative litigation). One way to distinguish corporate claims from personal claims is to ask whether the special rules that apply to derivative suits make sense in the context of the particular claim. For instance, is the case one in which it makes sense to require the shareholder to make a demand on the board before proceeding or one where any recovery should be paid to the corporation rather than the shareholders? Do the characterization rules in the following cases reflect these considerations?

ROSE v. SCHANTZ
Wisconsin Supreme Court
56 Wis. 2d 222, 201 N.W.2d 593 (1972)

This is an appeal from an order overruling defendants-appellants' demurrer to the complaint. Plaintiff-respondent, Robert H. Rose, a stockholder in U.S. Controls Corporation, commenced this action on December 30, 1970. The complaint alleged two causes of action: one, a stockholder's derivative action brought on behalf of the corporation; the other, a direct action brought in plaintiff's own behalf as a stockholder.

Plaintiff alleged that defendants Schantz and Nemmers, as officers and directors, threatened to act in violation of their duties as such, and sought an injunction prohibiting the threatened acts. . . . The complaint states that the defendants threatened to pay corporate obligations before they became due, redeem stock in the corporation, and allow defendant Schantz to resign as president of the corporation. This is alleged to be part of a scheme or plan to deplete the corporation of its cash reserves, thereby rendering it incapable of continuing in business, and enabling defendant Schantz to successfully engage in a competing business.

The trial court issued an order restraining defendants from paying debentures before due, from redeeming the company's stock, and from releasing the president of the company, Schantz, from any liability he may have to the corporation. . . .

* * *

Robert W. HANSEN, Justice.

The demurrer here challenged: (1) The derivative cause of action; (2) the direct stockholder action; and (3) the joinder of causes of actions and parties. Each involves a separate area of inquiry, and will be so approached.

Derivative Action

We deal here with the statutory restrictions surrounding the bringing of stockholder's derivative actions. Particularly, we deal with sec. 180.405(1)(b), Stats., requiring in any such action that:

> (1) No action may be instituted or maintained in the right of any domestic or foreign corporation by the holder or holders of shares or of voting trust certificates representing shares of such corporation unless:
>
> * * *
>
> (b) The plaintiff alleges in the complaint with particularity his efforts to secure from the board of directors such action as he desires and alleges further that he has either informed the corporation or such board of directors in writing of the ultimate facts of each cause of action against each such defendant director or delivered to the corporation or such board of directors a true copy of the complaint which he proposes to file, and the reasons for his failure to obtain such action *or the reasons for not making such effort.* [Emphasis supplied.]
>
> * * *

We affirm the trial court's ruling that stating the reasons in the complaint for not making the effort to secure action or give notice is sufficient, on test by demurrer, as to compliance with the requirements of sec. 180.405(1)(b), Stats. The order overruling the demurrer to the derivative cause of action is affirmed.

Direct Cause of Action

This brings us to the challenge by demurrer to plaintiff's pleaded "alternative cause of action." This is a direct action brought on his own behalf as a stockholder.[4]

---

[4]   Plaintiff's amended complaint, as "ALTERNATE CAUSE OF ACTION," alleges:

THIRTEEN: Plaintiff re-alleges herein all those allegations contained in paragraphs 5 through 11 of the within complaint as though specifically set forth herein.

Appellants contend that this type of direct action is barred in Wisconsin. Respondents contend that, for a breach of fiduciary duty owed to shareholders, a direct action can be brought by a stockholder in this state. The answer is that in the present case the allegations made by this plaintiff and contained in this complaint do not support a direct action by a stockholder.

It is true the fiduciary duty of a director is owed to the individual stockholders as well as to the corporation. Directors in this state may not use their position of trust to further their private interests. Thus, where some individual right of a stockholder is being impaired by the improper acts of a director, the stockholder can bring a direct suit on his own behalf because it is his individual right that is being violated.

However, it is also true in this state that: "Rights of action accruing to a corporation belong to the corporation, and an action at law or in equity, cannot be maintained by the members as individuals . . . ."

So the question to be asked is, Whose right is sought to be enforced by the alternative cause of action? It appears to us that the only direct injury alleged is to the corporation. It is the corporation's funds that allegedly are to be used to pay off debts before due and to redeem stock. It is the corporation that allegedly will have its working capital impaired. It is the corporation that allegedly will no longer be able to stay in business. At least, the primary injury set forth is to the corporation, not the individual stockholder bringing the suit.

That such primary and direct injury to a corporation may have a subsequent impact on the value of the stockholders' shares is clear, but that is not enough to create a right to bring a direct, rather than derivative, action. Where the injury to the corporation is the primary injury, and any injury to stockholders secondary, it is the derivative action alone that can be brought and maintained. That is the general rule, and, if it were to be abandoned, there would be no reason left for the concept of derivative actions for the redress of wrongs to a corporation. Given an option to proceed by either direct or derivative action, stockholders could be expected to prefer the direct action. Statutes, like sec. 180.405, Stats. providing controls over derivative suits would wither on an unused vine. In the case before us, the plaintiff does not have either option or opportunity to pursue the direct action road to recovery. The demurrer to the alternative cause of action, the direct stockholders' action, should have been sustained. The order overruling this portion of defendant's demurrer must be reversed.

FOURTEEN: That as directors of the defendants, U.S. Controls Corporation, the defendants Spencer C. Schantz and Erwin Nemmers occupy a position of trust and confidence and stand in a fiduciary relationship toward the plaintiff who is a stockholder of the defendant, U.S. Controls Corporation.

FIFTEEN: That if allowed to act as has been previously alleged said defendants Spencer Schantz and Erwin Nemmers would thereby use their positions of trust and confidence to further their private interests, in conflict with a free and impartial discharge of their duties toward the plaintiff, and would thereby cause irreparable harm to the plaintiff, for which there would be no adequate remedy in law.

NOTES AND QUESTIONS

(1) **Plaintiffs' preferences for direct actions.** Why did the plaintiff in *Rose* seek to characterize his "alternate cause of action" as direct? One reason might be that he was seeking to avoid the possibility that he would be out of court for failing to make a demand on the board of directors in connection with his derivative count. As discussed in Section 10.05, the demand requirement is one of the devices developed for screening derivative actions in light of the special problems that arise when individual shareholders take control of corporate litigation. The directors' refusal to pursue a corporate claim in response to a demand may have the effect of blocking the shareholder from prosecuting the particular claim on the corporation's behalf.

(2) **The ALI *Principles*.** The ALI *Principles* are largely consistent with the approach taken by the court in *Rose*. Under ALI *Principles* § 7.01, a shareholder who can prevail "only by showing an injury or breach of duty to the corporation," must proceed derivatively, but a shareholder who can prevail without such a showing can proceed directly. Section 7.01(c) allows a shareholder to "commence and maintain direct and derivative actions simultaneously, and any special restrictions or defenses pertaining to the maintenance, settlement, or dismissal of either action should not apply to the other."[4]

(3) **The nature of the relief.** Should it be significant in terms of whether the action in *Rose* must be brought derivatively that plaintiff is seeking injunctive relief— *i.e.*, that he is not seeking compensation or the recovery of funds in which creditors should arguably share? Note that where the plaintiff shareholder is not seeking compensation or the recovery of funds, there is no danger that creditors of the firm will be bypassed if the shareholder plaintiff is permitted to proceed directly and relief is granted to the shareholders, rather than to the corporation.

(4) **Closely held versus publicly held firms.** Should it matter to characterization of the action whether the corporation is closely held? On the one hand, derivative recovery may matter more to creditors in a closely held than in a publicly held corporation because in close corporations, recovery is more likely to involve a significant percentage of assets. But direct recovery may matter more to close corporation shareholders who cannot easily "cash in" the award by selling stock.[5] In addition, direct recovery by shareholders of close corporations may be relatively easy to fashion since close corporation shareholders do not frequently transfer their interests in the firm out. Are these considerations adequately reflected in ALI *Principles* § 7.01(d)? That section provides as follows:

---

[4]   For a case considering the rules that apply when direct and derivative claims are combined by shareholders of closely held corporations, see *Wessin v. Archives Corp.*, 592 N.W.2d 460 (Minn. 1999) (special derivative pleading requirements applicable to derivative claims).

[5]   *See Crosby v. Beam*, 548 N.E.2d 217 (Ohio 1989) (citing the latter problem in allowing a claim for unreasonable salaries in a close corporation to be brought directly). *But see Weston v. Weston Paper Manufacturing Co.*, 658 N.E.2d 1058 (Ohio 1996) (refusing to extend *Crosby* to case involving privately held company that had about 100 shareholders and 361,533 outstanding shares).

In the case of a closely held corporation, the court in its discretion may treat an action raising derivative claims as a direct action, . . . if it finds that to do so will not (i) unfairly expose the corporation or the defendants to a multiplicity of actions, (ii) materially prejudice the interests of creditors of the corporation, or (iii) interfere with a fair distribution of the recovery among all interested persons.[6]

IN RE PAXSON COMMUNICATION CORPORATION SHAREHOLDERS LITIGATION
Delaware Chancery Court
2001 Del. Ch. LEXIS 95 (2001)

CHANDLER, Chancellor

This action arises out of the alleged rejection of a cash offer for Paxson Communications Corporation ("Pax" or the "Company") from Fox Network ("Fox") and the later acceptance by Pax of a series of agreements (the "NBC Transactions") with the National Broadcasting Company, Inc. ("NBC"). The plaintiffs allege that Fox made an all cash offer of $20 per share for Pax common stock (the "Fox Offer") that was summarily rejected by the directors and/or senior officers of Pax [(the "Individual Defendants")]. Shortly after the alleged Fox Offer, NBC invested $415 million in Pax in exchange for convertible preferred stock, certain warrants, and the right to purchase certain shares owned by Pax's controlling stockholder, Lowell W. Paxson.

Based on these events, the plaintiffs . . . assert a direct claim, arguing that the defendants abdicated their duty to evaluate and fairly respond to the Fox Offer with a view towards maximizing shareholder value and thereby depriving the Company's shareholders of a substantial premium that Fox (or perhaps another potential bidder) might have been willing to provide ("Claim I"). . . .

I. FACTUAL BACKGROUND

Defendant Pax is a Delaware corporation with its headquarters in West Palm Beach, Florida. Pax is a network television broadcasting company that owns and operates the largest group of broadcast television stations in the United States. Pax is a publicly traded company whose Class A common stock trades on the American Stock Exchange. Pax's capital structure also includes Class B common stock. The Class B stock, beneficially

---

[6] For cases applying the ALI's close corporation exception, see *G & N Aircraft, Inc. v. Boehm*, 703 N.E.2d 665 (Ind. App. 1998), *Orsi v. Sunshine Art Studios, Inc.*, 874 F. Supp. 471 (D. Mass. 1995), *Barth v. Barth*, 659 N.E.2d 559 (Ind. 1995), and *Richards v. Bryan*, 879 P.2d 638 (Kan. Ct. App. 1994). *See also Wulf v. Mackey*, 899 P.2d 755 (Or. App. 1995) (permitting minority shareholder in three-shareholder firm to bring breach of fiduciary duty claim directly even though the plaintiff did not suffer a personal harm distinct from the harm suffered by the corporation). For cases rejecting the ALI rule on direct actions by shareholders of close corporations, see *Landstrom v. Shaver*, 561 N.W.2d 1 (S.D. 1997); *Wessin v. Archives Corp*, 592 N.W.2d 460 (Minn. 1999); *Small v. Sussman*, 713 N.E.2d 1216 (Ill. App. 1999); *Simmons v. Miller*, 544 S.E.2d 666 (Va. 2001). For a case refusing to use Delaware's "special injury" rule to characterize all close corporation suits as direct, see *Bagdon v. Bridgestone/Firestone, Inc.*, 916 F.2d 379 (7th Cir. 1990).

owned entirely by Pax Chairman Lowell Paxson, is identical to the Class A stock except that each Class B share possesses ten votes per share. Class A shares possess one vote per share. . . . Mr. Paxson controls approximately 75% of Pax's voting power.

On or about August 9, 1999, Pax issued a press release announcing that it had formally retained Salomon Smith Barney ("Salomon") to explore potential strategic alternatives for the Company. . . .

The plaintiffs contend that shortly after issuing this press release, Pax received an unsolicited offer from Fox to acquire Pax for approximately $20.00 per share. They further allege that Pax responded to the Fox Offer with a counter-offer of $26.00 per share, but failed to enter into a genuine negotiating process with Fox aimed at selling the Company. As Pax common stock had traded between $6.00 and $17.4375 over the preceding twelve months, the plaintiffs conclude that this aborted attempt to sell Pax deprived them as Pax shareholders of a substantial premium.

On September 15, 1999, Pax entered into the NBC Transactions. These three agreements included an investment agreement (the "Investment Agreement"), a call option agreement (the "Call Agreement"), and a stockholder agreement (the "Stockholder Agreement"). In the aggregate, NBC and its affiliates paid approximately $415 million for the rights they received in the NBC transactions.

In the first of these transactions, the Investment Agreement, Pax agreed to: (i) sell 41,500 shares of newly created preferred stock in Pax to a wholly owned subsidiary of NBC ("NBC Sub I"), convertible at any time into 31,896,032 shares of Pax Class A common stock for an initial conversion price of $13.01 per share; (ii) issue a warrant ("Warrant A") to another wholly owned subsidiary of NBC ("NBC Sub II") to purchase up to 13,065,507 shares of Pax common stock at an exercise price of $12.60 per share; and (iii) issue a warrant ("Warrant B") to NBC Sub II to purchase another 18,966,620 shares of Pax common stock at an exercise price equal to the average closing prices of the Class A common stock for the 45 consecutive trading days before the warrant exercise date, subject to a minimum exercise price of $22.50 per share during the three years after September 15, 1999. Subject to certain conditions and limitations, Warrants A and B are exercisable for ten years from September 15, 1999.

Concurrently with the Investment Agreement, a wholly owned subsidiary of NBC entered into the Call Agreement with Lowell Paxson, personally, and certain entities controlled by him. By the terms of the Call Agreement, the NBC subsidiary was granted the right (the "Call Right") to purchase all, but not less than all, of Mr. Paxson's 8,311,639 shares of Pax's Class B common stock (the "Call Shares"). Under the Call Agreement, the NBC subsidiary may purchase the Call Shares at a price equal to the greater of (i) the average of the closing sale prices of the Class A common stock for the 45 consecutive trading days ending on the trading date immediately preceding the date of exercise of the Call Right; and (ii) $22.50 per share for any exercise of the Call Right within three years of September 15, 1999, or $20.00 per share if the Call Right is exercised thereafter.

The third of the NBC transactions, the Stockholder Agreement, provided, among other things, for NBC to have representation on the Pax Board if permitted by applicable law. The Stockholder Agreement also requires NBC's consent for Pax to take certain actions, including the adoption of a shareholder's rights plan, amendments to Pax's organizational documents, and issuances of stock or other securities.

If NBC converts the newly created preferred shares, exercises both warrants, and purchases Lowell Paxson's Class B shares, NBC would own approximately 49% of the equity in Pax and control almost 70% of its voting power.

II. ANALYSIS

* * *

B. Claim I

Claim I purports to be a class action claim for breach of fiduciary duty. The defendants insist that Claim I is in fact a derivative claim that can be brought only on the Company's behalf and, therefore, must be dismissed for failure to state a direct claim.

The Delaware courts are often faced with the complex task of distinguishing derivative claims from individual claims. The distinction between the rights of the corporation as opposed to the individual rights of shareholders is often "a narrow one" that can have extremely important consequences for litigation. Among these consequences are:

> the possible dismissal for an unjustified failure to demand that the board institute litigation; the general inability of a derivative plaintiff to engage in discovery relevant to the demand issue when dismissal on such grounds is sought; [and,] the ability of a special litigation committee of the board to terminate even a properly instituted derivative action as to which demand has been shown to be futile. [citation omitted]

Although there is no standard test that shall be mechanistically applied in all cases to determine whether a given claim is derivative or direct, probably the most-cited formulation is that of former Chancellor Brown in *Moran v. Household International, Inc.*:

> To set out an individual action, the plaintiff must allege either "an injury which is separate and distinct from that suffered by other shareholders," . . . or a wrong involving a contractual right of a shareholder, such as the right to vote, or to assert majority control, which exists independently of any right of the corporation.[11]

The Supreme Court has made clear that although Chancellor Brown's *Moran* formulation may serve as "a quite useful guide," that test is not conclusive. Rather, Delaware courts must ultimately look "to whether the plaintiff has alleged 'special' injury, in whatever form." [citation omitted]

In this case, the plaintiffs assert that they have suffered two distinct, direct injuries that each bestow standing on the plaintiffs to bring direct claims against the defendants. Plaintiffs point to the dilution of their ownership interest, earnings per share and voting power due to the effect of the NBC Transactions. Additionally, plaintiffs argue that the Pax Board's failure to pursue the Fox Offer in favor of the NBC Transactions resulted in the loss of the

---

[11]   490 A.2d 1059, 1070 (1985), *aff'd*, Del.Supr., 500 A.2d 1346 (1986) (quoting 12b FLETCHER CYCLOPEDIA OF CORPORATIONS, § 5921, at 452 (perm. ed., rev. vol. 1984)).

opportunity for the shareholders to receive optimum value for their investment in Pax. I address each of these contentions in turn.

First, the plaintiffs argue that "it is well-settled that equity dilution and diminution of one's voting power constitutes a direct injury to the shareholders and not the corporation." They contend that the NBC Transactions will dilute the equity and voting power of the plaintiff shareholders should NBC Sub I convert its 41,500 shares of preferred stock into 31,896,032 shares of common stock and NBC Sub II exercise its warrants to purchase a total of 32,032,127 shares of Pax common stock.

Plaintiffs point to . . . *In re Tri-Star Pictures, Inc. Litigation*[15] . . . to support the proposition that their dilution claim is direct rather than derivative. Their reliance on [Tri-Star], however, is misplaced. In *Tri-Star*, the plaintiffs, former stockholders of Tri-Star Pictures, Inc. ("Tri-Star"), challenged an assets for stock transaction between Tri-Star and Coca-Cola Company ("Coca-Cola"), a 36.8% stockholder of Tri-Star before the transaction. The complaint alleged that Coca-Cola had wrongfully manipulated the transaction to receive an excessive amount of Tri-Star shares in exchange for assets having a lower value. As a result of the transaction, Coca-Cola obtained an 80% stock interest in Tri-Star and the public shareholders, who had formerly owned 43.4% of the common equity, now owned only 20% of Tri-Star's equity. Because Coca-Cola, a significant stockholder of Tri-Star before the transaction, did not suffer a similar dilution of their percentage ownership or their voting power as compared to the plaintiffs, the Supreme Court held that the plaintiffs had suffered a special injury not shared equally by all shareholders. This rendered the plaintiffs' claims direct and not derivative in nature.

. . . *Tri-Star* . . . stand[s] for the proposition that dilution claims are individual in nature where a significant stockholder's interest is increased "at the sole expense of the minority." *Tri-Star* [has] no application, in my opinion, where the entity benefiting from the allegedly diluting transaction, NBC, is a third party rather than an existing significant or controlling stockholder. This identical distinction was also made by Vice Chancellor Jacobs in *Turner v. Bernstein*.[24] In that case, Vice Chancellor Jacobs noted that a claim of stock dilution and a corresponding reduction in a stockholder's voting power states a direct claim

> only in transactions where a significant stockholder sells its assets to the corporation in exchange for the corporation's stock, and influences the transaction terms so that the result is (i) a decrease (or "dilution") of the asset value and voting power of the stock held by the public stockholders and (ii) a corresponding increase (or benefit) to the shares held by the significant stockholder.

Under this principle, to the extent that any alleged decrease in the asset value and voting power of plaintiffs' shares of Pax results from the issuance of new equity to a third party (NBC), plaintiff's dilution theory as a basis for a direct claim fails and any individual claim for dilution must be dismissed. . . .

---

[15]   15 Del. Supr., 634 A.2d 319 (1993).

[24]   1999 Del. Ch. LEXIS 18, *44-45, Del. Ch., C.A. No. 16190, Jacobs, V.C. (Feb. 9, 1999). *See also In re Ply Gem Indus., Inc. Shareholders Litig.*, 2001 Del. Ch. LEXIS 84, Del. Ch., Consol. C.A. No. 15779-NC, Noble, V.C. (June 26, 2001).

In the plaintiffs' second attempt to support a direct claim, they allege that the defendants' failure to properly explore the Fox Offer, and later engage in serious negotiations with Fox, deprived the plaintiffs of the opportunity to realize the optimum value for their Pax stock. This, according to the plaintiffs, caused them to suffer individual injury. . . . This argument fails . . . .

. . . [T]he plaintiffs have failed to distinguish these facts from the numerous cases that have previously held that allegations that directors wrongfully failed to pursue business combinations are derivative in nature. Vice Chancellor Hartnett's opinion in *Sumers v. Beneficial Corporation* is representative of this line of authority.[30] In *Sumers*, the plaintiff alleged that directors of Beneficial Corporation announced that the corporation was for sale and then "summarily and arbitrarily rejected, without timely disclosure to the public shareholders," acquisition offers made at substantial premiums over the market price. The Court held that

> the complaint in the present suit . . . does not state any claim of breach of contractual rights, nor any facts which, if true, would constitute a special or individual cause of action. Plaintiffs' injury, if any, is the same as the injury to all other stockholders of [the corporation].

In the present case, the plaintiffs have represented to the Court that "the Class B stock is identical to the Class A stock except for voting power. The economic attributes are identical." They have failed to identify any significant difference between the facts in this matter and those found in the *Sumers* line of cases.

* * *

III. CONCLUSION

Based on all the foregoing reasons, I conclude that the complaint in the present suit alleges claims that are solely derivative in nature. Due to the plaintiffs' failure to comply with the demand requirements of Court of Chancery Rule 23.1, the complaint is therefore dismissed.

An Order has been entered consistent with the determination reached in this memorandum opinion.

NOTES AND QUESTIONS

(1) **The Delaware "special injury" test.** As discussed in *Paxson*, a claim must involve a "special injury" to the shareholders in order to be brought directly rather than derivatively. *In re Tri-Star Pictures, Inc. Litigation*,[7] summarized and discussed in *Paxson*, is one of the Delaware Supreme Court's most important and most controversial

---

[30] 1988 Del. Ch. LEXIS 35, Del. Ch., C.A. No. 8788, mem. op., Hartnett, V.C. (Mar. 9, 1988). [citations omitted]

[7] 634 A.2d 319 (Del. 1993).

applications of the "separate and distinct" prong of the special injury test. *Tri-Star* lets shareholders bring direct actions when they suffer "separate and distinct" from other shareholders, even when the principal injury is to the corporation (as was arguably the case in *Tri-Star*). Delaware courts have differed in their interpretation of *Tri-Star*, with some permitting direct actions whenever the injury suffered affects some shareholders but not others,[8] while others have limited *Tri-Star* to its facts (*i.e.*, cases where a significant shareholder sells its assets to the corporation in exchange for stock).[9]

(2) **Contractual rights of shareholders as special injuries.** The Delaware Supreme Court also applied its "special injury" test in *Lipton v. News International, PLC*,[10] where News sued because its takeover bid for control of Warner was thwarted by a transfer of shares to a party friendly to incumbent management, Chris-Craft. The court held that the suit was individual, stating:

> News has not suffered any distinct harm merely by virtue of its 7% stock interest in Warner, because as of the time of the complaint News had not indicated a desire to use its holdings to gain control of the corporation. However . . ., News alleges harm to one of its contractual rights. Specifically, it contends that the Warner/Chris-Craft exchange agreement violated its voting rights by securing for Warner management veto power over all shareholder actions subject to the 80% supermajority voting requirement. We find that this allegation constitutes special injury to News. . . .

When is a particular right "contractual" within the meaning of *Lipton*? Why are the voting rights that News sought to enforce any more "contractual" than the fiduciary duties at issue in *Rose*?[11]

(3) **Takeover defenses as special injuries.** As is noted in *Lipton*, a shareholder who owns a substantial block of stock which it intends to use to gain control may suffer a separate and distinct injury when corporate managers adopt takeover defenses aimed at entrenching themselves in office. Accordingly, potential bidders for control of Delaware corporations may challenge these takeover defenses in direct actions. Should

---

[8]   *See, e.g., Odyssey Partners v. Fleming Co.*, 1998 Del. Ch. LEXIS 40, 1998 WL 155543 (Del. Ch. 1998) (direct action permitted where controlling shareholder allegedly engaged in course of dealing that culminated with its purchase of all the corporation's assets at a foreclosure sale for inadequate value); *Barbieri v. Swing-N-Slide Corp.*, 21 DEL. J. CORP. L. 1073 (Del. Ch. 1996) (shareholders can sue directly where directors' privileged access to non-public information insulated them from injury suffered by other shareholders in connection with corporation's self tender).

[9]   *See, e.g., Turner v. Bernstein*, 1999 Del. Ch. LEXIS 18, 1999 WL 66532 (Del. Ch. 1999) (discussed in *Paxson*); *Katz v. Halperin*, 1996 Del. Ch. LEXIS 13, 1996 WL 66006 (Del. Ch. 1996) (distinguishing *Tri-Star* in case where controlling shareholder was alleged to have benefited from converting loan into corporate stock at an inadequate price).

[10]   514 A.2d 1075 (1986).

[11]   For another case dealing with "contractual" rights of shareholders, see *Siegman v. Palomar Medical Technologies, Inc.*, 1998 WL 118201 (Del. Ch. 1998) (claim by common stockholder that issuance of new *series* of preferred stock was not valid under charter provision, which only authorized the issuance of new *classes* of preferred stock, was individual in nature).

the nature of the bidder's injury be determinative? Or should it matter more that characterizing the action as "direct" allows bidders to escape having to make a demand on target management (*see* Section 10.04 below) during a fast-moving takeover battle? *In re Gaylord Container Corporation Shareholders Litigation*, which limits direct actions challenging takeover defenses to shareholders who are actively engaged in a battle for control,[12] notes that the direct-derivative distinction may not matter at the "pre-transaction" stage of litigation, when courts will ordinarily excuse demand, but may matter at the "post-transaction" stage, particularly if a merger or other transaction has denied shareholders of standing to maintain a derivative action (*see* Section 10.04).

§ 10.03 Standing

In order to minimize the risk of "strike" suits by nominal shareholders discussed in Section 10.01[C][2], courts and legislatures have imposed several roadblocks to screen out "bad" derivative suits. These roadblocks include standing rules which focus on certain attributes of plaintiffs that indicate they are perversely motivated to bring derivative suits that are against the shareholders' interests, requirements that plaintiffs post security at the outset of derivative litigation to cover defendants' reasonable costs and attorneys' fees, and requirements that plaintiffs serve a demand on the board of directors before commencing a derivative suit, requesting the board to sue on the corporation's behalf or take the other actions specified in the shareholder's complaint. Standing rules are discussed immediately below; statutes requiring security for expenses and demands on board of directors are discussed in Sections 10.04 and 10.05, respectively.

The rules discussed in this and ensuing sections are usually embodied in statutory provisions, one of the most important of which is Federal Rule 23.1. Federal Rule 23.1 governs derivative actions brought in federal court and serves as the model for several state provisions:

> **Rule 23.1 Derivative Actions by Shareholders.** In a derivative action brought by one or more shareholders or members to enforce a right of a corporation or of an unincorporated association, the corporation or association having failed to enforce a right which may properly be asserted by it, the complaint shall be verified and shall allege (1) that the plaintiff was a shareholder or member at the time of the transaction of which he complains or that his share or membership thereafter devolved on him by operation of law, and (2) that the action is not a collusive one to confer jurisdiction on a court of the United States which it would not otherwise have. The complaint shall also allege with particularity the efforts, if any, made by the plaintiff to obtain the action he desires from the directors or comparable authority and, if necessary, from the shareholders or members, and the reasons for his fail-

---

[12] 747 A.2d 71 (Del. Ch. 1999).

ure to obtain the action or for not making the effort. The derivative action may not be maintained if it appears that the plaintiff does not fairly and adequately represent the interests of the shareholders or members similarly situated in enforcing the right of the corporation or association. The action shall not be dismissed or compromised without the approval of the court, and notice of the proposed dismissal or compromise shall be given to shareholders or members in such manner as the court directs.

[A] Nature of Plaintiff's Interest

The statutes vary as to type of interest in the corporation that the plaintiff must hold to bring a derivative suit. Some statutes require the plaintiff to be a shareholder of record, others simply a "shareholder," and still others explicitly allow suits by those who have merely an equitable interest in the stock, including pledgees and trust beneficiaries. The courts generally permit suit by beneficial holders where the statute is ambiguous.[13] Neither the statutes nor the courts have permitted derivative suits by creditors, although a trustee in bankruptcy can bring corporate actions on behalf of creditors.[14] Some courts have permitted so-called "double derivative" suits—that is, derivative suits brought by a shareholder in a parent, or a parent of the parent, of a subject corporation.[15] Also, some jurisdictions let non-shareholder directors and officers bring derivative suits.

[B] Time of Shareholding

[1] Plaintiff Must Have Been a Shareholder at the Time of the Wrong ("Contemporaneous Shareholder Requirement")

Rule 23.1 includes the typical requirement that the plaintiff have been a shareholder "at the time of the transaction of which he complains . . . ." *See also* Del. G.C.L. § 327. This is the so-called "contemporaneous ownership" requirement which is believed to have originated in *Home Fire Insurance Co. v. Barber.*[16] The rule prevents

---

[13] *See, e.g., West Virginia v. Wilson*, 189 W. Va. 739, 434 S.E.2d 411 (1993) (holding under Delaware law that employee stock ownership plan participants were equitable shareholders who had standing to sue derivatively under Delaware law).

[14] *See* Note, *Creditors' Derivative Suits on Behalf of Solvent Corporations*, 88 YALE L.J. 1299 (1979).

[15] *See Brown v. Tenney*, 125 Ill. App. 2d 348, 532 N.E.2d 230 (1988); Painter, *Double Derivative Suits and Other Remedies with Regard to Damaged Subsidiaries*, 36 IND. L.J. 143, 147-49 (1961); Comment, *The Dilemma of the Double Derivative Suit*, 83 Nw. U. L. REV. 729 (1989).

[16] 67 Neb. 644, 93 N.W. 1024 (1903). For a more recent application of the rule, see *7547 Partners v. Beck*, 682 A.2d 160 (Del. 1996) (shareholder derivative suit alleging that directors of Boston Chicken, Inc. authorized initial public offering and simultaneous private placement at grossly inadequate price dismissed because the alleged wrongs took place at the time the directors agreed to the pricing, before the shareholder-plaintiffs acquired their shares in the IPO). For an important extension of the rule, see *Bangor Punta Operations, Inc. v. Bangor & Aroostook Railroad*, 417 U.S. 703

unjust enrichment by those who purchase the security at prices which already reflect the wrong, as well as the practice of buying and speculating in lawsuits. But these reasons do not justify barring suits by all non-contemporaneous owners. As a result, several statutory exceptions to the contemporaneous ownership rule have evolved.[17] First, because involuntary non-contemporaneous owners cannot be said to be speculating in litigation, Rule 23.1 and other statutes exempt from the contemporaneous ownership rule those whose shares "thereafter devolved on [them] by operation of law." Second, several cases broadly define "the transaction of which he claims" or similar statutory language and hold that plaintiff purchased while the transaction or wrong was "continuing." Third, some statutes attempt to define situations in which permitting suit by non-contemporaneous owners would not be inequitable.[18] ALI *Principles* § 7.02(a)(1) permits suit by non-contemporaneous owners as long as they purchased before the wrong was publicly disclosed or known to them, in which case the buyer's price presumably does not reflect the wrong and the shareholder is presumably not speculating in litigation.[19]

The "contemporaneous ownership" rule, however, does not usually stop shareholders who purchased after the wrong from sharing in the recovery. As a result, even with the "contemporaneous ownership" rule, latecomers to the corporation may receive a windfall. At the same time, shareholders *at the time of the wrong* who sold prior to judgment may go without a remedy since any recovery in a derivative action is paid to the corporation.[20] As discussed in Section 10.01, this anomaly casts doubt on the compensatory role of the derivative remedy.

(1974) (where controlling shareholder, who acquired 98.3% of corporation's stock from alleged wrongdoer at a fair price, would have been barred from maintaining a shareholder derivative action by "contemporaneous ownership" requirement, equitable principles prevent the controlling shareholder from causing the corporation, itself, to maintain the action). For a recent application and discussion of the *Bangor Punta* doctrine, see *Midland Food Services LLC v. Castle Hill Holdings V LLC*, 1999 Del. Ch. LEXIS 162, 1999 WL 550360 (Del. Ch., July 16, 1999).

[17] There have also been case law exceptions. See *Shaev v. Wyly*, 1998 WL 13858 (Del. Ch. 1998) (where plaintiff became shareholder of subsidiary only because parent declared stock dividend, the purpose of contemporaneous ownership requirement, to prevent the purchasing of shares for the purpose of bringing a derivative action, would not be served by preventing plaintiff's suit); *Kaplus v. First Continental Corp.*, 711 So. 2d 108 (Fla. App. 1998) (recognizing exception to contemporaneous ownership rule for former spouse who obtained shares in marital dissolution because it was "highly unlikely that two parties who are in the throes of a divorce would collude with each other and intentionally transfer stock for the sole purpose of enabling one of the parties to bring a derivative action").

[18] *See* Pa. Stat. Ann. tit. 15 § 1516 (permitting suit if there is a strong claim and to prevent "serious injustice"); Cal. [Corporations] Code Ann. § 800(b)(1) (permitting suit if there is a strong claim, no other claim is likely to be brought, the plaintiff purchased prior to disclosure of the wrong, precluding an action would unjustly enrich defendant, and the relief will not unjustly enrich the corporation or any shareholders).

[19] *See Aurora Credit Servs., Inc. v. Liberty West Dev., Inc.*, 970 P.2d 1273 (Utah 1998) (exception to contemporaneous ownership requirement where corporation fraudulently concealed wrongdoing and reasonable shareholder purchasing after wrongdoing would not have discovered it); *Rifkin v. Platt*, 824 P.2d 32 (Colo. Ct. App. 1991) (buyer may sue on behalf of corporation for pre-acquisition fraud not reflected in purchase price).

[20] The plight of the former shareholder is mitigated by the possible availability of a direct action based, for example, on a nondisclosure or misrepresentation of the wrong which induced the shareholder's sale of stock. *See Britt v. Cyril Bath Co.*, 417 F.2d 433 (6th Cir. 1969).

[2] Plaintiff Must Be a Shareholder at the Time of the Litigation

In addition to owning shares at the time of the wrong, derivative plaintiffs must hold their shares at the time of filing the complaint and throughout the suit. Some courts, however, have taken steps to moderate the effect of this rule. See, for example, *Steiner v. Meyerson*,[21] allowing a new plaintiff to intervene in a derivative suit where the original plaintiff had sold his shares and dismissing the suit would prejudice the interests of the corporation and the other shareholders.

This requirement is particularly troublesome in connection with mergers and other corporate combinations where shareholders are forced to surrender their shares for consideration that does not include stock in the corporation surviving the combination. Examples of such transactions include "freeze-out" mergers in which the merged shareholders receive cash or debt for their interests, "triangular" mergers in which the merged corporation becomes a wholly-owned subsidiary of the parent, and transactions where the corporation sells all of its assets and then liquidates. If the current shareholder requirement were strictly applied to these transactions, corporations could eliminate shareholder derivative suits, even after those suits had been properly commenced, simply by entering one the above-described corporate combinations. To handle this problem, some jurisdictions give standing to certain merged-out plaintiffs.[22] Should cashed-out shareholders be treated any differently from any other injured shareholders who sold their shares prior to disclosure or recovery? These shareholders are not necessarily without a remedy even if they cannot sue derivatively. They may be able to have the value of their derivative claims included in the fair value of their stock as determined in an appraisal proceeding,[23] enjoin the merger if it is being done for the purpose of eliminating the derivative claim,[24] or bring a direct claim,[25] as where plaintiffs attack the consideration received in the merger.[26] In addition, cashed-out shareholders may have

---

[21]   1997 Del. Ch. LEXIS 88, 1997 WL 349169 (Del. Ch. 1997).

[22]   *See Shelton v. Thompson*, 544 So. 2d 845 (Ala. 1989); *Gaillard v. Natomas Co.*, 173 Cal. App. 3d 410, 219 Cal. Rptr. 74 (1985) (applying the California statute discussed above in footnote 12); *Schreiber v. Carney*, 447A.2d 17 (Del. Ch. 1982) (derivative claim permitted where a "triangular" merger merely reorganized the old corporation); *Alford v. Shaw*, 398 S.E.2d 445 (N.C. 1990) (interpreting statute as not requiring that shareholders remain such through litigation). *See also* the "double derivative" cases discussed in footnote 15. Other courts have denied standing to shareholders whose corporations disappeared in mergers. *See Fischer v. CF & I Steel Corp.*, 599 F. Supp. 340 (S.D.N.Y. 1984); *Lewis v. Anderson*, 477 A.2d 1040 (Del. 1984).

[23]   *See Gabhart v. Gabhart*, 370 N.E.2d 345, 357 (Ind. 1977).

[24]   *See Coleman v. Taub*, 638 F.2d 628 (3d Cir. 1981); *Merritt v. Colonial Foods, Inc.*, 505 A.2d 757 (Del. Ch. 1986).

[25]   *See Lochhead v. Alacano*, 697 F. Supp. 406 (D. Utah 1988) (issuance of stock options diluted plaintiff's shares, hence reducing what plaintiff received in merger). *Compare Kramer v. Western Pacific Indus., Inc.*, 546 A.2d 348 (Del. 1988) (attack on pre-merger golden parachutes and excessive fees and expenses were unconnected with merger price itself and so were derivative).

[26]   *Parnes v. Bally Entertainment Corp.*, 722 A.2d 1243 (Del. 1999) (holding that "[a] stockholder who directly attacks the fairness or validity of a merger alleges an injury to the stockholders, not the corporation, and may pursue such a claim even after the merger at issue has been consummated," but noting "that it is often difficult to determine whether the stockholder is challenging the merger itself, or alleged wrongs associated with the merger, such as the award of

a remedy under the federal securities laws if the proxy statement related to the cash-out merger failed adequately to disclose the effect of the merger on the shareholders' derivative suits.[27]

[C] Plaintiff is Subject to Personal Defenses

Derivative actions have been dismissed where the plaintiff engaged in conduct, including acquiescence in the wrong, which would constitute a defense if the action were brought by the plaintiff individually, or where the plaintiff purchased from a wrongdoer or from someone who acquiesced in the wrong.[28] Should these facts matter, given that plaintiff is suing on a corporate rather than personal cause of action? Perhaps the courts are seeking to avoid unjust enrichment of the plaintiff,[29] or suits by inadequate representatives.

[D] Fair and Adequate Representation

In addition to the standing rules discussed above, derivative suit statutes like Rule 23.1 require that plaintiffs fairly and adequately represent the interests of the shareholders. In *Kamen v. Kemper Financial Services, Inc.*,[30] Judge Easterbrook considered whether a plaintiff who held little stock and delegated the investigation and prosecution of the suit to counsel could "fairly and adequately" represent the shareholders within the meaning of Fed. R. Civ. Proc. 23.1. Judge Easterbrook concluded that she could, even though no other shareholder had joined in the suit and 82% of the shares present and voting at a duly convened shareholders' meeting had ratified the challenged action (the amount of fees paid to a mutual fund's manager):

---

golden parachute employment contracts"); *cf. In re First Interstate Bancorp Consol. Shareholder Litigation*, 1998 Del. Ch. LEXIS 185, 1998 WL 731600 (Del. Ch. 1998) (breach of fiduciary duty claim involving waste of corporate assets cannot be pursued in direct action simply because breach occurred in connection with a merger); *Golaine v. Edwards*, 1999 Del. Ch. LEXIS 237, 1999 WL 1271882 (Del. Ch. 1999) (former shareholder cannot challenge propriety of $20 million payment to shareholder-adviser in connection with merger because "there is nothing in the complaint that supports the notion that [the shareholder-adviser] took anything off the table that would have otherwise gone to all the . . . stockholders," so plaintiff cannot carry his burden under *Parnes* of pleading "that the merger terms were tainted by unfair dealing").

[27]   *See Lichtenberg v. Besicorp Group, Inc.*, 1999 U.S. Dist. LEXIS 3879, 1999 WL 178796 (S.D.N.Y. 1999) (after concluding that merger terms should be modified to reflect those "that the shareholders would have demanded had they been fully informed," court ordered corporation's interest in derivative suits to be transferred to new corporation in which minority shareholders retained an interest, thereby preserving the shareholders' ability to maintain their derivative claims).

[28]   *See, e.g., Wallad v. Access BIDCO, Inc.*, 600 N.W.2d 664 (Mich. App. 1999) (director and minority shareholder who voted in favor of provisions that allowed contested transactions to occur).

[29]   *See Courtland Manor, Inc. v. Leeds*, 347 A.2d 144 (Del. Ch. 1975).

[30]   908 F.2d 1338, 1349-50, *rev'd on other grounds*, 500 U.S. 90 (1991).

. . . Kamen is no less adequate a representative than are most plaintiffs in class actions. Securities actions, like many suits under Rule 23, are lawyers' vehicles. Investors diversify their holdings, so it is no surprise that Kamen, like most plaintiffs in securities cases, does not hold very much stock in the defendants and has delegated the investigation and prosecution of the suit to counsel. Class actions are valuable precisely because they allow the vindication of claims too small to prosecute individually but worth litigating in the aggregate. . . . When defendants' counsel took Kamen's deposition and learned that she knew little about either the Fund or the case and had given counsel free reign, they learned only that this case fits the norm. . . .

Magistrate Balog's conclusion that Kamen has only a private grievance misses the point. Kamen is not trying to get even because she bears a grudge—say, because a member of the Fund's board trampled her petunias. She seeks a higher rate of return on her investment. So do all other shareholders in the Fund. It may well be that most other shareholders believe that the Fund's special services are worth the 0.2% cost, but shareholders have a common interest in ensuring that the Fund pays Kemper no more than the extra services are worth. *Commonality of interest is the essence of adequate representation.* . . .

Judge Easterbrook went on to note that "commonality" did not mean that Kamen's interests had to be identical to those of other class members. Thus, the fact that Kamen's passive investment strategy did not require the extra services that Kemper's higher fees made possible did not preclude her from serving as class representative. Judge Easterbrook wrote: "Agency costs of this kind, . . . are not the same as concrete conflict of interest between the 'representative' and other members of the class."

What kinds of facts support characterizing a plaintiff as an inadequate representative? Compare *Recchion v. Kirby*,[31] barring a derivative suit by a former employee who was also pursuing a wrongful discharge claim, who participated in some of the wrongful corporate conduct alleged in his complaint, and who owned only one share of stock with *EyeSite, Inc. v. Blackburn*,[32] allowing a dissenting shareholder in a closely held corporation to sue all of the other shareholders.[33]

---

[31]   637 F. Supp. 1309 (W.D. Pa. 1986).

[32]   796 S.W.2d 160 (Tex. 1990).

[33]   For a good review of the relevant factors and case law, see *Davis v. Comed, Inc.*, 619 F.2d 588 (6th Cir. 1980). Recent cases considering the adequacy of class representatives include *Miller v. Material Sciences Corp.*, 1999 U.S. Dist. LEXIS 10628, 1999 WL 495490 (N.D. Ill. 1999) (class representative "needs to have only a limited understanding of and a minimal interest in the litigation, as well as a basic understanding of the class composition"), and *In re Fuqua Industries, Inc. Shareholder Litigation*, 1999 Del. Ch. LEXIS 216, 1999 WL 988724 (Del. Ch. 1999) (plaintiff whose deposition testimony "suggests an attention span deficit and fatigue" and who "was unable to articulate [an] understanding [of her claim] with any particularity and . . . was obviously confused about basic facts regarding her suit" is nonetheless a fair and adequate representative in a derivative suit).

NOTE AND QUESTIONS

An alternative rule: barring claims by small shareholders. In general, how well do the standing rules discussed in this section screen out the "bad" "strike" suits from meritorious derivative litigation? Evaluate the following alternative rule: "Only those who own X% of the corporation's stock may bring a derivative suit." Wouldn't this ensure that only suits likely to be a net benefit to the corporation would be brought? What might be the costs of such a rule? If this type of rule is a good idea, what should the percentage be? Once it is accepted that a shareholder who owns only a single share of stock can bring a derivative suit, do the other distinctions made by the standing rules make sense?

§ 10.04 Security for Expenses and Assessment of Costs Against Plaintiff

Statutes in many jurisdictions require derivative plaintiffs under certain circumstances on defendant's motion to post security at the outset of the suit to cover defendant's reasonable costs and attorneys' fees. This is supposed to curb "strike" suits by forcing plaintiff to internalize the costs of meritless litigation.[34] Many of these statutes provide for a court order requiring the posting of security unless plaintiff holds more than 5% of an outstanding class of stock or stock worth more than $25,000. Some let courts deny security when necessary to avoid "undue hardship" or "serious injustice."[35] The California Code provides for security if the court determines, after a hearing, "that there is no reasonable possibility that the prosecution of the cause of action . . . will benefit the corporation or its shareholders."[36]

Although the security-for-costs statutes provide that the court may give defendants recourse to the security upon termination of the action, they do not include any standards to guide such recourse. Thus, if security is required, the plaintiff may have to cover defendants' costs and attorneys' fees even if the action was brought in good faith. Conversely, plaintiffs who were not required to post security need not cover defendants' costs even for meritless actions.

Coffee & Schwartz (at 314) criticize security-for-cost statutes on the ground that it is difficult to determine accurately whether a suit is of the "strike" variety at the outset of the litigation, which is when the important determination must be made under a security-for-costs provision. Moreover, the security for costs increases the incentive of plaintiff's counsel to accept an early, inadequate settlement rather than pushing ahead to trial, where defeat can cost plaintiff not only her attorney's fee, but defendant's costs as well.

---

[34] *See Edited Transcript of Proceedings of the Conference on Remedies Under the ALI Proposals: Law and Economics*, 71 CORNELL L. REV. 409-11 (1986).

[35] *See, e.g.,* Pa. Stat. Ann. tit. 15, § 1782.

[36] Cal. Corporations Code Ann. § 800(c).

Plaintiffs may be able to avoid security-for-costs statutes by bringing a direct suit, suing in a jurisdiction that does not have a security-for-costs requirement,[37] suing under a federal statute,[38] or joining plaintiffs owning enough shares to avoid application of the statutes. As to the last alternative, a derivative plaintiff may meet defendant's motion for security with a request for a shareholder list and a solicitation of possible plaintiffs. Since this would serve to publicize plaintiff's claims, the threat of this procedure is itself enough to deter many defendants from moving for security even when it may be required under the applicable statute.

QUESTION

Is a properly designed security-for-costs statute a good compromise between generally allowing nominal holders to sue and restricting standing only to relatively large shareholders?

§ 10.05 Necessity of Demand on Directors

Sections 10.05-10.07 discuss four subjects that are related in the sense that they all deal with the role of intra-corporate procedures in the maintenance of a derivative suit: (1) demand on the directors (Section 10.05); (2) the directors' powers to block or terminate derivative litigation (Section 10.06); (3) demand on the shareholders (Section 10.07); and (4) the shareholders' powers to block or terminate derivative litigation (Section 10.07).

In general, as a prerequisite to maintaining the suit, the derivative plaintiff must either (1) serve a demand upon the board of directors asking the board to sue on the corporation's behalf or take the action requested in the complaint or (2) show facts supporting excuse of such demand. Although demand appears to be only a pleading requirement under Federal Rule 23.1, the rule is substantive in the sense that the plaintiff may be precluded from maintaining a derivative suit if she fails to establish facts justifying her failure to request action from the board.

This Section considers the precise circumstances under which the directors' views must be sought before a derivative suit is commenced. Subsection [A] discusses the leading approach—the Delaware *Aronson* rule—while subsection [B] discusses alternatives to *Aronson*, including a universal demand requirement.

---

[37] Security for costs statutes are regarded as procedural for conflict of laws purposes and thus are not applied outside the enacting state. *See Berkwitz v. Humphrey*, 130 F. Supp. 142 (N.D. Ohio 1955). Plaintiff may not, however, avoid a forum state's security statute by suing on a state claim in federal court, since the statute is regarded as substantive for *Erie* purposes and will be applied. *See Cohen v. Beneficial Industrial Loan Corp.*, 337 U.S. 541 (1949).

[38] Federal rules are applied in federal question litigation, and there is no federal security-for-costs requirement.

[A] The *Aronson* Test

STARRELS v. FIRST NATIONAL BANK OF CHICAGO
United States Court of Appeals, Seventh Circuit
870 F.2d 1168 (1989)

ESCHBACH, Senior Circuit Judge.

This appeal challenges the district court's dismissal with prejudice of the appellant's third amended and consolidated complaint. In essence, this is a shareholder derivative and class action suit asserting that the directors and officers of First Chicago Corporation ("FCC") and First National Bank of Chicago ("FNBC") have egregiously mismanaged the affairs of the corporations. The appellant raises two contentions on appeal.

* * *

II

The appellant . . . argues that a demand was excused because it would have been futile.

* * *

In the case before us, the appellant does not claim that the directors were in any way interested in the transactions of which she complains. Rather, Bernstein asserts that the directors' actions were not the product of proper business judgment. Therefore, we need to examine Bernstein's third amended and consolidated complaint only to see if it raises a reasonable doubt that the directors exercised proper business judgment. Under Delaware law, this requires us to look at both the substantive due care (substance of the transaction) as well as the procedural due care (an informed decision) used by the directors.

The appellant makes several allegations challenging the substantive due care used by the directors. In her third amended and consolidated complaint, Bernstein lists numerous transactions which she claims were not the product of proper business judgment. First, she alleges that FNBC and FCC, acting under the domination, direction, or control of the officers and directors, entered into a series of loans and a contract with companies affiliated with Nelson Bunker Hunt and W. Herbert Hunt, which resulted in losses totaling more than one hundred million dollars. She particularly complains that FNBC did not require collateral for some of these loans. Nowhere in her complaint, however, does Bernstein allege specific facts showing that these loans were "devoid of a legitimate corporate purpose." *See Pogostin,* 480 A.2d at 626. At most, her allegations merely show with hindsight that these loans were a mistake.

Bernstein's third amended and consolidated complaint also criticizes FCC's decision to purchase a 44.5% interest in a Brazilian bank and to guarantee the Brazilian bank's deposits. This investment resulted in significant losses to FCC. Her complaint, however, also notes that the investment was purportedly made in order to facilitate lending to multinational corporations in local currency. Clearly, this is a valid reason to invest in a foreign bank. Moreover, the complaint fails to allege with particularity any improper motive or conflict of

interest on the part of the directors and officers in deciding to make this investment. Therefore, this transaction can hardly be considered "so egregious on its face that [it] cannot
meet the test of business judgment." *Aronson* [*v. Lewis*,] 473 A.2d [805] at 815 [1984].

The third amended and consolidated complaint further alleges impropriety in the
awarding of $ 1.5 million in bonuses to top management. *See* Complaint, at 15-16. The com-
plaint, however, is void of any specific allegations of fact showing why these bonuses were
improper; for example, the complaint lacks facts which would support a claim that these
bonuses amounted to a waste of corporate assets. Indeed, we note that Delaware corporate
law gives directors broad powers to provide suitable compensation for a corporation's officers. *See* Del. Code Ann. tit. 8, § 122(5). Thus, the appellant has failed to create a reasonable doubt about whether these bonuses were the product of the directors' business
judgment.

Bernstein's third amended and consolidated complaint also criticizes the directors' procedural due care in entering into the challenged transactions. She alleges that many of these
transactions were "made without regard for adequate approval, or review auditing procedures." She further alleges that, in deciding to invest in the Brazilian bank, the directors
"failed to take steps to fully comprehend the financial situation" of the Brazilian bank and
did not "adequately study the situation." Notably absent from her complaint, however, are
specific facts describing what steps the directors did not take in informing themselves or
how they could have better informed themselves before entering into the challenged transactions. Thus, these bare conclusory allegations are not enough to cast a doubt on whether
these transactions were the products of the directors' business judgment.

Contrary to the appellant's claim, her third amended and consolidated complaint does
not allege with particularity facts which would have excused her from making a demand
upon the directors. . . .

* * *

III

For all the foregoing reasons, the judgment of the district court is AFFIRMED.

EASTERBROOK, Circuit Judge, concurring.
Delaware excuses demand on directors in a derivative suit when

> under the particularized facts alleged, a reasonable doubt is created that: (1) the
> directors are disinterested and independent [or] (2) the challenged transaction
> was otherwise the product of a valid exercise of business judgment.

Aronson v. Lewis, 473 A.2d 805, 814 (Del. 1984). *See also Pogostin v. Rice*, 480 A.2d 619,
624-25 (Del. 1984); *Grobow v. Perot*, 539 A.2d 180, 183, 186 (Del. 1988). The court uses
this standard, and I join its opinion. Having applied Delaware's law as best we can, we
might move on to other business. This case illustrates, however, the difficulty courts have
had with the rule of *Aronson*. . . .

* * *

Part (1) of [the *Aronson*] inquiry asks whether the directors' business decision not to sue would be respected. Part (2) asks whether the original decision is sheltered from liability by the business judgment rule. *Aronson*, *Pogostin*, and *Grobow* tell us that if the shareholder satisfies either part of the inquiry, demand is unnecessary. Yet this cuts even a disinterested board out of the process whenever there is a serious question about the status of the challenged conduct, denying the firm the initial opportunity to make a business decision whether to pursue litigation although there may be no reason to doubt the integrity of the board's decision.

If the original decision—that is, the decision to engage in "the challenged transaction"—was the product of a "valid exercise of business judgment," then the directors cannot in good faith authorize litigation. Only if there is a "reasonable doubt" about the application of the business judgment rule to the decision to undertake the "challenged transaction" may the firm litigate in its own name. The upshot of *Aronson* is that whenever the board may pursue litigation, demand is unnecessary; but when litigation would be an abuse of process, demand is required so that the board can make up its mind. Why should demand be excused when it might be useful and required only when the outcome is fore doomed? Judge Seitz, who served on the chancery court of Delaware for 20 years (and was Chancellor for 15) wrote in *Lewis v. Curtis*, 671 F.2d 779, 786 (3d Cir. 1982), that a plaintiff need not allege that the challenged transaction was unprotected by the business judgment rule and that courts should inquire instead whether the board could make a valid business judgment in response to a demand. That inquiry is more in line with the rationales of the demand requirement limned in *Aronson* than is the rule stated in *Aronson*.

Most of the "challenged transaction[s]" in today's case were authorized by managers who do not sit on the board. Some were down a considerable distance in the corporate hierarchy. Why would the exposure of these employees of the firm to liability (on the ground that their deeds are not sheltered by the business judgment rule) eliminate the need to make demand on the board? The board of a corporation wants as much as any shareholder to prevent and punish delicts by subordinate managers—probably they want to do so even more urgently, because members of the board are likely to hold larger stakes in the firm than are shareholder-plaintiffs. *See* Harold Demsetz & Kenneth Lehn, *The Structure of Corporate Ownership: Causes and Consequences*, 93 J. POL. ECON. 1155 (1985). This board, in particular, was concerned about these gaffes, in particular. Counsel informed us at oral argument that heads have rolled as a result of the transactions against which the complaint rails, and that some suits have been filed. Ironically, the fact that the board "did something" should be the magic arrow in plaintiff's quiver, for it suggests that the transactions were not sheltered by the business judgment rule. Such a topsy-turvy approach generates little other than mirth, however, which may be why the plaintiff did not pursue the point, and why this court can write that a sequence of events that had led to legal action did not create even a "reasonable doubt" about the protection of the business judgment rule.

Self-contradiction is not the only problem with the formulation of *Aronson*. The reference to "reasonable doubt" summons up the standard applied in criminal law. It is a demanding standard, meaning at least a 90% likelihood that the defendant is guilty. If "reasonable doubt" in the *Aronson* formula means the same thing as "reasonable doubt" in criminal law, then demand is excused whenever there is a 10% chance that the original transaction is not protected by the business judgment rule. Why should demand be excused on such a slight showing? Surely not because courts want shareholders to file suit whenever there is an 11% likelihood that the business judgment rule will not protect a transaction. *Aronson* did not say, and later cases have not supplied the deficit. If "reasonable doubt" in corporate law means something different from "reasonable doubt" in criminal law, however, what is the difference? Why use the same term for two different things?

A final oddment in the *Aronson* approach. Rule 23.1 and its parallel in Delaware practice require the court to determine at the pleading stage whether demand was necessary. This requires courts to adjudicate the merits on the pleadings, for a decision that the business judgment rule shelters the challenged conduct is "the merits" in derivative litigation, and under *Aronson* also shows that demand was necessary. It is a bobtailed adjudication, without evidence. If facts suggesting (at the one-in-ten level) that the business judgment rule will not prevent recovery have come to light, the investor may plead them and litigate further, setting the stage for still another decision about the scope of the business judgment rule. *See Grobow*, 539 A.2d at 186-87 (noting the link between the demand requirement and the need for discovery). If facts of this character would come to light only with discovery, then demand is necessary and plaintiff may not litigate at all—for in Delaware a demand-required case is one the board may elect to prevent or dismiss under *Zapata*. The amount of information in the public domain is unrelated to the ability of the board to make a business judgment concerning litigation, is unrelated indeed to any function of the demand requirement. Why should the board acquire the power to dismiss under *Zapata* just because the plaintiff needs discovery and so cannot make the required showing "with particularity" in the complaint? *Aronson* and its successors do not discuss the point.

* * *

NOTES AND QUESTIONS

(1) **The *Aronson* test: directors' self-interest.** With regard to the first prong of *Aronson*, concerning the directors' disinterest and independence, that all of the board members are defendants is not necessarily enough to disable them from acting disinterestedly on the demand.[39] Allegations that outside directors were "dominated" by wrongdoing insiders or "acquiesced" in their actions may or may not be enough.[40]

---

[39] *See Silver v. Allard*, 16 F. Supp. 2d 966 (N.D. Ill. 1998); *In re Baxter International Inc. Shareholders Litigation*, 654 A.2d 1268 (Del. Ch. 1995).

[40] Compare *International Equity Capital Growth Fund, L.P. v. Clegg*, 23 Del. J. Corp. L. 259 (Del. Ch. 1997) (demand excused where defendant owned 56% of the stock, had the "power to designate and to remove members of the board if he felt so moved," and had in fact used that power to remove directors who had exercised independent judgment); *Professional Management Associates, Inc. v. Coss*, 574 N.W.2d 107 (Minn. App. 1998) (demand excused where two of the other four directors were also officers whose employment and compensation were influenced by the defendant CEO) (Delaware law); *Mizel v. Connelly*, 1999 Del. Ch. LEXIS 157, 1999 WL 550369 (Del. Ch. 1999) (domination sufficiently alleged where defendant was company's largest shareholder (32.7% stake) and board chairman and two of four allegedly independent directors were employees of the company who were paid substantial salaries ($620,000 and $239,000)); and *Harbor Finance Partners v. Huizenga*, 1999 Del. Ch. LEXIS 220, 1999 WL 1059757 (Del. Ch. 1999) (reasonable doubt as to director's independence established where (1) director [Hudson] was brother-in-law of party

Beneville v. York[41] holds that demand is excused under the first prong of *Aronson* when at least half of the board is interested.

(2) The *Aronson* test: "valid business judgments." With regard to *Aronson's* second prong, concerning whether the challenged transaction was the product of a valid business judgment, should the court's determination depend upon the nature of the business decision challenged? Consider the following:

> Logic suggests a sharp distinction between a transaction completely undirected to a corporate purpose and one which, while perhaps vulnerable to criticism, is of a character that could be thought to serve the interests of the company. If the transaction attacked was one solely for the benefit of minority, interested directors—taking out a sham loan, trading in worthless real estate—the approval of the other, nominally disinterested, directors is prima facie inexplicable. If a director goes along with a colleague in an act on its face advantageous only to that colleague and not to the corporation, this in itself is a circumstance, or particularity, supporting the claim that he is under that colleague's control. It may be assumed that he would remain so when the directorate votes on plaintiff's demand. . . . It does not follow, however, that a director who merely made an erroneous business judgment in connection with what was plainly a corporate act will "refuse to do [his] duty in behalf of the corporation if [he] were act to do so."[42]

Consistent with this test, some influential commentators have proposed rejecting Part (2) of the *Aronson* test and permitting part (1) to be satisfied by a showing of an irrational business judgment.[43]

(3) *Rales v. Blasband*. How should demand futility be assessed when the board on whom demand is made did not make the challenged business decision, as where a majority of the directors making the decision has been replaced, or where the subject of the derivative suit is not a business decision of the board? In *Rales v. Blasband*,[44] the Delaware Supreme Court held that, rather than apply the two-pronged *Aronson* test, a court should restrict itself to examining whether

---

[Huizenga] whose shares in another corporation [AutoNation] were being acquired by corporation [Republic], (2) business ties between parties extended back over 30 years, (3) Hudson was management subordinate of Huizenga for many of those years, and (4) parties had a "long-standing pattern of mutually advantageous business relations" that made it unlikely that Hudson could impartially consider a demand that Republic file suit against Huizenga), *with Benerofe v. Cha*, 1998 Del. Ch. LEXIS 28, 1998 WL 83081 (Del. Ch. 1998) (that corporation has one controlling shareholder does not, as a matter of law, establish that directors are dominated or controlled by that shareholder unless plaintiff can show that director is beholden to the controlling shareholder for personal or other reasons, such as for continued employment or substantial remuneration).

[41] 796 A.2d 80 (Del. Ch. 2000).

[42] *In re Kauffman Mutual Fund Actions*, 479 F.2d 257, 265 (1st Cir.), *cert. denied*, 414 U.S. 857 (1973).

[43] Block, Radin & Rosenzweig, *The Role of the Business Judgment Rule in Shareholder Litigation at the Turn of the Decade*, 45 Bus. Law. 469, 486 (1990).

[44] 634 A.2d 927 (Del. 1993).

the board that would be addressing the demand can impartially consider its merits without being influenced by improper considerations. Thus, a court must determine whether or not the particularized factual allegations of a derivative stockholder complaint create a reasonable doubt that, *as of the time the complaint is filed*, the board of directors could have properly exercised its independent and disinterested business judgment in responding to a demand. If the derivative plaintiff satisfies this burden, then demand will be excused as futile.[45]

In re Abbott Laboratories Derivative Shareholder Litigation[46] holds that the *Rales* standard is satisfied, in a case where the subject of a derivative suit is not a business decision by the board, where the complaint pleads conduct which permits the court to conclude that there is a substantial likelihood that the directors will be held liability.

(4) **The need for particularity.** *Greenwald v. Batterson*[47] emphasized the need for particularity in allegations establishing demand futility under *Aronson*:

> A plaintiff-shareholder may successfully plead pre-suit demand futility [under the first prong of *Aronson*] by alleging [among other things] that "the 'sole or primary purpose' of the challenged board action was to perpetuate the directors in control of the corporation." . . . However, the mere allegation that directors have taken action to entrench themselves, without an allegation that the directors believed themselves vulnerable to removal from office, will not excuse demand.

* * *

> [Under the second prong of *Aronson*,] the plaintiff is required to "plead particularized facts creating a reasonable doubt as to the 'soundness' of the challenged transaction sufficient to rebut the presumption that the business judgment rule attaches to the transaction." . . . Plaintiff faces a substantial burden, as the second prong of the *Aronson* test is "directed to extreme cases in which despite the appearance of independence and disinterest a decision is so extreme or curious as to itself raise a legitimate ground to justify further inquiry and judicial review."

(5) **The decision to make a demand.** There may be significant costs to making demand, at least in jurisdictions that treat the making of a demand as a concession of the board's disinterestedness in responding to the demand. (This "concession" theory is discussed further in the *Kamen* excerpt in Section 10.05[B] and in Note 3 following

---

[45]   634 A.2d at 934 (emphasis added).

[46]   126 F. Supp. 2d 535 (N.D. Ill. 2000).

[47]   1999 Del. Ch. LEXIS 158, 1999 WL 596276 (Del. Ch. 1999).

Kamen.) Are there any costs to the plaintiff of *not* making a demand? Note that even if the suit is dismissed for failure to make a demand, the plaintiff may be able to replead with demand,[48] or another plaintiff could refile claiming the same cause of action. But a plaintiff who, without reasonable cause, files without demand may be liable for costs.[49]

(6) **Evaluation of *Aronson*.** Do you agree with Judge Easterbrook's criticisms of *Aronson*? It follows from the discussion in Note 5 that, under *Aronson*, plaintiffs rarely will make a demand unless ultimately forced to do so. *Aronson* therefore effectively results in an early judicial determination of the merits of the case on the basis of the pleadings alone. On the one hand, courts may not be able to tell, based on the pleadings, whether the board can make a valid business judgment in response to a demand. On the other hand, can *Aronson* be rationalized on the ground that the demand-futility hearing operates as a kind of "early warning" of trivial lawsuits—that is, a way to spot weak cases at a relatively early stage?

[B] Alternatives to *Aronson*: Universal Demand

One alternative to *Aronson* is the rule of *Lewis v. Curtis*, discussed in *Starrels*. Under that approach, courts inquire only as to whether the board could make a valid business judgment in response to a demand. Another is a rule of universal demand, like that set forth in ALI *Principles* § 7.03 and Model Act § 7.42. Under that approach, demand on the board is only excused if "the plaintiff makes a specific showing that irreparable injury to the corporation would otherwise result." The relative merits of these two alternatives are considered in the following case.

KAMEN v. KEMPER FINANCIAL SERVICES
United States Court of Appeals, Seventh Circuit
908 F.2d 1338, *rev'd*, 500 U.S. 90 (1991)

[This case is a suit under §§ 20(a) and 36(b) of the Investment Company Act of 1940 against a money market mutual fund and its investment advisor, challenging the management fee charged by the advisor. The trial court dismissed plaintiff's claim under § 20(a) of the Investment Company Act on the ground that plaintiff had failed to make a demand on the board in compliance with F.R.C.P. Rule 23.1.]

---

[48]   *See Abramowitz v. Posner*, 513 F. Supp. 120, 124-25 (S.D.N.Y. 1981), *aff'd*, 672 F.2d 1025 (2d Cir. 1982); *Markowitz v. Brody*, 90 F.R.D. 542, 563 (S.D.N.Y. 1981). *But see Grossman v. Johnson*, 674 F.2d 115, 125-26 (1st Cir.), *cert. denied*, 459 U.S. 838 (1982); *Shlensky v. Dorsey*, 574 F.2d 131, 141-42 (3d Cir. 1978).

[49]   *See Blumenthal v. Teets*, 155 Ariz. 123, 745 P.2d 181 (Ariz. Ct. App. 1987).

EASTERBROOK, J.:

Kamen's complaint as finally amended alleges that she did not make a demand on the board of directors because the seven independent directors (of the ten-member board) "receive aggregate remuneration of approximately $300,000 a year for serving as directors of the Fund and all of the other funds in the Kemper group" and therefore "are dependent upon and subservient to" Kemper. It alleges in addition that demand would be futile because the Fund solicited the proxies, so a demand would request that the directors sue themselves, and that because the Fund has asked for the dismissal of the suit on the merits the directors obviously are not interested in pursuing the claims. Judge Nordberg thought these allegations insufficient to excuse a demand under Rule 23.1, as do we.

[The court assumed without deciding that Rule 23.1 was applicable to this claim, and held that the circumstances under which the plaintiff might be excused from making a demand were a matter of federal common law. The Supreme Court reversed as to the application of state law, as discussed in Note 1 following this case.]

The scope of the demand requirement depends on why demand ever is required. The demand rule could reflect a hope that the dispute will go away without litigation, that the board of directors will "do something" (or persuade the putative plaintiff that suit is pointless). Demand then initiates a form of alternative dispute resolution, much like mediation. Steps to control the volume of litigation are welcome, yet the demand rule creates more litigation than it prevents. It is difficult to identify cases in which the board's response to a demand satisfied the shareholder and thus prevented litigation; even if the board acts the shareholder may believe the board did too little. It is easy to point to hundreds of cases, including this one, in which the demand requirement was itself the centerpiece of the litigation. An approach uncertain in scope and discretionary in operation—that is, any rule except one invariably requiring or excusing demand—promotes litigation. When the stakes are high (as they frequently are in cases of this character), even a small disagreement between the parties about the application of a legal rule makes it difficult to resolve disagreements amicably.

A stronger rationale for the demand requirement is the one Hawes gives—that it allows directors to make a business decision about a business question: whether to invest the time and resources of the corporation in litigation. Firms must make operational decisions; if these misfire, they must decide what to do next. Each decision must be made with the interests of the corporation at heart. Whether to buy a particular combination of services at a particular price is a business decision. So too the decision to file a lawsuit about the price or pursue a different course, such as renegotiating the contract, changing the level of services, even finding a new adviser. Even doing nothing is justified when the resources of top managers required to act exceed the injury to the firm; when "something must be done," acts short of litigation could have net benefits exceeding those of litigation. If the directors run the show, then they must control litigation (versus other remedies) to the same extent as they make the initial business decision.

Choosing between litigation and some other response may be difficult, depending on information unavailable to courts and a sense of the situation in which business executives are trained. Managers who make such judgment calls poorly ultimately give way to superior executives; no such mechanism "selects out" judges who try to make business decisions. In the long run firms are better off when business decisions are made by business specialists, even granting the inevitable errors. If principles such as the "business judgment rule" preserve room for managers to err in making an operational decision, so too they preserve room to err in deciding what remedies to pursue.

Consider now why plaintiffs may resist making demand. (a) Delay in starting the litigation while the board ponders may injure the firm, perhaps because the statute of limitations is about to expire, perhaps because a questionable transaction is about to occur and it will be hard to unscramble the eggs if it happens before the court can act. (b) Demand may be futile, in the sense that the members of the board are interested in the transaction and unwilling to sue themselves, or because they are so set against litigation that their minds are closed. (c) Demand may be pointless, in the sense that a substantive rule prevents the corporation from controlling the litigation. . . . (d) Demand may sometimes be imprudent from the plaintiff's perspective. Counsel who fear that the board will sue may hesitate before making a demand, because if the firm sues counsel will not reap the legal fees of victory. Or counsel may think that the board will pursue a strategy in litigation that his client disapproves, or settle for too little.

We will return to these four. Perhaps the most serious difficulty with demand from the perspective of plaintiffs is the link between the making of demand and the standard courts apply to the directors' decision not to sue. In Delaware, the Mother Court of corporate law, any shareholder who makes a demand is deemed to concede that demand was required. If demand is required, then the disinterested members of the board are deemed to possess the ability to refuse to sue or control the litigation, provided their decisions are sufficiently reasoned to come within the capacious bounds of the business judgment doctrine. *Zapata Corp. v. Maldonado,* 430 A.2d 779 (Del. 1981). Except in extraordinary cases, then, tendering a demand to the board puts the plaintiff out of court under Delaware law. No wonder plaintiffs stoutly resist making demands.

Federal courts have never embraced Delaware's link between the making of a demand and special deference to the board's decision not to sue. We think it would be unwise to do so. When the standard of review depends on the existence of a demand, plaintiffs have extraordinarily strong reasons not to make a demand, and corporations extraordinarily strong reasons to insist on one. Demand then becomes a threshold issue in every derivative suit, one that must be resolved in advance of discovery and on the basis of a good deal of speculation. . . . [T]he plaintiff will assert that the board is unreasonable. Why ask persons with closed minds? The board will proclaim that Solomonic wisdom would be applied if only plaintiff would ask, while simultaneously asserting that the suit has no conceivable merit. It is not a pretty picture, but it is an extended and expensive one, made more so by some peculiarities in the way Delaware phrases its standards. . . .

Four reasons remain why demand may be inappropriate: (a) exigencies of time; (b) futility; (c) irrelevance given a substantive rule; (d) the risk that demand will lead to suit and so deprive counsel of fees that might have been obtained were it necessary to file a derivative suit. We may at once discard (d) as a legal excuse. Cases in category (c) obviously never require demand. Cases in category (a) justify filing the complaint before receiving the board's answer to the demand but do not justify failure to make a demand. When time is tight, the investor should make demand at the same time he files the complaint. Category (b), futility, is the usual sticking point. The plaintiff asserts that the board is interested or intransigent; the board asserts that it is reasonable and wise. Courts predictably have great difficulty deciding who is right when, as is usual, it must decide such questions on the pleadings.

At least in principle the rationale of the demand requirement implies a futility exception. If courts would not respect the directors' decision not to file suit, then demand would be an empty formality. When all directors have a financial stake in the transaction, their decision not to sue themselves would carry little weight with a court. Or perhaps all of the directors are so ensnarled in the transaction that even when only the duty of care is at stake, their judgment could not be respected. Again demand seems an empty gesture. Courts dispense with futile gestures.

"In principle" is an important qualifier. In practice the futility exception to the demand rule has produced gobs of litigation. It is this exception that has sapped the potential role of the demand requirement as an alternative dispute resolution mechanism. Hundreds of cases opine on whether demand is or is not futile. . . . The time has come to do away with it. If demand is useful, then let the investor make one; if indeed futile, the board's response will establish that soon enough. In either case, the litigation may proceed free of arguments about whether a demand should have been made in the first place. The virtue of simplification may be seen by considering three of the common battles about the meaning of "futility."

1. The plaintiff may say that some or all of the members of the board approved or are interested in the transaction and that demand is futile because they will not sue themselves or contest their own acts. Although directors are unlikely to sue themselves, they may well take some action to palliate the consequences of poorly conceived acts, including their own. Directors want the venture to succeed, and if shown how they can improve its prospects, are likely to act. One mistake at the time of the initial decision does not imply that the member of the board opposes remedial action. Even when the "action" involves suit against some of their number, this does not disable the board. The ALI properly observes, *id.* at 70-71, that the board may appoint a minority of disinterested members to evaluate the demand and act for the corporation. In the extreme case in which all members are implicated, the board may expand its size and authorize the new members to act for the firm. Of course it may choose to do none of these things, but if so it will just decline the demand. Making a demand is cheap, especially so when the board is disabled from acting. Why prefer extended, costly litigation to the cheap and quick expedient of a demand?

2. The board may be determined not to sue. Perhaps by the time the judge comes to consider whether plaintiff should have made a demand, the defendant will have moved to dismiss the case on the merits. Any demand in such a case would be doomed to failure, and even at an earlier stage it may be transparent that the directors want nothing to do with litigation. This application of the "futility" exception has both a practical and a conceptual difficulty. The practical one is that it is difficult to tell in advance just what position the firm would take if asked; disputes about the demand requirement usually are resolved before the defendants plead to the merits. It is easy for the plaintiffs to say (and for the defendants to deny) that the board has a closed mind; it is much harder to tell who is right.

The conceptual difficulty is that even an adamant unwillingness to sue may reflect the merits. Boards ought not pursue silly or frivolous claims. So certain knowledge that the board is unwilling to authorize litigation may reflect only confidence that the case is feeble or injurious to the firm and other investors. Why should the plaintiffs be authorized to sue, and without so much as a request to the board, just because the complaint is all heat and no light? Once more the ALI hit the nail on the head when observing that a formulation of the futility rule that inquires whether a demand would prompt the board to correct a wrong "assumes that there is a wrong to be corrected. The director's antagonism to an action may well be justified and flow from a sound judgment that the action is either not meritorious or would otherwise subject the corporation to serious injury." *Id.* at 69. A decision not to file a weak lawsuit would be protected by the business judgment rule, so it makes perfect sense to ask for the board's perspective.

3. A plaintiff may insist that even the independent directors are toadies, so that their judgment could not be respected. Perhaps they are friends of the putative defendants; perhaps they draw hefty directors' fees and fear loss of their offices if they authorize suit; perhaps they believe that the courts have no business supervising corporate affairs and would not authorize litigation no matter how meritorious (and no matter how little their regard for holding onto their offices). If demand is futile in fact for any of these reasons, then the board will say no with dispatch and the case may proceed. As we have broken the link between the demand and the standard of review, the plaintiff may employ this arsenal of arguments to argue that the decision not to sue ought not be respected; the board will stand on the business judgment rule. The court will resolve the question on the merits rather than trying to treat it as a procedural hurdle. Framing questions about the independence of the directors as exceptions to the demand requirement diverts attention from the real issues.

Kamen's complaint pursues all three of these arguments for futility and has all the weaknesses we have identified. . . .

* * *

We conclude that precedent does not prevent us from holding that claims of futility should be tested by making the demand rather than by arguing about hypotheticals. If the firm declines to sue, the court can decide whether the board's decision is entitled to respect under state corporate law, which applies in light of the holding of *Burks*. As we have rejected *Zapata,* the making or failure to make a demand will not alter the business judgment standard that ordinarily applies to corporate decisions. Courts now may focus on the question whether the board's actual decision should be given force, rather than on hypothetical inquiries. "Futility" is the only reason Kamen gives for not making a demand on her claim under Sec. 20(a). As this is an unsatisfactory reason, we agree with the district court's decision that the claim must be dismissed for failure to make a required demand.

NOTES AND QUESTIONS

(1) **State versus federal law.** *Kemper* was reversed on the ground that the state law demand requirement, including the futility exception, applies unless this would frustrate federal policy.[50] The Supreme Court reasoned that the demand rule bears on the allocation of power in corporations, a matter that is normally governed by state law.

---

[50] 500 U.S. 90 (1991); 939 F.2d 548 (1991) (dismissal on remand, applying Maryland law).

(2) **Evaluation of alternatives.** Consider which of the following demand rules makes the most sense: (1) plaintiff must always make demand; (2) plaintiff need never make demand; (3) the rule of *Lewis v. Curtis*, discussed in *Starrels*; (4) the *Aronson* rule; (5) none of the above? *Marx v. Akers*[51] rejected both the universal demand approach of the ALI and the Delaware approach under *Aronson* (because the "reasonable doubt" standard of *Aronson* "has provoked criticism as confusing and overly subjective"). Instead, the Court said demand would be excused as futile when a complaint alleges with particularity that "a majority of the board of directors" is interested in the challenged transaction," "the board of directors did not fully inform themselves about the challenged transaction to the extent reasonably appropriate under the circumstances," or "the challenged transaction was so egregious on its face that it could not have been the product of sound business judgment of the directors." *Knox v. Rosenberg*,[52] interpreted Maryland law "to excuse presuit demand if either (1) a majority of the current board of directors faces liability for participation in the alleged wrongdoing, or (2) a majority of the current board of directors is dominated and controlled by the alleged wrongdoer." How different are these approaches from each other or from *Aronson*? Despite criticisms of the *Aronson* rule, courts continue to adopt it.[53]

(3) **The "Concession" Theory.** In *Kamen*, Judge Easterbrook says the most serious difficulty with demand in Delaware is that any shareholder who makes a demand is deemed to concede that demand was required and, therefore, that the board possesses the ability to refuse to sue or control the litigation. *Grimes v. Donald*[54] suggests that Judge Easterbrook's description of the consequences of making a demand in Delaware may no longer be correct:

> Simply because the composition of the board provides no basis ex ante for the stockholder to claim with particularity and consistently with Rule 11 that it is reasonable to doubt that a majority of the board is either interested or not independent, it does not necessarily follow ex post that the board in fact acted independently, disinterestedly or with due care in response to the demand. *A board or a committee of the board may appear to be independent, but may not always act independently.* If a demand is made and rejected, the board rejecting the demand is entitled to the presumption of the business judgment rule unless the stockholder can allege facts with particularity creating a reasonable doubt that the board is entitled to the benefit of the presumption. *If there is reason to doubt that the board acted independently* or with due care in responding to the demand, the stockholder may have the basis ex post to claim wrongful refusal. The stockholder then has the right to

---

[51]   88 N.Y.2d 189, 200 (1996).

[52]   Civ. Action. No. H-99-0123 (S.D. Tex., Sept. 28, 1999).

[53]   *See, e.g., In re PSE & G Shareholder Litigation*, 810 A.2d 295 (N.J. 2002) (accepting *Aronson* standard for derivative suits involving New Jersey corporations).

[54]   673 A.2d 1207, 1219 (Del. 1996) (footnotes omitted and emphasis added).

bring the underlying action with the same standing which the stockholder would have had, ex ante, if demand had been excused as futile.

How does this holding square with the "early warning" rationale of *Aronson* discussed in Note 6 following *Starrels*?

§ 10.06   Director Power to Block or Terminate Derivative Litigation

The question of the board's power to block or terminate derivative litigation arises in two contexts: (1) where the directors, in response to a demand, determine that a derivative suit is not in the best interests of the corporation and should not be pursued ("demand required cases"); and (2) where the directors, based on a recommendation of a "special litigation committee" composed of outside directors, determine that derivative litigation properly commenced after demand was excused should not be continued ("demand excused cases"). Courts have long assumed that directors have some power to block derivative suits in demand required cases. As the Delaware Supreme Court noted in *Grimes v. Donald* (*see* Note 3 immediately above), the board's decision not to sue in a demand required case will be respected under Delaware law, provided the board acted "independently, disinterestedly and with due care in response to the demand." Courts also have recognized the power of directors to halt derivative litigation in demand excused cases based upon reports prepared by special litigation committees, even where the suits are against members of the board.

The issue of the board's power to block or halt derivative suits goes to the heart of the derivative remedy. Recall that an important purpose of the derivative remedy is to bypass a wrongdoing board that cannot be expected to sue itself. Thus, an expansive power of directors to block or halt derivative suits could lead to the demise of the derivative suit as a viable remedy. At the same time, an excessively limited power of directors to block or terminate derivative litigation could lead to an unacceptable increase in the level of strike litigation. How should these countervailing concerns be balanced? The following materials consider the standards that apply in cases where directors seek to dismiss properly commenced derivative suits through the device of the special litigation committee.

ZAPATA CORP. v. MALDONADO

Delaware Supreme Court

430 A.2d 779 (1981)

[In the transaction complained of by the plaintiff, the Zapata board, in 1974, accelerated the exercise date of a company stock option plan, allegedly in anticipation of a tender offer shortly to be announced for the company's own shares. This acceleration permitted certain insiders, including some members of the board, to exercise their options when the market price was almost $7 below the tender offer price. While the exercise price (and hence the consideration received by the corporation) was not affected by the acceleration of the exercise date, the defendants did avoid substantial taxes, and the corporation lost a corresponding deduction. That is because the insiders' tax liability and the corporation's deduction was determined based on the difference between the exercise price and the market price on the date of exercise.].

QUILLEN, Justice:

This is an interlocutory appeal from an order entered on April 9, 1980, by the Court of Chancery denying appellant-defendant Zapata Corporation's (Zapata) alternative motions to dismiss the complaint or for summary judgment. The issue to be addressed has reached this Court by way of a rather convoluted path.

In June, 1975, William Maldonado, a stockholder of Zapata, instituted a derivative action in the Court of Chancery on behalf of Zapata against ten officers and/or directors of Zapata, alleging, essentially, breaches of fiduciary duty. Maldonado did not first demand that the board bring this action, stating instead such demand's futility because all directors were named as defendants and allegedly participated in the acts specified. In June, 1977, Maldonado commenced an action in the United States District Court for the Southern District of New York against the same defendants, save one, alleging federal security law violations as well as the same common law claims made previously in the Court of Chancery.

By June, 1979, four of the defendant-directors were no longer on the board, and the remaining directors appointed two new outside directors to the board. The board then created an "Independent Investigation Committee" (Committee), composed solely of the two new directors, to investigate Maldonado's actions, as well as a similar derivative action then pending in Texas, and to determine whether the corporation should continue any or all of the litigation. The Committee's determination was stated to be "final, . . . not . . . subject to review by the Board of Directors and . . . in all respects . . . binding upon the Corporation."

Following an investigation, the Committee concluded, in September, 1979, that each action should "be dismissed forthwith as their continued maintenance is inimical to the Company's best interests . . . ." Consequently, Zapata moved for dismissal or summary judgment in the three derivative actions. On January 24, 1980, the District Court for the Southern District of New York granted Zapata's motion for summary judgment, *Maldonado v. Flynn*, S.D.N.Y., 485 F. Supp. 274 (1980), holding, under its interpretation of Delaware law, that the Committee had the authority, under the "business judgment" rule, to require the termination of the derivative action. Maldonado appealed that decision to the Second Circuit Court of Appeals.

On March 18, 1980, the Court of Chancery, in a reported opinion, the basis for the order of April 9, 1980, denied Zapata's motions, holding that Delaware law does not sanction this means of dismissal. More specifically, it held that the "business judgment" rule is not a grant of authority to dismiss derivative actions and that a stockholder has an individual right to maintain derivative actions in certain instances. *Maldonado v. Flynn*, Del. Ch., 413 A.2d 1251 (1980) (herein *Maldonado*). Pursuant to the provisions of Supreme Court Rule 42, Zapata filed an interlocutory appeal with this Court shortly thereafter.

. . . We limit our review in this interlocutory appeal to whether the Committee has the power to cause the present action to be dismissed.

* * *

. . . [T]he focus in this case is on the power to speak for the corporation as to whether the lawsuit should be continued or terminated. As we see it, this issue in the current appellate posture of this case has three aspects: the conclusions of the Court below concerning the continuing right of a stockholder to maintain a derivative action; the corporate power under Delaware law of an authorized board committee to cause dismissal of litigation instituted for the benefit of the corporation; and the role of the Court of Chancery in resolving conflicts between the stockholder and the committee.

Accordingly, we turn first to the Court of Chancery's conclusions concerning the right of a plaintiff stockholder in a derivative action. We find that its determination that a stockholder, once demand is made and refused, possesses an independent, individual right to continue a derivative suit for breaches of fiduciary duty over objection by the corporation, *Maldonado*, 413 A.2d at 1262-63, as an absolute rule, is erroneous. . . .

* * *

. . . Generally disputes pertaining to control of [a derivative] suit arise in two contexts.

Consistent with the purpose of requiring a demand, a board decision to cause a derivative suit to be dismissed as detrimental to the company, after demand has been made and refused, will be respected unless it was wrongful.[10] . . . A claim of a wrongful decision not to sue is thus the first exception and the first context of dispute. Absent a wrongful refusal, the stockholder in such a situation simply lacks legal managerial power. Compare *Maldonado*, 413 A.2d at 1259-60.

But it cannot be implied that, absent a wrongful board refusal, a stockholder can never have an individual right to initiate an action. For, as is stated in *McKee* [v. *Rogers*, Del. Ch., 156 A. 191 (1931)], a "well settled" exception exists to the general rule.

> [A] stockholder may sue in equity in his derivative right to assert a cause of action in behalf of the corporation, *without prior demand* upon the directors to sue, when it is apparent that a demand would be futile, that the officers are under an influence that sterilizes discretion and could not be proper persons to conduct the litigation.

156 A. at 193 (emphasis added). This exception, the second context for dispute, is consistent with the Court of Chancery's statement below, that "[t]he stockholder's individual right to bring the action does not ripen, however, . . . unless he can show a demand to be futile." *Maldonado*, 413 A.2d at 1262.

These comments in *McKee* and in the opinion below make obvious sense. A demand, when required and refused (if not wrongful), terminates a stockholder's legal ability to ini-

---

[10] In other words, when stockholders, after making demand and having their suit rejected, attack the board's decision as improper, the board's decision falls under the "business judgment" rule and will be respected if the requirements of the rule are met. . . . That situation should be distinguished from the instant case, where demand was not made, and the power of the board to seek a dismissal, due to disqualification, presents a threshold issue. . . . We recognize that the two contexts can overlap in practice.

tiate a derivative action. But where demand is properly excused, the stockholder does possess the ability to initiate the action on his corporation's behalf.

These conclusions, however, do not determine the question before us. Rather, they merely bring us to the question to be decided. It is here that we part company with the Court below. Derivative suits enforce corporate rights and any recovery obtained goes to the corporation. . . . We see no inherent reason why the "two phases" of a derivative suit, the stockholder's suit to compel the corporation to sue and the corporation's suit (citation omitted), should automatically result in the placement in the hands of the litigating stockholder sole control of the corporate right throughout the litigation. To the contrary, it seems to us that such an inflexible rule would recognize the interest of one person or group to the exclusion of all others within the corporate entity. Thus, we reject the view of the Vice Chancellor as to the first aspect of the issue on appeal.

The question to be decided becomes: When, if at all, should an authorized board committee be permitted to cause litigation, properly initiated by a derivative stockholder in his own right, to be dismissed? As noted above, a board has the power to choose not to pursue litigation when demand is made upon it, so long as the decision is not wrongful. If the board determines that a suit would be detrimental to the company, the board's determination prevails. Even when demand is excusable, circumstances may arise when continuation of the litigation would not be in the corporation's best interests. Our inquiry is whether, under such circumstances, there is a permissible procedure under 141(a) by which a corporation can rid itself of detrimental litigation. If there is not, a single stockholder in an extreme case might control the destiny of the entire corporation. This concern was bluntly expressed by the Ninth Circuit in *Lewis v. Anderson*, 9th Cir., 615 F.2d 778, 783 (1979), *cert. denied*, ___ U.S. ___, 101 S. Ct. 206, 66 L. Ed. 2d 89 (1980): "To allow one shareholder to incapacitate an entire board of directors merely by leveling charges against them gives too much leverage to dissident shareholders." But, when examining the means, including the committee mechanism examined in this case, potentials for abuse must be recognized. This takes us to the second and third aspects of the issue on appeal.

Before we pass to equitable considerations as to the mechanism at issue here, it must be clear that an independent committee possesses the corporate power to seek the termination of a derivative suit. Section 141(c) allows a board to delegate all of its authority to a committee. Accordingly, a committee with properly delegated authority would have the power to move for dismissal or summary judgment if the entire board did.

Even though demand was not made in this case and the initial decision of whether to litigate was not placed before the board, Zapata's board, it seems to us, retained all of its corporate power concerning litigation decisions. If Maldonado had made demand on the board in this case, it could have refused to bring suit. Maldonado could then have asserted that the decision not to sue was wrongful and, if correct, would have been allowed to maintain the suit. The board, however, never would have lost its statutory managerial authority. The demand requirement itself evidences that the managerial power is retained by the board. When a derivative plaintiff is allowed to bring suit after a wrongful refusal, the board's authority to choose whether to pursue the litigation is not challenged although its conclusion—reached through the exercise of that authority—is not respected since it is wrongful. Similarly, Rule 23.1, by excusing demand in certain instances, does not strip the board of its corporate power. It merely saves the plaintiff the expense and delay of making a futile demand resulting in a probable tainted exercise of that authority in a refusal by the board or in giving control of litigation to the opposing side. But the board entity remains empowered under § 141(a) to make decisions regarding corporate litigation. The problem is one of member disqualification, not the absence of power in the board.

The corporate power inquiry then focuses on whether the board, tainted by the self-interest of a majority of its members, can legally delegate its authority to a committee of two disinterested directors. We find our statute clearly requires an affirmative answer to this question.

Our focus now switches to the Court of Chancery which is faced with a stockholder assertion that a derivative suit, properly instituted, should continue for the benefit of the corporation and a corporate assertion, properly made by a board committee acting with board authority, that the same derivative suit should be dismissed as inimical to the best interests of the corporation.

At the risk of stating the obvious, the problem is relatively simple. If, on the one hand, corporations can consistently wrest bona fide derivative actions away from well-meaning derivative plaintiffs through the use of the committee mechanism, the derivative suit will lose much, if not all, of its generally-recognized effectiveness as an intra-corporate means of policing boards of directors. . . . If, on the other hand, corporations are unable to rid themselves of meritless or harmful litigation and strike suits, the derivative action, created to benefit the corporation, will produce the opposite, unintended result. . . . It thus appears desirable to us to find a balancing point where bona fide stockholder power to bring corporate causes of action cannot be unfairly trampled on by the board of directors, but the corporation can rid itself of detrimental litigation.

As we noted, the question has been treated by other courts as one of the "business judgment" of the board committee. If a "committee, composed of independent and disinterested directors, conducted a proper review of the matters before it, considered a variety of factors and reached, in good faith, a business judgment that [the] action was not in the best interest of [the corporation]," the action must be dismissed. See, e.g., *Maldonado v. Flynn, supra,* 485 F. Supp. at 282, 286. The issues become solely independence, good faith, and reasonable investigation. The ultimate conclusion of the committee, under that view, is not subject to judicial review.

We are not satisfied, however, that acceptance of the "business judgment" rationale at this stage of derivative litigation is a proper balancing point. While we admit an analogy with a normal case respecting board judgment, it seems to us that there is sufficient risk in the realities of a situation like the one presented in this case to justify caution beyond adherence to the theory of business judgment.

The context here is a suit against directors where demand on the board is excused. We think some tribute must be paid to the fact that the lawsuit was properly initiated. It is not a board refusal case. Moreover, this complaint was filed in June of 1975 and, while the parties undoubtedly would take differing views on the degree of litigation activity, we have to be concerned about the creation of an "Independent Investigation Committee" four years later, after the election of two new outside directors. Situations could develop where such motions could be filed after years of vigorous litigation for reasons unconnected with the merits of the lawsuit.

Moreover, notwithstanding our conviction that Delaware law entrusts the corporate power to a properly authorized committee, we must be mindful that directors are passing judgment on fellow directors in the same corporation and fellow directors, in this instance, who designated them to serve both as directors and committee members. The question naturally arises whether a "there but for the grace of God go I" empathy might not play a role. And the further question arises whether inquiry as to independence, good faith and reasonable investigation is sufficient safeguard against abuse, perhaps sub-conscious abuse.

* * *

Whether the Court of Chancery will be persuaded by the exercise of a committee power resulting in a summary motion for dismissal of a derivative action, where a demand has not been initially made, should rest, in our judgment, in the independent discretion of the Court of Chancery. We thus steer a middle course between those cases which yield to the independent business judgment of a board committee and this case as determined below which would yield to unbridled plaintiff stockholder control. In pursuit of the course, we recognize that "[t]he final substantive judgment whether a particular lawsuit should be maintained requires a balance of many factors—ethical, commercial, promotional, public relations, employee relations, fiscal as well as legal." [citation omitted]. But we are content that such factors are not "beyond the judicial reach" of the Court of Chancery which regularly and competently deals with fiduciary relationships, disposition of trust property, approval of settlements and scores of similar problems. We recognize the danger of judicial overreaching but the alternatives seem to us to be outweighed by the fresh view of a judicial outsider. Moreover, if we failed to balance all the interests involved, we would in the name of practicality and judicial economy foreclose a judicial decision on the merits. At this point, we are not convinced that is necessary or desirable.

After an objective and thorough investigation of a derivative suit, an independent committee may cause its corporation to file a pretrial motion to dismiss in the Court of Chancery. The basis of the motion is the best interests of the corporation, as determined by the committee. The motion should include a thorough written record of the investigation and its findings and recommendations. Under appropriate Court supervision, akin to proceedings on summary judgment, each side should have an opportunity to make a record on the motion. As to the limited issues presented by the motion noted below, the moving party should be prepared to meet the normal burden under Rule 56 that there is no genuine issue as to any material fact and that the moving party is entitled to dismiss as a matter of law. The Court should apply a two-step test to the motion.

First, the Court should inquire into the independence and good faith of the committee and the bases supporting its conclusions. Limited discovery may be ordered to facilitate such inquiries. The corporation should have the burden of proving independence, good faith and a reasonable investigation, rather than presuming independence, good faith and reasonableness. If the Court determines either that the committee is not independent or has not shown reasonable bases for its conclusions, or, if the Court is not satisfied for other reasons relating to the process, including but not limited to the good faith of the committee, the Court shall deny the corporation's motion. If, however, the Court is satisfied under Rule 56 standards that the committee was independent and showed reasonable bases for good faith findings and recommendations, the Court may proceed, in its discretion, to the next step.

The second step provides, we believe, the essential key in striking the balance between legitimate corporate claims as expressed in a derivative stockholder suit and a corporation's best interests as expressed by an independent investigating committee. The Court should determine, applying its own independent business judgment, whether the motion should be granted. This means, of course, that instances could arise where a committee can establish its independence and sound bases for its good faith decisions and still have the corporation's motion denied. The second step is intended to thwart instances where corporate actions meet the criteria of step one, but the result does not appear to satisfy its spirit, or where corporate actions would simply prematurely terminate a stockholder grievance deserving of further consideration in the corporation's interest. The Court of Chancery of course must carefully consider and weigh how compelling the corporate interest in dismissal is when faced with a non-frivolous lawsuit. The Court of Chancery should, when appropriate, give special consideration to matters of law and public policy in addition to the corporation's best interests.

If the Court's independent business judgment is satisfied, the Court may proceed to grant the motion, subject, of course, to any equitable terms or conditions the Court finds necessary or desirable.

The interlocutory order of the Court of Chancery is reversed and the cause is remanded for further proceedings consistent with this opinion.

NOTES AND QUESTIONS

(1) **Demand required versus demand excused.** In contrast to its approach in "demand excused" cases, *Zapata* holds that courts should review board determinations not to sue in "demand required" cases under the relatively deferential standards of the business judgment rule.[55] Do you agree with this distinction between "demand required" and "demand excused" cases? There is authority for applying a *Zapata*-type test irrespective of whether demand is required or excused.[56] On the other hand, an argument for a dual standard is that the demand-made standard is generally applied only after a preliminary judicial determination on the pleadings that the board is capable of dealing with the matter and exercised reasonable business judgment in the transaction.

(2) **The standard under universal demand.** Where a universal demand requirement as in ALI *Principles* § 7.03 is adopted so that demand is required in virtually all cases, there is no longer a prior judicial screening that justifies special deference to board determinations not to sue in response to demands. Thus, ALI *Principles* §§ 7.08-.10 do not differentiate between demand-required and demand-refused cases in reviewing director motions to dismiss.

---

[55] For decisions discussing the application of the business judgment rule in "demand required" cases, see *Scattered Corp. v. Chicago Stock Exchange*, 701 A.2d 70 (Del. 1997), and *Grimes v. Donald*, 673 A.2d 1207 (Del. 1996).

[56] *See Alford v. Shaw*, 320 N.C. 465, 358 S.E.2d 323 (1987) (applying *Zapata*-type test).

(3) **Disinterested review.** What showing of board conflict of interest should be enough to establish a lack of independence under *Zapata* or similar tests? ALI *Principles* § 1.23(c) makes clear that a director is not disqualified from serving on a special litigation committee merely by the fact that the director participated in the decision that gave rise to the action. Also, the courts generally have held that special litigation committees were independent although defendant directors appointed them.[57] Do these situations present special risks of bias that are not present whenever a board committee passes on litigation against comembers? For good examples of cases considering the independence of special litigation committees, see *Kaplan v. Wyatt*[58] and *Lewis v. Fuqua*.[59] In *Kaplan*, the court found a two-member special litigation committee, which voted to terminate derivative litigation against the corporation's Chairman and CEO, to be independent under *Zapata*, even though (1) one of the two members was on the board at the time of the challenged transaction (though he abstained from voting on the challenged transaction), (2) that member owned a 50% interest in a firm that transacted business with the corporation, and (3) that member had, in the past, expressed sympathy for oil company executives, such as the defendant. But in *Lewis*, the court held that the defendants had failed to establish the independence of a one-man special litigation committee where (1) the committee member was a member of the corporation's board of directors at the time the challenged actions took place, (2) he was one of the defendants in the suit, (3) he had numerous political and financial dealings with the principal defendant, the CEO of the corporation, (4) he was the president of a university which had received a $10 million pledge from the corporation and the CEO, and (5) the CEO had, in the past, made several contributions to the university and was a member of its board of trustees.[60] For a detailed consideration of the independence of a special litigation committee outside of Delaware, see *Eihorn v. Culea*.[61]

(4) **Comparison with standards of independence for determining whether a demand is futile.** Should the standards for determining the independence of special litigation committees be the same as those used for determining whether a demand must be made on the board prior to suit? If the question in the demand situation is only whether a relatively costless demand may produce a constructive response from the

---

[57] See *Strougo v. Padegs*, 27 F. Supp. 2d 442 (S.D.N.Y. 1998); *Abella v. Universal Leaf Tobacco Co., Inc.*, 546 F. Supp. 795 (E.D. Va. 1982); *Stein v. Bailey*, 531 F. Supp. 684 (S.D.N.Y. 1982); *Genzer v. Cunningham*, 498 F. Supp. 682 (E.D. Mich. 1980); *Maldonado v. Flynn*, 485 F. Supp. 274 (S.D.N.Y. 1980), *modified*, 671 F.2d 729 (2d Cir. 1982); *Rosengarten v. ITT*, 466 F. Supp. 817 (S.D.N.Y. 1979); *Auerbach v. Bennett*, 47 N.Y.2d 619, 393 N.E.2d 994, 419 N.Y.S.2d 920 (1979). For a leading case contra, see *Miller v. Register and Tribute Syndicate, Inc.*, 336 N.W.2d 709 (Iowa 1983).

[58]   499 A.2d 1184 (Del. 1985).

[59]   502 A.2d 962 (Del. Ch. 1985).

[60]   For cases other than *Lewis* that refused on this ground to allow termination, see *Clark v. Lomas & Nettleton Financial Corp.*, 625 F.2d 49 (5th Cir. 1980), *cert. denied*, 450 U.S. 1029 (1981) (principal defendant was a major shareholder); *Galef v. Alexander*, 615 F.2d 51 (2d Cir. 1980) (outside directors who voted to terminate allegedly acquiesced and participated in the wrongful conduct).

[61]   612 N.W.2d 78 (Wis. 2000).

board, rather than whether the board's judgment should be trusted to the extent of foreclosing judicial scrutiny, perhaps a looser standard of independence should apply in the demand context. Thus, in *Grossman v. Johnson*,[62] the court held that the Supreme Court's dictum in an earlier case[63] to the effect that independent directors could not dismiss a suit brought under this particular statutory provision did not preclude giving the directors a chance to exercise their independent judgment.[64] On the other hand, in *Kaplan v. Wyatt*,[65] the Delaware Supreme Court held that the same standards of independence apply in the demand and termination contexts (see n.1 to the court's opinion). This arguably makes sense if the function of the demand excuse hearing is an early determination of whether the suit should proceed (*see* Note 6 following *Starrels* and Note 1, above).

(5) **Good faith.** The special litigation committee's decision must be made in good faith in the sense that it must be based on a thorough review of relevant data after due deliberation. An important feature of board review in the recent cases has been the appointment of a prestigious, irreproachable and expensive "special counsel."[66] For an example of a board review that did not pass, see *Peller v. The Southern Co.*,[67] where the plaintiff sued for mismanagement in the firm's construction of a power plant after the state's Public Service Commission had found in a rate case that the company had imprudently misspent almost a billion dollars, of which the company was forced to bear $300 million. The committee relied on retained counsel and on summarized rather than recorded interviews.[68] For an example of board review that did pass scrutiny, see *Kaplan v. Wyatt*, discussed in Note 3, above, where the committee retained legal counsel and accountants who had no prior dealings with the corporation, interviewed 140 people throughout the world, and prepared a 150-page report on the disputed transactions.

(6) **Independent judicial review.** A critical point of disagreement among the courts and commentators concerns whether a court should substitute its own judgment

---

[62]   674 F.2d 115 (1st Cir.), *cert. denied*, 459 U.S. 838 (1982).

[63]   *Burks v. Lasker*, 441 U.S. 471, 484 (1979).

[64]   See also to the same effect, *Weiss v. Temporary Investment Fund, Inc.*, 692 F.2d 928 (3d Cir. 1982), *vacated and remanded*, 464 U.S. 1001 (1984). For a case reaching a contrary conclusion in the same context, see *Fox v. Reich & Tang, Inc.*, 692 F.2d 250 (2d Cir. 1982), *aff'd*, 464 U.S. 523 (1984). The Supreme Court affirmed *Fox* and vacated and remanded *Weiss* on the ground that FRCP Rule 23.1 does not apply to a suit under § 36(b) of the Investment Company Act of 1940 because the corporation has no claim under that section.

[65]   *Supra* footnote 58.

[66]   *See* DeMott, *Defending the Quiet Life: The Role of Special Counsel in Director Terminations of Derivative Suits*, 56 Notre Dame L. Rev. 850 (1981).

[67]   707 F. Supp. 525 (N.D. Ga. 1988), *aff'd*, 911 F.2d 1532 (11th Cir. 1990).

[68]   For a more recent example of a board review that failed to pass muster, see *Electra Investment Trust PLC v. Crews*, 1999 Del. Ch. LEXIS 36, 1999 WL 135239 (Del. Ch. 1999) (special litigation committee (1) failed to investigate at all a matter involving a $2600 payment for the defendant's child support payments, deeming the amount in question too small; (2) merely accepted the defendant's explanation regarding the failure of the firm's auditor to issue an opinion; and (3) failed to investigate disputed travel and entertainment expenses, apart from discussing the matter with the defendant).

as to whether the suit should be maintained for that of independent directors who have made a thorough review. *Zapata* is a leading case favoring court power to review the substance as well as the procedure of a board decision not to sue.[69] Some cases hold that the court must review the substance of the board's decision,[70] while others (such as *Kaplan v. Wyatt*, discussed in Note 3, above) hold that substantive review is discretionary. A leading case against reviewability of a decision by an independent board not to sue is *Auerbach v. Bennett*.[71] *Alford v. Shaw*, *supra* footnote 70, discusses the difficulty of the issue and the choices available to the courts. The North Carolina Court of Appeals refused to accord any weight to the committee's decision. The Supreme Court reversed originally on the ground that the *Auerbach* business judgment approach should be applied,[72] later changing its mind and applying a *Zapata*-type test[73] and ultimately affirming dismissal on the basis of the special litigation committee report.[74] *In re PSE & G Shareholder Litigation*[75] carves out a middle ground between *Zapata* and *Auerbach*, applying a "modified business judgment rule," which places the initial burden on the corporation to demonstrate that the members of the special litigation committee (1) were independent and disinterested, (2) acted in good faith and with due care in their investigation of the shareholder's allegations, and that (3) the committee's decision was reasonable.

(7) **Policy considerations related to the need for independent judicial review: the "empathy" problem.** The commentators generally have supported some court review of board decisions to terminate derivative suits. **Coffee & Schwartz** argue that decisions to dismiss derivative suits ought to be entitled to less protection than other board decisions because the former decisions are made under less time pressure; decisions to terminate are more amenable to judicial review since the litigation committee creates a written record; the disinterestedness of the directors making the decision is more suspect than with respect to other business decisions; and the outside directors who make the decision probably need not in any event fear liability.

---

[69]   For holdings consistent with *Zapata*, see *Peller v. The Southern Co.*, *supra* footnote 67; *Abella v. Universal Leaf Tobacco Co.*, *supra* footnote 57; *Watts v. Des Moines Register & Tribune*, 525 F. Supp. 1311 (S.D. Iowa 1981).

[70]   *See Joy v. North*, 692 F.2d 880 (2d Cir. 1982); *Alford v. Shaw*, 320 N.C. 465, 358 S.E.2d 323 (1987).

[71]   *See supra* footnote 57. For holdings consistent with *Auerbach*, see *Genzer v. Cunningham*, *supra* footnote 57; *Gall v. Exxon Corp.*, 418 F. Supp. 508 (S.D.N.Y. 1976); *Black v. Nu-Aire, Inc.*, 426 N.W.2d 203 (Minn. Ct. App. 1988); *Cuker v. Mikalauskas*, 692 A.2d 1042 (Pa. 1997); and *In re Hirsch v. Jones Intercable, Inc.*, 984 P.2d 629 (Colo. 1999) (role of court is "limited to inquiring into the independence and good faith of the committee," because most courts outside of Delaware "are ill-equipped and infrequently called on to evaluate what are and must be essentially business judgments"). *See also Skoglund v. Brady*, 541 N.W.2d 17 (Minn. App. 1995) (trial court "properly refrained from conducting a substantive review of the special litigation committee's recommendation and properly limited its review to determining whether the special litigation committee was independent and conducted its review in good faith").

[72]   318 N.C. 289, 349 S.E.2d 41 (1986).

[73]   *See* Cox, *Heroes in the Law: Alford v. Shaw*, 66 N.C. L. Rev. 565 (1988).

[74]   398 S.E.2d 445 (N.C. 1990).

[75]   801 A.2d 295 (N.J. 2002).

With respect to whether the directors comprising the special litigation committee are truly disinterested, consider the discussion in *Zapata* of "there but for the grace of God go I empathy." This "empathy" exacerbates the independence problems that generally exist in connection with decisions by public corporation boards of directors (see, generally, the discussion of board selection and membership in Section 7.07[A]). **Coffee & Schwartz** argue:[76]

> Others have collected the empirical evidence that board members are still typically selected and regularly dismissed by the company's senior management. At first glance, this vulnerability of board members might seem to apply equally to all board decisions, and therefore not distinguish the special case of a decision not to sue. But shades of difference exist, and this process of director selection and socialization, which incumbent management dominates, may cause even the outside director to perceive his role, once litigation is commenced, as that of a buffer by which to shelter and protect management from hostile and litigious stockholders. In particular, a derivative action evokes a response of group loyalty, so that even a "maverick" director may feel compelled to close ranks and protect his fellows from the attack of the "strike suiter." As a result, an outside director independent enough to oppose the chief executive officer with respect to a proposed transaction that he thinks is unfair or unwise may still be unable to tell the same officer that he thinks a suit against him has sufficient merit to proceed. The latter vote would be a far more personal and stigmatizing form of opposition. In short, prospective rejections can be diplomatic and couched in terms of the appearances of impropriety, but a refusal to protect one's peers once events have transpired is seen as disloyal treachery.

For an acute example of the "empathy" problem, see *Rosengarten v. ITT*,[77] in which some members of the litigation committee passing on a questionable payments suit were directors of other companies which had been accused of making questionable payments, and one had been named as a defendant in such a suit.[78] But *Peller v. The Southern Co.*, discussed in Note 5, rejected the argument that the litigation committee was not independent because its members had similar backgrounds to the defendants, reasoning that this was the inevitable result of staffing the committee with experts.

On the other hand, consider the following, from **Fischel & Bradley** (at 273-74):[79]

---

[76] 81 COLUM. L. REV. at 283. Copyright 1982 by the Directors of the Columbia Law Review Association, Inc. All rights reserved.

[77] 466 F. Supp. 817 (S.D.N.Y. 1979).

[78] For judicial acceptance of the argument that the "empathy" problem necessitates court review of board decisions not to sue, *see*, in addition to *Zapata*, *Joy v. North*, *supra* footnote 70; *Lasker v. Burks*, 567 F.2d 1208, 1212 (2d Cir. 1978), *rev'd on other gds.*, 441 U.S. 471 (1979).

[79] Copyright © 1986 by Cornell Law Review. Reprinted by permission.

It is thus incorrect to conclude that the "structural bias" of the board ... demonstrates the need for more vigorous enforcement of derivative suits. This argument represents a form of the Nirvana fallacy: it compares imperfect incentives of corporate managers and their agents with a mythical perfect enforcement scheme and concludes, not surprisingly, that perfect enforcement dominates. But the relevant question is which of two very imperfect classes of decision makers—managers allegedly involved in wrongdoing or individuals named by them to serve on special litigation committees on the one hand or shareholders with a small economic stake in the venture represented by plaintiffs' attorneys and judges on the other hand— is more likely to make decisions that increase the value of the firm.

(8) **The nature of judicial review.** Assuming there should be some judicial review of the decision not to sue, what should be the nature of the review? The initial question is whether the court is limited to the findings in the special litigation committee's report, or whether it can make its own findings or rely on evidence outside the report. ALI *Principles* § 7.10(a)(2) lets the court, in cases involving breach of the duty of fair dealing, determine whether "the board or committee reasonably concluded that dismissal was in the best interests of the corporation, based on grounds that the court deems to warrant reliance."

(9) **The standard of review.** To the extent the court draws its own conclusions from the committee's findings, what standard of review should the court apply? Consider the standard actually applied by *Zapata*. One possible approach is to reverse a board decision to terminate only under a standard similar to that applied under the business judgment rule (*see* Section 9.03[A]) above—that is, where the directors have committed a gross abuse of discretion.[80] Another approach is to reverse a board decision if it is unreasonable,[81] as ALI *Principles* § 7.10(a)(2) suggests for cases involving breach of the duty of fair dealing.

Joy v. North, supra footnote 70, at 892, established the following standard for summary judgment based on a board decision not to sue:

> [T]he burden is on the moving party, as in motions for summary judgment generally, to demonstrate that the action is more likely than not to be against the interests of the corporation.

* * *

---

[80]   *See Cramer v. General Telephone & Electronics Corp.*, 582 F.2d 259, 275 (3d Cir. 1978), *cert. denied*, 439 U.S. 1129 (1979); Block, Prussin & Wachtel, *Dismissal of Derivative Actions Under the Business Judgment Rule:* Zapata *One Year Later*, 38 Bus. Law. 401, 416-17 (1983); *see also* ALI *Principles* § 7.10(a)(1) (court should dismiss a claim alleging breach of a director's duty of care if the committee's determination satisfies the requirements of the business judgment rule).

[81]   *See PSE & G Shareholder Litigation, supra* footnote 75.

Where the court determines that the likely recoverable damages discounted by the probability of a finding of liability are less than the costs to the corporation in continuing the action, it should dismiss the case. The costs which may properly be taken into account are attorney's fees and other out-of-pocket expenses related to the litigation and time spent by corporate personnel preparing for and participating in the trial. The court should also weigh indemnification which is mandatory under corporate by-laws, private contract or Connecticut law, discounted of course by the probability of liability for such sums.

* * *

Where, having completed the above analysis, the court finds a likely net return to the corporation which is not substantial in relation to shareholder equity, it may take into account two other items as costs. First, it may consider the impact of distraction of key personnel by continued litigation. Second, it may take into account potential lost profits which may result from the publicity of a trial.

Judicial scrutiny of special litigation committee recommendations should thus be limited to a comparison of the direct costs imposed upon the corporation by the litigation with the potential benefits. We are mindful that other less direct costs may be incurred, such as a negative impact on morale and upon the corporate image. Nevertheless, we believe that such factors, with the two exceptions noted, should not be taken into account. Quite apart from the elusiveness of attempting to predict such effects, they are quite likely to be directly related to the degree of wrongdoing, a spectacular fraud being generally more newsworthy and damaging to morale than a mistake in judgment as to the strength of consumer demand.

Under this test, suppose the plaintiff claims the directors made a major miscalculation that cost the corporation $50 million, but as to which there is a 95% chance that the decision is protected by the business judgment rule. Should the court insist that the action proceed if expected direct costs are less than $2.5 million?

Carlton Investments v. TLC Beatrice International Holdings[82] held, in applying *Zapata*'s second step, that a special litigation committee is "not required to attempt to maximize returns from the lawsuit," but can "legitimately sacrifice present compensation in the settlement if its good faith, informed judgment indicates to it that that course is best for the corporation."

(10) **Relevance of type of claim.** Many of the court decisions upholding negative decisions by litigation committees have involved questionable payments that served the corporation's rather than the directors' personal interests. Dismissal in these cases

---

[82]   1997 Del. Ch. LEXIS 86, 1997 WL 305829 (Del. Ch. 1997).

may reflect the courts' uneasiness with holding directors liable in this situation. On the other hand, many of the cases not upholding board decisions involved alleged self-dealing by board members.[83] The court in *Joy* expressly limited its rule on reviewability to cases involving "direct financial harm to the corporation and a consequent diminishing of shareholders' investment."[84] ALI *Principles* § 7.10 applies a lower standard of review to duty-of-care claims not involving a knowing and culpable law violation than to duty-of-loyalty claims. Even if such a distinction is warranted as to the underlying duty, does it follow that a different standard of review should be applied to board refusal to sue for breach of the duty? The ALI rule also precludes board dismissal of a suit that would permit a defendant "to retain a significant improper benefit" if the defendant controls the corporation or obtained the benefit by fraud or without a vote by disinterested directors or shareholders, unless "the likely injury to the corporation from continuation of the action convincingly outweighs any adverse impact on the public interest from dismissal of the action." Does this test give enough discretion to the board to dismiss litigation that alleges improper benefit but is nevertheless a waste of the corporation's resources?

(11) **Federal versus state law.** Where a federal claim is involved the Supreme Court's decision in *Burks v. Lasker, supra* footnote 63, requires the court to apply state law standards as to whether the board's refusal to sue should be upheld unless such standards would frustrate federal policy. It is not enough that dismissal would bar a federal remedy.[85] However, in *Galef v. Alexander, supra* footnote 60, at 62-64, the court held that federal policies were frustrated despite the availability of a direct action.

(12) **Discovery.** Some courts have denied dismissal in order to give the plaintiff an opportunity to take further discovery limited to the propriety of the board's refusal to sue.[86] How should discovery be limited in connection with a motion for summary judgment under the *Zapata* rule? In *Watts v. Des Moines Register and Tribune, supra* footnote 69, the court allowed 30 days of further discovery on the question of whether there was an adequate basis for the litigation committee's decision to dismiss the suit under the "final prong" of *Zapata*.[87] *Levine v. Smith*[88] held that discovery should be denied in a demand-refused case.

---

[83] *See, e.g., Joy v. North, supra* footnote 70; *Galef v. Alexander, supra* footnote 60; *Zapata v. Maldonado.*

[84] 692 F.2d at 892.

[85] *See, e.g., Abbey v. Control Data Corp.,* 603 F.2d 724, 732 (8th Cir. 1979), *cert. denied,* 444 U.S. 1017 (1980) (noting the remoteness of federal policy under the proxy laws from the claimed injury); *Genzer v. Cunningham, supra,* 498 F. Supp. at 692 (noting the availability of a direct action under the federal proxy laws).

[86] *See Gall v. Exxon Corp., supra* footnote 71; *In re PSE & G Shareholder Litigation,* 315 N.J. Super. 323 (N.J. Super. 1998).

[87] *See also In re PSE & G Shareholder Litigation,* 315 N.J. Super. 323 (N.J. Super. 1998) (permitting discovery on "the narrow issue of what steps directors took to inform themselves of the shareholder demand and the reasonableness of the decision," but holding that plaintiffs "may not have discovery on the merits of their claim nor may they require defendants to procure documents which were utilized in making decisions which resulted in alleged mismanagement").

[88] 591 A.2d 194 (Del. 1991).

(13) **Policy review.** The rules on director power to block or halt derivative litigation result in a tangled and lengthy procedure, as Chancellor Brown discussed at some length in his *Kaplan v. Wyatt* opinion.[89] Consider the tortuous course of a hypothetical litigation, which could be called the "Corporate Litigation Game."

Square 1:	Plaintiff files suit without making a demand.
Square 2:	Defendants move to dismiss for lack of a demand.
Square 3:	Motion denied. (If motion is granted, revisit Square 1 after demand and then skip to Square 4, with possible variations in later squares.)
Square 4:	Corporation organizes Special Litigation Committee, which makes its investigation and writes a report.
Square 5:	The corporation moves to dismiss on the basis of the SLC report.
Square 6:	Plaintiff moves for discovery on the report. After several hearings and many briefs, the court grants limited discovery.
Square 7:	Briefing and hearings on motion to dismiss.
Square 8:	Motion to dismiss denied.
Square 9:	Motion for summary judgment on the merits of plaintiff's claim.
Square 10:	Motion denied.
Square 11:	Trial on plaintiff's claim.
Square 12:	Settlement in mid-trial.
Square 13:	Hearings on adequacy of settlement, motions for leave to intervene, etc. (*see* Section 10.10, below).

Are there viable alternatives that would screen out "strike" suits without destroying the derivative suit as a device for disciplining management? One possibility is to give no effect to board decisions to block or terminate derivative suits, at least where the suit is against the board itself—that is, to do away with the demand requirement and the special litigation committee. The board could then secure dismissal in at least three ways: (1) obtaining a shareholder vote to terminate the litigation (*see* Section 10.07); (2) obtaining pre-trial dismissal on the merits; or (3) settling with the defendant (*see* Section 10.10). Dismissal on the merits may be unlikely at a preliminary phase of the suit. The third (settlement) option is similar to a board refusal to sue except that it requires the plaintiff's consent. Thus, if the board cannot dismiss the derivative suit apart from settlement, it must pay the plaintiff to go away. If the derivative remedy invites non-meritorious "strike" litigation, mandating settlement with the plaintiff could hurt the corporation.

---

[89] 484 A.2d 501 (Del. Ch. 1984).

A second alternative is to uphold board dismissals without a complex and protracted judicial review. This would effectively do away with derivative litigation and return control of corporate litigation to the board instead of delegating it in some cases to individual shareholders. The downside to this alternative is that the potential benefits of judicial monitoring of board decisions would be lost. But are these potential benefits worth the cost? Among other things, intensive judicial oversight of the board dismissal process encourages the board to dispose of the case more cheaply by paying off the plaintiff in a settlement, thereby encouraging "strike" litigation. Also recall the various monitoring and contractual devices discussed in Section 9.01 that tend to prevent directors from running wild with the shareholders' money, and that constrain them to take action against the occasional bad apple who does engage in fraud.

Finally, note that either of the above alternatives could be viewed merely as default rules, subject to contrary provision in the articles of incorporation. Why not let the shareholders opt out of the derivative remedy? Consider the discussion of opting out of fiduciary duties in Section 9.09.

REFERENCES

Buxbaum, *Conflict-of-Interests Statutes and the Need for Demand on Directors in Derivative Actions*, 68 CAL. L. REV. 1122 (1980).

Coffee & Schwartz, *The Survival of the Derivative Suit: An Evaluation and a Proposal for Legislative Reform*, 81 COLUM. L. REV. 261 (1981).

Cox, *Searching for the Corporation's Voice in Derivative Suit Litigation: A Critique of Zapata and the ALI Project*, 1982 DUKE L.J. 959.

Cox & Munsinger, *Bias in the Boardroom: Psychological Foundations and Legal Implications of Corporate Cohesion*, 48 LAW & CONTEMP. PROBS. 83 (1985).

Dent, *The Power of Directors to Terminate Shareholder Litigation: The Death of the Derivative Suit?*, 75 NW. U. L. REV. 96 (1980).

Duesenberg, *The Business Judgment Rule and Shareholder Derivative Suits: A View from the Inside*, 60 WASH. U. L.Q. 311 (1982).

Fischel, *The "Race to the Bottom" Revisited: Reflections on Recent Developments in Delaware's Corporation Law*, 76 NW. U. L. REV. 913 (1982).

Fischel & Bradley, *The Role of Liability Rules and the Derivative Suit in Corporate Law: A Theoretical and Empirical Analysis*, 71 CORNELL L. REV. 261 (1986).

PROBLEM

WTR Corporation is a large corporation, the stock of which is traded on the New York Stock Exchange. WTR has approximately 50,000 shareholders, none of whom owns more than 1% of the stock. The board consists of 15 members, of whom six are key executives in the company and nine are executives of other corporations.

As a result of a generally weak stock market, the price of WTR stock had declined precipitously to only half the exercise price of executive stock options granted a few years before. The WTR directors, purportedly acting pursuant to the terms of the stock option plan, decided to lower the exercise price of the options by approximately 50%. The purpose of this move as expressed in corporate proxy materials was to preserve the company's stock option plan, as a viable way of attracting and retaining key executives. As a result of the changes in the plan, the six executive-directors received options covering a total of almost 200,000 shares for a total price of some $2,000,000 less than the previous exercise price. The change in the stock option plan was unanimously approved by the nine "outside" members of the board who were not covered by the option plan. Although the original stock option plan was approved by the shareholders, the changes were not.

You represent a WTR shareholder who wishes to bring a derivative suit for damages arising out of the change in the stock option plan. You have concluded that there is some basis for a state law cause of action based on breach of the directors' fiduciary duties and a federal claim for misrepresentations and nondisclosures in proxy statements issued in connection with the original approval of the plan and in subsequent proxy statements issued in connection with director elections. Assume the relevant jurisdiction has enacted a rule governing derivative suits which is identical to Federal Rule 23.1 but that the law of the relevant jurisdiction governing the matters discussed in this section is unsettled.

(a) Advise the shareholder as to the likelihood that the board will be able to block his suit.

(b) Assuming your client decides to sue, would you make a demand on the directors?

(c) If you would not make a demand upon the directors, what would you allege in your complaint with respect to excuse?

§ 10.07 Demand on Shareholders and Effect of Shareholder Refusal to Sue

This Section considers three interrelated issues: (1) the effect of prior shareholder approval of the challenged transaction; (2) the effect of a shareholder vote to terminate a derivative suit; and (3) the necessity of serving a demand on the shareholders as a precondition of the right to maintain a derivative suit.

[A] Effect of Shareholder Approval

Shareholder approval of director fraud does not place the transaction beyond judicial scrutiny, although shareholder approval may be fully effective as to a breach of a duty of care claim.[90] Even where the shareholder vote is disinterested and made after full disclosure, the transaction may be overturned if plaintiff successfully bears the bur-

---

90   *See In re Wheelabrator Technologies, Inc. Shareholders Litigation*, 663 A.2d 1194 (Del. Ch. 1995).

den of proving that the transaction was grossly unfair.[91] Where the shareholder vote is interested, the burden of proving fairness of the challenged transaction remains with the defendant. *See* Section 9.04[C].

[B] Effect of Shareholder Termination

It does not necessarily follow from the fact that shareholder approval of a transaction is inconclusive that a shareholder vote to terminate a derivative suit will also be inconclusive. There is, in fact, authority for the proposition that the shareholders may terminate a derivative suit.[92] ALI *Principles* § 7.11 recommends dismissal of derivative suits upon the vote of disinterested shareholders, provided that a resolution recommending dismissal has been properly adopted by the board and dismissal would not constitute a waste of corporate assets. **Leavell** (at 335) compared relying on the shareholders to eliminate bad derivative suits to "dealing with the problem of pigeons on a window ledge by giving your eight-year-old son a loaded shot-gun." But why shouldn't the owners of the corporation be able to have the final say on whether suit is brought?

[C] Requirement of Demand on Shareholders

Some cases appear to tie the demand requirement to the question of whether the shareholders may ratify or terminate the suit.[93] But even if shareholders can effectively ratify or terminate, it does not necessarily follow that a demand on the shareholders should be required. The courts could hold that a demand requirement would excessively burden the plaintiff—particularly in a publicly held corporation—so that any vote to block the transaction should be obtained by the defendants.[94] Conversely, some courts have held that, even if the shareholders could not terminate the action, the plaintiff maybe required to make a demand.[95] ALI *Principles* § 7.03(c) provides that demand on the shareholders is not required.

---

[91]   *See Michelson v. Duncan*, 407 A.2d 211, 224-25 (Del. 1979); *Schreiber v. Pennzoil Co.*, 419 A.2d 952, 957 (Del. Ch. 1980).

[92]   *See S. Solomont & Sons Trust Inc. v. New England Theatres Operating Corp.*, 326 Mass. 99, 93 N.E.2d 241 (1950).

[93]   *See Mayer v. Adams*, 37 Del. Ch. 298, 141 A.2d 458 (Del. 1958).

[94]   *See Gottesman v. General Motors Corporation*, 268 F.2d 194 (2d Cir. 1959) (demand excused where the defendant owned a large, but not demonstrably controlling block of stock, and there were a large number of shareholders); *Weiss v. Sunasco, Inc.*, 316 F. Supp. 1197 (E.D. Pa. 1970) (demand excused where there were a large number of shareholders, and the history of the litigation demonstrated the unlikelihood that plaintiff could obtain an intracorporate remedy).

[95]   *See Bell v. Arnold*, 175 Colo. 277, 487 P.2d 545 (1971); *Claman v. Robertson*, 164 Ohio St. 61, 128 N.E.2d 429 (1955).

REFERENCES

Leavell, *The Shareholders as Judges of Alleged Wrongs by Directors*, 35 TUL. L. REV. 331 (1961).

Comment, *The Demand and Standing Requirements in Stockholder Derivative Actions*, 44 U. CHI. L. REV. 168 (1976).

Comment, *Shareholder Validation of Directors' Frauds: The Non-Ratification Rule v. The Business Judgment Rule*, 58 NW. L. REV. 807 (1964).

§ 10.08 Potential Conflicts Inherent in the Corporation's Role in a Derivative Suit

In a derivative suit, corporate managers frequently are defendants and yet at the same time control the corporation, the party in whose right the derivative suit is brought. Managers may try to use their power not only to seek dismissal of the suit on *Zapata* grounds (*see* Section 10.06), but also to assert defenses on behalf of the corporation (which is a party defendant), to structure a settlement so as to favor defendants and plaintiff's counsel at shareholder expense, and to obtain indemnification of litigation expenses.

Managers' power is constrained by legal rules intended to minimize the impact of the potential conflict of interest, such as those governing board termination of the suit. Also, the corporation is precluded from asserting defenses that do not involve the protection of specific corporate interests. For example, the corporation ordinarily may not defend the suit on the merits. However, it may move to dismiss for plaintiff's failure to make a demand on the directors or shareholders (if required) since this is a contention that the suit has frustrated intra-corporate procedures. ALI *Principles* § 7.05(a)(4) would also let the corporation "oppose injunctive relief directly affecting its material interests."[96] As to the other matters affected by management's conflicting interests, settlements are overseen by the court (*see* Section 10.10), and indemnification is restricted by statute (*see* Section 10.12).

These legal rules do not always fully protect the shareholders from the adverse effects of management's conflicting interests in derivative suits. For example, the corporation may raise certain defenses that technically protect the interests of the corporation and therefore are legally proper, but that are nevertheless not, as a practical matter, in the best interests of the corporation. Court supervision of settlements does not always prevent unwise settlements, and the rules regarding indemnification leave much room within which management may maneuver.

---

[96] For discussions of which defenses the corporation may raise, see *Otis & Co. v. Pennsylvania R. Co.*, 57 F. Supp. 680 (E.D. Pa. 1944); *Ireland v. Wynkoop*, 36 Colo. App. 205, 539 P.2d 1349 (1975); Washington, *Stockholders' Derivative Suits: The Company's Role, and a Suggestion*, 25 CORNELL L.Q. 361 (1940); Note, *Defenses in Shareholders' Derivative Suits—Who May Raise Them?*, 66 HARV. L. REV. 342 (1952).

In order fully to protect the shareholders against detrimental conflicts of interest, perhaps the corporation and individual defendants should be required to have separate counsel. Some cases support disqualifying attorneys from representing both corporate and individual defendants, at least where fraud is alleged against the individual defendants.[97] Some commentators argue that dual representation should virtually always be forbidden.[98] Case law support for this broad rule is mixed.[99] Arguably there will always be a conflict between the interests of the corporation and those of the individual defendants. On the other hand, multiple counsel arguably should not be required where the claims against the insider defendants are frivolous. Moreover, since the corporation may ultimately be required to pay the defendants' litigation costs (*see* Section 10.12), perhaps it should be permitted to pursue the lower-cost alternative of joint representation.

§ 10.09 Miscellaneous Procedural Matters

[A] Jurisdiction Over Non-Resident Directors

In state court derivative suits, the main jurisdiction problem is obtaining service of process on both the corporation, which is a necessary party, and on all of the other defendants. Even if the plaintiff seeks to enjoin a transaction rather than damages from individual directors, jurisdiction over the directors may be necessary so that the injunction binds the acting parties. For example, *Young v. Colgate-Palmolive Co.*[100] barred a derivative action seeking to prevent the adoption of a "poison pill," where jurisdiction over the directors could not be obtained. The court said that in a direct suit, such as one for the payment of dividends, jurisdiction over the corporation would suffice, since a direct suit seeks action only from the corporation. Is this a fair distinction?[101]

Delaware law attempts to alleviate the problem illustrated by *Young* by giving Delaware courts jurisdiction in certain cases over nonresident directors of Delaware cor-

---

[97]   *See Cannon v. U.S. Acoustics Corp.*, 398 F. Supp. 209 (N.D. Ill. 1975), *modified and aff'd on this point*, 532 F.2d 1118 (7th Cir. 1976); *In re Conduct of Kinsey*, 294 Or. 544, 660 P.2d 660 (1983).

[98]   *See* Bishop, THE LAW OF CORPORATE OFFICERS AND DIRECTORS: INDEMNIFICATION AND INSURANCE § 4.05 (1982); Note, *Independent Representation for Corporate Defendants in Derivative Suits*, 74 YALE L.J. 524 (1965).

[99]   The rule is supported by dictum in *Messing v. FDI, Inc.*, 439 F. Supp. 776, 782 (D.N.J. 1977). For a case refusing to disqualify counsel from representing both the corporation and independent directors in a derivative suit, see *Scott v. New Drug Services*, 1990 WL 135932 (Del. Ch. 1990). The same counsel may represent both the corporation and individual defendants where the corporation is a passive party in a governance dispute between two factions of shareholders. *See Schmidt v. Magnetic Head Corporation*, 468 N.Y.S. 2d 649, 97 A.D. 2d 151 (1983).

[100]   790 F.2d 567 (7th Cir. 1986).

[101]   For other recent cases on jurisdiction over individual defendants in derivative suits, see *Farr v. Designer Phosphate and Premix International, Inc.*, 777 F. Supp. 890 (D. Kan. 1991) (shareholder action against non-resident directors dismissed for lack of jurisdiction under Kansas long-arm); *Anderson v. Heartland Oil & Gas, Inc.*, 819 P.2d 1192 (Kan. 1991) (corporate officers constitutionally subject to state's long-arm statute because of corporation's business in state).

porations who were elected after the date of the statute.[102] But the Supreme Court has not yet directly considered whether such a statute is constitutional under *Shaffer v. Heitner*,[103] in which the Supreme Court held unconstitutional on due process grounds a Delaware statute that permitted seizure of stock of a Delaware corporation owned by a nonresident in order to compel that person's appearance in the state.

[B] Choice of Law

[1] Federal or State Law?

In a federal diversity suit, *Erie R. Co. v. Tompkins*[104] generally requires a federal court to apply state "substantive" law. In *Cohen v. Beneficial Industrial Loan Corp.*,[105] the Supreme Court held that a federal court was required to apply a local state security-for-costs statute, reasoning that the statute created a new liability for costs. There is authority for the proposition that state law determines generally a shareholder's right to bring or maintain a derivative action.[106] This is consistent with the "forum shopping" policy of *Erie*, since the right to sue is clearly "outcome-determinative." Also, many state rules regarding derivative suits, including those concerning the effect of a director decision to terminate, regulate internal corporate governance, and so are arguably substantive rather than procedural.

Does state law control the shareholders' right to sue even against an inconsistent standing rule in Federal Rule 23.1?[107] By adopting Rule 23.1, Congress and the Supreme Court arguably have made a judgment that the matters covered by that rule are "procedural" rather than "substantive."[108] Thus, in *Overberger v. BT Financial Corp.*,[109] the court applied as "procedural" the requirement inferred from Federal Rule 23.1 that a shareholder must continue to hold shares throughout the course of the litigation, even though no such requirement existed under state law.[110]

In a federal action arising under federal law, such as a securities law claim, *Erie* does not apply. The question in such a case is whether the state rule under consideration

---

[102] Del. Code. Ann. tit. 10, § 3114.

[103] 433 U.S. 186 (1977).

[104] 304 U.S. 64 (1938).

[105] 337 U.S. 541 (1949).

[106] *See Galef v. Alexander*, 615 F.2d 51, 58 (2d Cir. 1980).

[107] *See Jacobs v. Adams*, 601 F.2d 176, 179 (5th Cir. 1979) (noting the uncertainty on this point).

[108] *See Hanna v. Plummer*, 380 U.S. 460, 471 (1965).

[109] 106 F.R.D. 438 (W.D. Pa. 1985).

[110] For a more recent decision reaching the same result, see *Kona Enterprises, Inc. v. Estate of Bishop*, 179 F.3d 767 (9th Cir. 1999) (continuous share ownership requirement of Fed R. Civ. P. 23.1 procedural for *Erie* purposes).

is inconsistent with the federal law. If there is inconsistency, the Supremacy Clause requires the application of federal law.[111]

[2] Which State's Law?

In corporate law cases, if the issue involves the "internal affairs" of the corporation, the applicable law is usually that of the state of incorporation.[112] The "internal affairs" category clearly includes questions as to the scope of insiders' fiduciary duties.[113] It arguably also includes questions concerning the demand requirement because demand relates to the process of decision-making within the corporation.[114] In *Rosenmiller v. Borden*,[115] the court applied Delaware law to a Delaware corporation despite a shareholders' agreement that selected New York law. In a federal diversity action, the question as to which state's law to apply is determined according to the forum state's conflict of law rules.[116]

REFERENCES

Note, *The Internal Affairs Doctrine: Theoretical Justifications and Tentative Explanations for its Continued Primacy*, 115 HARV. L. REV. 1480 (2002).
Kozyris, *Corporate Wars and Choice of Law*, 1985 DUKE L.J. 1.
Ribstein, *Choosing Law by Contract*, 18 J. CORP. L. 245 (1993).

§ 10.10 Settlement and Related Dismissal Problems

Settlements of derivative suits put a corporation's shareholders at risk because none of the parties involved in the settlement negotiations—the shareholder plaintiff, the plaintiff's attorney, or the corporate managers—has the incentive to vigorously represent the corporation's interests. The shareholder plaintiff gets only a *pro rata* share of any

---

[111] *See Levitt v. Johnson*, 334 F.2d 815 (1st Cir. 1964), *cert. denied*, 379 U.S. 961 (1965) (federal law controls as to shareholder demand requirement), and *Burks v. Lasker*, 441 U.S. 471 (1979) (citing *Levitt* as an example of a case in which federal policy was held to have been significantly threatened by an "unreasonable" state rule).

[112] *See Draper v. Paul N. Gardner Defined Plan Trust*, 625 A.2d 859 (Del. 1993) (defendant not prejudiced by dismissing derivative suit and moving it to California since California is bound to apply the law of the state of incorporation).

[113] *See Robert A. Wachsler, Inc. v. Florafax Intern., Inc.*, 778 F.2d 547 (10th Cir. 1985) (applying the law of the state of incorporation rather than of the state where the contract was made in a case involving enforcement of an insider's contract with the corporation).

[114] *See Galef v. Alexander, supra*, 615 F.2d at 58, and cases cited therein. *See also West Virginia v. Wilson*, 189 W. Va. 739, 434 S.E.2d 411 (1993) (applying law of state of incorporation—Delaware—in determining whether employee stock ownership plan participants had standing to bring a derivative suit).

[115] 607 A.2d 465 (Del. Ch. 1991). For discussion of *Rosenmiller*, see Ribstein, *Delaware, Lawyers, and Contractual Choice of Law*, 19 DEL. J. CORP. L. 999, 1023 (1994).

[116] *See Klaxon Co. v. Stentor Elec. Mfg. Co.*, 313 U.S. 487 (1941).

recovery paid to the corporation and therefore may have a minimal stake in the litigation. The plaintiff's attorney, whose main financial interest in the case is her fee, may be willing to accept a small settlement even though a much larger recovery may have been obtained after trial. As Judge Friendly has noted, "[a] relatively small settlement may well produce an allowance [for attorney's fees] bearing a higher ratio to the cost of the work than a much larger recovery obtained only after extensive discovery, a long trial and an appeal" and a settlement avoids the risk that "years of costly effort by the [attorney] and his staff" will be lost if the defendants prevail.[117] For their part, the corporation's managers may be willing to agree to settlements even in non-meritorious cases that pay large fees to plaintiffs' lawyers and little to the corporation in order in exchange for the plaintiffs' lawyers' promise not to oppose generous indemnification for the managers.

Thus, bargaining among plaintiff, plaintiff's counsel, and corporate managers may produce settlements in which the corporation gets little apart from a vague "therapeutic" adjustment of procedures, while corporate managers and plaintiff's counsel secure generous indemnification and large fee awards. For example, in *Polk v. Good*,[118] the court approved the settlement of a suit complaining of a "greenmail" with an agreement that the shareholders could decide how certain stock could be voted and that the plaintiffs' discovery material would be disclosed. Plaintiffs' attorney received $700,000 fees plus expenses. Indeed, one study found that in approximately 30% of settlements the size of which could be determined, the corporation received no money.[119]

At one time, derivative plaintiffs could, like plaintiffs in other litigation, dismiss their suits without following any special procedure.[120] The primary relief available to class members aggrieved by settlements of derivative suits was the recovery of any private payments made to the shareholder plaintiffs.[121] It is now the rule in most jurisdictions that before a derivative suit is dismissed pursuant to settlement there must be notice to the shareholders and judicial approval of the settlement.[122] Judicial approval follows a hearing, where other shareholders may appear and object to the settlement.

The following case is an example of the standards applied by the courts in reviewing settlements.

---

[117] *Saylor v. Lindsley*, 456 F.2d 896, 900-901 (2d Cir. 1972).

[118] 507 A.2d 531 (Del. 1986).

[119] Grath, Nagel & Plager, *Empirical Research and the Shareholders' Derivative Suit: Toward a Better Informed Debate*, 48 LAW & CONTEMP. PROBS. 137 (1985).

[120] *See Manufacturer's Mutual Fire Ins. Co. v. Hopson*, 176 Misc. 220, 25 N.Y.S.2d 502 (1940), *aff'd*, 262 A.D. 731, 29 N.Y.S.2d 139 (1941), *aff'd*, 288 N.Y. 668, 43 N.E.2d 71 (1942).

[121] *See Clarke v. Greenberg*, 296 N.Y. 146, 71 N.E.2d 443 (1947).

[122] *See, e.g.*, Federal Rule 23.1.

ROSENFELD v. BLACK
United States District Court, Southern District of New York
336 F. Supp. 84 (1972)

GURFEIN, District Judge.

A settlement of this derivative stockholders' action is presented to the Court for approval pursuant to Fed. R. Civ. P. 23.1. The settlement was effected after the decision of the Court of Appeals for the Second Circuit, reversing the grant of summary judgment for the defendants in the District Court, thus sending the case back for trial.

* * *

The Facts

In 1967, The Lazard Fund, Inc. (Fund) merged into Moody's Capital Fund, Inc. (Moody's Capital), and the shareholders of the fund selected Moody's Advisors and Distributors, Inc. (Advisors) as the successor to Lazard Freres & Co. (Lazard) as investment adviser.

* * *

Contemporaneous with the merger agreement, there was executed on April 5, 1967 an agreement between Lazard and D&B [Dun & Bradstreet, Inc., Moody's parent], mentioned above, in which Lazard gave certain commitments to D&B and was to receive in return 75,000 shares of D&B stock.

* * *

The Issues

The thrust of the attack has been on the receipt of the 75,000 D&B shares by Lazard.
. . .

The theory of the action was that the Lazard-D&B agreement was a fraud designed to cover an unlawful sale of Lazard's advisory contract, with a secret undertaking by Lazard to use its influence to induce Fund stockholders to approve D&B's subsidiary as the new investment adviser.

* * *

Chief Judge Friendly in the Court of Appeals, . . . held that the Investment Company Act incorporated by implication the common law rule that a fiduciary may not sell its office for personal gain. The Court laid down a prophylactic rule forbidding the investment adviser from receiving "personal gain" on a transfer of the advisory contract. The use of the proxy machinery in favor of the successor was apparently enough to prevent the retiring adviser from being paid a consideration in connection therewith. The Court of Appeals did not, of course, consider the question whether the various covenants undertaken by Lazard were a mere sham to conceal the true nature of the payment, as the plaintiffs contended. That is a question of fact which has been remanded for trial. The Court of Appeals also held that there was a triable issue of fact with respect to the alleged deficiencies of the proxy statement.

In the meantime, Mr. Justice Marshall had extended the time for filing a petition for a writ of *certiorari* to afford this Court an opportunity to consider the reasonableness of the settlement. At the end of the extension, on December 10, 1971, the defendants filed their petition for *certiorari*.

The Settlement

The settlement of the derivative suits is itself quite simple. Lazard is to pay to the Fund one million dollars in cash. The money has been escrowed. All the defendants are to be released from all claims "by reason of, or in connection with, or which arise out of, any matters set forth or referred to in any of the complaints [in the consolidated action]." The settlement also purports to dismiss on the merits all actions which could have been brought by stockholders of the Moody's Capital and the Lazard Fund. In short, for the million dollar payment Lazard and its directors are to get complete absolution for their activities relating to the merger and to the approval by the stockholders of the advisory contract for the D&B subsidiary.

* * *

The general rules governing the approval by the Court of the reasonableness of a settlement under Rule 23.1 are well known. . . . As Judge Wyatt observed, "[a]pproval should be given if the settlement offered is fair, reasonable and adequate. . . . The most important factor is the strength of the case for plaintiffs on the merits, balanced against the amount offered in settlement. This factor is sometimes referred to as the likelihood of success" (*ibid*).

* * *

I

Eminent counsel have forged this settlement out of lengthy negotiations. The litigating posture of each is made uncertain by the overhanging possibility of the grant of certiorari by the Supreme Court. It is common ground that the decision of the Second Circuit announced a new doctrine of fiduciary responsibility in the mutual fund industry. No matter how logical the extension of *Meinhard v. Salmon*, 249 N.Y. 458, 464, 164 N.E. 545 (1928) to the charges here, the interdiction of any profit to the retiring adviser is a giant step forward. This is made manifest by a comparison with the earlier decision of the Ninth Circuit in *S.E.C. v. Insurance Securities, Inc.*, 254 F.2d 642, *cert. denied*, 358 U.S. 823, 79 S. Ct. 38, 3 L. Ed. 2d 64 (1958), a decision upon which Judge Mansfield relied. Although the distinction of that case by Judge Friendly—that it arose under Section 36 of the Act and would have required a finding of "gross misconduct or gross abuse of trust"—is unquestionably sound, Judge Friendly did not hesitate to say that, in any event, the Second Circuit was not in agreement with the Ninth Circuit on the underlying view of the propriety of what Lazard did (445 F.2d at 1346). There is, in my view, an essential conflict between the circuits. While one would hesitate normally to assume the role of handicapper in the certiorari sweepstakes, in this case the Court must, under the requirements of Rule 23.1, assess the odds. My assessment is that because of the importance of the case to a large industry, the shifting views of the SEC, the novelty of the result, the large number of pending suits, and the conflicting views of the Circuits (*see* Supreme Court Rule 19(1)(b)), there is a good chance that *certiorari* will be granted. At least a wise plaintiff might fear that result and adjust his thinking accordingly.

Assuming that *certiorari* is denied, and that *certiorari* is not granted in some other case from another circuit, the case is still only at the threshold of resolution. Summary judgment has been denied to the defendants but the issues of fact have been remanded for trial. The question is again one of assessment of probabilities.

While the Court of Appeals held that a claim for relief was stated if the 75,000 shares, or any part, were to be paid to Lazard for ensuring the succession of D&B's subsidiary, it did not purport to determine the facts. The defendants have tendered rather strong affidavits by persons of reputation, including Curtiss E. Frank, then President of D&B, affirming that the negotiations with Lazard were at arms' length, that it was D&B which insisted on the negative covenant and the other clauses, and that the total consideration was paid for these covenants.

The plaintiffs, on the other hand, contend that these convenants were a sham to cover up payment for the secret help of Lazard in getting the investment advisory contract for Advisors.

* * *

In any event, the burden of persuasion is heavy to overcome the direct testimony of the principals to the negotiations, who must be branded as less than honest witnesses if the plaintiffs are to prevail.

* * *

All this is grist for the mill of litigation. The trial of this action would be sharply contested on these issues on which the plaintiffs might lose. I would hesitate to substitute my own judgment on the likely outcome, even if I were permitted to do so, for the judgment of an intrepid trial lawyer like the general counsel for the plaintiffs.

* * *

II

Having analyzed the risks of combat, we must now consider whether the assumptions of the plaintiffs as to the maximum recovery upon a trial were adequately calculated.

The main thrust of the objectors is directed to the question of recoverable damages. They contend that the appraisal of Goldman, Sachs & Co. of the worth of the 75,000 D&B shares at the time of the contract on May 5, 1967 at approximately $18 a share, is unsupportable. They point out that the market price was then about $40 a share and that it was conceded in the notice of settlement given to stockholders that the value of the shares, without restrictions, would have been three million dollars ($40 per share). They argue that the restrictions should not be taken into account, because by the end of the five years Lazard would have had the right to dividends, the right to have the shares registered, and would have been released from the investment commitment.

That approach is not realistic. In assessing damages, the value of the shares would, in all likelihood and as discussed below, be measured at the time of the allegedly illegal transaction. The right to receive the 75,000 shares by Lazard was at that time restricted in several ways.

* * *

These restrictions are real. Their negative effect may not be precisely measurable in dollars, but the financial community has found ways to reach approximations that pass muster in the marketplace. I do not have to assume that the $18 valuation put on the shares by Goldman Sachs is precise, or even entirely objective. The Wall Street firms, even the most reputable houses, must, for obvious reasons, be suspected of taking in one another's washing, and of giving the honest benefit of the doubt to the beleaguered competitor. Yet the objectors have come up with no different appraisal, and their arguments all assume that damages would not be measured at the time of the original transaction. As we have seen, even a $40 valuation on that basis makes a maximum recovery of about three million dollars—for which a settlement of one million dollars cash, in view of the perils still to be surmounted by the plaintiffs, seems not unreasonable.

* * *

For the reasons stated, the settlement is approved and the decree will be signed as presented.

Decision on counsel fees and other related matters will be reserved and may be disposed of at the foot of the decree.

NOTES AND QUESTIONS

(1) **Standard of judicial review.** The standard of judicial review of derivative suit settlements was articulated by the Delaware Supreme Court in *Polk v. Good*:[123] "[T]he Chancellor . . . is not required to decide any of the issues on the merits. Instead, he . . . exercises a form of business judgment to determine the overall reasonableness of the settlement." Compare the standard of review of a director decision to terminate derivative litigation discussed in Section 10.06. Should the standards differ? There is also a procedural component to settlement review. In *In re Oracle Securities Litigation*,[124] the court rejected the settlement because the special committee recommending it failed to retain independent counsel and the in-house counsel recommending settlement may have been biased.

(2) **Relevant factors.** ALI *Principles* § 7.14(b) provides that "the court should approve a proposed settlement or other disposition if the balance of corporate interests warrants approval and the settlement or other disposition is consistent with public policy. In evaluating a proposed settlement, the court should place special weight on the net benefit, including pecuniary and non-pecuniary elements, to the corporation."

How does this test deal with settlements in which the corporation receives no monetary consideration? Consider two troublesome types of cases: first, a settlement that benefits the corporation only by saving substantial additional litigation expense in

---

[123] 507 A.2d 531, 536 (Del. 1986).

[124] 829 F. Supp. 1176 (N.D. Cal. 1993).

return for payment of plaintiffs' attorneys' fees and defendants' indemnification; and, second, a settlement like that in *Polk* discussed in Note 1 above, consisting solely of an exchange of attorneys' fees for corporate "therapeutics." As to the first type of settlement, Comment (e) to ALI *Principles* § 7.14 states that "little weight can be given" to the benefit of avoiding further wasteful or disruptive litigation. Do you agree with this position? Is it consistent with the "black letter" of § 7.14(b) quoted above? As to the second type of settlement, Comment (e) notes that the value of non-pecuniary relief should be considered, but cautions that "therapeutic relief can sometimes represent means by which the parties can increase the apparent value of the settlement . . . ." As to both types of settlement, Comment (f) requires the court to consider the adequacy of the settlement in the light of any payments of plaintiff's attorneys' fees and indemnification of defendants. For discussion of the rules applicable to attorneys' fee awards and indemnification, see Sections 10.11 and 10.12 below.[125]

In reviewing the adequacy of a proposed settlement, the court also may consider conflicts of interest between the class representative who negotiated the settlement and the other shareholders. *In re Banyan Mortgage Investment Fund Shareholders Litigation*[126] rejected a proposed settlement that would trigger the repurchase of shares owned by the class representatives, but not of other class members where "there [was] no indication . . . that purchase of the representatives' shares [was] motivated by a valid corporate purpose or [was] in any way justified by the unique position the representatives occup[ied] as shareholders."[127]

Should courts be less willing to approve settlements when the objector is a substantial shareholder? *In re MAXXAM, Inc./Federal Development Shareholders Litigation*[128] rejected a settlement where the objector was the corporation's leading non-management shareholder, the owner of approximately 14% of the corporation's shares, and one of the plaintiffs in the derivative suit. The court reasoned, in part, as follows:

> [T]his case has the unmistakable footprint of an effort by the defendants to negotiate a settlement with an adversary that they preferred, in order to extinguish claims being pressed by the adversary whom they disfavored, and to relegate that disfavored adversary to the status of an objector to the settlement. . . . Although the exclusion of a significant party litigant from the settlement negotiations will not, in and of itself, invalidate a proposed settlement, that approach, because of its inherent potential for abuse, will cause the settlement to be carefully scrutinized.[129]

---

[125] For a case in which plaintiff's fees and indemnification payments were considered in connection with a review of a settlement, see *Shlensky v. Dorsey*, 574 F.2d 131 (3d Cir. 1978).

[126] 1997 Del. Ch. LEXIS 123, 1997 WL 428584 (Del. Ch. 1997).

[127] *Cf. Lacos Land Company v. Arden Group, Inc.*, 1986 Del. Ch. LEXIS 495, 1986 WL 14525 (Del. Ch. 1986) (enhanced benefits justified where class representatives occupied unique position and settlement agreement provided "substantially all that the complaint sought").

[128] 659 A.2d 760 (Del. Ch. 1995).

[129] *Id.* at 777.

(3) **Constraints on settlement review.** Most derivative suit settlements are approved.[130] This may be explained less by the standard employed by the court than by the problems inherent in court review of settlements. Judge Friendly has said, "[o]nce a settlement is agreed, the attorneys for the plaintiff stockholders link arms with their former adversaries to defend the joint handiwork."[131] The only adversaries pressing arguments against the settlement are the objectors or intervenors who enter the suit after notice of settlement has been sent to the shareholders. The objector is in a difficult position because she is awarded attorneys' fees only in the unlikely event that she improves the settlement.[132] Not only is the settlement hearing rarely a truly adversarial proceeding, but the court is limited in the extent to which it can hear important facts bearing on the reasonableness of the settlement without turning the hearing into the trial the participants seek to avoid. In this connection, ALI *Principles* § 7.14(c) provides that "objecting shareholders should have a reasonable opportunity to contest a proposed settlement . . ., including an opportunity with the court's approval to present and to cross-examine witnesses," but at the same time Comment (c) cautions that "settlement review should not become a virtual trial on the merits."

(4) **Effect of judicially approved settlement.** Like involuntary dismissal on the merits, a judicially approved settlement generally bars litigation by other shareholders of the same claims.[133] However, a shareholder may be able to obtain relief from the judgment on the grounds, among others, of mistake, newly discovered evidence or fraud.[134] In addition, the judgment can generally be attacked "collaterally" in another case, if the shareholder can show inadequacy of notice or of representation, fraudulent misrepresentation, or nondisclosure.[135] It has been suggested that, in light of the courts' difficulties in effectively reviewing settlements, settlements should be readily subject to collateral attack unless the derivative plaintiff was a fully adequate representative.[136] How do you suppose application of such a rule would affect the settlement process?

---

[130] For examples of of rejected derivative suit settlements, see *In re MAXXAM, Inc./Federal Development Shareholders Litigation, supra* footnote 128; *Krasner v. Dreyfus Corp.*, 500 F. Supp. 36 (S.D.N.Y. 1980) (approved after modification, 90 F.R.D. 665 (S.D.N.Y. 1981)); *Fricke v. Daylin, Inc.*, 66 F.R.D. 90 (E.D.N.Y. 1975). *See also Polar International Brokerage Corp. v. Reeve*, 187 F.R.D. 108 (S.D.N.Y. 1999) (rejecting proposed settlement of securities class action, which provided $200,000 to class counsel and no pecuniary relief to plaintiff shareholders, because independent valuation opinion to help shareholders decide on tender offer was "virtually worthless" to the class).

[131] *Allegheny Corp. v. Kirby*, 333 F.2d 327, 347 (2d Cir. 1964), *aff'd en banc*, 340 F.2d 311 (2d Cir. 1965), *cert. dismissed sub nom. Holt v. Allegheny Corp.*, 384 U.S. 28 (1966).

[132] For a case awarding fees to counsel for objectors who proposed settlement, see *In re Resorts International Shareholders Litigation*, 1990 WL 154154 (Del. Ch. 1990).

[133] For a discussion of the effect of a judicially supervised judgment, see Haudek, *The Settlement and Dismissal of Stockholders' Actions—Part II: The Settlement*, 23 Sw. L.J. 765, 807-13 (1969).

[134] Federal Rules of Civil Procedure, Rule 60(b).

[135] *See Smith v. Allegheny Corp.*, 394 F.2d 381, 391 (2d Cir.), *cert. denied*, 393 U.S. 939 (1968); *Stella v. Kaiser*, 218 F.2d 64, 65 (2d Cir. 1954), *reh'g denied*, 221 F.2d 115, *cert. denied*, 350 U.S. 835 (1955).

[136] *See* Note, *Res Judicata in the Derivative Action: Adequacy of Representation and the Inadequate Plaintiff*, 71 MICH. L. REV. 1042 (1973).

The effect of the settlement may be tricky where a single set of facts gives rise to both state and federal claims, particularly when the federal claims arise under provisions of the Securities Exchange Act of 1934, such as § 10(b) and Rule 10b-5, as to which § 27 of the 1934 Act vests exclusive jurisdiction in the federal courts. Should settlements approved by state courts that purport to release all claims arising out of a particular set of facts have the effect of extinguishing federal claims over which state courts lack jurisdiction? *Matsushita Electrical Industrial Co., Ltd. v. Epstein*[137] held that a class action settlement approved by the Delaware Chancery Court was entitled to full faith and credit, even though it released claims under the 1934 Act that were within the exclusive jurisdiction of the federal courts.

(5) **Settlement between corporation and defendants.** Because the derivative plaintiff brings suit on the corporation's claim, it may be settled by the corporation (that is, by the board of directors) without the derivative plaintiff's concurrence. In *Wolf v. Barkes*,[138] Judge Friendly held that such an "overhead" settlement was not governed by Rule 23.1 (then Rule 23(c)): since the settlement, by itself, did not result in the dismissal or compromise of the derivative suit, neither notice nor court approval was required. Judge Friendly reasoned that the primary purpose of the notice and court approval requirements was to restrict private settlements with the plaintiff and that application of the federal derivative suit rule should be limited to settlements in which the court's process was being used to terminate the derivative claim. Plaintiff argued that the effect of a settlement directly with the defendants was the same as that of dismissal of the derivative claim because the release obtained by defendants in the settlement would now serve as a defense against the derivative suit. Judge Friendly rejected that argument noting, among other things, that the plaintiff could attack the validity of the release in a new derivative action.

Even though the parties are not required to submit "overhead" settlements for court approval under Rule 23.1, the parties may elect to do so if they want the settlement to result in an immediate dismissal of the derivative action. In *Clark v. Lomas & Nettleton Financial Corp.*,[139] the parties made such an election, but the appellate court reversed the district court's approval of the settlement, holding that board approval of the settlement was tainted by domination by the principal defendant.

ALI *Principles* § 7.15 rejects the approach taken by Rule 23.1. It provides that "overhead" settlements may be entered into only with approval of the court. To be approved, the overhead settlement must be entered into by an independent board after a thorough inquiry and the court must find that "the balance of corporate interests warrants approval and the settlement or release is consistent with public policy."

---

[137] 516 U.S. 367 (1996).

[138] 348 F.2d 994 (2d Cir.), *cert. denied*, 382 U.S. 941 (1965).

[139] 625 F.2d 49 (5th Cir. 1980), *cert. denied*, 450 U.S. 1029 (1981).

(6) **Involuntary dismissal.** *Papilsky v. Berndt*[140] applied the notice requirements of Rule 23.1 to a dismissal resulting from plaintiff's failure to comply with discovery. This holding prevents the plaintiff from privately settling the case and avoiding Rule 23.1 by obtaining dismissal under a rule that does not require notice (in this case Federal Rule 41(b)).

(7) **Summing up.** Does, and can, judicial approval of derivative suit settlements deal adequately with the problem of abusive settlements? Can courts reviewing settlements effectively block abusive settlements, while at the same time not unduly preventing efficient ones?[141] If judicial approval of settlements is inadequate, what options are available to deal with abusive settlements and the problems they create? For example, should courts be more generous in letting directors terminate the action without settlement? Alternatively, perhaps the director-defendants would not have been so willing to enter into abusive settlements if they could be sure of being protected by indemnification, insurance or advances (*see* Section 10.12) or defended by corporate counsel (*see* Section 10.08). If the problem is that plaintiff was bought off cheaply for fees, perhaps the solution is better incentives for plaintiff's attorney through the standard for awarding fees (*see* Section 10.11). Finally, in light of the concern that derivative suits may often conclude in inadequate settlements for the corporation, we are left with the pervasive question: Is the derivative remedy a net benefit to the corporation?

§ 10.11 Fees and Other Aspects of Compensating Plaintiff's Counsel

[A] General Rules

The plaintiff in a class or derivative action may be entitled to an award of attorneys' fees. Questions concerning compensation of plaintiff's counsel are important to the derivative remedy because the attorney is often the driving force behind the litigation (*see* Section 10.01[C][2]).

The attorneys' fee rule is an exception to the general American rule that the parties are not entitled to be reimbursed for attorneys' fees. The exception originated in cases in which plaintiff created or preserved a monetary fund. The award of fees mitigates the "free rider" problem that exists whenever a plaintiff captures only a portion of the benefits that result from his suit. The attorneys' fee can, therefore, be seen as a reward to encourage monitoring of corporate agents by derivative plaintiffs and their lawyers.

---

[140] 466 F.2d 251 (2d Cir.), *cert. denied*, 409 U.S. 1077 (1972).

[141] Note, in this regard, that there is reason to believe that most derivative suits *should be* settled, since defendants have more information about their behavior than do plaintiffs and therefore are more likely than not to be innocent and to prevail at trial. *See* Hylton, *Asymmetric Information and the Selection of Disputes for Litigation*, 22 J. LEG. STUD. 187 (1993).

Modern cases have extended the exception to the American rule to situations in which there has been a non-pecuniary benefit to the corporation.[142] With respect to what constitutes a sufficient non-pecuniary benefit, one court held that merely obtaining an accounting was sufficient even if this accounting did not reveal a cause of action for damages.[143] For other examples of the award of fees for non-pecuniary benefits, see the *Polk* case discussed in the Notes and Questions following the *Rosenfeld* excerpt (Section 10.10). The lawyer may obtain a fee even without filing a lawsuit[144] or if, after filing, plaintiff's claim is rendered moot by the defendant's action.[145]

Bird v. Lida, Inc.[146] allowed reimbursement of costs for benefits achieved without litigation (but following the making of a demand upon the board) where the plaintiff establishes "at least" the following elements: "(1) the presentation of a meritorious corporate claim by a shareholder, (2) the expenditure of funds or credit by the shareholder investigating such claim, (3) action by the board that confers a quantifiable financial benefit on the corporation, (4) which action is causally related to the making of the shareholder demand." But *Waterside Partners v. C. Brewer and Company*[147] rejected a fee award for a plaintiff who launched a proxy contest in conjunction with a derivative suit because the corporate benefit resulted from the proxy contest rather than the litigation.

---

[142] *See, e.g., Neese v. Richter*, 428 N.E.2d 36 (Ind. App. 1981); *Bosch v. Meeker Coop. Light & Power Ass'n*, 257 Minn. 362, 101 N.W.2d 423 (1960). For recent cases considering attorney fee awards where settlements failed to produce any pecuniary benefits, see *Seinfeld v. Robinson*, 676 N.Y.S.2d 579 (N.Y. App. 1998) (approving fee award for settlement requiring general counsel to approve contracts between the corporation and private investigators); *Kaplan v. Rand*, 192 F.3d 60 (2d Cir. 1999) (rejecting fee award for settlement requiring, among other things, shareholder access to report prepared by corporation's Task Force on Equality and Fairness because report was public document available from the court and presumably on the internet); and *In re Golden State Bancorp, Inc. Shareholders Litigation*, 2000 Del. Ch. LEXIS 8, 2000 WL 62964 (Del. Ch. 2000) (approving fee award of $500,000, significantly less than $1.325 million requested, for "therapeutic" settlement providing current financial statements and an updated fairness opinion for shareholders who would vote on merger).

[143] *Neese v. Richter*, 428 N.E.2d 36 (Ind. App. 1981). *But see Thorpe v. CERBCO, Inc.*, 1997 Del. Ch. LEXIS 18, 1997 WL 67833 (Del. Ch. 1997) (refusing to compensate plaintiff's counsel for the creation of a new rule of law, in a case which had only resulted in a small damages award for the corporation).

[144] *See, e.g., Gold v. Schwab*, 187 Cal. App. 3d 1296, 232 Cal. Rptr. 643 (1987) (fee permitted where attorney's re-litigation letter resulted in $8.4 million being paid to shareholders of acquired company). It also may not be necessary to obtain a fund, at least in the conventional sense. *See O'Neill v. Church's Fried Chicken, Inc.*, 910 F.2d 263 (11th Cir. 1990) (successful acquiror must pay attorneys' fees in suit against former management for entrenchment that resulted in increased price to former shareholders).

[145] *See United Vanguard Fund, Inc. v. Takecare, Inc.*, 693 A.2d 1076 (Del. 1997) (stating that, to qualify for an award of fees in such circumstances: "(1) the suit [must have been] meritorious when filed; (2) the action taken by defendants which produced the benefit to the shareholders [must have been] taken before there was a judicial resolution of the conflict; and (3) the resulting benefit to the shareholder [must have been] causally related to the lawsuit"); *see also In re First Interstate Bancorp Consolidated Shareholder Litigation*, 1999 Del. Ch. LEXIS 178, 1999 WL 693165 (Del. Ch. 1999) (fee approved where lawsuit challenging friendly merger rendered moot by acceptance of higher hostile bid); *Rovner v. Health-Chem Corp.*, 1998 Del. Ch. LEXIS 65, 1998 WL 227908 (Del. Ch. 1998) (fee approved where lawsuit was dismissed after company modified agreement that formed basis of suit); *In re American Real Estate Partners, L.P. Litigation*, 1997 Del. Ch. LEXIS 171, 1997 WL 770718 (Del. Ch. 1997) (fee approved where lawsuit was rendered moot as a result of defendants' decision to modify the terms of challenged offering).

[146] 681 A.2d 399, 403, 405 (Del. Ch. 1996).

[147] 739 A.2d 768 (Del. 1999).

The court must determine the amount of any fee. Although the parties may specify an amount in a settlement agreement, the effect of such an agreement is simply that the defendants will not contest a request for that amount or less.

Fees in derivative suits traditionally were set according to a "salvage" rule—that is, the fee was, at least in theory, measured by the amount of settlement. Under the emerging modern rule the emphasis is on the amount of time spent by the attorney. This time is multiplied by an hourly rate to produce a "lodestar" figure, which is then adjusted to reflect such elements as risk and difficulty.[148] In practice, the difference between the "salvage" and "lodestar" rules may be mostly a matter of emphasis. For example, in *Sugarland Industries, Inc. v. Thomas*,[149] the court rejected application of a rigid lodestar formula, but nevertheless reduced the fee from 20% to 5% of the award to avoid giving the attorneys a windfall that did not result from their efforts.[150]

Boyer v. Wilmington Materials, Inc.[151] cited the following factors as bearing on the reasonableness of a fee request for plaintiff's counsel in a successful derivative action: "(1) the results achieved; (2) the amount of time and effort applied to the case by plaintiff's counsel, (3) the relative complexities of the litigation, (4) the skills applied to their resolution by counsel, (5) the contingent nature of the fee and (6) the standing and ability of plaintiff's counsel." The court also said it considers "the amount of the award requested as it compares to previous awards made by Delaware courts." Based on these factors, the court decided to award 1/3 of corporate benefit achieved to plaintiff's counsel, noting that this was at the "very top of the range" that Delaware courts would award.

[B] Theoretical Considerations Underlying Compensation of Plaintiff's Counsel

The question of how to properly align plaintiff's and counsel's incentives has been extensively discussed by **Coffee** in several articles listed in the References. The following discussion draws on these articles. In considering the suggestions discussed below, note particularly how they bear on meritorious suits.

---

[148] Two leading cases espousing the modern rule are *Detroit v. Grinnell Corp.*, 495 F.2d 448 (2d Cir. 1974), and *Lindy Bros. Builders, Inc. v. American Radiator & Standard Sanitary Corp.*, 487 F.2d 161 (3d Cir. 1973). For examples of the application of this rule in shareholders' suits, see *Shlensky v. Dorsey*, 574 F.2d 131, 150-51 (3d Cir. 1978); *In re Baldwin-United Corporation Litigation*, CCH Fed. Sec. L. Rep. ¶ 92,918 (S.D.N.Y. 1986); *Weiss v. Drew Nat'l Corp.*, 465 F. Supp. 548, 552-555 (S.D.N.Y. 1979); *Lyons v. Scitex Corp.*, 987 F. Supp. 271 (S.D.N.Y. 1997); and *In re Bausch & Lomb, Inc. Securities Litigation*, 183 F.R.D. 78 (W.D.N.Y. 1998).

[149] 420 A.2d 142 (Del. 1980).

[150] *Cf. Goldberger v. Integrated Resources Inc.*, 209 F.3d 43 (2d Cir. 2000) (attorneys' fees in common fund cases may be awarded either as a percentage of the recovery or by the lodestar method of calculating reasonable hours and rates, but under either method, a court "should continue to be guided by traditional criteria," including time and labor, the magnitude and complexity, risk, quality of representation, the fee's relationship to the settlement, and public policy).

[151] 1999 Del. Ch. LEXIS 81, 1999 WL 342326 (Del. Ch., May 17, 1999).

Compensating counsel based on hours worked might seem to result in wasted hours, as the attorney builds time to pad the fee. But this ignores the fact that counsel does not know whether she will achieve a successful outcome that entitles her to a fee. The real problem is that, if the attorney is entitled to no more than compensation for her time even for a successful outcome, she may be inclined to accept a settlement that provides such compensation with certainty, even though a larger recovery might have been obtained after a trial. This is because settlement avoids the risk that "years of costly effort by the [attorney] and his staff"[152] will be lost if the defendants prevail after a trial. Thus, when attorneys are compensated based on hours worked, the attorney's incentives are misaligned with the shareholders' interests. Compensating the attorney according to hours spent presents other problems as well, particularly including the difficulty of accounting for hours and determining the appropriate hourly rate.

The problem of misaligned incentives may not be completely cured even if the attorney's fee is a percentage of recovery, as under the "salvage" approach. Although the attorney who is compensated in this way potentially has more to gain by going forward with the case, at some point additional hours spent will not increase recovery (and the attorney's likely fee) more than other uses of the attorney's time. Moreover, the attorney still loses everything from an adverse judgment and therefore faces the same incentive discussed above to accept a relatively small settlement in order to avoid the risk of losing everything in a trial. Shareholders, however, are not concerned with the risk of losing everything in a particular case since they hold a diversified portfolio of investments. Also, unlike their lawyers, shareholders have not invested non-recoverable time and expense into the case.

Plaintiffs' lawyers could respond to a salvage-based fee by filing more actions than they can prepare adequately (and thereby diversifying away the risk of losing any particular case), or by skewing their selection of cases toward easy winners. The former approach could increase non-meritorious litigation, while the latter would reduce meritorious derivative suits.

Finally, in determining whether compensation rules produce optimal incentives, it is necessary to consider all costs and benefits. **Kraakman, Park & Shavell** point out that compensating plaintiffs out of recoveries does not reflect either the deterrent value of law suits or the potential effects of suits on liability insurance premia.

It follows, therefore, that neither compensating according to the value of the recovery nor according to hours billed (nor by a combination of both as under the "lodestar" approach) produces an entirely satisfactory alignment of incentives.

---

[152] *Saylor v. Lindsley*, 456 F.2d 896, 900-01 (2d Cir. 1972).

[C] Other Approaches to Aligning the Interests of Plaintiff's Attorney and the Shareholders

Are there other potential approaches, apart from the method of compensation, that might better align the interests of counsel and shareholders? Evaluate the following alternatives.

[1] Formation of Plaintiff "Firms"

Coffee (48 LAW & CONTEMP. PROBS. 57-67) discusses the possibility of reducing the risk faced by counsel for plaintiffs in derivative actions by facilitating the formation of "firms" of plaintiffs' counsel for a given suit that would spread the risks of the action. This would reduce counsel's incentive to respond to the risk of loss at trial by accepting an early settlement. This suggestion also addresses the "strike" suit problem that arises when individual lawyers seek to file more cases than they can possibly handle in order to diversify away the risk of loss in particular cases: "firms" can diversify litigation risks by filing many suits, while still being able to adequately prosecute the claims and select a range of types of suits.

[2] Prohibiting Simultaneous Negotiation of the Settlement and the Fee

Prohibiting simultaneous negotiation of both the amount of the settlement and the amount of the fee would reduce the ability of plaintiff's counsel and defendants to agree to a settlement that provided only cosmetic value for the shareholders in exchange for a disproportionately high fee for plaintiff's counsel. But can the parties knowledgeably negotiate the settlement without knowing the size of the plaintiff's attorney's fee? A more serious problem is whether a prohibition on the contents of negotiations can be effectively policed. If, as appears to be the case, structuring of the settlement in this way is mutually beneficial to plaintiff's counsel and defendants, they probably can find some way to engage in simultaneous negotiations, such as by using subtle "signals."

[3] Non-Pecuniary Settlements

A third way to better align the incentives of counsel and shareholders is to address directly what is perhaps the most serious single problem: the settlement that exchanges a fee for plaintiff's attorneys for non-pecuniary relief for the corporation. Viewed at the time of settlement, this method of settlement is beneficial because it offers defendants a cheap way out of costly litigation. However, a rule barring settlements where fees are exchanged for non-pecuniary benefits might actually be better for defendants since it makes it more difficult to obtain the fee that motivates plaintiff's counsel to file derivative suits in the first instance. But defendants may find other ways to ransom themselves from non-meritorious suits even if fees for non-pecuniary relief are banned. If so, banning "strike" settlements may prolong rather than deter costly litigation. Moreover, banning fees for non-pecuniary settlements may discourage some suits that ought to be brought, including those that challenge changes in governance rules that infringe shareholder rights.

[4] Tightening Screening Rules

Can the interests of plaintiffs' counsel be better aligned with those of the class by tightening the screening and other rules regarding the bringing of the derivative suit? Attempting through "standing" rules (*see* Section 10.03) to distinguish "nominal" and other shareholders may be fruitless, since a shareholder would need a very large shareholding to substantially benefit from recovery other than via attorneys' fees. Requiring the posting of a security for costs (*see* Section 10.04) only increases the risk to plaintiff's counsel, which is one of the reasons for misalignment of incentives.

Perhaps the most effective way to cut down on "strike" suits by improperly motivated lawyers is giving the board the ability to dismiss derivative actions through a special litigation committee rather than forcing it to settle with plaintiff's counsel. In general, the more costly it is for the board to terminate the suit—*i.e.*, the later the stage of the litigation at which termination occurs—the more leverage plaintiff's counsel has to obtain a "bribe" to go away. But giving the board greater powers to terminate derivative suits carries the risk that directors will use that power to terminate suits that further the shareholders' interests.

[5] Selling Lawsuits to Lawyers

Why not permit auction of the right to prosecute a derivative suit to the highest bidder? This would unite the economic interest in the action and the right to fees in the same person, eliminating the problem of misalignment of incentives. Of course, this approach would constitute unethical champerty and maintenance, but realistically, these problems exist in the derivative suit as it exists now, since the attorney is the real party in interest. **Coffee** considered and rejected this approach (48 LAW & CONTEMP. PROBS. at 77-79). He raises the objection that the auction would deprive the first attorney to file of any reward for the search, thus deterring search. But as Coffee notes (*id.* at 79, 86 COLUM. L. REV. at 682), plaintiff's search costs are minimal because they are subsidized by the mandatory disclosure system of the federal securities laws and the cause of action is usually revealed in the financial press. Others, including **Macey & Miller,** have advocated the auction approach.

In re Oracle Securities Litigation[153] applies the related approach of having attorneys bid competitively for the right to be lead counsel. The court evaluated the structure

---

[153] 132 F.R.D. 538 (N.D. Cal. 1990).

of the fee, favoring decreasing rates with larger recoveries to prevent "windfalls." It rejected the argument that the contingency fee should increase with greater recovery to minimize incentive to settle early and cheaply because this could give the class less for a higher recovery, would deprive it of economies of effort from larger recoveries, and would not necessarily reward increased effort. Are these considerations persuasive? The court also rejected a premium for first-year settlement because this would encourage "sell-out settlement." Finally, the court rejected an argument that the winning bid was too low to provide adequate incentives for good work on the ground that the attorney was also subject to reputational constraints.

[6] Eliminating the Derivative Suit

An even more radical approach to solving the plaintiff attorney incentive problem is to let firms opt out of the derivative remedy. A primary reason for the derivative suit is that directors lack appropriate incentives to prosecute the corporation's right of action against insiders. We can now see that the incentives of individual shareholders, or more accurately their lawyers, are also imperfect. The question then becomes whether directors or plaintiff's counsel are the better monitors. If the directors fail to act on a cause of action that is likely to yield a significant net benefit for the corporation—either in terms of direct recovery or deterrence of future wrongdoing—a shareholder or outsider can purchase control, cause the action to be pursued, and realize a profit through the increase in value of his shares resulting from successful prosecution of the action. A large shareholder may be able to accomplish the same result through a proxy contest. Of course, the costs of acquiring control or pursuing a proxy contest mean that many beneficial suits will not be pursued in this way. But, again, the critical question involves a comparison of imperfect alternatives.

[D] The ALI Approach

ALI *Principles* § 7.17 does not accept any of the above approaches. It provides that compensation of plaintiff's attorney shall be "reasonable," "but in no event . . . exceed a reasonable proportion of the value of the relief (including any non-pecuniary relief) obtained by the plaintiff." This does not preclude either a lodestar (as long as it is not disproportionate to the relief) or a salvage fee. There is no prohibition of simultaneous negotiation or of fees for non-pecuniary settlements as long as these are assigned some value.

REFERENCES

Coffee, *Understanding the Plaintiff's Attorney: The Implications of Economic Theory for Private Enforcement of Law Through Class and Derivative Actions*, 86 COLUM. L. REV. 669 (1986).

Coffee, *The Unfaithful Champion: The Plaintiff as Monitor in Shareholder Litigation*, 48 LAW & CONTEMP. PROBS. 5 (1985).

Coffee, *Rescuing the Private Attorney General: Why the Model of the Lawyer as Bounty Hunter is Not Working*, 42 MD. L. REV. 215 (1983).

Kraakman, Park & Shavell, *When are Shareholder Suits in Shareholder Interests?*, 83 GEO. L.J. 1733 (1994).

Macey & Miller, *A Reply to Thomas & Hansen*, 87 NW. U. L. REV. 458 (1993).

Macey & Miller, *The Plaintiffs' Attorney's Role in Class Action and Derivative Litigation: Economic Analysis and Recommendations for Reform*, 58 U. CHI. L. REV. 1 (1991).

Thomas & Hansen, *Auctioning Class Action and Derivative Lawsuits: A Critical Analysis*, 87 NW. U. L. REV. 423 (1992).

§ 10.12 Indemnification and Insurance

This Section discusses two devices that operate to defuse shareholders' remedies against errant insiders—indemnification and insurance.

[A] Indemnification

Managers may be indemnified for costs they incur in serving the corporation, including expenses incurred in connection with litigation commenced against them by the corporation's shareholders. This obviously reduces the deterrent effect of derivative litigation. On the other hand, indemnification may be a reasonable price to pay to encourage risk-averse managers to serve.

[1] Common Law

Pre-statutory case law was unclear as to the extent of the corporation's ability and obligation to indemnify corporate directors in connection with their defense of share-holders' suits. Some cases went so far as to hold that a corporation could not indemnify a director for the costs of successfully defending a derivative suit since this defense did not benefit the corporation.[154] Others upheld indemnification, noting, among other things, the importance of attracting competent officers and directors.[155]

---

[154] *See New York Dock Co. v. McCollom*, 173 Misc. 106, 16 N.Y.S.2d 844 (Sup. Ct. 1939); *Griesse v. Lang*, 37 Ohio App. 553, 175 N.E. 222 (1931).

[155] *See Solimine v. Hollander*, 129 N.J. Eq. 264, 19 A.2d 344 (Ch. 1941); *In re E.C. Warner Co.*, 232 Minn. 207, 45 N.W.2d 388 (1950). For a review of the common law of indemnification, see J. Bishop, THE LAW OF CORPORATE OFFICERS AND DIRECTORS: INDEMNIFICATION AND INSURANCE, 5.03 at 5-7 to 5-14 (1982).

[2] Statutes

Because of the case authority wholly opposing a right to indemnification, because even the cases favoring indemnification left unanswered many questions as to the scope of the corporation's right and obligation to indemnify, and because this is an issue as to which substantial predictability and certainty are necessary, the subject of indemnification has largely been taken over by statutory provisions.

Several distinctions are relevant in interpreting indemnification statutes. First, it is important to distinguish statutory provisions setting forth "standard forms" from statutory provisions setting forth limitations on *opting out* of standard forms. Most indemnification statutes include both types of provisions. Second, it is necessary to distinguish between statutes that *compel* indemnification in certain situations and those that merely *permit* it. And third, it is important to determine the extent to which the statute in question is *exclusive* in that it invalidates broader bylaw or charter provisions.

In considering the usefulness of standard form indemnification provisions, keep in mind that indemnification is only one of several comparable ways of limiting agents' exposure to litigation risks. Compare (a) directly waiving fiduciary duties or liability for certain acts (*see* Section 9.09); (b) permitting the agent to insure at her own or the firm's expense; (c) providing counsel and other direct litigation assistance at the firm's expense (*see* Section 10.08); and (d) limiting certain remedies (in particular, the derivative remedy). In evaluating these alternatives, consider the fact that indemnification may not kick in until the corporate agents have actually had to pay litigation expenses, an arguably less effective way to address managerial risk aversion than more direct ways of limiting the exposure of managers. Also consider that, with indemnification, when the smoke clears, liability has circled back to the corporation (or its insurer) so that perhaps only the lawyers come out ahead.

[3] Role of Bylaw and Charter Provisions

Many corporations have charter or bylaw provisions concerning indemnification. Whether the relevant statute controls if it is inconsistent with a bylaw or charter provision depends on the answers to two questions. First, does the statute *compel* indemnification in certain situations? If so, the statute may control if its terms are more generous than the charter or bylaw provision. And second, to what extent is the statutory provision on indemnification *exclusive* in the sense that it invalidates broader indemnification rights granted under the corporate charter or bylaws? Some statutes include explicit "non-exclusivity" language. For example, Del. G.C.L. § 145(f) provides that "[t]he indemnification . . . provided by, or granted pursuant to, the other subsections of this section shall not be deemed exclusive of any other rights to which those seeking indemnification may be entitled . . . ." However, some cases have refused to enforce broader charter indemnification despite this language. *Waltuch v. Conticommodity Services, Inc.*[156] held that Del. G.C.L. § 145(a), which gives the corporation the power to indem-

---

[156] 88 F.3d 87 (2d Cir. 1996).

nify officers and directors who act in good faith, invalidates a corporate charter provision requiring the indemnification of officers and directors who act in bad faith notwithstanding DEL. G.C.L. §145(f). *VonFeldt v. Stifel Financial Corporation*[157] endorsed this result, reasoning that, "[w]hile § 145(f) permits indemnification on terms other than as set forth in the rest of § 145, such other indemnification must be consistent with the policies expressed in the other parts of § 145," including § 145(a) and (b) which limit indemnification to situations where the officer or director acts in good faith. Similarly, *TLC Beatrice International Holdings, Inc. v. CIGNA Insurance Co.*[158] held that the non-exclusivity language of Del. G.C.L. § 145(f) could not be used to indemnify a defendant in a derivative suit for amounts paid in settling even an entirely non-meritorious claim because doing so would circumvent the limitations on indemnification in Del. G.C.L. § 145(b). The court reasoned that, "[t]o permit directors and officers to receive indemnity for settlement payments in derivative suits under corporate bylaw and pursuant to § 145(f), when such indemnification is unauthorized by § 145(b), would ignore the carefully structured system of risk sharing crafted by the Delaware legislature."[159]

The "non-exclusivity" provision of the New York Business Corporation Law (N.Y. Bus. Corp. Law § 721) avoids some of the uncertainty arising under Del. G.C.L. § 145(f) by expressly providing that that "no indemnification may be made to or on behalf of any director or officer if a judgment or other final adjudication adverse to the director or officer establishes that his acts were committed in bad faith or were the result of active and deliberate dishonesty and were material to the cause of action so adjudicated . . . ." *Biondi v. Beekman Hill House Apartment Corporation*[160] barred indemnification of a director who had been held liable for punitive damages in an action alleging illegal discrimination on the basis of race under a bylaw provision calling for indemnification "if such director or officer acted in good faith, for a purpose which he reasonably believed to be in the best interest of the Corporation" because director's bad faith toward the corporation had been conclusively established in the underlying action.

In general, why shouldn't the corporation have the power to vary the terms of the statute without limitation? This question raises the same issues as other forms of opt-out from fiduciary duties discussed in Section 9.09. In particular, do the efficient securities markets and the market for corporate control adequately discipline indemnification arrangements? Should the standards for indemnification differ from those regarding opting out of managers' duties?[161]

---

[157] 1999 Del. Ch. LEXIS 131, 1999 WL 413393 (Del. Ch. 1999).

[158] 1999 U.S. Dist. LEXIS 605, 1999 WL 33454 (S.D.N.Y. 1999).

[159] For a case permitting indemnification by contract under Del. G.C.L. § 145(f), in circumstances where indemnifcation was not expressly authorized or required by other provisions of Del. G.C.L. § 145, see *Cochran v. Stifel Financial Corp.*, 2000 WL 1847676 (Del. Ch. 2000) (indemnification of employee of *subsidiary* in circumstances where indemnification would be mandatory for officer or director of *parent* under Del. G.C.L. § 145(c)), *aff'd in part and rev'd in part, on other grounds*, 2002 WL 1316240 (Del. 2002).

[160] 94 N.Y.2d 659 (2000).

[161] For comparisons of indemnification and opt-out provisions, see De Mott, *Limiting Directors' Liability*, 66 WASH. U. L.Q. 295 (1988). Note that the MBCA was changed in 1994 to align the two standards. *See* MBCA §§ 2.02(b)(4)-(5), 8.51.

[4] Specific Indemnification Situations

In applying statutory, charter and bylaw indemnification provisions, it is helpful to identify certain distinctions made in these provisions according to what is being indemnified and the circumstances surrounding the indemnification, and to compare the approach of each provision to each of these distinguishable situations.

[a] Type of Cost Reimbursed

Distinguish expenses of litigation and amounts paid by the defendant to satisfy an adverse judgment or settlement. The rules are much more liberal as to indemnification of the former type of cost.

[b] The Disposition of the Suit in Connection with which Indemnification Is Being Made

Distinguish the following: (1) defendant wins on the merits; (2) defendant wins on a procedural point; (3) defendant settles the case; (4) defendant loses. There should be no question from a policy standpoint as to the corporation's power to indemnify the defendant's expenses in situation (1); the only question here is as to whether the corporation may refuse to do so.[162]

Situations (2) and (3) are more troublesome because the defendant may have breached a duty to the corporation and indemnification might nullify the remedy for this breach of duty. Moreover, a settlement that trades indemnification for plaintiff's attorneys' fees is one of the main "strike" suit risks. (Is the appropriate solution to this problem to ban indemnification for settlement, or to permit indemnification (or waiver) of liability on the merits?) On the other hand, to refuse indemnification in these situations might prolong litigation while directors seek a favorable adjudication on the merits.

Assuming that the corporation should not necessarily be able to indemnify in situations (2) and (3), how should the cases in which there should and should not be indemnification be distinguished? If the distinction turns on a determination as to whether the defendant has breached a duty to the corporation, who should make this determination? May the board make the determination?

As to situation (4)—the defendant loses the suit—indemnification seemingly would defeat the purposes of liability. But is it clear that there should never be indemnification in this situation? If a losing defendant may be indemnified in some cases, how

---

[162] For a case involving the distinction between situations (1) and (2), see *Harris v. Resolution Trust Corp.*, 939 F.2d 926 (11th Cir. 1991) (no mandatory indemnification where hung jury on one count). Del. G.C.L. § 145(c) does not distinguish between situations (1) and (2). *See, e.g., Perconti v. Thornton Oil Corp.*, 2002 WL 982419 (Del. Ch. 2002) (requiring indemnification of officer who was indicted but not convicted for embezzling funds from the corporation because officer was successful "on the merits or otherwise").

should the decision to indemnify be made? Should the same procedures as are employed in cases that are settled or won on procedural points be trusted in this situation?

[c]   Whether the Action Is Brought by a Third Party or by or on Behalf of the Corporation

In a third-party suit it may not be clear that the director or officer is being sued as such.[163] If the insider is being sued in connection with dealings wholly unrelated to the corporation, there would be no justification for corporate expenditures in her defense. If the defendant is being sued because of her insider status, arguably there should be no indemnification where the director has breached a duty owed to the corporation. Should there be reimbursement of expenses or of the amount of liability or settlement where there was no breach of duty to the corporation?

[d]   The Identity of the Defendant

Statutes vary as to whether officers and employees can be indemnified. Compare Del. G.C.L. § 145 and MBCA § 8.56. Why distinguish directors from other agents? If anything, shouldn't the power to indemnify be greater as to lower level agents who have less ability to manipulate board decisions?[164]

PROBLEMS

Assume the same basic fact situation as *Zapata* (*see* Section 10.06). Assume further that all of the current directors are defendants—some on the basis of having directly benefited from the change in the exercise date and the others on the basis of having approved or acquiesced in the change. You are counsel for Zapata Corporation. Answer each of the questions below under each of these assumptions concerning the governing indemnification rules: (a) The Model Business Corporation Act §§ 8.50-8.59 applies; (b) Del. G.C.L. § 145 applies and there is no applicable bylaw; (c) Del. G.C.L. § 145 applies and the corporation has adopted the following bylaw:

---

[163] *See Heffernan v. Pacific Dunlop GNB Corp.*, 965 F.2d 369 (7th Cir. 1992) (director could be indemnified for a suit under § 12(a)(2) of the Securities Act of 1933 because the director's liability depended in part on his status as such and because the right of indemnification under Delaware law is broadly drawn to encourage people to be directors).

[164] For cases construing the meaning of the term "agent" in indemnification statutes, see *Cochran v. Stifel Corporation*, 2000 Del. Ch. LEXIS 69, 2000 WL 431629 (Del. Ch., Apr. 6, 2000) (person who serves as director, officer or employee of subsidiary is not automatically an agent of the parent for purposes of Del. G.C.L. § 145(c)); *Channel Lumber Co. v. Porter Simon*, 93 Cal. Rptr. 2d 482 (Cal. App. 2000) (outside attorney hired to pursue litigation on corporation's behalf, who is later sued by corporate client for legal malpractice, is not an "agent" of the corporation for indemnification purposes; since corporations cannot represent themselves in court, lawyer must be acting as independent contractor).

Any person who was or is a party or is threatened to be made a party to any threatened, pending or completed action, suit or proceeding, whether civil, criminal, administrative or investigative (including any action by or in the right of the Corporation), by reason of the fact that he is or was a director, officer, employee or agent of the Corporation, or is or was serving at the request of the Corporation as a director, officer, employee or agent of another corporation, partnership, joint venture, trust or other enterprise, shall be indemnified by the Corporation against expenses (including reasonable attorney's fees), judgments, fines and amounts paid in settlement actually and reasonably incurred by him in connection with such action, suit or proceeding, if he acted in good faith and in a manner he reasonably believed to be in or not opposed to the best interests of the Corporation (and with respect to any criminal action or proceeding, if he had no reasonable cause to believe his conduct was unlawful), to the maximum extent permitted by, and in the manner provided by, the Delaware General Corporation Law.

(d) same as (c), except the Model Business Corporation Act applies and the last line of the bylaw refers to that statute.

(1) The court ultimately refuses to uphold the attempted termination by the directors, and the case goes to trial. The result is a judgment of joint and several liability on the part of the entire board, including the inside directors who were covered by the option plan and the outside directors who were not covered, in the amount of the excess tax liability incurred by the corporation. Advise the board whether there is some way the corporation may validly reimburse any of the directors for legal fees and for amounts paid in satisfaction of the judgment, and, if so, specify which directors may be reimbursed, for what amounts they may be reimbursed, and what procedures must be followed.

(2) The parties have negotiated, and the board has unanimously approved, a settlement agreement pursuant to which the inside directors will pay to the corporation a portion of its excess tax liability and the corporation will pay the attorneys' fees incurred by all the director-defendants. Advise the corporation with respect to any legal problems presented by the indemnification provision in the settlement agreement.

(3) The court on remand has dismissed the suit on the basis of the board's recommendation, and this dismissal was affirmed on appeal. One of the defendant officer-directors has been fired and removed from the board for incompetence. Advise the board whether the corporation must reimburse the removed defendant for the legal fees he incurred.

REFERENCES

De Mott, *Limiting Directors' Liability*, 66 WASH. U. L.Q. 295 (1988).
Oesterle, *Limits on a Corporation's Protection of its Directors and Officers from Personal Liability*, 1983 WIS. L. REV. 513.

[B] Insurance

Insurance against the expense of shareholder suits has become quite common in recent years.[165] One reason for insurance coverage is that there are some legal gaps in the indemnification protection a corporation may provide to its directors. The gap that most concerns directors is the prohibition against reimbursing amounts paid where the director has been adjudicated liable to the corporation. Although liability to the corporation is rare, cautious executives fear even a remote possibility of a ruinous judgment for an unintentional mistake. Even where a particular expense is technically indemnifiable, the corporation may be unwilling or unable to pay. Inability to pay is a particular risk since a foundering company is most likely to be the subject of shareholder litigation. Unwillingness to pay is a real possibility where the directors have been replaced as a result of a hostile takeover or proxy contest. Apart from these gaps in protection, insurance helps the corporation guard against a sudden huge indemnification expense.

The typical "d & o," or "directors' and officers'" insurance policy consists of two parts. One part reimburses the corporation for indemnification payments it makes to directors and officers, while the other covers the directors and officers themselves. The policy covers both litigation expenses and amounts paid by the directors and officers as settlements or judgments. As with all insurance policies, the exclusions are particularly important. The policies do not protect directors and officers who have received "personal profit" or have engaged in "dishonesty." The latter term may extend very generally to breach of the directors' duty of loyalty and to recklessly false statements. Also, the policy does not cover risks that are uninsurable under applicable law, perhaps including intentional or gross misconduct.[166] But some courts have upheld insurance against punitive damages[167] and legal expenses incurred in defending intentional misconduct cases.[168]

Although the scope of the policy exclusions may be unclear, it is clear that d & o policies reimburse directors in at least one important respect where no indemnification is available—for amounts paid to satisfy adverse judgments or settlements by directors

---

[165] *See* Oster, *Directors' Insurance Fees Get Fatter*, WALL ST. J., July 12, 2002 at C1, reporting that 97% of all public companies provided such coverage in 2001.

[166] *See, e.g., Northwestern National Casualty Co. v. McNulty*, 307 F.2d 432 (5th Cir. 1962).

[167] *See, e.g., Lazenby v. Universal Underwriters Ins. Co.*, 214 Tenn. 639, 383 S.W.2d 1 (1964).

[168] *See Flintkote Co. v. Lloyd's Underwriters*, 176 N.Y.L.J. 6 (N.Y. Sup. Ct. 1969), *aff'd*, 56 A.D.2d 743, 391 N.Y.S.2d 1005 (1st Dept. 1977).

who have breached their duty of care to the corporation. Such insurance is expressly permitted by many indemnification statutes.[169]

While at first blush the provisions permitting insurance may seem inconsistent with those prohibiting indemnification, the apparent inconsistency is explained by some important differences between insurance and indemnification. First, the insurance payment is not made by the corporation, so the shareholders are compensated for the insiders' misconduct. Second, insurers have a strong incentive to supervise their insureds carefully, and director misconduct may result in higher premiums and in possible discontinuance of coverage.[170] Insurers have a powerful weapon in supervising officers and directors: any misrepresentation or nondisclosure of information concerning a covered risk may result under policy provisions in denial of coverage not only of the directors responsible for the misrepresentation or nondisclosure but of other directors to whom the dishonesty may be imputed. Third, standard insurance policies force directors to bear some of the risk of their misconduct through a substantial deductible and through coinsurance of about five percent of the loss in excess of the deductible.

Beginning in late 1984, a number of forces combined to create what many called a "crisis" in the availability of "d & o" insurance. D & O insurance not only became more expensive and less available during the "crisis," but insurers offered less protection.[171] An immediate effect of the insurance "crisis" was the moves toward statutory limitation of liability discussed above in Section 9.03[C]. One possible cause of the "crisis" was the significant increase in unpredictability of the application of the business judgment rule caused by the *Van Gorkom* decision (*see* **Romano**). Another may have been the courts' increasingly broad interpretations of "d & o" policies, including extension of policy coverage to suits by corporations against their employees.[172]

News reports suggest we may be on the verge of a new insurance crisis in 2002. Accounting problems at such firms as Enron, Global Crossing, and WorldCom have

---

[169] *See, e.g.,* N.Y. Bus. Corp. L. § 727(a)(3); Del. G.C.L. § 145(g); MBCA § 8.57. *See also* ALI *Principles* §§ 7.20(a)(4) and (b)(2).

[170] For evidence that liability insurance is employed as a device for monitoring managers, see Holderness, *Liability Insurers as Corporate Monitors,* 10 INT'L REV. L. & ECON. 115 (1990).

[171] *See Unocal Corp. v. Superior Court,* 244 Cal. Rptr. 540 (Cal. App. 1988) (opinion ordered not published) (insurer sued for having unannounced plan to cancel policies at first hint of a takeover to coerce insureds into substituting a less protective policy).

[172] *See National Union Fire Insurance Co. v. Seafirst Corp.,* 662 F. Supp. 36 (W.D. Wash. 1986). This extension of coverage permitted banks to shift some of their huge loan losses to insurers. *See* Bailey, *New Suit Filed by Continental Illinois Corp.,* WALL ST. J., Nov. 18, 1985, p. 16. In *American Casualty Co. of Reading v. Baker,* 758 F. Supp. 1340 (C.D. Cal. 1991), the court held that a d & o policy exclusion for actions by regulatory agencies protected an insurer from having to indemnify for a claim against a director of a failed bank by the Federal Deposit Insurance Corporation and Reconstruction Trust Corporation. Also in *Olympic Club v. Underwriters at Lloyd's of London,* 991 F.2d 497 (9th Cir. 1993), a d & o insurer was not liable for defense costs of discrimination by a private club because the action was based on the club's policies rather than the directors' wrongful acts, and the insurance policy protects the directors, not the club. The dissent noted that the suit was really based on a breach of duty by the directors to prevent violation.

lead to dramatic increases in both premiums and deductibles, particularly for firms in the telecommunications industry.[173]

REFERENCES

Johnston, *Corporate Indemnification and Liability Insurance for Directors and Officers*, 33 Bus. Law. 1993 (1978).

Romano, *What Went Wrong With Directors' and Officers' Liability Insurance?*, 14 Del. J. Corp. L. 1 (1989).

§ 10.13 Remedies in Unincorporated Firms

As discussed in Section 10.01, the derivative remedy is designed for firms with centralized management in which passive members may need to override managers' control over the firm's litigation in order to discipline managers' fiduciary breaches. Such a remedy may be unnecessarily costly in a "standard form partnership," given partners' direct participation in management. Subsection A discusses the partnership substitute—the accounting remedy. As discussed in subsections B and C, remedies are less clear in limited partnerships and LLCs, since these business forms share both partnership and corporate characteristics.

[A] The Accounting Remedy

The *exclusive* remedy for breach of fiduciary duty, as well as for other types of claims, in both general and limited partnerships[174] traditionally has been the partner's right to a formal accounting under UPA § 22 (and RUPA § 405). A formal accounting determines all of the rights and liabilities of the partners in a single proceeding. *See* **Bromberg & Ribstein**. The exclusivity rule is based at least partly on the historical "aggregate" nature of partnership, in which the firm is treated as an aggregation of the individual members. It is also supported by the practical consideration that members in a very closely held firm are likely to have claims against each other which should be resolved together in a single proceeding.

There is ordinarily no right in an accounting proceeding to recover attorneys' fees as in a derivative suit (*see* Section 10.11, above).[175] Thus, the right to an accounting may

---

[173] *See* Oster, *Directors' Insurance Fees Get Fatter*, Wall St. J., July 12, 2002 at C1, reporting premium increases ranging from 100% to 300%, along with new co-insurance requirements, for telecommunications firms, and greatly increased deductibles for securities firms.

[174] The general partnership remedies apply to both general and limited partnerships through UPA § 6(2) and RULPA § 1106.

[175] Courts may allow recovery in some cases, however, where the proceeding has created a fund. *See Cauble v. Handler*, 503 S.W.2d 362 (Tex. Civ. App. 1973); **Bromberg & Ribstein**, § 6.08, n.97.

afford little comfort in a large partnership where the interests of the individual partners are too small to justify the expense of such a proceeding.

The accounting "exclusivity" rule has been breaking down.[176] Revised UPA § 405(b) not only eliminates the exclusivity rule, but also provides that "a partner may maintain an action against the partnership or another person for legal or equitable relief, with or without an accounting . . . ." This language may be broad enough to allow a partner to bring a derivative-type suit.[177]

[B] Limited Partnership Derivative Suits

The accounting remedy may not be appropriate in limited partnerships because these partnerships typically have only one or two general partners, and limited partners are unlikely to have contribution obligations that give rise to cross claims that need to be resolved in a special proceeding.

Are corporate-type derivative suits appropriate in limited partnerships? Limited partners, to be sure, are even further removed from management than corporate shareholders because of the limited partnership "control rule." *See* Section 6.03. Yet general partners' personal liability and limited partners' default right to cash out of the firm arguably make derivative remedies less necessary in the limited partnership than in the corporate context.

Courts once denied derivative suits in limited partnerships, partly because of the partnership accounting exclusivity rule. Also, even if a limited partner may bring a derivative suit, she might lose her limited liability status on the ground that participation in the action constitutes taking part in the control of the business (*see* Section 6.03).

The derivative suit remedy now is expressly permitted under Article 10 of the Revised Uniform Limited Partnership Act and of ULPA (2001). Also, Rule 23.1 of the Federal Rules of Civil Procedure recognizes the existence of a derivative suit remedy in "unincorporated associations." The limited partnership derivative suit is similar to and involves many of the same questions as the corporate derivative suit discussed above.

[C] Limited Liability Companies

Should LLCs be treated like general partnerships or like limited partnerships regarding derivative and other remedies? Many LLCs have partnership-type decentralized management. Nevertheless, many LLC statutes and the Uniform Act (§§ 1101-

---

[176] *See Sertich v. Moore*, 162 Ariz. 407, 783 P.2d 1199 (1989) (eliminating the accounting exclusivity rule, reasoning that the rule has outlived its usefulness in light of, among other things, modern pleading and joinder rules and the court's power to appoint a master to sort out complex transactions).

[177] *See* Ribstein, *The Revised Uniform Partnership Act: Not Ready for Prime Time*, 49 Bus. Law. 45, 61-62 (1993).

1104) also provide for derivative suits. Some statutes include a provision which permits a suit by a majority of the disinterested members in both member-managed and manager-managed LLCs. State variations are discussed in **Ribstein & Keatinge.** Is this provision an appropriate alternative to the derivative suit in partnerships and LLCs?

[D] Contracting Around Remedies in Partnerships and LLCs

Partnerships and LLCs may be able to contract around statutory derivative remedies. There is no explicit rule against such contracts in the UPA or RULPA. *Lenz v. Associated Inns and Restaurants Co. of America*[178] enforced a provision in the partnership agreement that waived the partners' claims for an accounting remedy. Should it be easier for partnerships and LLCs to waive a default derivative remedy than for corporations to do so? If so, might a publicly held firm effectively waive the derivative remedy by organizing as a limited partnership or LLC?

REFERENCES

Bromberg & Ribstein, BROMBERG & RIBSTEIN ON PARTNERSHIP, §§ 5.05, 6.08 and 15.05.
Ribstein & Keatinge, RIBSTEIN & KEATINGE ON LIMITED LIABILITY COMPANIES, Ch. 10.

---

[178] 833 F. Supp. 362 (S.D.N.Y.1993).

CHAPTER 11

Distributions to Owners:
Duties to Owners and Creditors

§ 11.01 Introduction

The principal attribute of investments in firms is their return, which consists of distributions by the business to the owners and the increase or decrease in the value of the investment. This Chapter discusses legal rules relating to the former component of return. It discusses only distributions made pursuant to ownership relationships by a going concern, and not distributions to owners and others made on account of employment or extension of credit, or distributions by a liquidating business. As to the latter, see, generally, Sections 4.04 and 5.05. Most of the Chapter discusses corporate dividends. Section 11.08 deals with partnership distributions.

The law of distributions can be understood as part of the nexus of contracts among the classes of claimants whose contracts comprise the firm. The classes have different, and often opposing, interests in distributions. As discussed below in this Section, the contracts among them represent tradeoffs that accommodate these different interests.

[A] Interests of Common Shareholders

The board of directors generally has the discretion whether to declare payment of dividends to the common shareholders or to retain earnings in the business. The principal question in this context is the extent to which directors' discretion is constrained by their fiduciary duties. Analysis of this question requires an understanding of how dividends affect the common shareholders and whether legal duties are necessary to ensure that the board's distribution decisions are in the shareholders' interest.

[1] The "Irrelevance Theorem"

At first blush common shareholders might seem to have a strong interest in maximizing the firm's distributions. In fact, it is not clear whether or how this is true. A leading theory states that under certain assumptions the amount of dividends a corporation pays does not affect the total returns on the corporation's stock.[1] Instead, residual

---

[1] *See* Miller & Modigliani, *Dividend Policy, Growth, and the Valuation of Shares*, 34 J. Bus. 411 (1961).

claimants are concerned only with the level of a firm's earnings. This is the "irrelevance theorem."

A central intuition of the "irrelevance" theorem is that the payment of dividends does not reduce the firm's ability to make favorable investments. Although paying dividends depletes the firm's cash, a company that has favorable investment opportunities can always raise the money by borrowing or selling equity. Note how this assumes that changes in capital structure, as by taking on new debt, will not affect a firm's value. Thus, dividend irrelevance is a companion of the capital-structure-irrelevance theory discussed in Section 7.01[G].

Even accepting the independence of investment and dividends, shareholders might seem to prefer having the firm's earnings "in hand" rather than reinvested in the company. But shareholders can always declare "homemade dividends" by selling some of their equity. If, for example, earnings have increased the value of the firm by 5%, shareholders who want these earnings in hand can simply sell 5% of their holdings in the company, thereby taking the earnings out in the form of capital gains. Compare the analogous concept of "homemade leverage" suggested in proving the irrelevance of capital structure (*see* Section 7.01[G]).

The irrelevance theorem, however, is based on a number of assumptions. Among other things, the theory assumes efficient markets, no taxes, and no institutional considerations that would cause some holders to prefer dividends. As the following subsections illustrate, when these assumptions are relaxed, the conclusion that dividends do not matter no longer holds.[2]

[2] The Role of Taxes

The irrelevance theory assumes no taxes. But corporate income generally is taxed to shareholders when distributed as a dividend,[3] in contrast with partnerships and Subchapter S corporations in which income is generally taxed to owners when earned by the firm. Thus, shareholders may prefer that the corporation retain earnings. However, shareholders that are corporations can deduct at least 70% of dividend income, and often 100%, if they are at least 80% shareholders (I.R.C. § 243). This, for the most part, prevents the same income from being taxed more than twice (*i.e.*, when earned by the corporation and when distributed to shareholders). Close corporation shareholders may be able to take some funds out of the corporation as salaries or interest which are tax-deductible by the corporation.

---

[2] For evidence that dividends matter, see, *e.g.*, DeAngelo, DeAngelo & Skinner, *Dividends and Losses*, 47 J. Fin. 1837 (1992) (managers are reluctant to reduce dividends, and do not do so unless the company is actually losing money).

[3] A distribution is not taxable to the shareholder as a dividend if the corporation has no earnings and profits. *See* §§ 301 and 316 of the Internal Revenue Code. There is some complicated law on this. *See* Andrews, *"Out of Its Earnings and Profits": Some Reflection on the Taxation of Dividends*, 69 Harv. L. Rev. 1403 (1956).

[3]　Information, Transaction Costs and Market Efficiency

The irrelevance theory assumes no information or transaction costs. But as with the "no taxes" assumption, the facts are sometimes otherwise. For example, because information is costly to produce, markets probably do not reflect all information about firms—that is, they are not "strong form" efficient (*see* Section 7.01[F]). Management may, therefore, use dividend decisions to "signal" how the company is doing.[4] Also, transaction costs or institutional limitations on the sale of stock may effectively preclude shareholders from creating "homemade dividends" by selling their shares. Accordingly, shareholders who would like to liquidate some of their investment may sometimes prefer dividends to earnings retention. This is particularly true in close corporations, where there is no ready market for the shares.

[4]　Manager/Shareholder Conflicts

If dividends matter to common shareholders, the next question is whether directors can be trusted to make distribution decisions that are consistent with shareholder interests. Managers and shareholders may have conflicting interests regarding distributions (*see* **Brudney**). Managers may want to retain rather than distribute earnings because such a policy: (1) causes the firm to grow, thereby enhancing managerial power and compensation; (2) reduces the risk of bankruptcy, thereby alleviating concerns of managers who have much of their financial capital and all of their human capital invested in the firm; and (3) may serve the interests of controlling shareholders to whom managers are beholden. Thus, directors may pursue a dividend policy that is more aligned with the interests of creditors than of shareholders.

On the other hand, there are reasons to believe that the conflict of interest between managers and shareholders in regard to dividends is not serious (*see* **Fischel**). First, shareholders may not be injured even by self-interested earnings retention because corporations may develop "clienteles" of shareholders based on their dividend preferences. For example, firms with controlling shareholders who prefer no dividends would attract a clientele of like-minded shareholders. Second, shareholders are protected by market and contractual devices that operate to constrain director decision-making generally. For example, managers whose dividend decisions injure shareholders, like managers who are deficient in other ways, are subject to removal in the market for control by acquirors who stand to profit by increasing distributions.

Managers may adopt an established policy of distributing income in order to reduce agency costs arising from excessive retention of earnings, and thereby avoid ouster (**Easterbrook**). Alternatively, managers may do a "leveraged buyout" which effectively replaces outside shareholders with creditors, and replaces a dividend "pol-

---

[4]　*See* Asquith & Mullins, *Impact of Initiating Dividend Payments on Shareholders' Wealth*, 46 J. Bus. 77 (1983).

icy" with a contractual commitment to make distributions in the form of interest and repayment of principal.[5]

[B] Preferred Shareholders' Interests in Receiving Dividends

Where there are two or more classes of stock, "preferred" shareholders are usually entitled to receive dividends at a specified rate (usually expressed as a percentage of the face value of the preferred stock) before any payment is made to the "common" shareholders. The rights of holders of preferred stock are normally set forth in the certificate of incorporation. *See* Section 11.05. Dividends are much more important to preferred shareholders than to common shareholders because preferred holders normally do not have a residual claim on the firm's assets. There is an obvious conflict of interest between the directors, who are elected by the common shareholders, and the preferred shareholders. But, as discussed in Sections 11.05-06, the courts generally refuse to recognize fiduciary duties to preferred holders.

[C] Protection of Creditors and Other Fixed Claimants From Excessive Distributions

Corporate managers have the incentive to take actions on behalf of shareholders that injure bondholders. First, managers may distribute assets to shareholders, thereby increasing the risk that the corporation will be unable to repay its debt, and so decreasing the value of the debt. This is, of course, the primary reason for legal restrictions on dividends. Second, managers may substitute more risky assets for less risky ones. Riskier investments may be more valuable to shareholders, who reap the big payoffs, than to bondholders (*see* Section 3.02[C]). Fixed claimants are protected from excessive distribution by corporation statutes and insolvency statutes, as well as by their contracts (Section 11.03). As discussed in Section 11.04, there is a lively debate concerning whether creditors should also be protected by fiduciary duties.

Dividend restrictions, however, carry costs as well as benefits. As discussed above, distributing dividends may decrease self-interested retention of earnings by managers. Thus, dividend restrictions may increase agency costs between managers and shareholders.

Financial markets can discipline firms' selection of indenture covenants in particular contexts. For example, **Smith & Warner** found that distributions were more restricted for firms with higher debt/equity ratios, where the potential injury to creditors, and therefore the benefit of the restriction to creditors, is greater.

---

[5]   For a case in which the court recognized directors' incentives to increase payouts in refusing to impose liability for excessive distributions, see *In re C-T of Virginia, Inc.*, 953 F.2d 637 (4th Cir. 1992).

REFERENCES

Brudney, *Dividends, Discretion and Disclosure*, 66 VA. L. REV. 85 (1980).
Easterbrook, *Two Agency-Cost Explanations of Dividends*, 74 AM. ECON. REV. 650 (1984).
Fischel, *The Law and Economics of Dividend Policy,* 67 VA. L. REV. 699 (1981).
Smith & Warner, *On Financial Contracting: An Analysis of Bond Covenants*, 7 J. FIN. ECON. 117 (1979).

§ 11.02 Accounting and Corporate Distributions

[A] Basic Accounting Procedures

The rules regarding distributions to owners refer to a substantial extent to the amounts in various accounts computed in accordance with accounting procedures. The following is a very brief introduction to these procedures.

Each business transaction is normally recorded initially in two separate books—the journal and the ledger. The journal describes transactions chronologically, while the ledger groups transactions into categories. In each book, each transaction is recorded twice—as a debit on the left side and as a credit on the right. Credits are additions to liabilities or to owners' equity and subtractions from assets, while debits increase assets and reduce liabilities or owners' equity. This practice of characterizing each transaction as both a debit and a credit is called "double entry" bookkeeping. The underlying principle is that at any given time a business can be described by the following equation:

Assets = Liabilities + Owner Equity.

Thus, any change in one element of the equation must result in an offsetting change in another.

Accountants record expenses, such as rents and salaries, and revenues, including sales, in "temporary" or "SUB-T" accounts. At the end of the year the expense and revenue accounts are transferred in summary form, or "closed," to the company's income statement.

At the end of each accounting period, the "bottom line" of the income statement, or total revenues less total expenses, is transferred, or "closed," to the balance sheet as additions to or subtractions from owners' equity. Accounts other than these "temporary" accounts are closed directly to the balance sheet by adjusting assets, liabilities, or owners' equity. For a description of the balance sheet, see Section 3.02[B].

[B] Role of Accounting Rules

The corporation's financial statements are prepared by accountants according to the rules of their profession, often referred to as "Generally Accepted Accounting Principles," or "GAAP." To what extent do these accounting standards control the corporation's legal obligations with regard to distributions?

There are many situations in which legal, rather than accounting, rules control. To begin with, the statutes sometimes use legal terms, such as "surplus" and "capital surplus," that are different from those employed by accountants in the preparation of financial statements. Even where the statute is silent or ambiguous, courts may reject the accountant's approach because accounting and law have different goals. Accountants are concerned primarily with accurately disclosing the financial health of the enterprise, while legal rules are concerned with the substantive conduct of the corporation's business. Thus, a distribution may be consistent with the best interests of the corporation (and therefore accepted by the courts) even if it exceeds the amount accountants would disclose in a particular balance sheet or income statement "account" out of which the applicable statute allows distributions to be made.

On the other hand, for several reasons, accounting principles usually are controlling. First, some terms and concepts in corporation statutes were deliberately borrowed from accounting terminology, indicating that an accounting approach should be used in applying these terms. Second, accounting rules provide the only guidance with respect to problems which are not explicitly addressed by the corporation statutes or by case law (*see* **Hackney** at 819-23). Third, as a practical matter, directors are usually well advised to rely on their accountants because the directors are generally held liable only where they have authorized a dividend in bad faith, and reliance on an accountant's opinion may preclude such a finding. *See* Note 2, Section 11.03.

REFERENCE

Hackney, *Accounting Principles in Corporation Law*, 30 LAW & CONTEMP. PROBS. 791 (1965).

§ 11.03 Statutory Restrictions on the Payment of Dividends

An important general question regarding dividend restrictions in corporation statutes is their overall function in the nexus of contracts among corporate claimants. In reading the following materials, consider whether legal restrictions on dividends are necessary in light of the availability of protection under specific contracts and other creditor-protection rules, such as piercing the corporate veil; and whether the statutes appropriately accommodate the common shareholders' interests, including minimizing agency costs between shareholders and managers (*see* Section 11.01).

[A] Traditional Corporation Statutes: Overview

Corporation statutes generally limit the amount of distributions to shareholders to particular funds or accounts defined in the statutes. These funds are simply numbers computed in a prescribed manner, rather than amounts of money which are actually available for distribution. Thus, a corporation that owns a single asset such as a building and has only a small amount of liabilities may have a very large "surplus" fund available for the payment of dividends but no cash in the bank. The purpose of statutory restrictions on dividends is to protect creditors from being injured by excessive distributions of assets to owners.

This subsection briefly reviews three types of state corporation statutory provisions that traditionally dominated corporate law. As discussed in Note 1 below, these traditional approaches are being superseded by a more streamlined approach to regulating corporate distributions. Nevertheless, traditional statutes remain as constraints on board conduct in many states, including Delaware. Moreover, an analysis of these statutes is instructive in evaluating both modern statutes and contractual provisions.

[1] Balance Sheet Surplus

The Delaware statute includes a leading example of the type of provision that limits the amount of distributions to particular funds or accounts. Under the first part of § 170(a), the "fund" available for dividends is "surplus." Surplus is computed under § 154 by subtracting the total of "capital" and liabilities from assets. "Capital" consists of the par value of the corporation's stock or other amount allocated by the board to the capital account (not the amount of consideration received for the corporation's stock). *See* Section 3.02[D], above. Capital and surplus are both represented on the corporation's balance sheet as subcategories of shareholders' equity. "Surplus" created by the issuance of stock is referred to by accountants as "paid in surplus" or "capital in excess of par." (See the balance sheet in Section 3.02[B] above.) Note that statutory "surplus" is much broader than these terms since it is not determined solely with reference to the consideration received for stock.

Although the "capital" component of shareholders' equity is, at least theoretically, a "cushion" for creditors, this cushion often provides little actual comfort for creditors. First, the directors have substantial discretion under § 154 to determine what will be initially allocated to capital. Second, under § 244(a)(4), the directors may, in certain cases, reduce capital amounts in excess of par. Third, the par value of issued stock (and therefore the "surplus" available for dividends) may be changed by certificate amendment under § 242.

[2] Earned Surplus

The Model Business Corporation Act at one time referred to the basic fund for distributions as "earned surplus," defined as accumulated income and losses. Earned surplus is generally referred to by accountants as "retained earnings" and is represented on the balance sheet as a subcategory of shareholders' equity. (See the balance sheet in Section 3.02[B]). The earned surplus test reflects modern accounting's emphasis on the income statement (from which earned surplus is derived) rather than the balance sheet as the more realistic picture of the company's economic health. It also reflects a movement toward dividend limits that depend on the economic health of the enterprise rather than on "capital" and "surplus," which had become wholly arbitrary numbers.

The earned surplus test has ended up providing little more comfort for creditors than the approach tied to balance sheet surplus. First, under statutes like the old version of the MBCA, distributions out of "capital surplus" (defined as the excess of the net assets of the corporation over stated capital and earned surplus) can be made without a shareholder vote if such distributions have been "pre-authorized" in the articles of incorporation. Second, the earned surplus limitation can be circumvented through a "quasi-reorganization," in which a corporation eliminates a deficit in its earned surplus account by making a transfer from its capital surplus account.

[3] Nimble Dividends

Statutes both of the balance sheet type (*see* Del. G.C.L. § 170(a)) and of the earned surplus type may permit distributions out of current earnings. These distributions are referred to as "nimble dividends" because they are payable out of an earnings figure that is "closed out" from the income statement to the balance sheet and disappears into a deficit. Such provisions enable a corporation with a large deficit to attract capital by being able to pay a dividend in its first good year.

PROBLEM

Advise the corporation the balance sheet of which is included in Section 3.02[B], above, as to the maximum dividend it may pay (1) upon a favorable vote of the board of directors; and (2) upon a favorable vote of the board and the shareholders, consistently with Delaware law, assuming there are no relevant provisions in the certificate of incorporation.

[B] Specific Problems of Operation

The following are a very few of the large number of problems that may arise in applying statutory provisions like those summarized in the preceding subsection. The situations discussed below are intended both to indicate the complexity involved and to suggest an approach to resolving the problems. In reading the following materials, consider carefully the respective roles of accounting rules, statutory interpretation and policy considerations.

[1] Unrealized Appreciation

Accounting Approach:

When a corporation purchases an asset, the asset is generally debited at cost to the asset column. There is an offsetting credit either to assets (if, for example, the asset was purchased for cash) or to liabilities (if, for example, the asset was purchased on credit) or to owners' equity (if, for example, the asset was turned over to the corporation in exchange for stock). If the asset is tangible, such as a building or equipment, it is "depreciated." A similar process, called "amortization," is used for intangible assets. Each year a portion of the cost of the asset is offset as an expense against revenues and, consequently, reduces the amount of income which is "closed" to the owners' equity side of the balance sheet. Accumulated depreciation is also shown as offsetting the cost of the asset on the asset side of the balance sheet.

Through this process, net income reflects the cost of the use of the asset in a given year and the balance sheet shows how much of the cost of the asset has yet to be "written off" as an expense. Thus, an asset on a modern balance sheet is simply a sum of future expenses. The asset continues to be recorded at cost less accumulated depreciation even if it is actually appreciating in value. In accounting terminology, the appreciation in value is not recognized on the books of the company until it is realized when the asset is involved in a sale or exchange.

Legal Approach:

Under Del. G.C.L. § 154 surplus is defined with reference to "net assets." The question insofar as unrealized appreciation is concerned is whether the dollar amount of net assets is current value or cost. In *Randall v. Bailey*,[6] directors were held not liable for authorizing a distribution where there was a surplus if unrealized appreciation (which was "recognized" on the corporation's financial statements) was taken into account. The statute applied in *Randall*, unlike Del. G.C.L. § 154, explicitly referred to the "value" of the corporation's assets (although there is some question whether the provision in which that term appeared was relevant to the particular issue at hand).

What should be the approach under a Delaware-type provision? Should the law follow the "cost" approach of modern accounting? An argument against following the accounting approach is that corporation statutes should be interpreted to give the directors flexibility in distributing earnings. Consider, for example, the Easterbrook argument, discussed in Section 11.01[A][4] above, that an established dividend policy can increase the value of a corporation's stock because it helps minimize agency costs. The board may have to pay dividends out of unrealized appreciation in order to preserve an agency-cost-reducing high-dividend policy and therefore protect the corporation's stock price. Easterbrook says that this consideration may explain the flexible approach in *Randall*.[7]

---

[6]   23 N.Y.S.2d 173 (Sup. Ct. 1940), *aff'd*, 288 N.Y. 280, 43 N.E.2d 43 (1942).

[7]   *See* Easterbrook, *Two Agency Cost Explanations of Dividends*, 74 AM. ECON. REV. 650, 655 n.23 (1984).

There are several arguments in favor of following the accounting approach. First, the conservative accounting approach is consistent with the creditor-protection policy of the dividend statutes because it reduces the risk that dividends will be based on inflated asset values. Second, basing dividends on something other than GAAP would involve the practical problems of two sets of financial statements and would expose directors to a greater risk of liability. Third, a dividend based on inflated asset value might violate a corporation or creditor protection statute employing an "equitable" insolvency test. *See* Note 3, below. This, in fact, was probably the case in the situation involved in *Randall*.

Klang v. Smith's Food & Drug Centers, Inc.[8] held that balance sheet net worth does *not* control for purposes of determining whether a repurchase of stock causes an impairment of the corporation's capital for purposes of Del. G.C.L. § 160, which restricts corporate share repurchases (*see* Section 11.07). The court reasoned that "[t]he General Assembly enacted [Del. G.C.L. § 160] to prevent boards from draining corporations of assets to the detriment of creditors and the long-term health of the corporation" and that "[a]llowing corporations to revalue assets and liabilities to reflect current realities complies with the statute and serves well the policies behind the statute." The court's rationale suggests that the Delaware Supreme Court would also allow unrealized appreciation to be considered in determining "net assets" under Del. G.C.L. § 154.

The question under an earned surplus test is whether unrealized appreciation constitutes "earned surplus." Again, the statute is ambiguous. The arguments discussed above also would apply here. There is an additional argument against including unrealized appreciation in earned surplus which does not apply under a Balance Sheet Surplus test: since the shift to the earned surplus test was based in part on accounting practice, perhaps this indicates a legislative intent to apply accounting principles (*see* **Hackney** (1965) at 821).[9]

The question under a nimble dividend provision is whether unrealized appreciation is "net profits" in the year in which the appreciation is recognized on the corporation's financial statements. *See* Del. G.C.L. § 170(a). The same arguments against including unrealized appreciation in earned surplus would apply to inclusion in net profits, since the latter is a component of the former. Also, there is arguably a need for greater conservatism with respect to the nimble dividend provision: such a provision usually comes into play only when there is otherwise a deficit, and the account out of which dividends are paid only reflects a single year's possibly aberrational performance. As was noted in connection with earned surplus, recognition of unrealized appreciation may, as a result of higher depreciation charges, reduce net income, and hence the fund for nimble dividends, in subsequent years.

---

[8]   702 A.2d 150 (Del. 1997).

[9]   Note that if unrealized appreciation is recognized by "writing up" the value of the asset on the books of the corporation, depreciation charges would have to increase, thus reducing net income (and hence earned surplus) in future years. *See* **Hackney** (1957) at 1381.

[2] Unrealized Diminution in Value

Accounting Approach:

Under generally accepted accounting principles, unrealized diminution in value is recognized as to some assets including marketable securities and inventories. The apparent inconsistency with the treatment of unrealized appreciation is explained by the principle of conservatism underlying accounting theory.

Legal Approach:

The *Randall* case, discussed above, held that unrealized diminution in value, like unrealized appreciation, affected the amount available for distributions under a balance sheet surplus test. What approach should be taken under a provision like Del. G.C.L. § 154 which, unlike the provision applied in *Randall*, does not refer to "value"? As discussed above with respect to unrealized appreciation, perhaps the statutes should be interpreted to give directors more flexibility than is available under conservative accounting convention. Thus, directors should not necessarily be bound to revalue assets downward for dividend purposes in all the situations in which devaluation is required under generally accepted accounting principles.[10]

If unrealized diminution in value must be taken into account in some circumstances, does the devaluation affect earned surplus or capital surplus? The definition of earned surplus in the old version of the MBCA arguably includes unrealized diminution in value just as it does unrealized appreciation. But there are some arguments in favor of reflecting unrealized diminution in value in earned rather than capital surplus that do not apply to unrealized appreciation. For instance, if the policy of conservatism compels taking unrealized diminution into account, it follows that such diminution should reduce the primary distribution account—earned surplus—and not merely the "fall back" account.

As with unrealized appreciation, if unrealized diminution reduces earned surplus, it should also reduce "net income" and hence the fund available for nimble dividends. Also as with respect to unrealized appreciation, there is arguably a greater need for conservatism with respect to the nimble dividend fund than with respect to earned surplus which would point toward taking the unrealized diminution in value into account. This is, in fact, the approach of Del. G.C.L. § 170(a).

[C] Other Limitations on Dividends under Traditional Corporation Statutes

Even if there is "surplus" available for a distribution, the statutes discussed above may prohibit a distribution that violates one of two types of provisions. The first type of provision prohibits the payment of dividends when the corporation is or would be ren-

---

[10] *See also* **Kummert** (1966) at 156-57 (arguing that accounting principles may be unduly conservative as applied in this context).

dered insolvent. The second type of prohibition relates to liquidation preferences of pre-ferred stock. Preferred stockholders may have a contractual right to receive a certain amount upon liquidation of the corporation prior to the distribution of assets to common shareholders. Preferred shareholders may expect that the amount of this "preference" will not be dissipated by the corporation. This expectation is protected, at least in part, under both the Delaware and old Model Acts. Delaware G.C.L. § 170(a) applies only with respect to nimble dividends, and then only to the extent of the stated capital of the preferred shares. Thus, $1 par preferred having a liquidation preference of $100 per share is protected only up to $1 per share. The old Model Act, on the other hand, only limits distributions from capital surplus.

NOTES AND QUESTIONS

(1) **Modern statutory approaches to dividend regulation.** Under the traditional corporation statutes discussed above, the propriety of a dividend is determined with ref-erence to various "funds" defined in the statutes. This approach presents several prob-lems, including uncertainties in computing the various funds and the ease with which they can be manipulated. These problems have given rise to new statutory approaches to dividend regulation that prohibit a distribution when the corporation is insolvent in the "equity" sense of not being able to pay its debts as they come due, and also when the corporation's assets fall below a certain point in relation to liabilities and liquidation preferences. See, for example, MBCA § 6.40. Does the modern MBCA approach bet-ter accommodate the interests of creditors and common shareholders than did the tra-ditional statutes? Why do you suppose Delaware, normally a leader in providing state-of-the-art corporate law, adheres to the traditional approach?

(2) **Liabilities for improper payment of dividends.** Directors who fail to dissent from dividend declarations may be liable to the corporation for improper distributions under the corporation statutes. Delaware G.C.L. § 174(a) permits suit against the direc-tors both by the corporation and (on dissolution or insolvency) by creditors. Under most statutes, directors have a good faith defense. See, e.g., Del. G.C.L. §§ 141(e); 172. Also, directors usually have a right of action against fellow directors who agreed to the dividends (see, e.g., Del. G.C.L. § 174(b)), as well as against shareholders who received the distributions *with knowledge of the illegality (see, e.g.,* Del. G.C.L. § 174(c)). In addition, state common law may provide for a corporate cause of action against a shareholder who has received a dividend that impaired the legal capital of the corpora-tion or that rendered the corporation insolvent. In the latter situation, the shareholder may be strictly liable.[11]

(3) **Regulation of dividends under creditor protection statutes.** Dividends are regulated not only under state corporation law, but also under statutes dealing generally with creditors' rights. For instance, the payment of dividends may be limited by the Uni-

---

[11]   *See Wood v. National City Bank,* 24 F.2d 661 (2d Cir. 1928).

form Fraudulent Conveyance Act (the "UFCA"), which has been adopted in about half the states and in the federal bankruptcy code (*see* 11 U.S.C. § 548). Under the UFCA, a dividend may be deemed fraudulent as to creditors, if the corporation is insolvent when the dividend is paid, is rendered insolvent by the payment of the dividend, or is left with unreasonably small capital to conduct its business. The UFCA defines "insolvent" in the "balance sheet" sense of having debts that exceed the value of the corporation's assets. Unlike state corporation law, which generally bases shareholder liability on knowledge of the illegality, shareholders can be held liable under the UFCA irrespective of their knowledge of any illegality. In a state that has adopted the UFCA, the trustee in bankruptcy may sue either under the UFCA by way of 11 U.S.C. § 544(b), which permits the trustee to pursue state law claims on behalf of creditors, or under 11 U.S.C. § 548 (the bankruptcy code's version of the UFCA), which has a longer statute of limitations.

(4) **Contracts protecting creditors.** In addition to the various statutory protections discussed in this section, creditors may bargain for contractual limitations on the ability for their debtors to distribute assets to owners in credit agreements with banks and in "indentures" with trustees for the corporation's bondholders.

PROBLEMS

(1) Assume that the balance sheet in Section 3.02[B] represents the financial condition of Manufacturing Corporation as of the close of fiscal year 1999. In fiscal year 2000, Corporation loses $10,000,000, and in fiscal years 2001 and 2002 Corporation earns $2,000,000 each year. Answer the Problem at the end of Section 11.03[A] for 2000, 2001 and 2002. In answering for each year, assume the corporation paid no dividends in the previous years.

(2) Again assume the balance sheet in Section 3.02[B] represents Manufacturing Corporation's 1999 financial condition. How would your answer to the Problem at the end of Section 11.03[A] be affected if Manufacturing Corporation's machinery is appraised at $100,000 less than the cost figure represented on the balance sheet?

REFERENCES

Clark, *Duties of the Corporate Debtor to its Creditors*, 90 HARV. L. REV. 505 (1977).

Fiflis, Kripke & Foster, ACCOUNTING FOR BUSINESS LAWYERS: TEACHING MATERIALS (3d ed. 1984).

Hackney, *Accounting Principles in Corporation Law*, 30 LAW & CONTEMP. PROBS. 791 (1965).

Hackney, *The Financial Provisions of the Model Business Corporation Act*, 70 HARV. L. REV. 1357 (1957).

Klein, Anderson & McGuinness, *The Call Provision of Corporate Bonds: A Standard Form in Need of Change*, 18 J. CORP. L. 653 (1993).

Kummert, *State Statutory Restrictions on Financial Distributions by Corporations to Share-holders: Part II*, 59 WASH. L. REV. 185 (1984).

Kummert, *The Financial Provisions of the New Washington Business Corporation Act, Part II*, 42 WASH. L. REV. 119 (1966).

Manning & Hanks, LEGAL CAPITAL (3d ed. 1990).

§ 11.04 Fiduciary Duty and Good Faith Protection of Creditors and Other Fixed Claimants

Creditors are protected from harmful distributions by corporation statutes, express contracts, the doctrine of piercing the corporate veil, and creditor-protection statutes, particularly the law of fraudulent conveyances. The following principal case and notes discuss whether creditors also should be protected by fiduciary duties.

KATZ v. OAK INDUSTRIES, INC.
Delaware Court of Chancery
508 A.2d 873 (1986)

ALLEN, Chancellor.

* * *

Plaintiff is the owner of long-term debt securities issued by Oak Industries, Inc. ("Oak"), a Delaware corporation; in this class action he seeks to enjoin the consummation of an exchange offer and consent solicitation made by Oak to holders of various classes of its long-term debt. As detailed below that offer is an integral part of a series of transactions that together would effect a major reorganization and recapitalization of Oak. The claim asserted is in essence, that the exchange offer is a coercive device and, in the circumstances, constitutes a breach of contract. This is the Court's opinion on plaintiff's pending application for a preliminary injunction.

I.

The background facts are involved even when set forth in the abbreviated form the decision within the time period currently available requires.

Through its domestic and foreign subsidiaries and affiliated entities, Oak manufactures and markets component equipments used in consumer, industrial and military products (the "Components Segment"); produces communications equipment for use in cable television systems and satellite television systems (the "Communications Segment") and manufactures and markets laminates and other materials used in printed circuit board applications (the "Materials Segment"). During 1985, the Company has terminated certain other unrelated businesses. As detailed below, it has now entered into an agreement with Allied-Signal, Inc. for the sale of the Materials Segment of its business and is currently seeking a buyer for its Communications Segment.

Even a casual review of Oak's financial results over the last several years shows it unmistakably to be a company in deep trouble. During the period from January 1, 1982 through September 30, 1985, the Company has experienced unremitting loses from operations; on net sales of approximately $1.26 billion during that period it has lost over $335 million. As a result its total stockholders' equity has first shriveled (from $260 million on 12/31/81 to $85 million on 12/31/83) and then disappeared completely (as of 9/30/85 there was a $62 million deficit in its stockholders' equity accounts). Financial markets, of course, reflected this gloomy history.[2]

Unless Oak can be made profitable within some reasonably short time it will not continue as an operating company. Oak's board of directors, comprised almost entirely of outside directors, has authorized steps to buy the company time. In February, 1985, in order to reduce a burdensome annual cash interest obligation on its $230 million of then outstanding debentures, the Company offered to exchange such debentures for a combination of notes, common stock and warrants. As a result, approximately $180 million principal amount of the then outstanding debentures were exchanged. Since interest on certain of the notes issued in that exchange offer is payable in common stock, the effect of the 1985 exchange offer was to reduce to some extent the cash drain on the Company caused by its significant debt.

About the same time that the 1985 exchange offer was made, the Company announced its intention to discontinue certain of its operations and sell certain of its properties. Taking these steps, while effective to stave off a default and to reduce to some extent the immediate cash drain, did not address Oak's longer-range problems. Therefore, also during 1985 representatives of the Company held informal discussions with several interested parties exploring the possibility of an investment from, combination with or acquisition by another company. As a result of these discussions, the Company and Allied-Signal, Inc. entered into two agreements. The first, the Acquisition Agreement, contemplates the sale to Allied-Signal of the Materials Segment for $160 million in cash. The second agreement, the Stock Purchase Agreement, provides for the purchase by Allied-Signal for $15 million cash of 10 million shares of the Company's common stock together with warrants to purchase additional common stock.

The Stock Purchase Agreement provides as a condition to Allied-Signal's obligation that at least 85% of the aggregate principal amount of all of the Company's debt securities shall have tendered and accepted the exchange offers that are the subject of this lawsuit. Oak has six classes of such long term debt.[3]

If less than 85% of the aggregate principal amount of such debt accepts the offer, Allied-Signal has an option, but no obligation, to purchase the common stock and war-

---

[2] The price of the company's common stock has fallen from over $30 per share on December 31, 1981 to approximately $2 per share recently. The debt securities that are the subject of the exchange offer here involved (*see* n.3 for identification) have traded at substantial discounts.

[3] The three classes of debentures are: 13.65% debentures due April 1, 2001, 10 1/2% convertible subordinated debentures due February 1, 2002, and 11 7/8% subordinated debentures due May 15, 1998. In addition, as a result of the 1985 exchange offer the company has three classes of notes which were issued in exchange for debentures that were tendered in that offer. Those are: 13.5% senior notes due May 15, 1990, 9 5/8% convertible notes due September 15, 1991, and 11 5/8% notes due September 15, 1990.

rants contemplated by the Stock Purchase Agreement. An additional condition for the closing of the Stock Purchase Agreement is that the sale of the Company's Materials Segment
contemplated by the Acquisition Agreement shall have been concluded.

Thus, as part of the restructuring and recapitalization contemplated by the Acquisition
Agreement and the Stock Purchase Agreement, the Company has extended an exchange
offer to each of the holders of the six classes of its long-term debt securities. These pending exchange offers include a Common Stock Exchange Offer (available only to holders of
the 9 5/8% convertible notes) and the Payment Certificate Exchange Offers (available to
holders of all six classes of Oak's long-term debt securities). The Common Stock Exchange
Offer currently provides for the payment to each tendering note holder of 407 shares of the
Company's common stock in exchange for each $1,000 9 5/8% note accepted. The offer is
limited to $38.6 million principal amount of notes (out of approximately $83.9 million outstanding).

The Payment Certificate Exchange Offer is an any and all offer. Under its terms, a
payment certificate, payable in cash five days after the closing of the sale of the Materials
Segment to Allied-Signal, is offered in exchange for debt securities. The cash value of the
Payment Certificate will vary depending upon the particular security tendered. In each
instance, however, that payment will be less than the face amount of the obligation. The cash
payments range in amount, per $1,000 of principal, from $918 to $655. These cash values
however appear to represent a premium over the market prices for the Company's debentures
as of the time the terms of the transaction were set.

The Payment Certificate Exchange Offer is subject to certain important conditions
before Oak has an obligation to accept tenders under it. First, it is necessary that a minimum
amount ($38.6 million principal amount out of $83.9 total outstanding principal amount) of
the 9 5/8% notes be tendered pursuant to the Common Stock Exchange Offer. Secondly, it
is necessary that certain minimum amounts of each class of debt securities be tendered,
together with consents to amendments to the underlying indentures.[4]

Indeed, under the offer one may not tender securities unless at the same time one
consents to the proposed amendments to the relevant indentures.

The condition of the offer that tendering security holders must consent to amendments in the indentures governing the securities gives rise to plaintiff's claim of breach of
contract in this case. Those amendments would, if implemented, have the effect of removing significant negotiated protections to holders of the Company's long-term debt including
the deletion of all financial covenants. Such modification may have adverse consequences
to debt holders who elect not to tender pursuant to either exchange offer.

Allied-Signal apparently was unwilling to commit to the $15 million cash infusion
contemplated by the Stock Purchase Agreement, unless Oak's long-term debt is reduced by
85% (at least that is a condition of their obligation to close on that contract). Mathematically,
such a reduction may not occur without the Company reducing the principal amount of outstanding debentures (that is the three classes of outstanding notes constitute less than 85%

---

[4]   The holders of more than 50% of the principal amount of each of the 13.5% notes, the 9 5/8% notes and the
11 5/8% notes and at least 66 2/3% of the principal amount of the 13.65% debentures, 10 1/2% debentures, and 11 7/8%
debentures, must validly tender such securities and consent to certain proposed amendments to the indentures governing those securities.

of all long-term debt). But existing indenture covenants (*see* Offering Circular, pp. 38-39) prohibit the Company, so long as any of its long-term notes are outstanding, from issuing any obligation (including the Payment Certificates) in exchange for any of the debentures. Thus, in this respect, amendment to the indentures is required in order to close the Stock Purchase Agreement as presently structured.

Restrictive covenants in the indentures would appear to interfere with effectuation of the recapitalization in another way. Section 4.07 of the 13.50% Indenture provides that the Company may not "acquire" for value any of the 9 5/8% Notes or 11 5/8% Notes unless it concurrently "redeems" a proportionate amount of the 13.50% Notes. This covenant, if unamended, would prohibit the disproportionate acquisition of the 9 5/8% Notes that may well occur as a result of the Exchange Offers; in addition, it would appear to require the payment of the "redemption" price for the 13.50% Notes rather than the lower, market price offered in the exchange offer.

In sum, the failure to obtain the requisite consents to the proposed amendments would permit Allied-Signal to decline to consummate both the Acquisition Agreement and the Stock Purchase Agreement.

* * *

II.

Plaintiff's claim that the Exchange Offers and Consent Solicitation constitutes a threatened wrong to him and other holders of Oak's debt securities[6] appear to be summarized in paragraph 16 of his Complaint:

> The purpose and effect of the Exchange Offers is [1] to benefit Oak's common stockholders at the expense of the Holders of its debt securities, [2] to force the exchange of its debt instruments at unfair price and at less than face value of the debt instruments [3] pursuant to a rigged vote in which debt Holders who exchange, and who therefore have no interest in the vote, must consent to the elimination of protective covenants for debt Holders who do not wish to exchange.

As amplified in briefing on the pending motion, plaintiff's claim is that no free choice is provided to bondholders by the exchange offer and consent solicitation. Under its terms, a rational bondholder is "forced" to tender and consent. Failure to do so would face a bondholder with the risk of owning a security stripped of all financial covenant protections and for which it is likely that there would be no ready market. A reasonable bondholder, it is suggested, cannot possibly accept those risks and thus such a bondholder is coerced to tender and thus to consent to the proposed indenture amendments.

---

[6] It is worthy of note that a very high percentage of the principal value of Oak's debt securities are owned in substantial amounts by a handful of large financial institutions. Almost 85% of the value of the 13.50% Notes is owned by four such institutions (one investment banker owns 55% of that issue); 69.1% of the 9 5/8% Notes are owned by four financial institutions (the same investment banker owning 25% of that issue) and 85% of the 11 5/8% Notes are owned by five such institutions. Of the debentures, 89% of the 13.65% debentures are owned by four large banks; and approximately 45% of the two remaining issues is owned by two banks.

It is urged this linking of the offer and the consent solicitation constitutes a breach of a contractual obligation that Oak owes to its bondholders to act in good faith. Specifically, plaintiff points to three contractual provisions from which it can be seen that the structuring of the current offer constitutes a breach of good faith. Those provisions (1) establish a requirement that no modification in the term of the various indentures may be effectuated without the consent of a stated percentage of bondholders; (2) restrict Oak from exercising the power to grant such consent with respect to any securities it may hold in its treasury; and (3) establish the price at which and manner in which Oak may force bondholders to submit their securities for redemption.

III.

In order to demonstrate an entitlement to the provisional remedy of a preliminary injunction it is essential that a plaintiff show that it is probable that his claim will be upheld after final hearing; that he faces a risk of irreparable injury before final judgment will be reached in the regular course; and that in balancing the equities and competing hardships that preliminary judicial action may cause or prevent, the balance favors plaintiff.

I turn first to an evaluation of the probability of plaintiff's ultimate success on the merits of his claim. I begin that analysis with two preliminary points. The first concerns what is not involved in this case. To focus briefly on this clears away much of the corporation law case law of this jurisdiction upon which plaintiff in part relies. This case does not involve the measurement of corporate or directorial conduct against that high standard of fidelity required of fiduciaries when they act with respect to the interests of the beneficiaries of their trust. Under our law—and the law generally—the relationship between a corporation and the holders of its debt securities, even convertible debt securities, is contractual in nature. [citations omitted] Arrangements among a corporation, the underwriters of its debt, trustees under its indentures and sometimes ultimate investors are typically thoroughly negotiated and massively documented. The rights and obligations of the various parties are or should be spelled out in that documentation. The terms of the contractual relationship agreed to and not broad concepts such as fairness define the corporation's obligation to its bondholders.[7]

Thus, the first aspect of the pending Exchange Offers about which plaintiff complains—that "the purpose and effect of the Exchange Offers is to benefit Oak's common stockholders at the expense of the Holders of its debt"—does not itself appear to allege a cognizable legal wrong. It is the obligation of directors to attempt, within the law, to maximize the long-run interests of the corporation's stockholders; that they may sometimes do so "at the expense" of others (even assuming that a transaction which one may refuse to enter into can meaningfully be said to be at his expense) does not for that reason constitute a breach of duty. It seems likely that corporate restructurings designed to maximize shareholder values may in some instances have the effect of requiring bondholders to bear greater risk of loss and thus in effect transfer economic value from bondholders to stockholders.

---

[7]   To say that the broad duty of loyalty that a director owes to his corporation and ultimately its shareholders is not implicated in this case is not to say, as the discussion below reflects, that as a matter of contract law a corporation owes no duty to bondholders of good faith and fair dealing. *See* RESTATEMENT OF LAW, CONTRACTS 2D, § 205 (1979). Such a duty, however, is quite different from the congeries of duties that are assumed by a fiduciary. *See generally*, Bratton, *The Economics and Jurisprudence of Convertible Bonds*, 1984 WIS. L. REV. 667.

[citations omitted] But if courts are to provide protection against such enhanced risk, they will require either legislative direction to do so or the negotiation of indenture provisions designed to afford such protection.

The second preliminary point concerns the limited analytical utility, at least in this context, of the word "coercive" which is central to plaintiff's own articulation of his theory of recovery. If, pro arguendo, we are to extend the meaning of the word coercion beyond its core meaning—dealing with the utilization of physical force to overcome the will of another—to reach instances in which the claimed coercion arises from an act designed to affect the will of another party by offering inducements to the act sought to be encouraged or by arranging unpleasant consequences for an alternative sought to be discouraged, then—in order to make the term legally meaningful at all—we must acknowledge that some further refinement is essential. Clearly some "coercion" of this kind is legally unproblematic. Parents may "coerce" a child to study with the threat of withholding an allowance; employers may "coerce" regular attendance at work by either docking wages for time absent or by rewarding with a bonus such regular attendance. Other "coercion" so defined clearly would be legally relevant (to encourage regular attendance by corporal punishment, for example). Thus, for purposes of legal analysis, the term "coercion" itself—covering a multitude of situations—is not very meaningful. For the word to have much meaning for purposes of legal analysis, it is necessary in each case that a normative judgment be attached to the concept ("inappropriately coercive" or "wrongfully coercive," etc.). But, it is then readily seen that what is legally relevant is not the conclusory term "coercion" itself but rather the norm that leads to the adjective modifying it.

In this instance, assuming that the Exchange Offers and Consent Solicitation can meaningfully be regarded as "coercive" (in the sense that Oak has structured it in a way designed—and I assume effectively so—to "force" rational bondholders to tender), the relevant legal norm that will support the judgment whether such "coercion" is wrongful or not will, for the reasons mentioned above, be derived from the law of contracts. I turn then to that subject to determine the appropriate legal test or rule.

Modern contract law has generally recognized an implied covenant to the effect that each party to a contract will act with good faith towards the other with respect to the subject matter of the contract. The contractual theory for this implied obligation is well stated in a leading treatise:

> If the purpose of contract law is to enforce the reasonable expectations of parties induced by promises, then at some point it becomes necessary for courts to look to the substance rather than to the form of the agreement, and to hold that substance controls over form. What courts are doing here, whether calling the process "implication" of promises, or interpreting the requirements of "good faith", as the current fashion may be, is but a recognition that the parties occasionally have understandings or expectations that were so fundamental that they did not need to negotiate about those expectations. When the court "implies a promise" or holds that "good faith" requires a party not to violate those expectations, it is recognizing that sometimes silence says more than words, and it is

understanding its duty to the spirit of the bargain is higher than its duty to the technicalities of the language.

CORBIN ON CONTRACTS (Kaufman Supp. 1984), § 570.

It is this obligation to act in good faith and to deal fairly that plaintiff claims is breached by the structure of Oak's coercive exchange offer. Because it is an implied contractual obligation that is asserted as the basis for the relief sought, the appropriate legal test is not difficult to deduce. It is this: is it clear from what was expressly agreed upon that the parties who negotiated the express terms of the contract would have agreed to proscribe the act later complained of as a breach of the implied covenant of good faith—had they thought to negotiate with respect to that matter. If the answer to this question is yes, then, in my opinion, a court is justified in concluding that such act constitutes a breach of the implied covenant of good faith.

With this test in mind, I turn now to a review of the specific provisions of the various indentures from which one may be best able to infer whether it is apparent that the contracting parties—had they negotiated with the exchange offer and consent solicitation in mind—would have expressly agreed to prohibit contractually the linking of the giving of consent with the purchase and sale of the security.

IV.

Applying the foregoing standard to the exchange offer and consent solicitation, I find first that there is nothing in the indenture provisions granting bondholders power to veto proposed modifications in the relevant indenture that implies that Oak may not offer an inducement to bondholders to consent to such amendments. Such an implication, at least where, as here, the inducement is offered on the same terms to each holder of an affected security, would be wholly inconsistent with the strictly commercial nature of the relationship.

Nor does the second pertinent contractual provision supply a ground to conclude that defendant's conduct violates the reasonable expectations of those who negotiated the indentures on behalf of the bondholders. Under that provision Oak may not vote debt securities held in its treasury. Plaintiff urges that Oak's conditioning of its offer to purchase debt on the giving of consents has the effect of subverting the purpose of that provision; it permits Oak to "dictate" the vote on securities which it could not itself vote.

The evident purpose of the restriction on the voting of treasury securities is to afford protection against the issuer voting as a bondholder in favor of modifications that would benefit it as issuer, even though such changes would be detrimental to bondholders. But the linking of the exchange offer and the consent solicitation does not involve the risk that bondholder interests will be affected by a vote involving anyone with a financial interest in the subject of the vote other than a bond holder's interest. That the consent is to be given concurrently with the transfer of the bond to the issuer does not in any sense create the kind of conflict of interest that the indenture's prohibition on voting treasury securities contemplates. Not only will the proposed consents be granted or withheld only by those with a financial interest to maximize the return on their investment in Oak's bonds, but the incentive to consent is equally available to all members of each class of bondholders. Thus the "vote" implied by the consent solicitation is not affected in any sense by those with a financial conflict of interest.

In these circumstances, while it is clear that Oak has fashioned the exchange offer and consent solicitation in a way designed to encourage consents, I cannot conclude that that offer violates the intendment of any of the express contractual provisions considered or, applying the test set out above, that its structure and timing breaches an implied obligation of good faith and fair dealing.

One further set of contractual provisions should be touched upon: Those granting to Oak a power to redeem the securities here treated at a price set by the relevant indentures. Plaintiff asserts that the attempt to force all bondholders to tender their securities at less than the redemption price constitutes, if not a breach of the redemption provision itself, at least a breach of an implied covenant of good faith and fair dealing associated with it. The flaw, or at least one fatal flaw, in this argument is that the present offer is not the functional equivalent of a redemption which is, of course, an act that the issuer may take unilaterally. In this instance it may happen that Oak will get tenders of a large percentage of its outstanding long-term debt securities. If it does, that fact will, in my judgment, be in major part a function of the merits of the offer (*i.e.*, the price offered in light of the Company's financial position and the market value of its debt). To answer plaintiff's contention that the structure of the offer "forces" debt holders to tender, one only has to imagine what response this offer would receive if the price offered did not reflect a premium over market but rather was, for example, ten percent of market value. The exchange offer's success ultimately depends upon the ability and willingness of the issuer to extend an offer that will be a financially attractive alternative to holders. This process is hardly the functional equivalent of the unilateral election of redemption and thus cannot be said in any sense to constitute a subversion by Oak of the negotiated provisions dealing with redemption of its debt.

Accordingly, I conclude that plaintiff has failed to demonstrate a probability of ultimate success on the theory of liability asserted.

V.

An independent ground for the decision to deny the pending motion is supplied by the requirement that a court of equity will not issue the extraordinary remedy of preliminary injunction where to do so threatens the party sought to be enjoined with irreparable injury that, in the circumstances, seems greater than the injury that plaintiff seeks to avoid.

* * *

For the foregoing reasons plaintiff's application for a preliminary injunction shall be denied.

NOTES AND QUESTIONS

(1) **Judicial recognition of fiduciary duties to creditors.** Most courts have, like *Katz*, refused to recognize fiduciary duties to creditors and other fixed claimants, particularly preferred shareholders.[12] Other cases have apparently recognized fiduciary

---

[12] *See Metropolitan Life Ins. Co. v. RJR Nabisco, Inc.*, 716 F. Supp. 1526 (S.D.N.Y. 1989); *Kirschner Brothers Oil, Inc. v. Natomas Co.*, 185 Cal. App. 3d 784, 229 Cal. Rptr. 899 (1986) (preferred shareholders); *Simons v. Cogan*, 549 A.2d 300 (Del. 1988); *Revlon, Inc. v. MacAndrews & Forbes Holdings*, 506 A.2d 173 (Del. 1986) (debt holders);

duties in this situation, but fall short of being clear authority for a fiduciary duty rule. For example, in *Fox v. MGM Grand Hotels, Inc.*,[13] one of several cases involving restructurings of MGM, bondholders complained of a "spinoff" of MGM's film business to common shareholders (in other words, stock in the film subsidiary was distributed directly to the shareholders). The court found a breach of fiduciary duty but no damage because the company continued to pay its debts, despite the fact that the spinoff reduced the value of the bonds by raising the risk of nonpayment.

(2) **Judicial recognition of fiduciary duties to holders of convertible securities.** Several leading "fiduciary duty" cases involve convertible securities. In *Green v. Hamilton International Corp.*,[14] the corporation exercised its contractual right to redeem convertible securities, thereby letting shareholders appropriate gains from a forthcoming merger. However, the corporation did not disclose the impending merger, which would have given the holders the opportunity to convert their securities to common stock and avoid redemption. Similarly, *Zahn v. Transamerica Corp.*[15] held that the corporation's redemption of "Class A Common" without disclosing the corporation's plan to liquidate was a breach of duty. *Pittsburgh Terminal Corp. v. Baltimore & Ohio R.R. Co.*[16] held that the corporation should have notified convertible holders prior to a spinoff in order to give the holders the opportunity to participate in the spinoff by converting.

(3) **Judicial recognition of fiduciary duties to preferred shareholders.** It is not clear whether preferred shareholders should be treated as "fixed claimants" for purposes of applying the "no fiduciary duty" rule. In *Jedwab v. MGM Grand Hotels, Inc.*,[17] Chancellor Allen, who decided *Katz*, held that preferred shareholders were entitled to a "fair" allocation of the proceeds of a merger, although they had no "legal" right to consideration equivalent to that received by the common. But in *HB Korenvaes Investments, L.P. v. Marriott Corporation*,[18] Chancellor Allen held that there was no breach of fiduciary duty to preferred shareholders by reason of a special dividend to common stockholders where the contract specifically provided for protection of preferred in this situation through conversion rights. *Moore Business Forms, Inc. v. Cordant Holdings Corp.*[19] attempted to reconcile *Jedwab* and *HB Korenvaes Investments*, concluding that: "Whether or not a given claim asserted by preferred stockholders is governed by contract or fiduciary principles depends on whether the dispute arises from rights and

---

Rothschild International Corp. v. Liggett Group Inc., 474 A.2d 133 (Del. 1984) (preferred); *Harff v. Kerkorian*, 324 A.2d 215 (Del. Ch. 1974) (dismissing complaint by bondholders on fraud and fiduciary duty theories), *aff'd in part, rev'd in part*, 347 A.2d 133 (Del. 1975) (reversing dismissal of fraud allegations).

[13]   137 Cal. App. 3d 524, 187 Cal. Rptr. 141 (1983).

[14]   437 F. Supp. 723 (S.D.N.Y. 1977).

[15]   162 F.2d 36 (3d Cir. 1947).

[16]   680 F.2d 933 (3d Cir. 1982), *cert. denied*, 459 U.S. 1056 (1982).

[17]   509 A.2d 584 (Del. Ch. 1986).

[18]   19 Del. J. Corp. L. 736 (Del. Ch. 1993).

[19]   21 Del. J. Corp. L. 279 (Del. Ch. 1995).

obligations created by contract or from 'a right or obligation that is not by virtue of a preference but is shared equally with the common.'"[20]

Preferred share contracts have assumed importance recently as a device used in providing venture capital to start-up firms. **Bratton** (2002) provides an overview of the literature and a discussion of duties that are or (in the author's view) should be owed to preferred shareholders in this situation.

(4) **Policy analysis of fiduciary duties to creditors, holders of convertible debt, and preferred stockholders.** Why should fixed claimants' contracts be treated differently from those of residual claimants, who are clearly owed fiduciary duties of care and loyalty? Fiduciary duties might seem to be equally appropriate for both categories of investors, since both types of claims involve potential agency costs: Just as managers may be motivated to act contrary to the interests of the common shareholders, so they may, in representing the interests of the shareholders, act contrary to creditors' interests.

The important difference between residual and fixed claimants is that residual claimants' contracts delegate significant discretion to managers. Among other things, managers may decide whether to distribute earnings to the shareholders or retain them in the business. Interpreting the bounds of managers' discretion therefore involves a "gap" that the courts fill by applying fiduciary duties. Otherwise, the parties would be put to the considerable expense of specifying how managers should exercise their wide discretion. By contrast, managers lack discretion with respect to the funds provided by creditors—i.e., creditors are owed regular principal and interest payments. Accordingly, there is no comparable gap in creditors' contracts to be filled with fiduciary duties.

Of course, managers may still harm creditors through actions that increase the creditors' risk, such as investing in risky projects or distributing assets to shareholders. Creditors' contracts can and do provide for specific protection from wealth-decreasing actions by managers and residual claimants, such as the credit agreement and indenture terms relating to distributions referred to in Note 4 in Section 11.03. But contracts cannot wholly anticipate or eliminate risk. This was poignantly illustrated by the highly leveraged restructurings of the late 1980s that could not be predicted when the creditors' contracts were written.

Does it follow that creditors should have some fiduciary duty protection? Some creditors' contracts deliberately exclude fiduciary duties by, for example, providing other mechanisms to protect creditors. For example, convertible debt holders have an equity-like right to participate in the success of the company. This reduces the conflict

---

[20] For other cases involving the question of whether fiduciary duties were owed to preferred shareholders, *see Sanders v. Devine*, 1997 Del. Ch. LEXIS 131, 1997 WL 599539 (Del. Ch. 1997) (preferred shareholders who received the liquidation preference provided for in certificate of designations have no cause of action for breach of fiduciary duty in connection with cash-out merger); *Winston v. Mandor*, 710 A.2d 835 (Del. Ch. 1997) (no breach of fiduciary duty action where the "corporate actions complained of are expressly contemplated by a certificate [provision]"); *Jackson National Life Insurance Company v. Kennedy*, 741 A.2d 377 (Del. Ch. 1999) (fiduciary duty of loyalty is a right shared equally between the common and preferred stockholders, so preferred stockholders can bring an action based on, among other things, allegations that the preferred did not receive a fair allocation of the proceeds from a sale of assets).

of interest between bondholders and shareholders by decreasing equity's ability to capture all the gains from high-risk investments. A redemption feature, however, lets the
shareholders appropriate some future gains by paying off the convertible holders (*see*
Smith & Warner at 141-42). When such a redemption feature is included, convertible
holders cannot have their cake (the safety of debt) and eat it too (have all the gains of
equity). The duty to disclose discussed in Note 2 above arguably contradicts this scheme
by giving holders of convertible debt the same right to share in the proceeds of the
transaction that they would have had as straight equity holders.

More generally, fiduciary duties to creditors impose sig ~ificant costs on firms. If
fiduciary duties are implied, firms risk costly litigation whene` ~ they redeem con-
vertible securities or engage in other corporate transactions. This may deter transactions
that would benefit all of the firm's claim holders. Moreover, markets protect creditors
from opportunism even in the absence of fiduciary duties and specific contractual protections. A corporation that mistreats its fixed claimants must pay for that mistreatment
in the form of higher borrowing costs and demands for more costly restrictive covenants
the next time it enters the financial markets to borrow or sell preferred stock. These
increased costs are ultimately borne by equity. Thus, it does not necessarily follow from
the fact that creditors can be hurt by management and equity holders that their contracts
should be interpreted to include fiduciary duties.

(5) **Good faith and interpretation of the contract.** The *Katz* case, while not
imposing fiduciary duties, nevertheless apparently espoused a relatively expansive view
of interpreting bond contracts.[21] For two leading cases on bond contract interpretation,
see *Broad v. Rockwell Intern. Corp.*,[22] and *Sharon Steel Corp. v. Chase Manhattan
Bank, N.A.*[23] The **Bratton** articles discuss various approaches to interpreting bond and
preferred share contracts.

(6) **Coercion problem.** How serious was the "coercion" problem in *Katz*? The
bondholders in fact had little choice but to consent to the proposal out of fear that they
would be worse off if they voted no and the others accepted. To be sure, the bondholders were simply making a business decision, rather than being threatened at the point of
a gun. But this misses the plaintiff's point that the managers can, in effect, structure the
proposal to force the holders to accept even though, if the bondholders could effectively
coordinate with each other, they would insist on a better deal. On the other hand, two
commentators showed that, despite theoretical concerns about bondholders' consenting
to covenant changes against their interest, the evidence shows that bondholders actually
gain from bond modifications.[24] The writers suspect that bondholders are able to coordinate to defeat disadvantageous proposals.

---

[21] For a more recent exposition of Chancellor Allen's views on the good faith obligation, see *Credit Lyonnais
Bank, N.V. v. MGM-Pathe Communications Co.*, 17 DEL. J. CORP. L. 1099 (Del. Ch. 1991) (finding bad faith under the
Katz standard).

[22] 642 F.2d 929 (5th Cir. 1981).

[23] 691 F.2d 1039 (2d Cir. 1982), *cert. denied*, 460 U.S. 1012 (1983).

[24] *See* Kahan & Tuckman, *Do Bondholders Lose from Junk Bond Covenant Changes*, 66 J. BUS. 499 (1993).

(7) **Duties on insolvency.** There has been much debate on whether managers or equity owe duties to creditors in insolvency.[25] Chancellor Allen outlined potential problems in this area in *Credit Lyonnais Bank, N.V. v. MGM-Pathe Communications Co.*[26] This case involved the reverse situation of the duties of managing creditors to shareholders. In holding that members of an executive committee that was running a very heavily leveraged firm under a corporate governance agreement did not breach their duty to defendant, a 98% shareholder, by, among other things, refusing to sell certain assets, Chancellor Allen noted:[27]

> In these circumstances where the company was in bankruptcy until May 28 and even thereafter the directors labored in the shadow of that prospect, Mr. Ladd and his associates were appropriately mindful of the potential differing interests between the corporation and its 98% shareholder. At least where a corporation is operating in the vicinity of insolvency, a board of directors is not merely the agent of the residual risk bearers, but owes its duty to the corporate enterprise.[55] The Ladd management was not disloyal in not immediately facilitating whatever asset sales were in the financial best interest of the controlling stock-holder. In managing the business affairs of MGM, Mr. Ladd, and those he appointed owed their supervening loyalty to MGM, the corporate entity. It was not disloyal for them to consider carefully the corporation's interest in the UIP transaction, in the UK cinemas sale and in other proposed transactions. This I conclude they did. Mr. Parretti had gotten himself into a corner. He needed to liquidate assets to raise capital. Ladd and his team could reasonably suspect that he might be inclined to accept fire-sale prices. But the MGM board or its executive committee had an obligation to the community of interest that sustained the corporation, to exercise judgment in an informed, good faith effort to maximize the corporation's long-term wealth creating capacity. . . .

In footnote 55, the court said:

> The possibility of insolvency can do curious things to incentives, exposing creditors to risks of opportunistic behavior and creating complexities for directors. Consider, for example, a solvent corporation having a single asset, a judgment for $51 million against a solvent debtor. The judgment is on appeal and thus subject to modification or reversal. Assume that the only liabilities of the company are to bondholders in the amount of $12 million. Assume that the array of probable outcomes of the appeal is as follows:

---

[25] The law is outlined in **Varallo & Finkelstein**.

[26] 17 DEL. J. CORP. L. 1099 (Del. Ch. 1991).

[27] *Id.* at 34.

Expected Value	
25% chance of affirmance ($51mm)	$12.75
70% chance of modification ($4mm)	2.8
5% chance of reversal ($0)	0
Expected Value of Judgment on Appeal	$15.55

Thus, the best evaluation is that the current value of the equity is 3.55 million. ($15.55 million expected value of judgment on appeal—$12 million liability to bondholders). Now assume an offer to settle at $12.5 million (also consider one at $17.5 million). By what standard do the directors of the company evaluate the fairness of these offers? The creditors of this solvent company would be in favor of accepting either a $12.5 million offer or a $17.5 million offer. In either event they will avoid the 75% risk of insolvency and default. The stockholders, however, will plainly be opposed to acceptance of a $12.5 million settlement (under which they get practically nothing). More importantly, they very well may be opposed to acceptance of the $17.5 million offer under which the residual value of the corporation would increase from $3.5 to $5.5 million. This is so because the litigation alternative, with its 25% probability of a $39 million outcome to them . . . has an expected value to the residual risk bearer of $9.75 million ($39 million x 25% chance of affirmance), substantially greater than the $5.5 million available to them in the settlement. While in fact the stockholders' preference would reflect their appetite for risk, it is possible (and with diversified shareholders likely) that shareholders would prefer rejection of both settlement offers. But if we consider the community of interests that the corporation represents it seems apparent that one should in this hypothetical accept the best settlement offer available providing it is greater than $15.55 million, and one below that amount should be rejected. But that result will not be reached by a director who thinks he owes duties directly to shareholders only. It will be reached by directors who are capable of conceiving of the corporation as a legal and economic entity. Such directors will recognize that in managing the business affairs of a solvent corporation in the vicinity of insolvency, circumstances may arise when the right (both the efficient and the fair) course to follow for the corporation may diverge from the choice that the stockholders (or the creditors, or the employees, or any single group interested in the corporation) would make if given the opportunity to act. . . . .

Does it follow from this analysis that the managers should be held liable if they do sell the assets at "fire sale" prices in order to aid the desperate 98% shareholder?[26]

---

[28] For other cases on the duties of directors of insolvent corporations, see *LaSalle National Bank v. Perelman*, 82 F. Supp. 2d 279 (D. Del. 2000) (officers and directors of insolvent corporation have a "fiduciary duty to act in the best interest of the *estate as a whole*, including its creditors, equity interest holders and other parties in interest," so officers and directors cannot be held liable simply because their actions impair the value of the creditors' collateral (emphasis added)); *Odyssey Partners, L.P. v. Fleming Companies*, 735 A.2d 386 (Del. Ch. 1999) (stockholder complaints

REFERENCES

Bratton, *Venture Capital on the Downside: Preferred Stock and Corporate Control*, 100 MICH. L. REV. 891 (2002).

Bratton, *Corporate Debt Relationships: Legal Theory in a Time of Restructuring*, 1989 DUKE L.J. 92.

Bratton, *The Economics and Jurisprudence of Convertible Bonds*, 1984 WIS. L. REV. 667 (1984).

Bratton, *The Interpretation of Contracts Governing Corporate Debt Relationships*, 5 CARDOZO L. REV. 371 (1984).

Brudney, *Corporate Bondholders and Debtor Opportunism: In Bad Times and Good*, 105 HARV. L. REV. 1821 (1992).

Coffee & Klein, *Bondholder Coercion: The Problem of Constrained Choice in Debt Tender Offers and Recapitalizations*, 58 U. CHI. L. REV. 1207 (1991).

McDaniel, *Bondholders and Stockholders*, 13 J. CORP. L. 205 (1988).

Mitchell, *The Fairness Rights of Corporate Bondholders*, 65 N.Y.U. L. REV. 1165 (1990).

Ribstein, *Takeover Defenses and the Corporate Contract*, 78 GEO. L.J. 71 (1989).

Smith & Warner, *On Financial Contracting: An Analysis of Bond Covenants*, 7 J. FIN. ECON. 117 (1979).

Varallo & Finkelstein, *Fiduciary Obligations of Directors of the Financially Troubled Company*, 48 BUS. LAW. 239 (1992).

§ 11.05 Preferred's Contractual Right to Receive Distributions

So far we have been concerned with statutory restrictions on distributions. This section discusses preferred shareholders' contractual rights to distributions, which are generally set forth in the certificate of incorporation. Preferred dividend rights can be either cumulative or noncumulative. Holders of cumulative preferred shares are entitled to be paid a specific distribution per period before any payment is made to other shareholders. This right "cumulates" in the sense that no distribution may be made until the preferred shareholders have been paid amounts earned but not paid in all past periods. Noncumulative preferred shareholders, on the other hand, have no, or only limited, rights to distributions earned but not paid in prior years.

Much of the case law concerning contractual rights to distributions has concerned noncumulative preferred stock. Directors, who are usually elected by the common shareholders, may avoid distributions to noncumulative preferred holders in order to give the common shareholders a larger share of the earnings. As discussed in Section

---

that board should have filed for bankruptcy, rather than allowing foreclosure action, rejected because board of insolvent corporation was "obligated to consider and protect interests other than those of stockholders;" the effect of corporate action on "shareholders, creditors and other corporate constituencies" had to be balanced).

11.04, the courts generally have declined to go beyond the letter of the contract and impose on the board a fiduciary duty to declare dividends.[29] But instruments defining the rights of preferred stockholders may provide for other protections, including permitting preferred stockholders to elect a specified number of directors after a certain number of preferred dividends have been missed. In *Baron v. Allied Artists Pictures Corp.*,[30] the preferred shareholders had taken control of the board under such a provision. The corporation had mostly lost money on "B" pictures. (These were not named in the opinion, but research discloses that they included "Attack of the 50 Foot Woman," "Day of the Triffids," "Not of this Earth," and "World Without End.") After the preferreds took over, the corporation hit the jackpot with "Cabaret" and "Papillon." Common shareholders then sued to have control returned to them, claiming that the corporation could now pay enough dividends to the preferred to end the latter's right to control under the certificate. The court declined to interfere with the board's discretion absent a clearer showing of accumulation of unnecessary retained earnings.

Did the court properly interpret the preferreds' contract in *Baron*? As Chancellor Allen discussed in *Credit Lyonnais* (Note 7 following *Katz* in Section 11.04), there is a clear conflict of interest between the equity holders and the fixed claimants (here, the preferred). If fixed claimants control the board they would tend to be more risk-averse than the common shareholders would want them to be. This is particularly a problem in movie companies, in which the board has a wide range of investment choices along the scale of risk. Therefore, perhaps, the residual claimants agreed to a "takeover" by preferred only so long as the agency problem cut the other way—that is, while the company was in poor financial condition. Or did the court just not want to see any more films like "Attack of the 50 Foot Woman"?[31]

---

[29] *See Guttman v. Illinois Central Railroad Co.*, 189 F.2d 927 (2d Cir.), *cert. denied*, 342 U.S. 867 (1951) (stating that the preferred shareholders are not "wards of the judiciary," but also noting that the board of directors was largely controlled by a shareholder which held a majority of the preferred stock); *Kern v. Chicago & Eastern Illinois Railroad Co.*, 6 Ill. App. 3d 247, 285 N.E.2d 501 (1972) (holding that earnings of a subsidiary were not available for distribution by the parent); *L.L. Constantin & Co. v. R.P. Holding Corp.*, 56 N.J. Super. 411, 153 A.2d 378 (1959) (relying on a statutory provision that made dividend decisions matters of director discretion). *See contra Sanders v. Cuba Railroad Co.*, 21 N.J. 78, 120 A.2d 849 (1956) (a leading case espousing the New Jersey "dividend credit" rule permitting noncumulative preferred shareholders to share in retained earnings from prior years but declining to enter judgment for the plaintiffs on the showing made in the instant case); *Arizona Western Insurance Co. v. L.L. Constantin & Co.*, 247 F.2d 388 (3d Cir.), *cert. denied*, 355 U.S. 905 (1957) (finding a right to dividends under the same provisions construed in *Constantin* cited above).

[30] 337 A.2d 653 (Del. Ch. 1975), *app. dismissed*, 365 A.2d 136 (Del. 1976).

[31] For another case involving the transfer of control to creditors pursuant to a loan agreement, see *In re Bicoastal Corp.*, 600 A.2d 343 (Del. 1991) (enforcing secured creditor's contract right to elect majority of board triggered by failure to repay debt by specified date).

§ 11.06 Directors' Fiduciary Duty to Declare Dividends on Common Stock

In the absence of a conflict of interest, distribution decisions are subject to the business judgment rule discussed in Section 9.03, and will normally be upheld by the courts. This follows from the "irrelevance" theory and the availability of "homemade leverage" discussed in Section 11.01. If the distribution is approved by directors who are subject to a conflict of interest, the self-dealing rule (*see* Section 9.04) is applicable and the burden of proving fairness is shifted to the directors. The courts have, however, refused to apply the self-dealing rule unless the conflict is clearly shown.[32] One possible conflict situation is where a distribution is made to holders of one of two classes of stock by a board of directors controlled by the owner of the recipient class. *See Sinclair*, Section 9.07.

There are, however, important practical and legal distinctions between public and close corporations with regard to dividend policy, which may make a different set of rules appropriate in the latter context. Because close corporation stock is not readily marketable, close corporation shareholders often cannot declare "homemade dividends." Also, close corporation shareholders often devote a substantial portion of their capital, as well as their livelihoods, to the corporation, and therefore may not have the option of investing in corporations with more suitable distribution policies. These circumstances create the possibility of a "freeze-out" of close corporation shareholders through nonpayment of dividends.

Close corporation shareholders may deal with dividend problems by entering into agreements that control director discretion to declare dividends. *See* Section 5.03. In the absence of such an agreement, a court may give relief on a conventional breach of fiduciary theory.[33] Also, the *Donahue* case (Section 5.05[D]), which holds that controlling shareholders who sell their stock to the corporation must extend an "equal opportunity" to the minority, may be applicable to dividend payments to the majority.[34] And unfair withholding of dividends may constitute an oppressive "freeze out" triggering a right to dissolution or buyout under the corporation statute. *See Gardstein v. Kemp & Beatley*, Section 5.05[C].

---

[32] *See, e.g., Burton v. Exxon Corp.*, 583 F. Supp. 405 (S.D.N.Y. 1984); *Kamin v. American Express Co.*, 86 Misc. 2d 809, 383 N.Y.S.2d 807 (Sup. Ct.), *aff'd mem.*, 54 A.D.2d 654, 387 N.Y.S.2d 993 (1976).

[33] For cases holding in favor of a remedy where dividends were withheld in a close corporation, see *Dodge v. Ford*, discussed in Section 9.03[A]; *Smith v. Atlantic Properties, Inc.*, 422 N.E.2d 798 (Mass. App. Ct. 1981); *Miller v. Magline, Inc.*, 76 Mich. App. 284, 256 N.W.2d 761 (1977).

[34] *See Alaska Plastics, Inc. v. Cappock*, 621 P.2d 270 (Alaska 1980) (recognizing possibility of a remedy but denying relief in the instant case).

§ 11.07 Repurchases of Stock

Corporations often distribute assets by buying their own shares. They may do so for several reasons: (1) distribution of earnings (either through repurchase or dividend) is optimal because the corporation lacks investment opportunities with a return high enough to justify retaining earnings; (2) to eliminate undesirable shareholders; (3) to provide liquidity for the selling shareholders in a close corporation; (4) as a takeover defense; and (5) as a method of "signalling" management's information as to the company's prospects.

Like distributions in the form of dividends, share repurchases can injure creditors. Not surprisingly, therefore, they are subject to statutory rules discussed below, and to contractual constraints like those discussed in Note 4 in Section 11.03.

Repurchases raise a number of issues regarding possible injury to shareholders that are discussed elsewhere:

(1) A repurchase that is not open to all shareholders arguably injures the excluded shareholders by denying them an equal opportunity to sell. *See* Section 5.05[D]. This is a problem in a public corporation only if the repurchase is above current market price.

(2) Repurchases can entrench management in a public corporation by eliminating an active suitor for control, or by making it costly or impossible for an acquirer to buy enough shares to take control of the company.

(3) Management can use a repurchase to send a deliberately false positive signal about future earnings, perhaps to raise the sale price of their own stock.[35]

(4) Managers might be able to use their inside information and corporate information to engineer a buyout of the company for less than it is worth.

Although a repurchase of stock involves a distribution of the corporation's assets to shareholders, a share repurchase also returns an "asset," of sorts, to the corporation—the shareholder's stock. If the repurchase were accounted for as the acquisition of an asset, the expenditure of money or incurrence of a liability in connection with the purchase would be offset by adding the price paid for the stock to the assets column. However, under both accounting convention and most statutes, a share repurchase is treated as a distribution of assets to the shareholders. The statutes are concerned with the repurchase's potential for reducing stated capital, which is supposed to be the irreducible "cushion" for shareholders and creditors. Thus, Del. G.C.L. § 160(a)(1) forbids the impairment of capital by means of a repurchase of non-preferred stock. However, the provision does not specify how to account for the purchase. Under § 244(a)(2), upon cancellation (referred to as "retirement") of the stock, the directors may reduce

---

[35] *See* Bagwell & Shoven, *Cash Distributions to Shareholders*, 3 J. ECON. PERSP. 129 (1989) (showing that share repurchases increased sharply relative to dividends during the period 1977-1987, and theorizing that the increase is attributable to an increase in management's knowledge of how to use repurchases effectively as a takeover defense and signal of prospective earnings); Buckley, *When the Medium is the Message: Corporate Buy Backs as Signals*, 65 IND. L.J. 493 (1990).

some or all of the capital represented by the stock. The two sections together suggest that the repurchase may result in a reduction of capital *surplus*.

Under the Revised Model Act there is no longer any such concept as "capital." A share repurchase, like a dividend, is a "distribution" and is therefore subject to the same restrictions as are applicable to other distributions.

The statutory limitations on share repurchases may be troublesome when the shares of a corporation are purchased in a leveraged buyout and the corporation is later shown to be insolvent.[36]

§ 11.08 Distributions by Partnerships and LLCs

The Uniform Partnership Act does not explicitly regulate distributions by the partnership. The partnership agreement generally provides for a method of determining what a partner may withdraw from the business at any given time. This is normally done by means of a "drawing" or "income" account. Under an agreement that provides for drawing accounts, partnership income is credited in the agreed-upon proportions to the drawing accounts of the partners, and each partner may withdraw the amount in that account. The amount in the partner's capital account, on the other hand, is normally not subject to withdrawal.

The statutes regulating limited partnerships limit the rights of limited partners to receive distributions from the partnership. The rationale for such limitations is that creditors may not recover against limited partners as they may against the partners in a general partnership and therefore must be protected against depletion of the assets of the business. Under the Uniform Limited Partnership Act, limited partners may receive their agreed share of profits subject to the proviso under § 15 that such payments may not reduce the assets of the partnership below liabilities. Section 16(1)(a) provides that limited partners may not be repaid any part of their capital contributions unless the partnership has sufficient assets to pay its liabilities. A partner who unlawfully receives part of her capital contribution may be held liable to the partnership under § 17(2)(b).

Revised Uniform Limited Partnership Act (RULPA) § 607 carries forward the limitations of §§ 15 and 16 of the original Act with respect to payments to limited partners, but the liability under § 608 for excessive return of partners' contributions is more limited than that under ULPA § 17(2)(b). ULPA (2001) §§ 508-509 are similar.

Most limited liability company statutes include provisions on excessive distributions similar to those in the limited partnership acts in effect in the respective jurisdictions. However, some statutes have eliminated such provisions. *See* **Ribstein & Keatinge**.

---

[36] *See Matter of Munford, Inc.*, 97 F.3d 456 (11th Cir. 1996) (rejecting the argument that Georgia's stock distribution and repurchase statutes "only apply in circumstances where the directors take assets of the corporation and either distribute them to shareholders or use them to repurchase shares," but not in cases where control of the company changes hands and the directors determine the source of the assets used).

Limited partnership and LLC statutes largely duplicate protection creditors receive under fraudulent conveyance statutes from distributions by insolvent firms. Moreover, it is not clear why these statutes should offer protection beyond that in the fraudulent conveyance laws. In particular, why should states allow recovery of distributions made by solvent firms? Although a firm that is close to insolvency may rapidly decline toward bankruptcy, there are also costs connected with imposing liability on members for distributions by a solvent firm, including impeding transferability of shares to the extent the liability is carried over to successor members and forcing managers excessively to retain earnings in the firm. *See* **Ribstein.**

Finally, most limited liability partnership (LLP) statutes do *not* include restrictions on distributions, similar to the general partnership statutes on which they are based. *See* **Bromberg & Ribstein.**

QUESTION

Should LLCs and limited partnerships be distinguished from the standpoint of restrictions on distributions? Is there any justification for distinguishing LLPs from other limited liability partnership-type entities in this respect?

REFERENCES

BROMBERG & RIBSTEIN ON LLPs, RUPA AND ULPA, Ch. 4.

Ribstein, *An Applied Theory of Limited Partnership*, 37 EMORY L.J. 889 (1987).

Ribstein & Keatinge, RIBSTEIN & KEATINGE ON LIMITED LIABILITY COMPANIES § 6.05.

CHAPTER 12

Federal Regulation of the Issuance and Trading of Securities and Duties with Respect to Inside Information

§ 12.01 Introduction

This Chapter provides an overview of the federal regulation of securities transactions under the Securities Act of 1933 (the "1933 Act") and the Securities Exchange Act of 1934 (the "1934 Act"). Section 12.02 provides an overview of the 1933 Act, Section 12.03 provides an overview of the 1934 Act, and the remaining sections explore, in greater detail, the laws (state and federal) related to purchases and sales of stock by "insiders" (that is, those who, by reason of their corporate position or otherwise, have an information advantage over others in the market).

§ 12.02 The Securities Act of 1933

[A] Introduction

The 1933 Act is concerned primarily with the initial issuance of securities by the corporations. In very general terms, the 1933 Act requires the filing with the Securities and Exchange Commission of a "registration statement" and the delivery to purchasers of a "prospectus" in connection with certain transactions involving the sale of a "security." For our purposes, the most important provisions of the Act are those dealing with the operation of the Act, the substance of disclosure, coverage, and liability.

Section 5 lays out the operation of the Act. In general, it prohibits efforts to sell until disclosure materials are available and then requires delivery of the disclosure materials when the stock is offered or sold. Section 6 sets forth details regarding filing the registration statement, while Section 8 deals with SEC review of the contents of the disclosure materials. The substance of disclosure—that is, what must be included in the prospectus and registration statement—is covered in §§ 7 and 10. The details of disclosure are left for determination by the SEC. The coverage of the Act is dealt with primarily in § 2(a)(1) which defines "security," and §§ 3 and 4 which describe transactions and securities to which the filing and delivery requirements do not apply. Sections 11 and 12 provide for civil liability for violations of the Act.

[B] The Operation of the 1933 Act

The 1933 Act is intended to ensure that purchasers have complete information about publicly offered stocks and to protect the public from being stampeded into buying stock by incomplete and misleading sales talk. The Act therefore requires disclosure of reliable information and inhibits other disclosure.

The heart of the 1933 Act is § 5 which operates through §§ 2(a)(3), 2(a)(10) and 10. These provisions are, in turn, interpreted in various SEC rules (rules promulgated under the 1933 Act are codified at 17 C.F.R. § 230), and SEC opinions. Section 5 states what can and cannot be done (1) before the filing of the registration statement (the "pre-filing period"); (2) after filing but before the effective date (the "waiting period"); and (3) after the effective date (the "post-effective period").

[1] The Pre-Filing period

During the pre-filing period, the Act prohibits most selling efforts (*see* § 5(c), forbidding any "offers to sell," and § 5(a)(1) prohibiting actual sales). This term "offer to sell" is defined broadly in § 2(a)(3) to include "every attempt or offer to dispose of, or solicitation of an offer to buy, a security . . . ." Thus, § 5(c)'s prohibition reaches any premature selling effort (referred to as "gun-jumping"), not just formal offers to sell.[1] This ensures that issuers will not blunt the effectiveness of the standard disclosure document—the statutory prospectus—by antecedent statements.

But an issuer and its underwriter cannot lie wholly dormant during the pre-filing period. Accordingly, the act permits preliminary negotiations with or among "underwriters," including the execution of the letter of intent (*see* § 2(a)(3), third sentence, and § 2(a)(11)), and the dissemination of certain information about companies that are in registration (*see, e.g.,* Rules 135, 137, 138 and 139, as well as Securities Act Release No. 5009 (Oct. 7, 1969) and Securities Act Release No. 5180 (Aug. 16, 1971)). The latter rules and releases attempt to distinguish legitimate activities, such as promoting the issuer's products, from forbidden selling efforts.

[2] The Waiting Period

During the waiting period, the Act continues to prohibit actual sales of securities (*see* §§ 5(a)(1) and 2(a)(3)). However, the Act permits offers to sell (*see* § 5(c), which forbids offers only during the pre-filing period), so long as those offers take the form of: (1) oral communications; (2) written communications meeting the requirements of § 10 (*see* § 5(b)(1), requiring that "prospectuses"—broadly defined in § 2(a)(10) to include almost all written communications—meet the requirements of § 10); (3) preliminary

---

[1]   *See Carl M. Loeb, Rhoades & Co.,* 38 S.E.C. 843 (1959) (where the SEC interpreted the term "offer to sell" to include communications "of a character calculated, by arousing and stimulating investor and dealer interest . . . , to set in motion the processes of distribution.").

and summary prospectuses governed by Rules 430, 430A, 431;[2] and (4) "tombstone advertisements," which are black-bordered announcements of offerings (*see* § 2(a)(10)(b) which excludes such advertisements from the definition of prospectus and Rule 134 which interprets this provision).[3] "Free writing"—*i.e.*, the use of written communications not meeting the requirements of § 10 or falling within Rules 134, 430, 430A, or 431—is not permitted during the waiting period.

[3] The Post-Effective Period

During the post-effective period, the Act permits sales of securities (*see* § 5(a)(1) whose prohibition on sales does not apply if a registration statement is in effect), but only if they are accompanied by delivery of the final prospectus described by § 10(a) (*see* §§ 5(b)(2) and 5(b)(1)).[4] In addition, during the post-effective period, offers to sell can be made by way of written sales materials that do not satisfy the requirements of § 10, so long as those offers are preceded or accompanied by a copy of the final prospectus (*see* § 2(a)(10)(a), providing an exemption from the definition of the term "prospectus" and therefore from the requirements of § 5(b)(1)). Section 4(3), which is interpreted in Rule 174, suspends the obligations of dealers to deliver prospectuses with respect to secondary sales of securities after the appropriate period of time has passed (0, 25, 40, or 90 days, depending on the circumstances).[5]

[C] The Contents of the Prospectus

The elaborate regulatory scheme described above is intended to ensure that investors' decisions to buy new issues are based on the full disclosure in the prospectus. What must be disclosed in the prospectus is therefore crucial to an understanding of the 1933 Act.

In general, the 1933 Act disclosure requirements are designed to reduce issuers' uncertainty and costs of compliance by specifying affirmative disclosure requirements

---

[2]   The act *does not require* any communication with the purchaser prior to the actual sale of the security. However, to ensure investors get information during the waiting period, the SEC has promulgated Rule 460, which provides that the SEC will not "accelerate" the effective date of the prospectus unless some effort has been made to deliver preliminary and final prospectuses to underwriters, dealers and investors identified as prospective purchasers. Also, 1934 Act Rule 15c2-8 requires that those selling new issues have prospectuses and that they deliver copies to investors.

[3]   Rule 134 is concerned with what is not a prospectus, Rule 135 with what is not an offer, and Rules 430, 430A, 431 with what is a permitted prospectus.

[4]   Under § 5(b)(2), the security itself must be accompanied by a final prospectus if it is sent through interstate commerce. Also, since the confirmation slip the securities broker must send in connection with a sale is deemed to be a prospectus under § 2(a)(10), it cannot be delivered under § 5(b)(1) unless it is accompanied or preceded by a final prospectus. See the discussion of the "free-writing" privilege under § 2(a)(10)(a), which immediately follows in the text.

[5]   Note that if the security is trading in an efficient market, disclosures to the "market," such as the reports required under the 1934 Act, will arguably cause swift adjustments in market price, rendering prospectus delivery unnecessary.

in detailed forms with prior review by the SEC. But this specificity is compromised to some extent by the fact that the SEC may impose sanctions and the courts may impose liability under the 1933 Act for nondisclosure of material facts that were not specifically required to be disclosed by any form.[6]

The contents of the prospectus are determined by statutory, regulatory and judicial rules. Section 7 of the Act provides that the registration statement shall contain the information in Schedule A, which is an addendum to the statute, or such other information as the SEC shall provide. (The registration statement is what is filed with the SEC while the prospectus is what is actually given to the investor. The registration statement includes all of the prospectus plus some additional information and documents.) The SEC's basic form, Form S-1, mostly refers to Regulation S-K which governs disclosures required by both the 1933 and 1934 Acts. The Commission has prescribed other forms which reduce the required disclosure where the cost would be prohibitive given the size of the issuer or the offering or where investors have less need for mandatory disclosures.

Prospectuses generally disclose only "hard" historical information, such as accounting data and resumes of management, rather than "soft" information, such as management projections, asset valuations and plans (other than as relevant to use of proceeds). The distinction is based on the Act's concern with puffery by promoters of securities, although it has the effect of denying investors some potentially useful data. Discussion and litigation of this issue caused the SEC to recognize the importance of "soft" information and therefore to act to encourage (but not require) its use in 1933 Act prospectuses. SEC Rule 175 provides a "safe harbor" for statements containing soft information, provided the statements are made or reaffirmed with a "reasonable basis" and are disclosed "in good faith." Congress later added a statutory safe harbor for soft information to the 1933 Act as part of the Private Securities Litigation Act of 1995. Section 27A provides that issuers and parties acting on behalf of issuers cannot be held liable in private actions under the 1933 Act, with respect to "forward looking statements" (as defined), if (A) the forward looking statement is accompanied by "meaningful cautionary statements identifying important factors that could cause actual results to differ materially from those in the forward looking statements" or (B) the plaintiff fails to prove that the forward looking statement is made with "actual knowledge" that the statement was false or misleading. Subsection 27A(b) contains a list of statements that are ineligible for the statutory safe harbor, including statements made in connection with "initial public offerings."

Section 8 of the 1933 Act provides for an initial review of the registration statement by the SEC. Under that Section, the registration statement becomes effective twenty days after filing with the Commission. The Commission may, however, issue orders under § 8(b) or 8(d), after due notice and hearing, suspending or preventing the effectiveness of a registration statement. Because of the many prospectuses filed yearly

---

[6]   *See* Rule 408 and § 11 of the 1933 Act.

with the SEC, the SEC usually exercises its power informally. It now reviews registration statements of first-time registrants and only some registration statements filed by companies that are already "public" and filing reports under the 1934 Act. Other registration statements filed with the SEC may become effective without any SEC review. When the SEC reviews a registration statement and believes changes should be made, it will send to the issuer's counsel a "deficiency letter" outlining the suggested changes. This will lead to a discussion between the SEC and counsel and, in turn, to a document the SEC accepts. While registrants are not specifically required by any statute to obey SEC deficiency letters, they do so because the Commission can institute potentially costly formal proceedings under § 8, because corporate counsel need to maintain good relations with the SEC, and because of the SEC's informal power to "accelerate" the effective date of the registration statement discussed in the next paragraph.

Under § 8(a), each amendment to the registration statement restarts the twenty-day period prior to effectiveness. Registrants therefore depend on the SEC to "accelerate" the effectiveness of the registration statement so they can begin selling as soon as the final amendment to the registration statement is filed.[7] The power to accelerate gives the SEC the clout to insist on things that may or may not be required by the statute, such as the delivery of preliminary prospectuses. Rule 461 promulgated under the 1933 Act details the circumstances under which the SEC will accelerate.

A customary review of a registration statement by the SEC, together with informal discussions concerning revisions, takes more than the twenty days contemplated by the statute. To accommodate the SEC's time schedule, at the time of the initial filing of the registration statement, issuers also file "delaying amendments" with the SEC pursuant to SEC Rule 473, which prevent registration statements from becoming effective before the SEC has completed its review.

One of the major problems cited by early critics of 1933 Act disclosure requirements is the extent to which the disclosures required under the 1933 Act duplicate those under the 1934 Act for public corporations (defined under § 12 of the 1934 Act), including requirements under § 13 of the 1934 Act to file with the SEC Form 10-K annual reports, Form 10-Q quarterly reports, and Form 8-K current reports, and under § 14 to send annual reports to shareholders. An influential law review article,[8] and a subsequent SEC study that culminated in what is commonly known as the "Wheat Report"[9] called for coordination of 1933 and 1934 Act disclosure requirements. These studies directly led to, among other things, loosening of restrictions on release of information during registration and prospectus delivery requirements in connection with offerings by com-

---

[7]   Prior to 1987, virtually all registration statements had to be amended at the last minute to add the price, which depends on day-to-day market conditions. However, in 1987, the SEC adopted Rule 430A, which permits registration statements in most cash offerings to be declared effective without a price term, as long as the price amendment is filed shortly after the effective date and added by sticker to prospectuses delivered to investors with the confirmation of sale.

[8]   Cohen, *Truth in Securities Revisited*, 79 HARV. L. REV. 1340 (1966).

[9]   DISCLOSURE TO INVESTORS—A REAPPRAISAL OF ADMINISTRATIVE POLICIES UNDER THE 1933 AND 1934 SECURITIES ACTS (1969).

panies already subject to 1934 Act reporting requirements; abbreviated 1933 Act registration statements for relatively seasoned, well-financed companies that had been reporting under the 1934 Act; Regulation S-K, which prescribed a single set of disclosure rules for both 1933 and 1934 Act disclosure documents; and exemption of secondary sales of securities of 1934 Act reporting companies under Rule 144 (*see* Subsection [F] below).

The SEC later further coordinated 1933 and 1934 Act disclosure requirements by promulgating Forms S-1, which requires the delivery of a full prospectus, S-2 and S-3 for registering securities under the 1933 Act. Form S-1 to purchasers; Form S-2, which allows information with respect to the issuer to be delivered in the form of the company's annual report to shareholders; and Form S-3, which permits satisfaction of 1933 Act requirements by delivery of a brief document that refers the investor to the company's 1934 Act filings for information about the issuer and its business. Only more seasoned issuers may use Forms S-2 and S-3, and use of Form S-3 is subject to additional qualifications relating to the extent of the market for the corporation's stock and the riskiness of the offering.

[D] Civil Liability under the 1933 Act

There are four specific civil liability provisions in the 1933 Act: (1) § 12(a)(1), which impose liability for offers or sales in violation of § 5; and (2) §§ 11, 12(a)(2) and 17(a), which impose liability for misrepresentation and nondisclosure. Section 17(a) is very similar to Rule 10b-5, which will be discussed in Section 12.03 below. The Private Securities Litigation Reform Act of 1995 added § 27 to the 1933 Act setting forth procedural rules for private actions arising under the 1933 Act designed to minimize wasteful litigation.

[1] Section 12(a)(1)

Section 12(a)(1) imposes liability for violations of § 5. Recall that § 5 makes it unlawful to offer securities before a registration statement has been filed, limits the type of written sales materials that can be used after a registration statement has been filed but before it becomes effective, and requires the delivery of a prospectus included in an effective registration statement before a security can be sold. Section 12(a)(1) liability can be imposed even if defendant does not know or have reason to know that she is violating § 5 and has not engaged in wrongdoing vis-a-vis the particular plaintiff. For example, if a premature offer or an impermissible writing is made or sent to a prospective investor who is wholly unrelated to the plaintiff, the plaintiff may still sue on the basis that she purchased a security that was offered in violation of § 5.

[2] Section 12(a)(2)

The 1933 Act remedies for misrepresentation and non-disclosure are best considered in light of the requirements for common law fraud liability: scienter, or defendant's knowledge of being engaged in fraud; privity, or at least knowledge or foreseeability of harm to the plaintiff; reliance; and materiality. All of the 1933 Act misrepresentation provisions require proof of materiality which was discussed in Section 7.03 in the context of proxy materials.[10]

Unlike a common law fraud action, the plaintiff need not prove scienter to recover under § 12(a)(2). However, the defendant has a defense if he can show that he did not know, and in the exercise of reasonable care, could not have known of the misrepresentation or omission. This defense has been interpreted as imposing on the defendant a duty of investigation, or due diligence obligation, similar to that imposed under § 11.[11] In addition, under the Private Securities Litigation Reform Act of 1995, the defendant has a "negative causation" defense (*see* § 12(b)) pursuant to which defendant may reduce its liability by showing that some or all of the amount recoverable is attributable other than to false or misleading statements.[12]

Although the plainitff need not prove scienter in an action under § 12(a)(2), the plaintiff does have to show privity in the sense of a purchase from the defendant.[13] The privity requirement under § 12(a)(2) is particularly significant in light of the fact that the immediate seller of the security is often an ordinary broker or dealer who is able to prove lack of knowledge and reasonable care. *Pinter v. Dahl*[14] held that § 12(a)(1) "sellers" include only those who actually sell securities or at least solicit sales for personal gain. *Pinter* has been extended to § 12(a)(2).[15]

Section 12(a)(2) does not explicitly require plaintiff to prove reliance. The "by means of" language of § 12(a)(2) does, however, require plaintiff to prove some causal relationship between the fraud and the purchase, and so bars recovery where the plaintiff continues purchasing securities after learning the true facts.[16]

The broad language of § 12(a)(2) was once thought to provide a remedy for all persons who purchased securities sold by means of written or oral misrepresentations,

---

[10]   Although the Supreme Court has not passed on the precise issue, the proxy test of *TSC Industries, Inc. v. Northway, Inc.*, 426 U.S. 438 (1975), discussed in Subsection 7.03[C], is probably also applicable in the 1933 Act context. *See* Rule 405, promulgated under the 1933 Act.

[11]   *See Sanders v. John Nuveen & Co., Inc.*, 619 F.2d 1222 (7th Cir. 1980), *cert. denied*, 450 U.S. 1005 (1981) (Justices Powell and Rehnquist dissenting from the denial of certiorari on the ground that the effect of the Court of Appeals decisions is unjustifiably to impose a higher due diligence duty under § 12(a)(2) than under § 11).

[12]   For a recent case upholding a "loss causation" defense in an action under section 12(a)(2), see *Goldkrantz v. Griffin*, 1999 U.S. Dist. LEXIS 4445, 1999 WL 191540 (S.D.N.Y., Apr. 6, 1999).

[13]   *See Collins v. Signetics Corp.*, 605 F.2d 110 (3d Cir.), *cert. denied*, 439 U.S. 930 (1978).

[14]   486 U.S. 622 (1988).

[15]   *See Wilson v. Saintine Exploration & Drilling Corp.*, 872 F.2d 1124 (2d Cir. 1989).

[16]   *See Jackson v. Oppenheim*, 533 F.2d 826 (2d Cir. 1976); *Ross v. Warner*, Fed. Sec. L. Rep. (CCH) ¶ 97,735 (S.D.N.Y 1980).

not just those who purchased securities in public offerings.[17] However, *Gustafson v. Alloyd Co., Inc.*[18] held that the terms "prospectus and oral communication," as used in § 12(a)(2), refer only to documents and statements "related to public offerings by an issuer or its controlling shareholder." While *Gustafson* suggests that § 12(a)(2) no longer applies to private transactions, such as sales by issuers of unregistered securities under the private offering exemption of § 4(2) and sales by investors under the exemptions from registration provided by §§ 4(1) and 4(4) and Rules 144 and 144A (*see* Subsection [F] below), it does not mean that purchasers in such transactions are necessarily without a remedy under the federal securities laws. Among other things, purchasers may sue under § 10(b) and Rule 10b-5 of the 1934 Act if they can establish that the defendant acted with scienter. In addition, some lower courts have held that purchasers have a private action for damages under § 17(a) of the 1933 Act based on a showing of negligence.[19]

[3] Section 11

Section 11 is the most important liability provision under the 1933 Act. Section 11 is intended to deter false and incomplete 1933 Act registration statements by substantially eliminating many of the common law fraud roadblocks to recovery with respect to misrepresentations in these documents.

Plaintiff's *prima facie* case under § 11 normally consists merely of proof of the purchase of stock covered by a registration statement containing a material misstatement or omitting a material fact. Thus, in the usual case, plaintiff may recover without showing any reliance on the registration statement.[20] If, however, the plaintiff purchased the stock when later financial information about the issuer has become available, the last part of § 11(a) would condition liability on proof of reliance, though reliance can be established without proof that the plaintiff actually read the registration statement.

Section 11 draws a peculiar line. One who makes an open-market purchase of stock in an already public company that has just made a public offering is just as likely

---

[17] *See Metromedia Co. v. Fugazy*, 983 F.2d 350 (2d Cir. 1992), *cert. denied*, 113 S. Ct. 2445 (1993) (subjecting private placement transaction to § 12(2)); *Haralson v. E.F. Hutton Group, Inc.*, 919 F.2d 1014 (5th Cir. 1990) (same). For other cases subjecting private placement transactions to § 12(a)(2), see *Nor-Tex Agencies, Inc. v. Jones*, 482 F.2d 1093 (5th Cir. 1973), *cert. denied*, 415 U.S. 977 (1974); *Pacific Dunlop Holdings, Inc. v. Allen & Co., Inc.*, 993 F.2d 578 (7th Cir. 1993), *cert. granted*, 114 S. Ct. 907, *cert. dismissed*, 114 S. Ct. 1146 (1994).

[18] 513 U.S. 561 (1995).

[19] *See, e.g., Stephenson v. Calpine Conifers II, Ltd.*, 652 F.2d 808 (9th Cir. 1981), *overruled in In re Washington Public Power Supply System Securities Litigation*, 823 F.2d 1349 (9th Cir. 1987); *Kirshner v. United States*, 603 F.2d 234 (2d Cir. 1978), *cert. denied*, 442 U.S. 909 (1979); *Hanraty v. Ostertag*, 470 F.2d 1096 (10th Cir. 1972). Other courts have refused to imply a private remedy under § 17(a). *See Maldonado v. Dominguez*, 137 F.3d 1 (1st Cir. 1998); *Landry v. All American Assurance Co.*, 688 F.2d 381 (5th Cir. 1982); *Shull v. Dain, Kalman & Quail, Inc.*, 561 F.2d 152 (8th Cir. 1977), *cert. denied*, 434 U.S. 1086 (1978).

[20] *See Gibb v. Delta Drilling Co.*, 104 F.R.D. 59 (N.D. Tex. 1984).

to be buying newly offered stock that is subject to a registration statement and covered under § 11 as other previously-issued stock of the same class. Thus, two plaintiffs may be precisely similarly situated in the sense that they had the same information and placed their orders at the same time, but only the plaintiff who proves that she purchased stock issued under the defective registration statement may recover under § 11.[21]

Section 11 lowers the privity hurdle by providing that plaintiff may recover from all of those persons listed in § 11(a). This means that the plaintiff can recover from directors, underwriters, and (if material misrepresentations or omissions are found in the issuer's audited financial statements) accountants, as well as from the issuer and, under § 15, "controlling persons."[22]

A plaintiff who proves a purchase of "covered" stock and a material misstatement or omission is entitled to damages as computed under § 11(e), unless defendant proves one of the defenses described below. Plaintiff is entitled to recover the difference between the amount paid for the stock up to the public offering price and the "value" of the stock at the time of suit or, if the plaintiff sold, the sale price (except that if plaintiff sells after the suit is brought at a price lower than the value at the time of suit, the value at the time of suit controls).[23] Plaintiff therefore bears the risk that damages will be reduced by a rise in the price of the stock before the suit is brought, while defendant cannot gain by stalling the suit once it is filed.

Defendant has two main defenses under § 11. The most important is the "due diligence" defense under § 11(b), which is made available to all defendants listed in § 11(a) other than the issuer. Section 11(b) allows defendants to escape liability if they can show that they conducted an adequate investigation of the registration statement, though the extent of the required investigation differs depending upon whether the defendant is expert (like an accountant) or a non-expert (like a director or an underwriter). Experts satisfy their due diligence obligations under § 11(b) if they conduct a reasonable investigation of the portions of the registration statement they prepare. Non-experts have a duty to investigate the entire registration statement, but their duty is more easily satisfied with respect to those portions of the registration that are prepared

---

[21]   *See Barnes v. Osofsky*, 373 F.2d 269 (2d Cir. 1967); *Kirkwood v. Taylor*, 590 F. Supp. 1375 (D. Minn. 1984); *Gibb v. Delta Drilling Co., supra* footnote 20; *McFarland v. Memorex Corp.*, 493 F. Supp. 631 (N.D. Calif. 1980). *In Re WRT Energy Securities Litigation*, 1997 U.S. Dist. LEXIS 14009, 1997 WL 576023 (S.D.N.Y. 1997), eliminated the disparate treatment of similarly situated open-market purchasers by denying all open-market purchasers standing to assert claims under § 11. The court said this result was a logical extension of the Supreme Court's *Gustafson* decision, which limited § 12(a)(2) suits to those investors who purchase their securities from issuers in public offerings. Other courts have disagreed with this extension of *Gustafson*. *See, e.g., Joseph v. Wiles*, 223 F.3d 1155 (10th Cir. 2000); *Hertzberg v. Dignity Partners, Inc.*, 191 F.3d 1076 (9th Cir. 1999) (purchasers in after-market can sue under § 11 so long as they can trace their shares to the pubic offering); *Schwartz v. Celestial Seasonings, Inc.*, 178 F.R.D. 545 (D. Colo. 1998) (same); *In re WebSecure, Inc. Securities Litigation*, 182 F.R.D. 364 (D. Mass. 1998) (same). *But see Warden v. Crown Am. Realty Trust*, 1998 U.S. Dist. LEXIS 16194, 1998 WL 725946 (W.D. Pa. 1998) (following *WRT*).

[22]   For an interpretation of "controlling person" in the § 11 context, see *In re Diasonics Litigation*, 599 F. Supp. 447 (N.D. Cal. 1984).

[23]   For a discussion of "value" under § 11(e), see *Beecher v. Able*, 435 F. Supp. 397 (S.D.N.Y. 1977).

by experts (*e.g.*, the audited financial statements). Until *Escott v. Barchris Construction Corp.*,[24] it was only surmised that § 11(b) compelled distinctions among various kinds of defendants beyond the distinction between experts and non-experts specified in the statute. *Escott* was the first case to so hold and is still the leading case on the question of what duties are imposed under § 11. SEC Rule 176 attempts to clarify the due diligence duty by identifying relevant factors.

The defendant also has a "causation" defense under the "provided, that . . ." clause in the middle of § 11(e). Under this provision, defendant may avoid liability by proving that the stock price fell and that plaintiff was damaged for reasons unrelated to the misrepresentations in the prospectus, such as general market conditions.[25]

Section 11(g) caps defendants' total liability and § 11(e) limits underwriters' liability. Since liability is generally joint and several under § 11(f) (except for "outside directors" who do not "knowingly" violate the 1933 Act's requirements), plaintiff may pursue the "deep pocket," such as a large accounting firm, for the entire amount of the judgment. The defendant may then try to obtain contribution, except that one who was "actively" liable, in the sense of having actually made a misrepresentation, may not recover from a merely "passive" defendant, such as an outside director, who simply failed to investigate.

[E] Coverage of the 1933 Act: Definition of a Security

The 1933 Act imposes duties and liabilities in connection with transactions involving the offer or sale of a "security," which is defined in § 2(a)(1). ("Security" is defined virtually identically in the 1933 and 1934 Acts, although there is a minor difference in connection with loans.) This subsection examines the meaning of that term.

Plaintiffs have attempted to persuade the courts to include the instruments involved in a great variety of fraudulent transactions within the definition of a security. Plaintiffs have the incentive to do so because the civil remedies for fraud under the federal securities laws (*e.g.*, §§ 12(a)(2) and 17 of the 1933 Act) often involve fewer obstacles to recovery than do the comparable remedies under the common law, and because an unregistered "security" transaction may be rescindable under § 12(a)(1), even if the seller has misrepresented nothing and disclosed everything.

In defining "security," the courts must determine not simply whether a transaction involves fraud but whether it involves the particular type of fraud Congress intended to regulate by means of the securities laws. One pervasive issue that confronts courts in this task is that of form versus substance. That is, courts must determine whether parties should be able to, in effect, opt out of the securities laws by changing the form of their transactions.

---

[24]   283 F. Supp. 643 (S.D.N.Y. 1968).

[25]   For cases dealing with this defense, see *Collins, supra*, 605 F.2d 110 (3d Cir. 1979); *Akerman v. Oryx Communications*, 609 F. Supp. 363 (S.D.N.Y. 1984); *Beecher, supra* footnote 23.

Landreth Timber v. Landreth[26] held that an instrument that had the usual attributes of stock was a "security" within the meaning of § 2(a)(1). Thus, a corporation's sale of its own shares will involve an offer and sale of a security for purposes of the 1933 Act. But the law is less clear with respect to other entities such as general partnerships, limited partnerships, and limited liability companies. On the one hand, partnership and LLC interests are not included in § 2(a)(1)'s list of instruments that are presumptively securities for purposes of the 1933 Act. On the other hand, § 2(a)(1)'s definition includes open-ended terms, such as "investment contract" and "any interest or instrument commonly known as a 'security'"—terms broad enough to cover at least some interests investors may not ordinarily consider securities.

To decide whether interests other than corporate stock constitute securities for purposes of the federal securities laws, courts generally start with *SEC v. W.J. Howey Co.*,[27] which held that an "investment contract" for purposes of the 1933 Act means a contract, transaction or scheme that "involves [1] an investment of money [2] in a common enterprise [3] with profits [4] to come solely from the efforts of others." *Howey* held that a sale of trees in a citrus grove, coupled with a contact to harvest and market the fruit produced by those trees, constituted a security under the Act.

Since *Howey*, the federal courts have spilt considerable ink interpreting the various elements of the Court's "investment contract" test. For our purposes, the "efforts of others" factor is the most important, because this factor generally determines whether a partnership or LLC interest constitutes a security. The "efforts of others" factor matters because an investment in another's management skills is particularly difficult to evaluate. Investors must estimate expected returns on the basis of numerous factors relating to past performance. The complexity of the determination arguably justifies special disclosure rules. There is also reason to believe that investors will make certain systematic errors in judgment, such as too readily assuming that recent past results will continue. This may justify rules requiring measured and guarded statements of fact.

An investment in a limited partnership is generally considered sufficiently passive to be a "security."[28] On the other hand, an interest in a general partnership or joint venture may not be, even where the partners or venturers are passive and rely on managers. In the leading case, *Williamson v. Tucker*,[29] a promoter had arranged the sale of approximately fifteen interests in each of three joint ventures that owned portions of a tract of land. Each agreement gave joint venturers substantial control over the enterprise in the form of a unanimous consent requirement for a number of actions affecting the property and a supermajority voting requirement with respect to others. The joint venture interests were sold by means of promotional materials that emphasized the possibility of

---

[26]　471 U.S. 681 (1985).

[27]　328 U.S. 293 (1946).

[28]　*See SEC v. Murphy*, 626 F.2d 633 (9th Cir. 1980).

[29]　645 F.2d 404 (5th Cir. 1981).

appreciation in value and that the promoter would manage the property, have the land rezoned, and ultimately pursue sale or development. The trial court dismissed plaintiffs' securities law claims on the ground that the interests were not securities, but the Fifth Circuit reversed and remanded, stating the following test:

> [A]n investor who claims his general partnership or joint venture interest is an investment contract has a difficult burden to overcome. On the face of a partnership agreement, the investor retains substantial control over his investment and an ability to protect himself from the managing partner or hired manager. Such an investor must demonstrate that, in spite of the partnership form which the investment took, he was so dependent on the promoter or on a third party that he was in fact unable to exercise meaningful partnership powers. A general partnership or joint venture interest can be designated a security if the investor can establish, for example, that (1) an agreement among the parties leaves so little power in the hands of the partner or venturer that the arrangement in fact distributes power as would a limited partnership; or (2) the partner or venturer is so inexperienced and unknowledgeable in business affairs that he is incapable of intelligently exercising his partnership or venture powers; or (3) the partner or venturer is so dependent on some unique entrepreneurial or managerial ability of the promoter or manager that he cannot replace the manager of the enterprise or otherwise exercise meaningful partnership or venture powers.

Although the court doubted that there was a security because of the substantial expertise of the plaintiffs and lack of a showing as to any unique expertise on the part of the promoter, the court held that plaintiffs had met their very slight burden in opposing a motion for dismissal for want of subject matter jurisdiction.

Cases since *Williamson* have gone in different directions on the question of whether a general partnership interest is a "security." Some follow *Williamson* by examining characteristics of the individual partners; some completely or partially reject such evidence, holding that general partnerships are virtually *per se* non-securities; and some occupy a middle ground, rejecting examination of the plaintiff's actual knowledge and expertise and focusing on the partners' powers under the agreement, yet leaving the door open to evidence that would bear on plaintiffs' ability to exercise powers under the agreement. A further complication is whether a limited liability company interest, which combines partnership-type management with corporate-type limited liability, should be treated like a general partnership, a limited partnership, or a corporation.[30]

Other elements of *Howey*'s investment contract test—beyond the "efforts of others factor"—have also been the subject of extensive litigation. *United Housing Foundation, Inc. v. Forman*[31] upheld a dismissal of securities law claims brought by tenants

---

[30]   For a discussion of the partnership and LLC cases, *see* Ribstein, *Form and Substance in the Definition of a "Security": The Case Of Limited Liability Companies*, 51 WASH. & LEE L. REV. 807 (1994).

[31]   421 U.S. 837 (1975).

of a huge cooperative housing project, reasoning in part that there was no "expectation of profits" and that the plaintiffs had purchased a place to live rather than a "security." The Court rejected deductibility of tax benefits, the bargain rental price of the apartments, and the remote possibility of net income from leased commercial space as "profit" that would qualify under the *Howey* test. Expectation of profit matters because statements about expected returns are susceptible to overstatement, and therefore amenable to 1933 Act constraints. Fraud about the merit of an apartment, on the other hand, concerns readily verifiable facts. Although liability for misrepresentation may be appropriate, 1933 Act regulation of the format and nature of disclosures is not.[32]

International Brotherhood of Teamsters v. Daniel[33] held that an employee's participation in a pension plan did not involve the sale of a "security" to the employee, in part because the employee's labor was exchanged primarily for salary, rather than for the alleged "security" (*i.e.*, pension benefits). The Court therefore apparently recognized the possibility that an investment of labor rather than money could satisfy the *Howey* test under other circumstances, but held that an investment involves an exchange of some consideration for the "security." However, it is not clear why investment of anything of value, including labor, is not enough to trigger coverage of the securities laws.

Finally, some courts have held that the "common enterprise" aspect of *Howey* is satisfied only when there is "horizontal" commonality in the sense that the fortunes of many investors are pooled.[34] In this situation, requiring issuer disclosure helps economize on information costs by making duplicative research by investors unnecessary. Also, investors in a one-on-one bargaining situation probably have enough leverage to require disclosure, so that mandatory disclosure requirements may be unnecessary or wasteful. But other courts have held that it is enough for a "common enterprise" that there is "vertical" commonality, defined as dependence on promoters' efforts (and therefore overlapping the "efforts of others" requirement),[35] or as a link between the promoter's and investor's success.[36]

---

[32] For recent decisions applying the expectation of profit element of the *Howey* test, see *Teague v. Bakker*, 139 F.3d 892 (4th Cir. 1998) (interests in partnerships formed to provide lodging benefits in religious vacation park not securities because investors were attracted primarily by the prospect of acquiring use of the lodging, rather than by the prospect of financial returns), and *SEC v. ETS Payphones, Inc.*, 300 F.3d 1281 (11th Cir. 2002) (fixed lease payments earned under sale-leaseback contract for payphone not "profits" under *Howey*).

[33] 439 U.S. 551 (1979).

[34] *See Hirk v. Agri-Research Council, Inc.*, 561 F.2d 96 (7th Cir. 1977).

[35] *See SEC v. Koscot Interplanetary, Inc.*, 497 F.2d 473 (5th Cir. 1974).

[36] *See Brodt v. Bache*, 595 F.2d 459 (9th Cir. 1978).

[F] Exemptions from Registration under the 1933 Act

[1] In General

Even if a transaction involves a "security," it is possible to escape the stringent registration requirements of the 1933 Act through the exemptions from registration available under that Act. There are two general categories of exemptions from registration under the 1933 Act: exemptions for particular types of securities under §§ 3(a)(2) through 3(a)(8); and exemptions for particular types of transactions under §§ 3(9) through 3(a)(12) and §§ 4(1) through 4(6). The securities acquired in exempt transactions do not receive a permanent exemption from the Act and, therefore, unlike exempt securities, can only be resold if they are registered or are sold in another exempt transaction. An exemption under § 3 or 4 is not an exemption from all provisions of the securities laws. For example, the general anti-fraud provisions of the 1933 Act, §§ 12(a)(2) and 17(a), as well as § 10(b) of the 1934 Act, reach most sales of securities, regardless of whether an exemption from registration is available under § 3 or § 4.

The following discussion of exemptions focuses on the exemptions that are of the greatest every-day importance—those for private placements, small issues, and secondary sales. There are, however, many other important exemptions, including exemptions for (i) *Intrastate offerings* (§ 3(a)(11); Rule 147), where the entire distribution is offered only to people who reside in the state in which the issuer is located; (ii) *Regulation A offerings* (§ 3(b); Rules 251-263), which requires a registration process that is similar to, though slightly less burdensome than, the standard 1933 Act registration process for securities sold in relatively small offerings; (iii) *Regulation S offerings* (Rules 901-905) for securities sold in transactions outside the United States.

[2] Private Offering Exemption

Section 4(2) of the 1933 Act exempts "transactions by an issuer not involving any public offering." In an important early interpretation of § 4(2), *SEC v. Ralston Purina Co.*,[37] the Supreme Court held that a corporation could not claim the "nonpublic offering" exemption simply because it restricted offering of its stock to "key employees," defined as any "individual who especially influences others or who advises others, a person whom the employees look to in some special way . . . ." (Over a four-year period, the company had sold over $2,000,000 of stock to several hundred such employees without registration.) The court said:[38]

> Keeping in mind the broadly remedial purpose of federal securities legislation, imposition of the burden of proof on an issuer who would plead the exemption seems to us fair and reasonable. Agreeing, the court below

---

[37] 346 U.S. 119 (1953).

[38] 346 U.S. at 126-27.

thought the burden met primarily because of the respondent's purpose in singling out its key employees for stock offerings. But once it is seen that the exemption question turns on the knowledge of the offerees, the issuer's motives, laudable though they may be, fade into irrelevance. The focus of inquiry should be on the need of the offerees for the protections afforded by registration. The employees here were not shown to have access to the kind of information which registration would disclose. The obvious opportunities for pressure and imposition make it advisable that they be entitled to compliance with § 5.

After years of SEC and judicial attempts to define which offerees needed the protection of the Act, the SEC promulgated Rule 146 which insulated from liability transactions where (1) issuers had reasonable grounds to believe and did believe that all purchasers were able to evaluate the investment or, as to wealthy purchasers, were represented by someone who could make this evaluation on their behalf; (2) offerees were furnished with, or at least had "access" to, 1933 Act-type information; (3) there was no general solicitation made by, or on behalf of, the issuer; (4) there were sales to fewer than thirty-five purchasers; and (5) the issuer filed with the SEC a notice of sale and placed restrictions on disposition of the stock. Rule 146, however, did not end judicial interpretation of the scope of the 4(2) exemption. Several aspects of the Rule itself were unclear, particularly including the sophistication requirement and the meaning of "access" to information. Rule 146 has been superseded by Rule 506, which is part of Regulation D (discussed below), although the earlier case law continues to be relevant in interpreting Rule 506 and in interpreting the Section 4(2) exemption where Rule 506 does not apply (as, for example, where the issuer has failed to file a notice of offering).

[3] Regulation D and Related Rules Governing Small Issues

Registration under the 1933 Act is particularly burdensome for small companies. First, the per-dollar cost of compliance is quite large for relatively small issues of stock. Second, while established, publicly held companies are continually compiling and updating information to fulfill their reporting requirements under the 1934 Act, companies that have not previously gone public must compile much of the information needed for a 1933 Act registration statement for the first time.

During the late 1970s and early 1980s, both the SEC and Congress alleviated the burdens faced by small businesses in complying with the 1933 Act. The SEC first adopted Rule 240 (the basis for current rule Rule 504, discussed below), Rule 242 (the basis of current Rule 505, discussed below); and Form S-18 (a simplified form for registration of public offerings of less than $5 million available to issuers that have not previously gone public); and raised the ceiling for Regulation A offerings. In 1980, Congress passed the Small Business Investment Incentive Act of 1980 which added §§ 4(6) and 2(a)(15) to the 1933 Act and raised the ceiling in § 3(b) on the SEC's powers to adopt exemptions for small offerings.

In 1982, the SEC promulgated Regulation D (Rules 501-506). Regulation D exempts offerings that comply with its terms from the registration requirements of § 5. It replaces Rule 146, as well as Rules 240 and 242.

Rule 501 is the definitional section of the regulation. Among the most important definitions is that of "accredited investor." The "accredited investor" concept, which was introduced in Rule 242 and later incorporated in the 1933 Act itself (*see* §§ 2(a)(15) and 4(6)), defines certain classes of purchasers who are able to protect themselves because they have, or are able to incur the expense of obtaining, information about the issuer.

Rule 502 includes provisions that apply generally to the Regulation D exemptions. Rule 502(b) specifies the information required to be delivered to investors in a Regulation D offering. In general, Regulation D adjusts the duty to provide information according to the size of the offering, whether the issuer is a reporting company under the 1934 Act, and whether the purchasers need the protection of the 1933 Act (*i.e.,* are "accredited"). Rule 502(c) regulates how the offering may be made, and Rule 502(d) requires the issuer to ensure that a limited offering does not become more general through resales by the initial purchasers.

Rule 503 requires the filing of notices to permit monitoring of exempt offerings. Failure to comply with any one of the multiple filing requirements does not necessarily result in loss of the exemption under Rules 507 and 508.

Rule 504 exempts offerings of under $1,000,000 (aggregating all sales within a year in reliance on any small offering exemption). The issuer need not disclose under Rule 502(b) to qualify for the exemption, but must comply with the limitations regarding manner of offering and resales in Rules 502(c) and (d), unless the securities are registered under a state law requiring public filing and delivery of a disclosure document to investors before sale, or exempted under a state law restricting sales to accredited investors. Companies reporting under the 1934 Act may not use the exemption. The rule's rationale is that the per dollar cost of disclosure is particularly high for very small offerings while the need for protection of investors is low because of the small total amount involved. This rationale does not apply to reporting companies which must in all events compile information to comply with 1934 Act requirements.

Rule 505 exempts offerings of up to $5,000,000 (aggregating all sales within a year in reliance on any small offering exemption). In order to qualify for the exemption, the issuer must make disclosure to all non-accredited investors in accordance with Rule 502(b) and must comply with the manner of offering and resale limitations of Rules 502(c) and (d). There may be no more than thirty-five non-accredited purchasers.

Rule 506 is the successor to the Rule 146 private offering. There is no dollar limitation on this exemption. As with Rule 505 offerings, information must be furnished to non-accredited investors in accordance with Rule 502(b), the issuer must comply with Rules 502(c) and (d), and there may be no more than thirty-five non-accredited purchasers. The tradeoff under Rule 506 for the ability to raise large amounts of money is that non-accredited investors must, either individually or together with their "purchaser representatives," meet a sophistication test under Rule 506(b)(2)(ii). "Purchaser representative" is defined in Rule 501 to include only those who may be relied on to objectively and adequately guide the investor.

[4] Secondary Transactions

This Section discusses sales by shareholders as distinguished from the issuer. Although such sales may involve the same supposed dangers to investors as do sales by the issuer, registration requirements can impose greater burdens on shareholders than on issuers, and restricting the alienation of stock might adversely affect the liquidity of the capital markets. Thus, it is necessary to balance the need to protect investors against the burdens imposed by the regulation.

Section 4(1) exempts transactions by one who is not an "issuer," "underwriter" or "dealer." This Section exempts most sales by shareholders (as opposed to issuers) from the registration requirements of § 5 since, in the ordinary case, a shareholder will not be an issuer, underwriter, or dealer, as those terms are defined in §§ 2(a)(4), 2(a)(11), and 2(a)(12), respectively.

In some instances, however, the selling shareholder who distributes securities (or the party who sells for the selling shareholder) may be an "underwriter" under § 2(a)(11). This occurs mainly in two situations: first, where the shareholder has purchased from an issuer, as in a private placement, "with a view to . . . the distribution of any security" (*see* § 2(a)(11)); and second, where the selling shareholder is control person (see the last sentence of § 2(a)(11) which defines "issuer" for purposes of § 2(a)(11) to include one who controls or is controlled by the issuer and therefore makes anyone who sells for the control person in connection with a distribution an "underwriter"). In each of these cases, since the sale will involve an "underwriter," the Section 4(1) exemption will not be available. However, the transaction still may be exempt under some other provision of the 1933 Act, including Section 4(4) covering "brokers' transactions."

These provisions raise the following questions, among others:

(1) How much stock constitutes a "distribution" under § 2(a)(11)? In other words, must a controlling person register the sales through a broker of 10 shares of his stock? (The broker would be an "underwriter" if the sales are a "distribution" under § 2(a)(11).) What about the sale of 1000 shares to an institutional investor that plainly does not need the protection of the securities laws?

(2) Suppose a company sells a substantial amount of stock in a private offering and, after a period of time, a purchaser of the stock resells. Under what circumstances will the two transactions be connected into a single "distribution"? Note that, if the second sale is not a step in a distribution beginning with the company, the second seller is not an "underwriter" under § 2(a)(11). Thus, unless the second seller is a controlling person (and hence an "issuer" under § 2(a)(11)) and sells through another person, the transaction is not one by an "underwriter."

(3) If a transaction is one by an "underwriter," under what circumstances will it be an exempt "brokers' transaction" under § 4(4)).

(4) If the transaction is within § 4(4), does the exemption cover both the broker and others who are participating in the distribution?

Question 3, above, was addressed by the SEC in *Ira Haupt & Co.*,[39] which found a violation of the Act where those in control of a company sold a substantial percentage of their holdings through a single broker over a six-month period and the broker was fully aware of the scope of the intended sale. The Commission said that a "distribution" had taken place and that, since the broker had participated in the distribution, the broker was an "underwriter." The broker was denied the brokers' exemption, irrespective of whether it engaged in "solicitation," on the ground that the § 4(4) exemption was not intended to extend to participants in a distribution.

Haupt left several unanswered questions. First, there remained question 1, above, as to how much stock had to be sold before a "distribution" would be deemed to have taken place. Second, *Haupt* involved a broker who was clearly aware of what was going on. Could a broker who had simply executed a customer's telephone order be deemed to be an "underwriter" and not entitled to the § 4(4) exemption, even if he had no idea that the customer was engaging in a "distribution" of stock?

In Rule 154 (which has been superseded by Rule 144), the SEC attempted to answer the questions left open by *Haupt*. Rule 154 established a volume limitation on sales which would not constitute a "distribution," and also provided that only a broker who "is not aware" that a distribution is going on is entitled to the 4(4) exemption.

United States v. Wolfson[40] addressed question 4, above: where a controlling person had engaged in what was clearly a distribution through a number of brokers who were entitled to the brokers' exemption (since they were not aware that a distribution was taking place), the court held that the exemption applied only to the broker and not to the defendant.

Question 2 was dealt with in a series of cases which, focusing on the words "with a view to" in § 2(a)(11), examined the purchaser's intent as of the time of purchase. In some cases, the purchaser's intent was determined by considering whether the resale resulted from a change in the seller's circumstances. In other cases, the purchaser's intent was determined based upon the amount of time that he held the stock prior to the sale. For instance, in *United States v. Sherwood*,[41] the court held that a resale after a two-year holding period did not result in underwriter status absent evidence showing that the purchase was "with a view to" distribution.

Rule 144, promulgated in 1972, addresses all of the questions listed above. Rule 144, like Regulation D, is a "safe harbor" rule. Thus, sales by security holders within the

---

[39]   23 S.E.C. 589 (1946).

[40]   405 F.2d 779 (2d Cir. 1968).

[41]   175 F. Supp. 480 (S.D.N.Y. 1959).

Rule will not result in liability. On the other hand, transactions that do not conform to the rule do not necessarily violate the Act. *See* Subsection (j). However, since Rule 144 is influential in any interpretation of Section 4(1), and since Rule 144 provides clear standards, one would usually be ill-advised to violate the Rule. Rule 144 makes three major distinctions:

(1) Between controlling persons ("affiliates") and others. Controlling persons are better able to obtain registration and there is a greater risk that they are trading on inside information.

(2) Between large and small volume transactions. Small volume transactions do not generally involve high pressure sales tactics, have little effect on the market, and are more costly per share to register.

(3) With respect to "restricted" stock (*i.e.*, stock which was acquired in a transaction or chain or transactions not involving a public offering), between such stock that has and has not been held for a significant length of time. A holding period ensures that secondary sales will not convert a private offering into a public offering.

In general, Rule 144 allows restricted stock that is held by non-affiliates to be sold so long as the following conditions are satisfied: (1) there is current public information available regarding the issuer (*see* Rule 144(c)); (2) the stock being sold has been out of the hands of the issuer or an affiliate for at least one year (Rule 144(d)); (3) the amount sold does not exceed the volume limitations of Rule 144(e); (4) the stock is sold in brokers' transactions within the meaning of § 4(4) or to a "market maker"; and (5) in cases of sales in excess of a certain amount, the seller files a notice pursuant to Rule 144(h). Alternatively, under Rule 144(k), restricted stock can be sold by non-affiliates without limitation so long as two years have passed since the securities were acquired from an issuer or an affiliate.

Similar rules apply to sales by affiliates except that: (1) affiliates can sell stock that is not restricted stock without regard for the holding period requirements of Rule 144(d); (2) affiliates are subject to somewhat stricter limitations regarding the volume of securities that can be sold (*see* Rule 144(e)); and (3) affiliates cannot make use of Rule 144(k).

Rule 144 allows security holders to resell securities that were purchased in private placements under § 4(2) or in limited offerings under Regulation D, so long as volume limitations, among others, are observed. An important type of transaction that falls outside of Rule 144 (and of § 4(2) and Regulation D, since those exemptions covers sales by issuers only) is a private sale by a non-issuer that would be a private offering if it were a sale by the issuer. For years this was handled under an informal "Section 4(1½)" exemption that was recognized by the SEC. In 1990, the SEC promulgated Rule 144A to deal with this situation. Rule 144A provides a safe harbor for resales to certain institutional investors and dealers of securities that are not of the same class as securities traded the public markets. This rule significantly increases the liquidity of privately placed securities.

[G] State Securities Regulation

Every state has a "blue sky" law that regulates the sale of securities within the state. In general, blue sky laws require registration of securities dealers and of sales of stock. Blue sky laws differ substantially from state to state, with some including so-called "merit regulation" that goes beyond merely requiring full disclosure and gives the administrator the discretion to block offerings which are unfair to investors. Because of this variation, an attorney advising in connection with a public offering to which state blue sky laws apply (see the immediately following paragraph) must be sure that the offering complies with the statute of each state in which securities will be sold.

The National Securities Markets Improvement Act of 1996 amended § 18 of the 1933 Act to allocate regulatory responsibility between federal and state governments based on the nature of the securities offering. Under revised § 18, certain offerings, such as those of securities listed, or authorized for listing, on the New York Stock Exchange, the American Stock Exchange, or the National Market System of the Nasdaq Stock Market, are deemed to be exclusively national in character and are therefore subject only to federal regulation. But smaller, regional, and intrastate securities offerings remain subject to state blue sky regulation.

§ 12.03 The Securities Exchange Act of 1934

While the 1933 Act is concerned primarily with the initial issuance of securities by corporations and other business entities, the 1934 Act focuses on trading markets. The following subsections summarize the principal features of 1934 Act regulation, with an emphasis on the duties of issuers and others under § 10(b) and Rule 10b-5.

[A] Overview of the 1934 Act

The 1934 responded to alleged flaws in the trading markets described during the hearings that led to the securities laws. These included massive trading by corporate insiders, the issuance of false press releases, unscrupulous securities brokers and a lack of reliable public information. The effect of these practices on stock prices was magnified by widespread trading through margin accounts in which the investors had very little equity.

The 1934 Act was a multifarious attack on these alleged problems. Some of its provisions create a comprehensive scheme of regulation of securities brokers and dealers (*see* §§ 15 and 15A) and securities exchanges (§§ 5, 6, 8 and 19). Section 7 establishes rules for the purchase of securities on margin. Sections 9 and 10 prohibit various forms of manipulation. Section 16 provides a remedy for insider trading and §§ 12, 13 and 14 ensure a continuous flow of information concerning publicly traded securities.

The 1934 Act has been amended numerous times since its adoption, with the most recent amendments being adopted as part of the Sarbanes-Oxley Act of 2002. Enacted in response to the Enron collapse and accounting scandals at WorldCom and other companies, the Sarbanes-Oxley Act seeks to further the stated goals of increasing corporate responsibility, providing enhanced penalties for accounting and auditing improprieties at public companies, and protecting investors by improving the accuracy and reliability of corporate disclosures under the federal securities laws. The Sarbanes-Oxley Act features, as its centerpiece, a new Public Company Accounting Oversight Board with responsibility for regulating accountants who provide audit services to pubic companies. Other features of the Sarbanes-Oxley Act are discussed below.

[B] Express Disclosure Requirements under the 1934 Act

Section 12 of the 1934 Act requires the filing of a one-time registration statement for the company's securities; § 13 requires the filing of annual, quarterly and current reports with the SEC; and § 14 requires that certain material be filed and sent to shareholders in connection with annual and special shareholder meetings. Section 18 of the 1934 Act provides for liability for misrepresentations and omissions in documents filed with the SEC. Under § 18, a plaintiff who purchased or sold securities in reliance on the filed documents may recover without proof of scienter, but the defendant is permitted a "good faith" defense. Compare the elements of the implied action under § 10(b) and Rule 10b-5, discussed in subsection [D] below.

Issuers and others also have express disclosure requirements under the Williams Act in connection with tender offers and other bids for control. *See* Chapter 13. Among other things, the target board must make a recommendation to the shareholders as to whether they should accept or reject the bid.

Documents required to be filed under the 1934 Act generally have to be submitted electronically by direct transmission, magnetic tape or diskette. These documents are generally available for inspection without charge at the SEC's website (www.sec.gov) and at the issuer's own website.

The Sarbanes-Oxley Act of 2002 attempts to enhance the quality of issuer disclosures under the 1934 Act by, among other things, (1) requiring independent audit committees to oversee the work of company's outside auditors (§ 301); (2) requiring chief executive officers and chief financial officers to certify, among other things, the accuracy and completeness of the company's annual and quarterly financial reports (§ 302), with penalties of up to 20 years imprisonment for false certifications (§ 906); and (3) creating a new federal felony for securities fraud at public companies with a maximum penalty of 25 years imprisonment (§ 807).

[C] Implied Duties under § 10(b) and Rule 10b-5

In addition to the express duties already discussed, issuers and others have implied duties under the 1934 Act. These duties arise primarily under § 10(b) and Rule 10b-5. Section 10(b) makes it unlawful for any person

> To use or employ, in connection with the purchase or sale of any security . . . , any manipulative or deceptive device or contrivance in contravention of such rules and regulations as the Commission may prescribe as necessary or appropriate for the protection of investors,

while Rule 10b-5 provides that

> It shall be unlawful for any person, directly or indirectly . . . , (a) To employ any device, scheme, or artifice to defraud, . . . or (c) To engage in act, practice or course of dealing which operates or would operate as a fraud or deceit upon any person, in connection with the purchase or sale of any security.

[1] Misleading Statements

Section 10(b) and Rule 10b-5 have long been interpreted to include a duty to refrain from making materially misleading public statements. This duty applies to all persons who make statements "in connection with the purchase or sale of any security." In *Securities and Exchange Commission v. Texas Gulf Sulphur Co.*,[42] the court held that Rule 10b-5's reach is not limited to those who engage in securities transactions following public misstatements, but extends to any person who makes an assertion "in a manner reasonably calculated to influence the investing public." Thus, a public company (or an officer or employee acting on its behalf) that issues a misleading press release may be liable for violating § 10(b) and Rule 10b-5, even though the company itself did not purchase or sell any securities.

For a misleading public statement to constitute a violation of § 10(b) and Rule 10b-5, the statement must be "material" and must be made with the requisite intent to deceive or "scienter." The Supreme Court has held that the materiality standard under § 10(b) and Rule 10b-5 is the same as under § 14(a) of the 1934 Act—*i.e.*, the *TSC* materiality standard discussed above in Section 7.03.[43]

With respect to intent, *Ernst & Ernst v. Hochfelder*[44] held that "a private cause of action for damages will not lie under § 10(b) and Rule 10b-5 in the absence of any allegation of 'scienter'—intent to deceive, manipulate or defraud." *Hochfelder* clarifies that a merely negligent defendant is not liable for damages under § 10(b) and Rule 10b-5. But the opinion leaves unanswered several important questions: First, is there liability where the defendant was more than negligent but lacked actual knowledge of falsity or subjective intent to defraud? Second, is a negligent defendant subject to injunctive relief in an action by the SEC? Third, what is the requisite level of culpabil-

---

[42]   401 F.2d 833 (2d Cir. 1968), *cert. denied*, 394 U.S. 976 (1969).

[43]   *See Basic Incorporated v. Levinson*, 485 U .S. 224 (1988).

[44]   425 U.S. 185 (1976).

ity under other general antifraud provisions of the securities laws, including § 17(a) of the 1933 Act, which is very similar to Rule 10b-5?

The Supreme Court addressed the second and third questions in *Aaron v. SEC*.[45] In that case, the SEC sought injunctive relief under § 10(b) of the 1934 Act and § 17(a) of the 1933 Act against a brokerage firm that had negligently failed to supervise its employees in connection with a public offering. The Court held that injunctive relief could not be obtained by the SEC under § 10(b) in an action based upon negligence. However, the Supreme Court refused to extend the scienter requirement of *Hochfelder* to SEC actions under § 17(a)(2) and (3) of the 1933 Act. In differentiating between §§ 17(a) and 10(b), *Aaron* relied on the absence from § 17(a)(2) and (3) of the fraud-type language found in § 10(b). But *Aaron* did not consider whether private parties could seek damages under § 17(a) for conduct that does not meet the *Hochfelder* scienter requirement.[46]

With respect to the first question (*i.e.*, the precise meaning of "scienter"), the post-*Hochfelder* decisions have held that proof of recklessness is sufficient to satisfy the Supreme Court's standard.[47] For an often-cited definition of recklessness in the 10b-5 context, see *Franke v. Midwestern Oklahoma Development Authority*:[48]

> [R]eckless conduct may be defined as . . . highly unreasonable [conduct], involving not merely simple, or even inexcusable negligence, but an extreme departure from the standards of ordinary care, and which presents a danger of misleading buyers or sellers that is either known to the defendant or is so obvious that the actor must have been aware of it.

To deter frivolous lawsuits, the Private Securities Litigation Reform Act of 1995 added special pleading rules for private actions alleging violations of the 1934 Act, including § 10(b) and Rule 10b-5. Under these rules, the complaint must "state with particularity the facts giving rise to a strong inference that the defendant acted with the required state of mind" (*see* § 21D(b)(2)).[49]

---

[45]   446 U.S. 680 (1980).

[46]   The courts have generally held against such a remedy. *See, e.g., Maldonado v. Dominguez*, 137 F.3d 1 (1st Cir. 1998); *Stephenson v. Paine Webber Jackson & Curtis*, 839 F.2d 1095 (5th Cir. 1988); *In re Washington Public Power Supply System Securities Litigation*, 823 F.2d 1349 (9th Cir. 1987); *Mann v. Oppenheimer & Co.*, 517 A.2d 1056 (Del. 1986).

[47]   *See, e.g., Rolf v. Blyth, Eastman Dillon & Co., Inc.*, 570 F.2d 38, 44-47 (2d Cir. 1978), *cert. denied*, 439 U.S. 1039 (1978).

[48]   428 F. Supp. 719, 725 (W.D. Okla. 1976).

[49]   Prior to the adoption of the 1995 Act, courts had differed on the appropriate pleading standard. *Compare Stern v. Leucadia National Corp.*, 844 F.2d 997 (2d Cir. 1988) (plaintiff must allege specific facts that give rise to a "strong inference" that the defendants possessed the requisite fraudulent intent), *with In re GlenFed, Inc. Securities Litigation*, 42 F.3d 1541 (9th Cir. 1994) (plaintiff is required to allege with particularity the circumstances constituting the fraud, but state of mind can be more generally averred).

Courts have split on the meaning of the "strong inference" language of new § 21D(b)(2). Many courts, following the pre-Reform Act Second Circuit precedents, have held that a plaintiff satisfies the "strong inference" requirement by alleging specific facts that either (1) constitute circumstantial evidence of either reckless or conscious behavior or (2) establish a motive to commit fraud and an opportunity to do so.[50] But other courts have held that, in adopting new § 21D(b)(2), Congress intended to strengthen existing pleading standards, rather than merely to codify the Second Circuit approach. For instance, several courts have ruled that the "strong inference" requirement of new § 21D(b)(2) is not necessarily satisfied by allegations that merely establish a motive and opportunity to commit fraud.[51] And at least one held that the "strong inference" test is only satisfied if the plaintiff pleads facts that "constitute strong circumstantial evidence of *deliberately* reckless or *conscious* misconduct"; suggesting that allegations of simple recklessness no longer suffice.[52]

[2] Duty to Speak

Basic v. Levinson[53] said that "[s]ilence, absent a duty to disclose, is not misleading under 10b-5." Accordingly, § 10(b) and Rule 10b-5 do not generally require corporations to disclose information simply because investors might find that information significant. However, there are more limited instances in which a duty to disclose may arise. The most important of these are examined below.

Exchange-imposed duties. Stock exchange rules impose additional affirmative disclosure requirements on listed companies. For example, the New York Stock Exchange Company Manual requires disclosure of merger negotiations when "unusual market activity" indicates leaks, or when disclosures are made to outsiders. It also requires disclosure of information tipped to securities analysts (§ 202.02) and, more generally, of "news or information which might reasonably be expected to materially affect the market for [the company's] securities" (§ 202.05). *State Teachers Retirement Board v. Fluor Corp.*[54] held that there was no implied right of action for violation of an earlier version of this provision.

---

[50] *See, e.g., Novak v. Kasaks*, 216 F.3d 300 (2d Cir. 2000); *In re Advanta Corp. Securities Litigation*, 180 F.3d 525 (3d Cir. 1999).

[51] *See, e.g., Greebel v. FTP Software*, 194 F.3d 185 (1st Cir. 1999); *In re Comshare, Inc. Securities Litigation*, 183 F.3d 542 (6th Cir. 1999); *Bryant v. Avado Brands, Inc.*, 187 F.3d 1271 (11th Cir. 1999).

[52] *See In re Silicon Graphics, Inc. Securities Litigation*, 183 F.3d 970 (9th Cir. 1999) (emphasis added). The Ninth Circuit repudiated this interpretation of *Silicon Graphics* in *Howard v. Everex Systems, Inc.*, 228 F.3d 1057 (9th Cir. 2000). *See also Greebel v. FTP Software*, 194 F.3d 185 (1st Cir. 1999) (rejecting argument that PSLRA requires more than simple recklessness to show scienter); *In re Advanta Corp. Securities Litigation*, 180 F.3d 525 (3d Cir. 1999) (same); *In re Comshare, Inc. Securities Litigation*, 183 F.3d 542 (6th Cir. 1999) (same); *Bryant v. Avado Brands, Inc.*, 187 F.3d 1271 (11th Cir. 1999) (same).

[53] 485 U.S. 224 (1988).

[54] 654 F.2d 843 (2d Cir. 1981).

Misleading statements. There is a duty under the federal securities laws to refrain from making statements that omit material facts necessary to make the statements made not misleading. This point is particularly important in light of the obligation of exchange-listed companies to respond to requests by the exchange to comment on the company's price movements. In this situation, the company must say something. When does that "something" become materially misleading because of the omission of certain facts? To reduce the risk of liability for material omissions, firms may respond to a request for information by saying they have "no comment." This course of action was approved in *In re Carnation Co.*[55] and, apparently, by the Supreme Court in *Basic.* But unless the company always responds to inquiries by saying "no comment," doesn't a "no comment" response amount to the confirmation of the rumors that the company wishes to avoid? If so, exchange queries essentially leave the company that wishes to maintain secrecy with no choice but to disclose or answer evasively or misleadingly.

Duty to correct. Even if the company's statement is initially true, there may be a duty to correct the statement in the light of subsequent events. In *In re Revlon, Inc.,*[56] the SEC said Revlon had a duty of prompt disclosure as to negotiations it entered into two days after telling shareholders in a recommendation statement under SEC Rule 14d-9 that it "may undertake" negotiations. An amendment of the recommendation statement six days after entering into the negotiations was not timely. Similarly, *In re Time Warner, Inc. Securities Litigation*[57] held that defendants, who had hyped the prospect of a strategic alliance with a partner who would infuse billions of dollars of capital into the company, had a duty to disclose problems in the alliance negotiations as those problems developed.[58] But *Stransky v. Cummins Engine Co., Inc.*[59] rejected any duty to update projections that were accurate when made, as distinguished from a "duty to correct," statements rendered untrue by subsequently discovered information. *San Leandro Emergency Medical Profit Sharing Plan v. Philip Morris Companies, Inc.*[60] held that Philip Morris had no duty to disclose a new marketing plan to reduce the price of Marlboro cigarettes by $.40 per pack, where reasonable investors could not conclude that Philip Morris had committed itself to a particular marketing strategy or foreclosed other alternatives.[61]

---

[55]   Exch. Act Rel. No. 22214, 33 S.E.C. Docket 1025 Fed. Sec. L. Rep. (CCH) ¶ 83,801 (1985).

[56]   Exch. Act Rel. 23320, Fed. Sec. L. Rep. (CCH) ¶ 84,006 (1986).

[57]   9 F.3d 259 (2d Cir. 1993).

[58]   *See also Weiner v. Quaker Oats Co.*, 129 F.3d 310 (3d Cir. 1997) (defendant whose prior statements could have induced a reasonable investor to expect that company's debt-to-total capitalization ratio would remain unchanged had duty to disclose possible increase of debt ratio that would result from planned acquisition); *Shaw v. Digital Equipment Corp.*, 82 F.3d 1194 (1st Cir. 1996) (issuer in public offering has duty to disclose inside information that "the quarter in progress at the time of the public offering will be an extreme departure from the range of results which could be anticipated based on [previously disclosed information]").

[59]   51 F.3d 1329, 1331-32 (7th Cir. 1995).

[60]   75 F.3d 801, 810 (2d Cir. 1996).

[61]   *See also In re International Business Machines Corporate Securities Litigation*, 163 F.3d 102 (2d Cir. 1998) (holding that there was no duty to update statements that issuer's "dividend is safe," because "the statements . . . were not material and 'lack the sort of definite positive projections that might require later correction'").

Misleading statements made by others. Some cases raise the question whether a company's silence is, in effect, a "statement" endorsing the accuracy of comments made by others. *Elkind v. Liggett & Myers, Inc.*[62] held that an issuer had no duty to disclose internal projections that were less optimistic than those being made by analysts. Although the company had reviewed and commented on some analysts' reports, it did nothing to suggest that it endorsed the accuracy of the analysts' earnings projections.[63]

Regulation FD. This rule, discussed in Note 6 following *Dirks* in Section 12.05 requires a public disclosure of information disclosed to securities analysts.

[D] Civil Remedies for Breach of Disclosure Duties under Rule 10b-5

Although there is no express remedy in the 1934 Act for private parties who have been injured by violations of § 10(b) and Rule 10b-5, the courts have implied a remedy. The first case to do so was *Kardon v. National Gypsum Co.*[64] The court reasoned, in part, that an implied private remedy should be presumed to be consistent with legislative intent absent evidence of an intent to deny a remedy. The Supreme Court approved the implied right of action under § 10(b) and Rule 10b-5 in *Superintendent of Insurance v. Bankers Life & Casualty Co.*,[65] and in *Herman & MacLean v. Huddleston*[66] held that the implied remedy will lie even where the plaintiff also has an express remedy under another provision of the securities laws. The Supreme Court's current approach to implication of remedies is more restrictive (*see* Section 7.03[D]).

Having found an implied private remedy for violations of § 10(b) and Rule 10b-5, the courts were left to determine the rules governing that remedy. The primary source of these rules has been the common law of deceit, not only because the language of both 10(b) and 10b-5 seems to point in that direction, but also because § 10(b) and Rule 10b-5 offer no other guidelines. The common law rules may not, however, be wholly appropriate in the 10b-5 context. First, an argument could be made that the securities laws, and hence the 10(b) and 10b-5 "catchalls," were intended to provide more protection for investors than had been available under the common law. Second, the common law rules were developed primarily in cases arising out of face-to-face transactions between a plaintiff and defendant, while 10b-5 cases often involve numerous plaintiffs whose trades were remote from the defendant. What differences between the Rule 10b-5 and common law fraud remedies are revealed in the following subsections? What factors account for these differences?

---

[62]   635 F.2d 156 (2d Cir. 1980).

[63]   *See also In re Syntex Corp. Securities Litig.*, 95 F.3d 922 (9th Cir. 1996) (no liability where corporation's CEO responded to inquiries regarding analysts' projections by emphasizing that analysts' estimates should not be attributed to the corporation).

[64]   69 F. Supp. 512 (E.D. Pa. 1946).

[65]   404 U.S. 6, 13 n.9 (1971).

[66]   459 U.S. 375 (1983).

[1] Purchaser-Seller Requirement

Under the common law of fraud, a defendant may be held liable not only for inducing a transaction, but also for inducing the plaintiff to retain his stock. *See* RESTATEMENT (SECOND) TORTS § 525 (1976). *Blue Chip Stamps v. Manor Drug Stores,*[67] however, held that one who neither purchased nor sold stock may not maintain a private cause of action for damages under § 10(b) and Rule 10b-5. In that case, defendant had been required under an antitrust decree to offer part of its business to retailers that had used its stamp service. Plaintiff, a retailer who declined to buy stock under the antitrust decree, claimed that the prospectus for the offering was misleadingly pessimistic in order to facilitate a later public offering at a higher price. In upholding the trial court's dismissal, the Supreme Court cited evidence of Congressional intent to limit the remedy under Rule 10b-5 to purchasers and sellers. The Court also reasoned that a purchaser-seller standing rule would reduce vexatious litigation by denying standing to those who made the difficult-to-verify claim that they *would have* purchased or sold but for the violation of Rule 10b-5. The Court declined to create an exception where "would-be" purchasers were a limited class defined in the antitrust decree, in part because the Court favored a clear, predictable rule. Some cases have permitted a cause of action where there was clearly a securities transaction but plaintiff was arguably not directly a party to it.[68] Whether the purchaser-seller standing requirement applies to private actions seeking injunctive relief (rather than damages) remains unclear.[69]

[2] Reliance: Transaction Causation

As in common law deceit, the plaintiff must prove that she purchased or sold in reliance on the misrepresentation. Reliance is distinguishable from materiality in that materiality tests the significance of the misrepresentation from the point of view of the reasonable investor, while reliance tests the significance of the misrepresentation to the particular plaintiff.

Some courts require that reliance be reasonable.[70] Such a requirement, however, is arguably unnecessary since misrepresentations must be significant to the "reasonable" investor under the materiality standard to be actionable. Accordingly, in *Teamsters Local 282 Pension Fund v. Angelos,*[71] Judge Easterbrook refused to impose a general

---

[67] 421 U.S. 723 (1975).

[68] *See Grubb v. F.D.I.C.*, 868 F.2d 1151 (10th Cir. 1989) (plaintiff formed corporation to buy bank, paying half the cash and guaranteeing half the loan); *United Department Stores, Inc. v. Ernst & Whinney*, 713 F. Supp. 518 (D.R.I. 1989) (shareholders loaned cash to corporation that corporation used to buy shares of another company).

[69] *See, e.g., Trump Hotels & Casino Resorts, Inc. v. Mirage Resorts Inc.*, 140 F.3d 478 (3d Cir. 1998) (plaintiff who did not allege that he had any intention of purchasing bonds had no standing to seek injunctive relief based on misstatements related to proposed bond offering, even assuming that Third Circuit precedent conferring standing to seek injunctive relief on non-selling and non-purchasing plaintiffs survived *Blue Chip Stamps*).

[70] *See, e.g., Herpich v. Wallace*, 430 F.2d 792, 818 n.12 (5th Cir. 1970).

[71] 762 F.2d 522 (7th Cir. 1985).

duty on plaintiffs to show that they made a reasonable investigation of the defendant's statements, reasoning that an action would generally lie so long as the *TSC* materiality standard was satisfied and so long as the falsehood or omission did not concern things known to the plaintiff equally or better than to the defendant.[72]

In *List v. Fashion Park, Inc.*,[73] the court mitigated the reliance requirement in a case involving a complete failure to disclose, as distinguished from an affirmative misrepresentation, by holding that the plaintiff need only prove that he would have acted differently if the fact had been disclosed, rather than that he was lured into the transaction by defendant's conduct. The court noted that a contrary rule would limit the 10b-5 remedy to face-to-face transactions, contrary to Congress' intent to regulate the public markets.[74] The plaintiff's burden in a pure nondisclosure case was further lightened in *Affiliated Ute Citizens of Utah v. United States*,[75] where the Court held that the plaintiff could recover in such a case without any affirmative proof of reliance.[76]

[3] Reliance: Fraud-on-the-Market

The reliance requirement has been eroded even in cases involving affirmative misrepresentations. Two factors have contributed to this erosion. First, many Rule 10b-5 claims are brought as class actions on behalf of purchasers or sellers who were adversely affected by defendant's misrepresentations. The claims are maintainable as class actions under Rule 23 of the Federal Rules of Civil Procedure only if questions common to the class predominate over those concerning individual class members. Since common questions may be held not to predominate if each class member must prove reliance on the misrepresentation and many of the individual claims are not large enough to justify individual actions, plaintiffs' attorneys have struggled to find some way around the reliance requirement.

Second, the traditional reliance requirement has been eroded by the growing acceptance of the Efficient Capital Markets Hypothesis, discussed in Section 7.01[F]. The "semi-strong" version of ECMH holds that public disclosures are quickly reflected in market prices. If this is true, an investor who never saw the misrepresentation is nevertheless injured to the extent that the misrepresentation adversely affected the price of his transaction.

---

[72] *See also Banca Cremi, S.A. v. Alex Brown & Sons, Inc.*, 132 F.3d 1017 (4th Cir. 1997) (holding that reliance must be "justified," rather than reasonable, so a plaintiff would only be precluded from maintaining an action if "he possesse[d] information sufficient to call a misrepresentation into question, but nevertheless close[d] his eyes to a known risk").

[73] 340 F.2d 457 (2d Cir. 1965).

[74] *Id.* at 462.

[75] 406 U.S. 128 (1972).

[76] *Cf. Binder v. Gillespie*, 184 F.3d 1059 (9th Cir. 1999) (*Affiliated Ute* presumption of reliance only applies in case involving both misrepresentations and omissions if case can be characterized "as one that primarily alleges omissions").

The mechanism for skirting the reliance requirement in misrepresentation cases is the "fraud on the market" theory adopted in *Basic, Inc. v. Levinson*.[77] Under that theory, the plaintiff is entitled to a rebuttable presumption of reliance if he proves that: (1) the defendant made public misrepresentations; (2) the misrepresentations were material; (3) the shares were traded on an efficient market; and (4) the plaintiff traded the shares between the time the misrepresentations were made and the time the truth was revealed.

The presumption is rebutted by "[a]ny showing that severs the link between the alleged misrepresentation and either the price received (or paid) by the plaintiff, or his decision to trade at a fair market price." The former link might be severed by showing that correct information entered the market. As to the link between the misrepresentation and the plaintiff's transaction, if a plaintiff willingly bought (or sold) stock knowing that it had been inflated (or deflated) by fraud, it is hard to see how the plaintiff has been damaged. What if the plaintiff simply believed that the stock price was wrong, but was unaware, or at least not fully aware, of the fraud?

For an illuminating post-*Basic* opinion on what markets are "efficient" for purposes of the fraud on the market theory, see *Cammer v. Bloom*,[78] where the court allowed plaintiffs to use the fraud-on-the-market theory in connection with securities traded over-the-counter. The court rejected "bright-line" tests based on the distinction between OTC and exchange-listed stocks or on whether the security was eligible to register on SEC's Form S-3 which is used by the largest, most "seasoned" companies. The court held that the following facts were relevant to the efficiency of the market for the firm's stock: average weekly trading volume; whether the security is "followed" by a significant number of securities analysts; whether the stock has numerous "market makers" (securities traders who announce their willingness to trade the stock); whether the company is eligible to use SEC Form S-3, or is ineligible only because it has not been public long enough; and the relationship shown between a corporation's stock price and corporate events.[79]

What is left of reliance after *Basic*? Has *Basic* turned the plaintiff's case into one of simply proving that the defendant's misstatements or omissions impacted stock price—*i.e.*, "loss causation." If so, does *Basic* invite the filing of a class action lawsuit whenever there is a sharp decline in the market price of a company's stock? This concern led some commentators to suggest eliminating the fraud-on-the-market theory as a partial remedy for defendants who claim that they have become "victims of an epi-

---

[77]   485 U.S. 224 (1988).

[78]   711 F. Supp. 1264 (D.N.J. 1989).

[79]   The *Cammer v. Bloom* factors were cited approvingly in *Binder v. Gillespie*, 184 F.3d 1059 (9th Cir. 1999), where the court refused to find an efficient market because the evidence showed the presence of only one of the five factors—that the security had market makers and arbitrageurs. *Cf. In re NationsMart Corporation Securities Litigation*, 130 F.3d 309 (8th Cir. 1997) (plaintiffs can not employ fraud on the market theory with respect to stock traded on the NASDAQ market where they do not "allege specific facts showing that a large number of people could buy or sell the stock; that trading information on the stock was widely available; and that the market rapidly reflected new information in price").

demic of baseless litigation that confuses stock market volatility with securities fraud."[80] Although the initial version of the Private Securities Litigation Reform Act of 1995 took up this invitation, the final version settled for less dramatic limitations on private actions under the 1934 Act, including, among other things, a requirement the lead plaintiff in a class action be the person or group with the largest financial interest in the case, a bar on discovery and other proceedings during the pendency of a motion to dismiss, a requirement (discussed above) that the complaint state with particularity facts giving rise to a strong inference that the defendant acted with the required state of mind, and a new statutory safe harbor for forward looking statements. These provisions can be found at §§ 21D and 21E of the 1934 Act.

[4] Reliance: Fraud-Created-the-Market

If the stock is not traded on an "efficient market" for purposes of the fraud-on-the-market theory, the plaintiff may still be able to avoid the reliance requirement by using the "fraud created the market" theory of *Shores v. Sklar*.[81] *Shores* was a suit by purchasers of a new issue of municipal bonds that were not traded in an efficient market on the theory that the bonds would have been unmarketable without the defendant's fraud. In other words, although the plaintiffs could not prove that they relied on the integrity of the market price in an inefficient market, they could show that they relied on the marketability of the bonds. *Ross v. Bank South, N.A.*[82] held that this theory has survived the Supreme Court's articulation of the efficient-market basis of the fraud-on-the-market theory in *Basic*.[83]

[5] Damages

The general rule is that the appropriate measure of damages in Rule 10b-5 cases involving open market trading is the "out-of-pocket" rule, under which the plaintiff receives the difference between the price she paid or received for her stock and the price she would have paid or received in a market unaffected by the misrepresentation.[84] This difference can be calculated by (1) measuring the change in the stock's

---

[80] *See* Grundfest, *Disimplying Private Rights of Action under the Federal Securities Laws: The Commission's Authority*, 107 HARV. L. REV. 963, 972, 1013 & n.265 (1994).

[81] 647 F.2d 462 (5th Cir. 1981) (en banc), *cert. denied*, 459 U.S. 1102 (1983), *appeal after remand*, 844 F.2d 1485 (11th Cir. 1988).

[82] 885 F.2d 723 (11th Cir. 1989).

[83] However, there were two concurring opinions by four judges in *Ross* expressing doubts about *Shores*. It has been held that *Shores* does not apply where the fundamental marketability of the securities is established by continued trading even after the fraud is disclosed. *See Ross v. Bank South, N.A., supra; Abell v. Potomac Insurance Co.*, 858 F.2d 1104 (5th Cir. 1988).

[84] *See Huddleston v. Herman & MacLean*, 640 F.2d 534, 554-556 (5th Cir. 1981), *rev'd in part on other grounds*, 459 U.S. 375, 103 S. Ct. 683 (1983); *Green v. Occidental Petroleum Corp.*, 541 F.2d 1335, 1341-46 (9th Cir.

price over the period when the truth was disclosed; and (2) separating out movements that are not attributable to disclosure. Finance theory, and specifically the Capital Assets Pricing Model (*see* Section 7.01[E]), can be used in making these determinations: Price movements not attributable to disclosure can be separated out by showing the expected stock price based on the stock's "beta" and the movement of the market as a whole during the period of the misrepresentation. For greater precision, the effects of industry-wide movements can be separated out by determining the fluctuation of stocks in the same industry over the relevant period and the historic relationship between the prices of those stocks and of the stock being analyzed.

The Private Securities Litigation Reform Act of 1995 added § 21D(b)(4) of the 1934 Act, which places on the plaintiff the "burden of proving that the act or omission of the defendant alleged to violate [the 1934 Act] caused the loss for which the plaintiff seeks to recover." This suggests a legislative endorsement of the "out of pocket" measure of damages typically applied in Rule 10b-5 cases. It also added § 21D(e) limiting plaintiff's award in a private action under the 1934 Act to the difference between the purchase or sale price and the security's mean trading price during the 90-day period following dissemination of information correcting the misstatement or omission. This provision appears to be based on the questionable assumption that markets systematically overreact to bad news.

[6] Waiver

Like most provisions of the federal securities laws, § 10(b) and Rule 10b-5 are mandatory—that is, parties cannot agree to waive compliance with their requirements.[85] Parties might be able to reduce their risk of liability. For example, in *Harsco Corporation v. Segui*,[86] Harsco agreed to buy all of Multiserv's outstanding stock and some of Multiserv's subordinated debt pursuant to a written purchase agreement. The agreement included 14 pages of single-spaced representations and warranties made by the sellers, as well as a "no other representations" clause, which stated that the sellers "shall not be deemed to have made . . . any representation or warranty other than as expressly made . . . in [the agreement]" (section 2.05), and a merger clause, which provided that the agreement "contains the entire agreement between the parties" (section 7.02). After the transaction closed, Harsco sued, alleging violations of Rule 10b-5, but the district court dismissed the complaint. The Second Circuit affirmed based on the district court's

---

1976) (Sneed, J., concurring). *But see McMahan & Co. v. Wherehouse Entertainment Inc.*, 65 F.3d 1044 (2d Cir. 1995) (holding that "benefit of the bargain" damages might be available in an action under Rule 10b-5 where the purchaser of bonds alleged that the conditions under which bonds would be repurchased by the issuer at a 6.25% premium over par had been misstated in the prospectus).

[85] *See, e.g., In re Discovery Zone Securities Litigation*, 181 F.R.D. 582 (N.D. Ill. 1998) (agreement purporting to limit the circumstances under which purchaser of securities could recover for breach of representation or warranty did not bar action for securities fraud because "[a] waiver of future unknown securities fraud claims under the 1934 Act is explicitly precluded by statute").

[86] 91 F.3d 337 (2d Cir. 1996).

findings that: (1) the case was based on representations not included in the purchase agreement; and (2) Harsco was precluded from establishing "reasonable reliance" on such representations by virtue of sections 2.05 and 7.02 of the purchase agreement. But the Second Circuit qualified its holding by noting that, "[i]n different circumstances (*e.g.*, if there were but one vague seller's representation [rather than 14 pages of repre-sentations]) a 'no other representations' clause might be toothless and run afoul of [the anti-waiver provisions of § 29(a) of the 1934 Act]." *Rissman v. Rissman*[87] goes beyond *Harsco*, holding that non-reliance clauses in written stock-purchase agreements preclude any possibility of damages under the federal securities laws for prior oral statements.

In the context of international securities transactions, where foreign entities sell securities to U.S. investors, the courts have enforced provisions of international securities agreements (1) requiring the rights and obligations of U.S. purchasers to be determined under the laws of the seller's jurisdiction, and (2) providing courts in the seller's jurisdic-tion with *exclusive* jurisdiction to resolve any disputes arising out of the investment.[88]

[E] Responsibilities of Collateral Participants

There are often several participants other than the issuer involved in a corporate misrepresentation or nondisclosure, including the directors, accountants, underwriters, and attorneys. The SEC and plaintiffs' attorneys have long sought to hold each of these participants in the disclosure process liable because, when the financial balloon bursts, it is usually more remunerative to pursue a large accounting, law, or underwriting firm than the tattered remnants of the issuer. These claims raise a number of issues under the securities laws.

[1] Who Is Liable?

Suits against participants in a corporate fraud may be divided into two general cat-egories. In the first type of case, the defendant has made a representation that was used in connection with the sale of securities. These cases often involve accountants' certi-fications of financial statements or attorneys' opinions. The main issue in these cases is usually whether the defendant acted with the requisite scienter. (*See* Subsection [C][1] above.) The second type of case, discussed in this subsection, concerns the liability of those who assist in the misstatements of others, including those who simply stand by and do nothing.

---

[87]   213 F.3d 381 (7th Cir. 2000) (Easterbrook, J.).

[88]   *See, e.g., Richards v. Lloyd's of London,* 135 F.3d 1289 (9th Cir. 1998) (en banc), holding that such provisions do not contravene any "strong public policy" embodied in the anti-waiver provisions of the federal securities laws, *Haynsworth v. Lloyd's of London,* 121 F.3d 956 (5th Cir. 1997) (same), and *Lipcon v. Underwriters at Lloyd's, London,* 148 F.3d 1285 (11th Cir. 1998) (same). Five other circuits (the Second, Fourth, Fifth, Seventh, and Tenth) have reached the same result.

Until the Supreme Court's 1994 decision in *Central Bank of Denver v. First Inter-state Bank of Denver*,[89] federal courts generally held that those who assisted in the mis-statements of others could be held liable if the plaintiff established: (1) the existence of a securities law violation by the primary party; (2) knowledge of the violation on the part of the aider and abettor; and (3) substantial assistance by the aider and abettor in the achievement of the primary violation.[90] Thus, accountants, lawyers, and banks could be held liable for the 10b-5 violations of their clients and customers.

In *Central Bank*, however, the Supreme Court held that private civil liability did not extend to those who did not themselves engage in the manipulative or deceptive practice, but merely aided and abetted the violation. Focusing on the language of statute, the Court noted that § 10(b) authorized the SEC to proscribe manipulative or deceptive devices and contrivances, but did not mention aiding and abetting. The Court found the absence of such language conclusive: "Because the text of § 10(b) does not prohibit adding and abetting, we hold that a private plaintiff may not maintain an aiding and abetting suit under § 10(b)." Nevertheless, collateral participants might still be held liable under the following theories:[91]

Primary liability for collateral participant's misrepresentations and omissions. As the Court noted in *Central Bank*, "[a]ny person or entity, including a lawyer, accoun-tant, or bank, who employees a manipulative device or makes a material misstatement (or omission) on which a purchaser or seller of securities relies may be liable as a pri-mary violator under 10b-5 . . . ." This means that the collateral participant who makes an affirmative misstatement (*see* Subsection [C][1]]) or who remains silent in the face of a duty to speak (*see* Subsection [C][2]) might still be held liable to a purchaser or seller of securities who can establish all of the other requirements for an action under Rule 10b-5 (*see* Subsection [D]). Thus, accountants who certify incomplete or inaccu-rate financial statements and attorneys who issue incorrect opinion letters clearly remain at risk.[92]

Primary liability for statements made by others. In re Kendall Square Research Corporation Securities Litigation[93] dismissed allegations that accountants reviewed

---

[89]　511 U.S. 164 (1994).

[90]　*See, e.g., Metge v. Baehler*, 762 F.2d 621 (8th Cir. 1985).

[91]　These theories are likely to be tested in litigation against accountants, lawyers and investment bankers in the Enron matter. *See Newby v. Enron Corporation*, Civil Action No. H-01-3624 (S.D. Texas).

[92]　For a post-*Central Bank* decision allowing a suit against accountants based on the accountants' certification of the issuer's financial statements, see *In re Kendall Square Research Corporation Securities Litigation*, 868 F. Supp. 26 (D. Mass. 1994) (denying dismissal of count alleging that accountants falsely represented that issuer's financial state-ments fairly represented issuer's financial position in conformity with Generally Accepted Accounting Principles and had been audited in accordance with Generally Accepted Auditing Standards). For a post-*Central Bank* decision allowing a suit against a seller's attorney who allegedly made misstatements and incomplete statements to purchasers of securities, see *Rubin v. Schottenstein, Zox & Dunn*, 143 F.3d 263 (6th Cir. 1998) (en banc) (attorney who chooses to speak must "speak fully and truthfully" and purchasers can reasonably rely on attorney's statements without seeking independent confirmations, at least in transactions of modest size).

[93]　868 F. Supp. 26 (D. Mass. 1994).

and approved misleading statements made by the issuer in its quarterly financial reports and in its prospectuses for two stock offerings, holding that only "those who make a material misstatement or omission or commit a manipulative act, are subject to private suit under § 10(b)."[94] But *In re Software Toolworks Inc. Securities Litigation*[95] held that accountants could be held liable based on allegations that they participated in the drafting of two misleading letters that the issuer sent to the SEC.

Respondeat superior; conspiracy. Prior to *Central Bank,* collateral participants were sometimes held liable in § 10(b) actions under the common law doctrine of *respondeat superior.* Also some pre-*Central Bank* decisions permitted plaintiffs to recover against defendants on a common law conspiracy theory. However, the dissent in *Central Bank* stated that the majority's rationale appears to "sweep away" these decisions.[96]

Control person liability. While *Central Bank* arguably eliminates the common law theories of secondary liability discussed in the immediately preceding paragraph, collateral participants are still subject to "control person" liability under § 20(a) of the 1934 Act and § 15(b) of the 1933 Act. But a "control person" can escape liability under the federal securities laws by showing she "had no knowledge of or reasonable grounds to believe in the existence of the facts by reason of which . . . liability . . . is alleged to exist" (in the case of the 1933 Act) or by showing she "acted in good faith and did not directly or indirectly induce the act or acts constituting the violation or cause of action" (in the case of the 1934 Act). Also, the requisite level of "control" will generally only be found when the defendant *both* controls the day-to-day affairs of the primary violator and has the power to exercise control over the challenged transaction.[97] Control per-

---

[94]   For a similar holding, see *Vosgerichian v. Commodore Int'l,* 862 F. Supp. 1371 (E.D. Pa. 1994) (holding accountant not primarily liable for statements made by company despite allegations that company consulted with accountant and accountant advised or concurred with the company's decision). *See also Shapiro v. Cantor,* 123 F.3d 717 (2d Cir. 1997) (allegations that accountants "provide 'significant' or 'substantial' assistance to the representations of others" not sufficient to establish primary liability for violations of § 10(b)); *Brown v. Benchmark Power Corporation,* 94 F.3d 650 (9th Cir. 1996) (accountant not liable in action under § 10(b) when draft financial statements were included in private placement memorandum without accountant's authorization). The Second Circuit placed even tighter limits on suits against accounting firms in *Wright v. Ernst & Young, LLP,* 152 F.3d 169 (2d Cir. 1998). There, the court held that "a secondary actor cannot incur primary liability under the [1934] Act for a statement not attributed to that actor at the time of its dissemination." Accordingly, the court dismissed a suit based on a press release that "did not attribute any assurances to [the defendant] and, in fact, did not mention [the defendant] at all."

[95]   38 F.3d 1078 (9th Cir. 1994).

[96]   For cases holding that liability for conspiracy is inconsistent with *Central Bank,* see *Dinsmore v. Squadron, Ellenoff, Plesent, Sheinfeld & Sorkin,* 135 F.3d 837 (2d Cir. 1998), and *In re Glenfed Inc. Securities Litigation,* 60 F.3d 591 (9th Cir. 1995). The courts are divided on the question of whether the *respondeat superior* theory of liability survives *Central Bank. Compare Pollack v. Laidlaw Holdings, Inc.,* 1995 Fed. Sec. L. Rep. ¶ 98,741 (S.D.N.Y. 1995) (concluding that "[u]nlike aiding and abetting liability . . . liability of a principal based upon apparent authority has long been recognized by the federal courts"), *with ESI Montgomery County, Inc. v. Montenay International Corp.,* 1996 U.S. Dist. LEXIS 592, 1996 WL 22979 (S.D.N.Y. 1996) (holding that *Central Bank* precludes finding a corporation vicariously liable for the acts of its officers). If *respondeat superior* liability does not survive *Central Bank,* can corporations, which only act through agents, ever be held liable for violations of § 10(b) and Rule 10b-5?

[97]   For a good discussion of the meaning on "control" for purposes of "control person" liability under the federal securities laws, see *Brown v. Mendel,* 864 F. Supp. 1138 (M.D. Ala. 1994) (defendant is liable as a controlling person under section 20(a) if he or she "had the power to control the general affairs of the entity primarily liable at the time the entity violated the securities laws . . . [and] had the requisite power to directly or indirectly control or influence the specific corporate policy which resulted in the primary liability"), *aff'd sub nom. Brown v. The Enstar Group, Inc.,* 84

son liability therefore may not be very useful in cases against outside directors or professionals, such as attorneys, accountants, or investment bankers.[98]

The Private Securities Litigation Reform Act of 1995: SEC injunctive actions; cease and desist orders; administrative penalties; Rule 102(e) proceedings. In addition to being subject to civil actions by investors, collateral participants also remain subject to a variety of actions by the SEC. Although the rationale of *Central Bank* seemed broad enough to sweep away the SEC's powers to pursue aiders and abettors of § 10(b) violations in § 21(d) injunctive actions, Congress restored the SEC's § 21(d) powers over aiders and abettors in the Private Securities Litigation Reform Act of 1995 (*see* § 20(f) of the 1934 Act). In addition, the SEC may: (a) issue a cease and desist order under § 21C against any person "that is, was, or would be a cause of" a primary violation of the 1934 Act, "due to an act or omission the person knew or should have known would contribute to such violation"; (b) impose a civil penalty under § 21B on any broker or dealer who has willfully violated or willfully "aided, abetted, . . . or procured" a violation of the federal securities laws; and (c) suspend from practice before the SEC, pursuant to Rule 102(e) of the SEC's rules of practice, any person who was "willfully violated, or willfully aided and abetted the violation of any provision of the federal securities laws." Aiders and abettors of violations of the federal securities laws are also subject to potential criminal prosecution under 18 U.S.C. § 2, the general aiding and abetting statute applicable to all federal criminal offenses.[99]

[2] Proportionate Liability

The Private Securities Litigation Reform Act adds § 21D(f) of the 1934 Act, which adopts a scheme of proportionate liability under which defendants who do not "knowingly" violate the securities laws are generally held liable only "for the portion of the judgment that corresponds to [their] percentage of responsibility."[100] The prior rule

---

F.3d 393 (11th Cir. 1996), *cert. denied*, 117 S. Ct. 950 (1997). Some courts have adopted broader definitions of control. *See, e.g., Converse, Inc. v. Norwood Venture Corp.*, 1997 U.S. Dist. LEXIS 19106, 1997 WL 742534 (S.D.N.Y. 1997) (defining a "control person" as "one having 'the possession, direct or indirect, of the power to direct or cause the direction of management and policies of a person, whether through the ownership of voting securities, by contract or otherwise'").

[98]   *But see In re Intelligent Electronics Inc. Securities Litigation*, 1996 U.S. Dist. LEXIS 7674, 1996 WL 304852 (E.D. Pa. 1996) (allegations that accounting firm "could have refused to certify [issuer's] consolidated financial statements" and that "bad publicity brought on by such a refusal would no doubt have harmed the [issuer]" sufficient to defeat motion to dismiss claim that accounting firm should be held liable for issuer's misstatements as a control person).

[99]   Aiders and abettors may also be held liable under the provisions of state securities laws. *See, e.g., Iowa ex rel. Goettsch v. Diacide Distributors Inc.*, 561 N.W.2d 369 (Iowa 1997) (Iowa securities laws construed to permit action by state securities regulators against aiders and abettors even though statute does not expressly provide for such an action).

[100]   Section 21D(f)(4) provides that parties who do not "knowingly" violate the securities laws can be held liable for the share of the judgment that cannot be collected from other defendants. If the plaintiff has a net worth of less than $200,000 and the damages recoverable are at least 10% of the plaintiff's net worth, then all defendants are jointly

under 10b-5 was that all defendants were held jointly and severally liable for all damages, regardless of their degree of responsibility for the violation.

[3] Contribution and Indemnification

In *Musick, Peeler & Garrett v. Employers Insurance of Wausau*,[101] the Supreme Court held that an insurer could seek contribution from co-defendants for liabilities incurred as a result of a suit under Rule 10b-5. The Court reasoned that this is how Congress would have addressed the issue if 10b-5 were an express remedy, looking to §§ 9 and 18 of the 1934 Act which expressly provide for contribution. Compare the reasoning in *Central Bank*, below, concerning liability for aiding and abetting.

By contrast, federal courts have rejected claims for indemnification against liabilities incurred in suits under Rule 10b-5. *Eichenholtz v. Brennan*[102] rejected an implied right to indemnity against liabilities arising under provisions of the federal securities laws (including, but not limited to, Rule 10b-5) because "indemnification runs counter to the policies underlying the 1933 and 1934 Acts" and "there is no indication that Congress intended that indemnification be available under the Acts." The court also rejected an underwriter's claim for indemnification under the express provisions of its underwriting agreement, finding that claims for indemnification "run counter to the policies underlying the federal securities acts," even "in cases, as here, where an underwriter was merely negligent [and] played a 'de minimis' role in the public offering at issue." The court reasoned that "enforc[ing] an underwriter indemnification provision . . . would effectively eliminate the underwriter's incentive to fulfill its investigative obligation and therefore "the statute would fail to serve the prophylactic purpose that . . . underwriters make some reasonable attempt to verify data submitted to them."[103]

§ 12.04 Regulation of Insider Trading under State Law

The obligation of corporate insiders and others to refrain from trading based on nonpublic information is governed primarily by federal law. As Section 12.05 explains, the Securities and Exchange Commission first explicitly recognized a federal duty to refrain from insider trading in 1961 in *Cady, Roberts & Co.*,[104] holding that sales by corporate insiders based on nonpublic information constituted violations of § 10(b) and Rule 10b-5.

---

and severally liable. Otherwise, parties who do not "knowingly" violate the securities laws are held liable for the uncollectible share of the judgment in proportion to their percentage of responsibility, though the total excess liability under this provision cannot exceed 50% of the party's proportionate share of the total damages.

[101] 508 U.S. 286 (1993).

[102] 52 F.3d 478, 483-85 (3d. Cir. 1995).

[103] *But cf. Fromer v. Yogel*, 50 F. Supp. 2d 227 (S.D.N.Y. 1999) (approving implied right of action for indemnification under § 10(b) for party that is guilty of no more than ordinary negligence).

[104] 40 S.E.C. 907 (1961).

This Section begins the discussion of insider trading with coverage of state law remedies. The coverage of state law should be viewed as a backdrop for the consideration in Section 12.05 of federal remedies under § 10(b) and Rule 10b-5. The Chapter concludes in Section 12.06 with a discussion of liability for insider trading under § 16(b) of the 1934 Act.

Subsection [A] below covers state law remedies of purchasers and sellers, while subsection [B] below covers state law remedies available to the corporation itself.

[A] Remedies of Purchasers and Sellers

One may be subject to liability under the common law of fraud for affirmatively misstating facts to the other party to a transaction. However, the extent of common law liability to purchasers or sellers of securities for simply failing to disclose information is far less clear. Consider the following excerpt:[105]

> [T]he law cannot hope to put all parties to every contract on an equality as to knowledge experience skill, and shrewdness; even if it could, would such be a just and equitable law? It would certainly not be consistent with the present economic order. At one time, the Roman law taking the same high stand insisted upon a rigid equality between the parties contracting and demanded a full disclosure by each party of all the material facts known to him and equally accessible to the other. Bower quotes Cicero's case of conscience to this effect: a man takes corn from Alexandria to Rhodes where there is a famine and sells it to the Rhodians at famine prices keeping back from them the fact that on the voyage he had passed ships loaded with provisions making for the famished city, and then he sails away with the profits. But as Verplanck says in his essay on contracts: "It certainly cannot be essential to the making of a fair bargain, that before I can deal with my indolent neighbor, I should communicate to him all my private plans, my long sighted views of the future state of the market, my surmises—in short, all the results of that knowledge and address which have been the hard earned acquisitions of my own industry and activity." It is pointed out that it is neither just to the individual nor is it a wise social policy to follow because it tends to discourage industry and training.[106]

There are, however, several types of cases in which liability has been imposed for failure to disclose facts:

---

[105] Keeton, *Fraud-Concealment and Nondisclosure*, 15 TEX. L. REV. 22-23 (1936). Published originally in 15 TEX. L. REV. 1 (1936). Copyright © 1936 by the Texas Law Review Association. Reprinted by permission.

[106] For a more extensive discussion of the point noted at the end of the Keeton excerpt—that a general duty of disclosure would discourage productive activity, see Kronman, *Mistake, Disclosure, Information, and the Law of Contracts*, 7 J. LEG. STUD. 1 (1978).

(1) Where defendant's affirmative representation was misleading because it was incomplete.[107]

(2) Where defendant, dealing face-to-face with the other party, failed to disclose a fact that was not readily discoverable by the other party and was so basic he would have expected it to have been disclosed. In this situation, silence is a tacit representation of nonexistence of the fact.[108]

(3) Where defendant actively concealed facts from the other party.[109]

(4) Where defendant owed a fiduciary duty to the plaintiff.[110]

The following are two leading cases on the corporate insider's common law duty to disclose to shareholders.

STRONG v. REPIDE
United States Supreme Court
213 U.S. 419 (1909)

[Defendant insider, acting through an agent, purchased plaintiff's stock. Additional facts appear in the opinion.]

Mr. Justice PECKHAM . . . delivered the opinion of the court.

The question in this case . . . is whether . . . it was the duty of the defendant, acting in good faith, to disclose to the agent of the plaintiff the facts bearing upon or which might affect the value of the stock.

If it were conceded, for the purpose of the argument, that the ordinary relations between directors and shareholders in a business corporation are not of such a fiduciary nature as to make it the duty of a director to disclose to a shareholder the general knowledge which he may possess regarding the value of the shares of the company before he purchases any from a shareholder, yet there are cases where, by reason of the special facts, such duty exists. The supreme courts of Kansas and of Georgia have held the relationship existed in the cases before those courts because of the special facts which took them out of the general rule, and that under those facts the director could not purchase from the shareholder his shares without informing him of the facts which affected their value. *Stewart v. Harris*,

---

[107] *See Peek v. Gurney* (1893) L.R. 6 H.L. 377 above; RESTATEMENT (SECOND) TORTS §§ 529, 551(2)(b) (1976).

[108] *See Jim Short Ford Sales, Inc. v. Washington*, 384 So. 2d 83, 86-87 (Ala. 1980); *Rzepka v. Farm Estates, Inc.*, 83 Mich. App. 702, 269 N.W.2d 270 (1978); RESTATEMENT (SECOND) TORTS § 551(2)(e) (1976) (Illustration 3 of which is the classic example of the house riddled with termites); Keeton, *supra*, 15 TEX. L. REV. at 37-38.

[109] *See* RESTATEMENT (SECOND) TORTS § 550 (1976).

[110] *See Hotchkiss v. Fischer*, 136 Kan. 530, 16 P.2d 531 (1932); RESTATEMENT (SECOND) TORTS § 551(2)(a) (1976). For a modern case that refused to recognize a fiduciary duty in this situation, see *Goodman v. Poland*, 395 F. Supp. 660, 678-80 (D. Md. 1975). On the other hand, in *Bailey v. Vaughan*, 359 S.E.2d 599 (W. Va. 1987), the court upheld a cause of action by a shareholder who sold stock to an agent acting for a director as undisclosed principal. The director allegedly failed to disclose offers to buy the company. The court held that a director can be held liable for soliciting the purchase of stock from a shareholder and failing to disclose special information that would influence the value of the stock. The court rationalized the cases denying liability in this situation as not involving special information.

69 Kansas, 498; S.C., 77 Pac. Rep. 277; *Oliver v. Oliver*, 118 Georgia, 362; S.C., 45 S.E. Rep. 232. The case before us is of the same general character. On the other hand, there is the case of *Board of Commissioners v. Reynolds*, 44 Indiana, 509-515, where it was held (after referring to cases) that no relationship of a fiduciary nature exists between a director and a shareholder in a business corporation. Other cases are cited to that effect by counsel for defendant in error. These cases involved only the bare relationship between director and shareholder. It is here sought to make defendant responsible for his actions, not alone and simply in his character as a director, but because, in consideration of all the existing circumstances above detailed, it became the duty of the defendant, acting in good faith, to state the facts before making the purchase. That the defendant was a director of the corporation is but one of the facts upon which the liability is asserted, the existence of all the others in addition making such a combination as rendered it the plain duty of the defendant to speak. He was not only a director, but he owned three-fourths of the shares of its stock, and was, at the time of the purchase of the stock, administrator general of the company, with large powers, and engaged in the negotiations which finally led to the sale of the company's lands (together with all the other friar lands) to the Government at a price which very greatly enhanced the value of the stock. He was the chief negotiator for the sale of all the lands, and was acting substantially as the agent of the shareholders of his company by reason of his ownership of the shares of stock in the corporation and by the acquiescence of all the other shareholders, and the negotiations were for the sale of the whole of the property of the company. By reason of such ownership and agency, and his participation as such owner and agent in the negotiations then going on, no one knew as well as he the exact condition of such negotiations. No one knew as well as he the probability of the sale of the lands to the Government. No one knew as well as he the probable price that might be obtained on such sale. The lands were the only valuable asset owned by the company. Under these circumstances and before the negotiations for the sale were completed the defendant employs an agent to purchase the stock, and conceals from the plaintiff's agent his own identity and his knowledge of the state of the negotiations and their probable result, with which he was familiar as the agent of the shareholders and much of which knowledge he obtained while acting as such agent and by reason thereof. The inference is inevitable that at this time he had concluded to press the negotiations for a sale of the lands to a successful conclusion, else why would he desire to purchase more shares which, if no sale went through, were, in his opinion, worthless, because of the failure of the Government to properly protect the lands in the hands of their then owners? The agent of the plaintiff was ignorant in regard to the state of the negotiations for the sale of the land, which negotiations and their probable result were a most material fact affecting the value of the shares of stock of the company, and he would not have sold them at the price he did had he known the actual state of the negotiations as to the lands and that it was the defendant who was seeking to purchase the stock. Concealing his identity when procuring the purchase of the stock, by his agent, was in itself strong evidence of fraud on the part of the defendant. Why did he not ask Jones,* who

---

*   [Plaintiff's agent.—Ed.]

occupied an adjoining office, if he would sell? But by concealing his identity he could by such means the more easily avoid any questions relative to the negotiations for the sale of the lands and their probable result, and could also avoid any actual misrepresentations on that subject, which he evidently thought were necessary in his case to constitute a fraud. He kept up the concealment as long as he could, by giving the check of a third person for the purchase money. Evidence that he did so was objected to on the ground that it could not possibly even tend to prove that the prior consent to sell had been procured by the subsequent check given in payment. That was not its purpose. Of course, the giving of the check could not have induced the prior consent, but it was proper evidence as tending to show that the concealment of identity was not a mere inadvertent omission, an omission without any fraudulent or deceitful intent, but was a studied and intentional omission to be characterized as part of the deceitful machinations to obtain the purchase without giving any information whatever as to the state and probable result of the negotiations, to the vendor of the stock, and to in that way obtain the same at a lower price. After the purchase of the stock he continued his negotiations for the sale of the lands, and finally, he says, as administrator general of the company, under the special authority of the shareholders, and as attorney in fact he entered into the contract of sale December 21, 1903. The whole transaction gives conclusive evidence of the overwhelming influence defendant had in the course of the negotiations as owner of a majority of the stock and as agent for the other owners, and it is clear that the final consummation was in his hands at all times. If under all these facts he purchased the stock from the plaintiff, the law would indeed be impotent if the sale could not be set aside or the defendant cast in damages for his fraud.

The Supreme Court of the islands, in holding that there was no fraud in the purchase, said that the responsibility of the directors of a corporation to the individual stockholders did not extend beyond the corporate property actually under the control of the directors; that they did not owe any duty to the members in respect to their individual stock, which would prevent them from purchasing the same in the usual manner. While this may in general be true, we think it is not an accurate statement of the case, regard being had to the facts above mentioned.

* * *

GOODWIN v. AGASSIZ
Massachusetts Supreme Judicial Court
283 Mass. 358, 186 N.E. 659 (1933)

RUGG, Chief Justice. A stockholder in a corporation seeks in this suit relief for losses suffered by him in selling shares of stock in Cliff Mining Company by way of accounting, rescission of sales, or redelivery of shares.

* * *

. . . The facts thus displayed are these: The defendants, in May, 1926, purchased through brokers on the Boston stock exchange seven hundred shares of stock of the Cliff Mining Company which up to that time the plaintiff had owned. Agassiz was president and director and MacNaughton a director and general manager of the company. They had certain knowledge, material as to the value of the stock, which the plaintiff did not have. The plaintiff contends that such purchase in all the circumstances without disclosure to him of that knowledge was a wrong against him. That knowledge was that an experienced geologist had formulated in writing in March, 1926, a theory as to the possible existence of copper deposits under conditions prevailing in the region where the property of the company was located. That region was known as the mineral belt in Northern Michigan, where are located mines of several copper mining companies. Another such company, of which the defendants were officers, had made extensive geological surveys of its lands. In consequence of recommendations resulting from that survey, exploration was started on property of the Cliff Mining Company in 1925. That exploration was ended in May, 1926, because completed unsuccessfully, and the equipment was removed. The defendants discussed the geologist's theory shortly after it was formulated. Both felt that the theory had value and should be tested, but they agreed that, before starting to test it, options should be obtained by another copper company of which they were officers on land adjacent to or nearby in the copper belt, that if the geologist's theory were known to the owners of such other land there might be difficulty in securing options, and that theory should not be communicated to any one unless it became absolutely necessary. Thereafter, options were secured which, if taken up, would involve a large expenditure by the other company. The defendants both thought, also that, if there was any merit in the geologist's theory, the price of Cliff Mining Company stock in the market would go up. Its stock was quoted and bought and sold on the Boston Stock Exchange. Pursuant to agreement, they bought many shares of that stock through agents on joint account. The plaintiff first learned of the closing of exploratory operations on property of the Cliff Mining Company from an article in a paper on May 15, 1926, and immediately sold his shares of stock through brokers. It does not appear that the defendants were in any way responsible for the publication of that article. The plaintiff did not know that the purchase was made for the defendants and they did not know that his stock was being bought for them. There was no communication between them touching the subject. The plaintiff would not have sold his stock if he had known of the geologist's theory. The finding is express that the defendants were not guilty of fraud, that they committed no breach of duty owed by them to the Cliff Mining Company, and that that company was not harmed by the nondisclosure of the geologist's theory, or by their purchases of its stock, or by shutting down the exploratory operations.

The contention of the plaintiff is that the purchase of his stock in the company by the defendants without disclosing to him as a stockholder their knowledge of the geologist's theory, their belief that the theory was true, had value, the keeping secret the existence of the theory, discontinuance by the defendants of exploratory operations begun in 1925 on property of the Cliff Mining Company and their plan ultimately to test the value of the theory, constitute actionable wrong for which he as stockholder can recover.

The trial judge ruled that conditions may exist which would make it the duty of an officer of a corporation purchasing its stock from a stockholder to inform him as to knowledge possessed by the buyer and not by the seller, but found, on all the circumstances developed by the trial and set out at some length by him in his decision, that there was no fiduciary relation requiring such disclosure by the defendants to the plaintiff before buying his stock in the manner in which they did.

The question presented is whether the decree dismissing the bill rightly was entered on the facts found.

The directors of a commercial corporation stand in a relation of trust to the corporation and are bound to exercise the strictest good faith in respect to its property and business. . . . The contention that directors also occupy the position of trustee toward individual stockholders in the corporation is plainly contrary to repeated decisions of this court and cannot be supported.

* * *

The principle thus established is supported by an imposing weight of authority in other jurisdictions. . . . A rule holding that directors are trustees for individual stockholders with respect to their stock prevails in comparatively few states; but in view of our own adjudications it is not necessary to review decisions to that effect. . . .

While the general principle is as stated, circumstances may exist requiring that transactions between a director and a stockholder as to stock in the corporation be set aside. The knowledge naturally in the possession of a director as to the condition of a corporation places upon him a peculiar obligation to observe every requirement of fair dealing when directly buying or selling its stock. Mere silence does not usually amount to a breach of duty, but parties may stand in such relation to each other that an equitable responsibility arises to communicate facts. . . . Purchases and sales of stock dealt in on the stock exchange are commonly impersonal affairs. An honest director would be in a difficult situation if he could neither buy nor sell on the stock exchange shares of stock in his corporation without first seeking out the other actual ultimate party to the transaction and disclosing to him everything which a court or jury might later find that he then knew affecting the real or speculative value of such shares. Business of that nature is a matter to be governed by practical rules. Fiduciary obligations of directors ought not to be made so onerous that men of experience and ability will be deterred from accepting such office. Law in its sanctions is not coextensive with morality. It cannot undertake to put all parties to every contract on an equality as to knowledge, experience, skill and shrewdness. It cannot undertake to relieve against hard bargains made between competent parties without fraud. On the other hand, directors cannot rightly be allowed to indulge with impunity in practices which do violence to prevailing standards of upright business men. Therefore, where a director personally seeks a stockholder for the purpose of buying his shares without making disclosure of material facts within his peculiar knowledge and not within reach of the stockholder, the transaction will be closely scrutinized and relief may be granted in appropriate instances. *Strong v. Repide*, 213 U.S. 419, 29 S. Ct. 521, 53 L. Ed. 853. . . .

* * *

The precise question to be decided in the case at bar is whether on the facts found the defendants as directors had a right to buy stock of the plaintiff, a stockholder. Every element of actual fraud or misdoing by the defendants is negatived by the findings. . . . The facts found afford no ground for inferring fraud or conspiracy. The only knowledge possessed by the defendants not open to the plaintiff was the existence of a theory formulated in a thesis by a geologist as to the possible existence of copper deposits where certain geological conditions existed common to the property of the Cliff Mining Company and that of other mining companies in its neighborhood. This thesis did not express an opinion that copper deposits would be found at any particular spot or on property of any specified owner. Whether that theory was sound or fallacious, no one knew, and so far as appears has never been demonstrated. The defendants made no representations to anybody about the theory. No facts found placed upon them any obligation to disclose the theory. A few days after the thesis expounding the theory was brought to the attention of the defendants, the annual report by the directors of the Cliff Mining Company for the calendar year 1925, signed by Agassiz for the directors, was issued. It did not cover the time when the theory was formulated. The report described the status of the operations under the exploration which had been begun in 1925. At the annual meeting of the stockholders of the company held early in April, 1926, no reference was made to the theory. It was then at most a hope, possibly an expectation. It had not passed the nebulous stage. No disclosure was made of it. The Cliff Mining Company was not harmed by the nondisclosure. There would have been no advantage to it, so far as appears, from a disclosure. The disclosure would have been detrimental to the interests of another mining corporation in which the defendants were directors. In the circumstances there was no duty on the part of the defendants to set forth to the stockholders at the annual meeting their faith, aspirations and plans for the future. Events as they developed might render advisable radical changes in such views. Disclosure of the theory, if it ultimately was proved to be erroneous or without foundation in fact, might involve the defendants in litigation with those who might act on the hypothesis that it was correct. The stock of the Cliff Mining Company was bought and sold on the stock exchange. The identity of buyers and seller of the stock in question in fact was not known to the parties and perhaps could not readily have been ascertained. The defendants caused the shares to be bought through brokers on the stock exchange. They said nothing to anybody as to the reasons actuating them. The plaintiff was no novice. He was a member of the Boston stock exchange and had kept a record of sales of Cliff Mining Company stock. He acted upon his own judgment in selling his stock. He made no inquiries of the defendants or of other officers of the company. The result is that the plaintiff cannot prevail.

Decree dismissing bill affirmed with costs.

NOTES AND QUESTIONS

(1) **Remedy for insider trading in face-to-face transactions.** *Strong* and *Goodwin* mark a departure from the traditional common law rule that directors owed no fiduciary duty to shareholders with respect to transactions in the corporation's shares. However, the "special facts" rule endorsed in the two cases is not a general duty on the part of directors to refrain from insider trading. Among other things, *Goodwin* makes clear that the "special facts" rule does not apply when directors buy or sell shares over an exchange, rather than in face-to-face transactions with shareholders.

(2) **Insider trading and public securities markets.** In order to fully understand *Goodwin* and the federal cases discussed in Section 12.05 below, it is important to keep in mind that, on public securities markets, buyers and sellers do not know with whom

they are dealing. If the stock is listed for trading on an exchange, an investor's order is usually relayed to a broker on the floor who goes to the "post" where that stock is traded. At the post the broker either directly matches her customer's order with one held by another broker or gives the order to the securities trader who is the "specialist" for the stock. The specialist uses an order "book" to match buy ("bid") and sell ("offer") orders and also buys and sells for her own account. Exchange rules requiring the specialist to maintain an orderly market occasionally may mean that the specialist buys or sells for her own account. If the stock is traded "over-the-counter," the broker punches a request for information into a "NASDAQ" (National Association of Securities Dealers Automated Quotation System) terminal, which displays bids and offers of securities firms that are "making a market" in the stock. The broker then telephones a particular market maker and executes the transaction with him. NASDAQ market makers thus perform the same function for over-the-counter stocks as do specialists for listed stocks— that is, matching buy and sell orders as agents and buying and selling for their own accounts to make an orderly market.

[B] Liability to the Corporation

Insider traders occasionally have been held liable to their corporations under state law. In the leading case of *Diamond v. Oreamuno*,[111] the court upheld a derivative complaint seeking insider profits realized from a sale prior to the disclosure of negative information. The court relied on the agent's duty to account for profits from use of the employer's property, including information (*see* Section 9.06), and on the fact that insider trading may damage the corporation by adversely affecting its public image and the marketability of its stock. The *Diamond* court relied in part on *Brophy v. Cities Service Co.*,[112] which upheld a complaint alleging that an insider had purchased his company's stock knowing that the company was about to buy a substantial quantity of its own stock and then sold on the subsequent rise in price caused by the company's purchases. (Is this situation distinguishable from that in *Diamond*?)

The *Diamond* theory of liability was applied in *Schein v. Chasen*,[113] to the tipping of inside information by an insider, but that result was eventually overturned.[114] *Diamond* was held inapplicable to trading by non-insiders in *Walton v. Morgan Stanley & Co.*[115] and *Frigitemp Corp. v. Financial Dynamics Fund*.[116] It was also held inapplica-

---

[111] 24 N.Y.2d 494, 301 N.Y.S.2d 78, 248 N.E.2d 910 (1969).

[112] 31 Del. Ch. 241, 70 A.2d 5 (1949).

[113] 478 F.2d 817 (2d Cir. 1973).

[114] *Schein* was vacated by the Supreme Court pending resolution of the issue by the Florida Supreme Court (*Lehman Brothers v. Schein*, 416 U.S. 386 (1974)). The Florida court refused to recognize a cause of action in this situation (*Schein v. Chasen*, 313 So. 2d 739 (Fla. 1975)), and the judgment for defendants in the federal district court was accordingly affirmed (*Schein v. Chasen*, 519 F.2d 453 (2d Cir. 1975)).

[115] 623 F.2d 796 (2d Cir. 1980).

[116] 524 F.2d 275 (2d Cir. 1975).

ble to insider trading that did not involve material non-public information in *Thomas v. Roblin Industries, Inc.*[117] Finally, *Diamond* was wholly rejected in *Freeman v. Decio.*[118] For a discussion of the *Diamond* theory and its history in the courts, see **Hazen**.

Note that there is some question as to whether plaintiff must show that the corporation has been harmed, and what harm must be shown. In *Frankel v. Slotkin,*[119] the court in an action under New Jersey common law granted summary judgment against a derivative plaintiff and for insiders who allegedly bought the corporation's stock on the basis of inside information, holding that the plaintiff had failed adequately to allege injury to the corporation.

ALI *Principles* § 5.04 states a general rule against insider misuse of "corporate property, material non-public corporate information, or corporate position" to secure a pecuniary benefit. For the application of these rules to trading securities on inside information, see Comment d(2) to ALI *Principles* § 5.04. The liability is waivable by the company, except to the extent that the liability is incurred in connection with a violation of law, such as trading in the corporation's securities through the use of inside information. The corporation therefore could allocate the benefit from the information, like other corporate benefits, to the insider in the nature of compensation.

ALI *Principles* § 5.04 permits actions not only by the corporation, but also by shareholders with whom the insider deals. The remedy is available whether or not the insider has "special facts" (*see Strong v. Repide*; Section 12.04[A]), and whether or not the transaction is impersonal (*compare Goodwin v. Agassiz*; Section 12.04[A]). But Comment c(5) to § 5.04 suggests that the shareholder can sue only if "directly harmed . . . by the improper conduct (for example, through purchase of shares . . . by the director or senior executive . . . .)." Is the trading shareholder's action based on the same theory as the corporation's action? What should happen to the shareholder's action if the corporation has authorized the insider's trade?

REFERENCE

Hazen, *Corporate Insider Trading: Reawakening the Common Law*, 39 WASH. & LEE L. REV. 845 (1982).

---

[117] 520 F.2d 1393 (3d Cir. 1975).

[118] 584 F.2d 186 (7th Cir. 1978).

[119] 984 F.2d 1328 (2d Cir. 1993).

§ 12.05 Regulation of Insider Trading under § 10(b) and Rule 10b-5

[A] Basic Rule: Trading by Insiders in Shares of Their Companies

In *Cady, Roberts & Co.*,[120] the SEC first explicitly recognized a federal duty to refrain from insider trading. In *Cady*, the SEC disciplined a broker who had made open-market sales of stock in the Curtiss-Wright Corporation for the accounts of his wife and several customers, holding that these sales constituted violations of § 10(b), Rule 10b-5 and § 17(a) of the 1933 Act. The broker had acted immediately after learning by telephone from a member of the Curtiss-Wright board, who was also a member of the selling broker's firm, that the board had reduced the Curtiss-Wright dividend. The SEC, in an opinion by Chairman William Cary, stated in part:

> We have already noted that the anti-fraud provisions are phrased in terms of "any person" and that a special obligation has been traditionally required of corporate insiders, *e.g.*, officers, directors and controlling stockholders. These three groups, however, do not exhaust the classes of persons upon whom there is such an obligation. Analytically, the obligation rests on two principal elements: first, the existence of a relationship giving access, directly or indirectly, to information intended to be available only for a corporate purpose and not for the personal benefit of anyone, and second, the inherent unfairness involved where a party takes advantage of such information knowing it is unavailable to those with whom he is dealing. . . . Intimacy demands restraint lest the uninformed be exploited.

The obligation recognized in *Cady, Roberts* arguably goes beyond state law liability for insider trading. (*See* Section 12.04 and, particularly, *Goodwin v. Agassiz*.) What justifies this broad federal duty? If there is a federal interest in a fair and fully informed securities market, why limit the duty to those with "access"? Why not a general duty not to trade on unequal information? These questions are discussed in Subsection 12.05[D]. *Cady* left open several questions about the scope of the new federal obligation:

> (1) When is the information material? What about information that is less significant than the unexpected dividend cut in *Cady*?
>
> (2) When is the information nonpublic? In *Cady*, the broker clearly intended to "beat the market." What if the information was already circulating to some extent, or if the trader reasonably believed it was?
>
> (3) Who owes a duty? The information in *Cady* was tipped by a director, some of the sales were for the benefit of the tipper-director's customers, and all of the sales had some connection with tipper-director's firm. Does the

---

[120] 40 S.E.C. 907 (1961).

proscription necessarily travel with the information in the sense that anyone who receives the information, directly or indirectly, is forbidden from using it? Does the duty extend to others who are neither insiders in the firm whose stock they are trading nor tippees of insiders?

These questions are addressed in the following cases.

SEC v. TEXAS GULF SULPHUR CO.
United States Court of Appeals, Second Circuit
401 F.2d 833 (1968) (en banc), *cert. denied*, 394 U.S. 976 (1969)

[This action for injunctive and other relief was brought against Texas Gulf Sulphur Company (TGS) and a number of TGS officers, directors and employees. The SEC claimed violations of § 10(b) and Rule 10b-5 in connection with (1) an allegedly misleading April 12 press release issued by TGS; and (2) trading and tipping by the insiders. The part of the opinion excerpted here deals with the insider trading issue.]

WATERMAN, Circuit Judge:

THE FACTUAL SETTING

This action derives from the exploratory activities of TGS begun in 1957 on the Canadian Shield in eastern Canada. In March of 1959, aerial geophysical surveys were conducted over more than 15,000 square miles of this area by a group led by defendant Mollison, a mining engineer and a Vice President of TGS. The group included defendant Holyk, TGS's chief geologist, defendant Clayton, an electrical engineer and geophysicist, and defendant Darke, a geologist. These operations resulted in the detection of numerous anomalies, *i.e.*, extraordinary variations in the conductivity of rocks, one of which was on the Kidd 55 segment of land located near Timmins, Ontario.

On October 29 and 30, 1963, Clayton conducted a ground geophysical survey on the northeast portion of the Kidd 55 segment which confirmed the presence of an anomaly and indicated the necessity of diamond core drilling for further evaluation. Drilling of the initial hole, K-55-1, at the strongest part of the anomaly was commenced on November 8 and terminated on November 12 at a depth of 655 feet. Visual estimates by Holyk of the core of K-55-1 indicated an average copper content of 1.15% and an average zinc content of 8.64% over a length of 599 feet. This visual estimate convinced TGS that it was desirable to acquire the remainder of the Kidd 55 segment, and in order to facilitate this acquisition TGS President Stephens instructed the exploration group to keep the results of K-55-1 confidential and undisclosed even as to other officers, directors, and employees of TGS. The hole was concealed and a barren core was intentionally drilled off the anomaly. Meanwhile, the core of K-55-1 had been shipped to Utah for chemical assay which, when received in early December, revealed an average mineral content of 1.18% copper, 8.26% zinc, and 3.94% ounces of silver per ton over a length of 602 feet. These results were so remarkable that neither Clayton, an experienced geophysicist, nor four other TGS expert witnesses, had ever seen or heard of a comparable initial exploratory drill hole in a base metal deposit. So, the trial court concluded, "There is no doubt that the drill core of K-55-1 was unusually good and that it excited the interest and speculation of those who knew about it." By March 27, 1964, TGS decided that the land acquisition program had advanced to such a point that the company might well resume drilling, and drilling was resumed on March 31.

During this period, from November 12, 1963 when K-55-1 was completed, to March 31, 1964 when drilling was resumed, certain of the individual defendants . . . and persons . . . said to have received "tips" from them, purchased TGS stock or calls thereon. Prior to these transactions these persons had owned 1135 shares of TGS stock and possessed no calls; thereafter they owned a total of 8235 shares and possessed 12,300 calls.

On February 20, 1964, also during this period, TGS issued stock options to 26 of its officers and employees whose salaries exceeded a specified amount five of whom were the individual defendants Stephens, Fogarty, Mollison, Holyk, and Kline. Of these, only Kline was unaware of the detailed results of K-55-1, but he, too, knew that a hole containing favorable bodies of copper and zinc ore had been drilled in Timmins. At this time, neither the TGS Stock Option Committee nor its Board of Directors had been informed of the results of K-55-1, presumably because of the pending land acquisition program which required confidentiality. All of the foregoing defendants accepted the options granted them.

When drilling was resumed on March 31, hole K-55-3 was commenced 510 feet west of K-55-1 and was drilled easterly at a 457 angle so as to cross K-55-1 in a vertical plane. Daily progress reports of the drilling of this hole K-55-3 and of all subsequently drilled holes were sent to defendants Stephens and Fogarty (President and Executive Vice President of TGS) by Holyk and Mollison. Visual estimates of K-55-3 revealed an average mineral content of 1.12% copper and 7.93% zinc over 641 of the hole's 876-foot length. On April 7, drilling of a third hole, K-55-4, 200 feet south of and parallel to K-55-1 and westerly at a 457 angle, was commenced and mineralization was encountered over 366 of its 579-foot length. Visual estimates indicated an average content of 1.14% copper and 8.24% zinc. Like K-55-1, both K-55-3 and K-55-4 established substantial copper mineralization on the eastern edge of the anomaly. On the basis of these findings relative to the foregoing drilling results, the trial court concluded that the vertical plane created by the intersection of K-55-1 and K-55-3, which measured at least 350 feet wide by 500 feet deep extended southward 200 feet to its intersection with K-55-4, and that "There was real evidence that a body of commercially mineable ore might exist."

On April 8, TGS began with a second drill rig to drill another hole, K-55-6, 300 feet easterly of K-55-1. This hole was drilled westerly at an angle of 607 and was intended to explore mineralization beneath K-55-1. While no visual estimates of its core were immediately available, it was readily apparent by the evening of April 10 that substantial copper mineralization had been encountered over the last 127 feet of the hole's 569-foot length. On April 10, a third drill rig commenced drilling yet another hole, K-55-5, 200 feet north of K-55-1, parallel to the prior holes, and slanted westerly at a 457 angle. By the evening of April 10 in this hole, too, substantial copper mineralization had been encountered over the last 42 feet of its 97-foot length.

Meanwhile, rumors that a major ore strike was in the making had been circulating throughout Canada. On the morning of Saturday, April 11, Stephens at his home in Greenwich, Conn. read in the New York Herald Tribune and in the New York Times unauthorized reports of the TGS drilling which seemed to infer a rich strike from the fact that the drill cores had been flown to the United States for chemical assay. Stephens immediately contacted Fogarty at his home in Rye, N.Y., who in turn telephoned and later that day visited Mollison at Mollison's home in Greenwich to obtain a current report and evaluation of the drilling progress. The following morning, Sunday, Fogarty again telephoned Mollison, inquiring whether Mollison had any further information and told him to return to Timmins with Holyk, the TGS Chief Geologist, as soon as possible "to move things along." With the aid of one Carroll, a public relations consultant, Fogarty drafted a press release designed to quell the rumors, which release, after having been channeled through Stephens and Huntington, a TGS attorney, was issued at 3:00 P.M. on Sunday, April 12, and which appeared in the morning newspapers of general circulation on Monday, April 13. It read in pertinent part as follows:

> NEW YORK, April 12—The following statement was made today by Dr. Charles F. Fogarty, executive vice president of Texas Gulf Sulphur Company, in regard to the company's drilling operations near Timmins, Ontario, Canada. Dr. Fogarty said:
>
> During the past few days, the exploration activities of Texas Gulf Sulphur in the area of Timmins, Ontario, have been widely reported in the press, coupled with rumors of a substantial copper discovery there. These reports exaggerate the scale of operations, and mention plans and statistics of size and grade of ore that are without factual basis and have evidently originated by speculation of people not connected with TGS.
>
> The facts are as follows. TGS has been exploring in the Timmins area for six years as part of its overall search in Canada and elsewhere for various minerals—lead, copper, zinc, etc. During the course of this work, in Timmins as well as in Eastern Canada, TGS has conducted exploration entirely on its own, without the participation by others. Numerous prospects have been investigated by geophysical means and a large number of selected ones have been core-drilled. These cores are sent to the United States for assay and detailed examination as a matter of routine and on advice of expert Canadian legal counsel. No inferences as to grade can be drawn from this procedure.
>
> Most of the areas drilled in Eastern Canada have revealed either barren pyrite or graphite without value; a few have resulted in discoveries of small or marginal sulphide ore bodies.
>
> Recent drilling on one property near Timmins has led to preliminary indications that more drilling would be required for proper evaluation of this prospect. The drilling done to date has not been conclusive, but the statements made by many outside quarters are unreliable and include information and figures that are not available to TGS.
>
> The work done to date has not been sufficient to reach definite conclusions and any statement as to size and grade of ore would be premature and possibly misleading. When we have progressed to the point where reasonable and logical conclusions can be made, TGS will issue a definite

statement to its stockholders and to the public in order to clarify the Timmins project.

* * *

The release purported to give the Timmins drilling results as of the release date, April 12. From Mollison, Fogarty had been told of the developments through 7:00 P.M. on April 10, and of the remarkable discoveries made up to that time, detailed supra, which discoveries, according to the calculations of the experts who testified for the SEC at the hearing, demonstrated that TGS had already discovered 6.2 to 8.3 million tons of proven ore having gross assay values from $26 to $29 per ton. TGS experts, on the other hand, denied at the hearing that proven or probable ore could have been calculated on April 11 or 12 because there was then no assurance of continuity in the mineralized zone.

The evidence as to the effect of this release on the investing public was equivocal and less than abundant. On April 13 the New York Herald Tribune in an article head-noted "Copper Rumor Deflated" quoted from the TGS release of April 12 and backtracked from its original April 11 report of a major strike but nevertheless inferred from the TGS release that "recent mineral exploratory activity near Timmins, Ontario, has provided preliminary favorable results, sufficient at least to require a step-up in drilling operations." Some witnesses who testified at the hearing stated that they found the release encouraging. On the other hand, a Canadian mining security specialist, Roche, stated that "earlier in the week [before April 16] we had a Dow Jones saying that they [TGS] didn't have anything basically," and a TGS stock specialist for the Midwest Stock Exchange became concerned about his long position in the stock after reading the release. The trial court stated only that "While, in retrospect, the press release may appear gloomy or incomplete, this does not make it misleading or deceptive on the basis of the facts then known."

* * *

While drilling activity ensued to completion, TGS officials were taking steps toward ultimate disclosure of the discovery. On April 13, a previously-invited reporter for *The Northern Miner*, a Canadian mining industry journal, visited the drillsite, interviewed Mollison, Holyk and Darke, and prepared an article which confirmed a 10 million ton ore strike. This report, after having been submitted to Mollison and returned to the reporter unamended on April 15, was published in the April 16 issue. A statement relative to the extent of the discovery, in substantial part drafted by Mollison, was given to the Ontario Minister of Mines for release to the Canadian media. Mollison and Holyk expected it to be released over the airways at 11 P.M. on April 15th, but, for undisclosed reasons, it was not released until 9:40 A.M. on the 16th. An official detailed statement, announcing a strike of at least 25 million tons of ore, based on the drilling data set forth above, was read to representatives of American financial media from 10:00 A.M. to 10:10 or 10:15 A.M. on April 16, and appeared over Merrill Lynch's private wire at 10:29 A.M. and, somewhat later than expected, over the Dow Jones ticker tape at 10:54 A.M.

* * *

During the period of drilling in Timmins, the market price of TGS stock fluctuated but steadily gained overall. On Friday, November 8, when the drilling began, the stock closed at

17 3/8; on Friday, November 15, after K-55-1 had been completed, it closed at 18. After a slight decline to 16 3/8 by Friday, November 22, the price rose to 20 7/8 by December 13, when the chemical assay results of K-55-1 were received, and closed at a high of 24 1/8 on February 21, the day after the stock options had been issued. It had reached a price of 26 by March 31, after the land acquisition program had been completed and drilling had been resumed, and continued to ascend to 30 1/8 by the close of trading on April 10, at which time the drilling progress up to then was evaluated for the April 12th press release. On April 13, the day on which the April 12 release was disseminated, TGS opened at 30 1/8, rose immediately to a high of 32 and gradually tapered off to close at 30 7/8. It closed at 30 1/4 the next day, and at 29 3/8 on April 15. On April 16, the day of the official announcement of the Timmins discovery, the price climbed to a high of 37 and closed at 36 3/8. By May 15, TGS stock was selling at 58 1/4.

[The trial court held that only defendants Clayton and Crawford had violated Rule 10b-5 since the drilling results were not material until April 9, only Clayton, Crawford and Coates traded after that date, and Coates' trade followed public disclosure.].

I. THE INDIVIDUAL DEFENDANTS

A. Introductory

* * *

Rule 10b-5 was promulgated pursuant to the grant of authority given the SEC by Congress in Section 10(b) of the Securities Exchange Act of 1934 (15 U.S.C. § 78j(b)). By that Act Congress purposed to prevent inequitable and unfair practices and to insure fairness in securities transactions generally, whether conducted face-to-face, over the counter, or on exchanges. . . .

* * *

The Act and the Rule apply to the transactions here, all of which were consummated on exchanges. . . . Whether predicated on traditional fiduciary concepts, *see, e.g., Hotchkiss v. Fisher*, 136 Kan. 530, 16 P.2d 531 (Kan.1932), or on the "special facts" doctrine, *see, e.g., Strong v. Repide*, 213 U.S. 419, 29 S. Ct. 521, 53 L. Ed. 853 (1909), the Rule is based in policy on the justifiable expectation of the securities marketplace that all investors trading on impersonal exchanges have relatively equal access to material information. . . . The essence of the Rule is that anyone who, trading for his own account in the securities of a corporation has "access, directly or indirectly, to information intended to be available only for a corporate purpose and not for the personal benefit of anyone" may not take "advantage of such information knowing it is unavailable to those with whom he is dealing," *i.e.*, the investing public. *Matter of Cady, Roberts & Co.*, 40 SEC 907, 912 (1961). Insiders, as directors or management officers are, of course, by this Rule, precluded from so unfairly dealing, but the Rule is also applicable to one possessing the information who may not be strictly termed an "insider" within the meaning of Sec. 16(b) of the Act. *Cady, Roberts, supra*. Thus, anyone in possession of material inside information must either disclose it to the investing public, or, if he is disabled from disclosing it in order to protect a corporate confidence, or he chooses not to do so, must abstain from trading in or recommending the securities concerned while such inside information remains undisclosed. So, it is here no justification for insider activity that disclosure was forbidden by the legitimate corporate objective of acquiring options to purchase the land surrounding the exploration site; if the information was, as the SEC contends, material, its possessors should have kept out of the market until disclosure was accomplished. *Cady, Roberts, supra* at 911.

B. Material Inside Information

An insider is not, of course, always foreclosed from investing in his own company merely because he may be more familiar with company operations than are outside investors. An insider's duty to disclose information or his duty to abstain from dealing in his company's securities arises only in "those situations which are essentially extraordinary in nature and which are reasonably certain to have a substantial effect on the market price of the security if [the extraordinary situation is] disclosed." Fleischer, *Securities Trading and Corporate Information Practices: The Implications of the Texas Gulf Sulphur Proceeding*, 51 VA. L. REV. 1271, 1289.

Nor is an insider obligated to confer upon outside investors the benefit of his superior financial or other expert analysis by disclosing his educated guesses or predictions.

* * *

The only regulatory objective is that access to material information be enjoyed equally, but this objective requires nothing more than the disclosure of basic facts so that outsiders may draw upon their own evaluative expertise in reaching their own investment decisions with knowledge equal to that of the insiders.

This is not to suggest, however, as did the trial court, that "the test of materiality must necessarily be a conservative one, particularly since many actions under Section 10(b) are brought on the basis of hindsight," 258 F. Supp. 262 at 280, in the sense that the materiality of facts is to be assessed solely by measuring the effect the knowledge of the facts would have upon prudent or conservative investors. As we stated in *List v. Fashion Park, Inc.*, 340 F.2d 457, 462, "The basic test of materiality . . . is whether a *reasonable* man would attach importance . . . in determining his choice of action in the transaction in question . . . ." (Emphasis supplied.) This, of course, encompasses any fact "which in reasonable and objective contemplation *might* affect the value of the corporation's stock or securities . . . ." *List v. Fashion Park, Inc., supra* at 462, quoting from *Kohler v. Kohler Co.*, 319 F.2d 634, 642, 7 A.L.R.3d 486 (7 Cir. 1963). (Emphasis supplied.) Such a fact is a material fact and must be effectively disclosed to the investing public prior to the commencement of insider trading in the corporation's securities. The speculators and chartists of Wall and Bay Streets are also "reasonable" investors entitled to the same legal protection afforded conservative traders. Thus, material facts include not only information disclosing the earnings and distributions of a company but also those facts which affect the probable future of the company and those which may affect the desire of investors to buy, sell, or hold the company's securities.

In each case, then, whether facts are material within Rule 10b-5 when the facts relate to a particular event and are undisclosed by those persons who are knowledgeable thereof will depend at any given time upon a balancing of both the indicated probability that the event will occur and the anticipated magnitude of the event in light of the totality of the company activity. Here, notwithstanding the trial court's conclusion that the results of the first drill core, K-55-1, were "too 'remote' . . . to have had any significant impact on the market, *i.e.*, to be deemed material," 258 F. Supp. at 283, knowledge of the possibility, which surely was more than marginal, of the existence of a mine of the vast magnitude indicated by the remarkably rich drill core located rather close to the surface (suggesting mineability by the less expensive open-pit method) within the confines of a large anomaly (suggesting an extensive region of mineralization) might well have affected the price of TGS stock and would certainly have been an important fact to a reasonable, if speculative, investor in deciding whether he should buy, sell, or hold. After all, this first drill core was "unusually good and . . . excited the interest and speculation of those who knew about it." 258 F. Supp. at 282.

Our disagreement with the district judge on the issue does not, then, go to his findings of basic fact, as to which the "clearly erroneous" rule would apply, but to his understanding of the legal standard applicable to them. . . . Our survey of the facts found below conclusively establishes that knowledge of the results of the discovery hole, K-55-1, would have been important to a reasonable investor and might have affected the price of the stock.[12]

On April 16, The Northern Miner, a trade publication in wide circulation among mining stock specialists, called K-55-1, the discovery hole, "one of the most impressive drill holes completed in modern times." Roche, a Canadian broker whose firm specialized in mining securities, characterized the importance to investors of the results of K-55-1. He stated that the completion of "the first drill hole" with "a 600 foot drill core is very very significant . . . anything over 200 feet is considered very significant and 600 feet is just beyond your wildest imagination." He added, however, that it "is a natural thing to buy more stock once they give you the first drill hole." Additional testimony revealed that the prices of stocks of other companies, albeit less diversified, smaller firms, had increased substantially solely on the basis of the discovery of good anomalies or even because of the proximity of their lands to the situs of a potentially major strike.

Finally, a major factor in determining whether the K-55-1 discovery was a material fact is the importance attached to the drilling results by those who knew about it. In view of other unrelated recent developments favorably affecting TGS, participation by an informed person in a regular stock-purchase program, or even sporadic trading by an informed person, might lend only nominal support to the inference of the materiality of the K-55-1 discovery; nevertheless, the timing by those who knew of it of their stock purchases and their purchases of short-term calls—purchases in some cases by individuals who had never before purchased calls or even TGS stock—virtually compels the inference that the insiders were influenced by the drilling results. This insider trading activity, which surely constitutes highly pertinent evidence and the only truly objective evidence of the materiality of the K-55-1 discovery, was apparently disregarded by the court below in favor of the testimony of defendants' expert witnesses, all of whom "agreed that one drill core does not establish an

---

[12] We do not suggest that material facts must be disclosed immediately; the timing of disclosure is a matter for the business judgment of the corporate officers entrusted with the management of the corporation within the affirmative disclosure requirements promulgated by the exchanges and by the SEC. Here, a valuable corporate purpose was served by delaying the publication of the K-55-1 discovery. We do intend to convey, however, that where a corporate purpose is thus served by withholding the news of a material fact, those persons who are thus quite properly true to their corporate trust must not during the period of non-disclosure deal personally in the corporation's securities or give to outsiders confidential information not generally available to all the corporations' stockholders and to the public at large.

ore body, much less a mine," 258 F. Supp. at 282-283. Significantly, however, the court below, while relying upon what these defense experts said the defendant insiders ought to have thought about the worth to TGS of the K-55-1 discovery, and finding that from November 12, 1963 to April 6, 1964 Fogarty, Murray, Holyk and Darke spent more than $100,000 in purchasing TGS stock and calls on that stock, made no finding that the insiders were motivated by any factor other than the extraordinary K-55-1 discovery when they bought their stock and their calls. No reason appears why outside investors, perhaps better acquainted with speculative modes of investment and with, in many cases, perhaps more capital at their disposal for intelligent speculation, would have been less influenced, and would not have been similarly motivated to invest if they had known what the insider investors knew about the K-55-1 discovery.

Our decision to expand the limited protection afforded outside investors by the trial court's narrow definition of materiality is not at all shaken by fears that the elimination of insider trading benefits will deplete the ranks of capable corporate managers by taking away an incentive to accept such employment. Such benefits, in essence, are forms of secret corporate compensation, . . . derived at the expense of the uninformed investing public and not at the expense of the corporation which receives the sole benefit from insider incentives. Moreover, adequate incentives for corporate officers may be provided by properly administered stock options and employee purchase plans of which there are many in existence. In any event, the normal motivation induced by stock ownership, *i.e.*, the identification of an individual with corporate progress, is ill-promoted by condoning the sort of speculative insider activity which occurred here; for example, some of the corporation's stock was sold at market in order to purchase short-term calls upon that stock, calls which would never be exercised to increase a stockholder equity in TGS unless the market price of that stock rose sharply.

The core of Rule 10b-5 is the implementation of the Congressional purpose that all investors should have equal access to the rewards of participation in securities transactions. It was the intent of Congress that all members of the investing public should be subject to identical market risks,—which market risks include, of course the risk that one's evaluative capacity or one's capital available to put at risk may exceed another's capacity or capital. The insiders here were not trading on an equal footing with the outside investors. They alone were in a position to evaluate the probability and magnitude of what seemed from the outset to be a major ore strike; they alone could invest safely, secure in the expectation that the price of TGS stock would rise substantially in the event such a major strike should materialize, but would decline little, if at all, in the event of failure, for the public, ignorant at the outset of the favorable probabilities would likewise be unaware of the unproductive exploration, and the additional exploration costs would not significantly affect TGS market prices. Such inequities based upon unequal access to knowledge should not be shrugged off as inevitable in our way of life, or, in view of the congressional concern in the area, remain uncorrected.

We hold, therefore, that all transactions in TGS stock or calls by individuals apprised of the drilling results of K-55-1 were made in violation of Rule 10b-5. Inasmuch as the visual evaluation of that drill core (a generally reliable estimate though less accurate than a chemical assay) constituted material information, those advised of the results of the visual evaluation as well as those informed of the chemical assay traded in violation of law. The geologist Darke possessed undisclosed material information and traded in TGS securities. Therefore we reverse the dismissal of the action as to him and his personal transactions. The trial court also found, 258 F. Supp. at 284, that Darke, after the drilling of K-55-1 had been completed and with detailed knowledge of the results thereof, told certain outside individuals that TGS "was a good buy." These individuals thereafter acquired TGS stock and calls. The trial court also found that later, as of March 30, 1964, Darke not only used his material knowledge for his own purchases but that the substantial amounts of TGS stock and calls purchased by these outside individuals on that day, . . . was "strong circumstantial evidence that Darke must have passed the word to one or more of his 'tippees' that drilling on the Kidd 55 segment was about to be resumed." 258 F. Supp. at 284. Obviously if such a resumption were to have any meaning to such "tippees," they must have previously been told of K-55-1.

Unfortunately, however, there was no definitive resolution below of Darke's liability in these premises for the trial court held as to him, as it held as to all the other individual defendants, that this "undisclosed information" never became material until April 9. As it is our holding that the information acquired after the drilling of K-55-1 was material, we, on the basis of the findings of direct and circumstantial evidence on the issue that the trial court has already expressed, hold that Darke violated Rule 10b-5 (3) and Section 10(b) by "tipping" and we remand, pursuant to the agreement of the parties, for a determination of the appropriate remedy. As Darke's "tippees" are not defendants in this action, we need not decide whether, if they acted with actual or constructive knowledge that the material information was undisclosed, their conduct is as equally violative of the Rule as the conduct of their insider source, though we note that it certainly could be equally reprehensible.

* * *

C. When May Insiders Act?

Appellant Crawford, who ordered the purchase of TGS stock shortly before the TGS April 16 official announcement, and defendant Coates, who placed orders with and communicated the news to his broker immediately after the official announcement was read at the TGS-called press conference, concede that they were in possession of material information. They contend, however, that their purchases were not proscribed purchases for the news had already been effectively disclosed. We disagree.

Crawford telephoned his orders to his Chicago broker about midnight on April 15 and again at 8:30 in the morning of the 16th, with instructions to buy at the opening of the Midwest Stock Exchange that morning. The trial court's finding that "he sought to, and did, 'beat the news,'" 258 F. Supp. at 287, is well documented by the record. The rumors of a major ore strike which had been circulated in Canada and, to a lesser extent, in New York, had been disclaimed by the TGS press release of April 12, which significantly promised the public an official detailed announcement when possibilities had ripened into actualities. The abbreviated announcement to the Canadian press at 9:40 A.M. on the 16th by the Ontario Minister of Mines and the report carried by The Northern Miner, parts of which had sporadically reached New York on the morning of the 16th through reports from Canadian affiliates to a few New York investment firms, are assuredly not the equivalent of the official 10-15 minute announcement which was not released to the American financial press until after

10:00 A.M. Crawford's orders had been placed before that. Before insiders may act upon material information, such information must have been effectively disclosed in a manner sufficient to insure its availability to the investing public. Particularly here, where a formal announcement to the entire financial news media had been promised in a prior official release known to the media, all insider activity must await dissemination of the promised official announcement.

Coates was absolved by the court below because his telephone order was placed shortly before 10:20 A.M. on April 16, which was after the announcement had been made even though the news could not be considered already a matter of public information. 258 F. Supp. at 288. This result seems to have been predicated upon a misinterpretation of dicta in *Cady, Roberts*, where the SEC instructed insiders to "keep out of the market until the established procedures for public release of the information are carried out instead of hastening to execute transactions in advance of, and in frustration of, the objectives of the release," 40 SEC at 915. The reading of a news release, which prompted Coates into action, is merely the first step in the process of dissemination required for compliance with the regulatory objective of providing all investors with an equal opportunity to make informed investment judgments. Assuming that the contents of the official release could instantaneously be acted upon,[18] at the minimum Coates should have waited until the news could reasonably have been expected to appear over the media of widest circulation, the Dow Jones broad tape, rather than hastening to insure an advantage to himself and his broker son-in-law.[19]

* * *

MOORE, Circuit Judge (dissenting) (with whom Chief Judge LUMBARD concurs):

* * *

Wanting the knowledge requisite to making our own appraisal of the significance of the core, we must depend upon the experts. A correct decision in this case may well hang upon their testimony and its credibility because what these observers knew or should have known between November 12, 1963 and April 9, 1964 is basic to a determination of what, if anything, should have been disclosed or whether it was "material."

---

[18] Although the only insider who acted after the news appeared over the Dow Jones broad tape is not an appellant and therefore we need not discuss the necessity of considering the advisability of a "reasonable waiting period" during which outsiders may absorb and evaluate disclosures, we note in passing that, where the news is of a sort which is not readily translatable into investment action, insiders may not take advantage of their advance opportunity to evaluate the information by acting immediately upon dissemination. In any event, the permissible timing of insider transactions after disclosures of various sorts is one of the many areas of expertise for appropriate exercise of the SEC's rule-making power, which we hope will be utilized in the future to provide some predictability of certainty for the business community.

[19] The record reveals that news usually appears on the Dow Jones broad tape 2-3 minutes after the reporter completes dictation. Here, assuming that the Dow Jones reporter left the press conference as early as possible, 10:10 A.M., the 10-15 minute release (which took at least that long to dictate) could not have appeared on the wire before 10:22, and for other reasons unknown to us did not appear until 10:54. Indeed, even the abbreviated version of the release reported by Merrill Lynch over its private wire did not appear until 10:29. Coates, however, placed his call no later than 10:20.

For the defendants, Dean Forrester, Dean of the College of Mines of the University of Arizona and Director of the Arizona Bureau of Mines, said that "one hole is evidence of what you encounter only in that hole" and that even after K-55-3 was drilled in April 1964, it was "much more likely that the materials exposed in those two holes will extend for, let's say two feet outside the limits of the hole than it is likely that it will extend 25 feet or that it will extend 50 feet."

Dr. Park, former Dean of the School of Earth Sciences at Stanford, admitted that K-55-1 was "an interesting one, a good one" but that there was not "any evidence at all for any discussion of extent, from one drill hole." Dr. Lacy, head of the mining department of the University of Arizona, was of the opinion that "There is no basis for making any sort of prediction out from the hole."

Wiles, a consulting mining engineer, conceded that K-55-1 was a remark-able drill hole but that he could not estimate therefrom the probabilities of finding a commercially mineable body of ore, adding that he had had "the misfortune of having found a very attractive first hole and after drilling 52 around it got no more ore." Walkey, the manager of the Kamkotia, a mine some 12 miles distant from the Timmins property, testified that the geological composition of the Kamkotia and TGS areas was similar but that he could neither estimate nor say the chances were good of proving a substantial body of ore as a result of K-55-1.

Even the Commission's experts, Adelstein and Pennebaker, would not estimate what ore, if any, might lie beyond the 1 1/8 inch core. . . .

From this testimony, the trial court found:

> However, all the experts agreed that one drill core does not establish an ore body, much less a mine. Defendants' experts unanimously concluded that there is no way even to estimate the probabilities that one drill core will lead to the discovery of an ore body. 258 F. Supp. at 282.

Despite the experts' virtually uncontradicted testimony, despite Rule 52(a) and despite the Supreme Court's statement of the law, the majority choose to reject the trial court's findings as to the results of the first drill core, K- 55-1, and to substitute their own expertise in the mining engineering field by holding that "knowledge of the possibility which surely was more than marginal of the existence of a mine of the vast magnitude indicated by the remarkably rich drill core located rather close to the surface (suggesting mineability by the less expensive open-pit method) within the confines of a large anomaly (suggesting an extensive region of mineralization) might well have affected the price of TGS stock and would certainly have been an important fact to a reasonable, if speculative, investor in deciding whether he should buy, sell or hold."

* * *

The final question to be answered is: were these officers and employees disqualified as the result of possessing information gleaned by the first drill core from purchasing TGS stock? The number of possibilities for Congressional legislation and Commission rulings are legion. They extend over a gamut between definite extremes. At one extreme is a rule that no officer or employee or any member of their families shall own stock of the company for which they work or purchase stock if he possesses "material" inside information. This assumption raises the question of what is material and who is to make such a determination. Materiality must depend upon the facts and their resolution is for the fact-finder, court or jury. The majority state that the K-55-1 drilling results were material because they "might well have affected the price of TGS stock." But such a statement could be made of almost any fact related to TGS. If a labor strike had kept its plants idle for months, encouraging news of a possible settlement hoped for by the TGS labor negotiators might cause the negotiators to buy. Their belief that the strike would be protracted might cause them to sell. Either announcement might well have affected the market and would to those who bought or sold have seemed misleading and deceptive if the anticipated event did not come to pass. Yet the requirement of hourly bulletins to the press from the conference room would not be compatible with common sense. Scores of day by day intra-company situations come to mind which in the individual opinions of company officers or employees might well affect the price of TGS stock, each individual reacting according to his own judgment. However, companies listed on a national exchange can scarcely broadcast to the nation on a daily basis their hopes and/or expectations from the developments in, for example, their research departments. An even more striking illustration would be found within the structure of a large pharmaceutical company where discoveries of panaceas to cure human disease occupies [sic] the workdays of thousands of scientists. Premature announcements of important discoveries would be branded as false and misleading if unfulfilled and all stock purchases made during the course of the research, if ultimately successful would be said to have been made with the advantage of inside information. At the other extreme is an equally easy-to-resolve *Cady, Roberts* situation where a definite fact (the reduction of the dividend) was known by an insider, who participated in the meeting where the decision had already been made, whose knowledge of the probable reaction of the market to such an announcement, namely, a substantial sell-off, caused him to leave the meeting ahead of everyone else and before the potential buyers learned of the bad news to foist his selling orders on the market and his stock on uninformed purchasers. Between these extremes there should be a rule of reason.

Faced with this problem, the trial court selected a period from November 12, 1963 (the first information) to some date after drilling was resumed when it might reasonably be said that a body of commercially mineable ore might exist. The trial court, accepting the Commission's experts' version, fixed 7:00 p.m. on April 9, 1964 as the time when TGS had material information which "if disclosed, would have had a substantial impact on the market price of TGS stock" but also found that "the drilling results up to 7:00 p.m. on April 9th did not provide such material information." These findings are clearly supported by the proof upon which the court relied.

Practically all TGS stock in question here was purchased between November 12, 1963 and April 8, 1964. What were the motives behind each of the purchases? Obviously, a subjective approach presents difficulties. A myriad of reasons would be given—hope that a commercially profitable mine would be found if further exploration proved the ore to be as promising as the core of K-55-1 (November 12, 1963); the development of a phosphate project and potash mine (November 15, 1963); the prediction of security analysts that there would be a turnabout in the price of sulphur stocks; the acquisition of Canadian oil properties (December 16, 1963); the new high level of free world sulphur use and output (December 30, 1963); the launching of the world's largest liquid sulphur tanker (December 30,

1963); the entry into service of a large liquid sulphur tanker for domestic shipments (January 18, 1964); the sulphur expansion program in Canada (February 8, 1964); the new four-year high in sales reached in 1963 (February 20, 1964); and the $2 per ton price increase for sulphur (April 1, 1964).

There can be little doubt but that those familiar with the results of K-55-1 were influenced thereby in making their purchases. The conclusion of the majority is based primarily on this assumption. They call it "a major factor in determining whether the K-55-1 discovery was a material fact" and say that this "virtually compels the inference that the insiders were influenced by the drilling results." To them, completely disregarding the trial court's findings and substituting themselves as a jury, these purchases are "the only truly objective evidence of the materiality of the K-55-1 discovery." In so holding, they confuse the inducing motive of the individual purchaser with knowledge of material facts which ought to be revealed to the public at large. The inconsistency of the majority's position is immediately apparent. Those who purchased were apparently willing on the basis of the inconclusive first hole and other information to risk a certain amount of their funds in TGS stock, hopeful that future developments would be favorable. Their motive for purchase does not establish the materiality of the facts which influenced them. However, the importance of this case to the corporate and financial community centers around the news release, its timing and its content. It is unfortunate that the atmosphere surrounding this important issue has been so colored and in the collective mind of the majority so contaminated by the comparatively insignificant stock purchase issue.

The resolution, if such be possible, of the many problems presented in this field should be by rule, as definite as possible, formulated in the light of reality and not retroactive in effect as here. . . . The companies, the securities of which are listed on exchanges, their employees and investing public alike should have some knowledge of the rules which will govern their actions. They should not be forced, despite an exercise of the best judgment, to act at their peril or refrain in terrorem from acting. As to a waiting period after the information regarded as "material" has been disclosed, any such time period should be specifically fixed by Congressional or Commission rule not retroactive in application. There is no proof here that the purchases of the defendants, even if motivated by hopes not then solidly grounded, raised or lowered the market or were manipulative, misleading, deceptive or were accomplished by false or fraudulent devices. The trial court after hearing and seeing the witnesses has resolved these factual issues and in my opinion its decision should be sustained.

* * *

NOTES AND QUESTIONS

(1) **The definition of materiality.** In *TSC Industries, Inc. v. Northway, Inc.*,[2] the Supreme Court clarified the standard of materiality for cases arising under § 14(a) of the

---

[121] 426 U.S. 438, 449 (1975).

1934 Act. (*See* Section 7.03.) *Basic Inc. v. Levinson*[122] extended the *TSC* standard of materiality to cases arising under § 10(b) and Rule 10b-5. How does the *TSC* standard differ from the standard employed in *TGS*? Would information about the K-55-1 hole have been material under the *TSC* standard?

(2) **Relevance of expert testimony.** Why did the appellate court reject the expert testimony as to the significance of K-55-1 which was relied on by the trial court? Did the appellate court overstep the bounds of appellate review, as Judge Moore charged, or did the trial court and Second Circuit disagree over the applicable legal rule as to materiality?

(3) **Materiality and securities analysts.** A particular problem in determining materiality in the insider trading context is that the insider is often an expert who pieces together a "mosaic" of information consisting of both public and nonpublic information and general expertise.[123] Thus, a specific inside, nonpublic fact that is insignificant to an ordinary investor may be material to an expert when combined with the expert's other information.[124] For example, suppose a securities analyst, having thoroughly studied the market, has concluded that one of three large companies—A, B or C—may make a bid for T. Analyst learns through an insider tip that the chief executive of T is visiting A corporation. Is this material, inside information? Measuring materiality with reference to the insider's other information would introduce intolerable unpredictability. More likely, the test is the significance of the information to the ordinary investor. This has the effect of providing wide leeway for insiders to trade.[125]

PROBLEMS

(1) Apex Construction Corporation has total assets of $1 billion and earnings in its most recent fiscal year of $100 million. On April 1, Apex submits its bid for a very large construction contract in Africa. It is one of ten companies bidding. Under the Apex bid, the company would receive total revenues of $1 billion over a ten-year period. Opinion is divided in the company as to whether the company will be awarded the contract and how profitable the contract will be. On June 1, Apex learns that it is one of three finalists for the project. On July 1, Apex learns that it has been awarded the contract. Opinion in the company is still divided as to whether the contract will be profitable. Smith, a vice president of Apex, is fully aware of all of the above facts. None of the facts have been publicly disclosed. Smith seeks your advice as to whether he may

---

[122] 485 U.S. 224 (1988).

[123] *See Elkind v. Liggett & Myers, Inc.*, 635 F.2d 156, 165 (2d Cir. 1980).

[124] Lorie, *Insider Trading: Rule 10b-5, Disclosure, and Corporate Privacy: A Comment*, 9 J. Leg. Stud. 819, 821 (1980).

[125] *See* Carlton & Fischel, *Regulation of Insider Trading*, 35 Stan. L. Rev. 857, 886 (1983).

purchase Apex stock (a) on April 1; (b) on June 1; (c) on July 1. What advice would you give as of each of these dates?[126]

(2) Apex issues a press release at 10:00 a.m. on July 2 announcing that it has been awarded the contract and making reasonably full disclosure as to the terms of the contract and its significance for Apex. The announcement appears on the Dow Jones "broad tape" at 10:30, is announced on television and radio newscasts beginning at 2:00 p.m., and appears in the evening newspapers. Smith asks for your advice as to whether he may purchase Apex stock (a) at 10:15; (b) at 10:30; (c) at 10:45; (d) at noon. What advice would you give as of each of these times?

CHIARELLA v. UNITED STATES
United States Supreme Court
445 U.S. 222 (1980)

Mr. Justice POWELL delivered the opinion of the Court.

The question in this case is whether a person who learns from the confidential documents of one corporation that it is planning an attempt to secure control of a second corporation violates § 10(b) of the Securities Exchange Act of 1934 if he fails to disclose the impending takeover before trading in the target company's securities.

I

Petitioner is a printer by trade. In 1975 and 1976, he worked as a "markup man" in the New York composing room of Pandick Press, a financial printer. Among documents that petitioner handled were five announcements of corporate takeover bids. When these documents were delivered to the printer, the identities of the acquiring and target corporations were concealed by blank spaces or false names. The true names were sent to the printer on the night of the final printing.

The petitioner, however, was able to deduce the names of the target companies before the final printing from other information contained in the documents. Without disclosing his knowledge, petitioner purchased stock in the target companies and sold the shares immediately after the takeover attempts were made public.[1]

By this method, petitioner realized a gain of slightly more than $30,000 in the course of 14 months. Subsequently, the Securities and Exchange Commission (Commission or SEC) began an investigation of his trading activities. In May 1977, petitioner entered into a consent decree with the Commission in which he agreed to return his profits to the sellers of the shares. On the same day, he was discharged by Pandick Press.

---

[126] These facts are loosely drawn from *State Teachers Retirement Board v. Fluor Corp.*, 654 F.2d 843 (2d Cir. 1981).

[1] Of the five transactions, four involved tender offers and one concerned a merger. 588 F.2d 1358, 1363, n.2 (CA2 1978).

In January 1978, petitioner was indicted on 17 counts of violating § 10(b) of the Securities Exchange Act of 1934 (1934 Act) and SEC Rule 10b-5. After petitioner unsuccessfully moved to dismiss the indictment, he was brought to trial and convicted on all counts.

* * *

II

* * *

This case concerns the legal effect of the petitioner's silence. The District Court's charge permitted the jury to convict the petitioner if it found that he willfully failed to inform sellers of target company securities that he knew of a forthcoming takeover bid that would make their shares more valuable. In order to decide whether silence in such circumstances violates § 10(b), it is necessary to review the language and legislative history of that statute as well as its interpretation by the Commission and the federal courts.

Although the starting point of our inquiry is the language of the statute, *Ernst & Ernst v. Hochfelder*, 425 U.S. 185, 197 (1976), § 10(b) does not state whether silence may constitute a manipulative or deceptive device. Section 10(b) was designed as a catchall clause to prevent fraudulent practices. 425 U.S. at 202, 206. But neither the legislative history nor the statute itself affords specific guidance for the resolution of this case. When Rule 10b-5 was promulgated in 1942, the SEC did not discuss the possibility that failure to provide information might run afoul of § 10(b).

The SEC took an important step in the development of § 10(b) when it held that a broker-dealer and his firm violated that section by selling securities on the basis of undisclosed information obtained from a director of the issuer corporation who was also a registered representative of the brokerage firm. In *Cady, Roberts & Co.*, 40 S.E.C. 907 (1961), the Commission decided that a corporate insider must abstain from trading in the shares of his corporation unless he has first disclosed all material inside information known to him. The obligation to disclose or abstain derives from

> [a]n affirmative duty to disclose material information[, which] has been traditionally imposed on corporate "insiders," particularly officers, directors, or controlling stockholders. We, and the courts have consistently held that insiders must disclose material facts which are known to them by virtue of their position but which are not known to persons with whom they deal and which, if known, would affect their investment judgment. *Id.* at 911.

The Commission emphasized that the duty arose from (i) the existence of a relationship affording access to inside information intended to be available, only for a corporate purpose, and (ii) the unfairness of allowing a corporate insider to take advantage of that information by trading without disclosure. *Id.* at 912, and n.15.

That the relationship between a corporate insider and the stockholders of his corporation gives rise to a disclosure obligation is not a novel twist of the law. At common law, misrepresentation made for the purpose of inducing reliance upon the false statement is fraudulent. But one who fails to disclose material information prior to the consummation of a transaction commits fraud only when he is under a duty to do so. And the duty to disclose arises when one party has information "that the other [party] is entitled to know because of a fiduciary or other similar relation of trust and confidence between them." In its *Cady, Roberts* decision, the Commission recognized a relationship of trust and confidence between the shareholders of a corporation and those insiders who have obtained confidential information by reason of their position with that corporation.[10] This relationship gives rise to a duty to disclose because of the "necessity of preventing a corporate insider from . . . tak[ing] unfair advantage of the uninformed minority stockholders."

The federal courts have found violations of § 10(b) where corporate insiders used undisclosed information for their own benefit. *E.g.*, *SEC v. Texas Gulf Sulphur Co.*, 401 F.2d 833 (CA2 1968), *cert. denied*, 404 U.S. 1005 (1971). The cases also have emphasized, in accordance with the common-law rule, that "[t]he party charged with failing to disclose market information must be under a duty to disclose it." Accordingly, a purchaser of stock who has no duty to a prospective seller because he is neither an insider nor a fiduciary has been held to have no obligation to reveal material facts.

* * *

Thus, administrative and judicial interpretations have established that silence in connection with the purchase or sale of securities may operate as a fraud actionable under § 10(b) despite the absence of statutory language or legislative history specifically addressing the legality of nondisclosure. But such liability is premised upon a duty to disclose arising from a relationship of trust and confidence between parties to a transaction. Application of a duty to disclose prior to trading guarantees that corporate insiders, who have an obligation to place the shareholder's welfare before their own, will not benefit personally through fraudulent use of material, nonpublic information.[12]

III

In this case, the petitioner was convicted of violating § 10(b) although he was not a corporate insider and he received no confidential information from the target company. Moreover, the "market information" upon which he relied did not concern the earning power or operations of the target company, but only the plans of the acquiring company. Petitioner's use of that information was not a fraud under § 10(b) unless he was subject to an

---

[10] The dissent of Mr. Justice BLACKMUN suggests that the "special facts" doctrine may be applied to find that silence constitutes fraud where one party has superior information to another. This Court has never so held. In *Strong v. Repide*, 213 U.S. 419, 431-434 (1909), this Court applied the special-facts doctrine to conclude that a corporate insider had a duty to disclose to a shareholder. In that case, the majority shareholder of a corporation secretly purchased the stock of another shareholder without revealing that the corporation, under the insider's direction, was about to sell corporate assets at a price that would greatly enhance the value of the stock. The decision in *Strong v. Repide* was premised upon the fiduciary duty between the corporate insider and the shareholder. *See Pepper v. Litton*, 308 U. S. 295, 307, n.15 (1939).

[12] "Tippees" of corporate insiders have been held liable under § 10(b) because they have a duty not to profit from the use of inside information that they know is confidential and know or should know came from a corporate insider, *Shapiro v. Merrill Lynch, Pierce, Fenner & Smith, Inc.*, 495 F.2d 228, 237-238 (CA2 1974). The tippee's obligation has been viewed as arising from his role as a participant after the fact in the insider's breach of a fiduciary duty. Subcommittees of American Bar Association Section of Corporation, Banking, and Business Law, Comment Letter on Material, Non-Public Information (Oct. 15, 1973), reprinted in BNA, Securities Regulation & Law Report No. 233, pp. D-1, D-2 (Jan. 2, 1974).

affirmative duty to disclose it before trading. In this case, the jury instructions failed to specify any such duty.

* * *

We cannot affirm petitioner's conviction without recognizing a general duty between all participants in market transactions to forgo actions based on material, nonpublic information. Formulation of such a broad duty, which departs radically from the established doctrine that duty arises from a specific relationship between two parties, should not be undertaken absent some explicit evidence. As we have seen, no such evidence emerges from the language or legislative history of § 10(b). Moreover, neither the Congress nor the Commission ever has adopted a parity-of-information rule.

* * *

We see no basis for applying such a new and different theory of liability in this case. As we have emphasized before, the 1934 Act cannot be read "more broadly than its language and the statutory scheme reasonably permit." Section 10(b) is aptly described as a catchall provision, but what it catches must be fraud. When an allegation of fraud is based upon nondisclosure, there can be no fraud absent a duty to speak. We hold that a duty to disclose under § 10(b) does not arise from the mere possession of nonpublic market information. The contrary result is without support in the legislative history of § 10(b) and would be inconsistent with the careful plan that Congress has enacted for regulation of the securities markets. . . .

IV

In its brief to this Court, the United States offers an alternative theory to support petitioner's conviction. It argues that petitioner breached a duty to the acquiring corporation when he acted upon information that he obtained by virtue of his position as an employee of a printer employed by the corporation. The breach of this duty is said to support a conviction under § 10(b) for fraud perpetrated upon both the acquiring corporation and the sellers.

We need not decide whether this theory has merit for it was not submitted to the jury.

* * *

Because we cannot affirm a criminal conviction on the basis of a theory not presented to the jury, . . . we will not speculate upon whether such a duty exists, whether it has been breached, or whether such a breach constitutes a violation of § 10(b).

The judgment of the Court of Appeals is
Reversed.

Mr. Chief Justice Burger, dissenting.

I believe that the jury instructions in this case properly charged a violation of § 10(b) and Rule 10b-5, and I would affirm the conviction.

I

As a general rule, neither party to an arm's-length business transaction has an obligation to disclose information to the other unless the parties stand in some confidential or fiduciary relation. . . .

This rule permits a businessman to capitalize on his experience and skill in securing and evaluating relevant information; it provides incentive for hard work, careful analysis, and astute forecasting. But the policies that underlie the rule also should limit its scope. In particular, the rule should give way when an informational advantage is obtained, not by superior experience, foresight, or industry, but by some unlawful means. One commentator has written:

> [T]he way in which the buyer acquires the information which he conceals from the vendor should be a material circumstance. The information might have been acquired as the result of his bringing to bear a superior knowledge, intelligence, skill or technical judgment; it might have been acquired by mere chance; or it might have been acquired by means of some tortious action on his part. *Any time information is acquired by an illegal act it would seem that there should be a duty to disclose that information.*

Keeton, *Fraud—Concealment and Non-Disclosure*, 15 TEX. L. REV. 1, 25-26 (1936) (emphasis added).

I would read § 10(b) and Rule 10b-5 to encompass and build on this principle: to mean that a person who has misappropriated nonpublic information has an absolute duty to disclose that information or to refrain from trading.

The language of § 10(b) and of Rule 10b-5 plainly support such a reading. By their terms, these provisions reach any person engaged in any fraudulent scheme. This broad language negates the suggestion that congressional concern was limited to trading by "corporate insiders" or to deceptive practices related to "corporate information." Just as surely Congress cannot have intended one standard of fair dealing for "white collar" insiders and another for the "blue collar" level. The very language of § 10(b) and Rule 10b-5 "by repeated use of the word 'any' [was] obviously meant to be inclusive."

The history of the statute and of the Rule also supports this reading. The antifraud provisions were designed in large measure "to assure that dealing in securities is fair and without undue preferences or advantages among investors." H.R. Conf. Rep. No. 94-229, p. 91 (1975). These provisions prohibit "those manipulative and deceptive practices which have been demonstrated to fulfill no useful function." S. Rep. No. 792, 73d, Cong., 2d Sess., 6 (1934). An investor who purchases securities on the basis of misappropriated nonpublic information possesses just such an "undue" trading advantage; his conduct quite clearly serves no useful function except his own enrichment at the expense of others.

This interpretation of § 10(b) and Rule 10b-5 is in no sense novel. It follows naturally from legal principles enunciated by the Securities and Exchange Commission in its seminal *Cady, Roberts* decision. 40 S.E.C. 907 (1961). There, the Commission relied upon two factors to impose a duty to disclose on corporate insiders: (1) ". . . access . . . to information intended to be available only for a corporate purpose *and not for the personal benefit of anyone*" (emphasis added); and (2) the unfairness inherent in trading on such information when it is inaccessible to those with whom one is dealing. Both of these factors are present whenever a party gains an informational advantage by unlawful means. Indeed, in *In re Blyth & Co.*, S.E.C. 1037 (1969), the Commission applied its *Cady, Roberts* decision in just such a context. In that case a broker-dealer had traded in Government securities on the basis of confidential Treasury Department information which it received from a Federal Reserve Bank employee. The Commission ruled that the trading was "improper use of inside information" violative of § 10(b) and Rule 10b-5. 43 S.E.C. at 1040. It did not hesitate to extend *Cady, Roberts* to reach a "tippee" of a Government insider.

Finally, it bears emphasis that this reading of § 10(b) and Rule 10b-5 would not threaten legitimate business practices. So read, the antifraud provisions would not impose a duty on a tender offeror to disclose its acquisition plans during the period in which it "tests the water" prior to purchasing a full 5% of the target company's stock. Nor would it proscribe "warehousing." . . . Likewise, market specialists would not be subject to a disclose-or-refrain requirement in the performance of their everyday market functions. In each of these instances, trading is accomplished on the basis of material, nonpublic information, but the information has not been unlawfully converted for personal gain.

II

The Court's opinion, as I read it, leaves open the question whether § 10(b) and Rule 10b-5 prohibit trading on misappropriated nonpublic information.[4] Instead, the Court apparently concludes that this theory of the case was not submitted to the jury.

* * *

The Court's reading of the District Court's charge is unduly restrictive. Fairly read as a whole and in the context of the trial, the instructions required the jury to find that Chiarella obtained his trading advantage by misappropriating the property of his employer's customers.

* * *

In sum, the evidence shows beyond all doubt that Chiarella, working literally in the shadows of the warning signs in the printshop, misappropriated—stole to put it bluntly— valuable nonpublic information entrusted to him in the utmost confidence. He then exploited his ill-gotten informational advantage by purchasing securities in the market. In my view, such conduct plainly violates § 10(b) and Rule 10b-5. Accordingly, I would affirm the judgment of the Court of Appeals.

* * *

[Justice STEVENS concurred. He agreed with the plurality that petitioner's conviction was erroneously based on breach of a duty owed to the sellers, but stated that a violation of Rule 10b-5 might be predicated on breach of a duty owed to the acquiring company. Justice BRENNAN also concurred, stating that he joined in Part I of Justice BURGER's opinion, but agreeing with the majority that BURGER's theory had not been presented to the jury. Justice BLACKMUN, joining with Justice MARSHALL, dissented, presenting a theory of Rule 10b-5 liability similar to the theory discussed in Professor Brudney's article discussed in Section 12.05[D], below.]

---

[4]   There is some language in the Court's opinion to suggest that only "a relationship between petitioner and the sellers . . . could give rise to a duty [to disclose]." The Court's holding, however, is much more limited, namely, that mere possession of material nonpublic information is insufficient to create a duty to disclose or to refrain from trading. Accordingly, it is my understanding that the Court has not rejected the view, advanced above, that an absolute duty to disclose or refrain arises from the very act of misappropriating nonpublic information.

NOTES AND QUESTIONS

(1) **The holding in** *Chiarella.* Precisely what did the Court decide in *Chiarella?* Did it conclude that a "duty to disclose arising from a relationship of trust and confidence between parties to a transaction" was a prerequisite to liability? Or simply that the parity-of-information theory embodied in the indictment was too broad?

(2) **Source and nature of the duty to disclose.** Where does the "duty to disclose" come from? Is the Court referring to state law duties? Note the limitations on that duty discussed in Section 12.04. If there is an independent federal duty, why does it depend on a "relationship of trust and confidence"? Why is there not a federal duty to refrain from conduct that will harm the integrity of the markets? How extensive should such a duty be? For a discussion of these questions, which the Court avoided in *Chiarella*, see Section 12.05[D].

(3) **The "misappropriation" theory.** A version of the "misappropriation" theory advocated by Justice Burger, imposing restrictions on certain "outsiders" who trade based on nonpublic material information, was subsequently adopted by the Supreme Court in *United States v. O'Hagan.*[127] *See* Section 12.05[C].

[B] Tippees

The *Chiarella* plurality (*see* footnote 12) suggested that tippees, as well as insiders, had a duty to disclose as participants in the insider's breach. Does this mean that insider status is communicated, like a disease, with the information? If not, how should the liability of tippees be limited? The Supreme Court addressed this issue in the following case.

DIRKS v. SEC
United States Supreme Court
463 U.S. 646 (1983)

Justice POWELL delivered the opinion of the Court.

Petitioner Raymond Dirks received material nonpublic information from "insiders" of a corporation with which he had no connection. He disclosed this information to investors who relied on it in trading in the shares of the corporation. The question is whether Dirks violated the antifraud provisions of the federal securities laws by this disclosure.

I

In 1973, Dirks was an officer of a New York broker-dealer firm who specialized in providing investment analysis of insurance company securities to institutional investors. On March 6, Dirks received information from Ronald Secrist, a former officer of Equity Funding of America. Secrist alleged that the assets of Equity Funding, a diversified corporation primarily engaged in selling life insurance and mutual funds, were vastly overstated

---

[127] 521 U.S. 642 (1997).

as the result of fraudulent corporate practices. Secrist also stated that various regulatory agencies had failed to act on similar charges made by Equity Funding employees. He urged Dirks to verify the fraud and disclose it publicly.

Dirks decided to investigate the allegations. He visited Equity Funding's headquarters in Los Angeles and interviewed several officers and employees of the corporation. The senior management denied any wrongdoing, but certain corporation employees corroborated the charges of fraud. Neither Dirks nor his firm owned or traded any Equity Funding stock, but throughout his investigation he openly discussed the information he had obtained with a number of clients and investors. Some of these persons sold their holdings of Equity Funding securities, including five investment advisers who liquidated holdings of more than $16 million.[2]

While Dirks was in Los Angeles, he was in touch regularly with William Blundell, the Wall Street Journal's Los Angeles bureau chief. Dirks urged Blundell to write a story on the fraud allegations. Blundell did not believe, however, that such a massive fraud could go undetected and declined to write the story. He feared that publishing such damaging hearsay might be libelous.

During the two-week period in which Dirks pursued his investigation and spread word of Secrist's charges, the price of Equity Funding stock fell from $26 per share to less than $15 per share. This led the New York Stock Exchange to halt trading on March 27. Shortly thereafter California insurance authorities impounded Equity Funding's records and uncovered evidence of the fraud. Only then did the Securities and Exchange Commission (SEC) file a complaint against Equity Funding[3] and only then, on April 2, did the Wall Street Journal publish a front-page story based largely on information assembled by Dirks. Equity Funding immediately went into receivership.

The SEC began an investigation into Dirks' role in the exposure of the fraud. After a hearing by an administrative law judge, the SEC found that Dirks had aided and abetted violations of § 17(a) of the Securities Act of 1933, 15 U.S.C. § 77q(a), § 10(b) of the Securities Exchange Act of 1934, 15 U.S.C. § 78j(b), and SEC Rule 10b-5, 17 CFR § 240.10b-5 (1982), by repeating the allegations of fraud to members of the investment community who later sold their Equity Funding stock Recognizing, . . . however, that Dirks "played an important role in bringing [Equity Funding's] massive fraud to light," 21 S.E.C. Docket at 1412,[8] the SEC only censured him.

---

[2]   Dirks received from his firm a salary plus a commission for securities transactions above a certain amount that his clients directed through his firm. *See* 21 S.E.C. Docket at 1402, n.3. But "[i]t is not clear how many of those with whom Dirks spoke promised to direct some brokerage business through [Dirks' firm] to compensate Dirks, or how many actually did so." 220 U.S. App. D.C. at 316, 681 F.2d at 831. The Boston Company Institutional Investors, Inc., promised Dirks about $25,000 in commissions, but it is unclear whether Boston actually generated any brokerage business for his firm. *See* App. 199, 204-205; 21 S.E.C. Docket at 1404, n.10; 220 U.S. App. D.C. at 316, n.5, 681 F.2d at 831, n.5.

[3]   As early as 1971, the SEC had received allegations of fraudulent accounting practices at Equity Funding. Moreover, on March 9, 1973, an official of the California Insurance Department informed the SEC's regional office in Los Angeles of Secrist's charges of fraud. Dirks himself voluntarily presented his information at the SEC's regional office beginning on March 27.

[8]   Justice BLACKMUN's dissenting opinion minimizes the role Dirks played in making public the Equity Funding fraud. The dissent would rewrite the history of Dirks' extensive investigative efforts. *See, e.g.,* 21 S.E.C. at 1412 ("It is clear that Dirks played an important role in bringing [Equity Funding's] massive fraud to light, and it is also true that

Dirks sought review in the Court of Appeals for the District of Columbia Circuit. The court entered judgment against Dirks.

* * *

II

. . . In *Chiarella*, we accepted the two elements set out in *Cady, Roberts* for establishing a Rule 10b-5 violation: "(i) the existence of a relationship affording access to inside information intended to be available only for a corporate purpose, and (ii) the unfairness of allowing a corporate insider to take advantage of that information by trading without disclosure." 445 U.S. at 227. In examining whether *Chiarella* had an obligation to disclose or abstain, the Court found that there is no general duty to disclose before trading on material nonpublic information, and held that "a duty to disclose under § 10(b) does not arise from the mere possession of nonpublic market information." *Id.* at 235. Such a duty arises rather from the existence of a fiduciary relationship. *See id.* at 227-235.

Not "all breaches of fiduciary duty in connection with a securities transaction," however, come within the ambit of Rule 10b-5. *Santa Fe Industries, Inc. v. Green*, 430 U.S. 462, 472 (1977). There must also be "manipulation or deception." *Id.* at 473. In an inside-trading case this fraud derives from the "inherent unfairness involved where one takes advantage" of "information intended to be available only for a corporate purpose and not for the personal benefit of anyone." *In re Merrill Lynch, Pierce, Fenner & Smith, Inc.*, 43 S.E.C. 933, 936 (1968). Thus, an insider will be liable under Rule 10b-5 for inside trading only where he fails to disclose material nonpublic information before trading on it and thus makes "secret profits." *Cady, Roberts*, 40 S.E.C. at 916, n. 31.

III

We were explicit in *Chiarella* in saying that there can be no duty to disclose where the person who has traded on inside information "was not [the corporation's] agent, . . . was not a fiduciary, [or] was not a person in whom the sellers [of the securities] had placed their trust and confidence." 445 U.S. at 232. Not to require such a fiduciary relationship, we recognized, would "depar[t] radically from the established doctrine that duty arises from a specific relationship between two parties" and would amount to "recognizing a general duty between all participants in market transactions to forgo actions based on material, nonpublic information." *Id.* at 232, 233. This requirement of a specific relationship between the shareholders and the individual trading on inside information has created analytical difficulties for the SEC and courts in policing tippees who trade on inside information. Unlike insiders who have independent fiduciary duties to both the corporation and its shareholders, the typical tippee has no such relationships.[14] In view of this absence, it has been unclear how a tippee acquires the *Cady, Roberts* duty to refrain from trading on inside information.

---

he reported the fraud allegation to [Equity Funding's] auditors and sought to have the information published in the Wall Street Journal."); 681 F.2d at 829 (Wright, J.) ("Largely thanks to Dirks one of the most infamous frauds in recent memory was uncovered and exposed, while the record shows that the SEC repeatedly missed opportunities to investigate Equity Funding.").

[14] Under certain circumstances, such as where corporate information is revealed legitimately to an underwriter, accountant, lawyer, or consultant working for the corporation, these outsiders may become fiduciaries of the shareholders. The basis for recognizing this fiduciary duty is not simply that such persons acquired nonpublic corporate

A

The SEC's position, as stated in its opinion in this case, is that a tippee "inherits" the *Cady, Roberts* obligation to shareholders whenever he receives inside information from an insider.

> In tipping potential traders, Dirks breached a duty which he had assumed as a result of knowingly receiving confidential information from [Equity Funding] insiders. Tippees such as Dirks who receive non-public material information from insiders become "subject to the same duty as [the] insiders." *Shapiro v. Merrill Lynch, Pierce, Fenner & Smith, Inc.* [495 F.2d 228, 237 (CA2 1974) (quoting *Ross v. Licht*, 263 F. Supp. 395, 410 (SDNY 1967)]. Such a tippee breaches the fiduciary duty which he assumes from the insider when the tippee knowingly transmits the information to someone who will probably trade on the basis thereof. . . . Presumably, Dirks' informants were entitled to disclose the [Equity Funding] fraud in order to bring it to light and its perpetrators to justice. However, Dirks—standing in their shoes—committed a breach of the fiduciary duty which he had assumed in dealing with them, when he passed the information on to traders.

21 S.E.C. Docket at 1410, n. 42.

This view differs little from the view that we rejected as inconsistent with congressional intent in *Chiarella*. In that case, the Court of Appeals agreed with the SEC and affirmed *Chiarella's* conviction, holding that "[a]nyone—corporate insider or not—who regularly receives material nonpublic information may not use that information to trade in securities without incurring an affirmative duty to disclose." *United States v. Chiarella*, 588 F.2d 1358, 1365 (CA2 1978) (emphasis in original). Here, the SEC maintains that anyone who knowingly receives nonpublic material information from an insider has a fiduciary duty to disclose before trading.[15]

---

information, but rather that they have entered into a special confidential relationship in the conduct of the business of the enterprise and are given access to information solely for corporate purposes. *See SEC v. Monarch Fund*, 608 F.2d 938, 942 (CA2 1979); *In re Investors Management Co.*, 44 S.E.C. 633, 645 (1971); *In re Van Alystne, Noel & Co.*, 43 S.E.C. 1080, 1084-1085 (1969); *In re Merrill Lynch, Pierce, Fenner & Smith, Inc.*, 43 S.E.C. 933, 937 (1968); *Cady, Roberts*, 40 S.E.C. at 912. When such a person breaches his fiduciary relationship, he may be treated more properly as a tipper than a tippee. *See Shapiro v. Merrill Lynch, Pierce, Fenner & Smith, Inc.*, 495 F.2d 228, 237 (CA2 1974) (investment banker had access to material information when working on a proposed public offering for the corporation). For such a duty to be imposed, however, the corporation must expect the outsider to keep the disclosed nonpublic information confidential, and the relationship at least must imply such a duty.

[15] Apparently, the SEC believes this case differs from *Chiarella* in that Dirks' receipt of inside information from Secrist, an insider, carried Secrist's duties with it, while Chiarella received the information without the direct involvement of an insider and thus inherited no duty to disclose or abstain. The SEC fails to explain, however, why the receipt of nonpublic information from an insider automatically carries with it the fiduciary duty of the insider. As we emphasized in *Chiarella*, mere possession of nonpublic information does not give rise to a duty to disclose or abstain; only a specific relationship does that. And we do not believe that the mere receipt of information from an insider creates such a special relationship between the tippee and the corporation's shareholders.

Apparently recognizing the weakness of its argument in light of *Chiarella*, the SEC attempts to distinguish that case factually as involving not "inside" information, but rather "market" information, *i.e.*, "information generated within the company relating to its assets or earnings." Brief for Respondent 23. This Court drew no such distinction in *Chiarella* and, as THE CHIEF JUSTICE noted, "[i]t is clear that § 10(b) and Rule 10b-5 by their terms and by their history

In effect, the SEC's theory of tippee liability in both cases appears rooted in the idea that the antifraud provisions require equal information among all traders. This conflicts with the principle set forth in *Chiarella* that only some persons, under some circumstances, will be barred from trading while in possession of material nonpublic information. . . .

Imposing a duty to disclose or abstain solely because a person knowingly receives material nonpublic information from an insider and trades on it could have an inhibiting influence on the role of market analysts, which the SEC itself recognizes is necessary to the preservation of a healthy market.[17] It is commonplace for analysts to "ferret out and analyze information," 21 S.E.C. at 1406,[18] and this often is done by meeting with and questioning corporate officers and others who are insiders. And information that the analysts obtain normally may be the basis for judgments as to the market worth of a corporation's securities. The analyst's judgment in this respect is made available in market letters or otherwise to clients of the firm. It is the nature of this type of information, and indeed of the markets themselves, that such information cannot be made simultaneously available to all of the corporation's stockholders or the public generally.

B

The conclusion that recipients of inside information do not invariably acquire a duty to disclose or abstain does not mean that such tippees always are free to trade on the information. The need for a ban on some tippee trading is clear. Not only are insiders forbidden by their fiduciary relationship from personally using undisclosed corporate information to their advantage, but they may not give such information to an outsider for the same improper purpose of exploiting the information for their personal gain. *See* 15 U.S.C. § 78t(b) (making it unlawful to do indirectly "by means of any other person" any act made unlawful by the federal securities laws). Similarly, the transactions of those who knowingly participate with the fiduciary in such a breach are "as forbidden" as transactions "on behalf of the trustee himself." *Mosser v. Darrow*, 341 U.S. 267, 272 (1951). As the Court explained in *Mosser*,

---

make no such distinction." 445 U.S. at 241, n. 1 (dissenting opinion). *See* ALI Fed. Sec. Code § 1603, Comment (2)(j) (Proposed Official Draft 1978).

[17]　The SEC expressly recognized that "[t]he value to the entire market of [analysts'] efforts cannot be gainsaid; market efficiency in pricing is significantly enhanced by [their] initiatives to ferret out and analyze information, and thus the analyst's work redounds to the benefit of all investors." 21 S.E.C. at 1046. The SEC asserts that analysts remain free to obtain from management corporate information for purposes of "filling in the 'interstices in analysis' . . . ." Brief for Respondent 42 (quoting *Investors Management Co.*, 44 S.E.C. at 646). But this rule is inherently imprecise, and imprecision prevents parties from ordering their actions in accord with legal requirements. Unless the parties have some guidance as to where the line is between permissible and impermissible disclosures and uses, neither corporate insiders nor analysts can be sure when the line is crossed. *Cf. Adler v. Klawans*, 267 F. 2d 840, 845 (CA2 1959) (Burger, J., sitting by designation).

[18]　On its facts, this case is the unusual one. Dirks is an analyst in a broker-dealer firm, and he did interview management in the course of his investigation. He uncovered, however, startling information that required no analysis or exercise of judgment as to its market relevance. Nonetheless, the principle at issue here extends beyond these facts. The SEC's rule—applicable without regard to any breach by an insider—could have serious ramifications on reporting by analysts of investment views. Despite the unusualness of Dirks' "find," the central role that he played in uncovering the fraud at Equity Funding, and that analysts in general can play in revealing information that corporations may have reason to withhold from the public, is an important one. Dirks' careful investigation brought to light a massive fraud at the corporation. And until the Equity Funding fraud was exposed, the information in the trading market was grossly inaccurate. But for Dirks' efforts, the fraud might well have gone undetected longer. *See* n. 8, *supra*.

a contrary rule "would open up opportunities for devious dealings in the name of the others that the trustee could not conduct in his own." 341 U.S. at 271. *See SEC v. Texas Gulf Sulphur Co.*, 446 F.2d 1301, 1308 (CA2), *cert. denied*, 404 U.S. 1005 (1971). Thus, the tippee's duty to disclose or abstain is derivative from that of the insider's duty. . . .

Thus, some tippees must assume an insider's duty to the shareholders not because they receive inside information, but rather because it has been made available to them improperly. And for Rule 10b-5 purposes, the insider's disclosure is improper only where it would violate his *Cady, Roberts* duty. Thus, a tippee assumes a fiduciary duty to the shareholders of a corporation not to trade on material nonpublic information only when the insider has breached his fiduciary duty to the shareholders by disclosing the information to the tippee and the tippee knows or should know that there has been a breach. As Commissioner Smith perceptively observed in *Investors Management Co.*: "[T]ippee responsibility must be related back to insider responsibility by necessary finding that the tippee knew the information was given to him in breach of a duty by a person having a special relationship to the issuer not to disclose the information . . . ." 44 S.E.C. at 651 (concurring in the result). Tipping thus properly is viewed only as a means of indirectly violating the *Cady, Roberts* disclose-or-abstain rule.[21]

C

In determining whether a tippee is under an obligation to disclose or abstain, it thus is necessary to determine whether the insider's "tip" constituted a breach of the insider's fiduciary duty. All disclosures of confidential corporate information are not inconsistent with the duty insiders owe to shareholders. In contrast to the extraordinary facts of this case, the more typical situation in which there will be a question whether disclosure violates the insider's *Cady, Roberts* duty is when insiders disclose information to analysts. . . . In some situations, the insider will act consistently with his fiduciary duty to shareholders, and yet release of the information may affect the market. For example, it may not be clear—either to the corporate insider or to the recipient analyst—whether the information will be viewed as material nonpublic information. Corporate officials may mistakenly think the information already has been disclosed or that it is not material enough to affect the market. Whether disclosure is a breach of duty therefore depends in large part on the purpose of the disclosure. This standard was identified by the SEC itself in *Cady, Roberts*: a purpose of the securities laws was to eliminate "use of inside information for personal advantage." 40 S.E.C. at 912, n. 15. Thus, the test is whether the insider personally will benefit, directly or indirectly, from his disclosure. Absent some personal gain, there has been no breach of duty to stockhold-

---

[21]   We do not suggest that knowingly trading on inside information is ever "socially desirable or even that it is devoid of moral considerations." Dooley, *Enforcement of Insider Trading Restrictions*, 66 VA. L. REV. 1, 55 (1980). Nor do we imply an absence of responsibility to disclose promptly indications of illegal actions by a corporation to the proper authorities—typically the SEC and exchange authorities in cases involving securities. Depending on the circumstances, and even where permitted by law, one's trading on material nonpublic information is behavior that may fall below ethical standards of conduct. But in a statutory area of the law such as securities regulation, where legal principles of general application must be applied, there may be "significant distinctions between actual legal obligations and ethical ideals." SEC, Report of the Special Study of Securities Markets, H.R. Doc. No. 95, 88th Cong., 1st Sess., pt. 1, pp. 237-238 (1963). . . .

ers. And absent a breach by the insider, there is no derivative breach. As Commissioner Smith stated in *Investors Management Co.*: "It is important in this type of case to focus on policing insiders and what they do . . . rather than on policing information per se and its possession . . . ." 44 S.E.C. at 648 (concurring in the result).

The SEC argues that, if inside-trading liability does not exist when the information is transmitted for a proper purpose but is used for trading, it would be a rare situation when the parties could not fabricate some ostensibly legitimate business justification for transmitting the information. We think the SEC is unduly concerned. In determining whether the insider's purpose in making a particular disclosure is fraudulent, the SEC and the courts are not required to read the parties' minds. Scienter in some cases is relevant in determining whether the tipper has violated his *Cady, Roberts* duty. But to determine whether the disclosure itself "deceive[s], manipulate[s], or defraud[s]" shareholders, *Aaron v. SEC*, 446 U.S. 680, 686 (1980), the initial inquiry is whether there has been a breach of duty by the insider. This requires courts to focus on objective criteria, *i.e.*, whether the insider receives a direct or indirect personal benefit from the disclosure, such as a pecuniary gain or a reputational benefit that will translate into future earnings. . . . There are objective facts and circumstances that often justify such an inference. For example, there may be a relationship between the insider and the recipient that suggests a quid pro quo from the latter, or an intention to benefit the particular recipient. The elements of fiduciary duty and exploitation of nonpublic information also exist when an insider makes a gift of confidential information to a trading relative or friend. The tip and trade resemble trading by the insider himself followed by a gift of the profits to the recipient.

Determining whether an insider personally benefits from a particular disclosure, a question of fact, will not always be easy for courts. But it is essential, we think, to have a guiding principle for those whose daily activities must be limited and instructed by the SEC's inside-trading rules, and we believe that there must be a breach of the insider's fiduciary duty before the tippee inherits the duty to disclose or abstain. In contrast, the rule adopted by the SEC in this case would have no limiting principle.

IV

Under the inside-trading and tipping rules set forth above, we find that there was no actionable violation by Dirks.[25] It is undisputed that Dirks himself was a stranger to Equity Funding, with no preexisting fiduciary duty to its shareholders.[26] He took no action, directly

---

[25] Dirks contends that he was not a "tippee" because the information he received constituted unverified allegations of fraud that were denied by management and were not "material facts" under the securities laws that required disclosure before trading. He also argues that the information he received was not truly "inside" information, *i.e.*, intended for a confidential corporate purpose, but was merely evidence of a crime. The Solicitor General agrees. *See* Brief for United States as *Amicus Curiae* 22. We need not decide, however, whether the information constituted "material facts," or whether information concerning corporate crime is properly characterized as "inside information." For purposes of deciding this case, we assume the correctness of the SEC's findings, accepted by the Court of Appeals, that petitioner was a tippee of material inside information.

[26] Judge Wright found that Dirks acquired a fiduciary duty by virtue of his position as an employee of a broker-dealer. *See* 220 U.S. App. D.C. at 325-327, 681 F.2d at 840-842. The SEC, however, did not consider Judge Wright's novel theory in its decision, nor did it present that theory to the Court of Appeals. The SEC also has not argued Judge Wright's theory in this Court. *See* Brief for Respondent 21, n. 27. The merits of such a duty are therefore not before the Court. *See SEC v. Chenery Corp.*, 332 U. S. 194, 196-197 (1947).

or indirectly, that induced the shareholders or officers of Equity Funding to repose trust or confidence in him. There was no expectation by Dirks' sources that he would keep their information in confidence. Nor did Dirks misappropriate or illegally obtain the information about Equity Funding. Unless the insiders breached their *Cady, Roberts* duty to shareholders in disclosing the nonpublic information to Dirks, he breached no duty when he passed it on to investors as well as to the Wall Street Journal.

It is clear that neither Secrist nor the other Equity Funding employees violated their *Cady, Roberts* duty to the corporation's shareholders by providing information to Dirks.[27] The tippers received no monetary or personal benefit for revealing Equity Funding's secrets, nor was their purpose to make a gift of valuable information to Dirks. As the facts of this case clearly indicate, the tippers were motivated by a desire to expose the fraud. In the absence of a breach of duty to shareholders by the insiders, there was no derivative breach by Dirks. Dirks therefore could not have been "a participant after the fact in [an] insider's breach of a fiduciary duty." *Chiarella*, 445 U.S. at 230, n. 12.

V

We conclude that Dirks, in the circumstances of this case, had no duty to abstain from use of the inside information that he obtained. The judgment of the Court of Appeals therefore is

Reversed.

---

[27]   In this Court, the SEC appears to contend that an insider invariably violates a fiduciary duty to the corporation's shareholders by transmitting nonpublic corporate information to an outsider when he has reason to believe that the outsider may use it to the disadvantage of the shareholders. "Thus, regardless of any ultimate motive to bring to public attention the derelictions at Equity Funding, Secrist breached his duty to Equity Funding shareholders." Brief for Respondent 31. This perceived "duty" differs markedly from the one that the SEC identified in *Cady, Roberts* and that has been the basis for federal tippee-trading rules to date. In fact, the SEC did not charge Secrist with any wrongdoing, and we do not understand the SEC to have relied on any theory of a breach of duty by Secrist in finding that Dirks breached his duty to Equity Funding's shareholders. . . .

The dissent argues that "Secrist violated his duty to Equity Funding shareholders by transmitting material nonpublic information to Dirks with the intention that Dirks would cause his clients to trade on that information." By perceiving a breach of fiduciary duty whenever inside information is intentionally disclosed to securities traders, the dissenting opinion effectively would achieve the same result as the SEC's theory below, *i.e.*, mere possession of inside information while trading would be viewed as a Rule 10b-5 violation. . . .

. . . [T]o constitute a violation of Rule 10b-5, there must be fraud. *See Ernst & Ernst v. Hochfelder*, 425 U.S. 185, 199 (1976) (statutory words "manipulative," "device," and "contrivance . . . connot[e] intentional or willful conduct designed to *deceive or defraud* investors by controlling or artificially affecting the price of securities") (emphasis added). There is no evidence that Secrist's disclosure was intended to or did in fact "deceive or defraud" anyone. Secrist certainly intended to convey relevant information that management was unlawfully concealing, and—so far as the record shows—he believed that persuading Dirks to investigate was the best way to disclose the fraud. Other efforts had proved fruitless. Under any objective standard, Secrist received no direct or indirect personal benefit from the disclosure.

The dissenting opinion focuses on shareholder "losses," "injury," and "damages," but in many cases there may be no clear causal connection between insider trading and outsiders' losses. In one sense, as market values fluctuate and investors act on inevitably incomplete or incorrect information, there always are winners and losers; but those who have "lost" have not necessarily been defrauded. On the other hand, inside trading for personal gain is fraudulent, and is a violation of the federal securities laws. *See* Dooley, *supra*, at 39-41, 70. Thus, there is little legal significance to the dissent's argument that Secrist and Dirks created new "victims" by disclosing the information to persons who traded. In fact, they prevented the fraud from continuing and victimizing many more investors.

Justice BLACKMUN, with whom Justice BRENNAN and Justice MARSHALL join, dissenting.

The Court today takes still another step to limit the protections provided investors by § 10(b) of the Securities Exchange Act of 1934. *See Chiarella v. United States*, 445 U.S. 222, 246 (1980) (dissenting opinion). The device employed in this case engrafts a special motivational requirement on the fiduciary duty doctrine. This innovation excuses a knowing and intentional violation of an insider's duty to shareholders if the insider does not act from a motive of personal gain. Even on the extraordinary facts of this case, such an innovation is not justified. . . .

The Court holds . . . that Dirks is not liable because Secrist did not violate his duty; according to the Court, this is so because Secrist did not have the improper purpose of personal gain. In so doing, the Court imposes a new, subjective limitation on the scope of the duty owed by insiders to shareholders. The novelty of this limitation is reflected in the Court's lack of support for it. . . .

The fact that the insider himself does not benefit from the breach does not eradicate the shareholder's injury. . . . It makes no difference to the shareholder whether the corporate insider gained or intended to gain personally from the transaction; the shareholder still has lost because of the insider's misuse of nonpublic information. The duty is addressed not to the insider's motives, but to his actions and their consequences on the shareholder. Personal gain is not an element of the breach of this duty.[11] . . . I do not join this limitation of the scope of an insider's fiduciary duty to shareholders.[13]

---

[11] The Court seems concerned that this case bears on insiders' contacts with analysts for valid corporate reasons. It also fears that insiders may not be able to determine whether the information transmitted is material or nonpublic. When the disclosure is to an investment banker or some other adviser, however, there is normally no breach because the insider does not have scienter: he does not intend that the inside information be used for trading purposes to the disadvantage of shareholders. Moreover, if the insider in good faith does not believe that the information is material or nonpublic, he also lacks the necessary scienter. *Ernst & Ernst v. Hochfelder*, 425 U.S. 185, 197 (1976). In fact, the scienter requirement functions in part to protect good faith errors of this type. *Id.* at 211, n. 31.

Should the adviser receiving the information use it to trade, it may breach a separate contractual or other duty to the corporation not to misuse the information. Absent such an arrangement, however, the adviser is not barred by Rule 10b-5 from trading on that information if it believes that the insider has not breached any duty to his shareholders. *See Walton v. Morgan Stanley & Co.*, 623 F.2d 796, 798-799 (CA2 1980).

The situation here, of course, is radically different. *Ante*, at n. 17 (Dirks received information requiring no analysis "as to its market relevance"). Secrist divulged the information for the precise purpose of causing Dirks' clients to trade on it. I fail to understand how imposing liability on Dirks will affect legitimate insider-analyst contacts.

[13] Although I disagree in principle with the Court's requirement of an improper motive, I also note that the requirement adds to the administrative and judicial burden in Rule 10b-5 cases. Assuming the validity of the requirement, the SEC's approach—a violation occurs when the insider knows that the tippee will trade with the information, Brief for SEC 31—can be seen as a presumption that the insider gains from the tipping. The Court now requires a case-by-case determination, thus prohibiting such a presumption.

The Court acknowledges the burdens and difficulties of this approach, but asserts that a principle is needed to guide market participants. I fail to see how the Court's rule has any practical advantage over the SEC's presumption. The Court's approach is particularly difficult to administer when the insider is not directly enriched monetarily by the trading he induces. For example, the Court does not explain why the benefit Secrist obtained—the good feeling of exposing a fraud and his enhanced reputation—is any different from the benefit to an insider who gives the information as a gift to a friend or relative. Under the Court's somewhat cynical view, gifts involve personal gain. *See ibid.* Secrist surely gave Dirks a gift of the commissions Dirks made on the deal in order to induce him to disseminate the information. The distinction between pure altruism and self-interest has puzzled philosophers for centuries; there is no reason to believe that courts and administrative law judges will have an easier time with it . . . .

The improper purpose requirement not only has no basis in law, but it rests implicitly on a policy that I cannot accept. The Court justifies Secrist's and Dirks' action because the general benefit derived from the violation of Secrist's duty to shareholders outweighed the harm caused to those shareholders. . . .

Although Secrist's general motive to expose the Equity Funding fraud was laudable, the means he chose were not. Moreover, even assuming that Dirks played a substantial role in exposing the fraud,[15] he and his clients should not profit from the information they obtained from Secrist. Misprision of a felony long has been against public policy. . . . A person cannot condition his transmission of information of a crime on a financial award. As a citizen, Dirks had at least an ethical obligation to report the information to the proper authorities. The Court's holding is deficient in policy terms not because it fails to create a legal norm out of that ethical norm, *see ibid.*, but because it actually rewards Dirks for his aiding and abetting. . . .

In my view, Secrist violated his duty to Equity Funding shareholders by transmitting material nonpublic information to Dirks with the intention that Dirks would cause his clients to trade on that information. Dirks, therefore, was under a duty to make the information publicly available or to refrain from actions that he knew would lead to trading. Because Dirks caused his clients to trade, he violated § 10(b) and Rule 10b-5. Any other result is a disservice to this country's attempt to provide fair and efficient capital markets.

I dissent.

NOTES AND QUESTIONS

(1) **The Equity Funding fraud.** The Equity Funding fraud was unprecedented in size. Ultimately, it was determined that Equity Funding had misrepresented the face amount of insurance policies by billions of dollars. With respect to Dirks' role in uncovering the fraud, consider the following additional facts, summarized from Dirks' account in Dirks & Gross, The Great Wall Street Scandal (1974).

Equity Funding, at the time of Secrist's disclosure to Dirks, was one of Wall Street's highest fliers and was the darling of analysts and institutional investors. Secrist had gone to Dirks because of what he heard about Dirks' very high credibility and Dirks' ability, because of his influence with large institutional investors, to put selling pressure on Equity Funding stock. Secrist believed that a sudden drop in the price of Equity Funding stock would force an investigation by regulators and prevent insiders from liquidating their holdings and escaping with the loot. [Why might sales by Dirks' clients cause the price to drop?] Secrist had a habit of injuring his own credibility. For example, while Secrist told Dirks that he had resigned from Equity Funding, Dirks determined shortly thereafter that Secrist had been fired. Dirks' associate, who listened

---

[15]   The Court uncritically accepts Dirks' own view of his role in uncovering the Equity Funding fraud. *See ante*, at n. 17. It ignores the fact that Secrist gave the same information at the same time to state insurance regulators, who proceeded to expose massive fraud in a major Equity Funding subsidiary. The fraud surfaced before Dirks ever spoke to the SEC.

with Dirks to Secrist's first extended account of the fraud, concluded that there was a 10% chance the story was true and Dirks himself put the odds at no more than half. Dirks believes he was particularly receptive to Secrist's story because he had long believed in the existence of fraud in the financial markets and had wanted to expose one.

There were many indications during the period immediately preceding ultimate public disclosure of the incredibility of Secrist's story: Goldblum's (Equity Funding's chief executive) vehement denial of the allegations and veiled threats of a libel suit against Dirks; a strong positive press release by Equity Funding; a strong recommendation of the stock by a large brokerage firm (Hayden, Stone); the certification of Equity Funding's financial statements by a major accounting firm (Seidman and Seidman); and the SEC's failure to act on a tip from the California Department of Insurance, the first place Secrist had gone with his story.

(2) **Unverified allegations as material, inside information.** Did Dirks breach his duty under 10b-5 even under the broad theory advocated by the SEC? Was Dirks' information material? Was it inside? Consider footnote 25 to the majority opinion. Did Dirks have the requisite scienter as to these elements?

(3) **The source and nature of a tippee's duty.** Because *Dirks* applies the same theory of insider trading applied by the plurality in *Chiarella*, it raises the same questions about the basis of that theory. Review Note 2 following *Chiarella* in Section 12.05[A]. Specifically, why shouldn't it be enough to establish a 10b-5 violation that Dirks knowingly or recklessly used material, inside information? Why does a federal violation depend on a breach of fiduciary duty by Dirks' tipper? Is a showing of "personal benefit" enough to establish such a breach under state law? If the duty arises under federal law, why should "personal benefit" be necessary. Why isn't it enough to establish a breach of duty that Secrist knew Dirks would trade on the information and actually intended for him to do so? See footnote 27 to the majority opinion and footnote 11 to the dissent.

(4) **The "personal gain" test.** Does this test provide, in the majority's words, a "guiding principle for those whose daily activities must be limited and instructed by the SEC's inside-trading rules"? Compare footnote 13 to the dissenting opinion. Was it clear that the Secrist-Dirks tip was not within the rule? What about a gift of inside information? This is what is often referred to as "The Big Chill" scenario—one of the characters in that movie, to help out another one, divulges valuable inside formation. Consider *SEC v. Switzer*.[128] Barry Switzer, then the Oklahoma football coach, while sunbathing at a track meet, overheard a corporate executive friend of his discussing with the friend's wife an impending business trip to arrange the sale of a company. Switzer and a number of tippees and remote tippees profited from purchases and sales of the

---

[128] 590 F. Supp. 756 (W.D. Okla. 1984).

company's stock based on the nonpublic information. The court denied relief because the executive did not breach a duty by revealing the information for gain and, in all events, the traders did not have the requisite level of knowledge of any breach of duty. What if Switzer had reason to know that the executive knew he was there—for example, because the executive glanced quickly at him? Should Switzer conclude that the executive had intended to reap a personal benefit by making a gift of the information? The court found that the executive did not know Switzer was there, needed to talk to his wife about child care arrangements, and was not very "impressed" by Switzer. How would Switzer know these facts?

(5) **Insider trading and the traditional role of securities analysts.** An important consideration underlying the Supreme Court's decision in *Dirks* is the role of securities analysts in the process of dissemination of corporate information. A securities analyst closely follows a small number of companies and issues reports on these companies to her employer, typically an investment banking firm, bank, investment advisory firm, mutual fund, insurance company or pension fund. Analysts' traditional role is to uncover information that is not already reflected in the market price of the stock. Regulation of trading by analysts may deter this efficiency-enhancing process. The problem of determining materiality of inside information when analysts pierce together a "mosaic" of public and private information is discussed in Note 3 following *Texas Gulf Sulphur.*

(6) **The changing role and regulation of analysts.** Analysts' role has changed somewhat since *Dirks*. Particularly since the rise of mutual funds and deregulation of brokers' commissions, analysts have had a harder time earning their pay solely from research. One effect has been that analysts increasingly rely on the firms they follow for information. These firms, in turn, often cultivate the following of analysts because a good "press" favorably affects the price of the corporation's stock. This used to include giving analysts the nonpublic information they crave. But the SEC barred this practice in 2000 with adoption of Regulation FD.[129]

Under Regulation FD, whenever an issuer or any person acting on the issuer's behalf discloses any material nonpublic information regarding the issuer or its securities to a securities professional, such as an analyst, or to a holder of the issuer's securities who can be expected to buy or sell based on the information, the issuer is required: (1) in the case of an intentional disclosure, to make public disclosure of that information simultaneously; or (2) in the case of non-intentional disclosure, to make public disclosure of that information promptly. The issuer is exempt from making public disclosure of material nonpublic information if the information about the issuer or its securities is supplied only to a person who owes a duty of trust or confidence to the issuer, such as an attorney, investment banker, or accountant, or to a person who expressly agrees to maintain the confidentiality of the information. A stated purpose of

---

[129] 17 C.F.R. § 243.100 et seq.

Regulation FD is to ensure, "to the maximum extent possible . . . that all investors . . . have access to an issuer's material disclosures at the same time."[130] Regulation FD would appear to conflict with *Dirks* because it renders disclosure by corporate insiders unlawful even when the disclosure does not involve a breach of fiduciary duty by the insider. To handle this problem, Regulation FD provides that "[n]o failure to make a public disclosure required solely by [Regulation FD] shall be deemed to be a violation of Rule 10b-5."

Analysts also have been used to sell securities underwritten by the investment banking firms that employ them. This practice drew scrutiny in light of the corporate accounting scandals of 2002. Merrill Lynch reached a $100 million settlement with the State of New York after a state investigation found that Merrill Lynch analysts often provided overly optimistic research reports about the stock of the firm's investment banking clients. Under the settlement, Merrill Lynch agreed to take a series of steps to separate its investment banking and research departments, including changing the methods for evaluating and compensating analysts.[131] Section 501 of the Sarbanes-Oxley Act of 2002 requires the SEC (or the exchanges or the NASD, if the SEC elects) to adopt rules that "address the conflicts of interest that can arise when securities analysts recommend equity securities in research reports and public appearances." The rules must be designed to more fully separate securities analysts from investment bankers, so the prospect of investment banking business does not influence analyst recommendations. The rules also must require securities analysts to disclose conflicts of interest.

(7) **Tippee liability based on tips related to tender offers.** Section 14(e) of the 1934 Act gives the SEC rulemaking authority with respect to tender offers. Acting under this authority, the SEC has adopted Rule 14e-3, which bars trading based on non-public material information *related to tender offers*, provided the trader knows or has reason to know that the information is nonpublic and has been acquired directly or indirectly from the bidder, the target, or any person acting on either's behalf. Unlike *Dirks*, Rule 14e-3 does not require any showing that the disclosure or trading involves a breach of fiduciary duty. *United States v. O'Hagan*[132] rejected a challenge that the SEC exceeded its authority in adopting Rule 14e-3. The Court held that § 14(e) confers broader rulemaking authority than does § 10(b) because § 14(e) specifically authorizes the SEC to "define, and prescribe means reasonably designed to prevent," fraudulent, deceptive, or manipulative acts or practices.

(8) **Tippee liability under the misappropriation theory.** Suppose a tipper legitimately confides in a tippee, who then abuses this confidence by trading on the information. The tippee's trading would not constitute a 10b-5 violation under *Dirks*, but it

---

[130] *See* SEC Release No. 33-7787, 71 SEC Docket 732 (Dec. 20, 1999).

[131] *See* Gasperino, *Merrill Lynch to Pay Big Fine, Increase Oversight of Analysts*, WALL ST. J., May 22, 2002 at A1.

[132] 521 U.S. 642 (1997).

might constitute a violation of 10b-5 under the "misappropriation" theory discussed in Subsection 12.05[C], below.

PROBLEM

Computo Corporation has been a beneficiary of stock market interest in technology stocks, and the price of its stock has risen steadily on consistent earnings increases. Computo is in the process of a new stock offering, which is being handled by the large brokerage firm of Smith and Company. Executives at Computo have discovered a rapid softening in demand for their products due to intensifying competition, as a result of which the company's internal short-term earnings projections have been revised drastically downward. The executives informed the underwriting department of Smith and Company of this development so that Smith would have up-to-date information in connection with the proposed stock offering. The underwriting department then passed the information to Smith's institutional sales department, which is responsible for sale of securities to large institutional investors.

Investors, Inc., a large investment company, is a customer of Smith's institutional sales department and has made substantial purchases through Smith. Gray, the chief securities trader at Investors, heard a rumor at an analysts' luncheon of problems at Computo, in which Investors had a substantial stock position. Knowing that Smith was working on Computo's underwriting, Gray called a broker at Smith to get current information. That broker divulged the information that the underwriting department had received from Computo.

You are the attorney for Investors. Advise the company whether sale of its Computo stock at this point would present any legal problems.[133] Would it make a difference if Gray had not called the broker but had simply observed that Smith was selling some of its inventory of Computo shares?

[C] "Outsider" Trading: The Misappropriation Theory

Subsections [A] and [B] dealt with the traditional category of insider trading defendants under 10b-5—those who have some direct or (as with tippees) derivative connection with the company whose shares they are trading. Federal liability in this situation may differ, but is not far removed, from insider trading liability under state law. But it has never been clear that federal liability should stop here. Why not liability for "outsiders"—those unrelated to the company whose shares they are trading—who have some special information not known by the rest of the market.[134] *Chiarella* forecloses

---

[133] For a similar fact situation, see *Investors Management Co., Inc.*, 33 S.E.C. 633 (1971).

[134] For an early discussion of this question, see Fleischer, Mundheim & Murphy, *An Initial Inquiry into Responsibility to Disclose Market Information*, 121 U. PA. L. REV. 798 (1973).

any duty on outsiders arising solely from the possession of material nonpublic information. But *Chiarella* refused to consider whether outsiders might come under a duty to refrain from trading based on a "misappropriation" theory like that advocated by Justice Burger in his dissent in *Chiarella*. After several Courts of Appeals accepted the "misappropriation" theory, the Supreme Court addressed the theory in the following case.

UNITED STATES v. O'HAGAN
United States Supreme Court
521 U.S. 642 (1997)

GINSBURG, J., delivered the opinion of the Court, in which STEVENS, O'CONNOR, KENNEDY, SOUTER, and BREYER, JJ., joined, and in Parts I, III, and IV of which SCALIA, J., joined. SCALIA, J., filed an opinion concurring in part and dissenting in part. THOMAS, J., filed an opinion concurring in the judgment in part and dissenting in part, in which REHNQUIST, C.J., joined.

This case concerns the interpretation and enforcement of § 10(b) and § 14(e) of the Securities Exchange Act of 1934, and rules made by the Securities and Exchange Commission pursuant to these provisions, Rule 10b-5 and Rule 14e-3(a). Two prime questions are presented. The first relates to the misappropriation of material, nonpublic information for securities trading; the second concerns fraudulent practices in the tender offer setting. In particular, we address and resolve these issues: (1) Is a person who trades in securities for personal profit, using confidential information misappropriated in breach of a fiduciary duty to the source of the information, guilty of violating § 10(b) and Rule 10b-5? (2) Did the Commission exceed its rulemaking authority by adopting Rule 14e-3(a), which proscribes trading on undisclosed information in the tender offer setting, even in the absence of a duty to disclose? Our answer to the first question is yes, and to the second question, viewed in the context of this case, no.

I

Respondent James Herman O'Hagan was a partner in the law firm of Dorsey & Whitney in Minneapolis, Minnesota. In July 1988, Grand Metropolitan PLC (Grand Met), a company based in London, England, retained Dorsey & Whitney as local counsel to represent Grand Met regarding a potential tender offer for the common stock of the Pillsbury Company, headquartered in Minneapolis. Both Grand Met and Dorsey & Whitney took precautions to protect the confidentiality of Grand Met's tender offer plans. O'Hagan did no work on the Grand Met representation. Dorsey & Whitney withdrew from representing Grand Met on September 9, 1988. Less than a month later, on October 4, 1988, Grand Met publicly announced its tender offer for Pillsbury stock.

On August 18, 1988, while Dorsey & Whitney was still representing Grand Met, O'Hagan began purchasing call options for Pillsbury stock. Each option gave him the right to purchase 100 shares of Pillsbury stock by a specified date in September 1988. Later in August and in September, O'Hagan made additional purchases of Pillsbury call options. By the end of September, he owned 2,500 unexpired Pillsbury options, apparently more than any other individual investor. *See* App. 85, 148. O'Hagan also purchased, in September 1988, some 5,000 shares of Pillsbury common stock, at a price just under $39 per share. When Grand Met announced its tender offer in October, the price of Pillsbury stock rose to nearly $60 per share. O'Hagan then sold his Pillsbury call options and common stock, making a profit of more than $4.3 million.

The Securities and Exchange Commission (SEC or Commission) initiated an investigation into O'Hagan's transactions, culminating in a 57-count indictment. The indictment alleged that O'Hagan defrauded his law firm and its client, Grand Met, by using for his own trading purposes material, nonpublic information regarding Grand Met's planned tender offer. *Id.* at 8. . . .

* * *

II

We address first the Court of Appeals' reversal of O'Hagan's convictions under § 10(b) and Rule 10b-5. . . .

A

* * *

Liability under Rule 10b-5, our precedent indicates, does not extend beyond conduct encompassed by § 10(b)'s prohibition. . . .

Under the "traditional" or "classical theory" of insider trading liability, § 10(b) and Rule 10b-5 are violated when a corporate insider trades in the securities of his corporation on the basis of material, nonpublic information. Trading on such information qualifies as a "deceptive device" under § 10(b), we have affirmed, because "a relationship of trust and confidence [exists] between the shareholders of a corporation and those insiders who have obtained confidential information by reason of their position with that corporation." *Chiarella v. United States*, 445 U.S. 222, 228 (1980). That relationship, we recognized, "gives rise to a duty to disclose [or to abstain from trading] because of the 'necessity of preventing a corporate insider from . . . taking unfair advantage of . . . uninformed . . . stockholders.'" *Id.* at 228-229 (citation omitted). The classical theory applies not only to officers, directors, and other permanent insiders of a corporation, but also to attorneys, accountants, consultants, and others who temporarily become fiduciaries of a corporation. *See Dirks v. SEC*, 463 U.S. 646, 655, n. 14 (1983).

The "misappropriation theory" holds that a person commits fraud "in connection with" a securities transaction, and thereby violates § 10(b) and Rule 10b-5, when he misappropriates confidential information for securities trading purposes, in breach of a duty owed to the source of the information. *See* Brief for United States 14. Under this theory, a fiduciary's undisclosed, self-serving use of a principal's information to purchase or sell securities, in breach of a duty of loyalty and confidentiality, defrauds the principal of the exclusive use of that information. In lieu of premising liability on a fiduciary relationship between company insider and purchaser or seller of the company's stock, the misappropriation theory premises liability on a fiduciary-turned-trader's deception of those who entrusted him with access to confidential information.

The two theories are complementary, each addressing efforts to capitalize on non-public information through the purchase or sale of securities. The classical theory targets a corporate insider's breach of duty to shareholders with whom the insider transacts; the misappropriation theory outlaws trading on the basis of nonpublic information by a corporate "outsider" in breach of a duty owed not to a trading party, but to the source of the information. The misappropriation theory is thus designed to "protect the integrity of the securities markets against abuses by 'outsiders' to a corporation who have access to confidential information that will affect the corporation's security price when revealed, but who owe no fiduciary or other duty to that corporation's shareholders." *Ibid*.

In this case, the indictment alleged that O'Hagan, in breach of a duty of trust and confidence he owed to his law firm, Dorsey & Whitney, and to its client, Grand Met, traded on the basis of nonpublic information regarding Grand Met's planned tender offer for Pillsbury common stock. App. 16. This conduct, the Government charged, constituted a fraudulent device in connection with the purchase and sale of securities.

B

We agree with the Government that misappropriation, as just defined, satisfies § 10(b)'s requirement that chargeable conduct involve a "deceptive device or contrivance" used "in connection with" the purchase or sale of securities. We observe, first, that misappropriators, as the Government describes them, deal in deception. A fiduciary who "[pretends] loyalty to the principal while secretly converting the principal's information for personal gain," Brief for United States 17, "dupes" or defrauds the principal. *See* Aldave, *Misappropriation: A General Theory of Liability for Trading on Nonpublic Information*, 13 HOFSTRA L. REV. 101, 119 (1984).

* * *

Deception through nondisclosure is central to the theory of liability for which the Government seeks recognition. As counsel for the Government stated in explanation of the theory at oral argument: "To satisfy the common law rule that a trustee may not use the property that [has] been entrusted [to] him, there would have to be consent. To satisfy the requirement of the Securities Act that there be no deception, there would only have to be disclosure." Tr. of Oral Arg. 12; *see* generally RESTATEMENT (SECOND) OF AGENCY §§ 390, 395 (1958) (agent's disclosure obligation regarding use of confidential information).[6]

The misappropriation theory advanced by the Government is consistent with *Santa Fe Industries, Inc. v. Green*, 430 U.S. 462 (1977), a decision underscoring that § 10(b) is not an all-purpose breach of fiduciary duty ban; rather, it trains on conduct involving manipulation or deception. *See id*. at 473-476. In contrast to the Government's allegations in this case, in *Santa Fe Industries*, all pertinent facts were disclosed by the persons charged with violating

---

[6]   Under the misappropriation theory urged in this case, the disclosure obligation runs to the source of the information, here, Dorsey & Whitney and Grand Met. Chief Justice Burger, dissenting in *Chiarella*, advanced a broader reading of § 10(b) and Rule 10b-5; the disclosure obligation, as he envisioned it, ran to those with whom the misappropriator trades. 445 U. S. at 240 ("a person who has misappropriated nonpublic information has an absolute duty to disclose that information or to refrain from trading"); *see also id*. at 243, n. 4. The Government does not propose that we adopt a misappropriation theory of that breadth.

§ 10(b) and Rule 10b-5, *see id.* at 474; therefore, there was no deception through nondisclosure to which liability under those provisions could attach, *see id.* at 476. Similarly, full disclosure forecloses liability under the misappropriation theory: Because the deception essential to the misappropriation theory involves feigning fidelity to the source of information, if the fiduciary discloses to the source that he plans to trade on the nonpublic information, there is no "deceptive device" and thus no § 10(b) violation—although the fiduciary-turned-trader may remain liable under state law for breach of a duty of loyalty.[7]

We turn next to the § 10(b) requirement that the misappropriator's deceptive use of information be "in connection with the purchase or sale of [a] security." This element is satisfied because the fiduciary's fraud is consummated, not when the fiduciary gains the confidential information, but when, without disclosure to his principal, he uses the information to purchase or sell securities. The securities transaction and the breach of duty thus coincide. This is so even though the person or entity defrauded is not the other party to the trade, but is, instead, the source of the nonpublic information. *See* Aldave, 13 HOFSTRA L. REV. at 120 ("a fraud or deceit can be practiced on one person, with resultant harm to another person or group of persons"). A misappropriator who trades on the basis of material, nonpublic information, in short, gains his advantageous market position through deception; he deceives the source of the information and simultaneously harms members of the investing public. *See id.* at 120-121, and n. 107.

The misappropriation theory targets information of a sort that misappropriators ordinarily capitalize upon to gain no-risk profits through the purchase or sale of securities. Should a misappropriator put such information to other use, the statute's prohibition would not be implicated. The theory does not catch all conceivable forms of fraud involving confidential information; rather, it catches fraudulent means of capitalizing on such information through securities transactions.

The Government notes another limitation on the forms of fraud § 10(b) reaches: "The misappropriation theory would not . . . apply to a case in which a person defrauded a bank into giving him a loan or embezzled cash from another, and then used the proceeds of the misdeed to purchase securities." Brief for United States 24, n. 13. In such a case, the Government states, "the proceeds would have value to the malefactor apart from their use in a securities transaction, and the fraud would be complete as soon as the money was obtained." *Ibid.* In other words, money can buy, if not anything, then at least many things; its misappropriation may thus be viewed as sufficiently detached from a subsequent securities transaction that § 10(b)'s "in connection with" requirement would not be met. *Ibid.*

The dissent's charge that the misappropriation theory is incoherent because information, like funds, can be put to multiple uses, misses the point. The Exchange Act was enacted in part "to insure the maintenance of fair and honest markets," 15 U.S.C. § 78b, and there is no question that fraudulent uses of confidential information fall within § 10(b)'s prohibition if the fraud is "in connection with" a securities transaction. It is hardly remarkable that

---

[7]   Where, however, a person trading on the basis of material, nonpublic information owes a duty of loyalty and confidentiality to two entities or persons—for example, a law firm and its client—but makes disclosure to only one, the trader may still be liable under the misappropriation theory.

a rule suitably applied to the fraudulent uses of certain kinds of information would be stretched beyond reason were it applied to the fraudulent use of money.

The dissent does catch the Government in overstatement. Observing that money can be used for all manner of purposes and purchases, the Government urges that confidential information of the kind at issue derives its value *only* from its utility in securities trading. *See* Brief for United States 10, 21; *post* (several times emphasizing the word "only"). Substitute "ordinarily" for "only," and the Government is on the mark.

* * *

The misappropriation theory comports with § 10(b)'s language, which requires deception "in connection with the purchase or sale of any security," not deception of an identifiable purchaser or seller. The theory is also well-tuned to an animating purpose of the Exchange Act: to insure honest securities markets and thereby promote investor confidence. *See* 45 Fed. Reg. 60,412 (1980) (trading on misappropriated information "undermines the integrity of, and investor confidence in, the securities markets"). Although informational disparity is inevitable in the securities markets, investors likely would hesitate to venture their capital in a market where trading based on misappropriated nonpublic information is unchecked by law. An investor's informational disadvantage vis-a-vis a misappropriator with material, nonpublic information stems from contrivance, not luck; it is a disadvantage that cannot be overcome with research or skill. . . .

In sum, considering the inhibiting impact on market participation of trading on misappropriated information, and the congressional purposes underlying § 10(b), it makes scant sense to hold a lawyer like O'Hagan a § 10(b) violator if he works for a law firm representing the target of a tender offer, but not if he works for a law firm representing the bidder. The text of the statute requires no such result.[9] The misappropriation at issue here was properly made the subject of a § 10(b) charge because it meets the statutory requirement that there be "deceptive" conduct "in connection with" securities transactions.

C

The Court of Appeals rejected the misappropriation theory primarily on two grounds. First, as the Eighth Circuit comprehended the theory, it requires neither misrepresentation nor nondisclosure. *See* 92 F.3d at 618. As we just explained, however, deceptive nondisclosure is essential to the § 10(b) liability at issue. Concretely, in this case, "it [was O'Hagan's] failure to disclose his personal trading to Grand Met and Dorsey, in breach of his duty to do so, that made his conduct 'deceptive' within the meaning of [§] 10(b)." Reply Brief 7.

---

[9]   As noted earlier, however, the textual requirement of deception precludes § 10(b) liability when a person trading on the basis of nonpublic information has disclosed his trading plans to, or obtained authorization from, the principal—even though such conduct may affect the securities markets in the same manner as the conduct reached by the misappropriation theory. Contrary to the dissent's suggestion—the fact that § 10(b) is only a partial antidote to the problems it was designed to alleviate does not call into question its prohibition of conduct that falls within its textual proscription. Moreover, once a disloyal agent discloses his imminent breach of duty, his principal may seek appropriate equitable relief under state law. Furthermore, in the context of a tender offer, the principal who authorizes an agent's trading on confidential information may, in the Commission's view, incur liability for an Exchange Act violation under Rule 14e-3(a).

Second and "more obvious," the Court of Appeals said, the misappropriation theory is not moored to § 10(b)'s requirement that "the fraud be 'in connection with the purchase or sale of any security.'" *See* 92 F.3d at 618 (quoting 15 U.S.C. § 78j(b)). According to the Eighth Circuit, three of our decisions reveal that § 10(b) liability cannot be predicated on a duty owed to the source of nonpublic information: *Chiarella v. United States*, 445 U.S. 222 (1980); *Dirks v. SEC*, 463 U.S. 646 (1983); and *Central Bank of Denver, N. A. v. First Interstate Bank of Denver, N. A.*, 511 U.S. 164 (1994). . . . We read the statute and our precedent differently, and note again that § 10(b) refers to "the purchase or sale of any security," not to identifiable purchasers or sellers of securities.

* * *

In sum, the misappropriation theory, as we have examined and explained it in this opinion, is both consistent with the statute and with our precedent. Vital to our decision that criminal liability may be sustained under the misappropriation theory, we emphasize, are two sturdy safeguards Congress has provided regarding scienter. To establish a criminal violation of Rule 10b-5, the Government must prove that a person "willfully" violated the provision. *See* 15 U.S.C. § 78ff(a). Furthermore, a defendant may not be imprisoned for violating Rule 10b-5 if he proves that he had no knowledge of the rule. *See ibid.*[13] O'Hagan's charge that the misappropriation theory is too indefinite to permit the imposition of criminal liability, *see* Brief for Respondent 30-33, thus fails not only because the theory is limited to those who breach a recognized duty. In addition, the statute's "requirement of the presence of culpable intent as a necessary element of the offense does much to destroy any force in the argument that application of the [statute]" in circumstances such as O'Hagan's is unjust. *Boyce Motor Lines, Inc. v. United States*, 342 U.S. 337, 342 (1952).

The Eighth Circuit erred in holding that the misappropriation theory is inconsistent with § 10(b). The Court of Appeals may address on remand O'Hagan's other challenges to his convictions under § 10(b) and Rule 10b-5.

III

[In this part of the opinion, the Court held that the SEC did not exceed its authority under § 14(e) of the 1934 Act when it adopted Rule 14e-3(a), which prohibits trading while in possession of material, non-public information relating to a tender offer even if the trading at issue does not entail a breach of fiduciary duty. The Court therefore refused to reverse O'Hagan's conviction for violating § 14(e).]

* * *

The judgment of the Court of Appeals for the Eighth Circuit is reversed, and the case is remanded for further proceedings consistent with this opinion.

It is so ordered.

---

[13]   The statute provides no such defense to imposition of monetary fines. *See ibid.*

Justice SCALIA, concurring in part and dissenting in part.

. . . I do not agree . . . with Part II of the Court's opinion, containing its analysis of respondent's convictions under § 10(b) and Rule 10b-5.

* * *

While the Court's explanation of the scope of § 10(b) and Rule 10b-5 would be entirely reasonable in some other context, it does not seem to accord with the principle of lenity we apply to criminal statutes (which cannot be mitigated here by the Rule, which is no less ambiguous than the statute). [citations omitted] In light of that principle, it seems to me that the unelaborated statutory language: "to use or employ in connection with the purchase or sale of any security . . . any manipulative or deceptive device or contrivance," § 10(b), must be construed to require the manipulation or deception of a party to a securities transaction.

Justice THOMAS, with whom THE CHIEF JUSTICE joins, concurring in the judgment in part and dissenting in part.

* * *

Unlike the majority . . . I cannot accept the Commission's interpretation of when a deceptive device is "used . . . in connection with" a securities transaction. . . .

* * *

What the embezzlement analogy does not do . . . is explain how the relevant fraud is "used or employed, in connection with" a securities transaction. And when the majority seeks to distinguish the embezzlement of funds from the embezzlement of information, it becomes clear that neither the Commission nor the majority has a coherent theory regarding § 10(b)'s "in connection with" requirement.

* * *

. . . The touchstone required for an embezzlement to be "used or employed, in connection with" a securities transaction is not merely that it "coincide" with, or be consummated by, the transaction, but that it is *necessarily* and *only* consummated by the transaction. . . .

* * *

. . . [T]he relevant distinction is not that the misappropriated information *was* used for a securities transaction (the money example met that test), but rather that it could *only* be used for such a transaction. . . . .

. . . Although the majority claims that the fraud in a financial embezzlement case is complete as soon as the money is obtained, and before the securities transaction is consummated, that is not uniformly true, and thus cannot be the Government's basis for claiming that such embezzlement does not violate the securities laws. It is not difficult to imagine an embezzlement of money that takes place via the mechanism of a securities transaction—for example where a broker is directed to purchase stock for a client and instead purchases such stock—using client funds—for his own account. The unauthorized (and presumably undisclosed) transaction is the very act that constitutes the embezzlement and the "securities transaction and the breach of duty thus coincide." What presumably distinguishes monetary embezzlement for the Government is thus that it is not *necessarily* coincident with a securities transaction, not that it *never* lacks such a "connection."

Once the Government's construction of the misappropriation theory is accurately described and accepted—along with its implied construction of § 10(b)'s "in connection with" language—that theory should no longer cover cases, such as this one, involving fraud on the source of information where the source has no connection with the other participant in a securities transaction. It seems obvious that the undisclosed misappropriation of confidential information is not necessarily consummated by a securities transaction. In this case, for example, upon learning of Grand Met's confidential takeover plans, O'Hagan could have done any number of things with the information: He could have sold it to a newspaper for publication, *see* Tr. of Oral Arg. 36; he could have given or sold the information to Pillsbury itself, *see id.* at 37; or he could even have kept the information and used it solely for his personal amusement, perhaps in a fantasy stock trading game.

Any of these activities would have deprived Grand Met of its right to "exclusive use" of the information and, if undisclosed, would constitute "embezzlement" of Grand Met's informational property. Under *any* theory of liability, however, these activities would not violate § 10(b) and, according to the Commission's monetary embezzlement analogy, these possibilities are sufficient to preclude a violation under the misappropriation theory even where the informational property *was* used for securities trading. That O'Hagan actually did use the information to purchase securities is thus no more significant here than it is in the case of embezzling money used to purchase securities. In both cases the embezzler *could have* done something else with the property, and hence the Commission's necessary "connection" under the securities laws would not be met.[2] If the relevant test under the "in connection with" language is whether the fraudulent act is *necessarily* tied to a securities transaction, then the misappropriation of confidential information used to trade no more violates § 10(b) than does the misappropriation of funds used to trade. As the Commission concedes that the latter is not covered under its theory, I am at a loss to see how the same theory can coherently be applied to the former.

The majority makes no attempt to defend the misappropriation theory as set forth by the Commission. . . . Having rejected the Government's description of its theory, the majority then engages in the "imaginative" exercise of constructing its own misappropriation theory from whole cloth. Thus, we are told, if we merely "substitute 'ordinarily' for 'only'" when describing the degree of connectedness between a misappropriation and a securities transaction, the Government would have a winner. *Ibid.* Presumably, the majority would similarly edit the Government's brief to this Court to argue for only an "ordinary," rather than an "*inherent* connection between the deceptive conduct and the purchase or sale of a security." Brief for United States 21 (emphasis added).

---

[2]   Indeed, even if O'Hagan or someone else thereafter used the information to trade, the misappropriation would have been complete before the trade and there should be no § 10(b) liability. The most obvious real-world example of this scenario would be if O'Hagan had simply tipped someone else to the information. The mere act of passing the information along would have violated O'Hagan's fiduciary duty and, if undisclosed, would be an "embezzlement" of the confidential information, regardless of whether the tippee later traded on the information.

* * *

Whether the majority's new theory has merit, we cannot possibly tell on the record before us. There are no findings regarding the "ordinary" use of misappropriated information, much less regarding the "ordinary" use of other forms of embezzled property. The Commission has not opined on the scope of the new requirement that property must "ordinarily" be used for securities trading in order for its misappropriation to be "in connection with" a securities transaction. We simply do not know what would or would not be covered by such a requirement, and hence cannot evaluate whether the requirement embodies a consistent and coherent interpretation of the statute. Moreover, persons subject to this new theory, such as respondent here, surely could not and cannot regulate their behavior to comply with the new theory because, until today, the theory has never existed. In short, the majority's new theory is simply not presented by this case, and cannot form the basis for upholding respondent's convictions.

In upholding respondent's convictions under the new and improved misappropriation theory, the majority also points to various policy considerations underlying the securities laws, such as maintaining fair and honest markets, promoting investor confidence, and protecting the integrity of the securities markets. But the repeated reliance on such broad-sweeping legislative purposes reaches too far and is misleading in the context of the misappropriation theory. It reaches too far in that, regardless of the overarching purpose of the securities laws, it is not illegal to run afoul of the "purpose" of a statute, only its letter. The majority's approach is misleading in this case because it glosses over the fact that the supposed threat to fair and honest markets, investor confidence, and market integrity comes not from the supposed fraud in this case, but from the mere fact that the information used by O'Hagan was nonpublic.

As the majority concedes, because "the deception essential to the misappropriation theory involves feigning fidelity to the source of information, if the fiduciary discloses *to the source* that he plans to trade on the nonpublic information, there is no 'deceptive device' and thus no § 10(b) violation." (Emphasis added). Indeed, were the source expressly to authorize its agents to trade on the confidential information—as a perk or bonus, perhaps—there would likewise be no § 10(b) violation. Yet in either case—disclosed misuse or authorized use—the hypothesized "inhibiting impact on market participation," would be identical to that from behavior violating the misappropriation theory: "Outsiders" would still be trading based on nonpublic information that the average investor has no hope of obtaining through his own diligence.

The majority's statement that a "misappropriator who trades on the basis of material, nonpublic information, in short, *gains his advantageous market position through deception; he deceives the source of the information and simultaneously harms members of the investing public*," (emphasis added), thus focuses on the wrong point. Even if it is true that trading on nonpublic information hurts the public, it is true whether or not there is any deception of the source of the information. Moreover, as we have repeatedly held, use of nonpublic information to trade is not itself a violation of § 10(b). *E.g.*, *Chiarella*, 445 U.S. at 232-233. Rather, it is the use of fraud "in connection with" a securities transaction that is forbidden. Where the relevant element of fraud has no impact on the integrity of the subsequent transactions as distinct from the nonfraudulent element of using nonpublic information, one can reasonably question whether the fraud was used in connection with a securities transaction.

And one can likewise question whether removing that aspect of fraud, though perhaps laudable, has anything to do with the confidence or integrity of the market.

* * *

NOTES AND QUESTIONS

(1) **Consistency with prior law.** Does the Court's theory square with the Supreme Court's position in *Santa Fe* that the federal securities laws do not encompass state law fiduciary breaches? Also, how does the version of the misappropriation theory adopted in *O'Hagan* differ from the version suggested by Justice Burger in his dissent in *Chiarella*? See footnote 6 to the majority opinion in *O'Hagan*.

(2) **Scope of the theory.** Does the majority opinion adequately distinguish insider trading from ordinary embezzlement? Do you agree with Justice Thomas' qualification of the theory?

(3) **The roles of disclosure and consent.** What are the roles of disclosure and consent? Does *O'Hagan* mean that you can trade on stolen information as long as you disclose that you're doing so? *See* **Painter, et al.**, below. To whom must you disclose? Must O'Hagan disclose both to his firm and the client? See footnote 7 to the majority's opinion.

(4) **The misappropriation theory and market participants.** Must the misappropriation involve a market participant? Might the Court have affirmed the Fourth Circuit's reversal of the conviction in *United States v. Bryan*,[135] which involved misappropriation from the West Virginia Lottery? If so, is an occasional trader a market participant?

(5) **Materiality in misappropriation cases.** Must the misappropriated information be material? Assuming materiality is necessary, what should the standard be? Assuming *TSC Industries, Inc. v Northway, Inc.* applies to misappropriators (*see* Note 1 following *Texas Gulf Sulphur* in Section 12.05[A]), does it take into account that the insider may have legitimately acquired all but a small piece of his information? Note that O'Hagan acted initially on the basis of rumors of the impending Grand Met bid for Pillsbury that he heard from his broker.

(6) **The scienter standard.** What is the scienter standard for civil and criminal liability? Does culpability depend on knowledge of the law, as Justice Breyer suggested during oral argument?[136]

---

[135] 58 F.3d 933 (4th Cir. 1995).

[136] *See* Transcript of Oral Argument, 1997 WL 182584, at 34.

(7) **Relationships giving rise to duties not to misappropriate information.** One of the most difficult questions that arises in connection with the misappropriation theory is whether an outsider has a sufficient relationship with a third party to create a duty not to trade based on information obtained through that relationship. For instance, does a doctor have a duty to refrain from trading based on information obtained from a patient? Consider the following pre-*O'Hagan* decision.

UNITED STATES v. CHESTMAN

United States Court of Appeals, Second Circuit

947 F.2d 551 (1991), *cert. denied*, 503 U.S. 1004 (1992)

MESKILL, J.

A jury found Chestman guilty of thirty-one counts of insider trading and perjury . . . . A panel of this Court reversed Chestman's convictions in their entirety. 903 F.2d 75 (2d Cir. 1990).

On en banc reconsideration, we conclude that the Rule 14e-3(a) convictions should be affirmed and that the Rule 10b-5 and mail fraud convictions should be reversed. . . .

BACKGROUND

Robert Chestman is a stockbroker. Keith Loeb first sought Chestman's services in 1982, when Loeb decided to consolidate his and his wife's holdings in Waldbaum, Inc. (Waldbaum), a publicly traded company that owned a large supermarket chain. During their initial meeting, Loeb told Chestman that his wife was a granddaughter of Julia Waldbaum, member of the board of directors of Waldbaum and the wife of its founder. Julia Waldbaum also was the mother of Ira Waldbaum, the president and controlling shareholder of Waldbaum from 1982 to 1986, Chestman executed several transactions involving Waldbaum restricted and common stock for Keith Loeb. To facilitate some of these trades, Loeb sent Chestman a copy of his wife's birth certificate, which indicated that his wife's mother was Shirley Waldbaum Witkin.

On November 21, 1986, Ira Waldbaum agreed to sell Waldbaum to the Great Atlantic and Pacific Tea Company (A&P). The resulting stock purchase agreement required Ira to tender a controlling block of Waldbaum shares to A&P at a price of $50 per share. Ira told three of his children, all employees of Waldbaum, about the pending sale two days later, admonishing them to keep the news quiet until a public announcement. He also told his sister, Shirley Witkin, and nephew, Robert Karin about the sale, and offered to tender their shares along with his controlling block of shares to enable them to avoid the administrative difficulty of tendering after the public announcement. He cautioned them "that [the sale was] not to be discussed," that it was to remain confidential.

In spite of Ira's counsel, Shirley told her daughter Susan Loeb, on November 24 that Ira was selling the company. Shirley warned Susan not to tell anyone except her husband, Keith Loeb, because disclosure could ruin the sale. The next day, Susan told her husband about the pending tender offer and cautioned him not to tell anyone because "it could possibly ruin the sale."

The following day, November 26, Keith Loeb telephoned Robert Chestman at 8:59 a.m. Unable to reach Chestman, Loeb left a message asking Chestman to call him "ASAP." According to Loeb, he later spoke with Chestman between 9:00 a.m. and 10:30 a.m. that morning and told Chestman that he had "some definite, some accurate information" that Waldbaum was about to be sold at a "substantially higher" price than its market value. Loeb asked Chestman several times what he thought Loeb should do. Chestman responded that he could not advise Loeb what to do "in a situation like this" and that Loeb would have to make up his own mind.

That morning Chestman executed several purchases of Waldbaum stock. At 9:49 a.m., he bought 3,000 shares for his own account at $24.65 per share. Between 11:31 a.m. and 12:35 p.m., he purchased an additional 8,000 shares for his clients' discretionary accounts at prices ranging from $25.75 to $26.00 per share. One of the discretionary accounts was the Loeb account, for which Chestman bought 1,000 shares.

Before the market closed at 4:00 p.m., Loeb claims that he telephoned Chestman a second time. During their conversation Loeb again pressed Chestman for advice. Chestman repeated that he could not advise Loeb "in a situation like this," but then said that, based on his research, Waldbaum was "buy." Loeb subsequently ordered 1,000 shares of Waldbaum stock.

Chestman presented a different version of the day's events. Before the SEC and at trial, he claimed that he had purchased Waldbaum stock based on his own research. He stated that his purchases were consistent with previous purchases of Waldbaum stock and other retail food stocks and were supported by reports in trade publications as well as the unusually high trading volume of the stock on November 25. He denied having spoken to Loeb about Waldbaum stock on the day of the trades.

At the close of trading on November 26, the tender offer was publicly announced. Waldbaum stock rose to $49 per share the next business day. In December 1986, Loeb learned that the National Association of Securities Dealers had started an investigation concerning transactions in Waldbaum stock. Loeb contacted Chestman who, according to Loeb, "reassured" him that Chestman had bought the stock for Loeb's account based on his research. Loeb called Chestman again in April 1987 after learning of an SEC investigation into the trading of Waldbaum stock. Chestman again stated that he bought the stock based on research. Similar conversations ensued. After one of these conversations, Chestman asked Loeb what his "position" was. Loeb replied, "I guess it's the same thing." Loeb subsequently agreed, however, to cooperate with the government. The terms of his cooperation agreement required that he disgorge the $25,000 profit from his purchase and sale of Waldbaum stock and pay a $25,000 fine. . . .

DISCUSSION

[The court held SEC Rule 14e-3 was a valid exercise of the SEC's rulemaking authority, and upheld Chestman's conviction under that rule. As noted earlier, the Supreme Court upheld Rule 14e-3 in *O'Hagan*.]

* * *

B. Rule 10b-5

Chestman's Rule 10b-5 convictions were based on the misappropriation theory, which provides that "one who misappropriates nonpublic information in breach of a fiduciary duty and trades on that information to his own advantage violates Section 10(b) and Rule 10b-5." *SEC v. Materia*, 745 F.2d 197, 203 (2d Cir. 1984), *cert. denied*, 471 U.S. 1053 (1985). With respect to the shares Chestman purchased on behalf of Keith Loeb, Chestman was convicted of aiding and abetting Loeb's misappropriation of nonpublic information in breach of a duty Loeb owed to the Waldbaum family and to his wife Susan. As to the shares Chestman purchased for himself and his other clients, Chestman was convicted as a "tippee" of that same misappropriated information. Thus, while Chestman is the defendant in this case, the alleged misappropriator was Keith Loeb. The government agrees that Chestman's.convictions cannot be sustained unless there was sufficient evidence to show that (1) Keith Loeb breached a duty owed to the Waldbaum family or Susan Loeb based on a fiduciary or similar relationship of trust and confidence, and (2) Chestman knew that Loeb had done so. We have heretofore never applied the misappropriation theory—and its predicate requirement of a fiduciary breach—in the context of family relationships.

* * *

1. Traditional Theory of Rule 10b-5 Liability

The traditional theory of insider trader liability derives principally from the Supreme Court's holdings in *Chiarella*, 445 U.S. 222, and *Dirks v. SEC*, 463 U.S. 646 (1983). . . .

Binding these strands of Rule 10b-5 liability are two principles—one, the predicate act of fraud must be traceable to a breach of duty to the purchasers or sellers of securities; two, a fiduciary duty does not run to the purchasers or sellers solely as a result of one's possession of material nonpublic information.

2. Misappropriation Theory

* * *

[Under the misappropriation theory], the fiduciary relationship question takes on special importance. This is because a fraud-on-the-source theory of liability extends the focus of Rule 10b-5 beyond the confined sphere of fiduciary/shareholder relations to fiduciary breaches of any sort, a particularly broad expansion of 10b-5 liability if the add-on, a "similar relationship of trust and confidence," is construed liberally. One concern triggered by this broadened inquiry is that fiduciary duties are circumscribed with some clarity in the context of shareholder relations but lack definition in other contexts. . . .

3. Fiduciary Duties and Their Functional Equivalent

Against this backdrop, we turn to our central inquiry—what constitutes a fiduciary or similar relationship of trust and confidence in the context of Rule 10b-5 criminal liability? We begin by noting two factors that do not themselves create the necessary relationship.

First, a fiduciary duty cannot be imposed unilaterally by entrusting a person with confidential information. . . .

Second, marriage does not, without more, create a fiduciary relationship. . . . Although spouses certainly may by their conduct become fiduciaries, the marriage relationship alone does not impose fiduciary status. In sum, more than the gratuitous reposal of a secret to another who happens to be a family member is required to establish a fiduciary or similar relationship of trust and confidence.

We take our cues as to what is required to create the requisite relationship from the securities fraud precedents and the common law. *See Chiarella*, 445 U.S. at 227-30. The common law has recognized that some associations are inherently fiduciary. Counted among these hornbook fiduciary relations are those existing between attorney and client, executor and heir, guardian and ward, principal and agent, trustee and trust beneficiary, and senior corporate official and shareholder. . . . While this list is by no means exhaustive, it is clear that the relationships involved in this case—those between Keith and Susan Loeb and between Keith Loeb and the Waldbaum family—were not traditional fiduciary relationships.

That does not end our inquiry, however. The misappropriation theory requires us to consider not only whether there exists a fiduciary relationship but also whether there exists a "similar relationship of trust and confidence." As the term "similar" implies, a "relationship of trust and confidence" must share the essential characteristics of a fiduciary association. Absent reference to the adjective "similar," interpretation of a "relationship of trust and confidence" becomes an exercise in question begging. . . .

A fiduciary relationship involves discretionary authority and dependency: One person depends on another—the fiduciary—to serve his interests. In relying on a fiduciary to act for his benefit, the beneficiary of the relation may entrust the fiduciary with custody over property of one sort or another. Because the fiduciary obtains access to this property to serve the ends of the fiduciary relationship, he becomes duty-bound not to appropriate the property for his own use. What has been said of an agent's duty of confidentiality applies with equal force to other fiduciary relations: "an agent is subject to a duty to the principal not to use or to communicate information confidentially given him by the principal or acquired by him during the course of or on account of his agency." RESTATEMENT (SECOND) OF AGENCY 395 (1958). These characteristics represent the measure of the paradigmatic fiduciary relation-ship. A similar relationship of trust and confidence consequently must share these qualities.

In [*United States v.*] *Reed*, 601 F. Supp. 685 [S.D.N.Y. 1985], the district court confronted the question whether these principal characteristics of a fiduciary relationship—dependency and influence—were necessary factual prerequisites to a similar relationship of trust and confidence. There a member of the board of directors of Amax, Gordon Reed, disclosed to his son on several occasions confidential information concerning a proposed tender offer for Amax. Allegedly relying on this information, the son purchased Amax stock call options. The son was subsequently indicted for violating, among other things, Rule 10b-5 based on breach of a fiduciary duty arising between the father and son. The son then moved to dismiss the indictment, contending that he did not breach a fiduciary duty to his father. The district court sustained the indictment.

Both the government and Chestman rely on *Reed*. The government draws on *Reed's* application of the misappropriation theory in the family context and its expansive construction of relationships of trust and confidence. Chestman, without challenging the holding in *Reed*, argues that *Reed* cannot sustain his Rule 10b-5 convictions because, unlike

Reed senior and junior, Keith and Susan Loeb did not customarily repose confidential business information in one another. Neither party challenges the holding of *Reed*. And we
decline to do so *sua sponte*. To remain consistent with our interpretation of a "'similar relationship of trust and confidence," however, we limit *Reed* to its essential holding: the
repeated disclosure of business secrets between family members may substitute for a factual
finding of dependence and influence and thereby sustain a finding of the functional equivalent of a fiduciary relationship. We note, in this regard, that *Reed* repeatedly emphasized
that the father and son "frequently discussed business affairs." *Id.* at 690; *see also id.* at 705,
709, 717-18.

We recognize, as *Reed* did, that equity has occasionally established a less rigorous
threshold for a fiduciary-like relationship in order to right civil wrongs arising from non-
compliance with the statute of frauds, statute of wills and parol evidence rule. . . . Useful as
such an elastic and expedient definition of confidential relations, *i.e.*, relations of trust and
confidence, may be in the civil context, it has no place in the criminal law. A "suitable
occasion" test for determining the presence of criminal fraud would offend not only the rule
of lenity but due process as well. . . .

4. Application of the Law of Fiduciary Duties

The alleged misappropriator in this case was Keith Loeb. According to the government's theory of prosecution, Loeb breached a fiduciary duty to his wife Susan and the
Waldbaum family when he disclosed to Robert Chestman information concerning a pending tender offer for Waldbaum stock. Chestman was convicted as an aider and abettor of the
misappropriation and as a tippee of the misappropriated information. Conviction under
both theories, the government concedes, required the government to establish two critical
elements—Loeb breached a fiduciary duty to Susan Loeb or to the Waldbaum family and
Chestman knew that Loeb had done so.

* * *

We have little trouble finding the evidence insufficient to establish a fiduciary relationship or its functional equivalent between Keith Loeb and the Waldbaum family. The government presented only two pieces of evidence on this point. The first was that Keith was
an extended member of the Waldbaum family, specifically the family patriarch's (Ira Waldbaum's) "nephew-in-law." The second piece of evidence concerned Ira's discussions of the
business with family members. "My children," Ira Waldbaum testified, "have always been
involved with me and my family and they know we never speak about business outside of
the family." His earlier testimony indicates that the "family" to which he referred were his
"three children who were involved in the business."

Lending this evidence the reasonable inferences to which it is entitled, it falls short of
establishing the relationship necessary for fiduciary obligations. Kinship alone does not create the necessary relationship. The government proffered nothing more to establish a fiduciary-like association. It did not show that Keith Loeb had been brought into the family's
inner circle, whose members, it appears, discussed confidential business information either
because they were kin or because they worked together with Ira Waldbaum. Keith was not
an employee of Waldbaum and there was no showing that he participated in confidential
communications regarding the business. The critical information was gratuitously commu-

nicated to him. The disclosure did not serve the interests of Ira Waldbaum, his children or the Waldbaum company. Nor was there any evidence that the alleged relationship was characterized by influence or reliance of any sort. Measured against the principles of fiduciary relations, the evidence does not support a finding that Keith Loeb and the Waldbaum family shared either a fiduciary relation or its functional equivalent.

The government's theory that Keith breached a fiduciary duty of confidentiality to Susan suffers from similar defects. The evidence showed: Keith and Susan were married; Susan admonished Keith not to disclose that Waldbaum was the target of tender offer; and the two had shared and maintained confidences in the past.

Keith's status as Susan's husband could not itself establish fiduciary status. Nor, absent a pre-existing fiduciary relation or an express agreement of confidentiality, could the coda—"Don't tell." That leaves the unremarkable testimony that Keith and Susan had shared and maintained generic confidences before. The jury was not told the nature of these past disclosures and therefore it could not reasonably find a relationship that inspired fiduciary, rather than normal marital obligations.

In the absence of evidence of an explicit acceptance by Keith of a duty of confidentiality, the context of the disclosure takes on special import. While acceptance may be implied, it must be implied from a pre-existing fiduciary-like relationship between the parties: Here the government presented the jury with insufficient evidence from which to draw a rational inference of implied acceptance. Susan's disclosure of the information to Keith served no purpose, business or otherwise. The disclosure also was unprompted. Keith did not induce her to convey the information through misrepresentation or subterfuge. Superiority and reliance, moreover, did not mark this relationship either before or after the disclosure of the confidential information. Nor did Susan's dependence on Keith to act in her interests for some purpose inspire the disclosure. The government failed even to establish a pattern of sharing business confidences between the couple. The government, therefore, failed to offer sufficient evidence to establish the functional equivalent of a fiduciary relation.

In sum, because Keith owed neither Susan nor the Waldbaum family a fiduciary duty or its functional equivalent, he did not defraud them by disclosing news of the pending tender offer to Chestman. Absent a predicate act of fraud by Keith Loeb, the alleged misappropriator, Chestman could not be derivatively liable as Loeb's tippee or as an aider and abettor. Therefore, Chestman's Rule 10b-5 convictions must be reversed. . . .

CONCLUSION

Accordingly, we affirm the Rule 14e-3(a) convictions and reverse the Rule 10b-5 and mail fraud convictions. The reversal of these convictions does not warrant reconsideration of the sentence since the sentences on the Rule 10b-5 and mail fraud convictions are concurrent with the sentences in the Rule 14(e)-3(a) counts. The panel's reversal of the perjury conviction remains intact.

WINTER, Circuit Judge (joined by OAKES, Chief Judge, NEWMAN, KEARSE, and MCLAUGHLIN, Circuit Judges), concurring in part and dissenting in part:

. . . I respectfully dissent . . . from the reversals of [Chestman's] convictions under Section 10(b) and under the mail fraud statute, 18 U.S.C. § 1341 (1988).

* * *

. . . I believe that family members who have benefited from the family's control of the corporation are under a duty not to disclose confidential corporate information that comes to them in the ordinary course of family affairs. In the case of family-controlled corporations, family and business affairs are necessarily intertwined, and it is inevitable that from time to time normal familial interactions will lead to the revelation of confidential corporate matters to various family members. Indeed, the very nature of familial relationships may cause the disclosure of corporate matters to avoid misunderstandings among family members or suggestions that a family member is unworthy of trust.

Under my colleagues' theory, the disclosure of family corporate information can be avoided only by family members extracting formal, express promises of confidentiality or by elderly mothers in poor health refusing to tell their daughters about mysterious travels. If disclosure is made, daughters may not disclose their mother's doings or potential financial benefits to the daughters' husbands without a formal, express promise of confidentiality. If, for example, Susan had earlier shared with Keith her concerns about her mother's mysterious travels before learning of their purpose, she would not have been able to tell him what she later learned about those travels no matter how persistently he asked. For my colleagues in the majority, the critical gap in the government's case was that Susan did not testify either that on this occasion Keith agreed not to disclose the pending acquisition by A&P or that prior confidential communications between her and her husband had involved the Waldbaum's corporation.

I have no lack of sympathy with my colleagues' concern about the difficulty of drawing lines in this area. Nevertheless, the line they draw seems very unrealistic in that it expects family members to behave like strangers toward each other. It also leads to the perverse and circular result that where family business interests are concerned, family members must act as if there are no mutual obligations of trust and confidence because the law does not recognize such obligations. Under such a regime, parents and children must conceal their comings and goings, family members must cease to speak when a son-in-law enters a room, and offended members of the family must understand that such conduct is always related only to business. . . .

I thus believe that a family member (i) who has received or expects (*e.g.*, through inheritance) benefits from family control of a corporation, here gifts of stock, (ii) who is in a position to learn confidential corporate information through ordinary family interactions, and (iii) who knows that under the circumstances both the corporation and the family desire confidentiality, has a duty not to use information so obtained for personal profit where the use risks disclosure. The receipt or expectation of benefits increases the interest of such family members in corporate affairs and thus increases the chance that they will learn confidential information. Disclosure in the present case occurred in the course of a discussion that included, inter alia, an examination of the benefits of the A&P acquisition to Susan, Keith and their children. Susan's warning to Keith about secrecy was clearly intended to protect the corporation as well as the family and clearly had originated with Ira Waldbaum. In such circumstances, Susan's saying "Don't tell" is enough for me. Not to have such a rule means that a family-controlled corporation with public shareholders is subject to greater risk of disclosure of confidential information than is a corporation that is entirely publicly owned.

I see no room for argument over whether there was sufficient evidence for the jury to find that Chestman knew Keith Loeb was violating an obligation. The record fairly brims with Chestman's consciousness that Keith Loeb was behaving improperly. . . .

MINER, Circuit Judge, concurring:

. . . I write only to comment upon the "familial relationship" rule of insider trading proposed by Judge Winter in his partially dissenting opinion. . . .

It seems to me . . . that family discourse would be inhibited, rather than promoted, by a rule that would automatically assure confidentiality on the part of a family member receiving non-public corporate information. What speaker, secure in the knowledge that a relative could be prosecuted for insider trading, would reveal to that relative anything remotely connected with corporate dealings? Given the uncertainties surrounding the definition of insider trading, a term as yet unclarified by Congress, what family members would want to receive any information whatsoever that might bear on the family business? How could family news be disseminated freely in an atmosphere where the members must be ultra-sensitive to whether "both the corporation and the family" are seeking some measure of confidentiality "under the circumstances."

The difficulty of identifying those who would be covered by the proposed familial rule adds an additional element of uncertainty to what already are uncertain crimes. It is not clear just who would be subject to the duty of confidentiality: family members "who have received or expect[] . . . benefits from family control of a corporation" belong to a very broad category indeed. Here, those who have received gifts of stock are included. But does the category include those who have received only small amounts of stock? Does it matter what proportion the stock bears to the total issued and outstanding shares? Does the category include one who expects to receive stock through inheritance but never receives any? Does it include grandchildren who expect ultimately to inherit assets purchased with the proceeds of the sale of the family-controlled corporation? The net would be spread wider than appropriate in a criminal context. . . .

It is important to note that in the case at bar we deal with an attenuated trail of family confidences in which information was received without any assurance of confidentiality by the receiver and without any prior sharing of business information within the family. . . .

I would await further instructions from Congress before sailing into this uncharted area.

NOTES AND QUESTIONS

(1) **Relationships giving rise to a duty to refrain from insider trading.** Do you agree with the majority or the dissent in *Chestman*? Is it possible to draw a principled distinction between Loeb and a corporate employee, or is the court just trying to draw a bright line? Perhaps the furthest extension of the misappropriation theory so far is *United States v. Willis*,[137] in which the court held that a psychiatrist violated Rule 10b-5

---

[137] 737 F. Supp. 269 (S.D.N.Y. 1990).

by trading in Bank of America stock on information from his patient that the patient's husband (Sanford Weill, the former president of American Express) was involved in an effort to become chief executive of Bank of America. The defendant's breach of duty was based on his Hippocratic oath: "Whatsoever things I see or hear concerning the life of men, in my attendance on the sick or even apart therefrom, which ought not to be noised abroad, I will keep silence thereon, counting such things to be as sacred secrets." The patient was injured because she had a "property interest in a continuing course of psychiatric treatment." It seems unlikely that Hippocrates could have foreseen this use of his oath. Dr. Willis settled the SEC's civil case by paying $136,580.[138] Does *Willis* survive *Chestman*? Note in this regard that the defendant was allowed to withdraw his guilty plea in light of *Chestman*, but he again pleaded guilty.[139]

(2) **Rule 10b5-2.** Rule 10b5-2 reduces the uncertainty surrounding relationships that give rise to a duty not to misappropriate information by providing a non-exclusive definition of circumstances in which a person has a duty of trust or confidence for purposes of the misappropriation theory. Under the rule, a relation of trust and confidence is deemed to exist in the following circumstances:

(1) Whenever a person agrees to maintain information in confidence;

(2) Whenever the person communicating the material nonpublic information and the person to whom it is communicated have a history, pattern, or practice of sharing confidences, such that the recipient of the information knows or reasonably should know that the person communicating the material nonpublic information expects that the recipient will maintain its confidentiality; or

(3) Whenever a person receives or obtains material nonpublic information from his or her spouse, parent, child, or sibling; provided, however, that the person receiving or obtaining the information may demonstrate that no duty of trust or confidence existed with respect to the information, by establishing that he or she neither knew nor reasonably should have known that the person who was the source of the information expected that the person would keep the information confidential, because of the parties' history, pattern, or practice of sharing and maintaining confidences, and because there was no agreement or understanding to maintain the confidentiality of the information.

Would Loeb have a duty of trust and confidence under Rule 10b5-2?

---

[138] *See Psychiatrist Agrees to Settle Charges of Insider Trading*, WALL ST. J., Jan. 15, 1991, at B7.

[139] For a later opinion in the case, see *United States v. Willis*, 778 F. Supp. 205 (S.D.N.Y. 1991) (government need not prove breach of confidential relationship between husband and wife, only between doctor and patient, and government could show such a relationship here).

(3) **Tippees and the misappropriation theory.** As *Chestman* makes clear, tippees who trade on misappropriated information may be held liable for violating Rule 10b-5. However, the tippee must know of his tipper's breach. *See* Section 12.05[B]. In *United States v. Libera*,[140] the court held that a tippee could be convicted for insider trading, even if the tipper did not know the tippee intended to use the misappropriated information to engage in insider trading. The court reasoned that "[t]o allow a tippee to escape liability solely because the government cannot prove to a jury's satisfaction that the tipper knew exactly what misuse would result from the tipper's wrongdoing would not fulfill the purpose of the misappropriation theory, which is to protect property rights in information."[141] For a post-*O'Hagan* case applying *Libera*, see *United States v. Falcone*.[142] Both cases involved use of information about an "Inside Wall Stree." column in *Business Week* magazine.

REFERENCES

Painter, Krawiec & Williams, *Don't Ask, Just Tell: Insider Trading after* United States v.
    O'Hagan, 84 VA. L. REV. 153 (1998).
Ribstein, *Federalism and Insider Trading*, 6 SUP. CT. ECON. REV. 123 (1998).

[D] The Economics of Insider Trading

What should be the scope of the duty to refrain from trading on material, non-public information? The cases have displayed some confusion about the appropriate theory. The Supreme Court cases say that liability may be based either on breach of a fiduciary duty between the insider and those with whom the insider trades or upon a "misappropriation" from the source of the information. Both theories, however, are problematic. The fiduciary duty theory is not clearly grounded in either federal or state law and, as Justice Thomas points out in his dissent in *O'Hagan*, the "misappropriation" theory is difficult to tie to the goals of the securities laws. In short, there is a theoretical vacuum. It is, therefore, particularly appropriate to consider what guidance can be provided by economic analysis. Specifically, what are the costs and benefits of insider trading, and of the regulation of insider trading? In light of these costs and benefits, what is the best rule? The seminal work in this area is **Manne**. As is clear from the following discussion, many other academics have joined the debate.

---

[140] 989 F.2d 596 (2d Cir. 1993).

[141] 989 F.2d at 600.

[142] 257 F.2d 226 (2d Cir. 2001).

[1] Costs of Insider Trading

Unfairness and protection against a rigged market

Many people instinctively believe that insider trading is "just not fair," and that any market in which a substantial amount of insider trading occurs is "rigged." Because ordinary investors will avoid a "rigged" market, it seems to follow that regulation of insider trading is necessary to ensure the continued liquidity of our capital markets.[143] But do you suppose investors would favor prohibition of insider trading if it were shown that the average returns of non-insider investors would be unchanged or even decrease if everybody were required to trade on equal information? Investors might favor market egalitarianism, but they would want to know how much "fairness" will cost them.

Moreover, even if market egalitarianism were a worthwhile goal, it is probably not attainable. Some market participants, such as securities analysts, have inherent advantages over others because they invest time and money in acquiring information and expertise about stocks. Also, insider trading prohibitions are likely to be porous. For example, insiders can use their information to trade in the stock of their firm's competitors, suppliers, or customers. *See* **Ayres & Bankman**. If we permit inequalities like this, we must recognize that investors inevitably play in a "rigged" game, and that any attempt to regulate insider trading necessarily shifts advantages from one set of market participants to another. For example, prohibiting trading by corporate insiders increases the advantage of market professionals, such as securities analysts. Any such shifting must be justified by some benefit to investors.

Harm to buyers and sellers

Buyers and sellers are hurt when an insider induces them to trade when they would not otherwise have done so. This justifies liability in the situation in *Strong v. Repide*, Section 12.04[A], where the parties trade in face-to-face transactions. In open market insider trading cases, however, the defendant does not cause the other party to trade. How does this trading harm other participants in the market?

Commentators have argued that permitting insider trading gives insiders incentives to delay disclosure so that they can profit from trading while the market is uninformed.[144] But even trading insiders have strong counter-incentives to promptly disclose positive information—among other reasons, because delaying disclosure increases the likelihood of a takeover bid for the company. Also, insiders cannot profit from favorable information unless they do disclose, so any delay will be short-lived. Although the risk of delay is greater as to negative information, here, too, any delay resulting from insider trading is likely to be short-lived because the incentive to delay evaporates as soon as the insider has sold. *See* **Scott** at 810-11.

---

[143] *See* Schotland, *Unsafe at Any Price: A Reply to Manne, Insider Trading and the Stock Market*, 53 VA. L. REV. 1425, 1440-41 (1967).

[144] *Id.* at 1448-49.

Another way insider trading might affect buyers and sellers is through its effect on stock prices. Trading by insiders can cause the stock price to move up or down depending on whether the information is positive or negative. This is because the insiders' trades, even if small in terms of volume of shares traded, may be treated as a signal of information about the stock.[145] Insider trades can be observed from reports filed under Rule 144 or Section 16(a) of the 1934 Act (*see* Section 12.06, below), information from which is published in the financial press.[146]

If insider trading does affect stock prices, the price movement might lure some to sell to take advantage of an upswing or buy stock that has suddenly become cheaper. Such traders may be harmed by insider trading in a "but-for" causation sense. But should they have a remedy? Note that an investor who was unaware of the insider trading was simply trying to second-guess the market, a foolhardy course of action in light of the Efficient Market Hypothesis. *See* **Dooley** at 34-36.

If traders are not misled by changes in stock prices attributable to insider trading, what about harm to buyers in a market that is rising because of insider trading and sellers in a market that is falling? Note that their complaint is that their trading price was closer to the "true" value of the stock than it would have been without insider trading. Note also that "losses" to the injured investors will be exactly offset by the "gains" to those who got better prices because of the insider trading. *See* **Manne** at 98-110.

A final argument that buyers and sellers are harmed is that insider trading causes market makers and specialists on exchanges to alter their "spreads" between "bid" and "ask" prices in order to compensate for their disadvantage vis-a-vis insider traders. But this just means that outsiders are compensated for the risk that insiders are trading at the same time. If so, the injury would be to the market as a whole in the form of reduced trading.[147]

Effect on managerial conduct

It has been argued that insider trading gives corporate insiders perverse incentives to manage the corporation so as to maximize their opportunities to trade on inside information. Among other things, managers may declare dividends or invest in projects, such as takeovers or research and development, that cause dramatic swings in stock price.[148] Insider trading may also encourage delays in transmitting information between

---

[145] *See* Hirschey & Zaima, *Insider Trading, Ownership Structure and the Market Assessment of Corporate Sell-Offs*, 44 J. FIN. 971 (1989) (showing that where insiders were net purchasers in the six-month period prior to a corporate sell-off, the ultimate market reaction to the sell-off was highly positive).

[146] For discussions of this effect of insider trading on share prices, see Carney, *Signalling and Causation in Insider Trading*, 36 CATH. U. L. REV. 863 (1987); Gilson & Kraakman, *The Mechanisms of Market Efficiency*, 70 VA. L. REV. 549, 569-72 (1984). For evidence that insider trading affect stock prices, see Meulbroek, *An Empirical Analysis of Illegal Insider Trading*, 47 J. FIN. 1661 (1992) (finding an abnormal return on an insider trading day averaging 3%, and that almost half the pre-announcement stock price run-up observed before takeovers occurs on insider trading days).

[147] For a discussion of the use of this theory in *O'Hagan*, see Ribstein, *Federalism and Insider Trading*, 6 SUP. CT. ECON. REV. 123 (1998).

[148] *See* Schotland, *supra*, 53 VA. L. REV. 1452.

hierarchical levels, inhibit efficient delegation of tasks and impair cooperation between inside and outside directors.[149] Thus, insider trading may cause investors to question the quality of a firm's management.[150] On the other hand, perverse incentives of managers to manage so as to maximize their opportunities to trade on inside information are checked by such devices as state law fiduciary duties and firms' internal contracts.

Harm to owners of information

Insider trading regulation can be defended on the same ground as other protection of property rights. Like any theft of property, insider trading denies owners of information the full payoff from their investment. For example, executives, lawyers or investment bankers who use their position with a potential bidder to trade on information about an impending takeover might reduce the value of the bidder's information by raising the price of the acquisition. Preventing information users from capitalizing on their information not only harms the owners of the information, but also injures society by reducing incentives to acquire information. *See* **Easterbrook**; **Scott** at 814-815; **Macey**; **Wolfson**.

[2] Benefits of Insider Trading

Incentives for information search

The prices of publicly traded securities accurately reflect the value of traded firms only if information is extensively produced and rapidly disseminated. *See* Section 7.01[F]. Market participants, including securities analysts, search for information only to the extent that they are rewarded for their activities. Unless these participants can trade on information not shared by the rest of the market, they will not take the trouble to find the information, to the detriment of the entire market. *See* **Brudney** at 341-42; **Carlton & Fischel** at 871; **Dooley** at 63; **Hirshleifer**; **Lorie** at 822; and **Scott** at 813.

Increasing dissemination of information

Although, as noted above, insider trading has been blamed for delays in disclosure, it might actually speed dissemination of information to the market. Some facts, such as technological breakthroughs, mineral discoveries and merger negotiations cannot be directly disclosed without damaging the corporation. Thus, without insider trading, market prices would move in sudden jumps as corporate events are disclosed. Insider trading on the basis of these events can move stock prices in the "correct" direction during the period in which the basic facts about corporate events must remain undisclosed. Moreover, such "disclosable" but "soft" facts as management earnings projections are

---

[149] *See* Haft, *The Effect of Insider Trading Rules on the Internal Efficiency of the Large Corporation*, 80 MICH. L. REV. 1051 (1982).

[150] *See Diamond v. Oreamuno*, 23 N.Y.2d 494, 301 N.Y.S.2d 78, 81-82, 248 N.E.2d 910, 912-13 (1969).

more credible, and therefore more informative, if they are disclosed selectively through analysts than if they are disclosed publicly. Analysts serve as a valuable "filter" because they evaluate and monitor management's disclosures, and back up their evaluations and monitoring with their reputations for accuracy.[151]

Insider trading as management compensation

Manne (at 111-58) and **Carlton & Fischel** (at 870-78) argue that inside information is a legitimate form of executive compensation. As discussed in Section 9.05, it is difficult to design an executive compensation system that effectively reduces agency problems by motivating managers to act consistently with the firm's interests. Indeed, one study shows that executive pay in publicly traded firms is highly uncorrelated with the returns of the firm.[152] This discourages the best managers from working for public firms. One way public firms could reduce this problem is by allocating their rights in firm-related information to corporate insiders. This would motivate insiders to create valuable projects for public firms by allowing them to trade on stock price increases from these developments.

Cox (at 650-56) and **Schotland** (at 1453-57) have strongly criticized insider trading as management compensation. First, the trading insiders may not be the ones responsible for the favorable developments who deserve to be rewarded for them. Second, insider trading provides perverse as well as good incentives: insiders gain from investing in risky projects that produce significant stock price swings, and can profit from bad as well as from good information. Third, profits from insider trading have a high degree of variance (*i.e.*, risk) because insiders face a significant chance that they will gain nothing from their access to inside information. Accordingly, the ability to use or sell inside information may be more valuable to the firm than to its risk-averse executives, who may prefer to be paid in straight salary or bonuses.

The advantages and disadvantages of inside information as management compensation are likely to vary from firm to firm. In some firms, more conventional forms of compensation may motivate relatively poorly—for example, by inducing managers to manage too conservatively. In these firms, insider trading may be a valuable form of compensation precisely because it encourages executives to take risks. In other companies, the potential perverse incentives of insider trading may be great. Also, firms vary in their ability to minimize the effects of these perverse incentives through other monitoring devices (such as direct supervision of managers by their colleagues) and to ensure that those who profit from insider trading are only those who "deserve" to do so.

---

[151] *See* **Carlton & Fischel** at 868. For evidence of this benefit of insider trading, see John & Lang, *Insider Trading Around Dividend Announcements: Theory and Evidence*, 46 J. FIN. 1361 (1991) (insider trading around dividend announcements has explanatory power as an alternative signal competing with and helping the market interpret dividend announcements; dividend increase may be bad news for firms with large investment opportunities). **Kahan** argues that this price-accuracy benefit of insider trading is limited, noting among other things that it would not improve the accuracy of stock pricing at the critical point at which firms sell their stock in public offerings.

[152] *See* Jensen & Murphy, *Performance Pay and Top Management Incentives*, 98 J. POL. ECON. 225 (1990).

[3] Regulatory Costs

Even if the costs of insider trading outweigh its benefits, the costs of regulating insider trading may exceed the benefits. Insider trading regulation involves certain direct costs, including the SEC's enforcement costs, the legal expenses of private parties, and the costs to the judicial system. The costs of investigation are compounded by traders' use of such devices as foreign accounts. Insider trading regulation also involves substantial indirect costs. Rules designed to deter insider trading by, for example, imposing huge criminal and civil penalties also deter some legitimate trading, reducing general market liquidity. One possible response to these costs is to reduce insiders' profits by requiring them to disclose their trades before trading. *See* **Fried.**

[4] The Need for Mandatory Federal Regulation

Assuming insider trading does in fact result in harm to certain groups of people, is federal regulation necessary? Issuers, law firms, investment bankers and others that are injured by insider trading could adopt rules against it and discipline their employees as a matter of state contract or agency law. Even without specific contract terms, rules against misuse of corporate property and corporate opportunities now protect firms from insider trading. These may be standard form rules that firms can generally opt out of (*see* Section 9.09) or at least waive in specific cases through disinterested director or shareholder vote (*see* Section 9.04).

An important advantage of regulating insider trading by contract or by state law rules that can be altered is that it permits variation among firms. For example, using insider trading as a form of compensation might make sense for some firms but not for others. Thus, even if insider trading is costly for many firms, banning insider trading for all firms may not be efficient.

The argument for federal regulation of insider trading depends to some extent on the existence of externalities—that is, insiders' ability to impose the costs of insider trading on outside investors. But if outside investors perceive that they will be damaged by insider trading, they can bid down the stocks of firms in which insider trading is likely to occur. The market for control can discipline these firms: bidders can take over "insider-trading" firms at a price that reflects investors' condemnation of the practice and turn them into "insider-trading-free" firms that trade at a higher price. Indeed, even without the market for control, if outside investors condemn insider trading, many insiders will also regard the practice as immoral and unethical and not engage in it. This group will seek to demonstrate to the market that their firms are free of insider trading so that they are not punished along with the inside traders. *See* **Dooley** at 43-44.

The pro-regulatory counter to these arguments is that investors cannot distinguish the two types of firms, and accordingly will bid down all firms. This will cause investment capital to be misallocated to "bad" firms that tolerate insider trading. Note that this argument assumes that "signaling" by firms to show that they are free of insider trading is very costly or ineffective.

Firms might also favor federal regulation because it provides a cheaper enforcement mechanism than ordinary contractual rules. Federal law enforcement agencies and correction facilities can detect and punish insider trading at a relatively low marginal cost through facilities that are already in place to deal with other crimes. *See* **Easterbrook** at 333-34. But shouldn't firms that do not want to detect and punish insider trading be permitted to opt out?

[5] Conclusion

The foregoing analysis suggests that mandatory federal regulation is justified under the following set of circumstances: (1) The costs of insider trading exceed its benefits; (2) the costs of regulating insider trading do not exceed the net costs of insider trading; and (3) the costs of mandatory federal regulation do not exceed the costs of regulation by contract or under state law. Should we insist that this set of circumstances be verified empirically before regulating, or negated empirically before changing the current regulatory regime?[153] Should the fact that most firms have not attempted to regulate insider trading by contract be taken as an indication that firms do not consider such regulation to be in their interests?

[6] Insider Trading Regulation Explained: An Interest Analysis

The above discussion concerns whether we should have insider trading regulation. There is a separate question of why such regulation exists. The economic theory of regulation pioneered by Professor George J. Stigler explains laws and administrative rules in terms of interest groups.[154] In very simple terms, people will "pay" for regulation when the benefits they can reap from doing so exceed their costs. Payment for SEC regulation of insider trading, for example, could come in the form of campaign contributions to politicians who would increase funding of and support laws favorable to the SEC. The costs of forming effective coalitions depend on the logistics of forming interest groups that can act effectively to procure regulation.

To explain insider trading regulation under the economic theory of regulation, consider who is helped and who is hurt by the regulation. A case can be made in light of the above discussion that ordinary investors are not helped by insider trading regulations. Indeed, ordinary investors may be harmed by such regulation to the extent that they would favor insider trading as a means of compensating corporate insiders. But ordinary investors are not an effective interest group because they are such a large and diverse group that it would be very costly for them to form an effective coalition.

---

[153] For contrasting views on this issue, compare **Carlton & Fischel** (regulation of insider trading lacks empirical support) with **Cox** at 644-45 (burden should be on those seeking to change the regulatory status quo).

[154] Stigler, *The Economics of Regulation*, 59 J. POL. ECON. 213 (1961).

Both market professionals and corporate insiders might be able to gain from inside information. Moreover, both groups already have organizations (such as the Business Roundtable for corporate executives and the National Association of Securities Dealers for market professionals) that can act as effective lobbying groups. Why don't both groups vigorously oppose insider trading regulation? **Haddock & Macey** (in their Journal of Law & Economics article) suggest that *Chiarella*, by requiring breach of fiduciary duty as a prerequisite to insider trading liability, immunized many "outsider" market professionals. This left the outsiders free to press for vigorous enforcement of insider trading regulation against insiders, thereby eliminating their chief competition for information.

[7] The Search for the Appropriate Rule

The above discussion indicates that neither a rule permitting all trading on information advantages nor one wholly prohibiting such trading is clearly efficient. While a case can be made for dealing with insider trading exclusively by contract or state law, that sort of regime seems unlikely to be accepted. Assuming that some federal mandatory rule should be adopted, what should that rule be?

Should it be the *Chiarella-Dirks* "fiduciary duty" test. This test assumes that insiders have a fiduciary duty not to trade on corporate information, and therefore arguably protects the corporation's property right in its information. But should the corporation be precluded from conveying its property right to insiders as compensation? If the corporation has conveyed this property right, should it matter that the insider has reaped a "personal benefit" by tipping the information?[155]

What about the *O'Hagan* "misappropriation" theory? This can be seen as the logical extension of the "fiduciary duty" test since it protects property rights of all information-owners, and not merely the corporation whose stock the insider is trading. But does it justify federal mandatory liability under § 10(b) and Rule 10b-5?

PROBLEM

In each of the following situations, (a) under which of the alternative theories of liability listed above, if any, would the transaction be actionable? (b) is liability justified in light of the considerations discussed in Subsection 12.05[D]?

(1) Offeror Corporation purchases stock in Target without disclosing that it is about to announce a tender offer for Target's stock which will cause the stock to rise in value.

(2) An officer of Offeror, learning of the takeover, buys stock in Target.

---

[155] For commentary criticizing *Dirks* along these lines, see, *e.g.*, **Carlton & Fischel** at 885.

(3) An officer of Target, who learns of the impending offer when an Offeror executive contacts her seeking to negotiate a friendly takeover, purchases stock in Target.

(4) The investment banker of Offeror in (1) purchases stock in Target at Offeror's request. Offeror makes this request to ensure the success of the impending offer by placing a maximum number of Target shares in "friendly" hands.

(5) Brokerage firm makes an exhaustive investigation of a company, concludes that the stock is undervalued, and makes a substantial purchase.

(6) Brokerage firm makes its purchase in (5) knowing that it is about to recommend the stock to its customers and that the stock will rise on the basis of its recommendation.

(7) An SEC employee sells stock knowing that the SEC is about to announce an investigation of the issuer which will probably adversely affect the stock price.

(8) A large department store chain purchases stock in a small manufacturer of appliances knowing that it is about to place a very substantial order for the company's products.

(9) A friend of a corporate insider, knowing the public information that the firm is expecting to hear important information concerning government action on one of its products, sells when she hears from her broker that the insider is selling large amounts of stock.

REFERENCES

Ayres & Bankman, *Substitutes for Insider Trading,* 54 STAN. L. REV. 235 (2001).

Brudney, *Insiders, Outsiders, and Informational Advantages Under the Federal Securities Laws*, 93 HARV. L. REV. 322 (1979).

Carlton & Fischel, *Regulation of Insider Trading*, 35 STAN. L. REV. 857 (1983).

Carney, *Signalling and Causation in Insider Trading*, 36 CATH. U. L. REV. 863 (1987).

Dooley, *Enforcement of Insider Trading Restrictions*, 66 VA. L. REV. 1 (1980)

Easterbrook, *Insider Trading, Secret Agents, Evidentiary Privileges and the Production of Information*, 1981 SUP. CT. REV. 309.

Fried, *Reducing the Profitability of Corporate Insider Trading through Pretrading Disclosure*, 71 S. CAL. L. REV. 303 (1998).

Gilson & Kraakman, *The Mechanisms of Market Efficiency*, 70 VA. L. REV. 549 (1984).

Haddock & Macey, *A Coasian Model of Insider Trading*, 80 NW. U. L. REV. 1449 (1986).

Haddock & Macey, *Regulation on Demand: A Private Interest Model, With an Application to Insider Trading Regulation*, 30 J. L. & ECON. 311 (1986).

Hirshleifer, *The Private and Social Value of Information and the Reward to Incentive Activity*, 61 AM. ECON. REV. 561 (1971).

Kahan, *Securities Laws and the Social Costs of "Inaccurate" Stock Prices*, 41 DUKE L.J. 977 (1992).

Lorie, *Insider Trading: Rule 10b-5, Disclosure and Corporate Privacy: A Comment*, 9 J. LEG. STUD. 819 (1980).

Macey, *From Fairness to Contract: The New Direction of the Rules Against Insider Trading*, 13 HOFSTRA L. REV. 9 (1984).

Manne, INSIDER TRADING AND THE STOCK MARKET (1966).

Schotland, *Unsafe at Any Price: A Reply to Manne, Insider Trading and the Stock Market*, 53 VA. L. REV. 1425 (1967).

Scott, *Insider Trading: Rule 10b-5, Disclosure and Corporate Privacy*, 9 J. LEG. STUD. 801 (1980).

Wolfson, *Trade Secrets and Secret Trading*, 25 SAN DIEGO L. REV. 95 (1988).

[E] Remedies

The SEC may take one of three types of actions:

(1) An administrative proceeding against broker-dealers and other professionals who are directly subject to the agency's control. Such a proceeding may result in, among other things, censure, license revocation, or the imposition of a civil penalty of up to $500,000 per violation. *See* § 15(b)(4) and (6) and § 21B of the 1934 Act. Examples of this type of proceeding include *Cady, Roberts* and *Dirks*.

(2) Sue to enjoin the conduct and for other ancillary relief, including civil penalties, under § 21(d) of the 1934 Act. *See, e.g., Texas Gulf Sulphur*. Section 21A of the 1934 Act authorizes civil penalties in such actions of up to $1,000,000, or three times the profit gained or the loss avoided as a result of the insider trading, whichever is greater. Proceedings under § 21(d) often seek disgorgement of the insider's profit and are concluded quickly by means of a consent decree.

(3) Refer the matter to the Justice Department for criminal action under § 21(d)(1) of the 1934 Act. *See Chiarella*. Prior to 2002, maximum criminal penalties under § 32(a) of the 1934 Act were $1,000,000 and 10 years in prison for natural persons and $2,500,000 for other entities. The Sarbanes-Oxley Act of 2002 increases the maximum criminal penalties to $5,000,000 and 20 years in prison for natural persons and $25,000,000 for other entities (*see* § 1106 of the Act).

Rule 10b-5 actions also may be brought by private parties asserting the implied right of action established in *Kardon v. National Gypsum Co.*[156] *See* Section 12.03[D]. Who should be able to sue for insider trading, and what should be the measure of damages, in a private action under Rule 10b-5? An early case attempted to force insider trading into the face-to-face mold by apparently holding that a cause of action would lie only between matched buyers and sellers.[157] This approach would hinge recovery on the

---

[156] 69 F. Supp. 512 (E.D. Pa. 1946).

[157] *See Joseph v. Farnsworth Radio & Television Corp.*, 99 F. Supp. 701 (S.D.N.Y. 1951), *aff'd*, 198 F.2d 883 (2d Cir. 1952).

pure chance that an outsider was matched with an insider in an anonymous market transaction, and would also create tremendous proof problems for plaintiffs.

Shapiro v. Merrill Lynch, Pierce, Fenner & Smith, Inc.[158] upheld a cause of action against a tippee and its tippers on behalf of all investors who bought stock during the time of the defendants' wrongdoing. On remand,[159] the district court defined the appropriate plaintiff class as those who bought during the period beginning with the first illegal transactions and ending on the day of public announcement, rejecting defendants' argument that the class period should end one day earlier when the insider trading had ceased.

There are a number of problems with the *Shapiro* theory. First, both the appellate and district courts in *Shapiro* reasoned that the relevant breach of duty was failure to disclose, so that all investors who were injured by the nondisclosure should have a cause of action. Does this make sense? Isn't the offense the trading rather than the nondisclosure? See the discussion of *Fridrich*, below. Second, *Shapiro* seems to permit potentially draconian recovery. If the traditional fraud "out of pocket" measure of damages is applied, a single illegal tip could result in enormous liability to thousands of investors who traded between the tip and the disclosure.

Elkind v. Liggett & Myers, Inc.,[160] modified the *Shapiro* approach. The court held that investors who traded between the time of the illegal tip and eventual disclosure were entitled to the difference between their purchase price and the price the stock reached following disclosure of the true facts. However, the court limited the total recovery of the plaintiff class to the profits realized by the defendant's tippee.[161] Section 20A of the 1934 Act now codifies the result in *Elkind*.

In *Fridrich v. Bradford*,[162] the court held that investors could not recover from alleged insider traders without proof that the trading had caused the investors' injury. The court held that no such proof had been made in that case and did not explain how plaintiff could prove such a link. How might plaintiffs show that they were harmed by insider trading? Consider the discussion in Section 12.05[D][1]. Recall that insider trading may have no, or only a very slight effect, on stock price. Even if outside investors are able to show such an effect, can they show injury? Should an investor be able to recover simply because she bought at a price that was elevated by insider trad-

---

[158] 495 F.2d 228 (2d Cir. 1974). *Kardon* reasoned, in part, that an implied private remedy should be presumed to be consistent with legislative intent absent evidence of an intent to deny a remedy. The Supreme Court approved the implied right of action under § 10(b) in *Superintendent of Insurance v. Bankers Life & Casualty Co.*, 404 U.S. 6, 13 n.9 (1971). The Supreme Court's current approach to implication of private remedies is more restrictive (*see* Section 7.03[D]).

[159] 1975 Fed. Sec. L. Rep. ¶ 95,377 (S.D.N.Y. Dec. 9, 1975).

[160] 635 F.2d 156 (2d Cir. 1980).

[161] For discussions and applications of the *Elkind* approach, see *Wilson v. Comtech Telecommunications Corp.*, 648 F.2d 88, 94 (2d Cir. 1981); Wang, *The "Contemporaneous" Traders Who Can Sue an Insider Trader*, 38 HASTINGS L.J. 1175 (1987); Special Development, *Damages for Insider Trading in the Open Market: A New Limitation on Recovery Under Rule 10b-5*, 34 VAND. L. REV. 797 (1981).

[162] 542 F.2d 307 (6th Cir. 1976), *cert. denied*, 429 U.S. 1053 (1977).

ing? Should an investor recover if she proves that she sold because of a price increase caused by insider trading, or bought because of a price decrease?

What should be the remedy for insider trading under the "misappropriation" theory? In *Moss v. Morgan Stanley, Inc.*,[163] the court denied recovery sought by a class of investors who sold stock in a prospective target company during trading in target stock by an employee of the investment banker of a prospective bidder. The court held that, even if the defendant breached a duty owed to his employer, he breached none to the target shareholders. *Moss* was effectively reversed by the Insider Trading and Securities Fraud Enforcement Act of 1988, which, among other things, added § 20A to the 1934 Act.

Even under *Moss*, the owner of the information who was victimized by the insider trading could sue. In one case the court held that a corporation making a distribution to its shareholders could not sue for insider trading that supposedly increased the amount of the distribution by raising the corporation's stock price.[164] In *Litton Industries, Inc. v. Lehman Bros. Kuhn Loeb, Inc.*,[165] the court denied a remedy to a bidder that alleged that the target's stock price was increased by trading on information misappropriated by an employee of the bidder's investment banker. The court held that, because the transaction was at a negotiated price, and because the target board was not influenced by market price movements, the plaintiff failed to prove that the insider trading caused it to pay a higher price. (If the target board ignored market fluctuations, did it breach its fiduciary duty in setting the price?) *Litton Industries* was reversed on appeal on the ground that loss causation should have been left to the jury.[166]

NOTES AND QUESTIONS

(1) **Motivation for the trader's transaction.** Should an insider be forbidden, for example, to sell stock in order to raise badly needed cash or to follow through on a predetermined investment plan simply because he happened to have inside information that had no effect on his investment decision? If a defense is to be allowed in this situation, what should the insider be required to prove? *SEC v. MacDonald*[167] held that, in light of the positive nature of the nonpublic information in relation to the very negative public information, the nonpublic information must have motivated the insider's purchase.

---

[163] 719 F.2d 5 (2d Cir. 1983), *cert. denied*, 465 U.S. 1025 (1984).

[164] *FMC Corp. v. Boesky*, 36 F.3d 255 (2d Cir. 1994). The court reasoned that any excess inured to the benefit of corporation's shareholders, the corporation had no legitimate interest in short-changing public shareholders by maintaining confidential information regarding the value of its stock, and the corporation failed to demonstrate that it paid more than stock was worth.

[165] 709 F. Supp. 438 (S.D.N.Y. 1989).

[166] 967 F.2d 742 (2d Cir. 1992). On the causation issue, see Schwert, *Mark-up Pricing in Mergers and Acquisitions*, National Bureau of Economic Research Working Paper, 1994 (finding that pre-bid runup in takeover price does not substitute for post-bid increase, implying that insider trading does not raise price of acquisition).

[167] 1981 Fed. Sec. L. Rep. (CCH) ¶ 98,009 (D.R.I. April 23, 1981).

SEC v. Adler[168] held that the insider had to be given the opportunity to show that the inside information was not a factor in his trading, such as by showing a pre-existing plan to trade. However, it established a presumption of use that insiders would have to rebut. *United States v. Smith*[169] reached a similar result, but noted that the presumption of use in *Adler* did not apply to a criminal prosecution. Rule 10b5-1, adopted in 2000, provides that a purchase or sale of a security is deemed to be "on the basis of" material nonpublic information if the person making the purchase or sale was "aware" of the material non-public information when the person made the purchase or sale. But the rule provides affirmative defenses where the trade resulted from a pre-existing contract, instruction, or previously-adhered-to written plan, or where the person making the investment decision on behalf of the trader was not aware of the information.

(2) **The Chinese wall.** In an attempted takeover of McGraw, Hill by American Express, an American Express executive sat on the McGraw, Hill board and wallowed in inside information. American Express, meanwhile, was buying McGraw, Hill stock and maneuvering for a takeover. The director claimed that he had built a "Chinese wall" around himself such that the director's inside information did not reach American Express. This claim has been made in analogous situations by large brokerage companies. Should this defense be allowed or should it be conclusively presumed that information of a director is communicated to the company of which he is an executive?

(3) **In pari delicto.** Suppose a purported insider induces someone to buy stock in a company by claiming that she has inside information. In fact, the information is untrue and the "tippee" sues the "tipper" under Rule 10b-5 for misrepresentation. Should the tippee be barred from recovery because he was "in equal fault" with the defendant? What approach is suggested by *Dirks*? *Bateman Eichler, Hill Richards, Inc. v. Berner*[170] held that the *pari delicto* defense bars only actions where the plaintiff bears "at least substantially equal responsibility" for the violation and where precluding the suit would not "significantly interfere" with enforcement of the securities laws. Under this rule, a tippee is not barred from recovering against a broker-dealer. The tippee's liability is only derivative of the tipper's and the tippee commits a wrong only against trading shareholders. The tipper, on the other hand, breaches a fiduciary duty to the issuer as well as committing fraud against the tippee. Also, *pari delicto* would frustrate enforcement of the securities laws because it would impede detection, and because deterrence is more effective when directed against corporate insiders and broker-dealers who are advised by counsel and are more likely to be aware of the law.

(4) **Conflicting duties.** In *Cady, Roberts, Dirks* and other cases, the SEC has rejected the argument that an investment adviser owes a "higher" fiduciary duty to use

---

[168] 137 F.3d 1325 (11th Cir. 1998).

[169] 155 F.3d 1051 (9th Cir. 1998).

[170] 472 U.S. 299 (1985).

inside information for the benefit of the client than he owes to the anonymous market not to use the information. Do you agree? What are the considerations on each side?

§ 12.06 Liability for Insider Trading under § 16(b)

[A] Introduction

Section 16(b) holds officers, directors, and 10% shareholders of public corporations (*i.e.*, corporations whose equity securities are required to be registered under § 12 of the 1934 Act[171]) liable to the corporation when they engage in "short-swing" transactions—*i.e.*, purchases and sales of securities within a six-month period. Section 16(b) is based on a presumption that one or both of the trades in the short-swing transaction resulted from the misuse of non-public information. It therefore allows relief even if no actual misuse of inside information can be shown. Any shareholder of the corporation has standing to sue for a violation of § 16(b).[172]

Section 16(b) permits recovery for the insider's profits rather than merely for the injury to the corporation. The profits have been held to be computable by matching the highest sale prices with the lowest purchase prices during the relevant six-month period.[173] This means that the insider may bear substantially greater liability than if profits were computed more conventionally—by subtracting total costs from total receipts. This measure of damages obviously is intended to deter the proscribed conduct.

Section 16(a) facilitates enforcement of § 16(b) by requiring officers, directors, and large shareholders to report their transactions. Under the pre-2002 version of § 16(a) and Rule 16a-3, an initial statement of beneficial ownership on Form 3 had to be filed within 10 days after the person became an officer, director or 10% shareholder subject to the requirements of § 16(a). Thereafter, a statement of changes in beneficial ownership on Form 4 had to be filed within 10 days after the close of each calendar month, if there had been any change in beneficial ownership during that month (except for changes resulting from certain transactions that are exempt from § 16(b) liability), and an annual statement on Form 5 had to be filed within 45 days after the corporation's fiscal year end disclosing transactions not previously reported on Forms 3 and 4. The Sarbanes-Oxley Act of 2002 amends § 16(a) to, among other things, require changes in beneficial ownership to be reported before the end of the second business day following the ownership change (unless the SEC determines that reporting within a 2-day period is not feasible). Sarbanes-Oxley also requires the SEC to make such filings

---

[171] Generally, this includes corporations whose shares are registered for trading on a national securities exchange and corporations with more than $10 million in assets and more than 500 shareholders of record. *See* § 12(a) & (g) of the 1934 Act and Rule 12g-1 thereunder.

[172] For a broad interpretation of the standing rule extending it to a shareholder whose interest was exchanged in a merger, see *Gollust v. Mendell*, 501 U.S. 115 (1991).

[173] *See Smolowe v. Delendo Corp.*, 136 F.2d 231 (2d Cir. 1943).

available on a publicly accessible internet site not later than the end of the business day following the filing.

Fox suggests a theoretical basis for understanding and applying § 16(b). Applying portfolio theory, Fox argues that an insider will hold the market portfolio so long as he lacks inside information about his company. Once he acquires inside information, however, he will either increase or decrease (depending on whether the news is good or bad) both his proportional holdings of the issuers' shares relative to other available risky securities and the absolute number of shares that he holds. In other words, the insider will "dediversify." Fox argues that § 16(b) deters insider trading by increasing the time that an insider must remain "dediversified" in order to profit from inside information: without § 16(b), the insider would seek to rediversify his portfolio by readjusting his holdings of the issuer's shares as soon as the inside information became public; with § 16(b), the insider must remain dediversified for at least six months. But Fox notes that § 16(b) may deter "good" as well as "bad" trades by insiders (*i.e.*, trades not motivated by inside information). This suggests that insiders will choose to hold a smaller proportion of an issuer's shares than they would absent § 16(b). As a result, even assuming that insider trading is harmful, the costs of § 16(b)—increased agency costs due to decreased stock ownership by insiders—could exceed the benefits.

Other commentators have different views of the actual motivations for § 16. **Thel** argues that § 16 was intended to regulate management manipulation of corporate activities rather than insider trading. **Okamoto** says that § 16(b) was intended to deter corporate actors from sending false signals to the market through stock trading.

[B] Who Is an Insider?

Not every titular officer is an "officer" for 16(b) purposes after an examination of their actual duties.[174] On the other hand, plaintiff can recover without showing that one who is an "officer" had access to inside information.[175]

In *Chemical Fund, Inc. v. Xerox Corp.*,[176] an owner of more than 10% of a class of convertible debentures was held not to be a 10% owner for § 16(b) purposes since the relevant class of securities from the standpoint of power in the corporation and access to information was the stock into which the debentures were convertible.[177] On the other hand, in *Newmark v. RKO General, Inc.*,[178] an option to purchase more than 50%

---

[174] *Compare C.R.A. Realty Corp. v. Crotty*, 878 F.2d 562 (2d Cir. 1989) (vice president is not an "officer" under § 16(b)), *with Winston v. Federal Express Corp.*, 853 F.2d 455 (6th Cir. 1988) (vice president was a § 16(b) "officer" because he did not adequately rebut the presumption of access to inside information arising from his position).

[175] *See National Medical Enterprises, Inc. v. Small*, 680 F.2d 83 (9th Cir. 1982).

[176] 377 F.2d 107 (2d Cir. 1967).

[177] *See also Levner v. Saud*, 1994 WL 570748 (S.D.N.Y.) (holder of option to convert preferred stock into common stock held not to be beneficial owner of common stock subject to option because, under terms of standstill agreement, option was not presently exerciseable due to material contingencies beyond the option holder's control), *aff'd*, 61 F.3d 8 (2d Cir. 1995).

[178] 425 F.2d 348 (2d Cir. 1970), *cert. denied*, 400 U.S. 854 (1970), *reh'g denied*, 400 U.S. 920 (1970).

of a corporation's stock was held to confer insider status. More generally, Rule 16a-1(a) defines beneficial ownership to include sole or shared voting or investment power with respect to a security, so interests far short of legal ownership suffice for purposes of determining whether a person is a § 16(b) insider. Note also that courts generally reject defendants' arguments to characterize separate types of securities as a single class for purposes of determining whether a defendant is a 10% shareholder.[179]

In *Feder v. Martin Marietta Corp.*,[180] the chief executive officer of Martin Marietta (Bunker) sat on the board of Sperry Rand during a portion of a MM's short-swing transaction in Sperry stock. The court held that MM was an insider for § 16(b) purposes because it concluded that Bunker was MM's "deputy" on the Sperry board. The court found persuasive in support of this "deputization theory" the facts that Bunker controlled MM, sat on the Sperry board in order to protect MM's financial interest in Sperry, and served with MM's approval. However, *Blau v. Lehman*[181] refused to find "deputization" under the facts of that case.

[C] What Transactions Are Attributable to the Insider?

CBI INDUSTRIES, INC. v. HORTON
United States Court of Appeals, Seventh Circuit
682 F.2d 643 (1982)

POSNER, Circuit Judge.

Section 16(b) of the Securities Exchange Act of 1934, 15 U.S.C. § 78p(b), provides, so far as is immediately relevant here, that if a corporate director sells shares in his company and then, within six months, buys shares in the company, "any profit realized by him" shall be recoverable in a suit by the company. Thus, if a director sold 1000 shares in his company for $60 a share and within six months bought 1000 shares for $40, the company could sue him for $20,000, his "profit" on the transaction (more realistically, the loss he averted by selling when he did). We have to decide in this case whether the "him" includes his grown children, when they are beneficiaries of a trust of which the director is a co-trustee.

Horton, the defendant in this case, is a director of CBI Industries, Inc., the plaintiff. Along with the Continental Illinois National Bank and Trust Company of Chicago he is co-trustee of a trust (actually two trusts, but to make this opinion simpler we shall treat them

---

[179] *See, e.g., Schaffer v. Dickstein & Co., L.P.*, 1996 U.S. Dist. LEXIS 4009, 1996 WL 148335 (S.D.N.Y. 1996) (court refuses to consider preferred stock and common stock as a single class, even though preferred stock conferred voting rights, dividend rights, and was convertible into common stock on a one-to-one basis); *Morales v. New Valley Corporation*, 936 F. Supp. 119 (S.D.N.Y. 1996) (court rejects argument that holders of 34% of corporation's "B Convertible Stock" should not be subject to § 16(b) because their stock represents only .46% of the voting power of all classes of stock), *aff'd sub nom. Morales v. Freund*, 163 F.3d 763 (2d Cir. 1999).

[180] 406 F.2d 260 (2d Cir. 1969).

[181] 368 U.S. 403 (1962).

as one) created many years ago by his mother for the benefit of his two sons. In the period relevant to this case they were full-time students, 19 and 22 years old, living apart from Horton most of the time. The original assets of the trust consisted entirely of CBI stock. The trustees were authorized but not required to retain the stock, and the record does not reveal the present composition of the trust's assets. In 1980 Horton sold on the open market 3000 shares of CBI stock that he owned himself; and within six months he bought (again on the open market), this time for the trust, 2000 shares of the stock at a lower price than he had sold his own stock. The difference in price, multiplied by 2000, is $25,000—the amount CBI sued Horton for, and recovered below. 530 F. Supp. 784 (N.D. Ill. 1982).

If Horton had bought the shares for his own account he would indisputably have violated section 16(b) and the company would have been entitled to his $25,000 "profit." But that is because the $25,000 would have been his to do with as he liked; it would have been "profit realized by him," in the language of the statute. The $25,000 that the trust may be said to have gained from the purchase of the shares at a price lower than the price at which Horton had earlier sold his own shares (gained, that is, by waiting to buy until the price fell) did not become his to use as he wished, but was for the exclusive use of his sons. It is true that as the family-member co-trustee, Horton had, within very broad limits, the power to manage the trust; for when a bank is a co-trustee with a member of the family of the grantor and the beneficiaries, it ordinarily defers to the family member's wishes, and did so here. But Horton did not have the power to divert the income of the trust to himself. That would clearly have violated the terms of the trust, and even a somnolent bank trustee would have been jarred awake by an attempt at such a diversion. Moreover, since the trust beneficiaries were, in contemplation of law at least, adults, *see, e.g., Waldron v. Waldron*, 13 Ill. App. 3d 964, 301 N.E.2d 167 (1973), Horton could not have looked to the income of the trust to fulfill his legal obligation of support, thereby replacing personal income that he would otherwise have had to devote to the boys—he no longer had any such obligation. (In any event, if he had used trust income to fulfill a legal obligation, the income so used would have been taxed to him rather than to the trust, a result that he would almost certainly want to avoid and that therefore was unlikely to occur, and so far as appears did not occur.) Finally, it is of little significance that Horton is the first in a series of contingent remaindermen of the trust. If both boys die without issue before they reach the age of 25, all of the assets of the trust will go to him. The probability of this happening could be calculated, and the result of this calculation could be multiplied by $25,000 to yield the expected value to Horton of the trust's profit from the challenged transaction, but no one has made this calculation and we suspect it would yield a number too minute to motivate CBI to sue.

If Horton did have a pecuniary interest in the trust's $25,000 "profit," the fact that the stock was not purchased in his name would not be decisive. In *Whiting v. Dow Chem. Co.*, 523 F.2d 680, 682 (2d Cir. 1975), the wife of a corporate director sold stock in his company less than six months before he bought shares in it at a lower price, and the difference in price was held to be a profit realized by him. But her income was considerably larger than his and was used to pay many of their joint living expenses, so that in effect the defendant was treating her money, including proceeds from transactions in the stock of the company of which he was a director, as if it were his. But so far as appears Horton does not—and under the terms of the trust he may not—treat the trust income this way. In *Whittaker v. Whittaker Corp.*, 639 F.2d 516, 523 (9th Cir. 1981), the defendant's mother had given him a general power of attorney which he used, among other things, "to freely borrow large sums of money from her while never having to consider paying the money back, posting adequate security or even paying any interest that might accrue." In fact, he "felt free to utilize his mother's assets exactly as if they were his own." He thus had a direct pecuniary stake in the profits from the insider trading that he did in her name. . . . If Horton had like access to the trust assets, or if, as in *Whiting,* those assets were used to pay his living expenses, then a profit realized by the trust would be realized "by him" within the meaning of the statute; otherwise the statute would be so easily avoidable as to be virtually a dead letter.

But we cannot stop here. Having regard for the purpose and not merely the language of section 16(b), we must consider whether the words "profit realized by him" should be read more broadly—as broadly as the temptations that led Congress to enact the statute in the first place can be conceived. The preamble to section 16(b) describes the statutory purpose as "preventing the unfair use of information which may have been obtained" by the classes of corporate insiders specified in section 16(b). This suggests, what is anyway obvious, that the framers were concerned that corporate insiders would be tempted to use inside information to make short-term speculative profits; and the temptation is there whether the beneficiary is the insider himself or his children, grown or otherwise. A person's "wealth," in a realistic though not pecuniary sense, is increased by increasing the pecuniary wealth of his children—even if no part of their increased wealth is used to reduce any legal obligation of support that he may owe them, even if they never spend a nickel on him, even if he has no financial relations with them at all—provided only that he has the normal human feelings toward his children. To limit "profit realized by him" to purely pecuniary receipts thus seems, in the case of Mr. Horton, to ignore human nature.

But taking a "realistic" approach to the interpretation of these words would result in placing greater restrictions on corporate insiders than Congress can plausibly be thought to have intended in 1934, when notions of conflict of interest were less exacting than they are today. We asked CBI's counsel at oral argument whether in his view it would have made any difference to Horton's liability if the trust beneficiaries had been Horton's godsons rather than his sons. Counsel said it would not, but that it would be a different matter if the beneficiary were Horton's alma mater. But some men love their colleges as much as their godsons. An argument that the district court found persuasive (*see* 530 F. Supp. at 787 and n.2)—that an increase in the income of the trust would save Horton money by reducing the "voluntary gifts" he would "need" to make to his children—would apply with equal force if the beneficiary of the trust had been Horton's alma mater.

Thus the implication of holding Horton liable in this case would be that neither he nor any corporate insider could manage or control (or, we suppose, influence, *see Whiting, supra,* 523 F.2d at 688-89) an investment portfolio containing the stock of his company without being in jeopardy of violating section 16(b). *Blau v. Lehman,* 368 U.S. 403, 82 S. Ct. 451, 7 L. Ed. 2d 403 (1962), where the Supreme Court refused to treat a profit realized by the defendant's partnership as profit realized by him, is authority against going so far; and even if we could distinguish *Blau,* we would not feel free to impute the morality of the 1980s to the Congress of the 1930s.

It would moreover be arbitrary to take CBI's suggestion and use as a cut-off point the definition of beneficial owner in Rule 16a-8 of the Securities and Exchange Commission. Section 16(a) of the Act defines as one type of corporate insider subject to the statute anyone who is "directly or indirectly the beneficial owner" of more than 10 percent of any class of any registered equity security, and the rule defines a beneficial owner for purposes of section 16(a) as including a trustee of a trust for a member of the trustee's "immediate family," defined in turn as including a child of any age. 17 C.F.R. § 240.16a-8(e)(1). But the purpose of this definition is unrelated to the issue in the present case. It is to figure out who has a large enough stake in the corporation to be deemed an insider. For this purpose the adding up of family interests is eminently reasonable. But Horton is not an insider by virtue of being a beneficial owner, directly or indirectly, of more than 10 percent of the stock of CBI, but by virtue of being a director. Rule 16a-8 is irrelevant.

We hold that profit realized by a corporate insider means direct pecuniary benefit to the insider, as in the factual settings of *Whiting* and *Whittaker*; it is not enough that ties of affinity or consanguinity between the nominal recipient and the insider make it likely that the insider will experience an enhanced sense of well-being as a result of the receipt, or will be led to reduce his gift- giving to the recipient. . . . The test of "some direct or indirect benefit" in *Altamil Corp. v. Pryor*, 405 F. Supp. 1222, 1227 (S.D. Ind. 1975), relied on by the district court in this case, is therefore disapproved, though we express no view on how that case should have been decided under the standard we adopt today.

To prevail in this case, CBI therefore would have to show that the trust was a sham; that despite its terms Horton was able to use income or assets of the trust to pay his personal expenses. CBI has made no effort to prove a direct pecuniary benefit to Horton. But we shall leave it to the district judge to decide, in the first instance at least, whether it should be given a chance to try to prove liability under the standard adopted in this opinion.

Strictly speaking, we need not resolve Horton's alternative contention that even if he derived sufficient benefit indirectly from the $25,000 profit made by the trust to have violated section 16(b), he should not be held liable for the entire profit; his reasoning is that the benefit to him must have been a lesser amount since there is no contention that he could divert the whole $25,000 to his own use. But as this issue could become important in the event that CBI wants, and the district judge grants it, an opportunity to try to establish liability under the standard of direct pecuniary benefit that we adopt today, we shall discuss it briefly. The standard of direct pecuniary benefit excludes by definition any attempt to monetize the emotional satisfaction that Horton might derive from a transaction that increased the wealth of his sons. But it does not exclude an attempt to measure any direct pecuniary benefit he may have received from the transaction even if that benefit was less than $25,000. It does not even exclude the possibility of computing the actuarial value of the increase in his contingent remainder due to the profit to the trust—for an expected value is a form of direct pecuniary benefit.

We thus reject the view that the profit nominally received by a third party must be attributed to the insider either entirely or not at all.

* * *

The judgment of the district court is reversed and the case remanded for further proceedings consistent with this opinion.

REVERSED AND REMANDED.

WOOD, Circuit Judge dissenting in part.

It is for me a very close question, but I prefer the approach labeled and rejected by the majority as "realistic" even though it does have some shortcomings. Section 16(a) defines a beneficial owner as including a trustee of a trust for members of the "immediate family." That, of course, applies to a different aspect of the insider problem, but I view it as at least a sparse clue as to what 16(b) may mean. I prefer to read 16(b) a little more broadly so as to include "immediate family" in its proscriptions. Therefore, I respectfully dissent on that issue, but I concur in the majority's analysis of the pecuniary benefit issue.

NOTES AND QUESTIONS

(1) **The holding in *CBI*.** Is the court's holding consistent with the definition of "beneficial owner" under § 16(a)? Is there a justification for attributing purchases of the type involved in *CBI* to the insider for purposes of determining insider status under § 16(a), while not attributing these purchases to the insider for purposes of determining the existence of a short-swing transaction under 16(b)? As to the relationship between 16(a) and 16(b), see also the *Whiting* case discussed in *CBI* and in Note 2, below. Is the court's test of attributing benefit to insiders consistent with the *Dirks* "personal benefit" test (*see* Section 12.05[B])? Should there be a stricter test of "benefit" under 16(b) than in 10b-5 cases?

(2) **Attributing transactions to insiders.** *Whiting v. Dow Chemical Co.*, discussed in *CBI*, held that the insider was a "beneficial owner" of the stock sold by his wife. The court relied in part on an SEC interpretation of § 16(a) to the effect that an insider must report securities trades where he has received "benefits substantially equivalent to ownership." Such benefits were present in *Whiting* by reason of the circumstances discussed in *CBI*. The *Whiting* court also noted that defendant had sufficient control over his wife's transactions to justify imputing the transactions to him in that the husband and wife had engaged in joint financial planning. Moreover, a "beneficial owner" must be charged "with all the profits or none, in the absence of a way to measure benefit. . . . The whole profit is 'his' profit . . . because the shares are 'his' by the statutory 'beneficial owner' concept . . . and because he is a person in a position to obtain inside information."[182] How does the approach in *Whiting* differ from that in *CBI*? Which approach represents the better interpretation of § 16?

[D] When Must the Insider Be An Insider?

Section 16(b) distinguishes between officers and directors on the one hand and 10% shareholders on the other. The rationale for the distinction is that the former type of insider is more likely to have inside information and to be able to use it. Thus, an offi-

---

[182] *See* 523 F.2d at 689.

cer or director may be held liable under 16(b) even if she had such status only as of the date of purchase[183] or only as of the date of sale,[184] though Rules 16a-2(a) and (c) limit the circumstances in which this will happen. But under the "exemptive clause," or last sentence of § 16(b), large shareholders are liable only if they are 10% holders at both ends of the short swing.

Foremost-McKesson, Inc. v. Provident Securities Co.[185] held that the purchase by which one becomes a 10% holder may not be included as part of a short-swing transaction. *Reliance Electric Co. v. Emerson Electric Co.*[186] held that a large holder could liquidate in "steps" and avoid liability as to the last transaction even though it was clear that the shareholder was deliberately attempting to evade liability. But *The Reece Corp. v. Walco National Corp.*[187] refused to extend *Reliance* to a situation in which both "steps" were sold to the same buyer and were negotiated and priced as a single transaction.

PROBLEM

Henry is the chief executive officer of Corporation. Fred is Henry's 13-year-old son who lives with and is wholly supported by Henry. Henry and Fred have a joint checking account. Henry makes periodic deposits to the account and Fred deposits his earnings from his paper route. Henry does not make withdrawals from the account, although he has the legal right to do so. Father and son have agreed that the account will constitute Fred's sole source of money for entertainment and other nonessentials—in other words, that the account is to constitute Fred's "allowance." The purpose of the account is to teach Fred how to manage money. Henry thought it would be a good idea to teach Fred finance by having him invest in the stock of Corporation. After securing Fred's agreement with this plan, Henry purchased some Corporation stock and paid for the stock by withdrawing money from the joint account. Henry is holding the stock in his name as trustee for Fred. Three months after this transaction, Corporation stock has risen substantially in value. Henry needs to raise some money to pay taxes and would like to sell some of the Corporation stock in his personal portfolio. Advise Henry as to whether the sale at this time would raise any legal problems.

[E]   What Are a "Purchase" and a "Sale"?

There are many different ways to obtain or divest oneself of corporate securities in addition to exchanging cash and stock. When will such transactions be "purchases"

---

[183] *See Feder v. Martin Marietta Corp.*, 406 F.2d 260 (2d Cir. 1969), *cert denied*, 396 U.S. 1036 (1970).

[184] *See Adler v. Klawans*, 267 F.2d 840 (2d Cir. 1959).

[185] 423 U.S. 232 (1976).

[186] 404 U.S. 418 (1972).

[187] Fed. Sec. L. Rep. (CCH) ¶ 98,289 (S.D.N.Y. 1981).

or "sales" for purposes of § 16(b)? We will discuss mergers as one important example of the 16(b) purchase-sale problem. As discussed in Section 13.02, in a merger two corporations become one, with shareholders of the "disappearing" corporation receiving shares in the "surviving" corporation. The relevant questions under § 16(b) with respect to mergers are: (1) is the merger a purchase or sale? and (2) may transactions in the two different securities be "matched"?

In *Kern County Land Co. v. Occidental Petroleum Corp.*,[188] Occidental Petroleum Corporation had acquired, by June 8, 1967, more than 10% of the stock of Kern County Land Company in a tender offer. In order to escape the clutches of Occidental, the Kern management agreed to a merger with Tenneco. In the merger, which was closed on August 30, Occidental's Kern stock was converted by operation of law into a right to receive Tenneco stock. On December 11, 1967, Occidental sold its Tenneco stock to Tenneco under Tenneco's exercise of an option that had been entered into on June 2.

The Court held that a merger was an "unorthodox" transaction which, unlike the exchange of cash for stock, was not clearly within 16(b). Such an unorthodox transaction is included within 16(b) only if inclusion is consistent with underlying legislative intent—that is, only where the transaction involves the possibility of the type of speculative abuse § 16(b) was intended to curb. In the present case, there was no such possibility since (1) Occidental had no control over the transaction; and (2) as a contestant for control of Old Kern, Occidental was in an adversary relationship with management and therefore lacked any access to inside information. Thus, the merger could not be matched with the tender offer purchases. The Court also held that Occidental did not sell its Tenneco stock at the time of the option contract (June 2), but rather on December 11 when the option was exercised.

Texas International Airlines v. National Airlines Inc.[189] refused to extend *Kern* to a cash resale of target stock by a frustrated bidder to the winning bidder just prior to a merger in which the target was the disappearing corporation and the winning bidder was the survivor. Do you agree with this result?

QUESTION

Is *CBI's* approach to the interpretation of § 16(b) consistent with that in *Kern*? Should the interpretation of § 16(b) be more literal when the effect of literalness is to *exclude* a transaction from coverage (as in *CBI*) than where the effect would be to *include* it (as in *Kern*)?

---

[188] 411 U.S. 582 (1973).

[189] 714 F.2d 533 (5th Cir. 1983).

[F] "Waiver" of § 16(b)

Like most provisions of the securities laws, § 16(b) is mandatory—that is, parties that are subject to the rule cannot, in terms, opt out of it. But is there any way that the provision can, like many "mandatory" state law provisions, be avoided by planning and drafting? Consider the "step" transaction in *Reliance. See also Sterman v. Ferro Corp.,*[190] where a corporation repurchased its shares from a company that had purchased a "stake" preparatory to a possible takeover. The seller renegotiated a proposed price to include an additional amount that exactly compensated it for its 16(b) liability. The court held that this was not a waiver that contravened § 29(a) of the 1934 Act.

REFERENCES

Fox, *Insider Trading Deterrence Versus Managerial Incentives: A Unified Theory of Section 16(b)*, 92 MICH. L. REV. 2088 (1994).

Okamoto, *Rereading Section 16(b) of the Securities and Exchange Act*, 27 GA. L. REV. 183 (1992).

Ribstein, *The Application of Section 16(b) of the Securities Exchange Act of 1934 to Tender Offers*, 31 SW. L.J. 503 (1977).

Thel, *The Genius of Section 16: Regulating the Management of Publicly Held Companies*, 42 HASTINGS L.J. 391 (1991).

---

[190] 785 F.2d 162 (6th Cir. 1986).

CHAPTER 13

Corporate Acquisitions: An Overview

The next three Chapters discuss the law and policy of corporate acquisitions. Corporate acquisitions can occur in two general ways: (1) as corporate-level transactions in which a target corporation merges into, consolidates with, or sells its assets to, an acquiring corporation (*see* Section 13.02); or (2) as shareholder-level transactions in which an acquirer takes control of a target either by convincing the target company's shareholders to grant it a sufficient number of proxies to replace the target's board of directors (*see* Section 13.03) or by purchasing, directly from the target's shareholders, a controlling interest in the target firm's stock (*see* Section 13.04). For the purposes of the discussion in this and subsequent Chapters, corporate-level transactions are referred to as "corporate combinations" and shareholder-level transactions are referred to as "control acquisitions."

This Chapter begins by reviewing the economic background of corporate acquisitions (*see* Section 13.01). It then goes on to consider in greater detail the basic methods of combining corporations and acquiring control from shareholders (*see* Sections 13.02, 13.03, and 13.04). Legal standards governing management decisions impeding and approving acquisitions of the corporation are considered in Chapters 14 and 15.

§ 13.01 Economic Considerations

When a corporation is acquired through a purchase of a controlling block of stock or through a corporate combination, the shareholders of the acquired firm almost always receive a substantial premium over the current market price of their shares. The payment of this "control premium" indicates either that the acquired firm is worth more as a result of the acquisition—that is, the acquisition *creates* wealth; or that, in acquiring control, the acquirer is able to appropriate the wealth of others, such as shareholders, creditors, employees, or taxpayers—that is, the acquisition *redistributes* wealth. Which proposition is more accurate bears on how the law should approach takeovers. The following materials examine these two competing explanations for control acquisitions.

[A] Wealth-Creation Explanations for Corporate Acquisitions

This Subsection examines two reasons why corporate acquisitions may increase the value of the acquired firms: synergy and gains from changing the acquired firm's capital structure.

[1] Synergy

One possible explanation for the premium in corporate acquisitions is that the purchaser will use the assets of the acquired company more productively than current management. Because the market may not have been aware of the possibility of this more productive use of the acquired firm's assets, or may have discounted the probability that it would occur because, for example, of management resistance or opposition by regulatory agencies, the pre-acquisition market price may not reflect the full value of the company in this alternative use. Therefore, the purchaser can profit from the acquisition even though it pays a premium over the pre-acquisition market price. The concept of increasing the value of assets through acquisition is referred to generally as "synergy." There are a number of possible sources of synergy, including the following:

(a) *"Horizontal" economies of scale.* The potential for horizontal economies of scale exists when the cost per unit of production falls as more units are produced. For example, it might cost only twice as much to make three times more of a chemical in a much larger vat, or workers might commit fewer errors if they perform more specialized tasks on a larger number of products. Therefore, an acquisition may produce synergy if, for example, it will result in increased production at a given location.

(b) *"Scope" economies of production.* The potential for "scope" economies of production exists when the costs per unit of production can be reduced by combining the manufacture of different products that draw on the same resources. For example, when Philip Morris bought Kraft, it was hoping to profit by selling the products of the two companies through the same distribution network.

(c) *Vertical integration.* Firms can also reduce costs through "vertical integration"—that is, by combining Firm A, the owner of Resource A, with Firm B, the owner of Resource B. Vertical integration can reduce costs by eliminating a resource owner's ability to extract extra benefits from another party that depends on this resource, as in the situation involving the printing press and the newspaper in Section 1.02[E].

[2] Gains in Restructurings

The synergies discussed above are only possible when the purchaser offers the target firm new managers or assets. Thus, gains from synergies cannot explain corporate acquisitions such as "leveraged management buy-outs" that accomplish no more than a change in the acquired firm's capital structure.

In a typical leveraged management buyout, a group consisting of incumbent management (which invests personal savings, borrowed funds and deferred compensation in the buyout) and a leveraged buyout promoter, such as Kohlberg, Kravis Roberts & Co., forms a new corporation whose purpose is to acquire the target. The new corporation is funded mostly by debt, including bank loans and super-subordinated high yield bonds. It then generally undertakes a two-step transaction: first, the new corporation purchases a controlling interest in the stock of the target corporation from the public shareholders, often through a public tender offer; second, the new corporation uses the control it has acquired to cause the two corporations to merge in a transaction where the remaining public shareholders of the target receive cash or additional bonds for their shares. When the smoke clears, the post-buyout firm is controlled by the same management team that controlled the target, but the public shareholders have been eliminated, the stock is largely held by management and the leveraged buyout promoter, and the post-buyout company has a much higher ratio of debt to equity.

This sort of restructuring offers a number of potential benefits (see the **Jensen** articles). First, by concentrating equity shares in management and the promoters, the leveraged management buyout can give managers better incentives to maximize profits because managers will have much of their wealth and credit tied up in the firm's stock. The leveraged buyout promoter also has more expertise and better incentive to monitor than the widely dispersed public shareholders it replaces.

Second, by creating a capital structure consisting mostly of debt, the leveraged management buyout can reduce agency costs. The heavy periodic principal and interest payments the new company must make may be a better mechanism for disciplining management than the combination of fiduciary duties, market for control and other devices that align manager and shareholder incentives in the publicly held firm. Managers of public companies with low debt-equity ratios have substantial discretion over how to use cash that is not needed to pay expenses.

[B] Wealth-Redistribution Explanations for Corporate Acquisitions

The preceding Subsection suggests that acquirers purchase target companies at a premium over the market price because they profit by making changes that increase the value of the acquired firm. However, not all commentators accept this benign explanation for corporate acquisitions. In particular, some argue that acquirers purchase target companies at a premium because, by acquiring control, they are able to appropriate the wealth of others, such as shareholders, creditors, employees, or taxpayers. Some of the principal arguments along these lines are examined below.

[1] Injuries to Acquirer Shareholders

Shareholders of the acquiring company may be harmed by takeovers if bidder-managers systematically pay too much for targets. But why would bidder-managers pay too much? One possible reason is that managers of acquiring companies, by using corporate funds for acquisitions rather than returning them to shareholders as dividends, may be seeking to increase their own power, stature or compensation. Or managers may be trying to reduce the risks of their own undiversified portfolio by expanding into other businesses, providing diversification that ordinary shareholders do not need.[1]

---

[1]   *See* Amihud & Lev, *Risk Reduction as a Managerial Motive for Conglomerate Mergers*, 12 BELL J. ECON. 605 (1981).

To the extent that inefficient acquisitions result from managerial error, there is an obvious antidote: the market for corporate control. Firms that make inefficient acquisitions may themselves become potential targets for takeovers if bidders can profit by dismantling these companies and selling off the pieces. This will be the case when the assets comprising the firm may be used more profitably in other companies—that is, where greater synergies are available elsewhere. The prospect of these so-called "bust-up takeovers" thus disciplines incumbent management's decision to acquire and maintain control over new assets.[2]

[2] Injuries to Target Shareholders

Target shareholders might see their wealth transferred to bidders if the market "undervalues" the target. This could occur where, for example, managers acquiring the company in a management buyout have inside information or the ability to exert pressure on the board that results in favoritism in a bidding contest. However, the data does not support the hypothesis that takeover gains by acquirers result from market "undervaluation" of targets (*see, e.g.,* **Jarrell, Brickley & Netter**).

[3] Injuries to Target "Stakeholders"

A third group that may be harmed by takeovers consists of target "stakeholders," such as employees and creditors. For example, takeovers, which are usually decided by shareholders, may increase the risks of existing creditors by leaving the firm perilously close to insolvency or harm employees by lowering wages and benefits.[3]

On the other hand, there are some arguments raising questions about whether stakeholders are really harmed by takeovers. First, the new owners are subject to the same constraints in using the firm's assets as were the old owners, including contracts with creditors, employees and others. Second, while some acquisitions may involve costs for stakeholders, they also bring offsetting benefits. For example, all participants in the enterprise potentially share in the benefits of increased management efficiency that may result from a leveraged buyout. In other words, high debt deters managers from the sort of profligate investments that can get a firm into trouble.

---

[2]   Evidence shows that the market for control disciplines errors by acquirer-managers. *See* Mitchell & Lehn, *Do Bad Bidders Become Good Targets?*, 98 J. POL. ECON. 372 (1990) (firms that announced acquisitions from 1982–86 that produced negative stock price reactions were more likely to be taken over than were other firms; on average, the stock price reaction to acquisitions by firms that eventually became targets was negative, while the reaction to acquisitions by non-target firms was positive).

[3]   *See, e.g.,* Coffee, *The Uncertain Case for Takeover Reform: An Essay on Stockholders, Stakeholders and Bust-Ups*, 1988 WIS. L. REV. 435.

[4] Injuries to Consumers and Other Non-Shareholders

Consumers of the acquirer's and the target's products may be harmed by takeovers if takeovers reduce competition among firms. This complex problem will be left to another course. For present purposes, it is enough to point out that at least part of the recent boom in takeovers is attributable to reduced enforcement of the antitrust laws beginning in the Reagan administration.

Leveraged buyouts may also harm taxpayers or, more accurately, the United States Treasury by reducing tax collections. In most situations, shareholders gain if the firm's capital structure is altered so that funds generated by the firm are paid out in the form of tax deductible interest on debt, rather than being retained by the firm or distributed as dividends on equity.

Finally, takeovers may harm society more generally if, for example, the takeovers themselves, or the threat of takeovers, reduce socially beneficial investments in research and development. This may occur if share prices do not reflect the long term value added by these activities. The data, however, does not support the hypothesis that takeovers are motivated by such "market myopia."[4]

REFERENCES

Jarrell, Brickley & Netter, *The Market for Corporate Control: Empirical Evidence Since 1980*, 3 J. ECON. PERSP. 49 (1988).

Jensen, *Eclipse of the Public Corporation*, HARV. BUS. REV. 61 (Sept.–Oct. 1989).

Jensen, *Agency Costs of Free Cash Flow, Corporate Finance, and Takeovers*, 76 AM. ECON. REV. 323 (1986).

Lehn & Poulsen, *Leveraged Buyouts: Wealth Created or Wealth Redistributed?*, in PUBLIC POLICY TOWARD CORPORATE MERGERS (M. Weidenbaum & K. Chilton, eds., 1987).

Muscarella & Vetsuypens, *Efficiency and Organizational Structure: A Study of Reverse LBOs*, 45 J. FIN. 1389 (1990).

Romano, *A Guide to Takeovers: Theory, Evidence, and Regulation*, 9 YALE J. REG. 119 (1992).

---

[4] *See, e.g.*, Hall, *The Effect of Takeover Activity on Corporate Research and Development*, in CORPORATE TAKEOVERS: CAUSES AND CONSEQUENCES (Auerbach, ed. 1988) (showing some evidence that takeovers do not "punish" r & d); Meulbrook, Mitchell, Mulherin, Netter & Poulsen, *Shark Repellents and Managerial Myopia: An Empirical Test*, 98 J. POL. ECON. 1108 (1990) (finding that research and development actually decreased relative to the rest of the market in firms that adopted anti-takeover amendments, contrary to the hypothesis that decreasing the takeover threat would make managers focus more on the long term).

§ 13.02 Corporate Combinations

[A] Introduction

This Section is concerned with corporate acquisitions that are structured as mergers, consolidations, and asset sales. Although the focus here is on corporate combinations that accomplish the combination of two previously unaffiliated businesses, it should be understood that corporate combinations can be used for other purposes as well. For example, corporate combinations can be used to make changes within a single business as (1) when a corporation merges into a new corporate entity that has the same shareholders and directors as the first in order to effect a change in the company's jurisdiction of incorporation or (2) when a parent corporation combines with a company it has been operating as a subsidiary in order to force minority shareholders of the subsidiary to accept cash or some other form of consideration for their shares (*see* Section 15.02, below).

Corporate combinations generally must be approved by the boards of directors of the participating corporations before they become effective. But unlike many other business decisions entrusted to the board, corporate combinations often involve substantial changes in the rights of some or all of the shareholders. For instance, shareholders of one or more of the corporations participating in the transaction may have their shares converted into securities of a different firm, cash, or a combination of both. Thus, special procedures and remedies beyond board approval may be necessary to protect the shareholders. The special procedures prescribed under state law for corporate combinations are introduced in Subsection [B] below. Legal remedies available to shareholders aggrieved by the terms of corporate combinations, including appraisal rights, state law fiduciary duties, and remedies under the federal securities laws, are considered in detail in Chapter 15.

[B] Forms of Corporate Combinations and Procedures

The principal state law procedures for corporate combinations include voting by shareholders and the right of shareholders who disagree with the combination to dissent from the transaction and receive, in cash, a judicially-determined fair value for their shares (*i.e.*, appraisal rights). *See* Del. G.C.L. § 262(d)-(k) for a description of procedures related to appraisal rights. Whether shareholders of any or all the corporations participating in the combination get voting rights or appraisal rights or both generally depends upon how the combination is structured. The rules related to a number of different transaction structures are reviewed below.

[1] Sales of Assets

One way for corporations to combine is to have one corporation purchase all, or substantially all, of the assets of the other. The selling corporation may then either liquidate and distribute the consideration received to its shareholders (after satisfying the claims of any creditors) or continue to exist and hold the consideration received on its shareholders' behalf.

In a sale of assets, the shareholders of the purchaser generally do not get voting rights or appraisal rights. *See, e.g.*, Del. G.C.L. §§ 262(b) and 271. However, when the purchaser issues stock in exchange for the assets, a shareholder vote may be required or advisable under several circumstances, including the following: (1) the number of shares issued exceeds the number authorized in the charter and therefore the transaction cannot be effected without a shareholder-approved charter amendment; (2) the transaction is "interested" or otherwise might involve a breach of fiduciary duty (*see* Section 9.04); or (3) applicable stock exchange rules require shareholder approval on the theory that the issuance presents a substantial risk of dilution.[5]

On the other hand, a sale of assets does frequently require the approval of the seller's shareholders. *See, e.g.*, Del. G.C.L. § 271(a), which requires approval by a majority vote of all affected shareholders (not just a majority of those shareholders present and voting at the meeting), whenever the sale involves "all or substantially all," of the seller's assets.[6] Compare MBCA § 12.02 (a), which requires shareholder approval only if the transaction "would leave the corporation without a significant continuing business activity," with assets representing 25% of the firms total assets and income being conclusively deemed significant. In addition, most states provide appraisal rights to shareholders of the selling firm who dissent from substantial asset sales. See, for example, MBCA § 13.02(a)(3). The Delaware Act, however, does not grant appraisal rights in this situation. *See* Del. G.C.L. §§ 262(b)-(c), which only make appraisal rights available for certain mergers and consolidations, but which allow charter amendments extending appraisal rights to sales of all or substantially all the assets of the corporation.

[2] Mergers and Consolidations

A second way for corporations to combine is to merge or consolidate with one another. A merger involves a combination of two or more corporate entities such that one or more of the corporations wholly disappears and one survives. A consolidation is similar except that all of the constituent corporations disappear into a new corporation. (Henceforth "merger" will refer to both mergers and consolidations.) The surviving corporation in a merger that is accomplished pursuant to procedures prescribed in the

---

[5]   *See, e.g.,* New York Stock Exchange Company Manual, A-283, A-284.

[6]   As to the meaning of "all or substantially all," compare *Gimbel v. Signal Companies, Inc.*, 316 A.2d 599 (Del. Ch.), *aff'd, per curiam*, 316 A.2d 619 (Del. Sup. Ct. 1974) (sale by a conglomerate of a subsidiary that represented 26% of the parent's assets, 41% of its net worth, and 15% of its revenues held not to involve a sale of "all or substantially all" of the corporation's assets), with *Katz v. Bregman*, 431 A.2d 1274 (Del. Ch. 1981) (sale of a subsidiary that contributed 51% of assets, 44.9% of sales, and 52.4% of pretax net income and which historically constituted the parent's major line of business held to require shareholder approval).

applicable corporation law acquires all of the rights and liabilities of the constituent corporations. *See, e.g.*, Del. G.C.L. § 259.

Unlike a typical sale of assets, which may not have a dramatic impact on the rights of the purchaser's shareholders, a merger usually substantially affects the rights of shareholders of all of the constituent corporations. Thus, the corporation statutes generally require approval of mergers by the boards and shareholders of both the surviving and disappearing corporations. *See* Del. G.C.L. § 251(a)-(d). In addition, the shareholders of all of the constituent corporations are generally entitled to appraisal rights. *See* Del. G.C.L. § 262(b).

[3] "Short Form" and "Small Scale" Mergers

Many modern corporation statutes provide for special types of mergers, such as "short form" mergers and "small scale mergers." In these special types of mergers, voting rights and appraisal rights are denied to the shareholders of one or both of the constituent corporations.

In a "short form" merger, a parent corporation owning at least 80%-90% of its subsidiary's stock merges with its subsidiary. Since the parent corporation controls the subsidiary's board of directors, as well as the subsidiary's stock, corporation statutes generally permit the merger to take place without a formal vote of the subsidiary's board or shareholders (*see, e.g.*, Del. G.C.L. § 253), though subsidiary shareholders other than the parent corporation are generally granted appraisal rights (*see, e.g.*, Del. G.C.L. § 262(b)(3)). In addition, since a short form merger has limited consequences for the parent corporation's shareholders, shareholders of the parent corporation are generally denied both voting rights and appraisal rights.

In a "small scale" merger, one corporation absorbs another in a transaction where shareholders of the first corporation end up owning the vast majority (typically, at least 5/6) of the stock of the survivor. Since this type of merger does not substantially dilute the interest of the first corporation's shareholders, these shareholders are entitled neither to a vote nor to appraisal rights. *See, e.g.*, Del. G.C.L. § 251(f).[7] However, unlike shareholders involved in a "short-form" merger, the shareholders of the disappearing corporation in a small scale merger are entitled both to appraisal rights and to a vote.

---

[7]   *See also* Cal. Corp. C. § 1201(b); *cf. ALI Principles* § 7.21(a) (no appraisal rights in business combinations, including mergers, if persons who were shareholders of the corporation immediately before the combination own 60% or more of the total voting power of the surviving corporation).

[4] Problems of Traditional Forms of Combination and Alternative Transaction Structures

Each of the above forms of business combination presents advantages and disadvantages. For instance, a purchase of assets is generally subject to fewer corporate law formalities than a merger: while a sale of assets generally does not trigger voting or appraisal rights in the transferee's shareholders and, depending on the applicable corporation statute, may not trigger appraisal rights in the transferor shareholders, a merger generally triggers voting and appraisal rights on the part of the shareholders of both corporations. (But see the discussion of the "*de facto* merger" doctrine in Section 15.01[D] below.) In addition, unlike the surviving corporation in a merger, a purchaser of assets need not assume the liabilities of the selling corporation. But these advantages over mergers come at a cost. In particular, a purchase of assets requires substantial paperwork in connection with recorded deeds and titles and assignment of contract rights—paperwork which is not necessary in connection with mergers since the surviving corporation in a merger acquires all the rights of the disappearing corporations by operation of law (*see* Del. G.C.L. § 259). In addition, a purchase of assets may trigger liabilities under creditor protection statutes, including those dealing with fraudulent conveyances and bulk sales. These problems have led corporate planners to seek out other acquisition structures that avoid the problems of both. Some of theses alternative acquisition structures considered below.

[a] Purchases of Controlling Stock Interests

One alternative is to have the acquiring corporation purchase a controlling stock interest in the target and operate the target as a subsidiary. This alternative, which is discussed in greater detail in Section 13.04 below, avoids the substantial paperwork of the asset sale since it does not involve the transfer of title of any of the target's assets; it also avoids the substantial corporate law formalities of the merger since neither shareholders of the acquiring corporation nor shareholders of the target corporation obtain voting or appraisal rights in connection with the transaction. But purchasing a controlling stock interest has problems of its own: since buying every share of stock is not practical with respect to a public corporation because of the problem of holdouts, the purchaser of control will have to operate the subsidiary subject to burdensome conflict-of-interest rules (*see Sinclair* and related notes in Section 9.07) or undertake a costly "squeeze out" merger following the acquisition of the controlling stock interest in which the remaining minority shareholders of the subsidiary are forced to surrender their shares for cash, new securities, or a combination of both. (The rules relating to squeeze out mergers are discussed below at Section 15.02.)

[b] Triangular Mergers

Another alternative to the standard forms of corporate combinations is the triangular merger. In this type of transaction, the acquiring corporation creates a subsidiary and then either merges the target into the subsidiary (a "forward" triangular merger) or merges the subsidiary into the target ("reverse" triangular merger). (The decision as to whether to use the forward or reverse method depends on whether there is some reason, such as ownership of franchises or contract rights, for preserving the target entity.) The triangular merger retains the main benefit of ordinary mergers—the acquisition of the target's assets and liabilities by operation of law—but generally avoids some of the burdensome corporate law formalities—voting rights and appraisal rights for shareholders of the acquiring corporation, which is not, itself, a party to the merger. The validity of this type of transaction may be in question under statutes that require the surviving corporation in a merger to issue its own shares, since in a triangular merger the subsidiary usually issues shares of the parent to the shareholders of the disappearing firm. This, however, is not a problem under Del. G.C.L. § 251(b)(5), which permits constituent corporations in a merger to issue the securities "of any other corporation."

[c] Compulsory Share Exchanges

A transaction that accomplishes the same result as a triangular merger is the compulsory share exchange, in which the shareholders of the target corporation vote to exchange all outstanding shares for those of the acquiring corporation. *See, e.g.*, MBCA § 11.03. This device, however, has not been widely adopted by the states.

[5] Tax Consequences of Choice of Form of Combination

An important tax question in connection with a corporate combination is whether the shareholders of one or more of the constituent corporations will be deemed for tax purposes to have sold their stock. If shareholders are deemed to have sold their stock in connection with a corporate combination, they will be forced to "recognize" a taxable gain on the difference between the sale price and their "basis" in the stock.

The Internal Revenue Code incorporates the idea that when a shareholder merely continues her interest in a business she should not be required to recognize gain even if the entity in which she holds her interest substantially changes form or is absorbed by a different entity. Section 368(a)(1)(A) through (G) of the Code describes seven types of "reorganizations" that are entitled to nonrecognition treatment. These transactions commonly are referred to according to the subsection in which they are described. Subsections A through C deal with the types of combinations with which we are primarily concerned here—those involving amalgamation of previously unaffiliated businesses as distinguished from changes in a single business.

In general, as long as shareholders receive only voting stock in a reorganization, they will be deemed merely to be continuing their interests in their investments and will not be required to recognize gain. The principal question concerns the amount of consideration other than voting stock—particularly assumption of liabilities and cash—that may be paid before all gain must be recognized. (Note that even a "tax-free" reorganization may result in some tax liability to the extent that the shareholders receive consideration other than voting stock.) While the rules are complicated, the important point to remember in the present connection is that in a Type A reorganization—a statutory merger—the shareholders may receive as much as half of the consideration in non-equity consideration before the transaction loses its non-recognition status. In a Type B reorganization—an acquisition of stock—the consideration must consist entirely of voting stock. In a Type C reorganization—a purchase of assets—non-equity consideration may comprise up to 20% of the consideration. Thus, a merger permits more tax flexibility while preserving non-recognition status than do other forms of business combination. For this reason it is often the preferred form from a tax standpoint.

[6] Combinations Involving Non-Corporate Forms

The partnership laws have not traditionally provided for mergers and other forms of combinations. Partnerships could accomplish transactions that were equivalent to mergers by customized agreements. However, Article 9 of the Revised Uniform Partnership Act now includes provisions for conversions between general and limited partnership (§§ 902-904) and for mergers of partnerships (§§ 905-908). Also, many LLC acts provide for mergers between LLCs and other types of business entities, including general and limited partnerships and corporations. *See* ULLCA, Article 9.

These provisions raise two types of issues which are not present in corporate merger provisions. First, when a firm converts into or merges with a form of business association which provides for different rules regarding liability of the members, how does the transaction affect the liability of the members of the constituent firms? Second, in "cross-entity" mergers or conversions, which statute controls in the event of conflict? For example, suppose the general partnership statute provides for voting rights for both constituents of a merger or conversion between a general and a limited partnership. Does the general partnership merger or conversion provision or the limited partnership voting rule apply in determining the requisite vote by the limited partnership?

§ 13.03 Control Acquisitions: Proxy Contests

Section 13.02 was concerned with corporate acquisitions that were structured as corporate-level transactions, such as mergers and asset sales which, among other things, require the consent of the target firm's directors. But, as noted in the introduction to Chapter 13, corporate acquisitions can also be structured as shareholder-level transactions—that is, transactions in which an acquirer takes control of a target by dealing directly with the target's shareholders. Perhaps the most basic of these shareholder-level transactions is the proxy contest in which the acquirer solicits from the target's shareholders the power to vote (but not ownership of) a sufficient number of shares to replace the target corporation's board of directors. Proxy contests may be waged as ends in themselves—that is, as a way for one firm to capture working control of the board of directors of another. Alternatively, proxy contestants may propose corporate combinations or tender offers. In the latter case, the role of the proxy contest is to give the acquiring firm the board control necessary to allow the corporate combination or tender offer to proceed.

One of the most difficult questions concerning proxy contests is the extent to which each side may be reimbursed for their expenses of soliciting proxies. In modern proxy contests, these expenses can be considerable. In the absence of specific statutory or charter rules regarding proxy expenses, the courts in effect supply a standard form contract that determines the extent to which the board can approve payment or reimbursement of incumbent and insurgent expenses without a shareholder vote. In determining the standard form, it is relevant to consider the beneficial changes in corporate governance often accomplished through proxy contests. But more proxy contests are not necessarily better if other devices, such as fiduciary duties, employment markets, and the market for corporate control, can achieve the same results at lower cost to the corporation.

Analyze the following questions in light of these general considerations:

(1) *Should incumbent directors have the power to approve payment by the corporation of the expenses of soliciting proxies in support of management positions and the management slate of directors?* Allowing managers to fight proxy contests with the corporation's money arguably reduces the likelihood that proxy contests will lead to beneficial changes in corporate governance. If incumbents have unfettered power to spend money for their own reelection, incumbents may run for reelection even if only they, and not the corporation, stand to gain from their retention. But consider the effect of a rule that requires the incumbents to bear all of the cost of their own reelection unless the shareholders voted otherwise. Under such a rule, incumbents would incur the expense of a proxy contest only if this expense was less than the expected benefit to them of reelection. Thus, incumbents might not stand for reelection even if the corporation would gain from their continued services (*see* **Easterbrook & Fischel** at 413).

(2) *Should all insurgents (winners and losers) be entitled to reimbursement for their proxy expenses?* The benefits of a change in governance effected by a proxy contest will be enjoyed by all of the shareholders, but the costs will be borne solely by the dissidents unless they are compensated. This suggests that there will be underproduction of beneficial proxy contests if dissident shareholders are not entitled to reimbursement. But if dissidents do not bear any of their own expenses, the result may be overproduction of proxy contests.

(3) *Should only winning insurgents be able to obtain reimbursement?* One way to deal with the overproduction problem would be to permit reimbursement only of winning insurgents. But many proxy contests that do not immediately cause a change in control ultimately lead to beneficial changes in governance that increase shareholder

value. This suggests that many "losing" dissidents make positive contributions to corporate governance that will be underproduced if only "winning" dissidents are reimbursed. On the other hand, perhaps even winning dissidents should not be reimbursed. As long as there is a significant chance that insurgents will have to bear substantial expense in mounting a proxy contest, proxy contests probably will be fought mostly by those who have substantial investments in the firm. Such shareholders arguably do not need reimbursement to encourage them to launch beneficial proxy contests (*see* **Easterbrook & Fischel** at 414).

(4) *Should incumbent directors be permitted to vote expenses for losing insurgents?* On the surface it would seem that there is no problem with letting incumbent directors authorize payment of the expenses incurred by losing dissidents. The adversary relationship between incumbents and dissidents ensures that the directors will not approve dissidents' expenses unless there is some corporate benefit. But incumbents may want to buy peace for themselves, at shareholder expense, by paying off dissidents who agree not to vigorously press their case. On the other hand, a policy letting incumbent-directors reimburse dissident expenses may be beneficial because it encourages dissidents to commence such contests in the first instance.

The courts have stressed the following factors in determining whether to approve the payment of proxy expenses out of the corporate treasury: (1) whether the expenses are being paid to incumbent management or to insurgents; (2) whether the expenses have been approved only by the board of directors or by the shareholders as well; (3) whether the expenses relate to a contest involving a "policy" dispute or to a "personnel" dispute;[3] (4) whether the expenses are necessary expenses of organizing a meeting, sending legally required proxy statements and annual reports, and soliciting sufficient proxies to produce a quorum at the meeting, on the one hand, or expenses of using professional proxy solicitors, public relations counsel, and high-priced lawyers to help ensure victory, on the other;[9] and (5) with respect to reimbursement of insurgent expenses, whether the insurgents won or lost.

Rosenfeld v. Fairchild Engine and Airplane Corp.[10] upheld dismissal of a shareholder's complaint seeking repayment to the corporation of $261,522 paid to both sides in a proxy contest—$106,000 spent by the old board while in office; $28,000 paid to the old board by the new board after winning the contest; and $127,000 paid by the new board to reimburse its own expenses. The seven-member court was divided along several lines. The three-member plurality opinion distinguished between "policy" and "personnel" disputes, holding the expenses properly reimbursable to the contestants because

---

[8]   *See Steinberg v. Adams*, 90 F. Supp. 604 (S.D.N.Y. 1950) (holding that, under Delaware law, reasonable expenses in a "policy" dispute were reimbursable for both sides); *see also Hibbert v. Hollywood Park, Inc.*, 457 A.2d 339 (Del. 1983).

[9]   *See In re Zickl*, 73 N.Y.S.2d 181 (Sup: Ct. N.Y. Co. 1947) (approving expenses of a proxy solicitation firm); and *Levin v. Metro-Goldwyn-Mayer*, 264 F. Supp. 797 (S.D.N.Y. 1967) (refusing to enjoin management's use of corporate employees and proxy soliciting firms to solicit proxies); *Rosenfeld*, discussed immediately below.

[10]   309 N.Y. 168, 128 N.E.2d 291 (1955).

the case involved a "policy" dispute over the propriety of the incumbent president's employment contract rather than simply a "personnel" dispute over who should run the corporation. The remaining four members of the court concluded that, irrespective of whether the dispute was over policy or personnel, unreasonable expenses would not be reimbursable. Both the concurring opinion of Judge Desmond and the three-member dissenting opinion cited with approval *Lawyers' Advertising Co. v. Consolidated Ry. Lighting & Refrigerating Co.*,[11] which distinguished the expenses of mailing customary proxy material for the purpose of facilitating shareholder voting, and "the unusual expense of publishing advertisements or . . . of dispatching special messengers."[12] But Judge Desmond disagreed with the three dissenters over the burden of proof and voted to uphold dismissal on the ground that the plaintiff had failed to prove the unreasonableness of specific expenses.

Modern practice as to the reimbursement of proxy expenses does not seem to be consistent with *Rosenfeld*. Both incumbents and insurgents readily resort to the kind of expensive proxy solicitation techniques, including the use of professional soliciting firms and newspaper advertisements, reimbursement for which was apparently condemned by a majority of the *Rosenfeld* court. Moreover, insurgents are commonly reimbursed by director, rather than shareholder, vote.

REFERENCES

Aranow & Einhorn, PROXY CONTESTS FOR CORPORATE CONTROL Chs. 20-22 (2d ed. 1968).
Easterbrook & Fischel, *Voting in Corporate Law*, 26 J.L. & ECON. 395 (1983).
Eisenberg, THE STRUCTURE OF THE CORPORATION Chs. 9 and 10 (1976).

§ 13.04 Control Acquisitions: Stock Purchases

In proxy contests, dissident shareholders obtain control of the corporation's board of directors by convincing other shareholders to vote with them for a new slate of dissident-approved directors. Proxy contests, however, suffer from one principal flaw (at least from the point of view of the dissident shareholders who organize them): they allow dissident shareholders to keep only that portion of the gains from a change in control that corresponds with their ownership share in the firm. Acquiring control by purchasing stock solves this problem.

[A] Purchase of a Control Block

If a controlling block of stock is concentrated in the hands of a relatively small group of shareholders, one might acquire a controlling interest in the firm's stock by one

---

[11]   187 N.Y. 395, 80 N.E. 199 (1907).

[12]   187 N.Y. at 399, 80 N.E. at 201.

or more private purchases. Corporate shareholders generally have no power to veto transfers of shares, even if these share transfers involve controlling interests. By contrast, partners can veto new members (*see* UPA § 18(g), RUPA § 401(i)), and close corporation shareholders may agree to a veto power (*see* Section 5.03). This subsection considers what duties are imposed on shareholders who sell controlling stock interests absent such an agreement.

[1] Meaning of Control

The corporation technically is controlled by the owners of all of the shares. However, as Berle & Means pointed out in their 1932 landmark work, THE MODERN CORPORATION AND PRIVATE PROPERTY, it is possible to control a corporation without owning all of its stock. Statutes and charters generally give the power to make important decisions and to elect directors to the owners of a majority of the stock. In a large public corporation with dispersed, passive shareholders, a large minority shareholder may have substantial power to elect directors and influence corporate decisions because of the difficulty and expense of mustering a large opposition block. This is often referred to as "working control."

[2] Policy Issues

Whether shareholders should have duties with respect to sales of control blocks of stock involves two conflicting principles. On the one hand, corporate stock traditionally has been regarded as property which its owners ought to be able to trade freely. In fact, free trade of stock is essential to a healthy capital market. On the other hand, some commentators believe that permitting controlling shareholders to reap a premium over market price for sales of control blocks of stock is unfair. Professor **Berle** first suggested shareholder liability for the control premium in his book cited above,[13] and developed the idea in subsequent articles cited in the References. The following passage summarizes his views:[14]

> By its corporation statute, the state grants each corporation capacity to choose a board of directors for management of its affairs. It directs exercise of that capacity through the stockholder's vote. By the certificate of incorporation, it gives the incorporators power to assign the vote evenly among all shares outstanding or evenly among all the shares of a specified class or classes. By statute in most states, and by general doctrine, the rights of each share of stock within each class must be identical. It is wholly impractical to require a unanimous vote to elect directors; consequently in all normal situations a majority is authorized to elect the directors prevailing over the votes

---

[13] Berle & Means, *supra* at 216-17 (rev. ed. 1968).

[14] 50 CORNELL L.Q. at 637-638. Copyright © 1965 by Cornell University. All rights reserved.

of the minority. Essentially, this is nothing more than a device to assure continued management and functioning; it is a corporate power, though exercised by individual stockholders. It does not authorize or permit a management thus constituted to distinguish between majority and minority shareholders: management power does not include that privilege. The position of a majority shareholder, with his capacity to control, is thus not a "property right" in the same sense as is his right to participate in dividends, or in liquidation or the like. His control power is really adventitious, a by-product of the corporate capacity to choose a board of directors by less than unanimity. This is why the control power—capacity to choose a management—is a corporate asset, not an individual one.

Like **Berle**, **Andrews** also takes the view that a control premium represents an extra advantage that in fairness ought not to be wholly appropriated by the controlling shareholder. Andrews, however, proposes a slightly different rule than does Berle. Instead of treating control as a corporate asset which may not be sold by an individual shareholder, Andrews proposes a right of equal opportunity in the sale of corporate shares. The following is a statement of Andrews' proposed rule:[15]

> [W]henever a controlling stockholder sells his shares, every other holder of shares (of the same class) is entitled to have an equal opportunity to sell his shares, or a pro rata part of them in substantially the same terms. Or in terms of the correlative duty: before a controlling stockholder may sell his shares to an outsider he must assure his fellow stockholders an equal opportunity to sell their shares, or as high a proportion of theirs as he ultimately sells of his own.

Andrews also offers some practical arguments in favor of an equal opportunity rule. One of his principal arguments is that an equal opportunity rule will discourage transactions involving a risk of harm to the corporation without unduly discouraging beneficial takeovers. This argument assumes that the control purchaser will be willing and able either to purchase all of the shares or to persuade the control holder to sell only a *pro rata* portion of his investment if and only if the transfer of control is likely to be beneficial to the corporation.

[3] The Traditional Rule

The cases have reflected both of the conflicting principles just discussed. Consistent with the principle of "free trade," the courts generally have held that there is no lia-

---

[15]   78 HARV. L. REV. 515-16, Copyright © 1965 by The Harvard Law Review Association.

bility merely for receiving a control premium.[16] On the other hand, the courts have been alert to find other bases for shareholder liability when control blocks of stock are sold. In many cases, it is difficult to avoid the conclusion that the ostensible theory of liability is merely a "cover" for liability for receipt of a control premium. The following are the theories of liability most commonly applied in sale-of-control cases.

[a] Duty to Disclose

The sale of control may involve three steps: (1) an offer addressed to a major or controlling shareholder to purchase all of the stock or assets of the corporation; (2) a purchase by that shareholder of additional stock from one or more other shareholders without disclosure of the offer; and (3) a sale by the major or controlling shareholder at a premium price. Courts have imposed liability on the controlling shareholder in such cases on the basis of a breach of a fiduciary duty to disclose the third party's offer to the controlling shareholder.[17] In light of doubts about corporate insiders' state law duties to disclose (*see* Section 12.04), the courts' willingness to impose liability in the sale-of-control setting may, therefore, be partly attributable to the courts' distaste for the control premium.

[b] Duty to Investigate

Several courts have imposed liability on a seller of control for failure to investigate a purchaser who later looted the corporation.[18] But since a duty of care is generally not imposed on controlling shareholders, the control premium itself is one possible explanation for liability in these cases.

The duty to investigate depends on whether the seller has notice of the possibility of looting by the purchasers. In cases involving corporations primarily owning marketable securities and other easily sold assets, the courts have indicated that the mere payment of a premium is an important circumstance putting the defendant on notice.[19]

---

[16] *See, e.g., Clagett v. Hutchison*, 583 F.2d 1259 (4th Cir. 1978); *McDaniel v. Painter*, 418 F.2d 545 (10th Cir. 1969); *Ritchie v. McGrath*, 1 Kan. App. 2d 481, 571 P.2d 17 (1977); *Tryon v. Smith*, 191 Or. 172, 229 P.2d 251 (1951); *Thompson v. Hambrick*, 508 S.W.2d 949 (Tex. Civ. App. 1974).

[17] *See, e.g., Childs v. RIC Group, Inc.*, 331 F. Supp. 1078 (N.D. Ga. 1970); *Low v. Wheeler*, 207 Cal. App. 2d 477, 24 Cal. Rptr. 538 (Cal. Ct. App. 1962); *Jacobson v. Yaschik*, 249 S.C. 577, 155 S.E.2d 601 (1967); *Bailey v. Vaughan*, 359 S.E.2d 599 (W. Va. 1987).

[18] *See Insuranshares Corp. v. Northern Fiscal Corp.*, 35 F. Supp. 22 (E.D. Pa. 1940); *De Baun v. First Western Bank & Trust Co.*, 46 Cal. App. 3d 686, 120 Cal. Rptr. 354 (1975); *Harris v. Carter*, 582 A.2d 222 (Del. Ch. 1990); *Gerdes v. Reynolds*, 28 N.Y.S.2d 622 (Sup. Ct. N.Y. Co. 1941).

[19] *See Gerdes* and *Insuranshares, supra.*

However, the courts are considerably more reluctant to impose liability under this theory in cases involving industrial corporations.[20]

The following cases illustrate the extent of the seller's duty to investigate.

1. *De Baun v. First Western Bank & Trust Co.*[21] affirmed the imposition of liability in connection with a sale by defendant bank of a controlling interest in Alfred S. Johnson, Inc., to one Mattison. The court stated the facts in part as follows:

> Here Bank was the controlling majority shareholder of Corporation. As it was negotiating with Mattison, it became directly aware of facts that would have alerted a prudent person that Mattison was likely to loot the corporation. Bank knew from the Dun & Bradstreet report that Mattison's financial record was notable by the failure of entities controlled by him. Bank knew that the only source of funds available to Mattison to pay it for the shares he was purchasing lay in the assets of the corporation. The after-tax net income from the date of the sale would not be sufficient to permit the payment of dividends to him which would permit the making of payments. An officer of Bank possessed personal knowledge that Mattison, on at least one occasion, had been guilty of a fraud perpetrated on Bank's predecessor in interest and had not satisfied a judgment Bank held against him for damages flowing from that conduct.

2. *Swinney v. Keebler Co.*[22] reversed the imposition of liability in connection with the sale by defendant Keebler of a controlling interest in Meadors, Inc., a candy manufacturer, to Atlantic Services, Inc. despite the following facts stated by the court:

> (1) no one from Atlantic had any experience in the candy business, (2) at the time the contract was executed no one from Atlantic had inspected the "Meadors operation," (3) by the time of the closing, only Atlantic's accountant had examined Meadors to "any appreciable extent and he was interested principally in the books and inventory," (4) Meadors had no market of its own and the "profit as shown could not have been accepted at face value by an outsider," (5) prior to the closing Atlantic had no negotiations with Meadors' key employees concerning the continuation of the business, (6) the sale was consummated with dispatch, and (7) Atlantic had inquired as to the availability of Meadors' funds for payment of the purchase price.

[c] Sale of Office

While stock is the property of the shareholder and thus arguably may be traded without restriction, the courts have held that officers and directors are fiduciaries and

---

[20] For examples of such cases in which liability was denied, see *Clagett v. Hutchison*, 583 F.2d 1259 (4th Cir. 1978); *Harman v. Willbern*, 520 F.2d 1333 (10th Cir. 1975); *Swinney v. Keebler Co.*, 480 F.2d 573 (4th Cir. 1973); *Levy v. American Beverage Corp.*, 265 A.D. 208, 38 N.Y.S.2d 517 (1942).

[21] 46 Cal. App. 3d 696, 700, 120 Cal. Rptr. 354, 362 (1975).

[22] 480 F.2d 573, 580 (4th Cir. 1973).

may not sell their offices for private gain. Thus, the seller of a control block of stock may be held liable if he is found to have received a premium price which includes payment for the his resignation from office or other official action, including assistance in selecting a successor.[23] In this connection, recall that directors may fill vacancies in the board that are created by the death or resignation of a member and that the incumbent board, including appointed replacements, will control the proxy machinery in connection with the next scheduled election of directors.[24]

Although the fact that the seller resigns her directorship or procures other resignations is suspicious, this does not necessarily indicate that the seller has received a "bribe" for official action. Since a purchaser of a controlling stock interest could procure replacement of the board in due course, a requirement that the seller of control linger to the end would exalt form over substance. Thus, if a transaction involves sale of a controlling stock interest, courts will generally not impose liability for sale of office. For example, courts have imposed liability in cases involving premium sales of 4% and 3% stock interests, respectively,[25] but have declined to hold sellers liable in cases involving premium sales of 44.3%, 28.3% and 9.7%.[26]

[d] Corporate Opportunity

Liability has also been imposed on control sellers in a variety of cases in which the premium price appears to have involved a clear diversion of an opportunity from the corporation or from the minority shareholders. For example, courts have found selling shareholders liable: where the insider sold at a premium to an outsider who had approached him with a proposition that the corporation sell its assets;[27] where the insider sold at a premium after rejecting an earlier agreement calling for a general offer addressed to all of the shareholders (in both of these cases, the insiders bought stock from minority shareholders without disclosing the pending offers from outsiders, thus bringing the cases within category (a), above);[28] and where a premium sale by insiders

---

[23] For a clear case of this type, see *Porter v. Healy*, 244 Pa. 427, 91 A. 428 (1914).

[24] *See Rosenfeld v. Black*, 445 F.2d 1337, 1344 (2d Cir. 1971), *cert. denied*, 409 U.S. 802 (1972), which discusses an analogous problem in connection with investment advisors for investment companies.

[25] *See Brecher v. Gregg*, 89 Misc. 2d 457, 392 N.Y.S.2d 776 (1975); *In re Caplan's Petition*, 20 A.D.2d 301, 246 N.Y.S.2d 913, *aff'd*, 14 N.Y.2d 679, 249 N.Y.S.2d 877 (1964).

[26] *See Cooke v. Oolie*, 26 DEL. J. CORP. L. 609 (Del. Ch. 2000); *Essex Universal Corp. v. Yates*, 305 F.2d 572 (2d Cir. 1962), and *Carter v. Muscat*, 21 A.D.2d 543, 251 N.Y.S.2d 378 (1st Dept. 1964). *Cooke v. Oolie* generally rejects liability for sale of control in Delaware unless the sale of control involves the misuse of corporate information, the outright sale of a corporate office, or a sale to a looter.

[27] *Commonwealth Title Ins. & Trust Co. v. Seltzer*, 227 Pa. 410, 76 A. 77 (1910); *see also Thorpe v. Cerbco*, 676 A.2d 436 (Del. 1996). In *Thorpe*, the court accepted the general principle that a shareholder has a right to sell for a premium, but nonetheless held that controlling shareholders breached their duty of loyalty by entering into negotiations to sell their stock to a third party who had contacted them to discuss the possibility of acquiring substantially all the corporation's assets. The court held that the controlling shareholders should have presented the opportunity to the corporation first, even though the controlling shareholders could have vetoed the proposed asset sale under Del. G.C.L. § 271.

[28] *Thompson v. Hambrick*, 508 S.W.2d 949 (Tex. Civ. App. 1974).

was followed by a lower offer to the other shareholders and the outsider was seeking the assets of the company through its purchase of control.[29]

On the other hand, the court denied liability where the outsider approached the president and 70% shareholder with a plan to buy 100% of the stock of the company, bought the 70% interest at a premium price, and then dealt directly with the minority shareholders in purchasing the remainder.[30] Should it make a difference if the outsider initially had proposed a general offer to all the shareholders at the same price, or if a purchase of assets had immediately followed the purchase of stock?[31]

[4] Toward a Broader Rule of Recovery in Sale-of-Control Transactions

The following case has been widely cited as pointing the way toward a broader rule of recovery in sale-of-control cases than is available under the traditional rule. In reading the case, consider carefully how far the court has gone toward establishing a remedy for sale-of-control.

PERLMAN v. FELDMANN
United States Court of Appeals, Second Circuit
219 F.2d 173, *cert. denied*, 349 U.S. 952 (1955)

CLARK, Chief Judge.

This is a derivative action brought by minority stockholders of Newport Steel Corporation to compel accounting for, and restitution of, allegedly illegal gains which accrued to defendants as a result of the sale in August, 1950, of their controlling interest in the corporation. The principal defendant, C. Russell Feldmann, who represented and acted for the others, members of his family,[1] was at that time not only the dominant stockholder, but also the chairman of the board of directors and the president of the corporation. Newport, an Indiana corporation, operated mills for the production of steel sheets for sale to manufacturers of steel products, first at Newport, Kentucky, and later also at other places in Kentucky and Ohio. The buyers, a syndicate organized as Wilport Company, a Delaware corporation, consisted of end-users of steel who were interested in securing a source of supply in a market becoming ever tighter in the Korean War. Plaintiffs contend that the consideration paid for

---

[29] *Dunnett v. Arn*, 71 F.2d 912 (10th Cir. 1934).

[30] *Tryon v. Smith*, 191 Or. 172, 229 P.2d 251 (1951).

[31] For a discussion of this case, see Jennings, *Trading in Corporate Control*, 44 CALIF. L. REV. 1, 23-25 (1956). For a case similar to *Tryon* but including some additional, aggravating circumstances, see *Brown v. Halbert*, 271 Cal. App. 2d 252, 76 Cal. Rptr. 781 (1969) (imposing liability).

[1] The stock was not held personally by Feldmann in his own name, but was held by the members of his family and by personal corporations. The aggregate of stock thus had amounted to 33% of the outstanding Newport stock and gave working control to the holder. The actual sale included 55,552 additional shares held by friends and associates of Feldmann, so that a total of 37% of the Newport stock was transferred.

the stock included compensation for the sale of a corporate asset, a power held in trust for the corporation by Feldmann as its fiduciary. This power was the ability to control the allocation of the corporate product in a time of short supply, through control of the board of directors; and it was effectively transferred in this sale by having Feldmann procure the resignation of his own board and the election of Wilport's nominees immediately upon consummation of the sale.

. . . Plaintiffs argue here, as they did in the court below, that in the situation here disclosed the vendors must account to the non-participating minority stockholders for that share of their profit which is attributable to the sale of the corporate power. Judge Hincks denied the validity of the premise, holding that the rights involved in the sale were only those normally incident to the possession of a controlling block of shares, with which a dominant stockholder, in the absence of fraud or foreseeable looting, was entitled to deal according to his own best interests. Furthermore, he held that plaintiffs had failed to satisfy their burden of proving that the sales price was not a fair price for the stock per se. Plaintiffs appeal from these rulings of law which resulted in the dismissal of their complaint.

The essential facts found by the trial judge are not in dispute. Newport was a relative newcomer in the steel industry with predominantly old installations which were in the process of being supplemented by more modern facilities. Except in times of extreme shortage Newport was not in a position to compete profitably with other steel mills for customers not in its immediate geographical area. Wilport, the purchasing syndicate, consisted of geographically remote end-users of steel who were interested in buying more steel from Newport than they had been able to obtain during recent periods of tight supply. The price of $20 per share was found by Judge Hincks to be a fair one for a control block of stock, although the over-the-counter market price had not exceeded $12 and the book value per share was $17.03. But this finding was limited by Judge Hincks' statement that "[w]hat value the block would have had if shorn of its appurtenant power to control distribution of the corporate product, the evidence does not show." It was also conditioned by his earlier ruling that the burden was on plaintiffs to prove a lesser value for the stock.

Both as director and as dominant stockholder, Feldmann stood in a fiduciary relationship to the corporation and to the minority stockholders as beneficiaries thereof.

* * *

It is true, as defendants have been at pains to point out, that this is not the ordinary case of breach of fiduciary duty. We have here no fraud, no misuse of confidential information, no outright looting of a helpless corporation. But on the other hand, we do not find compliance with that high standard which we have just stated and which we and other courts have come to expect and demand of corporate fiduciaries. The actions of defendants in siphoning off for personal gain corporate advantages to be derived from a favorable market situation do not betoken the necessary undivided loyalty owed by the fiduciary to his principal.

The corporate opportunities of whose misappropriation the minority stock-holders complain need not have been an absolute certainty in order to support this action against Feldmann. If there was possibility of corporate gain, they are entitled to recover.

. . . [I]n *Irving Trust Co. v. Deutsch*, 2 Cir., 73 F.2d 121, 124, an accounting was required of corporate directors who bought stock for themselves for corporate use, even though there was an affirmative showing that the corporation did not have the finances itself to acquire the stock. Judge Swan speaking for the court pointed out that "The defendants' argument, contrary to *Wing v. Dillingham* [5 Cir., 239 F. 54], that the equitable rule that fiduciaries should not be permitted to assume a position in which their individual interests might be in conflict with those of the corporation can have no application where the corporation is unable to undertake the venture, is not convincing. If directors are permitted to justify their conduct on such a theory, there will be a temptation to refrain from exerting their strongest efforts on behalf of the corporation since, if it does not meet the obligations, an opportunity of profit will be open to them personally."

This rationale is equally appropriate to a consideration of the benefits which Newport might have derived from the steel shortage. In the past Newport had used and profited by its market leverage by operation of what the industry had come to call the "Feldmann Plan." This consisted of securing interest-free advances from prospective purchasers of steel in return for firm commitments to them from future production. The funds thus acquired were used to finance improvements in existing plants and to acquire new installations. In the summer of 1950 Newport had been negotiating for cold-rolling facilities which it needed for a more fully integrated operation and a more marketable product, and Feldmann plan funds might well have been used toward this end.

Further, as plaintiffs alternatively suggest, Newport might have used the period of short supply to build up patronage in the geographical area in which it could compete profitably even when steel was more abundant. Either of these opportunities was Newport's, to be used to its advantage only. Only if defendants had been able to negate completely any possibility of gain by Newport could they have prevailed. It is true that a trial court finding states: "Whether or not, in August, 1950, Newport's position was such that it could have entered into 'Feldmann Plan' type transactions to procure funds and financing for the further expansion and integration of its steel facilities and whether such expansion would have been desirable for Newport, the evidence does not show." This, however, cannot avail the defendants, who—contrary to the ruling below—had the burden of proof on this issue, since fiduciaries always have the burden of proof in establishing the fairness of their dealings with trust property.

. . . Defendants seek to categorize the corporate opportunities which might have accrued to Newport as too unethical to warrant further consideration. It is true that reputable steel producers were not participating in the gray market brought about by the Korean War and were refraining from advancing their prices, although to do so would not have been illegal. But Feldmann plan transactions were not considered within this self-imposed interdiction; the trial court found that around the time of the Feldmann sale Jones & Laughlin Steel Corporation, Republic Steel Company, and Pittsburgh Steel Corporation were all participating in such arrangements. In any event, it ill becomes the defendants to disparage as unethical the market advantages from which they themselves reaped rich benefits.

We do not mean to suggest that a majority stockholder cannot dispose of his controlling block of stock to outsiders without having to account to his corporation for profits or even never do this with impunity when the buyer is an interested customer, actual or potential, for the corporation's product. But when the sale necessarily results in a sacrifice of this element of corporate good will and consequent unusual profit to the fiduciary who has caused the sacrifice, he should account for his gains. So in a time of market shortage, where a call on a corporation's product commands an unusually large premium, in one form or another, we think it sound law that a fiduciary may not appropriate to himself the value of this premium. Such personal gain at the expense of his co-venturers seems particularly reprehensible when made by the trusted president and director of his company. In this case the violation of duty seems to be all the clearer because of this triple role in which Feldmann appears, though we are unwilling to say, and are not to be understood as saying, that we should accept a lesser obligation for any one of his roles alone.

Hence to the extent that the price received by Feldmann and his co-defendants included such a bonus, he is accountable to the minority stockholders who sue here. RESTATEMENT, RESTITUTION §§ 190, 197 (1937)[.] And plaintiffs, as they contend, are entitled to a recovery in their own right, instead of in right of the corporation (as in the usual derivative actions), since neither Wilport nor their successors in interest should share in any judgment which may be rendered. *See Southern Pacific Co. v. Bogert*, 250 U.S. 483, 39 S. Ct. 533, 63 L. Ed. 1099. Defendants cannot well object to this form of recovery, since the only alternative, recovery for the corporation as a whole, would subject them to a greater total liability.

The case will therefore be remanded to the district court for a determination of the question expressly left open below, namely, the value of defendants' stock without the appurtenant control over the corporation's output of steel. We reiterate that on this issue, as on all others relating to a breach of fiduciary duty, the burden of proof must rest on the defendants. Judgment should go to these plaintiffs and those whom they represent for any premium value so shown to the extent of their respective stock interests.

The judgment is therefore reversed and the action remanded for further proceedings pursuant to this opinion.

SWAN, Circuit Judge (dissenting).

With the general principles enunciated in the majority opinion as to the duties of fiduciaries I am, of course, in thorough accord. But, as Mr. Justice Frankfurter stated in *Securities and Exchange Comm. v. Chenery Corp.*, 318 U.S. 80, 85, 63 S. Ct. 454, 458, 87 L. Ed. 626, "to say that a man is a fiduciary only begins analysis; it gives direction to further inquiry. To whom is he a fiduciary? What obligations does he owe as a fiduciary? In what respect has he failed to discharge these obligations?" My brothers' opinion does not specify precisely what fiduciary duty Feldmann is held to have violated or whether it was a duty imposed upon him as the dominant stockholder or as a director of Newport. Without such specification I think that both the legal profession and the business world will find the decision confusing and will be unable to foretell the extent of its impact upon customary practices in the sale of stock.

The power to control the management of a corporation, that is, to elect directors to manage its affairs, is an inseparable incident to the ownership of a majority of its stock, or sometimes, as in the present instance, to the ownership of enough shares, less than a majority, to control an election. Concededly a majority or dominant shareholder is ordinarily privileged to sell his stock at the best price obtainable from the purchaser. In so doing he acts on his own behalf, not as an agent of the corporation. If he knows or has reason to believe that the purchaser intends to exercise to the detriment of the corporation the power of management acquired by the purchase, such knowledge or reasonable suspicion will terminate the dominant shareholder's privilege to sell and will create a duty not to transfer the power of management to such purchaser. The duty seems to me to resemble the obligation which everyone is under not to assist another to commit a tort rather than the obligation of a fiduciary. But whatever the nature of the duty, a violation of it will subject the violator to liability for damages sustained by the corporation. Judge Hincks found that Feldmann had no reason to think that Wilport would use the power of management it would acquire by the purchase to injure Newport, and that there was no proof that it ever was so used. Feldmann did know, it is true, that the reason Wilport wanted the stock was to put in a board of directors who would be likely to permit Wilport's members to purchase more of Newport's steel than they might otherwise be able to get. But there is nothing illegal in a dominant shareholder purchasing from his own corporation at the same prices it offers to other customers. That is what the members of Wilport did, and there is no proof that Newport suffered any detriment therefrom.

My brothers say that "the consideration paid for the stock included compensation for the sale of a corporate asset," which they describe as "the ability to control the allocation of the corporate product in a time of short supply, through control of the board of directors; and it was effectively transferred in this sale by having Feldmann procure the resignation of his own board and the election of Wilport's nominees immediately upon consummation of the sale." The implications of this are not clear to me. If it means that when market conditions are such as to induce users of a corporation's product to wish to buy a controlling block of stock in order to be able to purchase part of the corporation's output at the same mill list prices as are offered to other customers, the dominant stockholder is under a fiduciary duty not to sell his stock, I cannot agree. For reasons already stated, in my opinion Feldmann was not proved to be under any fiduciary duty as a stockholder not to sell the stock he controlled.

Feldmann was also a director of Newport. Perhaps the quoted statement means that as a director he violated his fiduciary duty in voting to elect Wilport's nominees to fill the vacancies created by the resignations of the former directors of Newport. As a director Feldmann was under a fiduciary duty to use an honest judgment in acting on the corporation's behalf. A director is privileged to resign, but so long as he remains a director he must be faithful to his fiduciary duties and must not make a personal gain from performing them. Consequently, if the price paid for Feldmann's stock included a payment for voting to elect the new directors, he must account to the corporation for such payment, even though he honestly believed that the men he voted to elect were well qualified to serve as directors. He can not take pay for performing his fiduciary duty. There is no suggestion that he did do so, unless the price paid for his stock was more than its value. So it seems to me that decision must turn on whether finding 120 and conclusion 5 of the district judge are supportable on the evidence. They are set out in the margin.[1]

---

[1]   "120. The 398,927 shares of Newport stock sold to Wilport as of August 31, 1950, had a fair value as a control block of $20 per share. What value the block would have had if shorn of its appurtenant power to control distribution of the corporate product, the evidence does not show."

"5. Even if Feldmann's conduct in cooperating to accomplish a transfer of control to Wilport immediately upon the sale constituted a breach of a fiduciary duty to Newport, no part of the moneys received by the defendants in connection with the sale constituted profits for which they were accountable to Newport."

Judge Hincks went into the matter of valuation of the stock with his customary care and thoroughness. He made no error of law in applying the principles relating to valuation of stock. Concededly a controlling block of stock has greater sale value than a small lot. While the spread between $10 per share for small lots and $20 per share for the controlling block seems rather extraordinarily wide, the $20 valuation was supported by the expert testimony of Dr. Badger, whom the district judge said he could not find to be wrong. I see no justification for upsetting the valuation as clearly erroneous. Nor can I agree with my brothers that the $20 valuation "was limited" by the last sentence in finding 120. The controlling block could not by any possibility be shorn of its appurtenant power to elect directors and through them to control distribution of the corporate product. It is this "appurtenant power" which gives a controlling block its value as such block. What evidence could be adduced to show the value of the block "if shorn" of such appurtenant power, I cannot conceive, for it cannot be shorn of it.

* * *

The final conclusion of my brothers is that the plaintiffs are entitled to recover in their own right instead of in the right of the corporation. This appears to be completely inconsistent with the theory advanced at the outset of the opinion, namely, that the price of the stock "included compensation for the sale of a corporate asset." If a corporate asset was sold, surely the corporation should recover the compensation received for it by the defendants. Moreover, if the plaintiffs were suing in their own right, Newport was not a proper party.

* * *

I would affirm the judgment on appeal.

NOTES AND QUESTIONS

(1) **The nature of the "opportunity."** According to the court, one of the corporate opportunities" of which the sale of control might have deprived Newport was the building of local patronage during the period of short supply. (The other corporate opportunity was, of course, the opportunity to receive "Feldmann Plan" loans.) Historically, steel industry prices were determined according to a "multiple basing point" system which permitted sales to nearby and remote customers at the same prices. Under pressure from the Federal Trade Commission, the steel industry, at the time of the Feldmann sale, was about to change to an "fob (free on board)" system under which prices would depend on distance from the factory. The new system, as the court indicated, would force competition more on a local than on a national basis.[32]

(2) **Pre-case history.** Feldmann's career did not begin with Newport Steel. An early company formed by Feldmann was a pioneer in diesel engines and a predecessor

---

[32]   *See* Hayes, *Sale of Control of a Corporation: Who Gets the Premium?*, 4 J. Corp. L. 243, 252-53 (1979).

of General Motor's diesel division. Feldmann later pioneered in the auto radio business, forming a company that was a predecessor of Philco. Feldmann's interest in Newport began in 1946. In 1950, Newport began merger negotiations with another company. The termination of these negotiations resulted in a suit under § 10(b) of the 1934 Act and SEC Rule 10b-5 [33] in which plaintiffs claimed that Feldmann broke off merger negotiations in order to realize a higher price for his own stock, and the court upheld dismissal on the ground of plaintiff's lack of standing as a purchaser or seller of securities. After these negotiations, Feldmann rejected a number of offers for his stock, finally accepting the offer that was the basis of *Perlman*. Prior to accepting this offer, Feldmann investigated the buying group. At the first annual shareholder meeting following the Wilport purchase, Newport shareholders approved the sale of steel to the new controlling group at prevailing market prices. In 1953, prior to the Second Circuit's opinion in *Perlman*, Wilport sold its interest to Merritt-Chapman & Scott, a company run by a controversial wheeler-dealer named Louis Wolfson. MCS made an offer to all shareholders at the same price ($10.50 per share), which was accepted by all but 5.3% of the public shareholders.

(3) **Post-case history.** Following the Second Circuit's decision, Newport Steel Corporation, which was now controlled by Merritt-Chapman, petitioned for a rehearing, claiming that the judgment should be on behalf of the corporation rather than the noncontrolling shareholders. The petition was denied per curiam. A private, prehearing memorandum by Judge Clark in connection with the petition for rehearing provides an intriguing glimpse into the thought processes of the judge who wrote the *Perlman* decision: "Practically our result is the only one which has meaning in any attempt to hold these trade buccaneers to a modicum of morality."[34]

(4) **The decision on remand.** On remand,[35] the court determined the enterprise value of Newport, hearing expert witnesses for plaintiff who minimized this value and expert witnesses for defendant who tried to maximize it. The per share enterprise value was determined to be $14.67. The court characterized the premium as the difference between that and $20, or $5.33 per share. This amount was multiplied by 400,000, the number of shares sold by Feldmann, and then reduced by approximately 37%, Feldmann group's proportionate ownership of the company before its sale to Wilport. The resulting figure, $1,339,769.62, was to be shared by Merritt-Chapman as the successor of the shareholders who were excluded from Feldmann's sale and the few public shareholders who had not tendered in response to Merritt-Chapman's general offer. The case ultimately was settled for $1,150,000, of which $488,329.73 went to the attorneys. Merritt-

---

[33]   *Birnbaum v. Newport Steel Corp.*, 193 F.2d 461 (2d Cir.), *cert. denied*, 343 U.S. 956 (1952).

[34]   The above facts concerning Feldmann and the subsequent history of the case are drawn in large part from Deutsch, Perlman v. Feldmann: *A Case Study in Contemporary Corporate Legal History*, 8 U. MICH. J. L. REF. 1 (1974). That article is interesting not only for its background data on *Perlman*, but for the nearly cosmic significance it attaches to the case.

[35]   154 F. Supp. 436 (D. Conn. 1957).

Chapman received approximately $600,000 with the remaining $60,000 going to those public shareholders who had not tendered in response to the general offer.

(5) **Analyzing the court's theory.** The *Perlman* court held that there was a sale of a corporate asset. In analyzing this theory, consider the following questions:

(a) If the purchasers of control (Wilport) managed the company in their own interests so as to deprive the corporation of the valuable opportunities mentioned in *Perlman*, would the minority shareholders have a cause of action against the controlling shareholders? *See Sinclair v. Levien*, Section 9.07. If a remedy would lie in this situation, how did the premium sale transfer control of a corporate asset?

(b) Why did defendant have the burden of establishing the nonexistence of the "Feldmann plan" opportunity that the plaintiff claimed was denied to Newport as a result of the sale of control? Although the court said that "fiduciaries always have the burden of proof in establishing the fairness of their dealings with trust property," this assumes the Feldmann group had, in fact, transferred trust property in connection with the sale of their stock. Compare *Sinclair v. Levien*, Section 9.07, which rejected a claim that a controlling shareholder had denied the corporation valuable opportunities by causing the payment of excessive dividends because the plaintiff failed to establish the existence of the opportunities.

(6) **The nature of the remedy: derivative or direct?** There is a distinction between derivative recovery on behalf of the corporation and individual and direct recovery by the plaintiff class (*see* Section 10.01). What forms of recovery would be consistent with the **Berle** and **Andrews** theories discussed in subsection [2] above? *Perlman* was a derivative suit. Why, then, did the *Perlman* court order payment directly to the shareholders? The courts sometimes order such recovery in a derivative suit in order to avoid unjust enrichment of a stockholder who purchased at a depressed price following the wrongdoing, or to avoid indirect recovery by wrongdoers.[36] Is *Perlman* an appropriate case for such recovery? Note, in this regard, that requiring the Feldmann group to repay the entire control premium to the corporation would, in effect, allow Merritt-Chapman, Wilport's successor who presumably was not harmed by any of Wilport's actions as a controlling shareholder of Newport, to share in the recovery. But allowing the plaintiffs to recover in their personal capacities for the misappropriation of a corporate asset leaves creditors who might have benefited from the proceeds from the sale of that asset unprotected. Is Feldmann reaping a windfall by being assessed only a *pro rata* share of the control premium?

(7) **Other sale of control cases.** *Honigman v. Green Giant Co.*[37] upheld a recapitalization in which the former holders of 100% of the voting power—the Class A

---

[36]   *See Jannes v. Microwave Communications, Inc.*, 385 F. Supp. 759 (N.D. Ill. 1974); *Matthews v. Headley Chocolate Co.*, 130 Md. 523, 100 A. 645 (1917); *Young v. Columbia Oil Co.*, 110 W. Va. 364, 158 S.E. 678 (1931).

[37]   208 F. Supp. 754 (D. Minn. 1961), *aff'd*, 309 F.2d 667 (8th Cir. 1962), *cert. denied*, 372 U.S. 941 (1963).

shareholders—gave up most of their control to Class B shareholders in exchange for a larger share in the assets of the company. The plan was approved by the holders of 92.3% of the Class B stock. The courts rejected plaintiff's argument that the Class A shareholders were receiving an impermissible control premium. Also, the lower court noted that the corporation would benefit from the recapitalization in that its business operations no longer would be inhibited by reason of a capital structure that included a class of nonvoting stock. Is *Honigman* inconsistent with *Perlman*? *Donahue v. Rodd Electrotype Co., Inc.*, Section 5.05[D], gave a minority shareholder in a close corporation the right to have her shares purchased by the corporation on the same basis that the corporation had purchased the shares of a controlling shareholder. Does the rationale of the *Donahue* case extend to the public corporation setting? Finally, *Jones v. H.F. Ahmanson & Co.*[38] held that the controlling shareholders breached a duty to the minority when they formed a holding company and then made a public offering of holding company stock, thereby creating a public market for the controlling shareholders' interest in the corporation. The court reasoned that the opportunity to take advantage of the public market was one that belonged to all the shareholders.

(8) **Defining "control."** *Treadway Companies, Inc. v. Care Corp.*[39] refused to impose liability for a premium over market price realized on a stock sale by a 14% shareholder (the largest single interest in the corporation) who was also a director. The court said that a controlling shareholder might have a duty to account for a control premium, but noted that the lower court had found that defendant did not, in fact, have control. *In re Sea-Land Corp. Shareholders Litigation*[40] held that a defeated bidder did not breach a fiduciary duty when it sold its 39.5% stake to the successful bidder for a premium in a transaction in which the other shareholders did not participate. The court reasoned that, although the selling shareholder had substantial leverage, domination is necessary to trigger a fiduciary duty. The selling shareholder's lack of domination was apparent from the very fact that the incumbent board had rejected its bid.

(9) **Federal liability.** The Williams Act requires disclosures to the shareholders in connection with the transfer of control through a tender offer, which may include certain "street sweeps," or unpublicized private purchases. Full disclosure is also required under § 14(a) of the 1934 Act in connection with the election of directors following the transfer of control, and under § 14(f) in connection with the seriatim resignation of directors that often accompanies the transfer of control. In addition, the sale of control may sometimes be accompanied by deceptive conduct that constitutes a violation of § 10(b) and Rule 10b-5, though such conduct will only give rise to a private right of action if the plaintiff is a purchaser or seller of stock.[41] For instance, liability has been

---

[38]   1 Cal. 3d 93, 81 Cal. Rptr. 592, 460 P.2d 464 (1969).

[39]   638 F.2d 357 (2d Cir. 1980).

[40]   Fed. Sec. L. Rep. (CCH) ¶ 93,923 (Del. Ch. 1988).

[41]   See the discussion of *Blue Chip Stamps* in Section 12.03[D][1] above.

recognized: (a) where the control sellers have remained in office and perpetrated a fraud on the corporation;[42] (b) where the sale of control was followed by a tender offer at a much lower price and the tendering shareholders, as well as those by shareholders who were forced out in a subsequent merger, alleged that they might not have sold if the higher price paid to the controlling shareholders had been disclosed;[43] and (c) where the control-seller purchased stock from noncontrolling shareholders without disclosing the higher pending offer.

(10) **Policy analysis.** Should there be liability for reaping a control premium or a duty to share the premium with minority holders? One way to analyze this question is to consider whether minority shareholders would be likely to bargain for this result prior to the transaction. **Easterbrook & Fischel** conclude that the parties would not reach such a bargain because forbidding unequal gain-sharing prevents transfers of control that will ultimately benefit all of the shareholders. The buyer purchases control because it expects to profit by using its control to improve the company through synergistic gains of the type discussed in Section 13.01, a result which benefits all shareholders. But such beneficial transactions are unlikely to take place if the seller cannot reap the full control premium, because the seller is unlikely to be willing to give up his control block without special compensation for the benefits allowed under *Sinclair v. Levien*, Section 9.07.

On the other hand, as discussed above in Subsection [2], **Andrews** argues that an equal opportunity rule will discourage transactions involving a risk of harm to the corporation, since harmful transactions are less likely where the seller must retain a portion of her shares or the purchaser must purchase 100% of the corporation's stock. If this is true, minority shareholders may want to foreclose even some beneficial control transfers in order to prevent detrimental control transfers. Easterbrook & Fischel respond to this point by noting that investors normally hold diversified portfolios of securities, and therefore are equally likely to be holding shares in the control purchaser, control seller or subject corporation.

The quandary about whether the transfer is likely to be beneficial or detrimental to the minority shareholders is illustrated by *Perlman* itself. The court saw a possibly detrimental transaction in which the control buyer sought to reap for itself the benefits of the "Feldmann Plan." But Newport also may have been trying to gain an assured market for its product during a time of uncertainty and change in the steel industry. Alternatively, Newport may have been trying to take advantage of Wilport's experience in the steel industry to increase the value of the company.

(11) **The evidence.** The question of whether control transfers are more likely to be beneficial than detrimental can be tested empirically. Some studies show positive

---

[42]   *See Drachman v. Harvey*, 453 F.2d 722 (2d Cir. 1971) (panel), *rev'd on rehearing*, 453 F.2d 736 (2d Cir. 1972) (en banc).

[43]   *Vine v. Beneficial Finance Co.*, 374 F.2d 627 (2d Cir. 1967).

returns to non-selling shareholders at the time of block sales.[44] Indeed, in the *Perlman* situation itself, Newport stock increased 13% during the week the Feldmann sale was announced, 38% during the two months of negotiations of the block sale, and 98% during the year of the sale, all as compared with the rest of the market.[45]

(12) **An alternative approach.** A middle-road argument would seek to identify as breaches of duty certain types of control transactions in which there is most likely to be harm to minority shareholders. **Elhauge** asserts that this is the function of rules such as the duty to investigate and the prohibition on sale of office.

PROBLEM

Client owns 35% of the stock of Mining Corporation, which is the only large block of stock. Mining Corporation is a publicly owned company, the stock of which is traded nationally over-the-counter. By virtue of his stock ownership, Client is able to elect a majority of Mining's board of directors.

Client is approached by Oil Corporation with an offer to buy Client's stock for 50% more than the current market price. As a condition of the deal, Oil is insisting that, upon payment for the shares, Client procure the resignation of his nominees on the board.

Client investigates Oil and determines that it is a very reputable company. It is clear that Oil wants an interest in Mining because Mining has potentially valuable molybdenum reserves that Oil needs to hedge against fluctuations in oil supplies and prices.

Client would like your advice as to potential legal problems in connection with the proposed deal. What advice would you give? Assume that the relevant jurisdiction has accepted the "traditional" theories of liability for sale of control, but has neither endorsed nor rejected *Perlman*.

REFERENCES

Andrews, *The Stockholder's Right to Equal Opportunity in the Sale of Shares*, 78 HARV. L. REV. 505, 515-16 (1965).

Bayne, *A Philosophy of Corporate Control*, 112 U. PA. L. REV. 22 (1963) (and many other articles by the same author).

---

[44]   *See* Barclay & Holderness, *Negotiated Block Trades and Corporate Control*, 46 J. FIN. 861 (1991) (finding variation in stock price reaction depending on whether block purchaser takes control, management does not resist blockholder, or block purchaser eventually fully buys firm, suggesting that specific skills and expertise of blockholders rather than just concentration of ownership is important; and showing that block trade may itself be corporate control event rather than just preceding other type of transaction); Holderness & Sheehan, *The Role of Majority Shareholders in Publicly Held Corporations: An Exploratory Analysis*, 20 J. FIN. ECON. 317 (1988) (reporting that announcements of majority block trades were accompanied by positive abnormal stock returns).

[45]   *See* Barclay & Holderness, *supra* footnote 44.

Berle, *The Price of Power: Sale of Corporate Control*, 50 CORNELL L.Q. 628 (1965).

Berle, *"Control" in Corporate Law*, 58 COLUM. L. REV. 1212 (1958).

Easterbrook & Fischel, *Corporate Control Transactions*, 91 YALE L.J. 698 (1982).

Elhauge, *The Triggering Function of Sale of Control Doctrine*, 59 U. CHI. L. REV. 1465 (1992).

Hazen, *Transfers of Corporate Control and Duties of Controlling Shareholders—Common Law, Tender Offers, Investment Companies—And a Proposal for Reform*, 125 U. PA. L. REV. 1023 (1977).

Jennings, *Trading in Corporate Control*, 44 CAL. L. REV. 1 (1956).

[B] Tender Offers

In most publicly owned corporations, share ownership is widely dispersed and, therefore, control cannot be obtained by purchasing shares from a small number of shareholders. Accordingly, most dissidents seeking to acquire a controlling interest in a target firm's stock proceed by making a public offer to purchase shares from any and all holders. Such a public offer is typically referred to as a "tender offer."

[1] Business Background: What Is a Tender Offer?

Tender offers generally involve three stages. In the first stage, the tender offeror typically buys a "stake" in the target through ordinary open market purchases. As this "stake" is purchased before the market is aware that a bidder is seeking control, it can be obtained before the price of the target's stock rises to reflect the increased likelihood that shareholders will be able to sell their stock at a premium price. This initial "stake" reduces the bidder's average cost of purchases, provides a hedge against the risk of a competing offer (because any such offer will increase the market value of the stake), and facilitates access to shareholder lists and other corporate information.

In the second stage, the tender offeror places a newspaper advertisement to buy more shares at a price that is always significantly above current market. This offer typically is contingent upon the tender by shareholders of enough shares to give the bidder control. At this point, shareholders can (1) do nothing; (2) sell their stock in the open market, most likely to an "arbitrageur," who buys with the intent of tendering in the tender offer (the arbitrageur will generally pay a price that is somewhat lower than the tender offer price since the arbitrageur takes the risk that the bid will not succeed); or (3) tender their stock to a bidder.

In the third stage, the bidder uses the controlling interest it obtained in the tender offer to cause the acquired firm to merge with a new corporation that is wholly-owned by the bidder. Under the terms of the merger (which is known as a "squeeze out"), minority shareholders will be forced to exchange their shares in the acquired firm for cash, new securities, or a combination of both, leaving the bidder with 100% ownership of the target.

[2] An Overview of Tender Offer Regulation

[a] State Corporation Law

Under state corporate law shares are generally freely transferable, so that the formal power to decide whether or not a tender offer succeeds is lodged in the shareholders. However, corporate managers can exercise their substantial powers to manage the corporation's business in ways that make tender offers more costly for acquirers, thereby reducing shareholders' opportunities to participate in tender offers. Thus, the thorniest state law tender offer issues relate to the clash between management's broad state law powers to run the company, and shareholders' right to transfer their shares. These issues are considered in Section 14.03, below.

[b] Federal Law

When tender offers first became widely used in the 1960s, they were seen mostly as a tool by corporate "raiders" and as a threat to the continuity of "fine old" established companies. Even before tender offers were invented, hostile takeovers had an image defined in the 1933 film "Dinner at Eight": The genteel incumbent manager John Barrymore pitted against the uncouth Wallace Beery. This image has not changed, as evidenced by the machinations of the Michael Douglas and Danny De Vito characters in "Wall Street" and "Other People's Money," respectively. This attitude, to a large degree, is reflected in the federal laws dealing with tender offers.

The principal federal statute regulating tender offers is the Williams Act, adopted in 1968 as a series of amendments to the Securities and Exchange Act of 1934. Among other things, the Williams Act: (1) requires disclosure by any person or group that acquires 5% of a class of securities, thus limiting the initial "stake" that a bidder can acquire before the market becomes aware of the increased likelihood of a premium bid (*see* Exchange Act § 13(d)(1)); (2) requires disclosure by bidders upon the making of a tender offer (*see* Exchange Act § 14(d)(1)) and upon the seriatim resignation of directors that often accompanies a transfer of control (*see* Exchange Act § 14(f)); and (3) regulates the substantive terms of a bidder's offer to shareholders, primarily to prevent bidders from rushing target shareholders into quick decisions (*see* Exchange Act §§ 14(d)(5)-(7)). In addition, the Williams Act added Exchange Act § 14(e), which is a general antifraud provision that applies specifically to tender offers, and Exchange Act § 14(d)(4), which requires target management to comply with SEC rules in connection with recommendations to shareholders concerning whether to accept the tender offer. Many of the provisions of the Williams Act are implemented in SEC rules contained in Exchange Act Regulations 13D, 14D, and 14E.

The general scheme of federal securities regulation discussed in Chapters 12 also applies in the tender offer setting. For instance, Exchange Act § 10(b) and Rule 10b-5 forbid misleading statements by bidders, incumbent management and others; Exchange Act § 14(a) requires complete disclosures in connection with management defensive tactics that involve proxy solicitations, including, for example, the charter amendments discussed in Section 14.03, below; and the Securities Act of 1933 requires complete disclosure when the bidder offers its securities (rather than cash) in exchange for target stock.[46] In addition, a losing bidder may be liable under Exchange Act § 16(b) for buying more than 10% of the target's stock and then reselling that stock within six months.[47]

Laws other than those dealing explicitly with securities transactions may also apply to tender offers. For example, federal antitrust laws may apply to agreements among competing bidders or between bidders and incumbent managers that have the effect of restraining competition for control of a company's stock,[48] and bidders may be able to sue competing bidders for tortious interference with a merger.[49]

---

[46]   See Feit v. Leasco Data Processing Equipment Corp., 332 F. Supp. 544 (E.D.N.Y. 1971).

[47]   See Ribstein, The Application of Section 16(b) of the Securities Exchange Act of 1934 to Tender Offers, 31 Sw. L.J. 503 (1977).

[48]   See Finnegan v. Campeau Corp., 915 F.2d 824 (2d Cir. 1990) (denying antitrust claim on the basis of Williams Act provision for "group" bids); Rock, Antitrust and the Market for Corporate Control, 77 CALIF. L. REV. 1365 (1989) (arguing for application of the antitrust laws).

[49]   See NBT Bankcorp, Inc. v. Fleet/Norstar Financial Group, Inc., 159 A.D.2d 902, 553 N.Y.S.2d 864 (1990), appeal dism'd, 76 N.Y.2d 886, 561 N.Y.S.2d 546, 562 N.E.2d 871 (stock manipulation).

CHAPTER 14

Corporate Acquisitions:
Takeover Defenses

Incumbent managers generally do not like unsolicited offers to acquire their firms. This should not be surprising since acquisitions by outsiders often threaten the positions of incumbent managers in the firm. Accordingly, managers frequently take steps to reduce the likelihood that an unfriendly outsider will acquire control of the firm. Among other things, they rebuff proposals for corporate combinations from unwanted suitors, advance the dates set for shareholders meetings to reduce a would-be acquirer's time for soliciting proxies, and put into place "poison pills," "shark repellent" charter amendments, "lock-ups" and "no-shops" that have the effect of increasing the cost to bidders of hostile tender offers. This Chapter considers the law and policy of these takeover defenses.

§ 14.01 Corporate Combinations

Corporate statutes give directors the power to evaluate and reject proposed corporate combinations such as merger and asset sales. For example, Del. G.C.L. §§ 251(b) and 271(a) provide that mergers and sales of all, or substantially all, a corporation's assets must be approved by the board of directors, and Del. G.C.L. §§ 251(d) and 271(b) provide that agreements to merge or sell assets may be terminated by the board notwithstanding approval of the agreement by the stockholders.

These rules may seem surprising, since directors might be expected to reject corporate combinations that are consistent with shareholders' interests but inconsistent with their own. However, directors who reject proposed corporate combinations that are consistent with shareholder interests may be liable for breach of fiduciary duty if their actions fall outside the protections of the business judgment rule (*see* Section 9.03). Also, a rejected suitor can go over the directors' heads and propose a shareholder-level transaction such as a hostile tender offer or a proxy contest. The critical question, discussed in Sections 14.02 and 14.03, is whether directors also can block these alternative forms of corporate acquisitions.

§ 14.02 Proxy Contests

[A] Director Power to Control the Meeting Date and Set Voting Rules

Corporate statutes do not expressly give incumbent managers the power to impede proxy contests. However, in leaving the details of shareholders meetings to the corporate bylaws (*see, e.g.*, Del. G.C.L. § 211), corporate statutes do give incumbent managers powers they can use toward that end. For example, if, as is often the case, the corporate bylaws grant the directors the exclusive power to call shareholder meetings, the directors may simply refuse to call a meeting, thereby forcing the insurgents to wait until the company's next scheduled annual meeting to advance their proposal. The directors also can use their powers in the corporate bylaws to delay or cancel a meeting if they think they need more time to solicit shareholder support, or to advance the date for a meeting so as to reduce the insurgents' time for soliciting shareholder support. Since management already has inherent advantages in a proxy contest because of its superior ability to identify and communicate with shareholders, these management tactics may significantly discourage dissident appeals to shareholders.

Directors' power to manipulate the timing of shareholders' meetings to their own advantage is limited where the bylaws give both shareholders and corporate officers powers to call meetings[1] and where the charter fails to abrogate the shareholders' power to act by written consent *without a meeting*. See Del. G.C.L. § 228, providing that shareholders can act by written consent without a meeting "[u]nless otherwise provided in the certificate of incorporation." But directors can use their power to amend the bylaws to eliminate or condition provisions giving shareholders and others the right to call meetings. In addition, even though the power to act by written consent under Del. G.C.L. § 228 can only be taken away by a shareholder-approved charter amendment, the Delaware Supreme Court has held that the directors can adopt bylaws that defer consummation of shareholder action by consent until a ministerial review of the consents has been completed.[2] The following materials consider the extent to which management can use its powers over shareholder meetings and consents to prevent or deter shareholder action.

---

[1]   *See Republic Corporation v. Carter*, 22 A.D.2d 29, 253 N.Y.S.2d 280, *aff'd*, 15 N.Y.2d 661, 255 N.Y.S.2d 875, 204 N.E.2d 206 (1964) (holding that neither the board nor a successor to the president could cancel a meeting called by the president where the applicable bylaw permitted the president to call meetings and did not provide for a power of cancellation, reasoning that, even though the board was superior to the president in authority, the bylaw expressed the shareholders' intention that meetings called by the president should not be cancellable).

[2]   *See Datapoint Corp. v. Plaza Securities Co.*, 496 A.2d 1031 (Del. 1985), discussed at Note 2 following the *Schnell* excerpt, below.

SCHNELL v. CHRIS-CRAFT INDUSTRIES, INC.
Delaware Supreme Court
285 A.2d 437 (1971)

HERRMANN, Justice (for the majority of the Court):

This is an appeal from the denial by the Court of Chancery of the petition of dissident stockholders for injunctive relief to prevent management from advancing the date of the annual stockholders' meeting from January 11, 1972, as previously set by the by-laws, to December 8, 1971.

* * *

It will be seen that the Chancery Court considered all of the reasons stated by management as business reasons for changing the date of the meeting; but that those reasons were rejected by the Court below in making the following findings:

I am satisfied, however, in a situation in which present management has disingenuously resisted the production of a list of its stockholders to plaintiffs or their confederates and has otherwise turned a deaf ear to plaintiffs' demands about a change in management designed to lift defendant from its present business doldrums, management has seized on a relatively new section of the Delaware Corporation Law for the purpose of cutting down on the amount of time which would otherwise have been available to plaintiffs and others for the waging of a proxy battle. Management thus enlarged the scope of its scheduled October 18 directors' meeting to include the by-law amendment in controversy after the stockholders committee had filed with the S.E.C. its intention to wage a proxy fight on October 16.

Thus plaintiffs reasonably contend that because of the tactics employed by management (which involve the hiring of two established proxy solicitors as well as a refusal to produce a list of its stockholders, coupled with its use of an amendment to the Delaware Corporation Law to limit the time for contest), they are given little chance, because of the exigencies of time, including that required to clear material at the S.E.C., to wage a successful proxy fight between now and December 8. . . .

In our view, those conclusions amount to a finding that management has attempted to utilize the corporate machinery and the Delaware Law for the purpose of perpetuating itself in office; and, to that end, for the purpose of obstructing the legitimate efforts of dissident stockholders in the exercise of their rights to undertake a proxy contest against management. These are inequitable purposes, contrary to established principles of corporate democracy. The advancement by directors of the by-law date of a stockholders' meeting, for such purposes, may not be permitted to stand. Compare *Condec Corporation v. Lunkenheimer Company*, Del. Ch., 230 A.2d 769 (1967).

When the by-laws of a corporation designate the date of the annual meeting of stockholders, it is to be expected that those who intend to contest the reelection of incumbent management will gear their campaign to the by-law date. It is not to be expected that management will attempt to advance that date in order to obtain an inequitable advantage in the contest.

Management contends that it has complied strictly with the provisions of the new Delaware Corporation Law in changing the by-law date. The answer to that contention, of course, is that inequitable action does not become permissible simply because it is legally possible.

We are unable to agree with the conclusion of the Chancery Court that the stockholders' application for injunctive relief here was tardy and came too late. The stockholders learned of the action of management unofficially on Wednesday, October 27, 1971; they filed this action on Monday, November 1, 1971. Until management changed the date of the meeting, the stockholders had no need of judicial assistance in that connection. There is no indication of any prior warning of management's intent to take such action; indeed, it appears that an attempt was made by management to conceal its action as long as possible. Moreover, stockholders may not be charged with the duty of anticipating inequitable action by management, and of seeking anticipatory injunctive relief to foreclose such action, simply because the new Delaware Corporation Law makes such inequitable action legally possible.

Accordingly, the judgment below must be reversed and the cause remanded, with instructions to nullify the December 8 date as a meeting date for stock-holders; to reinstate January 11, 1972 as the sole date of the next annual meeting of the stockholders of the corporation; and to take such other proceedings and action as may be consistent herewith regarding the stock record closing date and any other related matters.

WOLCOTT, Chief Justice (dissenting):

I do not agree with the majority of the Court in its disposition of this appeal. The plaintiff stockholders concerned in this litigation have, for a considerable period of time, sought to obtain control of the defendant corporation. These attempts took various forms.

In view of the length of time leading up to the immediate events which caused the filing of this action, I agree with the Vice Chancellor that the application for injunctive relief came too late.

I would affirm the judgment below on the basis of the Vice Chancellor's opinion.

NOTES AND QUESTIONS

(1) **Right to hold an annual meeting.** Under Delaware G.C.L. § 211(c), a shareholder can petition the Chancery Court to order an annual meeting of the shareholders if there is a failure to hold the meeting within 30 days after the designated date or, if no date has been designated, if a period of 13 months has passed since the last annual meeting. *Saxon Industries, Inc. v. NKFW Partners*[3] granted a shareholder's petition for an annual meeting of a company that was reorganizing in bankruptcy. The court held that the mere possibility that a proxy contest might scare away a buyer and threaten the reorganization was not enough to rebut the strong presumption in favor of the share-

---

[3]   498 A.2d 1298 (Del. 1985).

holders' right to a meeting under § 211.[4] *Hoschett v. TSI International Software, Ltd.*[5] concluded that Del. G.C.L. § 211's mandatory requirement of an annual meeting of shareholders could not be satisfied by shareholder action by written consent under Del. G.C.L. § 228(a), unless the shareholder consent was unanimous. Some cases, unlike *Schnell,* allow directors to reschedule annual meetings to their own advantage. *See, e.g., MAI Basic Four, Inc. v. Prime Computer, Inc.,*[6] where the board delayed an annual meeting to give it time to respond to a bid for the company. Issues similar to those presented by *Schnell* also arise in connection with special meetings of the shareholders.[7]

(2) **Bylaws affecting shareholder action by consent.** *Datapoint Corp. v. Plaza Securities Co.*[8] overturned a director-approved bylaw limiting the effectiveness of action by shareholder consent for 45 days, holding that the directors could not delay operation of consents simply in order to prevent quick "midnight raids." *Datapoint* left open the possibility that the directors might "defer consummation of shareholder action by consent . . . until a ministerial-type review has been performed." But *Allen v. Prime Computer Inc.*[9] overturned the board's adoption, in the face of a hostile takeover, of a minimum 20-day delay in the effectiveness of shareholder action by consent, finding that the unexplained 20-day delay did more than simply defer consummation of shareholder action until a ministerial review had been performed.

(3) **Other director moves thwarting shareholder action.** Director power to defeat or deter shareholder action may include strategies such as issuing new shares to dilute the voting power of a dissident holder. Some courts have employed an analysis similar to that of *Schnell* to invalidate these attempts by directors to influence the out-

---

[4]   For other cases indicating the importance of the annual meeting, see *Aprahamian v. HBO & Co.,* 531 A.2d 1204 (Del. Ch. 1987) (directors could not cancel an annual meeting for which proxies had already been solicited in connection with a proxy contest, even though the directors had themselves planned to put into action the dissidents' sale proposal); *Speiser v. Baker,* 525 A.2d 1001 (DEL. CH. 1987) (management's claim that a shareholder petitioning for an annual meeting was attempting to use the meeting to unfairly seize control did not defease the shareholder's right to the meeting); *Phillips v. Insituform of N.A.,* 13 DEL. J. CORP. L. 774 (Del. Ch. 1987) (management failed to show that their failure to hold the annual meeting at the time provided in the by laws or within the time required by statute was justified by an important corporate purpose); *Byrne v. Lord,* 1995 Fed. Sec. L. Rep. ¶ 98,987 (Del. Ch. 1995) (directors' inability to solicit proxies under the federal securities laws because company lacked audited financial statements does not defeat shareholders' right to annual meeting under Del. G.C.L. § 211, particularly when the inability to obtain audited financial statements was the directors' fault). For a criticism of *Aprahamian* as unduly limiting management's flexibility in rescheduling meetings, see Comment, *Postponing the Delaware Corporation Annual Meeting,* 38 EMORY L.J. 207 (1989).

[5]   683 A.2d 43 (Del. Ch. 1996).

[6]   15 DEL. J. CORP. L. 690 (Del. Ch. 1989).

[7]   *See, e.g., Wyser-Pratte v. Smith,* 1997 Del. Ch. LEXIS 41, 1997 WL 153806 (Del. Ch. 1997) (permitting directors to designate a record date that was only 12 days before the special meeting sought by dissident shareholders allegedly so that management could enlist allies to purchase shares and vote them on behalf of management).

[8]   496 A.2d 1031 (Del. 1985).

[9]   540 A.2d 417 (Del. 1988).

come of shareholder action.[10] Other courts have analyzed these and similar strategies using the framework established in the following case.

BLASIUS INDUSTRIES, INC. v. ATLAS CORPORATION
Delaware Court of Chancery
564 A.2d 651 (1988)

ALLEN, Chancellor.

* * *

I.

Blasius Acquires a 9% Stake in Atlas.

Blasius is a new stockholder of Atlas. It began to accumulate Atlas shares for the first time in July, 1987. On October 29, it filed a Schedule 13D with the Securities Exchange Commission disclosing that, with affiliates, it then owed 9.1% of Atlas' common stock. It stated in that filing that it intended to encourage management of Atlas to consider a restructuring of the Company or other transaction to enhance shareholder values. It also disclosed that Blasius was exploring the feasibility of obtaining control of Atlas, including instituting a tender offer or seeking "appropriate" representation on the Atlas board of directors.

Blasius has recently come under the control of two individuals, Michael Lubin and Warren Delano . . . .

* * *

The prospect of Messrs. Lubin and Delano involving themselves in Atlas' affairs, was not a development welcomed by Atlas' management. Atlas had a new CEO, defendant Weaver, who had, over the course of the past year or so, overseen a business restructuring of a sort. . . .

The Blasius Proposal of a Leverage Recapitalization or Sale.

Immediately after filing its 13D on October 29, Blasius' representatives sought a meeting with the Atlas management. Atlas dragged its feet. A meeting was arranged for December 2, 1987 following the regular meeting of the Atlas board. . . .

At that meeting, Messrs. Lubin and Delano suggested that Atlas engage in a leveraged restructuring and distribute cash to shareholders. . . .

Immediately following the meeting, the Atlas representatives expressed among themselves an initial reaction that the proposal was infeasible. On December 7, Mr. Lubin sent a letter detailing the proposal. . . .

---

[10]   *See, e.g., Phillips v. Insituform of N.A.*, 13 DEL. J. CORP. L. 774 (Del. Ch. 1987), and *Condec Corporation v. Lunkenheimer Co.*, 230 A.2d 769 (Del. 1967), where the courts invalidated board actions issuing enough new stock to permit the boards to retain control.

Atlas Asks Its Investment Banker to Study the Proposal.

This written proposal was distributed to the Atlas board on December 9 and Goldman Sachs was directed to review and analyze it.

The proposal met with a cool reception from management. On December 9, Mr. Weaver issued a press release expressing surprise that Blasius would suggest using debt to accomplish what he characterized as a substantial liquidation of Atlas at a time when Atlas' future prospects were promising. . . .

Blasius attempted on December 14 and December 22 to arrange a further meeting with the Atlas management without success. . . . A meeting after the first of the year was proposed.

The Delivery of Blasius' Consent Statement.

On December 30, 1987, Blasius caused Cede & Co. (the registered owner of its Atlas stock) to deliver to Atlas a signed written consent (1) adopting a precatory resolution recommending that the board develop and implement a restructuring proposal, (2) amending the Atlas bylaws to, among other things, expand the size of the board from seven to fifteen members—the maximum number under Atlas' charter, and (3) electing eight named persons to fill the new directorships. . . .

The reaction was immediate. Mr. Weaver conferred with Mr. Masinter, the Company's outside counsel and a director, who viewed the consent as an attempt to take control of the Company. They decided to call an emergency meeting of the board, even though a regularly scheduled meeting was to occur only one week hence, on January 6, 1988. The point of the emergency meeting was to act on their conclusion (or to seek to have the board act on their conclusion) "that we should add at least one and probably two directors to the board . . ." (Tr. 85, Vol. II). A quorum of directors, however, could not be arranged for a telephone meeting that day. A telephone meeting was held the next day. At that meeting, the board voted to amend the bylaws to increase the size of the board from seven to nine and appointed John M. Devaney and Harry J. Winters, Jr. to fill those newly created positions. Atlas' Certificate of Incorporation creates staggered terms for directors; the terms to which Messrs. Devaney and Winters were appointed would expire in 1988 and 1990, respectively.

The Motivation of the Incumbent Board In Expanding the Board and Appointing New Members.

In increasing the size of Atlas' board by two and filling the newly created positions, the members of the board realized that they were thereby precluding the holders of a majority of the Company's shares from placing a majority of new directors on the board through Blasius' consent solicitation, should they want to do so. Indeed the evidence establishes that that was the principal motivation in so acting.

The conclusion that, in creating two new board positions on December 31 and electing Messrs. Devaney and Winters to fill those positions the board was principally motivated to prevent or delay the shareholders from possibly placing a majority of new members on the board, is critical to my analysis of the central issue posed by the first filed of the two pending cases. If the board in fact was not so motivated, but rather had taken action completely independently of the consent solicitation, which merely had an incidental impact upon the possible effectuation of any action authorized by the shareholders, it is very unlikely that such action would be subject to judicial nullification. . . . The board, as a general matter, is under no fiduciary obligation to suspend its active management of the firm while the consent solicitation process goes forward.

* * *

The January 6 Rejection of the Blasius Proposal.

On January 6, the board convened for its scheduled meeting. At that time, it heard a full report from its financial advisor concerning the feasibility of the Blasius restructuring proposal. . . .

* * *

The board then voted to reject the Blasius proposal. . . .

II.

Plaintiff attacks the December 31 board action as a selfishly motivated effort to protect the incumbent board from a perceived threat to its control of Atlas. Their conduct is said to constitute a violation of the principle, applied in such cases as *Schnell v. Chris Craft Industries*, Del.Supr., 285 A.2d 437 (1971), that directors hold legal powers subjected to a supervening duty to exercise such powers in good faith pursuit of what they reasonably believe to be in the corporation's interest. . . .

* * *

III

* * *

While I am satisfied that the evidence is powerful, indeed compelling, that the board was chiefly motivated on December 31 to forestall or preclude the possibility that a majority of shareholders might place on the Atlas board eight new members sympathetic to the Blasius proposal, it is less clear with respect to the more subtle motivational question: whether the existing members of the board did so because they held a good faith belief that such shareholder action would be self-injurious and shareholders needed to be protected from their own judgment.

On balance, I cannot conclude that the board was acting out of a self-interested motive in any important respect on December 31. I conclude rather that the board saw the "threat" of the Blasius recapitalization proposal as posing vital policy differences between itself and Blasius. It acted, I conclude, in a good faith effort to protect its incumbency, not selfishly, but in order to thwart implementation of the recapitalization that it feared, reasonably, would cause great injury to the Company.

The real question the case presents, to my mind, is whether, in these circumstances, the board, even if it is acting with subjective good faith (which will typically, if not always, be a contestable or debatable judicial conclusion), may validly act for the principal purpose of preventing the shareholders from electing a majority of new directors. The question thus posed is not one of intentional wrong (or even negligence), but one of authority as between the fiduciary and the beneficiary (not simply legal authority, *i.e.*, as between the fiduciary and the world at large).

IV.

It is established in our law that a board may take certain steps—such as the purchase by the corporation of its own stock—that have the effect of defeating a threatened change in corporate control, when those steps are taken advisedly, in good faith pursuit of a corporate interest, and are reasonable in relation to a threat to legitimate corporate interests posed by the proposed change in control.* . . . Does this rule—that the reasonable exercise of good faith and due care generally validates, in equity, the exercise of legal authority even if the act has an entrenchment effect—apply to action designed for the primary purpose of interfering with the effectiveness of a stockholder vote? Our authorities, as well as sound principles, suggest that the central importance of the franchise to the scheme of corporate governance, requires that, in this setting, that rule not be applied and that closer scrutiny be accorded to such transaction.

1. Why the deferential business judgment rule does not apply to board acts taken for the primary purpose of interfering with a stockholder's vote, even if taken advisedly and in good faith.

A. The question of legitimacy.

* * *

. . . [W]hether the vote is seen functionally as an unimportant formalism, or as an important tool of discipline, it is clear that it is critical to the theory that legitimates the exercise of power by some (directors and officers) over vast aggregations of property that they do not own. Thus, when viewed from a broad, institutional perspective, it can be seen that matters involving the integrity of the shareholder voting process involve consideration not present in any other context in which directors exercise delegated power.

B. Questions of this type raise issues of the allocation of authority as between the board and the shareholders.

The distinctive nature of the shareholder franchise context also appears when the matter is viewed from a less generalized, doctrinal point of view. From this point of view, as well, it appears that the ordinary considerations to which the business judgment rule originally responded are simply not present in the shareholder voting context. That is, a decision by the board to act for the primary purpose of preventing the effectiveness of a shareholder vote inevitably involves the question who, as between the principal and the agent, has authority with respect to a matter of internal corporate governance. That, of course, is true in a very specific way in this case which deals with the question who should constitute the board of directors of the corporation, but it will be true in every instance in which an incumbent board seeks to thwart a shareholder majority. A board's decision to act to prevent the shareholders from creating a majority of new board positions and filling them does not

---

*   [*See infra* Section 14.03.—Ed.]

involve the exercise of the corporation's power over its property, or with respect to its rights or obligations; rather, it involves allocation, between shareholders as a class and the board, of effective power with respect to governance of the corporation. . . . Judicial review of such action involves a determination of the legal and equitable obligations of an agent towards his principal. This is not, in my opinion, a question that a court may leave to the agent finally to decide so long as he does so honestly and competently; that is, it may not be left to the agent's business judgment.

2. What rule does apply: per se invalidity of corporate acts intended primarily to thwart effective exercise of the franchise or is there an intermediate standard?

Plaintiff argues for a rule of per se invalidity once a plaintiff has established that a board has acted for the primary purpose of thwarting the exercise of a shareholder vote. . . .

* * *

. . . A per se rule that would strike down, in equity, any board action taken for the primary purpose of interfering with the effectiveness of a corporate vote would have the advantage of relative clarity and predictability. It also has the advantage of most vigorously enforcing the concept of corporate democracy. The disadvantage it brings along is, of course, the disadvantage a per se rule always has: it may sweep too broadly.

In two recent cases dealing with shareholder votes, this court struck down board acts done for the primary purpose of impeding the exercise of stockholder voting power. In doing so, a per se rule was not applied. Rather, it was said that, in such a case, the board bears the heavy burden of demonstrating a compelling justification for such action.

* * *

In my view, our inability to foresee now all of the future settings in which a board might, in good faith, paternalistically seek to thwart a shareholder vote, counsels against the adoption of a per se rule invalidating, in equity, every board action taken for the sole or primary purpose of thwarting a shareholder vote, even though I recognize the transcending significance of the franchise to the claims to legitimacy of our scheme of corporate governance. It may be that some set of facts would justify such extreme action.[5] This, however, is not such a case.

---

[5]   . . . Assume an acquiring company buys 25% of the target's stock in a small number of privately negotiated transactions. It then commences a public tender offer for 26% of the company stock at a cash price that the board, in good faith, believes is inadequate. Moreover, the acquiring corporation announces that it may or may not do a second-step merger, but if it does one, the consideration will be junk bonds that will have a value, when issued, in the opinion of its own investment banker, of no more than the cash being offered in the tender offer. . . . Assume, for purposes of the hypothetical, that . . . just as the tender offer is closing, the board locates an all cash deal for all shares at a price materially higher than that offered by the acquiring corporation. Would the board of the target corporation be justified in issuing sufficient shares to the second acquiring corporation to dilute the 51% stockholder down so that it no longer had a practical veto over the merger or sale of assets that the target board had arranged for the benefit of all shares? It is not necessary to now hazard an opinion on that abstraction. The case is clearly close enough, however, . . . , to demonstrate, to my mind at least, the utility of a rule that permits, in some extreme circumstances, an incumbent board to act in good faith for the purpose of interfering with the outcome of a contemplated vote. . . .

3. Defendants have demonstrated no sufficient justification for the action of December 31 which was intended to prevent an unaffiliated majority of shareholders from effectively exercising their right to elect eight new directors.

The board was not faced with a coercive action taken by a powerful shareholder against the interests of a distinct shareholder constituency (such as a public minority). It was presented with a consent solicitation by a 9% shareholder. Moreover, here it had time (and understood that it had time) to inform the shareholders of its views on the merits of the proposal subject to stockholder vote. The only justification that can, in such a situation, be offered for the action taken is that the board knows better than do the shareholders what is in the corporation's best interest. . . . It may be that the Blasius restructuring proposal was or is unrealistic and would lead to injury to the corporation and its shareholders if pursued. . . . The board certainly viewed it that way, and that view, held in good faith, entitled the board to take certain steps to evade the risk it perceived. It could, for example, expend corporate funds to inform shareholders and seek to bring them to a similar point of view. . . . But there is a vast difference between expending corporate funds to inform the electorate and exercising power for the primary purpose of foreclosing effective shareholder action. A majority of the shareholders, who were not dominated in any respect, could view the matter differently than did the board. If they do, or did, they are entitled to employ the mechanisms provided by the corporation law and the Atlas certificate of incorporation to advance that view. They are also entitled, in my opinion, to restrain their agents, the board, from acting for the principal purpose of thwarting that action.

I therefore conclude that, even finding the action taken was taken in good faith, it constituted an unintended violation of the duty of loyalty that the board owed to the shareholders. . . . That action will, therefore, be set aside by order of this court.

* * *

NOTES AND QUESTIONS

(1) **Triggering *Blasius* scrutiny.** *Blasius* established a new "compelling justification" standard for board actions taken "for the primary purpose of interfering with a stockholder's vote, even if taken advisedly and in good faith." *Hilton Hotels Corp. v. ITT Corp.*[11] relied on *Blasius* to enjoin the board's plan, adopted in response to a tender offer and proxy context, to split the corporation into three new entities, one of which would hold nearly all of the firm's assets and would be managed by a board with staggered terms, all without obtaining shareholder approval.[12]

---

[11]   978 F. Supp. 1342 (D. Nev. 1997).

[12]   *See also IBS Fin. Corp. v. Seidman & Assocs., L.L.C.*, 136 F.3d 940 (3d Cir. 1998), where the court of appeals, applying *Blasius* in the absence of New Jersey authority, invalidated a resolution reducing the board's size from 7 to 6. The court found that the resolution was motivated by a desire to hinder the efforts of a group of shareholders to gain board representation.

(2) **The *Stroud* qualification.** *Stroud v. Grace*[13] apparently limited the circumstances in which *Blasius* scrutiny would be applied to "situations where boards of directors deliberately employed various legal strategies either to frustrate or completely disenfranchise a shareholder vote." Since *Stroud*, the courts generally have limited *Blasius* to board action that has the effect of either completely precluding effective shareholder action or snatching victory from an insurgent at the last moment. For example, in *State of Wisconsin Investment Board v. Peerless Systems Corp.*,[14] the board sought to adjourn an annual meeting after it became clear that its proposal would fail if the polls were allowed to close. On the other hand, *Golden Cycle, L.L.C. v. Allan*[15] refused to block the board from acting on March 30, 1998 to set that date as the record date for a bidder's consent solicitation announced on March 24 for the purpose of replacing the incumbent board. The plaintiff argued that, by acting hastily to set the March 30 record date, the board eliminated a large number of voters who purchased the corporation's shares in response to the plaintiff's March 23 offer to purchase all the corporation's outstanding stock. The court held that the board did not have to show a "compelling justification" for its action because "[t]here is nothing about the action taken here remotely comparable to the action taken in *Blasius*. . . . [T]here is no suggestion in the record that these problems will *preclude* or even substantially interfere with the ability of the [corporation's] stockholders to remove and replace the entire board, should they choose to do so. For these reasons, the application of the *Blasius* standard to this case is unwarranted."

MM Companies, Inc. v. Liquid Audio, Inc.[16] appears to expand the circumstances in which *Blasius* may be applied. In response to a dissident shareholder's effort to obtain two seats on the corporation's five-member, staggered board of directors at the corporation's annual meeting, the Liquid Audio board adopted a bylaw expanding the board to seven members and appointing two additional directors. The court found that the primary purpose for the expansion was to diminish the influence of the dissident shareholder's two nominees on a five-member board "by eliminating either the possibility of a deadlock on the board or of the dissident controlling the Board, if one or two Director Defendants resigned from the Board." Although the bylaw did not preclude the dissident from obtaining the two board seats sought at the annual meeting, the court nonetheless held that *Blasius* applied because "defensive action . . . [that] compromised the essential role of corporate democracy in maintaining the proper allocation of power between the shareholders and the Board . . . was taken in the context of a contested election for successor directors."

(3) **The "compelling justification" test.** Once *Blasius* is triggered, the board must establish a "compelling justification" for its action. See footnote 5 to the court's

---

[13]   606 A.2d 75, 91-92 (Del. 1992).

[14]   2000 WL 1805376 (Del. Ch. 2000).

[15]   1998 Del. Ch. LEXIS 80, 1998 WL 276224 (Del. Ch. 1998).

[16]   813 A.2d 1118 (2003).

opinion where Chancellor Allen suggests that board action thwarting a shareholder vote might be permitted if necessary to defeat an inadequately priced takeover bid and give shareholders the opportunity to accept a "more fairly priced alternative." Should the question whether the board has the power to act in this situation depend on its motives or reasons?

PROBLEM

On April 1, Smith, a substantial shareholder in Widget Corporation, made a Schedule 14B filing notifying management of Smith's intent to wage a proxy contest for control of the Corporation at the next annual meeting, scheduled for June 30. On May 1, the board passed a bylaw repealing the June date for the meeting and leaving the date to be fixed at the discretion of the board. The board also added a bylaw requiring that, to be eligible for office, non-incumbent nominees for board positions must submit information about themselves to the corporation's secretary at least 70 days prior to the meeting. Smith was notified of these bylaw provisions immediately after they were passed. Later that month, Smith requested a shareholder list, indicating his continuing intention to wage a proxy campaign. It is July 30. The Widget board is meeting on August 1. Management intends to fix the shareholder meeting date for October 3 which, in light of the 70-day notice rule, will effectively foreclose the election of any new directors. You are counsel for the corporation. Advise the board whether, under Delaware law, its proposed action presents any legal problems.[17]

[B] Shareholder Lists

Another way that incumbent managers can defend against proxy contests is to delay dissident access to shareholder lists, thereby maximizing incumbent management's advantages relating to the identification and communication with shareholders. The general law regarding production of shareholder lists is discussed above in Section 7.05. Additional rules designed to deal with director delaying tactics in the midst of takeovers are discussed below.

[1] State Law

Several state law rules are designed to help get the shareholder list into the dissident's hands quickly.[18] Some statutes place the burden of proving improper purpose for

---

[17] *See Lerman v. Diagnostic Data, Inc.*, 421 A.2d 906 (Del. Ch. 1980); *see also Shoen v. Amerco*, 1994 WL 715895 (D. Nev.).

[18] For a discussion of management delaying tactics, see Comment, *Protecting the Shareholders' Right to Inspect the Share Register in Corporate Proxy Contests for the Election of Directors*, 50 S. CAL. L. REV. 1273 (1977).

gaining access to shareholder lists on the corporation rather than on the petitioner in certain circumstances. *See, e.g.,* Del. G.C.L. § 220 (burden on corporation where request is for a stock list, as distinguished from other books and records). *See also Chavco Investment Co., Inc. v. Pybus,*[19] which upheld the granting of a shareholder's request for books and records without a jury trial, where the corporation failed to allege in its answer specific facts as to improper purpose and the shareholder had alleged a proper purpose. The statute in that case was silent on the burden of proof. The main significance of the locus of the burden is in connection with summary disposition of the request. If the corporation is able to insist on a full trial, critical solicitation time may pass before the issue is resolved.

Other statutes address concerns regarding management delay by mandating an "expedited" resolution of requests for records (*see* MBCA § 16.04(b)), providing for assessment of costs and attorney fees against the corporation if it cannot prove that its resistance was in good faith (*see* MBCA § 16.04(c)), or providing for penalties for improper refusals to deliver lists—often 10% of the value of the petitioner's shares.[20] Penalty provisions are unlikely to be effective, particularly given management's possible right to be indemnified by the corporation. The Model Act dropped a penalty provision because it was "arbitrary and . . . seldom actually enforced." *See* Official Comment to Chapter 16, Subchapter A. Another way to address management recalcitrance is to enjoin the shareholders' meeting to permit use of the list.[21]

Quickly gaining access to the shareholder lists may not be enough if the lists are not in usable form or do not provide needed information. For instance, in the 1982 takeover contest involving Bendix, Martin-Marietta, Allied and United, Bendix, prior to a crucial shareholder vote, made its shareholder list available to an opposing proxy solicitor in the form of a stack of 10,000 pages with three names on each page and required the proxy solicitor to photocopy the list.[22] But *Hatleigh Corp. v. Lane Bryant, Inc.*[23] required the corporation to produce, not only computer tapes and daily transfer sheets setting forth fully current information on stock holdings, but also a breakdown of the brokerage firms holding stock in the name of a single nominee, which information was readily available to the corporation.[24]

---

[19]   613 S.W.2d 806 (Tex. Civ. App. 1981).

[20]   *See Chavco Investment Co., Inc. v. Pybus,* 613 S.W.2d 806 (Tex. Civ. 1981), awarding $2650 in attorneys' fees under a provision in the Texas statute giving the court discretion to make such an award.

[21]   *See Susquehanna Corp. v. General Refractories Co.,* 356 F.2d 985 (3d Cir.), *aff'd per curiam,* 250 F. Supp. 797 (E.D. Pa. 1966).

[22]   *See Dirty Tricks Abound in Takeover Business as Well as in Politics,* WALL ST. J., Sept. 22, 1982 at 1, 24.

[23]   428 A.2d 350 (Del. Ch. 1981).

[24]   For other such cases, see *Sadler v. NCR Corp.,* 928 F.2d 48 (2d Cir. 1991) (requiring a corporation to provide lists of brokerage firms and other record owners holding shares for customers in "street" name, and of beneficial owners of shares who have consented to disclosure of their identities); *Emerald Isle Associates v. Polaroid Corp.,* 559 A.2d 278 (Del. Ch. 1989) (requiring production of a shareholder list five months after a previous list had been produced, even though the insurgent had been receiving periodic transfer sheets, because of the many transfers during a "turbulent" takeover battle, and because the insurgent should have access to the same information as the incumbent board).

Courts may enforce a shareholder's right to stock lists by a writ of mandamus in the state courts, or in federal court through a mandatory injunction.[25]

[2] Federal Law

If the corporation is subject to federal proxy regulation, SEC Rule 14a-7 gives a shareholder the right to compel management either to produce a list of shareholders or to mail the shareholder's proxy materials to the shareholders at the shareholder's request.[26] Although there is no proper purpose limitation or right of refusal under Rule 14a-7, this remedy provides little help to contestants. Not only may management choose to mail the dissident's proxy materials to shareholders instead of providing access to the list the dissident needs to solicit effectively, but management receives the dissident's proxy materials before they are mailed to shareholders and can therefore neutralize them in its own materials.[27]

§ 14.03 Tender Offers

As noted in Section 13.04, the shareholders formally have the ultimate power to decide whether tender offers succeed. However, corporate managers can, with or without shareholder approval, take actions that make tender offers more costly for acquirers. This Section reviews the law and policy of tender offer defenses: subsection [A] summarizes some of the more popular tender offer defenses; subsection [B] examines whether these defenses enhance shareholder welfare; and subsection [C] considers the applicable legal standards governing the adoption of tender offer defenses.

[A] Types of Defensive Tactics

Defenses against tender offers come in two flavors: those that require the approval of the shareholders and those that do not. These two categories of defenses are discussed separately below.

[1] Shareholder-Approved Defenses

The following are some of the many kinds of shareholder-approved charter amendments and recapitalization plans that can reduce the firm's vulnerability to

---

[25] *See Rockwell v. SCM Corp.*, 496 F. Supp. 1123 (S.D.N.Y. 1980).

[26] The option belongs to the requesting security holder in the case of going private or limited partnership "roll up" transactions. *See* Rule 14a-7(b).

[27] *See* Aranow & Einhorn, PROXY CONTESTS FOR CORPORATE CONTROL 33-39 (2d ed. 1968).

takeover. Note particularly the tradeoffs between costs and benefits of various structures that make some more appropriate than others for particular firms (*see* **Ribstein** at 90-94).

[a] Charter Amendments Impeding Transfers of Board Control

Incumbent managers can reduce their vulnerability to takeovers by securing shareholder support for charter amendments that impair bidders' ability to take control of the corporation's board of directors. First, the charter might eliminate the shareholders' power to act by written consent. If the bylaws also do not give shareholders the power to call a shareholders' meeting, the bidder cannot replace the corporation's board of directors before the corporation's next scheduled annual meeting.

Second, the charter might provide for a "staggered" or "classified" board. *See* Del. G.C.L. § 141(d). Under typical staggered board provisions, only a fraction of the firm's directors (generally 1/3) are elected at each annual meeting. Unless the certificate provides otherwise, the shareholders cannot remove "staggered" directors without cause (*see* Del. G.C.L. § 141(k)(i)). Thus, it might take a bidder as long as two years to take control of, and three years to completely replace, a three-class board, provided the board does not voluntarily resign in the meantime. **Bebchuk, Coates and Subramanian** is an important study showing the significant effect of staggered board provisions in conjunction with other anti-takeover devices.

Third, the charter might provide for cumulative voting. *See* Del. G.C.L. § 214. Under cumulative voting provisions, minority shareholders who own at least a certain amount of shares are assured of the power to elect one or more directors. This prevents a bidder from removing the entire board with a simple majority of stock, although it also lets a bidder with a minority of shares obtain some seats on the board and thereby influence policy and obtain information.

[b] Charter Amendments Creating Barriers to "Second-Step" Transactions

As discussed in Section 13.04, successful tender offers in which bidders acquire a controlling interest in a target's stock are often followed by "squeeze out" mergers or "second-step" transactions in which bidders use their newly-acquired control to cause the target to merge with a new corporation that is wholly owned by the bidder. The target's minority shareholders must exchange their shares for cash, new securities or a combination of both. The bidder thereby avoids having to operate the target subject to burdensome conflict of interest rules (*see* **Sinclair** and the related notes in Section 9.07).

The charter can limit use of this technique by requiring a high shareholder vote on the second-step merger, perhaps unless the merger is at a "fair" price or has been approved by a majority of disinterested directors.[28] This will effectively prevent tender offers where the bidder's costs of operating the target as a majority, but not wholly owned, subsidiary are sufficiently high.

[c] Recapitalizations Allocating Voting Power to Incumbent Managers

Managers may avoid the risk of unfriendly takeovers altogether if they own stock that carries the power to elect all or most of the board. Managers could accomplish this goal by purchasing a majority of the equity shares, but this would be costly and would probably force them to forego portfolio diversification. They could accomplish the same result more cheaply through a shareholder-approved recapitalization or charter amendment that establishes a dual class common voting structure. Under this structure, high-vote stock is allocated to management or a controlling family, while low-vote stock is allocated to the corporation's other shareholders. As a result, those holding a minority interest in the firm's earnings and assets—incumbent managers or a controlling family—hold the majority of votes. Many family-controlled media companies, such as Dow Jones and the Washington Post, have adopted this structure.

The SEC once acted to curtail issuance of dual-class common stock except in certain situations, particularly including initial public offerings, but its rule was invalidated on the ground that it exceeded the SEC's power to regulate disclosure as distinguished from internal corporate management.[29] At the request of the Chairman of the SEC, the major securities exchanges adopted a rule providing that common shareholders' voting rights "cannot be disparately reduced or restricted through any corporate action or issuance . . . ."[30]

[d] Leveraged (Management) Buyout

As noted in Subsection [C] above, another way for management to own stock carrying the power to elect all or most of the board is to purchase a majority of the equity shares. This can be accomplished through a leveraged buyout in which the outside shareholders are replaced with creditors who have only limited governance powers. **Gilson** discusses some considerations relevant to why a firm might choose a leveraged buyout rather than a shift to a dual class voting structure as a means of entrenching management, including whether the firm has favorable investment opportunities that would make it costly to have too much debt.

---

[28] For a case interpreting a supermajority voting provision, see *Berlin v. Emerald Partners*, 552 A.2d 482 (Del. 1988).

[29] *See The Business Roundtable v. SEC*, 905 F.2d 406 (D.C. Cir. 1990).

[30] *See* New York Stock Exchange, *Uniform Voting Rights Policy—Request for Comment* 1 (Feb. 3, 1994); SEC Release No. 34-35121, 1994 SEC LEXIS 4072, Dec. 19, 1994.

[2] Director-Approved Defenses

The board has the power under corporate statutes and charters to engage in many acts that make takeovers more difficult. Some examples of steps boards can take on their own authority are reviewed below.

[a] Bylaw Provisions

Incumbent managers can use their powers to amend the corporate bylaws without shareholder consent to eliminate bylaw provisions that give shareholders the power to call shareholder meetings at which the board can be replaced. If the shareholders cannot call meetings, bidders could not immediately exercise any votes they acquire in a tender offer, assuming the corporate charter denies the shareholders the power to act by written consent without a meeting.

[b] Stock Repurchases and Stock Issuances

Managers can cause the corporation to purchase shares owned by a bidder or potential bidder or cause the corporation to issue additional shares (provided these are authorized in the charter) to friendly shareholders. The former approach uses payments from the corporate treasury to induce bidders or prospective bidders to abandon their plans to take over the target. The latter approach uses the voting rights attached to corporate stock to make it more difficult for the bidder to buy enough shares to take control. Defensive stock issuances are especially useful in conjunction with charter provisions requiring supermajority shareholder approval for corporate action, such as the charter amendments creating barriers to "second-step" transactions discussed at Subsection [A][1][b] above.

Where the stock is purchased for a premium, this has been referred to as "greenmail," implying that it is almost as bad as paying "blackmail." It has been argued that greenmail can actually aid the functioning of the market for control by rewarding bidders who gather information about potential targets but are unable to actually acquire control. **Macey & McChesney** discuss other theories and data on greenmail. Although the greenmailer is enough of a threat that the managers have an incentive to buy it off, it might accept management's "bribe" when it discovers that the target is not worth as much as it originally thought. Also, greenmail may signal that the managers have not found a "white knight" that will ride in to buy the target company while preserving the managers' jobs, thereby encouraging other firms to enter the bidding.[31]

---

[31] *See* McChesney, *Transaction Costs and Corporate Greenmail: Theory, Empirics and a Mickey Mouse Case Study*, 14 MANAGERIAL & DECISION ECON. 131 (1993) (Walt Disney's payment of greenmail to the "raider" Saul Steinberg induced departure of first bidder, but others quickly appeared; during the delay board restructured firm to the benefit of Disney shareholders).

[c] Defensive Acquisitions

Incumbent managers can cause the corporation to purchase other firms and thereby make it more costly for bidders to digest the target, as by increasing the price or triggering antitrust or regulatory problems.

[d] Poison Pills

Managers have the power to issue preferred stock, debt, or rights to purchase additional securities as long as these are authorized in the charter (*see, e.g.*, Del. G.C.L. § 151(a)). Pursuant to this power, managers can issue so-called "poison pill" rights and distribute them to the existing shareholders as a dividend. These instruments give the corporation's existing shareholders rights to buy additional stock at deeply discounted prices or to sell shares to the target or the bidder on favorable terms in the event that certain triggering events occur.

Poison pills initially were of the "flip-over" variety. Such pills were typically triggered by the second-step transaction in which the bidder uses its newly-acquired control to squeeze out the target's remaining minority shareholders. Holders of "flip-over" poison pill rights are generally entitled to either sell stock to, or acquire stock from, the *bidder*—that is, the rights against the target provided in the instrument issued to the shareholders "flip-over" into rights against the bidder once the second-step transaction takes place. This makes the "squeeze out" prohibitively expensive for a bidder. A bidder can avoid them by avoiding the second step, but then the bidder must operate the target as a subsidiary, subject to burdensome conflict of interest rules (*see Sinclair* and the related Notes in Section 9.07), and possibly unpleasant tax and accounting consequences.

Flip-in poison pills overcome this problem because they typically are triggered when the bidder acquires a threshold stake of 10% to 20% of the target's stock rather than when a second-step transaction occurs. Once triggered, all holders of flip-in poison pill rights, *other than the bidder*, generally get the opportunity to purchase stock from, or sell stock to, the *target* on extremely favorable terms, thus diluting the value of the bidder's stake in the target.

Boards of directors generally reserve the right to redeem the poison pill until the bidder acquires a sufficient threshold stake in the firm (*e.g.*, more than 10 to 20 percent of the firm's stock). A bidder therefore can attempt to avoid a poison pill by waging a proxy contest for control of the board before it acquires a level of stock ownership that would make the pill non-redeemable. If the proxy contest is successful, the bidder can use its power on the board to remove the poison pill.

In order to block this strategy, some companies added "dead-hand" or "no-hand" provisions to their poison pills. Under a "dead-hand" provision, the poison pill can only be redeemed or amended by the vote of a majority of the directors who were members of the board *prior to the adoption of the poison pill*; under a "no-hand" provision, the poison pill becomes non-amendable and non-redeemable (either permanently or for a limited period of time) when the board members who implemented the poison pill no longer constitute a majority of the board. These pills are discussed in *Carmody* and *Quickturn*, excerpted in Section 14.03[D] below.

There was early evidence that shareholders were hurt by poison pills (*see, e.g.*, **Jarrell, Brickley & Netter**). However, the effect of poison pills and other defensive tactics on stock prices is difficult to measure because announcement of the poison pill also may carry, in addition to the negative information about management entrenchment, positive information that the adopting company is a potential target. More importantly, the effect of poison pills depends on other takeover defenses and governance devices that are in place. For more recent analyses taking this context into account, see **Bebchuk**; **Coates & Subramanian** (effect of poison pills in conjunction with staggered boards); **Coates** (effect of the "shadow" or pre-authorized poison pills in place prior to actual adoption of the poison pill or other takeover defenses); and **Kahan** (effect of poison pills on general shareholder welfare depends on board independence and incentive compensation).

Pension funds and other large shareholders have offered resolutions that ask the board to rescind or require shareholder approval of poison pills, some of which have garnered significant votes. The effect of such shareholder action is discussed below in Note 7 following *Quickturn* in Section 14.03[D].

[e] Lock-Ups and No-Shops

Incumbent managers may cause their companies to enter into "lock-up" and "no-shop" agreements with favored bidders. Devices that "lock-up" a sale of the corporation can come in many shapes and forms, including options that give the favored bidder the ability to purchase assets of the target company at below market prices if another bidder acquires control of the target ("asset lock-ups") and cancellation fees that are triggered if the transaction with the favored bidder is terminated. Asset lock-ups and cancellation fees give the friendly bidder an advantage over other bidders by, in effect, giving it liquidated damages if the acquisition is not completed. No-shops prevent target companies from cooperating with, or furnishing information to, other bidders. Other types of lock-ups include agreements to sell key assets, known as "crown jewels," to a favored bidder if a competing bidder should acquire control, agreements to reimburse favored bidders for expenses or other charges incurred in connection with unsuccessful takeover bids, and agreements granting a favored bidder the right to acquire a large amount of target stock at a pre-auction price. The policy question concerning lock-ups is whether they help target shareholders by promoting an auction, or hurt the shareholders by, among other things, favoring management's over shareholders' interests in picking a winner. **Coates & Subramanian** is a comprehensive study of the effects of lock-ups on target firms.

[B] Policy Issues Concerning Defenses to Tender Offers

Do takeover defenses enhance the welfare of target shareholders? On the one hand, takeover defenses would seem to harm target shareholders to the extent shareholders are denied the substantial premium over the market price of their shares when a bidder purchases control. On the other hand, (1) premiums received by shareholders of targets might be higher, (2) takeover bids might be more frequent, and (3) targets might be better run, if incumbent managers can defend against takeovers. The principal arguments along these lines are discussed in the following materials.

[1] Shareholder Disadvantages in Tender Offers

The arguments for takeover defenses focus on problems that shareholders face in responding to a bidder's purchase offer. Shareholders, it is argued, will sell for too low a price due, among other things, to their lack of information or inability to coordinate with each other. These arguments are explored below.

[a] Information

A tender offer confronts target shareholders with the following questions: (1) If I sell, will I miss out on a higher offer? (2) If I do not sell, will the offer be defeated and the stock retreat to pre-tender offer levels? (3) If I do not sell and the offer is successful, will new management improve or harm the company? (4) If I remain a shareholder and the company improves, will I share in the bounty, or will I be victimized or squeezed out at a bargain price as a helpless minority shareholder? The target shareholder therefore needs information on such matters as the current value of the target and the plans and track record of the bidder. Her plight is complicated by the fact that there is only a limited "window" in which she has an opportunity to take advantage of the bidder's willingness to buy at an elevated price.[32] Managers may be better able than shareholders to assess the "hidden value" of target companies that is not reflected in current share price (**Black & Kraakman**). But are these informational problems so severe that incumbent managers should be given the power to block or impede tender offers? Note that incumbent managers can disclose this information to target shareholders, and shareholders can simply refuse to tender their shares if they think they need more information.

[b] The Extra Value of Minority Shares

The price at which some security holders value their shares may be higher than what a bidder must pay for simple majority control. The shareholders who are unwilling to trade at the price offered by the bidder can be called "extramarginal" because the

---

[32] *See* Cohen, *Why Tender Offers? The Efficient Market Hypothesis, The Supply of Stock, and Signalling*, 19 J. Leg. Stud. 113 (1989).

price at which they want to sell is above that of the "marginal" share that transfers control. It follows that tender offer defenses might be necessary to prevent a bidder from acquiring control at a price that is lower than the holders of as many as 49% of the shares think their stock is worth.[33] For example, some investors may have developed special relationships or contracts with managers (*see* **Baysinger & Butler**) or derive special value from voting, as in a family-held business or a baseball team.[34] But note that shareholders can protect this value through dual class common stock (*see* Section 14.03[A][1]). On the other hand, shareholders may simply be more optimistic than their fellow shareholders about the value of the firm. But then who is to say that they are right? And if they are so sure, why can't they assemble their own higher bid?

[c]   The Prisoners' Dilemma

The bidder may be able to "force" the shareholders to tender below the price at which they would sell if they were "free" to choose. This problem arises because the shareholders must act individually, in ignorance of what their fellow shareholders will do, so that it is difficult for the shareholders to coordinate their actions. As a result, the bidder may be able, by playing the shareholders off against each other, to buy the company for less than a single owner would demand. This problem is referred to in game theory as the "prisoner's dilemma."

Imagine two co-defendant prisoners, locked in separate cells, each having information about their crime, the concealment of which will lead to acquittal. The prosecutor promises Prisoner A a reduced sentence in exchange for the information. If A refuses, the prosecutor may be able to get the information from Prisoner B, so that B will get the deal while A will not. A fears that B will squeal because B irrationally fears that A will squeal first, so A beats B to the punch. Thus, both are convicted, although neither would have been had they both remained silent.[35]

In the takeover setting, target shareholders may be confronted with a prisoners' dilemma if the "prosecutor" (that is, the bidder) can promise a lighter sentence for "squealing" (that is, tendering) than for remaining silent (that is, holding). The bidder can offer a relatively high price to those shareholders who accept the tender offer, while threatening those who do not with a low price in a second tier merger or with the unenviable status of a minority shareholder in a corporation that the bidder will run for its own benefit. For example, assume a corporation equally owned by two shareholders who, like the prisoners, cannot communicate with each other. Each believes the corporation is worth $80 ($40 each). A bidder might offer to buy just over half of the stock

---

[33]   For opposing positions on the "extramarginality" point, compare **Stout** with **Bradford** and **Sidak & Woodward**.

[34]   *See* Demsetz & Lehn, *The Structure of Corporate Ownership: Causes and Consequences*, 93 J. POL. ECON. 1155, 1162, 1170 (1985).

[35]   For a real-life example of a prisoners' dilemma involving actual prisoners, see *Page v. United States*, 884 F.2d 300 (7th Cir. 1989). For a movie example, see "L.A. Confidential."

from the two shareholders on a *pro rata* basis for $50, while obtaining the remainder in a second-tier merger for $25. Both shareholders tender their shares to the bidder for an aggregate price of $75 (instead of holding out for $80) so as to avoid the possibly of having to accept the $25 price for their entire interest in the firm. Takeover defenses may therefore be necessary to prevent bidders from exploiting the inability of target shareholders to coordinate their responses to the bid.

There are several potential answers to this justification for takeover defenses, some of which were discussed by Chancellor Allen in *Katz*, Section 11.04. Target shareholders are, in fact, making a free choice, albeit from limited alternatives, when they choose to tender their shares. Also, their dilemma is not as bad as it might look because shareholders can assume that there is a floor below which their fellow shareholders (many of whom will be sophisticated arbitrageurs) will not be so dumb as to tender— probably substantially higher than the pre-tender offer trading price.

The chief risk to target shareholders from the prisoners' dilemma outlined above therefore seems to be that they will end up with a premium over pre-tender offer market that is not as great as the premium they could get if they were acting as a single owner. This risk troubles some commentators, particularly Lucian **Bebchuk**.[36] But this higher price probably results from synergy or management discipline attributable to the bid itself. Thus, the question is whether the rules governing tender offers and takeover defenses should ensure that all these gains are allocated to the target shareholders. Consider the discussion in the next subsection.

[d] Creating an Auction

Competition among bidders creates a higher price for a target's shares. But auctions do not necessarily develop spontaneously. Bidders need information concerning the value of the target and the "fit" of the two companies to make a prudent bid. Potential acquirers will be reluctant to enter the bidding if they must expend substantial resources to develop a bid but, at the same time, stand a good chance of losing the contest. Management can encourage an auction by reducing bidders' costs and risks. For example, incumbent managers can provide information to bidders, enter into "lockup" or "no-shop" agreements with the first bidder that ensure benefits even if it is outbid, or use takeover defenses such as "poison pills" to stall a first bidder so that a second bidder has time to develop its offer.

But strong management steps are not always necessary for auctions to develop, particularly since the SEC requires a minimum 20-day bid period.[37] For example, potential bidders may develop information about entire industries that allows them to step quickly and cheaply into specific takeover battles. Moreover, auctions may not be good

---

[36] For arguments against the Bebchuk position, see Bradford, 67 NEB. L. REV. at 512-18.

[37] SEC Exchange Act Rule 14e-1(a).

for target shareholders, since raising the price may reduce the likelihood that any bid will emerge.

The advisability of facilitating auctions has been extensively debated by, among others, **Bebchuk, Gilson** (1981 and 1982), **Easterbrook & Fischel**, and **Schwartz**. In general, when the auction raises the price for the shareholders, it also raises the price of the first bidder's initial "stake" in the target (*see* Section 13.04[B][1]). Accordingly, auctions may actually increase the likelihood of takeover bids by rewarding those who specialize in identifying targets but do not wish to acquire firms themselves. Whether auctions are necessary to reward those who specialize in information-gathering depends partly on whether information-gatherers can profit from their investment in information other than by transferring their stakes in auctions—for example, by selling their information directly to bidders who specialize in acquiring, rather than identifying, targets. Also, it is not clear whether auctions are necessary to ensure that the target goes to the one who can make the best use of it, since the first buyer can always sell it to someone else.

[2] Effect of Tender Offers on Managers

As discussed above in Section 13.01[B], takeovers may impose costs on non-shareholder groups or "stakeholders," including employees, creditors and others. **Haddock, Macey & McChesney** suggest that tender offers can discourage managers from investing time and energy in developing human capital that will have little value outside the firm. For example, managers might choose not to invest extra time in learning about a product line that is unique to their company if this expertise will not help them in the job market when they are displaced by a tender offer. Also, the market for control tends to reduce the value to managers of deferred compensation. Thus, exposing managers to takeover risk can increase the cost of managerial services, deter managers from learning skills that would be helpful to the shareholders, and make it more difficult to align manager and shareholder interests through incentive compensation. These problems may outweigh the benefits of the incentive effects of the market for control and may provide a justification for at least some takeover defenses, such as "golden parachute" compensation agreements (*see* Section 9.05[B][6]; **Knoeber**).

[3] Fashioning the Appropriate Rule

In regulating tender offer defenses, it is important to balance the benefits of tender offer defenses discussed above against the potential costs to shareholders and others. These tradeoffs can be expressed in a formula: Market value of firm = Value under current management + (Probability of control change x Change in value from control change) (*see* **Ruback**). For example, a takeover defense that enhances the managers' ability to auction the company may increase the current value of the firm if it lowers the probability of an acquisition but raises the eventual premium.

It is important to keep in mind that the cost-benefit tradeoffs of defending against takeovers vary from firm to firm. For example, firms with strong "internal" monitoring and incentive devices such as large institutional shareholders, active outside directors and well-designed incentive compensation do not have as much need for monitoring by the market for control, and therefore can better afford to entrench managers than firms that are dominated by a single powerful executive.[38] Accordingly, general rules requiring management passivity in all cases are suspect.[39] An alternative approach would recognize that different rules are appropriate for different corporations and give effect to the contract fashioned by the particular corporation (*see* **Ribstein**). The above policy arguments would then be legally relevant primarily from the perspective of interpreting ambiguous contracts or providing standard form terms where the parties have not explicitly agreed. Does this indicate that the shareholders should ultimately have control over which takeover defenses are adopted? *See* Note 7 following the *Quickturn* excerpt in Section 14.03[D].

REFERENCES

Bainbridge, *Director Primacy in Corporate Takeovers: Preliminary Reflections*, 54 STAN. L. REV. 791 (2002).

Baysinger & Butler, *Antitakeover Amendments, Managerial Entrenchment, and the Contractual Theory of the Corporation*, 71 VA. L. REV. 1257 (1985).

Bebchuk, *Toward Undistorted Choice and Equal Treatment in Corporate Takeovers*, 98 HARV. L. REV. 1693 (1985).

Bebchuk, *The Case for Facilitating Competing Tender Offers*, 95 HARV. L. REV. 1028 (1982).

Bebchuk, Coates & Subramanian, *The Powerful Antitakeover Force of Staggered Boards: Theory, Evidence, and Policy*, 54 STAN. L. REV. 887 (2002).

Black & Kraakman, *Delaware's Takeover Law: The Uncertain Search for Hidden Value*, 96 Nw. U. L. REV. 521 (2002).

Carney, *Shareholder Coordination Costs, Shark Repellent Amendments, and Takeout Mergers: The Case Against Fiduciary Duties*, 1983 AM. B. FOUND. RES. J. 341.

Coates, *Takeover Defenses in the Shadow of the Pill: A Critique of the Scientific Evidence*, 79 TEX. L. REV. 271 (2000).

Coates & Subramanian, *A Buy-Side Model of M&A Lockups: Theory and Evidence*, 53 STAN. L. REV. 307 (2000).

---

[38] *See* Morck, Shleifer & Vishny, *Alternative Mechanisms for Corporate Control*, 79 AM. ECON. REV. 842 (1989); **Kahan**.

[39] Easterbrook & Fischel, 94 HARV. L. REV. 1161, at first proposed a rule of complete management passivity in the face of a bid apart from the release of information concerning the merits of the offer. Any actions "set in motion" before the managers could know of a takeover attempt presumptively do not violate this rule, while actions taken after the managers had such knowledge would be presumptively violative. Both authors later endorsed shareholder-approved defensive control policies. *See* Easterbrook & Jarrell, *Separate Statement to Report of Recommendations of the SEC Advisory Committee on Tender Offers* 16-18, reprinted in Fed. Sec. L. Rep. (CCH) at 70 (special edition no. 1028) (July 15, 1983); Fischel, *Organized Exchanges and the Regulation of Dual Class Common Stock*, 54 U. CHI. L. REV. 119 (1987).

Coffee, *Shareholders vs. Managers: The Strain in the Corporate Web*, 85 MICH. L. REV. 1 (1986).

Cramton & Schwartz, *Using Auction Theory to Inform Takeover Regulation*, 7 J. L. ECON. & ORG. 27 (1991).

Easterbrook & Fischel, *Auctions and Sunk Costs in Tender Offers*, 35 STAN. L. REV. 1 (1982).

Easterbrook & Fischel, *The Proper Role of a Target's Management in Responding to a Tender Offer*, 94 HARV. L. REV. 1161 (1981).

Gilson, *Seeking Competitive Bids Versus Pure Passivity in Tender Offer Defense*, 35 STAN. L. REV. 51 (1982).

Gilson, *A Structural Approach to Corporations: The Case Against Defensive Tactics in Tender Offers*, 33 STAN. L. REV. 819 (1981).

Haddock, Macey & McChesney, *Property Rights in Assets and Resistance to Tender Offers*, 73 VA. L. REV. 701 (1987).

Jarrell, Brickley & Netter, *Market for Corporate Control: Empirical Evidence Since 1980*, 2 J. ECON. PERSP. 49 (1988).

Kahan, *How I Learned to Stop Worrying and Love the Pill: Adaptive Responses to Takeover Law*, 69 U. CHI. L. REV. 973 (2002).

Knoeber, *Golden Parachutes, Shark Repellents and Hostile Tender Offers*, 76 AM. ECON. REV. 155 (1986).

Macey & McChesney, *A Theoretical Analysis of Greenmail*, 95 YALE L.J. 13 (1985).

Ribstein, *Takeover Defenses and the Corporate Contract*, 78 GEO. L.J. 71 (1989).

Ruback, *An Overview of Takeover Defenses*, in MERGERS AND ACQUISITIONS (A. Auerbach, ed. 1988).

Schwartz, *The Fairness of Tender Offer Prices in Utilitarian Theory*, 17 J. LEG. STUD. 165 (1988).

Sidak & Woodward, *Takeover Premiums, Appraisal Rights, and the Price Elasticity of a Firm's Publicly Traded Stock*, 25 GA. L. REV. 783 (1991).

Stout, *Are Takeover Premiums Really Premiums? Market Price, Fair Value and Corporate Law*, 99 YALE L.J. 1235 (1990).

[C] Legal Standards Governing Shareholder-Approved Defenses

Tender offer defenses that have been expressly approved by the shareholders, like the charter amendments and recapitalization plans discussed in Subsection [A][1] above, are not generally susceptible to legal challenge. It has been argued, however, that shareholders should not have unlimited power to authorize the adoption of entrenchment mechanisms. The primary concern is that entrenchment-seeking managers will be able to manipulate passive, uninformed shareholders into approving the device even if it will reduce shareholder wealth.

In particular, where a company with one class of voting stock "recapitalizes" into a dual-class company by offering the shareholders the choice between high vote or high dividend stock, the shareholders may ignore the possible loss of a takeover premium that accompanies a decision to accept high dividend stock instead of high vote stock. Shareholders may assume that their individual decisions will not determine whether incumbent managers obtain voting control of the corporation as a result of the recapitalization. On the other hand, shareholder decisions to accept high dividend stock instead of high vote stock may simply reflect an accurate judgment that the dividend rights acquired are worth more than the voting rights surrendered. Management also might play a "chicken" game with shareholders by threatening to mismanage the company if the shareholders defeat the recapitalization.[40] But management's propensity to engage in such a game should be checked by managements' own substantial investments in the firm.[41] See also the discussions of market constraints on shareholder voting, at Note 2 following *Fliegler* in Section 9.04[B].

Williams v. Geier[42] considered the legal standards that would apply to a shareholder-approved, dual class common stock recapitalization. The court held that the directors' decision to recommend the charter amendment implementing the recapitalization plan under Del. G.C.L. § 242(b)(1) should be judged under the deferential standards of the business judgment rule rather than under *Unocal* (*see* Section 14.03[D]), finding that "[a] *Unocal* analysis should be used only when a board *unilaterally* (*i.e.*, without stockholder approval) adopts defensive measures in reaction to a perceived threat."[43] The Court also rejected the application of *Blasius* standard (*see* Section 14.02[A]), because stockholders had been given a full and fair opportunity to vote on the recapitalization. Finally, the Court refused to apply the entire fairness test for interested director transactions (*see* Section 9.04) because 7 of the 10 directors who approved the dual class common stock recapitalization were independent of the controlling shareholders who potentially stood to benefit from the plan.[44] Also, *In re Gaylord Container Corp. Shareholders Litigation*[45] refused to apply heightened scrutiny to shareholder-approved antitakeover charter amendments adopted on the eve of a corporate restructuring that reduced the controlling shareholder's voting power from 62% to 12%, although the controlling shareholder dominated the shareholder vote. The court noted that the charter amendments had been authorized by a board dominated by disinterested, independent directors.

QUESTION

If shareholder approval of entrenchment moves is a problem, why not leave it to the shareholders to enact voting rules that prevent approval of such moves?

---

[40] *See* **Gilson; Gordon; Ruback.** For a counter argument, see **Romano.**

[41] *See* **Romano.**

[42] 671 A.2d 1368 (Del. 1996).

[43] *Id.* at 1377 (emphasis added).

[44] *Id.* at 1377 n.9.

[45] 2000 Del. Ch. LEXIS 16, 2000 WL 128910 (Del. Ch. 2000).

REFERENCES

Gilson, *Evaluating Dual Class Common Stock: The Relevance of Substitutes*, 73 VA. L. REV. 807 (1987).

Gordon, *The Mandatory Structure of Corporate Law*, 89 COLUM. L. REV. 1549 (1989).

Gordon, *Ties That Bond: Dual Class Common Stock and the Problem of Shareholder Choice*, 75 CAL. L. REV. 1 (1987).

Romano, *Answering the Wrong Question: The Tenuous Case for Mandatory Corporate Laws*, 89 COLUM. L. REV. 1599 (1989).

Ruback, *Coercive Dual Class Exchange Offers*, 20 J. FIN. ECON. 153 (1988).

[D] Legal Standards Governing Director-Approved Tender Offer Defenses

The most troublesome questions concerning the state law of tender offers relate to the directors' power to reduce the firm's vulnerability to takeovers through entrenchment devices that do not require shareholder approval under literal terms of corporate statutes or charters. *See* Section 14.03[A][2]. The courts generally have adopted a very broad view of the directors' power, but have limited directors' exercise of their power through a fiduciary duty analysis.

How strictly should the courts scrutinize defensive board moves? Where the board is acting to protect its tenure, perhaps the court should treat the transaction as one in which the board is subject to a conflict of interest. *See* Section 9.04. But this rule would subject many management actions to strict judicial scrutiny. Also, for reasons discussed in Section 14.03[B], shareholders may sometimes want directors to actively defend against takeovers. These considerations support giving broad leeway to such director decisions even if they may have an entrenchment effect. Consistent with these competing considerations, the courts have attempted to find some intermediate level of review between loose business judgment rule scrutiny and tighter self-dealing rules.

As you read the following notes and cases, consider the following general questions. First, what level of judicial scrutiny is appropriate for director entrenchment decisions? And second, is case-by-case review of management discretion under a fiduciary duty analysis appropriate, or would it be better to interpret the corporate contract as not giving the board the power to make certain types of decisions?

[1] The "Motive" Test

Early takeover defense cases applied the business judgment rule unless the plaintiff could show that the directors were primarily serving their own interest in holding onto their jobs rather than the interests of the corporation. In *Johnson v. Trueblood*,[46]

---

[46]   629 F.2d 287, 292-93 (3d Cir. 1980).

Judge Seitz stated the Delaware rule to be that the business judgment rule applies unless:

> . . . the plaintiff . . . make[s] a showing from which a fact-finder might infer that impermissible motives predominated in the making of the decision in question.
>
> The plaintiffs' theory that "a" motive to control is sufficient to rebut the rule is inconsistent with [the purpose of the business judgment rule]. Because the rule is designed to validate certain transactions despite conflicts of interest, the plaintiffs' rule would negate that purpose, at least in many cases. As already noted, control is always arguably "a" motive in any action taken by a director. Hence plaintiffs could always make this showing and thereby undercut the purpose of the rule.

Under this approach, courts applied the business judgment rule if the defensive maneuver had a business purpose other than to defeat the takeover or if the bid could hurt the company.[47] The "motive" approach gave the directors great latitude in opposing takeovers as long as they could find (as they nearly always did) some non-entrenchment purpose. But the takeover defenses to which the "motive" test was applied, such as greenmail and defensive acquisitions, were relatively mild.

[2] The *Unocal* and *Revlon* Rules

Beginning in the mid-1980s, the takeover game took on a different look. Of particular importance was the development of the high yield or "junk" bond market, primarily by Michael Milken at Drexel Burnham.[48] Because Milken could summon a network of bond buyers on short notice, he was able to issue letters to bidders that said Drexel was "highly confident" that the necessary financing for the takeover was in place. For a time, at least, these letters displaced bank loan commitments, and therefore opened the door to takeovers that banks had been unwilling to finance. An important point was reached when Ronald Perelman took over Revlon, establishing that virtually anybody could take over virtually any company without succumbing to the relatively weak takeover defenses of the earlier era. As illustrated by the following cases, the new takeover technology led both to escalation in defensive weaponry and to stronger legal rules.

---

[47] *See, e.g., Panter v. Marshall Field & Co.*, 646 F.2d 271 (7th Cir.), *cert. denied*, 454 U.S. 1092 (1981) (defensive acquisitions had non-entrenchment purpose); *Northwest Industries, Inc. v. The B.F. Goodrich Co.*, 301 F. Supp. 706 (N.D. Ill. 1969); *Cheff v. Mathes*, 199 A.2d 548 (Del. 1964) (greenmail payment approved to raider who threatened the survival of the corporation and whose potential bid was causing unrest among employees and others); *Kors v. Carey*, 39 Del. Ch. 47, 158 A.2d 136 (1960) (approving buyout of bidder who threatened management policy and company's established relationships with customers).

[48] For a colorful history, see Bruck, THE PREDATORS' BALL (1988).

UNOCAL CORPORATION v. MESA PETROLEUM CO.
Delaware Supreme Court
493 A.2d 946 (1985)

MOORE, Justice.

We confront an issue of first impression in Delaware—the validity of a corporation's self-tender for its own shares which excludes from participation a stockholder making a hostile tender offer for the company stock.

The Court of Chancery granted a preliminary injunction to the plaintiffs, Mesa Petroleum Co., Mesa Asset Co., Mesa Partners II, and Mesa Eastern, Inc. (collectively "Mesa"),[1] enjoining an exchange offer of the defendant, Unocal Corporation (Unocal), for its own stock. The trial court concluded that a selective exchange offer, excluding Mesa, was legally impermissible. We cannot agree with such a blanket rule. . . .

I.

The factual background of this matter bears a significant relationship to its ultimate outcome.

On April 8, 1985, Mesa, the owner of approximately 13% of Unocal's stock, commenced a two-tier "front-loaded" cash tender offer for 64 million shares, or approximately 37%, of Unocal's outstanding stock at a price of $54 per share. The "back-end" was designed to eliminate the remaining publicly held shares by an exchange of securities purported worth $54 per share. However, pursuant to an order entered by the United States District Court for the Central District of California on April 26, 1985, Mesa issued a supplemental proxy statement to Unocal's stockholders disclosing that the securities offered in the second-step merger would be highly subordinated, and that Unocal's capitalization would differ significantly from its present structure. Unocal has rather aptly termed such securities "junk bonds."

Unocal's board consists of eight independent outside directors and six outsiders. It met on April 13, 1985, to consider the Mesa tender offer. Thirteen directors were present and the meeting lasted nine and one-half hours. . . . The board . . . received a presentation from Peter Sachs on behalf of Goldman Sachs & Co. (Goldman Sachs) and Dillon, Read & Co. (Dillon Read) discussing the bases for their opinions that the Mesa proposal was wholly inadequate. Mr. Sachs opined that the minimum cash value that could be expected from a sale or orderly liquidation for 100% of Unocal's stock was in excess of $60 per share. . . .

Mr. Sachs also presented various defensive strategies available to the board if it concluded that Mesa's two-step tender offer was inadequate and should be opposed. One of the devices outlined was a self-tender by Unocal for its own stock with a reasonable price range of $70 to $75 per share. The cost of such a proposal would cause the company to incur $6.1-6.5 billion of additional debt, and a presentation was made informing the board of Unocal's ability to handle it. . . .

The eight outside directors, comprising a clear majority of the thirteen members present, then met separately with Unocal's financial advisors and attorneys. Thereafter, they

---

[1]   T. Boone Pickens, Jr., is President and Chairman of the Board of Mesa Petroleum and President of Mesa Asset and controls the related Mesa entities.

unanimously agreed to advise the board that it should reject Mesa's tender offer as inadequate, and that Unocal should pursue a self-tender to provide the stockholders with a fairly priced alternative to the Mesa proposal. The board then reconvened and unanimously adopted a resolution rejecting as grossly inadequate Mesa's tender offer. Despite the nine and one-half hour length of the meeting, no formal decision was made on the proposed defensive self-tender.

On April 15, the board met again with four of the directors present by telephone and one member still absent. This session lasted two hours. . . . [At that meeting,] the directors unanimously approved the exchange offer. Their resolution provided that if Mesa acquired 64 million shares of Unocal stock through its own offer (the Mesa Purchase Condition), Unocal would buy the remaining 49% [later reduced to 29%—Ed.] outstanding for an exchange of debt securities having an aggregate par value of $72 per share. The board resolution also stated that the offer would be subject to other conditions . . . including the exclusion of Mesa from the proposal (the Mesa exclusion). . . .

Unocal's exchange offer was commenced on April 17, 1985, and Mesa promptly challenged it by filing this suit in the Court of Chancery. On April 22, the Unocal board met again and was advised by Goldman Sachs and Dillon Read to waive the Mesa Purchase Condition as to 50 million shares. This recommendation was in response to a perceived concern of the shareholders that, if shares were tendered to Unocal, no shares would be purchased by either offeror. The directors were also advised that they should tender their own Unocal stock into the exchange offer as a mark of their confidence in it.

Another focus of the board was the Mesa exclusion. Legal counsel advised that under Delaware law Mesa could only be excluded for what the directors reasonably believed to be a valid corporate purpose. The directors' discussion centered on the objective of adequately compensating shareholders at the "backend" of Mesa's proposal, which the latter would finance with "junk bonds." To include Mesa would defeat that goal, because, under the proration aspect of the exchange offer (49%), every Mesa share accepted by Unocal would displace one held by another stockholder. Further, if Mesa were permitted to tender to Unocal, the latter would in effect be financing Mesa's own inadequate proposal.

* * *

. . . [O]n April 22, 1985, Mesa amended its complaint in this action to challenge the Mesa exclusion. . . . [On May 8, the Chancellor preliminarily enjoined the Unocal exchange offer. This appeal followed.]

II.

The issues we address involve these fundamental questions: Did the Unocal board have the power and duty to oppose a takeover threat it reasonably perceived to be harmful to the corporate enterprise, and if so, is its action here entitled to the protection of the business judgment rule?

* * *

III.

We begin with the basic issue of the power of a board of directors of a Delaware corporation to adopt a defensive measure of this type. Absent such authority, all other questions are moot. Neither issues of fairness nor business judgment are pertinent without the basic underpinning of a board's legal power to act.

The board has a large reservoir of authority upon which to draw. Its duties and responsibilities proceed from the inherent powers conferred by 8 Del. C. Sec. 141(a), respecting management of the corporation's "business and affairs." Additionally, the powers here being exercised derive from 8 Del. C. Sec. 160(a), conferring broad authority upon a corporation to deal in its own stock. From this it is now well established that in the acquisition of its shares a Delaware corporation may deal selectively with its stockholders, provided the directors have not acted out of a sole or primary purpose to entrench themselves in office. *Cheff v. Mathes*, Del. Supr., 199 A.2d 548, 554 (1964).

Finally, the board's power to act derives from its fundamental duty and obligation to protect the corporate enterprise, which includes stockholders, from harm reasonably perceived, irrespective of its source. [citations omitted] Thus, we are satisfied that in the broad context of corporate governance, including issues of fundamental corporate change, a board of directors is not a passive instrumentality.[8]

Given the foregoing principles, we turn to the standards by which director action is to be measured. In *Pogostin v. Rice*, Del. Supr., 480 A.2d 619 (1984), we held that the business judgment rule, including standards by which director conduct is judged, is applicable in the context of a takeover. *Id.* at 627. The business judgment rule is a "presumption that in making a business decision the directors of a corporation acted on an informed basis, in good faith and in the honest belief that the action taken was in the best interests of the company." *Aronson v. Lewis*, Del. Supr., 473 A.2d 805, 812 (1984). A hallmark of the business judgment rule is that a court will not substitute its judgment for that of the board if the latter's decision can be "attributed to any rational business purpose." *Sinclair Oil Corp. v. Levien*, Del. Supr., 280 A.2d 717, 720 (1971).

When a board addresses a pending takeover bid it has an obligation to determine whether the offer is in the best interests of the corporation and its shareholders. In that respect a board's duty is no different from any other responsibility it shoulders, and its decisions should be no less entitled to the respect they otherwise would be accorded in the realm of business judgment.

There are, however, certain caveats to a proper exercise of this function. Because of the omnipresent specter that a board may be acting primarily in its own interests, rather than those of the corporation and its shareholders, there is an enhanced duty which calls for judicial examination at the threshold before the protections of the business judgment rule may be conferred.

This Court has long recognized that:

> We must bear in mind the inherent danger in the purchase of shares with corporate funds to remove a threat to corporate policy when a threat to control is involved. The directors are of necessity confronted with a conflict of interests, and an objective decision is difficult.

---

[8]   Even in the traditional areas of fundamental corporate change, *i.e.*, charter, amendments [8 Del. C. Sec. 242(b)], mergers [8 Del. C. Secs. 251(b), 252(c), 253(a), and 254(d)], sale of assets [8 Del. C. Sec. 271(a)], and dissolution [8 Del. C. Sec. 275(a)], director action is a prerequisite to the ultimate disposition of such matters. *See also Smith v. Van Gorkom*, Del. Supr. 488 A.2d 858, 888 (1985).

Bennett v. Propp, Del. Supr., 187 A.2d 405, 409 (1962). In the face of this inherent conflict directors must show that they had reasonable grounds for believing that a danger to corporate policy and effectiveness existed because of another person's stock ownership. *Cheff v. Mathes*, 199 A.2d at 554-55. However, they satisfy that burden by showing "good faith and reasonable investigation . . . ." *Id.* at 555. Furthermore, such proof is materially enhanced, as here, by the approval of a board comprised of a majority of outside independent directors who have acted in accordance with the foregoing standards. . . .

A.

In the board's exercise of corporate power to forestall a takeover bid our analysis begins with the basic principle that corporate directors have a fiduciary duty to act in the best interests of the corporation's stockholders. As we have noted, their duty of care extends to protecting the corporation and its owners from other shareholders.[10]

But such powers are not absolute. A corporation does not have unbridled discretion to defeat any perceived threat by any Draconian means available.

The restriction placed upon a selective stock repurchase is that the directors may not have acted solely or primarily out of a desire to perpetuate themselves in office. *See Cheff v. Mathes*, 199 A.2d at 556; *Kors v. Carey*, 158 A.2d at 140. Of course, to this is added the further caveat that inequitable action may not be taken under the guise of law. *Schnell v. Chris-Craft Industries, Inc.*, Del. Supr., 285 A.2d 437, 439 (1971). The standard of proof established in *Cheff v. Mathes* . . . is designed to ensure that a defensive measure to thwart or impede a takeover is indeed motivated by a good faith concern for the welfare of the corporation and its stockholders, which in all circumstances must be free of any fraud or other misconduct. *Cheff v. Mathes*, 199 A.2d at 554-55. However, this does not end the inquiry.

B.

A further aspect is the element of balance. If a defensive measure is to come within the ambit of the business judgment rule, it must be reasonable in relation to the threat posed. This entails an analysis by the directors of the nature of the takeover bid and its effect on the corporate enterprise. Examples of such concerns may include: inadequacy of the price offered, nature and timing of the offer, questions of illegality, the impact on "constituencies" other than shareholders (*i.e.*, creditors, customers, employees, and perhaps even the community generally), the risk of nonconsummation, and the quality of securities being offered in the exchange. [citation omitted] While not a controlling factor, it also seems to us that a board may reasonably consider the basic stockholder interests at stake, including those of short term speculators, whose actions may have fueled the coercive aspect of the offer at the expense of the long term investor.[11]

---

[10]   It has been suggested that a board's response to a takeover threat should be a passive one. Easterbrook & Fischel, *supra*, 36 Bus. Law. at 1750. However, that clearly is not the law of Delaware, and as the proponents of this rule of passivity readily concede, it has not been adopted either by courts or state legislatures. Easterbrook & Fischel, *supra*, 94 Harv. L. Rev. at 1194.

[11]   There has been much debate respecting such stockholder interests. One rather impressive study indicates that the stock of over 50 percent of target companies, who resisted hostile takeovers, later traded at higher market prices than the rejected offer price, or were acquired after the tender offer was defeated by another company at a price higher than the offer price. *See* Lipton, *supra* 35 Bus. Law. at 106-109, 132-133. Moreover, an update by Kidder Peabody & Com-

Here the threat posed was viewed by the Unocal board as a grossly inadequate two-tier coercive tender offer coupled with the threat of greenmail. Specifically, the Unocal directors had concluded that the value of Unocal was substantially above the $54 per share offered in cash at the front end. Furthermore, they determined that the subordinated securities to be exchanged in Mesa's announced squeeze out of the remaining shareholders in the "back-end" merger were "junk bonds" worth far less than $54. It is now well-recognized that such offers are a classic coercive measure designed to stampede shareholders into tendering at the first tier, even if the price is inadequate, out of fear of what they will receive at the back end of the transaction.

Wholly beyond the coercive aspect of an inadequate two-tier tender offer, the threat was posed by a corporate raider with a national reputation as a "greenmailer."[13]

In adopting the selective exchange offer, the board stated that its objective was either to defeat the inadequate Mesa offer or, should the offer still succeed, provide the 49% of its stockholders, who would otherwise be forced to accept "junk bonds," with $72 worth of senior debt. We find that both purposes are valid.

However, such efforts would have been thwarted by Mesa's participation in the exchange offer. First, if Mesa could tender its shares, Unocal would effectively be subsidizing the former's continuing effort to buy Unocal stock at $54 per share. Second, Mesa could not, by definition, fit within the class of shareholders being protected from its own coercive and inadequate tender offer.

Thus, we are satisfied that the selective exchange offer is reasonably related to the threats posed. It is consistent with the principle that "the minority stockholder shall receive the substantial equivalent in value of what he had before." *Sterling v. Mayflower Hotel Corp.*, Del. Supr., 93 A.2d 107, 114 (1952). [additional citation omitted]. This concept of fairness, while stated in the merger context, is also relevant in the area of tender offer law. Thus, the board's decision to offer what it determined to be the fair value of the corporation to the 49% of its shareholders, who would otherwise be forced to accept highly subordinated "junk bonds," is reasonable and consistent with the directors' duty to ensure that the minority stockholders receive equal value for their shares.

V.

Mesa contends that it is unlawful, and the trial court agreed, for a corporation to discriminate in this fashion against one shareholder. It argues correctly that no case has ever sanctioned a device that precludes a raider from sharing in a benefit available to all other

---

pany of this study, involving the stock prices of target companies that have defeated hostile tender offers during the period from 1973 to 1982 demonstrates that in a majority of cases the target's shareholders benefited from the defeat. The stock of 81% of the target's studies has, since the tender offer, sold at prices higher than the tender offer price. When adjusted for the time value of money, the figure is 64%. *See* Lipton & Brownstein, *supra* ABA Institute at 10. The thesis being that this strongly supports application of the business judgment rule in response to takeover threats. There is, however, a rather vehement contrary view. *See* Easterbrook & Fischel, *supra* 36 BUS. LAW. at 1739-1745.

[13] The term "greenmail" refers to the practice of buying out a takeover bidder's stock at a premium that is not available to other shareholders in order to prevent the takeover. The Chancery Court noted that "Mesa has made tremendous profits from its takeover activities although in the past few years it has not been successful in acquiring any of the target companies on an unfriendly basis." Moreover, the trial court specifically found that the actions of the Unocal board were taken in good faith to eliminate both the inadequacies of the tender offer and to forestall the payment of "greenmail."

stockholders. However, as we have noted earlier, the principle of selective stock repurchases by a Delaware corporation is neither unknown nor unauthorized. *Cheff v. Mathes*, 199 A.2d at 554. The only difference is that heretofore the approved transaction was the payment of "greenmail" to a raider or dissident posing a threat to the corporate enterprise. All other stockholders were denied such favored treatment, and given Mesa's past history of greenmail, its claims here are rather ironic.

* * *

. . . [G]iven the nature of the threat posed here the response is neither unlawful nor unreasonable. If the board of directors is disinterested, has acted in good faith and with due care, its decision in the absence of an abuse of discretion will be upheld as a proper exercise of business judgment.

To this Mesa responds that the board is not disinterested, because the directors are receiving a benefit from the tender of their own shares, which because of the Mesa exclusion, does not devolve upon all stockholders equally. [citation omitted] However, Mesa concedes that if the exclusion is valid, then the directors and all other stockholders share the same benefit. The answer of course is that the exclusion is valid, and the directors' participation in the exchange offer does not rise to the level of a disqualifying interest. The excellent discussion in *Johnson v. Trueblood*, 620 F.2d at 292-293, of the use of the business judgment rule in takeover contests also seems pertinent here.

* * *

Mesa also argues that the exclusion permits the directors to abdicate the fiduciary duties they owe it. However, that is not so. The board continues to owe Mesa the duties of due care and loyalty. But in the face of the destructive threat Mesa's tender offer was perceived to pose, the board had a supervening duty to protect the corporate enterprise, which includes the other shareholders, from threatened harm.

Mesa contends that the basis of this action is punitive, and solely in response to the exercise of its rights of corporate democracy.

Nothing precludes Mesa, as a stockholder, from acting in its own self-interest. However, Mesa, while pursuing its own interests, has acted in a manner which a board consisting of a majority of independent directors has reasonably determined to be contrary to the best interests of Unocal and its other shareholders. In this situation, there is no support in Delaware law for the proposition that, when responding to a perceived harm, a corporation must guarantee a benefit to a stockholder who is deliberately provoking the danger being addressed. There is no obligation of self-sacrifice by a corporation and its shareholders in the face of such a challenge.

Here, the Court of Chancery specifically found that the "directors' decision [to oppose the Mesa tender offer] was made in the good faith belief that the Mesa tender offer is inadequate." . . . [W]e are satisfied that Unocal's board has met its burden of proof. *Cheff v. Mathes*, 199 A.2d at 555.

VI.

In conclusion, there was directional power to oppose the Mesa tender offer, and to undertake a selective stock exchange made in good faith and upon a reasonable investigation pursuant to a clear duty to protect the corporate enterprise. Further, the selective stock repurchase plan chosen by Unocal is reasonable in relation to the threat that the board rationally and reasonably believed was posed by Mesa's inadequate and coercive two-tier tender offer. Under those circumstances the board's action is entitled to be measured by the standards of the business judgment rule. Thus, unless it is shown by a preponderance of the evidence that the directors' decisions were primarily based on perpetuating themselves in office, or some other breach of fiduciary duty such as fraud, overreaching, lack of good faith, or being uninformed, a Court will not substitute its judgment for that of the board.

In this case that protection is not lost merely because Unocal's directors have tendered their shares in the exchange offer. Given the validity of the Mesa exclusion, they are receiving a benefit shared generally by all other stockholders except Mesa. In this circumstance the test of *Aronson v. Lewis*, 473 A.2d at 812, is satisfied. *See also Cheff v. Mathes*, 199 A.2d at 554. If the stockholders are displeased with the action of their elected representatives, the powers of corporate democracy are at their disposal to turn the board out. . . .

With the Court of Chancery's findings that the exchange offer was based on the board's good faith belief that the Mesa offer was inadequate, that the board's action was informed and taken with due care, that Mesa's prior activities justify a reasonable inference that its principle objective was greenmail, and implicitly, that the substance of the offer itself was reasonable and fair to the corporation and its stockholders if Mesa were included, we cannot say that the Unocal directors have acted in such a manner as to have passed an "unintelligent and unadvised judgment." . . .

NOTES AND QUESTIONS

(1) **The effect of the Unocal exchange offer.** Assuming the initial 29% Unocal exchange offer was fully subscribed, 29% of Unocal's equity, which was trading at approximately $46 per share immediately before Unocal's exchange offer closed, would be replaced with $72 in senior debt. Assume a beginning market value of $46,000 (1000 shares @ $46). If each of 290 shares is replaced by $72 in debt, the remaining 710 shares would be worth about $25,000, or about $35 per share. If the new debt and equity were allocated *pro rata* among the original shareholders, there would be no change in market value of each original shareholder's total interest (debt and equity) in the firm unless the new capital structure affected the firm's value. But if the debt is given to one group of shareholders, the excluded equity holders suffer a loss in value of approximately $11 per share ($46 – $35). Thus, Mesa, the owner of 23.7 million shares of Unocal stock, stood to loose approximately $260 million if it purchased enough shares to trigger Unocal's exchange offer. In the end, Unocal and Mesa settled by entering into a standstill agreement under which Unocal agreed to include 7.7 million of the Unocal shares owned by Mesa in its $72 exchange offer. Nonetheless, when Mesa's legal, investment banking, and other expenses were taken into account, Mesa still suffered an estimated $100 million loss on its $1.1 billion investment in Unocal shares.[49]

---

[49]   *See How T. Boone Pickens Finally Met His Match: Unocal's Fred Hartley*, WALL ST. J., May 24, 1985, at 1.

(2) **The purpose of the Unocal exchange offer.** Unocal's exchange offer clearly protected Unocal shareholders from the "two-tier" nature of the Mesa tender offer: under the terms of Unocal's exchange offer for 29% of its shares, shareholders who did not tender their stock to Mesa would be guaranteed a $72 per share price for approximately 60% (*i.e.*, 29/49) of their shares if Mesa acquired 51% control of Unocal. But Mesa would still suffer dilution if it had offered to purchase all Unocal shares, including those acquired in a second-step merger, for the same $54 per share price, thus curing the "two-tier" problem. This is because some shareholders might still tender to Unocal in the hope they would have all or some of their stock exchanged for $72 in debt, even though the $54 per share value of a 100% Mesa offer exceeded the $46 per share value of the partial Unocal offer (29% x $72 + 71% x $35). Thus, Mesa was faced with a Hobson's Choice: substantially increase the price it paid for all of the company's stock (thereby persuading all of the shareholders to tender to Mesa), or stand pat and end up buying diluted shares. Unocal could force this choice by threatening to transfer some of the value of Mesa's stake to its other shareholders through its selective exchange offer. One empirical study supports the hypothesis that the Unocal defense was both effective and contrary to shareholder interests.[50]

(3) **Federal response to *Unocal*.** State law reaction to the specific move in *Unocal* was preempted by the adoption of SEC Rule 14d-10, which prohibits discriminatory self-tenders. But while SEC Rule 14d-10 prohibits discriminatory self-tenders, it does not prohibit the use of "flip-in" poison pills which have a very similar effect (*see* Section 14.03[A][2][d]).

(4) **Flip-over poison pills: *Moran v. Household International, Inc.*** The Delaware Supreme Court's next significant pronouncement on director-approved tender offer defenses came in *Moran v. Household International, Inc.*,[51] where the court considered the validity of a "flip-over" poison pill (*see* Section 14.03[A][2][d]). The court described the "pill" in that case as follows:

> . . . There are two triggering events that can activate the Rights. The first is the announcement of a tender offer for 30 percent of Household's shares ("30% trigger") and the second is the acquisition of 20 percent of Household's shares by any single entity or group ("20% trigger").
>
> If an announcement of a tender offer for 30 percent of Household's shares is made, the Rights are issued and are immediately exercisable to purchase 1/100 share of new preferred stock for $100 and are redeemable by the Board for $.50 per Right. If 20 percent of Household's shares are acquired by anyone, the Rights are issued and become non-redeemable and are exercisable to purchase 1/100 of a share of preferred. If a Right is not

---

[50]   *See* Kamma, Weintrop & Weir, *Investors' Perceptions of the Delaware Supreme Court Decision in* Unocal v. Mesa, 20 J. FIN. ECON. 419 (1988) (value of Delaware firms that were targets of hostile tender offers at the time of the *Unocal* decision fell on the announcement of the Supreme Court's decision).

[51]   500 A.2d 1346 (Del. 1985).

exercised for preferred, and thereafter, a merger or consolidation occurs, the Rights holder can exercise each Right to purchase $200 of the common stock of the tender offeror for $100. This "flip-over" provision of the Rights Plan is at the heart of this controversy.

Like *Unocal*, *Moran* considered both whether the board had the power to adopt the defense at issue in the case and whether the board's action was consistent with its fiduciary duties to its shareholders. In holding that the rights plan did not exceed the board's power, the court rejected the argument that Household's rights plan usurped the stockholders' rights to receive tender offers. The court reasoned that there were many ways around the plan, including tendering for control but foregoing the "second step" merger that triggered the rights (as, the court noted, Sir James Goldsmith had done in connection with his takeover of Crown Zellerbach), tendering with a high minimum condition of shares and rights, tendering and soliciting consents to remove the board and redeem the rights, and tendering for more than half the shares and causing the firm to self-tender for the rights. The court also rejected the argument that the rights plan "fundamentally restricted the stockholders' rights to conduct a proxy contest," reasoning that the rights plan had no effect on proxy contests where the contestant did not purchase more than 20% of the shares.

In holding that the board had not breached its fiduciary duties under the *Unocal* test, the court concluded that the plan was a good faith effort to prevent two-tier, bust-up takeovers and was "reasonable in relation to the threat posed." But the court also noted that the case involved a mechanism that was adopted in advance of an actual takeover and pointed out that the board might have a duty to redeem the rights plan in response to a particular bid.

As to the court's reasoning that the bidder could tender for the rights or buy control and cause the company to self-tender for the rights, target shareholders, before they give up control over their rights, probably will demand to be paid enough to compensate them for the value of the flip-over feature—that is, the opportunity to buy discounted bidder stock. A leading commentator, who testified in *Moran*, pointed out that the *Moran* pill (assuming a transaction that triggered the flip-over) locked up the corporation against anything less than a 200% premium bid.[52] But perhaps the shareholders would realize that if they held out for this price, there would be no takeover at all.

(5) **Flip-in poison pills.** Poison pill rights plans have been through significant evolution since *Moran*. The first important variation was the "flip-in" right, which permits target shareholders other than the bidder to buy discounted target stock in the event that the bidder acquires a specified percentage of target stock (*see* Section 14.03[A][2][d]). Flip-in poison pills raise some issues not present in connection with flip-over poison pills. First, to be effective, flip-over poison pills must discriminate among shareholders in the same class (*i.e.*, the bidder does not get to exercise flip-in

---

[52] *See* Jensen, *Takeovers: Their Causes and Consequences*, 2 J. Econ. Persp. 21 (1988).

rights).[53] Second, flip-in plans are more potent than flip-over plans since they are activated upon mere acquisition of a substantial block of stock and, therefore, cannot be avoided simply by foregoing a second-step merger. In *Dynamics Corporation of America v. CTS Corporation*,[54] Judge Posner invalidated a flip-in plan permitting target shareholders to buy target securities at 25% of their market value upon a shareholder's purchase of 15% or more of target's stock. He reasoned in part that *Dynamics* posed a minimal threat because it was not even going for control.

(6) **Fiduciary duty: standard of judicial review.** In light of the facts discussed in Notes 1 and 2, above concerning the broad purpose and strong effect of the *Unocal* exchange offer, how seriously does the court intend its "enhanced business judgment rule" in *Unocal* to be taken? Is the court just applying the same business judgment rule that applies to all board actions (*see* Section 9.03) to board-approved responses to hostile bids? Or is it really restricting application of the business judgment rule to moves that respond to particular types of threats, and that do so proportionately to the threat posed by the takeover? Some later cases held that a board can refuse to order redemption of poison pill rights at least while an auction was continuing.[55] Also, *Ivanhoe Partners v. Newmont Mining Corp.*[56] approved a "standstill agreement" between a target and one of two potential suitors under which the suitor could buy up to 49.9% of the target's stock and obtain 40% board representation, but could not transfer its interest to a third party that was not bound by the standstill agreement and had to vote for the board's nominees for the remaining board positions. The court stressed that the board had reasonably responded to the threat of two potentially coercive bids. Other cases ordered redemption of poison pill rights where refusal to do so would have effectively stopped a *non-coercive* bid.[57] However, the continued validity of these latter Chancery Court decisions was subsequently called into question by the Delaware Supreme Court in *Paramount Communications, Inc. v. Time Incorporated*,[58] excerpted below in Section 14.03[D][3].

Even if the board's action complies with the *Unocal* test, the board must still exercise due care in order to be entitled to the protection of the business judgment rule (*see* Section 9.03). This has been a significant issue in many takeover defense cases. See, for example, *Hanson Trust PLC v. MLSCM Acquisition, Inc.*[59] which invalidated a lockup given by the SCM board in connection with a management buyout engineered by a unit

---

[53]   Courts have sometimes invalidated flip-in plans on this ground. *See, e.g., Amalgamated Sugar Co. v. NL Indus., Inc.*, 644 F. Supp. 1229 (S.D.N.Y. 1986).

[54]   794 F.2d 250 (7th Cir. 1986), *rev'd on other grounds*, 481 U.S. 69 (1987).

[55]   *See, e.g., TW Services, Inc. v. SWT Acquisition Corp.*, Fed. Sec. L. Rep. (CCH) ¶ 94,334 (Del. Ch. 1989); *MAI Basic Four, Inc. v. Prime Computer, Inc.*, Fed. Sec. L. Rep. (CCH) ¶ 94,179 (Del. Ch. 1988).

[56]   535 A.2d 1334 (Del. 1987).

[57]   *See Grand Metropolitan PLC v. The Pillsbury Co.*, 558 A.2d 1049 (Del. Ch. 1988); *City Capital Associates L.P. v. Interco Inc.*, 551 A.2d 787 (Del. Ch. 1988).

[58]   571 A.2d 1140 (Del. 1990).

[59]   781 F.2d 264 (2d Cir. 1986).

of Merrill, Lynch. (In addition to the lockup, Merrill Lynch received a bounty of many millions of dollars in actual or potential fees for initiating the deal and to compensate it in case the deal fell through—a "hello" fee, a "hello-again" fee and a "goodbye" fee.) The court criticized such things as the absence of a fair value opinion by the investment banker that had advised the board, the extent of director reliance on the investment banker's advice, and the lack of an independent negotiating committee. All of this was enough to shift to SCM the burden of proof as to whether the transaction should be preliminarily enjoined, including the burden of rebutting plaintiff's evidence that the sale was for too low a price.

(7) **Board power to act.** In addition to the fiduciary duty issues raised by moves like those in *Unocal* and *Moran*, there are also significant issues concerning the board's power to act under the statute and other governance documents. In *Unocal*, the court held that Unocal's selective exchange offer was within the board's power to repurchase stock under Delaware G.C.L. § 160(a). Note, however, that the selective repurchase distributed the corporation's assets unequally among shareholders in the same class, contrary to the general rule that shareholders shall be treated equally within classes. *See* Del. G.C.L. § 151(a). Is the *Unocal* court's greenmail analogy a persuasive rebuttal on this point? Further, the effect of the repurchase, because of its discriminatory nature, was to fundamentally change the shareholders' rights by preventing the shareholders from transferring control. Consider the summary in Note 4 above of the *Moran* court's response to the argument that the Household poison pill rights plan usurped the shareholders' rights to receive tender offers.

Moran held that the rights plan was authorized by Del. G.C.L. §§ 151(g) and 157 despite appellants' arguments that § 157 was not intended to authorize anti-takeover moves, that the rights were "shams" because they were never intended to be exercised, and that § 157 does not authorize the issuance of rights to purchase the shares of another firm. As to the first argument, the court declined to read such a limitation into the statute. With respect to the second argument, the court said it was enough that the rights can be exercised. (But is it likely that any shareholders would ever exercise the rights to buy preferred stock at $10,000 per share? The value of the rights is indicated by the $.50 redemption price.) As to the third argument, the court found persuasive an analogy to "anti-dilution" provisions commonly found in instruments protecting the rights of holders of convertible securities. Do you agree? In finding the rights plan within the board's power, the court also noted the board's general power to manage under Delaware § 141(a).

(8) **Protecting stakeholders.** To what extent may the directors adopt takeover defenses that injure the shareholders but protect non-shareholder interests? Although some cases purport to recognize such a power, they do not let the board entirely disregard shareholder interests. For example, *Unocal* and its progeny let the board have regard for other corporate constituencies, but only where there are rationally related benefits to the shareholders. Consider the discussion of this issue in *Revlon* excerpted below.

ALI *Principles* § 6.02(b)(2) allows the board, in determining whether to block a bid, to "have regard for interests or groups (other than shareholders) with respect to which the corporation has a legitimate concern if to do so would not significantly disfavor the long-term interests of shareholders." Some state statutes permit directors to consider the interests of non-shareholder constituencies. *See* Note 4 following *CTS* in Section 14.03[E]. To the extent that these statutes permit the directors to disregard shareholder interests in favor of the interests of other groups, they may override case law limitations on the exercise of director discretion.

Should directors be able to adopt defensive moves that help "stakeholders," while injuring shareholders? Managers surely must obey specific laws, such as plant closing laws, that protect various corporate constituencies injured by takeovers. They also must comply with contracts with non-shareholder groups. For example, consumer cooperatives must be run for the benefit of their consumer-owners, and cannot be sold without the consumer-owners' consent. Employees are protected by collective bargaining agreements. Creditors can, and have, contracted for bond covenants (called "poison puts") that give them a right of redemption in the event of certain types of takeovers. The question is whether managers should be able to exercise their discretion to confer protection on non-shareholder groups beyond what is required by their contracts or applicable regulation.

Some writers assert that stakeholders have rights under "implied contracts." For example, **Shliefer & Summers** argue that firms try to minimize contracting costs with labor and other groups through long-term implicit contracts backed up by managers who develop life-long credibility as "enforcers" of these "contracts." If managers cannot resist hostile takeovers for the benefit of stakeholders, stakeholders might mistrust implicit bargains, thereby raising the firm's bargaining costs. The question is whether the benefits to stakeholders and the corresponding reduction in the costs of bargaining with them are likely to offset increased agency costs to shareholders by removing the discipline of the takeover market. Note that stakeholders would not necessarily gain as much as shareholders lose because, if managers could ignore profits, they would be free to serve their own interests at the expense of all these groups.

What is the appropriate balancing point? Should the board be able to rebuff a takeover under circumstances where stakeholders would be benefited and shareholders would be hurt as long as shareholders' loss is not material?

(9) **Toward a test for directors' takeover defenses.** What should be directors' duties in responding to takeovers? A *Unocal*-type "enhanced business judgment rule" can make litigation of defensive moves quite costly because these duties generate complex, fact-specific issues. Incumbent managers, who usually do not bear litigation costs, have an incentive to push questions into court, thereby deterring potential bidders who may incur substantial costs from the entrenching moves and associated litigation. An alternative would be to apply a "limited power" approach under which the board would not be allowed to preclude shareholders from transferring control, but would be subject to the ordinary business judgment rule with respect to acts that fall short of such preclusion (*see* **Ribstein**). This would ensure that the board is immune from judicial second-guessing, but only as long as its actions are ultimately subject to market scrutiny. Is

Delaware law, as ultimately expressed in *Time* and *QVC*, below, consistent with the latter approach?

REFERENCES

Allen, *Our Schizophrenic Conception of the Business Corporation*, 14 CARDOZO L. REV. 261 (1992).

Carney, *The Corporate Stakeholder Conference: Introduction*, 43 U. TORONTO L.J. 297 (1993).

Carney, *Does Defining Constituencies Matter?*, 59 U. CIN. L. REV. 385 (1990).

Coffee, *The Uncertain Case for Takeover Reform: An Essay on Stockholders, Stakeholders and Bust-Ups*, 1988 WIS. L. REV. 435.

Easterbrook & Fischel, *The Proper Role of a Target's Management in Responding to a Tender Offer*, 94 HARV. L. REV. 1161 (1982).

Macey, *An Economic Analysis of the Various Rationales for Making Shareholders the Exclusive Beneficiaries of Corporate Fiduciary Duties*, 21 STETSON L. REV. 23 (1991).

Macey, *Externalities, Firm-Specific Capital Investments and the Legal Treatment of Fundamental Corporate Changes*, 1989 DUKE L.J. 173.

O'Connor, *The Human Capital Era: Reconceptualizing Corporate Law to Facilitate Labor Management Cooperation*, 78 CORNELL L. REV. 899 (1993).

O'Connor, *Restructuring the Corporation's Nexus of Contracts: Recognizing a Fiduciary Duty to Protect Displaced Workers*, 69 N.C. L. REV. 1189 (1991).

Ribstein, *Takeover Defenses and the Corporate Contract*, 78 GEO. L.J. 71 (1989).

Shleifer & Summers, *Breach of Trust in Hostile Takeovers*, *in* CORPORATE TAKEOVERS: CAUSES AND CONSEQUENCES (Auerbach, ed. 1988).

REVLON INC. v. MACANDREWS & FORBES HOLDINGS, INC.
Delaware Supreme Court
506 A.2d 173 (1986)

MOORE, Justice:

In this battle for corporate control of Revlon, Inc. (Revlon), the Court of Chancery enjoined certain transactions designed to thwart the efforts of Pantry Pride, Inc. (Pantry Pride) to acquire Revlon. The defendants are Revlon, its board of directors, and Forstmann Little & Co. and the latter's affiliated limited partnership (collectively Forstmann). The injunction barred consummation of an option granted Forstmann to purchase certain Revlon assets (the lock-up option), a promise by Revlon to deal exclusively with Forstmann in the face of a takeover (the no-shop provision), and the payment of a $25 million cancellation fee to Forstmann if the transaction was aborted. . . .

In our view, lock-ups and related agreements are permitted under Delaware law where their adoption is untainted by director interest or other breaches of fiduciary duty. The actions taken by the Revlon directors, however, did not meet this standard. Moreover, while concern for various corporate constituencies is proper when addressing a takeover threat, that principle is limited by the requirement that there be some rationally related benefit accruing to the stockholders. We find no such benefit here.

Thus, under all the circumstances we must agree with the Court of Chancery that the enjoined Revlon defensive measures were inconsistent with the directors' duties to the stockholders. Accordingly, we affirm.

I.

The somewhat complex maneuvers of the parties necessitate a rather detailed examination of the facts. The prelude to this controversy been in June, 1985, when Ronald O. Perelman, chairman of the board and chief executive officer of Pantry Pride, met with his counterpart at Revlon, Michel C. Bergerac, to discuss a friendly acquisition of Revlon by Pantry Pride. Perelman suggested a price in the range of $40-50 per share, but the meeting ended with Bergerac dismissing those figures as considerably below Revlon's intrinsic value. All subsequent Pantry Pride overtures were rebuffed, perhaps in part based on Mr. Bergerac's strong personal antipathy to Mr. Perelman.

Thus, on August 14, Pantry Pride's board authorized Perelman to acquire Revlon, either through negotiation in the $42-$43 per share range, or by making a hostile tender offer at $45. Perelman then met with Bergerac and outlined Pantry Pride's alternate approaches. Bergerac remained adamantly opposed to such schemes and conditioned any further discussions of the matter on Pantry Pride executing a standstill agreement prohibiting it from acquiring Revlon without the latter's prior approval.

On August 19, the Revlon board met specially to consider the impending threat of a hostile bid by Pantry Pride.[3]

At the meeting, Lazard Freres, Revlon's investment banker, advised the directors that $45 per share was a grossly inadequate price for the company. Felix Rohatyn and William Loomis of Lazard Freres explained to the board that Pantry Pride's financial strategy for acquiring Revlon would be through "junk bond" financing followed by a break-up of Revlon and the disposition of its assets. With proper timing, according to the experts, such transactions could produce a return to Pantry Pride of $60 to $70 per share, while a sale of the company as a whole would be in the "mid 50" dollar range. Martin Lipton, special counsel for Revlon, recommended two defensive measures: first, that the company repurchase up to 5 million of its nearly 30 million outstanding shares; and second, that it adopt a Note Purchase Rights Plan. Under this plan, each Revlon shareholder would receive as a dividend one Note Purchase Right (the Rights) for each share of common stock, with the Rights entitling the holder to exchange one common share for a $65 principal Revlon note at 12% interest with a one-year maturity. The Rights would become effective whenever anyone acquired beneficial ownership of 20% or more of Revlon's shares, unless the purchaser acquired all the company's stock for cash at $65 or more per share. In addition, the Rights would not be available to the acquiror, and prior to the 20% triggering event the Revlon board could redeem the rights for 10 cents each. Both proposals were unanimously adopted.

---

[3]　There were 14 directors on the Revlon board. Six of them held senior management positions with the company, and two others held significant blocks of its stock. Four of the remaining six directors were associated at some point with entities that had various business relationships with Revlon. On the basis of this limited record, however, we cannot conclude that this board is entitled to certain presumptions that generally attach to the decisions of a board whose majority consists of truly outside independent directors. [citations omitted]

Pantry Pride made its first hostile move on August 23 with a cash tender offer for any and all shares of Revlon at $47.50 per common share and $26.67 per preferred share, subject to (1) Pantry Pride's obtaining financing for the purchase, and (2) the Rights being redeemed, rescinded or voided.

The Revlon board met again on August 26. The directors advised the stockholders to reject the offer. Further defensive measures also were planned. On August 29, Revlon commenced its own offer for up to 10 million shares, exchanging for each share of common stock tendered one Senior Subordinated Note (the Notes) of $47.50 principal at 11.75% interest, due 1995, and one-tenth of a share of $9.00 Cumulative Convertible Exchangeable Preferred Stock valued at $100 per share. Lazard Freres opined that the notes would trade at their face value on a fully distributed basis. Revlon stockholders tendered 87 percent of the outstanding shares (approximately 33 million), and the company accepted the first 10 million shares on a pro rata basis. The new Notes contained covenants which limited Revlon's ability to incur additional debt, sell assets, or pay dividends unless otherwise approved by the "independent" (non-management) members of the board.

At this point, both the Rights and the Note covenants stymied Pantry Pride's attempted takeover. The next move came on September 16, when Pantry Pride announced a new tender offer at $42 per share, conditioned upon receiving at least 90% of the outstanding stock. Pantry Pride also indicated that it would consider buying less than 90%, and at an increased price, if Revlon removed the impeding Rights. While this offer was lower on its face than the earlier $47.50 proposal, Revlon's investment banker, Lazard Freres, described the two bids as essentially equal in view of the completed exchange offer.

The Revlon board held a regularly scheduled meeting on September 24. The directors rejected the latest Pantry Pride offer and authorized management to negotiate with other parties interested in acquiring Revlon. Pantry Pride remained determined in its efforts and continued to make cash bids for the company, offering $50 per share on September 27, and raising its bid to $53 on October 1, and then to $56.25 on October 7.

In the meantime, Revlon's negotiations with Forstmann and the investment group Adler & Shaykin had produced results. The Revlon directors met on October 3 to consider Pantry Pride's $53 bid and to examine possible alternatives to the offer. Both Forstmann and Adler & Shaykin made certain proposals to the board. As a result, the directors unanimously agreed to a leveraged buyout by Forstmann. The terms of this accord were as follows: each stockholder would get $56 cash per share; management would purchase stock in the new company by the exercise of their Revlon "golden parachutes"; Forstmann would assume Revlon's $475 million debt incurred by the issuance of the Notes; and Revlon would redeem the Rights and waive the Notes covenants for Forstmann or in connection with any other offer superior to Forstmann's. . . .

When the merger, and thus the waiver of the Notes covenants, was announced, the market value of these securities began to fall. The Notes, which originally traded near par, around 100, dropped to 87.50 by October 8. One director later reported (at the October 12 meeting) a "deluge" of telephone calls from irate noteholders, and on October 10 the Wall Street Journal reported threats of litigation by these creditors.

Pantry Pride countered with a new proposal on October 7, raising its $53 offer to $56.25, subject to nullification of the Rights, a waiver of the Notes covenants, and the election of three Pantry Pride directors to the Revlon board. On October 9, representatives of

Pantry Pride, Forstmann and Revlon conferred in an attempt to negotiate the fate of Revlon, but could not reach agreement. At this meeting Pantry Pride announced that it would engage in fractional bidding and top any Forstmann offer by a slightly higher one. It is also significant that Forstmann, to Pantry Pride's exclusion, had been made privy to certain Revlon financial data. Thus, the parties were not negotiating on equal terms. Again privately armed with Revlon data, Forstmann met on October 11 with Revlon's special counsel and investment banker. On October 12, Forstmann made a new $57.25 per share offer, based on severalconditions. The principal demand was a lock-up option to purchase Revlon's Vision Care and National Health Laboratories divisions for $525 million, some $100-$175 million below the value ascribed to them by Lazard Freres, if another acquiror got 40% of Revlon's shares. Revlon also was required to accept a no-shop provision. The Rights and Notes covenants had to be removed as in the October 3 agreement. There would be a $25 million cancellation fee to be placed in escrow, and released to Forstmann if the new agreement terminated or if another acquiror got more than 19.9% of Revlon's stock. Finally, there would be no participation by Revlon management in the merger. In return, Forstmann agreed to support the par value of the Notes, which had faltered in the market, by an exchange of new notes. Forstmann also demanded immediate acceptance of its offer, or it would be withdrawn. The board unanimously approved Forstmann's proposal because: (1) it was for a higher.price than the Pantry Pride bid, (2) it protected the noteholders, and (3) Forstmann's financing was firmly in place.[7]

The board further agreed to redeem the rights and waive the covenants on the preferred stock in response to any offer above $57 cash per share. The covenants were waived, contingent upon receipt of an investment banking opinion that the Notes would trade near par value once the offer was consummated.

Pantry Pride, which had initially sought injunctive relief from the Rights plan on August 22, filed an amended complaint on October 14 challenging the lock-up, the cancellation fee, and the exercise of the Rights and the Notes covenants. Pantry Pride also sought a temporary restraining order to prevent Revlon from placing any assets in escrow or transferring them to Forstmann. Moreover, on October 22, Pantry Pride again raised its bid, with a cash offer of $58 per share conditioned upon nullification of the Rights, waiver of the covenants, and an injunction of the Forstmann lock-up.

On October 15, the Court of Chancery prohibited the further transfer of assets, and eight days later enjoined the lock-up, no-shop, and cancellation fee provisions of the agreement. The trial court concluded that the Revlon directors had breached their duty of loyalty by making concessions to Forstmann, out of concern for their liability to the noteholders, rather than maximizing the sale price of the company for the stockholders' benefit. *MacAndrews & Forbes Holdings, Inc v. Revlon, Inc.*, 501 A.2d at 1249-50.

---

[7]   Actually, at this time about $400 million of Forstmann's financing was still subject to two investment banks using their "best efforts" to organize a syndicate to provide the balance. Pantry Pride's entire financing was not firmly committed at this point either, although Pantry Pride represented in an October 11 letter to Lazard Freres that its investment banker, Drexel Burnham Lambert, was highly confident of its ability to raise the balance of $350 million. Drexel Burnham had a firm commitment for this sum by October 18.

II.

To obtain a preliminary injunction, a plaintiff must demonstrate both a reasonable probability of success on the merits and some irreparable harm which will occur absent the injunction. . . .

A.

We turn first to Pantry Pride's probability of success on the merits. . . . "[W]hen a board implements anti-takeover measures there arises "the omnipresent specter that a board may be acting primarily in its own interests, rather than those of the corporation and its shareholders . . . ." *Unocal Corp. v. Mesa Petroleum Co.*, 493 A.2d at 954. This potential for conflict places upon the directors the burden of proving that they had reasonable grounds for believing there was a danger to corporate policy and effectiveness, a burden satisfied by a showing of good faith and reasonable investigation. *Id.* at 955. In addition, the directors must analyze the nature of the takeover and its effect on the corporation in order to ensure balance—that the responsive action taken is reasonable in relation to the threat posed. *Id.*

B.

The first relevant defensive measure adopted by the Revlon board was the Rights Plan, which would be considered a "poison pill" in the current language of corporate takeovers . . . .

The Revlon board approved the Rights Plan in the face of an impending hostile takeover bid by Pantry Pride at $45 per share, a price which Revlon reasonably concluded was grossly inadequate. . . . In adopting the Plan, the board protected the shareholders from a hostile takeover at a price below the company's intrinsic value, while retaining sufficient flexibility to address any proposal deemed to be in the stockholders' best interests.

To that extent the board acted in good faith and upon reasonable investigation. Under the circumstances it cannot be said that the Rights Plan as employed was unreasonable, considering the threat posed. Indeed, the Plan was a factor in causing Pantry Pride to raise its bids from a low of $42 to an eventual high of $58. . . .

* * *

C.

The second defensive measure adopted by Revlon to thwart a Pantry Pride takeover was the company's own exchange offer for 10 million of its shares. . . .

The Revlon directors concluded that Pantry Pride's $47.50 offer was grossly inadequate. In that regard the board acted in good faith, and on an informed basis, with reasonable grounds to believe that there existed a harmful threat to the corporate enterprise. The adoption of a defensive measure, reasonable in relation to the threat posed, was proper and fully accorded with the powers, duties, and responsibilities conferred upon directors under our law. [citations omitted]

D.

However, when Pantry Pride increased its offer to $50 per share, and then to $53, it became apparent to all that the break-up of the company was inevitable. The Revlon board's authorization permitting management to negotiate a merger or buyout with a third party was a recognition that the company was for sale. The duty of the board had thus changed from the preservation of Revlon as a corporate entity to the maximization of the company's value at a sale for the stockholders' benefit. This significantly altered the board's responsibilities under the *Unocal* standards. It no longer faced threats to corporate policy and effectiveness, or to the stockholders' interests, from a grossly inadequate bid. The whole question of defensive measures became moot. The directors' role changed from defenders of the corporate bastion to auctioneers charged with getting the best price for the stockholders at a sale of the company.

III.

This brings us to the lock-up with Forstmann and its emphasis on shoring up the sagging market value of the Notes in the face of threatened litigation by their holders. Such a focus was inconsistent with the changed concept of the directors' responsibilities at this stage of the developments. The impending waiver of the Notes covenants had caused the value of the Notes to fall, and the board was aware of the noteholders' ire as well as their subsequent threats of suit. The directors thus made support of the Notes an integral part of the company's dealings with Forstmann, even though their primary responsibility at this stage was to the equity owners.

* * *

The Revlon board argued that it acted in good faith in protecting the noteholders because *Unocal* permits consideration of other corporate constituencies. Although such considerations may be permissible, there are fundamental limitations upon that prerogative. A board may have regard for various constituencies in discharging its responsibilities, provided there are rationally related benefits a to the stockholders. *Unocal*, 493 A.2d at 955. However, such concern for non-stockholder interests is inappropriate when an auction among active bidders is in progress, and the object no longer is to protect or maintain the corporate enterprise but to sell it to the highest bidder.

Revlon also contended that by *Gilbert v. El Paso Co.*, Del. Ch., 490 A.2d 1050, 1054-55 (1984), it had contractual and good faith obligations to consider the noteholders. However, any such duties are limited to the principle that one may not interfere with contractual relationships by improper actions. Here, the rights of the noteholders were fixed by agreement, and there is nothing of substance to suggest that any of those terms were violated. The Notes covenants specifically contemplated a waiver to permit sale of the company at a fair price. The Notes were accepted by the holders on that basis, including the risk of an adverse market effect stemming from a waiver. Thus, nothing remained for Revlon to legitimately protect, and no rationally related benefit thereby accrued to the stockholders. Under such circumstances we must conclude that the merger agreement with Forstmann was unreasonable in relation to the threat posed.

A lock-up is not per se illegal under Delaware law. Such options can entice other bidders to enter a contest for control of the corporation, creating an auction for the company and maximizing shareholder profit. Current economic conditions in the takeover market are such that a "white knight" like Forstmann might only enter the bidding for the target company if it receives some form of compensation to cover the risks and costs involved. However, while those lock-ups which draw bidders into the battle benefit shareholders, similar measures which end an active auction and foreclose further bidding operate to the shareholders' detriment.

* * *

The Forstmann option had a . . . destructive effect on the auction process. Forstmann had already been drawn into the contest on a preferred basis, so the result of the lock-up was not to foster bidding, but to destroy it. The board's stated reasons for approving the transaction were: (1) better financing, (2) noteholder protection, and (3) higher price. As the Court of Chancery found, and we agree, any distinctions between the rival bidders' methods of financing the proposal were nominal at best, and such a consideration has little or no significance in a cash offer for any and all shares. The principal object, contrary to the board's duty of care, appears to have been protection of the noteholders over the shareholders' interests.

While Forstmann's $57.25 offer was objectively higher than Pantry Pride's $56.25 bid, the margin of superiority is less when the Forstmann price is adjusted for the time value of money. In reality, the Revlon board ended the auction in return for very little actual improvement in the final bid. The principal benefit went to the directors, who avoided personal liability to a class of creditors to whom the board owed no further duty under the circumstances. Thus, when a board ends an intense bidding contest on an insubstantial basis and where a significant by-product of that action is to protect the directors against a perceived threat of personal liability for consequences stemming from the adoption of previous defensive measures, the action cannot withstand the enhanced scrutiny which *Unocal* requires of director conduct. *See Unocal*, 493 A.2d at 954-55.

. . . The no-shop provision, like the lock-up option, while not per se illegal, is impermissible under the *Unocal* standards when a board's primary duty becomes that of an auctioneer responsible for selling the company to the highest bidder. The agreement to negotiate only with Forstmann ended rather than intensified the board's involvement in the bidding contest.

It is ironic that the parties even considered a no-shop agreement when Revlon had dealt preferentially, and almost exclusively, with Forstmann throughout the contest. After the directors authorized management to negotiate with other parties, Forstmann was given every negotiating advantage that Pantry Pride had been denied: cooperation from management, access to financial data, and the exclusive opportunity to present merger proposals directly to the board of directors. Favoritism for a white knight to the total exclusion of a hostile bidder might be justifiable when the latter's offer adversely affects shareholder interests, but when bidders make relatively similar offers, or dissolution of the company becomes inevitable, the directors cannot fulfill their enhanced *Unocal* duties by playing favorites with the contending factions. Market forces must be allowed to operate freely to bring the target's shareholders the best price available for their equity.[16]

---

[16]   By this we do not embrace the "passivity" thesis rejected in *Unocal*. *See* 493 A.2d at 954-55, nn. 8-10. The directors' role remains an active one, changed only in the respect that they are charged with the duty of selling the company at the highest price attainable for the stockholders' benefit.

Thus, as the trial court ruled, the shareholders' interests necessitated that the board remain free to negotiate in the fulfillment of that duty.

The court below similarly enjoined the payment of the cancellation fee, pending a resolution of the merits, because the fee was part of the overall plan to thwart Pantry Pride's efforts. We find no abuse of discretion in that ruling.

* * *

V.

In conclusion, the Revlon board was confronted with a situation not uncommon in the current wave of corporate takeovers. A hostile and deter-mined bidder sought the company at a price the board was convinced was inadequate. The initial defensive tactics worked to the benefit of the shareholders, and thus the board was able to sustain its Unocal burdens in justifying those measures. However, in granting an asset option lock-up to Forstmann, we must conclude that under all the circumstances the directors allowed considerations other than the maximization of shareholder profit to affect their judgment, and followed a course that ended the auction for Revlon, absent court intervention, to the ultimate detriment of its shareholders. No such defensive measure can be sustained when it represents a breach of the directors' fundamental duty of care. *See Smith v. Van Gorkom*, Del. Supr., 488 A.2d 858, 874 (1985). In that context the board's action is not entitled to the deference accorded it by the business judgment rule. The measures were properly enjoined. The decision of the Court of Chancery, therefore, is

Affirmed.

NOTES AND QUESTIONS

(1) **The Revlon battle.** The Revlon-Pantry Pride battle was one of the more colorful and costly takeover contests. It was a classic case of conflicting styles and philosophies. Revlon was founded in 1932 by Charles and Joseph Revson and Charles R. Lachman. Michel Bergerac had taken over in 1974 and diversified Revlon into a multibillion dollar health care-cosmetics conglomerate. At the time of the takeover contest, his "perks" included $1.3 million in salary and bonus, and use of a Boeing 727 equipped with a kitchen, bedroom, living room, backgammon board, and gun rack. When Bergerac claimed that Ronald Perelman of Pantry Pride had offered to "greatly improve my life style" if he did not resist Perelman's initial overture, Perelman responded, "I don't think that could ever be improved on." Perelman was a 42-year-old upstart who owned a much smaller conglomerate, MacAndrews & Forbes Holdings, which specialized in "bust-up" takeovers: It acquired companies and profited by selling off their divisions for more than the value of the combined company. Perelman saw in Revlon an opportunity for this kind of profit.

Revlon's all-out defense was led by, among others, Felix Rohatyn of Lazard Freres & Company, a leading figure in the bailout of New York City; Martin Lipton, the inventor of the "poison pill" and 100 lawyers at the firm of Wachtell, Lipton, Rosen & Katz; Arthur L. Liman, the counsel to the "Iran-gate" committee; and a Revlon board that encompassed both New York Post gossip columnist Suzy Knickerbocker and Judge Simon H. Rifkin. Both sides in the contest had reportedly adopted the slogan "It ain't over 'til the fat lady sings," with Revlon even printing up t-shirts with that slogan. [Apparently the "fat lady" turned out to be the Delaware Supreme Court.] In the end, advisers for both sides earned over $100 million in fees, including over $60 million for Drexel Burnham alone, but not including Forstmann Little's $25.million fee, which was disapproved by the Delaware court. Bergerac was consoled with $36 million in stock and severance payments, but was apparently not happy. He said: "Here we built a great American corporation. Then through this process the stock ended up in the hands of the arbitrageurs, who forced the sale of the company. And junk bond financing made it all possible."[60]

The Revlon battle was a major victory for Kohlberg Kravis, Drexel Burnham and their "junk bond" arsenal over the less highly leveraged sort of financing used by Forstmann, Little. "Junk bonds" dominated takeovers for the next four years, culminating in the $30 billion RJR Nabisco takeover, also engineered by Kohlberg Kravis. *See* Note 7, below.

(2) **The *Revlon* duty.** *Revlon* added further complication to the law governing takeover defenses when it held that, on the Revlon board's authorization of negotiations for a buyout or merger, "[t]he directors' role changed from defenders of the corporate bastion to auctioneers charged with getting the best price for the stockholders in a sale of the company." This special duty to maximize shareholder interests may be even more stringent than the enhanced business judgment test under *Unocal*. This duty may be based on the concern that the takeover will lock up control in a close-knit group or leave the corporation closely held without shareholder approval. But is the *Revlon* duty triggered by all sales of control? For further consideration of this issue, see *Time* and *QVC*, excerpted in Subsection [3] below.

(3) **Lockups.** As discussed in Section 14.03[A][2][e], devices that "lock-up" a sale of the corporation or otherwise give one bidder an advantage over other bidders come in a variety of shapes and forms, including the low-priced asset lock-up, cancellation fee, and no-shop that the Revlon board granted to Forstmann Little. Another example is the million-share sale to the Pritzkers in *Van Gorkom*, Section 9.03[B]. Lockups and related devices might encourage auctions because they draw bidders into control contests by reducing their risk of losing expenses sunk into making a bid. Compare **Ayres** and **Schwartz**. Was this the case in *Revlon*? (On the more general question of whether management should have an active role in facilitating auctions, see subsection 14.03[B][1][d].) As discussed in Section 14.03[A][2][e], the general policy question is whether the benefits of lock-ups in promoting auctions outweighs potential costs, including those of letting managers reap "side payments" from favored bidders. *See* **Coates & Subramanian**.

---

[60]   The above account is based on, and the quotes are from, Cole, *High-Stakes Drama at Revlon*, N.Y. TIMES, Nov. 11, 1985, at 23, 36.

(4) **The board's power to act: the relationship between lock-ups and share-holder approval of sales of control.** Some lock-up devices can have the effect of selling the company to the favored bidder without shareholder approval. So should directors be denied the power to grant lock-ups without shareholder approval irrespective of whether they increase shareholder wealth? If so, should the same analysis apply to no-shops? Note that no-shops do not impose a penalty on the target company if the favored bidder does not acquire control. They also arguably are consistent with statutory provisions like Del. G.C.L. §§ 251 and 271, which appear to give the board the power to screen transactions by permitting shareholder approval only of those transactions that are submitted by the board. *Hills Stores Co. v. Bozic*[61] refused to apply the *Blasius* "compelling justification" standard (*see* Section 14.02[A]) to devices that penalize the corporation when shareholders reject managers' recommendation, at least where the financial penalty is not so large as to constitute a coercive influence. The court reasoned that there was no need to add *Blasius* to tests already available under *Unocal*, *Revlon*, and *Brazen*.[62]

(5) **Board power to act: tortious interference with merger agreements.** The board's power with regard to sales of control has been considered where the board entered into a no-shop agreement with a bidder that bound it to recommend that the shareholders approve a sale to that bidder but the board ultimately sided with a competing bidder.[63] The question in these cases is whether the winning bidder is liable for tortious interference with the no shop agreement. *Jewel Companies v. Pay Less Drug Stores Northwest*[64] upheld a claim for interference with a merger agreement that the shareholders had not approved. The court held that the board can at least bind itself not to accept a competing offer until the shareholders have voted on the initial agreement, but did not decide whether the board could bind itself to recommend the initial proposal even if it later receives a better offer, and remanded for a determination of whether the corporation was in fact so bound under the agreement at issue. The court relied in part on a provision in the applicable California Corporation Code that appeared to recognize a third-party breach of contract claim if the merger was abandoned prior to shareholder vote.

On the other hand, *ConAgra, Inc v. Cargill, Inc.*[65] held that summary judgment should have been entered for defendant Cargill on a claim that Cargill had interfered

---

[61]   2000 Del. Ch. LEXIS 28, 2000 WL 238007 (Del. Ch., Feb. 22, 2000).

[62]   *Brazen v. Bell Atlantic Corp.*, 695 A.2d 43 (Del. 1997), applies to liquidated damages. *See* Note 8 following the *QVC* excerpt in Section 14.03[D][3] below.

[63]   The case may present the threshold issue of whether there was an agreement. In *Pennzoil Co. v. Texaco, Inc.*, (151st Judicial District of Texas, 1985), *aff'd,* 729 S.W.2d 768 (Tex. Civ. App. 1987), Texaco lost a judgment on a jury verdict for $11.12 billion for interfering with a Pennzoil-Getty handshake "agreement in principle" to merge. For discussions of this issue see Epstein, *The Pirates of Pennzoil*, REGULATION (December, 1985); Tempkin, *When Does the "Fat Lady" Sing?: An Analysis of Agreements in Principle*, in CORPORATE ACQUISTIONS, 55 FORD. L. REV. 125 (1986).

[64]   741 F.2d 1555 (9th Cir. 1984).

[65]   222 Neb. 136, 382 N.W.2d 576 (1986).

with a merger agreement between ConAgra and MBPXL. The MBPXL board canceled the shareholder meeting scheduled for approval of the ConAgra merger and recommended that the shareholders accept Cargill's friendly tender offer. The court held that a shareholder vote was required to bind the corporation to a merger under Delaware G.C.L. § 251. Moreover, the merger agreement provided that the directors' obligation to effectuate the merger was subject to their "continuing duties to their respective shareholders," which included a duty to continue to act in the shareholders' best interests after entering into the initial agreement and, therefore, to recommend higher offers. Thus, even if the directors were bound to submit the ConAgra proposal to the shareholders, there was insufficient evidence that any such inaction was the proximate cause of ConAgra's loss, since it was highly unlikely that the shareholders would have accepted the ConAgra offer. There was a strong dissent, relying largely on *Jewel*. Similarly, *NBT Bancorp Inc. v. Fleet/Norstar Financial Group Inc.*[66] rejected claims that Norstar tortiously interfered with a merger agreement between NBT Bancorp and Central National Bank by making a higher offer that led the Central board to cancel the shareholder meeting and withdraw its recommendation of the merger. The court held, in part, that there was no breach of contract on which to base the tortuous interference claim.

(6) **Fiduciary duty analysis of lock-ups and related devices.** Despite the potential impact of lock-ups on shareholder power to approve sales of the company, the courts apparently have upheld the board's power to enter into lock-ups and related devices that favor one bidder over another, and have instead considered favoritism of selected bidders as a fiduciary duty problem. Several courts have invalidated lockups where, as in *Revlon*, they had the effect of ending an auction in favor of the bidder selected by incumbent management.[67] *Mills Acquisition Co. v. MacMillan, Inc.*[68] held that the directors could justify a lockup or similar device by showing that shareholder interests were enhanced and that the board's favoritism was "reasonable in relation to the advantage sought to be achieved, or conversely, to the threat which a particular bid allegedly poses to stockholder interests."[69] How might this test have been satisfied in the *Revlon* setting? For further discussion of the board's duty in entering into lockups and related agreements, see *Paramount Communications, Inc. v. QVC Network, Inc.*, excerpted below.

(7) **The management buyout.** Commentators, particularly including **Brudney & Chirelstein**, long have suggested that courts should scrutinize closely sales of control to groups that include incumbent managers, as in the typical leveraged management buyout. These transactions arguably involve special problems of insider conflict of

---

[66]   67 N.Y.2d 614 (1996).

[67]   *See, e.g., Hanson Trust PLC v. MLSCM Acquisition, Inc.*, 781 F.2d 264 (2d Cir. 1986) (invalidating lock-up although it succeeded in eliciting a higher bid and board made an extensive inquiry as to value and procured an investment banker's valuation).

[68]   559 A.2d 1261 (Del. 1989).

[69]   559 A.2d at 1288.

interest, potential abuse of inside information, and the need to ensure the other bidders can compete on a level playing field with the management group. Consistently with this analysis, *Mills Acquisition*, discussed in Note 6 above, applied to a management buyout the "entire fairness" rule that is generally applicable to self-dealing transactions. *See* Section 9.04. In *Mills Acquisition*, the court found that heightened judicial scrutiny was necessary because insiders participating in the buyout had concealed from the board material information about advantages given to the management group and the board failed actively to oversee the auction process. On the other hand, *Barkan v. Amsted Industries, Inc.*[70] refused to apply the entire fairness standard to a management buyout where the independent special committee charged with overseeing the process had acted with due diligence and in good faith.

ALI *Principles* § 5.15 prescribes rules for management buyouts structured as either tender offers or corporate combinations, such as mergers. It provides that interested directors have the burden of proving the transaction is fair unless the buyout is approved by disinterested directors and shareholders, the transaction is publicly disclosed, and potential competing bidders are given information and a reasonable opportunity to submit competing bids. Comment (a)(2) to § 5.15 states that this procedure is "designed to allow the market to operate as the primary check on the fairness of a management buyout." California Corporation Code § 1203, requires, among other things, an independent appraisal of the management's proposal and disclosure to and consideration by shareholders of competing offers.

Do these procedures make sense? **Macey** argues that auctions should not be *required* in management buyouts because they do not necessarily lead to a better price than a negotiated sale to incumbent management. Consistently with Macey's view, the Delaware Supreme Court has stated that, even in the management buyout context, "there is no single blueprint that a board must follow to fulfill its duties."[71] In *Barkan*, the court approved a management buyout even though the special committee was instructed *not* to engage in an active search for alternatives to the MBO.

The 1989 $30 billion RJR Nabisco LBO illustrates the difficulties inherent in applying the special rules applicable to management buyouts.[72] After the chief executive proposed a management buyout, a special RJR board committee, advised closely by outside counsel, attempted to run an auction "by the book." In order to level the bidding playing field, the management group had to provide information to outside bidders. But the outsiders discovered that the executives could not be forced to embrace them with open arms, but instead suffered "collective memory loss."[73] The board also dithered about closing the auction. First management appeared to have won, but bidding was reopened to permit assessment of an outside bid by First Boston that raised difficult tax

---

[70]   567 A.2d 1279 (Del. 1989).

[71]   *Barkan*, 567 A.2d at 1286.

[72]   This transaction is described in entertaining detail in Burroughs & Helyar, Barbarians at the Gate (1990).

[73]   *Id.* at 304.

issues. Then the leading outside bidder, Kohlberg, Kravis Roberts & Co., appeared to have won, but the management group forced the contest to continue by putting an apparently higher bid on the table. In the end, the board had 30 minutes (a time limit set by KKR) to choose between a management bid valued (by management) at $112 per share and a KKR bid valued (by KKR) at $109. The bids involved complex, hard-to-value securities and numerous subtle differences, particularly concerning protecting employees. The board chose the KKR bid, a decision the court subsequently upheld based on findings that the special committee was independent and acted in good faith after gathering all material information reasonably available under the circumstances.[74]

REFERENCES

Ayres, *Analyzing Stock Lock-Ups: Do Target Treasury Sales Foreclose or Facilitate Takeover Auctions?*, 90 COLUM. L. REV. 682 (1990).

Berkovitch, Bradley & Khanna, *Tender Offer Auctions, Resistance Strategies and Social Welfare*, 5 J.L. ECON. & ORG. 395 (1989).

Brudney & Chirelstein, *A Restatement of Corporate Freezeouts*, 87 YALE L.J. 1354 (1978).

Brudney, *A Note on "Going Private,"* 61 VA. L. REV. 1019 (1975).

Coates & Subramanian, *A Buy-Side Model of M&A Lockups: Theory and Evidence*, 53 STAN. L. REV. 307 (2000).

Macey, *Auction Theory, MBOs and Property Rights in Corporate Assets*, 25 WAKE FOREST L. REV. 85 (1990).

Schwartz, *Defensive Tactics and Optimal Search*, 5 J.L. ECON. & ORG. 413 (1989).

[3] Strategic Mergers and Transfers of Control

PARAMOUNT COMMUNICATIONS, INC. v. TIME INCORPORATED
Delaware Supreme Court
571 A.2d 1140 (1990)

HORSEY, Justice:

Paramount Communications, Inc. ("Paramount") and two other groups of plaintiffs ("Shareholder Plaintiffs"), shareholders of Time Incorporated ("Time"), a Delaware corporation, separately filed suits in the Delaware Court of Chancery seeking a preliminary injunction to halt Time's tender offer for 51% of Warner Communication, Inc.'s ("Warner") outstanding shares at $70 cash per share. The court below consolidated the cases and, following the development of an extensive record, after discovery and an evidentiary hearing, denied plaintiffs' motion. . . .

* * *

---

[74]   *See In re RJR Nabisco, Inc. Shareholder Litigation*, 14 DEL. J. CORP. L. 1132 (Del. Ch. 1989).

The principal ground for reversal, asserted by all plaintiffs, is that Paramount's June 7, 1989 uninvited all-cash, all-shares, "fully negotiable" (though conditional) tender offer for Time triggered duties under *Unocal Corp. v. Mesa Petroleum Co.*, Del. Supr., 493 A.2d 946 (1985), and that Time's board of directors, in responding to Paramount's offer, breached those duties. As a consequence, plaintiffs argue that in our review of the Time board's decision of June 16, 1989 to enter into a revised merger agreement with Warner, Time is not entitled to the benefit and protection of the business judgment rule.

Shareholder Plaintiffs also assert a claim based on *Revlon v. MacAndrews & Forbes Holdings, Inc.*, Del. Supr. 506 A.2d 173 (1986). They argue that the original Time-Warner merger agreement of March 4, 1989 resulted in a change of control which effectively put Time up for sale, thereby triggering *Revlon* duties. Those plaintiffs argue that Time's board breached its *Revlon* duties by failing, in the face of the change of control, to maximize shareholder value in the immediate term.

* * *

I

Time is a Delaware corporation with its principal offices in New York City. Time's traditional business is publication of magazines and books; however, Time also provides pay television programming through its Home Box Office, Inc. and Cinemax subsidiaries. In addition, Time owns and operates cable television franchises through is subsidiary, American Television and Communication Corporation. During the relevant time period, Time's board consisted of sixteen directors. Twelve of the directors were "outside," nonemployee directors. Four of the directors were also officers of the company. . . .

As early as 1983 and 1984, Time's executive board began considering expanding Time's operations into the entertainment industry. In 1987, Time established a special committee of executives to consider and propose corporate strategies for the 1990s. The consensus of the committee was that Time should move ahead in the area of ownership and creation of video programming. . . . Some of Time's outside directors, especially Luce and Temple, had opposed this move as a threat to the editorial integrity and journalistic focus of Time.[4] Despite this concern, the board recognized that a vertically integrated video enterprise to complement Time's existing HBO and cable networks would better enable it to compete on a global basis.

* * *

On August 11, 1987, Gerald M. Levin, Time's vice chairman and chief strategist, wrote J. Richard Munro a confidential memorandum in which he strongly recommended a strategic consolidation with Warner. In June 1988, Nicholas and Munro sent to each outside director a copy of the "comprehensive long-term planning document" prepared by the com-

---

[4]   The primary concern of Time's outside directors was the preservation of the "Time Culture." They believed that Time had become recognized in this country as an institution built upon a foundation of journalistic integrity. Time's management made a studious effort to refrain from involvement in Time's editorial policy. Several of Time's outside directors feared that a merger with an entertainment company would divert Time's focus from news journalism and threaten the Time Culture.

mittee of Time executives that had been examining strategies for the 1990s. The memo included reference to and a description of Warner as a potential acquisition candidate.

. . . On July 21, 1988, Time's board met, with all outside directors present. The meeting's purpose was to consider Time's expansion into the entertainment industry on a global scale. Management presented the board with a profile of various entertainment companies in addition to Warner, including Disney, 20th Century Fox, Universal, and Paramount.

Without any definitive decision on choice of a company, the board approved in principle a strategic plan for Time's expansion. The board gave management the "go-ahead" to continue discussions with Warner concerning the possibility of a merger. . . .

The board's consensus was that a merger of Time and Warner was feasible, but only if Time controlled the board of the resulting corporation and thereby preserved a management committed to Time's journalistic integrity. To accomplish this goal, the board stressed the importance of carefully defining in advance the corporate governance provisions that would control the resulting entity. Some board members expressed concern over whether such a business combination would place Time "in play." The board discussed the wisdom of adopting further defensive measures to lessen such a possibility.[5]

Of a wide range of companies considered by Time's board as possible merger candidates, Warner Brothers, Paramount, Columbia, M.C.A., Fox, MGM, Disney, and Orion, the board, in July 1988, concluded that Warner was the superior candidate for such a consolidation. . . .

* * *

From the outset, Time's board favored an all-cash or cash and securities acquisition of Warner as the basis for consolidation. Bruce Wasserstein, Time's financial advisor, also favored an outright purchase of Warner. However, Steve Ross, Warner's CEO, was adamant that a business combination was only practicable on a stock-for-stock basis. Warner insisted on a stock swap in order to preserve its shareholders' equity in the resulting corporation. Time's officers, on the other hand, made it abundantly clear that Time would be the acquiring corporation and that Time would control the resulting board. Time refused to permit itself to be cast as the "acquired" company.

Eventually Time acquiesced in Warner's insistence on a stock-for-stock deal, but talks broke down over corporate governance issues. Time wanted Ross' position as a co-CEO to be temporary and wanted Ross to retire in five years. Ross, however, refused to set a time for his retirement and viewed Time's proposal as indicating a lack of confidence in his leadership. Warner considered it vital that their executives and creative staff not perceive Warner as selling out to Time. . . .

* * *

Warner and Time resumed negotiations in January 1989. . . . Ross agreed to retire in five years and let Nicholas succeed him. Negotiations resumed and many of the details of

---

[5]   Time had in place a panoply of defensive devices, including a staggered board, a "poison pill" preferred stock rights plan triggered by an acquisition of 15% of the company, a fifty-day notice period for shareholder motions, and restrictions on shareholders' ability to call a meeting or act by consent.

the original stock-for-stock exchange agreement remained intact. In addition, Time's senior management agreed to long-term contracts.

Time insider directors Levin and Nicholas met with Warner's financial advisors to decide upon a stock exchange ratio. Time's board had recognized the potential need to pay a premium in the stock ratio in exchange for dictating the governing arrangement of the new Time-Warner. Levin and outside director Finkelstein were the primary proponents of paying a premium to protect the "Time Culture." The board discussed premium rates of 10%, 15% and 20%. Wasserstein also suggested paying a premium for Warner due to Warner's rapid growth rate. The market exchange of ratio of Time stock for Warner stock was .38 in favor of Warner. Warner's financial advisors informed its board that any exchange rate over .400 was a fair deal and any exchange rate over .450 was "one hell of a deal." The parties ultimately agreed upon an exchange rate favoring Warner of .465. On that basis, Warner stockholders would own slightly over 61% of the common stock of Time-Warner.

On March 3, 1989, Time's board, with all but one director in attendance, met and unanimously approved the stock-for-stock merger with Warner. Warner's board likewise approved the merger. The agreement called for Warner to be merged into a wholly-owned Time subsidiary with Warner becoming the surviving corporation. The common stock of Warner would then be converted into common stock of Time at the agreed upon ratio. Thereafter, the name of Time would be changed to Time-Warner, Inc.

The rules of the New York Stock Exchange required that Time's issuance of shares to effectuate the merger be approved by a vote of Time's stockholders. . . . The Chancellor concluded that the agreement was the product of "an arms-length negotiation between two parties seeking individual advantage through mutual action."

* * *

At its March 3, 1989 meeting, Time's board adopted several defensive tactics. Time entered an automatic share exchange agreement with Warner. Time would receive 17,292,747 shares of Warner's outstanding common stock (9.4%) and Warner would receive 7,080,016 shares of Time's outstanding common stock (11.1%). Either party could trigger the exchange. Time sought out and paid for "confidence" letters from various banks with which it did business. In these letters, the banks promised not to finance any third-party attempt to acquire Time. Time argues these agreements served only to preserve the confidential relationship between itself and the banks. The Chancellor found these agreements to be inconsequential and futile attempts to "dry up" money for a hostile takeover. Time also agreed to a "no-shop" clause, preventing Time from considering any other consolidation proposal, thus relinquishing its power to consider other proposals, regardless of their merits. Time did so at Warner's insistence. Warner did not want to be left "on the auction block" for an unfriendly suitor, if Time were to withdraw from the deal.

* * *

Time representatives lauded the lack of debt to the United States Senate and to the President of the United States. Public reaction to the announcement of the merger was positive. Time-Warner would be a media colossus with international scope. The board scheduled the stockholder vote for June 23; and a May 1 record date was set. On May 24, 1989, Time sent out extensive proxy statements to the stockholders regarding the approval vote on the merger. . . . Time's board was unanimously in favor of the proposed merger with Warner; and, by the end of May, the Time-Warner merger appeared to be an accomplished fact.

On June 7, 1989, these wishful assumptions were shattered by Paramount's surprising announcement of its all-cash offer to purchase all outstanding shares of Time for $175 per share. The following day, June 8, the trading price of Time's stock rose from $126 to $170 per share. Paramount's offer was said to be "fully negotiable."[8]

Time found Paramount's "fully negotiable" offer to be in fact subject to at least three conditions. First, Time had to terminate its merger agreement and stock exchange agreement with Warner, and remove certain other of its defensive devices, including the redemption of Time's shareholder rights. Second, Paramount had to obtain the required cable franchise transfers from Time in a fashion acceptable to Paramount in its sole discretion. Finally, the offer depended upon a judicial determination that section 203 of the General Corporate Law of Delaware (The Delaware Anti-Takeover Statute) was inapplicable to any Time-Paramount merger. While Paramount's board had been privately advised that it could take months, perhaps over a year, to forge and consummate the deal, Paramount's board publicly proclaimed its ability to close the offer by July 5, 1989. Paramount executives later conceded that none of its directors believed that July 5th was a realistic date to close the transaction.

On June 8, 1989, Time formally responded to Paramount's offer. Time's chairman and CEO, J. Richard Munro, sent an aggressively worded letter to Paramount's CEO, Martin Davis. Munro's letter attacked Davis' personal integrity and called Paramount's offer "smoke and mirrors." Time's nonmanagement directors were not shown the letter before it was sent. However, at a board meeting that same day, all members endorsed management's response as well as the letter's content.

Over the following eight days, Time's board met three times to discuss Paramount's $175 offer. The board viewed Paramount's offer as inadequate and concluded that its proposed merger with Warner was the better course of action. Therefore, the board declined to open any negotiations with Paramount and held steady its course toward a merger with Warner.

In June, Time's board of directors met several times. . . . During the course of these meeting, Time's financial advisors informed the board that, on an auction basis, Time's per share value was materially higher than Warner's [sic] $175 per share offer. On this basis, the board concluded that Paramount's $175 offer was inadequate.

At these June meetings, certain Time directors expressed their concern that their stockholders would not comprehend the long-term benefits of the Warner merger. Large quantities of Time shares were held by institutional investors. The board feared that even though there appeared to be wide support for the Warner transaction, Paramount's cash premium would be a tempting prospect to these investors. In mid-June, Time sought permission from the New York Stock Exchange to alter its rules and allow the Time-Warner merger to proceed without stockholder approval. Time did so at Warner's insistence. The

---

[8]   Subsequently, it was established that Paramount's board had decided as early as March 1989 to move to acquire Time. However, Paramount management intentionally delayed publicizing its proposal until Time had mailed to its stockholders its Time-Warner merger proposal along with the required proxy statements.

New York Stock Exchange rejected Time's request on June 15; and on that day, the value of Time stock reached $182 per share.

The following day, June 16, Time's board met to take up Paramount's offer. The board's prevailing belief was that Paramount's bid posed a threat to Time's control of its own destiny and retention of the "Time Culture." Even after Time's financial advisors made another presentation of Paramount and its business attributes, Time's board maintained its position that a combination with Warner presented greater potential for Time. Warner provided Time with a much desired production capability and an established international marketing chain. Time's advisors presented the board with various options, including defensive measures. . . .

At the same meeting, Time's board decided to recast its consolidation with Warner into an outright cash and securities acquisition of Warner by Time; and Time so informed Warner. Time accordingly restructured its proposal to acquire Warner as follows: Time would make an immediate all-cash offer for 51% of Warner's outstanding stock at $70 per share. The remaining 49% would be purchased at some later date for a mixture of cash and securities worth $70 per share. To provide the funds required for its outright acquisition of Warner, Time would assume 7-10 billion dollars worth of debt, thus eliminating one of the principal transaction-related benefits of the original merger agreement. . . .

Warner agreed but insisted on certain terms. Warner sought a control premium and guarantees that the governance provisions found in the original merger agreement would remain intact. . . . The Chancellor found the initial Time-Warner transaction to have been negotiated at arms length and the restructured Time-Warner transaction to have resulted from Paramount's offer and its expected effect on a Time shareholder vote.

On June 23, 1989, Paramount raised its all-cash offer to buy Time's outstanding stock to $200 per share. Paramount still professed that all aspects of the offer were negotiable. Time's board met on June 26, 1989 and formally rejected Paramount's $200 per share second offer. . . .

II

The Shareholder Plaintiffs first assert a *Revlon* claim. They contend that the March 4 Time-Warner agreement effectively put Time up for sale, triggering *Revlon* duties, requiring Time's board to enhance short-term shareholder value and to treat all other interested acquirors on an equal basis. The Shareholder Plaintiffs base this argument on two facts: (i) the ultimate Time-Warner exchange ratio of .465 favoring Warner, resulting in Warner shareholders' receipt of 62% of the combined company; and (ii) the subjective intent of Time's directors as evidenced in their statements that the market might perceive the Time-Warner merger as putting Time up "for sale" and their adoption of various defensive measures.

The Shareholder Plaintiffs further contend that Time's directors, in structuring the original merger transaction to be "takeover-proof," triggered *Revlon* duties by foreclosing their shareholders from any prospect of obtaining a control premium. In short, plaintiffs argue that Time's board's decision to merge with Warner imposed a fiduciary duty to maximize immediate share value and not erect unreasonable barriers to further bids. Therefore, they argue, the Chancellor erred in finding: that Paramount's bid for Time did not place Time "for sale"; that Time's transaction with Warner did not result in any transfer of control;

and that the combined Time-Warner was not so large as to preclude the possibility of the stockholders of Time-Warner receiving a future control premium.

Paramount asserts only a *Unocal* claim in which the shareholder plaintiffs join. Paramount contends that the Chancellor, in applying the first part of the *Unocal* test, erred in finding that Time's board had reasonable grounds to believe that Paramount posed both a legally cognizable threat to Time shareholders and a danger to Time's corporate policy and effectiveness. Paramount also contests the court's finding that Time's board made a reasonable and objective investigation of Paramount's offer so as to be informed before rejecting it. Paramount further claims that the court erred in applying *Unocal*'s second part in finding Time's response to be "reasonable." Paramount points primarily to the preclusive effect of the revised agreement which denied Time shareholders the opportunity both to vote on the agreement and to respond to Paramount's tender offer. Paramount argues that the underlying motivation of Time's board in adopting these defensive measures was management's desire to perpetuate itself in office.

The Court of Chancery posed the pivotal question presented by this case to be: Under what circumstances must a board of directors abandon an in-place plan of corporate development in order to provide its shareholders with the option to elect and realize an immediate control premium? As applied to this case, the question becomes: Did Time's Board, having developed a strategic plan of global expansion to be launched through a business combination with Warner, come under a fiduciary duty to jettison its plan and put the corporation's future in the hands of its shareholders?

While we affirm the result reached by the Chancellor, we think it unwise to place undue emphasis upon long-term versus short-term corporate strategy. Two key predicates underpin our analysis. First, Delaware law imposes on a board of directors the duty to manage the business and affairs on the corporation. 8 Del. C. § 141(a). This broad mandate includes a conferred authority to set a corporate course of action, including time frame, designed to enhance corporate profitability. Thus, the question of "long-term" versus "short-term" values is largely irrelevant because directors, generally, are obliged to charter a course for a corporation which is in its best interest without regard to a fixed investment horizon. Second, absent a limited set of circumstances as defined under *Revlon*, a board of directors, while always required to act in an informed manner, is not under any per se duty to maximize shareholder value in the short term, even in the context of a takeover.[12] In our view, the pivotal question presented by this case is: "Did Time, by entering into the proposed merger with Warner, put itself up for sale?" A resolution of that issue through application of *Revlon* has a significant bearing upon the resolution of the derivative *Unocal* issue.

A.

We first take up plaintiffs' principal *Revlon* argument, summarized above. In rejecting this argument, the Chancellor found the original Time-Warner merger agreement not to constitute a "change of control" and concluded that the transaction did not trigger *Revlon*

---

[12]   In endorsing this finding, we tacitly accept the Chancellor's conclusion that it is not breach of faith for directors to determine that the present stock market price of shares is not representative of true value or that there may indeed be several market values for any corporation's stock. We have so held in another context. *See Van Gorkom*, 488 A.2d at 876.

duties. The Chancellor's conclusion is premised on a finding that "[b]efore the merger agreement was signed, control of the corporation existed in a fluid aggregation of unaffiliated shareholders representing a voting majority—in other words, in the market." The Chancellor's findings of fact are supported by the record and his conclusion is correct as a matter of law. However, we premise our rejection of plaintiffs' *Revlon* claim on different grounds, namely, the absence of any substantial evidence to conclude that Time's board, in negotiating with Warner, made the dissolution or breakup of the corporate entity inevitable, as was the case in *Revlon*.

Under Delaware law there are, generally speaking and without excluding other possibilities, two circumstances which may implicate *Revlon* duties. The first, and clearer one, is when a corporation initiates an active bidding process seeking to sell itself or to effect a business reorganization involving a clear break-up of the company. *See, e.g., Mills Acquisition Co. v. Macmillan, Inc.,* Del. Supr., 559 A.2d 1261 (1988). However, *Revlon* duties may also be triggered where, in response to a bidder's offer, a target abandons its long-term strategy and seeks an alternative transaction also involving the breakup of the company.[13] Thus, in *Revlon*, when the board responded to Pantry Pride's offer by contemplating a "bust-up" sale of assets in a leveraged acquisition, we imposed upon the board a duty to maximize immediate shareholder value and an obligation to auction the company fairly. If, however, the board's reaction to a hostile tender offer is found to constitute only a defensive response and not an abandonment of the corporation's continued existence, *Revlon* duties are not triggered, though *Unocal* duties attach.[14] [citation omitted]

The plaintiffs insist that even though the original Time-Warner agreement may not have worked "an objective change of control," the transaction made a "sale" of Time inevitable. Plaintiffs rely on the subjective intent of Time's board of directors and principally upon certain board members' expressions of concern that the Warner transaction *might* be viewed as effectively putting Time up for sale. Plaintiffs argue that the use of a lock-up agreement, a no-shop clause, and so-called "dry-up" agreements prevented shareholders from obtaining a control premium in the immediate future and thus violated *Revlon*.

We agree with the Chancellor that such evidence is entirely insufficient to invoke *Revlon* duties; and we decline to extend *Revlon*'s application to corporate transactions simply because they might be construed as putting a corporation either "in play" or "up for sale." [citations omitted] The adoption of structural safety devices alone does not trigger *Revlon*. Rather, as the Chancellor stated, such devices are properly subject to a *Unocal* analysis.

---

[13]   As we stated in *Revlon*, in both such cases, "[t]he duty of the board [has] changed from the preservation of . . . [the] corporate entity to the maximization of the company's value at a sale for the stockholder's benefit. . . . [The board] no longer face[s] threats to corporate policy and effectiveness, or to the stockholders' interests, from a grossly inadequate bid." *Revlon v. MacAndrews & Forbes Holdings, Inc.,* Del. Supr., 506 A.2d 173, 182 (1986).

[14]   Within the auction process, any action taken by the board must be reasonably related to the threat posed or reasonable in relation to the advantage sought, *see Mills Acquisition Co. v. Macmillan, Inc.,* Del. Supr., 559 A.2d 1261, 1288 (1988). Thus, a *Unocal* analysis may be appropriate when a corporation is in a *Revlon* situation and *Revlon* duties may be triggered by a defensive action taken in response to a hostile offer. Since *Revlon*, we have stated that differing treatment of various bidders is not actionable when such action reasonably relates to achieving the best price available for the stockholders. *Macmillan*, 559 A.2d at 1286-87.

Finally, we do not find in Time's recasting of its merger agreement with Warner from a share exchange to a share purchase a basis to conclude that Time had either abandoned its strategic plan or made a sale of Time inevitable. The Chancellor found that although the merged Time-Warner company would be large (with a value approaching approximately $30 billion), recent takeover cases have proven that acquisition of the combined company might nonetheless be possible. *In Re: Time Incorporated Shareholder Litigation*, Del. Ch., C.A. No. 10670, Allen, C. (July 14, 1989), slip op. at 56. The legal consequence is that *Unocal* alone applies to determine whether the business judgment rule attaches to the revised agreement. Plaintiffs' analogy to *Macmillan* thus collapses and plaintiffs' reliance on *Macmillan* is misplaced.

B.

We turn now to plaintiffs' *Unocal* claim. We begin by noting, as did the Chancellor, that our decision does not require us to pass on the wisdom of the board's decision to enter into the original Time-Warner agreement. That is not a court's task. Our task is simply to review the record to determine whether there is sufficient evidence to support the Chancellor's conclusion that the initial Time-Warner agreement was the product of a proper exercise of business judgment. *Macmillan*, 559 A.2d at 1288.

We have purposely detailed the evidence of the Time board's deliberative approach, beginning in 1983-84, to expand itself. Time's decision in 1988 to combine with Warner was made only after what could be fairly characterized as an exhaustive appraisal of Time's future as a corporation. After concluding in 1983-84 that the corporation must expand to survive, and beyond journalism into entertainment, the board combed the field of available entertainment companies. By 1987 Time had focused upon Warner; by late July 1988 Time's board was convinced that Warner would provide the best "fit" for Time to achieve its strategic objectives. The record attests to the zealousness of Time's executives, fully supported by their directors, in seeing to the preservation of Time's "culture," *i.e.*, its perceived editorial integrity in journalism. We find ample evidence in the record to support the Chancellor's conclusion that the Time board's decision to expand the business of the company through its March 3 merger with Warner was entitled to the protection of the business judgment rule. [citation omitted]

The Chancellor reached a different conclusion in addressing the Time-Warner transaction as revised three months later. He found that the revised agreement was defense-motivated and designed to avoid the potentially disruptive effect that Paramount's offer would have had on consummation of the proposed merger were it put to a shareholder vote. Thus, the court declined to apply the traditional business judgment rule to the revised transaction and instead analyzed the Time board's June 16 decision under *Unocal*. The court ruled that *Unocal* applied to all director actions taken, following receipt of Paramount's hostile tender offer, that were reasonably determined to be defensive. Clearly that was a correct ruling and no party disputes that ruling.

In *Unocal*, we held that before the business judgment rule is applied to a board's adoption of a defensive measure, the burden will lie with the board to prove (a) reasonable grounds for believing that a danger to corporate policy and effectiveness existed; and (b) that the defensive measure adopted was reasonable in relation to the threat posed. *Unocal*, 493 A.2d 946. Directors satisfy the first part of the *Unocal* test by demonstrating good faith and reasonable investigation. We have repeatedly stated that the refusal to entertain an offer may comport with a valid exercise of a board's business judgment. [citations omitted]

Unocal involved a two-tier, highly coercive tender offer. In such a case, the threat is obvious: shareholders may be compelled to tender to avoid being treated adversely in the second stage of the transaction. Accord Ivanhoe, 535 A.2d at 1344. In subsequent cases the Court of Chancery has suggested that an all-cash, all-shares offer, falling within a range of values that a shareholder might reasonably prefer, cannot constitute a legally recognized "threat" to shareholder interests sufficient to withstand a Unocal analysis. AC Acquisitions Corp. v. Anderson, Claytone Co., Del. Ch., 519 A.2d 103 (1986); see Grand Metropolitan, PLC v. Pillsbury Co., Del. Ch., 558 A.2d 1049 (1988); City Capital Associates v. Interco, Inc., Del. Ch., 551 A.2d 787 (1988). In those cases, the Court of Chancery determined that whatever threat existed related only to the shareholders and only to price and not to the corporation.

From those decisions by our Court of Chancery, Paramount and the individual plaintiffs extrapolate a rule of law that an all-cash, all-shares offer with values reasonably in the range of acceptable price cannot pose any objective threat to a corporation or its shareholders. Thus, Paramount would have us hold that only if the value of Paramount's offer were determined to be clearly inferior to the value created by management's plan to merge with Warner could the offer be viewed—objectively—as a threat.

Implicit in the plaintiffs' argument is the view that a hostile tender offer can pose only two types of threats: the threat of coercion that results from a two-tier offer promising unequal treatment for nontendering shareholders; and the threat of inadequate value from an all-shares, all-cash offer at a price below what a target board in good faith deems to be the present value of its shares. [citations omitted] Since Paramount's offer was all-cash, the only conceivable "threat," plaintiffs argue, was inadequate value. We disapprove of such a narrow and rigid construction of Unocal, for the reasons which follow.

Plaintiffs' position represents a fundamental misconception of our standard of review under Unocal principally because it would involve the court in substituting its judgment as to what is a "better" deal for that of a corporation's board of directors. To the extent that the Court of Chancery has recently done so in certain of its opinions, we hereby reject such approach as not in keeping with a proper Unocal analysis. [citations omitted]

The usefulness of Unocal as an analytical tool is precisely its flexibility in the face of a variety of fact scenarios. Unocal is not intended as an abstract standard; neither is it a structured and mechanistic procedure of appraisal. Thus, we have said that directors may consider, when evaluating the threat posed by a takeover bid, the "inadequacy of the price offered, nature and timing of the offer, questions of illegality, the impact on constituencies other than shareholders, the risk of nonconsummation and the quality of securities being offered in the exchange." 493 A.2d at 955. The open-ended analysis mandated by Unocal is not intended to lead to a simple mathematical exercise: that is, of comparing the discounted value of Time-Warner's expected trading price at some future date with Paramount's offer and determining which is the higher. Indeed, in our view, precepts underlying the business judgment rule militate against a court's engaging in the process of attempting to ap-praise and evaluate the relative merits of a long-term versus a short-term investment goal for shareholders. To engage in such an exercise is a distortion of the Unocal process and, in particular, the application of the second part of Unocal's test, discussed below.

In this case, the Time board reasonably determined that inadequate value was not the only legally cognizable threat that Paramount's all-cash, all-shares offer could present. Time's board concluded that Paramount's eleventh hour offer posed other threats. One concern was that Time shareholders might elect to tender into Paramount's cash offer in ignorance or a mistaken belief of the strategic benefit which a business combination with Warner might produce. Moreover, Time viewed the conditions attached to Paramount's offer as introducing a degree of uncertainty that skewed a comparative analysis. Further, the timing of Paramount's offer to follow issuance of Time's proxy notice was viewed as arguably designed to upset, if not confuse, the Time stockholders' vote. Given this record evidence, we cannot conclude that the Time board's decision of June 6 that Paramount's offer posed a threat to corporate policy and effectiveness was lacking in good faith or dominated by motives of either entrenchment or self-interest.

Paramount also contends that the Time board had not duly investigated Paramount's offer. Therefore, Paramount argues, Time was unable to make an informed decision that the offer posed a threat to Time's corporate policy. Although the Chancellor did not address this issue directly, his findings of fact do detail Time's exploration of the available entertainment companies, including Paramount, before determining that Warner provided the best strategic "fit." In addition, the court found that Time's board rejected Paramount's offer because Paramount did not serve Time's objectives or meet Time's needs. Thus, the record does, in our judgment, demonstrate that Time's board was adequately informed of the potential benefits of a transaction with Paramount. We agree with the Chancellor that the Time board's lengthy pre-June investigation of potential merger candidates, including Paramount, mooted any obligation on Time's part to halt its merger process with Warner to reconsider Paramount. Time's board was under no obligation to negotiate with Paramount. *Unocal*, 493 A.2d at 954-55; *see also Macmillan*, 559 A.2d at 1285 n.35. Time's failure to negotiate cannot be fairly found to have been uninformed. The evidence supporting this finding is materially enhanced by the fact that twelve of Time's sixteen board members were outside independent directors. *Unocal*, 493 A.2d at 955; *Moran v. Household Intern., Inc.*, Del. Supr., 500 A.2d 1346, 1356 (1985).

We turn to the second part of the *Unocal* analysis. The obvious requisite to determining the reasonableness of a defensive action is a clear identification of the nature of the threat. As the Chancellor correctly noted, this "requires an evaluation of the importance of the corporate objective threatened; alternative methods of protecting that objective; impacts of the 'defensive' action, and other relevant factors." *In re: Time Incorporated Shareholder Litigation*, Del. Ch., C.A. 565 A.2d 281 (1989). It is not until both parts of the *Unocal* inquiry have been satisfied that the business judgment rule attaches to defensive actions of a board of directors. *Unocal*, 493 A.2d at 954.[18] As applied to the facts of this case, the question is whether the record evidence supports the Court of Chancery's conclusion that the restructuring of the Time-Warner transaction, including the adoption of several preclusive defensive measures, was a reasonable response in relation to a perceived threat.

---

[18] Some commentators have criticized *Unocal* by arguing that once the board's deliberative process has been analyzed and found not to be wanting in objectivity, good faith or deliberateness, the so-called "enhanced" business judgment rule has been satisfied and no further inquiry is undertaken. *See generally* Johnson & Siegel, *Corporate Mergers: Redefining the Role of Target Directors*, 136 U. PA. L. REV. 315 (1987). We reject such views.

Paramount argues that, assuming its tender offer posed a threat, Time's response was unreasonable in precluding Time's shareholders from accepting the tender offer or receiving a control premium in the immediately foreseeable future. Once again, the contention stems, we believe, from a fundamental misunderstanding of where the power of corporate governance lies. Delaware law confers the management of the corporate enterprise to the stockholders' duly elected board representatives. 8 Del. C. § 141(a). The fiduciary duty to manage a corporate enterprise includes the selection of a time frame for achievement of corporate goals. That duty may not be delegated to the stockholders. *Van Gorkom*, 488 A.2d at 873. Directors are not obliged to abandon a deliberately conceived corporate plan for a short-term shareholder profit unless there is clearly no basis to sustain the corporate strategy. *See, e.g., Revlon*, 506 A.2d 173.

Although the Chancellor blurred somewhat the discrete analyses required under *Unocal*, he did conclude that Time's board reasonably perceived Paramount's offer to be a significant threat to the planned Time-Warner merger and that Time's response was not "overly broad." We have found that even in light of a valid threat, management actions that are coercive in nature or force upon shareholders a management-sponsored alternative to a hostile offer may be struck down as unreasonable and nonproportionate responses. [citations omitted]

Here, on the record facts, the Chancellor found that Time's responsive action to Paramount's tender offer was not aimed at "cramming down" on its shareholders a management-sponsored alternative, but rather had as its goal the carrying forward of a pre-existing transaction in an altered form.[19] Thus, the response was reasonably related to the threat. The Chancellor noted that the revised agreement and its accompanying safety devices did not preclude Paramount from making an offer for the combined Time-Warner company or from changing the conditions of its offer so as not to make the offer dependent upon the nullification of the Time-Warner agreement. Thus, the response was proportionate. We affirm the Chancellor's rulings as clearly supported by the record. Finally, we note that although Time was required, as a result of Paramount's hostile offer, to incur a heavy debt to finance its acquisition of Warner, that fact alone does not render the board's decision unreasonable so long as the directors could reasonably perceive the debt load not to be so injurious to the corporation as to jeopardize its well being.

CONCLUSION

Applying the test for grant or denial of preliminary injunctive relief, we find plaintiffs failed to establish a reasonable likelihood of ultimate success on the merits. Therefore, we affirm.

---

[19]   The Chancellor cited *Shamrock Holdings, Inc. v. Polaroid Corp.*, Del. Ch., 559 A.2d 257 (1989), as a closely analogous case. In that case, the Court of Chancery upheld, in the face of a takeover bid, the establishment of an employee stock ownership plan that had a significant antitakeover effect. The Court of Chancery upheld the board's action largely because the ESOP had been adopted prior to any contest for control and was reasonably determined to increase productivity and enhance profits. The ESOP did not appear to be primarily a device to affect or secure corporate control.

NOTES AND QUESTIONS

(1) **The value of Time.** The valuation of Time in connection with the *Time* case provided an interesting sideshow. The facts are set forth in the Chancery Court opinion.[75] Analysts presented trading ranges for Time-Warner ranging from $90–$175 per share—*i.e.*, none higher than Paramount's first bid. Time's advisers predicted that the trading range would increase between 1990 and 1993, reaching $208–$402 in 1993. The Chancery court (*id.* at ¶ 93,273) characterized that as a "range that a Texan might feel at home on." Meanwhile, Time's advisers fixed Time's value for purposes of setting the exchange ratio of the original merger at $189.88 to $212.25. Note that Warner's value was fixed at between $64.39 and $72.87. Based on that value for Warner and the exchange ratio of .465 of a Time share for each Warner share, the value of Time would have been only about $150 per share. But a premium was built into Warner's share price that was not built into Time's. As Warner's financial advisors told the Warner board, Warner got "one hell of a deal." In any event, whatever the analysts thought would be the case, Time actually traded in the range between about $120 per share and, as of early 1990, around $90. In light of this trading range, as compared with the Paramount offer, one writer called the Time-Warner merger a good deal only under the "Time value of money theory."[76]

In September, 1992, Time-Warner stock split 4 for 1. In addition, 1992 saw the ouster of Nicholas Nicholas, who had replaced Richard Munro as co-CEO of Time-Warner in 1990, the death of Stephen Ross, and the appointment of Gerald Levin (formerly a Vice Chairman of Time) as the new leader of Time-Warner. During 1994, Time-Warner stock traded in the $31 to $43 range, still well below Paramount's split-adjusted bid of $50 per share.

In January 2000, America Online announced plans to acquire Time-Warner for approximately $90 per share in America Online stock. When the transaction closed in January 2001, the new AOL Time Warner shares exchanged for each Time-Warner share had declined in value to approximately $70. By December 2002, these shares had a market value of less than $16.

(2) **The relevance of stock price.** In footnote 12 to its opinion, the court again endorsed the view expressed in *Van Gorkom* that directors can decide that the present stock value does not represent its true value (*see* Note 6 following *Van Gorkom* in Section 9.03[B]). Can you see a difference from this standpoint between the Time board's rejection of Paramount's bid and the Trans Union board's acceptance of Pritzker's $55 bid?

(3) ***Unocal* revisited.** In the light of *Time*, what is left of *Unocal*'s apparently special rule for takeover defenses—*i.e.*, that the defensive move respond proportionately to the threat posed by the takeover? As discussed in Note 6 following *Unocal*, this was left

---

[75]   Fed. Sec. L. Rep. (CCH) ¶ 94,514.

[76]   Crovitz, *Can Takeover Targets Just Say No to Stockholders?*, WALL ST. J., March 7, 1990, at A19.

unclear both by *Unocal* and by post-*Unocal* cases. First, in considering whether a "threat" existed for *Unocal* purposes, the court explicitly rejected the idea that the board could defend only against bids that were "structurally" coercive, as in *Unocal* (*i.e.*, the two-tier bid that creates the prisoners' dilemma described in Section 14.03[B][1][c]) or "substantively" coercive in the sense of inadequacy of price. The Paramount bid was all-cash and, as discussed in Notes 1 and 2, at a lofty price. Second, with respect to "proportionality," the court approved the restructured Time-Warner transaction even though it was almost certain to defeat the Paramount bid. Moreover, in footnote 19, the court approved *Shamrock Holdings*, where stock issuances and repurchases prevented the bidder from obtaining the 85% control necessary to avoid the effect of Delaware's anti-takeover statute.[77] Where is the *Unocal* line now drawn? Note that the challenged action in *Time* was simply the completion of a plan to acquire Warner, not the refusal to redeem a poison pill. The court condemned "management actions that are coercive in nature or force upon shareholders a management-sponsored alternative . . . ." We will revisit this question following the *QVC* excerpt below.

(4) **Revlon revisited.** As discussed in Note 2 following *Revlon*, heightened judicial scrutiny may be appropriate when a transaction locks up control in a close-knit group or leaves the company closely held. But *Time* seemed to cast doubt on the application of a special *Revlon* duty to those cases. To be sure, the proposed stock for stock merger of Time and Warner in which shareholders of Warner would end up owning approximately 61% of the combined entity would not have lodged control of the corporation in a close-knit group or left the corporation closely held. But the court "premise[d] [its] rejection of plaintiffs' *Revlon* argument on broader grounds, namely, the absence of any substantial evidence to conclude that Time's board, in negotiating with Warner, made the dissolution or breakup of the corporate entity inevitable, as was the case in *Revlon*." This statement led many to believe that *Revlon* scrutiny would not be triggered by a "strategic" merger that did not contemplate a "break-up" of the corporation or an abandonment of the corporation's long term strategy even if it shifted control from the open market to a single shareholder or related group of shareholders. This interpretation of *Revlon*, however, was put to rest in the following case.

---

[77] *See* Del. G.C.L. § 203 and the related discussion in Note 7 following the *CTS* excerpt in Section 14.03[E].

PARAMOUNT COMMUNICATIONS INC. v. QVC NETWORK INC.
Delaware Supreme Court
637 A.2d 34 (1994)

VEASEY, Chief Justice.

* * *

QVC and certain stockholders of Paramount commenced separate actions (later consolidated) in the Court of Chancery seeking preliminary and permanent injunctive relief against Paramount, certain members of the Paramount Board, and Viacom. This action arises out of a proposed acquisition of Paramount by Viacom through a tender offer followed by a second-step merger (the "Paramount-Viacom transaction"), and a competing unsolicited tender offer by QVC. The Court of Chancery granted a preliminary injunction. . . . We affirm[]. . . .

* * *

I. FACTS

* * *

Paramount is a Delaware corporation with its principal offices in New York City. . . . The majority of Paramount's stock is publicly held by numerous unaffiliated investors. Paramount owns and operates a diverse group of entertainment businesses. . . .

* * *

Viacom is a Delaware corporation with its headquarters in Massachusetts. Viacom is controlled by Sumner M. Redstone ("Redstone"), its Chairman and Chief Executive Officer, who owns indirectly approximately 85.2 percent of Viacom's voting Class A stock and approximately 69.2 percent of Viacom's nonvoting Class B stock through National Amusements, Inc. ("NAI"), an entity 91.7 percent owned by Redstone. Viacom has a wide range of entertainment operations. . . .

QVC is a Delaware corporation with its headquarters in West Chester, Pennsylvania. . . . Barry Diller ("Diller"), the Chairman and Chief Executive Officer of QVC, is also a substantial stockholder. QVC sells a variety of merchandise through a televised shopping channel. . . .

Beginning in the late 1980s, Paramount investigated the possibility of acquiring or merging with other companies in the entertainment, media, or communications industry. Paramount considered such transactions to be desirable, and perhaps necessary, in order to keep pace with competitors in the rapidly evolving field of entertainment and communications. . . .

Although Paramount had considered a possible combination of Paramount and Viacom as early as 1990, recent efforts to explore such a transaction began at a dinner meeting between Redstone and [Martin S.] Davis[, Paramount's Chairman and Chief Executive Officer ("Davis")], on April 20, 1993. Robert Greenhill ("Greenhill"), Chairman of Smith Barney Shearson Inc. ("Smith Barney"), attended and helped facilitate this meeting. After several more meetings between Redstone and Davis, serious negotiations began taking place in early July.

It was tentatively agreed that Davis would be the chief executive officer and Redstone would be the controlling stockholder of the combined company, but the parties could not reach agreement on the merger price and the terms of a stock option to be granted to Viacom. With respect to price, Viacom offered a package of cash and stock (primarily Viacom Class B nonvoting stock) with a market value of approximately $61 per share, but Paramount wanted at least $70 per share.

Shortly after negotiations broke down in July 1993, two notable events occurred. First, Davis apparently learned of QVC's potential interest in Paramount, and told Diller over lunch on July 21, 1993, that Paramount was not for sale. Second, the market value of Viacom's Class B nonvoting stock increased from $46.875 on July 6 to $57.25 on August 20. . . .

On August 20, 1993, discussions between Paramount and Viacom resumed when Greenhill arranged another meeting between Davis and Redstone. After a short hiatus, the parties negotiated in earnest in early September, and performed due diligence with the assistance of their financial advisors, Lazard Freres & Co. ("Lazard") for Paramount and Smith Barney for Viacom. On September 9, 1993, the Paramount Board was informed about the status of the negotiations and was provided information by Lazard, including an analysis of the proposed transaction.

On September 12, 1993, the Paramount Board met again and unanimously approved [a merger agreement (the "Original Merger Agreement")] . . . whereby Paramount would merge with and into Viacom. The terms of the merger provided that each share of Paramount common stock would be converted into 0.10 shares of Viacom Class A voting stock, 0.90 shares of Viacom Class B nonvoting stock, and $9.10 in cash. In addition, the Paramount Board agreed to amend its "poison pill" Rights Agreement to exempt the proposed merger with Viacom. The Original Merger Agreement also contained several provisions designed to make it more difficult for a potential competing bid to succeed. We focus, as did the Court of Chancery, on three of these defensive provisions: a "no-shop" provision (the "No-Shop Provision"), the Termination Fee, and the Stock Option Agreement.

First, under the No-Shop Provision, the Paramount Board agreed that Paramount would not solicit, encourage, discuss, negotiate, or endorse any competing transaction unless: (a) a third party "makes an unsolicited written, bona fide proposal, which is not subject to any material contingencies relating to financing"; and (b) the Paramount Board determines that discussions or negotiations with the third party are necessary for the Paramount Board to comply with its fiduciary duties.

Second, under the Termination Fee provision, Viacom would receive a $100 million termination fee if: (a) Paramount terminated the Original Merger Agreement because of a competing transaction; (b) Paramount's stockholders did not approve the merger; or (c) the Paramount Board recommended a competing transaction.

The third and most significant deterrent device was the Stock Option Agreement, which granted to Viacom an option to purchase approximately 19.9 percent (23,699,000 shares) of Paramount's outstanding common stock at $69.14 per share if any of the triggering events for the Termination Fee occurred. In addition to the customary terms that are normally associated with a stock option, the Stock Option Agreement contained two provisions that were both unusual and highly beneficial to Viacom: (a) Viacom was permitted to pay for the shares with a senior subordinated note of questionable marketability instead of cash, thereby avoiding the need to raise the $1.6 billion purchase price (the "Note Feature"); and (b) Viacom could elect to require Paramount to pay Viacom in cash a sum equal to the difference between the purchase price and the market price of Paramount's stock (the "Put Feature"). Because the Stock Option Agreement was not "capped" to limit its maximum dollar value, it had the potential to reach (and in this case did reach) unreasonable levels.

After the execution of the Original Merger Agreement and the Stock Option Agreement on September 12, 1993, Paramount and Viacom announced their proposed merger. In a number of public statements, the parties indicated that the pending transaction was a virtual certainty. Redstone described it as a "marriage" that would "never be torn asunder" and stated that only a "nuclear attack" could break the deal. Redstone also called Diller and John Malone of Tele-Communications Inc., a major stockholder of QVC, to dissuade them from making a competing bid.

Despite these attempts to discourage a competing bid, Diller sent a letter to Davis on September 20, 1993, proposing a merger in which QVC would acquire Paramount for approximately $80 per share, consisting of 0.893 shares of QVC common stock and $30 in cash. QVC also expressed its eagerness to meet with Paramount to negotiate the details of a transaction. When the Paramount Board met on September 27, it was advised by Davis that the Original Merger Agreement prohibited Paramount from having discussions with QVC (or anyone else) unless certain conditions were satisfied. In particular, QVC had to supply evidence that its proposal was not subject to financing contingencies. . . .

On October 5, 1993, QVC provided Paramount with evidence of QVC's financing. The Paramount Board then held another meeting on October 11, and decided to authorize management to meet with QVC. . . . Discussions proceeded slowly, however, due to a delay in Paramount signing a confidentiality agreement. In response to Paramount's request for information, QVC provided two binders of documents to Paramount on October 20.

On October 21, 1993, QVC filed this action and publicly announced an $80 cash tender offer for 51 percent of Paramount's outstanding shares (the "QVC tender offer"). Each remaining share of Paramount common stock would be converted into 1.42857 shares of QVC common stock in a second-step merger. The tender offer was conditioned on, among other things, the invalidation of the Stock Option Agreement, which was worth over $200 million by that point. QVC contends that it had to commence a tender offer because of the slow pace of the merger discussions and the need to begin seeking clearance under federal antitrust laws.

Confronted by QVC's hostile bid, which on its face offered over $10 per share more than the consideration provided by the Original Merger Agreement, Viacom realized that it would need to raise its bid in order to remain competitive. Within hours after QVC's tender offer was announced, Viacom entered into discussions with Paramount concerning a revised transaction. These discussions led to serious negotiations concerning a comprehensive amendment to the original Paramount-Viacom transaction. In effect, the opportunity for a "new deal" with Viacom was at hand for the Paramount Board. With the QVC hostile bid offering greater value to the Paramount stockholders, the Paramount Board had considerable leverage with Viacom.

At a special meeting on October 24, 1993, the Paramount Board approved [an amended merger agreement ("the Amended Merger Agreement")] . . . and an amendment to the Stock Option Agreement. The Amended Merger Agreement was, however, essentially the same as the Original Merger Agreement, except that it included a few new provisions. One provision related to an $80 per share cash tender offer by Viacom for 51 percent of Paramount's stock, and another changed the merger consideration so that each share of Para-mount would be converted into 0.20408 shares of Viacom Class A voting stock, 1.08317 shares of Viacom Class B nonvoting stock, and 0.20408 shares of a new series of Viacom convertible preferred stock. The Amended Merger Agreement also added a provision giving Paramount the right not to amend its Rights Agreement to exempt Viacom if the Paramount Board determined that such an amendment would be inconsistent with its fiduciary duties because another offer constituted a "better alternative." Finally, the Paramount Board was given the power to terminate the Amended Merger Agreement if it withdrew its recommendation of the Viacom transaction or recommended a competing transaction.

Although the Amended Merger Agreement offered more consideration to the Paramount stockholders and somewhat more flexibility to the Paramount Board than did the Original Merger Agreement, the defensive measures designed to make a competing bid more difficult were not removed or modified. In particular, there is no evidence in the record that Paramount sought to use its newly-acquired leverage to eliminate or modify the No-Shop Provision, the Termination Fee, or the Stock Option Agreement when the subject of amending the Original Merger Agreement was on the table.

Viacom's tender offer commenced on October 25, 1993, and QVC's tender offer was formally launched on October 27, 1993. Diller sent a letter to the Paramount Board on October 28 requesting an opportunity to negotiate with Paramount, and Oresman [Paramount's Executive Vice President, Chief Administrative Officer, and General Counsel] responded the following day by agreeing to meet. The meeting, held on November 1, was not very fruitful. . . .

On November 6, 1993, Viacom unilaterally raised its tender offer price to $85 per share in cash and offered a comparable increase in the value of the securities being proposed in the second-step merger. At a telephonic meeting held later that day, the Paramount Board agreed to recommend Viacom's higher bid to Paramount's stockholders.

QVC responded to Viacom's higher bid on November 12 by increasing its tender offer to $90 per share and by increasing the securities for its second-step merger by a similar amount. In response to QVC's latest offer, the Paramount Board scheduled a meeting for November 15, 1993. Prior to the meeting, Oresman sent the members of the Paramount Board a document summarizing the "conditions and uncertainties" of QVC's offer. One director testified that this document gave him a very negative impression of the QVC bid.

At its meeting on November 15, 1993, the Paramount Board determined that the new QVC offer was not in the best interests of the stockholders. The purported basis for this conclusion was that QVC's bid was excessively conditional. The Paramount Board did not communicate with QVC regarding the status of the conditions because it believed that the No-Shop Provision prevented such communication in the absence of firm financing. Several Paramount directors also testified that they believed the Viacom transaction would be more advantageous to Paramount's future business prospects than a QVC transaction.[7] Although a number of materials were distributed to the Paramount Board describing the Viacom and QVC transactions, the only quantitative analysis of the consideration to be received by the stockholders under each proposal was based on then-current market prices of the securities involved, not on the anticipated value of such securities at the time when the stockholders would receive them.[8]

The preliminary injunction hearing in this case took place on November 16, 1993. On November 19, Diller wrote to the Paramount Board to inform it that QVC had obtained financing commitments for its tender offer and that there was no antitrust obstacle to the offer. On November 24, 1993, the Court of Chancery issued its decision granting a preliminary injunction in favor of QVC and the plaintiff stockholders.[*] This appeal followed.

II. APPLICABLE PRINCIPLES OF ESTABLISHED DELAWARE LAW

. . . [T]here are rare situations which mandate that a court take a more direct and active role in overseeing the decisions made and actions taken by directors. In these situations, a court subjects the directors' conduct to enhanced scrutiny to ensure that it is reasonable. The decisions of this Court have clearly established the circumstances where such enhanced scrutiny will be applied. *E.g., Unocal*, 493 A.2d 946; *Moran v. Household Int'l, Inc.*, Del. Supr., 500 A.2d 1346 (1985); *Revlon*, 506 A.2d 173. . . . The case at bar implicates two such circumstances: (1) the approval of a transaction resulting in a sale of control, and (2) the adoption of defensive measures in response to a threat to corporate control.

A. The Significance of a Sale or Change of Control

When a majority of a corporation's voting shares are acquired by a single person or entity, or by a cohesive group acting together, there is a significant diminution in the voting power of those who thereby become minority stockholders. . . .

In the absence of devices protecting the minority stockholders,[12] stockholder votes are likely to become mere formalities where there is a majority stockholder. . . .

In the case before us, the public stockholders (in the aggregate) currently own a majority of Paramount's voting stock. Control of the corporation is not vested in a single person,

---

[7]   This belief may have been based on a report prepared by Booz-Allen and distributed to the Paramount Board at its October 24 meeting. The report, which relied on public information regarding QVC, concluded that the synergies of a Paramount-Viacom merger were significantly superior to those of a Paramount-QVC merger. QVC has labeled the Booz-Allen report as a "joke."

[8]   The market prices of Viacom's and QVC's stock were poor measures of their actual values because such prices constantly fluctuated depending upon which company was perceived to be the more likely to acquire Paramount.

[*]   [Under the terms of the Chancery Court's injunction, Paramount was enjoined from taking any action to facilitate the consummation of the Viacom tender offer. In addition, both Viacom and Paramount were enjoined from taking any action to exercise any provision of the Stock Option Agreement.—Ed.]

[12]   Examples of such protective provisions are supermajority voting provisions, majority of the minority requirements, etc. Although we express no opinion on what effect the inclusion of any such stockholder protective devices would have had in this case, we note that this Court has upheld, under different circumstances, the reasonableness of a standstill agreement which limited a 49.9 percent stockholder to 40 percent board representation. *Ivanhoe*, 535 A.2d at 1343.

entity, or group, but vested in the fluid aggregation of unaffiliated stockholders. In the event the Paramount-Viacom transaction is consummated, the public stockholders will receive cash and a minority equity voting position in the surviving corporation. Following such consummation, there will be a controlling stockholder who will have the voting power to: (a) elect directors; (b) cause a break-up of the corporation; (c) merge it with another company; (d) cash-out the public stockholders; (e) amend the certificate of incorporation; (f) sell all or substantially all of the corporate assets; or (g) otherwise alter materially the nature of the corporation and the public stockholders' interests. Irrespective of the present Paramount Board's vision of a long-term strategic alliance with Viacom, the proposed sale of control would provide the new controlling stockholder with the power to alter that vision.

Because of the intended sale of control, the Paramount-Viacom transaction has economic consequences of considerable significance to the Paramount stockholders. Once control has shifted, the current Paramount stockholders will have no leverage in the future to demand another control premium. As a result, the Paramount stockholders are entitled to receive, and should receive, a control premium and/or protective devices of significant value. There being no such protective provisions in the Viacom-Paramount transaction, the Para-mount directors had an obligation to take the maximum advantage of the current opportunity to realize for the stockholders the best value reasonably available.

B. The Obligations of Directors in a Sale or Change of Control Transaction

The consequences of a sale of control impose special obligations on the directors of a corporation.[13] In particular, they have the obligation of acting reasonably to seek the transaction offering the best value reasonably available to the stockholders. The courts will apply enhanced scrutiny to ensure that the directors have acted reasonably. . . .

In the sale of control context, the directors must focus on one primary objective—to secure the transaction offering the best value reasonably available for the stockholders—and they must exercise their fiduciary duties to further that end. . . .

In pursuing this objective, the directors must be especially diligent. . . . In particular, this Court has stressed the importance of the board being adequately informed in negotiating a sale of control: "The need for adequate information is central to the enlightened evaluation of a transaction that a board must make." *Barkan*, 567 A.2d at 1287. This requirement is consistent with the general principle that "directors have a duty to inform themselves, prior to making a business decision, of all material information reasonably available to them." [citations omitted] Moreover, the role of outside, independent directors becomes particularly important because of the magnitude of a sale of control transaction and the possibility, in certain cases, that management may not necessarily be impartial. . . .

Barkan teaches some of the methods by which a board can fulfill its obligation to seek the best value reasonably available to the stockholders. . . . These methods are designed to

---

[13] We express no opinion on any scenario except the actual facts before the Court, and our precise holding herein. Unsolicited tender offers in other contexts may be governed by different precedent. For example, where a potential sale of control by a corporation is not the consequence of a board's action, this Court has recognized the prerogative of a board of directors to resist a third party's unsolicited acquisition proposal or offer. . . . The decision of a board to resist such an acquisition, like all decisions of a properly-functioning board, must be informed, *Unocal*, 493 A.2d at 954-55, and the circumstances of each particular case will determine the steps that a board must take to inform itself, and what other action, if any, is required as a matter of fiduciary duty.

determine the existence and viability of possible alternatives. They include conducting an auction, canvassing the market, etc. Delaware law recognizes that there is "no single blue-print" that directors must follow. . . .

In determining which alternative provides the best value for the stockholders, a board of directors is not limited to considering only the amount of cash involved, and is not required to ignore totally its view of the future value of a strategic alliance. . . . Instead, the directors should analyze the entire situation and evaluate in a disciplined manner the consideration being offered. Where stock or other non-cash consideration is involved, the board should try to quantify its value, if feasible, to achieve an objective comparison of the alternatives.[14] In addition, the board may assess a variety of practical considerations relating to each alternative including:

> [an offer's] fairness and feasibility; the proposed or actual financing for the offer, and the consequences of that financing; questions of illegality; . . . the risk of non-consummation; . . . the bidder's identity, prior background and other business venture experiences; and the bidder's business plans for the corporation and their effects on stockholder interests.

Macmillan, 559 A.2d at 1282 n. 29. These considerations are important because the selection of one alternative may permanently foreclose other opportunities. While the assessment of these factors may be complex, the board's goal is straightforward: Having informed themselves of all material information reasonably available, the directors must decide which alternative is most likely to offer the best value reasonably available to the stockholders

C. Enhanced Judicial Scrutiny of a Sale or Change of Control Transaction

Board action in the circumstances presented here is subject to enhanced scrutiny. Such scrutiny is mandated by: (a) the threatened diminution of the current stockholders' voting power; (b) the fact that an asset belonging to public stockholders (a control premium) is being sold and may never be available again: and (c) the traditional concern of Delaware courts for actions which impair or impede stockholder voting rights . . . .

The key features of an enhanced scrutiny test are: (a) a judicial determination regarding the adequacy of the decisionmaking process employed by the directors, including the information on which the directors based their decision; and (b) a judicial examination of the reasonableness of the directors' action in light of the circumstances then existing. The directors have the burden of proving that they were adequately informed and acted reasonably.

Although an enhanced scrutiny test involves a review of the reasonableness of the substantive merits of a board's actions, a court should not ignore the complexity of the directors' task in a sale of control. There are many business and financial considerations implicated in investigating and selecting the best value reasonably available. The board of directors is the corporate decisionmaking body best equipped to make these judgments.

---

[14]   When assessing the value of non-cash consideration, a board should focus on its value as of the date it will be received by the stockholders. Normally, such value will be determined with the assistance of experts using generally accepted methods of valuation. . . .

Accordingly, a court applying enhanced judicial scrutiny should be deciding whether the directors made a reasonable decision, not a perfect decision. . . .

D. *Revlon* and *Time-Warner* Distinguished

The Paramount defendants and Viacom assert that the fiduciary obligations and the enhanced judicial scrutiny discussed above are not implicated in this case in the absence of a "break-up" of the corporation. . . . This argument is based on their erroneous interpretation of our decisions in *Revlon* and *Time-Warner*.

In *Revlon*, we reviewed the actions of the board of directors of Revlon, Inc. . . ., which had rebuffed the overtures of Pantry Pride, Inc. and had instead entered into an agreement with Forstmann Little & Co. . . . providing for the acquisition of 100 percent of Revlon's outstanding stock by Forstmann and the subsequent break-up of Revlon. . . .

It is true that one of the circumstances bearing on . . . [our holdings in *Revlon*] was the fact that "the break-up of the company . . . had become a reality which even the directors embraced." *Id.* at 182. It does not follow, however, that a "break-up" must be present and "inevitable" before directors are subject to enhanced judicial scrutiny and are required to pursue a transaction that is calculated to produce the best value reasonably available to the stockholders. . . .

* * *

Although *Macmillan* and *Barkan* are clear in holding that a change of control imposes on directors the obligation to obtain the best value reasonably available to the stockholders, the Paramount defendants have interpreted our decision in *Time-Warner* as requiring a corporate break-up in order for that obligation to apply. The facts in *Time-Warner*, however, were quite different from the facts of this case, and refute Paramount's position here. In *Time-Warner*, the Chancellor held that there was no change of control in the original stock-for-stock merger between Time and Warner because Time would be owned by a fluid aggregation of unaffiliated stockholders both before and after the merger. . . . Moreover, the transaction actually consummated in *Time-Warner* was not a merger, as originally planned, but a sale of Warner's stock to Time.

In our affirmance of the Court of Chancery's well-reasoned decision, this Court held that "The Chancellor's findings of fact are supported by the record and *his conclusion is correct as a matter of law*." 571 A.2d at 1150 (emphasis added). Nevertheless, the Paramount defendants here have argued that a break-up is a requirement and have focused on the following language in our Time-Warner decision:

> However, we premise our rejection of plaintiffs' Revlon claim on different grounds, namely, the absence of any substantial evidence to conclude that Time's board, in negotiating with Warner, made the dissolution or break-up of the corporate entity inevitable, as was the case in *Revlon*.
>
> Under Delaware law there are, generally speaking and *without excluding other possibilities,* two circumstances which may implicate *Revlon* duties. The first, and clearer one, is when a corporation *initiates an active bidding process seeking to sell itself* or to effect a business reorganization involving a clear breakup of the company. However, *Revlon* duties may also be triggered where,

in response to a bidder's offer, a target abandons its long-term strategy and seeks an alternative transaction involving the breakup of the company.

Id. at 1150 (emphasis added).

The Paramount defendants have misread the holding of *Time-Warner*. Contrary to their argument, our decision in *Time-Warner* expressly states that the two general scenarios discussed in the above-quoted paragraph are not the only instances where "Revlon duties" may be implicated. The Paramount defendants' argument totally ignores the phrase "without excluding other possibilities." Moreover, the instant case is clearly within the first general scenario set forth in *Time-Warner*. The Paramount Board, albeit unintentionally, had "initiated an active bidding process seeking to sell itself" by agreeing to sell control of the corporation to Viacom in circumstances where another potential acquiror (QVC) was equally interested in being a bidder.

* * *

III. BREACH OF FIDUCIARY DUTIES BY PARAMOUNT BOARD

We now turn to duties of the Paramount Board under the facts of this case and our conclusions as to the breaches of those duties which warrant injunctive relief.

A. The Specific Obligations of the Paramount Board

Under the facts of this case, the Paramount directors had the obligation: (a) to be diligent and vigilant in examining critically the Paramount-Viacom transaction and the QVC tender offers; (b) to act in good faith; (c) to obtain, and act with due care on, all material information reasonably available, including information necessary to compare the two offers to determine which of these transactions, or an alternative course of action, would provide the best value reasonably available to the stockholders; and (d) to negotiate actively and in good faith with both Viacom and QVC to that end.

* * *

These obligations necessarily implicated various issues, including the questions of whether or not those provisions and other aspects of the Paramount-Viacom transaction (separately and in the aggregate): (a) adversely affected the value provided to the Paramount stockholders; (b) inhibited or encouraged alternative bids; (c) were enforceable contractual obligations in light of the directors' fiduciary duties; and (d) in the end would advance or retard the Paramount directors' obligation to secure for the Paramount stockholders the best value reasonably available under the circumstances.

The Paramount defendants contend that they were precluded by certain contractual provisions including the No-Shop Provision, from negotiating with QVC or seeking alternatives. Such provisions, whether or not they are presumptively valid in the abstract, may not validly define or limit the directors' fiduciary duties under Delaware law or prevent the Paramount directors from carrying out their fiduciary duties under Delaware law. To the extent such provisions are inconsistent with those duties, they are invalid and unenforceable. . . .

Since the Paramount directors had already decided to sell control, they had an obligation to continue their search for the best value reasonably available to the stockholders. This continuing obligation included the responsibility, at the October 24 board meeting and thereafter, to evaluate critically both the QVC tender offers and the Paramount-Viacom transaction to determine if: (a) the QVC tender offer was, or would continue to be, conditional; (b) the QVC tender offer could be improved; (c) the Viacom tender offer or other aspects of the Paramount-Viacom transaction could be improved; (d) each of the respective offers would be reasonably likely to come to closure, and under what circumstances; (e) other material information was reasonably available for consideration by the Paramount directors; (f) there were viable and realistic alternative courses of action; and (g) the timing constraints could be managed so the directors could consider these matters carefully and deliberately.

B. The Breaches of Fiduciary Duty by the Paramount Board

The Paramount directors made the decision on September 12, 1993, that, in their judgment, a strategic merger with Viacom on the economic terms of the Original Merger Agreement was in the best interests of Paramount and its stockholders. Those terms provided a modest change of control premium to the stockholders. The directors also decided at that time that it was appropriate to agree to certain defensive measures (the Stock Option Agreement, the Termination Fee, and the No-Shop Provision) insisted upon by Viacom as part of that economic transaction. Those defensive measures, coupled with the sale of control and subsequent disparate treatment of competing bidders, implicated the judicial scrutiny of *Unocal, Revlon, Macmillan*, and their progeny. We conclude that the Paramount directors' process was not reasonable, and the result achieved for the stockholders was not reasonable under the circumstances.

When entering into the Original Merger Agreement, and thereafter, the Paramount Board clearly gave insufficient attention to the potential consequences of the defensive measures demanded by Viacom. The Stock Option Agreement had a number of unusual and potentially "draconian"[19] provisions, including the Note Feature and the Put Feature. Furthermore, the Termination Fee, whether or not unreasonable by itself, clearly made Paramount less attractive to other bidders, when coupled with the Stock Option Agreement. Finally, the No-Shop Provision inhibited the Paramount Board's ability to negotiate with other potential bidders, particularly QVC which had already expressed an interest in Paramount.[20]

Throughout the applicable time period, and especially from the first QVC merger proposal on September 20 through the Paramount Board meeting on November 15, QVC's interest in Paramount provided the opportunity for the Paramount Board to seek significantly higher value for the Paramount stockholders than that being offered by Viacom. QVC persistently demonstrated its intention to meet and exceed the Viacom offers, and frequently expressed its willingness to negotiate possible further increases.

---

[19]   The Vice Chancellor so characterized the Stock Option Agreement. . . . We express no opinion whether a stock option agreement of essentially this magnitude, but with a reasonable "cap" and without the Note and Put Features, would be valid or invalid under other circumstances. . . .

[20]   We express no opinion whether certain aspects of the No-Shop Provision here could be valid in another context. Whether or not it could validly have operated here at an early stage solely to prevent Paramount from actively "shopping" the company, it could not prevent the Paramount directors from carrying out their fiduciary duties in considering unsolicited bids or in negotiating for the best value reasonably available to the stockholders. . . .

The Paramount directors had the opportunity in the October 23-24 time frame, when the Original Merger Agreement was renegotiated, to take appropriate action to modify the improper defensive measures as well as to improve the economic terms of the Paramount-Viacom transaction. Under the circumstances existing at that time, it should have been clear to the Paramount Board that the Stock Option Agreement, coupled with the Termination Fee and the No-Shop Clause, were impeding the realization of the best value reasonably available to the Paramount stockholders. Nevertheless, the Paramount Board made no effort to eliminate or modify these counterproductive devices, and instead continued to cling to its vision of a strategic alliance with Viacom. Moreover, based on advice from the Paramount management, the Paramount directors considered the QVC offer to be "conditional" and asserted that they were precluded by the No-Shop Provision from seeking more information from, or negotiating with, QVC.

By November 12, 1993, the value of the revised QVC offer on its face exceeded that of the Viacom offer by over $1 billion at then current values. This significant disparity of value cannot be justified on the basis of the directors' vision of future strategy, primarily because the change of control would supplant the authority of the current Paramount Board to continue to hold and implement their strategic vision in any meaningful way. Moreover, their uninformed process had deprived their strategic vision of much of its credibility. . . .

When the Paramount directors met on November 15 to consider QVC's increased tender offer, they remained prisoners of their own misconceptions and missed opportunities to eliminate the restrictions they had imposed on themselves. Yet, it was not "too late" to reconsider negotiating with QVC. The circumstances existing on November 15 made it clear that the defensive measures, taken as a whole, were problematic: (a) the No-Shop Provision could not define or limit their fiduciary duties; (b) the Stock Option Agreement had become "draconian"; and (c) the Termination Fee, in context with all the circumstances, was similarly deterring the realization of possibly higher bids. Nevertheless, the Paramount directors remained paralyzed by their uninformed belief that the QVC offer was "illusory." This final opportunity to negotiate on the stockholders' behalf and to fulfill their obligation to seek the best value reasonably available was thereby squandered.

* * *

V. CONCLUSION

* * *

For the reasons set forth herein, the . . . Order of the Court of Chancery has been AFFIRMED, and this matter has been REMANDED for proceedings consistent herewith.
. . .

NOTES AND QUESTIONS

(1) **Lock-ups under** *QVC*. Paramount used a particularly strong lock-up that took the form of a stock option that gave Viacom the right to purchase approximately 24 million shares of Paramount stock for $69.14 per share (the price of Viacom's offer under the original merger agreement) if the Viacom-Paramount merger was not com-

pleted. Paramount in effect would have to pay Viacom liquidated damages equal to 24 million times the difference between a competing bidder's successful offer and $69.14 (or approximately $480 million dollars in the case of QVC's final offer of $90 per share). The *QVC* court, while it invalidated this stock option as unreasonable, stated in footnote 19 that it was not deciding "whether a stock option agreement of essentially this magnitude, but with a reasonable 'cap' and without Note and Put Features, would be valid or invalid under other circumstances . . . ." Subsequent cases indicate that lock-ups of up to 3% of transaction value will ordinarily be upheld.[78]

(2) **No-shops under *QVC*.** In addition to the stock option, the Paramount board also agreed to a stringent no-shop agreement under which Paramount could not "solicit, encourage, discuss, negotiate, or endorse any competing transaction" unless, among other things, the third party making the competing offer made a written proposal which was not subject to any financing contingency. The court invalidated that provision, finding that it unreasonably inhibited the Paramount board's ability to negotiate with others. Does this mean the board must actively seek out competing bidders and conduct auctions before selling the firm? *See* footnote 20 to the court's opinion. *Matador Capital Management Corporation v. BRC Holdings, Inc.*[79] upheld a provision barring the target corporation from soliciting additional offers or providing information to third parties until the board received "an unsolicited bona fide written Acquisition Proposal" that appeared more favorable than the original bidder's offer, because the provision "operate[d] merely to afford some protection to prevent disruption of the agreement by proposals from third parties that are neither bona fide nor likely to result in a higher transaction."[80]

(3) **Structuring the decision-making process.** How would you advise a board in a similar position to the Paramount board to structure its decision-making process in light of *QVC*? Must the board conduct an even-handed auction in which it seeks out competing bidders before it sells the company? *See* Note 2 above. If it needn't actively seek out competing bidders, what duties does the board have with respect to those bidders who make unsolicited offers? And finally, assuming that competing bids are made, what information should the board gather before approving a sale? In this regard, precisely how was the information gathered by the Paramount board inadequate to support its decision to select Viacom over QVC?

---

[78]   *See, e.g., Golden Cycle, L.L.C. v. Allan*, 1998 Del. Ch. LEXIS 237, 1998 WL 892631 (Del. Ch. 1998) (termination fee of slightly less than 3% of transaction value); *Goodwin v. Live Entertainment, Inc.*, 1999 Del. Ch. LEXIS 5, 1999 WL 64265 (Del. Ch. 1999) (termination fee equal to 3.125% of transaction value); *McMillan v. Intercargo Corp.*, 768 A.2d 492 (Del. Ch. 2000) (termination fee equal to 3.5% of transaction value).

[79]   1998 Del. Ch. LEXIS 225, 1998 WL 842286 (Del. Ch. 1998).

[80]   *See also Golden Cycle, L.L.C. v. Allan*, 1998 Del. Ch. LEXIS 237, 1998 WL 892631 (Del. Ch. 1998) (board permitted to establish process for selling company and need not negotiate with party who refuses to abide by that process). For cases questioning no-shops in transactions not triggering *Revlon* duties, see Note 8, below.

(4) **Effect on sales of control.** Does *QVC* alter the duties of directors in connection with sales of control or does it merely apply standards set forth in earlier cases, such as *Revlon* or *Van Gorkom*? Recall that *Van Gorkom* closely scrutinized the director-approved sale of Trans Union in part because it found that the board's "market test" of the terms of the transaction was inadequate. Is a market test *necessary* under *QVC*? Is it *sufficient*? *In re Pennaco Energy, Inc.*[81] upheld the board's decision to sell the corporation without first actively canvassing the market, because the transaction was structured to ensure an effective post-agreement check. The court noted, among other things, (1) a relatively weak no-shop that permitted Pennaco to talk and provide information to any party that could reasonably be expected to make a superior offer, (2) a termination fee at the traditional 3% level, (3) the buyer's agreement not to commence a tender offer for at least two weeks to give potential buyers "breathing room" to make competing bids," and (4) publicity designed to give the marketplace knowledge of Pennaco's ability to speak with others.

(5) **Effect on other takeover defenses.** Does *QVC* change director duties under *Unocal* and *Time* with respect to takeover defenses other than those involving a sale of control? In particular, does it impose on target boards who have not decided to sell the company any special duty to negotiate with those who make or threaten to make unsolicited takeover offers? Consider, in this regard, footnote 13 to the court's opinion. **Cunningham & Yablon** argued that *QVC* imposed on managers a "unified" duty to achieve best value reasonably available in all takeover actions. But **Kahan** suggested that courts would impose only process-type review unless the board is selling the company or changing control in other than a pre-planned, "strategic"-type transaction as in the *Time*.

The **Kahan** view is supported by *In re Santa Fe Pacific Corp. Shareholder Litigation*,[82] which, in rejecting the plaintiffs' *Revlon* claims, stated that the "Plaintiffs have failed to state a claim that the Board had a duty to *seek the transaction offering the best value reasonably available to the stockholders*" (emphasis added) that arose under the sale-of-control circumstances identified in *QVC*. Also, *Unitrin, Inc. v. American General Corp.*[83] held that the Chancery Court erred in interpreting *Unocal's* proportionality prong to require that a defensive response be "necessary." Instead, the Court said, "[a]n examination of the cases applying *Unocal* reveals a direct correlation between findings of proportionality or disproportionality and the judicial determination of whether a defensive response was *draconian* because it was either *coercive* or *preclusive* in character." (Emphasis added.) It defined "preclusive" as making the bidder's success "mathematically impossible or realistically unattainable." If a response is neither coercive nor preclusive, the Court concluded, "the Unocal proportionality test requires the focus of enhanced judicial scrutiny to shift to the 'range of reasonableness'" test of

---

[81]   787 A.2d 691 (Del. Ch. 2001).

[82]   669 A.2d 59 (Del. 1995).

[83]   651 A.2d 1361, 1385-89 (Del. 1995).

QVC. Under that test, a defensive measure must be upheld if the court finds that the board made a reasonable, though perhaps imperfect, decision. The court remanded for an evaluation under this standard of the Unitrin board's authorization of a repurchase of shares that would increase its directors' holdings from 23% to 28% of its stock, giving them the power to block a merger with a 15% shareholder under a charter provision that required a 75% stockholder vote for mergers with interested shareholders. *Moore Corp. Ltd. v. Wallace Computer Services, Inc.*[84] upheld refusal to redeem a poison pill in response to a hostile bid as not coercive or preclusive because the bidder could wage a proxy contest for control if its ownership stayed below the pill's 20% trigger level.

Unitrin and *Moore* suggest that a defensive response, including a failure to redeem a poison pill, will not be deemed preclusive under *Unocal* if a proxy contest remains a viable alternative. For a critique of the Delaware Supreme Court's apparent preference for elections over market transactions such as tender offers, see **Gilson**. Is a proxy contest a viable alternative to a tender offer when the target firm has a classified board of directors? For a recent case suggesting that it is not, see *Hilton Hotels Corp. v. ITT Corp.*, discussed in Note 1 following *Blasius* in Section 14.02[A]. What if the target company has a "dead-hand" or "no-hand" poison pill (*see* Section 14.03[A][2][d]), which prevents an acquirer-controlled board elected after a successful proxy fight from redeeming the pill? The latter issue is discussed further in Subsection [4] below.

(6) **Triggering *QVC*.** If *QVC* does impose a special duty, when, exactly, does this duty arise? Does the duty apply whenever the director action insulates the action from the discipline of the market for control? Can courts readily identify these situations? For example, *In re Lukens Inc. Shareholders Litigation*[85] applied *Revlon* duties where 62% of the merger consideration was cash and 38% was shares of common stock of a widely held corporation with no controlling shareholder.

(7) **The impact of *Cinerama*.** Assume that the devices designed to ensure that no third party interfered with the Viacom-Paramount merger worked, so that QVC never made a bid for Paramount. Would Paramount shareholders have been able to recover damages in a derivative suit against the Paramount directors based on allegations that the directors breached their fiduciary duties to the shareholders by approving a merger agreement that included the no-shop, the termination fee, and the stock option? Consider *Cinerama v. Technicolor, Inc.*,[86] which held that, although target directors breached their fiduciary duties to the shareholders by approving a sale of the company without adequately canvassing the market, they carried their burden of establishing entire fairness. How might this bear on directors' duties in connection with sales of control?

---

[84] 907 F. Supp. 1545, 1563 (D. Del. 1995).

[85] 1999 Del. Ch. LEXIS 233, 1999 WL 1135143 (Del. Ch., Dec. 1, 1999).

[86] 663 A.2d 1156 (Del. 1995) (discussed in Note 3 following *Technicolor* in Section 9.03[D]).

(8) **Protecting strategic mergers.** Does *QVC* mean that "strategic" mergers that do not contemplate a "break-up" of the corporation or an abandonment of the corporation's long term strategy and that do not shift control to a single shareholder or related group of shareholders get the protection of the business judgment rule? Some decisions have balked at stringent deal-protection provisions in this context. *Brazen v. Bell Atlantic Corp.*[87] upheld a stock-for-stock merger agreement that provided for a reciprocal termination fee of $550 million to compensate either party if the merger did not occur because of certain enumerated events, including a party's receipt of a competing offer. However, the Delaware Supreme Court rejected the Chancery Court's reliance on the business judgment rule, instead testing the termination fee under the legal standards applicable to liquidated damages provisions generally—that is, actual damages from terminating the merger agreement were uncertain and the $550 million amount was reasonable. This suggests that a "reasonableness" test may be applied to termination fee provisions even when there is no sale of control under *QVC*. For further consideration of rules related to strategic mergers, see *Omnicare,* immediately below.

(9) **Evaluation and analysis of *QVC*: director power vs. fiduciary duty.** Compare the court's approach in *QVC* with one that focuses on the directors' power under the corporate statute and charter. Where the corporate statute appears to give shareholders the ultimate power to decide on sales of the company, and where there is no alteration of this rule in the corporate charter, should courts deny directors the power to enter into lock-ups and related devices that, in effect, sell the company without shareholder approval irrespective of whether directors breached a fiduciary duty? Conversely, should a transaction in which the directors are not effectively selling control be analyzed under the standard business judgment rule (*see* Section 9.03)? *See* **Ribstein** and Note 9 following the *Unocal* excerpt in Section 14.03[D][2].

The following case revisits the legal standards that apply to "strategic" mergers that have the effect of fending off a competing bid. Although these transactions do not necessarily trigger enhanced scrutiny under *Revlon* and *QVC*, this case indicates that devices employed to protect the deals from being upset by a competing transaction may make the transaction vulnerable to attack.

OMNICARE, INC. v. NCS HEALTHCARE, INC.
Supreme Court of Delaware
2003 Del. LEXIS 195 (April 4, 2003)

[This case arose out of competing bids for NCS Healthcare, Inc. ("NCS") by Genesis Health Ventures, Inc. ("Genesis") and Omnicare, Inc. ("Omnicare"). Jon H. Outcalt, Chairman of the NCS board of directors, owned 202,063 shares of NCS Class A common stock and 3,476,086 shares of Class B common stock. Kevin B. Shaw, President, CEO and a

---

[87]   695 A.2d 43 (Del. 1997).

director of NCS, owned 28,905 shares of NCS Class A common stock and 1,141,134 shares of Class B common stock. The other two board members were Boake A. Sells, a graduate of the Harvard Business School and former Chairman and CEO at Revco Drugstores, and Richard L. Osborne, a full-time professor at the Weatherhead School of Management at Case Western Reserve University.

[Beginning in late 1999, due to adverse conditions in the health care industry, NCS began having problems collecting accounts receivables, causing its stock to decline. As a result, NCS began to explore strategic alternatives. In February 2000, NCS retained UBS Warburg, L.L.C. to identify potential acquirers and possible equity investors, but by October had only received one non-binding indication of interest for $190 million, which was substantially less than the face value of NCS's senior debt. In the summer of 2001, NCS invited Omnicare, Inc. to begin discussions with Brown Gibbons (NCS' new financial advisor) regarding a possible transaction. On July 20, Joel Gemunder, Omnicare's President and CEO, proposed to acquire NCS in a bankruptcy sale for $225 million, later increased to $270 million, but in any event lower than the face value of NCS's outstanding debt. In October 2001, Omnicare affirmed that it was not interested in a transaction other than an asset sale in bankruptcy. Moreover, Omnicare entered into secret discussions regarding an asset sale with a representative of NCS' noteholders committee.

[In January 2002 this committee contacted Genesis regarding a possible transaction. Genesis executed a confidentiality agreement and began a due diligence review. Genesis had previously lost a bidding war to Omnicare in a different transaction, resulting in bitter feelings between the companies' principals and Genesis' insistence on exclusivity agreements and lock-ups in any potential transaction with NCS.

[By early 2002, NCS' operating performance was improving, and NCS formed an "Independent Committee" of board members (Sells and Osborne) who were neither NCS employees nor major NCS stockholders, to pursue a transaction that could produce some recovery for NCS' shareholders. The Independent Committee initially sought a "stalking-horse merger partner" to obtain the highest possible value in any transaction. But Genesis made it clear that it did not want to be a "stalking horse." In June 2002, Genesis offered to negotiate a transaction that would take place outside of bankruptcy, conditioned on NCS' execution of an exclusivity agreement as the first step towards a completely locked up transaction that would preclude a higher bid from Omnicare. Following NCS' execution of the requested exclusivity agreement (originally scheduled to expire on July 19, but subsequently extended to July 31), the parties began negotiating a merger agreement that would provide NCS shareholders with $24 million in Genesis stock.

[As negotiations between NCS and Genesis neared completion in late July, Omnicare suspected that a deal was in the offing that would pose a competitive threat. On July 26, 2002, Omnicare proposed a transaction in which Omnicare would retire NCS' senior and subordinated debt at par plus accrued interest, and pay the NCS stockholders $3 cash for their shares, conditioned on negotiating a merger agreement and completing due diligence. However, the Independent Committee concluded that discussions with Omnicare would constitute a breach of NCS' exclusivity agreement with Genesis and risk causing Genesis to abandon merger discussions. On July 27, Genesis responded to the news of the Omnicare offer by proposing substantially improved terms, increasing by 80% the ratio of Genesis stock to be exchanged for NCS stock on the condition that the transaction be approved by midnight July 28.

[On July 28, the Independent Committee unanimously recommended the transaction in a meeting that lasted less than an hour, but that the Court of Chancery determined left the directors fully informed of all material facts. This was followed by full Board approval, based on the conclusion that "balancing the potential loss of the Genesis deal against the uncertainty of Omnicare's letter, results in the conclusion that the only reasonable alternative for the Board of Directors is to approve the Genesis transaction."]

[As the Court described the key agreements:] Among other things, the NCS/Genesis merger agreement provided the following:

—NCS stockholders would receive 1 share of Genesis common stock in exchange for every 10 shares of NCS common stock held;

—NCS would submit the merger agreement to NCS stockholders regardless of whether the NCS board continued to recommend the merger;

—NCS would not enter into discussions with third parties concerning an alternative acquisition of NCS, or provide non-public information to such parties, unless, among other things, the NCS board believed in good faith that the proposal was or was likely to result in an acquisition on terms superior to those contemplated by the NCS/Genesis merger agreement; and

—If the merger agreement were to be terminated, under certain circumstances NCS would be required to pay Genesis a $6 million termination fee and/or Genesis' documented expenses, up to $5 million.

Voting Agreements

Outcalt and Shaw, in their capacity as NCS stockholders, entered into voting agreements with Genesis. NCS was also required to be a party to the voting agreements by Genesis. Those agreements provided, among other things, that:

—Outcalt and Shaw were acting in their capacity as NCS stockholders in executing the agreements, not in their capacity as NCS directors or officers;

—Neither Outcalt nor Shaw would transfer their shares prior to the stockholder vote on the merger agreement;

—Outcalt and Shaw agreed to vote all of their shares in favor of the merger agreement; and

—Outcalt and Shaw granted to Genesis an irrevocable proxy to vote their shares in favor of the merger agreement.

—The voting agreement was specifically enforceable by Genesis.

The merger agreement further provided that if either Outcalt or Shaw breached the terms of the voting agreements, Genesis would be entitled to terminate the merger agreement and potentially receive a $6 million termination fee from NCS. Such a breach was impossible since Section 6 provided that the voting agreements were specifically enforceable by Genesis.

[On July 29, 2002, hours after the NCS/Genesis transaction was executed, Omnicare restated its proposal and faxed a draft merger agreement. Later that morning, Omnicare issued a press release publicly disclosing the proposal. On August 1, 2002, Omnicare filed a lawsuit attempting to enjoin the NCS/Genesis merger, and announced its intention to launch a tender offer for NCS' shares at a price of $3.50 per share. On October 6, 2002, Omnicare irrevocably committed itself to acquire NCS Class A and Class B shares for $3.50 per share cash.

[On October 21, 2002, the NCS board withdrew its recommendation that the stockholders vote in favor of the NCS/Genesis merger agreement, and NCS' financial advisor withdrew its fairness opinion. But pursuant to the Genesis merger agreement, the NCS board was still bound to submit the merger to a stockholder vote. In an SEC filing, the NCS board explained that, although it would recommend against the merger, its success was assured because "(1) the existing contractual obligations to Genesis currently prevent NCS from accepting the Omnicare irrevocable merger proposal; and (2) the existence of the voting agreements entered into by Messrs. Outcalt and Shaw, whereby Messrs. Outcalt and Shaw agreed to vote their shares of NCS Class A common stock and NCS Class B common stock in favor of the Genesis merger, ensure NCS stockholder approval of the Genesis merger." Omnicare sued to prevent consummation of the Genesis transaction.]

HOLLAND, Justice, for the majority:

* * *

. . . This Court has held that a board's decision to enter into a merger transaction that does not involve a change in control is entitled to judicial deference pursuant to the procedural and substantive operation of the business judgment rule. When a board decides to enter into a merger transaction that will result in a change of control, however, enhanced judicial scrutiny under *Revlon* is the standard of review.

* * *

The Court of Chancery's decision to review the NCS board's decision to merge with Genesis under the business judgment rule rather than the enhanced scrutiny standard of *Revlon* is not outcome determinative for the purposes of deciding this appeal. We have assumed arguendo that the business judgment rule applied to the decision by the NCS board to merge with Genesis. We have also assumed arguendo that the NCS board exercised due care when it: abandoned the Independent Committee's recommendation to pursue a stalking horse strategy, without even trying to implement it; executed an exclusivity agreement with Genesis; acceded to Genesis' twenty-four hour ultimatum for making a final merger decision; and executed a merger agreement that was summarized but never completely read by the NCS board of directors.

Deal Protection Devices Require Enhanced Scrutiny

* * *

There are inherent conflicts between a board's interest in protecting a merger transaction it has approved, the stockholders' statutory right to make the final decision to either approve or not approve a merger, and the board's continuing responsibility to effectively exercise its fiduciary duties at all times after the merger agreement is executed. These competing considerations require a threshold determination that board-approved defensive devices protecting a merger transaction are within the limitations of its statutory authority and consistent with the directors' fiduciary duties. Accordingly, in *Paramount v. Time*, we held that the business judgment rule applied to the Time board's original decision to merge with Warner. We further held, however, that defensive devices adopted by the board to protect the original merger transaction must withstand enhanced judicial scrutiny under the *Unocal* standard of review, even when that merger transaction does not result in a change of control.

Enhanced Scrutiny Generally

* * *

In *QVC*, we explained that the application of an enhanced judicial scrutiny test involves a judicial "review of the reasonableness of the substantive merits of the board's actions." In applying that standard, we held that "a court should not ignore the complexity of the directors' task" in the context in which action was taken. Accordingly, we concluded that a court applying enhanced judicial scrutiny should not decide whether the directors made a perfect decision but instead should decide whether "the directors' decision was, on balance, within a range of reasonableness."

In *Unitrin*, we explained the *"ratio decidendi* for the 'range of reasonableness' standard" when a court applies enhanced judicial scrutiny to director action pursuant to our holding in *Unocal*. It is a recognition that a board of directors needs "latitude in discharging its fiduciary duties to the corporation and its shareholders when defending against perceived threats." "The concomitant requirement is for judicial restraint." Therefore, if the board of directors' collective defensive responses are not draconian (preclusive or coercive) and are "within a 'range of reasonableness,' a court must not substitute its judgment for the board's [judgment]." The same *ratio decidendi* applies to the "range of reasonableness" when courts apply *Unocal*'s enhanced judicial scrutiny standard to defensive devices intended to protect a merger agreement that will not result in a change of control.

* * *

When the focus of judicial scrutiny shifts to the range of reasonableness, *Unocal* requires that any defensive devices must be proportionate to the perceived threat to the corporation and its stockholders if the merger transaction is not consummated. Defensive devices taken to protect a merger agreement executed by a board of directors are intended to give that agreement an advantage over any subsequent transactions that materialize before the merger is approved by the stockholders and consummated. This is analogous to the favored treatment that a board of directors may properly give to encourage an initial bidder when it discharges its fiduciary duties under *Revlon*.

Therefore, in the context of a merger that does not involve a change of control, when defensive devices in the executed merger agreement are challenged *vis-a-vis* their effect on a subsequent competing alternative merger transaction, this Court's analysis in *Macmillan* is didactic. In the context of a case of defensive measures taken against an existing bidder, we stated in *Macmillan*:

> In the face of disparate treatment, the trial court must first examine whether the directors properly perceived that shareholder interests were enhanced. In any event the board's action must be reasonable in relation to the advantage sought to be achieved [by the merger it approved], or conversely, to the threat which a [competing transaction] poses to stockholder interests. If on the basis of this enhanced *Unocal* scrutiny the trial court is satisfied that the test has been met, then the directors' actions necessarily are entitled to the protections of the business judgment rule.

The latitude a board will have in either maintaining or using the defensive devices it has adopted to protect the merger it approved will vary according to the degree of benefit or detriment to the stockholders' interests that is presented by the value or terms of the subsequent competing transaction.

* * *

These Deal Protection Devices Unenforceable

* * *

Pursuant to the judicial scrutiny required under *Unocal*'s two-stage analysis, the NCS directors must first demonstrate "that they had reasonable grounds for believing that a danger to corporate policy and effectiveness existed . . . ." To satisfy that burden, the NCS directors are required to show they acted in good faith after conducting a reasonable investigation. The threat identified by the NCS board was the possibility of losing the Genesis offer and being left with no comparable alternative transaction.

The second stage of the *Unocal* test requires the NCS directors to demonstrate that their defensive response was "reasonable in relation to the threat posed." This inquiry involves a two-step analysis. The NCS directors must first establish that the merger deal protection devices adopted in response to the threat were not "coercive" or "preclusive," and then demonstrate that their response was within a "range of reasonable responses" to the threat perceived. . . .

. . . In this case, the deal protection devices of the NCS board were *both* preclusive and coercive.

This Court enunciated the standard for determining stockholder coercion in the case of *Williams v. Geier*. A stockholder vote may be nullified by wrongful coercion "where the board or some other party takes actions which have the effect of causing the stockholders to vote in favor of the proposed transaction for some reason other than the merits of that transaction." . . .

. . . In this case, the Court of Chancery did not expressly address the issue of "coercion" in its *Unocal* analysis. It did find as a fact, however, that NCS's public stockholders (who owned 80% of NCS and overwhelmingly supported Omnicare's offer) will be forced to accept the Genesis merger because of the structural defenses approved by the NCS board. Consequently, the record reflects that any stockholder vote would have been robbed of its effectiveness by the impermissible coercion that predetermined the outcome of the merger without regard to the merits of the Genesis transaction at the time the vote was scheduled to be taken. Deal protection devices that result in such coercion cannot withstand *Unocal*'s enhanced judicial scrutiny standard of review because they are not within the range of reasonableness.

Although the minority stockholders were not forced to vote for the Genesis merger, they were required to accept it because it was *a fait accompli*. The record reflects that the defensive devices employed by the NCS board are preclusive and coercive in the sense that they accomplished *a fait accompli*. In this case, despite the fact that the NCS board has withdrawn its recommendation for the Genesis transaction and recommended its rejection by the stockholders, the deal protection devices approved by the NCS board operated in concert to have a preclusive and coercive effect. Those tripartite defensive measures—the Section 251(c) provision, the voting agreements, and the absence of an effective fiduciary out clause—made it "mathematically impossible" and "realistically unattainable" for the Omnicare transaction or any other proposal to succeed, no matter how superior the proposal.

The deal protection devices adopted by the NCS board were designed to coerce the consummation of the Genesis merger and preclude the consideration of any superior transaction. The NCS directors' defensive devices are not within a reasonable range of responses to the perceived threat of losing the Genesis offer because they are preclusive and coercive. Accordingly, we hold that those deal protection devices are unenforceable.

Effective Fiduciary Out Required

The defensive measures that protected the merger transaction are unenforceable not only because they are preclusive and coercive but, alternatively, they are unenforceable because they are invalid as they operate in this case. Given the specifically enforceable irrevocable voting agreements, the provision in the merger agreement requiring the board to submit the transaction for a stockholder vote and the omission of a fiduciary out clause in the merger agreement completely prevented the board from discharging its fiduciary responsibilities to the minority stockholders when Omnicare presented its superior transaction. "To the extent that a [merger] contract, or a provision thereof, purports to require a board to act or not act in such a fashion as to limit the exercise of fiduciary duties, it is invalid and unenforceable."

* * *

Under the circumstances presented in this case, where a cohesive group of stockholders with majority voting power was irrevocably committed to the merger transaction, "[e]ffective representation of the financial interests of the minority shareholders imposed upon the [NCS board] an affirmative responsibility to protect those minority shareholders' interests." The NCS board could not abdicate its fiduciary duties to the minority by leaving it to the stockholders alone to approve or disapprove the merger agreement because two stockholders had already combined to establish a majority of the voting power that made the outcome of the stockholder vote a foregone conclusion.

The Court of Chancery noted that Section 251(c) of the Delaware General Corporation Law now permits boards to agree to submit a merger agreement for a stockholder vote, even if the Board later withdraws its support for that agreement and recommends that the stockholders reject it.[80] The Court of Chancery also noted that stockholder voting agreements are permitted by Delaware law. In refusing to certify this interlocutory appeal, the Court of Chancery stated "it is simply nonsensical to say that a board of directors abdicates its duties to manage the 'business and affairs' of a corporation under Section 141(a) of the DGCL by agreeing to the inclusion in a merger agreement of a term authorized by § 251(c) of the same statute."

Taking action that is otherwise legally possible, however, does not *ipso facto* comport with the fiduciary responsibilities of directors in all circumstances. . . .

Genesis admits that when the NCS board agreed to its merger conditions, the NCS board was seeking to assure that the NCS creditors were paid in full and that the NCS stockholders received the highest value available for their stock. In fact, Genesis defends its "bulletproof" merger agreement on that basis. We hold that the NCS board did not have authority to accede to the Genesis demand for an absolute "lock-up."

The directors of a Delaware corporation have a continuing obligation to discharge their fiduciary responsibilities, as future circumstances develop, after a merger agreement is announced. Genesis anticipated the likelihood of a superior offer after its merger agreement was announced and demanded defensive measures from the NCS board that *completely* protected its transaction. Instead of agreeing to the absolute defense of the Genesis merger from a superior offer, however, the NCS board was required to negotiate a fiduciary out clause to protect the NCS stockholders if the Genesis transaction became an inferior offer. By acceding to Genesis' ultimatum for complete protection *in futuro*, the NCS board disabled itself from exercising its own fiduciary obligations at a time when the board's own judgment is most important, *i.e.* receipt of a subsequent superior offer.

* * *

The NCS board was required to contract for an effective fiduciary out clause to exercise its continuing fiduciary responsibilities to the minority stockholders.[88] The issues in this appeal do not involve the general validity of either stockholder voting agreements or the authority of directors to insert a Section 251(c) provision in a merger agreement. In this case, the NCS board combined those two otherwise valid actions and caused them to operate in concert as an absolute lock up, in the absence of an effective fiduciary out clause in the Genesis merger agreement.

In the context of this preclusive and coercive lock up case, the protection of Genesis' contractual expectations must yield to the supervening responsibility of the directors to discharge their fiduciary duties on a continuing basis. The merger agreement and voting agreements, as they were combined to operate in concert in this case, are inconsistent with

---

[80]   Section 251(c) was amended in 1998 to allow for the inclusion in a merger agreement of a term requiring that the agreement be put to a vote of stockholders whether or not their directors continue to recommend the transaction. Before this amendment, Section 251 was interpreted as precluding a stockholder vote if the board of directors, after approving the merger agreement but before the stockholder vote, decided no longer to recommend it. *See Smith v. Van Gorkom*, 488 A.2d 858, 887-88 (Del. 1985).

[88]   *See Paramount Communications Inc. v. QVC Network Inc.*, 637 A.2d at 42-43. Merger agreements involve an ownership decision and, therefore, cannot become final without stockholder approval. Other contracts do not require a fiduciary out clause because they involve business judgments that are within the *exclusive* province of the board of directors' power to manage the affairs of the corporation. *See Grimes v. Donald*, 673 A.2d 1207, 1214-15 (Del. 1996).

the NCS directors' fiduciary duties. To that extent, we hold that they are invalid and unenforceable.

* * *

VEASEY, Chief Justice, with whom STEELE, Justice, joins dissenting:

The beauty of the Delaware corporation law, and the reason it has worked so well for stockholders, directors and officers, is that the framework is based on an enabling statute with the Court of Chancery and the Supreme Court applying principles of fiduciary duty in a common law mode on a case-by-case basis. Fiduciary duty cases are inherently fact-intensive and, therefore, unique. This case is unique in two important respects. First, the peculiar facts presented render this case an unlikely candidate for substantial repetition. Second, this is a rare 3-2 split decision of the Supreme Court.

* * *

The process by which this merger agreement came about involved a joint decision by the controlling stockholders and the board of directors to secure what appeared to be the only value-enhancing transaction available for a company on the brink of bankruptcy. The Majority adopts a new rule of law that imposes a prohibition on the NCS board's ability to act in concert with controlling stockholders to lock up this merger. The Majority reaches this conclusion by analyzing the challenged deal protection measures as isolated board actions. The Majority concludes that the board owed a duty to the NCS minority stockholders to refrain from acceding to the Genesis demand for an irrevocable lock-up notwithstanding the compelling circumstances confronting the board and the board's disinterested, informed, good faith exercise of its business judgment.

Because we believe this Court must respect the reasoned judgment of the board of directors and give effect to the wishes of the controlling stockholders, we respectfully disagree with the Majority's reasoning that results in a holding that the confluence of board and stockholder action constitutes a breach of fiduciary duty. The essential fact that must always be remembered is that this agreement and the voting commitments of Outcalt and Shaw concluded a lengthy search and intense negotiation process in the context of insolvency and creditor pressure where no other viable bid had emerged. Accordingly, we endorse the Vice Chancellor's well-reasoned analysis that the NCS board's action before the hostile bid emerged was within the bounds of its fiduciary duties under these facts.

We share with the Majority and the independent NCS board of directors the motivation to serve carefully and in good faith the best interests of the corporate enterprise and, thereby, the stockholders of NCS. It is now known, of course, after the case is over, that the stockholders of NCS will receive substantially more by tendering their shares into the topping bid of Omnicare than they would have received in the Genesis merger, as a result of the post-agreement Omnicare bid and the injunctive relief ordered by the Majority of this Court. Our jurisprudence cannot, however, be seen as turning on such ex post felicitous results. Rather, the NCS board's good faith decision must be subject to a real-time review of the board action before the NCS-Genesis merger agreement was entered into.

* * *

It is regrettable that the Court is split in this important case. One hopes that the Majority rule announced here—though clearly erroneous in our view—will be interpreted narrowly and will be seen as *sui generis*. By deterring bidders from engaging in negotiations like those present here and requiring that there must always be a fiduciary out, the universe of potential bidders who could reasonably be expected to benefit stockholders could shrink or disappear. Nevertheless, if the holding is confined to these unique facts, negotiators may be able to navigate around this new hazard.

Accordingly, we respectfully dissent.

STEELE, Justice, dissenting:

I respectfully dissent from the majority opinion, join the Chief Justice's dissent in all respects and dissent separately in order to crystallize the central focus of my objection to the majority view.

* * *

We should not encourage proscriptive rules that invalidate or render unenforceable precommitment strategies negotiated between two parties to a contract who will presumably, in the absence of conflicted interest, bargain intensely over every meaningful provision of a contract after a careful cost benefit analysis. Where could this plain common sense approach be more wisely invoked than where a board, free of conflict, fully informed, supported by the equally conflict-free holders of the largest economic interest in the transaction, reaches the conclusion that a voting lockup strategy is the best course to obtain the most benefit for all stockholders?

This fundamental principle of Delaware law so eloquently put in the Chief Justice's dissent, is particularly applicable here where the NCS board had no alternative if the company were to be saved. If attorneys counseling well-motivated, careful, and well-advised boards cannot be assured that their clients' decision—sound at the time but later less economically beneficial only because of post-decision, unforeseeable events—will be respected by the courts, Delaware law, and the courts that expound it, may well be questioned. I would not shame the NCS board, which acted in accordance with every fine instinct that we wish to encourage, by invalidating their action approving the Genesis merger because they failed to insist upon a fiduciary out. . . .

* * *

Lockup provisions attempt to assure parties that have lost business opportunities and incurred substantial costs that their deal will close. I am concerned that the majority decision will remove the certainty that adds value to any rational business plan. Perhaps transactions that include "force-the-vote" and voting agreement provisions that make approval a foregone conclusion will be the only deals invalidated prospectively. Even so, therein lies the problem. Instead of thoughtful, retrospective, restrained flexibility focused on the circumstances existing at the time of the decision, have we now moved to a bright line regulatory alternative?

For the majority to articulate and adopt an inflexible rule where a board has discharged both its fiduciary duty of loyalty and care in good faith seems a most unfortunate turn. Does the majority mean to signal a mandatory, bright line, *per se* efficient breach analysis *ex post* to all challenged merger agreements? Knowing the majority's general, genuine concern to do equity, I trust not. If so, our courts and the structure of our law that we have strived so hard to develop and perfect will prevent a board, responsible under Delaware law to make precisely the kind of decision made here, in good faith, free of self interest, after exercising scrupulous due care from honoring its contract obligations.

Therefore, I respectfully dissent.

NOTES AND QUESTIONS

(1) **The rule in *Omnicare*.** Although the Court assumed for the sake of argument that *Revlon* duties do not apply in stock-for-stock mergers, it required enhanced scrutiny of the lock-up under *Unocal*. Does, or should, this scrutiny of deal protection devices in stock-for-stock mergers differ from the scrutiny of similar devices in change-of-control transactions under *Revlon* and *QVC*?

(2) **Reconciling *Omnicare* with *Paramount v. Time*.** Is the lock-up in *Omnicare* any more preclusive or coercive than the steps taken by Time to ensure its shareholders wouldn't have an opportunity to block a merger with Warner (*i.e.*, restructuring the stock-for-stock merger as a cash tender offer to avoid a shareholder vote)? Couldn't Omnicare have launched a bid for a combined NCS-Genesis just as Paramount might have launched a bid for a combined Time-Warner?

(3) **Reconciling *Omnicare* with *QVC*.** Is an absolute lock-up a *per se* violation of fiduciary duty under *Revlon* and *QVC*, or do these cases just require the kind of case-by-case analysis of absolute lock-ups Chief Justice Veasey advocates in his *Omnicare* dissent? Does, or should, *Omnicare*'s *per se* rule extend to change-of-control transactions?

(4) **Fiduciary outs for other contracts.** Should "fiduciary outs" be required in contracts not involving mergers or sales of control? *See* footnote 88 to the *Omnicare* opinion.

REFERENCES

Cunningham & Yablon, *Delaware Fiduciary Duty Law after* QVC *and* Technicolor*: A Unified Standard (and the End of* Revlon *Duties?)*, 49 Bus. Law. 1593 (1994).

Gilson, Unocal *Fifteen Years Later (And What We Can Do About It)*, 26 Del. J. Corp. L. 491 (2001).

Kahan, Paramount *or Paradox: The Delaware Supreme Court's Takeover Jurisprudence*, 19 J. Corp. L. 583 (1994).

Ribstein, *Takeover Defenses and the Corporate Contract*, 78 Geo. L.J. 71 (1989).

[4] Dead-Hand and No-Hand Poison Pills

The poison pill, particularly the flip-in poison pill, has proven to be an extremely popular and formidable defense. In the pill's twenty-year history, not a single bidder has willingly triggered the flip-in or flip-over rights associated with a poison pill and the Delaware courts have only rarely ordered poison pills to be redeemed. This means that target boards can "just say no" to hostile takeovers by deploying and refusing to redeem poison pills with little fear that bidders will purchase control from the firm's share-holders or that courts will object. However, as noted earlier in Section 14.03[A][1][d]), directors typically reserve the right to redeem poison pills as long as no shareholder acquires the designated threshold stake in the firm. Accordingly, a determined bidder can attempt to avoid a poison pill by waging a proxy contest for control of the target board before it acquires a level of stock ownership sufficient to render the pill non-redeemable. If the proxy contest is successful, the bidder can use its newly won control to remove the pill so the bid can proceed.

To counter this strategy, some firms began adding "dead-hand" or "no-hand" pro-visions to their poison pills. Under the typical dead-hand provision, a poison pill can be redeemed only by the vote of a majority of the directors who were members of the board prior to the adoption of the poison pill (i.e., "continuing directors"); under the typ-ical "no-hand" provision, the poison pill becomes non-redeemable (either permanently or for a limited period of time) when the board members who deployed the poison pill (or their designated successors) no longer constitute a majority of the board. The legal-ity of dead-hand and no-hand provisions is considered in the following cases.

CARMODY v. TOLL BROTHERS, INC.

Delaware Court of Chancery

723 A.2d 1180 (1998)

Jacobs, Vice Chancellor.

At issue on this Rule 12(b)(6) motion to dismiss is whether a most recent innovation in corporate antitakeover measures—so-called "dead hand" poison pill rights plan—is sub-ject to legal challenge on the basis that it violates the Delaware General Corporation Law and/or the fiduciary duties of the board of directors who adopted the plan. . . .

I. FACTS

A. Background Leading to Adoption of the Plan

The firm whose rights plan is being challenged is Toll Brothers (sometimes referred to as "the company"), a Pennsylvania-based Delaware corporation that designs, builds, and markets single family luxury homes in thirteen states and five regions in the United States. The company was founded in 1967 by brothers Bruce and Robert Toll, who are its Chief Executive and Chief Operating Officers, respectively, and who own approximately 37.5% of Toll Brothers' common stock. The company's board of directors has nine members, four of whom (including Bruce and Robert Toll) are senior executive officers. The remaining five members of the board are "outside" independent directors.

* * *

. . . For some time [the home building] industry has been undergoing consolidation through the acquisition process . . . . Inherent in any such expansion-through- acquisition environment is the risk of a hostile takeover. To protect against that risk, the company's board of directors adopted the Rights Plan.

B. The Rights Plan

* * *

1. The Rights Plan's "Flip In" and "Flip Over" Features

* * *

. . . The dilutive mechanism of the Rights is "triggered" by certain defined events. One such event is the acquisition of 15% or more of Toll Brothers' stock by any person or group of affiliated or associated persons. Should that occur, each Rights holder (except the acquiror and its affiliates and associates) becomes entitled to buy two shares of Toll Brothers common stock or other securities at half price. . . . [T]his so-called "flip in" feature of the Rights Plan would massively dilute the value of the holdings of the unwanted acquiror.

* * *

The complaint alleges that the purpose and effect of the company's Rights Plan, as with most poison pills, is to make any hostile acquisition of Toll Brothers prohibitively expensive, and thereby to deter such acquisitions unless the target company's board first approves the acquisition proposal. The target board's "leverage" derives from [a] critical feature found in most rights plans: the directors' power to redeem the Rights at any time before they expire, on such conditions as the directors "in their sole discretion" may establish. To this extent there is little to distinguish the company's Rights Plan from the "standard model." What is distinctive about the Rights Plan is that it authorizes only a specific, defined category of directors—the "Continuing Directors"—to redeem the Rights. The dispute over the legality of this "Continuing Director" or "dead hand" feature of the Rights Plan is what drives this lawsuit.

2. The "Dead Hand" Feature of the Rights Plan

In substance, the "dead hand" provision operates to prevent any directors of Toll Brothers, except those who were in office as of the date of the Rights Plan's adoption (June 12, 1997) or their designated successors, from redeeming the Rights until they expire on June 12, 2007. That consequence flows directly from the Rights Agreement's definition of a "Continuing Director," which is:

> (i) any member of the Board of Directors of the Company, while such person is a member of the Board, who is not an Acquiring Person, or an Affiliate [as defined] or Associate [as defined] of an Acquiring Person, or a representative or nominee of an Acquiring Person or of any such Affiliate or Associate, and was

a member of the Board prior to the date of this agreement, or (ii) any Person who subsequently becomes a member of the Board, while such Person is a member of the Board, who is not an Acquiring Person, or an Affiliate [as defined] or Associate [as defined] of an Acquiring Person, or a representative or nominee of an Acquiring Person or of any such Affiliate or Associate, if such Person's nomination for election or election to the Board is recommended or approved by a majority of the Continuing Directors.

According to the complaint, this "dead hand" provision has a twofold practical effect. First, it makes an unsolicited offer for the company more unlikely by eliminating a proxy contest as a useful way for a hostile acquiror to gain control, because even if the acquiror wins the contest, its newly-elected director representatives could not redeem the Rights. Second, the "dead hand" provision disenfranchises, in a proxy contest, all shareholders that wish the company to be managed by a board empowered to redeem the Rights, by depriving those shareholders of any practical choice except to vote for the incumbent directors. Given these effects, the plaintiff claims that the only purpose that the "dead hand" provision could serve is to discourage future acquisition activity by making any proxy contest to replace incumbent board members an exercise in futility.

II. OVERVIEW OF THE PROBLEM AND THE PARTIES' CONTENTIONS

* * *

A. Overview

The critical issue on this motion is whether a "dead hand" provision in a "poison pill" rights plan is subject to legal challenge on the basis that it is invalid as ultra vires, or as a breach of fiduciary duty, or both. Although that issue has been the subject of scholarly comment, it has yet to be decided under Delaware law, and to date it has been addressed by only two courts applying the law of other jurisdictions.[10]

* * *

III. ANALYSIS

* * *

B. The Validity of the "Dead Hand" Provision

1. The Invalidity Contentions

The plaintiff's complaint attacks the "dead hand" feature of the Toll Brothers poison pill on both statutory and fiduciary duty grounds. The statutory claim is that the "dead hand" provision unlawfully restricts the powers of future boards by creating different classes of directors—those who have the power to redeem the poison pill, and those who do not.

---

[10]   The jurisdictions that have directly addressed the legality of the dead hand poison pill are New York, *see Bank of New York Co., Inc. v. Irving Bank Corp., et. al.,* N.Y. Sup.Ct., 139 Misc.2d 665, 528 N.Y.S.2d 482 (1988), and the United States District Court for the Northern District of Georgia, *see Invacare Corp. v. Healthdyne Technologies. Inc.,* N.D. Ga., 968 F. Supp. 1578 (1997) (applying Georgia law). . . .

Under 8 Del. C. §§ 141(a) and (d), any such restrictions and director classifications must be stated in the certificate of incorporation. The complaint alleges that because those restrictions are not stated in the Toll Brothers charter, the "dead hand" provision of the Rights Plan is ultra vires and, consequently, invalid on its face.

The complaint also alleges that even if the Rights Plan is not ultra vires, its approval constituted a breach of the Toll Brothers board's fiduciary duty of loyalty in several respects. It is alleged that the board violated its duty of loyalty because (a) the "dead hand" provision was enacted solely or primarily for entrenchment purposes; (b) it was also a disproportionate defensive measure, since it precludes the shareholders from receiving tender offers and engaging in a proxy contest, in contravention of the principles of *Unocal Corp. v. Mesa Petroleum Co.* ("*Unocal*"), as elucidated in *Unitrin, Inc. v. American General Corp.* ("*Unitrin*") and (c) the "dead hand" provision purposefully interferes with the shareholder voting franchise without any compelling justification, in derogation of the principles articulated in *Blasius Indus. v. Atlas Corp.* ("*Blasius*").

* * *

2. The Statutory Invalidity Claims

Having carefully considered the arguments and authorities marshaled by both sides, the Court concludes that the complaint states legally sufficient claims that the "dead hand" provision of the Toll Brothers Rights Plan violates 8 Del. C. §§ 141(a) and (d). There are three reasons.

First, it cannot be disputed that the Rights Plan confers the power to redeem the pill only upon some, but not all, of the directors. But under § 141(d), the power to create voting power distinctions among directors exists only where there is a classified board, and where those voting power distinctions are expressed in the certificate of incorporation. Section 141(d) pertinently provides:

> . . . The certificate of incorporation may confer upon holders of any class or series of stock the right to elect 1 or more directors who shall serve for such term, and have such voting powers as shall be stated in the certificate of incorporation. The terms of office and voting powers of the directors elected in the manner so provided in the certificate of incorporation may be greater than or less than those of any other director or class of directors . . . .

The plain, unambiguous meaning of the quoted language is that if one category or group of directors is given distinctive voting rights not shared by the other directors, those distinctive voting rights must be set forth in the certificate of incorporation. In the case of Toll Brothers (the complaint alleges), they are not.

Second, § 141(d) mandates that the "right to elect 1 or more directors who shall . . . have such [greater] voting powers" is reserved to the stockholders, not to the directors or a subset thereof. Absent express language in the charter, nothing in Delaware law suggests that some directors of a public corporation may be created less equal than other directors, and certainly not by unilateral board action. Vesting the pill redemption power exclusively in the Continuing Directors transgresses the statutorily protected shareholder right to elect the directors who would be so empowered. For that reason, and because it is claimed that the

Rights Plan's allocation of voting power to redeem the Rights is nowhere found in the Toll Brothers certificate of incorporation, the complaint states a claim that the "dead hand" feature of the Rights Plan is ultra vires, and hence, statutorily invalid under Delaware law.

Third, the complaint states a claim that the "dead hand" provision would impermissibly interfere with the directors' statutory power to manage the business and affairs of the corporation. That power is conferred by 8 Del. C. § 141(a), which mandates:

> The business and affairs of every corporation organized under this chapter shall be managed by or under the direction of a board of directors, except as may be otherwise provided in this chapter or in its certificate of incorporation . . . .

The "dead hand" poison pill is intended to thwart hostile bids by vesting shareholders with preclusive rights that cannot be redeemed except by the Continuing Directors. Thus, the one action that could make it practically possible to redeem the pill—replacing the entire board—could make that pill redemption legally impossible to achieve. The "dead hand" provision would jeopardize a newly-elected *future* board's ability to achieve a business combination by depriving that board of the power to redeem the pill without obtaining the consent of the "Continuing Directors," who (it may be assumed) would constitute a minority of the board. In this manner, it is claimed, the "dead hand" provision would interfere with the board's power to protect fully the corporation's (and its shareholders') interests in a transaction that is one of the most fundamental and important in the life of a business enterprise.

* * *

. . . [The defendants' argument that the "dead hand" provision is tantamount to a delegation to a special committee, consisting of the Continuing Directors, of the power to redeem the pill] rests upon an analogy that has no basis in fact. In adopting the Rights Plan, the board did not, nor did it purport to, create a special committee having the exclusive power to redeem the pill. The analogy also ignores fundamental structural differences between the creation of a special board committee and the operation of the "dead hand" provision of the Rights Plan. The creation of a special committee would not impose long term structural power-related distinctions between different groups of directors of the same board. The board that creates a special committee may abolish it at any time, as could any successor board. On the other hand, the Toll Brothers "dead hand" provision, if legally valid, would embed structural power-related distinctions between groups of directors that no successor board could abolish until after the Rights expire in 2007.

For these reasons, the statutory invalidity claims survive the motion to dismiss.

3. The Fiduciary Duty Invalidity Claims

Because the plaintiffs statutory invalidity claims have been found legally cognizable, the analysis arguably could end at this point. But the plaintiff also alleges that the board's adoption of the "dead hand" feature violated its fiduciary duty of loyalty. For the sake of completeness, that claim is addressed as well.

The duty of loyalty claim, to reiterate, has two prongs. The first is that the "dead hand" provision purposefully interferes with the shareholder voting franchise without any compelling justification, and is therefore unlawful under *Blasius*. The second is that the "dead hand" provision is a "disproportionate" defensive measure, because it either precludes or materially abridges the shareholders' rights to receive tender offers and to wage a proxy contest to replace the board. Under *Unocal/Unitrin*, in such circumstances the board's approval of the "dead hand" provision would not enjoy the presumption of validity conferred by the business judgment review standard, and therefore would be found to constitute a breach of fiduciary duty.

I conclude, for the reasons next discussed, that both fiduciary duty claims are cognizable under Delaware law.

a) The *Blasius* Fiduciary Duty Claim

The validity of antitakeover measures is normally evaluated under the *Unocal/Unitrin* standard. But where the defensive measures purposefully disenfranchise shareholders, the board will be required to satisfy the more exacting *Blasius* standard, which our Supreme Court has articulated as follows:[39]

> A board's unilateral decision to adopt a defensive measure touching "upon issues of control" that purposefully disenfranchises its shareholders is strongly suspect under *Unocal*, and cannot be sustained without a "compelling justification."

The complaint alleges that the "dead hand" provision purposefully disenfranchises the company's shareholders without any compelling justification. The disenfranchisement would occur because even in an election contest fought over the issue of the hostile bid, the shareholders will be powerless to elect a board that is both willing and able to accept the bid, and they "may be forced to vote for [incumbent] directors whose policies they reject because only those directors have the power to change them."

A claim that the directors have unilaterally "create[d] a structure in which shareholder voting is either impotent or self defeating" is necessarily a claim of purposeful disenfranchisement. Given the Supreme Court's rationale for upholding the validity of the poison pill in *Moran*, and the primacy of the shareholder vote in our scheme of corporate jurisprudence, any contrary view is difficult to justify. In *Moran*, the Supreme Court upheld the adoption of a poison pill, in part because its effect upon a proxy contest would be "minimal," but also because if the board refused to redeem the plan, the shareholders could exercise their prerogative to remove and replace the board. In *Unocal* the Supreme Court reiterated that view—that the safety valve which justifies a board being allowed to resist a hostile offer a majority of shareholders might prefer, is that the shareholders always have their ultimate recourse to the ballot box. Those observations reflect the fundamental value that the shareholder vote has primacy in our system of corporate governance because it is the "ideological underpinning upon which the legitimacy of directorial power rests." . . .

The defendants contend that the complaint fails to allege a valid stockholder disenfranchisement claim, because the Rights Plan does not on its face limit a dissident's ability to propose a slate or the shareholders' ability to cast a vote. The defendants also urge that even if the Plan might arguably have that effect, it could occur only in a very specific and unlikely context, namely, where (i) the hostile bidder makes a fair offer that it is willing to

---

[39] *Stroud v. Grace*, Del.Supr., 606 A.2d 75, 92 n. 3 (1992).

keep open for more than one year, (ii) the current board refuses to redeem the Rights, and (iii) the offeror wages two successful proxy fights and is committed to wage a third.

This argument, in my opinion, begs the issue and is specious. It begs the issue because the complaint does not claim that the Rights Plan facially restricts the shareholders' voting rights. What the complaint alleges is that the "dead hand" provision will either preclude a hostile bidder from waging a proxy contest altogether, or, if there should be a contest, it will coerce those shareholders who desire the hostile offer to succeed to vote for those directors who oppose it—the incumbent (and "Continuing") directors. Besides missing the point, the argument is also specious, because the hypothetical case the defendants argue must exist for any disenfranchisement to occur, rests upon the unlikely assumption that the hostile bidder will keep its offer open for more than one year. Given the market risks inherent in financed hostile bids for public corporations, it is unrealistic to assume that many bidders would be willing to do that.

For these reasons, the plaintiffs *Blasius*-based breach of fiduciary duty claim is cognizable under Delaware law.

b) The *Unocal/Unitrin* Fiduciary Duty Claim

The final issue is whether the complaint states a legally cognizable claim that the inclusion of the "dead hand" provision in the Rights Plan was an unreasonable defensive measure within the meaning of *Unocal*. I conclude that it does.

* * *

The complaint at issue here is far from conclusory. Under *Unitrin*, a defensive measure is disproportionate (*i.e.*, unreasonable) if it is either coercive or preclusive. The complaint alleges that the "dead hand" provision "disenfranchises shareholders by forcing them to vote for incumbent directors or their designees if shareholders want to be represented by a board entitled to exercise its full statutory prerogatives." That is sufficient to claim that the "dead hand" provision is coercive. The complaint also alleges that that provision "makes an offer for the Company much more unlikely since it eliminates use of a proxy contest as a possible means to gain control . . . [because] . . . any directors elected in such a contest would still be unable to vote to redeem the pill"; and "renders future contests for corporate control of Toll Brothers prohibitively expensive and effectively impossible." A defensive measure is preclusive if it makes a bidder's ability to wage a successful proxy contest and gain control either "mathematically impossible" or "realistically unattainable." These allegations are sufficient to state a claim that the "dead hand" provision makes a proxy contest "realistically unattainable," and therefore, is disproportionate and unreasonable under *Unocal*.

IV. CONCLUSION

The Court concludes that for the reasons discussed above, the complaint states claims under Delaware law upon which relief can be granted.[52] . . .

---

[52] For the sake of clarity, it must be emphasized that the "dead hand" provision at issue here is of unlimited duration; that is, it remains effective during the entire life of the poison pill. There are also "dead hand" provisions of limited duration (*e.g.*, six months), which are sometimes referred to as "diluted" or "deferred redemption" provisions. Some commentators have urged that such limited duration "dead hand" provisions stand on a different footing and

QUICKTURN DESIGN SYSTEMS, INC. v. SHAPIRO
Delaware Supreme Court
721 A.2d 1281 (1998)

HOLLAND, Justice:

This is an expedited appeal from a final judgment entered by the Court of Chancery. The dispute arises out of an ongoing effort by Mentor Graphics Corporation ("Mentor"), a hostile bidder, to acquire Quickturn Design Systems, Inc. ("Quickturn"), the target company. The plaintiffs-appellees are Mentor and an unaffiliated stockholder of Quickturn. The named defendants-appellants are Quickturn and its directors.

In response to Mentor's tender offer and proxy contest to replace the Quickturn board of directors, as part of Mentor's effort to acquire Quickturn, the Quickturn board . . . amended the Quickturn shareholder rights plan ("Rights Plan") by adopting a "no hand" feature of limited duration (the "Delayed Redemption Provision" or "DRP"). . . .

* * *

In this appeal, Quickturn argues that the Court of Chancery erred in finding that Quickturn's directors breached their fiduciary duty by adopting the Delayed Redemption Provision. . . .

STATEMENT OF FACTS

* * *

Mentor Tender Offer and Proxy Contest

On August 12, 1998, Mentor announced an unsolicited cash tender offer for all outstanding common shares of Quickturn at $12.125 per share, a price representing an approximate 50% premium over Quickturn's immediate pre-offer price, and a 20% discount from Quickturn's February 1998 stock price levels. Mentor's tender offer, once consummated, would be followed by a second step merger in which Quickturn's nontendering stockholders would receive, in cash, the same $12.125 per share tender offer price.

Mentor also announced its intent to solicit proxies to replace the board at a special meeting. Relying upon Quickturn's then-applicable by-law provision governing the call of special stockholders meetings, Mentor began soliciting agent designations from Quickturn stockholders to satisfy the by-law's stock ownership requirements to call such a meeting.

Quickturn Board Meetings

Under the Williams Act, Quickturn was required to inform its shareholders of its response to Mentor's offer no later than ten business days after the offer was commenced. During that ten day period, the Quickturn board met three times, on August 13, 17, and 21,

---

should be upheld; others have argued the contrary. *See* Lese, 96 COL. L.REV. at 2210; and Gordon, 19 CARDOZO L. REV. at 542. In any event, this case does not involve the validity of a "dead hand" provision of limited duration, and nothing in this Opinion should be read as expressing a view or pronouncement on that subject.

1998. During each of those meetings, it considered Mentor's offer and ultimately decided how to respond.

* * *

The Quickturn board held its third and final meeting in response to Mentor's offer on August 21, 1998. Again, the directors received extensive materials and a further detailed analysis performed by H & Q. The focal point of that analysis was a chart entitled "Summary of Implied Valuation." That chart compared Mentor's tender offer price to the Quickturn valuation ranges generated by H & Q's application of five different methodologies. The chart showed that Quickturn's value under all but one of those methodologies was higher than Mentor's $12.125 tender offer price.

Quickturn's Board Rejects Mentor's Offer as Inadequate

After hearing the presentations, the Quickturn board concluded that Mentor's offer was inadequate, and decided to recommend that Quickturn shareholders reject Mentor's offer. . . .

Quickturn's Defensive Measures

At the August 21 board meeting, the Quickturn board . . . amended Quickturn's shareholder Rights Plan by eliminating its "dead hand" feature and replacing it with the Deferred Redemption Provision, under which no newly elected board could redeem the Rights Plan for six months after taking office, if the purpose or effect of the redemption would be to facilitate a transaction with an "Interested Person" (one who proposed, nominated or financially supported the election of the new directors to the board).[15] Mentor would be an Interested Person.

. . . The effect of the DRP would be to delay the ability of a newly-elected, Mentor-nominated board to redeem the Rights Plan or "poison pill" for six months, in any transaction with an Interested Person. . . .

* * *

DELAYED REDEMPTION PROVISION VIOLATES FUNDAMENTAL DELAWARE LAW

In this appeal, Mentor argues that the judgment of the Court of Chancery should be affirmed because the Delayed Redemption Provision is invalid as a matter of Delaware law. According to Mentor, the Delayed Redemption Provision, like the "dead hand" feature in the

---

[15]   The amended Rights Plan pertinently provides that: "[I]n the event that a majority of the Board of Directors of the Company is elected by stockholder action at an annual or special meeting of stockholders, then until the 180th day following the effectiveness of such election (including any postponement or adjournment thereof), the Rights shall not be redeemed if such redemption is reasonably likely to have the purpose or effect of facilitating a Transaction with an Interested Person."

An "Interested Person" is defined under the amended Rights Plan as "any Person who (i) is or will become an Acquiring Person if such Transaction were to be consummated or an Affiliate or Associate of such a Person, and (ii) is, or directly or indirectly proposed, nominated or financially supported, a director of [Quickturn] in office at the time of consideration of such Transaction who was elected at an annual or special meeting of stockholders."

Rights Plan that was held to be invalid in *Toll Brothers*, will impermissibly deprive any newly elected board of both its statutory authority to manage the corporation under 8 Del.C. § 141(a) and its concomitant fiduciary duty pursuant to that statutory mandate. We agree.

Our analysis of the Delayed Redemption Provision in the Quickturn Rights Plan is guided by the prior precedents of this Court with regard to a board of directors authority to adopt a Rights Plan or "poison pill." In *Moran*, this Court held that the "inherent powers of the Board conferred by 8 Del.C. § 141(a) concerning the management of the corporation's 'business and affairs' provides the Board additional authority upon which to enact the Rights Plan." Consequently, this Court upheld the adoption of the Rights Plan in *Moran* as a legitimate exercise of business judgment by the board of directors. In doing so, however, this Court also held "the rights plan is not absolute":

> When the Household Board of Directors is faced with a tender offer and a request to redeem the Rights [Plan], they will not be able to arbitrarily reject the offer. They will be held to the same fiduciary standards any other board of directors would be held to in deciding to adopt a defensive mechanism, the same standards as they were held to in originally approving the Rights Plan.

In *Moran*, this Court held that the "ultimate response to an actual takeover bid must be judged by the Directors' actions at the time and nothing we say relieves them of their fundamental duties to the corporation and its shareholders." Consequently, we concluded that the use of the Rights Plan would be evaluated when and if the issue arises.

One of the most basic tenets of Delaware corporate law is that the board of directors has the ultimate responsibility for managing the business and affairs of a corporation. Section 141(a) requires that any limitation on the board's authority be set out in the certificate of incorporation. The Quickturn certificate of incorporation contains no provision purporting to limit the authority of the board in any way. The Delayed Redemption Provision, however, would prevent a newly elected board of directors from completely discharging its fundamental management duties to the corporation and its stockholders for six months. While the Delayed Redemption Provision limits the board of directors' authority in only one respect, the suspension of the Rights Plan, it nonetheless restricts the board's power in an area of fundamental importance to the shareholders—negotiating a possible sale of the corporation. Therefore, we hold that the Delayed Redemption Provision is invalid under Section 141(a), which confers upon any newly elected board of directors full power to manage and direct the business and affairs of a Delaware corporation.

In discharging the statutory mandate of Section 141(a), the directors have a fiduciary duty to the corporation and its shareholders. This unremitting obligation extends equally to board conduct in a contest for corporate control. The Delayed Redemption Provision prevents a newly elected board of directors from completely discharging its fiduciary duties to protect fully the interests of Quickturn and its stockholders.

This Court has recently observed that "although the fiduciary duty of a Delaware director is unremitting, the exact course of conduct that must be charted to properly discharge that responsibility will change in the specific context of the action the director is taking with regard to either the corporation or its shareholders." This Court has held "[t]o the extent that a contract, or a provision thereof, purports to require a board to act or not act in such a fashion as to limit the exercise of fiduciary duties, it is invalid and unenforceable."

The Delayed Redemption Provision "tends to limit in a substantial way the freedom of [newly elected] directors' decisions on matters of management policy." Therefore, "it violates the duty of each [newly elected] director to exercise his own best judgment on matters coming before the board."

In this case, the Quickturn board was confronted by a determined bidder that sought to acquire the company at a price the Quickturn board concluded was inadequate. Such situations are common in corporate takeover efforts. In *Revlon*, this Court held that no defensive measure can be sustained when it represents a breach of the directors' fiduciary duty. A fortiori, no defensive measure can be sustained which would require a new board of directors to breach its fiduciary duty. In that regard, we note Mentor has properly acknowledged that in the event its slate of directors is elected, those newly elected directors will be required to discharge their unremitting fiduciary duty to manage the corporation for the benefit of Quickturn and its stockholders.

Conclusion

The Delayed Redemption Provision would prevent a new Quickturn board of directors from managing the corporation by redeeming the Rights Plan to facilitate a transaction that would serve the stockholders' best interests, even under circumstances where the board would be required to do so because of its fiduciary duty to the Quickturn stockholders. Because the Delayed Redemption Provision impermissibly circumscribes the board's statutory power under Section 141(a) and the directors' ability to fulfill their concomitant fiduciary duties, we hold that the Delayed Redemption Provision is invalid. . . .

NOTES AND QUESTIONS

(1) **The statutory invalidity claims in *Carmody*.** *Carmody* invalidated the dead-hand provision in Toll Brothers' poison pill partly on the ground that the provision would interfere with the full board's statutory power to manage the business and affairs of the corporation under Del. G.C.L. § 141(a). Do you agree? How does the delegation of authority to "Continuing Directors" in Toll Brother's poison pill differ from a permitted delegation to a committee of directors under Del. G.C.L. § 141(c)? Is Del. G.C.L. § 141(c) limited to *revocable* delegations, as the Vice Chancellor suggests? *See* **Letsou**.

(2) **The fiduciary duty claims in *Carmody*.** *Carmody* also found legally cognizable claims that the Toll Brothers board violated its fiduciary duties under *Blasius* and *Unocal* when it adopted the disputed dead-hand provision. With respect to the *Blasius* claim, the court said that shareholders "may be forced to vote for [incumbent] directors whose policies they reject because only those directors have the power to change them." With respect to the *Unocal* claim, the court noted that the dead-hand provision could render "future contests for corporate control of Toll Brothers prohibitively expensive and effectively impossible." Does this overstate the effect of the dead-hand provision? Note that Toll Brothers already had a classified board of directors, so shareholders who disagreed with the incumbents would not be under any immediate pressure to support incumbents, even if shareholders wanted to preserve board power to redeem

the poison pill. The Continuing Directors who would remain on Toll Brothers' classified board also retained the power, and presumably the duty, to redeem the poison pill in response to a non-threatening bid. Why wasn't this enough to prevent the pill from having a "draconian" impact under *Unocal* and *Unitrin*?

(3) *Carmody* **and slow-hand poison pills.** While *Carmody* invalidated Toll Brothers' dead-hand provision, the Vice Chancellor reserved judgment with respect to "slow-hand" provisions—*i.e.*, no-hand provisions which merely suspend, but do not eliminate, the board's power to redeem a poison pill following an insurgent's successful proxy contest. *See* footnote 52 to the court's opinion. The Vice Chancellor presumably reasoned that a "slow-hand" provision of limited duration (*e.g.*, six months) would pose less of a problem under Del. G.C.L. § 141(a) since the board's loss of power would be temporary. A newly elected board eventually could redeem the pill, and future control contests would not be "effectively impossible." Accordingly, a "slow-hand" poison pill would be less vulnerable under *Blasius* and *Unocal*.

(4) *Quickturn* **and slow-hand poison pills.** *Quickturn* declined to take the route to validity suggested by *Carmody* and instead held that a slow-hand poison pill—even one that suspended a board's redemption powers for just six months—impermissibly restricted the board's fundamental power to negotiate a sale of the corporation under Del. G.C.L. § 141(a). The court found it unnecessary to consider the plaintiff's *Blasius* and *Unocal* arguments, thereby preserving its perfect record of never invalidating a takeover defense under *Unocal*.

(5) **The impact of** *Quickturn* **on ordinary poison pills.** Does the decision in *Quickturn* threaten ordinary poison pills? Recall that *all* poison pills, even those without dead-hand or no-hand provisions, at some point become non-redeemable and therefore eliminate the board's fundamental power to sell the corporation. *See* **Letsou**. But in *Leonard Loventhal Account v. Hilton Hotels Corp.*,[88] the Delaware Supreme Court made clear that its prior decisions upholding poison pills, including *Moran v. Household International, Inc.* (*see* Note 4 following *Unocal* in Section 14.03[D][2]), remain good law.

(6) **Dead-hand and no-hand poison pills outside of Delaware.** While dead-hand and no-hand poison pills, seem clearly out of bounds for Delaware corporations, they may still be used by corporations in other states. For example, *Invacare Corporation v. Healthdyne Technologies, Inc.*[89] upheld a dead-hand provision included in a Georgia corporation's poison pill largely because § 624 of the Georgia Business Corporation Act gave the board the authority "to determine, *in its sole discretion*, the terms and conditions of . . . rights, options or warrants." (Emphasis added.) Similarly, *AMP Incorporated v. Allied Signal Inc.*[90] upheld a Pennsylvania corporation's no-hand poison pill, because § 2513 of the Pennsylvania Business Corporation Law explicitly permits

---

[88]   780 A.2d 245 (Del. 2001).

[89]   968 F. Supp. 1578 (N.D. Ga. 1997).

[90]   1998 U.S. Dist. LEXIS 15617, 1998 WL 778348 (E.D. Pa. 1998).

corporations to adopt poison pills with "such terms as are fixed by the board of directors." But the *AMP* court qualified its decision by noting that "[t]he non-redemption and non-amendable features of the AMP shareholder rights plan are finite in time. Were this not so, it would mitigate towards a finding of lack of good faith or self-dealing." For an earlier decision upholding a continuing director provision, see *Bank of New York Co. v. Irving Bank Corp.*[91]

(7) **Shareholder bylaw amendments.** Can shareholders act directly to amend corporate bylaws to remove director-approved takeover defenses? As discussed in Note 5 following the *Medical Committee* excerpt in Section 7.04[C], *International Brotherhood of Teamsters General Fund v. Fleming Companies* held that shareholders did have this power under the Oklahoma corporation statute, which is similar to Delaware's. The shareholders' power, of course, depends significantly on the language of the applicable state corporation statute. *Invacare*, discussed in Note 6 above, did not allow a shareholder-approved bylaw that would compel removal of a dead hand poison pill because of the statute's "sole discretion" language. Delaware G.C.L. § 141(a) gives directors the general power to manage unless the articles or statute otherwise provide. The reference to the statute may or may not include Del. G.C.L. § 109, which permits a shareholder bylaw unless otherwise limited by law—which may or may not refer back to § 141.

The Delaware courts have not yet spoken on the use of shareholder bylaws to remove takeover defenses. **Coates & Faris** argue that such bylaws are unlikely to survive, because, like the deferred redemption provision invalidated in *Quickturn*, they restrict the board's authority concerning the possible sale of the corporation and prevent boards from taking actions they believe are in the shareholder's best interests. The SEC has accepted this argument as a basis for blocking shareholder use of Rule 14a-8 to propose bylaws requiring the dismantling of takeover defenses, at least for Delaware corporations.[92] But even if such broad bylaws are invalid, might different types of shareholder bylaws survive? What about a bylaw that facilitates a special meeting of the shareholders where the board can be replaced, if the board fails to redeem a poison pill? Or a bylaw setting forth procedural rules making it more difficult for a board to act during a takeover battle? *See* **Coates & Faris**.

Even if shareholders can act, might directors have the last word, as by amending a shareholder bylaw or adopting their own bylaws per Del. G.C.L. § 109 or § 216? *See* **Hamermesh** and **Coates & Faris**. Would directors choose to exercise such a power, even if it exists? *See* **Coates & Faris**.

As a matter of policy, should the shareholders have the last word? Consider the problems afflicting shareholder voting discussed in Note 2 following *Fliegler* in Section 9.04[B]. *See also* **Macey** and **Gordon**. Should it matter what director action the shareholders are reversing? For example, should the shareholders have the specific power to reverse dead hand pills, which themselves arguably represent a change in the share-

---

[91]   528 N.Y.S.2d 482 (N.Y. Sup. Ct. 1988).

[92]   *See, e.g., Toy's R Us, Inc,* 2002 WL 1058521 (S.E.C. No-Action Letter).

holders' pre-existing power? *See* **Gordon.** Might problems with shareholder voting be cured by special procedural rules, such as those concerning convening shareholder meetings? *See* **Hamermesh.**

PROBLEM

Technoroid Corporation is a widely held Delaware corporation whose 200 million common shares are listed on the New York Stock Exchange. Technoroid has nine directors, three of whom are employed full time by the company and own 25% of the stock, and six who are not otherwise associated with the company. Institutional investors own another 50% of Technoroid's shares. The board is staggered so that three directors are elected each year. Technoroid has a "flip-in" poison pill rights in place which permit Technoroid's shareholders to buy Technoroid stock at $5 per share once someone has bought more than 20% of Technoroid stock. The rights can be redeemed by the board (whether consisting of current or new directors), but only until someone buys more than 5% of the company's stock.

Technoroid has experienced several years of earnings declines and is currently trading for $10 per share, which is near the stock's ten-year low. Instaroid Corporation, a consumer products company, sees an opportunity to profit by taking control of Technoroid, selling off some product lines that don't fit with Technoroid's main products, and branching into related products. It has presented to Technoroid management a friendly $15 per share takeover, making it clear that Instaroid will make a hostile bid if it is rebuffed, but that it is prepared to go higher if it can be convinced that the company is worth more. Technoroid management has learned that Instaroid has bought a 4.9% "stake" in Technoroid. Instaroid is well-financed and can be expected to make an all-cash tender offer for all of Technoroid's shares.

Technoroid management believes that Instaroid's plan would thwart some long-term strategies and product development that are about to bear fruit. It is planning to meet to discuss how to defeat this threat. It has asked you, its outside counsel, to come up with some ideas. Technoroid's long-time investment banking firm is prepared to issue an opinion supporting the board's reasoning and stating that the "intrinsic value" of Technoroid is $20 per share.

You have come up with the following ideas. First, amend the bylaws to require a 67% vote of the shareholders to remove the staggered board provision.

Second, and alternatively, do a leveraged buyout at $20 per share, arranged by the leveraged buyout promoter Forstburg, Krattle, in which Technoroid would merge with a newly-created private firm. Most of the equity of the new, heavily leveraged firm would be owned by Forstburg and by the incumbent managers, who would invest substantial personal assets and stock options and other deferred compensation. Forstburg does not like to invest in LBO proposals without some protection from an ensuing bidding war. Accordingly, it will not agree to promote the LBO unless it gets an option to buy 10 million shares of Technoroid stock at $10 per share.

Would these alternatives be enforceable in light of all of the case law in Section 14.03[D]?

REFERENCES

Coates & Faris, *Second-Generation Shareholder Bylaws: Post*-Quickturn *Alternatives*, 56 Bus. Law. 1323 (2001).

Gordon, *"Just Say Never?" Poison Pills, Deadhand Pills, and Shareholder-Adopted Bylaws: An Essay for Warren Buffett,* 19 Cardozo L. Rev. 511 (1997).

Hamermesh, *Corporate Democracy and Stockholder-Adopted By-Laws: Taking Back the Street?,* 73 Tulane L. Rev. 409 (1998).

Letsou, *Are Dead Hand (and No Hand) Poison Pills Really Dead?,* 68 U. Cin. L. Rev. 1101 (2000).

Macey, *The Legality and Utility of the Shareholder Rights Bylaw,* 26 Hofstra L. Rev. 835 (1998).

[E] State Anti-Takeover Statutes

Corporate statutes generally let companies adopt devices that make takeovers more difficult, including staggered boards and supermajority voting on mergers (*see* Section 14.03[A]). Beginning in the late 1970s, state legislators started adding statutes that substantially impeded tender offers by, among other things, providing for lengthy notice periods and approval by state regulators. In 1982, the validity of all of these statutes was cast in considerable doubt by the Supreme Court's decision in *Edgar v. MITE Corp.*[93] A majority of the Court held that the Illinois statute unconstitutionally burdened interstate commerce. A plurality also held that the statute was unconstitutional under the Supremacy Clause because it conflicted with the Williams Act, which is aimed solely at protecting shareholders from coercive takeovers rather than protecting the jobs of incumbent managers.

After *MITE*, state legislatures passed a "second generation" of state anti-takeover statutes that sought to avoid Commerce and Supremacy Clause problems by eliminating notice periods and administrative approval and by applying the statutes only to corporations incorporated in the enacting state. The most prominent of the early second generation statutes were control share acts that prevented bidders who cross certain specified thresholds of ownership (*e.g.*, 20%, 33⅓%, and 50%) from voting their shares unless a majority of disinterested shareholders approve. Since bidders are unlikely to commit millions of dollars to buying shares at a premium if they might not carry voting rights, control share acts—like flip-in poison pills—effectively preclude the takeover of corporations to which they apply. The constitutionality of one control share statute is considered in the following case.

---

[93]   457 U.S. 624 (1982).

CTS CORPORATION v. DYNAMICS CORPORATION OF AMERICA
United States Supreme Court
481 U.S. 69 (1987)

Justice POWELL delivered the opinion of the Court.

This case presents the questions whether the Control Share Acquisitions Chapter of the Indiana Business Corporation Law, Ind. Code Sec. 23-1-42-1 *et seq.* (Supp. 1986), is pre-empted by the Williams Act, 82 Stat. 454, as amended, 15 U.S.C. Sec. 78m(d)-(e) and 78n(d)-(f) (1982 ed. and Supp. III), or violates the Commerce Clause of the Federal Constitution, Art. I, Sec. 8, cl. 3.

I

A

On March 4, 1986, the Governor of Indiana signed a revised Indiana Business Corporation Law, Ind., Code Sec. 23-1-17-1 *et seq.* (Supp. 1986). That law included the Control Share Acquisitions Chapter (Indiana Act or Act). Beginning on August 1, 1987, the Act will apply to any corporation incorporated in Indiana, Sec. 23-1-17-3(a), unless the corporation amends its articles of incorporation or bylaws to opt out of the Act, Sec. 23-1-42-5. Before that date, any Indiana corporation can opt into the Act by resolution of its board of directors. Sec. 23-1-17-3(b). The act applies only to "issuing public corporations." The term "corporation" includes only businesses incorporated in Indiana. *See* Sec. 23-1-20-5. An "issuing public corporation" is defined as:

a corporation that has:

(1) one hundred (100) or more shareholders;

(2) its principal place of business, its principal office, or substantial assets within Indiana; and

(3) either:

    (A) more than ten percent (10%) of its shareholders resident in Indiana;

    (B) more than ten percent (10%) of its shares owned by Indiana residents; or

    (C) ten thousand (10,000) shareholders resident in Indiana.

Sec. 23-1-42-4(a).[1]

The Act focuses on the acquisition of "control shares" in an issuing public corporation. Under the Act, an entity acquires "control shares" whenever it acquires shares that, but for the operation of the Act, would bring its voting power in the corporation to or above any of three thresholds: 20%, 33-1/3%, or 50%. Sec. 23-1-42-1. An entity that acquires control shares does not necessarily acquire voting rights. Rather, it gains those rights only "to the extent granted by resolution approved by the shareholders of the issuing public corporation." Sec. 23-1-42-9(a). Section 9 requires a majority vote of all disinterested[2] shareholders hold-

---

[1]   These thresholds are much higher than the 5% threshold Acquisition requirement that brings a tender offer under the coverage of the Williams Act. *See* 15 U.S.C. Sec. 78n(d)(1).

[2]   "Interested shares" are shares with respect to which the acquiror, an officer or an inside director of the corporation "may exercise or direct the exercise of the voting power of the corporation in the election of directors." Sec. 23-1-42-3. If the record date passes before the acquiror purchases shares pursuant to the tender offer, the purchased shares

ing each class of stock for passage of such a resolution. Sec. 23-1-42-9(b). The practical effect of this requirement is to condition acquisition of control of a corporation on approval of a majority of the pre-existing disinterested shareholders.

The shareholders decide whether to confer rights on the control shares at the next regularly scheduled meeting of the shareholders, or at a specially scheduled meeting. The acquiror can require management of the corporation to hold such a special meeting within 50 days if it files an acquiring person statement,[4] requests the meeting, and agrees to pay the expenses of the meeting. *See* Sec. 23-1-42-7. If the shareholders do not vote to restore voting rights to the shares, the corporation may redeem the control shares from the acquiror at fair market value, but it is not required to do so. Sec. 23-1-42- 10(b). Similarly, if the acquiror does not file an acquiring person statement with the corporation, the corporation may, if its bylaws or articles of corporation so provide, redeem the shares at any time after 60 days after the acquiror's last acquisition. Sec. 23-1-42-10(a).

B.

On March 10, 1986, appellee Dynamics Corporation of America (Dynamics) owned 9.6% of the common stock of appellant CTS Corporation, an Indiana corporation. On that day, six days after the Act went into effect, Dynamics announced a tender offer for another million shares in CTS; purchase of those shares would have brought Dynamics' ownership interest in CTS to 27.5%.

* * *

On March 27, the Board of Directors of CTS, an Indiana corporation, elected to be governed by the provisions of the Act, *see* Sec. 23-1-17-3.

Dynamics sought a temporary restraining order, a preliminary injunction, and declaratory relief against CTS's use of the Act. On April 9, the District Court ruled that the Williams Act pre-empts the Indiana Act and granted Dynamics' motion for declaratory relief. 637 F. Supp. 389 (N.D. Ill. 1986).

* * *

A week later, on April 17, the District Court issued an opinion accepting Dynamics' claim that the Act violated the Commerce Clause.

---

will not be "interested shares" within the meaning of the Act; although the acquiror may own the shares on the date of the meeting, it will not "exercise . . . the voting power" of the shares.

As a practical matter, the record date usually will pass before shares change hands. Under SEC regulations, the shares cannot be purchased until 20 business days after the offer commences. 17 CFR Sec. 240.14e-1(a) (1986). If the acquiror seeks an early resolution of the issue—as most acquirors will—the meeting required by the Act must be held no more than 50 calendar days after the offer commences, about three weeks after the earliest date on which the shares could be purchased. *See* Sec. 23-1-42-7. The Act requires management to give notice of the meeting "as promptly as reasonably practical . . . to all shareholders of record as of the record date set for the meeting." Sec. 23-1-42-8(a). It seems likely that management of the target corporation would violate this obligation if it delayed setting the record date and sending notice until after 20 business days had passed. Thus, we assume that the record date usually will be set before the date on which federal law first permits purchase of the shares.

    [4] An "acquiring person statement" is an information statement describing, inter alia, the identity of the acquiring person and the terms and extent of the proposed acquisition. *See* Sec. 23-1-42-6.

* * *

CTS appealed the District Court's holdings on these claims to the Court of Appeals for the Seventh Circuit. . . . On April 23—23 days after Dynamics' first contested application of the Act in the District Court—the Court of Appeals issued an order affirming the judgment of the District Court. . . .

* * *

. . . We . . . now reverse.

II

The first question in this case is whether the Williams Act pre-empts the Indiana Act. As we have stated frequently, absent an explicit indication by Congress of an intent to pre-empt state law, a state statute is pre-empted only "'where compliance with both federal and state regulations is a physical impossibility . . .' [citation omitted], or where the state 'law stands as an obstacle to the accomplishment and execution of the full purposes and objectives of Congress.'" [citations omitted] Because it is entirely possible for entities to comply with both the Williams Act and the Indiana Act, the state statute can be pre-empted only if it frustrates the purposes of the federal law.

A

Our discussion begins with a brief summary of the structure and purposes of the Williams Act. Congress passed the Williams Act in 1968 in response to the increasing number of hostile tender offers. Before its passage, these transactions were not covered by the disclosure requirements of the federal securities laws. . . . The Williams Act, backed by regulations of the Securities and Exchange Commission (SEC), imposes requirements in two basic areas. First, it requires the offeror to file a statement disclosing information about the offer, including: the offeror's background and identity; the source and amount of the funds to be used in making the purchase; the purpose of the purchase, including any plans to liquidate the company or make major changes in its corporate structure; and the extent of the offeror's holdings in the target company.

Second, the Williams Act, and the regulations that accompany it, establish procedural rules to govern tender offers. For example, stockholders who tender their shares may withdraw them during the first 15 business days of the tender offer and, if the offeror has not purchased their shares, any time after 60 days from commencement of the offer. The offer must remain open for at least 20 business days. If more shares are tendered than the offeror sought to purchase, purchases must be made on a pro rata basis from each tendering shareholder. Finally, the offeror must pay the same price for all purchases; if the offering price is increased before the end of the offer, those who already have tendered must receive the benefit of the increased price.

B

The Indiana Act differs in major respects from the Illinois statute that the Court considered in *Edgar v. MITE Corp.*, 457 U.S. 624, 102 S. Ct. 2629, 73 L. Ed. 2d 269 (1982). After reviewing the legislative history of the Williams Act, Justice White, joined by Chief

Justice Burger and Justice Blackmun (the plurality), concluded that the Williams Act struck a careful balance between the interests of offerors and target companies, and that any state statute that "upset" this balance was pre-empted. *Id.* at 632-634, 102 S. Ct. at 2635-2636.

The plurality then identified three offending features of the Illinois statute. Justice White's opinion first noted that the Illinois statute provided for a 20-day precommencement period. During this time, management could disseminate its views on the upcoming offer to shareholders, but offerors could not publish their offers. The plurality found that this provision gave management "a powerful tool to combat tender offers." *Id.* at 635, 102 S. Ct. at 2637. This contrasted dramatically with the Williams Act; Congress had deleted express precommencement notice provisions from the Williams Act. According to the plurality, Congress had determined that the potentially adverse consequences of such a provision on shareholders should be avoided. Thus, the plurality concluded that the Illinois provision "frustrate[d] the objectives of the Williams Act." *Id.* The second criticized feature of the Illinois statute was a provision for a hearing on a tender offer that, because it set no deadline allowed management "'to stymie indefinitely a takeover,'" *id.* at 637, 102 S. Ct. at 2638 (quoting *MITE Corp. v. Dixon*, 633 F.2d 486, 494 (CA 1980). The plurality noted that "'delay can seriously impede a tender offer,'" 457 U.S. at 637, 102 S. Ct. at 2638 (quoting *Great Western United Corp. v. Kidwell*, 577 F.2d 1256, 1277 (CA5 1978) (per Wisdom, J.)), and that "Congress anticipated that investors and the takeover offeror would be free to go forward without unreasonable delay," 457 U.S. at 639, 102 S. Ct. at 2639. Accordingly, the plurality concluded that this provision conflicted with the Williams Act. The third troublesome feature of the Illinois statute was its requirement that the fairness of tender offers would be reviewed by the Illinois Secretary of State. Noting that "Congress intended for investors to be free to make their own decisions," the plurality concluded that "'[t]he state thus offers investor protection at the expense of investor autonomy—an approach quite in conflict with that adopted by Congress.'" *Id.* at 639-640, 102 S. Ct. at 2639 (quoting *MITE Corp. v. Dixon, supra,* at 494).

C

As the plurality opinion in *MITE* did not represent the views of a majority of the Court, we are not bound by its reasoning. We need not question that reasoning, however, because we believe the Indiana Act passes muster even under the broad interpretation of the Williams Act articulated by Justice White in *MITE.* As is apparent from our summary of its reasoning, the overriding concern of the *MITE* plurality was that the Illinois statute considered in that case operated in favor of management against offerors, to the detriment of shareholders. By contrast, the statute now before the Court protects the independent shareholder against both of the contending parties. Thus, the Act furthers a basic purpose of the Williams Act, "'plac[ing] investors on an equal footing with the takeover bidder,'" *Piper v. Chris-Craft Industries*, 430 U.S. at 30, 97 S. Ct. at 943 (quoting the Senate Report accompanying the Williams Act, S. Rep. No. 550, 90th Cong., 1st Sess, 4 (1967)).

The Indiana Act operates on the assumption, implicit in the Williams Act, that independent shareholders faced with tender offers often are at a disadvantage. By allowing such shareholders to vote as a group, the Act protects them from the coercive aspects of some tender offers. If, for example, shareholders believe that a successful tender offer will be followed by a purchase of nontendering shares at a depressed price, individual shareholders may tender their shares—even if they doubt the tender offer is in the corporation's best interest—to protect themselves from being forced to sell their shares at a depressed price. As the SEC explains: "The alternative of not accepting the tender offer is virtual assurance that, if the offer is successful, the shares will have to be sold in the lower priced, second step." *Two-Tier Tender Offer Pricing and Non-Tender Offer Purchase Programs*, SEC Exchange Act Rel., No. 21079 (June 21, 1984), [1984 Transfer Binder] CCH Fed. Sec. L. Rep. p. 83,637, p. 86,916 (footnote omitted) (hereinafter SEC Release No. 21-79). *See* Lowenstein, *Pruning Deadwood in Hostile Takeovers: A Proposal for Legislation*, 83 COLUM. L. REV. 249, 307-309 (1983). In such a situation under the Indiana Act, the shareholders as a group, acting in the corporation's best interest, could reject the offer, although individual shareholders might be inclined to accept it. The desire of the Indiana Legislature to protect shareholders of Indiana corporations from this type of coercive offer does not conflict with the Williams Act. Rather, it furthers the federal policy of investor protection.

In implementing its goal, the Indiana Act avoids the problems the plurality discussed in *MITE*. Unlike the *MITE* statute, the Indiana Act does not give either management or the offeror an advantage in communicating with the shareholders about the impending offer. The Act also does not impose an indefinite delay on tender offers. Nothing in the Act prohibits an offeror from consummating an offer on the 20th business day, the earliest day permitted under applicable federal regulations. Nor does the Act allow the state government to interpose its views of fairness between willing buyers and sellers of shares of the target company. Rather, the Act allows shareholders to evaluate the fairness of the offer collectively.

D

The Court of Appeals based its finding of pre-emption on its view that the practical effect of the Indiana Act is to delay consummation of tender offers until 50 days after the commencement of the offer. 794 F.2d at 263. As did the Court of Appeals, Dynamics reasons that no rational offeror will purchase shares until it gains assurance that those shares will carry voting rights. Because it is possible that voting rights will not be conferred until a share-holder meeting 50 days after commencement of the offer, Dynamics concludes that the Act imposes a 50-day delay. This, it argues, conflicts with the minimum period for which a tender offer may be held open. We find the alleged conflict illusory.

The Act does not impose an absolute 50-day delay on tender offers, nor does it preclude an offeror from purchasing shares as soon as federal law permits. If the offeror fears an adverse shareholder vote under the Act, it can make a conditional tender offer, offering to accept shares on the condition that the shares receive voting rights within a certain period of time. The Williams Act permits tender offers to be conditioned on the offeror's subsequently obtaining regulatory approval. . . . There is no reason to doubt that this type of conditional tender offer would be legitimate as well.

Even assuming that the Indiana Act imposes some additional delay, nothing in *MITE* suggested that any delay imposed by state regulation, however short, would create a conflict with the Williams Act. The plurality argued only that the offeror should "be free to go forward without *unreasonable* delay." 457 U.S. at 639, 102 S. Ct. at 2639 (emphasis added). In that case, the Court was confronted with the potential for indefinite delay and presented with no persuasive reason why some deadline could not be established. By contrast, the Indiana Act provides that full voting rights will be vested—if this eventually is to occur—within 50 days after commencement of the offer. This period is within the 60-day maximum period Congress established for tender offers in 15 U.S.C. Sec. 78n(d)(5). We cannot say that a delay within that congressionally determined period is unreasonable.

Finally, we note that the Williams Act would pre-empt a variety of state corporate laws of hitherto unquestioned validity if it were construed to pre-empt any state statute that may limit or delay the free exercise of power after a successful tender offer. State corporate laws commonly permit corporations to stagger the terms of their directors. [citations omitted] By staggering the terms of directors, and thus having annual elections for only one class of directors each year, corporations may delay the time when a successful offeror gains control of the board of directors. Similarly, state corporation laws commonly provide for cumulative voting. [citations omitted] By enabling minority shareholders to assure themselves of representation in each class of directors, cumulative voting provisions can delay further the ability of offerors to gain untrammeled authority over the affairs of the target corporation. [citation omitted]

In our view, the possibility that the Indiana Act will delay some tender offers is insufficient to require a conclusion that the Williams Act pre-empts the Act. The longstanding prevalence of state regulation in this area suggests that, if Congress had intended to pre-empt all state laws that delay the acquisition of voting control following a tender offer, it would have said so explicitly. The regulatory conditions that the Act places on tender offers are consistent with the text and the purposes of the Williams Act. Accordingly, we hold that the Williams Act does not pre-empt the Indiana Act.

III

As an alternative basis for its decision, the Court of Appeals held that the Act violates the Commerce Clause of the Federal Constitution. We now address this holding. On its face, the Commerce Clause is nothing more than a grant to Congress of the power "[t]o regulate Commerce . . . among the several states . . .," Art. I., Sec. 8, cl. 3. But it has been settled for more than a century that the Clause prohibits States from taking certain actions respecting interstate commerce even absent congressional action. *See, e.g., Cooley v. Board of Wardens,* 12 How. 299, 13 L. Ed. 996 (1852). The Court's interpretation of "these great silences of the Constitution," *H.P. Hood & Sons, Inc. v. Du Mond,* 336 U.S. 525, 535, 69 S. Ct. 657, 663, 93 L. Ed. 865 (1949), has not always been easy to follow. Rather, as the volume and complexity of commerce and regulation have grown in this country, the Court has articulated a variety of tests in an attempt to describe the difference between those regulations that the Commerce Clause permits and those regulations that it prohibits. [citation omitted]

A

The principal objects of dormant Commerce Clause scrutiny are statutes that discriminate against interstate commerce. [citations omitted] The Indiana Act is not such a statute. It has the same effects on tender offers whether or not the offeror is a domiciliary or resident of Indiana. Thus, it "visits its effects equally upon both interstate and local business," *Lewis v. BT Investment Managers, Inc., supra,* 447 U.S. at 36, 100 S. Ct. at 2015.

Dynamics nevertheless contends that the statute is discriminatory because it will apply most often to out-of-state entities. This argument rests on the contention that, as a practical matter, most hostile tender offers are launched by offerors outside Indiana. But this argument avails Dynamics little. "The fact that the burden of a state regulation falls on some interstate companies does not, by itself, establish a claim of discrimination against interstate commerce." *Exxon Corp. v. Governor of Maryland*, 437 U.S. 117, 126, 98 S.Ct. 2207, 2214, 57 L. Ed. 2d 91 (1978). . . . Because nothing in the Indiana Act imposes a greater burden on out-of-state offerors than it does on similarly situated Indiana offerors, we reject the contention that the Act discriminates against interstate commerce.

B

This Court's recent Commerce Clause cases also have invalidated statutes that adversely may affect interstate commerce by subjecting activities to inconsistent regulations.

* * *

The Indiana Act poses no such problem. So long as each State regulates voting rights only in the corporations it has created, each corporation will be subject to the law of only one State. No principle of corporation law and practice is more firmly established than a State's authority to regulate domestic corporations, including the authority to define the voting rights of shareholders. . . . Accordingly, we conclude that the Indiana Act does not create an impermissible risk of inconsistent regulation by different States.

C

The Court of Appeals did not find the Act unconstitutional for either of these threshold reasons. Rather, its decision rested on its view of the Act's potential to hinder tender offers. We think the Court of Appeals failed to appreciate the significance of Commerce Clause analysis of the fact that state regulation of corporate governance is regulation of entities whose very existence and attributes are a product of state law. As Chief Justice Marshall explained:

> A corporation is an artificial being, invisible, intangible, and existing only in contemplation of law. Being the mere creature of law, it possesses only those properties which the charter of its creation confers upon it, either expressly, or as incidental to its very existence. These are such as are supposed best calculated to effect the object for which it was created.

Trustees of Dartmouth College v. Woodward, 4 Wheat. 518, 636, 4 L. Ed. 518 (1819). *See First National Bank of Boston v. Bellotti*, 435 U.S. 765, 822-824, 98 S. Ct. 1407, 1439-1441, 55 L. Ed. 2d 707 (1978) (Rehnquist, J., dissenting). Every State in this country has enacted laws regulating corporate governance. By prohibiting certain transactions, and regulating others, such laws necessarily affect certain aspects of interstate commerce. This necessarily is truer with respect to corporations with shareholders in States other than the State of incorporation. Large corporations that are listed on national exchanges, or even regional exchanges, will have shareholders in many States and shares that are traded frequently. The markets that facilitate this national and international participation in ownership of corporations are essential for providing capital not only for new enterprises but also for established companies that need to expand their businesses. This beneficial free market system depends at its core upon the fact that a corporation—except in the rarest situations—is organized under, and governed by, the law of a single jurisdiction, traditionally the corporate law of the state of its incorporation.

These regulatory laws may affect directly a variety of corporate transactions. Mergers are a typical example. In view of the substantial effect that a merger may have on the shareholders' interests in a corporation, many States require supermajority votes to approve mergers. *See, e.g.*, MBCA Sec. 73 (requiring approval of a merger by a majority of all shares, rather than simply a majority of votes cast); RMBCA Sec. 11.03 (same). By requiring a greater vote for mergers than it required for other transactions, these laws make it more difficult for corporations to merge. State laws also may provide for "dissenters' rights" under which minority shareholders who disagree with corporate decisions to take particular actions are entitled to sell their shares to the corporation at fair market value. *See, e.g.*, MBCA Sec. 80-81; RMBCA Sec. 13.02. By requiring the corporation to purchase the shares of dissenting shareholders, these laws may inhibit a corporation from engaging in the specified transactions.[12]

It thus is an accepted part of the business landscape in this country for States to create corporations, to prescribe their powers, and to define the rights that are acquired by purchasing their shares. A State has an interest in promoting stable relationships among parties involved in the corporations it charters, as well as in ensuring that investors in such corporations have an effective voice in corporate affairs.

There can be no doubt that the Act reflects these concerns. The primary purpose of the Act is to protect the shareholders of Indiana corporations. It does this by affording shareholders when a takeover offer is made, an opportunity to decide collectively whether the resulting change in voting control of the corporation, as they perceive it, would be desirable. A change of management may have important effects on the shareholders' interests; it is well within the State's role as overseer of corporate governance to offer this opportunity. The autonomy provided by allowing shareholders collectively to determine whether the takeover is advantageous to their interests may be especially beneficial where a hostile tender offer may coerce shareholders into tendering their shares.

Appellee Dynamics responds to this concern by arguing that the prospect of coercive tender offers is illusory, and that tender offers generally should be favored because they reallocate corporate assets into the hands of management who can use them most effectively.

---

[12] Numerous other common regulations may affect both nonresident and resident shareholders of a corporation. Specified votes may be required for the sale of all of the corporation's assets. *See* MBCA Sec. 79; RMBCA Sec. 12.02. The election of directors may be staggered over a period of years to prevent abrupt changes in management. *See* MBCA Sec. 37; RMBCA Sec. 8.06. Various classes of stock may be created with differences in voting rights as to dividends and on liquidation. *See* MBCA Sec. 15; RMBCA Sec. 6.01(c). Provisions may be made for cumulative voting. *See* MBCA Sec. 33, par. 4; RMBCA Sec. 7.28. Corporations may adopt restrictions on payment of dividends to ensure that specified ratios of assets to liabilities are maintained for the benefit of the holders of corporate bonds or notes. *See* MBCA Sec. 45 (noting that a corporation's articles of incorporation can restrict payment of dividends); RMBCA Sec. 6.40 (same). Where the shares of a corporation are held in States other than that of incorporation, actions taken pursuant to these and similar provisions of state law will affect all shareholders alike wherever they reside or are domiciled.

Nor is it unusual for partnership law to restrict certain transactions. For example, a purchaser of a partnership interest generally can gain a right to control the business only with the consent of other owners. *See* Uniform Partnership Act Sec. 27, 6 U.L.A. 353 (1969); Uniform Limited Partnership Act Sec. 19 (1916 Act Sections 702, 704 (1976 draft), 6 U.L.A. 259, 261 (Supp. 1986). These provisions—in force in the great majority of the States—bear a striking resemblance to the Act at issue in this case.

... The Constitution does not require the States to subscribe to any particular economic theory. We are not inclined "to second-guess the empirical judgments of lawmakers concerning the utility of legislation," *Kassel v. Consolidated Freightways Corp.*, 450 U.S. at 679, 101 S. Ct. at 1321 (Brennan, J., concurring in judgment). In our view, the possibility of coercion in some takeover bids offers additional justification for Indiana's decision to promote the autonomy of independent shareholders.

Dynamics argues in any event that the State has "no legitimate interest in protecting the nonresident shareholders." . . . We agree that Indiana has no interest in protecting nonresident shareholders of nonresident corporations. But this Act applies only to corporations incorporated in Indiana. We reject the contention that Indiana has no interest in providing for the shareholders of its corporations the voting autonomy granted by the Act. Indiana has a substantial interest in preventing the corporate form from becoming a shield for unfair business dealing. Moreover, unlike the Illinois statute invalidated in *MITE*, the Indiana Act applies only to corporations that have a substantial number of shareholders in Indiana. *See* Ind. Code Sec. 23- 1-42-4(a)(3) (Supp. 1986). Thus, every application of the Indiana Act will affect a substantial number of Indiana residents, whom Indiana indisputably has an interest in protecting.

D

Dynamics' argument that the Act is unconstitutional ultimately rests on its contention that the Act will limit the number of successful tender offers. There is little evidence that this will occur. But even if true, this result would not substantially affect our Commerce Clause analysis. We reiterate that this Act does not prohibit any entity—resident or nonresident— from offering to purchase, or from purchasing, shares in Indiana corporations, or from attempting thereby to gain control. It only provides regulatory procedures designed for the better protection of the corporations' shareholders. We have rejected the "notion that the Commerce Clause protects the particular structure or methods of operation in a . . . market." *Exxon Corp. v. Governor of Maryland*, 437 U.S. at 127, 98 S. Ct. at 2215. The very commodity that traded in the securities market is one whose characteristics are defined by state law. Similarly, the very commodity that is traded in the "market for corporate control"—the corporation—is one that owes its existence and attributes to state law. Indiana need not define these commodities as other States do; it need only provide that residents and nonresidents have equal access to them. This Indiana has done. Accordingly, even if the Act should decrease the number of successful tender offers for Indiana corporations, this would not offend the Commerce Clause.

IV

On its face, the Indiana Control Share Acquisition Chapter evenhandedly determines the voting rights of shares of Indiana corporations. The Act does not conflict with the provisions or purposes of the Williams Act. To the limited extent that the Act affects interstate commerce, this is justified by the State's interests in defining the attributes of shares in its corporations and in protecting shareholders. Congress has never questioned the need for state regulation of these matters. Nor do we think such regulation offends the Constitution. Accordingly, we reverse the judgment of the Court of Appeals.

It is so ordered.

Justice SCALIA, concurring in part and concurring in the judgment.

I join Parts I, III-A, and III-B of the Court's opinion. However, having found, as those Parts do, that the Indiana Control Share Acquisitions Chapter neither "discriminates against interstate commerce," nor "create[s] an impermissible risk of inconsistent regulation by different States," I would conclude without further analysis that it is not invalid under the dormant Commerce Clause. While it has become standard practice at least since *Pike v. Bruce Church, Inc.*, 397 U.S. 137, 90 S. Ct. 844, 25 L. Ed. 2d 174 (1970), to consider, in addition to these factors, whether the burden on commerce imposed by a state statute "is clearly excessive in relation to the putative local benefits," *id*. at 142, 90 S. Ct. at 847, such an inquiry is ill suited to the judicial function and should be undertaken rarely if at all. . . .

* * *

I also agree with the Court that the Indiana control shares Act is not pre-empted by the Williams Act, but I reach that conclusion without entering into the debate over the purposes of the two statutes. The Williams Act is governed by the antipreemption provision of the Securities Exchange Act of 1934, which provides that nothing it contains "shall affect the jurisdiction of the securities commission (or any agency or officer performing like function) of any state over any security or any person insofar as it does not conflict with the provisions of this chapter or the rules and regulations thereunder." Unless it serves no function, that language forecloses pre-emption on the basis of conflicting "purpose" as opposed to conflicting "provision." . . .

I do not share the Court's apparent high estimation of the beneficence of the state statute at issue here. But a law can be both economic folly and constitutional. The Indiana Control Shares Acquisition Chapter is at least the latter. I therefore concur in the judgment of the Court.

Justice WHITE, with whom Justice BLACKMUN and Justice STEVENS join as to Part II, dissenting.

The majority today upholds Indiana's Control Share Acquisitions Chapter, a statute which will predictably foreclose completely some tender offers for stock in Indiana corporations. I disagree with the conclusion that the Chapter is neither pre-empted by the Williams Act nor in conflict with the Commerce Clause. The Chapter undermines the policy of the Williams Act by effectively preventing minority shareholders, in some circumstances, from acting in their own best interests by selling their stock. In addition, the Chapter will substantially burden the interstate market in corporate ownership, particularly if other States follow Indiana's lead as many already have done. The Chapter, therefore, directly inhibits interstate commerce, the very economic consequences the Commerce Clause was intended to prevent. The opinion of the Court of Appeals is far more persuasive than that of the majority today, and the judgment of that court should be affirmed.

I

The Williams Act expressed Congress' concern that individual investors be given sufficient information so that they could make an informed choice on whether to tender their stock in response to a tender offer. The problem with the approach the majority adopts today is that it equates protection of the individual investors, the focus of the Williams Act, with the protection of shareholders as a group. Indiana's Control Share Acquisitions Chapter undoubtedly helps protect the interests of a majority of the shareholders in any corporation subject to its terms, but in many instances, it will effectively prevent an individual investor from selling his stock at a premium. Indiana's statute, therefore, does not "furthe[r] the federal policy of *investor* protection" (emphasis added), as the majority claims.

* * *

The Control Share Acquisitions Chapter, by design, will frustrate individual investment decisions. Concededly, the Control Share Acquisitions Chapter allows the majority of a corporation's shareholders to block a tender offer and thereby thwart the desires of an individual investor to sell his stock. . . .

The majority claims that if the Williams Act pre-empts Indiana's Control Share Acquisitions Chapter, it also pre-empts a number of other corporate-control provisions such as cumulative voting or staggering the terms of directors. But this view ignores the fundamental distinction between these other corporate-control provisions and the Chapter: Unlike those other provisions, the Chapter is designed to prevent certain tender offers from ever taking place. It is transactional in nature, although it is characterized by the state as involving only the voting rights of certain shares. "[T]his Court is not bound by '[t]he name, description or characterization given [a challenged statute] by the legislature of the courts of the State,' but will determine for itself the practical impact of the law." *Hughes v. Oklahoma*, 441 U.S. 322, 336, 99 S. Ct. 1727, 1736, 60 L. Ed. 2d 250 (1979). The Control Share Acquisitions Chapter will effectively prevent minority shareholders in some circumstances from selling their stock to a willing tender offeror. It is the practical impact of the Chapter that leads to the conclusion that it is pre-empted by the Williams Act.

II

Given the impact of the Control Share Acquisition Chapter, it is clear that Indiana is directly regulating the purchase and sale of shares of stock in interstate commerce. Appellant CTS's stock is traded on the New York Stock Exchange, and people from all over the country buy and sell CTS's shares daily. Yet, under Indiana's scheme, any prospective purchaser will be effectively precluded from purchasing CTS's shares if the purchaser crosses one of the Chapter's threshold ownership levels and a majority of CTS's shareholders refuse to give the purchaser voting rights. This Court should not countenance such a restraint on interstate trade.

* * *

The State of Indiana, in its brief, admits that at least one of the Chapter's goals is to protect Indiana Corporations. The State notes that the Chapter permits shareholders "to determine . . . whether [a tender offeror] will liquidate the company or remove it from the State." Brief for Appellant in No. 86-97, p. 19. The State repeats this point later in its brief: "The Statute permits shareholders (who may also be community residents or employees or suppliers of the corporation) to determine the intentions of any offeror concerning the liquidation of the company or its possible removal from the State." *Id.* at 90. A state law which permits a majority of an Indiana corporation's stockholders to prevent individual investors, including out-of-state stockholders, from selling their stock to an out-of-state tender offeror and thereby frustrate any transfer of corporate control, is the archetype of the kind of state law that the Commerce Clause forbids.

* * *

NOTES AND QUESTIONS

(1) **The Indiana control share statute.** The Indiana statute involved in *CTS* was passed at the instance of James K. Baker, chairman of Arvin Industries Inc., based in Columbus, Indiana. The passage of the statute arose in part out of the battle of conflicting cultures that has been an important part of the takeover scene. Arvin was a typical "rust belt" manufacturer of automobile parts and other industrial products. It was a major employer and benefactor in the small middle-American town of Columbus, which had a population of only 30,000. On December 3, 1985, Arvin received a letter threatening a takeover from the Belzberg family of Canada, an immensely wealthy Jewish family of Polish origins famous for many takeover attempts and greenmail payments. Later that month, the Belzbergs threatened to make the tender offer on Christmas eve. Baker later recalled that Arvin executives responded: "We're all good gentiles here. . . . We like to be with our families on Dec. 24." Baker mentioned his problem to Bob Garton, a fellow Rotarian and fellow member of a gourmet cooking club, whose children had been classmates in junior high school. Garton happened to be president of the Indiana Senate. Indiana soon had an anti-takeover statute. Arvin and the Belzbergs ended up settling under an agreement pursuant to which Arvin bought out the Belzbergs' stock interest as well as a tire-valve company they owned.[94]

(2) **Reasons for state anti-takeover statutes.** Anti-takeover statutes have both political explanations and *post hoc* rationales. As to the political story, there is substantial evidence to the effect that, like the Indiana statute in *CTS,* many state anti-takeover statutes have been passed as the result of lobbying by managers of a dominant firm (*see* **Romano,** *Political Economy*), often to prevent the hostile takeover of specific corporations by publicly identified potential bidders.[95] Romano demonstrates that corporations that lobby for this type of statute tend to have high concentration ratios of ownership, and concludes that the shareholders of such corporations (primarily institutional investors) would most likely reject control-share-type provisions, which primarily serve to facilitate coordination by small shareholders. The Romano story helps explain why Delaware, normally a leader in corporate statutory provisions, was relatively late in passing an anti-takeover statute and even then passed a relatively weak one (*see* Del. G.C.L. § 203, discussed below). Delaware has no dominant corporation, and its corporations have relatively low concentration ratios.

---

[94] These facts are drawn from Miller, *How Indiana Shielded a Firm and Changed the Takeover Business,* WALL ST. J., July 1, 1987, at 1, 12.

[95] *See* Butler, *Corporation-Specific Anti-Takeover Laws and the Market for Corporate Charters,* 1988 WIS. L. REV. 365.

(3) **Justifications for state anti-takeover statutes: protecting shareholders.** How convincing is the shareholder-protection argument advanced by the majority in *CTS*? This depends, first, on whether shareholders need protection from the "coercion" inherent in partial or two-tier bids (*see* Section 14.03[B][1][c]); second, on whether such protection is appropriately provided by state anti-takeover statutes; and, third, whether the benefits of protection from coercion outweigh the costs of hampering the disciplinary effects of the market for control. Moreover, assuming that the shareholders of some corporations would want to adopt control share provisions, is it appropriate to impose this protection on all shareholders of covered corporations? Significantly, none of the state anti-takeover statutes condition application of the statute on shareholder approval. (While the Indiana statute at issue in *CTS* provided for an initial opt-in period, the directors determined whether the corporation opted for coverage during this period.) Thus, as Romano argued, those favoring state anti-takeover statutes apparently used the political process to bypass shareholder approval. Are the statutes justified because shareholders generally would prefer these statutes, so that applying the statutes without shareholder vote saves the cost of approval? Note that share prices decline on passage of these statutes,[96] which suggests that the statutes do not anticipate shareholder preferences. *See* **Booth, Bradford** and **Fischel** on this point.

(4) **Justifications for state anti-takeover statutes: protecting stakeholders.** An alternative justification for state anti-takeover statutes is that they protect non-shareholder "stakeholders," including employees, managers and local communities. Many Indiana-type statutes express such an intention (*see* **Coffee** and **Johnson & Millon**). Moreover, some state statutes explicitly permit or require directors to consider non-shareholder constituencies in making corporate control decisions.[97] Do you agree with this justification? Consider this question in light of Note 8 following *Unocal* in Section 14.03[D][2].

(5) **The Supremacy Clause argument.** Do you agree with the *CTS* Court's conclusion that the Indiana statute is valid on Supremacy Clause grounds? Is the Indiana statute consistent with the Williams Act because it fosters investor "autonomy"? Note that while the statute does address the supposed "coercion" problem, it does this by removing from an individual investor the right to transfer voting power without the other shareholders' consent. This tips the balance against bidders, contrary to the Williams Act. But as the majority points out, this argument also applies to many other

---

[96] *See* Hackle & Testani, *Second Generation State Takeover Statutes and Shareholder Wealth: An Empirical Study*, 97 YALE L.J. 1193 (1988); Karpoff & Malatesta, *The Wealth Effects of Second-Generation State Takeover Legislation*, 25 J. FIN. ECON. 291 (1989); Ryngaert & Netter, *Shareholder Wealth Effects of the Ohio Antitakeover Law*, 4 J.L. ECON. & ORG. 373 (1988); Ryngaert & Netter, *Shareholder Wealth Effects of the 1986 Ohio Antitakeover Law Revisited: Its Real Effects*, 6 J.L. ECON. & ORG. 253 (1990); **Sidak & Woodward**.

[97] *See, e.g.*, Ill. Ann. Stat. Ch. 32, § 8.85; Ind. Code § 23-1-35-1(d); Missouri § 351.347; N.Y. Bus. Corp. Law § 717(b) (McKinney's 1990); Ohio Rev. Code Ann. § 1701.59(e) (quoted in Note 6 following *Brehm v. Eisner* in Section 9.03[A]). Georgia Bus. Corp. Code § 14-2-202(b)(5) permits corporations to include non-shareholder constituency protection provisions in their charters.

corporate statutes that impede takeovers. Is the dissent's counterargument on this point persuasive? A further question is whether any of this matters under the Supremacy Clause. *See Amanda* below.

(6) **The Commerce Clause argument.** Four types of approaches to the Commerce Clause are discussed in *CTS*: discrimination, direct vs. indirect regulation, balancing, and danger of inconsistent regulation. As to whether the statute discriminates against interstate commerce, **Fischel** suggests that the question is arguably whether the statute is inefficient because the enacting state is "exporting" negative effects to other states. While both the *CTS* and *MITE* statutes applied by their terms equally to interstate and intrastate offers, shareholders and bidders, both statutes could be expected to have greater interstate than intrastate effects. Fischel argues that discriminatory intent, rather than merely effect, should control. As to whether the Indiana statute constitutes an impermissible direct regulation of interstate commerce, is the majority's distinction between regulation of the transfers themselves and defining the attributes of the share contract one of form or of substance?

Assuming some type of balancing test of interstate commerce effects is appropriate under the Commerce Clause (*contra* Justice Scalia's concurring opinion), how important is Indiana's "interest" in protecting "its" corporations? Does the "corporation" "belong" to Indiana any more than any other contract made under Indiana law (*e.g.*, a sales contract or a security agreement)? To the extent that Indiana is protecting shareholders, note that most of the shareholders of the corporations governed by the statute do not reside in Indiana. Also note that in evaluating Indiana's interest in enacting state anti-takeover statutes under a balancing test, the majority largely ignored the negative effects of such statutes on the market for control. *See* **Sidak & Woodward**. If the Commerce Clause calls for a balancing of state interests against effect on interstate commerce, is it appropriate to consider only whether the state has some *bona fide* interest in passing the statute, or to do a complete cost-benefit analysis of the statute?

Finally, as to the danger of inconsistent regulation, note the importance the court assigns to the fact that the Indiana statute in *CTS* applied to Indiana corporations. As discussed in Note 1 following the next case, a state anti-takeover statute's application only to locally incorporated firms apparently has been an important factor in post-*CTS* cases. This, in effect, affirms the private-ordering nature of corporate law in the sense that the parties to firms choose the applicable state law (*see* **Palmiter**).

(7) **Post-*CTS* developments.** The number and variety of so-called "second generation" anti-takeover statutes (*i.e.*, those passed in the wake of the *MITE* case) have greatly proliferated since *CTS*. Among the statutes that have gained in popularity in the post-*CTS* era are so-called "third generation" "business combination" statutes, like Del. G.C.L. § 203. These statutes are similar in their effect to flip-over poison pills—they prevent successful bidders from entering into "second-step" transactions and other business combinations between the bidder and the target unless the board that was in office prior to the takeover, disinterested shareholders approve, or (in the case of Delaware) the

bidder acquires 85% or more of the target's stock.[98] Business combination statutes give an acquiring corporation somewhat more flexibility than do control share statutes, since an acquirer can avoid the effect of the business combination statute by, among other things, operating the target as a subsidiary. But, as discussed in connection with flip-over poison pills (*see* Section 14.03[A][2][d]), the additional flexibility is illusory in many cases, because the inability to cash out minority shareholders can be very inconvenient for the acquiring company. The constitutionality of "business combination" anti-takeover statutes is considered below.

AMANDA ACQUISITION CORP. v. UNIVERSAL FOODS CORP.
United States Court of Appeals, Seventh Circuit
877 F.2d 496, *cert. denied*, 493 U.S. 955 (1989)

EASTERBROOK, Circuit Judge.

* * *

Wisconsin has a third-generation takeover statute. Enacted after *CTS*, it postpones the kinds of transactions that often follow tender offers (and often are the reason for making the offers in the first place). Unless the target's board agrees to the transaction in advance, the bidder must wait three years after buying the shares to merge with the target or acquire more than 5% of its assets. We must decide whether this is consistent with the Williams Act and Commerce Clause.

I

Amanda Acquisition Corporation is a shell with a single purpose: to acquire Universal Foods Corporation, a diversified firm incorporated in Wisconsin and traded on the New York Stock Exchange. Universal is covered by Wisconsin's anti-takeover law. . . .

. . . Amanda's financing is contingent on a prompt merger with Universal if the offer succeeds, so the offer is conditional on a judicial declaration that the law is invalid. . . .

No firm incorporated in Wisconsin and having its headquarters, substantial operations, or 10% of its shares or shareholders there may "engage in a business combination with an interested stockholder . . . for 3 years after the interested stockholder's stock acquisition date unless the board of directors of the [Wisconsin] corporation has approved, before the interested stockholder's stock acquisition date, that business combination or the purchase of stock," Wis. Stat. § 180.726(2). An "interested stockholder" is one owning 10% of the voting stock, directly or through associates (anyone acting in concert with it), § 180.726(1)(e). A "business combination" is a merger with the bidder or any of its affiliates, sale of more than 5% of the assets to bidder or affiliate, liquidation of the target, or a transaction by which

---

[98]   The provision exempting bidders who acquire 85% of a target's stock accentuates the effect of defensive moves that lock shares in friendly hands. See for example, *Shamrock Holdings, Inc. v. Polaroid Corp.*, 559 A.2d 278 (Del. Ch. 1989) (upholding under *Unocal* an all-out defensive strategy, including issuances of large blocks of stock to an ESOP and a friendly shareholder, that would have placed over a third of the company's stock in pro-management hands).

the target guarantees the bidder's or affiliates debts or passes tax benefits to the bidder or affiliate, § 180.726(1)(e). The law, in other words, provides for almost hermetic separation of bidder and target for three years after the bidder obtains 10% of the stock—unless the target's board consented before then. No matter how popular the offer, the ban applies: obtaining 85% (even 100%) of the stock held by non-management shareholders won't allow the bidder to engage in a business combination, as it would under Delaware law. [citations omitted] Wisconsin firms cannot opt out of the law, as may corporations subject to almost all other state takeover statutes. In Wisconsin it is management's approval in advance, or wait three years. Even when the time is up, the bidder needs the approval of a majority of the remaining investors, without any provision disqualifying shares still held by the managers who resisted the transaction, § 180.726(3)(b). The district court found that this statute "effectively eliminates hostile leveraged buyouts." As a practical matter, Wisconsin prohibits any offer contingent on a merger between bidder and target, a condition attached to about 90% of contemporary tender offers.

Amanda filed this suit seeking a declaration that this law is preempted by the Williams Act and inconsistent with the Commerce Clause. . . .

II

* * *

A

If our views of the wisdom of state law mattered, Wisconsin's takeover statute would not survive. Like our colleagues who decided *MITE* and *CTS*, we believe that antitakeover legislation injures shareholders. *MITE*, 633 F.2d at 496-98 and 457 U.S. at 643-44; *CTS*, 794 F.2d at 253-55. Managers frequently realize gains for investors via voluntary combinations (mergers). If gains are to be had, but managers balk, tender offers are investors' way to go over managers' heads. If managers are not maximizing the firm's value—perhaps because they have missed the possibility of a synergistic combination, perhaps because they are clinging to divisions that could be better run in other hands, perhaps because they are just not the best persons for the job—a bidder that believes it can realize more of the firm's value will make investors a higher offer. Investors tender; the bidder gets control and changes things. . . . The prospect of monitoring by would-be bidders, and an occasional bid at a premium, induces managers to run corporations more efficiently and replaces them if they will not.

* * *

B

Skepticism about the wisdom of a state's law does not lead to the conclusion that the law is beyond the state's power, however. . . . Unless a federal statute or the Constitution bars the way, Wisconsin's choice must be respected.

Amanda relies on the Williams Act of 1968, incorporated into §§ 13(d), (e) and 14(d)-(f) of the Securities Exchange Act of 1934, 15 U.S.C. §§ 78m(d), (e), 78n(d)-(f). The Williams Act regulates the conduct of tender offers. Amanda believes that Congress created an entitlement for investors to receive the benefit of tender offers, and that because Wisconsin's law makes tender offers unattractive to many potential bidders, it is preempted. *See MITE*, 633 F.2d at 490-99, and Justice White's views, 457 U.S. at 630-40.

Preemption has not won easy acceptance among the Justices for several reasons. First there is § 28(a) of the '34 Act, 15 U.S.C. § 78bb(a), which provides that "nothing in this chapter shall affect the jurisdiction of the securities commission . . . of any State over any security or any person insofar as it does not conflict with the provisions of this chapter or the rules and regulations thereunder." Although some of the SEC's regulations (particularly the one defining the commencement of an offer) conflict with some state takeover laws, the SEC has not drafted regulations concerning mergers with controlling shareholders, and the Act itself does not address the subject. States have used the leeway afforded by § 28(a) to carry out "merit regulation" of securities—"blue sky" laws that allow securities commissioners to forbid sales altogether, in contrast with the federal regimen emphasizing disclosure. So § 28(a) allows states to stop some transactions federal law would permit, in pursuit of an approach at odds with a system emphasizing disclosure and investors' choice. Then there is the traditional reluctance of federal courts to infer preemption of "state law in areas traditionally regulated by the States," *California v. ARC America Corp.*, 490 U.S. 93, 109 S. Ct. 1661, 1665, 104 L. Ed. 2d 86 (1989) . . . . States have regulated corporate affairs, including mergers and sales of assets, since before the beginning of the nation.

* * *

There is a big difference between what Congress enacts and what it supposes will ensue. Expectations about the consequences of a law are not themselves law. To say that Congress wanted to be neutral between bidder and target—a conclusion reached in many of the Court's opinions, *e.g.*, *Piper v. Chris-Craft Industries, Inc.*, 430 U.S. 1, 51 L. Ed. 2d 124, 97 S. Ct. 926 (1977)—is not to say that it also forbade the states to favor one of these sides. Every law has a stopping point, likely one selected because of a belief that it would be unwise (for now, maybe forever) to do more. . . . Nothing in the Williams Act says that the federal compromise among bidders, targets' managers, and investors is the only permissible one. . . . Like the majority of the Court in *CTS*, however, we stop short of the precipice. 481 U.S. at 78-87.

The Williams Act regulates the process of tender offers: timing, disclosure, proration if tenders exceed what the bidder is willing to buy, best-price rules. It slows things down, allowing investors to evaluate the offer and management's response. Best-price, proration, and short-tender rules ensure that investors who decide at the end of the offer get the same treatment as those who decide immediately, reducing pressure to leap before looking. After complying with the disclosure and delay requirements, the bidder is free to take the shares. *MITE* held invalid a state law that increased the delay and, by authorizing a regulator to nix the offer, created a distinct possibility that the bidder would be unable to buy the stock (and the holders to sell it) despite compliance with federal law. Illinois tried to regulate the process of tender offers, contradicting in some respects the federal rules. Indiana, by contrast, allowed the tender offer to take its course as the Williams Act specified but "sterilized" the acquired shares until the remaining investors restored their voting rights. Congress said nothing about the voting power of shares acquired in tender offers. Indiana's law reduced the benefits the bidder anticipated from the acquisition but left the process alone. So the Court, although accepting Justice White's views for the purpose of argument, held that Indiana's rules do not conflict with the federal norms.

* * *

Any bidder complying with federal law is free to acquire shares of Wisconsin firms on schedule. Delay in completing a second-stage merger may make the target less attractive, and thus depress the price offered or even lead to an absence of bids; it does not, however, alter any of the procedures governed by federal regulation. . . . Wisconsin's law is no different in effect from one saying that for the three years after a person acquires 10% of a firm's stock, a unanimous vote is required to merge. Corporate law once had a generally-applicable unanimity rule in major transactions, a rule discarded because giving every investor the power to block every reorganization stopped many desirable changes. . . . Wisconsin's more restrained version of unanimity also may block beneficial transactions, but not by tinkering with any of the procedures established in federal law.

Only if the Williams Act gives investors a right to be the beneficiary of offers could Wisconsin's law run afoul of the federal rule. No such entitlement can be mined out of the Williams Act, however. . . . Investors have no right to receive tender offers. More to the point—since Amanda sues as bidder rather than as investor seeking to sell—the Williams Act does not create a right to profit from the business of making tender offers. It is not attractive to put bids on the table for Wisconsin corporations, but because Wisconsin leaves the process alone once a bidder appears, its law may co-exist with the Williams Act.

C

The Commerce Clause, Art. I § 8 cl. 3 of the Constitution, grants Congress the power "to regulate Commerce . . . among the several States." For many decades the Court took this to be what it says: a grant to Congress with no implications for the states' authority to act when Congress is silent. . . . Limitations came from provisions, such as the Contract Clause, Art. I § 10 cl. 1 ("No State shall . . . pass any . . . Law impairing the Obligation of Contracts"), expressly denying the states certain powers. The Contract Clause has been held to curtail states' authority over corporations, see *Trustees of Dartmouth College v. Woodward*, 17 U.S. (4 Wheat.) 518, 4 L. Ed. 629 (1819), and it may have something to say about states' ability to limit the transferability of shares after they have been issued. *See* Henry N. Butler & Larry E. Ribstein, *State Anti-Takeover Statutes and the Contract Clause*, 57 U. CIN. L. REV. 611 (1988). Broad dicta in *Cooley v. Board of Wardens*, 53 U.S. (12 How.) 299, 13 L. Ed. 996 (1852), eventually led to holdings denying states the power to regulate interstate commerce directly or discriminatorily, or to take steps that had unjustified consequences in other states. Meanwhile the Court began to treat the Contract Clause as if it said that "No State shall pass any unwise Law impairing the Obligation of Contracts," so that divergent clauses have become homogenized. *Chicago Board of Realtors, Inc. v. Chicago*, 819 F.2d 732, 742-45 (7th Cir. 1987).

When state law discriminates against interstate commerce expressly—for example, when Wisconsin closes its border to butter from Minnesota—the negative Commerce Clause steps in. The law before us is not of this type: it is neutral between inter-state and intra-state commerce. Amanda therefore presses on us the broader, all-weather, be-reasonable vision of the Constitution. Wisconsin has passed a law that unreasonably injures investors, most of whom live outside of Wisconsin, and therefore it has to be unconstitutional, as Amanda sees things. Although *Pike v. Bruce Church, Inc.*, 397 U.S. 137, 25 L. Ed. 2d 174, 90 S. Ct. 844 (1970), sometimes is understood to authorize such general-purpose balancing, a closer examination of the cases may support the conclusion that the Court has looked for discrimination rather than for baleful effects. . . . At all events, although *MITE* employed the balancing process described in *Pike* to deal with a statute that regulated all firms having "contacts" with the state, *CTS* did not even cite that case when dealing with a statute regulating only the affairs of a firm incorporated in the state, and Justice Scalia's concurring opinion questioned its application. 481 U.S. at 95-96. The Court took a decidedly confined view of the judicial role: "We are not inclined 'to second-guess the empirical judgments of lawmakers concerning the utility of legislation,' *Kassel v. Consolidated Freightways Corp.*, 450 U.S. at 679 [101 S. Ct. 1309, 67 L. Ed. 2d 580] (Brennan, J., concurring in judgment)." 481 U.S. at 92. Although the scholars whose writings we cited in Part II.A conclude that laws such as Wisconsin's injure investors, Wisconsin is entitled to give a different answer to this empirical question—or to decide that investors' interests should be sacrificed to protect managers' interests or promote the stability of corporate arrangements.

Illinois's law, held invalid in *MITE*, regulated sales of stock elsewhere. Illinois tried to tell a Texas owner of stock in a Delaware corporation that he could not sell to a buyer in California. By contrast, Wisconsin's law, like the Indiana statute sustained by *CTS*, regulates the internal affairs of firms incorporated there. Investors may buy or sell stock as they please. . . .

Buyers of stock in Wisconsin firms may exercise full rights as investors, taking immediate control. No interstate transaction is regulated or forbidden. True, Wisconsin's law makes a potential buyer less willing to buy (or depresses the bid), but this is equally true of Indiana's rule. Many other rules of corporate law—supermajority voting requirements, staggered and classified boards, and so on—have similar or greater effects on some person's willingness to purchase stock. *CTS*, 481 U.S. at 89-90. States could ban mergers outright, with even more powerful consequences. . . . Wisconsin did not allow mergers among firms chartered there until 1947. We doubt that it was violating the Commerce Clause all those years. . . . Every rule of corporate law affects investors who live outside the state of incorporation, yet this has never been thought sufficient to authorize a form of cost-benefit inquiry through the medium of the Commerce Clause.

Wisconsin, like Indiana, is indifferent to the domicile of the bidder. A putative bidder located in Wisconsin enjoys no privilege over a firm located in New York. So too with investors: all are treated identically, regardless of residence. Doubtless most bidders (and investors) are located outside Wisconsin, but unless the law discriminates according to residence this alone does not matter. . . .

Wisconsin could exceed its powers by subjecting firms to inconsistent regulation. Because § 180.726 applies only to a subset of firms incorporated in Wisconsin, however, there is no possibility of inconsistent regulation. Here, too, the Wisconsin law is materially identical to Indiana's. *CTS*, 481 U.S. at 88-89. This leaves only the argument that Wisconsin's law hinders the flow of interstate trade "too much." *CTS* dispatched this concern by declaring it inapplicable to laws that apply only to the internal affairs of firms incorporated in the regulating state. 481 U.S. at 89-94. States may regulate corporate transactions as they choose without having to demonstrate under an un-focused balancing test that the benefits are "enough" to justify the consequences.

* * *

The three district judges who have considered and sustained Delaware's law delaying mergers did so in large measure because they believed that the law left hostile offers "a meaningful opportunity for success." *BNS, Inc. v. Koppers Co.*, 683 F. Supp. at 469. *See also RP Acquisition Corp.*, 686 F. Supp. at 482-84, 488; *City Capital Associates*, 696 F. Supp. at 1555. Delaware allows a merger to occur forthwith if the bidder obtains 85% of the shares other than those held by management and employee stock plans. If the bid is attractive to the bulk of the unaffiliated investors, it succeeds. Wisconsin offers no such opportunity, which Amanda believes is fatal.

Even in Wisconsin, though, options remain. Defenses impenetrable to the naked eye may have cracks. Poison pills are less fatal in practice than in name (some have been swallowed willingly), and corporate law contains self-defense mechanisms. . . . So too there are countermeasures to statutes deferring mergers. The cheapest is to lower the bid to reflect the costs of delay. Because every potential bidder labors under the same drawback, the firm placing the highest value on the target still should win. Or a bidder might take down the stock and pledge it (or its dividends) as security for any loans. That is, the bidder could operate the target as a subsidiary for three years. The corporate world is full of partially owned subsidiaries. If there is gain to be had from changing the debt-equity ratio of the target, that can be done consistent with Wisconsin law. The prospect of being locked into place as holders of illiquid minority positions would cause many persons to sell out, and the threat of being locked in would cause many managers to give assent in advance, as Wisconsin allows. (Or bidders might demand that directors waive the protections of state law, just as Amanda believes that the directors' fiduciary duties compel them to redeem the poison pill rights.) Many bidders would find lock-in unattractive because of the potential for litigation by minority investors, and the need to operate the firm as a subsidiary might foreclose savings or synergies from merger. So none of these options is a perfect substitute for immediate merger, but each is a crack in the defensive wall allowing some value-increasing bids to proceed.

At the end of the day, however, it does not matter whether these counter-measures are "enough." The Commerce Clause does not demand that states leave bidders a "meaningful opportunity for success." Maryland enacted a law that absolutely banned vertical integration in the oil business. No opportunities, "meaningful" or otherwise, remained to firms wanting to own retail outlets. *Exxon Corp. v. Governor of Maryland* held that the law is consistent with the Commerce Clause, even on the assumption that it injures consumers and investors alike. A state with the power to forbid mergers has the power to defer them for three years. . . . Wisconsin's law may well be folly; we are confident that it is constitutional.

AFFIRMED

NOTES AND QUESTIONS

(1) **Recent cases.** Post-*CTS* cases on state anti-takeover statutes that, like the one at issue in *Amanda*, regulate only the internal affairs of companies incorporated in the enacting state appear to be safe against attacks under the Supremacy and Commerce Clauses.[99] On the other hand, statutes that apply to corporations incorporated in other states or that regulate the tender offer process itself have been held unconstitutional.[100] Taken together, these cases suggest that application to locally incorporated firms determines constitutionality, at least under the Commerce Clause (*see* **Kozyris** and **Palmiter**).[101]

(2) **Should state anti-takeover statutes be federally preempted?** Whether or not state anti-takeover statutes are bad policy, it seems clear that little can be done about them under the Commerce Clause or Supremacy Clause. As illustrated by *Amanda*, a state legislature can go very far in restricting takeovers of locally incorporated firms without coming up against these constitutional restraints. One way of dealing with state anti-takeover statutes is through a federal law that, unlike the Williams Act, clearly pre-empts such state statutes. For example, **Bebchuk & Ferrell** would permit firms to opt into a federal takeover law by shareholder vote.[102] Such proposals raise important questions:

   a) Where would preemption stop? In particular, to what extent would a federal statute pre-empt state-law areas of internal governance such as staggered boards or the board's power to set meeting dates?

   b) To what extent might capital markets and the market for corporate charters "discipline" state anti-takeover statutes, at least in the long run?[103]

   c) Do the costs of leaving the terms of corporate contracts in state hands exceed those of federal regulation? In this regard, it is worth noting that Congress is not immune from the sort of interest group pressures that produce inefficient state laws.

---

[99] *See, e.g., WLR Foods, Inc. v. Tyson Foods, Inc.*, 65 F.3d 1172 (4th Cir. 1995), *cert. denied*, 116 S. Ct. 921 (1996).

[100] *See, e.g., Tyson Foods, Inc. v. McReynolds*, 865 F.2d 99 (6th Cir. 1989); *see also* Weiss, *What Lawyers Do When the Emperor Has No Clothes: Evaluating CTS Corp. v. Dynamics Corp. of America and its Progeny*, 78 GEO. L.J. 1655, 79 GEO. L.J. 211 (1990).

[101] See also in this regard Ribstein, *Choosing Law By Contract*, 18 J. CORP. L. 245 (1993) (arguing that all contractual choice of law, and not merely the contractual choice which underlies the internal affairs rule, should be constitutionally protected under the Commerce Clause).

[102] For criticism of this proposal, see Choi & Guzman, *Choice and Federal Intervention in Corporate Law*, 87 VA. L. REV. 961 (2001). For a rebuttal, see Bebchuk & Ferrell, *Federal Intervention to Enhance Shareholder Choice*, 87 VA. L. REV. 993 (2001).

[103] *See Amanda Acquisition*, 877 F.2d at 507; Butler, *supra*, 1988 WIS. L. REV. at 379; Romano, *Competition for Corporate Charters and the Lesson of Takeover Statutes*, 61 FORD. L. REV. 843 (1993).

(3) **Are state anti-takeover statutes unconstitutional under the Contract Clause?** There is an alternative way of dealing with state anti-takeover statutes. Article I, § 10, Clause 1 of the U.S. Constitution provides: "No State shall . . . pass any . . . Law impairing the Obligation of Contracts." As discussed in **Butler & Ribstein**, the contract clause argument raises three questions: (1) Is the corporation a "contract"? (2) Do state anti-takeover statutes impair this contract? (3) Are contract impairments by anti-takeover statutes unconstitutional?[104] The characterization of the corporation as a "contract" is a recurring theme of this book. Indeed, as discussed in Section 1.04, the *Dartmouth College* decision applied the Contract Clause to the corporation in the first important Contract Clause case. The impairment element focuses on the fact that state anti-takeover statutes, unlike other corporate governance provisions, are imposed on existing corporations without a shareholder vote. If governance terms are a contract, state anti-takeover statutes would seem to change, or "impair," these terms—substantially so, in light of the importance of the market for corporate control. On the other hand, how much of a difference do state anti-takeover statutes make given the prevalence of strong takeover defenses discussed in Section 14.03[A]? Also, might the impairment be justified as "reasonable" under the doctrine of *Home Building & Loan Association v. Blaisdell*.[105] This brings into play, to some extent, the policy arguments for and against these statutes.

(4) **The ultimate test: the Pennsylvania statute.** The Pennsylvania statute, enacted as a result of lobbying by a coalition of managers of large Pennsylvania corporations and labor unions, tested the limits of constitutionality and federal tolerance of state anti-takeover statutes by coming very close to banning hostile takeovers of Pennsylvania corporations. The statute includes the following provisions (all cites are to 15 Pennsylvania Cons. Stat. Ann.), which apply to existing Pennsylvania corporations, except those that opt out by director, but not shareholder, vote.

> (a) Directors may consider non-shareholder constituencies in discharging their duties (§ 515(a)).
> (b) Directors' actions in connection with control transactions need only satisfy a "good faith" test, and breach of directors' duties in such transactions must be proven by "clear and convincing evidence" (§ 515(d)).
> (c) Pursuant to Indiana-type control share acquisition provisions (§§ 2561-68), persons who buy or acquire voting power over 20% or more of the corporation's voting shares (including acquisitions through some proxy solicitations) cannot vote those shares without disinterested shareholder approval. In addition, those who acquired their stock within the past 12 months cannot vote on whether to confer voting rights on the control shares

---

[104] For endorsements of the application of Contract Clause analysis to state anti-takeover statutes, see Judge Easterbrook's opinion in *Amanda*, 877 F.2d at 505; McGee, *Mergers and Acquisitions: An Economic and Legal Analysis*, 22 CREIGHTON L. REV. 665 (1989).

[105] 290 U.S. 398 (1934).

and the control shareholder cannot even seek a shareholder vote unless it has firm financing (which is unlikely to be the case before the control-share vote). If the control shareholder cannot obtain financing or meet other requirements for obtaining a vote to confer voting rights within thirty days of making the acquisition, the shares may be redeemed by the board at any time within two years.

(d) Shareholders who buy or otherwise obtain voting power over 20% or more of the corporation's voting shares (again, including some acquisitions through proxy solicitations), or who even announce an intention to do so, must disgorge all profits from a sale of shares within 18 months (§§ 2571-76).

(e) Workers fired within two years after the company is put "in play" are entitled to up to 26 weeks' mandatory severance pay (§§ 2581-84). These provisions explain the unusual labor-management coalition that lobbied in favor of the statute.

Armstrong World Industries, Inc. v. Adams[106] held that a shareholder lacked standing to challenge the constitutionality of the Pennsylvania statute prior to a takeover, reasoning that any effect of the statute on the market value of the corporation's shares does not support a challenge to the constitutionality of legislation, and that even if takeovers had been deterred this would only affect potential offerors who are not parties to the action. Do you agree with this reasoning?[107]

(5) **The duty to waive the protection of state anti-takeover statutes.** Since directors usually can waive application of state anti-takeover statutes, just as they can redeem poison pill rights, litigation over state anti-takeover statutes ultimately sometimes focuses on the board's duty to opt out of the statute, just as in the poison pill context.

REFERENCES

Bebchuk & Ferrell, *Federalism and Corporate Law: The Race to Protect Managers from Takeovers*, 99 COLUM. L. REV. 1168 (1999).

Booth, *The Promise of State Takeover Statutes*, 86 MICH. L. REV. 1635 (1988).

Bradford, *Protecting the Shareholders from Themselves? A Policy and Constitutional Review of a State Takeover Statute*, 67 NEB. L. REV. 459 (1988).

---

[106] 961 F.2d 405 (3d Cir. 1992).

[107] See Pound, *On the Motives for Choosing a Corporate Governance Structure: A Study of Corporate Reaction to the Pennsylvania Takeover Law*, 8 J.L. ECON. & ORG. 656 (1992) (decision not to opt out of the statute shown to be more likely for firms that have lower internal incentives and more principal-agent slack, with lower insider ownership, that are prone to poor decisions on deployment of current resources, that have market valuations revealing low confidence in management, and that have adopted poison pills, all suggesting that the statute weakens market discipline of management).

Butler & Ribstein, *State Anti-Takeover Statutes and the Contract Clause*, 57 U. CIN. L. REV. 611 (1988).

Coffee, *The Uncertain Case for Takeover Reform: An Essay on Stockholders, Stakeholders and Bust-Ups*, 1988 WIS. L. REV. 435.

Fischel, *From* MITE *to* CTS*: State Anti-Takeover Statutes, The Williams Act, The Commerce Clause and Insider Trading*, 1987 SUP. CT. REV. 47 (1988).

Johnson & Millon, *Missing the Point About State Takeover Statutes*, 87 MICH. L. REV. 846 (1989).

Kozyris, *Some Observations on State Regulation of Multistate Takeovers—Controlling Choice of Law Through the Commerce Clause*, 14 DEL. J. CORP. L. 499 (1989).

Palmiter, *The* CTS *Gambit: Stanching the Federalization of Corporate Law*, 69 WASH. U. L.Q. 445 (1991).

Romano, *Competition for Corporate Charters and the Lesson of Takeover Statutes*, 61 FORDHAM L. REV. 843 (1993).

Romano, *The Political Economy of Takeover Statutes*, 73 VA. L. REV. 1 (1987).

Sidak & Woodward, *Corporate Takeovers, The Commerce Clause, and the Efficient Anonymity of Shareholders*, 84 NW. U. L. REV. 501 (1990).

CHAPTER 15

Corporate Acquisitions:
Appraisal Rights, Fiduciary Duties and
Other Shareholder Remedies

Corporate combinations (*i.e.*, mergers and asset purchases) often involve substantial changes in the rights of some or all of the shareholders affected by the transaction, such as the conversion of the shares of one or more of the corporations participating in the transaction into securities of a different firm, cash, or both. Moreover, since corporate combinations, unlike purchases of stock from individual shareholders, involve a decision by the corporation, shareholders may be forced into the transaction if enough of their fellow shareholders agree to it. Thus, special procedures and remedies may be necessary to protect the shareholders. Section 15.01 focuses on a particularly important state law procedure—the appraisal right. Section 15.02 and 15.03 discuss additional lines of shareholder protection—state law fiduciary duties and remedies under the federal securities laws.

§ 15.01 The Appraisal Right

One of the main state law procedures protecting shareholders is the appraisal right—that is, the right of shareholders who disagree with the combination to dissent from the transaction and receive a judicially-determined cash fair value for their shares. The circumstances under which the appraisal remedy is available to shareholders are discussed in Section 13.02, above.

[A] Introduction: Fundamental Changes and Vested Rights

In corporations fundamental changes, including corporate combinations, may be approved by a less than unanimous vote of the shareholders—often by a simple majority. *See* Section 5.01, above. Corporate law has evolved from a position in the early 1800s that a corporation, like a partnership, could not fundamentally change its form without the approval of all the shareholders. Under partnership law, each partner, at least in the absence of contrary agreement, may veto decisions that are extraordinary or contrary to the parties' agreement. *See* Uniform Partnership Act § 18(h), Revised UPA § 401(j), and Section 4.02[A], above. Consistent with this general voting rule, RUPA

§§ 902(b), 903(b) and 905(c) now specifically provide for approval of mergers and conversions by all partners.[1]

Gradually courts, and then legislatures, came to recognize the need for greater flexibility in widely held corporations, where the costs of a unanimity rule to the shareholders as a group often exceed the benefits of such a rule to minority holders (see the discussion of the costs and benefits of various voting rules in Section 4.01). Thus, the minority's veto was transformed into a right to receive cash. Rationales for the appraisal remedy are discussed in subsection 15.01[E], below.

REFERENCES

Carney, *Fundamental Corporate Changes, Minority Shareholders, and Business Purposes*, 1980 AM. B. FOUND. RES. J. 69.

Eisenberg, THE STRUCTURE OF THE CORPORATION (1976).

Letsou, *The Role of Appraisal in Corporate Law*, 39 B.C. L. REV. 1121 (1998).

Manning, *The Shareholder's Appraisal Remedy: An Essay for Frank Coker*, 72 YALE L.J. 223 (1962).

[B] Appraisal Right Procedures

For an example of a statutory provision outlining the procedures that dissenting shareholders must follow in order to secure appraisal rights, see Del. G.C.L. § 262. Under this provision, the corporation must notify shareholders as to whether the transaction is one in connection with which appraisal rights are available. (§ 262(d)(1)). Following notification of the availability of appraisal rights, shareholders who wish to take advantage of appraisal rights must not vote in favor of the transaction (§ 262(a)) and must, before the vote, give notice of intention to demand payment for their stock (§ 262(d)(1)). Although some older cases were very strict as to what the demand must state, more recently they have required only fair notice to the corporation of the shareholders' intentions.[2]

After the vote on the transaction the shareholder must initiate an appraisal proceeding within 120 days after the merger by filing a petition in the Court of Chancery (§ 262(e)). The court then determines, first, which petitioning shareholders are entitled to appraisal (§ 262(g)); and, second, the "fair value" of the shares of the petitioning shareholders (§ 262(h)). The surviving corporation must pay this amount, together with

---

[1]   Compare the discussion of partnership voting rules for registering as an LLP discussed in Note 3 of Section 6.05.

[2]   *See, e.g., Bell v. Kirby Lumber Corp.*, 413 A.2d 137, 149 (Del. 1980). *But see Pritchard v. Mead*, 455 N.W.2d 263 (Wis. Ct. App. 1990) (refusing to excuse shareholder's technical noncompliance with the appraisal statute); *Edgerly v. Hechinger*, 1998 Del. Ch. LEXIS 177, 1998 WL 671241 (Del. Ch. 1998) (demand inadequate where petitioner who held her shares in street name failed to correctly identify record holder).

interest (§ 262(i)), to the petitioning shareholders. Under § 262(j), the court may tax costs upon the parties as it "deems equitable in the circumstances."

This procedure poses substantial problems for the petitioning shareholders. Among other things, shareholders may fail to give the required pre-meeting notice to the corporation or mistakenly vote in favor of the transaction giving rise to appraisal rights; the proceedings may take several years, during which time the shareholders may not vote their stock or receive dividends (§ 262(k)); after sixty days has elapsed from the date of the merger, the shareholders may not withdraw their appraisal demand without the corporation's consent;[3] and, as discussed below, the shareholders must produce substantial evidence and are subject to great uncertainty as to the final outcome, including the taxing of costs of the proceeding.

The Model Act has provisions intended to remedy some of these problems. First, § 13.24 requires the corporation to remit what it believes to be fair value to the shareholders within 30 days after plaintiffs' demand, and provides for court proceedings only in cases of disagreement between the corporation and the dissenters as to what constitutes fair value (*see* §§ 13.26 and 13.30). Second, costs and expenses of the proceeding may be assessed against the corporation more readily under the Model Act than under the Delaware statute (*see* § 13.31), thereby encouraging quick resolution of appraisal rights. Third, § 13.30 provides for a single consolidated appraisal proceeding brought by the corporation.

ALI *Principles* § 7.23 recommends statutory adoption of many of the procedural reforms of the Model Act as well as additional procedures intended to make appraisal a more effective remedy for dissenting shareholders. Among other things, § 7.23 provides for only a single indication of dissent to trigger the appraisal right rather than both an indication of dissent before the vote and further action after the vote; assessment of costs and expenses against the corporation if payment is not made within 30 days of the transaction giving rise to the right of appraisal or if the tendered payment is "materially less" than what is ultimately determined to be the fair value of the dissenters' shares; and appointment of a lead counsel to represent dissenters who have not secured other representation.

[C] Determining "Fair Value" in an Appraisal Proceeding: The "Delaware Block" Approach

In an appraisal proceeding the court must determine the value (usually referred to in the statute as "fair value") of the dissenters' shares. The traditional rule, applied in the following materials, is the so-called "Delaware block" approach. Subsection 15.02[D], below, discusses the emerging trend toward recognition of other valuation techniques in appraisal proceedings. This trend is best understood by first looking at the traditional approach and the criticisms of that approach.

---

[3]   *See* § 262(k); *Dofflemyer v. W.F. Hall Printing Co.*, 432 A.2d 1198 (Del. 1981).

FRANCIS I. DUPONT & CO. v. UNIVERSAL CITY STUDIOS, INC.
Delaware Court of Chancery
312 A.2d 344 (1973)

DUFFY, Justice.

This is the decision upon exceptions to an Appraiser's final report determining the value of minority shares in a corporation absorbed in a short form merger.

A.

On March 25, 1966 Universal Pictures Co. (Universal) was merged into Universal City Studios, Inc. (defendant) under 8 Del. C. § 253 effected by MCA, Inc., the common parent. MCA owned 92% of Universal and 100% of defendant. The minority stockholders of Universal were offered $75 per share which plaintiffs rejected and then perfected their appraisal rights.

On March 29, 1973 the Appraiser filed a final report, in which he found the value of the Universal stock to be $91.47 per share. Both parties filed exceptions and this is the decision thereon after briefing and oral argument.

B.

The parties' ultimate disagreement is, of course, over the value of the stock. Plaintiffs submit that the true value is $131.89 per share, defendant says it is $52.36. The computations are as follows:

Plaintiffs

Value Factor	Value	Weight	Result
Earnings	$129.12	70%	$90.38
Market	144.36	20%	28.87
Assets	126.46	10%	12.64

Defendant

Value Factor	Value	Weight	Result
Earnings	$51.93	70%	$36.35
Dividends	41.66	20%	8.33
Assets	76.77	10%	7.68

Appraiser

Value Factor	Value	Weight	Result
Earnings	$92.89	80%	$74.31
Assets	85.82	20%	17.16
		Value Per Share	$91.47

The parties differ as to details of the report to which each assigns error, but their exceptions spring from fundamentally different views of several basic elements of the appraisal. These are, principally: (1) Universal's earnings and selection of the proper multiplier for capitalization of those earnings; (2) the correct asset value per share; (3) whether an independent dividend value should have been used; (4) whether a market value for Universal's stock should have been reconstructed; and (5) the correct weight to be given each of the value factors found to be relevant by the Appraiser.

C.

At the heart of the dispute is the different picture each side draws of the nature of Universal's business, its place in the broader industry of which that business was a part, and the prospects of the industry generally and of Universal in particular. The parties, apparently, agree that at the date of merger Universal was engaged in the production and distribution of feature motion pictures. But agreement ends there.

Defendant takes exception to the Appraiser's failure to find that in the years prior to merger the industry was declining and that Universal was ranked near its bottom. And it argues that Universal was in the business of producing and distributing feature motion pictures for theatrical exhibition. It contends that such business, generally, was in a severe decline at the time of merger and that Universal, in particular, was in a vulnerable position because it had failed to diversify, its feature films were of low commercial quality and, unlike other motion picture companies, substantially all of its film library had already been committed to distributors for television exhibition. In short, defendant pictures Universal as a weak ("wasting asset") corporation in a sick industry with poor prospects for revival.

The stockholders see a different company. They say that Universal's business was indeed the production and distribution of feature films, but not merely for theatrical exhibition. They argue that there was a dramatic increase in the television market for such feature films at the time of the merger. This new market, they contend, gave great new value to a fully amortized film library and significantly enhanced the value of Universal's current and future productions. They equate the television market to the "acquisition of a new and highly profitable business whose earnings potential was just beginning to be realized at the time of the merger." Finally, say plaintiffs, the theatrical market itself was recovering in 1966. Thus, they paint the portrait of a well situated corporation in a rejuvenated industry.

The Appraiser agreed with the stockholders that the theatrical market was recovering and that the new television market had favorable effects and would continue to provide a ready market for future films to be released by Universal. However, he declined to give the stockholders the benefit of all inferences as to specific value factors which they maintained those conclusions required.

D.

I first consider earnings. Both parties disagree, for different reasons, with the result of the Appraiser's analysis of Universal's earnings as a value factor. He concluded that Universal's earnings value should be derived by calculating the mean average of earnings per share for the years 1961 through 1965, the five years preceding the merger.[4] So doing, he arrived at average earnings of $5.77 per share. He then adopted a multiplier of 16.1, which

---

[4]   Those earnings per share were:

Year	EPS	Year	EPS
1961	$3.32	1964	6.32
1962	4.96	1965	8.02
1963	6.22		

is the average price earnings ratio of nine motion picture companies, to capitalize Universal's earnings.

The stockholders accept the multiplier selected by the Appraiser but argue that he should have used the 1965 earnings of $8.02 per share rather than the mean average of the five years preceding the merger.

Valuation of a going business is a complex task and nothing about it is more difficult than capitalizing earnings. Expert authorities disagree about the relative significance of past, present and projected earnings and as to whether some figure representative of the enterprise's true earning power can be fairly derived from such figures. But our law has settled upon a basic approach to be followed in appraisal proceedings.

It is established Delaware law that for appraisal purposes earnings are to be determined by averaging the corporation's earnings over a reasonable period of time. . . . The determination must be based upon historical earnings rather than on the basis of prospective earnings. *Application of Delaware Racing Association*, Del. Supr., 213 A.2d 203 (1965). The five-year period immediately preceding the merger is ordinarily considered to be the most representative and reasonable period of time over which to compute the average.

* * *

The stockholders argue that averaging past earnings is proper only when the earnings history has been erratic. In support of that proposition, Mr. Stanley Nabi, managing partner of a NYSE brokerage house and an investment and financial analyst, testified that the accepted practice among security analysts is to capitalize present earnings, and to give the trend of earnings important consideration in the selection of the multiplier. The stockholders argue that Universal's earnings history was not erratic but, in fact, had a steady and rapid growth. They contend that the Appraiser therefore should have used the current (1965) earnings as the figure to be capitalized.

This argument is not persuasive even if Mr. Nabi's testimony as to the accepted practice among security analysts for capitalizing earnings is conceded to be correct. Whatever that practice may currently be, the policy of Delaware law is that averaging earnings over the five years immediately preceding the merger should be the rule and not the exception. In short, a choice among alternative techniques for capitalizing earnings has been made and no persuasive conceptual reason has been shown to change that choice now.

The stockholders also argue that Universal's earlier earnings, particularly those of 1961, were not representative of Universal's earning power at the time of merger because television was a relatively minor factor in such earnings. They offered a number of alternatives to the Appraiser and, on the exceptions, press their contention that he should have used 1965 earnings of $8.02 per share.

I do not agree with the shareholders that the "pre-1965 earnings had become an anachronism" at the time of merger. I view Universal's situation at that time as one of change in the nature of its market, not in the fundamental nature of its business. It was undoubtedly clear at the time of merger that the new television market had contributed substantially to Universal's earnings and would continue to do so for at least the short term. It was also evident that television presented a relatively permanent new market. But I do not think it realistic to say that that market was of such a revolutionary character as to assure for time without end either a trend of increasing earnings or a comparatively high level of earnings. . . . The fact is that, with or without the television market, Universal's earning experience over the long term remains subject to the variables in its managerial and artistic talent, the ability and ingenuity of competitors and the uncertainties of public tastes in entertainment.

* * *

Universal's earnings over the five-year period were representative of the Company's experience in the broader context of its business of producing feature length films, whether for the theatrical market or for television, or both. An important purpose behind the practice of averaging over a five-year period is to balance extraordinary profits and/or losses which might distort the earnings data if a period of only one or two years was used. . . . It is for this reason that the use of such shorter periods by appraisers has generally not been permitted. . . . Similarly, an appraiser usually may not exclude years of unusual loss or profit, nor may he extend the period to be averaged so as to minimize their impact. . . . None of the five years immediately preceding the merger has been shown to be so extraordinary as to justify exclusion from the span to be averaged. As I have indicated, the very purpose of averaging is to balance out such years as 1961 when the Company's earnings were comparatively low.

I conclude, therefore, that the Appraiser correctly used the mean average of earnings for the five years immediately preceding the merger.

Defendant agrees that the earnings to be capitalized is the five-year average of $5.77 per share, but says that the Appraiser erred in adopting as a multiplier the industry price earnings ratio (16:1). It argues that even if such ratio were appropriate, the correct figure is not more than 12.7 and it contends that the maximum multiplier permitted under our case law is 10, except under special circumstances not present here. Plaintiffs do not except to the Appraiser's multiplier. Specifically, defendant says a multiplier of 9 is fair both in terms of Universal's prior history and its position in that industry.

Admittedly many of the cases and treatises approve a multiplier of 10 or thereabouts. But that is based largely on the economics and pricing outs structure of an earlier day and, under the circumstances here present, the use of any such number would be artificial.

Arguably, there is much to be said about the choice of any particular multiplier and the briefs cover it all. In the last analysis, I am not persuaded that the Court should reject the Appraiser's reasonable judgment in this matter. In accepting his choice, I note particularly the trend of Universal's earnings, the predictability of certain of its television income during the four years following merger . . . that valuation on a going concern basis as of a single date (of the merger) is the object of the appraisal, and the norm, therefore, is to determine the multiplier as of that date; determination of the multiplier by reference to the average experience of other companies in comparable businesses is a reasonable formulation in this case.

The earnings value (16.1 x $5.77 = $92.89) determined by the Appraiser will be approved.

E.

I turn now to asset value. Plaintiffs say that at the time of merger the net figure was $126.46, defendant says it was $76.77, the Appraiser determined it to be $85.82.

The parties have argued at some length their respective views of the adjustments which should be made to Universal's book value, but I do not propose to discuss each of these in detail. My view of the issues is reflected in the table and the comments which follow.

	Plaintiffs	Defendant	Appraiser	Court
(1) Book Value	$58.42	$57.94	$57.94	$58.42
(2) Increase in value of MCA stock	7.28	7.28	7.28	7.28
(3) Estimated future television revenue	22.84	20.26	20.26	22.84
(4) Future theatrical revenue from fully amortized pictures	32.17	0	0	0
(5) 30% network distribution fee (if disallowed; if 12½% allowed, $2.84)	5.40	0	0	2.84
(6) Present value discount on accounts payable after one year.	.34	.34	.34	.34
	$126.45	$85.82	$85.82	$91.72

* * *

Future theatrical revenue from fully amortized pictures: Plaintiffs argue that the Appraiser was mistaken in his conclusion that *Poole v. N.V. Deli Maatschappij*, Del. Supr., 243 A.2d 67 (1968), holds that asset value cannot be calculated on the basis of earnings. They argue that 1965 income from the films in question should be capitalized (with appropriate discounts) and an asset value determined. But I conclude that the Appraiser was correct, because in *Poole* the Court said that

> Any allowance for earning power of the assets . . . is best left to the court's consideration of earnings as an independent element of stock value and to the court's exercise of the weighting function.

* * *

I conclude that for appraisal purposes a share of Universal stock should be assigned an asset value of $91.72.

F.

The Appraiser declined to include market value of Universal stock as a value factor because there was not a reliable market for it and none could be constructed. Defendant agrees with that conclusion. Plaintiffs urged the Appraiser to find a reconstructed value of $144 a share.

The Delaware law is that in the absence of a reliable market for stock, a reconstructed market value "must be given consideration," if one can be made. Application of Delaware Racing Association, supra.

I agree with plaintiffs that, on a comparative basis, Universal's financial performance was more impressive than that of MCA, but I am not persuaded that a reliable basis for valuation can be established by applying MCA price earnings ratio to Universal's 1965 earnings. Certainly there was a market for MCA shares and Universal's earnings and experience contributed to whatever value that buyers and sellers in that market placed upon MCA at any given time. But to reach through the MCA curtain and find Universal, is to grasp at shadows, and to attempt to divine (in this case where we deal with hard dollars) what buyers would have paid for Universal had they the chance, is to substitute fantasy for fact. This simply involves too much speculation about too many intangibles. Accordingly, market value will not be included as an appraisal index.

G.

Defendant urged the Appraiser to capitalize the historical dividends of Universal and assign to them an independent value of $41.66 for appraisal purposes. He declined to do so. Plaintiffs agree.

I agree with the Appraiser's conclusion, . . . that dividends largely reflect the same value as earnings and so should not be separately considered.

H.

Finally, I consider the weighting factor, an issue as to which the parties are in least disagreement. The views of the Appraiser and the parties are as follows:

Value Factor	Plaintiffs	Defendant	Appraiser
Earnings	70%	70%	80%
Assets	10%	10%	20%
Market Value	20%	—	—
Dividend Distribution	—	20%	—

As this table shows, the parties agree on the weight which should be assigned to earnings and assets, respectively. They differ on allocation of the remaining 20% which each argues should be assigned to separate factors, both of which the Appraiser and the Court have rejected. The Appraiser, in effect, divided the 20% equally between the two components he used.

In my own view, a more precise division of that 20% should be made by applying to it a factor derived from the allocations about which the parties agree. I think this is particularly desirable because both sides agree that earnings are entitled to seven times as much weight as assets. Applying such factors (7/8 for earnings, 1/8 for assets) to the remaining 20%, I conclude that the earnings percentage should be increased by 17.5%, while the asset percentage should be increased by 2.5%.

* * *

I conclude that the value of a share of Universal stock on the date of merger should be determined to be as follows:

Value Factor	Value	Weight	Result
Earnings	$92.89	87.5%	$81.28
Assets	$91.72	12.5%	$11.46
	Value per share		$92.75

NOTE

The Chancellor's determination was affirmed on appeal. The following are excerpts from the opinion of the Delaware Supreme Court:

UNIVERSAL CITY STUDIOS, INC. v. FRANCIS I. DUPONT & CO.
Delaware Supreme Court
334 A.2d 216 (1975)

McNEILLY, Justice:

* * *

Universal City Studios, Inc. (appellant) assigns as error the earnings multiplier arrived at by the Appraiser and the Court of Chancery. Further, appellant contends that the Court below erred in the determination of the asset value of a share of Universal stock.

. . . The appellant contends that improper criteria were used by the Appraiser and the Court in determining the multiplier and that the figure is impermissably high. For this latter proposition, appellants cite Professor Dewing, whose works in the past have been accorded deferential treatment in Delaware. At page 388 of his work, THE FINANCIAL POLICY OF CORPORATIONS, (5th Ed. 1953), Professor Dewing states that a multiplier of 10 is the highest value that can be assigned to a business. We, however, do not find such a view to be persuasive, but instead concur with the findings of Swanton [v. State Guaranty Corp. 42 Del. Ch. 477, 215 A.2d 242 (1965)] (where a multiplier of 14 was fixed), which recognized that Professor Dewing's capitalization chart was not the "be-all and end-all," and it did not "freeze the subject matter for all time," especially since "contemporary financial history" reveals a "need for flexibility." (at 246).

Appellants contend that the Appraiser and the Chancellor looked solely to the price-earnings ratios of nine other motion picture companies on March 25, 1966, and averaged them together to arrive at a 16.1 multiplier. We agree with the appellant insofar as the 16.1 figure is arrived at through precise mathematical calculations involving the price-earnings ratios of these nine other companies. We disagree however that this was the sole consideration. . . .

The Chancellor included a table in the opinion which showed that in 1961, earnings per share were $3.32, and that the earnings steadily increased until in 1965, they were at $8.02 per share. The record shows that during these years, none of the companies except Disney could show a steady growth trend. Within the industry, there was pronounced volatility of earnings, with years of deficit and decline. Universal, on the other hand, was able to show a steady growth, even during the period of 1962 and 1963, when the industry was suffering greatly. As for the "predictability" of certain of its television income, the Chancellor was taking cognizance of the Appraiser's report, which specified that Universal was to receive "substantial future income" in the sum of over $48,000,000 as a result of the leasing of major portions of its film library to television networks. Such commitments were labeled "guaranteed" by the Appraiser, and he noted that they would result in net earnings from television of at least $16.63 per share over the following four years. Further income could be expected from renewal of television contracts as well as from release of future films and subsequent leases to television. The evidence presented was sufficient to warrant a departure from Dewing's capitalization chart. The steady upward trend in Universal's earnings and the vast amount of money guaranteed to inure to Universal are persuasive factors indicating future economic success and stability. . . . It is true that a corporation in the motion picture industry, such as Universal, is subject to the whims of public taste and the artistic talents of its employees. Fluctuation in earnings is indeed a trademark of the motion picture industry and Universal was as vulnerable to non-acceptance of its theatrical productions as any other company. However, as of the date of the merger, Universal had exhibited a better earnings picture than any other motion picture company and had, through its television contracts, provided a buffer which would tend to offset for several years any theatrical losses. Therefore a relatively high multiplier was warranted.

There are other factors not alluded to in the opinion which support a high multiplier in this case. The years of 1964 and 1965 showed a marked resurgence for the motion picture industry after a long period of slumping profits due to competition from television. The stock market reflected the turnaround of the industry by rising from the stock price index of 49 in 1963 (the mean price of Columbia, MGM, 20th Century Fox, United Artists, Paramount, Warner Brothers) to a mean of about $64 per share figure in 1966. Further, on March 25, 1966, the Dow Jones and Standard and Poors Indices showed an average price to earnings ratio of approximately 17.3, 17.4. Universal's growth rate during the years 1961 through 1965 amounted to 142 per cent or a compound rate of 25 per cent a year. This record, showing no yearly volatility, was far superior to those other companies within the industry and was also superior to the rate of growth of the stocks listed in the Dow Jones and Standard and Poors Indices.

* * *

As for the appellant's contention that error was committed below by the use of certain non-comparable companies in arriving at the 16.1 figure, we are not persuaded to reverse. The "imponderables of the valuation process" and the concomitant broad discretion traditionally granted to evaluators of corporate shares of stock, compel an acceptance of the method of determining a multiplier unless there is a clear abuse of discretion amounting to an error at law. . . . We accept the findings below that the companies used to initially provide a basis for the multiplier for Universal were in fact "comparable" to Universal. True, some of the companies were more diversified than Universal, and some produced more award winning movies than Universal. Nevertheless, all nine companies were heavily engaged in the production of distribution of motion pictures and were therefore subject to the same public moods and reactions that effected Universal. We note that, based on its past record and managerial plans for the future, Universal was in a position to suffer less than other companies from woes generally effecting the industry. We are not prepared to delineate one or more companies within the same industry as Universal, as being non-comparable, when influxes applicable to one are applicable to all, but register in varying degrees as measured by financial growth or depletion. *See David J. Greene & Co. v. Dunhill International, Inc.*, Del. Ch., 249 A.2d 427, 433 (1968). In that case, the Court admonished the Appraiser below for including in a group of companies, for purposes of ascertaining a multiplier based on comparability, five companies that were productive in a related field, but not within the industry. Nevertheless, the use of the price-earnings ratios of three companies which competed with the company under evaluation, "to a limited degree," was not found to have unwarranted effects in the choice of a multiplier.

From the foregoing, and after applying the standard of review applicable to the selection of earnings multipliers, we conclude that the 16.1 figure reached below is within the range of reason.

* * *

NOTES AND QUESTIONS

(1) **Universal City Studios' history.** Universal City Studios was founded in 1912 by Carl Laemle. The company's early history was illustrious, and included "All Quiet on the Western Front," "Dracula" and "Frankenstein." For a long period after 1930, however, Universal produced low-budget pictures. MCA acquired control in 1962. During the period immediately before and after the MCA acquisition, Universal produced some splashy and mostly successful films including "Teacher's Pet" (Doris Day and Clark Gable, 1958), "Pillow Talk" (Doris Day and Rock Hudson, 1959), "Spartacus" (Kirk Douglas, directed by Stanley Kubrick, 1960), "Lover Come Back" (Doris Day and Rock Hudson, 1962), "Charade" (1963), and "Send Me No Flowers" (Doris Day and Rock Hudson, 1964).[4]

---

[4]   For a good history of Universal, see Schatz, THE GENIUS OF THE SYSTEM (1988).

(2) **Pre-merger valuation.** In general, fair value for appraisal purposes is determined as of the time immediately prior to the merger. Note in this regard that Delaware G.C.L. § 262(h) provides that fair value is determined "exclusive of any element of value arising from the accomplishment or expectation of the merger or consolidation." This provision appears to preclude appraisal plaintiffs from sharing in expected gains from the merger. However, *Weinberger*, Section 15.02[D], suggests that some, though not all, merger gains can be included in fair value and *Cede & Co. v. Technicolor, Inc.*[5] permitted dissenting shareholders to share in post-merger gains at least to the extent that the plan producing those gains was conceived and implemented prior to the merger. Also, ALI *Principles* § 7.22(c) provides that the court may include a "proportionate share of any gain reasonably to be expected to result from the combination, unless special circumstances would make such an allocation unreasonable." Should the valuation standard prevent dissenting shareholders from sharing in the gains attributable to mergers, as Del. G.C.L. § 262(h) appears to suggest? Although a shareholder who is objecting to the merger seemingly should not share in gains from it, the shareholder usually is objecting to the *price* of the merger, not the merger itself. The better argument for the pre-merger-value rule is that shareholders may be willing to agree before any merger proposals come along to forego an opportunity to share in merger gains in order to encourage monitoring of the firm by potential bidders.[6]

(3) **Market substitutes for appraisal.** Some states have, in effect, adopted market price as the exclusive method of valuation for actively traded securities by providing, in their appraisal statutes, for the elimination of appraisal rights with respect to actively traded securities, thus substituting the market for appraisal rights. See, for example, Delaware G.C.L. § 262(b). However, some shareholders may effectively be shut out of the market, either because the size of their holdings makes it difficult for them to sell at the prevailing market price, or because of legal restrictions on sales such as those imposed by the Securities Act of 1933 or § 16(b) of the 1934 Act.[7] Some statutes deal specifically with these problems. For example, Cal. Corp. Code § 1300(b)(1) extends appraisal rights to actively traded shares where (i) the shares are subject to transfer restrictions imposed by the corporation itself or by law or regulation or (ii) demands for appraisal are filed with respect to five percent or more of the outstanding shares.

(4) **Combining valuation approaches.** Under the "Delaware block" approach applied in *Universal*, the court determines value according to three major valuation

---

[5]   684 A.2d 289 (Del. 1996).

[6]   For an analogous argument, see the discussion of auctions in Section 14.03[B][1][d].

[7]   For a discussion of the problems of substituting the market for appraisal rights, see **Eisenberg** at 79-84. For a criticism of the Delaware public-market exception based on shareholders' differing opinions of the value of their stock, see Stout, *Are Takeover Premiums Really Premiums? Market Price, Fair Value and Corporate Law*, 99 YALE L.J. 1235 (1990). For an argument against Professor Stout's position, see Sidak & Woodward, *Takeover Premiums, Appraisal Rights, and the Price Elasticity of a Firm's Publicly Traded Stock*, 25 GA. L. REV. 783 (1991).

methods and then assigns weights to each of the values to arrive at a single "fair value." The following Notes discuss first each of the valuation methods and then the problem of weighting.

(5) **Market price as the exclusive measure for actively traded stocks.** If shareholders in actively traded firms are not to be left to the market because of the problems with selling their stock discussed in Note 3, then perhaps at least market price should be the exclusive measure of value under the appraisal statute. Yet market price is only one of the three valuation methods that comprise the Delaware block method. This is consistent with statutory language like that in Del. G.C.L. § 262(h), which calls for a consideration of "all relevant factors" and uses the term "value" instead of "price." Thus, most courts have rejected market value as an exclusive test.[8] Is this appropriate for actively traded stocks traded in efficient securities markets? One problem with letting market price be the exclusive measure of value is that, according to the most commonly accepted form of the efficient market theory, market price does not reflect inside information (*see* Section 7.01[F]). Another problem is that the market price may have been affected at all relevant times by the terms of the transaction itself, so that disadvantageous terms may depress the price. Note 12, below, discusses how the price might be adjusted to deal with this problem.

(6) **Reconstructing a market price for stocks that are not actively traded.** Should market value have any role when the stock is not actively traded? *Gonsalves v. Straight Arrow Publishers Inc.*[9] rejected any role for market value where there were only six transactions involving the sale of the corporation's stock in the previous five years and, in every case, the corporation was the purchaser. But other cases, unlike *Universal*, have tried to "reconstruct" a market price for inactive stocks. For example, *Application of Delaware Racing Ass'n*[10] used as market value an arm's length offer adjusted to reflect a reduction in earnings during the period since the offer.[11]

(7) **Highest tender offer price as a minimum market value.** Comment (f) to ALI *Principles* § 7.22 recommends using the highest tender offer price as a floor where

---

[8]   For a strong statement of this approach, see *Endicott Johnson Corp. v. Bade*, 37 N.Y.2d 585, 590-91, 376 N.Y.S.2d 103, 108, 338 N.E.2d 614, 617 (1975); *see also Oakridge Energy Inc. v. Clifton*, 937 P.2d 130 (Utah 1997) (holding under Utah law that, although market value may be entitled to more weight than asset value or investment value, market value may not be used as the sole measure in valuation). *But see Armstrong v. Marathon Oil Co.*, 32 Oh. St. 3d 397, 513 N.E.2d 776 (1987) (holding that the market price in an active market on the day before the shareholder vote was conclusive as to "fair cash value" in connection with a merger between the target and the acquiring company, subject to a determination on remand of whether that price included appreciation from the prospective merger, noting in the latter connection defendant's evidence that the merger price was substantially higher than the range of comparable stocks). On remand in *Armstrong*, the court held in favor of a market value that was far below the consideration offered in the merger. This was affirmed on appeal, 66 Ohio App. 3d 127, 583 N.E. 2d 462 (Ohio Ct. App. 1990), *appeal dism'd*, 54 Ohio St. 3d 703, 561 N.E.2d 543 (Ohio 1990).

[9]   1998 Del. Ch. LEXIS 45, 1998 WL 155556 (Del. Ch. 1998).

[10]   42 Del. Ch. 406, 213 A.2d 203 (1965).

[11]   For other discussions of "reconstructed" market price, see *Piemonte v. New Boston Garden Corp.*, 377 Mass. 719, 387 N.E.2d 1145 (Mass. 1979); *Brown v. Hedahl's Q B & R, Inc.*, 185 N.W.2d 249 (N.D. 1971).

a tender offer is followed by a "second-step" merger. This approach addresses the use of a lower "second-step" to coerce the shareholders into accepting a low-ball first step tender offer. But note the possibility that such a rule could deter takeovers by depriving bidders of merger gains. *See* Note 2 above and Section 14.03[B][1][d].

(8) **Earnings value: general considerations.** Earnings valuation in the appraisal rights context is the same as the "capitalized earnings" approach to close corporation valuation discussed in (*see* Note 5 following *Piedmont Publishing* in Section 5.04[D]): a firm's value is approximated by determining a typical earnings figure and multiplying that figure by a "capitalizer." Typical earnings are conventionally determined by averaging the earnings for the five years prior to the merger, though in determining the earnings for any given year, the courts have tended to exclude large revenue or expense items that are unlikely to recur.[12] As in *Universal*, the "capitalizer" is generally drawn from "comparable" companies in the same industry.[13] Since the capitalization rate reflects expectations of future earnings, the more certain the firm's future earnings and the greater the expected growth rate, the greater the value of the investment and the higher the capitalizer. Courts have, for example, applied a higher capitalization rate to established businesses than to new businesses.[14] Although the courts generally ignore the trend of earnings in determining the typical earnings of a company, as did the courts in *Universal*, they often consider that factor in setting the appropriate capitalizer.[15]

(9) **Dividends and earnings value.** The above discussion of earnings value ignores whether earnings were paid to the shareholders in the form of dividends. Most courts have not given independent weight to dividends.[16] Although dividends may be "irrelevant" in publicly traded firms where shareholders can declare "homemade" dividends by selling some of their shares (*see* Section 11.01[A][1]), they may be quite important in closely held firms (see the *Gardstein* close corporation "oppression" case, Section 5.05[C]). Some courts have taken the lack of dividends into account in determining fair value.[17]

---

[12] Compare, in this regard, *In re Valuation of Common Stock of Libby, McNeill & Libby*, 406 A.2d 54, 68 (Sup. Jud. Ct. Me. 1979) (excluding amounts realized from sale of obsolete facilities), and *Gibbons v. Schenley Industries, Inc.*, 339 A.2d 460 (Del. Ch. 1975) (excluding gain from sale of franchise), with *Piemonte, supra* footnote 11 (permitting inclusion of payments from expansion teams admitted to the National Hockey League on the ground that the NHL had further expansion plans), and *Gonsalves v. Straight Arrow Publishers Inc.*, 1998 Del. Ch. LEXIS 45, 1998 WL 155556 (Del. Ch. 1998) (permitting inclusion of legal expenses incurred in connection with acquisition where company was in the business of diversification).

[13] For other recent examples, see *Gibbons* and *Libby*, *supra* footnote 12.

[14] *See Sporborg v. City Specialty Stores, Inc.*, 35 Del. Ch. 560, 123 A.2d 121 (Ch. 1956).

[15] *But see Gonsalves v. Straight Arrow Publishers Inc.*, 1998 Del. Ch. LEXIS 45, 1998 WL 155556 (Del. Ch. 1998) (selecting five-year period for computing earnings, but assigning greater weights to more recent years so that company's "less successful past [will not] prevent recognition of recent trends").

[16] See, in addition to *Universal, Felder v. Anderson, Clayton & Co.*, 39 Del. Ch. 76, 159 A.2d 278 (Ch. 1960); *In re Olivetti Underwood Corp.*, 246 A.2d 800 (Del. Ch. 1968); *Piemonte, supra* footnote 11.

[17] *See Swanton v. State Guaranty Corp.*, 42 Del. Ch. 477, 215 A.2d 242 (1965) (assigning a low weight to market value partly because it was artificially depressed by a poor dividend record).

(10) **Net asset value.** The corporation may valued as a holder of assets, which requires a valuation of the assets, rather than simply an acceptance of the "book value" on the corporation's balance sheet.[18] (The artificiality of book value is discussed above in Note 3 following *Piedmont Publishing* in Section 5.04[D]). Net asset value usually is computed, as in *Universal*, on the basis of an assumption of imminent liquidation, since a going concern assumption leaves little or no difference between net asset value and earnings value.[19] But since net asset value is determined from the perspective of what a third party would pay for the assets,[20] the courts have found it difficult to ignore earnings value in their computations.[21] Consider the approach taken in *Universal* to the valuation of the film library.

(11) **Factors determining weighting of different methods of valuation.** As in *Universal*, after the market value, earnings value, and net asset value are determined, a final "fair value" figure is computed by weighting the individual values. The process of weighting discards even the pretense of precision involved in determining each of the component values. The courts tend to approve weighting based on some combination of the reliability of each of the valuation figures and the type of business. The reliability factor often affects the weight given to market value.[22] The type of business factor often affects the relative weightings of earnings value and net asset value, with earnings value being assigned the larger weight when the purpose of the business is mainly to produce income and net asset value being assigned the larger weight when the purpose of the business is chiefly to hold assets.[23] What factors might explain the weights assigned in *Universal*?

---

[18]   For examples of cases distinguishing net asset value and book value, see *Libby, supra* footnote 12 (permitting the use of book value but giving it a low weight because of its lack of reliability), and *Heller v. Munsingwear, Inc.,* 33 Del. Ch. 593, 98 A.2d 774 (1953).

[19]   *See Poole v. N.V. Deli Maatschappij,* 243 A.2d 67 (Del. Sup. Ct. 1968); *Bell v. Kirby Lumber Corp.,* 413 A.2d 137 (Del. Sup. Ct. 1980).

[20]   *See Bell v. Kirby Lumber Corp., supra* footnote 19, 413 A.2d at 143.

[21]   *See, e.g., Sporborg v. City Specialty Stores, Inc., supra* footnote 14 (court upholds the determination of the value of rental property through capitalization of rentals); *see also Gibbons, supra* footnote 12, 339 A.2d at 472-73 (court assigns a zero weight to unproductive assets, reasoning that the value of assets depends on their capability of producing earnings).

[22]   *Compare Swanton, supra* footnote 17 (low weight given to artificially depressed market price) and *Piemonte, supra* footnote 11 (low weight given to reconstructed market price) with *Libby, supra* footnote 12 (40% weight given to market value where fairly active market but large controlling interest).

[23]   *Compare Swanton, supra* footnote 17; *Sporborg, supra* footnote 14; *Piemonte, supra* footnote 11; *Brown v. Hedahl's Q B & R, Inc., supra* footnote 11; and *Elk Yarn Mills v. 514 Shares of Common Stock of Elk Yarn Mills, Inc.,* 742 S.W.2d 638 (Tenn. Ct. App. 1987) (giving relatively high weight to asset value), *with Heller v. Munsingwear, Inc., supra* footnote 18 (giving a low weight to asset value). *See also Sarrouf v. New England Patriots Football Club, Inc.,* 397 Mass. 542, 492 N.E.2d 1122 (1986) (asset value emphasized rather than earnings value because the shareholders paid for the "celebrity" status of owning a professional sports team rather than exclusively for the team's earnings potential); *Gonsalves v. Straight Arrow Publishers Inc.,* 1998 Del. Ch. LEXIS 45, 1998 WL 155556 (Del. Ch. 1998) (asset value assigned no weight in valuing magazine publisher with few tangible assets).

Might Delaware's approach to weighting be another application of the general principle that target shareholders should not be entitled to share in gains produced by the transaction? Note that a bidder doing a "bust-up" merger seeks to capitalize on the difference between market price and the value of the underlying assets in a better use. Heavily weighting market price despite a higher asset value effectively assigns this difference to the acquirer. This point is recognized in Comment (d) to ALI *Principles* § 7.22, which states that the dissenters should not be entitled to a bust-up value that is higher than what a third party would pay for the entire company. Nevertheless, the ALI *Principles* § 7.22 does not exclude synergy gains from fair value. Are these two positions consistent?

(12) **An alternative approach: The Capital Assets Pricing Model.** Asset value and earnings value are simply alternative methods of reconstructing a market value where there is none that can be relied on. Neither is completely adequate, and weighting does not necessarily resolve this inadequacy. **Fischel** (at 893-94) suggests reconstructing a market price using the Capital Assets Pricing Model (*see* Section 7.01[E]). This could be done by determining the "beta," or systematic risk, of the stock, and the movement in the market of risky assets generally (as indicated by, for example, the Dow Jones or Standard & Poor's index) since the last "untainted" market price. To use Professor Fischel's example, suppose the market price before any effects from the acquisition was $100 on July 1, the merger was announced on January 1, during that period the market rose 5%, the "risk-free" rate of return was 2.5%, and the stock has a beta of 2. In this situation the stock "should" have appreciated 7.5% (2.5% + 2 x (5.0% − 2.5%)), and so "should" be worth $107.50. Do you agree with this approach? Does it adequately take into account events during the intervening period other than the merger that would affect value?

(13) **The minority discount.** Appraisal gives shareholders the fair value of their shares. Is it appropriate to determine this value by discounting the value of the firm to reflect the appraisal plaintiff's minority interest? The courts generally reject the minority discount in the context of close corporation oppression actions (*see* Note 9 following *Gardstein* in Section 5.05[C]). These actions are arguably intended to offset the weakness of the shareholder's minority position. Appraisal, like the oppression remedy, arguably is intended to protect minority holders. On the other hand, perhaps applying the minority discount would be consistent with the idea that gains from the transaction should not be allocated to the dissenters (*see* Notes 2 and 7, above, and Section 14.03[B][1][d]).[24] ALI *Principles* § 7.22 rejects a discount for minority status (*see*

---

[24] For cases refusing to disturb the trial court's application of the discount, see *King v. FTJ, Inc.*, 765 S.W.2d 301 (Mo. Ct. App. 1988); *Stanton v. Republic Bank of South Chicago*, 581 N.E.2d 678 (1991) (small discount in appraisal award for minority status and lack of marketability); *Weigel Broadcasting Company v. Smith*, 682 N.E.2d 745 (Ill. App. 1996). For cases refusing to apply the discount, see *Cavalier Oil Corp. v. Harnett*, 564 A.2d 1137 (Del. 1989); *Charland v. Country View Golf Club, Inc.*, 588 A.2d 609 (R.I. 1991); *MT Properties, Inc. v. CMC Real Estate Corp.*, 481 N.W.2d 383 (Minn. Ct. App. 1992); *Friedman v. Beway Realty Corp.*, 87 N.Y.2d 161 (1995) (rejecting discount for

Comment (e)). *Kleinwort Benson Ltd. v. Silgan Corp.*[25] goes one step further, holding that valuation methods that include an inherent minority discount must be adjusted upward to compensate for that discount.

(14) **Jury instructions.** An appraisal proceeding sometimes is tried to a jury rather than to a court, although some statutes do not permit jury trials.[26] It has been held that, although the appraiser should consider the three major factors of asset, earnings and market value, the court need instruct the jury only as to a "willing buyer-willing seller" standard that omits any reference to the three factors.[27] Is such an instruction consistent with the Delaware rule as to weighting discussed immediately above?

(15) **The role of the court.** If an appraisal proceeding is tried to the court rather than to a jury, must the court independently determine the value of the shares that are the subject of the appraisal proceeding or may the court simply accept the valuation of one of the competing experts, hook, line, and sinker? *Gonsalves v. Straight Arrow Publishers, Inc.*[28] concluded that the history of deference accorded to expert appraisers under Delaware law showed that the legislature now wanted the Chancery Court to engage in an "independent valuation exercise." Simply accepting one party's valuation over the other's was held to be at variance with this duty. But *M.G. Bancorporation v. LeBeau*[29] apparently limited *Gonsalves* by holding that "it is entirely proper for the Court of Chancery to adopt any one expert's model, methodology, and mathematical calculations, in toto, *if that valuation is supported by credible evidence and withstands a critical judicial analysis on the record.*"[30]

(16) **Fixing fair value by contract.** Should courts enforce charter provisions that fix fair value, or the method of determining fair value, for appraisal purposes? *In re Appraisal of Ford Holdings, Inc. Preferred Stock*[31] enforced a certificate of designation for a series of preferred stock that fixed the value to which a holder of preferred stock would be entitled in an appraisal action, reasoning that "[t]here is no utility in defining as forbidden any term thought advantageous to informed parties, unless that term vio-

---

minority status but allowing discount for lack of marketability); *HMO-W Inc. v. SSM Health Care System*, 611 N.W.2d 250 (Wis. 2000); *Swope v. Siegel-Robert, Inc.*, 243 F.3d 486 (8th Cir. 2001) (Missouri law). Courts have also generally rejected the use of discounts for illiquidity. *See, e.g., Lawson Mardon Wheaton Inc. v. Smith*, 734 A.2d 738 (N.J. 1999) (rejecting marketability discount, absent "extraordinary circumstances"); *Borruso v. Communications Telesystems International*, 1999 Del. Ch. LEXIS 197, 1999 WL 787864 (Del. Ch. 1999) (rejecting marketability discount, but acknowledging that discount might be justified based on testimony that privately held corporations sell at valuation multiples substantially lower than publicly held corporations). *But see Friedman v. Beway Realty Corp., supra* (allowing discount).

[25]   20 DEL. J. CORP. L. 1079 (Del. Ch. 1995).

[26]   *See, e.g.*, N.Y. Bus. Corp. L. § 623(h)(4).

[27]   *See Multitex Corp. v. Dickinson*, 683 F.2d 1325 (11th Cir. 1982).

[28]   701 A.2d 357 (Del. 1997).

[29]   737 A.2d 513 (Del. 1999).

[30]   737 A.2d at 526 (emphasis added).

[31]   698 A.2d 973 (Del. Ch. 1997).

lates substantive law." But the court limited its holding to cases involving preferred stock, which the court characterized as "very special case[s] . . . [because of] the essentially contractual nature of preferred stock." Does it make sense to enforce agreements by preferred stockholders related to appraisal proceedings, but not agreements by common stockholders? Isn't common stock also "essentially contractual" in nature?

PROBLEM

Fine Pictures, Inc., a medium-sized publicly held corporation, has agreed to merge with International Conglomerates, which owns 51% of Fine's stock. The stock of both Fine and International is traded on the New York Stock Exchange. Under the merger agreement, which is subject to shareholder approval, each Fine shareholder will receive one Conglomerate share having a current market price of $15 for each Fine share. A Fine shareholder seeks your advice as to whether he should dissent from the merger and pursue his right of appraisal. What advice would you give on the basis of the following facts you have been able to glean as to the value of the company, assuming the relevant jurisdiction applies the "Delaware block" approach?

Fine holds substantial assets consisting largely of prime southern California real estate, motion picture sets and equipment and a great many old movies. The book value of these assets (that is, the value of the assets less liabilities as reflected on the company's balance sheet) is approximately $35 per share. It is common knowledge in the industry that the value of the film library is rising rapidly because of the substantial new market for old movies opened up by cable television and video discs and cassettes. Another studio recently incorporated its film library (which is comparable in size to Fine's) and sold shares in the library to the public. Substituting this public offering price (adjusted for the slight difference in size between the libraries) for the book value of Fine's films would yield a total net asset value for Fine of $75 per share.

During the last five years Fine's earnings have steadily declined as the movie industry as a whole has become less profitable and the quality and quantity of Fine's offerings in particular have slipped. The past five years' earnings per share were, respectively, $3.00, $2.00, $1.00, $.50 and a loss of $2.00. The loss in the most recent year was caused by a very large write-off of the investment in the film "The Birth of the Universe" which opened to disastrous reviews and was withdrawn from distribution. Movie stocks as a whole are trading at an average price-earnings multiple of 10 times current earnings.

The market price of Fine stock is currently $15 per share, after having traded as high as $40 per share five years ago, as low as $10 per share a year ago, and at $20 per share just prior to the announcement of the merger. Approximately a year ago, International acquired its controlling interest in Fine in a tender offer for $15 per share. Immediately after acquiring control, International installed a much more aggressive management team.

Fine is currently filming only two movies. However, several films that are in the early planning stages feature major directors, writers and actors. New management has announced its intention of pursuing large-scale film projects that have the potential of becoming major hits. By utilizing the solid capital position of International, Fine will be able to pursue expensive projects after the merger that would have been beyond the means of the company prior to the takeover.

[D] Availability of Appraisal Rights: *De Facto* Mergers

As discussed in Section 13.02 above, the availability of voting and appraisal rights in corporate combinations depends on the type of transaction involved. Most statutes grant voting and appraisal rights to the shareholders of both the transferor and transferee corporations when the transaction is structured as an ordinary merger, but not when the transaction is structured as a sale of assets or as a triangular merger. Accordingly, corporate planners sometimes attempt to accomplish the effect of an ordinary merger through other means, such as a two step transaction consisting of a triangular merger followed by a short-form merger. Some courts have responded to these attempts with the so-called *"de facto* merger" doctrine pursuant to which a transaction may be characterized as an ordinary merger by the court even if the parties have attempted to characterize it as something else.

APPLESTEIN v. UNITED BOARD & CARTON CORP.
New Jersey Superior Court, Chancery Division
60 N.J. Super. 333, 159 A.2d 146, *aff'd*, 33 N.J. 72, 161 A.2d 474 (1960)

KILKENNY, J.S.C.

The parties herein, by written stipulation, have submitted for determination, as upon motions and cross-motions for partial summary judgment, a single limited issue. That issue is whether the agreement of July 7, 1959 among United Board and Carton Corporation, hereinafter referred to as "United," Interstate Container Corporation, hereinafter referred to as "Interstate," and Saul L. Epstein, hereinafter referred to as "Epstein," and the transaction set forth in the proxy solicitation statement, hereinafter called "proxy statement," dated September 22, 1959, amount to a merger, entitling dissenting stockholders of United to an appraisal of their stock, and is therefore invalid.

* * *

United is an active corporation of New Jersey, organized in 1912. Its business consists in the manufacture and sale of paperboard, folding boxes, corrugated containers and laminated board, in that relative order of importance. Its present authorized capital stock consists of 400,000 shares, of which 240,000 have already been issued and are held by a great number of stockholders, no one of whom holds in excess of 10% of the outstanding shares. There are 160,000 shares not yet issued. The United stock is publicly held, there being 1,086 shareholders of record as of September 22, 1959, and the stock is traded on the New York Stock Exchange. The book value of each share of stock, as indicated by the proxy statement, is approximately $31.97. The consolidated balance sheet of United and its wholly owned subsidiaries, as of May 31, 1958, shows total assets of $10,121,233, and total liabilities of $2,561,724, and a net total capital of $7,559,509. Its business is managed by the usual staff of officers and a board of directors consisting of seven directors.

Interstate was incorporated under the laws of New York in 1939. It owns several operating subsidiaries located in various parts of the northeastern section of the United States. It is engaged primarily in the manufacture and sale of corrugated shipping containers, and also containers which have the dual use of carriers and point of purchase displays. The major portion of its business is corrugated containers. Its corrugated board, other than that consumed by its own container operations, is used by outside plants for the manufacture of corrugated containers and, in some instances, for display items. Interstate has issued and outstanding 1,250 shares, all of which are owned and controlled by a single stockholder, Epstein, who thereby owns and controls Interstate. The consolidated balance sheet of Interstate and its subsidiaries, as of October 31, 1958, shows that its total assets are $7,956,424, and its total liabilities are $6,318,371, leaving a net total capital of $1,638,053.

* * *

United entered into a written agreement with Interstate and Epstein on July 7, 1959. In its language, it is not designated or referred to as a merger agreement, eo nomine. In fact, the word "merger" nowhere appears in that agreement. On the contrary, the agreement recites that it is an "exchange of Interstate stock for United Stock." Epstein agrees to assign and deliver to United his 1,250 shares of the common stock of Interstate solely in exchange for 160,000 as yet unissued shares of voting common stock (par value $10) of United. Thus, by this so-called "exchange of stock" United would wholly own Interstate and its subsidiaries, and Epstein would thereupon own a 40% stock interest in United. Dollarwise, on the basis of the book values of the two corporations hereinabove set forth, a combination of the assets and liabilities of United and Interstate would result in a net total capital of approximately $9,200,000, as against which there would be outstanding 400,000 shares, thereby reducing the present book value of each United share from about $1.97 to about $23, a shrinkage of about 28%. Epstein would contribute, book value-wise, the net total capital of Interstate in the amount of $1,638,053, for which he would receive a 40% interest in $9,200,000, the net total combined capital of United and Interstate, or about $3,680,000. The court is not basing its present decision upon the additional charge made by dissenting stockholders of United that the proposed agreement is basically unfair and inequitable. That is one of the reserved issues. The court recognizes that book values and real values are not necessarily the same thing, and, therefore, apparent inequities appearing from a comparison of the book values might be explained and justified.

The agreement of July 7, 1959 does not contemplate the continued future operation of Interstate, as a subsidiary corporation of United. Rather, it provides that United will take over all the outstanding stock of Interstate, that all of Interstate's "assets and liabilities will be recorded on the books of the Company (United)," and that Interstate will be dissolved. At the time of closing, Epstein has agreed to deliver the resignation of the officers and directors of Interstate and of its subsidiary corporations, so that, in effect, Interstate would have no officers, directors, or stockholders, other than United's. The agreement further stipulates that the by-laws of United shall be amended to increase the number of directors from 7 to 11. It provides for the filling of the additional directorships, it pre-ordains who will be the officers and new directors of United in the combined enterprise, and even governs the salaries to be paid. Epstein would become the president and a director of United and, admittedly, would be in "effective control" of United. As stated in the proxy statement, "The transaction will be accounted for as a 'pooling of interests' of the two corporations."

The stipulation of the parties removed from the court's present consideration not only the issue of the basic equity or fairness of the agreement, but also the legal effect and validity of the pre-determination of directorships, officers, salaries, and other similar terms of the bargain between the parties. The fairness of a merger agreement generally presents a question of a factual nature, ordinarily reserved for final hearing. If the alleged injustice of the project were the sole objection, I would be hesitant to substitute preliminarily my judgment for that of a transcendent majority of the stockholders.

* * *

The attorneys for the respective parties herein have conceded in the record that the proposed corporate action would be invalid if this court determines that it would constitute a merger of United and Interstate, entitling the dissenting stockholders of United to an appraisal of their stock. The notice of the stockholders' meeting and the proxy statement did not indicate that the purpose of the meeting was to effect a merger, and failed to give notice to the shareholders of their right to dissent to the plan of merger, if it were one, and claim their appraisal rights under the statute, as inferentially required by R.S. 14:12-3, N.J.S.A. Obviously, the notice of the meeting and proxy statement stressed the contrary, by labeling the proposed corporate action "an exchange of Interstate stock for United stock" rather than a merger, by its emphasis upon the need for a majority vote only, instead of the required two-thirds vote for a merger under the statute, and by the express declaration that dissenting stockholders would not be entitled to any rights of appraisal of their stock.

* * *

Despite the contrary representations by United to its stockholders in its proxy statement, United's present position is that the proposed corporate action in acquiring and absorbing Interstate is a merger. . . .

* * *

Looking, then, only to the single, crucial issue presently involved in this opinion—did the proposed corporate action by United constitute such a "merger" as would entitle dissenting stockholders of United to an appraisal of their shares of stock? Let us first state some general principles.

A merger of corporations is the absorption by one corporation of one or more usually smaller corporations, which lose their identity by becoming part of the large enterprise. While the statutory authorization for a merger or consolidation of corporations is set forth in the same section, R.S. 14:12-1, N.J.S.A. and the procedure to accomplish the result is the same in either instance, and dissenting stockholders have equivalent rights of appraisal of their shares in a merger or a consolidation, an academic distinction still exists between them. A merger of two corporations contemplates that one will be absorbed by the other and go out of existence, but the absorbing corporation will remain. In a consolidation, the two corporations unite and both go out of existence, and a new amalgamated corporate enterprise takes the place of the former corporations.

* * *

It is true that our present corporation law, R.S. 14:3-5, N.J.S.A., sanctions a corporate sale of all or substantially all of the property and assets of the selling corporation, with stockholder approval and appraisal rights in favor of objecting shareholders of the selling corporation. Likewise, our statute, R.S. 14:3-9, N.J.S.A., allows a corporate purchase of the property and stock of another corporation to be paid for in cash or the stock of the purchasing corporation. There is no dispute as to the existence of these present statutory devices for the sale and acquisition of corporate property and shares of stock. Hence, if the purchase by United of Interstate and its shares represented a bona fide utilization of the corporate power conferred by R.S. 14:3-9, N.J.S.A., and if the intended dissolution of Interstate represented a bona fide merger of a parent corporation with a wholly-owned corporation under N.J.S.A. 14:12-10, without more, United's dissenting shareholders would then have no right to an appraisal of their shares.

But when an authorized device, such as that provided for in a sale or purchase of assets, or a dissolution, is used to bring about a virtual consolidation or merger, minority stockholders may object on the ground that a direct method has been authorized for such a purpose. If consolidation or merger is permitted through a pretended sale of assets or dissolution, minority stockholders may be frozen out of their legal rights of appraisal. If the court is obliged to consider only the device employed, or the mere form of the trans-action, a corporate merger in fact can be achieved without any compliance with the statutory requirements for a valid merger, and without any regard for the statutory rights of dissenting shareholders. It would be strange if the powers conferred by our Legislature upon corporations under R.S. 14:3-9, N.J.S.A. for a purchase of the property and shares of another corporation and, under N.J.S.A. 14:12-10, for the merger of a parent corporation with a wholly-owned corporation can effect a corporate merger de facto, with all the characteristics and consequences of a merger, without any of the legislative safeguards and rights afforded to a dissenting shareholder in a de jure merger under R.S. 14:12-1 et seq., N.J.S.A. If that were so, we obtain the anomalous result of one part of the corporation law rendering nugatory another part of the same law in accomplishing the same result.

That the proposed corporate action is more than an "exchange of Interstate stock for United stock," as it is labeled in the agreement of July 7, 1959, and more than a purchase by United of Epstein's Interstate stock and the corporate properties of Interstate, pursuant to R.S. 14:3-9, N.J.S.A., is demonstrated by the following facts.

1. The exchange of stock is made expressly contingent upon stockholder approval of Proposal No. 2 increasing the number of directors of United from 7 to 11. Proxy statement, pp. 2 and 9. It is also so stipulated in paragraph 10 of the agreement.

2. United admits that by the exchange of stock Epstein will acquire 40% of United's outstanding stock "and effective control." Proxy statement, p. 3.

3. Epstein's "effective control" of United is made obvious by the fact that two directors of United's present board of seven "will resign as directors." Proxy statement, p. 9. The agreement of July 7, 1959 expressly provides in paragraph 9, "The resignations of George

Luttinger and Thomas V. Wade [two of United's directors] will be presented at the closing." This would leave United with only five of its present directors on the new enlarged board of 11 directors, which Proposal No. 2 insures as a contingent part of the deal. Thus, Epstein and the five new directors, presumably his associates and friends from Interstate, are assured a majority vote of six and control of the new 11-man board. It is clear that he who controls a majority of the board of directors generally controls the management and destiny of the corporation.

4. It is also pre-ordained by the agreement, in paragraph 9, who the new 11 directors will be. Reference to their names and to their present and past connection and relationship with Epstein and Interstate (Proxy statement, p. 10) shows that Epstein will really have "effective control" of the board and United, as the latter freely concedes.

5. While the proposed issuance by United to Epstein of 160,000 shares of United's total authorized 400,000 shares seems to give Epstein only a 40% stock interest in United, which by itself is substantial enough to control United as against the 1,086 other stock-holders, but still less than the combined 60% of those 1,086 present United shareholders, 8 of those 1,086 present United shareholders, who would become directors on the enlarged board, already own 49,200 shares of United. Therefore, Epstein's new 160,000 shares plus those 49,200 shares would add up to 209,200 shares of the total 400,000, or better than 50%. Even if we discount the shares now held by Stuhr (18,000), Marchini (8,200), Passannante (300), Peters (300), and Miller (1,000), a total of 27,800 shares, because they are presently five of United's seven directors, although Miller is also vice-president and general manager of Allcraft Container Division of Interstate, Epstein's working stockholder control of United under the proposed corporate action is abundantly clear. Combined with his real control of the board of directors, the conclusion is inescapable that control of the affairs of United would pass out of the present board of directors and out of the present majority of United's stockholders to Epstein and those associated with him in Interstate.

6. The proxy statement, p. 3, expressly recites: "The transaction will be accounted for as a 'pooling of interests' of the two corporations." Such a characterization is descriptive of a merger or consolidation of two corporations, rather than a mere exchange of stock or purchase of corporate assets.

7. It is intended that Interstate will be dissolved. Dissolution is always an element of merger or consolidation and it is not a necessary concomitant of a mere exchange of stock or purchase of corporate assets.

8. United expressly represents (proxy statement, p. 3) that Interstate's "assets and liabilities will be recorded on the books of the Company [United] as set forth in the pro forma balance sheet." Proxy statement, pp. F 24-25. This is indicative of the fact that United is assuming Interstate's liabilities, a necessary legal consequence of a merger or consolidation, as contrasted with the normal non-assumption of the debts of the selling corporation, in the absence of special agreement, upon a mere "sale-of-assets" transaction. . . .

9. Also, as a further evidence of Interstate's control and intervention in United's management,

> "It is contemplated that the present executive and operating personnel of Interstate will be retained in the employ of the Company [United]." Proxy statement, p. 9.

Thus, every factor present in a corporate merger is found in this corporate plan, except, perhaps, a formal designation of the transaction as a "merger." There is proposed: (1) a transfer of all the shares and all the assets of Interstate to United; (2) an assumption by United of Interstate's liabilities; (3) a "pooling of interests" of the two corporations; (4) the absorption of Interstate by United, and the dissolution of Interstate; (5) a joinder of officers and directors from both corporations on an enlarged board of directors; (6) the present executive and operating personnel of Interstate will be retained in the employ of United; and (7) the shareholders of the absorbed corporation, Interstate, as represented by the sole stockholder, Epstein, will surrender his 1,250 shares in Interstate for 160,000 newly issued shares in United, the amalgamated enterprise.

* * *

The courts of this State and of other jurisdictions have never hesitated in the past in finding that a particular corporate combination was in fact and in legal effect a merger or a consolidation, even though the transaction might have been otherwise labeled by the parties. . . . This is not a new legal philosophy, but is grounded upon the common sense observation that judges, as well as laymen, have the right, and often the duty, to call a spade a spade, and to follow the long established equitable maxim of looking to the substance rather than the form, whenever justice requires.

* * *

Where, as here, we have more than a simple purchase by United of the assets of Interstate, as noted above, the conclusion is fairly drawn that the transaction in question will cause United to alter its existing fundamental relationship with its present shareholders, and will result in shifting the working control of United to Epstein and his associates in Interstate. In substance, regardless of the form, the transaction in question would be a merger of United and Interstate, or what the court described in [*Farris v. Glen Alden Corp.*, 393 Pa. 427, 143 A.2d 25 (1958)], as a "de facto merger."

* * *

CONCLUSION

This court holds that the corporate combination of United and Interstate, contemplated by their executory contract of July 7, 1959, and explained in United's proxy solicitation statement of September 22, 1959, would be a practical or de facto merger, in substance and in legal effect, within the protective purview of N.J.S.A. 14:12-7. Accordingly, the shareholders of United are and were entitled to be notified and advised of their statutory rights of dissent and appraisal. The failure of the corporate officers of United to take these steps and to obtain stockholder approval of the agreement by the statutory two-thirds vote under R.S. 14:12-3, N.J.S.A. at a properly convened meeting of the stockholders would render the proposed corporate action invalid.

Therefore, there will be partial summary judgment on the single, limited issue submitted in accordance with this holding.

NOTES AND QUESTIONS

(1) **Holding in *Applestein*.** Could the parties have achieved the principal objectives of the transaction in *Applestein* without entering into a *de facto* merger under the rule of that case? If so, how? Might the court have reached a different result if the parties had provided that Interstate would be operated as a wholly owned subsidiary of United, rather than being dissolved?

(2) *Farris v. Glen Alden Corp.* In *Farris v. Glen Alden Corp.*,[32] perhaps the most noted *de facto* merger case, List, a large conglomerate, acquired a controlling interest in a much smaller mining corporation, Glen Alden. The companies then entered into a "reorganization" agreement which provided that Glen Alden would purchase with its newly issued stock the assets of the larger List; Glen Alden stock would be distributed by List to List shareholders; List's liabilities would be assumed by Glen Alden; List would be dissolved; and Glen Alden would change its name to List Alden. The court held that the transaction was a *de facto* merger of the two corporations, entitling Glen Alden shareholders to appraisal rights. As in *Applestein*, the court noted how similar in effect the transaction was to a statutory merger. The *Farris* court also noted that even if the transaction were, in fact, a sale of assets, the real seller was not List but Glen Alden, and that under this characterization of the transaction Glen Alden shareholders would have had appraisal rights under Pennsylvania law.

(3) **Triangular mergers as *de facto* mergers.** In *Terry v. Penn Central Corporation*,[33] the plaintiffs, shareholders of Penn Central, objected to a transaction in which Colt Industries would be merged into a wholly owned subsidiary of Penn Central, with Colt shareholders receiving a new series of Penn Central preferred stock. The plaintiffs argued that the *de facto* merger doctrine of *Farris* should be applied to the transaction to give Penn Central shareholders voting and appraisal rights. The court refused to apply the *de facto* merger doctrine to the case, finding, among other things, that the Pennsylvania legislature had expressed disapproval of the *Farris de facto* merger doctrine and that the doctrine should not be applied unless fraud or fraudulent unfairness could be shown.

(4) **Partnerships and other arrangements between corporations as *de facto* mergers.** The *de facto* merger doctrine was applied in *Good v. Lackawanna Leather Co.*[34] and in *Pratt v. Ballman-Cummings Furniture Co.*[35] In *Pratt*, the court characterized as a *de facto* merger a transaction in which plaintiff's corporation entered into a partnership with another resulting in a change in management, control and identity of plaintiff's corporation. However, in *Good*, an arrangement in which plaintiff's corpo-

---

[32]   393 Pa. 427, 143 A.2d 25 (1958).

[33]   688 F.2d 188 (3d Cir. 1981).

[34]   96 N.J. Super. 439, 233 A.2d 201 (Ch. Div. 1967).

[35]   254 Ark. 570, 495 S.W.2d 509 (1973).

ration entered into a long-term lease of its major asset and became a co-shareholder with another corporation in a third corporation was held not to be a *de facto* merger. In *Good*, the court emphasized that the corporations had retained separate control structures and that the transaction was beneficial to plaintiffs' corporation. In *Pratt*, on the other hand, not only was there virtual absorption by one corporation of the other, but the transaction was particularly detrimental to plaintiff's corporation

HARITON v. ARCO ELECTRONICS, INC.
Delaware Supreme Court
41 Del. Ch. 74, 188 A.2d 123 (1963)

SOUTHERLAND, Chief Justice.

This case involves a sale of assets under § 271 of the corporation law, 8 Del. C. It presents for decision the question presented, but not decided, in *Heilbrunn v. Sun Chemical Corporation*, Del., 150 A.2d 755. It may be stated as follows:

A sale of assets is effected under § 271 in consideration of shares of stock of the purchasing corporation. The agreement of sale embodies also a plan to dissolve the selling corporation and distribute the shares so received to the stockholders of the seller, so as to accomplish the same result as would be accomplished by a merger of the seller into the purchaser. Is the sale legal?

The facts are these:

The defendant Arco and Loral Electronics Corporation, a New York corporation, are both engaged, in somewhat different forms, in the electronic equipment business. In the summer of 1961 they negotiated for an amalgamation of the companies. As of October 27, 1961, they entered into a "Reorganization Agreement and Plan." The provisions of this Plan pertinent here are in substance as follows:

1. Arco agrees to sell all its assets to Loral in consideration (inter alia) of the issuance to it of 283,000 shares of Loral.

2. Arco agrees to call a stockholders meeting for the purpose of approving the Plan and the voluntary dissolution.

3. Arco agrees to distribute to its stockholders all the Loral shares received by it as a part of the complete liquidation of Arco.

At the Arco meeting all the stockholders voting (about 80%) approved the Plan. It was thereafter consummated.

Plaintiff, a stockholder who did not vote at the meeting, sued to enjoin the consummation of the Plan on the grounds (1) that it was illegal, and (2) that is was unfair. The second ground was abandoned. Affidavits and documentary evidence were filed, and defendant moved for summary judgment and dismissal of the complaint. The Vice Chancellor granted the motion and plaintiff appeals.

The question before us we have stated above. Plaintiff's argument that the sale is illegal runs as follows:

The several steps taken here accomplish the same result as a merger of Arco into Loral. In a "true" sale of assets, the stockholder of the seller retains the right to elect whether the selling company shall continue as a holding company. Moreover, the stockholder of the selling company is forced to accept an investment in a new enterprise without the right of appraisal granted under the merger statute. § 271 cannot therefore be legally combined with a dissolution proceeding under § 275 and a consequent distribution of the purchaser's stock. Such a proceeding is a misuse of the power granted under § 271, and a *de facto* merger results.

* * *

We now hold that the reorganization here accomplished through § 271 and a mandatory plan of dissolution and distribution is legal. This is so because the sale-of-assets statute and the merger statute are independent of each other. They are, so to speak, of equal dignity, and the framers of a reorganization plan may resort to either type of corporate mechanics to achieve the desired end. This is not an anomalous result in our corporation law. As the Vice Chancellor pointed out, the elimination of accrued dividends, though forbidden under a charter amendment (*Keller v. Wilson & Co.*, 21 Del. Ch. 391, 190 A. 115) may be accomplished by a merger. *Federal United Corporation v. Havender*, 24 Del. Ch. 318, 11 A.2d 331.

In *Langfelder v. Universal Laboratories*, D.C., 68 F. Supp. 209, Judge Leahy commented upon "the general theory of the Delaware Corporation Law that action taken pursuant to the authority of the various sections of that law constitute acts of independent legal significance and their validity is not dependent on other sections of the Act." 68 F. Supp. 211, footnote.

* * *

Plaintiff concedes, as we read his brief, that if the several steps taken in this case had been taken separately they would have been legal. That is, he concedes that a sale of assets, followed by a separate proceeding to dissolve and distribute, would be legal, even though the same result would follow. This concession exposes the weakness of his contention. To attempt to make any such distinction between sales under § 271 would be to create uncertainty in the law and invite litigation.

We are in accord with the Vice Chancellor's ruling, and the judgment below is affirmed.

NOTES AND QUESTIONS

(1) **Equal dignity of statutory provisions governing corporate combinations.** *Rath v. Rath Packing Co.*[36] held that a transaction in which Corporation A purchased the assets of Corporation B with its stock, A assumed B's liabilities, B was dissolved, and A stock was distributed to B shareholders, was subject to the merger statute and there-

---

[36]   257 Iowa 1277, 136 N.W.2d 410 (1965).

fore required the approval of two thirds of A's shareholders. The court rejected A's argument that the transaction was subject to the simple majority vote requirement of the certificate amendment section of the statute (because the authorization of the shares issued by Corporation A necessitated a certificate amendment), reasoning that the specific merger provision and the general certificate amendment provision of the corporation statute were not of "equal dignity." Can *Rath* be reconciled with *Hariton*?

(2) **Statutory versions of the *de facto* merger doctrine: the California Corporation Code.** The California Corporation Code grants voting and appraisal rights (*see* §§ 1201 and 1300) for shareholders of each corporation (including a parent corporation in a triangular mergers) participating in a "reorganization," unless the corporation's shareholders immediately before the reorganization receive more than five-sixths of the voting power of the surviving, acquiring, or parent corporation (*see* § 1201(b)). The term "reorganization" is defined in § 181:

"Reorganization" means:
(a) A merger pursuant to Chapter 11 (commencing with Section 1100) other than a short-form merger (a "merger reorganization");

(b) The acquisition by one domestic corporation, foreign corporation, or other business entity in exchange in whole or in part for its equity securities (or the equity securities of a domestic corporation, a foreign corporation, or an other business entity which is in control of the acquiring entity) of equity securities of another domestic corporation, foreign corporation, or other business entity if, immediately after the acquisition, the acquiring entity has control of such other corporation (an "exchange reorganization"); or

(c) The acquisition by one domestic corporation, foreign corporation, or other business entity in exchange in whole or in part for its equity securities (or the equity securities of a domestic corporation, foreign corporation, or other business entity which is in control of the acquiring entity) or for its debt securities (or debt securities of a domestic corporation, foreign corporation, or other business entity which is in control of the acquiring entity) which are not adequately secured and which have a maturity date in excess of five years after the consummation of the reorganization, or both, of all or substantially all of the assets of another domestic corporation, foreign corporation, or other business entity (a "sale-of-assets reorganization").

* * *

Legislative Committee Comment (1975)—Assembly
The new law treats the various methods of corporate fusion as different means to the same end. This approach is intended to codify the concept of the so-called "de facto merger" doctrine so that the rights of shareholders in a corporate combination do not depend upon the form in which the transaction is cast.

(3) **The ALI *Principles*.** Section 7.21 of the ALI *Principles*, which governs the availability of appraisal rights but not voting rights, is patterned after the California statute, but uses the term "business combination" in place of "reorganization." Section 7.21 provides that shareholders should be entitled to appraisal rights in business combinations "unless those persons who were shareholders of the corporation immediately before the combination own 60 percent or more of the total voting power of the surviving or issuing corporation immediately thereafter . . . ." Comment c.(1) to that section notes that "the term 'business combination'" in § 7.21(a) is intended to have approximately the same functional reach as the "*de facto*" merger doctrine . . . ."

(4) **Selecting among the alternatives.** Which approach to the *de facto* merger doctrine is preferable—that represented by *Hariton*, that of *Applestein*, or that of the California Corporation Code and the ALI *Principles*? The *Hariton* approach offers the benefit of a bright line rule; the *Applestein* approach offers the benefit of treating all functionally equivalent transactions in the same fashion; the California Corporation Code/ALI *Principles* approach attempts to do both.

(5) **Product liability of successor corporations; the step transaction doctrine.** The "*de facto* merger" doctrine discussed above should be distinguished from the developing doctrine of the same name under which successor corporations have been held liable for injuries caused by the predecessor's product. It should be obvious that the policy considerations relating to the survival of liabilities aspect of a merger differ from those relating to the appraisal and voting rights of shareholders. This policy difference is reflected in the application of a different rule in the products liability cases.[37] The *de facto* merger doctrine should also be distinguished from the "step-transaction" doctrine from tax law, which "treats the 'steps' in a series of formally separate but related transactions involving the transfer of property as a single transaction, if all the steps are substantially linked."[38] *Noddings Investment Group, Inc. v. Capstar Communications, Inc.*[39] borrowed the step-transaction doctrine from tax law to treat a spin-off of a subsidiary followed by a merger involving the parent as a single transaction for purposes of determining the rights of the parent's warrant holders. Is *Noddings* consistent with *Hariton*?

(6) ***De facto* mergers and conversions involving non-corporate firms.** Until recently, non-corporate business association statutes did not provide explicitly for mergers and conversions. Accordingly, partnership and other non-corporate firms developed contractual merger techniques. For example, as noted in Section 13.02[B][6], RUPA

---

[37] For some leading product liability cases, see *Knapp v. North American Rockwell Corp.*, 506 F.2d 361 (3d Cir. 1974), *cert. denied*, 421 U.S. 965 (1975); *Ray v. Alad Corp.*, 19 Cal. 3d 22, 560 P.2d 3, 136 Cal. Rptr. 574 (1977); *Nieves v. Bruno Sherman Corp.*, 86 N.J. 361, 431 A.2d 826 (1981); *Ramirez v. Amsted Industries*, 86 N.J. 332, 431 A.2d 811 (1981). For a more recent product liability case, see *Garcia v. Coe Manufacturing Co.*, 993 P.2d 243 (N.M. 1997) (extending successor liability to those "who have purchased the right to benefit from selling and servicing a product").

[38] *Greene v. United States*, 13 F.3d 577, 583 (2d Cir. 1994).

[39] 1999 Del. Ch. LEXIS 56, 1999 WL 182568 (Del. Ch. 1999).

Article 9 now provides for partnership mergers and conversions. RUPA § 908 also provides: "This article is not exclusive. Partnerships or limited partnerships may be converted or merged in any other manner provided by law." Does this mean (1) that any transaction involving a RUPA partnership that the parties characterize as a "merger" or "conversion" has the effect RUPA prescribes for the transaction even if the parties have not complied with RUPA formalities (*i.e.*, filings and merger agreements)? (2) that the agreement controls the effect of the transaction irrespective of whether the parties have complied with RUPA? (3) that to be effective, the merger or conversion must be sanctioned by some other statute? (4) none of the above?

[E] A Functional Analysis of Appraisal Rights

The appraisal remedy has been heavily criticized, most notably by **Folk** and **Manning**. Manning argues that the statutes make arbitrary distinctions between the situations in which the appraisal remedy is, and is not, available—that it makes no sense to distinguish, for example, between corporate dissolution and merger since both are fundamental changes in the corporation. Manning also says that appraisal rights unjustifiably deter beneficial corporate transactions since heavy demand for appraisal rights can threaten the liquidity of the surviving corporation, and since uncertainty as to the extent of demand for appraisal rights hinders planning of the transaction. Folk, like Manning, argues that the appraisal remedy is arbitrary. According to Folk, shareholders invest in management's business judgment and there is no more reason to permit them to "cash out" in reaction to a merger than as a result of any other significant management decision. Folk and Manning both conclude that shareholders who disagree with a proposed transaction should be remitted to the securities markets, as they are under statutes which eliminate the appraisal right with respect to actively traded securities (*see* Note 3 following *Universal City Studios* in Subsection [C], above).

Eisenberg defends the statutory appraisal right on the basis that they protect minority shareholders from fundamental change imposed by the majority. Thus, there is reason to distinguish, as the statutes do, between fundamental changes in the corporation and other business decisions; between fundamental changes that result from majority vote and those that result from external economic events; and between mergers and dissolution, since the latter does not force the minority to become shareholders in a different corporate entity. Eisenberg argues that the stock markets do not provide adequate recourse for the minority shareholders; and that appraisal rights do not unduly burden corporate transactions.

Like Eisenberg, **Fischel** also explains appraisal rights as a way to deal with majority-minority conflicts. Specifically, Fischel asserts that appraisal rights protect minority shareholders from self-interested actions of a coherent majority block. Under Fischel's and Eisenberg's explanation of appraisal rights, does it make sense to protect minority shareholders by both costly voting rights and costly appraisal rights? Specifically, would the cost of appraisal exceed the benefit if the majority were protected by a voting rule requiring approval by a majority of the minority shareholders?

Even if appraisal rights are useful in dealing with majority-minority conflicts, it is not clear this explains the appraisal provisions that have actually been included in corporate statutes. Appraisal rights are available even where majority-minority conflicts are unlikely, including negotiated mergers with unrelated firms. Also, appraisal rights are offered to shareholders in acquiring firms. On the other hand, some statutes do not offer appraisal rights in situations in which the minority needs protection. A prominent example is the Delaware-type exemption for publicly traded stock (*see* Note 3 following *Universal City Studios* in Subsection [C], above).

Letsou advances a "preference reconciliation" theory of appraisal that addresses some of these problems. This theory focuses on the capacity of appraisal rights to reconcile differing shareholder preferences with respect to corporate transactions that alter the risk, or "beta," of the firm's shares (*see* Section 7.01[E]). When shareholders lack effective access to capital markets, risk-altering transactions can make some shareholders better off, while leaving others worse off. Appraisal rights require the corporation to compensate shareholders who may be harmed by such transactions and place the net costs of providing that compensation on shareholders who otherwise gain. As a result, shareholders who gain from appraisal triggering transactions will only vote in favor of those transactions if their gains more than offset the net costs of compensating objectors. Unlike the theories discussed above, Letsou's theory is consistent with common statutory features like the "market out," the denial of appraisal rights to shareholders of acquiring firms, and the availability of appraisal rights where majority-minority conflicts are absent.

For another explanation of the appraisal remedy, see the **Kanda & Levmore** article cited in the References below.

REFERENCES

Eisenberg, THE STRUCTURE OF THE CORPORATION, Ch. 7 (1976).

Fischel, *The Appraisal Remedy in Corporate Law*, 1983 AM. BAR FOUND. RES. J. 875.

Folk, *De Facto Mergers in Delaware:* Hariton v. Arco Electronics, Inc., 49 VA. L. REV. 1261 (1963).

Kanda & Levmore, *The Appraisal Remedy and the Goals of Corporate Law*, 32 UCLA L. REV. 429 (1985).

Letsou, *The Role of Appraisal in Corporate Law*, 39 B.C. L. REV. 1121 (1998).

Manning, *The Shareholder's Appraisal Remedy: An Essay for Frank Coker*, 72 YALE L.J. 223 (1962).

Thompson, *Exit, Liquidity, and Majority Rule: Appraisal's Role in Corporate Law*, 84 GEO. L.J. 1 (1995).

Wertheimer, *The Shareholders' Appraisal Remedy and How Courts Determine Fair Value*, 47 DUKE L.J. 613 (1998).

§ 15.02 Judicial Review of Corporate Combinations

This Section discusses the extent to which shareholders who are unhappy with mergers or other corporate combinations have remedies in addition to the right of appraisal discussed in the preceding Section. There are two general questions: First, to what extent are the courts barred from any review of the transaction by the appraisal rights provision of the applicable corporate statute? In other words, to what extent are appraisal rights the exclusive remedy for disgruntled shareholders? Second, assuming the court may grant a "fairness" remedy in connection with a corporate combination, notwithstanding the existence of appraisal rights, under what circumstances will liability be imposed? In other words, what is the appropriate standard of judicial review of such transactions?

[A] Exclusivity of the Appraisal Remedy

[1] Policy Considerations

Should the appraisal remedy be exclusive? As long as the dissenters can claim the appraised value of their stock, they arguably have no real cause for complaint. But the appraisal remedy has several shortcomings. First, appraisal involves great cost and risk for the dissenters. There may be a substantial delay between the merger and the final resolution of the appraisal proceeding during which the dissenters lose control over and income from their investments, the outcome is unpredictable, and the evidence in an appraisal proceeding consists largely of costly expert testimony. Second, the traditional appraisal standard of valuation—the "Delaware block" approach—does not include any increase in value resulting from the merger (*see* Note 2 following *Universal City Studios* in Section 15.01[C] above). Third, only shareholders who qualify by dissenting from the merger and complying with other statutory procedures get appraisal, which effectively restricts the remedy to relatively large, sophisticated shareholders and limits the aggregate amount that the corporation will have to pay. Fourth, dissenting shareholders only get an amount based on the value of the overall enterprise, excluding any special value they attach to their shares (*see* Section 14.03[B][1][b]). In general, therefore, appraisal rights may not fully protect against "unfair" merger terms (*see* **Brudney & Chirelstein; Letsou**).

But even if the appraisal right is "incomplete" in providing a check against unfair merger terms, it does not necessarily follow that it should be supplemented by an action for breach of fiduciary duty. First, the supposed inadequacies of appraisal can be addressed by revising the rules regarding appraisal rather than offering an additional remedy. (This is, to some extent, the approach of *Weinberger*, Subsection [D] below). Second, costly appraisal rights reduce the reward for takeovers that can be reaped by acquiring companies, thereby possibly reducing monitoring by the market for control (*see* Notes 2, 7 and 13 following *Universal City Studios* in Section 15.01[C] above and Section 14.03[B][1][d]). Adding fiduciary duties to an "incomplete" appraisal right therefore may do more harm than good.

[2] Statutory Provisions

The availability of non-appraisal remedies for dissenting shareholders varies among jurisdictions. A merger or other corporate combination with statutory appraisal rights may be enjoined if the transaction is not conducted in conformity with statutory procedures. The important question is whether such a transaction may be attacked even if the applicable procedures have been followed.

The exclusivity of the appraisal remedy is determined in many jurisdictions by the language of the appraisal statute and the strictness with which the statute is interpreted by the courts. Some statutes explicitly reserve a non-appraisal remedy for unlawful or fraudulent transactions.[40] Others purport to exclude all remedies other than appraisal, but the courts are divided as to whether even such explicit language wholly bars other relief, at least where the transaction is fraudulent or unlawful.[41] Finally, California Corp. Code § 1312(b) carefully limits the non-appraisal remedy to suits involving "controlled" mergers (discussed immediately below) by shareholders who have not demanded appraisal.[42] This statutory prohibition of attacks on "validity" of a merger has been held to include actions for damages as well as for injunctive relief.[43]

The above discussion demonstrates that a shareholder may obtain at least injunctive relief from an unlawful or fraudulent merger even where the statute seems to provide that the appraisal right is "exclusive." This additional remedy matters for corporate planners, since the costs of litigation and delay resulting from a successful injunction action may be enormous. Thus, corporate transactions must be planned so as to minimize the risk of successful attack.

ALI *Principles* § 7.24-7.25 would settle some of the uncertainty about exclusivity by specifying the circumstances under which appraisal rights are exclusive. If appraisal rights conforming with the ALI's recommendations (*see id.* at § 7.22-7.23) are made available, they are exclusive: (1) in a transaction not involving a controlling share-

---

[40] *See, e.g.*, Model Business Corp. Act § 13.02(d); N.Y. Bus. Corp. L. § 623(k).

[41] *Compare Perl v. IU International Corp.*, 61 Hawaii 622, 607 P.2d 1036 (1980) (availability of injunctive relief recognized under Hawaii Rev. Stat. § 417-29, which then provided that "[t]he rights and remedies of any stockholder to object to or litigate as to any such merger or consolidation are limited to the right to receive the fair market value of his shares . . ."); *Galligan v. Galligan*, 741 N.E.2d 1217 (Ind. 2001) (availability of alternative relief recognized under Indiana statute providing that shareholder "may not challenge the corporate action creating . . . the shareholder's entitlement [to appraisal]," where plaintiff alleges that transaction triggering appraisal rights was not properly authorized under the state corporation law and the company's bylaws), *with Yanow v. Teal Industries*, 178 Conn. 262, 422 A.2d 311 (1979) (denying non-appraisal remedy in connection with short form merger under Conn. Gen. Stat. § 33-373(f), which provided that "[w]here the right to be paid the value of shares is made available to a shareholder by this section, such remedy shall be his exclusive remedy as holder of such shares against the corporate transactions described in this section," though the court left open the possibility that non-appraisal relief might be permitted with respect to a long form merger). *See also In re Jones & Laughlin Steel Corp.*, 488 Pa. 524, 412 A.2d 1099 (1980) (recognizing the availability of injunctive relief even though the appraisal statute, Pa. Stat. Ann. tit. 15, § 1515K, provides that "the rights and remedies prescribed by this section shall be exclusive"). For a more recent case applying *Jones & Laughlin*, see *Herskowitz v. Nutri/System, Inc.*, 857 F.2d 179 (3d Cir. 1988).

[42] *See Deutsch v. Blue Chip Stamps*, 172 Cal. Rptr. 21 (Cal. Ct. App. 1981) (applying California Corp. Code § 1312(b)).

[43] *Steinberg v. Amplica, Inc.*, 42 Cal. 3d 1198, 233 Cal. Rptr. 249, 729 P.2d 683 (1986).

holder, if shareholders approve the merger pursuant to applicable procedures after full disclosure (*see id.* at § 7.24); and (2) in a transaction involving controlling shareholders, if these qualifications are met and the directors who approve the transaction had "an adequate basis, grounded on substantial objective evidence, for believing that the consideration offered to the minority shareholders . . . constitutes fair value."

[B] Merger Fairness: In General

If a merger (or similar transaction) is subject to judicial scrutiny (*i.e.*, there is no appraisal right or the appraisal right is not exclusive), the level of judicial scrutiny of the substantive terms of the transaction depends on whether the transaction was negotiated at arms' length or approval was controlled to some extent by the other party to the transaction. Where the merger involves two corporations dealing at arms length, the courts have generally applied the "business judgment rule" as in *Van Gorkom* (*see* Section 9.03[B]) or, if the merger locks up control in a close-knit group or leaves the corporation closely held, heightened scrutiny under *Revlon* and *QVC* (*see* Section 14.03[D]). But where a parent corporation merges with a subsidiary in which the parent has a greater than 50% interest (*see Sterling,* below) or otherwise dominates the subsidiary,[44] the defendant normally has the considerably greater burden of proving that the terms were fair. ALI *Principles* §§ 7.24-7.25 provides similar rules. In a transaction that does not involve a controlling shareholder, § 7.24 requires proof that the transaction constituted waste. In a transaction that does involve a controlling shareholder, § 7.25 requires proof as to the fairness of the transaction. If the transaction was not approved by disinterested shareholders after full disclosure, the burden of proof as to fairness is on the controlling shareholders.

Vorenberg suggests that a less stringent standard should be applied to controlled mergers where appraisal rights are available, even if the merger has not been approved by disinterested shareholders. He argues that a strict standard of review makes corporate planning difficult, and that appraisal rights provide a check on abuse of director discretion comparable to that provided by disinterested shareholder ratification. Vorenberg draws the appropriate standard from *Gottlieb v. Heyden Chemical Corp.,*[45] in which the court illustrated the appropriate scope of judicial review as follows: "a man does not need to be a 'judge of horseflesh' to refrain from buying a Clydesdale for racing." ALI *Principles* § 7.25 adopts a modified version of the Vorenberg test, providing that the appraisal remedy is exclusive in controlled mergers if the directors approving the trans-

---

[44] *Compare Kahn v. Lynch Communication Systems, Inc.,* 638 A.2d 1110 (Del. 1994), *with In re Western National Corp. Shareholders Litigation,* 26 DEL. J. CORP. L. 806 (Del. Ch. 2000). In *Kahn,* the 43.3% shareholder's 5 designees sat on the corporation's 11-member board and asserted that other directors were required to comport with their demands, while the 46% shareholder in *Western National* had no designees on the corporation's board and only was alleged to have used its legitimate voting power as a shareholder to veto a previously proposed merger. *See also Puma v. Marriott,* Section 9.04[B].

[45] 33 Del. Ch. 177, 180, 91 A.2d 57, 58 (Sup. Ct. 1952).

action have an adequate basis for believing that the consideration offered constitutes fair value, disclosure is made to the minority shareholders, and the transaction is approved in accordance with law and the corporation's charter documents. The Delaware position on exclusivity of appraisal in controlled mergers is discussed below in Subsection [D].

STERLING v. MAYFLOWER HOTEL CORP.
Delaware Supreme Court
3 Del. Ch. 293, 93 A.2d 107 (1952)

SOUTHERLAND, Chief Justice.

The principal question presented is whether the terms of a proposed merger of Mayflower Hotel Corporation (herein "Mayflower") into its parent corporation, Hilton Hotels Corporation (herein "Hilton"), are fair to the minority stockholders of Mayflower.

The essential facts are these:

Mayflower and Hilton are both Delaware corporations. Mayflower's sole business is the ownership and operation of the Mayflower Hotel in Washington, D.C. It has outstanding 389,738 shares of common stock of $1 par value. Hilton and its subsidiary corporations are engaged in the business of owning, leasing, operating and managing hotel properties in many of the large centers of population in the country. Hilton has outstanding, in addition to an issue of Convertible Preference stock, 1,592,878 shares of common stock of $5 par value.

On December 18, 1946, Hilton acquired a majority of the outstanding shares of Mayflower. Thereafter it continued to make purchases of Mayflower stock. On or about February 4, 1952, it purchased 21,409 shares at a price of $19.10 a share, and on that date made an offer to all other minority stockholders to buy their shares at the same price. As of March 25, 1952, Hilton owned 321,883 shares, or nearly five-sixths of the outstanding stock.

From the time of the acquisition by Hilton of a majority interest in Mayflower, Hilton's management had contemplated a merger of Mayflower with Hilton. Soon after such acquisition, however, litigation ensued in the District of Columbia between Hilton and certain minority stockholders of Mayflower, not terminated until late in the year 1951. In the early part of 1950 the Mayflower directors discussed the question of ascertaining a fair basis of exchange of Mayflower stock for Hilton stock. All of the Mayflower directors (nine in number) were nominees of Hilton, and it was the view of the board (as well as of the Hilton board) that an independent study should be made by competent and disinterested financial analysts for the purpose of evolving a fair plan of exchange. Three of the members of the board (Messrs. Fleming, Folger and Baxter) had been directors before the acquisition by Hilton of its interest in Mayflower, and appear to have had little or no interest in Hilton. Messrs. Fleming and Folger were of opinion that although the study should be made no definite action should be taken upon the plan thereby to be developed until the Washington litigation should be finally terminated. The other directors deferred to this view.

In the early part of 1950 Standard Research Consultants, Inc., a subsidiary of Standard & Poor, was retained to make the study, and Mr. John G. Haslam, its Vice President, undertook the work. Later he submitted a study which determined a fair basis of exchange of Hilton stock for Mayflower stock to be three-fourths of a share of Hilton for one share of Mayflower. No action was taken on the basis of this study.

The Washington litigation having been finally terminated, Mr. Haslam on January 7, 1952, was again retained to continue and bring up to date his prior study and to develop a fair plan of exchange. Thereafter he submitted his final study (hereinafter referred to as "the Haslam report"), which embodies his conclusion that a fair rate of exchange would be share for share. A plan for a merger upon this basis was approved by the boards of directors of both corporations. The directors—at least the Mayflower directors—appear to have relied largely on the Haslam report to justify their action. A formal agreement of merger was entered into on March 14, 1952, providing for the merger of Mayflower (the constituent corporation) into Hilton (the surviving corporation), as authorized by the provisions of Section 59 of the General Corporation Law, Rev. Code of Del. 1935, par. 2091, as amended. Each outstanding share of Mayflower is converted into one share of Hilton. A separate agreement between Hilton and Mayflower provides that for a limited period Hilton will pay $19.10 a share for any Mayflower stock tendered to it by any minority stockholder. At stockholders' meetings held in April the requisite approval of the merger was obtained. At the Mayflower meeting 329,106 shares were voted in favor; 4,645 against. Holders of 35,191 shares of Mayflower who objected to the merger did not vote. The Hilton stockholders voted overwhelmingly to approve the merger.

On April 7, 1952, plaintiffs below (herein "plaintiffs"), holders of 32,295 shares of Mayflower stock, filed their complaint in the court below, seeking injunctive relief against the consummation of the merger, on the ground that the terms of the merger are grossly unfair to the minority stockholders of Mayflower, and that the Mayflower directors entered into the merger agreement in bad faith.

* * *

The Chancellor found no fraud or bad faith in the case and concluded that the plan was fair to the minority. . . . On June 18 he denied injunctive relief, and plaintiffs thereafter appealed.

Plaintiffs' principal contention here, as in the court below, is that the terms of the merger are unfair to Mayflower's minority stockholders. Plaintiffs invoke the settled rule of law that Hilton as majority stockholder of Mayflower and the Hilton directors as its nominees occupy in relation to the minority, a fiduciary position in dealing with Mayflower's property. Since they stand on both sides of the transaction, they bear the burden of establishing its entire fairness, and it must pass the test of careful scrutiny by the courts. . . . Defendants agree that their acts must meet this test. We therefore inquire whether the facts sustain the conversion ratio of share-for-share which forms the basis of the merger agreement.

As the Chancellor observed, the Haslam report forms the principal justification for the terms of the merger. We accordingly examine it.

. . . In Haslam's opinion the problem reduces to "a comparison of the operating trends of each of the corporations and of the investment characteristics of the two stock issues." A summary of some of the more important comparisons developed in the report is set forth in the margin.[1] On the basis of these comparisons, as well as upon consideration of the past history and future prospects of the two corporations, Haslam concludes that the financial record of Hilton has been substantially superior to that of Mayflower, and that purely upon a statistical basis it could be argued that Hilton should not offer better than three-fourths of a share of Hilton for one share of Mayflower. Nevertheless it is his opinion that, because of the problems incident to Hilton's control of Mayflower and the advantages incident to complete ownership, a share-for-share exchange will be fair and reasonable to all concerned.

* * *

The Haslam report contains no finding of net asset value—a factor nevertheless proper to be considered. Plaintiffs submitted affidavits containing an appraisal of the Mayflower Hotel (including land) and an estimate of reproduction cost (less depreciation) of the hotel proper. These affidavits indicate a value of upwards of $10,000,000. If plaintiffs' figure of a minimum value of $10,500,000 be accepted (it was accepted by the Chancellor), a share of Mayflower stock would have a liquidating or net asset value of about $27 a share. Defendants submitted an affidavit of J.B. Herndon, Jr., Vice President and Treasurer of Hilton, to the effect that two of the hotel properties of Hilton (the Conrad Hilton and the Palmer House in Chicago), which are carried on the books at $26,800,000, have a value of at least $60,000,000. Mr. Hilton gave some testimony to the same effect. If the indicated increase of $33,200,000 be accepted, there is added to Hilton's per share book value about $20, making an asset value of about $38 a share. Haslam submitted a comparison of "indicated values" of the hotel properties, arrived at by assuming rates of capitalization of earnings derived from plaintiffs' appraisal of the Mayflower Hotel and applying such rates to the Hilton earnings, and, by two different methods, arrived at figures of $30.56 and $40.82 as "indicated" net asset values of a share of Hilton stock. Plaintiffs submitted no evidence of value of the Hilton hotel properties.

Now, it will be noted that all of the comparisons above set forth except that of market value are in favor of Hilton. As for the market value of Mayflower stock, it appears to be

---

[1]   Comparisons drawn from Haslam report:

Average Earnings Per Share	Hilton	Mayflower
1947-1951 Average:		
Before income taxes and extraordinary items	4.31	2.17
After income taxes and extraordinary items	2.79	1.17
1951 to Nov. 30:		
Before income taxes and extraordinary items	4.22	3.14
After income taxes and extraordinary items	2.37	1.15
Dividends Per Share		
1947-1951 Average	1.07	.34
1951	1.20	.40
Book Value Per Share		
Nov. 30, 1951 Per books	18.26	14.38
Adjusted	18.42	13.08
Market Value Per share		
1950 average	12.88	11.25
1951 average	15.46	15.56
Approximate current price [at date of study]	14.75	16.25

conceded by all parties to be fictitious, that is, higher than would be justified in a free and normal market uninfluenced by Hilton's desire to acquire it and its policy of continued buying. At all events, that is the natural inference from the evidence. If we lay aside market value, and also disregard the comparison of book values—a factor, as the Chancellor said, of little relevancy in this case—we find three comparisons of various degrees of importance—earnings, dividends and net asset value—all in favor of Hilton.

If, therefore, we should accept the findings in the Haslam report and the principles on which it is based, and also accept the evidence bearing on comparative net asset value of Mayflower and Hilton stock, we should have to conclude that a share of Hilton stock has a value at least equal to a share of Mayflower stock, and that no unfair treatment of the Mayflower minority stockholders has been shown.

But we are confronted at the outset with the contention of the plaintiffs, basic to their case, that the Haslam report and the comparisons of value therein developed are wholly irrelevant to the issues before us. This contention, urged with much vigor—and repetition—is that the transaction here assailed is in substance a sale of assets by a fiduciary to himself. That the transaction is cast in the form of a merger, they say, is of no consequence; it is in effect a sale, and the only relevant comparison to be made is the comparison of the value of the transferred assets—worth $10,500,000—with the value of the consideration—389,738 shares of Hilton stock of a market value of $5,846,700; a disparity so shocking as to stamp the transaction as a fraud upon the Mayflower minority stockholders.

If plaintiffs' contention should be accepted it would follow that upon every merger of a subsidiary into its parent corporation that involves a conversion of the subsidiary's shares into shares of the parent, the market value of the parent stock issued to the stockholders of the subsidiary must equal the liquidating value of the subsidiary's stock. On its face this proposition is unsound, since it attempts to equate two different standards of value. In the case of many industrial corporations, and also in the instant case, there is a substantial gap between the market value and the liquidating value of the stock; and to apply to the merger of such corporations the proposition advanced by plaintiffs would be to bestow upon the stockholder of the subsidiary something which he did not have before the merger and could not obtain—the liquidating value of his stock.

* * *

What is the reasoning by which plaintiffs would lead us to sanction such a result?

* * *

[P]laintiffs say in effect: A merger is essentially a sale of assets; this transaction is a sale of assets by a fiduciary (Hilton) to itself for shares of stock worth shockingly less than the assets sold; therefore the transaction is a fraud. So runs the syllogism.

* * *

Plaintiffs' attempt to push to extremes the analogy drawn from a sale of assets leads them to a wholly untenable position, viz., that upon a merger a stockholder of a subsidiary is entitled to receive securities equal in value to the liquidating value of his stock. As we have already indicated, this proposition is unsound. Speaking generally, a merger effects an exchange of shares of stock in a going concern for shares in another going concern. In determining the fairness of the exchange, liquidating value is not the sole test of the value of either.

* * *

A similar rule obtains in ascertaining the value of stock in appraisal proceedings under the merger statute. In such cases the liquidating value of the stock is not the sole test of value; all relevant factors must be considered.

* * *

For the reasons above given, we find no error in this ruling.

The main question of law having been resolved against the plaintiffs, we turn to their remaining contentions.

Criticisms of the Haslam report.

Plaintiffs make some criticisms of the Haslam report designed to rebut or weaken its findings.

* * *

An argument of more substance is directed to the question of the net asset value of a share of Hilton.

Noting the omission in the Haslam report of any comparison of such values, plaintiffs develop the contention that the defendants, having the burden to justify the terms of the merger, have failed to sustain it, since no proper appraisal of Hilton's physical assets has been made. . . . As we have already held, net asset value is one of the factors to be considered in determining the fairness of a plan of merger. But the requirement that consideration be given to all relevant factors entering into the determination of value does not mean that any one factor is in every case important or that it must be given a definite weight in the evaluation. . . . The relative importance of several tests of value depends on the circumstances. Thus, in some cases net asset value may be quite important. . . . But in the case at bar it is of much less importance than the factors analysed in the Haslam report. We are dealing here with corporations engaged in the hotel business, whose capital is invested largely in fixed assets. The shares of such corporations are worth, from the viewpoint of an investor, what they can earn and pay. A comparison of net asset values may have some weight, but it is of much less importance than demonstrated capacity of the corporation to earn money and pay dividends. . . . In respect of earning power the superiority of Hilton stock is clearly shown. In these circumstances we deem the evidence adduced by defendants upon the issue of comparative net asset value to be sufficient to discharge whatever duty they were under in respect of the matter; and this notwith-standing the inconclusive nature of the "indicated values" arrived at by Haslam.

As we have already held, net asset value is one of the factors.

* * *

Hilton's offer to buy Mayflower stock at $19.10 a share.

The facts with respect to this offer are set forth above. The price derives from a purchase by Hilton in February, 1952, of 21,409 shares of Mayflower stock at $19.10 a share from a group headed by John E. Meyers, one of the interveners in the Washington litigation. A similar offer is now made to the remaining minority stockholders in connection with but not technically as a part of the plan of merger.

Upon these facts plaintiffs build an argument that the price thus voluntarily paid by Hilton, and still offered for Mayflower shares, shows the unfairness of converting one share of Mayflower into one share of Hilton. This argument assumes that the price in Hilton's offer is better evidence of value than the prices of the over-the-counter market and the values indicated by the Haslam report. This does not follow; on the contrary, the true inference would seem to be that, for whatever reason, Hilton paid for a large block of shares somewhat higher than real value. Messrs. Baxter and Fleming, two of the directors who had served under the prior management, are of the opinion that Mayflower stock is not worth $19.10 a share. After the Meyers purchase, Hilton may have determined to continue the offer to others in order to avoid any charge of having accorded the Meyers group special treatment. But Hilton's reasons for doing so are not here important; it is enough to say, as the Chancellor said, that the minority stockholders of Mayflower suffer no harm from the offer and have no ground of complaint.

Conclusion.

We have considered all of plaintiffs' objections to the fairness of the proposed merger, and find ourselves in accord with the Chancellor's conclusion that no fraud, or unfairness has been shown.

* * *

The order of the Court of Chancery of New Castle County dated June 18, 1952, is affirmed; and the cause is remanded to that court for further proceedings in conformity with this opinion.

NOTES AND QUESTIONS

(1) **Determining fairness: applying the appraisal standard.** In determining fairness of the price, the courts traditionally have followed the appraisal rights "fair value" approach discussed in Section 15.01[C]. Consider the *Sterling* court's refusal to rely solely on liquidation value and its minimization of the importance of net asset value. Another example of the use of the appraisal rights approach in fairness hearings is the treatment of merger gains. As noted in Section 15.01, merger gains historically have been excluded from "fair value" in an appraisal rights proceeding (*see* Note 2 following *Universal City Studios* in Section 15.01[C]). The courts traditionally refused in fairness hearings to hold that the minority was entitled to share in any additional value accruing to the defendant as a result of the merger.[46] However, as discussed below in Section 15.02[D], the courts now let minority shareholders share in merger gains, at

---

[46]   *See, e.g., Tanzer v. International General Industries, Inc.*, 402 A.2d 302 (Del. Ch. 1979).

least where the plan producing the gains was conceived and implemented prior to the merger.

(2) **The Brudney & Chirelstein approach.** Brudney & Chirelstein argue that valuation in a parent-subsidiary merger should be approached by considering what the subsidiary shareholders would receive in an arms' length merger with an unaffiliated third party. They contend that in an arms' length merger a portion of the merger gains would be allocated to the target on the basis of the relative sizes of the subsidiary and parent, consistent with the way trustees allocate savings and gains among multiple beneficiaries. **Lorne** criticizes the Brudney & Chirelstein formula, arguing, among other things, that the parent may be entitled to more of a gain than it would receive under the size-based formula. This would be so, for example, where the prospective merger gains are attributable to the parent's superior management. Do you agree with Brudney & Chirelstein's underlying assumption—that the subsidiary in a controlled merger is entitled to what it would receive in an arms' length merger? Keep in mind that a rule allocating merger gains to the minority shareholders may operate *ex ante* to discourage takeovers by denying takeover gains to acquiring companies (*see* Section 14.03[B][1][d], and Notes 2 and 7 following *Universal City Studios* in Section 15.01[C]).

(3) **The Brudney & Chirelstein formula applied.** The Brudney & Chirelstein formula was applied as follows in *Mills v. Electric Auto-Lite Co.,*[47] in which the court assessed the fairness of a merger of Mergenthaler and Auto-Lite into a new company, Eltra, in order to determine the appropriate relief for proxy violations in connection with the merger:

> . . . At the time of the merger there were 532,550 minority shares of Auto-Lite and 2,698,822 shares of Mergenthaler outstanding. During the first part of 1963 the average market price of Auto-Lite was $52.25 per share and the average market price of Mergenthaler was $24.875 per share. Thus, the premerger value of the minority holdings in Auto-Lite was 532,550 x $52.25 = $27,825,737 and the premerger value of Mergenthaler was 2,698,822 x $24.875 = $67,133,197. The combined premerger value of the two corporations was $27,825,737 + $67,133,197 = $94,958,934.
>
> In the month following the merger, Eltra common stock had an average market value of $25.25 per share. Eltra preferred stock had an average market value of $58.39 per 1.88 shares, the amount of stock which Auto-Lite shareholders had received for each share of Auto-Lite that they had held. The postmerger value of Eltra was therefore (2,698,822 x $25.25) + (532,550 x $58.39) = $68,145,255 + $31,095,594 = $99,240,849. The difference between the combined premerger value of Auto-Lite and Mergenthaler and the postmerger value of Eltra, which was $99,240,849 − $94,958,934 + $4,281,915, can be attributed to the synergism generated by the merger.

[47]   552 F.2d 1239, 1248 (7th Cir.), *cert. denied*, 434 U.S. 922 (1977).

According to the fairness formula devised by Professors Brudney and Chirelstein, the minority shareholders of Auto-Lite should have received Eltra stock worth at least as much as the premerger market value of their holdings in Auto-Lite and the synergism produced by the merger proportionate to the percentage of the combined premerger value of Auto-Lite and Mergenthaler which their holdings represented. The premerger value of the Auto-Lite minority shares was $27,825,737, which represented 29.3 percent of $94,958,934, the combined premerger value of Auto-Lite and Mergenthaler. Thus, to satisfy the constraints of fairness, the Auto-Lite minority shareholders should have received stock worth at least $27,825,737 + (.293 x $4,281,915) = $29,080,338. This would be equivalent to 1,151,696.5 shares of Eltra common at $25.25 per share. Had this many shares been distributed to the Auto-Lite minority shareholders, the exchange ratio would have been 1,151,696.5/532,550 = 2.16 to 1.

The Auto-Lite minority shareholders actually received preferred stock worth $58.39 on the market for each share of Auto-Lite that they had held. As a group, their Eltra holdings were worth 532,550 x $58,39 = $31,095,594. This was $31,095,594 – $29,080,338 = $2,015,256 more than fairness required. This result can be expressed in terms of Eltra common shares. Since the effective exchange ratio of the merger was 2.31 to 1, the property given the Auto-Lite minority was worth 2.31 – 2.16 = .15 shares of Eltra common per share of Auto-Lite more than what a fair amount would have been.

(4) **Procedural fairness.** In reviewing fairness, the courts have examined not only the price but also the procedure employed, comparable to the standard in business decisions generally discussed in Section 9.03. The specific problem in connection with controlled mergers is that because one party to the transaction is in a controlling position, standard majority rule may be unsatisfactory. *See* Notes 4-7 following *Kahn* in Section 15.02[D].

(5) **Choice of appraisal or fairness hearing.** In a jurisdiction in which appraisal is available but is not the dissenter's exclusive remedy, what, precisely, are the dissenter's alternatives? A shareholder who fails to comply with the appraisal procedures within the time allotted under the statute and instead pursues the fairness remedy beyond the injunction stage cannot select appraisal later on. If, however, the shareholder pursues appraisal, does this bar damages for unfairness? *Cede & Co. v. Technicolor, Inc.*[48] permitted an appraisal plaintiff to add a fraud claim two years after suing for appraisal. If the shareholder is able to pursue both remedies simultaneously, as appears to be the case in Delaware, an unfavorable result in one proceeding may have a *res judicata* or collateral estoppel effect on the other.[49] Thus, even where the dissent-

---

[48]   542 A.2d 1182 (Del. 1988).

[49]   *See Dofflemyer v. W. F. Hall Printing Co.*, 432 A.2d 1198 (Del. 1981) (shareholder pursuing both remedies unsuccessfully sought to withdraw from the appraisal proceeding, apparently in order to avoid such a result). *But cf. Cede*

ing shareholder may pursue both remedies simultaneously, he may eventually have to choose one remedy or the other.

REFERENCES

Brudney & Chirelstein, *Fair Shares in Corporate Mergers and Takeovers*, 88 HARV. L. REV. 297 (1974).

Letsou, *The Role of Appraisal in Corporate Law*, 39 B.C. L. REV. 1121 (1998).

Lorne, *Reappraisal of Fair Shares in Controlled Mergers*, 126 U. PA. L. REV. 955 (1978).

Vorenberg, *Exclusiveness of the Dissenting Stockholder's Appraisal Right*, 77 HARV. L. REV. 1189 (1964).

[C] Freezeout Transactions: Introduction and Historical Background

In a freeze out transaction, minority shareholders are expelled from an enterprise in a transaction in which they are forced to accept cash for their shares, unlike in *Sterling* where minority shareholders received stock in the surviving entity. This may be done, for example, by a merger, a dissolution followed by transfer of assets, or a reverse stock split. Some courts have held that such transactions must be accomplished for a legitimate purpose[50] and the majority may not appropriate an unfair share in the enterprise.[51]

Corporation statutes initially prohibited mergers in which shareholders received cash instead of shares. Corporations achieved the effect of freeze-out mergers under these statutes by issuing debt or redeemable preferred stock which would be redeemed or repaid in cash shortly after the merger.[52] Corporation statutes were eventually amended to permit payment of cash in mergers (*see* Del. G.C.L. § 251(b)(4)) and to permit "short-form" mergers in which small minorities could be frozen out without the formality of a shareholder vote (*see* Del. G.C.L. § 253 discussed in Section 13.02[B][3]). Early cases involving "short-form" mergers in which minority shareholders were "frozen out" for cash rejected challenges to these mergers, construing § 253 and similar provisions as expressly permitting elimination of minority shareholders.[53]

& *Co. v. Technicolor, Inc.*, 634 A.2d 345 (Del. 1993) (measure of recoverable loss in breach of fiduciary duty action is not necessarily limited to the difference between the price offered in merger and "true" value as determined in appraisal proceeding).

[50]   *See, e.g., In re Security Finance Co.*, 49 Cal. 2d 370, 317 P.2d 1 (1957).

[51]   *See, e.g., Lebold v. Inland Steamship Co.*, 82 F.2d 351 (7th Cir. 1936).

[52]   *See Matteson v. Ziebarth*, 40 Wash. 2d 286, 242 P.2d 1025 (1952) (holding that such a merger designed to circumvent limitations on freeze-outs was not unfair where it was done for the legitimate business reason of expelling a troublesome minority shareholder and thereby clearing the way for a necessary sale of the corporation). *But see Outwater v. Public Service Corp.*, 103 N.J. Eq. 461, 143 A. 729 (N.J. Ch. 1928) (refusing to uphold such a merger), *aff'd mem.*, 104 N.J. Eq. 490, 146 A. 916 (N.J. 1929).

[53]   *See, e.g., Stauffer v. Standard Brands Inc.*, 41 Del. Ch. 7, 187 A.2d 78 (Del. 1962); *Willcox v. Stern*, 18 N.Y.2d 195, 219 N.E.2d 401 (1966).

Notwithstanding these early cases, there was some sentiment against freeze-outs because of disadvantages of minority shareholders compared to the majority, including the need to recognize capital gains for tax purposes and find an alternative investment. This seems to require more than a *Sterling*-type examination of substantive fairness of price and procedure.[54] Minority shareholders initially sought protection in the federal courts under § 10(b) of the Securities Exchange Act of 1934 and Rule 10b-5. This tactic was ultimately unsuccessful in *Santa Fe Industries, Inc. v. Green*, Section 15.03[B], where the United States Supreme Court reasoned in part that the regulation of such matters as freeze-out mergers was appropriately a matter for state law.

Possibly picking up the "cue" from the United States Supreme Court, the Delaware Supreme Court, soon after the opinion in *Santa Fe*, upheld a complaint challenging a freezeout merger in *Singer v. The Magnavox Co.*[55] In *Singer*, a subsidiary of North American Phillips created expressly for the purpose had acquired 84.1% of the stock of Magnavox in a tender offer of $9 per share. The tender offer was ultimately not opposed by Magnavox management, many of whom received two-year employment contracts. A few months later, Magnavox was merged into a specially created subsidiary of the acquiring corporation for $9 per share. In the proxy materials issued in connection with the merger, the book value of the stock was stated to be $10.16. In reversing the trial court's dismissal of a shareholder's complaint challenging the merger, the Delaware Supreme Court reasoned in part as follows:[56]

> Defendants concede that they owe plaintiffs a fiduciary duty but contend that, in the context of the present transaction, they have met that obligation by offering fair value for the Magnavox shares. And, say defendants, plaintiffs' exclusive remedy for dissatisfaction with the merger is to seek an appraisal under § 262. We disagree. In our view, defendants cannot meet their fiduciary obligation to plaintiffs simply by relegating them to a statutory appraisal proceeding.
>
> At the core of defendants' contention is the premise that a shareholder's right is exclusively in the value of his investment, not its form. And, they argue, that right is protected by a § 262 appraisal which, by definition, results in fair value for the shares. This argument assumes that the right to take is coextensive with the power to take and that a dissenting stockholder has no legally protected right in his shares, his certificate or his company beyond a right to be paid fair value when the majority is ready to do this. Simply stated, such an argument does not square with the duty stated so eloquently and so forcefully by Chief Justice Layton in *Guth*.

---

[54]   For a discussion of the distinctions between freezeout and equity mergers, see Greene, *Corporate Freeze-out Mergers: A Proposed Analysis*, 28 STAN. L. REV. 487, 490-91 (1976).

[55]   380 A.2d 969 (Del. 1977).

[56]   380 A.2d at 977-78, 980.

We agree that, because the power to merge is conferred by statute, every stockholder in a Delaware corporation accepts his shares with notice thereof. See *Federal United Corporation v. Havender*, Del. Supr., 24 Del. Ch. 318, 11 A.2d 331, 338 (1940). . . . But it by no means follows that those in control of a corporation may invoke the statutory power conferred by § 251, a power which this Court in *Havender*, *supra*, said was "somewhat analogous to the right of eminent domain," 11 A.2d at 338, when their purpose is simply to get rid of a minority. On the contrary, as we shall ultimately conclude here, just as a minority shareholder may not thwart a merger without cause, neither may a majority cause a merger to be made for the sole purpose of eliminating a minority on a cashout basis.

Plaintiffs allege that defendants violated their respective fiduciary duties by participating in the tender offer and other acts which led to the merger and which were designed to enable Development and North American to, among other things:

> [C]onsummate a merger which did not serve any valid corporate purpose or compelling business need of Magnavox and whose sole purpose was to enable Development and North American to obtain sole ownership of the business and assets of Magnavox at a price determined by defendants which was grossly inadequate and unfair and which was designed to give Development and North American a disproportionate amount of the gain said defendants anticipated would be recognized from consummation of the merger.

Defendants contend, and the Court of Chancery agreed, that the "business purpose" rule does not have a place in Delaware's merger law. In support of this contention defendants cite: *Stauffer v. Standard Brands, Incorporated*, Del. Supr., 187 A.2d 78 (1962); *Federal United Corporation v. Havender*, *supra*; *David J. Greene & Co. v. Schenley Industries, Inc.*, Del. Ch. 281 A.2d 30 (1971); *Bruce v. E.L. Bruce Company*, 40 Del. Ch. 80, 174 A.2d 29 (1961); and *MacCrone v. American Capital Corporation*, D. Del. 51 F. Supp. 462 (1943).

Each of these cases involved an effort to enjoin or attack a merger and each was unsuccessful. To this extent they support defendants' side of the controversy. But none of these decisions involved a merger in which the minority was totally expelled via a straight "cash-for-stock" conversion in which the only purpose of the merger was, as alleged here, to eliminate the minority.

* * *

We hold, therefore, that a § 251 merger, made for the sole purpose of freezing out minority stockholders, is an abuse of the corporate process; and the complaint, which so alleges in this suit, states a cause of action for violation of a fiduciary duty for which the Court may grant such relief as it deems appropriate under the circumstances.

This is not to say, however, that merely because the Court finds that a cashout merger was not made for the sole purpose of freezing out minority stockholders, all relief must be denied to the minority stockholders in a § 251 merger.[11] On the contrary, the fiduciary obligation of the majority to the minority stockholders remains and proof of a purpose, other than such freeze-out, without more, will not necessarily discharge it. In such case the Court will scrutinize the circumstances for compliance with the *Sterling* rule of "entire fairness" and, if it finds a violation thereof, will grant such relief as equity may require. Any statement in *Stauffer* inconsistent herewith is held inapplicable to a § 251 merger.

* * *

Accordingly, as to this facet of the appeal, we reverse.

Less than a month after the *Singer* opinion, the Delaware Supreme Court resolved the issue left open in footnote 11 to *Singer*, holding in *Tanzer v. International General Industries*,[57] that justifiable business purpose includes benefit to the parent. In *Tanzer*, that benefit was the parent's increased ability to secure long-term debt financing if it increased its ownership of the subsidiary from 81% to 100%.[58] Then *Roland International Corp. v. Najjar*[59] extended the *Singer* business purpose requirement to freezeout mergers effected under the short-form merger statute. Justice Quillen, dissenting, noted that the plaintiff did not challenge defendant's right to cash him out of the corporation, but simply complained that the price was unfair—a claim that could be adequately redressed through the appraisal proceeding. In response to plaintiff's argument that the appraisal standard of valuation was unfair, Justice Quillen stated:[60]

Certainly this Court should not foster an unnecessary damage forum because of any judicial limitation placed on the statutory appraisal procedure. Rather, we should encourage this legislatively established valuation process to be

---

[11] Plaintiffs contend that a "business purpose" is proper in a merger only when it serves the interests of the subsidiary corporation; defendants contend, on the other hand, that if any such purpose is relevant, it is only that of the parent corporation. Since resolution of that question is not necessary to the disposition of this appeal, and since it was not central in the briefing and argument, we leave it to another day.

[57] 379 A.2d 1121 (Del. 1977).

[58] To the same effect, see *Alpert v. 28 Williams Street Corp.*, 63 N.Y.2d 557, 483 N.Y.S.2d 667, 473 N.E.2d 19 (1984); *Schulwolf v. Cerro Corp.*, 86 Misc. 2d 292, 380 N.Y.S.2d 957 (Sup. Ct. N.Y. Co. 1976) (combination would facilitate intercompany transactions); *Dower v. Mosser Industries, Inc.*, 648 F.2d 183 (3d Cir. 1981) (parent would be better able to provide needed financing to the subsidiary); *Polin v. Conductron Corp.*, 552 F.2d 797 (8th Cir.), *cert. denied*, 434 U.S. 857 (1977) (same).

[59] 407 A.2d 1032 (Del. 1979).

[60] *Id.* at 1040, n.12.

open to generally accepted techniques of evaluation used in other areas of business and law.

On this last point, see *Weinberger*, below.

Although the business purpose test was intended to ensure that the transaction would produce sufficient gains to justify cashing out the minority, it did not ensure that the cash-out price was fair (*see* **Carney**). Accordingly, the courts scrutinizing freeze-out mergers have, consistent with the guidance provided in *Singer*, retained a second-level "fairness" review similar to that discussed in Section 15.02[B]. For example, *Tanzer*, after finding a *bona fide* business purpose for the freeze-out, remanded for consideration of the "entire fairness" of the transaction.

The *Singer* business purpose requirement came under heavy attack. **Weiss** (670-71) criticized the business purpose rule as unclear and unpredictable in application, particularly in light of the additional requirement of "entire fairness." **Brudney & Chirelstein** criticized the requirement as unnecessary with respect to some freezeout mergers and insufficient protection with respect to others. They argued that a two-step takeover that begins with a tender offer and concludes with a freezeout merger should be permitted without regard to business purpose, though they would require that the minority shareholders of the subsidiary be given stock in the surviving corporation or, if that corporation was public, enough cash so that, taking into account tax effects and transaction costs, the shareholders could reenter the corporation without having been penalized by the merger. As to other types of freezeouts, Brudney & Chirelstein argued that, even if these mergers have a business purpose, it would nevertheless be unfair to permit termination of the minority shareholders' investment against their will. Criticism of *Singer* and erosion in cases like *Tanzer* led ultimately to its demise in Delaware and to a radical restructuring of the corporate law of mergers.

[D] A Reexamination of Merger Fairness and Appraisal Rights: *Weinberger* and Statutory Approaches

WEINBERGER v. UOP, INC.
Delaware Supreme Court
457 A.2d 701 (1983)

[The Signal Companies, Inc. sold its Signal Oil division in 1974 for $420 million in cash. In 1975, Signal used some of this cash to buy 50.5% of UOP in a tender offer for $21 per share—a price reached in arms' length bargaining with the UOP board. At the time of the offer, UOP stock had been trading at $14. By the end of 1975, seven Signal representatives sat on UOP's 13-member board. These included Signal's president (Shumway), board chairman (Walkup), director of planning (Arledge), and chief financial officer (Chitiea). Crawford, UOP's chief executive officer, had been a long-time Signal employee before joining UOP and was also a member of UOP's board.

[By February, 1978, Signal had concluded that the remaining 49.5% of UOP's stock was a good investment for Signal. On February 28, the executive committee of the Signal board authorized negotiations for the purchase of this stock for $20 to $21 per share (the stock was then trading for $14.50). Crawford was invited to this meeting and presented with this price range. The terms were subject to approval by the boards of directors of the two corporations at meetings scheduled March 6, only four business days away. During that time, Crawford spoke to UOP's non-Signal directors. Lehman Brothers, UOP's regular investment banker, was asked to render a fairness opinion and did a "due diligence" investigation. By March 6, Lehman had concluded that $20-$21 per share would be a fair price, and Crawford had informed Walkup that he felt the UOP "outside" directors would demand $21 per share.

[On March 6, the Signal and UOP boards approved the transaction at $21 per share, subject to the approval of a majority of UOP's outstanding minority stock voting on the merger and of at least two-thirds of all UOP shares. The UOP board decision was made after a discussion that occurred while Walkup and Crawford were out of the room. All of the Signal directors abstained from voting. At the UOP annual meeting on May 26, 56% of UOP's minority shareholders voted. 51.9% of the outstanding minority stock voted for the merger and 2.2% against.

[Plaintiff, a former UOP minority shareholder, sued to challenge the merger. The Chancery Court first dismissed the complaint for failure to state a cause of action on the ground that the transaction had been approved by a majority of the minority shares and that there were no allegations of abuse of control by the majority.[*] After the complaint was amended to add such allegations, the court held that the merger was fair and entered judgment for the defendants.[**]

[In the course of its second opinion, the Chancery Court rejected plaintiff's evidence that the UOP stock was worth $26 per share.]

MOORE, Justice:

* * *

Numerous points were raised by the parties, but we address only the following questions presented by the trial court's opinion:

1) The plaintiff's duty to plead sufficient facts demonstrating the unfairness of the challenged merger;

2) The burden of proof upon the parties where the merger has been approved by the purportedly informed vote of a majority of the minority shareholders;

3) The fairness of the merger in terms of adequacy of the defendants' disclosures to the minority shareholders;

4) The fairness of the merger in terms of adequacy of the price paid for the minority shares and the remedy appropriate to that issue; and

5) The continued force and effect of *Singer v. Magnavox Co.*, Del. Supr., 380 A.2d 969, 980 (1977), and its progeny.

---

[*]   [*Weinberger v. UOP, Inc.*, 409 A.2d 1262 (Del. Ch. 1979).]

[**] [*Weinberger v. UOP, Inc.*, 426 A.2d 1333 (Del. Ch. 1981).]

In ruling for the defendants, the Chancellor restated his earlier conclusion that the plaintiff in a suit challenging a cash-out merger must allege specific acts of fraud, misrepresentation, or other items of misconduct to demonstrate the unfairness of the merger terms to the minority. We approve this rule and affirm it.

The Chancellor also held that even though the ultimate burden of proof is on the majority shareholder to show by a preponderance of the evidence that the transaction is fair, it is first the burden of the plaintiff attacking the merger to demonstrate some basis for invoking the fairness obligation. We agree with that principle. However, where corporate action has been approved by an informed vote of a majority of the minority shareholders, we conclude that the burden entirely shifts to the plaintiff to show that the transaction was unfair to the minority. . . . But in all this, the burden clearly remains on those relying on the vote to show that they completely disclosed all material facts relevant to the transaction.

Here, the record does not support a conclusion that the minority stockholder vote was an informed one. Material information, necessary to acquaint those shareholders with the bargaining positions of Signal and UOP, was withheld under circumstances amounting to a breach of fiduciary duty. We therefore conclude that this merger does not meet the test of fairness, at least as we address that concept, and no burden thus shifted to the plaintiff by reason of the minority shareholder vote. Accordingly, we reverse and remand for further proceedings consistent herewith.

In considering the nature of the remedy available under our law to minority shareholders in a cash-out merger, we believe that it is, and hereafter should be, an appraisal under 8 Del. C. § 262 as hereinafter construed. . . . [T]o give full effect to section 262 within the framework of the General Corporation Law we adopt a more liberal, less rigid and stylized, approach to the valuation process than has heretofore been permitted by our courts. While the present state of these proceedings does not admit the plaintiff to the appraisal remedy per se, the practical effect of the remedy we do grant him will be co-extensive with the liberalized valuation and appraisal methods we herein approve for cases coming after this decision.

Our treatment of these matters has necessarily led us to a consideration of the business purpose rule announced in the trilogy of *Singer v. Magnavox Co., supra; Tanzer v. International General Industries, Inc.,* Del. Supr., 379 A.2d 1121 (1977); and *Roland International Corp. v. Najjar,* Del. Supr., 407 A.2d 1032 (1979). For the reasons hereafter set forth, we consider that the business purpose requirement of these cases is no longer the law of Delaware.

I

* * *

A.

A primary issue mandating reversal is the preparation by two UOP directors, Arledge and Chitiea, of their feasibility study for the exclusive use and benefit of Signal. This document was of obvious significance to both Signal and UOP. Using UOP data, it described the advantages to Signal of ousting the minority at a price range of $21-$24 per share. Mr. Arledge, one of the authors, outlined the benefits to Signal:[6]

---

[6]   The parentheses indicate certain handwritten comments of Mr. Arledge.

Purpose Of The Merger

1) Provides an outstanding investment opportunity for Signal—(Better than any recent acquisition we have seen.)

2) Increases Signal's earnings.

3) Facilitates the flow of resources between Signal and its subsidiaries—(Big factor—works both ways.)

4) Provides cost savings potential for Signal and UOP.

5) Improves the percentage of Signal's "operating earnings" as opposed to "holding company earnings."

6) Simplifies the understanding of Signal.

7) Facilitates technological exchange among Signal's subsidiaries.

8) Eliminates potential conflicts of interest.

Having written those words, solely for the use of Signal, it is clear from the record that neither Arledge nor Chitiea shared this report with their fellow directors of UOP. We are satisfied that no one else did either.

* * *

The Arledge-Chitiea report speaks for itself in supporting the Chancellor's finding that a price of up to $24 was a "good investment" for Signal. It shows that a return on the investment at $21 would be 15.7% versus 15.5% at $24 per share. This was a difference of only two-tenths of one percent, while it meant over $17,000,000 to the minority. Under such circumstances, paying UOP's minority shareholders $24 would have had relatively little long-term effect on Signal, and the Chancellor's findings concerning the benefit to Signal, even at a price of $24, were obviously correct.

* * *

Certainly, this was a matter of material significance to UOP and its shareholders. Since the study was prepared by two UOP directors, using UOP information for the exclusive benefit of Signal, and nothing whatever was done to disclose it to the outside UOP directors or the minority shareholders, a question of breach of fiduciary duty arises. This problem occurs because there were common Signal-UOP directors participating, at least to some extent, in the UOP board's decision-making processes without full disclosure of the conflicts they faced.[7]

* * *

---

[7] Although perfection is not possible, or expected, the result here could have been entirely different if UOP had appointed an independent negotiating committee of its outside directors to deal with Signal at arm's length. *See, e.g., Harriman v. E. I. du Pont de Nemours & Co.*, 411 F. Supp. 133 (D. Del. 1975). Since fairness in this context can be equated to conduct by a theoretical, wholly independent, board of directors acting upon the matter before them, it is unfortunate that this course apparently was neither considered nor pursued. *Johnston v. Greene*, Del. Supr., 121 A.2d 919, 925 (1956). Particularly in a parent-subsidiary context, a showing that the action taken was as though each of the contending parties had in fact exerted its bargaining power against the other at arm's length is strong evidence that the transaction meets the test of fairness. *Getty Oil Co. v. Skelly Oil Co.*, Del. Supr., 267 A.2d 883, 886 (1970); *Puma v. Marriott*, Del. Ch., 283 A.2d 693, 696 (1971).

Given the absence of any attempt to structure this transaction on an arm's length basis, Signal cannot escape the effects of the conflicts it faced, particularly when its designees on UOP's board did not totally abstain from participation in the matter. There is no "safe harbor" for such divided loyalties in Delaware. When directors of a Delaware corporation are on both sides of a transaction, they are required to demonstrate their utmost good faith and the most scrupulous inherent fairness of the bargain.

* * *

There is no dilution of this obligation where one holds dual or multiple directorships, as in a parent-subsidiary context. *Levien v. Sinclair Oil Corp.*, Del. Ch., 261 A.2d 911, 915 (1969). Thus, individuals who act in a dual capacity as directors of two corporations, one of whom is parent and the other subsidiary, owe the same duty of good management to both corporations, and in the absence of an independent negotiating structure (*see* n.7, *supra*), or the directors' total abstention from any participation in the matter, this duty is to be exercised in light of what is best for both companies. . . . The record demonstrates that Signal has not met this obligation.

C.

The concept of fairness has two basic aspects: fair dealing and fair price. The former embraces questions of when the transaction was timed, how it was initiated, structured, negotiated, disclosed to the directors, and how the approvals of the directors and the stockholders were obtained. The latter aspect of fairness relates to the economic and financial considerations of the proposed merger, including all relevant factors: assets, market value, earnings, future prospects, and any other elements that affect the intrinsic or inherent value of a company's stock. . . . However, the test for fairness is not a bifurcated one as between fair dealing and price. All aspects of the issue must be examined as a whole since the question is one of entire fairness. . . . However, in a non-fraudulent transaction we recognize that price may be the preponderant consideration outweighing other features of the merger. Here, we address the two basic aspects of fairness separately because we find reversible error as to both.

D.

Part of fair dealing is the obvious duty of candor[.] . . . With the well-established Delaware law on the subject, and the Court of Chancery's findings of fact here, it is inevitable that the obvious conflicts posed by Arledge and Chitiea's preparation of their "feasibility study," derived from UOP information, for the sole use and benefit of Signal, cannot pass muster.

The Arledge-Chitiea report is but one aspect of the element of fair dealing. How did this merger evolve? It is clear that it was entirely initiated by Signal. The serious time constraints under which the principals acted were all set by Signal. It had not found a suitable outlet for its excess cash and considered UOP a desirable investment, particularly since it was now in a position to acquire the whole company for itself. For whatever reasons, and they were only Signal's, the entire transaction was presented to and approved by UOP's board within four business days. Standing alone, this is not necessarily indicative of any lack of fairness by a majority shareholder. It was what occurred, or more properly, what did not occur, during this brief period that makes the time constraints imposed by Signal relevant to the issue of fairness.

The structure of the transaction, again, was Signal's doing. So far as negotiations were concerned, it is clear that they were modest at best. Crawford, Signal's man at UOP, never really talked price with Signal, except to accede to its management's statements on the subject, and to convey to Signal the UOP outside directors' view that as between the $20-$21 range under consideration, it would have to be $21. The latter is not a surprising outcome, but hardly arm's length negotiations. Only the protection of benefits for UOP's key employees and the issue of Lehman Brothers' fee approached any concept of bargaining.

As we have noted, the matter of disclosure to the UOP directors was wholly flawed by the conflicts of interest raised by the Arledge-Chitiea report. All of those conflicts were resolved by Signal in its own favor without divulging any aspect of them to UOP.

* * *

There was no disclosure of the circumstances surrounding the rather cursory preparation of the Lehman Brothers' fairness opinion. Instead, the impression was given UOP's minority that a careful study had been made.

* * *

Finally, the minority stockholders were denied the critical information that Signal considered a price of $24 to be a good investment. Since this would have meant over $17,000,000 more to the minority, we cannot conclude that the shareholder vote was an informed one. Under the circumstances, an approval by a majority of the minority was meaningless.

* * *

Given these particulars and the Delaware law on the subject, the record does not establish that this transaction satisfies any reasonable concept of fair dealing, and the Chancellor's findings in that regard must be reversed.

E.

Turning to the matter of price, plaintiff also challenges its fairness. His evidence was that on the date the merger was approved the stock was worth at least $26 per share. In support, he offered the testimony of a chartered investment analyst who used two basic approaches to valuation: a comparative analysis of the premium paid over market in ten other tender offer-merger combinations, and a discounted cash flow analysis.

In this breach of fiduciary duty case, the Chancellor perceived that the approach to valuation was the same as that in an appraisal proceeding. Consistent with precedent, he rejected plaintiff's method of proof and accepted defendants' evidence of value as being in accord with practice under prior case law. This means that the so-called "Delaware block" or weighted average method was employed wherein the elements of value, *i.e.*, assets, market price, earnings, etc., were assigned a particular weight and the resulting amounts added to determine the value per share. This procedure has been in use for decades. . . . However, to the extent it excludes other generally accepted techniques used in the financial community and the courts, it is now clearly outmoded. It is time we recognize this in appraisal and other stock valuation proceedings and bring out law current on the subject.

While the Chancellor rejected plaintiff's discounted cash flow method of valuing UOP's stock, as not corresponding with "either logic or the existing law" (426 A.2d at 1360), it is significant that this was essentially the focus, *i.e.*, earnings potential of UOP, of Messrs. Arledge and Chitiea in their evaluation of the merger. Accordingly, the standard "Delaware block" or weighted average method of valuation, formerly employed in appraisal and other stock valuation cases, shall no longer exclusively control such proceedings. We believe that a more liberal approach must include proof of value by any techniques or methods which are generally considered acceptable in the financial community and otherwise admissible in court, subject only to our interpretation of 8 Del. C. § 262(h), *infra*. . . . This will obviate the very structured and mechanistic procedure that has heretofore governed such matters.

* * *

It is significant that section 262 now mandates the determination of "fair" value based upon "all relevant factors." Only the speculative elements of value that may arise from the "accomplishment or expectation" of the merger are excluded. We take this to be a very narrow exception to the appraisal process, designed to eliminate use of pro forma data and projections of a speculative variety relating to the completion of a merger. But elements of future value, including the nature of the enterprise, which are known or susceptible of proof as of the date of the merger and not the product of speculation, may be considered. When the trial court deems it appropriate, fair value also includes any damages resulting from the taking, which the stockholders sustain as a class. If that was not the case, then the obligation to consider "all relevant factors" in the valuation process would be eroded.

* * *

Although the Chancellor received the plaintiff's evidence, his opinion indicates that the use of it was precluded because of past Delaware practice. While we do not suggest a monetary result one way or the other, we do think the plaintiff's evidence should be part of the factual mix and weighed as such. Until the $21 price is measured on remand by the valuation standards man-dated by Delaware law, there can be no finding at the present stage of these proceedings that the price is fair. Given the lack of any candid disclosure of the material facts surrounding establishment of the $21 price, the majority of the minority vote, approving the merger, is meaningless.

* * *

While a plaintiff's monetary remedy ordinarily should be confined to the more liberalized appraisal proceeding herein established, we do not intend any limitation on the historic powers of the Chancellor to grant such other relief as the facts of a particular case may dictate. The appraisal remedy we approve may not be adequate in certain cases, particularly where fraud, misrepresentation, self-dealing, deliberate waste of corporate assets, or gross and palpable overreaching are involved. . . . Under such circumstances, the Chancellor's powers are complete to fashion any form of equitable and monetary relief as may be appropriate, including rescissory damages. Since it is apparent that this long completed transaction is too involved to undo, and in view of the Chancellor's discretion, the award, if any, should be in the form of monetary damages based upon entire fairness standards, *i.e.*, fair dealing and fair price.

Obviously, there are other litigants, like the plaintiff, who abjured an appraisal and whose rights to challenge the element of fair value must be preserved.[8] Accordingly, the quasi-appraisal remedy we grant the plaintiff here will apply only to: (1) this case; (2) any case now pending on appeal to this Court; (3) any case now pending in the Court of Chancery which has not yet been appealed but which may be eligible for direct appeal to this Court; (4) any case challenging a cash-out merger, the effective date of which is on or before February 1, 1983; and (5) any proposed merger to be presented at a shareholders' meeting, the notification of which is mailed to the stockholders on or before February 23, 1983. Thereafter, the provisions of 8 Del. C. § 262, as herein construed, respecting the scope of an appraisal and the means for perfecting the same, shall govern the financial remedy available to minority shareholders in a cash-out merger. Thus, we return to the well established principles of *Stauffer v. Standard Brands, Inc.*, Del. Supr., 187 A.2d 78 (1962) and *David J. Greene & Co. v. Schenley Industries, Inc.*, Del. Ch., 281 A.2d 30 (1971), mandating a stockholder's recourse to the basic remedy of an appraisal.

III.

Finally, we address the matter of business purpose. The defendants contend that the purpose of this merger was not a proper subject of inquiry by the trial court. The plaintiff says that no valid purpose existed—the entire transaction was a mere subterfuge designed to eliminate the minority. The Chancellor ruled otherwise, but in so doing he clearly circumscribed the thrust and effect of *Singer. Weinberger v. UOP*, 426 A.2d at 1342-43, 1348-50.

* * *

The requirement of a business purpose is new to our law of mergers and was a departure from prior case law. *See Stauffer v. Standard Brands, Inc., supra; David J. Greene & Co. v. Schenley Industries, Inc., supra.*

In view of the fairness test which has long been applicable to parent-subsidiary mergers, *Sterling v. Mayflower Hotel Corp.*, Del. Supr., 93 A.2d 107, 109-10 (1952), the expanded appraisal remedy now available to shareholders, and the broad discretion of the Chancellor to fashion such relief as the facts of a given case may dictate, we do not believe that any additional meaningful protection is afforded minority shareholders by the business purpose requirement of the trilogy of *Singer, Tanzer, Najjar*, and their progeny. Accordingly, such requirement shall no longer be of any force or effect.

The judgment of the Court of Chancery, finding both the circumstances of the merger and the price paid the minority shareholders to be fair, is reversed. The matter is remanded for further proceedings consistent herewith.

---

[8]   Under 8 Del. C. § 262(a), (d) & (e), a stockholder is required to act within certain time periods to perfect the right to an appraisal.

RABKIN v. P.A. HUNT CHEMICAL CORPORATION
Delaware Supreme Court
498 A.2d 1099 (1985)

[This is a class action challenging the merger of Hunt and its majority stockholder, Olin Corporation. On March 1, 1983, Olin bought 63.4% of Hunt stock from Turner and Newall Industries, Inc. for $25 per share pursuant to an agreement that obligated Olin to pay at least that amount if the remaining interest were acquired within one year. Soon after the expiration of the one-year period, Olin obtained an investment banker's opinion that Hunt stock was worth $20 per share and made an offer at that price. The offer was accepted by a committee of outside directors of Hunt directors although the committee's financial adviser had found a range of values from $19 to $25 per share. The merger was approved by Hunt shareholders, but there was no requirement of approval by a majority of the minority share-holders. The Vice Chancellor dismissed the complaint on the ground that "[w]here . . . there are no allegations of non-disclosures or misrepresentations, Weinberger mandates that plaintiffs' entire fairness claims be determined in an appraisal proceeding."[*]]

MOORE, Justice:

* * *

. . . The trial court's narrow interpretation of *Weinberger* would render meaningless our extensive discussion of fair dealing found in that opinion. In *Weinberger*, we defined fair dealing as embracing "questions of when the transaction was timed, how it was initiated, structured, negotiated, disclosed to the directors, and how the approvals of the directors and the stockholders were obtained." 457 A.2d at 711. While this duty of fairness certainly incorporates the principle that a cash-out merger must be free of fraud or misrepresentation, *Weinberger*'s mandate of fair dealing does not turn solely on issues of deception. We par-ticularly noted broader concerns respecting the matter of procedural fairness. *Weinberger*, 457 A.2d at 711, 714. Thus, while "in a non-fraudulent transaction . . . price *may* be the pre-ponderant consideration," *id*. at 711 (emphasis added), it is not necessarily so.

Although the Vice Chancellor correctly understood *Weinberger* as limiting collateral attacks on cash-out mergers, her analysis narrowed the procedural protections which we still intended *Weinberger* to guarantee. Here, plaintiffs are not arguing questions of valuation which are the traditional subjects of an appraisal. Rather, they seek to enforce a contractual right to receive $25 per share, which they claim was unfairly destroyed by Olin's manipu-lative conduct.

While a plaintiff's mere allegation of "unfair dealing," without more, cannot survive a motion to dismiss, averments containing "specific acts of fraud, misrepresentation, or other items of misconduct" must be carefully examined in accord with our views expressed both here and in *Weinberger*. See 457 A.2d at 703, 711, 714.

---

* [*Rabkin v. Philip A. Hunt Chemical Corp.*, 480 A.2d 655, 660 (Del. Ch. 1984).]

III

A.

Having outlined the facts and applicable principles, we turn to the details of the Hunt-Olin merger and the plaintiffs' complaints to determine whether the specific acts of misconduct alleged are sufficient to withstand a motion to dismiss.

The Court of Chancery stated that "the gravamen of all the complaints appears to be that the cash-out price is unfair." *Rabkin*, 480 A.2d at 658. However, this conclusion, which seems to be more directed to issues of valuation, is neither supported by the pleadings themselves nor the extensive discussion of unfair dealing found in the trial court's opinion. There is no challenge to any method of valuation or to the components of value upon which Olin's $20 price was based. The plaintiffs want the $25 per share guaranteed by the one year commitment, which they claim was unfairly denied them by Olin's manipulations.

According to the Vice Chancellor's analysis, the plaintiff's complaints alleged three claims—"breach of the fiduciary duty of entire fairness, breach of fiduciary duty under *Schnell v. Chris-Craft Industries*, Del. Supr., 285 A.2d 437 (1971) and promissory estoppel." *Id.* at 659. The entire fairness claim was rejected on the ground that the plaintiff's exclusive remedy was an appraisal. *Id.* at 660. The *Schnell* analogy was repudiated on the theory that Olin had not impinged on any rights of the minority shareholders by letting the one-year commitment expire before consummating the merger. *Id.* at 661. The court also rejected what it categorized as the promissory estoppel claim on the grounds that the language allegedly forming the promise was too vague to constitute such an undertaking and that estoppel cannot be predicated upon a promise to do that which the promisor is already obliged to do. *Id.*

B.

In *Weinberger* we observed that the timing, structure, negotiation and disclosure of a cash-out merger all had a bearing on the issue of procedural fairness. 457 A.2d at 711. The plaintiffs contend inter alia that Olin breached its fiduciary duty of fair dealing by purposely timing the merger, and thereby unfairly manipulating it, to avoid the one-year commitment. In support of that contention plaintiffs have averred specific facts indicating that Olin knew it would eventually acquire Hunt, but delayed doing so to avoid paying $25 per share. Significantly, the trial court's opinion seems to accept that point:

> It is apparent that, from the outset, Olin anticipated that it would eventually acquire the minority interest in Hunt, Olin's chief executive officer expected as much when the Agreement was executed and, in evaluating the Agreement, Olin prepared computations based upon the assumption that it would acquire 100% of Hunt.

Rabkin, 480 A.2d at 657-58.

Consistent with this observation are the confidential Berardino memo to the three Olin and Hunt directors, Henske, Johnstone and Berry, about the disadvantages of paying a higher price during the one-year commitment; the deposition testimony of Olin's chief executive officer, Mr. Henske, that the one year commitment "Meant nothing"; and what could be considered a quick surrender by the Special Committee of Hunt directors in the face of Olin's proposal to squeeze out the minority at $20 per share.[7] While we do not pass on the merits of such questions, Olin's alleged attitude toward the minority, at least as it appears on the face of the complaints and their proposed amendments, coupled with the apparent absence of any meaningful negotiations as to price, all have an air reminiscent of the dealings between Signal and UOP in *Weinberger. See* 457 A.2d at 711. Certainly the Berardino memorandum, although not unusual as an Olin planning document, raises unanswered questions about the recognition by three of its recipients, all Hunt directors, of their undiminished duty of loyalty to Hunt.

* * *

These are issues which an appraisal cannot address, and at this juncture are matters that cannot be resolved by a motion to dismiss.

In our opinion the facts alleged by the plaintiffs regarding Olin's avoidance of the one-year commitment support a claim of unfair dealing sufficient to defeat dismissal at this stage of the proceedings. The defendants answer that they had no legal obligation to effect the cash-out merger during the one-year period. While that may be so, the principle announced in *Schnell v. Chris-Craft Industries* establishes that inequitable conduct will not be protected merely because it is legal. 285 A.2d at 439. At the very least the facts alleged import a form of overreaching, and in the context of entire fairness they deserve more considered analysis than can be accorded them on a motion to dismiss.

Similarly, the plaintiffs' pleas arising from the language in Olin's Schedule 13D (referred to by the trial court as the claim for promissory estoppel) should not have been dismissed on the ground that appraisal was the only remedy available to the plaintiffs challenging the entire fairness of the merger.

IV.

In conclusion, we find that the trial court erred in dismissing the plaintiffs' actions for failure to state a claim upon which relief could be granted. As we read the complaints and the proposed amendments, they assert a conscious intent by Olin, as the majority shareholder of Hunt, to deprive the Hunt minority of the same bargain that Olin made with Hunt's former majority shareholder, Turner and Newall. But for Olin's allegedly unfair manipulation, the plaintiffs contend, this bargain also was due them. In short, the defendants are charged with bad faith which goes beyond issues of "mere inadequacy of price." *Cole v. National Cash Credit Association*, Del. Ch., 156 A. 183, 187-88 (1931). In *Weinberger* we specifically relied on this aspect of *Cole* in acknowledging the imperfections of an appraisal where circumstances of this sort are present. *See* 457 A.2d at 714.

---

[7]   As we noted in *Weinberger*, the use of an independent negotiating committee of outside directors may have significant advantages to the majority stockholder in defending suits of this type. *See* 457 A.2d at 709-11; 709 n.7. The efficacy of that procedure was recently indicated by our opinion in *Rosenblatt v. Getty Oil Company*, Del. Supr., 493 A.2d 929, 937-39 (1985). However, we recognize that there may be serious practical problems in the use of such a committee as even *Rosenblatt* demonstrated. *See* 493 A.2d at 933-36. Thus, we do not announce any rule, even in the context of a motion to dismiss, that the absence of such a bargaining structure will preclude dismissal in cases bottomed on claims of unfair dealing.

Necessarily, this will require the Court of Chancery to closely focus upon *Weinberger's* mandate of entire fairness based on a careful analysis of both the fair price and fair dealing aspects of a transaction. *See* 457 A.2d at 711, 714. We recognize that this can present certain practical problems, since stockholders may invariably claim that the price being offered is the result of unfair dealings. However, we think that plaintiffs will be tempered in this approach by the prospect that an ultimate judgment in defendant's favor may have cost plaintiffs their unperfected appraisal rights. Moreover, our courts are not without a degree of sophistication in such matters. A balance must be struck between sustaining complaints averring faithless acts, which taken as true would constitute breaches of fiduciary duties that are reasonably related to and have a substantial impact upon the price offered, and properly dismissing those allegations questioning judgment factors of valuation. *Cole v. National Cash Credit Association*, 156 A. at 187-88. Otherwise, we face the anomalous result that stockholders who are eliminated without appraisal rights can bring class actions, while in other cases a squeezed-out minority is limited to an appraisal, provided there was no deception, regardless of the degree of procedural unfairness employed to take their shares. Without that balance, *Weinberger's* concern for entire fairness loses all force.

Accordingly, the decision of the Court of Chancery dismissing these consolidated class actions is REVERSED. The matter is REMANDED with directions that the plaintiffs be permitted to file their proposed amendments to the pleadings.

KAHN v. LYNCH COMMUNICATION SYSTEMS, INC.

Delaware Supreme Court
669 A.2d 79 (1995)

WALSH, Justice:

This is the second appeal in this shareholder litigation after a Court of Chancery ruling in favor of the defendants. The underlying dispute arises from a cash-out merger of Lynch Communications System, Inc. ("Lynch") into a subsidiary of Alcatel USA, Inc. ("Alcatel").

* * *

I

The facts underlying the derivative claims are set forth extensively in [*Kahn v. Lynch Communication Systems, Inc.*, Del. Supr., 638 A.2d 1110, 1112-13 (1994) ("*Lynch I*")] and we summarize them briefly for present purposes.

Lynch, a Delaware corporation, designed and manufactured electronic telecommunications equipment, primarily for sale to telephone operating companies. Alcatel, a holding company, is a subsidiary of Alcatel (S.A.), a French company involved in public telecommunications, business communications, electronics, and optronics. Alcatel (S.A.), in turn, is a subsidiary of Compagnie Generale d'Electricite ("CGE"), a French corporation with operations in energy, transportation, telecommunications and business systems.

In 1981, Alcatel acquired 30.6% of Lynch's common stock pursuant to a stock purchase agreement. As part of that agreement, Lynch amended its certificate of incorporation to require an 80% affirmative vote to approve any business combination. By the time of the events leading to the contested merger, Alcatel owned 43.3% of Lynch's outstanding stock and designated five of the eleven directors on Lynch's board of directors, two of the three members of the executive committee, and two of the four members of the compensation committee.

In the spring of 1986, Lynch determined that it needed to acquire fiber optics technology in order to remain competitive. Lynch management identified a target company, Telco Systems, Inc. ("Telco"), that had the needed technology. Telco was apparently amenable to acquisition by Lynch. Lynch had to obtain Alcatel's consent, however, since the supermajority voting provision gave Alcatel an effective veto over any business combination. Exercising this power, Alcatel vetoed the transaction and instead proposed a combination of Lynch and Celwave Systems, Inc. ("Celwave"), an indirect subsidiary of CGE that possessed fibre optics technology. Ellsworth F. Dertinger ("Dertinger"), chairman of the board and CEO of Lynch, stated that Celwave would not be of interest to Lynch if Celwave were not owned by Alcatel. Nevertheless, the Lynch Board unanimously adopted a resolution that established a committee of independent directors (the "Independent Committee") to negotiate with Celwave and recommend the terms and conditions on which a combination would be based.

On October 24, 1986, Alcatel's investment banking firm, Dillon, Read & Co., Inc. ("Dillon, Read") made a presentation to the Independent Committee in which it explained the benefits of a Lynch/Celwave combination and proposed a stock-for-stock merger. The Independent Committee's investment advisors reviewed the Dillon, Read report and placed a significantly lower value on Celwave than had Dillon, Read. Consequently, the Independent Committee decided that the proposal was unattractive to Lynch and made a recommendation against the Lynch/Celwave combination.

Reacting to the Independent Committee's recommendation, Alcatel withdrew the Celwave proposal and instead offered to acquire the Lynch shares it did not already own at $14 cash per share. In response, at its November 7th board meeting, the Lynch directors revised the mandate of the Independent Committee and authorized the same directors to negotiate the cash merger offer with Alcatel. Meeting on the same day, the Independent Committee decided that $14 per share was inadequate.

On November 12, the Independent Committee made a counteroffer of $17 per share. The parties negotiated for approximately two weeks, during which time Alcatel's highest offer was $15.50 per share. On November 24, 1986, the Independent Committee met with its financial and legal advisors and were informed by one of the committee members that Alcatel was "ready to proceed with an unfriendly tender at a lower price" if the $15.50 offer was not accepted. The Independent Committee, after consulting with its financial and legal advisors, voted unanimously to recommend that the Lynch board approve Alcatel's $15.50 cash per share merger. The Lynch board met later that day and, with Alcatel's nominees abstaining, approved the merger.

Kahn, a Lynch shareholder, brought suit, later certified as a class action, challenging Alcatel's acquisition of Lynch through a tender offer and cash-out merger. Kahn alleged the merger to be unfair in that Alcatel, as a controlling shareholder, breached its fiduciary duties to Lynch's minority shareholders. Specifically, Kahn charged that Alcatel dictated the terms of the merger; made false, misleading, and inadequate disclosures; and paid an unfair price.

[In the previous appeal, *Lynch I*, the Delaware Supreme Court concluded that Alcatel should be treated as a controlling shareholder even though it owned only 43.3% of Lynch's outstanding common stock, because Alcatel exercised "actual control over Lynch by dominating its corporate affairs." 638 A.2d at 1115. However, the Delaware Supreme Court held that the Chancery Court had improperly shifted to the plaintiff the burden of showing a lack of entire fairness. The court reasoned that such a shift in the burden of proof was not appropriate since the Independent Committee's negotiations did not result in something approximating arm's length negotiations. In particular, the court held that "the ability of the Committee effectively to negotiate at arm's length was compromised by Alcatel's threats to proceed with a hostile tender offer [at a lower price] if the $15.50 price [proposed by Alcatel] was not approved by the Committee." *Id.* at 1121. Accordingly, the case was remanded for a "redetermination of the entire fairness of the cash out merger to Kahn and the other Lynch minority shareholders with the burden of proof remaining on Alcatel, the dominant and interested shareholder." *Id.* at 1122.]

* * *

After [re-]examining the transaction for entire fairness [on remand], the Court of Chancery once again found for the defendants, holding that they had carried the burden of showing the entire fairness of the transaction. *See Cinerama, Inc. v. Technicolor, Inc.*, Del. Ch., 663 A.2d 1134, 1144 (1994). . . .

* * *

In this appeal from the 1995 decision of the Court of Chancery, Kahn raises several issues. First, he contends that the finding of fair dealing was inconsistent with our opinion in *Lynch I* and unsupported by the record. Specifically, Kahn asserts that the coercion of the Independent Committee constituted a *per se* breach of fiduciary duty which strongly compels a finding that the transaction was not entirely fair. In addition, the plaintiff charges that the initiation, timing and negotiation of the merger were unfair and also require a finding of unfair dealing.

Second, the plaintiff contends that Alcatel breached its fiduciary duty to Lynch's stockholders by not fully disclosing its conduct in negotiating the merger. Thus, according to the plaintiff, the Court of Chancery erred by not finding a breach of the duty of disclosure. Such a finding, it is argued, is itself proof of unfair dealing.

The third claim made by Kahn is a challenge to the determination that they received a fair price for their shares. Kahn insists that the evidence submitted by Alcatel did not sustain their burden of showing that the price was fair.

II

* * *

A.

At the outset we must confront the disagreement between the parties concerning the extent to which our decision in *Lynch I* limited the scope of the Court of Chancery's reexamination of the record on remand. Kahn argues that this Court's characterization of Alcatel's conduct as "coercive" was not accorded adequate consideration by the trial court in its entire fairness calculation. Alcatel contends to the contrary that this Court's evaluation of the record in *Lynch I* was done in the context of determining which party had the burden of proving entire fairness and that the Court of Chancery, on remand, was restricted procedurally, but not substantively, in its view of the trial evidence.

While we agree that our decision in *Lynch I* limited the range of findings available to the Court of Chancery upon remand, our previous review of the record focused upon the threshold question of burden of proof. Our reversal on burden of proof left open the question whether the transaction was entirely fair. *Lynch I*, 638 A.2d at 1122. . . .

* * *

B.

This Court will now review the Court of Chancery's entire fairness analysis upon remand. *Accord Cinerama, Inc. v. Technicolor, Inc.*, Del. Supr., 663 A.2d at 1172. The record reflects that the Court of Chancery followed this Court's mandate by applying a unified approach to its entire fairness examination. *Lynch I*, 638 A.2d at 1115. In doing so, the Court of Chancery properly considered "how the board of directors discharged all of its fiduciary duties with regard to each aspect of the non-bifurcated components of entire fairness: fair dealing and fair price." *Cinerama, Inc. v. Technicolor, Inc.*, Del. Supr., 663 A.2d at 1172.

In addressing the fair dealing component of the transaction, the Court of Chancery determined that the initiation and timing of the transactions were responsive to Lynch's needs. This conclusion was based on the fact that Lynch's marketing strategy was handicapped by the lack of a fiber optic technology. Alcatel proposed the merger with Celwave to remedy this competitive weakness but Lynch management and the non-Alcatel directors did not believe this combination would be beneficial to Lynch. Dertinger, Lynch's CEO, suggested to Alcatel that, under the circumstances, a cash merger with Alcatel will be preferable to a Celwave merger. Thus, the Alcatel offer to acquire the minority interests in Lynch was viewed as an alternative to the disfavored Celwave transaction.

Kahn argues that the Telco acquisition, which Lynch management strongly supported, was vetoed by Alcatel to force Lynch to accept Celwave as a merger partner or agree to a cash out merger with Alcatel. The benefits of the Telco transaction, however, are clearly debatable. Telco was not profitable and had a limited fiber optic capability. There is no assurance that Lynch's shareholders would have benefitted from the acquisition. More to the point, the timing of a merger transaction cannot be viewed solely from the perspective of the acquired entity. A majority shareholder is naturally motivated by economic self-interest in initiating a transaction. Otherwise, there is no reason to do it. Thus, mere initiation by the acquirer is not reprehensible so long as the controlling shareholder does not gain a financial advantage at the expense of the minority. *Cinerama, Inc., v. Technicolor, Inc.*, Del. Supr., 663 A.2d 1156, 1172 (1995); *Jedwab v. MGM Grand Hotels, Inc.*, Del. Ch., 509 A.2d 584, 599 (1986).

In support of its claim of coercion, Kahn contends that Alcatel timed its merger offer, with a thinly-veiled threat of using its controlling position to force the result, to take advantage of the opportunity to buy Lynch on the cheap. As will be discussed at greater length in our fair price analysis, *infra*, Lynch was experiencing a difficult and rapidly changing competitive situation. Its current financial results reflected that fact. Although its stock was trading at low levels, this may simply have been a reflection of its competitive problems. Alcatel is not to be faulted for taking advantage of the objective reality of Lynch's financial situation. Thus the mere fact that the transaction was initiated at Alcatel's discretion, does not dictate a finding of unfairness in the absence of a determination that the minority shareholders of Lynch were harmed by the timing. The Court of Chancery rejected such a claim and we agree.

C.

With respect to the negotiations and structure of the transaction, the Court of Chancery, while acknowledging that the Court in *Lynch I* found the negotiations coercive, commented that the negotiations "certainly were no less fair than if there had been no negotiations at all" 1995 decision at 4. The court noted that a committee of non-Alcatel directors negotiated an increase in price from $14 per share to $15.50. The committee also retained two investment banking firms who were well acquainted with Lynch's prospects based on their work on the Celwave proposal. Moreover, the committee had the benefit of outside legal counsel.

It is true that the committee and the Board agreed to a price which at least one member of the committee later opined was not a fair price. *Lynch I*, 638 A.2d at 1118. But there is no requirement of unanimity in such matters either at the Independent Committee level or by the Board. A finding of unfair dealing based on lack of unanimity could discourage the use of special committees in majority dominated cash-out mergers. Here Alcatel could have presented a merger offer directly to the Lynch Board, which it controlled, and received a quick approval. Had it done so, of course, it would have born the burden of demonstrating entire fairness in the event the transaction was later questioned. *See Weinberger v. UOP*, Del. Supr., 457 A.2d 701 (1983). Where, ultimately, it has been required to assume the same burden, it should fare no worse in a judicial review of the fairness of its negotiations with the Independent Committee.

Kahn asserts that the Court of Chancery did not properly consider our finding of coercion in *Lynch I*. Generally, as in this case, the burden rests on the party that engaged in coercive conduct to demonstrate the equity of their actions. *Lynch I*, 638 A.2d at 1121; *Unitrin, Inc. v. American General Corp.*, Del. Supr., 651 A.2d 1361, 1373, 1387 (1995) (holding that burden rests on board of directors which has taken draconian, *e.g.*, coercive, measures in response to hostile tender offer). Kahn challenges the Court of Chancery's finding of fair dealing by relying upon the holding in *Ivanhoe Partners v. Newmont Min. Corp.*, Del. Ch., 533 A.2d 585, 605-06 (1987), *aff'd*, Del. Supr., 535 A.2d 1334 (1988), for the proposition that coercion creates liability *per se*. *Ivanhoe* makes clear, however, that to be actionable, the coercive conduct directed at selling shareholders must be a "material" influence on the decision to sell. *Id.*; *see also Eisenberg v. Chicago Milwaukee Corp.*, Del. Ch., 537 A.2d 1051, 1061-62 (1987).

Where other economic forces are at work and more likely produced the decision to sell, as the Court of Chancery determined here, the specter of coercion may not be deemed material with respect to the transaction as a whole, and will not prevent a finding of entire fairness. In this case, no shareholder was treated differently in the transaction from any other shareholder nor subjected to a two-tiered or squeeze-out treatment. *See, e.g., Unocal Corp. v. Mesa Petroleum Co.*, Del. Supr., 493 A.2d 946, 956 (1985). Alcatel offered cash for all the minority shares and paid cash for all shares tendered. Clearly there was no coercion exerted which was material to this aspect of the transaction, and thus no finding of *per se* liability is required.

D.

As previously noted, in *Lynch I* this Court did not address the fair price aspect of the merger transaction since our remand required a reexamination of fair dealing at the trial level. The parties had presented extensive evidence at the original trial concerning the value of Lynch. Upon remand the Court of Chancery reassessed that evidence with the burden on Alcatel to prove the fairness of the cash-out merger price. *Accord Cinerama, Inc. v. Technicolor, Inc.*, Del. Ch., 663 A.2d 1134, 1142-44 (1994).

In considering whether Alcatel had discharged its burden with respect to fairness of price, the Court of Chancery placed reliance upon the testimony of Michael McCarty, a senior officer at Dillon Read, who prepared Alcatel's proposal to the Independent Committee. He valued Lynch at $15.50 to $16.00 per share—a range determined by using the closing market price of $11 per share of October 17, 1988 and adding a merger premium of 41 to 46%. Dillon Read's valuation had been prepared in October, 1986 in connection with the Lynch/Celwave combination proposed at a time when Lynch was experiencing a downward trend in earnings and prospects. Subsequent to the October valuation, Lynch management revised its three year forecast downward to reflect disappointing third quarter results.

The Court of Chancery also considered the valuation reports issued by both Kidder Peabody and Thompson McKinnon who were retained by the Independent Committee at the time of the Celwave proposal in October. At that time both bankers valued Lynch at $16.50 to $17.50 per share. These valuations, however, were made in response to Alcatel's Celwave proposal and were not, strictly speaking, fairness opinions. When Lynch later revised downward its financial forecasts based on poor third quarter operating results both firms opined that the Alcatel merger price was fair as of the later merger date.

* * *

The Court of Chancery's finding that Alcatel had successfully born the initial burden of proving the fairness of the merger price is fully supportable by the evidence tendered by the experts retained by Alcatel and by the Independent Committee. . . . Although the burden of proving fair price had shifted to Alcatel, once a sufficient showing of fair value of the company was presented, the party attacking the merger was required to come forward with sufficient credible evidence to persuade the finder of fact of the merit of a greater figure proposed. . . . The Court of Chancery was not persuaded that Kahn had presented evidence of sufficient quality to prove the inadequacy of the merger price. We find that ruling to be logically determined and supported by the evidence and accordingly affirm.

III

We next address the remaining question decided by the Court of Chancery in its 1993 decision but not resolved in *Lynch I*—whether Alcatel violated the duty of disclosure in its Offer to Purchase directed to Lynch shareholders. Kahn asserts that in light of this Court's finding that Alcatel used coercion to gain approval of the merger price by the Lynch board, the Offer to Purchase contained material omissions. To the contrary, Alcatel maintains that in both the Offer to Purchase and in its Schedule 13D filed with the Securities and Exchange Commission, Alcatel fully and clearly indicated that its option included a tender offer directly to stockholders if negotiations with the Lynch Board proved unsuccessful.

* * *

We begin our examination of the record below with the allegedly deficient documents. The Offer to Purchase, distributed to Lynch shareholders at the Board's behest and apparently under Alcatel's direction, described Alcatel's negotiation stance as follows:

> Discussions between representatives of Dillon Read on behalf of Alcatel USA and the Independent Committee and its financial advisors continued during the period from November 12 to November 20, 1986. During such discussions representatives of Alcatel USA informed the Independent Committee that, in the event the parties could not reach an agreement for a transaction, Alcatel USA would consider the options that were available to it at that time, including among other things, making an offer directly to the stockholders of the Company.

* * *

Kahn argues that Alcatel's description of its negotiating options was incomplete and misleading and should have conveyed the additional information that its "making an offer" would have been "far below the merger price of $15.50 per share." The narrow question thus becomes whether a reasonable shareholder would have considered the additional language "as having significantly altered the total mix of information made available." *Arnold v. Bancorp*, 650 A.2d at 1277.

Although the additional language may have rendered the Offer to Purchase somewhat more informative by "closing the circle" on the full extent of Alcatel's options, we agree with the Court of Chancery that such additional language was not required to describe the extent of Alcatel's bargaining power. . . . There can be little doubt that Alcatel intended to acquire the entire equity interest in Lynch and the description of negotiations contained in the Offer to Purchase described its efforts and the responses of the Lynch Board and the Independent Committee. . . .

* * *

The Court of Chancery's finding of no disclosure violation, which we endorse, though not determinative of entire fairness, is of "persuasive substantive significance." *Cinerama Inc. v. Technicolor, Inc.*, Del. Supr., 663 A.2d 1156, 1176 (1995). Such a determination precludes the award of damages *per se* bears directly upon the manner in which stockholder approval was obtained, and places this case in the category of "nonfraudulent transactions" in which price may be the preponderant consideration. *Id.* (quoting *Weinberger v. UOP, Inc.*, 457 A.2d at 711). Although the merger was not conditioned on a majority of the minority vote, we note that more than 94 percent of the shares were tendered in response to Alcatel's offer.

IV

. . . We find no error in the trial court's application of legal standards and accordingly affirm. . . .

NOTES AND QUESTIONS

(1) **When may plaintiff challenge fairness?** What kinds of cases might fall within *Weinberger*'s "fraud" and "self-dealing" categories? *Rabkin. Nebel v. Southwest Bancorp, Inc.*[61] stated that appraisal was not an adequate remedy "in merger cases that involve 'fraud, misrepresentation, self dealing, deliberate waste of corporate assets or gross and palpable overreaching,' because such conduct 'present[s] issues which an appraisal cannot address'" and because "misdisclosures or nondisclosures of material facts might warrant injunctive relief that would prevent the merger from taking place"; and in "'[c]ertain types of unfair dealing [cases], although not involving fraud or deception, [that are] . . . so egregious as to make it inequitable to relegate the minority shareholders to the appraisal remedy, even though as a practical matter the unfair dealing impacts only the merger price.'" ALI *Principles* § 7.25 makes the appraisal remedy exclusive in controlled mergers where the directors approving the transaction have an adequate basis for believing that the consideration offered to the minority constitutes fair value, disclosure is made to the minority shareholders, and the transaction is approved in accordance with law and the corporation's charter documents. From a policy standpoint, to what extent does *Weinberger*'s liberalized standard of valuation address the policy arguments against appraisal exclusivity discussed above in Subsection [A][1]?

Should plaintiffs also be permitted to challenge the fairness of short-form mergers under Del. G.C.L. § 253, just as in long-form mergers under § 251, the provision involved in *Rabkin*? *Glassman v. Unocal Exploration Corp.*[62] rejected a challenge to fair process and held appraisal was exclusive where a 96% majority shareholder formed a special committee of three independent directors to negotiate the merger price on behalf of the subsidiary's minority. The court reasoned:[63]

> . . . Under settled principles, a parent corporation and its directors
> undertaking a short-form merger are self-dealing fiduciaries who should be
> required to establish entire fairness, including fair dealing and fair price.

---

[61] 1999 WL 135259 (Del. Ch. 1999).

[62] 777 A.2d 242 (Del. 2001).

[63] *Id.* at 247-48.

The problem is that § 253 authorizes a summary procedure that is inconsistent with any reasonable notion of fair dealing. In a short-form merger, there is no agreement of merger negotiated by two companies; there is only a unilateral act—a decision by the parent company that its 90% owned subsidiary shall no longer exist as a separate entity. The minority stockholders receive no advance notice of the merger; their directors do not consider or approve it; and there is no vote. Those who object are given the right to obtain fair value for their shares through appraisal.

The equitable claim plainly conflicts with the statute. If a corporate fiduciary follows the truncated process authorized by § 253, it will not be able to establish the fair dealing prong of entire fairness. If, instead, the corporate fiduciary sets up negotiating committees, hires independent financial and legal experts, etc., then it will have lost the very benefit provided by the statute—a simple, fast and inexpensive process for accomplishing a merger. We resolve this conflict by giving effect the intent of the General Assembly. In order to serve its purpose, § 253 must be construed to obviate the requirement to establish entire fairness.

Unocal Exploration is potentially useful even to majority shareholders who own less than 90% of a subsidiary's stock, since such shareholders could freeze out the minority by combining a tender offer for 90% of the subsidiary's stock with a short-form merger under Del. G.C.L. § 253. The tender offer would be immune from fairness challenge under *Solomon v. Pathe Communications*,[64] which dismissed claims that directors breached their duty of fair dealing by not opposing a tender offer by the controlling shareholder at an allegedly inadequate price, while the short-form merger would be immune under *Unocal Exploration*. *Solomon* concluded that, "in the absence of coercion or disclosure violations, the adequacy of the price in a voluntary tender offer cannot be an issue."[65]

(2) **Post-*Weinberger* methods of valuation.** How does the court's new appraisal standard differ from the "Delaware block approach" discussed in Section 15.01[C]? Note that, even after *Weinberger*, the courts continue to be skeptical about the "discounted cash flow" method of valuation involved in *Weinberger* itself. In the *Weinberger* remand,[66] the court again rejected the plaintiff's evidence as to discounted cash flow. (The court also rejected plaintiff's rescission damages theory and awarded damages of only $1 per share.)[67] Also *Weinberger* apparently permits some but not all

---

[64]   672 A.2d 35 (Del. 1996).

[65]   *Id.* at 39.

[66]   10 DEL. J. CORP. L. 945 (Del. Ch. 1985).

[67]   For an exhaustive example of post-*Weinberger* valuation in which the court rejected a discounted cash flow valuation, see *Pinson v. Campbell-Taggart, Inc.*, 14 DEL. J. CORP. L. 1095 (Del. Ch. 1989). For a post-*Weinberger* application of discounted cash-flow, see *Cavalier Oil Corp. v. Harnett*, 564 A.2d 1137 (Del. 1989). For other post-*Weinberger* valuation cases, see *Kleinwort Benson Ltd. v. Silgan Corp.*, 20 DEL. J. CORP. L. 1079 (Del. Ch. 1995) (approving dis-

merger gains to be included in fair value. *Cede & Co. v. Technicolor, Inc.*[68] holds that post-merger gains must be included at least to the extent that the plan producing the gains was conceived and implemented by a controlling shareholder prior to the merger. In *Technicolor*, MacAndrews & Forbes Group (MAF) had acquired 82% of Technicolor in a tender offer. Immediately after acquiring control (but before the freeze-out merger), MAF began implementing a pre-conceived plan for how certain Technicolor assets would be sold. The court held that the fair value of the dissenter's shares had to be determined under MAF's business plan, rather than under the failed business plan in place prior to the tender offer. The court rejected policy arguments like those discussed in Note 2 following *Universal City Studios* in Section 15.01[C] because fair value under Delaware's appraisal statute had to be determined *as of the date of the merger*. Consider whether the court in *Technicolor* might have reached a different result if MAF had waited until after the merger to begin implementing its new business plan.[69] For a discussion of newer statutory approaches to "fair value," see Note 8 below.

(3) **Purpose of the valuation.** Should the purpose of a stock valuation affect the outcome—*e.g.*, where the valuation is being made in an appraisal proceeding rather than a breach of fiduciary duty action? In *M.P.M. Enterprises v. Gilbert*,[70] dissenters in an appraisal action contended that the court should have considered the merger price and prior offers for the corporation in determining the fair value of their shares. The dissenters relied on an earlier decision where the court had considered such evidence in connection with claims of minority shareholders that a board had breached its fiduciary duties in accepting an unfair merger price. The court rejected the dissenters' argument, concluding that "[a] fair price in the context of a breach of fiduciary duty claim will not always be a fair value in the context of determining going concern value" and that, "in an appraisal action, [the] merger price [and prior offers] must be accompanied by evidence tending to show that [they] represent[] the going concern value of the company rather than just the value of the company to one specific buyer."[71] Why should plaintiffs

---

counted cash flow and comparative market analysis methods of valuation, but holding that comparative market analysis value must be adjusted upward to compensate for inherent minority discount in market analysis, but not to reflect a control premium); *In the Matter of Shell Oil Co.*, 607 A.2d 1213 (Del. 1992) (discussing several valuation methods employed by parties' experts and urging chancery court to appoint neutral experts in stock appraisal cases); *In re Radiology Associates, Inc.*, 611 A.2d 485 (Del. Ch. 1991) (approving discounted cash flow value; also holding against awarding premium for tax advantages of Subchapter S because not "generally considered acceptable in the financial community," criticizing defendant's Delaware block valuation for failure to include asset valuation for goodwill and expectation of future business, and rejecting earnings approach because reliance on historical earnings unwarranted where reliable projections available).

   [68]   684 A.2d 289 (Del. 1996).

   [69]   For an application of the valuation principle stated in *Technicolor*, see *Onti, Inc. v. Integra Bank*, 1999 Del. Ch. LEXIS 130, 1999 WL 377829 (Del. Ch. 1999) (price paid in acquisition that followed shortly after cash-out merger could be taken into account in appraisal proceeding because plan for acquisition was effectively in place at the time of the cash-out merger).

   [70]   731 A.2d 790 (Del. 1999).

   [71]   *Id.* at 797.

in a breach of fiduciary duty action get a remedy based on the best price available, while appraisal dissenters get something less? *M.P.M.* arguably suggests that appraisal has a different purpose than ensuring that managers get the best possible price for shareholders in mergers and other corporate combinations. *See* **Letsou**.

(4) **Role of procedure in merger fairness.** As discussed in *Weinberger*, courts examine procedure as well as substance in assessing the fairness of a merger. Procedures are significant both in determining the placement of the burden and whether the burden of proof has been discharged. *See* ALI *Principles* § 7.25, discussed in the introduction to Subsection [B] above. In general, compare the procedures employed in *Sterling* and *Weinberger*. Would the *Weinberger* court have come to a different conclusion with respect to procedural fairness under the facts in *Sterling*?

(5) **Approval of controlled mergers by a majority of the minority shareholders.** Do you agree with the approach in *Weinberger* as to the effect of approval by a majority of the minority shareholders? **Brudney & Chirelstein** (*Fair Shares*, at 299-300) point out that, even where shareholders unaffiliated with the other party to the merger control enough votes to block the merger, the majority controls through the board the proxy machinery and which merger proposals are submitted to the shareholders. It has also been argued that a shareholder vote cannot ensure fairness since only direct negotiators are in a position to determine what the controlling shareholder is willing to pay.[72] Do these considerations support placing the burden of justification on the defendant even in the face of a majority-of-minority vote? *See also* the discussion of shareholder voting on interested transactions in Section 9.04[B][3].

(6) **Independent negotiating committees.** Another device that is intended to protect minority shareholders and ensure court approval is negotiation by a committee of directors who have no direct or indirect financial ties with the controlling shareholders. *See Puma*, Section 9.04[B][2] and footnote 7 to the *Weinberger* opinion. Should mergers negotiated by such committees be subject to less judicial scrutiny than other controlled mergers? If so, what standard of independence should the negotiating committee have to meet, and how should use of the committee affect the parent's disclosure obligation? Specifically, if Signal had employed an independent negotiating committee, should the *Weinberger* transaction have been upheld even without disclosure of the critical Arledge-Chittea memo?

Lynch I[73] (discussed in *Kahn v. Lynch Communication Systems, Inc.*, above) held that approval of a merger by an independent committee of directors shifts the burden of proof from the controlling or dominating shareholder to the challenging shareholder-plaintiff, but does not change the applicable legal standard of review from "entire fair-

---

[72]   *See* Chazen, *Fairness from a Financial Point of View in Acquisitions of Public Companies: Is "Third Party Sale Value" the Appropriate Standard?*, 36 Bus. Law. 1439, 1475 (1981).

[73]   638 A.2d 1110 (Del. 1994).

ness" to "business judgment."[74] However, the court clarified that the mere existence of an independent negotiating committee would not itself shift the burden of proof. Instead, the court concluded that the burden of proving entire fairness would only shift if the controlling or dominating shareholder could demonstrate: "[f]irst, [that it did] not dictate the terms of the merger . . . [;] [and] [s]econd, [that] the special committee [had] real bargaining power that it [could] exercise with the majority shareholder on an arm's-length basis."[75] The court held that these standards had not been satisfied because "the ability of the Committee effectively to negotiate at arm's length was compromised by [the dominating shareholder's] threats to proceed with a hostile tender offer [at a lower price] if the $15.50 price was not approved by the Committee."[76]

But even though *Lynch I* concluded that the independent committee lacked real bargaining power, the *Kahn* court nonetheless upheld the cash out of Lynch Communication's public shareholders. The court concluded that a cash out merger that is adequately disclosed to, and approved by, a majority of the minority shareholders constitutes a "'non-fraudulent transaction[]' in which price may be the preponderant consideration." If price is the "preponderant consideration" where a majority of minority shareholder approval is obtained, does a controlling shareholder who conditions a cash out merger on such approval obtain any real benefit from making use of an independent committee?

(7) **The use of independent appraisers.** Consider the extent to which the court in *Sterling* relied on the Haslam report. The independence of the appraiser has been challenged in some cases on the ground of the appraiser's financial self interest in the transaction. For example, in *Weinberger v. UOP, Inc.*,[77] the court held that the appraiser's investment banking relationship with the controlling shareholder was insufficient to show lack of independence. Similarly, *Tanzer v. International General Industries, Inc.*[78] held that facts that the appraiser stood to lose a $200,000 fee if the merger was not approved and that the SEC had questioned the appraiser's independence were insufficient to show that the price recommended by the appraiser was unfair.

(8) **Statutory approaches to "fair value."** Compare with *Weinberger* the following language from New York Business Corporation Law § 623(h)(4):

> In fixing the fair value of the shares, the court shall consider the nature of the
> transaction giving rise to the shareholder's right to receive payment for shares

---

[74] *But cf. In re Western National Shareholders Litigation*, 26 DEL. J. CORP. L. 806 (Del. Ch. 2000) (where 46% shareholder is not a controlling shareholder under *Lynch I*, approval of merger by independent committee results in application of business judgment rule, even where majority of full board of directors is conflicted).

[75] 638 A.2d at 1117 (quoting *Rabkin v. Olin Corp.*, 1990 WL 47648, slip op. at 14-15 (Del. Ch. 1990)).

[76] *Id.* The Delaware Chancery Court has criticized special committees for selecting financial and legal advisors who were recommended by parties beholden to the controlling shareholder. *See Kahn v. Dairy Mart Convenience Stores*, 21 DEL. J. CORP. L. 1143 (Del. Ch. 1996); *Kahn v. Tremont Corporation*, 21 DEL. J. CORP. L. 1161 (Del. Ch. 1996).

[77] 426 A.2d 1333 (Del. Ch. 1981), *rev'd and remanded on other grounds*, 457 A.2d 701 (Del. 1983).

[78] 402 A.2d 382 (Del. Ch. 1979) (on remand).

and its effects on the corporation and its shareholders, the concepts and methods then customary in the relevant securities and financial markets for determining fair value of shares of a corporation engaging in a similar transaction under comparable circumstances and all other relevant factors.[79]

The Model Act dissenters' rights provision states that "fair value" includes merger gains when "exclusion would be inequitable." *See* MBCA § 13.01(3). The Official Comment to the subsection says that "[t]he purpose of this exception . . . is to permit consideration of factors similar to those approved by the Supreme Court of Delaware in *Weinberger v. UOP, Inc.* . . . ."

ALI *Principles* § 7.22 proposes the use of "customary valuation concepts and techniques generally employed in the relevant securities and financial markets for similar businesses" and does not exclude merger gains. The Comments to Section 7.22 provide that, if the transaction is with a management group or controlling shareholders, the court should give substantial weight to the highest reasonable third-party price for the entire corporation, including a proportionate share of merger gains, unless allocating these gains to the dissenters is unreasonable under the circumstances. In disinterested transactions, the price accepted by the board is presumed to represent fair value, and the presumption can be rebutted only by clear and convincing evidence.

(9) **Statutory approaches to freezeouts.** In rejecting *Singer*, the Delaware Supreme Court in *Weinberger* appears to reject special rules for freeze-out mergers. Compare the approach to freeze-outs taken by the following statutes:

California

California prohibits freezeout mergers with majority-owned subsidiaries unless the merger is approved by a state agency or the parent owns 90% of each class of the subsidiary. *See* Calif. Corp. Code §§ 1101 and 1101.1.

Companies Act

England's Companies Act of 1985, §§ 428-30, permits a bidder whose offer was accepted by holders of at least 90% of the target's shares (other than those previously owned by the bidder) to require the holders of the remaining shares to sell their stock on the same terms as were offered to the accepting shareholders. If the bidder was a 10% holder prior to the offer, the freezeout must be approved not only by holders of 90% of the shares not already held by the bidder, but also by 75% of the shareholders. If the bidder has acquired 90% of the shares of the company, the remaining shareholders may require the bidder to purchase their shares.

---

[79] For an application of the New York statute, see *Cawley v. SCM Corp.*, 72 N.Y.2d 465, 534 N.Y.S.2d 344, 530 N.E.2d 1264 (1988) (holding that the corporation's increased tax deduction resulting from cash-out of incentive stock options in the merger should be taken into account in determining "fair value").

New Jersey

New Jersey § 14A: 10-9 is similar in some respects to § 209 of the Companies Act. Under the New Jersey provision, a corporation may acquire shares of another corporation by mailing an offer to all target shareholders. If holders of at least 90% of the target's shares (other than those previously held by the offeror) accept the offer within 120 days, the offeror must notify the remaining shareholders that they must either accept the offer or dissent and obtain the fair value of their shares. Shareholders who do not demand fair value within 20 days of the mailing of the notice are deemed to have accepted the offer. There is no provision for court-ordered relief from the provisions of the statute.

Evaluate each of these statutory approaches in light of the materials in Subsection 15.02[D].

PROBLEMS

(1) How, if at all, would your answer to the Problem at the end of Section 15.01[C] be different if Delaware law applied and the case were being decided after *Weinberger*?

(2) Assume the same facts as in the Problem at the end of Section 15.01[C]. You are counsel for International. Advise the corporation as to the likelihood that the merger will be enjoined under Delaware law.

REFERENCES

Brudney & Chirelstein, *A Restatement of Corporate Freezeouts*, 87 YALE L.J. 1354 (1978).

Brudney & Chirelstein, *Fair Shares in Corporate Mergers and Takeovers*, 88 HARV. L. REV. 297 (1974).

Carney, *Fundamental Corporate Changes, Minority Shareholders, and Business Purposes*, 1980 AM. B. FOUND. RES. J. 69.

Letsou, *The Role of Appraisal in Corporate Law*, 39 B.C. L. REV. 1121 (1998).

Weiss, *The Law of Take Out Mergers: A Historical Perspective*, 56 N.Y.U. L. REV. 624 (1981).

§ 15.03 Remedies under the Federal Securities Laws

This Section discusses federal securities law remedies for shareholders aggrieved by corporate combinations. Federal remedies are important to plaintiffs not only because they offer the possibility of a substantive cause of action in situations in which no remedy is available under state law, but also because the procedures available in connection with federal causes of action may be more advantageous to plaintiffs than those applicable to state remedies. A federal remedy may offer, among other things, an escape from a state security for costs statute (*see* Section 10.04) as well as broader service of process and choice of venue provisions. To avoid these remedies, the corporate planner must structure a corporate transaction to avoid not only state, but federal liability.

[A] 1934 Act Liability for Misleading Proxy Materials

Section 14(a) of the 1934 Act requires full disclosure in connection with proxy solicitations, including those made to secure approval of corporate combinations. We have discussed the problem of materiality under § 14(a) (*see* Section 7.03[C]) and some of the issues in connection with the private civil remedy under that provision (*see* Section 7.03[D]).

Section 10(b) of the 1934 Act and SEC Rule 10b-5 apply to all misrepresentations and omissions in connection with purchases and sales of stock, including misrepresentations in proxy materials used to solicit votes for corporate transactions that involve purchases or sales of stock. The definition of a 10b-5 purchase or sale is discussed in Note 8 following *Santa Fe* in Section 15.03[B]. For present purposes, it is enough to note that the exchange of shares of the disappearing corporation for shares of the surviving corporation in a merger has been held to involve a 10b-5 purchase and sale.[80]

Mills v. Electric Auto-Lite Co.[81] held that a private action under § 14(a) would lie where, due to supermajority voting requirements, the controlling shareholder lacked sufficient votes to secure approval of a merger. An important question in a Rule 10b-5 or § 14(a) cause of action based on misleading proxy materials is whether a remedy will lie even in the "controlled merger" situation in which the parent corporation holds enough votes in the subsidiary to secure approval of a merger of the two corporations even without the additional votes solicited by the allegedly misleading proxy materials. While the fact that the merger is "controlled" would make it easier to obtain relief under state law, this circumstance makes relief more difficult to obtain under federal law because the misleading proxy materials—the basis of the federal remedy—may not have caused the transaction for which the remedy is being sought. The following case addresses this issue.

---

[80] *See SEC v. National Securities, Inc.*, 393 U.S. 453 (1969).

[81] 396 U.S. 375 (1970).

VIRGINIA BANKSHARES, INC. v. SANDBERG
United States Supreme Court
501 U.S. 1083 (1991)

Justice SOUTER delivered the opinion of the Court.

* * *

The questions before us are whether a statement couched in conclusory or qualitative terms purporting to explain directors' reasons for recommending certain corporate action can be materially misleading within the meaning of Rule 14a-9, and whether causation of damages compensable under § 14(a) can be shown by a member of a class of minority shareholders whose votes are not required by law or corporate bylaw to authorize the corporate action subject to the proxy solicitation. We hold that knowingly false statements of reasons may be actionable even though conclusory in form, but that respondents have failed to demonstrate the equitable basis required to extend the § 14(a) private action to such shareholders when any indication of congressional intent to do so is lacking.

I

In December 1986, First American Bankshares, Inc. (FABI), a bank holding company, began a "freeze-out" merger, in which the First American Bank of Virginia (Bank) eventually merged into Virginia Bankshares, Inc., (VBI), a wholly owned subsidiary of FABI. VBI owned 85% of the Bank's shares, the remaining 15% being in the hands of some 2,000 minority shareholders. FABI hired the investment banking firm of Keefe, Bruyette & Woods (KBW) to give an opinion on the appropriate price for shares of the minority holders, who would lose their interests in the Bank as a result of the merger. Based on market quotations and unverified information from FABI, KBW gave the Bank's executive committee an opinion that $42 a share would be a fair price for the minority stock. The executive committee approved the merger proposal at that price, and the full board followed suit.

Although Virginia law required only that such a merger proposal be submitted to a vote at a shareholders' meeting, and that the meeting be preceded by circulation of a statement of information to the shareholders, the directors nevertheless solicited proxies for voting on the proposal at the annual meeting set for April 21, 1987.[3] In their solicitation, the directors urged the proposal's adoption and stated they had approved the plan because of its opportunity for the minority shareholders to achieve a "high" value, which they elsewhere described as a "fair" price, for their stock.

Although most minority shareholders gave the proxies requested, respondent Sandberg did not, and after approval of the merger she sought damages. . . . She pleaded two counts, one for soliciting proxies in violation of § 14(a) and Rule 14a-9, and the other for breaching fiduciary duties owed to the minority shareholders under state law. . . . The jury awarded Sandberg $18 a share, having found that she would have received $60 if her stock had been valued adequately. . . .

---

[3]   Had the directors chosen to issue a statement instead of a proxy solicitation, they would have been subject to an SEC antifraud provision analogous to Rule 14a-9. *See* 17 CFR 240.14c-6 (1990). *See also* 15 U.S.C. § 78n(c).

II

[In this portion of the opinion, the Court held that statements made by the directors could be actionable under § 14(a) and Rule 14a-9. For a discussion of this portion of the Court's opinion, see Note 5 following *International Paper* in Section 7.03[C].]

III

The second issue before us, left open in *Mills v. Electric Auto-Lite Co.*, 396 U.S. at 385, n.7 is whether causation of damages compensable through the implied private right of action under § 14(a) can be demonstrated by a member of a class of minority shareholders whose votes are not required by law or corporate by-law to authorize the transaction giving rise to the claim. *J.I. Case Co. v. Borak*, 377 U.S. 426 (1964), did not itself address the requisites of causation, as such, or define the class of plaintiffs eligible to sue under § 14(a). But its general holding, that a private cause of action was available to some shareholder class, acquired greater clarity with a more definite concept of causation in *Mills*, where we addressed the sufficiency of proof that misstatements in a proxy solicitation were responsible for damages claimed from the merger subject to complaint.

Although a majority stockholder in *Mills* controlled just over half the corporation's shares, a two-thirds vote was needed to approve the merger proposal. After proxies had been obtained, and the merger had carried, minority shareholders brought a *Borak* action. 396 U.S. at 379, 619. The question arose whether the plaintiffs' burden to demonstrate causation of their damages traceable to the § 14(a) violation required proof that the defect in the proxy solicitation had "a decisive effect on the voting." *Id.* at 385. The *Mills* Court avoided the evidentiary morass that would have followed from requiring individualized proof that enough minority shareholders had relied upon the misstatements to swing the vote. Instead, it held that causation of damages by a material proxy misstatement could be established by showing that minority proxies necessary and sufficient to authorize the corporate acts had been given in accordance with the tenor of the solicitation, and the Court described such a causal relationship by calling the proxy solicitation an "essential link in the accomplishment of the transaction." *Id.* In the case before it, the Court found the solicitation essential, as contrasted with one addressed to a class of minority shareholders without votes required by law or by-law to authorize the action proposed, and left it for another day to decide whether such a minority shareholder could demonstrate causation. *Id.* at 385, n.7.

In this case, respondents address *Mills'* open question by proffering two theories that the proxy solicitation addressed to them was an "essential link" under the *Mills* causation test.[9] They argue, first, that a link existed and was essential simply because VBI and FABI

---

[9]   Citing the decision in *Schlick v. Penn-Dixie Cement Corp.*, 507 F.2d 374, 382-383 (CA2 1974), petitioners characterize respondents' proffered theories as examples of so-called "sue facts" and "shame facts" theories. Brief for Petitioners 41; Reply Brief for Petitioners 8. "A 'sue fact' is, in general, a fact which is material to a sue decision. A 'sue decision' is a decision by a shareholder whether or not to institute a representative or derivative suit alleging a state-law cause of action." Gelb, *Rule 10b-5 and Santa Fe—Herein of Sue Facts, Shame Facts, and Other Matters*, 87 W. VA. L. REV. 189, 198, and n.52 (1985), quoting Borden, *"Sue Fact" Rule Mandates Disclosure to Avoid Litigation in State Courts*, 10 SEC'82, pp. 201, 204-205 (1982). *See also* Note, *Causation and Liability in Private Actions for Proxy Violations*, 80 YALE L.J. 107, 116 (1970) (discussing theories of causation). "Shame facts" are said to be facts which, had they been disclosed, would have "shamed" management into abandoning a proposed transaction. *See Schlick, supra*, at 384. *See also* Gelb, *supra*, at 197.

would have been unwilling to proceed with the merger without the approval manifested by the minority shareholders' proxies, which would not have been obtained without the solicitation's express misstatements and misleading omissions. On this reasoning, the causal connection would depend on a desire to avoid bad shareholder or public relations, and the essential character of the causal link would stem not from the enforceable terms of the parties' corporate relationship, but from one party's apprehension of the ill will of the other.

In the alternative, respondents argue that the proxy statement was an essential link between the directors' proposal and the merger because it was the means to satisfy a state statutory requirement of minority shareholder approval, as a condition for saving the merger from voidability resulting from a conflict of interest on the part of one of the Bank's directors, Jack Beddow, who voted in favor of the merger while also serving as a director of FABI. Brief for Respondents 43-44, 45-46. Under the terms of Va. Code § 13.1-691(A) (1989), minority approval after disclosure of the material facts about the transaction and the director's interest was one of three avenues to insulate the merger from later attack for conflict, the two others being ratification by the Bank's directors after like disclosure, and proof that the merger was fair to the corporation. On this theory, causation would depend on the use of the proxy statement for the purpose of obtaining votes sufficient to bar a minority shareholder from commencing proceedings to declare the merger void.[10]

Although respondents have proffered each of these theories as establishing a chain of causal connection in which the proxy statement is claimed to have been an "essential link," neither theory presents the proxy solicitation as essential in the sense of *Mills'* causal sequence, in which the solicitation links a directors' proposal with the votes legally required to authorize the action proposed. As a consequence, each theory would, if adopted, extend the scope of *Borak* actions beyond the ambit of *Mills*, and expand the class of plaintiffs entitled to bring *Borak* actions to include shareholders whose initial authorization of the transaction prompting the proxy solicitation is unnecessary. Assessing the legitimacy of any such extension or expansion calls for the application of some fundamental principles governing recognition of a right of action implied by a federal statute, the first of which was not, in fact, the considered focus of the *Borak* opinion. The rule that has emerged in the years since *Borak* and *Mills* came down is that recognition of any private right of action for violating a federal statute must ultimately rest on congressional intent to provide a private remedy, *Touche Ross & Co. v. Redington*, 442 U.S. 560, 575 (1979). From this the corollary follows that the breadth of the right once recognized should not, as a general matter, grow beyond the scope congressionally intended.

This rule and corollary present respondents with a serious obstacle, for we can find no manifestation of intent to recognize a cause of action (or class of plaintiffs) as broad as

---

[10]   The district court and court of appeals have grounded causation on a further theory, that Virginia law required a solicitation of proxies even from minority shareholders as a condition of consummating the merger. *See* 891 F.2d at 1120, n.1; App. 426. While the provisions of Va. Code §§ 13.1-718(A), (D), and (E) (1989) are said to have required the Bank to solicit minority proxies, they actually compelled no more than submission of the merger to a vote at a shareholders' meeting, § 13.1-718(E), preceded by issuance of an informational statement, § 13.1-718(D). There was thus no need under this statute to solicit proxies, although it is undisputed that the proxy solicitation sufficed to satisfy the statutory obligation to provide a statement of relevant information. On this theory causation would depend on the use of the proxy statement to satisfy a statutory obligation, even though a proxy solicitation was not, as such, required. In this Court, respondents have disclaimed reliance on any such theory.

respondents' theory of causation would entail. At first blush, it might seem otherwise, for the *Borak* Court certainly did not ignore the matter of intent. Its opinion adverted to the statutory object of "protection of investors" as animating Congress' intent to provide judicial relief where "necessary," *Borak*, 377 U.S. at 432 and it quoted evidence for that intent from House and Senate Committee Reports, *id.* at 431-32, *Borak's* probe of the congressional mind, however, never focused squarely on private rights of action, as distinct from the substantive objects of the legislation, and one member of the *Borak* Court later characterized the "implication" of the private right of action as resting modestly on the Act's "exclusively procedural provision affording access to a federal forum." *Bivens v. Six Unknown Fed. Narcotics Agents*, 403 U.S. 388, 403, n.4 (1971) (Harlan, J., concurring in judgment) (internal quotation marks omitted). [other citations omitted] In fact, the importance of enquiring specifically into intent to authorize a private cause of action became clear only later, see *Cort v. Ash*, 422 U.S., at 78, and only later still, in *Touche Ross*, was this intent accorded primacy among the considerations that might be thought to bear on any decision to recognize a private remedy. There, in dealing with a claimed private right under § 17(a) of the Act, we explained that the "central inquiry remains whether Congress intended to create, either expressly or by implication, a private cause of action." 442 U.S. at 575-576.

Looking to the Act's text and legislative history mindful of this heightened concern reveals little that would help toward understanding the intended scope of any private right. According to the House report, Congress meant to promote the "free exercise" of stockholders' voting rights, H.R. Rep. No. 1383, 73d Cong., 2d Sess., 14 (1934), and protect "[f]air corporate suffrage," *id.* at 13, from abuses exemplified by proxy solicitations that concealed what the Senate report called the "real nature" of the issues to be settled by the subsequent votes, S. Rep. No. 792, 73d Cong., 2d Sess., 12 (1934). While it is true that these reports, like the language of the Act itself, carry the clear message that Congress meant to protect investors from misinformation that rendered them unwitting agents of self-inflicted damage, it is just as true that Congress was reticent with indications of how far this protection might depend on self-help by private action. The response to this reticence may be, of course, to claim that § 14(a) cannot be enforced effectively for the sake of its intended beneficiaries without their participation as private litigants. *Borak, supra*, 377 U.S. at 432. But the force of this argument for inferred congressional intent depends on the degree of need perceived by Congress, and we would have trouble inferring any congressional urgency to depend on implied private actions to deter violations of § 14(a), when Congress expressly provided private rights of action in §§ 9(e), 16(b) and 18(a) of the same Act. *See* 15 U.S.C. §§ 78i(e), 78p(b) and 78r(a).[11]

The congressional silence that is thus a serious obstacle to the expansion of cognizable *Borak* causation is not, however, a necessarily insurmountable barrier. This is not the first effort in recent years to expand the scope of an action originally inferred from the Act without "conclusive guidance" from Congress, see *Blue Chip Stamps v. Manor Drug Stores*, 421

---

[11]   The object of our enquiry does not extend further to question the holding of either *J.I. Case Co. v. Borak*, 377 U.S. 426 (1964), or *Mills v. Electric Auto-Lite Co.*, 396 U.S. 375 (1970) at this date, any more than we have done so in the past, see *Touche Ross & Co. v. Redington*, 442 U.S. 560, 577 (1979). Our point is simply to recognize the hurdle facing any litigant who urges us to enlarge the scope of the action beyond the point reached in *Mills*.

U.S. at 737, and we may look to that earlier case for the proper response to such a plea for expansion. There, we accepted the proposition that where a legal structure of private statutory rights has developed without clear indications of congressional intent, the contours of that structure need not be frozen absolutely when the result would be demonstrably inequitable to a class of would-be plaintiffs with claims comparable to those previously recognized. Faced in that case with such a claim for equality in rounding out the scope of an implied private statutory right of action, we looked to policy reasons for deciding where the outer limits of the right should lie. We may do no less here, in the face of respondents' pleas for a private remedy to place them on the same footing as shareholders with votes necessary for initial corporate action.

A

Blue Chip Stamps set an example worth recalling as a preface to specific policy analysis of the consequences of recognizing respondents' first theory, that a desire to avoid minority shareholders' ill will should suffice to justify recognizing the requisite causality of a proxy statement needed to garner that minority support. It will be recalled that in *Blue Chip Stamps* we raised concerns about the practical consequences of allowing recovery, under § 10(b) of the Act and Rule 10b-5, on evidence of what a merely hypothetical buyer or seller might have done on a set of facts that never occurred, and foresaw that any such expanded liability would turn on "hazy" issues inviting self-serving testimony, strike suits, and protracted discovery, with little chance of reasonable resolution by pretrial process. *Id.* at 742-743. These were good reasons to deny recognition to such claims in the absence of any apparent contrary congressional intent.

The same threats of speculative claims and procedural intractability are inherent in respondents' theory of causation linked through the directors' desire for a cosmetic vote. Causation would turn on inferences about what the corporate directors would have thought and done without the minority shareholder approval unneeded to authorize action. A subsequently dissatisfied minority shareholder would have virtual license to allege that managerial timidity would have doomed corporate action but for the ostensible approval induced by a misleading statement, and opposing claims of hypothetical diffidence and hypothetical boldness on the part of directors would probably provide enough depositions in the usual case to preclude any judicial resolution short of the credibility judgments that can only come after trial. Reliable evidence would seldom exist. Directors would understand the prudence of making a few statements about plans to proceed even without minority endorsement, and discovery would be a quest for recollections of oral conversations at odds with the official pronouncements, in hopes of finding support for ex post facto guesses about how much heat the directors would have stood in the absence of minority approval. The issues would be hazy, their litigation protracted, and their resolution unreliable. Given a choice, we would reject any theory of causation that raised such prospects, and we reject this one.[12]

---

[12]   In parting company from us on this point, Justice KENNEDY emphasizes that respondents in this particular case substantiated a plausible claim that petitioners would not have proceeded without minority approval. FABI's attempted freeze-out merger of a Maryland subsidiary had failed a year before the events in question when the subsidiary's directors rejected the proposal because of inadequate share price, and there was evidence of FABI's desire to avoid any renewal of adverse comment. The issue before us, however, is whether to recognize a theory of causation generally, and

B

The theory of causal necessity derived from the requirements of Virginia law dealing with postmerger ratification seeks to identify the essential character of the proxy solicitation from its function in obtaining the minority approval that would preclude a minority suit attacking the merger. Since the link is said to be a step in the process of barring a class of shareholders from resort to a state remedy otherwise available, this theory of causation rests upon the proposition of policy that § 14(a) should provide a federal remedy whenever a false or misleading proxy statement results in the loss under state law of a shareholder plaintiff's state remedy for the enforcement of a state right. Respondents agree with the suggestions of counsel for the SEC and FDIC that causation be recognized, for example, when a minority shareholder has been induced by a misleading proxy statement to forfeit a state-law right to an appraisal remedy by voting to approve a transaction, *cf. Swanson v. American Consumers Industries, Inc.*, 475 F.2d 516, 520-521 (CA7 1973), or when such a shareholder has been deterred from obtaining an order enjoining a damaging transaction by a proxy solicitation that misrepresents the facts on which an injunction could properly have been issued. [citations omitted] Respondents claim that in this case a predicate for recognizing just such a causal link exists in Va. Code § 13.1-691(A)(2) (1989), which sets the conditions under which the merger may be insulated from suit by a minority shareholder seeking to void it on account of Beddow's conflict.

This case does not, however, require us to decide whether § 14(a) provides a cause of action for lost state remedies, since there is no indication in the law or facts before us that the proxy solicitation resulted in any such loss. The contrary appears to be the case. Assuming the soundness of respondents' characterization of the proxy statement as materially misleading, the very terms of the Virginia statute indicate that a favorable minority vote induced by the solicitation would not suffice to render the merger invulnerable to later attack on the ground of the conflict. The statute bars a shareholder from seeking to avoid a transaction tainted by a director's conflict if, inter alia, the minority shareholders ratified the transaction following disclosure of the material facts of the transaction and the conflict. Va. Code § 13.1-691(A)(2) (1989). Assuming that the material facts about the merger and Beddow's interests were not accurately disclosed, the minority votes were inadequate to ratify the merger under state law, and there was no loss of state remedy to connect the proxy solicitation with harm to minority shareholders irredressable under state law.[13] Nor is there a claim here that the statement misled respondents into entertaining a false belief that they had no chance to upset the merger, until the time for bringing suit had run out.[14]

---

our decision against doing so rests on our apprehension that the ensuing litigation would be exemplified by cases far less tractable than this. Respondents' burden to justify recognition of causation beyond the scope of *Mills* must be addressed not by emphasizing the instant case but by confronting the risk inherent in the cases that could be expected to be characteristic if the causal theory were adopted.

[13] In his opinion dissenting on this point, Justice KENNEDY suggests that materiality under Virginia law might be defined differently from the materiality standard of our own cases, resulting in a denial of state remedy even when a solicitation was materially misleading under federal law. Respondents, however, present nothing to suggest that this might be so.

[14] Respondents do not claim that any other application of a theory of lost state remedies would avail them here. It is clear, for example, that no state appraisal remedy was lost through a § 14(a) violation in this case. Respondent Weinstein and others did seek appraisal under Virginia law in the Virginia courts; their claims were rejected on the explicit

IV

The judgment of the Court of Appeals is reversed. It is so ordered.

[Four justices dissented from Part III of the Court's opinion. Justice STEVENS and Justice MARSHALL would have permitted an action for damages under § 14(a) whenever materially false or misleading statements were made in proxy statements; Justice KENNEDY and Justice BLACKMAN, on the other hand, concluded that the facts alleged in the complaint were sufficient to establish that FABI or VBI would have withdrawn or revised the merger proposal had all material facts been disclosed.]

NOTE

Other causation theories. The Court rejected both of the plaintiff's causation theories—that VBI and FABI would not have proceeded with the merger without the minority's vote solicited by the misleading proxy materials; and that the proxy statement made the merger harder to attack under state law. Prior to *Sandberg*, the courts had developed other § 14(a) causation theories—that disclosure would have caused such massive exercise of appraisal rights that the transaction would have to have been abandoned;[82] and that nondisclosure had deterred minority shareholders from exercising state law rights.[83] Do these theories survive *Sandberg*? For post-*Sandberg* opinions holding in favor of the loss-of-state-remedy theory of causation, see *Wilson v. Great American Indus, Inc.*,[84] and *Howing Co. v. Nationwide Corp.*[85]

[B] 10(b) and 10b-5 Liability Where There is No Proxy Solicitation

Section 10(b) and Rule 10b-5 have a potentially broader reach in some respects than does § 14(a). First, § 14(a) is limited to misconduct in connection with the solicitation of proxies, while 10(b) and 10b-5 apply to misconduct "in connection with the purchase or sale of any security." Thus, only the latter provisions provide a remedy

---

grounds that although "[s]tatutory appraisal is now considered the exclusive remedy for stockholders opposing a merger," App. to Pet. for Cert. 32a; *see Adams v. United States Distributing Corp.*, 34 S.E.2d 244 (Va. 1945), *cert. denied*, 327 U.S. 788, (1946), "dissenting stockholders in bank mergers do not even have this solitary remedy available to them," because "Va. Code § 6.1-43 specifically excludes bank mergers from application of § 13.1-730 [the Virginia appraisal statute]." App. to Pet. for Cert. 31a, 32a. Weinstein does not claim that the Virginia court was wrong and does not rely on this claim in any way. Thus, the § 14(a) violation could have had no effect on the availability of an appraisal remedy, for there never was one.

[82] *See Cole v. Schenley Industries, Inc.*, 563 F.2d 35 (2d Cir. 1977).

[83] *See Healey v. Catalyst Recovery of Pennsylvania, Inc.*, 616 F.2d 641, 647 (3d Cir. 1980) (causation established if there was "a reasonable probability that a shareholder could have used the information to obtain an injunction"); *Wright v. Heizer Corp.*, 560 F.2d 236 (7th Cir. 1977), *cert. denied*, 434 U.S. 1066 (1978) (causation established only if state action would have succeeded).

[84] 979 F.2d 924 (2d Cir. 1992).

[85] 972 F.2d 700 (6th Cir. 1992).

with respect to transactions that do not require shareholder approval. Such transactions would include short-form mergers (*see Santa Fe*, below) and sales of assets.

A second difference between § 10(b) and § 14(a) remedies is that, while 14(a), through SEC Rule 14a-9, prohibits misrepresentations and omissions in proxy materials, the "manipulative or deceptive device" language of § 10(b) and the "fraud" language of clauses 1 and 3 of Rule 10b-5 have a potentially broader reach. This raises the question, addressed in the following case, whether these provisions provide the basis for a broad federal remedy for corporate mismanagement that would supplement the state law of fiduciary duties.

SANTA FE INDUSTRIES, INC. v. GREEN
United States Supreme Court
430 U.S. 462 (1977)

Mr. Justice WHITE delivered the opinion of the Court.

The issue in this case involves the reach and coverage of § 10(b) of the Securities Exchange Act of 1934 and Rule 10b-5 thereunder in the context of a Delaware short-form merger transaction used by the majority stockholder of a corporation to eliminate the minority interest.

I

In 1936, petitioner Santa Fe Industries, Inc. (Santa Fe), acquired control of 60% of the stock of Kirby Lumber Corp. (Kirby), a Delaware corporation. Through a series of purchases over the succeeding years, Santa Fe increased its control of Kirby's stock to 95%; the purchase prices during the period 1968-1973 ranged from $65 to $92.50 per share. In 1974, wishing to acquire 100% ownership of Kirby, Santa Fe availed itself of § 253 of the Delaware Corporation Law, known as the "short-form merger" statute. Section 253 permits a parent corporation owning at least 90% of the stock of a subsidiary to merge with the subsidiary, upon approval by the parent's board of directors, and to make payment in cash for the shares of the minority stockholders. The statute does not require the consent of, or advance notice to, the minority stockholders. However, notice of the merger must be given within 10 days after its effective date, and any stockholder who is dissatisfied with the terms of the merger may petition the Delaware Court of Chancery for a decree ordering the surviving corporation to pay him the fair value of his shares, as determined by a court-appointed appraiser subject to review by the court. Del. Code Ann. tit. 8, §§ 253, 262 (1975 ed. and Supp. 1976).

Santa Fe obtained independent appraisals of the physical assets of Kirby—land, timber, buildings, and machinery—and of Kirby's oil, gas, and mineral interests. These appraisals, together with other financial information, were submitted to Morgan Stanley & Co. (Morgan Stanley), an investment banking firm retained to appraise the fair market value of Kirby stock. Kirby's physical assets were appraised at $320 million (amounting to $640 for each of the 500,000 shares); Kirby's stock was valued by Morgan Stanley at $125 per share. Under the terms of the merger, minority stockholders were offered $150 per share.

The provisions of the short-form merger statute were fully complied with. The minority stockholders of Kirby were notified the day after the merger became effective and were advised of their right to obtain an appraisal in Delaware court if dissatisfied with the offer of $150 per share. They also received an information statement containing, in addition to the relevant financial data about Kirby, the appraisals of the value of Kirby's assets and the Morgan Stanley appraisal concluding that the fair market value of the stock was $125 per share.

Respondents, minority stockholders of Kirby, objected to the terms of the merger, but did not pursue their appraisal remedy in the Delaware Court of Chancery.* Instead, they brought this action in federal court on behalf of the corporation and other minority stockholders, seeking to set aside the merger or to recover what they claimed to be the fair value of their shares. The amended complaint asserted that, based on the fair market value of Kirby's physical assets as revealed by the appraisal included in the information statement sent to minority shareholders, Kirby's stock was worth at least $772 per share. The complaint alleged further that the merger took place without prior notice to minority stockholders; that the purpose of the merger was to appropriate the difference between the "conceded pro rata value of the physical assets," App. 103a, and the offer of $150 per share—to "freez[e] out the minority stockholders at a wholly inadequate price," id. at 100a; and that Santa Fe, knowing the appraised value of the physical assets, obtained a "fraudulent appraisal" of the stock from Morgan Stanley and offered $25 above that appraisal "in order to lull the minority stockholders into erroneously believing that [Santa Fe was] generous." Id. at 103a. This course of conduct was alleged to be "a violation of Rule 10b-5 because defendants employed a 'device, scheme, or artifice to defraud' and engaged in an 'act, practice or course of business which operates or would operate as a fraud or deceit upon any person, in connection with the purchase or sale of any security.'" Id. Morgan Stanley assertedly participated in the fraud as an accessory by submitting its appraisal of $125 per share although knowing the appraised value of the physical assets.

* * *

II

Section 10(b) of the 1934 Act makes it "unlawful for any person . . . to use or employ . . . any manipulative or deceptive device or contrivance in contravention of [Securities and Exchange Commission rules]"; Rule 10b-5, promulgated by the SEC under § 10(b), prohibits, in addition to nondisclosure and misrepresentation, any "artifice to defraud" or any act "which operates or would operate as a fraud or deceit." The court below construed the term "fraud" in Rule 10b-5 by adverting to the use of the term in several of this Court's decisions in contexts other than the 1934 Act and the related Securities Act of 1933, 15 U.S.C. § 77a et seq. The Court of Appeals' approach to the interpretation of Rule 10b-5 is inconsistent with that taken by the Court last Term in Ernst & Ernst v. Hochfelder, 425 U.S. 185 (1976).

---

* [Other minority shareholders did pursue their appraisal remedy. See Bell v. Kirby Lumber Corp., 413 A.2d 137 (Del. 1980).—Ed.]

Ernst & Ernst makes clear that in deciding whether a complaint states a cause of action for "fraud" under Rule 10b-5, "we turn first to the language of § 10(b), for '[t]he starting point in every case involving construction of a statute is the language itself.'"

* * *

The language of § 10(b) gives no indication that Congress meant to prohibit any conduct not involving manipulation or deception.

* * *

III

It is our judgment that the transaction, if carried out as alleged in the complaint, was neither deceptive nor manipulative and therefore did not violate either § 10(b) of the Act or Rule 10b-5.

As we have indicated, the case comes to us on the premise that the complaint failed to allege a material misrepresentation or material failure to disclose. The finding of the District Court, undisturbed by the Court of Appeals, was that there was no "omission" or "misstatement" in the information statement accompanying the notice of merger. On the basis of the information provided minority shareholders could either accept the price offered or reject it and seek an appraisal in the Delaware Court of Chancery. Their choice was fairly presented, and they were furnished with all relevant information on which to base their decision.[14]

---

[14]   In addition to their principal argument that the complaint alleges a fraud under clauses (a) and (c) of Rule 10b-5, respondents also argue that the complaint alleges nondisclosure and misrepresentation in violation of clause (b) of the Rule. Their major contention in this respect is that the majority stockholder's failure to give the minority advance notice of the merger was a material nondisclosure, even though the Delaware short-form merger statute does not require such notice. Brief for Respondents 27. But respondents do not indicate how they might have acted differently had they had prior notice of the merger. Indeed, they accept the conclusion of both courts below that under Delaware law they could not have enjoined the merger because an appraisal proceeding is their sole remedy in the Delaware courts for any alleged unfairness in the terms of the merger. Thus, the failure to give advance notice was not a material nondisclosure within the meaning of the statute or the Rule. *Cf. TSC Industries, Inc. v. Northway, Inc.*, 426 U.S. 438 (1976).

[15]   The decisions of this Court relied upon by respondents all involved deceptive conduct as part of the Rule 10b-5 violation alleged. *Affiliated Ute Citizens v. United States*, 406 U.S. 128 (1972) (misstatements of material fact used by bank employees in position of market maker to acquire stock at less than fair value); *Superintendent of Insurance v. Bankers Life & Cas. Co.*, 404 U.S. 6, 9 (1971) ("seller [of bonds] was duped into believing that it, the seller, would receive the proceeds"). *Cf. SEC v. Capital Gains Research Bureau*, 375 U.S. 180 (1963) (injunction under Investment Advisers Act of 1940 to compel registered investment adviser to disclose to his clients his own financial interest in his recommendations).

We have been cited to a large number of cases in the Courts of Appeals, all of which involved an element of deception as part of the fiduciary misconduct held to violate Rule 10b-5. *E.g., Schoenbaum v. Firstbrook*, 405 F.2d 215, 220 (CA2 1968) (en banc), *cert. denied*, 395 U.S. 906 (1969) (majority stockholder and board of directors "were guilty of deceiving" the minority stockholders); . . . *Pappas v. Moss*, 393 F.2d 865, 869 (CA3 1968) ("if a 'deception' is required in the present context [of § 10(b) and Rule 10b-5], it is fairly found by viewing this fraud as though the 'independent' stockholders were standing in the place of the defrauded corporate entity," where the board of directors passed a resolution containing at least two material misrepresentations and authorizing the sale of corporate stock to the directors at a price below fair market value)[.]

We therefore find inapposite the cases relied upon by respondents and the court below, in which the breaches of fiduciary duty held violative of Rule 10b-5 included some element of deception.[15]

* * *

Those cases forcefully reflect the principle that "[§]10(b) must be read flexibly, not technically and restrictively" and that the statute provides a cause of action for any plaintiff who "suffer[s] an injury as a result of deceptive practices touching its sale [or purchase] of securities . . . ." *Superintendent of Insurance v. Bankers Life & Cas. Co.*, 404 U.S. 6, 12-13 (1971). But the cases do not support the proposition, adopted by the Court of Appeals below and urged by respondents here, that a breach of fiduciary duty by majority stockholders, without any deception, misrepresentation, or nondisclosure, violates the statute and the Rule.

It is also readily apparent that the conduct alleged in the complaint was not "manipulative" within the meaning of the statute. "Manipulation" is "virtually a term of art when used in connection with securities markets." *Ernst & Ernst*, 425 U.S. at 199. The term refers generally to practices, such as wash sales, matched orders, or rigged prices, that are intended to mislead investors by artificially affecting market activity. . . . No doubt Congress meant to prohibit the full range of ingenious devices that might be used to manipulate securities prices. But we do not think it would have chosen this "term of art" if it had meant to bring within the scope of § 10(b) instances of corporate mismanagement such as this, in which the essence of the complaint is that shareholders were treated unfairly by a fiduciary.

IV

The language of the statute is, we think, "sufficiently clear in its context" to be dispositive here, *Ernst & Ernst, supra*, at 201; but even if it were not, there are additional considerations that weigh heavily against permitting a cause of action under Rule 10b-5 for the breach of corporate fiduciary duty alleged in this complaint. Congress did not expressly provide a private cause of action for violations of § 10(b). Although we have recognized an implied cause of action under that section in some circumstances, *Superintendent of Insurance v. Bankers Life & Cas. Co., supra*, at 13 n.9, we have also recognized that a private cause of action under the antifraud provisions of the Securities Exchange Act should not be implied where it is "unnecessary to ensure the fulfillment of Congress' purposes" in adopting the Act. *Piper v. Chris-Craft Industries*, [430 U.S. 1 (1977)] at 41. . . . [T]he Court repeatedly has described the "fundamental purpose" of the Act as implementing a "philosophy of full disclosure"; once full and fair disclosure has occurred, the fairness of the terms of the transaction is at most a tangential concern of the statute. . . . As in *Cort v. Ash*, 422 U.S. 66, 80 (1975), we are reluctant to recognize a cause of action here to serve what is "at best a subsidiary purpose" of the federal legislation.

A second factor in determining whether Congress intended to create a federal cause of action in these circumstances is "whether 'the cause of action [is] one traditionally relegated to state law . . . .'" *Piper v. Chris-Craft Industries, Inc., ante*, at 40, quoting *Cort v. Ash, supra*, at 78. The Delaware Legislature has supplied minority shareholders with a cause of action in the Delaware Court of Chancery to recover the fair value of shares allegedly undervalued in a short-form merger. Of course, the existence of a particular state law remedy is not dispositive of the question whether Congress meant to provide a similar federal remedy, but as in *Cort* and *Piper*, we conclude that "it is entirely appropriate in this instance to relegate respondent and others in his situation to whatever remedy is created by state law." 422 U.S. at 84; *ante*, at 41.

The reasoning behind a holding that the complaint in this case alleged fraud under Rule 10b-5 could not be easily contained. It is difficult to imagine how a court could distinguish, for purposes of Rule 10b-5 fraud, between a majority stockholder's use of a short-form merger to eliminate the minority at an unfair price and the use of some other device, such as a long-form merger, tender offer, or liquidation, to achieve the same result; or indeed how a court could distinguish the alleged abuses in these going private transactions from other types of fiduciary self-dealing involving transactions in securities. The result would be to bring within the Rule a wide variety of corporate conduct traditionally left to state regulation. In addition to posing a "danger of vexatious litigation which could result from a widely expanded class of plaintiffs under Rule 10b-5," *Blue Chip Stamps v. Manor Drug Stores*, 421.U.S. at 740, this extension of the federal securities laws would overlap and quite possibly interfere with state corporate law. Federal courts applying a "federal fiduciary principle" under Rule 10b-5 could be expected to depart from state fiduciary standards at least to the extent necessary to ensure uniformity within the federal system.[16] Absent a clear indication of congressional intent, we are reluctant to federalize the substantial portion of the law of corporations that deals with transactions in securities, particularly where established state policies of corporate regulation would be overridden. As the Court stated in *Cort v. Ash*, *supra*: "Corporations are creatures of state law, and investors commit their funds to corporate directors on the understanding that, except where federal law *expressly* requires certain responsibilities of directors with respect to stockholders, state law will govern the internal affairs of the corporation." 422 U.S. at 84 (emphasis added).

We thus adhere to the position that "Congress by § 10(b) did not seek to regulate transactions which constitute no more than internal corporate mismanagement." *Superintendent of Insurance v. Bankers Life & Cas. Co.*, 404 U.S. at 12. There may well be a need for uniform federal fiduciary standards to govern mergers such as that challenged in this complaint. But those standards should not be supplied by judicial extension of § 10(b) and Rule 10b-5 to "cover the corporate universe."

The judgment of the Court of Appeals is reversed, and the case is remanded for further proceedings consistent with this opinion.

So ordered.

[Dissenting opinion of Justice BRENNAN and concurring opinions of Justices BLACKMUN and STEVENS omitted].

---

[16]   For example, some States apparently require a "valid corporate purpose" for the elimination of the minority interest through a short-form merger, whereas other States do not. *Compare Bryan v. Brock & Blevins Co.*, 490 F.2d 563 (CA5), *cert. denied*, 419 U.S. 844 (1974) (merger arranged by controlling stockholder for no business purpose except to eliminate 15% minority stockholder violated Georgia short-form merger statute), with *Stauffer v. Standard Brands, Inc.*, 41 Del. Ch. 7, 187 A.2d 78 (1962) (Delaware short-form merger statute allows majority stockholder to eliminate the minority interest without any corporate purpose and subject only to an appraisal remedy). Thus to the extent that Rule 10b-5 is interpreted to require a valid corporate purpose for elimination of minority shareholders as well as a fair price for their shares, it would impose a stricter standard of fiduciary duty than that required by the law of some States.

NOTES AND QUESTIONS

(1) **Federal liability for corporate transactions where there is no proxy solicitation.** Under *Santa Fe* there is no federal securities law remedy in connection with a corporate transaction when the facts are disclosed fully to the board and the shareholders. To what extent is there a federal remedy for the broad range of transactions that are approved by the directors only *without any disclosure to the shareholders*? This issue is discussed in the following notes.[86]

(2) **Transactions approved by uninformed directors.** The clearest situation for coverage by 10(b) and 10b-5 is one in which the entire board of directors is deceived by the defendant into purchasing or selling stock. A leading early case is *Hooper v. Mountain States Securities Corp.*,[87] in which the court held in favor of 10(b) liability on behalf of a corporation that had sold its stock for overvalued assets, rejecting the argument that a corporation is not an "investor" and therefore not entitled to the protection of the securities laws. *Ruckle v. Roto American Corp.*[88] permitted an injunction when a majority of the board had withheld facts from the minority.

(3) **Transactions approved by fully informed directors; nondisclosure to shareholders.** A somewhat less clear case for coverage by 10(b) and 10b-5 is one in which a transaction is approved by fully informed directors, but no disclosure is made to shareholders. In the leading case of *Schoenbaum v. Firstbrook*,[89] the Second Circuit recognized a cause of action in this situation. Plaintiff had sued derivatively under 10(b) on behalf of Banff Oil Ltd. In one of the transactions complained of, Banff sold stock to its allegedly controlling shareholder, Acquitaine, during a period in which no public disclosure had been made of material information concerning Banff's oil exploration activities. A Second Circuit panel initially affirmed the lower court's dismissal, stating in part:[90]

> The directors, who were authorized to act on behalf of the corporation in these transactions, were all concededly in full possession of the material information, and we find no basis, on the facts before us, for refusing to impute their knowledge to the corporation.
>
> A corporation can act only through its agents and officers and can know only what its agents and officers know. . . . In general, if the corporation's agents have not been deceived, neither has the corporation. However, as in other situations governed by agency principles, knowledge of the cor-

---

[86] *See* Ribstein, *The Scope of Federal Securities Law Liability for Corporate Transactions*, 33 Sw. L.J. 1129 (1980).

[87] 282 F.2d 195 (5th Cir. 1960), *cert. denied*, 365 U.S. 814 (1961).

[88] 339 F.2d 24 (2d Cir. 1964).

[89] 405 F.2d 215 (2d Cir. 1968) (en banc), *cert. denied*, 395 U.S. 906 (1969).

[90] 405 F.2d at 211-12.

poration's officers and agents is not imputed to it when there is a conflict between the interests of the officers and agents and the interests of the corporate principal. . . . Therefore, a corporation may be defrauded in a stock transaction even when all of its directors know all of the material facts, if the conflict between the interests of one or more of the directors and the interests of the corporation prevents effective transmission of material information to the corporation, in violation of Rule 10b-5(2). . . .

   While the purchaser in the Aquitaine transaction had three representatives on Banff's board of directors and was Banff's controlling shareholder, the Aquitaine representatives on the Banff board abstained from the authorization vote and shareholder ratification by Aquitaine was not required for the sale. Under these circumstances, we cannot refuse to impute the directors' knowledge to the corporation on the ground that directors participating in the corporate decision had a conflicting personal interest in the transaction.

On a rehearing en banc, the court reversed the dismissal, stating in part:[91]

In the present case it is alleged that Aquitaine exercised a controlling influence over the issuance to it of treasury stock of Banff for a wholly inadequate consideration. If it is established that the transaction took place as alleged it constituted a violation of Rule 10b-5, subdivision (3) because Aquitaine engaged in an "act, practice or course of business which operates or would operate as a fraud or deceit upon any person, in connection with the purchase or sale of any security." Moreover, Aquitaine and the directors of Banff were guilty of deceiving the stockholders of Banff (other than Aquitaine).

   The above excerpt from the en banc opinion indicates that the court found two independent bases for liability. The aspect of the *Schoenbaum* rule that apparently would permit liability without deception in "controlling influence" transactions clearly does not survive *Santa Fe*. Footnote 15 to the *Santa Fe* opinion, however, supports the aspect of the *Schoenbaum* rule that is based on nondisclosure to the minority shareholders. In the post-*Santa Fe* case of *Goldberg v. Meridor*,[92] the Second Circuit held in favor of a 10(b) remedy in connection with a transaction approved by a fully informed board when there was no disclosure to the shareholders and management had issued deceptive press releases to the shareholders.[93]

   (4) **The imputation of interested directors' knowledge to shareholders.** Under the *Schoenbaum-Goldberg* theory, the court must determine whether the informed directors are sufficiently interested that their knowledge may not be imputed to the

---

[91]   405 F.2d at 219-20.

[92]   567 F.2d 209 (2d Cir. 1977), *cert. denied,* 434 U.S. 1069 (1978).

[93]   For a case endorsing the *Goldberg* theory, see *Frankel v. Slotkin,* 984 F.2d 1328 (2d Cir. 1993).

shareholders. The courts will not impute the knowledge of a director who will reap a direct economic benefit from the transaction.[94] In *Kidwell, Penfold v. Meikle*,[95] the court held that such a benefit existed for directors who were interested in a company that stood to benefit from the transaction, but not for directors whose exposure to liability on personal guarantees would be decreased as a result of the transaction. Also, *Schoenbaum* held against imputing the knowledge of a director when the transaction in question is one with controlling shareholders. However, *Maldonado v. Flynn*[96] refused to extend this theory to a management-controlled corporation. *Maldonado* held imputable to the shareholders the knowledge of a director who might have lost legal fees from the corporation by opposing the directors who were benefiting directly from the transaction, and the knowledge of another director who depended on a management director to cover up his illegal insider trading. Finally, post-*Santa Fe* courts have imputed the knowledge of directors who acted to keep their jobs by approving corporate purchases of the shares of dissident shareholders.[97]

(5) **Other definitions of interest.** Compare the definition of "interest" in the context of the federal disclosure duty with the definitions of "interest" under state law in the contexts of director fiduciary duties generally (*see* Section 9.04); demand in and termination of derivative suits (*see* Sections 10.05 and 10.06); and fiduciary duties of management in resisting takeovers (*see* Section 14.03[D]). To the extent that there are differences between these definitions, are the differences justified?

(6) **Federalism and Part IV of *Santa Fe*.** Much of the *Santa Fe* opinion concerns the interpretation of the scope of the federal duty. Since federal law is concerned with disclosure, it seems to follow that the existence of a federal remedy turns on whether defendant breached a disclosure duty and whether this breach caused plaintiff's harm. Thus, footnote 14 to the *Santa Fe* opinion apparently permits a remedy when the plaintiff shows how he "might have acted differently"—for example, by bringing a state law action for breach of fiduciary duty. However, Part IV of *Santa Fe* looks more broadly at the interrelationship of state and federal law. This approach might deny a remedy that depends on a showing of a breach of state law—*i.e.*, by showing breach of a state law disclosure duty, or that breach of a federal duty interfered with plaintiff's state law remedy (*see* the Note following *Virginia Bankshares* in Section 15.03[A]). *See* **Ribstein**.[98]

---

[94] *See Dasho v. Susquehanna Corp.*, 380 F.2d 262 (7th Cir. 1967).

[95] 597 F.2d 1273 (9th Cir. 1979).

[96] 597 F.2d 789 (2d Cir. 1979). This case arose out of the same transaction as *Zapata*, Section 10.06.

[97] *See Brayton v. Ostrav*, Fed. Sec. L. Rep. (CCH) ¶ 99,128 (S.D.N.Y. 1983); *Seigal v. Merrick*, Fed. Sec. L. Rep. (CCH) ¶ 96,887 (S.D.N.Y. 1979); *Tyco Laboratories, Inc. v. Kimball*, 444 F. Supp. 292 (E.D. Pa. 1977); *Falkenberg v. Baldwin*, Fed. Sec. L. Rep. (CCH) ¶ 96,086 (S.D.N.Y. 1977).

[98] For a case that, consistent with this approach, seems to narrow the scope of the *Goldberg* rule, see *Field v. Trump*, 850 F.2d 938 (2d Cir. 1988) (holding that a cause of action for failure to disclose facts material to a state law fiduciary duty claim would lie only where those facts were needed to prevent irreparable injury and noting that *Goldberg* involved willful misconduct, so that the court did not have to closely examine state law).

(7) **The purchase and sale requirement under 10b-5.** Liability under 10b-5 depends not only on the deception element required by *Santa Fe*, but also on a purchase or sale of stock. In this sense, therefore, the 10b-5 remedy is narrower than that under 14(a), which provides a remedy for any corporate transaction resulting from misleading proxy material. The purchase or sale of stock is relevant in two respects in a 10b-5 cause of action. First, the plaintiff must be a purchaser or seller of stock in order to have standing to sue under 10b-5.[99] Second, Rule 10b-5 proscribes only conduct connected to a purchase or sale of stock.[100] The purchase-or-sale requirement is, therefore, an aspect of defendant's duty under 10b-5. The following Notes discuss separately the standing and duty aspects of the purchase-or-sale requirement.

(8) **Standing: plaintiff as purchaser or seller of stock.** The issue in connection with standing is what constitutes a purchase or sale of stock for 10b-5 purposes. *Vine v. Beneficial Finance Co.*[101] held that a plaintiff who had not personally engaged in a securities transaction was a seller when the corporation in which he was a shareholder merged into its controlling shareholder by means of a short-form freezeout merger. The court reasoned that plaintiff's shares had been converted by operation of law into something else—either a right to receive a certain amount of cash under the merger agreement or the right under the corporation statute to receive the appraised cash value of the stock. Is this holding consistent with *Blue Chip Stamps*?

The *Vine* "forced seller" rule has been applied in several cases in which the corporation was so substantially changed that plaintiff shareholders could be said to have sold stock in one corporation and bought stock in another.[102] On the other hand, the courts have refused to grant "forced seller" status when the transaction merely reduced the value of the plaintiff's interest in the corporation;[103] changes were made in controlling partnership agreement;[104] and the plaintiff lost working control of the corporation as a result of an agreement between two other shareholders.[105] Also, there has been no 10b-5 sale even when there was an actual exchange of stock in a merger, if the merger merely effected a minor reorganization of a single corporate business.[106] Are the differences between the cases in which a purchase or sale has, and has not, been recognized sensibly related to the policies underlying the 10b-5 cause of action? Should there be liability under 10b-5 for transactions by publicly held companies without regard to

---

[99] *See* the discussion of *Blue Chip Stamps* in Section 12.03[D][1].

[100] *See* Section 12.03[C][1].

[101] 374 F.2d 627 (2d Cir.), *cert. denied*, 389 U.S. 970 (1967).

[102] *See, e.g., Bailey v. Meister Brau, Inc.*, 535 F.2d 982 (7th Cir. 1976) (corporation liquidated).

[103] *See Tully v. Mott Supermarkets, Inc.*, 540 F.2d 187 (3d Cir. 1976).

[104] *See Abrahamson v. Fleschner*, 568 F.2d 862 (2d Cir. 1977), *cert. denied*, 436 U.S. 913 (1978).

[105] *See Canadian Javelin Ltd. v. Brooks*, 462 F. Supp. 190 (S.D.N.Y. 1978).

[106] *See, e.g., Rathborne v. Rathborne*, 683 F.2d 914 (5th Cir. 1982); *cf. Isquith v. Caremark International*, 136 F.3d 531 (7th Cir. 1998) (Posner, J.) (party who receives shares in corporate spin-off is not a "forced seller" because spin-off left plaintiff "with the same proportionate ownership of the same corporate assets," and therefore did not change the plaintiff's investment in a fundamental manner).

whether the specific transaction involved the purchase or sale of a security? *See* **Ribstein** at 1146-52, 1171-73.

(9) **Proscribed conduct: connection with securities transaction.** Even if the plaintiff is a purchaser or seller of securities, there is no violation of 10(b) or 10b-5 if the defendant's fraud did not have the requisite connection with a securities transaction.[107] A typical kind of case in which this issue is raised is one in which a shareholder sues derivatively to redress insider mismanagement. Here, the relevant purchase or sale for standing purposes is one by the corporation, rather than by the individual shareholders as in the "forced seller" cases discussed above. The courts have permitted a cause of action as long as the transaction complained of somehow involved the purchase or sale of stock, even if the securities aspect of the transaction was only incidental to the deception or other fraud. For example, some courts have recognized 10b-5 liability when the corporations exchanged their securities for overvalued property.[108] In this type of case, the fraud principally concerns the value of the property, and the wrong to the corporation would seem to be essentially the same whether the property is exchanged for the corporation's securities or for cash.[109]

In what may be the furthest extension of this approach, the Supreme Court recognized 10(b) and 10b-5 liability when insiders had purchased 100% of the stock of an insurance company and then had looted the corporation by appropriating the proceeds of a sale of the corporation's securities.[110] The Court noted that the corporation's board (which was controlled by the insiders) "was allegedly deceived into authorizing the sale by misrepresentation that the proceeds would be exchanged for a certificate of deposit of equal value."[111] The Court (in an opinion by Justice Douglas), said:[112]

> There certainly was an "act" or "practice" within the meaning of Rule 10b-5 which operated as "a fraud or deceit" on Manhattan, the seller of the Government bonds. To be sure, the full market price was paid for those bonds; but the seller was duped into believing that it, the seller, would receive the proceeds. We cannot agree with the Court of Appeals that "no investor [was] injured" and that the "purity of the security transaction and the purity of the trading process were unsullied." 430 F.2d at 361.

---

[107] *See Frymire-Brinati v. KPMG Peat Marwick*, 2 F.3d 183 (7th Cir. 1993) (holding that an audit of a financial statement was not in connection with sale of securities because auditor did not know the audit would be used to sell stock).

[108] *See, e.g., Rekant v. Desser*, 425 F.2d 872 (5th Cir. 1970); *Hooper v. Mountain States Securities Corp.*, 282 F.2d 195 (5th Cir. 1960).

[109] *See also Hoff v. Sprayregen*, 339 F. Supp. 369 (S.D.N.Y. 1971) (recognizing liability in a case in which the corporation had made an illegal payment to managers as a finder's fee in connection with the sale of stock).

[110] *See Superintendent of Insurance of New York v. Bankers Life & Casualty Co.*, 404 U.S. 6 (1971).

[111] 404 U.S. at 8 n.1.

[112] 404 U.S. at 9-13.

* * *

Manhattan was injured as an investor through a deceptive device which deprived it of any compensation for the sale of its valuable block of securities.

* * *

The Congress made clear that "disregard of trust relationships by those whom the law should regard as fiduciaries, are all a single seamless web" along with manipulation, investor's ignorance, and the like. H.R. Rep. No. 1383, 73d Cong., 2d Sess., 6.

* * *

We agree that Congress by § 10(b) did not seek to regulate transactions which constitute no more than internal corporate mismanagement. But we read § 10(b) to mean that Congress meant to bar deceptive devices and contrivances in the purchase or sale of securities whether conducted in the organized markets or face to face. And the fact that creditors of the defrauded corporate buyer or seller of securities may be the ultimate victims does not warrant disregard of the corporate entity. The controlling stockholder owes the corporation a fiduciary obligation—one "designed for the protection of the entire community of interests in the corporation—creditors as well as stockholders." *Pepper v. Litton*, 308 U.S. 295, 307. The crux of the present case is that Manhattan suffered an injury as a result of deceptive practices touching its sale of securities as an investor.

Is the *Bankers Life* theory of § 10(b) liability still viable after *Santa Fe*?

[C] Regulation of Corporate Combinations under 1933 Act

A corporate combination may involve a sale of stock for purposes of the Securities Act of 1933. SEC Rule 145 provides that a "sale" for purposes of § 2(a)(3) of the 1933 Act is involved where certain types of corporate combinations are submitted for shareholder approval. Such combinations include equity mergers and asset-for-stock transactions in which shares of the surviving corporation are distributed to shareholders of the target. According to the Preliminary Note to Rule 145, a shareholder's vote on a corporate combination "is in substance a new investment decision, whether to accept a new or different security in exchange for (the shareholder's) existing security." Compare the discussion in the Note immediately above, concerning the purchase-sale requirement under § 10(b) and Rule 10b-5.

It is important to note that Form S-4 permits registration of Rule 145 transactions by means of a proxy statement that complies with § 14 of the 1934 Act. Thus, a principal consequence of Rule 145 is that misleading statements in a proxy statement issued in connection with a Rule 145 transaction may trigger liability under the stringent standard of Section 11 of the 1933 Act as well as under §§ 10(b) and 14(a) of the 1934 Act.

PROBLEM

Assume the same basic facts as in the Problem at the end of Section 15.01[C], except that International has acquired 90% of Fine's stock in its initial tender offer and International's management is now considering effecting the merger with Fine through one of the following procedures:

(a) A merger pursuant to the Delaware "short form" merger statute (§ 253) that would be accomplished upon a vote of the International board and that would not require a proxy solicitation or the sending of proxy materials.

(b) A merger pursuant to the general Delaware merger statute (§ 251) that would be accomplished upon a vote of the Fine shareholders.

(c) Same procedure as (b) except that the transaction would be conditioned on the vote of a majority of the minority shareholders.

REFERENCE

Ribstein, *The Scope of Federal Securities Law Liability for Corporate Transactions*, 33 Sw. L.J. 1129 (1980).

Index

[References are to sections.]

LIQUIDATION

MANAGEMENT AND CONTROL

MARKET EFFICIENCY

MEETINGS

SUBCHAPTER S CORPORATIONS

SUBSIDIARIES (*See* PARENT AND SUBSIDIARY)

TAKEOVERS